THE LAST TSAR'S WARRIORS

Volume I: A – O

Andris J. Kursietis

# THE LAST TSAR'S WARRIORS

A Biographical Dictionary of the Senior Officers
of the Imperial Russian Armed Forces under Tsar Nikolai II
1894 - 1917

Volume I:  A – O

Aspekt Publishers

THE LAST TSAR'S WARRIORS - Volume I:  A – O

© Andris J. Kursietis
© 2017 Uitgeverij ASPEKT / Aspekt Publishers
Amersfoortsestraat 27, 3769 AD Soesterberg, The Netherlands
info@uitgeverijaspekt.nl – http://www.uitgeverijaspekt.nl

Cover: Maarten Bakker
Inside: Maarten Bakker

ISBN: 9789463382014
NUR: 680

All rights reserved. No reproduction copy or transmission of this publication  may be made without written permission.

## INDEX

Introduction ................................................................................. 1

Generals & Admirals of Imperial Russia, 1894 - 1917:
  Table of ranks ........................................................................... 4
  Alphabetical listing of Generals and Admirals (A - O) ….......………...… 5

List of Primary Sources ………………………………………...……… 596

  Alphabetical listing of Generals and Admirals (P - Z):  see Volume II

**Introduction**

In October 1894, Tsar Aleksandr III died at the early age of 49, and his son Nikolai ascended the throne of the Russian Empire as Nikolai II, Emperor and Autocrat of All the Russias. He inherited an empire that spanned three continents, almost 9 million square miles, extending from the Arctic Ocean in the north to the Black Sea in the south, from the Baltic Sea in the west to the Pacific Ocean in the east. As can be imagined, such a vast territory required a significantly-sized military to maintain order in the interior and to protect its borders from foreign aggressors. The size of the imperial armed forces can be judged by the fact that over 6,400 generals and admirals served the last Tsar of Russia during the 23-year period of his reign, 1894 – 1917. A study of the annual rank lists published by the Ministry of War shows that well over 1,000 generals were on active duty each year. This book attempts to provide an overview of the empire's military commanders, a task made all the more difficult by the lack of any detailed material in the English language, and the destruction of countless Russian-language records during the revolution in 1917 and the years that followed. Many senior officers were murdered by the revolutionaries, by unorganized mobs that did not keep records of whom they killed or when; others were lucky to flee the country and scatter to all corners of the planet, where they lived out their remaining years in obscurity and anonymity, wishing to avoid recognition and potential assassination by Communist agents. Accordingly, the dates when many of the generals and admirals listed in this book died have been lost to posterity, and the reader will frequently see a question mark in place of an officer's death date.

**The officers**
During the years of the last Tsar's reign, there were in effect three levels of flag rank in the Imperial Russian armed forces: *Major-General (Rear-Admiral)*; *Lieutenant-General (Vice-Admiral)*; *General of Infantry/Cavalry/ Artillery/Engineers (Admiral)*. A more complete listing of ranks is shown at the beginning of the next chapter of this book. The Russian army did include the rank of *General-Field Marshal (General-Admiral)*, but did not issue promotions to this rank after 1898 (Count Dmitry Milyutin was the last Russian officer to receive a field marshal's baton), other than bestowing honorary batons to several foreign princes (among which King Carol I of Romania was the last recipient, in 1912). The only holder of the rank of *General-Admiral* during the period covered by this book was Grand Duke Alexei Alexandrovich, who received the rank in 1883.

Interestingly, the supreme commander of the armed forces, Tsar Nikolai II, held only the rank of *Colonel* in the Russian army. This was the rank that he had reached in 1894 at the time of the death of his father. Nikolai loved his father deeply, and as a mark of respect towards him refused to accept any promotion within the Russian military thereafter. This essentially meant that although he was the supreme military commander, every single general and admiral who served under him was superior in rank! It should be noted, however, that in 1908 the United Kingdom bestowed the honorary rank of *Admiral of the Fleet* upon the Tsar, and in 1915 the honorary rank of *Field Marshal*.

Even a brief perusal of the list of officers named in this book provides a glimpse at the broad spectrum of ethnic origins of these men. During the history of the Russian Empire, help in developing the economy and military of the empire had been requested from many European nations. Scots, Irishmen, Frenchmen, Germans, Swedes and others answered the call, and many of their descendants rose to senior rank in the Russian armed forces. Officers such as *General of Infantry* Aleksandr Preskott, *Lieutenant-General* Aleksandr Aleksandrovich Lesli, *Lieutenant-General* Prince Lyudovik Karlovich Lyudovik-Napoleon, *General of Infantry* Nikolai Baron von der Osten-Driesen, *General of Infantry* Count Aleksandr Adlerberg and *General of Artillery* Konstantin Petrovich Fan-der-Flit, testify to the ethnic diversity of the Imperial Russian army. Moreover, the territories comprising the Russian Empire, for example Finland, Kurdistan, or Latvia also provided general officers such as *Lieutenant-General* Baron Karl-Gustav-Emil Mannerheim, *Major-General* Ali-Ashraf-Agha-Shamshadinov Ali-Agiraf-Bek, and *Major-General* Avgust Ernestovich Misin. A particularly interesting personality was *Lieutenant-General of Naval Engineers* Mikhail Mikhailovich Yegipteos, who was a member of an Ethiopian princely family, but also had Greek nationality.

As is usual in most armies, officers who reached flag rank were older in years. In the ranks of the Imperial Russian military, the normal peacetime retirement age for a *Major-General* was 60 years. Officers of higher rank had their retirements deferred to an older age, and senior advisers to the Tsar were often kept on the active duty rolls (rank lists published annually by the Ministry of War) well into their seventies. Not surprisingly, among both the youngest and oldest serving generals were the Romanov Grand Dukes, members of the extended family of the Tsar who owed their careers more to their family ties than anything else.

It should be noted that the biographical information contained in this book spans the careers of the officers from the time they were promoted to flag rank.

**Structure of the armed forces**
During peacetime, command of the army at the highest level was overseen by the Minister of War, with the Minister of the Navy holding an equivalent responsibility over the Navy. Their ministries were divided into several Main Directorates, all headed by senior officers. In addition, the army and navy both had general staffs that oversaw the day-to-day administration of the military.

The highest peacetime army unit was the Military District, of which there were twelve in number. These Military Districts remained active even during wartime, serving mainly as bases for conscription, especially during World War I. Upon mobilization in July 1914, troops from the Military Districts were used to create Armies which were then sent to the various theaters of operations. These armies were grouped under "Fronts" that were designated according to their respective theaters (for example, Northwestern Front).

Subordinated to the Military Districts in peacetime, and to the Armies during the war, were corps of various designations: Guards Corps, Grenadier Corps, Army (= infantry) Corps, and Cavalry Corps. These units comprised Divisions, which in turn were made up of Brigades. A typical Infantry Division comprised two Infantry Brigades and an Artillery Brigade, while Cavalry Divisons were composed of two Cavalry Brigades and a Horse Artillery Battalion.

The Russian Navy had three main spheres of activity: the Baltic Sea, Black Sea and the Pacific. After the Pacific Fleet was destroyed by the Japanese in 1905, naval operations in the Far East effectively ceased, and the focus of attention switched to the Baltic and Black Sea. During World War I, naval activities in the Baltic were mainly defensive in nature, while the Black Sea Fleet became dominant in its area of operations throughout the war.

**Conclusion**
During Nikolai's reign, Russia was involved in two significant conflicts, the Russo-Japanese War in 1904 -1905, and World War I. Despite the size of its armed forces, Russia was soundly beaten by the Japanese and forced to sue for peace. Unfortunately for the Russian Empire, any lessons learned from the poor showing of its army and navy in the fight against Japan were not put to constructive use. Although Russia possessed the largest army in the world, the initial battles of World War I on the Eastern Front resulted in yet another series of decisive defeats at the hands of the Germans, and matters did not improve as the war dragged on. A combination of poor training, inadequate supplies, abysmal morale, and ineffective leadership, both at the front and in the high command, led to the Russian army suffering significant losses for no military tactical or strategic gain.

A total of 15 million men served in the Russian Army during World War I, of which an estimated 1.8 million were killed and a further 2.8 million wounded. These are only approximations, with different sources providing figures ranging from 1.5 million dead to 2.2 million. The lack of accurate statistics is regrettable but not surprising given the chaotic conditions in the front lines and the change in regime in 1917. By most accounts over 2 million Russian soldiers were captured and became prisoners of war.

Eventually, this sapping of manpower and the ever-decreasing morale of the soldiers in the trenches led to conditions that were ripe for revolution, and that is indeed what occurred in February 1917. Tired of the sacrifices of war, both at home and in the front lines, the Russians revolted in protest, and within a week the last Russian emperor's reign was over. Bowing to the inevitable, on March 2, 1917 (date based on the Julian calendar that was still in use in Russia at that time), Nikolai II abdicated and the four-hundred year old Russian Empire was no more. The fate of the last Tsar and his family, and indeed of Russia itself, is well known.

# Generals & Admirals of Imperial Russia, 1894 - 1917

*This list includes all officers who held the rank of General or Admiral during 20 October 1894 - 2 March 1917\*, from the ascension of Tsar Nikolai II to the throne until the Russian Empire ceased to exist upon his abdication.*
*(\* These dates correspond to the Julian calendar that was in effect during the period in question.)*

Table of ranks

|  |  |
|---|---|
| Генерал-фельдмаршал | General Field Marshal |
| Генерал-адмирал | General-Admiral |
| | |
| Генерал от артиллерии | General of Artillery |
| Генерал от кавалерии | General of Cavalry |
| Инженер-генерал | General of Engineers |
| Генерал от инфантерии | General of Infantry |
| Генерал по адмиралтейству | General of the Admiralty |
| Генерал флота | General of the Fleet |
| Генерал корпуса гидрографов | General of the Hydrographic Corps |
| Адмирал | Admiral |
| Действительный тайный советник | Actual Privy Councillor |
| | |
| Генерал-лейтенант | Lieutenant-General |
| Генерал-лейтенант по адмиралтейству | Lieutenant-General of the Admiralty |
| Генерал-лейтенант флота | Lieutenant-General of the Fleet |
| Генерал-лейтенант корпуса гидрографов | Lieutenant-General of the Hydrographic Corps |
| Вице-адмирал | Vice-Admiral |
| Тайный советник | Privy Councillor |
| Протопресвитер военного и морского духовенства | Protopresbyter, army and naval clergy |
| | |
| Генерал-майор | Major-General |
| Генерал-майор по адмиралтейству | Major-General of the Admiralty |
| Генерал-майор флота | Major-General of the Fleet |
| Генерал-майор корпуса гидрографов | Major-General of the Hydrographic Corps |
| Контр-адмирал | Rear-Admiral |
| Действительный статский советник | Actual State Councillor |
| Главные священники округов | Chief District Chaplain |
| | |
| Полковник | Colonel |
| Капитан 1-го ранга | Captain 1$^{st}$ Class (Navy) |

*Note: The rank of* Генерал-адъютант *(General-Adjutant) was accorded to officers of General rank and was used as an honorable distinction for senior military officials, giving them the right to report directly to the Emperor.*

*Lieutenant-General* Pavel Konstantinovich **Abakanovich** (31 Dec 1855 - Nov 1917)
| | |
|---|---|
| 12 Nov 1907: | Promoted to *Major-General* |
| 12 Nov 1907 - 21 Nov 1908: | Commander, 2$^{nd}$ Brigade, 32$^{nd}$ Infantry Division |
| 21 Nov 1908 - 2 May 1913: | Commander, 2$^{nd}$ Brigade, 42$^{nd}$ Infantry Division |
| 2 May 1913 - 5 Aug 1914: | Attached to Irkutsk Military District |
| 8 My 1914 - 3 Apr 1915: | Commander, 77$^{th}$ Infantry Brigade |
| 3 Apr 1915 - 11 Aug 1915: | Commander, 53$^{rd}$ Infantry Division |
| 13 Jun 1915: | Promoted to *Lieutenant-General* |
| 12 Aug 1915: | Retired |

*Lieutenant-General* Stanislav Konstantinovich **Abakanovich** (23 Mar 1860 - 13 Mar 1914)
| | |
|---|---|
| 1 Jun 1904 - 19 Feb 1907: | Commander, 58$^{th}$ Infantry Regiment |
| 16 Feb 1905: | Promoted to *Major-General* |
| 19 Feb 1907 - 19 Feb 1914: | Commander, 1$^{st}$ Brigade, 15$^{th}$ Infantry Division |
| 19 Feb 1914 - 13 Mar 1914: | Commander, 27$^{th}$ Infantry Division |
| 13 Mar 1914: | Promoted to *Lieutenant-General* |

*Major-General* Aleksandr Ivanovich **Abakovsky** (11 Apr 1856 - ?)
| | |
|---|---|
| 3 Dec 1901 - 31 Mar 1909: | Office Chief to Grand Duke Vladimir Alexandrovich |
| 13 Apr 1908: | Promoted to *Major-General* |
| 31 Mar 1909 - 2 Mar 1917: | Official of the Imperial Court |

*Lieutenant-General* Aleksandr Aleksandrovich **Abaleshev** (23 Feb 1871 - 2 Sep 1918)
| | |
|---|---|
| 17 Dec 1911 - 24 Dec 1913: | Commander, 2$^{nd}$ Life Hussar Regiment |
| 21 Dec 1913: | Promoted to *Major-General* |
| 24 Dec 1913 - 24 Jun 1915: | Commander, Life Guards Uhlan Regiment |
| 24 Jun 1915 - 27 Jun 1916: | Commander, Special Guards Cavalry Brigade |
| 27 Jun 1916 - 3 Dec 1916: | Commander, 1$^{st}$ Brigade, 3$^{rd}$ Guards Cavalry Division |
| 3 Dec 1916 - 1917: | Commander, 2$^{nd}$ Guards Cavalry Division |
| 1917: | Promoted to *Lieutenant-General* |

*Lieutenant -General* Solomon Iosifovich **Abamelikov** (20 Nov 1853 - ?)
| | |
|---|---|
| 28 Apr 1906 - 20 Nov 1913: | Commander of Artillery, Fortress Kaunas |
| 6 Dec 1906: | Promoted to *Major-General* |
| 20 Nov 1913: | Promoted to *Lieutenant-General* |
| 20 Nov 1913: | Retired |

*Major-General* Prince Dmitry Rostomovich **Abashidze** (8 Sep 1856 - ?)
| | |
|---|---|
| 17 Sep 1912 - 29 Jul 1914: | At the disposal of the Minister of War |
| 3 Feb 1913: | Promoted to *Major-General* |
| 29 Jul 1914 - 8 Sep 1915: | Commander, Brigade, 12$^{th}$ Siberian Rifle Division |
| 8 Sep 1915 - 1917: | Reserve officer, 6$^{th}$ Army |

*Major-General* Konstantin Georgievich **Abashidze** (2 Jun 1856 - 7 Oct 1917)
| | |
|---|---|
| 3 Aug 1912: | Promoted to *Major-General* |
| 3 Aug 1912 - 12 May 1916: | Commander, 47$^{th}$ Artillery Brigade |
| 12 May 1916 - 1 Nov 1916: | Inspector of Artillery, XLVI. Army Corps |
| 1 Nov 1916 - 1917: | Reserve officer, Minsk Military District |

*Lieutenant-General* Dmitry Konstantinovich **Abatsiev** (3 Dec 1857 - 4 Jun 1936)
| | |
|---|---|
| 23 May 1904 - 9 Jul 1906: | Commander, Ussuri Cossack Regiment |
| 28 Mar 1906: | Promoted to *Major-General* |
| 9 Jul 1906 - 6 Jan 1907: | Attached to the Caucasus Military District |
| 6 Jan 1907 - 9 Oct 1912: | Commander, 2$^{nd}$ Brigade, 1$^{st}$ Caucasus Cossack Division |
| 9 Oct 1912: | Promoted to *Lieutenant-General* |
| 9 Oct 1912 - 14 Jun 1916: | Commander, 2$^{nd}$ Caucasus Cossack Division |
| 14 Jun 1916 - 15 Sep 1917: | Commanding General, VI. Caucasus Army Corps |
| 15 Sep 1917 - Oct 1917: | Reserve officer, Caucasus Military District |

*Vice-Admiral* Alexey Mikhailovich **Abaza** (30 Apr 1853 - 3 Feb 1917)
| | |
|---|---|
| 29 Nov 1899 - 10 Nov 1902: | Commander of the Naval Guards |
| 1 Apr 1901: | Promoted to *Rear-Admiral* |
| 10 Nov 1902 - 20 Jan 1903: | Deputy Chief, Ministry of Merchant Shipping and Ports |
| 20 Jan 1903 - 10 Oct 1903: | Acting Deputy Minister of Merchant Shipping and Ports |
| 10 Oct 1903 - 13 Jun 1905: | Head of Special Committee on the Far East |
| 13 Jun 1905 - 11 Jan 1910: | Admiral à la suite |
| 11 Jan 1910: | Promoted to *Vice-Admiral* |
| 11 Jan 1910: | Retired |

*Lieutenant-General* Viktor Afanasyevich **Abaza** (24 Jan 1831 - 6 Jul 1898)
| | |
|---|---|
| 1 Mar 1868 - 20 Jan 1874: | At the disposal of the Main Artillery Directorate |
| 20 Jan 1874: | Promoted to *Major-General* |
| 20 Jan 1874: | Retired |
| 4 Apr 1877 - 6 Jul 1898: | Recalled; At the disposal of the Main Artillery Directorate |
| 30 Aug 1893: | Promoted to *Lieutenant-General* |

*Major-General of the Admiralty* Vladimir Alekseyevich **Abaza** (3 Jun 1854 - 1916)
| | |
|---|---|
| ?: | Promoted to *Major-General of the Admiralty* |

*Major-General* Anatoly Nikolayevich **Abdulov** (9 Dec 1861 - ?)
| | |
|---|---|
| 31 Oct 1912 - 29 Apr 1915: | Military Judge, Caucasus Military District Court |
| 6 Dec 1912: | Promoted to *Major-General* |
| 29 Apr 1915 - 1917: | Military Judge, Western Front |

*Lieutenant-General* Nikolai Filippovich **Abdulov** (9 May 1833 - ?)
| | |
|---|---|
| 21 Aug 1894 - 8 Jul 1900: | Director, Volskaya Military School |
| 1 Jan 1895: | Promoted to *Major-General* |
| 8 Jul 1900: | Promoted to *Lieutenant-General* |
| 8 Jul 1900: | Retired |

*Major-General* Istlyam Isakovich **Abdurakhmanov** (24 Dec 1848 - Feb 1909)
| | |
|---|---|
| 11 May 1907 - 1909: | Staff Officer, Irkutsk Military District |
| 1909: | Promoted to *Major-General* |

*Rear-Admiral* Aleksandr Georgiyevich **Abramov** (17 Jan 1857 - ?)
| | |
|---|---|
| 13 Oct 1908 - 1 Nov 1911: | Chief of Section 1, Baltic Fleet Machinist School |
| 1 Nov 1911: | Promoted to *Rear-Admiral* |
| 1 Nov 1911: | Retired |

*Lieutenant-General* Fyodor Fyodorovich **Abramov** (21 Feb 1848 - 10 Aug 1913)
| | |
|---|---|
| 6 Dec 1902: | Promoted to *Major-General* |
| 6 Dec 1902 - 22 Apr 1904: | Military Commander, Rostov District |
| 22 Apr 1904 - 20 Jul 1904: | Ataman, 2$^{nd}$ Don District |
| 20 Jul 1904 - 18 May 1906: | Commander, 2$^{nd}$ Brigade, 4$^{th}$ Don Cossack Division |
| 1905: | Acting Commander, 4$^{th}$ Don Cossack Division |
| 18 May 1906 - 17 Jan 1910: | Commander, 1$^{st}$ Brigade, 1$^{st}$ Don Cossack Division |
| 17 Jan 1910: | Promoted to *Lieutenant-General* |
| 17 Jan 1910: | Discharged |

*Major-General* Fyodor Fyodorovich **Abramov** (23 Dec 1870 - 8 Mar 1963)
| | |
|---|---|
| 15 Jun 1912 - 10 Jan 1914: | Commander, 1$^{st}$ Uhlan Regiment |
| 10 Jan 1914: | Promoted to *Major-General* |
| 10 Jan 1914 - Jan 1915: | Commandant, Tver Cavalry School |
| Jan 1915 - Apr 1915: | Quartermaster-General, 12$^{th}$ Army |
| Apr 1915 - 12 Sep 1915: | Commander, Brigade, Cossack Division |
| 12 Sep 1915 - 21 Nov 1916: | Commander, 15$^{th}$ Cavalry Division |
| Nov 1916: | Promoted to *Lieutenant-General* |
| 21 Nov 1916 - Feb 1917: | Chief of Staff, Don Cossacks |
| 25 Apr 1917 - May 1917: | Commander, 2$^{nd}$ Turkestan Cossack Division |
| May 1917 - 25 Jun 1918: | Commander, 1$^{st}$ Don Cossack Division |

*Major-General* Sergey Mikhailovich **Abramov** (1 Nov 1867 - ?)
| | |
|---|---|
| 4 Sep 1914 - Jul 1916: | Military Judge, Turkestan Military District Court |
| 6 Dec 1915: | Promoted to *Major-General* |
| Jul 1916 - 1917: | Military Judge, Amur Military District Court |

*Major-General* Vladimir Nikolayevich **Abramov** (21 Jan 1862 - 2 Nov 1920)
| | |
|---|---|
| 14 Aug 1906 - 28 Feb 1908: | Military Judge, Irkutsk Military District Court |
| 1906: | Promoted to *Major-General* |
| 28 Feb 1908 - 28 Mar 1913: | Military Judge, Vilnius Military District Court |
| 28 Mar 1913 - 1917: | Military Judge, Odessa Military District Court |

*Major-General* Sergey Semyonovich **Abramovich-Baranovsky** (22 Apr 1866 - May 1941)
| | |
|---|---|
| 15 Nov 1902 - 1917: | Professor, Military Law Academy |
| 6 Dec 1909: | Promoted to *Major-General* |

*Lieutenant-General* Georgy Nazarovich **Abrezov** (23 Apr 1853 - 25 Jul 1917)
| | |
|---|---|
| 6 Dec 1907 - 1912: | Ataman, Mozdok Division, Terek Cossack Army |
| 18 Apr 1910: | Promoted to *Major-General* |
| 1912: | Promoted to *Lieutenant-General* |
| 1912: | Retired |

*Major-General* Nikolai Vladimirovich **Abutkov** (25 Jul 1873 - 7 Feb 1920)
25 Oct 1916 - 12 May 1917: Attached to the Headquarters, 4th Army
6 Dec 1916: Promoted to *Major-General*

*Major-General* Nikolai Adolfovich **Abzholtovsky** (30 Jan 1862 - 26 Dec 1919)
2 Jul 1913: Promoted to *Major-General*
2 Jul 1913 - 29 Jul 1914: Commander, 1st Brigade, 11th Infantry Division
29 Jul 1914 - 26 Apr 1916: Commander, 1st Brigade, 78th Infantry Division
26 Apr 1916 - Oct 1917: Commander, 3rd Rifle Division

*Major-General* Mikhail Alekseyevich **Adabash** (5 Aug 1864 - ?)
29 Jul 1909 - 25 Feb 1912: Commander, 6th Grenadier Regiment
25 Feb 1912: Promoted to *Major-General*
25 Dec 1912: Retired

*General of Infantry* Anton Sigismundovich **Adamovich** (16 Dec 1831 - 20 Jul 1911)
2 Feb 1872 - 27 Apr 1890: Military Judge, Kazan Military District Court
30 Aug 1882: Promoted to *Major-General*
27 Apr 1890 - 31 Aug 1890: Military Prosecutor, Moscow Military District
31 Aug 1890 - 1906: Chairman of the Military Tribunal, Odessa Military District
30 Aug 1893: Promoted to *Lieutenant-General*
1906: Promoted to *General of Infantry*
1906: Retired

*Lieutenant-General* Boris Viktorovich **Adamovich** (15 Nov 1870 - 22 Mar 1936)
22 May 1909 - 20 Sep 1914: Commandant, Vilnius Infantry Cadet School
14 Apr 1913: Promoted to *Major-General*
20 Sep 1914 - 3 Jul 1915: Commander, Kexholmsky Life Guards Regiment
Aug 1915 - 5 Jan 1916: Commander, 2nd Brigade, 3rd Guards Infantry Division
5 Jan 1916 - 13 Oct 1917: General for Special Purposes to the Minister of War
13 Oct 1917: Promoted to *Lieutenant-General*
13 Oct 1917: Retired

*General of Artillery* Leonid Yefremovich **Adamovich** (15 Apr 1832 - 8 Feb 1911)
19 Jul 1875 - 2 Nov 1876: Commander of Artillery, St. Petersburg Garrison
30 Aug 1875: Promoted to *Major-General*
2 Nov 1876 - 13 Oct 1878: Deputy Chief of Artillery of the Army
13 Oct 1878 - 2 Dec 1883: Deputy Commander of Artillery, St. Petersburg Military District
2 Dec 1883 - 22 Apr 1888: Commander of Artillery, XIV. Army Corps
30 Aug 1885: Promoted to *Lieutenant-General*
22 Apr 1888 - 15 Feb 1893: Commander of Artillery, Grenadier Corps
15 Feb 1893 - 17 Aug 1895: Commander of Artillery, St. Petersburg Military District
17 Aug 1895 - 10 Jan 1902: Commanding General, XVIII. Army Corps
6 Dec 1898: Promoted to *General of Artillery*
10 Jan 1902 - 3 Jan 1906: Member, Committee for Wounded Veterans
3 Jan 1906: Retired

*Major-General* Mikhail Yefremovich **Adamovich** (22 Jan 1839 - ?)
12 Sep 1885 - 6 Sep 1891:           Commander, 20$^{th}$ Dragoon Regiment
6 Sep 1891:                         Promoted to *Major-General*
6 Sep 1891 - Dec 1896:              Commander, 1$^{st}$ Brigade, 12$^{th}$ Cavalry Division

*Major-General* Viktor Mikhailovich **Adamovich** (6 Aug 1839 - 1903)
4 May 1898 - 1903:                  Chief of Moscow Military Hospital
6 Dec 1898:                         Promoted to *Major-General*

*Lieutenant-General* August-Karl-Mikhail Mikhailovich **Adaridi** (26 Aug 1859 - 15 Nov 1940)
19 Mar 1903 - 18 Jul 1905:          Commander, 98$^{th}$ Infantry Regiment
18 Feb 1905:                        Promoted to *Major-General*
18 Jul 1905 - 3 Oct 1906:           Attached to the General Staff
3 Oct 1906 - 29 Dec 1909:           Member, Military Commission on the history of the Russo-Japanese War
29 Dec 1909 - 2 Apr 1914:           Chief of Staff, XII. Army Corps
2 Apr 1914:                         Promoted to *Lieutenant-General*
2 Apr 1914 - 2 Feb 1915:            Commander, 27$^{th}$ Infantry Division
2 Feb 1915:                         Retired

*Major-General* Yevtikhy Konstantinovich **Adasovsky** (6 Apr 1846 - 23 Jan 1898)
25 Aug 1892 - 23 Jan 1898:          Commander of Artillery Training Polygon, St. Petersburg Military District
14 May 1896:                        Promoted to *Major-General*

*General of Cavalry* Nikolai Osipovich **Adelson** (30 Aug 1829 - 25 Feb 1901)
11 Aug 1874 - 25 Feb 1901:          Commandant of St. Petersburg
1 Jan 1878:                         Promoted to *Major-General*
30 Aug 1888:                        Promoted to *Lieutenant-General*
9 Apr 1900:                         Promoted to *General of Cavalry*

*General of Infantry* Count Aleksandr Aleksandrovich **Adlerberg** (11 Jul 1849 - 9 Apr 1931)
31 Oct 1899:                        Promoted to *Major-General*
31 Oct 1899 - 15 Feb 1900:          Commander, 1$^{st}$ Brigade, 20$^{th}$ Infantry Division
15 Feb 1900 - 27 Jun 1906:          Commander, 2$^{nd}$ Brigade, 23$^{rd}$ Infantry Division
27 Jun 1906 - 10 Jan 1907:          Commander, 24$^{th}$ Infantry Division
30 Jul 1906:                        Promoted to *Lieutenant-General*
10 Jan 1907 - 24 Jun 1908:          Commander, 2$^{nd}$ Guards Infantry Division
24 Jun 1908 - 15 May 1912:          Commanding General, II. Army Corps
24 Apr 1912:                        Promoted to *General of Infantry*
15 May 1912:                        Retired
5 Oct 1914 - 12 Aug 1915:           Reserve officer, Minsk Military District
12 Aug 1915 - 1916:                 At the disposal of the Supreme Commander-in-Chief
1916 - 28 Apr 1917:                 Inspector of Replacement Troops
28 Apr 1917:                        Retired

*Major-General* Aleksandr Aleksandrovich **Adrianov** (7 Dec 1861 - 9 Mar 1918)
| | |
|---|---|
| 10 Nov 1906 - 31 Oct 1907: | Military Judge, Moscow Military District Court |
| 22 Apr 1907: | Promoted to *Major-General* |
| 31 Oct 1907 - 14 Feb 1908: | Military Judge, St. Petersburg Military District Court |
| 14 Feb 1908 - 30 May 1915: | Mayor of Moscow |
| 30 May 1915 - Mar 1917: | General à la suite |

*Major-General* Lev Georgievich **Afanasyev** (22 Feb 1853 - 6 Jan 1911)
| | |
|---|---|
| 17 Apr 1901 - 6 Jan 1911: | Chairman, Kharkov Region Remount Commission |
| 6 Dec 1906: | Promoted to *Major-General* |

*Major-General* Lukyan Vasilievich **Afanasyev** (29 Jun 1869 - 1934)
| | |
|---|---|
| 1914 - 2 Feb 1916: | Commander, 27$^{th}$ Siberian Rifle Regiment |
| 21 Oct 1915: | Promoted to *Major-General* |
| 2 Feb 1916 - 29 Nov 1916: | Commander, 2$^{nd}$ Brigade, Caucasus Grenadier Division |
| 29 Nov 1916 - 1917: | Commander, 134$^{th}$ Infantry Division |

*Lieutenant-General* Mikhail Grigoryevich **Afanasyev** (6 Sep 1850 - ?)
| | |
|---|---|
| 4 Jun 1905 - 1912: | Quartermaster-General, Fortress Warsaw |
| 6 Dec 1908: | Promoted to *Major-General* |
| 1912: | Promoted to *Lieutenant-General* |
| 1912: | Retired |

*Lieutenant-General* Mikhail Yemelyanovich **Afanasyev** (23 Jan 1857 - 22 Feb 1936)
| | |
|---|---|
| 13 Feb 1903 - 27 Feb 1906: | Military Judge, Amur Military District Court |
| 28 Mar 1904: | Promoted to *Major-General* |
| 27 Feb 1906 - 15 Mar 1907: | Military Judge, Warsaw Military District Court |
| 15 Mar 1907 - 19 Apr 1909: | Military Judge, Amur Military District Court |
| 19 Apr 1909 - 12 Feb 1910: | Attached to the Ministry of Finance |
| 6 Dec 1911: | Promoted to *Lieutenant-General* |
| 6 Dec 1911 - 1917: | Deputy Administrator, Chinese Eastern Railway |

*Major-General* Nikolai Ivanovich **Afanasyev** (25 Dec 1837 - ?)
| | |
|---|---|
| 11 Sep 1892 - 1901: | Commander of Gendarmerie, Astrakhan Province |
| 18 Apr 1899: | Promoted to *Major-General* |

*Major-General* Nikolai Nikolayevich **Afanasyev** (9 May 1862 - ?)
| | |
|---|---|
| 26 May 1910 - 1913: | Chief of Tsarskoye Selo Military Housing Allocation Office |
| 1913: | Promoted to *Major-General* |
| 1913: | Retired |
| 9 Aug 1914 - 1917: | Recalled; Attached to the Ministry of War |

*Major-General of the Fleet* Nikolai Vasilyevich **Afanasyev** (2 Dec 1871 - ?)
| | |
|---|---|
| 1914 - 1917: | Deputy Chief, Mechanical Section, Main Directorate of Shipbuilding & Supply |
| 30 Jun 1915: | Promoted to *Major-General of the Fleet* |

*Major-General* Pavel Panteleimonovich **Afanasyev** (30 Aug 1865 - 1949)
Feb 1917 - 1917:                    Commander, Brigade, 184th Infantry Division
4 Mar 1917:                         Promoted to *Major-General*

*Major-General* Sergey Konstantinovich **Afanasyev** (8 Oct 1871 - ?)
1910 - 2 Oct 1915:                  Chief of Military Housing Allocation, Irkutsk Military District
22 Mar 1915:                        Promoted to *Major-General*
2 Oct 1915 - 1917:                  Section Chief, Main Directorate for Troop Billeting

*Lieutenant-General of Naval Engineers* Vasily Ivanovich **Afanasyev** (22 Dec 1843 - 1913)
1894 - 1906:                        Inspector of Mechanics, Naval Technical Committee
1897:                               Promoted to *Major-General of Naval Engineers*
1906:                               Promoted to *Lieutenant-General of Naval Engineers*
1906:                               Retired

*Lieutenant-General* Vasily Ivanovich **Afanasyev** (2 Mar 1848 - 19 May 1906)
10 Jul 1884 - 1 May 1897:           Section Chief, General Staff
30 Aug 1894:                        Promoted to *Major-General*
1 May 1897 - 11 Feb 1898:           Attached to the General Staff
11 Feb 1898 - 19 May 1906:          Head of the Troop Mobilization Committee
6 Dec 1900:                         Promoted to *Lieutenant-General*

*Lieutenant-General* Vasily Vasilievich **Afanasyev** (1 Jan 1838 - ?)
20 Jan 1892 - 1909:                 Chief of Mine Section, Electro-Technical Engineering Department
30 Aug 1892:                        Promoted to *Major-General*
6 Jun 1907:                         Promoted to *Lieutenant-General*
1909:                               Retired

*Lieutenant-General* Vladimir Dmitriyevich **Afanasyev** (1 Feb 1853 - ?)
3 Mar 1904:                         Promoted to *Major-General*
3 Mar 1904 - 4 May 1907:            Commander, 20th Artillery Brigade
4 May 1907 - 21 Mar 1908:           Commander of Artillery, II. Caucasus Army Corps
14 Oct 1907:                        Promoted to *Lieutenant-General*
21 Mar 1908 - 3 Apr 1917:           Commander of Artillery, Caucasus Military District
3 Apr 1917 - 18 Apr 1917:           Chief of Artillery Logistics, Caucasus Army
18 Apr 1917 - 24 Aug 1917:          Reserve officer, Caucasus Military District
24 Aug 1917:                        Dismissed

*Major-General* Vladimir Moiseyevich **Afanasyev** (14 Jun 1868 - ?)
16 Aug 1914 - 30 Jan 1916:          Commander, 328th Infantry Regiment
27 Aug 1915:                        Promoted to *Major-General*
30 Jan 1916 - 26 Nov 1916:          Reserve Officer, Kiev Military District
26 Nov 1916 - 5 Jun 1917:           Commander, Brigade, 115th Infantry Division
5 Jun 1917 - 27 Sep 1917:           Commander, 8th Rifle Division
27 Sep 1917 - ?:                    Commander, 10th Rifle Division

*Lieutenant-General* Kaetan Kaetanovich **Affanasovich** (29 May 1854 - ?)
| | |
|---|---|
| 16 Jun 1903 - 20 Jun 1908: | Military Judge, Kazan Military District Court |
| 6 Dec 1903: | Promoted to *Major-General* |
| 20 Jun 1908 - 28 May 1909: | Military Judge, St. Petersburg Military District Court |
| 28 May 1909 - 9 Mar 1912: | Military Prosecutor, Caucasus Military District |
| 6 Dec 1911: | Promoted to *Lieutenant-General* |
| 9 Mar 1912 - 1915: | Chairman of the Military Tribunal, Turkestan Military District |

*Lieutenant-General* Viktor Konstantinovich **Affanasovich** (8 Oct 1846 - 3 Jun 1908)
| | |
|---|---|
| 19 Apr 1895: | Promoted to *Major-General* |
| 19 Apr 1895 - 15 Nov 1901: | Deputy Chief of Staff, St. Petersburg Military District |
| 15 Nov 1901 - 23 Oct 1904: | Commander, 22$^{nd}$ Infantry Division |
| 6 Dec 1902: | Promoted to *Lieutenant-General* |
| 23 Oct 1904 - 27 May 1905: | Attached to the General Staff |
| 27 May 1905 - 1906: | At the disposal of the Minister of War |

*Lieutenant-General* Mikhail Yemelyanovich **Afonasyev** (23 Jan 1857 - 22 Mar 1936)
| | |
|---|---|
| 13 Feb 1903 - 27 Feb 1906: | Military Judge, Amur Military District Court |
| 28 Mar 1904: | Promoted to *Major-General* |
| 27 Feb 1906 - 15 Mar 1907: | Military Judge, Warsaw Military District Court |
| 15 Mar 1907 - 19 Apr 1909: | Military Judge, Amur Military District Court |
| 19 Apr 1909 - 12 Feb 1910: | At the disposal of the Minister of Finance |
| 12 Feb 1910 - 6 Dec 1911: | Military Judge, Amur Military District Court |
| 6 Dec 1911: | Promoted to *Lieutenant-General* |
| 6 Dec 1911 - 1917: | Deputy Director of the Chinese Eastern Railway |

*Major-General* Mikhail Aleksandrovich **Afrosimov** (19 Aug 1864 - ?)
| | |
|---|---|
| 1 Jan 1911 - 22 May 1916: | Commander, 27$^{th}$ Borderguard Brigade |
| 14 Apr 1913: | Promoted to *Major-General* |
| 22 May 1916 - 1917: | Reserve Officer, Kiev Military District |

*General of Artillery* Pyotr Petrovich **Agafonov** (25 Sep 1823 - 24 May 1898)
| | |
|---|---|
| 5 Sep 1877 - 9 Dec 1888: | Commander, 17$^{th}$ Artillery Brigade |
| 30 Aug 1879: | Promoted to *Major-General* |
| 9 Dec 1888 - 4 Jul 1892: | Commander of Artillery, II. Army Corps |
| 30 Aug 1889: | Promoted to *Lieutenant-General* |
| 4 Jul 1892 - 27 Nov 1893: | Unassigned |
| 27 Nov 1893 - 1895: | At the disposal of the Main Artillery Directorate |
| 1895: | Promoted to *General of Artillery* |
| 1895: | Retired |

*General of Infantry* Nikolai Yeremeyevich **Agapeyev** (6 May 1849 - ?)
| | |
|---|---|
| 24 Dec 1889 - 3 Jan 1899: | Quartermaster-General, Finland Military District |
| 14 May 1896: | Promoted to *Major-General* |
| 3 Jan 1899 - 28 Feb 1904: | Quartermaster-General, Vilnius Military District |
| 28 Feb 1904 - 7 May 1912: | Quartermaster-General, Caucasus Military District |
| 6 Dec 1904: | Promoted to *Lieutenant-General* |

7 May 1912:                        Promoted to *General of Infantry*
7 May 1912:                        Retired

*Lieutenant-General* Pyotr Yeremeyevich **Agapeyev** (9 Jul 1839 - ?)
18 Jun 1891:                       Promoted to *Major-General*
13 Jun 1891 - 22 Jun 1898:         Commander, 2nd Brigade, 7th Infantry Division
22 Jun 1898 - 20 Oct 1899:         Commander, 47th Reserve Infantry Brigade
6 Dec 1899:                        Promoted to *Lieutenant-General*
20 Oct 1899 - 16 Jun 1901:         Commander, 18th Infantry Division
16 Jun 1901 - 21 Oct 1902:         Commander, 10th Infantry Division
21 Oct 1902:                       Retired

*Major-General* Sergey Ivanovich **Agapeyev** (22 Aug 1868 - 23 Sep 1916)
12 Sep 1911 - 11 Nov 1914:         Commander, 4th Rifle Artillery Battalion
11 Nov 1914:                       Promoted to *Major-General*
11 Nov 1914:                       Retired

*Major-General* Vladimir Petrovich **Agapeyev** (9 Jun 1876 - 6 May 1956)
26 Jul 1915 - 10 Nov 1915:         Commander, 2nd Life Hussar Regiment
10 Nov 1915 - 21 Dec 1915:         Unassigned
16 Jul 1916:                       Promoted to *Major-General*
21 Dec 1915 - 24 Feb 1917:         Chief of Staff, VI. Cavalry Corps
24 Feb 1917 - 30 Aug 1917:         Chief of Staff, XXXV. Army Corps
30 Aug 1917 - 1918:                Chief of Staff, Polish Corps

*Major-General* Vsevolod Nikolayevich **Agapeyev** (20 Apr 1877 - 22 Feb 1948)
7 Oct 1916 - 9 Mar 1917:           Chief of Staff, 124th Infantry Division
6 Dec 1916:                        Promoted to *Major-General*
9 Mar 1917 - 18 Nov 1917:          Chief of Staff, Kiev Military District
18 Nov 1917:                       Dismissed

*Major-General* Aleksei Alekseyevich **Agapov** (14 Sep 1855 - 1912)
13 Aug 1906 - Sep 1908:            Director, Voronezh Cadet Corps
1906:                              Promoted to *Major-General*
Sep 1908:                          Dismissed

*Lieutenant-General* Pavel Osipovich **Agapov** (23 Aug 1862 - ?)
3 Nov 1906 - 13 Sep 1910:          Deputy Chief of Cossack Section, General Staff
6 Dec 1906:                        Promoted to *Major-General*
3 Mar 1910 - 1 Sep 1910:           Acting Chief of Cossack Section, General Staff
13 Sep 1910 - 12 Jan 1918:         Chief of Cossack Section, General Staff
14 Apr 1913:                       Promoted to *Lieutenant-General*

*Major-General* Pyotr Osipovich **Agapov** (6 Jun 1851 - 15 Feb 1910)
19 Sep 1903 - 15 Feb 1910:         Ataman, 3rd Detachment, Orenburg Cossack Army
6 Dec 1906:                        Promoted to *Major-General*

*General of Cavalry* Aleksandr Aleksandrovich **Agasi-Beck-Avsharov** (25 Sep 1833 - 29 Jan 1907)
17 Mar 18877 - 14 Jul 1883: Commander, 5<sup>th</sup> Uhlan Regiment
14 Jul 1883: Promoted to *Major-General*
14 Jul 1883 - 27 Apr 1885: Commander, 1<sup>st</sup> Brigade, 8<sup>th</sup> Cavalry Division
27 Apr 1885 - 3 Jun 1885: Commander, 2<sup>nd</sup> Brigade, 12<sup>th</sup> Cavalry Division
25 Jun 1885 - 3 May 1897: Commander, 6<sup>th</sup> Reserve Cavalry Brigade
14 May 1896: Promoted to *Lieutenant-General*
3 May 1897 - 3 Feb 1902: Commandant of the Officers Cavalry School
3 Feb 1902 - 14 Feb 1906: Attached to the Inspector-General of Cavalry
14 Feb 1906: Promoted to *General of Cavalry*
14 Feb 1906: Retired

*Major-General* Aleksei Petrovich **Ageyev** (16 Oct 1852 - ?)
27 Sep 1904: Promoted to *Major-General*
27 Sep 1904 - 1906: Commander of Artillery, Fortress Sveaborg

*Major-General* Aleksandr Apollonovich von **Agte** (3 Mar 1859 - ?)
14 Aug 1913 - 1915: Director, Irkutsk Cadet Corps
6 Dec 1913: Promoted to *Major-General*
1915: Retired

*Major-General* Antonin Apollonovich von **Agte** (8 Sep 1857 - 12 Jan 1919)
20 Dec 1911: Promoted to *Major-General*
20 Dec 1911 - 1917: Commander, Fortress Vladivostok Sapper Brigade

*Major-General* Ivan Apollonovich von **Agte** (22 Jan 1866 - 8 Feb 1922)
3 Apr 1913 - 1917: Military Judge, Kazan Military District Court
14 Apr 1913: Promoted to *Major-General*

*Major-General* Leonid Yulievich von **Akerman** (24 Jul 1852 - ?)
23 Aug 1905 - 21 Nov 1907: Commander, 35<sup>th</sup> Artillery Brigade
30 May 1907: Promoted to *Major-General*

*General of Infantry* Nikolai Yulievich **Akerman** (27 Apr 1840 - 28 Nov 1907)
10 Apr 1886 - 31 Aug 1888: Chief of Staff, Trans-Baikal Military District
30 Aug 1887: Promoted to *Major-General*
31 Aug 1888 - 24 Jul 1891: Commandant of Fortress Vladivostok
24 Jul 1891 - 7 Feb 1894: Chief of Staff, Fortress Kaunas
7 Feb 1894 - 19 Jun 1896: Commander, 58<sup>th</sup> Replacement Infantry Brigade
19 Jun 1896 - 8 May 1898: Commandant of Fortress Kerch
8 May 1898 - 27 Apr 1903: Commander, 2<sup>nd</sup> Infantry Division
6 Dec 1898: Promoted to *Lieutenant-General*
27 Apr 1903: Promoted to *General of Infantry*
27 Apr 1903: Retired

*Major-General* Aleksandr Konstantinovich **Akhmatov** (20 Aug 1867 - 7 Apr 1918)
6 Apr 1911 - 1918: Director, 2<sup>nd</sup> Orenburg Cadet Corps

25 Mar 1912:                          Promoted to *Major-General*

*General of Engineers* Veniamin Ivanovich **Akhsharumov** (18 Dec 1826 - Jun 1907)
14 Dec 1859 - Jun 1907:           Chairman of the Land Survey Office
17 Apr 1863:                          Promoted to *Major-General*
26 Feb 1873:                          Promoted to *Lieutenant-General*
9 Apr 1889:                           Promoted to *General of Engineers*

*Major-General* Ivan Vasilievich **Akhverdov** (29 Jul 1873 - 28 Apr 1931)
1 May 1915 - 11 May 1916:         Commander, 3rd Finnish Rifle Regiment
22 Oct 1915:                          Promoted to *Major-General*
11 May 1916 - 26 Jul 1916:        Chief of Staff, 127th Infantry Division
26 Jul 1916 - Feb 1917:           Chief of Staff, II. Caucasus Cavalry Corps

*Major-General* Nikolai Nikolayevich **Akhverdov** (15 Oct 1841 - 4 May 1908)
29 Nov 1897 - 26 Mar 1898:        Chief of Staff, 11th Replacement Cavalry Brigade
23 Mar 1898:                          Promoted to *Major-General*
26 Mar 1898 - 28 Nov 1901:        Commander, 6th Replacement Cavalry Brigade
28 Nov 1901 - May 1902:           Commander, 1st Replacement Cavalry Brigade
May 1902:                             Retired

*Major-General* Vladimir Nikolayevich **Akhverdov** (30 May 1847 - 24 Feb 1908)
9 Apr 1904 - 24 Feb 1908:         Intendant, Guards Corps
1908:                                 Promoted to *Major-General*

*Major-General* Yasen Aleksandrovich **Akhvlediani** (7 Apr 1852 - 1940)
18 Mar 1908 - 13 Jan 1911:        Commandant, Fortress Abbas-Tuman
6 Dec 1910:                           Promoted to *Major-General*
13 Jan 1911 - 1912:               Reserve officer
1912:                                 Retired

*Major-General* Isai Isaevich **Akimov** (5 Jul 1858 - 2 Mar 1917)
6 Apr 1911 - 11 Jan 1916:         Commander, 7th Mortar Artillery Regiment
23 Oct 1914:                          Promoted to *Major-General*
11 Jan 1916 - 2 May 1916:         Commander, 5th Artillery Brigade
2 May 1916 - 2 Mar 1917:          Commander, 1st Reserve Artillery Brigade

*Major-General* Mikhail Vasilievich **Akimov** (13 Oct 1867 - ?)
6 Dec 1915:                           Promoted to *Major-General*
6 Dec 1915 - 1917:                Deputy Quartermaster-General, Ministry of War

*General of Cavalry* Nikolai Agafonovich **Akimov** (30 Oct 1842 - ?)
3 Jan 1886 - 11 Mar 1894:         Brigade Commander, Crimean Borderguard
5 Apr 1892:                           Promoted to *Major-General*
11 Mar 1894 - 1 Jul 1899:         Commander, St. Petersburg Borderguard Brigade
1 Jul 1899 - 9 Mar 1901:          Commander, 5th Borderguard District
9 Apr 1900:                           Promoted to *Lieutenant-General*
9 Mar 1901 - 1 Dec 1908:          Commander, 1st Borderguard District

20 Dec 1908: Promoted to *General of Cavalry*
20 Dec 1908: Retired

*Lieutenant-General* Nikolai Isaevich **Akimov** (20 Nov 1844 - ?)
31 Jul 1899 - 29 Nov 1903: Commander of Engineers, Fortress Novogeorgiyevsk
9 Apr 1900: Promoted to *Major-General*
29 Nov 1903 - 1 Dec 1908: Deputy Commander of Engineers, Kiev Military District
1 Dec 1908 - 20 Dec 1908: Engineer Inspector, Omsk Military District
20 Dec 1908 - Jan 1911: Commander of Engineers, Vilnius Military District
29 Mar 1909: Promoted to *Lieutenant-General*
Jan 1911: Retired

*Major-General* Vladimir Nikolayevich **Akimov** (18 May 1856 - ?)
1910: Retired
12 Nov 1914 - 1917: Recalled; Special Assignments Officer to the Military Governor of Dagestan
12 Nov 1914: Promoted to *Major-General*

*Major-General* Konstantin Mikhailovich **Akinfiyev** (5 May 1833 - ?)
30 Oct 1885 - 25 Oct 1895: Commander, 130$^{th}$ Infantry Regiment
14 Nov 1894: Promoted to *Major-General*
25 Oct 1895 - 4 Dec 1895: Commander, 1$^{st}$ Brigade, 28$^{th}$ Infantry Division
4 Dec 1895 - 4 Mar 1896: Commander, 1$^{st}$ Brigade, 5$^{th}$ Infantry Division
4 Mar 1896 - 24 Oct 1899: Commander, 1$^{st}$ Brigade, 9$^{th}$ Infantry Division

*Lieutenant-General* Georgy Vasilievich **Akishev** (30 Jan 1858 - 22 Jun 1915)
1 Mar 1908 - 17 May 1910: Deputy Quartermaster-General, Kiev Military District
6 Dec 1909: Promoted to *Major-General*
17 May 1910 - 30 Jul 1914: Quartermaster-General, Warsaw Military District
30 Jul 1914 - 22 Jun 1915: Quartermaster-General, Army, Northwestern Front
14 May 1915: Promoted to *Lieutenant-General*

*Major-General* Aleksandr Fyodorovich **Akkerman** (4 Apr 1871 - ?)
25 Jul 1914 - 19 Apr 1915: Commander, 68$^{th}$ Artillery Brigade
19 Apr 1915 - 27 Apr 1917: Commander, 2$^{nd}$ Life Guards Artillery Brigade
1 Sep 1915: Promoted to *Major-General*
27 Apr 1917 - Oct 1917: Inspector of Artillery, XXXIV. Army Corps

*Lieutenant-General* Aleksandr Yulievich **Akkerman** (18 Aug 1850 - 19 Apr 1919)
13 Jun 1907: Promoted to *Major-General*
13 Jun 1907 - 31 Dec 1913: Commandant, Bryansk Arsenal
31 Dec 1913: Promoted to *Lieutenant-General*
31 Dec 1913: Retired

*Lieutenant-General* Yevgeny Yulievich **Akkerman** (18 Jan 1839 - 18 Jan 1912)
8 Aug 1891: Promoted to *Major-General*
8 Aug 1891 - 15 Dec 1894: Deputy Chief of Staff, Omsk Military District

15 Dec 1894 - 2 Jun 1898:        Commander, Omsk Regional Brigade
2 Jun 1898 - 1902:               Commandant of Fortress Kerch
6 Dec 1900:                      Promoted to *Lieutenant-General*
1902:                            Retired

*Major-General* Bogdan-Shchepan Napoleonovich **Akko** (26 Dec 1857 - ?)
27 Feb 1909 - 23 Feb 1913:       Commander, 22nd Borderguard Brigade
23 Feb 1913 - 1917:              Commander, 31st Borderguard Brigade
30 Jul 1915:                     Promoted to *Major-General*

*Lieutenant-General* Arseny Irodionovich **Aknov** (7 Apr 1843 - 18 Aug 1909)
15 Feb 1900:                     Promoted to *Major-General*
15 Feb 1900 - Apr 1903:          Commander, 2nd Brigade, 2nd Infantry Division
Apr 1903:                        Promoted to *Lieutenant-General*
Apr 1903:                        Retired

*Major-General* Germogen Semyonovich **Aksenov** (25 Apr 1862 - ?)
22 Mar 1914:                     Promoted to *Major-General*
22 Mar 1914 - 13 Aug 1914:       Commander, 2nd Brigade, 2nd Infantry Division
13 Aug 1914 - 1917:              POW, Germany

*Major-General* Mikhail Lvovich **Aksenov** (9 Jan 1860 - 8 Sep 1933)
16 Sep 1915 - 1917:              Commander, 2nd Vladivostok Fortress Artillery Brigade
10 Apr 1916:                     Promoted to *Major-General*

*Lieutenant-General* Vasily Andreyevich **Akulov** (16 Mar 1854 - Nov 1921)
26 Apr 1901 - 23 Jul 1907:       Commander, 1st Kuban Cossack Regiment
2 Dec 1906:                      Promoted to *Major-General*
23 Jul 1907 - 16 Mar 1913:       Commander, 2nd Brigade, 2nd Consolidated Cossack Division
16 Mar 1913:                     Promoted to *Lieutenant-General*
16 Mar 1913:                     Retired
9 Sep 1915 - 7 May 1916:         Reserve officer, Minsk Military District
7 May 1916 - 31 Mar 1917:        Special Assignments General, Omsk Military District

*Major-General* Vladimir Ivanovich **Akutin** (13 Jun 1861 - 27 Dec 1919)
9 Aug 1914 - 19 Nov 1916:        Commander, 4th Ural Cossack Regiment
16 May 1915:                     Promoted to *Major-General*
19 Nov 1916 - 29 Dec 1917:       Commander, 1st Brigade, Ural Cossack Division, Commandant, Bobruisk Garrison

*Protopresbyter* Yevgeny Petrovich **Akvilonov** (4 Nov 1861 - 30 Mar 1911)
29 Apr 1910:                     Promoted to *Protopresbyter*
29 Apr 1910 - 30 Mar 1911:       Chief, Directorate of the Orthodox Army and Naval Chaplaincy

*Lieutenant-General of the Naval Legal Corps* Vasily Nikolayevich **Alabyshev** (23 Dec 1858 - ?)
| | |
|---|---|
| 1901 - 16 Jul 1907: | Deputy Procurator, Port of Kronstadt |
| 1907: | Promoted to *Major-General of the Naval Legal Corps* |
| 16 Jul 1907 - 28 Nov 1911: | President of the Sevastopol Naval Court |
| 28 Nov 1911 - 1917: | President of the Naval Court, Port of Kronstadt |
| 14 Apr 1913: | Promoted to *Lieutenant-General of the Naval Legal Corps* |

*Major-General* Aleksandr Romanovich **Alakhverdov** (2 Jul 1858 - ?)
| | |
|---|---|
| 11 Jan 1912 - 1 Apr 1914: | Commander, 10$^{th}$ Dragoon Regiment |
| 1 Apr 1914: | Promoted to *Major-General* |
| 1 Apr 1914: | Retired |

*General of Artillery* Fyodor Konstantinovich **Albedil** (26 May 1836 - 1 Aug 1914)
| | |
|---|---|
| 28 Jun 1878 - 26 Jan 1897: | Director, 2$^{nd}$ Moscow Cadet Corps |
| 30 Aug 1881: | Promoted to *Major-General* |
| 26 Jan 1897 - 1905: | Special Assignments General, Main Directorate for Military Schools |
| 6 Dec 1899: | Promoted to *Lieutenant-General* |
| 1905: | Promoted to *General of Artillery* |
| 1905: | Retired |

*General-Field Marshal* Archduke **Albrecht** Friedrich Rudolf von Österreich-Teschen (3 Aug 1817 - 18 Feb 1895)
| | |
|---|---|
| ?: | Honorary Colonel-in-Chief, 14$^{th}$ Dragoon Regiment |
| ?: | Promoted to *General-Field Marshal* |

*General of Infantry* Prince Friedrich Wilhelm Nikolaus **Albrecht** von Preußen (8 May 1837 - 13 Sep 1906)
| | |
|---|---|
| 10 Mar 1875: | Promoted to *General of Infantry* à la suite |
| ?: | Honorary Colonel-in-Chief, 42$^{nd}$ Dragoon Regiment |

*Rear Admiral* Aleksandr Ivanovich **Aleksandrov** (5 Jun 1864 - 16 Dec 1917)
| | |
|---|---|
| 15 Sep 1909 - 1917: | Commandant, Sevastopol Naval Cadet School |
| 6 Dec 1915: | Promoted to *Rear Admiral* |
| 1917 - 16 Dec 1917: | Chief of Staff, Port of Sevastopol |

*Major-General* Ivan Aleksandrovich **Aleksandrov** (29 Mar 1845 - ?)
| | |
|---|---|
| 5 May 1906 - 1917: | Chief of Drawing & Lithography, Main Military Technical Directorate |
| 6 Dec 1907: | Promoted to *Major-General* |

*Lieutenant-General of the Naval Legal Corps* Ivan Ivanovich **Aleksandrov** (4 Nov 1859 - ?)
| | |
|---|---|
| 1907: | Promoted to *Major-General of the Naval Legal Corps* |
| 12 Mar 1907 - 28 Nov 1911: | Chairman of the Kronstadt Naval Court |
| 28 Nov 1911 - 15 Mar 1917: | Member, Main Naval Tribunal |
| 6 Dec 1912: | Promoted to *Lieutenant-General of the Naval Legal* |

| | Corps |
|---|---|
| 15 Mar 1917: | Retired |

*General of Engineers* Nikolai Fomich **Aleksandrov** (21 Oct 1851 - 14 Oct 1915)
| | |
|---|---|
| 18 Mar 1896 - 10 Feb 1898: | Deputy Chief Engineer, Amur Military District |
| 14 May 1896: | Promoted to *Major-General* |
| 10 Feb 1898 - 23 Apr 1904: | Commander of Engineers, Amur Military District |
| 6 Dec 1902: | Promoted to *Lieutenant-General* |
| 23 Apr 1904 - 2 Sep 1905: | Inspector of Engineers, 1st Manchurian Army |
| 2 Sep 1905 - 15 Oct 1906: | Chief Engineer to C-in-C of Land & Naval Forces operating against Japan |
| 15 Oct 1906 - 27 Nov 1908: | Commander of Engineers, Vilnius Military District |
| 27 Nov 1908 - 6 Feb 1909: | Commandant of Fortress Kovno |
| 6 Feb 1909 - 2 Aug 1909: | Inspector-General of Engineers |
| 29 Mar 1909: | Promoted to *General of Engineers* |
| 2 Aug 1909 - 21 Dec 1913: | Chief of Army Engineers |
| 21 Dec 1913: | Retired |

*Major-General* Nikolai Ivanovich **Aleksandrov** (23 Jun 1835 - ?)
| | |
|---|---|
| 14 Mar 1886: | Promoted to *Major-General* |
| 14 Mar 1886 - 1894: | Commander, Siberian Gendarmerie District |

*Major-General* Pyotr Stepanovich **Aleksandrov** (1 Jan 1854 - ?)
| | |
|---|---|
| 16 Dec 1914 - 24 Jul 1917: | Commander, Perm District Evacuation Points |
| 16 Feb 1917: | Promoted to *Major-General* |

*General of Engineers* Sergey Ivanovich **Aleksandrov** (20 Nov 1845 - ?)
| | |
|---|---|
| 1884 - 21 Mar 1894: | Commander of Engineers, Fortress Sveaborg |
| 30 Aug 1893: | Promoted to *Major-General* |
| 21 Mar 1894 - 13 Feb 1897: | Commander of Engineers, Fortress Kronstadt |
| 13 Feb 1897 - 17 Nov 1910: | Chief of Fortifications Construction, Kronstadt |
| 17 Apr 1905: | Promoted to *Lieutenant-General* |
| 17 Nov 1910: | Promoted to *General of Engineers* |
| 17 Oct 1910: | Retired |

*Major-General* Valentin Varukhovich **Aleksandrov** (1 Aug 1868 - 5 Apr 1933)
| | |
|---|---|
| 1916 - Jul 1916: | Commander, 237th Infantry Regiment |
| 14 Mar 1916: | Promoted to *Major-General* |
| Jul 1916 - 1917: | Commander, Brigade, 59th Infantry Division |

*Major-General* Vladimir Vladimirovich **Aleksandrov** (11 May 1842 - ?)
| | |
|---|---|
| 14 Jan 1898: | Promoted to *Major-General* |
| 14 Jan 1898 - 22 May 1902: | Commander, 1st Brigade, 43rd Infantry Division |

*Rear-Admiral* Aleksandr Ivanovich **Aleksandrovich** (5 Jun 1864 - 15 Dec 1917)
| | |
|---|---|
| 15 Sep 1914 - 1917: | Commandant, Sevastopol Cadet School |
| 6 Dec 1915: | Promoted to *Rear-Admiral* |
| 1917 - 15 Dec 1917: | Chief of Staff, Port of Sevastopol |

*Major-General* Ivan Petrovich **Aleksandrysky** (3 Nov 1859 - ?)
22 Jun 1912 - 10 May 1916: Section Chief, Main Artillery Directorate
6 Dec 1915: Promoted to *Major-General*
10 May 1916 - 1917: Chief of 3rd (Economic) Department, Main Artillery Directorate

*Major-General* Aleksandr Nikolayevich **Alekseyev** (3 Aug 1858 - ?)
23 Jun 1916 - 1 Dec 1916: Reserve officer, Minsk Military District
1 Dec 1916: Promoted to *Major-General*
1 Dec 1916: Retired

*Major-General* Aleksandr Petrovich **Alekseyev** (30 Jul 1841 - ?)
11 Jun 1890 - 19 Aug 1894: Commander, Life Guards Uhlan Regiment
30 Aug 1890: Promoted to *Major-General*
19 Aug 1894 - 1895: At the disposal of the Commanding General, Warsaw Military District

*Major-General* Aleksandr Yevdokimovich **Alekseyev** (9 May 1837 - 21 Dec 1898)
24 Nov 1888: Promoted to *Major-General*
24 Nov 1888 - 23 May 1894: Commander, 1st Brigade, 9th Infantry Division
23 May 1894 - 1895: Commander, 47th Reserve Infantry Brigade
1895: Retired

*Lieutenant-General* Anatoly Nikolayevich **Alekseyev** (6 Feb 1865 - 23 Dec 1922)
3 Jun 1915 - 7 May 1915: Commander, 2nd Cavalry Brigade
7 May 1915 - 7 Jan 1916: Commander, 3rd Cavalry Brigade
31 Aug 1915: Promoted to *Major-General*
7 Jan 1916 - 18 Apr 1917: Chief of Staff, Siberian Cossack Division
18 Apr 1917 - 9 Sep 1917: Commander, Siberian Cossack Division
9 Sep 1917 - Dec 1917: Commanding General, VI. Cavalry Corps
12 Oct 1917: Promoted to *Lieutenant-General*
Dec 1917 - Mar 1918: Chief of Staff, 9th Army

*Major-General* Ivan Filippovich **Alekseyev** (16 Sep 1847 - ?)
15 Sep 1904: Promoted to *Major-General*
15 Sep 1904 - 9 Oct 1906: Commander, 1st Brigade, 33rd Infantry Division

*General of Infantry* Konstantin Mikhailovich **Alekseyev** (22 Nov 1851 - 8 May 1917)
3 Jul 1899: Promoted to *Major-General*
3 Jul 1899 - 19 Jun 1900: Commander, 1st East Siberian Line Brigade
19 Jun 1900 - 17 Jul 1900: Commander, 2nd East Siberian Rifle Brigade
17 Jul 1900 - 22 Feb 1904: Commander, 5th East Siberian Rifle Brigade
22 Feb 1904 - 21 Jun 1905: Commander, 5th East Siberian Rifle Division
18 Jul 1904: Promoted to *Lieutenant-General*
17 Nov 1905 - 1 Jul 1906: Acting Governor-General of Irkutsk
19 Aug 1906 - 12 Apr 1907: Commander, 4th East Siberian Rifle Division
12 Apr 1907 - 5 May 1907: Attached to the General Staff

| | |
|---|---|
| 5 May 1907 - 5 Dec 1909: | Commander, 13th Infantry Division |
| 5 Dec 1909 - 3 Jun 1910: | Commanding General, VI. Army Corps |
| 3 Jun 1910 - 11 May 1912: | Commanding General, III. Caucasus Army Corps |
| 6 Dec 1910: | Promoted to *General of Infantry* |

*Major-General* Mikhail Pavlovich **Alekseyev** (31 Dec 1867 - ?)

| | |
|---|---|
| 16 Nov 1914: | Promoted to *Major-General* |
| 16 Nov 1914 - 29 Feb 1916: | Chief of Staff, VI. Army Corps |
| 29 Feb 1916 - 30 Aug 1916: | Quartermaster-General, 5th Army |
| 30 Aug 1916 - 18 Apr 1917: | Chief of Staff, Special Army |
| 18 Apr 1917 - 27 Jun 1917: | Quartermaster-General, Western Front |

*General of Infantry* Mikhail Vasilievich **Alekseyev** (3 Nov 1857 - 25 Sep 1918)

| | |
|---|---|
| 1 May 1903 - 30 Oct 1904: | Section Chief, General Staff |
| 30 Oct 1904: | Promoted to *Major-General* |
| 30 Oct 1904 - 27 Sep 1906: | Quartermaster-General, 3rd Manchurian Army |
| 27 Sep 1906 - 2 May 1907: | Quartermaster-General, General Staff |
| 2 May 1907 - 4 Sep 1907: | Commander, 2nd Brigade, 22nd Division |
| 4 Sep 1907 - 30 Aug 1908: | Quartermaster-General, General Staff |
| 30 Aug 1908 - 12 Jul 1912: | Chief of Staff, Kiev Military District |
| 30 Oct 1908: | Promoted to *Lieutenant-General* |
| 12 Jul 1912 - 19 Jul 1914: | Commanding General, XIII. Army Corps |
| 19 Jul 1914 - 22 Mar 1915: | Chief of Staff, Southwestern Front |
| 24 Sep 1914: | Promoted to *General of Infantry* |
| 22 Mar 1915 - 8 Apr 1915: | C-in-C, Northwestern Front |
| 8 Apr 1915 - 18 Aug 1915: | C-in-C, Western Front |
| 9 Apr 1916: | Promoted to *General-Adjutant* |
| 18 Aug 1915 - 10 Nov 1916: | Chief of Staff to the Supreme Commander-in-Chief |
| 10 Nov 1916 - 17 Feb 1917: | Sick leave |
| 11 Mar 1917 - 2 Apr 1917: | Acting Supreme Commander-in-Chief |
| 2 Apr 1917 - 21 May 1917: | Supreme Commander-in-Chief |
| 21 May 1917 - 30 Aug 1917: | Military adviser to the government |
| 30 Aug 1917 - 9 Sep 1917: | Chief of Staff to the Supreme Commander-in-Chief |
| 9 Sep 1917: | Resigned |

*Lieutenant-General* Nikolai Fomich **Alekseyev** (30 Nov 1851 - ?)

| | |
|---|---|
| 12 Mar 1907: | Promoted to *Major-General* |
| 12 Mar 1907 - 19 Oct 1910: | Commander, Irkutsk Engineer Brigade |
| 19 Oct 1910 - 1911: | Inspector of Field Engineers, Irkutsk Military District |
| 1911 - 30 Nov 1911: | Inspector of Engineers, Irkutsk Military District |
| 30 Nov 1911: | Promoted to *Lieutenant-General* |
| 30 Nov 1911: | Retired |

*Major-General* Nikolai Ivanovich **Alekseyev** (19 Apr 1868 - 13 Sep 1919)

| | |
|---|---|
| 15 Mar 1915 - 1917: | Commander, 38th Siberian Rifle Regiment |
| 9 Jul 1916: | Promoted to *Major-General* |

*Major-General* Nikolai Nikolayevich **Alekseyev** (25 Mar 1875 - 15 Sep 1955)
18 Sep 1916 - 5 May 1917: Quartermaster-General, 4th Army
6 Dec 1916: Promoted to *Major-General*
5 May 1917 - 22 Sep 1917: Commander, 3rd Turkestan Infantry Division
22 Sep 1917 - Oct 1917: Chief of Staff, 5th Army

*General of Artillery* Pavel Aleksandrovich **Alekseyev** (1 Aug 1836 - 14 Jul 1906)
23 Jun 1879 - 6 Dec 1897: Director, Vladimir-Kiev Cadet Corps
26 Feb 1881: Promoted to *Major-General*
6 Dec 1897: Promoted to *Lieutenant-General*
6 Dec 1897 - 1906: Special Assignments General, Directorate-General of Military Schools
1906: Promoted to *General of Artillery*
1906: Retired

*Vice-Admiral* Vasily Alekseyevich **Alekseyev** (14 Nov 1856 - ?)
26 Jul 1910: Promoted to *Rear-Admiral*
26 Jul 1910 - 21 Jan 1913: Commander, Port of Baku,
 Director of Lighthouses & Navigation, Caspian Sea
28 Jan 1913: Promoted to *Vice-Admiral*
28 Jan 1913: Retired

*Major-General* Vasily Alekseyevich **Alekseyev** (1858 - ?)
1907: Promoted to *Major-General*

*Major-General* Vasily Fyodorovich **Alekseyev** (16 Apr 1840 - ?)
18 Mar 1896 - 2 Sep 1910: Duty Staff Officer, Smolensk Regional Brigade
30 Jun 1908: Promoted to *Major-General*
2 Sep 1910: Retired

*Major-General* Vladimir Vasilyevich **Alekseyev** (25 Jun 1865 - ?)
? - 21 Jan 1916: Commander, 1st Finnish Rifle Regiment
25 Aug 1915: Promoted to *Major-General*
21 Jan 1916 - 29 Sep 1916: Commander, Brigade, 74th Infantry Division
29 Sep 1916 - 1917: Reserve officer, Petrograd Military District

*Major-General* Yakov Ivanovich **Alekseyev** (26 Nov 1872 - 1942)
8 May 1911 - 13 Mar 1917: Chief of Geodesic Office, Military Topographic Department, General Staff
10 Apr 1916: Promoted to *Major-General*
13 Mar 1917 - 1918: Acting Chief, Military Topographic Department, General Staff

*Admiral* Yevgeny Ivanovich **Alekseyev** (13 May 1843 - 27 May 1917)
1 Jan 1892: Promoted to *Rear-Admiral*
1 Jan 1892 - 6 Jan 1895: Deputy Chief of the Naval General Staff
16 May 1892 - 5 Oct 1892: Acting Chief of the Naval General Staff
29 Jul 1894 - 7 Oct 1894: Acting Chief of the Naval General Staff

| | |
|---|---|
| 3 Dec 1894 - 6 Jan 1895: | Acting Chief of the Naval General Staff |
| 6 Jan 1895 - 11 Aug 1897: | Commander, Pacific Squadron |
| 13 Apr 1897: | Promoted to *Vice-Admiral* |
| 11 Aug 1897 - 19 Aug 1899: | Senior Flagman, Black Sea Fleet |
| 1898: | Acting C-in-C, Black Sea Fleet |
| 1898 - 19Aug 1899: | Commander, Training Squadron, Black Sea Fleet |
| 19 Aug 1899 - 30 Jun 1903: | Commander of Forces, Kwantung Area, C-in-C of Naval Forces, Pacific |
| 6 May 1901: | Promoted to *General-Adjutant* |
| 6 Apr 1903: | Promoted to *Admiral* |
| 30 Jun 1903 - 6 Jun 1905: | Viceroy, Far East |
| 28 Jan 1904 - 12 Oct 1904: | C-in-C, Land & Naval Forces, Far East |
| 3 Apr 1904 - 22 Apr 1904: | Acting Commander, 1$^{st}$ Pacific Squadron |
| 6 Jun 1905 - 27 May 1917: | Member of the State Council |

*Lieutenant-General* Konstantin Alekseyevich **Alekseyevsky** (3 Sep 1855 - ?)
| | |
|---|---|
| 26 Oct 1908 - 20 Dec 1911: | Commander, 1$^{st}$ Fortress Vladivostok Artillery Brigade |
| 6 Dec 1909: | Promoted to *Major-General* |
| 20 Dec 1911 - 1917: | Commander of Artillery, Fortress Sveaborg |
| 6 Dec 1916: | Promoted to *Lieutenant-General* |

*Major-General* Pyotr Vasilievich **Alekseyevsky** (27 Oct 1843 - 4 Feb 1909)
| | |
|---|---|
| 23 Nov 1906 - 15 Jun 1907: | Deputy Intendant, St. Petersburg Military District |
| 6 Dec 1906: | Promoted to *Major-General* |
| 15 Jun 1907 - 4 Feb 1909: | Intendant, Amur Military District |

*Major-General* Konstantin Gavrilovich **Aleksinsky** (1 Sep 1866 - ?)
| | |
|---|---|
| 25 Jul 1914 - 25 Sep 1916: | Commander, 64$^{th}$ Artillery Brigade |
| 26 Jul 1915: | Promoted to *Major-General* |
| 25 Sep 1916 - 31 Oct 1916: | Deputy Inspector of Artillery, XLIV. Army Corps |
| 31 Oct 1916 - 31 Dec 1916: | Deputy Inspector of Artillery, Danube Army |
| 31 Dec 1916 - 1917: | Deputy Chief of Artillery, Romanian Front |
| 1917: | Chief of Logistics, Romanian Front |

*Major-General* Sampsony Georgievich **Alenich** (6 Feb 1839 - ?)
| | |
|---|---|
| 5 Mar 1901 - 1907: | Commander, 6$^{th}$ Infantry Regiment |
| 1907: | Promoted to *Major-General* |
| 1907: | Retired |

*Lieutenant-General* Baron Georgy Antonovich von **Alftan** (26 Oct 1828 - 23 Jan 1896)
| | |
|---|---|
| 12 May 1862 - 26 Jun 1873: | Governor of Oulu |
| 19 Jul 1863: | Promoted to *Major-General* |
| 26 Jun 1873 - 19 Sep 1888: | Governor of Nyuland |
| 19 Feb 1879: | Promoted to *Lieutenant-General* |
| 19 Sep 1888 - 20 Dec 1889: | Chief of Expeditionary Militia, Finnish Senate |
| 20 Dec 1889 - 23 Jan 1896: | Senator, Imperial Finnish Senate, Chief of Agriculture & Railways, Finnish Senate |

*General of Infantry* Vladimir Alekseyevich **Alftan** (17 Apr 1860 - 19 Dec 1940)
| | |
|---|---|
| 12 Nov 1905 - 1 Dec 1906: | Special Assignments General, Caucasus Military District |
| 6 Dec 1905: | Promoted to *Major-General* |
| 1 Dec 1906 - 15 Jun 1907: | Commandant, Fortress Mikhailov |
| 15 Jun 1907 - 5 May 1908: | Military Governor of Dagestan |
| 5 May 1908: | Retired |
| 31 Jul 1909 - 9 May 1914: | Recalled; Commander, 1st Brigade, 12th Infantry Division |
| 9 May 1914 - 19 Jul 1914: | Commander, 1st Brigade, 42nd Infantry Division |
| 19 Jul 1914: | Promoted to *Lieutenant-General* |
| 19 Jul 1914 - 3 Jun 1915: | Commander, 78th Infantry Division |
| 3 Jun 1915 - 5 Jul 1915: | Commanding General, XII. Army Corps |
| 5 Jul 1915 - 22 Aug 1915: | Commander, 65th Infantry Division |
| 22 Aug 1915 - 16 Apr 1916: | Commanding General, III. Army Corps |
| 16 Apr 1916: | Promoted to *General of Infantry* |
| 16 Apr 1916: | Retired |

*Major-General* Ali-Ashraf-Agha-Shamshadinov **Ali-Agiraf-Bek** (20 Mar 1851 - ?)
| | |
|---|---|
| 2 Jul 1886 - 2 Jan 1915: | Attached to the Caucasus Military District |
| 6 Dec 1914: | Promoted to *Major-General* |
| 2 Jan 1915 - 1917: | Reserve officer, Caucasus Military District |

*Lieutenant-General* Maksud **Alikhanov-Avarsky** (23 Nov 1846 - 3 Jul 1907)
| | |
|---|---|
| 16 Jun 1890 - 28 Nov 1906: | Attached to the Caucasus Military District |
| 14 Oct 1901: | Promoted to *Major-General* |
| 28 Nov 1906 - 3 Jul 1907: | Commander, 2nd Caucasus Cossack Division |
| 22 Apr 1907: | Promoted to *Lieutenant-General* |

*General of Artillery* Eris-Khan-Sultan-Girei **Aliyev** (20 Apr 1855 - 1920)
| | |
|---|---|
| 13 Nov 1903 - 13 Aug 1905: | Commander, 26th Artillery Brigade |
| 6 Dec 1903: | Promoted to *Major-General* |
| 13 Aug 1905 - 16 May 1906: | Attached to the C-in-C of Land & Naval Forces operating against Japan |
| 16 May 1906 - 14 Aug 1908: | Commander, 5th East Siberian Rifle Division |
| 6 Dec 1907: | Promoted to *Lieutenant-General* |
| 14 Aug 1908 - 8 Feb 1914: | Commanding General, II. Siberian Army Corps |
| 6 Dec 1913: | Promoted to *General of Artillery* |
| 8 Feb 1914 - 16 Nov 1917: | Commanding General, IV. Army Corps |

*Major-General* Ivan Nikolayevich **Alkalaev-Kalageorgy** (7 Jan 1848 - ?)
| | |
|---|---|
| 22 Feb 1904: | Promoted to *Major-General* |
| 22 Feb 1904 - Jul 1906: | Commander, 2nd Brigade, 8th East Siberian Rifle Brigade |

*General of Infantry* Yakov Kaykhosorovich **Alkhazov** (1 Jan 1826 - 3 Nov 1896)
| | |
|---|---|
| 30 Aug 1873: | Promoted to *Major-General* |
| 30 Aug 1873 - 12 Apr 1877: | Commander, 2nd Brigade, 19th Infantry Division |

| | |
|---|---|
| 12 Apr 1877 - 13 Dec 1878: | Commander, Kutaisi Detachment |
| 24 Oct 1877: | Promoted to *Lieutenant-General* |
| 13 Dec 1878 - 27 Feb 1883: | Commander, 41st Infantry Division |
| 27 Feb 1883 - 6 Jul 1885: | Commander, Caucasus Grenadier Division |
| 6 Jul 1885 -19 Oct 1894: | Commanding General, III. Army Corps |
| 30 Aug 1891: | Promoted to *General of Infantry* |
| 19 Oct 1894 - 3 Nov 1896: | Member of the Military Council |

*General of Infantry* Aleksandr Samoylovich **Aller** (24 Apr 1824 - 28 Jun 1895)
| | |
|---|---|
| 23 Nov 1865 - 9 Jun 1873: | Commander, St. Petersburg Grenadier Regiment |
| 30 Aug 1866: | Promoted to *Major-General* |
| 9 Jun 1873 - 26 Sep 1881: | Commander, 32nd Infantry Division |
| 30 Aug 1876: | Promoted to *Lieutenant-General* |
| 26 Sep 1881 - 1 Jan 1888: | Commanding General, VII. Army Corps |
| 1 Jan 1888 - 28 Jun 1895: | Member of the Military Council |
| 30 Aug 1890: | Promoted to *General of Infantry* |

*Major-General* Ivan Ivanovich **Almazov** (9 Jul 1855 - ?)
| | |
|---|---|
| 11 Aug 1910 - 9 Jul 1913: | Commander, 14th Mortar Artillery Battalion |
| 9 Jul 1913: | Promoted to *Major-General* |
| 9 Jul 1913: | Retired |

*Major-General* Aleksei Nikolayevich **Almedingen** (22 Feb 1855 - 30 Nov 1908)
| | |
|---|---|
| 1 Jan 1899 - Oct 1908: | Chief of Legal Department, Main Artillery Directorate |
| 13 Apr 1908: | Promoted to *Major-General* |
| Oct 1908: | Retired |

*Major-General* Dmitry Vasilievich **Altfater** (23 May 1874 - 15 Oct 1931)
| | |
|---|---|
| 23 Aug 1916 - 17 Mar 1917: | Commander, 36th Artillery Brigade |
| 6 Dec 1916: | Promoted to *Major-General* |
| 17 Mar 1917 - 26 Sep 1917: | Commander, 1st Life Guards Artillery Brigade |
| 26 Sep 1917 - ?: | Inspector of Artillery, XXXIX. Army Corps |

*General of Artillery* Mikhail Anton Sigizmund Georgievich **Altfater** (8 Oct 1840 - 24 Aug 1918)
| | |
|---|---|
| 11 Oct 1889: | Promoted to *Major-General* |
| 11 Oct 1889 - 14 Jan 1891: | Commander, 10th Artillery Brigade |
| 14 Jan 1891 - 6 Mar 1892: | Commander, 23rd Artillery Brigade |
| 6 Mar 1892 - 3 Jul 1899: | Deputy Chief of the Main Artillery Directorate |
| 28 Jan 1898: | Promoted to *Lieutenant-General* |
| 3 Jul 1899 - 6 Dec 1904: | Deputy Master-General of Ordnance, Chief of the Main Artillery Directorate |
| 6 Dec 1904 - 25 Oct 1917: | Member of the State Council |
| 6 Dec 1906: | Promoted to *General of Artillery* |

*Major-General* Konstantin Nikolayevich **Alyanchikov** (16 May 1874 - 17 Aug 1936)
| | |
|---|---|
| 14 May 1915 - 3 Feb 1916: | Commander, 28th Siberian Rifle Regiment |
| 6 Dec 1915: | Promoted to *Major-General* |

| | |
|---|---|
| 3 Feb 1916 - 8 Feb 1917: | Commander, Brigade, 127th Infantry Division |
| 8 Feb 1917 - 20 May 1917: | Commander, 1st Brigade, 5th Infantry Division |
| 20 May 1917 - 14 Aug 1917: | Commander, 129th Infantry Division |
| 14 Aug 1917 - 1918: | Reserve officer, Minsk Military District |

*Lieutenant-General* Apollinary Aleksandrovich **Alymov** (25 Jan 1857 - 20 Sep 1934)
| | |
|---|---|
| 9 Jul 1903 - 31 Aug 1907: | Commander, 34th Dragoon Regiment |
| 31 Aug 1907: | Promoted to *Major-General* |
| 31 Aug 1907 - 22 Oct 1910: | Commander, 2nd Brigade, 9th Cavalry Division |
| 22 Oct 1910 - 13 Mar 1916: | Commander, 3rd Reserve Cavalry Brigade |
| 31 Aug 1913: | Promoted to *Lieutenant-General* |
| 13 Mar 1916 - 2 May 1916: | Reserve officer, Kiev Military District |
| 2 May 1916 - 1917: | Special Assignments General, Omsk Military District |

*Major-General* Yakov Vasilievich **Amasysky** (5 Mar 1855 - ?)
| | |
|---|---|
| 12 Jul 1907 - 5 Mar 1913: | Commander, 9th Rifle Regiment |
| 5 Mar 1913: | Promoted to *Major-General* |
| 5 Mar 1913: | Retired |
| 14 Nov 1914 - 25 Mar 1915: | Recalled; Reserve officer, Caucasus Military District |
| 25 Mar 1915 - 12 Aug 1916: | Commander, Brigade, 66th Infantry Division |
| 12 Aug 1916 - 7 Oct 1916: | Commander, Don Cossack Infantry Brigade |
| 7 Oct 1916 - 9 Jun 1917: | Commander, 7th Caucasus Rifle Division |

*Major-General* Aleksandr Sergeyevich **Ambrazantsev-Nechayev** (6 Sep 1841 - ?)
| | |
|---|---|
| 16 Nov 1890 - 3 Jun 1896: | Commander, 32nd Dragoon Regiment |
| 25 Apr 1896: | Promoted to *Major-General* |
| 3 Jun 1896 - 16 Dec 1899: | Commander, 1st Brigade, 2nd Cavalry Division |
| 16 Dec 1899: | Retired |

*General of Cavalry* Prince Ivan Yegorovich **Amilokhvarov** (6 Jan 1829 - 27 Aug 1905)
| | |
|---|---|
| 30 Aug 1873: | Promoted to *Major-General* |
| 30 Aug 1873 - 21 Jan 1879: | Attached to the Caucasus Army |
| 21 Jan 1879 - 27 Jul 1881: | Commander, 3rd Caucasus Cavalry Division |
| 27 Jul 1881 - 10 Mar 1883: | Commander, 2nd Caucasus Cavalry Division |
| 10 Mar 1883 - 16 Jan 1893: | Commander, 1st Caucasus Cavalry Division |
| 15 May 1883: | Promoted to *Lieutenant-General* |
| 16 Jan 1893 - 11 Jun 1897: | Commanding General, Caucasus Army Corps |
| 14 May 1896: | Promoted to *General of Cavalry* |
| 11 Jun 1897 - 27 Aug 1905: | Special Assignments General, Caucasus Military District |
| 1901: | Promoted to *General-Adjutant* |
| 1904: | Acting Governor of Baku |

*Lieutenant-General* Baron Iogann-Fridrikh-Gustav Aleksandrovich **Aminov** (9 Aug 1844 - 26 Dec 1898)
| | |
|---|---|
| 14 Nov 1884 - 25 Nov 1888: | Commander, Life Guards 3rd Finnish Rifle Battalion |
| 24 Jul 1885: | Promoted to *Major-General* |
| 25 Nov 1888 - 26 Dec 1898: | Military Commander, Kuopio Province |

6 Dec 1895:                          Promoted to *Lieutenant-General*

*Lieutenant-General* Prince Mikhail Kaikhosrovich **Amiradzhibov** (2 Sep 1833 - 27 Nov 1903)
1871 - 22 Mar 1880:                  Commander, 156th Infantry Regiment
8 Nov 1877:                          Promoted to *Major-General*
22 Mar 1880 - 2 Sep 1882:            Commander, 1st Brigade, Caucasus Grenadier Division
2 Sep 1882 - 31 Aug 1884:            Transferred to the reserve
31 Aug 1884 - 21 Jul 1893:           Commander, 1st Brigade, Caucasus Grenadier Division
30 Aug 1893:                         Promoted to *Lieutenant-General*
21 Jul 1893 - 22 Mar 1899:           Commander, 39th Infantry Division
30 Aug 1893:                         Promoted to *Lieutenant-General*
22 Mar 1899 - 27 Nov 1903:           Commanding General, I. Caucasus Army Corps

*Vice-Admiral* Fyodor Ivanovich **Amosov** (11 Feb 1841 - 17 May 1905)
1893:                                Promoted to *Rear-Admiral*
1893 - 1898:                         Junior Flagman, 1st Division, Baltic Fleet
1898 - 12 Feb 1901:                  Junior Flagman, 2nd Division, Baltic Fleet
12 Feb 1901:                         Promoted to *Vice-Admiral*
12 Feb 1901:                         Retired

*Major-General* Vladimir Ivanovich **Amosov** (2 Jun 1842 - 12 Mar 1901)
29 Nov 1893:                         Promoted to *Major-General*
29 Nov 1893 - 17 Feb 1900:           Commander, 6th Reserve Artillery Brigade
17 Feb 1900 - 12 Mar 1901:           Commander of Artillery, II. Army Corps

*General of Artillery* Arkady Nikolayevich **Ananin** (23 Jan 1851 - ?)
1 Mar 1900 - 27 Sep 1904:            Commander of Artillery, Fortress Sveaborg
9 Apr 1900:                          Promoted to *Major-General*
27 Sep 1904 - 28 Mar 1906:           Commander of Artillery, Kazan Military District
28 Mar 1906 - 13 Mar 1909:           Commander of Artillery, Warsaw Military District
6 Dec 1906:                          Promoted to *Lieutenant-General*
13 Mar 1909 - 10 Nov 1916:           Commandant of Fortress Sevastopol
16 Oct 1914:                         Promoted to *General of Artillery*
10 Nov 1916 - 7 Jul 1917:            Reserve officer, Odessa Military District
7 Jul 1917:                          Retired

*Lieutenant-General* Konstantin Nikolayevich **Anchutin** (27 Apr 1840 - 30 Sep 1911)
5 Aug 1888:                          Promoted to *Major-General*
5 Aug 1888 - 16 May 1891:            Director of Polotsk Cadet Corps
16 May 1891 - 4 Feb 1903:            Director of Don Cadet Corps
4 Feb 1903 - 23 Feb 1908:            Deputy Chief of Military Schools
24 Feb 1903:                         Promoted to *Lieutenant-General*
23 Feb 1908:                         Retired

*Major-General* Aleksei Ivanovich **Andogsky** (8 Mar 1863 - ?)
8 May 1907 - 20 May 1910:            Military Judge, Irkutsk Military District Court
31 May 1907:                         Promoted to *Major-General*

20 May 1910 - 1917: Military Judge, Turkestan Military District Court

*Major-General* Aleksandr Aleksandrovich **Andreyev** (10 Apr 1870 - ?)
20 Jun 1910 - 2 Aug 1916: Deputy Chief, Main Artillery Proving Grounds
22 Mar 1915: Promoted to *Major-General*
2 Aug 1916 - 1917: Deputy Chief of Okhtenskaya Explosives Factory

*Major-General* Aleksandr Nikolayevich **Andreyev** (30 Oct 1869 - ?)
23 Jan 1916 - 18 Apr 1917: Intendant-General, Minsk Military District
6 Dec 1916: Promoted to *Major-General*

*Lieutenant-General* Aleksandr Petrovich **Andreyev** (20 Nov 1853 - ?)
1 Aug 1910: Promoted to *Major-General*
1 Aug 1910 - 20 Nov 1913: Commander, 9th Siberian Rifle Artillery Brigade
20 Nov 1913: Promoted to *Lieutenant-General*
20 Nov 1913: Retired

*Rear-Admiral* Andrey Parfonovich **Andreyev** (5 Sep 1855 - 7 Apr 1924)
18 Sep 1905 - 1906: Commander, 10th Naval Depot
1906 - 28 Aug 1906: Acting Chief of Staff, Port of Kronstadt
28 Aug 1906: Promoted to *Rear-Admiral*
28 Aug 1906: Retired

*Major-General* Andrey Petrovich **Andreyev** (24 Aug 1864 - ?)
18 Jul 1909 - 10 Jul 1916: Military Judge, Caucasus Military District Court
6 Dec 1909: Promoted to *Major-General*
10 Jul 1916 - 1917: Military Judge, V. Caucasus Army Corps

*General of the Naval Legal Corps* Ippolit Petrovich **Andreyev** (18 Dec 1844 - ?)
1896: Promoted to *Major-General of the Naval Legal Corps*
1896 - 1904: Military Judge, Port of Kronstadt Naval Court
1904: Promoted to *Lieutenant-General of the Naval Legal Corps*
1904 - 8 Jan 1907: Chairman of the Naval Court, Port of Sevastopol
8 Jan 1907 - 28 Nov 1911: Member, Supreme Naval Tribunal
6 Dec 1909: Promoted to *General of the Naval Legal Corps*
28 Nov 1911 - Jan 1914: Chairman, Supreme Naval Tribunal

*Major-General* Ivan Alekseyevich **Andreyev** (13 Nov 1856 - 1916)
28 Oct 1895 - Sep 1916: Commander, 1st Squadron, St. Petersburg Gendarmerie
29 Sep 1916: Posthumously promoted to *Major-General*

*Major-General* Ivan Nikanorovich **Andreyev** (4 Jan 1864 - ?)
18 Jul 1907 - 16 Dec 1914: Commander, 9th Horse Artillery Battalion
27 Sep 1914: Promoted to *Major-General*
16 Dec 1914 - 18 Feb 1917: Commander, 45th Artillery Brigade
18 Feb 1917 - 1917: Inspector of Artillery, III. Army Corps

*Lieutenant-General of the Naval Navigators Corps* Konstantin Petrovich **Andreyev** (2 Oct 1853 - 7 Jan 1919)
| | |
|---|---|
| 29 Nov 1893 - 31 Jul 1908: | Chief of Special Survey, Black Sea |
| 6 Dec 1904: | Promoted to *Major-General of the Naval Navigators Corps* |
| 31 Jul 1908 - 17 Sep 1908: | Reserve officer, Ministry of the Navy |
| 17 Sep 1908: | Promoted to *Lieutenant-General of the Naval Navigators Corps* |
| 17 Sep 1908: | Retired |

*Major-General* Konstantin Porfirievich **Andreyev** (11 Jan 1858 - ?)
| | |
|---|---|
| 14 Jul 1905: | Promoted to *Major-General* |
| 14 Jul 1905 - 5 Jan 1907: | Commander, 2nd Brigade, 7th Infantry Division |

*Major-General* Mikhail Nikanorovich **Andreyev** (17 Oct 1867 - ?)
| | |
|---|---|
| 10 Mar 1912: | Promoted to *Major-General* |
| 10 Mar 1912 - 8 Nov 1915: | Commander, 50th Artillery Brigade |
| 8 Nov 1915 - 25 Dec 1915: | Unassigned |
| 25 Dec 1915 - 7 Oct 1916: | Inspector of Artillery, X. Army Corps |
| 7 Oct 1916 - 19 Dec 1916: | Inspector of Artillery, Danube Army |
| 19 Dec 1916 - 8 Jun 1917: | Inspector of Artillery, 8th Army |
| 8 Jun 1917 - ?: | Commander, 50th Artillery Brigade |

*General of Infantry* Mikhail Semyonovich **Andreyev** (24 Feb 1848 - 1919)
| | |
|---|---|
| 26 Aug 1892 - 27 Jan 1894: | Attached to Kiev Military District |
| 30 Aug 1892: | Promoted to *Major-General* |
| 27 Jan 1894 - 1 Mar 1900: | Chief of Staff, I. Army Corps |
| 1 Mar 1900: | Promoted to *Lieutenant-General* |
| 1 Mar 1900 - 9 Jun 1904: | Commander, 23rd Infantry Division |
| 9 Jun 1904 - 30 Jan 1907: | Deputy Commanding General, Amur Military District |
| 30 Jan 1907 - 24 Jun 1908: | Commanding General, II. Army Corps |
| 13 Apr 1908: | Promoted to *General of Infantry* |
| 24 Jun 1908: | Retired |

*Lieutenant-General* Nikolai Petrovich **Andreyev** (17 May 1838 - 2 Sep 1927)
| | |
|---|---|
| 22 Mar 1902 - 1907: | Director of the Siberian Cadet Corps |
| 14 Apr 1902: | Promoted to *Major-General* |
| 1907: | Promoted to *Lieutenant-General* |
| 1907: | Retired |

*Major-General* Nikolai Petrovich **Andreyev** (21 Jun 1855 - ?)
| | |
|---|---|
| 13 Nov 1903 - 23 Apr 1907: | Commander, 1st Grenadier Artillery Brigade |
| 6 Dec 1903: | Promoted to *Major-General* |

*Admiral* Pavel Petrovich **Andreyev** (14 Jul 1843 - 18 Oct 1911)
| | |
|---|---|
| 1893: | Promoted to *Rear-Admiral* |
| 1893 - 1894: | Junior Flagman, Baltic Fleet |
| 1894 - 11 Jul 1896: | Chief of Staff, Port of Kronstadt |

| | |
|---|---|
| 11 Jul 1896 - 21 Feb 1898: | Commander, Mediterranean Squadron |
| 1899: | Promoted to *Vice-Admiral* |
| 1899 - 1901: | Senior Flagman, Black Sea Fleet, Commander, Training Squadron, Black Sea Fleet |
| 1901 - 1907: | Commander, 1st Division, Baltic Fleet |
| 1907: | Promoted to *Admiral* |
| 1907: | Retired |

*Lieutenant-General* Pyotr Andreyevich **Andreyev** (16 Dec 1859 - ?)
| | |
|---|---|
| 6 Dec 1907: | Promoted to *Major-General* |
| 6 Dec 1907 - 19 Jul 1914: | Commander, 1st Brigade, 8th Siberian Rifle Division |
| 19 Jul 1914 - 20 Oct 1915: | Commander, 13th Siberian Rifle Division |
| 22 Dec 1914: | Promoted to *Lieutenant-General* |
| 25 Oct 1915 - 1917: | Reserve officer, Petrograd Military District |

*General of Engineers* Pyotr Grigoryevich **Andreyev** (7 Jun 1812 - 22 Dec 1899)
| | |
|---|---|
| 28 Jul 1863 - 22 Dec 1899: | Professor, Nikolayev Engineering Academy |
| 20 Apr 1869: | Promoted to *Major-General* |
| 25 May 1878 - 22 Dec 1899: | Conference Member, Nikolayev Engineering Academy |
| 1 Dec 1880: | Promoted to *Lieutenant-General* |
| 30 Aug 1894: | Promoted to *General of Engineers* |

*Major-General* Pyotr Petrovich **Andreyev** (3 Feb 1845 - 1912)
| | |
|---|---|
| 21 Sep 1895 - 23 Dec 1897: | At the disposal of the Commanding General, Warsaw Military District |
| 14 May 1896: | Promoted to *Major-General* |
| 23 Dec 1897 - 14 Aug 1905: | At the disposal of the Commanding General, Finland Military District |
| 14 Aug 1905 - 1912: | At the disposal of the Commanding General, St. Petersburg Military District |

*Major-General* Sergey Mikhailovich **Andreyev** (23 Oct 1859 - 1925)
| | |
|---|---|
| 27 Jul 1907 - 4 Nov 1913: | Commander, Kineshemsky District |
| 14 Apr 1913: | Promoted to *Major-General* |
| 4 Nov 1913 - 1917: | Commander, Moscow Brigade |

*Major-General* Dmitry Ivanovich **Andrievsky** (6 Feb 1875 - 29 May 1951)
| | |
|---|---|
| 14 Jun 1915 - 10 Jul 1916: | Commander, 14th Turkestan Infantry Regiment |
| 19 Jan 1916: | Promoted to *Major-General* |
| 10 Jul 1916 - 3 Jun 1917: | Chief of Staff, 1st Kuban Cossack Infantry Brigade |
| 3 Jun 1917 - 1918: | Attached to the General Staff |

*Major-General* Vitaly Yevgenievich **Andro-de-Byui-Ginglyatt** (28 Jan 1854 - ?)
| | |
|---|---|
| 25 Mar 1904: | Promoted to *Major-General* |
| 25 Mar 1904 - 16 Jun 1904: | Commander, 1st Brigade, 4th East Siberian Division |
| 16 Jun 1904 - 29 Jul 1905: | Deputy Intendant, Manchurian Army |
| 29 Jul 1905 - 17 Jul 1906: | Chief Field Intendant |
| 17 Jul 1906 - 3 Oct 1907: | Commander, 1st Turkestan Rifle Brigade |

3 Oct 1907 - 28 Sep 1908: Transferred to the reserve
28 Sep 1908 - 30 Apr 1911: Section Chief, Intendant-General's Department
30 Apr 1911: Retired

*Lieutenant-General* Vladimir Yevgenievich **Andro-De-Byui-Ginglyatt** (12 Jan 1856 - ?)
15 Jul 1891 - 22 Dec 1913: Deputy Chief of the Gatchina Palace Administration
6 Dec 1906: Promoted to *Major-General*
22 Dec 1913- 2 Feb 1914: Chief of the Gatchina Palace Administration
2 Feb 1914 - Mar 1917: Member, Ministry of the Imperial Court
29 Jul 1917: Promoted to *Lieutenant-General*
29 Jul 1917: Dismissed

*Major-General* Ignaty Vikentievich **Andrushkevich** (4 Dec 1849 - 1905)
29 Jan 1900 - 1905: Commander of Fortress Artillery, Ivangorod
6 Dec 1901: Promoted to *Major-General*

*Major-General* Mitrofan Vasilievich **Andrussky** (15 Feb 1855 - 12 Jan 1937)
2 Feb 1913: Promoted to *Major-General*
2 Feb 1913 - 5 Apr 1915: Commander, 20$^{th}$ Artillery Brigade
5 Apr 1915 - 8 Jul 1917: Inspector of Artillery, IV. Caucasus Army Corps
8 Jul 1917: Retired

*Major-General of the Admiralty* Konstantin Klitovich **Andrzheyevsky** (1859 - 12 Apr 1908)
1904 - 24 Mar 1908: Captain, Destroyer "*Grozny*"
24 Mar 1908: Promoted to *Major-General of the Admiralty*
24 Mar 1908: Retired

*Major-General* Loggin Lukyanovich **Anichikhin** (8 Oct 1838 - 1914)
28 Sep 1889 - May 1905: Ataman, 1$^{st}$ Division, Ural Cossack Army
29 Jul 1891: Promoted to *Major-General*
May 1905: Retired

*Lieutenant-General* Mily Milievich **Anichkov** (20 Jan 1848 - ?)
15 Jun 1891 - Mar 1917: Chief of the Economic Section, Imperial Court
14 May 1896: Promoted to *Major-General*
2 Apr 1906: Promoted to *Lieutenant-General*

*Lieutenant-General* Aleksandr Nikanorovich **Anikeyev** (12 May 1851 - ?)
27 Nov 1904: Promoted to *Major-General*
27 Nov 1904 - 6 Jun 1907: Commander, 1$^{st}$ Brigade, 6$^{th}$ Infantry Division
6 Jun 1907 - 21 Jul 1910: Commander, 50$^{th}$ Replacement Infantry Brigade
21 Jul 1910 - 23 Jul 1911: Transferred to the reserve
23 Jul 1911: Promoted to *Lieutenant-General*
23 Jul 1911: Retired
11 Oct 1914 - 1917: Recalled; Commander, 5$^{th}$ Militia Corps

*General of Infantry* Pyotr Nikanorovich **Anikeyev** (26 Jan 1844 - ?)
3 Oct 1879 - 17 Jan 1894: Military Judge, Odessa Military District Court

| | |
|---|---|
| 30 Aug 1888: | Promoted to *Major-General* |
| 17 Jan 1894 - 18 Feb 1897: | Military Prosecutor, Kiev Military District |
| 18 Feb 1897 - 9 Jan 1906: | Chairman of the Military Tribunal, Moscow Military District |
| 6 Dec 1898: | Promoted to *Lieutenant-General* |
| 9 Jan 1906 - 1909: | Member, Supreme Military Tribunal |
| 22 Apr 1907: | Promoted to *General of Infantry* |
| 1909: | Retired |

*Lieutenant-General* Konstantin Andreyevich **Anisimov** (19 Apr 1850 - ?)
| | |
|---|---|
| 22 Nov 1900: | Promoted to *Major-General* |
| 22 Nov 1900 - 22 Feb 1904: | Commander, 2$^{nd}$ East Siberian Rifle Brigade |
| 22 Feb 1904 - 3 Dec 1908: | Commander, 2$^{nd}$ East Siberian Rifle Division |
| 6 Dec 1906: | Promoted to *Lieutenant-General* |
| 3 Dec 1908: | Retired |

*Major-General* Nikolai Silvestrovich **Anisimov** (30 Jul 1860 - ?)
| | |
|---|---|
| 31 Dec 1913 - 5 Sep 1916: | Commandant, Warsaw Artillery Depot |
| 22 Mar 1915: | Promoted to *Major-General* |
| 5 Sep 1916 - ?: | Commander, Kiev Artillery Depot |
| ? - 21 Oct 1917: | Commandant, Odessa Ensign School |

*Major-General* Fyodor Ivanovich **Annenkov** (15 Dec 1843 - 25 Jul 1903)
| | |
|---|---|
| 6 Dec 1902: | Promoted to *Major-General* |
| 6 Dec 1902 - 25 Jul 1903: | Attached to the General Staff |

*General of Infantry* Mikhail Nikolayevich **Annenkov** (23 Apr 1835 - 9 Jan 1899)
| | |
|---|---|
| 17 Jul 1867 - 10 Apr 1875: | Section Chief, Committee for Railway and Waterway Troop Movements, General Staff |
| 1 Jan 1869: | Promoted to *Major-General* |
| 10 Apr 1875 - 3 Apr 1877: | Member, Commission for the Study of Railways |
| 3 Apr 1877 - 6 Oct 1884: | Member, Committee for Troop Movements |
| 1 Jan 1878: | Promoted to *Lieutenant-General* |
| 6 Oct 1884 - 7 Dec 1889: | Section Chief, Ministry of Communications |
| 28 Jul 1888 - 4 Jul 1891: | Chief of the Transcaspian Railway |
| 4 Jul 1891 - 9 Jan 1899: | Member of the Military Council |
| 30 Aug 1892: | Promoted to *General of Infantry* |

*Major-General* Nikolai Yurievich **Anofriev** (4 Dec 1857 - 11 Mar 1920)
| | |
|---|---|
| 31 Oct 1914 - 12 Nov 1916: | Reserve officer, Kiev Military District |
| 12 Nov 1916: | Promoted to *Major-General* |
| 12 Nov 1916: | Retired |

*General of Artillery* Aleksei Vasilievich **Anosov** (8 Mar 1822 - 10 Apr 1906)
| | |
|---|---|
| 25 Jul 1868 - 25 Jan 1879: | Commander, 9$^{th}$ Artillery Brigade |
| 18 May 1875: | Promoted to *Major-General* |
| 25 Jan 1879 - 20 Aug 1882: | Commander of Artillery, Kharkov Military District |
| 20 Aug 1882 - 26 Mar 1890: | Commander of Artillery, XI. Army Corps |

6 May 1884: Promoted to *Lieutenant-General*
26 Mar 1890 - 21 Jul 1899: Commandant of Fortress Kiev
6 Dec 1899: Promoted to *General of Artillery*
21 Jul 1899 - 1905: Member, Committee for Wounded Veterans
1905: Retired

*Major-General* Nikolai Stepanovich **Anosov** (15 Sep 1866 - Jan 1920)
19 Mar 1914 - 17 Oct 1915: Commander, 30$^{th}$ Siberian Rifle Regiment
25 Jan 1915: Promoted to *Major-General*
17 Oct 1915 - 30 Jan 1916: Reserve officer, Petrograd Military District
30 Jan 1916 - 4 May 1917: Commander, 19$^{th}$ Replacement Infantry Brigade
4 May 1917 - 1 Jul 1917: Commander, 20$^{th}$ Infantry Division

*Major-General* Stepan Petrovich **Anosov** (1 Aug 1844 - ?)
1 Jan 1898 - 1901: Commander, 170$^{th}$ Infantry Regiment
1901: Promoted to *Major-General*
1901: Retired
1914 - 8 Apr 1915: Recalled; Reserve officer, Dvina Military District
8 Apr 1915 - 1917: Commander, 94$^{th}$ State Militia Brigade

*Lieutenant-General* Vladimir Vasilievich **Antipov** (12 Mar 1862 - ?)
6 Jul 1907 - 25 Jan 1915: Commandant, Vladimir Military School
31 Dec 1910: Promoted to *Major-General*
25 Jan 1915 - 18 Apr 1915: Commander, Brigade, 63$^{rd}$ Infantry Division
18 Apr 1915 - 18 May 1915: Commander, 63$^{rd}$ Infantry Division
18 May 1915 - 21 Dec 1915: Chief of Staff, Guards Corps
21 Dec 1915 - 6 Jul 1916: Chief of Staff, II. Guards Corps
6 Jul 1916 - 19 Apr 1917: Commander, 36$^{th}$ Infantry Division
29 Apr 1917: Promoted to *Lieutenant-General*

*Major-General* Aleksei Alekseyevich **Antonov** (3 Jan 1854 - ?)
27 Oct 1912 - 31 Aug 1917: Commandant, Tomylovskaya Artillery Depot
6 Dec 1912: Promoted to *Major-General*
31 Aug 1917: Dismissed

*Lieutenant-General* Nikolai Alekseyevich **Antonov** (16 Nov 1860 - ?)
21 Jan 1907 - 22 Apr 1917: Military Judge, Kiev Military District Court
22 Apr 1907: Promoted to *Major-General*
22 Apr 1917: Promoted to *Lieutenant-General*
22 Apr 1917: Retired

*Major-General* Kasyan Iustinovich **Antushevich** (29 May 1836 - ?)
12 May 1877 - 1894: Military Judge, Caucasus Military District Court
30 Aug 1887: Promoted to *Major-General*

*General of Infantry* Dmitry Gavrilovich **Anuchin** (9 Apr 1833 - 17 Jan 1900)
1867: Promoted to *Major-General*
10 Jun 1867 - 7 Dec 1879: Governor of Radom

| | |
|---|---|
| 13 Oct 1877: | Promoted to *Lieutenant-General* |
| 7 Dec 1879 - 1 Jan 1885: | Governor-General of Eastern Siberia, Commanding General, Eastern Siberian Military District |
| 1 Jan 1885 - 17 Jan 1900: | Senator |
| 30 Aug 1891: | Promoted to *General of Infantry* |

*Major-General* Aleksandr Vilgelmovich **Apel** (31 Mar 1870 - ?)
| | |
|---|---|
| 9 Aug 1914 - 1916: | Commander, 10th Pontoon Battalion |
| 10 Jul 1916: | Promoted to *Major-General* |

*Rear-Admiral* Nikolai Ivanovich **Apostoli** (1861 - 1937)
| | |
|---|---|
| 1910 - 1917: | Chief of Communications, Baltic Fleet |
| 1915: | Promoted to *Rear-Admiral* |

*Major-General* Pavel Pavlovich **Aprelev** (8 Jun 1865 - 24 Nov 1934)
| | |
|---|---|
| 26 Oct 1907 - 26 Jan 1914: | Commander, 7th Replacement Cavalry Regiment |
| 14 Apr 1913: | Promoted to *Major-General* |
| 26 Jan 1914 - 17 Nov 1916: | Commander, 1st Reserve Cavalry Brigade |
| 17 Nov 1916 - 1917: | Commander, 5th Reserve Cavalry Brigade |

*Lieutenant-General* Aleksandr Nikolayevich **Apukhtin** (1 Jan 1862 - 7 Jul 1928)
| | |
|---|---|
| 9 Mar 1905: | Promoted to *Major-General* |
| 9 Mar 1905 - 6 Jul 1905: | Commander, 2nd Brigade, 61st Infantry Division |
| 6 Jul 1905 - 27 Jan 1906: | Attached to the General Staff |
| 27 Jan 1906 - 19 Jul 1914: | Commander, 1st Brigade, 24th Infantry Division |
| 19 Jul 1914: | Promoted to *Lieutenant-General* |
| 19 Jul 1914 - 15 Apr 1917: | Commander, 68th Infantry Division |

*Lieutenant-General* Vladimir Aleksandrovich **Apushkin** (2 Nov 1868 - 1937)
| | |
|---|---|
| 16 Nov 1913 - Mar 1917: | Chief of Military Prison Branch, Military Justice Administration |
| 22 Mar 1915: | Promoted to *Major-General* |
| 22 Apr 1917: | Promoted to *Lieutenant-General* |

*Major-General* Vladimir Fyodorovich **Apushkin** (15 Jul 1855 - ?)
| | |
|---|---|
| 16 Jan 1909: | Promoted to *Major-General* |
| 16 Jan 1909 - 4 May 1911: | Commander, 40th Artillery Brigade |
| 4 May 1911: | Retired |

*Major-General* Aleksandr Petrovich **Arakantsev** (5 Sep 1855 - 10 Dec 1910)
| | |
|---|---|
| 22 Jun 1900 - 2 Jun 1910: | Commander, 18th Don Cossack Regiment |
| 2 Jun 1910: | Promoted to *Major-General* |
| 2 Jun 1910 - 10 Dec 1910: | Commander, 2nd Brigade, 12th Cavalry Division |

*Lieutenant-General* Bala-Kishi-Ali-Bek **Arablinsky** (30 Aug 1828 - 3 Jan 1902)
| | |
|---|---|
| 12 Mar 1887: | Promoted to *Major-General* |
| 12 Mar 1887 - 25 May 1888: | Commander, 1st Transcaspian Rifle Brigade |

| | |
|---|---|
| 25 May 1888 - 3 Aug 1898: | Commander, 2$^{nd}$ Brigade, 21$^{st}$ Infantry Division |
| 3 Aug 1898: | Promoted to *Lieutenant-General* |
| 3 Aug 1898: | Retired |

*Lieutenant-General* Fyodor Tikhonovich **Arakin** (13 Feb 1838 - ?)

| | |
|---|---|
| 19 Feb 1880: | Promoted to *Major-General* |
| 19 Feb 1880 - 6 Apr 1880: | General Staff Officer, General Staff |
| 6 Apr 1880 - 7 Sep 1887: | General Staff Officer, Main Intendant Directorate |
| 7 Sep 1887 - 7 May 1890: | Commander, 2$^{nd}$ Brigade, 31$^{st}$ Infantry Division |
| 7 May 1890 - Jan 1897: | Commander, 2$^{nd}$ (Archangel) Regional Brigade |
| 30 Aug 1890: | Promoted to *Lieutenant-General* |

*Lieutenant-General* Nikolai Dmitrievich **Arakin** (20 Sep 1862 - ?)

| | |
|---|---|
| 14 Aug 1906 - 24 Jun 1913: | Military Judge, Irkutsk Military District Court |
| 6 Dec 1906: | Promoted to *Major-General* |
| 24 Jun 1913 - May 1914: | Military Judge, Warsaw Military District Court |
| May 1914 - 21 Jul 1914: | Military Judge, Vilnius Military District Court |
| 21 Jul 1914 - ?: | Military Judge, 1$^{st}$ Army |
| ? - 17 Dec 1914: | Military Judge, Minsk Military District Court |
| 17 Dec 1914 - 22 Apr 1917: | Military Judge, Dvinsk Military District Court |
| 22 Apr 1917: | Promoted to *Lieutenant-General* |
| 22 Apr 1917: | Retired |

*Major-General* Georgy Alekseyevich **Arandarenko** (4 Feb 1846 - ?)

| | |
|---|---|
| 12 Sep 1899 - 4 Jun 1901: | Special Assignments General, Turkestan Military District |
| 6 Dec 1900: | Promoted to *Major-General* |
| 4 Jun 1901 - 9 Dec 1904: | Military Governor, Ferghana Province |
| 9 Dec 1904: | Retired |

*Lieutenant-General* Ivan Andreyevich **Arapov** (21 Nov 1844 - 11 Sep 1913)

| | |
|---|---|
| 8 May 1881 - 16 Sep 1894: | Member, Main Remount Board |
| 15 Sep 1884: | Promoted to *Major-General* |
| 16 Sep 1894 - 2 Jan 1895: | Transferred to the reserve |
| 2 Jan 1895 - 1911: | Member, Council of Ministers of Agriculture & State Property |
| 6 Dec 1904: | Promoted to *Lieutenant-General* |

*General of Cavalry* Konstantin Ustinovich **Arapov** (29 Mar 1831 - 28 Aug 1916)

| | |
|---|---|
| 24 Feb 1883 - 26 Jan 1885: | Marshal of the Imperial Peterhof Palace |
| 15 May 1883: | Promoted to *Major-General* |
| 23 Apr 1885 - 31 Jul 1892: | At the disposal of the Commanding General, St. Petersburg Military District |
| 31 Jul 1892 - 28 Aug 1916: | Member, Board of Trustees, Empress Maria Institutions |
| 30 Aug 1893: | Promoted to *Lieutenant-General* |
| 2 May 1893 - 28 Aug 1916: | Chief of Economic Management, St. Petersburg Alexander Institute |
| 28 Mar 1904: | Promoted to *General of Cavalry* |

1908: Promoted to *General-Adjutant*

*Lieutenant-General* Pyotr Ivanovich **Arapov** (12 Feb 1871 - 21 Jan 1930)
29 May 1910 - 3 Mar 1912: Commander, 2nd Life Dragoon Regiment
3 Mar 1912 - 12 Nov 1914: Commander, Life Guards Cuirassier Regiment
6 Dec 1912: Promoted to *Major-General*
12 Nov 1914 - 13 Jan 1915: Commander, 2nd Brigade, 2nd Guards Cavalry Division
13 Jan 1915 - 9 Aug 1915: Commander, 2nd Brigade, 1st Guards Cavalry Division
9 Aug 1915 - 7 May 1916: Commander, 1st Brigade, 1st Guards Cavalry Division
7 May 1916 - 27 Jun 1917: Unassigned
27 Jun 1916 - Oct 1917: Commander, 3rd Guards Cavalry Division
2 Apr 1917: Promoted to *Lieutenant-General*

*Major-General* Nikolai Mikhailovich **Arbuzov** (5 Dec 1846 - ?)
24 Oct 1900: Promoted to *Major-General*
24 Oct 1900 - 7 Feb 1901: Commander, 2nd Brigade, 36th Infantry Division
7 Feb 1901 - 12 Mar 1905: Commander, 1st Brigade, 7th Infantry Division
12 Mar 1905 - Jul 1906: Commander, 1st Brigade, 70th Infantry Division
Jul 1906: Retired

*General of Infantry* Vasily Alekseyevich **Arbuzov** (17 May 1858 - 27 Sep 1919)
14 Nov 1902 - 2 Jul 1908: Military Judge, St. Petersburg Military District Court
6 Dec 1902: Promoted to *Major-General*
2 Jul 1908 - 3 May 1909: Military Prosecutor, Vilnius Military District Court
6 Dec 1908: Promoted to *Lieutenant-General*
3 May 1909 - 4 Jun 1912: Military Prosecutor, St. Petersburg Military District Court
4 Jun 1912 - 13 Dec 1916: Chairman of the Military Tribunal, Warsaw Military District
13 Dec 1916: Promoted to *General of Infantry*
13 Dec 1916: Retired

*Major-General* Georgy Pavlovich **Ardzhevanidze** (24 Jan 1863 - 16 Jan 1940)
2 Apr 1916 - 30 Sep 1917: Commander, Brigade, 39th Infantry Division
15 Jun 1916: Promoted to *Major-General*

*Major-General* Apollon Ivanovich **Arens** (14 Nov 1860 - 23 Feb 1916)
14 Apr 1903 - Mar 1915: Military Lecturer, Nikolayev Engineering Academy
14 Apr 1913: Promoted to *Major-General*
Mar 1915 - 23 Feb 1916: Deputy Chief of Engineers, Front

*General of the Fleet* Yevgeny Ivanovich **Arens** (4 Jan 1856 - 5 Nov 1931)
Aug 1896 - 21 Aug 1910: Associate Professor, Nikolayev Naval Academy
6 May 1905: Promoted to *Major-General of the Admiralty*
6 Dec 1909: Promoted to *Lieutenant-General of the Admiralty*
21 Aug 1910 - 11 Nov 1916: Professor, Nikolayev Naval Academy
8 Apr 1913: Redesignated *Lieutenant-General of the Fleet*
6 Dec 1915: Promoted to *General of the Fleet*

11 Nov 1916:                    Retired

*Lieutenant-General* Aleksandr Pavlovich **Argamakov** (23 Mar 1842 - 1931)
5 Mar 1884 - 1903:              Inspector, Polotsk Cadet Corps
?:                              Promoted to *Major-General*
1903:                           Promoted to *Lieutenant-General*
1903:                           Retired

*Lieutenant-General* Konstantin Fyodorovich **Argamakov** (1 Mar 1836 - 16 Mar 1907)
30 Sep 1880 - 22 Oct 1885:      Commander of Guards Troops, St. Petersburg Military District
24 Jan 1881:                    Promoted to *Major-General*
22 Oct 1885 - 28 Apr 1893:      Commander, 2$^{nd}$ Brigade, 37$^{th}$ Infantry Division
30 Aug 1893:                    Promoted to *Lieutenant-General*
28 Apr 1893 - 1903:             Commandant of Fortress Sveaborg
1903:                           Retired

*Major-General* Nikolai Nikolayevich **Argamakov** (14 Nov 1870 - ?)
30 Mar 1916 - Oct 1917:         Commander, 1$^{st}$ Battalion, 3$^{rd}$ Finnish Rifle Artillery Brigade
9 Feb 1917:                     Promoted to *Major-General*

*Lieutenant-General* Prince David Luarsabovich **Argutinsky-Dolgorukov** (1 May 1843 - 1910)
28 Mar 1894:                    Promoted to *Major-General*
28 Mar 1894 - 12 Oct 1895:      Commander, 1$^{st}$ Brigade, 28$^{th}$ Infantry Division
12 Oct 1895 - 1 Feb 1900:       Commander, Kexholmsky Life Guards Regiment
1 Feb 1900 - 3 Aug 1900:        Commander, 1$^{st}$ Brigade, 3$^{rd}$ Guards Infantry Division
3 Aug 1900 - 22 Mar 1901:       Commander, 2$^{nd}$ Brigade, 3$^{rd}$ Guards Infantry Division
22 Mar 1901 - 2 May 1903:       Commander, 1$^{st}$ Brigade, 3$^{rd}$ Guards Infantry Division
2 May 1903:                     Promoted to *Lieutenant-General*
2 May 1903:                     Retired

*Major-General* Andrei Trofimovitch **Arkannikov** (4 Jul 1856 - 29 Oct 1916)
2 May 1903 - 1906:              At the disposal of the Chief of the General Staff
6 Dec 1904:                     Promoted to *Major-General*
1906:                           Retired

*Lieutenant-General* Aleksei Petrovich **Arkhangelsky** (5 Mar 1872 - 2 Nov 1959)
19 Sep 1910 - 24 Jul 1914:      Deputy Duty General, General Staff
6 Dec 1913:                     Promoted to *Major-General*
24 Jul 1914 - 17 Apr 1917:      Duty General, General Staff
17 Apr 1917 - 9 May 1917:       Duty General to the Supreme Commander-in-Chief
24 Aug 1917:                    Promoted to *Lieutenant-General*
9 May 1917 - 8 Dec 1917:        Chief of the General Staff

*Major-General* Ivan Mikhailovich **Arkhangelsky** (17 Jul 1855 - ?)
10 Mar 1911 - 1917:             Commandant, Benderski District

6 Dec 1914: Promoted to *Major-General*

*Lieutenant-General* Nikolai Aleksandrovich **Arkhangelsky** (2 Mar 1862 - ?)
21 Aug 1907 - 1917: Inspector of Military School Construction
29 Mar 1909: Promoted to *Major-General*
22 Mar 1915: Promoted to *Lieutenant-General*

*Lieutenant-General* Aleksandr Aleksandrovich **Arkhipov** (27 Dec 1858 - 30 Sep 1922)
2 Dec 1911: Promoted to *Major-General*
2 Dec 1911 - 3 Aug 1914: Commander, 1st Brigade, 2nd Infantry Division
3 Aug 1914 - 16 Apr 1916: Commander, 1st Brigade, 57th Infantry Division
16 Apr 1916 - 1917: General Assignments Officer, Irkutsk Military District
1917: Promoted to *Lieutenant-General*
1917: Retired

*Major-General* Aleksandr Lazarevich **Arkhipov** (26 Aug 1859 - ?)
1 Jan 1916 - 18 Oct 1917: Reserve officer, Kiev Military District
29 Sep 1916: Promoted to *Major-General*
18 Oct 1917: Retired

*Major-General* Nikolai Aleksandrovich **Arkhipov** (24 Aug 1857 - 24 Jun 1909)
15 Apr 1907: Promoted to *Major-General*
15 Apr 1907 - 24 Jun 1909: Commander, Life Guards Grenadier Regiment

*General of Infantry* Vladimir Aleksandrovich **Arkhipov** (11 Oct 1855 - ?)
30 Jun 1902: Promoted to *Major-General*
30 Jun 1902 - 24 Dec 1908: Chief of Military Communications, Odessa Military District
24 Dec 1908: Promoted to *Lieutenant-General*
24 Dec 1908 - 9 May 1914: Commander, 29th Infantry Division
9 May 1914: Promoted to *General of Infantry*
9 May 1914: Retired

*Major-General* Nikolai Georgievich **Arkhipovich** (6 Dec 1869 - ?)
Aug 1914 - 26 Jun 1915: Commander, 74th Infantry Regiment
16 Dec 1914: Promoted to *Major-General*
26 Jun 1915 - 1916: Chief of Staff, XXXIX. Army Corps
1916 - 25 Mar 1916: Commander, 2nd Brigade, 1st Border Infantry Division
25 Mar 1916 - 25 Oct 1916: Commander, Brigade, 3rd Border Infantry Division
25 Oct 1916 - 7 Jul 1917: Commander, 12th Siberian Rifle Division

*Lieutenant-General* Aleksandr Ioannikievich **Arpashev** (4 Mar 1845 - ?)
24 Mar 1908: Promoted to *Major-General*
24 Mar 1908 - 1912: Commander, Minsk Regional Brigade
1912: Promoted to *Lieutenant-General*
1912: Retired

*General of Artillery* Dmitry Gavrilovich **Arsenyev** (5 Nov 1840 - 9 Apr 1912)
| | |
|---|---|
| 1 Jun 1887 - 10 Feb 1890: | Commander, 11th Artillery Brigade |
| 1 Jul 1887: | Promoted to *Major-General* |
| 10 Feb 1890 - 18 Jun 1892: | Commander of Artillery, Amur Military District |
| 18 Jun 1892 - 11 Jun 1897: | Military Governor of Amur, Ataman, Amur Cossack Army |
| 14 May 1896: | Promoted to *Lieutenant-General* |
| 11 Jun 1897 - 6 Mar 1903: | Governor of Perm |
| 6 Mar 1903 - 24 Aug 1903: | Mayor of Odessa |
| 24 Aug 1903 - 1909: | Attached to the Minister of Internal Affairs |
| 1909: | Promoted to *General of Artillery* |
| 1909: | Retired |

*Admiral* Dmitry Sergeyevich **Arsenyev** (14 Sep 1832 - 14 Sep 1915)
| | |
|---|---|
| 29 Apr 1877: | Promoted to *Rear-Admiral* |
| 29 Apr 1977 - 27 Jun 1882: | Admiral à la suite |
| 27 Jun 1882 - 14 May 1896: | Commandant of the Naval Academy |
| 26 Feb 1887: | Promoted to *Vice-Admiral* |
| 14 May 1896: | Promoted to *Adjutant-General* |
| 14 May 1896 - 1 Apr 1901: | Member of the Admiralty Board |
| 9 Aug 1900: | Promoted to *Admiral* |
| 1 Apr 1901 - 14 Sep 1915: | Member of the State Council |

*Lieutenant-General* Yevgeny Konstantinovich **Arsenyev** (3 Nov 1873 - 29 May 1938)
| | |
|---|---|
| 12 Nov 1914: | Promoted to *Major-General* |
| 23 Nov 1914 - 19 Dec 1915: | Commander, Life Guards Cuirassier Regiment |
| 19 Dec 1915 - 10 Mar 1917: | Commander, 2nd Brigade, 2nd Guards Cavalry Division |
| 10 Mar 1917 - 15 Apr 1917: | Commander, 1st Guards Cavalry Division |
| 15 Apr 1917 - Oct 1917: | Commander, Guards Cavalry Corps |
| 29 Apr 1917: | Promoted to *Lieutenant-General* |

*General of Infantry* Leonid Konstantinovich **Artamonov** (25 Feb 1859 - 1 Jan 1932)
| | |
|---|---|
| 7 Feb 1901: | Promoted to *Major-General* |
| 7 Feb 1901 - 30 Oct 1903: | Commander, 2nd Brigade, 31st Infantry Division |
| 30 Oct 1903 - 22 Feb 1904: | Commander, 8th East Siberian Rifle Brigade |
| 22 Feb 1904 - 17 Oct 1904: | Commander, 8th East Siberian Rifle Division |
| 17 Oct 1904 - 4 Jul 1906: | Commander, 54th Infantry Division |
| 4 Jul 1906 - 7 Jul 1906: | Acting Commander, 8th East Siberian Rifle Division |
| 7 Jul 1906 - 14 Dec 1908: | Commander, 22nd Infantry Division |
| 22 Apr 1907: | Promoted to *Lieutenant-General* |
| 14 Dec 1908 - 31 Dec 1910: | Commandant of Kronstadt |
| 31 Dec 1910 - 5 Mar 1911: | Commandant of Fortress Kronstadt |
| 5 Mar 1911 - 17 Mar 1911: | Commanding General, XVI. Army Corps |
| 17 Mar 1911 - 18 Aug 1914: | Commanding General, I. Army Corps |
| 14 Apr 1913: | Promoted to *General of Infantry* |
| 18 Aug 1914 - 1915: | Reserve officer, Minsk Military District |
| 1915: | Commandant of Fortress Przemysl |
| 9 Apr 1916 - 29 Jan 1917: | Reserve officer, Petrograd Military District |

29 Jan 1917 - 12 Apr 1917: Acting Commander, 18th Siberian Rifle Division

*Major-General* Maksimilian Konstantinovich **Artamonov** (22 Oct 1854 - ?)
4 Feb 1896 - 1902: Military Judge, Kiev Military District Court
6 Dec 1900: Promoted to *Major-General*

*General of Infantry* Mikhail Konstantinovich **Artamonov** (20 Oct 1857 - ?)
30 Apr 1899 - 13 Jul 1902: Military Judge, Turkestan Military District Court
1 Jan 1901: Promoted to *Major-General*
13 Jul 1902 - 23 Jan 1906: Military Prosecutor, Amur Military District
23 Jan 1906 - 11 May 1917: Chairman of the Military Tribunal, Amur Military District
22 Apr 1907: Promoted to *Lieutenant-General*
11 May 1917: Promoted to *General of Infantry*
11 May 1917: Retired

*General of Infantry* Nikolai Dmitrievich **Artamonov** (26 Oct 1840 - 1918)
14 Oct 1878 - 6 Mar 1886: Map Editor, Military Topographical Department, General Staff
15 May 1883: Promoted to *Major-General*
6 Mar 1886 - 11 Mar 1903: Commandant, Military Topography School
30 Aug 1894: Promoted to *Lieutenant-General*
13 Feb 1901 - 11 Mar 1903: Member of the Training Committee, General Staff
11 Mar 1903 - 1 May 1903: Chief of the Military Topographical Section, General Staff
1 May 1903 - 3 Apr 1911: Chief of the Military Topographical Directorate, General Staff
6 Dec 1906: Promoted to *General of Infantry*
3 Apr 1911 - Mar 1918: Member of the Military Council
22 Jun 1918: Retired

*Major-General* Nikolai Nikolayevich **Artamonov** (11 Mar 1872 - 28 Oct 1937)
18 Apr 1910 - Jan 1918: Ministry of War representative, Omsk Military District
6 Dec 1916: Promoted to *Major-General*

*Major-General* Viktor Alekseyevich **Artamonov** (9 Oct 1873 - 23 Aug 1942)
14 Oct 1909 - Oct 1917: Military Attaché, Serbia
6 Dec 1915: Promoted to *Major-General*

*Major-General* Nikandr Pavlovich **Artemyev** (26 Jun 1854 - 6 Apr 1935)
7 Jul 1905 - 1912: Commander of Gendarmerie, Yaroslavl
6 Dec 1911: Promoted to *Major-General*
1912: Retired

*Lieutenant-General of the Naval Legal Corps* Pyotr Aleksandrovich **Artemyev** (3 Aug 1859 - 17 Mar 1916)
8 Dec 1908 - 17 Mar 1916: Military Judge, Vladivostok Naval Court
6 Dec 1909: Promoted to *Major-General of the Naval Legal Corps*

3 Nov 1914 - 17 Mar 1916:     Chairman, Vladivostok Naval Prize Court
1915:     Promoted to *Lieutenant-General of the Naval Legal Corps*

*Lieutenant-General* Vasily Vasilievich **Artemyev** (14 Jun 1860 - 17 Dec 1929)
5 Aug 1904 - 17 Apr 1907:     Commander, Railway Brigade
6 Dec 1904:     Promoted to *Major-General*
17 Apr 1907 - 11 Jun 1910:     Commander, $2^{nd}$ Turkestan Reserve Brigade
11 Jun 1910 - 31 Dec 1913:     Commander, $2^{nd}$ Rifle Brigade
31 Dec 1913:     Promoted to *Lieutenant-General*
31 Dec 1913 - 8 May 1915:     Commander, $52^{nd}$ Infantry Division
8 May 1915 - 31 Oct 1916:     Commanding General, XXXVIII. Army Corps
31 Oct 1916 - 14 Apr 1917:     Commanding General, XLVII. Army Corps
14 Apr 1917:     Transferred to the reserve, Moscow Military District

*Major-General* Aleksandr Mikhailovich **Artobolevsky** (3 Jan 1841 - ?)
24 Oct 1899:     Promoted to *Major-General*
24 Oct 1899 - 8 Jan 1901:     Commander, $2^{nd}$ Brigade, $14^{th}$ Infantry Division
8 Jan 1901:     Retired

*Rear-Admiral* Aleksey Nikolayevich **Artseulov** (1854 - 30 Oct 1910)
?:     Promoted to *Rear-Admiral*
1905:     Retired

*Major-General of Naval Engineers* Konstantin Nikolayevich **Artseulov** (1847 - 1919)
1900 - 1901:     Senior Shipbuilder, Port of Sevastopol
1901:     Promoted to *Major-General of Naval Engineers*
1901:     Retired

*Major-General* Adolf Feliksovich **Artsishevsky** (17 Jun 1829 - 10 Feb 1895)
18 Mar 1880 - 13 Dec 1881:     Commander, Taman Cossack Regiment
13 Dec 1881:     Promoted to *Major-General*
13 Dec 1881 - 14 May 1884:     Attached to Kuban Cossack Army
14 May 1884 - 10 Feb 1895:     Commander, $2^{nd}$ Brigade, Caucasus Cossack Division

*Major-General* Prince **Artsu-Chermoyev** (16 Jul 1825 - 27 Sep 1895)
24 Sep 1871:     Promoted to *Major-General*
24 Sep 1871 - 25 Dec 1872:     Unassigned
25 Sep 1872 - 27 Sep 1895:     Attached to Caucasus Military District

*Lieutenant-General* Vasily Nikolayevich **Artsybushev** (25 Jun 1834 - ?)
30 Aug 1876:     Promoted to *Major-General*
30 Aug 1876 - 14 May 1877:     Chairman of the Military Tribunal, Command Directorate
14 May 1877 - 19 Oct 1883:     Attached to the Commanding General, St. Petersburg Military District
19 Oct 1883 - Sep 1896:     Chief of St. Petersburg Nikolayev Military Hospital
30 Aug 1887:     Promoted to *Lieutenant-General*

*Major-General* Ivan Ignatievich **Artsyshevsky** (21 Jun 1844 - ?)
| | |
|---|---|
| 22 Mar 1895 - 18 Oct 1896: | Chief of Staff, Fortress Modlin |
| 25 Jul 1895: | Promoted to *Major-General* |
| 18 Oct 1896 - 13 Dec 1897: | Chief of Staff, XIX. Army Corps |
| 13 Dec 1897 - 10 Mar 1898: | Commander, 2nd Brigade, 10th Infantry Division |
| 10 Mar 1898 - 17 Nov 1899: | Chief of Staff, VI. Army Corps |
| 17 Nov 1899 - May 1904: | Commander, 2nd Brigade, 17th Infantry Division |

*Lieutenant-General* Tigran Danilovich **Aryutinov** (1 Jun 1858 - 10 Jan 1916)
| | |
|---|---|
| 5 Nov 1912: | Promoted to *Major-General* |
| 5 Nov 1912 - 29 Jul 1914: | Commander, 2nd Brigade, 1st Caucasus Cossack Division |
| 29 Jul 1914 - 10 Jan 1916: | Commander, 1st Terek Cossack Division |
| 6 Dec 1915: | Promoted to *Lieutenant-General* |

*Major-General* Dmitry Pavlovich **Aseyev** (20 Oct 1852 - Mar 1915)
| | |
|---|---|
| 16 Aug 1908: | Promoted to *Major-General* |
| 16 Aug 1908 - 25 Jul 1910: | Commander, 39th Artillery Brigade |
| 25 Jul 1910 - 23 Oct 1912: | Commander, Caucasus Grenadier Artillery Brigade |
| 23 Oct 1912: | Retired |
| 14 Nov 1914 - 6 Jan 1915: | Recalled; Reserve officer, Caucasus Military District |
| 6 Jan 1915 - Mar 1915: | Inspector of Artillery, IV. Caucasus Army Corps |

*Major-General* Mikhail Vasilyevich **Aseyev** (5 Oct 1863 - ?)
| | |
|---|---|
| 14 Nov 1914 - 18 Nov 1916: | Reserve officer, Kiev Military District |
| 18 Nov 1916: | Promoted to *Major-General* |
| 18 Nov 1916: | Dismissed |

*Major-General* Sergey Pavlovich **Aseyev** (12 Sep 1855 - ?)
| | |
|---|---|
| 14 Sep 1913 - 1917: | Military Commander, Nizhny Novgorod District |
| 6 Dec 1914: | Promoted to *Major-General* |

*Major-General* Viktor Pavlovich **Aseyev** (24 Feb 1851 - ?)
| | |
|---|---|
| 22 Feb 1904: | Promoted to *Major-General* |
| 22 Feb 1904 - Jul 1907: | Commander, 1st Brigade, 2nd East Siberian Rifle Division |

*Major-General* Vladimir Pavlovich **Aseyev** (27 Jan 1850 - ?)
| | |
|---|---|
| 18 Jun 1901: | Promoted to *Major-General* |
| 18 Jun 1901 - 2 Sep 1904: | Commander, 2nd Brigade, 14th Infantry Division |
| 2 Sep 1904 - 12 Jan 1905: | Commander, 1st Brigade, 52nd Infantry Division |
| 12 Jan 1905 - 1908: | Commander, 58th Reserve Infantry Brigade |

*General of Infantry* Baron Nikolai Pavlovich von **Asheberg** (28 May 1846 - ?)
| | |
|---|---|
| 14 Aug 1895: | Promoted to *Major-General* |
| 14 Aug 1895 - 16 Mar 1900: | Commander, 2nd Life Guards Rifle Battalion |
| 16 Mar 1900 - 8 Jul 1906: | Commander, St. Petersburg Regional Brigade |
| 1 Jan 1903: | Promoted to *Lieutenant-General* |

| | |
|---|---|
| 8 Jul 1906 - 26 Aug 1908: | Commanding General, XVIII. Army Corps |
| 26 Aug 1908 - 23 Aug 1912: | Deputy Commanding General, St. Petersburg Military District |
| 6 Dec 1908: | Promoted to *General of Infantry* |
| 23 Aug 1912 - 1917: | Member of the Military Council |
| 30 Aug 1914 - 18 Nov 1914: | Commanding General, Petrograd Military District |

*Major-General* Pavel Mikhailovich **Ashikhmanov** (5 Jun 1859 - ?)
| | |
|---|---|
| 31 Dec 1913 - 1917: | Commandant, Kremenchug Artillery Depot |
| 6 Dec 1914: | Promoted to *Major-General* |

*Vice-Admiral* Avramy Bogdanovich **Aslanbegov** (10 Sep 1822 - 7 Dec 1900)
| | |
|---|---|
| 1876 - Aug 1879: | Commander, 8th Naval Depot |
| 1 Jan 1878: | Promoted to *Rear-Admiral* |
| Aug 1879 - 1881: | Commander, Cruiser Squadron |
| 1881 - 1882: | Commander of Naval Forces, Pacific |
| 1883 - 8 Apr 1884: | Commander, Squadron |
| 8 Apr 1884 - 1898: | Junior Flagman, Baltic Fleet |
| 22 Sep 1887: | Promoted to *Vice-Admiral* |
| 1898: | Retired |

*Lieutenant-General* Konstantin Vladimirovich **Asmus** (12 May 1857 - 22 Feb 1916)
| | |
|---|---|
| 22 May 1910: | Promoted to *Major-General* |
| 22 May 1910 - 4 Apr 1915: | Chief of Staff, XIX. Army Corps |
| 4 Apr 1915 - 22 Feb 1916: | Commander, 27th Infantry Division |
| 18 Feb 1916: | Promoted to *Lieutenant-General* |

*General of Infantry* Viktor Karlovich **Aspelund** (16 May 1842 - 7 May 1912)
| | |
|---|---|
| 26 Dec 1892: | Promoted to *Major-General* |
| 26 Dec 1892 - 25 May 1899: | Commander, 1st Brigade, 35th Infantry Division |
| 25 May 1899 - 19 May 1900: | Commander, 55th Replacement Infantry Brigade |
| 19 May 1900 - 8 Apr 1904: | Commander, 3rd Infantry Division |
| 6 Dec 1900: | Promoted to *Lieutenant-General* |
| 8 Apr 1904 - 7 May 1912: | Member of the Committee for Wounded Veterans |
| 1908: | Promoted to *General of Infantry* |

*Major-General* **Assadul-Bek-Iedigarov** (20 Dec 1844 - ?)
| | |
|---|---|
| 12 Oct 1895: | Promoted to *Major-General* |
| 12 Oct 1895 - 1903: | Attached to the Caucasus Military District |

*Major-General* Konstantin Vasilievich **Asseyev** (20 May 1858 - Apr 1909)
| | |
|---|---|
| 24 Nov 1908: | Promoted to *Major-General* |
| 24 Nov 1908 - Jan 1909: | Commander, 1st Brigade, 19th Infantry Division |

*Lieutenant-General* Lev Georgiyevich **Astafyev** (29 Oct 1857 - 13 Feb 1911)
| | |
|---|---|
| 21 Aug 1905 - 13 Feb 1911: | Commander of Gendarmerie, Kurland Province |
| 2 Apr 1906: | Promoted to *Major-General* |
| 1911: | Promoted to *Lieutenant-General* |

*Major-General* Ivan Petrovich **Astakhov** (13 Jun 1863 - 26 Nov 1935)
26 Sep 1916: Promoted to *Major-General*
26 Sep 1916 - 17 Dec 1916: Commander, 38th Artillery Brigade
17 Dec 1916 - 18 Jun 1917: Commander, 7th Turkestan Rifle Artillery Brigade
18 Jun 1917 - 1918: Commander of Artillery, Don Army

*Lieutenant-General* Pyotr Fyodorovich **Astanin** (12 Jun 1852 - ?)
18 Jul 1905: Promoted to *Major-General*
18 Jul 1905 - 12 Jun 1912: Commander, 2nd Brigade, 25th Infantry Division
12 Jun 1912: Promoted to *Lieutenant-General*
12 Jun 1912: Retired

*Major-General* Aleksandr Vasilievich **Astashev** (19 Aug 1865 - 1919)
16 Aug 1914 - 6 Aug 1915: Commander, 249th Infantry Regiment
6 Aug 1915 - 19 Oct 1917: Commander, Brigade, 48th Infantry Division
11 Aug 1915: Promoted to *Major-General*

*General of Artillery* Andrei Adamovich **Atabekov** (5 Oct 1854 - 10 Sep 1918)
1 Mar 1900 - 31 Oct 1903: Commander, 1st Grenadier Artillery Brigade
9 Apr 1900: Promoted to *Major-General*
31 Oct 1903 - 5 Apr 1907: Commandant, Konstantinovsky Artillery School
6 Dec 1906: Promoted to *Lieutenant-General*
5 Apr 1907 - 21 Aug 1907: Commander of Artillery, XIX. Army Corps
21 Aug 1907 - 31 Jul 1910: Commander of Artillery, XVII. Army Corps
31 Jul 1910 - 21 Apr 1913: Inspector of Artillery, XVII. Army Corps
21 Apr 1913 - 18 May 1917: Commander of Artillery, Moscow Military District
10 Apr 1916: Promoted to *General of Artillery*
18 May 1917 - 1 Jan 1918: Reserve officer, Moscow Military District
1 Jan 1918: Dismissed

*Major-General* Avgust Vasilievich **Aurenius** (22 Mar 1850 - ?)
15 Aug 1898 - 9 Oct 1903: Commander, 3rd East Siberian Rifle Regiment
5 Feb 1903: Promoted to *Major-General*
9 Oct 1903 - 25 Jan 1904: Commander, 2nd Brigade, 44th Infantry Division

*Major-General* Prince Aleksandr Semyonov **Avalov** (8 Sep 1852 - 8 Mar 1916)
? - 1910: Commander, 30th Dragoon Regiment
1910: Promoted to *Major-General*
1910: Retired
8 Mar 1915 - 20 Sep 1915: Recalled; Commander, 228th Infantry Brigade
20 Sep 1915 - 8 Mar 1916: Reserve officer, Odessa Military District

*General of Cavalry* Nikolai Vasilievich **Avdeyev** (18 Apr 1852 - ?)
6 Mar 1900: Promoted to *Major-General*
6 Mar 1900 - 19 Nov 1907: Commander, 2nd Brigade, 10th Cavalry Division
19 Nov 1907: Promoted to *Lieutenant-General*
19 Nov 1907 - 14 Sep 1911: Commander, 2nd Consolidated Cossack Division

14 Sep 1911: Promoted to *General of Cavalry*
14 Sep 1911: Retired

*Admiral* Fyodor Karlovich **Avelan** (31 Aug 1839 - 17 Nov 1916)
1 Jan 1890 - 6 May 1891: Commandant, 3rd Naval Depot
1 Jan 1891: Promoted to *Rear-Admiral*
6 May 1891 - 1 Aug 1893: Chief of Staff, Kronstadt Naval Port
1 Aug 1893 - 7 Nov 1894: Commander, Mediterranean Squadron
7 Nov 1894 - 1 Jan 1895: Deputy Commander, 2nd Naval Division
1 Jan 1895 - 13 Jul 1896: Deputy Chief of the Main Naval Staff
21 May 1895 - 8 Sep 1895: Acting Chief of the Main Naval Staff
13 Jul 1896 - 4 Mar 1903: Chief of the Main Naval Staff
6 Dec 1896: Promoted to *Vice-Admiral*
7 Jun 1897 - 19 Jul 1897: Acting Minister of the Navy
8 Mar 1898 - 21 Apr 1898: Acting Minister of the Navy
12 Jul 1898 - 9 Sep 1898: Acting Minister of the Navy
17 Jun 1899 - 3 Aug 1899: Acting Minister of the Navy
3 Jul 1901 - 31 Aug 1901: Acting Minister of the Navy
4 Mar 1903 - 29 Jun 1905: Minister of the Navy
6 Apr 1903: Promoted to *General-Adjutant*
17 Apr 1905: Promoted to *Admiral*
29 Jun 1905: Retired
11 Oct 1914 - 17 Nov 1916: Member of the State Council

*Major-General* Karl Karlovich **Avellan** (2 Mar 1835 - 22 Feb 1897)
30 Jul 1894 - 22 Feb 1897: Commander, 5th Grenadier Regiment
14 May 1896: Promoted to *Major-General*

*Major-General* Mikhail Yakovlevich **Avenarius** (14 Apr 1854 - ?)
5 Nov 1906 - 16 Nov 1912: Director, Petersburg-Semyonovsky-Aleksandrovsky Military Hospital
6 Dec 1911: Promoted to *Major-General*
16 Nov 1912 - 22 Aug 1913: Reserve officer, St. Petersburg Military District
22 Aug 1913: Retired

*Major-General* Konstantin Ivanovich **Averin** (18 May 1840 - ?)
31 May 1888 - 14 Oct 1893: Junior Deputy Military Commander, Kuban Region, Ataman, Kuban Cossack Army
30 Aug 1890: Promoted to *Major-General*
14 Oct 1893 - 1897: Attached to the Kuban Cossack Army

*Major-General* Georgy Alekseyevich **Averkiyev** (18 Mar 1852 - ?)
2 Apr 1891 - 24 Oct 1900: Military Judge, Vilnius Military District Court
6 Dec 1898: Promoted to *Major-General*
24 Oct 1900 - 1908: Military Judge, Turkestan Military District Court

*Lieutenant-General* Pyotr Ivanovich **Averyanov** (5 Oct 1867 - 13 Oct 1937)
17 Apr 1908 - 6 Dec 1910: Commander, 16th Grenadier Regiment

| | |
|---|---|
| 6 Dec 1910: | Promoted to *Major-General* |
| 6 Dec 1910 - 27 Mar 1914: | Second Deputy Quartermaster-General, General Staff |
| 27 Mar 1914 - 20 Nov 1914: | Chief of Staff, Irkutsk Military District |
| 20 Nov 1914 - 10 Aug 1916: | Chief of the Main Mobilization Directorate of the General Staff |
| 10 Aug 1916 - 9 May 1917: | Chief of the General Directorate of the General Staff |
| 6 Dec 1916: | Promoted to *Lieutenant-General* |
| 9 May 1917 - 15 May 1917: | At the disposal of the Minister of War |
| 15 May 1917 - 1918: | Chief of Logistics, Caucasus Front |

*Major-General* Pyotr Aleksandrovich **Avgustov** (16 Aug 1862 - ?)
| | |
|---|---|
| 16 Mar 1914 - 9 Oct 1916: | Commander, 254$^{th}$ Infantry Regiment |
| 21 May 1915: | Promoted to *Major-General* |
| 9 Oct 1916 - 29 Jul 1917: | Reserve officer, Kiev Military District |
| 29 Jul 1917: | Dismissed |

*Major-General* Vladimir Vasilyevich **Avilov** (2 Feb 1870 - 22 May 1916)
| | |
|---|---|
| 11 Jan 1916 - 22 May 1916: | Commander, 2$^{nd}$ Battalion, 6$^{th}$ Field Artillery Brigade |
| 19 Oct 1916: | Posthumously promoted to *Major-General* |

*Lieutenant-General* Fyodor Aleksandrovich **Avinov** (19 Sep 1835 - 1903)
| | |
|---|---|
| 7 Apr 1886: | Promoted to *Major-General* |
| 7 Apr 1886 - 20 Dec 1892: | Commander, 2$^{nd}$ Brigade, 11$^{th}$ Infantry Division |
| 20 Dec 1892 - 2 Apr 1899: | Commander, 2$^{nd}$ Brigade, 3$^{rd}$ Grenadier Division |
| 2 Apr 1899 - 11 Sep 1902: | Commander, Tambov Regional Brigade |
| 6 Dec 1899: | Promoted to *Lieutenant-General* |
| 11 Sep 1902 - 1903: | At the disposal of the Commanding General, Moscow Military District |

*Lieutenant-General* Nikolai Aleksandrovich **Avinov** (17 Oct 1844 - 1911)
| | |
|---|---|
| 31 Dec 1892: | Promoted to *Major-General* |
| 31 Dec 1892 - 18 Feb 1898: | Commander, Turkestan Infantry Brigade |
| 18 Feb 1898 - 31 Aug 1900: | Commander, Finnish Rifle Brigade |
| 31 Aug 1900 - 20 May 1901: | Commander, 12$^{th}$ Infantry Division |
| 6 Dec 1900: | Promoted to *Lieutenant-General* |
| 1903: | Retired |

*General of Infantry* Sergey Aleksandrovich **Avinov** (7 Oct 1831 - 24 Dec 1906)
| | |
|---|---|
| 10 Dec 1865 - 10 Dec 1873: | Commander, 75$^{th}$ Infantry Regiment |
| 10 Dec 1873: | Promoted to *Major-General* |
| 10 Dec 1873 - 4 Apr 1874: | Unassigned |
| 4 Apr 1874 - 9 Jun 1875: | Commander, 2$^{nd}$ Brigade, 39$^{th}$ Infantry Division |
| 9 Jun 1875 - 22 Feb 1880: | Commander, 1$^{st}$ Brigade, Caucasus Grenadier Division |
| 22 Feb 1880 - 1 Dec 1883: | Commander, 20$^{th}$ Infantry Division |
| 10 May 1883: | Promoted to *Lieutenant-General* |
| 1 Dec 1883 - 2 Aug 1884: | Unassigned |
| 2 Aug 1884 - 16 Jul 1885: | Commander, 9$^{th}$ Infantry Division |
| 16 Jul 1885 - 8 Mar 1893: | Commander, Caucasus Grenadier Division |

| | |
|---|---|
| 8 Mar 1893 - 19 May 1895: | At the disposal of the Minister of War |
| 19 May 1895 - 24 Dec 1906: | Member, Committee for Wounded Veterans |
| 14 May 1896: | Promoted to *General of Infantry* |

*Lieutenant-General* Dmitry Ivanovich **Avramov** (26 May 1850 - ?)
| | |
|---|---|
| 1 Jun 1904: | Promoted to *Major-General* |
| 1 Jun 1904 - 13 Jul 1906: | Commander, 1st Brigade, 51st Infantry Division |
| 13 Jul 1906 - 2 Jul 1907: | Commander, 1st Brigade, 41st Infantry Division |
| 2 Jul 1907 - 2 Jun 1910: | Commander, 53rd Replacement Infantry Brigade |
| 2 Jun 1910: | Promoted to *Lieutenant-General* |
| 2 Jun 1910: | Retired |
| 8 Feb 1915 - 29 Jun 1915: | Recalled; Commander, 99th Militia Brigade |
| 29 Jun 1915 - 8 Jul 1915: | Attached to Fortress Modlin |
| 8 Jul 1915 - 11 Jun 1918: | POW, Germany |
| 18 Jun 1918: | Retired |

*Major-General* Ivan Petrovich **Avramov** (28 Jan 1831 - ?)
| | |
|---|---|
| 22 Apr 1888: | Promoted to *Major-General* |
| 22 Apr 1888 - 5 Jul 1895: | Commander, 1st Brigade, 19th Infantry Division |
| 5 Jul 1895 - 9 Oct 1899: | Commander, 1st Brigade, 14th Infantry Division |

*Lieutenant-General* Nikolai Alekseyevich **Aygustov** (1 Jan 1841 - 10 Jan 1918)
| | |
|---|---|
| 15 Oct 1895 - 17 Jul 1900: | Commander, 2nd East Siberian Brigade |
| 6 Dec 1895: | Promoted to *Major-General* |
| 17 Jul 1900 - 28 May 1903: | At the disposal of the Commanding General, Amur Military District |
| 28 May 1903 - Aug 1905: | Governor of Yenisei |
| 17 Apr 1905: | Promoted to *Lieutenant-General* |
| Aug 1905: | Retired |

*Major-General* Mitrofan Nikolayevich **Azaryev** (16 Nov 1869 - ?)
| | |
|---|---|
| 3 Nov 1914 - 21 Jun 1916: | Judge, Vladivostok Naval Prize Court |
| 22 Mar 1915: | Promoted to *Major-General* |
| 21 Jun 1916 - 1917: | Chairman, Vladivostok Naval Prize Court |

*Lieutenant-General* Nikolai Nikolayevich **Azaryev** (24 Feb 1848 - ?)
| | |
|---|---|
| 1902: | Promoted to *Major-General* |
| 8 May 1906: | Promoted to *Lieutenant-General* |

*Major-General* Nikolai Nikolayevich **Azaryev** (26 Sep 1865 - 1933)
| | |
|---|---|
| 24 Jul 1910 - 20 May 1915: | Commander, 14th Turkestan Rifle Regiment |
| 5 Jan 1915: | Promoted to *Major-General* |
| 20 May 1915 - 1917: | Commander, 4th Turkestan Rifle Division |

*Major-General of the Fleet* Pyotr Pavlovich **Azbelev** (27 Feb 1868 - 28 Feb 1933)
| | |
|---|---|
| 1912: | Promoted to *Major-General of the Admiralty* |
| ?: | Member, Commission for Air Force Organization |
| 8 Apr 1913: | Redesignated *Major-General of the Fleet* |

*Lieutenant-General* Aleksandr Feofilaktinovich **Babakin** (26 Aug 1848 - ?)
29 Dec 1899 - 27 Feb 1903:   Commander, 42nd Artillery Brigade
1 Jan 1900:                  Promoted to *Major-General*
27 Feb 1903 - 1904:          Attached to the Main Artillery Directorate
1904:                        Promoted to *Lieutenant-General*
1904:                        Retired

*Major-General* Nikolai Emmanuilovich **Babalykov** (30 Dec 1836 - 20 Feb 1905)
8 Oct 1881 - 1899:           Attached to the Kuban Cossack Army
6 Oct 1888:                  Promoted to *Major-General*
1899:                        Retired

*Major-General* Andrei Aleksandrovich **Babchenko** (24 Sep 1861 - ?)
24 May 1903 - 1912:          Commandant, Yaroslavl Cadet Corps
6 Dec 1906:                  Promoted to *Major-General*
1912:                        Retired

*Lieutenant-General* Georgy Pavlovich **Babich** (6 Apr 1862 - 15 Feb 1943)
19 Feb 1908 - 22 Apr 1916:   Chief of Gendarmerie, Orenburg Province
14 Apr 1913:                 Promoted to *Major-General*
22 Apr 1916:                 Promoted to *Lieutenant-General*

*Major-General* Ivan Pavlovich **Babich** (22 Jan 1850 - 1 Mar 1918)
17 Mar 1915 - 1916:          Commander, 3rd Regiment, Consolidated Kuban
                             Cossack Army
1916:                        Promoted to *Major-General*
1916:                        Retired

*General of Infantry* Mikhail Pavlovich **Babich** (23 Jul 1844 - 18 Oct 1918)
6 May 1899:                  Promoted to *Major-General*
6 May 1899 - 1 Dec 1906:     Deputy Commander, Kuban Region,
                             Deputy Commander, Kuban Cossack Army
1 Dec 1906 - 3 Feb 1908:     Military Governor, Kars Region
22 Apr 1907:                 Promoted to *Lieutenant-General*
3 Feb 1908 - 26 Mar 1917:    Commander, Kuban Region,
                             Commander, Kuban Cossack Army
17 Nov 1914:                 Promoted to *General of Infantry*
26 Mar 1917:                 Retired

*Major-General* Gavril Fyodorovich **Babiev** (18 Mar 1860 - 6 Feb 1921)
5 Feb 1913 - 7 Jun 1916:     Commander, 1st Regiment, Kuban Cossack Army
18 Nov 1915:                 Promoted to *Major-General*
7 Jun 1916 - 1917:           Commander, 1st Brigade, 1st Kuban Cossack Division

*Major-General* Mikhail Sergeyevich **Babikov** (13 Oct 1846 - ?)
24 Feb 1901:                 Promoted to *Major-General*
24 Feb 1901 - Dec 1904:      Commander, 16th Artillery Brigade

*Lieutenant-General* Nikolai Aleksandrovich **Babikov** (2 Dec 1866 - May 1920)
| | |
|---|---|
| 15 Jun 1910: | Promoted to *Major-General* |
| 15 Jun 1910 - 21 Dec 1910: | Commander, 2nd Brigade, 11th Infantry Division |
| 21 Dec 1910 - 19 Jul 1914: | Commander, 2nd Brigade, 15th Infantry Division |
| 19 Jul 1914 - 6 Sep 1914: | Quartermaster-General, 3rd Army |
| 6 Sep 1914 - 2 Oct 1914: | Commander, 2nd Brigade, 15th Infantry Division |
| 2 Oct 1914 - 31 Jul 1915: | Commander, 12th Infantry Division |
| 5 Oct 1914: | Promoted to *Lieutenant-General* |
| 31 Jul 1915 - 22 Aug 1915: | Reserve officer, Kiev Military District |
| 22 Aug 1915 - 20 Oct 1915: | Reserve officer, Petrograd Military District |
| 20 Oct 1915 - 6 Dec 1916: | At the disposal of the Minister of War |
| 6 Dec 1916 - 1917: | Director-General, Special Defense Council |

*General of the Naval Legal Corps* Andrei Aleksandrovich **Babitsyn** (28 Nov 1841 - 1914)
| | |
|---|---|
| 1 Jan 1892 - 1 Jul 1896: | Chairman, Nikolayev Naval Court |
| 17 Apr 1894: | Promoted to *Major-General of the Admiralty* |
| 1 Jul 1896 - 20 Oct 1903: | Chairman, Kronstadt Naval Court |
| 1 Apr 1901: | Promoted to *Lieutenant-General of the Admiralty* |
| 20 Oct 1903 - 28 Aug 1909: | Member, Supreme Naval Tribunal |
| 9 Aug 1909: | Promoted to *General of the Naval Legal Corps* |
| 28 Aug 1909 - 28 Nov 1911: | Chairman, Supreme Naval Tribunal |
| 28 Nov 1911: | Retired |

*Major-General* Sergey Ivanovich **Babkin** (18 Jan 1863 - ?)
| | |
|---|---|
| 1 Feb 1898 - 1910: | Attached to Main Cossack Directorate |
| 1910: | Promoted to *Major-General* |
| 1910: | Retired |
| 1914 - ?: | Recalled; Commander, 234th Infantry Brigade, Don Militia |

*Major-General* Aleksandr Artemievich **Babochkin** (1 Apr 1866 - 2 May 1944)
| | |
|---|---|
| 1914 - 5 May 1916: | Commander, 247th Infantry Regiment |
| 13 Jul 1915: | Promoted to *Major-General* |
| 5 May 1916 - 3 Jun 1917: | Commander, Brigade, 81st Infantry Division |
| 3 Jun 1917 - 1917: | Commander, 69th Infantry Division |

*Major-General* Aleksey Aleksandrovich **Babushkin** (1 Jan 1861 - 2 Jun 1936)
| | |
|---|---|
| 22 May 1912 - 19 Dec 1915: | Member, Grodno Fortress Steering Committee, Ministry of War |
| 6 Dec 1912: | Promoted to *Major-General* |
| 19 Dec 1915 - 1917: | Reserve officer, Dvinsk Military District |

*Major-General* Vasily Aleksandrovich **Babushkin** (24 Dec 1857 - ?)
| | |
|---|---|
| 31 Jul 1912 - Mar 1917: | Chief of Gendarmerie, Ryazan Province |
| 6 Dec 1913: | Promoted to *Major-General* |
| Mar 1917 - 30 Mar 1917: | Chief of Gendarmerie, Simbirsk Province |
| 30 Sep 1917: | Retired |

*Major-General* Konstantin Ivanovich **Bachevksy** (11 Oct 1851 - 19 Jun 1914)
| | |
|---|---|
| 21 Aug 1908: | Promoted to *Major-General* |
| 21 Aug 1908 - 1910: | Commander, 2nd Brigade, 8th East Siberian Rifle Division |
| 1910 - 18 Oct 1911: | Commander, 2nd Brigade, 8th Siberian Rifle Division |
| 18 Oct 1911: | Dismissed |

*Lieutenant-General* Aleksandr Lvovich **Bachinsky** (13 Jan 1852 - ?)
| | |
|---|---|
| 30 Nov 1903 - 29 Jul 1905: | Intendant, Amur Military District |
| 4 Jan 1905: | Promoted to *Major-General* |
| 29 Jul 1905 - 6 Feb 1906: | Intendant, Manchurian Army |
| 6 Feb 1906 - 12 Jun 1908: | Intendant, Moscow Military District |
| 12 Jun 1908 - 1911: | Deputy Intendant-General, Ministry of War |
| 24 Jan 1911: | Promoted to *Lieutenant-General* |
| 1911: | Dismissed |

*Lieutenant-General* Mikhail Lvovich **Bachinsky** (30 Sep 1858 - 24 Oct 1937)
| | |
|---|---|
| 20 Feb 1904 - 9 Mar 1905: | Commander, 36th East Siberian Rifle Regiment |
| 2 Jun 1904: | Promoted to *Major-General* |
| 9 Mar 1905 - 25 Apr 1905: | Commander, 2nd Brigade, 3rd East Siberian Rifle Division |
| 25 Apr 1905 - 16 May 1906: | Commander, 2nd Brigade, 5th East Siberian Rifle Division |
| 16 May 1906 - 18 Apr 1915: | Transferred to the Borderguards Corps |
| 18 Apr 1915 - 1917: | Commander, 11th Infantry Division |
| 8 May 1915: | Promoted to *Lieutenant-General* |
| 1917: | Commanding General, VII. Siberian Army Corps |

*Lieutenant-General* Edmund Karlovich von **Bader** (7 Jul 1843 - ?)
| | |
|---|---|
| 3 Jun 1887 - 3 Mar 1895: | Commander, 6th Dragoon Regiment |
| 14 Nov 1894: | Promoted to *Major-General* |
| 3 Mar 1895 - 30 Jan 1902: | Commander, 1st Brigade, 4th Cavalry Division |
| 30 Jan 1902 - 24 Dec 1903: | Commander, 11th Cavalry Division |
| 14 Apr 1902: | Promoted to *Lieutenant-General* |
| 24 Dec 1903 - Dec 1906: | Commander, 4th Cavalry Division |
| Dec 1906: | Retired |

*Major-General* Mikhail Vasilievich **Bagayev** (8 Nov 1855 - ?)
| | |
|---|---|
| 1904 - 1905: | Commander, 26th Don Cossack Regiment |
| 1905 - 1910: | Transferred to the reserve |
| 1910: | Retired |
| 1916: | Recalled; Promoted to *Major-General* |
| Dec 1916 - 1917: | Inspector of Hospitals, Petrograd |

*General of Artillery* Ivan Karlovich **Baggovut** (12 Apr 1862 - 9 Feb 1933)
| | |
|---|---|
| 13 Jun 1907: | Promoted to *Major-General* |
| 13 Jun 1907 - 14 Nov 1909: | Commander, 37th Artillery Brigade |
| 14 Nov 1909 - 27 May 1910: | Commander, 2nd Life Guards Artillery Brigade |

| | |
|---|---|
| 27 May 1910 - 18 Oct 1913: | Commander of Artillery, Don Cossack Army |
| 31 Dec 1911: | Promoted to *Lieutenant-General* |
| 18 Oct 1913 - 19 Jul 1914: | Inspector of Artillery, I. Army Corps |
| 19 Jul 1914 - 19 Dec 1914: | Commander, 74$^{th}$ Infantry Division |
| 19 Dec 1914 - 27 Jun 1915: | Special Purposes General, 3$^{rd}$ Army |
| 27 Jun 1915 - 26 May 1917: | Inspector of Artillery, XLII. Army Corps |
| 26 May 1917: | Promoted to *General of Artillery* |
| 26 May 1917: | Retired |

*General of Infantry* Karl Fyodorovich **Baggovut** (20 Oct 1810 - 8 Mar 1895)
| | |
|---|---|
| 20 Jun 1862 - 1 Nov 1882: | Commandant of Gatchina Palace |
| 30 Aug 1862: | Promoted to *Major-General* |
| 16 Apr 1872: | Promoted to *Lieutenant-General* |
| 1 Nov 1882 - 8 Mar 1895: | Director, Nikolaev Chesmenskaya Military Almshouses, Member, Committee for Wounded Veterans |
| 30 Aug 1886: | Promoted to *General of Infantry* |

*Lieutenant-General* Nikolai Nikolayevich **Baggovut** (13 Nov 1853 - 1924)
| | |
|---|---|
| 11 Jan 1900 - 10 Feb 1910: | Director, Streletsky Remount Farms |
| 17 Apr 1905: | Promoted to *Major-General* |
| 10 Feb 1910 - 20 Jan 1911: | Attached to the Ministry of War |
| 20 Jan 1911 - 15 Feb 1913: | Head of Remount Commission, Kharkov Region |
| 14 Apr 1913: | Promoted to *Lieutenant-General* |
| 15 Feb 1913 - 1917: | General for Special Purposes, Main Remount Office |

*Major-General* Ivan Sergeyevich **Bagramov** (7 Nov 1860 - 1921)
| | |
|---|---|
| 19 Sep 1910 - 14 Jan 1913: | Section Chief, Main Directorate of the General Staff |
| 25 Mar 1912: | Promoted to *Major-General* |
| 14 Jan 1913 - 1917: | Section Chief, General Staff |

*Major-General* Prince Aleksandr Petrovich **Bagration** (18 Jul 1862 - Dec 1920)
| | |
|---|---|
| ? - 2 Jul 1916: | Deputy Director of Troop Movement, Moscow-Smolensk Region |
| 2 Jul 1916: | Promoted to *Major-General* |
| 2 Jul 1916: | Dismissed |

*Lieutenant-General* Prince Dmitry Petrovich **Bagration** (13 Jun 1863 - 21 Oct 1919)
| | |
|---|---|
| 1 Jul 1909 - 25 May 1913: | Deputy Commandant, Cavalry School |
| 6 Dec 1909: | Promoted to *Major-General* |
| 25 May 1913 - 23 Aug 1914: | Member, Directorate-General for Remounts |
| 23 Aug 1914 - 20 Feb 1916: | Commander, 1$^{st}$ Brigade, Caucasus Native Cavalry Division |
| 20 Feb 196 - 15 Apr 1917: | Commander, Caucasus Native Cavalry Division |
| 12 Jul 1916: | Promoted to *Lieutenant-General* |
| 15 Apr 1917 - 30 Jun 1917: | Reserve officer, Kiev Military District |
| 30 Jun 1917 - 28 Aug 1917: | Commander, Caucasus Native Cavalry Division |
| 28 Aug 1917 - 2 Sep 1917: | Commanding General, Caucasus Native Corps |
| 2 Sep 1917 - 1918: | Reserve officer, Petrograd Military District |

*Lieutenant-General* Prince Aleksandr Iraklievich **Bagration-Mukhransky** (20 Jul 1853 - 19 Oct 1918)
| | |
|---|---|
| 10 Jul 1904: | Promoted to *Major-General* |
| 10 Jul 1904 - 4 Jul 1906: | Commander, Life Guards Horse Regiment |
| 4 Jul 1906 - 6 Apr 1917: | Reserve officer, Guards Cavalry |
| 6 Apr 1917: | Promoted to *Lieutenant-General* |
| 6 Apr 1917: | Retired |

*Lieutenant-General* Aleksei Konstantinovich **Baiov** (8 Feb 1871 - 8 May 1935)
| | |
|---|---|
| 3 Oct 1906 - 6 Sep 1914: | Professor, General Staff Academy |
| 6 Dec 1911: | Promoted to *Major-General* |
| 6 Sep 1914 - 30 Sep 1914: | Chief of Staff, VI. Siberian Army Corps |
| 30 Sep 1914 - 1 Apr 1915: | Chief of Staff, XXIV. Army Corps |
| 1 Apr 1915 - 6 Jun 1915: | Quartermaster-General, 3$^{rd}$ Army |
| 6 Jun 1915 - 8 Apr 1917: | Chief of Staff, 3$^{rd}$ Army |
| 6 Dec 1915: | Promoted to *Lieutenant-General* |
| 8 Apr 1917 - 19 Jun 1917: | Commander, 42$^{nd}$ Infantry Division |
| 19 Jun 1917 - 22 Oct 1917: | Professor, General Staff Academy |
| 22 Oct 1917 - 1918: | Commanding General, L. Army Corps |

*General of Infantry* Konstantin Alekseyevich **Baiov** (23 Apr 1839 - 10 May 1903)
| | |
|---|---|
| 12 Feb 1890: | Promoted to *Major-General* |
| 12 Feb 1890 - 7 Feb 1894: | Chief of Staff, IX. Army Corps |
| 7 Feb 1894 - 21 Jan 1899: | Commander, 60$^{th}$ Replacement Infantry Brigade |
| 21 Jan 1899 - 23 Apr 1902: | Commander, 40$^{th}$ Infantry Division |
| 6 Dec 1899: | Promoted to *Lieutenant-General* |
| 23 Apr 1902: | Promoted to *General of Infantry* |
| 23 Apr 1902: | Retired |

*Lieutenant-General* Konstantin Konstantinovich **Baiov** (4 Jul 1869 - 1920)
| | |
|---|---|
| 31 Jul 1910: | Promoted to *Major-General* |
| 31 Jul 1910 - Aug 1914: | Quartermaster-General, Vilnius Military District |
| Aug 1914 - 16 Sep 1914: | Quartermaster-General, 1$^{st}$ Army |
| 16 Sep 1914 - 21 Dec 1914: | Chief of Staff, 1$^{st}$ Army |
| 21 Dec 1914 - 25 Apr 1917: | Commander, 6$^{th}$ Infantry Division |
| 1 Aug 1915: | Promoted to *Lieutenant-General* |
| 25 Aug 1917 - 1918: | Commanding General, Dvinsk Military District |

*Vice-Admiral* Mikhail Koronatovich **Bakhirev** (17 Jul 1868 - 16 Jan 1920)
| | |
|---|---|
| 24 Dec 1914: | Promoted to *Rear-Admiral* |
| 24 Dec 1914 - 19 Dec 1915: | Commander, Cruiser Squadron, Baltic Fleet |
| 19 Dec 1915 - 23 May 1917: | Commander, Battleship Squadron, Baltic Fleet |
| 6 Dec 1916: | Promoted to *Vice-Admiral* |
| 21 Aug 1917 - 12 Jan 1918: | Chief of Naval Forces, Gulf of Riga |
| 12 Jan 1918: | Dismissed |

*Lieutenant-General* Vladimir Dmitrievich **Bakulin** (27 Jul 1857 - 13 Apr 1913)
| | |
|---|---|
| 23 Jan 1904 - 17 Nov 1907: | Commander, Life Guards Rifle Regiment |

| 17 Apr 1905: | Promoted to *Major-General* |
| 17 Nov 1907 - 19 Jan 1913: | Commander, 2nd Brigade, 2nd Guards Infantry Division |
| 1913: | Promoted to *Lieutenant-General* |
| 19 Jan 1913 - 13 Apr 1913: | Commander, Guards Rifle Brigade |

*Major-General* Vladimir Ivanovich **Bakurevich** (10 Jul 1849 - ?)
| 1 Feb 1908 - 1916: | President of the Military Board, Semirechensk Cossack Army |
| 6 Dec 1908: | Promoted to *Major-General* |

*Rear-Admiral* Mitrofan Yakovlevlich **Bal** (1851 - ?)
| 12 Nov 1901 - 1906: | Commander, 33rd Naval Depot |
| 10 Apr 1906: | Promoted to *Rear-Admiral* |

*Major-General of the Admiralty* Pyotr Petrovich **Bal** (21 Jun 1861 - ?)
| 29 Aug 1911: | Commander, Black Sea Reserve Mine Division |
| 1912: | Promoted to *Major-General of the Admiralty* |
| 1912: | Retired |

*Vice-Admiral* Vladimir Yakovlevlich **Bal** (25 Jun 1849 - ?)
| 1898 - 9 Sep 1902: | Commander, Battleship "Sinop" |
| 14 Apr 1902: | Promoted to *Rear-Admiral* |
| 9 Sep 1902 - 17 Feb 1903: | Chief of Staff, Black Sea Fleet |
| 17 Feb 1903 - 21 Apr 1903: | Reserve officer, Black Sea Fleet |
| 21 Apr 1903 - 16 Jan 1906: | Commandant, Port of Baku, Chief of Lighthouses & Navigation, Caspian Sea |
| 16 Jan 1906: | Promoted to *Vice-Admiral* |
| 16 Jan 1906: | Retired |

*Major-General* Semyon Vasilyevich **Balabin** (2 Feb 1843 - ?)
| 11 May 1882 - 24 Sep 1893: | Chief of Nobility, Rostov District, Don Region |
| 6 May 1891: | Promoted to *Major-General* |
| 24 Sep 1893 - 16 Dec 1894: | Member, Cossack Military Committee |
| 16 Dec 1894: | Resigned |

*Lieutenant-General* Zakhary Aleksandrovich **Balachinsky** (24 Mar 1852 - ?)
| 7 Sep 1904: | Promoted to *Major-General* |
| 7 Sep 1904 - 8 Apr 1906: | At the disposal of the C-in-C, 1st Manchurian Army |
| 8 Apr 1906 - 15 Jan 1912: | Commander, Kharkov Regional Brigade |
| 6 Dec 1908: | Promoted to *Lieutenant-General* |

*General of Infantry* Dmitry Vasilievich **Balanin** (26 Nov 1857 - Oct 1928)
| 2 Feb 1902: | Promoted to *Major-General* |
| 2 Feb 1902 - 11 Dec 1902: | Chief of Mobilization Section, Quartermaster-General's Department |
| 11 Dec 1902 - 9 Mar 1904: | Chief of Staff, XXI. Army Corps |
| 9 Mar 1904 - 17 Jun 1908: | Quartermaster-General, Kiev Military District |
| 17 Jun 1908: | Promoted to *Lieutenant-General* |

| | |
|---|---|
| 17 Jun 1908 - 2 Sep 1914: | Commander, 18th Infantry Division |
| 2 Sep 1914 - 20 Dec 1916: | Commanding General, XXVII. Army Corps |
| 6 Dec 1914: | Promoted to *General of Infantry* |
| 20 Dec 1916 - 5 Apr 1917: | C-in-C, 11th Army |
| 5 Apr 1917 - 4 May 1917: | Reserve officer, Kiev Military District |
| 4 May 1917: | Retired |

*Major-General* Ivan Stepanovich **Balashov** (27 Mar 1868 - ?)
| | |
|---|---|
| 29 Nov 1916 - 1917: | Duty General, 10th Army |
| 6 Dec 1916: | Promoted to *Major-General* |

*Lieutenant-General* Leonard Ivanovich **Balbashevsky** (6 Nov 1840 - 18 Mar 1913)
| | |
|---|---|
| 22 Oct 1883 - 23 Jan 1907: | Inspector of Engineering Works, Caucasus Military District |
| 6 Dec 1904: | Promoted to *Major-General* |
| 23 Jan 1907 - 1910: | Deputy Chief of Engineers, Caucasus Military District |
| 1910 - 7 Jun 1910: | Deputy Chief of Engineers, Kazan Military District |
| 7 Jun 1910: | Promoted to *Lieutenant-General* |
| 7 Jun 1910: | Retired |

*Major-General* Siluan Femistoklovich **Baldin** (22 Jul 1870 - 28 Apr 1961)
| | |
|---|---|
| 4 Aug 1914 - 1917: | Head of Mission to USA for purchase of military equipment |
| 22 Mar 1915: | Promoted to *Major-General* |

*Major-General* Ignaty Ivanovich **Balinsky** (18 Dec 1867 - Dec 1920)
| | |
|---|---|
| 6 Dec 1908 - 24 Sep 1917: | Chief of Bureau, Court of Grand Duke Nikolai Nikolayevich |
| 6 Dec 1916: | Promoted to *Major-General* |
| 24 Sep 1917: | Dismissed |

*Major-General* Ignaty Oktavievich **Balinsky** (10 Mar 1858 - ?)
| | |
|---|---|
| ? - 1 Jan 1911: | Commander, 7th Dragoon Regiment |
| 1 Jan 1911: | Promoted to *Major-General* |
| 1 Jan 1911 - 9 Nov 1911: | Commander, 2nd Brigade, 12th Cavalry Division |

*Major-General* Aleksandr Pavlovich **Balk** (7 Feb 1866 - 20 Oct 1957)
| | |
|---|---|
| 31 Dec 1906 - 1 Nov 1916: | Deputy Chief of Police, Warsaw |
| 6 Dec 1912: | Promoted to *Major-General* |
| 1 Nov 1916 - 27 Feb 1917: | Mayor of Petrograd |
| 27 Feb 1917 - 13 May 1917: | Unassigned |
| 13 May 1917: | Dismissed |

*Major-General* Count Sergey Sergeyevich de-**Balmen** (20 Feb 1848 - ?)
| | |
|---|---|
| 5 Nov 1889 - 1906: | Adjutant to the Commanding General, Kiev Military District |
| 1906: | Promoted to *Major-General* |
| 1906: | Retired |

11 Dec 1914 - 1917: Recalled; Reserve officer, Kiev Military District

*Lieutenant-General* Aleksandr Fyodorovich **Balts** (18 Nov 1841 - 30 Jun 1899)
12 Nov 1884 - 23 Oct 1889: Chief of Staff, Guards Corps
30 Aug 1885: Promoted to *Major-General*
23 Oct 1889 - 17 Jan 1894: At the disposal of the Chief of the General Staff
17 Jan 1894 - 30 Jun 1899: Intendant, Warsaw Military District
1 Jan 1895: Promoted to *Lieutenant-General*

*Lieutenant-General* Aleksandr Alekseyevich **Baltysky** (18 Jun 1870 - 7 Mar 1939)
20 May 1916 - 28 Aug 1917: Chief of Staff, 3rd Siberian Rifle Division
6 Dec 1916: Promoted to *Major-General*
28 Aug 1917 - 3 Oct 1917: Chief of Economic Section, 12th Army
1917: Promoted to *Lieutenant-General*

*General of Infantry* Pyotr Semyonovich **Baluyev** (21 Jun 1857 - 1923)
19 Feb 1904: Promoted to *Major-General*
19 Feb 1904 - 22 Oct 1904: Commander, 2nd Brigade, 16th Infantry Division
22 Oct 1904 - 9 Jul 1910: Chief of Staff, VI. Army Corps
9 Jul 1910: Promoted to *Lieutenant-General*
9 Jul 1910 - 31 Oct 1914: Commander, 17th Infantry Division
30 Aug 1914 - 9 Nov 1914: Acting Commanding General, VI. Army Corps
9 Oct 1914 - 6 Dec 1914: Unassigned
6 Dec 1914 - 18 Mar 1917: Commanding General, V. Army Corps
27 Sep 1915: Promoted to *General of Infantry*
10 Nov 1916 - 9 Jul 1917: C-in-C, Special Army
9 Jul 1917 - 2 Aug 1917: C-in-C, 11th Army
2 Aug 1917 - 12 Nov 1917: C-in-C, Western Front

*Major-General* Mikhail Yakovlevich **Balyasny** (5 Nov 1867 - ?)
18 Dec 1914 - 13 Aug 1915: Military Judge, General-Government of Galicia Military Court
22 Mar 1915: Promoted to *Major-General*
13 Aug 1915 - 1917: Military Judge, Amur Military District Court

*General of Artillery* Vladimir Frantsevich **Bandrovsky** (23 Sep 1848 - ?)
4 Mar 1903: Promoted to *Major-General*
4 Mar 1903 - 27 Nov 1904: Commander, 15th Artillery Brigade
27 Nov 1904 - 13 Aug 1905: Commander, 45th Artillery Brigade
13 Aug 1905 - 9 Nov 1905: Attached to the C-in-C of Land & Naval Forces operating against Japan
9 Nov 1905 - 9 May 1906: Commander of Artillery, II. Rifle Corps
9 May 1906 - 28 Jul 1910: Commander of Artillery, XVI. Army Corps
31 May 1907: Promoted to *Lieutenant-General*
28 Jul 1910 - 23 Sep 1911: Inspector of Artillery, XVI. Army Corps
23 Sep 1911: Promoted to *General of Artillery*
23 Sep 1911: Retired
1914 - 1917: Recalled; Commander, 2nd Militia Corps

*Major-General* Vladimir Aleksandrovich **Bankovsky** (19 Jul 1860 - ?)
| | |
|---|---|
| 17 Mar 1912 - 29 Sep 1916: | Commander, 11th Horse Artillery Battalion |
| 26 Sep 1916: | Promoted to *Major-General* |
| 29 Sep 1916 - 3 May 1917: | Commander, 3rd Artillery Brigade |
| 3 May 1917 - 1918: | Inspector of Artillery, XVII. Army Corps |

*General of Infantry* Yakov Fyodorovich **Barabash** (12 May 1838 - 17 Oct 1910)
| | |
|---|---|
| 12 Dec 1874 - 24 Jun 1884: | Chief of Staff, Primorsk Region |
| 6 May 1884: | Promoted to *Major-General* |
| 24 Jun 1884 - 8 Feb 1888: | Military Governor of the Trans-Baikal Region |
| 8 Feb 1888 - 4 Oct 1899: | Military Governor of the Turgay Region |
| 30 Aug 1894: | Promoted to *Lieutenant-General* |
| 4 Oct 1899 - 20 Mar 1906: | Governor of Orenburg, Ataman, Orenburg Cossack Army |
| 20 Mar 1906 - 17 Oct 1910: | Member of the Senate |
| 6 Dec 1906: | Promoted to *General of Infantry* |

*Major-General* Fyodor Samoilovich **Barakovsky** (17 Feb 1836 - ?)
| | |
|---|---|
| 17 Dec 1890 - 1901: | Chief of Tiflis Military Hospital |
| 14 May 1896: | Promoted to *Major-General* |

*Major-General* Aleksandr Nikolayevich **Baranov** (7 Feb 1851 - ?)
| | |
|---|---|
| 19 Dec 1915 - 1917: | Chief of Orenburg District Evacuation Points |
| 23 Jan 1917: | Promoted to *Major-General* |

*Major-General* Aleksandr Yevgrafovich **Baranov** (8 Oct 1832 - ?)
| | |
|---|---|
| 7 Sep 1883: | Promoted to *Major-General* |
| 7 Sep 1883 - 26 Jan 1894: | Special Assignments General, Turkestan Military District |
| 26 Jan 1894 - 14 Jan 1898: | Commander, 1st Brigade, 8th Infantry Division |
| 14 Jan 1898 - 23 Jul 1898: | Commander, 2nd Brigade, 6th Infantry Division |

*Lieutenant-General* Aleksandr Yevstafyevich **Baranov** (9 Jan 1837 - 27 Dec 1905)
| | |
|---|---|
| 17 Nov 1872 - 8 Nov 1878: | Commander, 158th Infantry Regiment |
| 8 Nov 1877: | Promoted to *Major-General* |
| 8 Nov 1878 - 1 Jan 1880: | Attached to the Caucasus Army |
| 1 Jan 1880 - 24 Sep 1881: | Military Commander, Simbirsk Region |
| 24 Sep 1881 - 27 Dec 1905: | Commander, 21st (Perm) Regional Brigade |
| 30 Aug 1886: | Promoted to *Lieutenant-General* |
| ?: | Acting Commanding General, Kazan Military District |

*Lieutenant-General* Nikolai Mikhailovich **Baranov** (25 Jul 1837 - 30 Jul 1901)
| | |
|---|---|
| Jan 1881 - Aug 1881: | Acting Governor of Kovno Province |
| 19 Feb 1881: | Promoted to *Major-General* |
| Aug 1881 - 31 Aug 1882: | Mayor of St. Petersburg |
| 31 Aug 1882 - 16 May 1897: | Governor of Nizhny Novgorod |
| 30 Aug 1893: | Promoted to *Lieutenant-General* |
| 16 May 1897 - 30 Jul 1901: | Senator |

*Lieutenant-General* Pyotr Mikhailovich **Baranov** (2 Sep 1860 - 1920)
| | |
|---|---|
| 15 Sep 1906 - 22 Nov 1908: | Commander, 215th Reserve Infantry Regiment |
| 11 Aug 1907: | Promoted to *Major-General* |
| 22 Nov 1908 - 2 May 1913: | Commander, 2nd Brigade, 32nd Infantry Division |
| 2 May 1913 - 19 Jul 1914: | Commander, 2nd Brigade, 42nd Infantry Division |
| 19 Jul 1914 - 30 Apr 1915: | Commander, 60th Infantry Division |
| 30 Aug 1914: | Promoted to *Lieutenant-General* |
| 30 Apr 1915 - 7 Jan 1916: | Commander, 3rd Militia Brigade |
| 7 Jan 1916 - 9 Jun 1916: | Commander, 127th Infantry Division |
| 9 Jun 1916 - 11 Aug 1916: | Reserve officer, Kiev Military District |
| 11 Aug 1916 - 10 Apr 1917: | Commander, 26th Infantry Division |
| 10 Apr 1917 - 8 May 1917: | Commanding General, IV. Siberian Army Corps |

*General of Cavalry* Pyotr Petrovich **Baranov** (9 May 1843 - 9 Dec 1924)
| | |
|---|---|
| 15 Apr 1891: | Promoted to *Major-General* |
| 15 Apr 1891 - 6 Mar 1897: | Commander, Life Guards Uhlan Regiment |
| 6 Mar 1897 - 1 Feb 1898: | Commander, 1st Brigade, 2nd Guards Cavalry Division |
| 1 Feb 1898 - 10 Feb 1902: | Court Marshal to Grand Duke Mikhail Nikolayevich |
| 1 Jan 1900: | Promoted to *Lieutenant-General* |
| 10 Feb 1902 - 3 Jan 1910: | Court Chamberlain to Grand Duke Mikhail Nikolayevich |
| 3 Jan 1910: | Promoted to *General-Adjutant* |
| 3 Jan 1910 - 6 Jul 1917: | General à la suite |
| 18 Apr 1910: | Promoted to *General of Cavalry* |
| 6 Jul 1917: | Retired |

*Major-General* Stepan Yakovlevich **Baranov** (20 Dec 1845 - 10 May 1918)
| | |
|---|---|
| 26 Feb 1909 - 1917: | Map Editor, Military Topographic Directorate |
| 18 Apr 1910: | Promoted to *Major-General* |

*Lieutenant-General* Valerian Mikhailovich **Baranov** (11 Jul 1856 - ?)
| | |
|---|---|
| 1 May 1903 - 2 Dec 1908: | Chief Secretary, General Staff |
| 6 Dec 1906: | Promoted to *Major-General* |
| 2 Dec 1908 - 19 Sep 1910: | Deputy Duty General, General Staff |
| 19 Sep 1910 - 8 Jan 1914: | Chief of Assignment Section, General Staff |
| 31 May 1913: | Promoted to *Lieutenant-General* |
| 8 Jan 1914 - 4 Jun 1917: | Chief of Pension Service, General Staff |
| 4 Jun 1917: | Dismissed |

*Major-General* Sergey Mikhailovich **Baranovich** (29 Jun 1867 - ?)
| | |
|---|---|
| 29 May 1912 - 4 Jul 1916: | Commander of Artillery, Fortress Mikhailovsky |
| 6 Dec 1913: | Promoted to *Major-General* |
| 4 Jul 1916 - 1917: | Commandant of Fortress Mikhailovsky |

*Major-General* Anton-Logvin Yuryevich **Baranovsky** (15 Mar 1854 - 31 May 1922)
| | |
|---|---|
| 9 Aug 1908 - 1911: | Commander, 25th Siberian Rifle Regiment |
| 1911: | Retired |
| 1915: | Recalled |

21 May 1916:                  Promoted to *Major-General*
17 Jun 1916 - 1917:           Reserve officer, Petrograd Military District

*Major-General* Erazm Fyodorovich **Baranovsky** (24 Feb 1846 - 25 Jan 1933)
23 Aug 1897 - 1905:           Deputy Commander, Izmaylov Borderguard Brigade
1905:                         Promoted to *Major-General*
1905:                         Retired

*Major-General* Grigory Yakovlevich **Baranovsky** (14 Jan 1843 - ?)
2 Apr 1894:                   Promoted to *Major-General*
2 Apr 1894 - 1895:            Chief of Staff, Fortress Kaunas

*Major-General* Leopold Valentinovich **Baranovsky** (29 Nov 1836 - 1910)
30 Nov 1892:                  Promoted to *Major-General*
30 Nov 1892 - 17 Feb 1900:    Commander, 10th Artillery Brigade

*Lieutenant-General* Lev Stepanovich **Baranovsky** (6 May 1855 - ?)
6 Jul 1907:                   Promoted to *Major-General*
6 Jul 1907 - 12 Aug 1907:     Commander, 1st Brigade, 44th Infantry Division
12 Aug 1907 - 5 Aug 1911:     Commander, 2nd Brigade, 36th Infantry Division
5 Aug 1911 - 19 Jul 1914:     Commander, 2nd Brigade, 41st Infantry Division
19 Jul 1914 - 25 Aug 1915:    Commander, 77th Infantry Division
19 Dec 1914:                  Promoted to *Lieutenant-General*
25 Aug 1915 - 25 Feb 1916:    Reserve officer, Minsk Military District
25 Feb 1916 - 7 Dec 1916:     Commander, 45th Infantry Division
7 Dec 1916 - 18 Oct 1917:     Reserve officer, Kiev Military District

*Lieutenant-General* Mikhail Nikolayevich **Baranovsky** (10 Jul 1847 - 15 Aug 1912)
22 Aug 1891 - 1905:           Professor, Mikhailovsky Artillery Academy
6 Dec 1895:                   Promoted to *Major-General*
2 Sep 1901 - 1905:            Member of the Artillery Committee, Main Artillery Directorate
6 Dec 1903:                   Promoted to *Lieutenant-General*
1905:                         Retired

*Major-General* Valentin Mikhailovich **Baranovsky** (19 Apr 1841 - ?)
14 Oct 1892 - 18 Oct 1896:    Commander, 115th Infantry Regiment
14 May 1896:                  Promoted to *Major-General*
18 Oct 1896 - 2 Feb 1902:     Commander, 1st Brigade, 32nd Infantry Division

*General of Cavalry* Vsevolod Stepanovich **Baranovsky** (26 Nov 1853 - Jul 1921)
29 Nov 1902 - 1 Nov 1907:     Military Judge, Kazan Military District Court
6 Dec 1902:                   Promoted to *Major-General*
1 Nov 1907 - 9 Apr 1909:      Military Judge, Moscow Military District Court
9 Apr 1909 - 1 Mar 1914:      Military Judge, Odessa Military District Court
1 Mar 1914 - 1916:            Senator; Member of the Economic Department, Finnish Senate
6 Apr 1914:                   Promoted to *Lieutenant-General*

| | |
|---|---|
| 1916: | Retired |
| 26 Oct 1917: | Promoted to *General of Cavalry* |

*General of Artillery* Count Mikhail Aleksandrovich **Barantsov** (10 Aug 1857 - 1921)
| | |
|---|---|
| 6 Apr 1903: | Promoted to *Major-General* |
| 6 Apr 1903 - 8 Jun 1906: | Commander, 3rd Life Guards Artillery Brigade |
| 8 Jun 1906 - 14 Apr 1909: | Transferred to the reserve |
| 14 Apr 1909 - 31 May 1914: | Commander of Artillery, Warsaw Military District |
| 12 Feb 1910: | Promoted to *Lieutenant-General* |
| 31 May 1914 - 7 Jan 1915: | Attached to the Inspector-General of Artillery |
| 7 Jan 1915 - 3 Nov 1915: | Inspector of Artillery, XXX. Army Corps |
| 3 Nov 1915 - 6 Apr 1917: | Commanding General, XI. Army Corps |
| 10 Apr 1916: | Promoted to *General of Artillery* |
| 6 Apr 1917 - 4 May 1917: | Reserve officer, Kiev Military District |
| 4 May 1917: | Retired |

*Major-General* Prince Konstantin Fyodorovich **Baratov** (11 Aug 1858 - ?)
| | |
|---|---|
| 17 Nov 1901 - 1 Jun 1906: | Commander, 12th Sapper Battalion |
| 5 Jan 1906: | Promoted to *Major-General* |
| 1 Jun 1906 - 1 Jun 1907: | Commander, Turkestan Sapper Brigade |

*General of Cavalry* Nikolai Nikolayevich **Baratov** (1 Feb 1865 - 22 Mar 1932)
| | |
|---|---|
| 29 Mar 1901 - 1 Jul 1907: | Commander, 1st Caucasus Cossack Regiment |
| 14 Aug 1905 - 17 Mar 1906: | Chief of Staff, Combined Cavalry Corps |
| 18 May 1906: | Promoted to *Major-General* |
| 1 Jul 1907 - 26 Nov 1912: | Chief of Staff, II. Caucasus Army Corps |
| 26 Nov 1912: | Promoted to *Lieutenant-General* |
| 26 Nov 1912 - 28 Apr 1916: | Commander, 1st Caucasus Cossack Division |
| Oct 1915 - 28 Apr 1916: | Commanding General, Expeditionary Cavalry Corps |
| 28 Apr 1916 - 24 Mar 1917: | Commanding General, I. Caucasus Cavalry Corps |
| 24 Mar 1917 - 25 Apr 1917: | Chief of Logistics, Caucasus Front, Commanding General, Caucasus Military District |
| 25 Apr 1917 - 7 Jul 1917: | Commanding General, V. Caucasus Army Corps |
| 7 Jul 1917 - 10 Jun 1918: | Commanding General, Caucasus Cavalry Corps, Persia |
| 8 Sep 1917: | Promoted to *General of Cavalry* |

*Major-General* Leonid Alekseyevich **Bardin** (21 Feb 1864 - 1 Aug 1936)
| | |
|---|---|
| 19 Jan 1915 - Feb 1917: | Commander of Railway Gendarmerie, Vladikavkaz |
| 1916: | Promoted to *Major-General* |

*General of Infantry* Prince Aleksandr Petrovich **Barklay de Tolly-Weymarn** (22 Dec 1824 - 8 May 1905)
| | |
|---|---|
| 2 Aug 1856 - 12 Dec 1863: | Commandant of the Imperial Headquarters |
| 30 Aug 1860: | Promoted to *Major-General* |
| 12 Dec 1863 - 30 Aug 1867: | Commander, Life Guards Pavlovsky Regiment |
| 30 Aug 1867: | Promoted to *Lieutenant-General* |
| 30 Aug 1867: | Promoted to *General-Adjutant* |
| 30 Aug 1867 - 10 Nov 1868: | General à la suite |

| | |
|---|---|
| 10 Nov 1868 - 1 Nov 1876: | Commander, 24th Infantry Division |
| 1 Nov 1876 - 19 Jan 1888: | Commanding General, I. Army Corps |
| 30 Aug 1882: | Promoted to *General of Infantry* |
| 19 Jan 1888 - 8 May 1905: | General à la suite |

*Major-General* Georgy Andreyevich **Barkovsky** (14 Apr 1870 - 10 Oct 1929)
| | |
|---|---|
| 13 Jul 1915 - 11 Feb 1917: | Commander, 297th Infantry Regiment |
| 10 Jul 1916: | Promoted to *Major-General* |
| 11 Feb 1917 - 1917: | Commander, Brigade, 75th Infantry Division |
| 1917: | Commander, 75th Infantry Division |

*General of Infantry* Ivan Fomich **Barkovsky** (28 Dec 1831 - 1917)
| | |
|---|---|
| 1 Apr 1879: | Promoted to *Major-General* |
| 3 Apr 1879 - 26 Jul 1899: | Chief of Statistics Department, Ministry of Railways |
| 19 Oct 1889: | Promoted to *Lieutenant-General* |
| 26 Jul 1899 - 1907: | Chief of Statistics & Cartography Department, Ministry of Railways, |
| | Member of the Technical Committee, Main Intendant Directorate, |
| | Member of the Military Training Committee, General Staff |
| 23 Jan 1904: | Promoted to *General of Infantry* |
| 1907: | Retired |

*Major-General* Vladimir Mikhailovich **Barkovsky** (23 Jul 1862 - 4 Jan 1915)
| | |
|---|---|
| 4 Jul 1913 - 4 Jan 1915: | Commander, 80th Infantry Regiment |
| 20 Jan 1915: | Posthumously promoted to *Major-General* |

*General of Infantry* Aleksandr Savelyevich **Barmin** (4 Sep 1837 - 1917)
| | |
|---|---|
| 21 Oct 1887: | Promoted to *Major-General* |
| 21 Oct 1887 - 23 Sep 1890: | Commander, 2nd Brigade, 25th Infantry Division |
| 23 Sep 1890 - 13 Jun 1894: | Deputy Chief of Staff, Caucasus Military District |
| 13 Jun 1894 - 5 Oct 1897: | Chief of Staff, Caucasus Military District |
| 14 May 1896: | Promoted to *Lieutenant-General* |
| 5 Oct 1897 - 2 Oct 1901: | Commander, 22nd Infantry Division |
| 2 Oct 1901: | Promoted to *General of Infantry* |
| 2 Oct 1901: | Retired |

*Major-General* Aleksandr Antonovich **Baronch** (24 Dec 1829 - ?)
| | |
|---|---|
| 15 Feb 1878 - 28 Apr 1885: | Commander, 12th Dragoon Regiment |
| 28 Apr 1885: | Promoted to *Major-General* |
| 28 Apr 1885 - 31 Jul 1895: | Commander, 2nd Brigade, 4th Cavalry Division |

*General of Artillery* Aleksandr Andreyevich **Barsov** (10 Jan 1823 - 27 Mar 1908)
| | |
|---|---|
| 1 Jul 1874: | Promoted to *Major-General* |
| 1 Jul 1874 - 18 Jan 1877: | Commander, 19th Artillery Brigade |
| 18 Jan 1877 - 6 Nov 1877: | Commander, Artillery Detachment Erivan |
| 6 Nov 1877 - 19 Mar 1878: | Commander of Artillery, IX. Army Corps |

| | |
|---|---|
| 19 Mar 1878 - 11 Apr 1878: | Commander of Artillery, Caucasus-Turkey Border Corps |
| 11 Apr 1878 - 28 Mar 1879: | Attached to the C-in-C, Caucasus Army |
| 28 Mar 1879 - 28 Aug 1889: | Commander of Artillery, XII. Army Corps |
| 15 May 1883: | Promoted to *Lieutenant-General* |
| 28 Aug 1889 - 28 Sep 1892: | Commander of Artillery, IX. Army Corps |
| 28 Sep 1892 - 6 Dec 1896: | Commanding General, IX. Army Corps |
| 14 May 1896: | Promoted to *General of Artillery* |
| 6 Dec 1896 - 19 Jun 1899: | Deputy Master-General of Ordnance, Chief of the Main Artillery Directorate |
| 19 Jun 1899 - 3 Jan 1906: | Member of the Military Council |
| 1 Jan 1906: | Retired |

*Major-General* Anatoly Fyodorovich **Barsov** (31 Oct 1867 - 13 Jun 1937)
| | |
|---|---|
| 15 Oct 1915 - 1917: | Chief of Office, Director of Army Aviation |
| 6 Dec 1915: | Promoted to *Major-General* |
| 1917 - 6 May 1917: | Chief of Staff, Inspector-General of the Air Force |
| 6 May 1917: | Dismissed |

*Major-General* Mikhail Vasilyevich **Barsov** (16 Feb 1857 - ?)
| | |
|---|---|
| 27 Mar 1900 - 1902: | Director, Siberian Cadet Corps |
| 1 Apr 1901: | Promoted to *Major-General* |
| 1902 - ?: | General for Special Assignments, Main Directorate for Military Schools |

*Major-General* Yevgeny Zakharovich **Barsukov** (16 Mar 1866 - 1 Jan 1957)
| | |
|---|---|
| 1910 - 1918: | Member of the Artillery Committee, Main Artillery Direcorate |
| 1914 - 5 Jan 1916: | Chief of Office, Inspector-General of Artillery |
| 6 Dec 1915: | Promoted to *Major-General* |
| 5 Jan 1916 - Dec 1917: | Chief of the Field Office, Inspector-General of Artillery |

*Vice-Admiral* Anton Antonovich **Bartashevich** (18 Jun 1848 - ?)
| | |
|---|---|
| 1899 - 1903: | Commander, Guards Naval Depot |
| 1902: | Promoted to *Rear-Admiral* |
| 1903 - 24 Apr 1906: | Junior Flagman, Baltic Fleet |
| 24 Apr 1906: | Promoted to *Vice-Admiral* |
| 24 Apr 1906: | Retired |

*Major-General* Aleksandr Dmitriyevich **Bartenev** (16 Aug 1858 - ?)
| | |
|---|---|
| 11 Jun 1910 - 31 Dec 1913: | Head of the Army & Navy Officers Assembly |
| 6 Dec 1910: | Promoted to *Major-General* |
| 31 Dec 1913 - 1917: | Commander, St. Petersburg Regional Brigade |

*General of Cavalry* Aleksandr Vladimirovich **Bartolomey** (3 Jul 1843 - 1916)
| | |
|---|---|
| 22 Jun 1886 - 21 Aug 1891: | Commander, 2$^{nd}$ Dragoon Regiment |
| 21 Aug 1891: | Promoted to *Major-General* |
| 21 Aug 1891 - 25 Sep 1892: | Deputy Chief of Staff, Kiev Military District |

| | |
|---|---|
| 25 Sep 1892 - 20 Dec 1892: | Duty General, Kiev Military District |
| 20 Dec 1892 - 31 Dec 1901: | Deputy Chief of Staff, Moscow Military District |
| 31 Dec 1901: | Promoted to *Lieutenant-General* |
| 31 Dec 1901 - 9 Oct 1906: | Commander, 1st Cavalry Division |
| 9 Oct 1906: | Promoted to *General of Cavalry* |
| 9 Oct 1906: | Retired |

*Major-General* Vsevolod Aleksandrovich **Bartolomey** (26 Aug 1867 - ?)
| | |
|---|---|
| 9 Apr 1911 - 1917: | Commander, 6th Sapper Battalion |
| 22 Dec 1916: | Promoted to *Major-General* |

*General of Infantry* Prince Aleksandr Anatolievich **Baryatinsky** (14 Aug 1846 - 16 Apr 1914)
| | |
|---|---|
| 19 Aug 1890: | Promoted to *Major-General* |
| 19 Aug 1890 - 4 Feb 1895: | Commander, Caucasus Native Rifle Brigade |
| 4 Feb 1895 - 10 Apr 1896: | Deputy Military Governor of Kutaisi |
| 10 Apr 1896 - 1907: | Military Governor of Dagestan |
| 6 Dec 1899: | Promoted to *Lieutenant-General* |
| 1907: | Promoted to *General of Infantry* |
| 1907: | Retired |

*Major-General* Prince Anatoly Vladimirovich **Baryatinsky** (7 Aug 1871 - 17 Mar 1924)
| | |
|---|---|
| 24 Sep 1914: | Promoted to *Major-General* |
| 24 Sep 1914 - Nov 1914: | Special Purposes General, 3rd Army |
| 11 Dec 1914 - 30 Dec 1915: | Special Purposes General, Southwestern Front |
| 30 Dec 1915 - 24 Apr 1917: | Commander, 2nd Brigade, Guards Rifle Division |
| 24 Apr 1917 - 1917: | Reserve officer, Kiev Military District |

*General of Infantry* Prince Vladimir Anatolievich **Baryatinsky** (19 Sep 1843 - 30 Nov 1914)
| | |
|---|---|
| 17 Apr 1879 - 1 Dec 1883: | Commander, Life Guards 4th Rifle Battalion |
| 1 Dec 1883 - 19 Dec 1883: | Unassigned |
| 19 Dec 1883: | Promoted to *Major-General* |
| 19 Dec 1883 - 6 Nov 1889: | Master of the Imperial Hunt |
| 6 Nov 1889 - 6 Dec 1889: | Attached to the Imperial Headquarters |
| 6 Dec 1889 - 8 Jul 1896: | Attached to the Imperial Court |
| 8 Jul 1896: | Promoted to *General-Adjutant* |
| 8 Jul 1896 - 30 Nov 1914: | Aide-de-Camp to Dowager Empress Maria Feodorovna |
| 13 Apr 1897: | Promoted to *Lieutenant-General* |
| 6 Dec 1906: | Promoted to *General of Infantry* |

*Major-General of the Fleet* Fyodor Yevgenyevich **Barykov** (1 Aug 1862 - ?)
| | |
|---|---|
| 1 May 1914 - 1917: | Commandant of the Naval Prison, Petrograd |
| 6 Dec 1915: | Promoted to *Major-General of the Fleet* |

*General of Artillery* Petr Aleksandrovich **Bashilov** (1 Oct 1819 - 29 Sep 1908)
| | |
|---|---|
| 5 Jan 1866 - 6 Feb 1870: | Commander, 1st Horse Artillery Brigade |
| 16 Apr 1867: | Promoted to *Major-General* |

| | |
|---|---|
| 6 Feb 1870 - 7 Feb 1877: | Commander of Artillery, Don Army |
| 30 Aug 1876: | Promoted to *Lieutenant-General* |
| 7 Feb 1877 - 19 Mar 1877: | Unassigned |
| 19 Mar 1877 - 22 Mar 1879: | Commander of Artillery, IV. Army Corps |
| 22 Mar 1879 - 27 Jun 1879: | Commander of Artillery, Occupation Forces in Bulgaria |
| 27 Jun 1879 - 26 Dec 1883: | Commander of Artillery, Finland Military District |
| 26 Dec 1883 - 27 Nov 1899: | Master-General of Ordnance, Member of the Artillery Committee, Main Artillery Directorate |
| 30 Aug 1891: | Promoted to *General of Infantry* |
| 27 Nov 1899 - 29 Sep 1908: | Member, Committee for Wounded Veterans |

*Major-General* Veniamin Ivanovich **Baskakov** (25 Mar 1861 - 11 Feb 1941)
| | |
|---|---|
| 18 Apr 1904 - 17 Apr 1905: | Chief of Staff, Orenburg Cossack Division |
| 17 Apr 1905: | Promoted to *Major-General* |
| 17 Apr 1905 - 7 Mar 1906: | Professor, Nikolayev General Staff Academy |
| 7 Mar 1906: | Retired |

*General of Infantry* Vladimir Onisimovich **Baskov** (26 May 1842 - 18 Apr 1909)
| | |
|---|---|
| 14 May 1879 - 20 Sep 1890: | Military Judge, St. Petersburg Military District Court |
| 30 Aug 1888: | Promoted to *Major-General* |
| 20 Sep 1890 - 7 Oct 1893: | Military Prosecutor, Moscow Military District Court |
| 7 Oct 1893 - 24 Sep 1905: | Chairman of the Military Tribunal, Kazan Military District |
| 6 Dec 1898: | Promoted to *Lieutenant-General* |
| 24 Sep 1905 - 10 Jun 1908: | Commandant, Military Law Academy |
| 20 Apr 1906 - 18 Apr 1909: | Member, Supreme Military Tribunal |
| 22 Apr 1907: | Promoted to *General of Infantry* |

*Major-General* Dmitry Ivanovich **Basnin** (26 Oct 1853 - 20 Oct 1916)
| | |
|---|---|
| 25 Aug 1904 - 21 Jan 1910: | Military Commander, Kishinev District |
| 21 Jan 1910: | Promoted to *Major-General* |
| 21 Jan 1910: | Retired |
| 5 Oct 1914 - 20 Sep 1915: | Recalled; Commander, 13th Militia Brigade |
| 20 Sep 1915 - 20 Oct 1916: | Commander, 112th Militia Brigade |

*Lieutenant-General* Nikita Mikhailovich **Batashev** (3 Sep 1854 - 1927)
| | |
|---|---|
| 14 Jan 1905: | Promoted to *Major-General* |
| 14 Jan 1905 - 19 Jul 1914: | Commander, 1st Brigade, 34th Infantry Division |
| 19 Jul 1914: | Promoted to *Lieutenant-General* |
| 19 Jul 1914 - 25 Aug 1914: | Commander, 71st Infantry Division |
| 25 Aug 1914 - 23 Mar 1915: | Commander, 34th Infantry Division |
| 23 Mar 1915 - 18 Aug 1915: | Commanding General, VIII. Army Corps |
| 19 Nov 1915 - 27 May 1916: | Commander of Reserves, Southwestern Front |
| 27 May 1916 - 1917: | Reserve officer, Kiev Military District |

*Lieutenant-General* Sergey Aleksandrovich **Batog** (24 Sep 1863 - ?)
| | |
|---|---|
| 5 Jun 1907 - 28 Mar 1908: | Military Judge, Kiev Military District Court |

6 Dec 1907: Promoted to *Major-General*
28 Mar 1908 - 17 Nov 1912: Military Judge, Odessa Military District Court
17 Nov 1912 - 29 Jul 1916: Military Prosecutor, Kiev Military District Court
10 Apr 1916: Promoted to *Lieutenant-General*
29 Jul 1916 - 1917: Military Judge, Southwestern Front

*Major-General* Aleksandr Aleksandrovich **Batorsky** (24 Oct 1850 - 11 Dec 1897)
7 Apr 1894 - 15 Mar 1897: Chief of Military Staff, Terek Cossack Army
14 May 1896: Promoted to *Major-General*
15 Mar 1897 - 11 Dec 1897: Governor of Yekaterinoslav

*Major-General* Nikolai Leontyevich **Batranets** (1 Aug 1872 - ?)
22 Dec 1915 - 25 Oct 1916: Commander, 43rd Infantry Regiment
20 Oct 1916: Promoted to *Major-General*
25 Oct 1917 - 12 May 1917: Reserve officer, Kiev Military District
12 May 1917 - 28 Aug 1917: Chief of Staff, XXVI. Army Corps
28 Aug 1917 - Dec 1917: Commander, 4th Rifle Division

*General of Infantry* Mikhail Ivanovich **Batyanov** (17 Oct 1835 - 5 Dec 1916)
23 Dec 1867 - 14 Jan 1878: Commander, 80th Infantry Regiment
16 May 1877: Promoted to *Major-General*
14 Jan 1878 - 28 Apr 1881: Commander, 2nd Brigade, 1st Grenadier Division
28 Apr 1881 - 5 Nov 1886: Commander, 3rd Rifle Brigade
5 Nov 1886 - 15 Aug 1888: Commander, 13th Infantry Division
25 Jul 1887: Promoted to *Lieutenant-General*
15 Aug 1888 - 3 Nov 1893: Commander, 23rd Infantry Division
3 Nov 1893 - 17 Feb 1896: Commanding General, XII. Army Corps
17 Feb 1896 - 12 Jan 1897: Unassigned
12 Jan 1897 - 1 Jan 1903: Commanding General, XVI. Army Corps
6 Dec 1899: Promoted to *General of Infantry*
1 Jan 1903 - 13 Mar 1905: Member of the Military Council
13 Mar 1905 - 3 Feb 1906: C-in-C, 3rd Manchurian Army
24 Nov 1911 - 1 Jan 1911: Member of the Military Council
1 Jan 1911: Retired

*Major-General* Nikolai Stepanovich **Batyushin** (26 Feb 1874 - 9 Feb 1957)
6 Oct 1915 - 3 Sep 1917: Special Purposes General, Northern Front
6 Dec 1915: Promoted to *Major-General*

*Major-General of the Fleet* Mikhail Konstantinovich **Batyushkov** (22 Sep 1860 - ?)
31 Mar 1908 - ?: Senior Deputy Captain, Port of Kronstadt
6 Dec 1913: Promoted to *Major-General of the Fleet*
1 Jan 1915 - 1917: Deputy Chief of the Admiralty Shipyards

*Lieutenant-General* Viktor Fyodorovich **Bauder** (17 Jan 1856 - ?)
14 Jan 1914: Promoted to *Major-General*
14 Jan 1914 - 13 Aug 1914: Commander, 2nd Brigade, 16th Infantry Division
13 Aug 1914 - 31 Jan 1915: Acting Commander, 16th Infantry Division

| | |
|---|---|
| 31 Jan 1915 - 17 Oct 1915: | Commander, 2nd Brigade, 16th Infantry Division |
| 17 Oct 1915 - 9 Aug 1916: | Commander, 4th Infantry Division |
| 9 Aug 1916: | Promoted to *Lieutenant-General* |
| 9 Aug 1916: | Dismissed from the service |

*Lieutenant-General* Aleksandr Fyodorovich **Bauer** (21 Jan 1852 - ?)

| | |
|---|---|
| 4 Mar 1905: | Promoted to *Major-General* |
| 4 Mar 1905 - 11 Sep 1906: | Commander, 2nd Brigade, 20th Infantry Division |
| 11 Sep 1906 - 15 Jun 1907: | General Staff Officer, Caucasus Military District |
| 15 Jun 1907 - 25 Nov 1913: | Commandant of Fortress St. Michael |
| 31 Dec 1910: | Promoted to *Lieutenant-General* |
| 25 Nov 1913 - 15 Mar 1915: | Commandant of Fortress Sveaborg |
| 15 Mar 1915 - 22 Apr 1917: | Commander, 20th Infantry Division |
| 22 Apr 1917 - ?: | Reserve officer, Moscow Military District |

*Lieutenant-General* Nikolai Fyodorovich **Bauer** (19 Jan 1841 - 24 Nov 1910)

| | |
|---|---|
| 31 Jan 1901 - 24 Nov 1910: | Company Commander, Palace Grenadiers |
| 12 Dec 1902: | Promoted to *Major-General* |
| 1910: | Promoted to *Lieutenant-General* |

*Rear-Admiral* Salvador Fyodorovich **Bauer** (2 Oct 1841 - 25 Oct 1895)

| | |
|---|---|
| 1892 - 25 Oct 1895: | Commander, 7th Naval Depot |
| 1894: | Promoted to *Rear-Admiral* |

*Lieutenant-General* Vladislav Frantsevich **Baufal** (12 Jul 1853 - 20 Nov 1914)

| | |
|---|---|
| 19 Jun 1905: | Promoted to *Major-General* |
| 19 Jun 1905 - 5 May 1906: | Commander, 2nd Brigade, 4th Rifle Division |
| 5 May 1906 - 7 Jul 1907: | Commander, 2nd Brigade, 34th Infantry Division |
| 7 Jul 1907 - 19 Sep 1914: | Commander, 4th Rifle Brigade |
| 19 Sep 1914 - 4 Nov 1914: | Commander, 3rd Grenadier Division |
| 1914: | Promoted to *Lieutenant-General* |
| 4 Nov 1914 - 20 Nov 1914: | Reserve officer, Kiev Military District |

*General of Cavalry* Arkady Vasilievich **Bauler** (9 Jan 1852 - ?)

| | |
|---|---|
| 15 Jul 1901: | Promoted to *Major-General* |
| 15 Jul 1901 - 30 Sep 1904: | At the disposal of the Commanding General, St. Petersburg Military District |
| 30 Sep 1904 - 1912: | Intendant, St. Petersburg Military District |
| 6 Dec 1907: | Promoted to *Lieutenant-General* |
| 1912: | Promoted to *General of Cavalry* |
| 1912: | Retired |

*Major-General* Eduard Eduardovich **Bauman** (12 May 1834 - ?)

| | |
|---|---|
| 28 Nov 1889: | Promoted to *Major-General* |
| 28 Nov 1889 - Jan 1895: | Commander, 3rd Siberian Artillery Brigade |

*Lieutenant-General* Aleksandr Trofimovich **Baumgarten** (16 Feb 1843 - 25 Jan 1901)

| | |
|---|---|
| 20 Jun 1888: | Promoted to *Major-General* |

| | |
|---|---|
| 20 Jun 1888 - 7 Aug 1888: | Commander, 3rd Grenadier Artillery Brigade |
| 7 Aug 1888 - 19 Dec 1890: | Commander, 28th Artillery Brigade |
| 19 Dec 1890 - 9 Nov 1895: | Commander, 1st Life Guards Artillery Brigade |
| 9 Nov 1895 - 29 Apr 1898: | Commander of Artillery, Caucasus Army Corps |
| 12 Feb 1897: | Promoted to *Lieutenant-General* |
| 29 Apr 1898 - 22 Jan 1899: | Commander of Artillery, Caucasus Military District |
| 22 Jan 1899 - 25 Jan 1901: | Member of the Artillery Committee, Main Artillery Directorate |

*Major-General* Fyodor-Otto-Aleksandr Fyodorovich **Baumgarten** (6 Apr 1855 - 1940)
| | |
|---|---|
| 1910: | Promoted to *Major-General* |

*Lieutenant-General* Karl Fyodorovich **Baumgarten** (26 Nov 1847 - ?)
| | |
|---|---|
| 27 Oct 1894 - 18 Jun 1903: | Commander of Engineers, Fortress Osovets |
| 6 Dec 1899: | Promoted to *Major-General* |
| 18 Jun 1903 - 13 Jan 1905: | Chief of Engineers, Fortress Warsaw |
| 13 Jan 1905 - 5 Jul 1905: | Member of the Engineering Committee, Main Engineering Directorate |
| 5 Jul 1905 - 9 May 1908: | Member, Main Fortress Committee |
| 6 Dec 1906: | Promoted to *Lieutenant-General* |

*Major-General* Leonid Fyodorovich **Baumgarten** (30 Sep 1843 - ?)
| | |
|---|---|
| 25 Jan 1900: | Promoted to *Major-General* |
| 25 Jan 1900 - Feb 1904: | Commander, 2nd Brigade, 14th Cavalry Division |

*General of Cavalry* Leonty Nikolayevich von **Baumgarten** (30 Jun 1853 - 24 Mar 1931)
| | |
|---|---|
| 17 Nov 1894 - 25 Nov 1896: | Commander, 13th Dragoon Regiment |
| 25 Nov 1896: | Promoted to *Major-General* |
| 25 Nov 1896 - 28 Nov 1897: | Commander, 1st Brigade, 10th Cavalry Division |
| 28 Nov 1897 - 10 Feb 1899: | Commander, 3rd Independent Cavalry Brigade, Consolidated Cavalry Division |
| 10 Feb 1899 - 26 Jan 1904: | Commander, Life Guards Uhlan Regiment |
| 26 Jan 1904 - 20 Aug 1904: | Transferred to the reserve |
| 20 Aug 1904 - 2 Oct 1905: | Commander, 1st Brigade, Siberian Cossack Division |
| 7 Feb 1905: | Promoted to *Lieutenant-General* |
| 2 Oct 1905 - 24 Jul 1907: | Commander, 2nd Independent Cavalry Brigade |
| 24 Jul 1907 - 4 May 1917: | Honorary Trustee, Empress Maria Institutions |
| 22 Mar 1915: | Promoted to *General of Cavalry* |
| 4 May 1917: | Dismissed |

*Lieutenant-General* Mikhail Georgiyevich **Bayev** (2 Jan 1837 - 1895)
| | |
|---|---|
| 3 Apr 1881 - 8 Jan 1888: | Special Assignments Officer for Quarantine and Customs Matters in the Caucasus, Ministry of Finance |
| 15 May 1883: | Promoted to *Major-General* |
| 8 Jan 1888 - 1895: | Chief of Customs Service, Bessarabia |
| 1895: | Promoted to *Lieutenant-General* |

*Major-General* Leonid Semyonovich **Baykov** (27 May 1858 - ?)
25 May 1911 - 1917: Chief of Gendarmerie, Kovno Province
14 Apr 1913: Promoted to *Major-General*

*Major-General* Lev Lvovich **Baykov** (15 Jun 1869 - 23 Nov 1938)
23 Mar 1913 - 14 Jan 1915: Commander, 53rd Infantry Regiment
16 Aug 1914: Promoted to *Major-General*
14 Jan 1915 - 1 Apr 1915: Commander, 2nd Brigade, 71st Infantry Division
1 Apr 1915 - 2 Nov 1916: Chief of Staff, XXXII. Army Corps
2 Nov 1916 - 19 Apr 1917: Commander, 115th Infantry Division
19 Apr 1917 - 24 Jun 1917: Reserve officer, Odessa Military District
24 Jun 1917 - 19 Apr 1918: Commander, 38th Infantry Division

*Lieutenant-General* Lev Matveyevich **Baykov** (6 May 1840 - ?)
7 Jan 1894 - 2 May 1896: Commander, 105th Infantry Regiment
14 Nov 1894: Promoted to *Major-General*
2 May 1896 - 6 May 1901: Commander, 1st Brigade, 5th Infantry Division
6 May 1901: Promoted to *Lieutenant-General*
6 May 1901: Retired

*Major-General* Aleksandr Prokofievich **Baykovsky** (2 Jan 1837 - ?)
23 Mar 1898: Promoted to *Major-General*
23 Mar 1898 - 14 Jan 1900: Commander, 2nd Brigade, 10th Infantry Division
14 Jan 1900: Retired

*Major-General* Vladimir Fyodorovich **Baymakov** (8 Feb 1867 - 24 Mar 1913)
? - 24 Mar 1913: Attached to Life Guards Pavlovsky Regiment
1913: Promoted to *Major-General*

*Lieutenant-General* Khalil Mustafovich **Bazarevsky** (25 Sep 1851 - ?)
15 Feb 1905 - 28 Sep 1911: Commander, 29th Artillery Brigade
5 Jan 1906: Promoted to *Major-General*
28 Sep 1911: Promoted to *Lieutenant-General*
28 Sep 1911: Retired

*Vice-Admiral* Aleksandr Aleksandrovich **Bazhenov** (4 Oct 1860 - ?)
10 Nov 1908 - 11 Oct 1911: Captain, Port of Kronstadt
6 Dec 1910: Promoted to *Rear-Admiral*
11 Oct 1911 - 1913: Chief of Staff, Port of Kronstadt
1913 - 1917: Commander, Amur Flotilla
22 Mar 1915: Promoted to *Vice-Admiral*

*Major-General of Naval Engineers* Aleksey Aleksandrovich **Bazhenov** (24 Nov 1870 - 23 Oct 1916)
27 Feb 1915 - 23 Oct 1916: Chief, Navy Shipbuilding Yard
30 Jul 1915: Promoted to *Major-General of Naval Engineers*

*Major-General* Boris Petrovich **Bazhenov** (31 Jul 1871 - ?)
| | |
|---|---|
| 30 Jul 1913: | Promoted to *Major-General* |
| 30 Jul 1913 - 19 Aug 1914: | Chief of Military Communications, St. Petersburg Military District |
| 19 Aug 1914 - Jan 1917: | Quartermaster-General, 6th Army |
| Jan 1917 - 16 Sep 1917: | Chief of Staff, XLII. Army Corps |
| 16 Sep 1917 - 1918: | Reserve officer, Petrograd Military District |

*Major-General of the Admiralty* Nikolai Romanovich **Bazhenov** (20 Apr 1854 - ?)
| | |
|---|---|
| 4 Jun 1907 - ?: | Chief of Naval Construction Training Commission |
| 6 Dec 1907: | Promoted to *Major-General of the Admiralty* |

*General of Infantry* Pyotr Nikolayevich **Bazhenov** (24 Nov 1840 - ?)
| | |
|---|---|
| 26 Jan 1885 - 19 Jun 1889: | Commander, 18th Dragoon Regiment |
| 19 Jun 1889: | Promoted to *Major-General* |
| 19 Jun 1889 - 1 Dec 1889: | Commander, 1st Brigade, 12th Cavalry Division |
| 1 Dec 1889 - 23 Jul 1891: | Chief of Staff, XIV. Army Corps |
| 23 Jul 1891 - 18 Mar 1897: | Commander, 2nd Brigade, 15th Cavalry Division |
| 18 Mar 1897 - 23 Jun 1899: | Commander, 2nd Cavalry Division |
| 6 Dec 1898: | Promoted to *Lieutenant-General* |
| 23 Jun 1899 - 20 Mar 1900: | Attached to the Commanding General, Warsaw Military District |
| 20 Mar 1900 - 24 Sep 1901: | Commander, 4th Infantry Division |
| 24 Sep 1901 - 14 Oct 1904: | At the disposal of the Chief of the General Staff |
| 14 Oct 1904 - 24 Sep 1905: | At the disposal of the C-in-C, 2nd Manchurian Army |
| 24 Sep 1905 - 23 Feb 1906: | At the disposal of the Chief of the General Staff |
| 23 Feb 1906 - 24 Mar 1908: | Commander, Minsk Regional Brigade |
| 24 Mar 1908: | Promoted to *General of Infantry* |
| 24 Mar 1908: | Retired |

*Lieutenant-General* Mikhail Nikolayevich **Bazilevsky** (8 Mar 1843 - 16 Dec 1903)
| | |
|---|---|
| 24 Oct 1899: | Promoted to *Major-General* |
| 24 Oct 1899 - Jan 1903: | Commander, 1st Brigade, 36th Infantry Division |
| Jan 1903: | Promoted to *Lieutenant-General* |
| Jan 1903: | Retired |

*Lieutenant-General* Platon Yevgenievich **Bazilevsky** (23 Mar 1856 - ?)
| | |
|---|---|
| 9 Sep 1898 - ?: | Commander of Engineers, Kwantung Region |
| 26 Feb 1901: | Promoted to *Major-General* |
| ? - 28 Jul 1906: | Commander of Engineers, Far East |
| 28 Jul 1906 - 19 Oct 1910: | Commander of Engineers, Amur Military District |
| 22 Apr 1907: | Promoted to *Lieutenant-General* |
| 19 Oct 1910 - 17 Apr 1913: | Commander of Engineers, Far East |
| 17 Apr 1913: | Retired |

*Major-General* Vladimir Nikolayevich **Bazilevsky** (25 Sep 1844 - 29 Jan 1898)
| | |
|---|---|
| 4 Apr 1894: | Promoted to *Major-General* |
| 4 Apr 1894 - 29 Jan 1898: | Commander, 2nd Brigade, 27th Infantry Division |

*Major-General* Yevgeny Yevgenievich **Bazilevsky** (3 Dec 1848 - ?)
15 Feb 1885 - 16 Nov 1892: Military Judge, Kiev Military District
30 Aug 1892: Promoted to *Major-General*
16 Nov 1892 - 24 Mar 1897: Military Prosecutor, Omsk Military District
24 Mar 1897 - 1902: Military Prosecutor, Kiev Military District

*Major-General* Prince Nikolai Vasilyevich **Bebutov** (8 May 1839 - 9 Feb 1904)
8 Feb 1877 - 9 Feb 1904: Staff Officer, Caucasus Military District
4 Jun 1895: Promoted to *Major-General*

*Lieutenant-General* Pavel Ivanovich **Bedo** (29 Jun 1839 - 1914)
2 Jul 1892: Promoted to *Major-General*
2 Jul 1892 - 23 Sep 1893: Deputy Commander of Artillery, Amur Military District
23 Sep 1893: Retired
19 May 1894 - 23 Dec 1898: Recalled; Commander, 28th Artillery Brigade
23 Dec 1898 - 24 Mar 1900: Deputy Commander of Artillery, Kiev Military District
24 Mar 1900: Promoted to *Lieutenant-General*
24 Mar 1900: Retired

*Lieutenant-General* Prince Konstantin Sergeyevich **Begildeyev** (25 Dec 1858 - 1920)
14 Jan 1905: Promoted to *Major-General*
14 Jan 1905 - 4 Sep 1911: Chief of Staff, II. Army Corps
4 Sep 1911: Promoted to *Lieutenant-General*
4 Sep 1911 - 6 Apr 1917: Commander, 9th Cavalry Division
?: Acting Commanding General, VII. Caucasus Army Corps
6 Apr 1917 - 1917: Reserve officer, Kiev Military District

*Lieutenant-General* Maksimilian Garaldovich **Bek** (22 Sep 1850 - ?)
29 Aug 1900 - 8 Mar 1913: Military Judge, Turkestan Military District
6 Dec 1901: Promoted to *Major-General*
8 Mar 1913: Promoted to *Lieutenant-General*
8 Mar 1913: Retired

*Lieutenant-General* Pyotr Petrovich **Bek** (19 Jun 1839 - 17 May 1912)
29 Mar 1892 - 1902: Commander of Gendarmerie, Kuban Region
13 Apr 1897: Promoted to *Major-General*
1902: Promoted to *Lieutenant-General*
1902: Retired

*Major-General* Soslan-Bek Sosurkoyevich **Bek-Buzarov** (4 Oct 1865 - May 1930)
9 Aug 1915 - 1917: Commander, 76th Infantry Regiment
31 Jan 1917: Promoted to *Major-General*
1917: Commander, Brigade, 19th Infantry Division

*Lieutenant-General* Alfred-Stanislav Vasilievich von **Bekker** (10 May 1847 - ?)
20 Sep 1901: Promoted to *Major-General*
20 Sep 1901 - 27 Feb 1907: Commander, St. Petersbug Life Guards Regiment

| | |
|---|---|
| 27 Feb 1907 - 19 May 1908: | Commander, 2nd Brigade, 3rd Guards Infantry Division |
| 19 May 1908: | Promoted to *Lieutenant-General* |
| 19 May 1908 - 2 Dec 1908: | Commander, 32nd Infantry Division |

*Vice-Admiral* Nikolai Aleksandrovich **Beklemishev** (18 Mar 1851 - 30 Jun 1913)
| | |
|---|---|
| 1903: | Promoted to *Rear-Admiral* |
| 1903 - 1905: | Deputy Commander, 2nd Naval Division |
| 1905 - 1906: | Commander of Training Detachment, Baltic Sea |
| 1907: | Deputy Commander, Baltic Fleet |
| 1907: | Acting Commander, Baltic Fleet |
| 17 Nov 1907 - 1913: | Member, Committee for Wounded Veterans |
| 29 Mar 1909: | Promoted to *Vice-Admiral* |

*Major-General of the Admiralty* Mikhail Nikolayevich **Beklemishev** (26 Sep 1858 - 18 Feb 1936)
| | |
|---|---|
| 1908 - 1909: | Chief of Diving Department, Naval Technical Committee |
| 1910: | Promoted to *Major-General of the Admiralty* |
| 1910: | Retired |

*Major-General of the Admiralty* Nikolai Nikolayevich **Beklemishev** (18 Mar 1857 - ?)
| | |
|---|---|
| 1902 - 1905: | Chief of Commercial Ports |
| 1905: | Promoted to *Major-General of the Admiralty* |
| 1905: | Retired |

*General of Cavalry* Vladimir Aleksandrovich **Bekman** (31 May 1848 - 26 Nov 1923)
| | |
|---|---|
| 31 Aug 1891: | Promoted to *Major-General* |
| 31 Aug 1891 - 2 Mar 1899: | Chief of Staff, XI. Army Corps |
| 2 Mar 1899 - 23 Nov 1904: | Commander, 8th Cavalry Division |
| 6 Dec 1899: | Promoted to *Lieutenant-General* |
| 23 Nov 1904 - 12 Jan 1905: | Commanding General, XII. Army Corps |
| 12 Jan 1905 - 9 Nov 1906: | Commanding General, XX. Army Corps |
| 9 Nov 1906 - 2 Feb 1908: | Commanding General, XXII. Army Corps |
| 6 Dec 1907: | Promoted to *General of Cavalry* |
| 2 Feb 1908 - 11 Nov 1909: | Governor-General of Finland |
| 11 Nov 1909 - Feb 1917: | Member of the State Council |

*Major-General* Alexander Nikolayevich **Beknev** (4 Feb 1852 - ?)
| | |
|---|---|
| 3 Nov 1903 - 1907: | Commander of Gendarmerie, Kostroma Province |
| 6 Dec 1903: | Promoted to *Major-General* |

*Lieutenant-General* Konstantin Nikolayevich **Bekov** (1 Jan 1856 - ?)
| | |
|---|---|
| 16 Jan 1913: | Promoted to *Major-General* |
| 16 Jan 1913 - 22 Apr 1915: | Commander, 2nd Brigade, Caucasus Grenadier Division |
| 22 Apr 1915 - 3 Nov 1915: | Commander, 1st Caucasus Rifle Brigade |
| 3 Nov 1915 - 1917: | Commander, 1st Caucasus Rifle Division |
| 6 Dec 1915: | Promoted to *Lieutenant-General* |

*Lieutenant-General* Vasily Ivanovich **Belenchenko** (1840 - 7 Feb 1909)
| | |
|---|---|
| 30 Jan 1888 - 21 Jun 1898: | Attached to the Ministry of War |
| 14 May 1896: | Promoted to *Major-General* |
| 21 Jun 1898 - 29 Jan 1909: | General for Special Assignments, Main Engineering Directorate |
| 6 Dec 1904: | Promoted to *Lieutenant-General* |

*Major-General* Grigory Moiseyevich **Beletsky** (10 Jan 1834 - ?)
| | |
|---|---|
| 19 Apr 1892 - 9 Sep 1895: | Commander, 1st Mortar Artillery Regiment |
| 9 Sep 1895: | Promoted to *Major-General* |
| 9 Sep 1895 - 29 Dec 1899: | Commander, 34th Artillery Brigade |

*Major-General* Iosif Donatovich **Belevich** (9 Oct 1866 - 16 Oct 1942)
| | |
|---|---|
| 4 Nov 1915 - 6 Jun 1917: | Commander, 45th Infantry Regiment |
| 13 Jan 1917: | Promoted to *Major-General* |
| 6 Jun 1917 - 1917: | Commander, Brigade, 12th Infantry Division |

*Major-General* Ivan Valerianovich **Belgard** (7 May 1860 - ?)
| | |
|---|---|
| 11 May 1902 - 12 Aug 1914: | Attached to Grand Duke Aleksandr Georgiyevich |
| 25 Mar 1912: | Promoted to *Major-General* |
| 12 Aug 1914 - 10 Jun 1917: | Attached to the C-in-C, Northwestern Front |
| 10 Jun 1917: | Dismissed |

*Major-General* Nikolai Valerianovich **Belgard** (22 Jan 1849 - ?)
| | |
|---|---|
| 6 Dec 1897: | Promoted to *Major-General* |
| 6 Dec 1897 - 26 Feb 1898: | Special Assignments General (5th Class), Ministry of War |
| 26 Feb 1898 - 1905: | Special Assignments General (4th Class), Ministry of War |

*General of Infantry* Valerian Aleksandrovich **Belgard** (6 Mar 1812 - 1897)
| | |
|---|---|
| Mar 1846 - Feb 1850: | Commander, Kuban Jaeger Regiment |
| 23 Sep 1849: | Promoted to *Major-General* |
| Feb 1850 - Dec 1854: | Commander, 1st Brigade, 20th Infantry Division |
| Dec 1854 - Jan 1857: | Commander, 2nd Reserve Infantry Division |
| Jan 1857 - Mar 1862: | Commander, 11th Infantry Division |
| 30 Aug 1858: | Promoted to *Lieutenant-General* |
| Mar 1862 - Oct 1863: | Commander, 3rd Grenadier Division |
| Oct 1863 - Jan 1864: | Commander, 2nd Grenadier Division |
| Jan 1864 - Dec 1865: | Commander, 7th Infantry Division |
| Dec 1865 - 1872: | Commandant of Dunaburg |
| 1872 - 1897: | Member, Committee for Wounded Veterans |
| 26 Nov 1878: | Promoted to *General of Infantry* |

*Major-General* Valerian Valerianovich **Belgard** (3 Jun 1855 - ?)
| | |
|---|---|
| 15 Jul 1897 - 1907: | Vice-Governor of Orel |
| 6 Dec 1903: | Promoted to *Major-General* |
| 1907: | Retired |

*Lieutenant-General* Vladimir Karlovich **Belgardt** (1 Jun 1863 - 18 Aug 1914)
| | |
|---|---|
| 24 Mar 1903 - 3 Oct 1907: | Commander, 54th Dragoon Regiment |
| 3 Oct 1907: | Promoted to *Major-General* |
| 3 Oct 1907 - 21 May 1912: | Commander, 1st Brigade, 14th Cavalry Division |
| 21 May 1912 - 18 Aug 1914: | Commander, 3rd Cavalry Division |
| 3 Oct 1913: | Promoted to *Lieutenant-General* |

*Major-General* Nikolai Vasilievich **Belikhov** (14 Apr 1859 - Jul 1914)
| | |
|---|---|
| 15 Jul 1910 - 31 Mar 1911: | Deputy Commander, 46th Artillery Brigade |
| 31 Mar 1911: | Promoted to *Major-General* |
| 31 Mar 1911 - 2 Apr 1913: | Commander, 48th Artillery Brigade |
| 2 Apr 1913 - Jul 1914: | Commander, 10th Artillery Brigade |

*Major-General* Sergey Petrovich **Belikov** (16 Sep 1850 - ?)
| | |
|---|---|
| 23 Dec 1901 - 1 Aug 1905: | Director, Aleksandr Military Academy |
| 14 Apr 1902: | Promoted to *Major-General* |
| 1 Aug 1905 - Jul 1908: | Director of Khabarovsk Cadet Corps |

*Major-General* Aleksandr Konstantinovich **Belinsky** (24 Nov 1869 - 24 Nov 1922)
| | |
|---|---|
| 23 Dec 1914 - 31 May 1916: | Commander, 2nd Siberian Rifle Regiment |
| 13 Nov 1915: | Promoted to *Major-General* |
| 31 May 1916 - 30 Apr 1917: | Commander, Brigade, 57th Infantry Division |
| 30 Apr 1917 - 19 Sep 1917: | Commander, 111th Infantry Division |

*Rear-Admiral* Mikhail Fyodorovich **Belkin** (1825 - 12 Feb 1909)
| | |
|---|---|
| ? - 1905: | Member, Volunteer Navy Committee |
| 1904: | Promoted to *Rear-Admiral* |
| 1905: | Retired |

*General of Infantry* Leonid Nikolayevich **Belkovich** (6 Mar 1859 - ?)
| | |
|---|---|
| 7 Sep 1905: | Promoted to *Major-General* |
| 7 Sep 1905 - 7 Oct 1905: | Commander, 2nd Brigade, 35th Infantry Division |
| 7 Oct 1905 - 15 May 1907: | Chief of Staff, Trans-Baikal Region |
| 15 May 1907 - 24 Apr 1909: | Commander, 1st Brigade, 4th East Siberian Rifle Division |
| 24 Apr 1909 - 19 Jul 1914: | Commander, 1st Brigade, 3rd Infantry Division |
| 19 Jul 1914: | Promoted to *Lieutenant-General* |
| 19 Jul 1914 - 26 Jul 1914: | Commander, 57th Infantry Division |
| 26 Jul 1914 - 5 Jul 1915: | Commander, 15th Infantry Division |
| 5 Jul 1915 - 13 Apr 1917: | Commanding General, XLI. Army Corps |
| 13 Apr 1917 - 20 Jun 1917: | C-in-C, 7th Army |
| 26 Jun 1917 - 19 Jul 1917: | Reserve officer, Kiev Military District |
| 19 Jul 1917 - 1918: | Reserve officer, Moscow Military District |
| 8 Sep 1917: | Promoted to *General of Infantry* |

*Major-General* Nikolai Nikolayevich **Belkovich** (7 Feb 1858 - ?)
| | |
|---|---|
| 11 Oct 1914 - 31 May 1917: | Commander, 1st Grenadier Artillery Brigade |
| 18 Apr 1915: | Promoted to *Major-General* |

31 May 1917 - 1917: Inspector of Artillery, XXIV. Army Corps

*Rear-Admiral* Aleksandr Andreyevich **Belogolovy** (18 May 1862 - 1927)
6 Apr 1914: Promoted to *Rear-Admiral*
Jul 1914 - Sep 1916: Chairman of the Standing Committee for Testing Naval Vessels
Sep 1916 - Oct 1917: Commandant of the Port of Petrograd

*Major-General* Ivan Anatolyevich **Belogorsky** (6 Nov 1870 - 1927)
29 Apr 1911 - 10 Aug 1914: Inspector of Classes, Orlovsky Bakhtin Cadet Corps
6 Dec 1913: Promoted to *Major-General*
10 Aug 1914 - 1917: Inspector of Classes, 2$^{nd}$ Tsar Peter the Great Cadet Corps

*Major-General* Valerian Yerofeyevich **Belolipetsky** (23 Dec 1869 - 1943)
29 Aug 1914 - 2 Nov 1916: Commander, 108$^{th}$ Infantry Regiment
10 Jul 1916: Promoted to *Major-General*
2 Nov 1916 - 4 Mar 1917: Commander, Brigade, 2$^{nd}$ Special Infantry Division
4 Mar 1917 - 19 Apr 1917: Commander, Brigade, 3$^{rd}$ Special Infantry Division
19 Apr 1917 - 8 May 1917: Commander, 18$^{th}$ Siberian Rifle Division
8 May 1917 - 1917: Commander, 18$^{th}$ Infantry Division

*Major-General* Valerian Iosifovich **Belolipsky** (15 Jan 1863 - ?)
17 Mar 1910 - Oct 1917: At the disposal of the Minister of War
6 Dec 1911: Promoted to *Major-General*

*Lieutenant-General* Prince Konstantin Esperovich **Beloselsky-Belozersky** (16 Jun 1843 - 26 May 1920)
1881 - 20 Oct 1894: Aide-de-Camp to Tsar Aleksandr III
30 Aug 1894: Promoted to *Major-General*
20 Oct 1894 - 16 Jul 1895: Attached to the Imperial Court
16 Jul 1895 - 14 May 1896: Transferred to the reserve
6 May 1896: Promoted to *General-Adjutant*
14 May 1896 - 16 Apr 1917: Attached to the Imperial Court
6 May 1906: Promoted to *Lieutenant-General*
16 Apr 1917: Retired

*Lieutenant-General* Prince Sergey Konstantinich **Beloselsky-Belozersky** (13 Jul 1867 - 20 Apr 1951)
10 Mar 1910: Promoted to *Major-General*
10 Mar 1910 - 24 Dec 1913: Commander, Life Guards Uhlan Regiment
24 Dec 1913 - 23 Nov 1914: Commander, 1$^{st}$ Brigade, 2$^{nd}$ Guards Cavalry Division
Nov 1914: Acting Commander, 2$^{nd}$ Guards Cavalry Division
23 Nov 1914 - 11 Jul 1915: Commander, 1st Brigade, 2$^{nd}$ Guards Cavalry Division
11 Jul 1915 - 29 Dec 1915: Commander, 3$^{rd}$ Don Cossack Division
29 Dec 1915 - 15 Apr 1917: Commander, Caucasus Cavalry Division
10 Apr 1916: Promoted to *Lieutenant-General*
15 Apr 1917 - Dec 1917: At the disposal of the Minister of War

*Major-General* Ivan Maksimovich **Belousov** (19 Jun 1869 - 24 Nov 1932)
16 Jul 1915 - 10 Nov 1916: Commander, 63rd Infantry Regiment
18 Jul 1916: Promoted to *Major-General*
10 Nov 1916 - 15 May 1917: Chief of Staff, 32nd Infantry Division
15 May 1917 - 27 Jul 1917: Chief of Staff, XXII. Army Corps
27 Jul 1917 - 1917: Chief of Staff, XXIII. Army Corps

*Major-General* Dmitry Vasilyevich **Belov** (8 Apr 1862 - ?)
16 Jun 1907 - 1917: Staff officer of assignments, General Government of Turkestan
6 Dec 1915: Promoted to *Major-General*
1917: Retired

*Lieutenant-General* Nikolai Vasilievich **Belov** (21 Jan 1857 - ?)
9 Jul 1905: Promoted to *Major-General*
9 Jul 1905 - 19 Jul 1914: Commander, 2nd Brigade, 33rd Infantry Division
19 Jul 1914 - 21 Oct 1915: Commander, 70th Infantry Division
19 Feb 1915: Promoted to *Lieutenant-General*
21 Oct 1915 - 6 Jul 1916: Commander, 40th Infantry Division
6 Jul 1916 - 1917: Reserve officer, Dvinsk Military District

*Major-General* Vasily Aleksandrovich **Belov** (27 Jan 1848 - 22 Jun 1905)
30 Mar 1902 - 22 Jun 1905: Commander of Artillery, Fortress St. Petersburg
14 Apr 1902: Promoted to *Major-General*

*Major-General* Vladimir Vladimirovich **Belov** (16 Jun 1857 - ?)
2 Jun 1904: Promoted to *Major-General*
2 Jun 1904 - 2 May 1907: Commander, Life Guards Moscow Regiment
2 May 1907 - 10 Aug 1908: Commander, 2nd Brigade, 1st Guards Infantry Division

*Major-General* Vladimir Vasilievich **Belovodsky** (15 Jul 1845 - 10 Dec 1901)
5 Oct 1882 - 9 Apr 1901: Clerk of the Chancellery, Main Artillery Directorate
14 May 1896: Promoted to *Major-General*
9 Apr 1901 - 10 Dec 1901: Deputy Commander of Artillery, Odessa Military District

*Lieutenant-General* Yulian Yulianovich **Belozor** (10 Jan 1862 - 1942)
22 Feb 1913: Promoted to *Major-General*
22 Feb 1913 - Nov 1914: Special Purposes General, Amur Military District
Nov 1914 - Feb 1915: Chief of the Medical Section, 9th Army
Feb 1915 - 26 Feb 1915: Acting Commander, Brigade, 3rd Grenadier Division
26 Feb 1915 - 12 Jul 1915: Commander, 2nd Rifle Brigade
12 Jul 1915 - 7 Apr 1917: Commander, 2nd Rifle Division
6 Dec 1915: Promoted to *Lieutenant-General*
7 Apr 1917 - Sep 1917: Commanding General, XL. Army Corps
Sep 1917: Acting C-in-C, 9th Army

*Major-General* Aleksey Petrovich **Belsky** (11 Mar 1857 - ?)
3 May 1907 - 15 Apr 1917: Chief of Gendarmerie, Warsaw
14 Apr 1913: Promoted to *Major-General*
15 Apr 1917 - 25 May 1917: Reserve officer, Moscow Military District
25 May 1917: Dismissed

*Lieutenant-General* Vladimir Alekseyevich **Beltsov** (6 Jul 1836 - 18 Feb 1897)
12 Apr 1874 - 26 Apr 1884: Commander of Engineers, Fortress Kiev
15 May 1883: Promoted to *Major-General*
26 Apr 1884 - 3 Feb 1894: Commander of Engineers, Vilnius Military District
30 Aug 1893: Promoted to *Lieutenant-General*
3 Feb 1894 - 18 Feb 1897: Commander of Engineers, Moscow Military District

*Major-General* Sergey Aleksandrovich **Bely** (6 Dec 1855 - 9 Nov 1910)
30 Dec 1906 - 1910: Commander, 3$^{rd}$ Battery, 4$^{th}$ Artillery Brigade
1910: Promoted to *Major-General*

*General of Artillery* Vasily Fyodorovich **Bely** (19 Jan 1854 - 7 Jan 1913)
5 Aug 1900 - 17 Jun 1906: Commander of Artillery, Fortress Kwantung
6 Dec 1903: Promoted to *Major-General*
17 Jun 1906 - 25 Apr 1911: Commander of Artillery, Fortress Vladivostok
12 Jun 1908: Promoted to *Lieutenant-General*
25 Apr 1911: Promoted to *General of Artillery*
25 Apr 1911: Retired

*Major-General* Aleksandr Vasilyevich **Belyakov** (8 Dec 1871 - 1946)
19 Oct 1914 - 2 Jun 1917: Commander, Life Guards Petrograd Regiment
22 Mar 1915: Promoted to *Major-General*
2 Jun 1917 - Oct 1917: Commander, 157$^{th}$ Infantry Division

*Major-General* Aleksey Petrovich **Belyavsky** (13 Feb 1867 - ?)
24 May 1913 - 17 Oct 1915: Commander, 61$^{st}$ Infantry Regiment
1 Sep 1915: Promoted to *Major-General*
17 Oct 1915 - 16 Apr 1917: Commander, 1$^{st}$ Brigade, 16$^{th}$ Infantry Division
16 Apr 1917 - Jul 1917: Commander, 16$^{th}$ Infantry Division
Jul 1917 - ?: Commander, 52$^{nd}$ Infantry Division

*General of Infantry* Nikolai Nikolayevich **Belyavsky** (1 Mar 1846 - ?)
3 May 1893: Promoted to *Major-General*
3 May 1893 - 21 Jul 1894: Deputy Chief of Staff, Turkestan Military District
21 Jul 1894 - 28 Aug 1897: Deputy Chief of Staff, Caucasus Military District
28 Aug 1897 - 27 Feb 1899: Chief of Staff, Turkestan Military District
27 Feb 1899 - 4 Dec 1904: Chief of Staff, Caucasus Military District
6 Dec 1900: Promoted to *Lieutenant-General*
4 Dec 1904 - 19 May 1906: Commandant of Fortress Libau
19 May 1906 - 1 Jan 1910: Commander, Warsaw Fortified Region
13 Apr 1908: Promoted to *General of Infantry*
1 Jan 1910 - 1 Jan 1916: Member of the Military Council

1 Jan 1916: Retired

*Major-General* Andrey Ivanovich **Belyayev** (9 Mar 1854 - ?)
11 Feb 1899 - 1905: Military Prosecutor, Turkestan Military District
6 Dec 1900: Promoted to *Major-General*

*Major-General of Naval Engineers* Ivan Yefimovich **Belyayev** (15 Jun 1867 - ?)
14 Nov 1908 - 1917: Deputy Chief of Izhorsk Factory
14 Jun 1913: Promoted to *Major-General of Naval Engineers*

*General of Infantry* Mikhail Alekseyevich **Belyayev** (23 Dec 1863 - Sep 1918)
5 Dec 1906 - 17 Mar 1909: Section Chief, General Staff
13 Apr 1908: Promoted to *Major-General*
17 Mar 1909 - 31 Dec 1910: Quartermaster-General, General Staff
31 Dec 1910 - 2 Aug 1914: Chief of Service Troops Section, General Staff
1912: Promoted to *Lieutenant-General*
2 Aug 1914 - 10 Aug 1916: Chief of the General Directorate of the General Staff
6 Dec 1914: Promoted to *General of Infantry*
23 Jun 1915 - 10 Aug 1916: Deputy Minister of War
10 Aug 1916 - 3 Jan 1917: Member of the Military Council
3 Jan 1917 - 2 Mar 1917: Minister of War
2 Mar 1917 - 2 Apr 1917: Unassigned
2 Apr 1917: Dismissed

*Major-General* Mikhail Timofeyevich **Belyayev** (18 Jul 1869 - 1951)
16 Mar 1914: Promoted to *Major-General*
16 Mar 1914 - 2 Oct 1916: Commander, 23rd Artillery Brigade
2 Oct 1916 - 1917: Inspector of Artillery, XXVIII. Army Corps

*Major-General* Nikolai Semyonovich **Belyayev** (4 Dec 1866 - ?)
20 Oct 1915 - 30 Nov 1916: Commander, 152nd Infantry Regiment
1916: Promoted to *Major-General*
30 Nov 1916 - 19 Apr 1917: Chief of Staff, 17th Infantry Division
19 Apr 1917 - 18 May 1917: Chief of Staff, XIII. Army Corps
18 May 1917 - Oct 1917: Commander, 70th Infantry Division

*Lieutenant-General* Sergey Timofeyevich **Belyayev** (29 Sep 1867 - 24 Feb 1923)
8 Aug 1908 - 28 Sep 1911: Permanent Member, Artillery Committee, Main Artillery Directorate
18 Apr 1910: Promoted to *Major-General*
28 Sep 1911 - 31 Mar 1914: Commander, 29th Artillery Brigade
31 Mar 1914 - 26 Sep 1914: Permanent Member, Artillery Committee, Main Artillery Directorate
26 Sep 1914 - 16 Apr 1916: Inspector of Artillery, XXIX. Army Corps
10 Apr 1916: Promoted to *Lieutenant-General*
16 Apr 1916 - 1917: Inspector of Artillery, 2nd Army

*Major-General* Sergey Vasilyevich **Belyayev** (20 Sep 1856 - ?)
18 Nov 1914 - 1917: Commander, Brigade, 83rd Infantry Division
24 May 1915: Promoted to *Major-General*

*General of Artillery* Timofey Mikhailovich **Belyayev** (26 Jan 1843 - 7 Oct 1915)
9 Jan 1890: Promoted to *Major-General*
9 Jan 1890 - 16 Mar 1892: Commander, 17th Artillery Brigade
16 Mar 1892 - 29 Aug 1895: Commander, 23rd Artillery Brigade
29 Aug 1895 - 13 Nov 1895: Commander, 2nd Life Guards Artillery Brigade
13 Nov 1895 - 14 Feb 1899: Commander, 1st Life Guards Artillery Brigade
14 Feb 1899 - 13 Apr 1899: Commander of Artillery, Caucasus Army Corps
13 Apr 1899 - 8 Jul 1901: Commander of Artillery, II. Caucasus Army Corps
6 Dec 1899: Promoted to *Lieutenant-General*
8 Jul 1901 - 3 Apr 1903: Commander, 11th Infantry Division
3 Apr 1903 - 6 Feb 1907: Commandant of Fortress Kronstadt
6 Feb 1907: Promoted to *General of Artillery*
6 Feb 1907: Retired
8 Feb 1911 - 1914: Recalled; Reserve officer, Life Guards Artillery Brigade

*Major-General* Vladimir Timofeyevich **Belyayev** (12 Jan 1872 - ?)
1916 - 1917: Commander, 2nd Special Artillery Brigade
1917: Promoted to *Major-General*

*Lieutenant-General* Vladimir Vasilievich **Belyayev** (1 Oct 1868 - ?)
6 Dec 1910: Promoted to *Major-General*
6 Dec 1910 - 9 Nov 1914: Chief Editor of "*Military Collection*" and "*Russian Invalid*"
9 Nov 1914 - 19 Jun 1915: Commander, 83rd Infantry Division
19 Jun 1915 - 8 Apr 1917: Chief of Staff, 12th Army
10 Apr 1916: Promoted to *Lieutenant-General*
8 Apr 1917: Dismissed

*Major-General* Mikhail Antonovich **Bem** (20 Jan 1858 - 4 Mar 1917)
8 Apr 1911: Promoted to *Major-General*
8 Apr 1911 - 9 Oct 1915: Commander, 1st Brigade, 38th Infantry Division
9 Oct 1915 - 17 Mar 1916: Reserve officer, Dvinsk Military District
17 Mar 1916 - 4 Mar 1917: Commander, 30th Replacement Infantry Brigade

*Major-General* Yevgeny Yulyevich **Bem** (1 Mar 1869 - 17 May 1951)
18 Nov 1916 - 1917: Reserve officer, Petrograd Military District
22 Dec 1916: Promoted to *Major-General*
1917: Commander, 18th Engineer Regiment
1917: Inspector of Engineers, Kiev Military District

*Lieutenant-General* Anastas Fyodorovich **Benderev** (25 Mar 1859 - 20 Nov 1946)
9 Mar 1910: Promoted to *Major-General*
9 Mar 1910 - 18 Feb 1914: Commander, 1st Brigade, 1st Turkestan Cossack Division
18 Feb 1914 - 17 Aug 1914: Quartermaster-General, Turkestan Military District

| | |
|---|---|
| 17 Aug 1914 - 19 Oct 1914: | Chief of Staff, I. Turkestan Army Corps |
| 19 Oct 1914 - 5 Dec 1914: | Chief of Staff, III. Army Corps |
| 5 Dec 1914 - 19 Mar 1916: | Commander, 1st Independent Cavalry Brigade |
| 19 Mar 1916 - 14 Jul 1917: | Commander, 121st Infantry Division |
| 3 Jul 1916: | Promoted to *Lieutenant-General* |
| 14 Jul 1917 - 1918: | Reserve officer, Caucasus Military District |

*Lieutenant-General* Vladimir Onufrievich **Beneskul** (15 Jul 1863 - 2 Apr 1917)

| | |
|---|---|
| 12 Feb 1908 - 5 May 1910: | Chief of Staff, XIX. Army Corps |
| 13 Apr 1908: | Promoted to *Major-General* |
| 5 May 1910 - 22 Dec 1914: | Chief of Staff, V. Army Corps |
| 4 Dec 1914: | Promoted to *Lieutenant-General* |
| 22 Dec 1914 - 2 Apr 1917: | Commander, 51st Infantry Division |

*General of Infantry* Arkady Semyonovich **Benevsky** (29 Mar 1840 - 3 Apr 1913)

| | |
|---|---|
| 20 Nov 1884 - 27 Feb 1886: | Commander, 2nd East Siberian Rifle Brigade |
| 30 Aug 1885: | Promoted to *Major-General* |
| 27 Feb 1886 - 14 Mar 1892: | Military Governor, Amur Region, Ataman, Amur Cossack Army |
| Aug 1891 - 14 Mar 1892: | Acting Governor-General of Priamursk |
| 14 Mar 1892 - 12 Mar 1894: | Chief of Staff, Kiev Military District |
| 30 Aug 1893: | Promoted to *Lieutenant-General* |
| 12 Mar 1894 - Aug 1898: | Deputy Chief of the General Staff |
| Aug 1898 - 12 Feb 1903: | Deputy Governor-General of Priamursk, Deputy Commanding General, Amur Military District, Ataman, Amur Cossack Army |
| 16 Feb 1901: | Promoted to *General of Infantry* |
| 12 Feb 1903 - Sep 1905: | Member of the Military Council |
| Sep 1905: | Retired |

*Lieutenant-General* Aleksandr Aleksandrovich **Benkendorf** (29 Aug 1848 - 1915)

| | |
|---|---|
| 31 Jul 1895: | Promoted to *Major-General* |
| 31 Jul 1895 - 19 Aug 1896: | Commander, 2nd Brigade, 4th Cavalry Division |
| 19 Aug 1896 - 28 Dec 1896: | Commander, 2nd Brigade, 12th Cavalry Division |
| 28 Dec 1896 - 7 Mar 1905: | Commander, 1st Brigade, 12th Cavalry Division |
| 7 Mar 1905 - 18 Jan 1907: | Commander, 12th Cavalry Division |
| 17 Apr 1905: | Promoted to *Lieutenant-General* |
| 18 Jan 1907 - 22 Apr 1907: | Unassigned |
| 22 Apr 1907: | Retired |

*General of Cavalry* Count Pavel Leopold Johann Stefan Konstantinovich **Benkendorf** (29 Mar 1853 - 28 Jan 1921)

| | |
|---|---|
| 25 Oct 1893 - 6 Dec 1912: | Court Marshal of the Imperial Court |
| 14 May 1896: | Promoted to *Major-General* |
| 1905: | Promoted to *General-Adjutant* |
| 22 Apr 1907: | Promoted to *Lieutenant-General* |
| 6 Dec 1912: | Promoted to *General of Cavalry* |
| 6 Dec 1912 - 1917: | Chief Marshal of His Majesty's Court |

10 Apr 1916 - 1917: Member of the State Council

*Major-General* Aleksandr Mikhailovich **Benua** (9 Aug 1862 - 1 Mar 1944)
19 Apr 1915 - 28 Apr 1917: Commander, 42nd Artillery Brigade
2 Feb 1916: Promoted to *Major-General*
28 Apr 1917 - 1918: Inspector of Artillery, XIX. Army Corps

*Major-General* Nikolai-Konstantin Konstantinovich **Benua** (21 Aug 1858 - Feb 1916)
9 Nov 1911: Promoted to *Major-General*
9 Nov 1911 - 8 Sep 1913: Commander, 1st Brigade, 12th Cavalry Division
8 Sep 1913: Retired
5 Oct 1914 - Feb 1916: Recalled; Commander, 52nd State Militia Brigade

*Lieutenant-General* Baron Sergey Ernestovich von **Ber** (11 Feb 1855 - ?)
4 Dec 1906: Promoted to *Major-General*
4 Dec 1906 - 7 Dec 1912: Attached to the Commanding General, Amur Military District
7 Dec 1912 - 21 Jan 1916: Commander, 1st Brigade, 32nd Infantry Division
11 Nov 1915: Promoted to *Lieutenant-General*
21 Jan 1916 - 11 Aug 1916: Commander, 125th Infantry Division
11 Aug 1916 - 1917: Reserve officer, Odessa Military District

*Major-General* Leonid Fyodorovich **Berdyayev** (16 Apr 1853 - ?)
25 May 1908: Promoted to *Major-General*
25 May 1908 - 20 Dec 1908: Commander of Artillery, Fortress Brest-Litovsk

*Lieutenant-General* Nikolai Sergeyevich **Berdyayev** (7 Sep 1856 - ?)
9 Jan 1903: Promoted to *Major-General*
9 Jan 1903 - 24 Mar 1904: General for Special Assignments, Vilnius Military District
24 Mar 1904 - 12 Oct 1904: Chief of Staff, III. Army Corps
12 Oct 1904 - 4 Jun 1906: General for Special Assignments, 2nd Manchurian Army
15 Jun 1905 - 14 Apr 1906: Chief of Staff, VII. Siberian Army Corps
4 Jun 1906 - 13 Feb 1909: Commander, 5th Rifle Brigade
13 Feb 1909: Promoted to *Lieutenant-General*
13 Feb 1909 - 21 Jul 1910: Commander, 32nd Infantry Division
21 Jul 1910 - 22 Dec 1914: Commander, 50th Infantry Division
22 Dec 1914 - 25 Feb 1916: Reserve officer, Dvinsk Military District
25 Feb 1916 - 6 Feb 1917: Reserve officer, Petrograd Military District
6 Feb 1917: Retired

*Lieutenant-General* Viktor Osipovich **Berens** (4 May 1843 - ?)
9 Apr 1897: Promoted to *Major-General*
9 Apr 1897 - 11 Aug 1900: Commander, Turkestan Artillery Brigade
11 Aug 1900 - 20 Dec 1900: Commander of Artillery, III. Siberian Army Corps
20 Dec 1900 - 2 Mar 1901: At the disposal of the Main Artillery Directorate
2 Mar 1901 - 4 Jun 1902: Commander of Artillery, Turkestan Military District
4 Jun 1902: Promoted to *Lieutenant-General*

4 Jun 1902: Retired

*Major-General* Pyotr Ivanovich **Beresnev** (1859 - 15 Sep 1913)
3 Jan 1909 - 1913: Military Commander, Atkarsky County
1913: Promoted to *Major-General*

*Lieutenant-General* Aleksandr Ivanovich **Berezovsky** (1 Dec 1867 - 15 Oct 1940)
24 Oct 1910 - 3 Mar 1915: Commander, 57th Infantry Regiment
28 Oct 1914: Promoted to *Major-General*
3 Mar 1915 - 30 May 1915: Commander, Brigade, 15th Infantry Division
30 May 1915 - 9 Sep 1916: Chief of Staff, X. Army Corps
9 Sep 1916 - 29 May 1917: Commander, 3rd Grenadier Division
29 May 1917: Promoted to *Lieutenant-General*
29 May 1917 - 1918: Commanding General, XXXI. Army Corps

*Lieutenant-General of the Admiralty* Anton Antonovich **Berezovsky** (16 Sep 1847 - 2 Apr 1917)
1902: Promoted to *Major-General of the Admiralty*
1902 - 1906: Chief of Waterways, Amur Basin
1906: Promoted to *Lieutenant-General of the Admiralty*
1906: Retired

*Major-General* Aleksandr Fyodorovich **Berg** (6 Mar 1827 - ?)
23 Jun 1877 - 1899: Inspector of Works, Engineering Department, Caucasus Military District
14 Nov 1894: Promoted to *Major-General*

*General of Infantry* Ivan Aleksandrovich **Berg** (19 Nov 1830 - 12 Apr 1900)
27 Jan 1883 - 6 Mar 1885: Chief of St. Petersburg Military Hospital
15 May 1883: Promoted to *Major-General*
6 Mar 1885 - 5 Jul 1893: Commander, 1st Brigade, 32nd Infantry Division
5 Jul 1893 - 1900: Commander, 22nd (Orenburg) Regional Brigade
30 Aug 1894: Promoted to *Lieutenant-General*
1900: Promoted to *General of Infantry*
1900: Retired

*Major-General* Mikhail Leontyevich **Berg** (6 Jun 1859 - 9 Mar 1919)
8 Jul 1915 - 1917: Commander, 18th Artillery Brigade
2 Feb 1916: Promoted to *Major-General*

*Vice-Admiral* Vladimir Reingoldovich von **Berg** (23 Nov 1842 - 2 Jan 1905)
17 Nov 1897: Promoted to *Rear-Admiral*
17 Nov 1897 - 9 Sep 1902: Director of Lighthouses, Caspian Sea, Port Commander, Baku
9 Sep 1902 - 26 Nov 1902: Junior Flagman
26 Nov 1902: Promoted to *Vice-Admiral*
26 Nov 1902: Retired

*Major-General* Ivan Avgustovich **Bergau** (23 Sep 1861 - ?)
18 Jun 1910 - 4 Jun 1913:    Commander, 199th Infantry Regiment
14 Apr 1913:    Promoted to *Major-General*
4 Jun 1913 - 14 Nov 1915:    Commander, 1st Brigade, 51st Infantry Division
14 Nov 1915 - 18 May 1917:    Commander, Brigade, 68th Infantry Division
18 May 1917 - ?:    Commander, 68th Infantry Division

*Vice-Admiral* Konstantin Vladislavovich **Bergel** (30 Aug 1855 - 1939)
31 Aug 1910:    Promoted to *Rear-Admiral*
31 Aug 1910 - 1913:    Commander, Amur Flotilla
1913:    Promoted to *Vice-Admiral*
1913:    Retired

*Lieutenant-General* Viktor-Aleksandr Albertovich **Berger** (29 Mar 1859 - ?)
4 Feb 1907 - 24 Jul 1917:    Military Judge, Kiev Military District Court
22 Apr 1907:    Promoted to *Major-General*
24 Jul 1917:    Promoted to *Lieutenant-General*
24 Jul 1917:    Dismissed

*Vice-Admiral* Nikolai Karlovich **Bergshtresser** (12 May 1855 - May 1919)
?:    Promoted to *Rear-Admiral*
1 Oct 1908 - 3 Jan 1911:    Commander, Port of Emperor Aleksandr III (Libau)
26 Dec 1910:    Promoted to *Vice-Admiral*

*Major-General* Yevgeny Aleksandrovich **Berkalov** (4 Jan 1878 - 1952)
1910 - Jul 1915:    Vice-Chairman, Commission on Naval Artillery Testing
6 Dec 1913:    Promoted to *Major-General*
Jul 1915 - Jan 1918:    First Deputy Chief of Artillery Section, Main Shipbuilding Directorate

*General of Engineers* Aleksandr Mavrikievich **Berkh** (29 Oct 1830 - 7 Mar 1909)
? - 5 Nov 1886:    Attached to Nikolayev Engineering Academy
1877:    Promoted to *Major-General*
5 Nov 1886 - 21 Oct 1904:    Member of the Engineer Committee, Main Engineering Directorate
30 Aug 1889:    Promoted to *Lieutenant-General*
21 Oct 1904 - 1906:    Member, Committee for Wounded Veterans
6 Dec 1904:    Promoted to *General of Engineers*
1906:    Retired

*Lieutenant-General of the Fleet* Boris Aleksandrovich **Berkh** (16 Jul 1858 - ?)
22 Oct 1901 - 27 Sep 1911:    Chief of Naval Construction Engineers, Port of Kronstadt
5 Jan 1909:    Promoted to *Major-General of the Fleet*
27 Sep 1911 - 1916:    Chief Inspector of Naval Construction
6 Dec 1913:    Promoted to *Lieutenant-General of the Fleet*

*General of Infantry* Georgy Eduardovich **Berkhman** (3 Apr 1854 - 2 Feb 1929)
| | |
|---|---|
| 27 Nov 1902: | Promoted to *Major-General* |
| 27 Nov 1902 - 29 Jul 1905: | Chief of Staff, II. Caucasus Army Corps |
| 29 Jul 1905 - 31 Jan 1907: | Quartermaster-General, Caucasus Military District |
| 31 Jan 1907 - 29 Jan 1913: | Chief of Staff, Caucasus Military District |
| 6 Dec 1907: | Promoted to *Lieutenant-General* |
| 29 Jan 1913 - 2 Jan 1914: | Commanding General, XXIV. Army Corps |
| 2 Jan 1914 - 11 Dec 1914: | Commanding General, II. Caucasus Army Corps |
| 6 Dec 1913: | Promoted to *General of Infantry* |
| 11 Dec 1914 - 4 Feb 1915: | Commanding General, I. Caucasus Army Corps |
| 4 Feb 1915 - 13 Nov 1916: | Attached to the C-in-C, Caucasus Army |
| 13 Nov 1916 - 5 Apr 1917: | Commanding General, XL. Army Corps |
| 5 Apr 1917 - 1918: | Reserve officer, Caucasus Military District |

*Lieutenant-General* Ivan Andreyevich **Berladin** (26 Apr 1850 - ?)
| | |
|---|---|
| 15 Dec 1900 - 1913: | Ataman, Cherkassy District, Don Cossack Army |
| 3 Oct 1902: | Promoted to *Major-General* |
| 1913: | Promoted to *Lieutenant-General* |
| 1913: | Retired |

*Major-General* Nikolai Nikolayevich **Bernatsky** (12 Apr 1860 - 13 Jan 1941)
| | |
|---|---|
| 21 Mar 1908 - Jul 1914: | Military Judge, Vilnius Military District Court |
| 6 Dec 1908: | Promoted to *Major-General* |
| Jul 1914 - 1918: | Military Judge, Dvinsk Military District Court |

*Major-General* Aleksandr Aleksandrovich **Berndt** (3 Jun 1869 - 5 Aug 1915)
| | |
|---|---|
| 7 Aug 1887 - 5 Aug 1915: | Staff Officer, 87th Infantry Regiment |
| 23 Jul 1916: | Posthumously promoted to *Major-General* |

*Lieutenant-General* Aleksandr Vladimirovich **Bernikov** (23 Mar 1846 - ?)
| | |
|---|---|
| 1 Jun 1889 - 21 Nov 1899: | Military Judge, Omsk Military District Court |
| 30 Aug 1890: | Promoted to *Major-General* |
| 21 Nov 1899 - 16 May 1902: | Military Judge, Siberian Military District Court |
| 16 May 1902 - 29 Jul 1905: | Deputy Intendant, Kazan Military District |
| 29 Jul 1905 - 1906: | Intendant, 2nd Manchurian Army |
| 2 Apr 1906: | Promoted to *Lieutenant-General* |

*Lieutenant-General* Nikolai Vladimirovich **Bernikov** (17 Jan 1853 - 1932)
| | |
|---|---|
| 3 Mar 1904: | Promoted to *Major-General* |
| 3 Mar 1904 - 17 May 1905: | Commander, 8th Artillery Brigade |
| 17 May 1905 - 13 Jun 1907: | Commander, 37th Artillery Brigade |
| 13 Jun 1907: | Promoted to *Lieutenant-General* |
| 13 Jun 1907 - 28 Jul 1910: | Commander of Artillery, XVIII. Army Corps |
| 28 Jul 1910 - 7 Apr 1917: | Inspector of Artillery, XVIII. Army Corps |

*Major-General* Emmanuil Ivanovich **Bernov** (19 Aug 1854 - 27 Jan 1907)
| | |
|---|---|
| 26 May 1897 - 28 Apr 1902: | Commander, 5th Life Dragoon Regiment |
| 28 Apr 1902: | Promoted to *Major-General* |

| | |
|---|---|
| 28 Apr 1902 - 18 Jun 1904: | Commander, His Majesty's Life Guards Cossack Regiment |
| 18 Jun 1904 - 28 Jun 1905: | At the disposal of the Commander, Amur Military District |
| 28 Jun 1905 - 5 Sep 1905: | Commander, 2nd Independent Cavalry Brigade |
| 5 Sep 1905 - 9 Jul 1906: | Commander, Ural- Zabaikalskaya Cossack Division |
| 9 Jul 1906 - 27 Jan 1907: | Attached to St. Petersburg Military District |

*Lieutenant-General* Yevgeny Ivanovich **Bernov** (28 Nov 1855 - 19 Sep 1917)
| | |
|---|---|
| Feb 1904 - 9 Jun 1907: | Commander, 22nd Dragoon Regiment |
| 9 Jun 1907: | Promoted to *Major-General* |
| 9 Jun 1907 - 3 Mar 1912: | Commander, Life Guards Cuirassier Regiment |
| 3 Mar 1912 - 20 Nov 1913: | Commander, 1st Brigade, 2nd Guards Cavalry Division |
| 20 Nov 1913 - 11 Dec 1914: | General à la suite |
| 11 Dec 1914 - Feb 1917: | Chief of Medical & Evacuation Sections, Supreme HQ |
| Feb 1917 - 9 Aug 1917: | Reserve officer, Petrograd Military District |
| 9 Aug 1917: | Promoted to *Lieutenant-General* |
| 9 Aug 1917: | Retired |

*Lieutenant-General* Ostap Andreyevich **Bertels** (24 Oct 1844 - ?)
| | |
|---|---|
| 29 Mar 1897: | Promoted to *Major-General* |
| 29 Mar 1897 - 20 Nov 1899: | Chief of Staff, X. Army Corps |
| 20 Nov 1899 - 21 Jun 1901: | Chief of Staff, IV. Army Corps |
| 21 Jun 1901 - 7 Mar 1904: | Commander, 60th Replacement Infantry Brigade |
| 7 Mar 1904 - 11 Dec 1906: | Commander, 36th Infantry Division |
| 28 Mar 1904: | Promoted to *Lieutenant-General* |
| 11 Dec 1906 - Jul 1908: | Commanding General, XX. Army Corps |
| Jul 1908: | Retired |

*Lieutenant-General* Pavel Vasiliyevich **Bertgold** (22 Mar 1841 - ?)
| | |
|---|---|
| 19 Jun 1886 - 3 Feb 1894: | Deputy Chief of Engineers, Vilnius Military District |
| 30 Aug 1888: | Promoted to *Major-General* |
| 3 Feb 1894 - 1898: | Chief of Engineers, Vilnius Military District |
| 14 May 1896: | Promoted to *Lieutenant-General* |

*Major-General* Grigory Mefodyevich **Beshenib** (14 Nov 1858 - ?)
| | |
|---|---|
| 25 Mar 1915 - 1917: | Reserve officer, Dvinsk Military District |
| 30 Jul 1915: | Promoted to *Major-General* |

*Rear-Admiral* Anatoly Ivanovich **Bestuzhev-Ryumin** (10 Dec 1873 - 23 Mar 1917)
| | |
|---|---|
| Feb 1916 - Feb 1917: | Commander, Special Purpose Detachment |
| 10 Nov 1916: | Promoted to *Rear-Admiral* |
| Feb 1917 - 23 Mar 1917: | Commander, Kola Region |

*General of Artillery* Vasily Nikolayevich **Bestuzhev-Ryumin** (14 Sep 1835 - 12 Feb 1910)
| | |
|---|---|
| 8 Oct 1876 - 16 Jan 1889: | Chief, Tula Imperial Arms Factory |
| 27 Mar 1877: | Promoted to *Major-General* |
| 16 Jan 1889 - 30 Mar 1909: | Inspector-General of Arms & Ammunition Factories |

30 Aug 1889:                    Promoted to *Lieutenant-General*
30 Mar 1909:                    Promoted to *General of Artillery*
30 Mar 1909:                    Retired


*Major-General* Karl-Artur Markovich **Beyerman** (3 Jul 1850 - ?)
13 Jul 1901 - 1907:             Attached to the Commanding General, Borderguard Corps
6 Apr 1903:                     Promoted to *Major-General*


*Major-General* Artur-Sevostyan Yemilyevich **Beymelburg** (16 Dec 1860 - ?)
8 Feb 1914:                     Promoted to *Major-General*
8 Feb 1914 - 24 May 1915:       Commander, 2nd Brigade, 27th Infantry Division
24 May 1915 - 12 Apr 1918:      POW, Germany
12 Apr 1918:                    Dismissed


*Lieutenant-General* Nikolai Aleksandrovich **Bezak** (28 Mar 1836 - 31 Mar 1897)
17 Sep 1875 - 15 Jun 1884:      Commander, 5th Battalion, Guards Corps Artillery Brigade
1 Jan 1878:                     Promoted to *Major-General*
1878 - 1880:                    Governor of Yaroslavl
1880 - 1882:                    Governor of Nizhny Novgorod
15 Jun 1884 - 22 Jul 1895:      Chief of the Main Directorate for Posts & Telegraphs
30 Aug 1886:                    Promoted to *Lieutenant-General*
22 Jul 1895 - 31 Mar 1897:      Member of the State Council


*Lieutenant-General* Aleksandr Alekseyevich **Bezkrovny** (26 Aug 1866 - 26 Apr 1948)
15 May 1912 - 5 Jun 1915:       Commander, 73rd Infantry Regiment
16 Feb 1915:                    Promoted to *Major-General*
5 Jun 1915 - 9 Sep 1916:        Chief of Staff, XXXVIII. Army Corps
9 Sep 1916 - 30 Nov 1916:       Attached to the C-in-C, 10th Army
30 Nov 1916 - 18 May 1917:      Chief of Staff, XX. Army Corps
17 Jul 1917 - ?:                Commanding General, XXII. Army Corps
23 Aug 1917:                    Promoted to *Lieutenant-General*


*Major-General* Vasily Lvovich **Bezladnov** (16 Oct 1859 - ?)
5 Dec 1905:                     Promoted to *Major-General*
5 Dec 1905 - 16 Oct 1914:       General for Special Assignments, Moscow Military District
16 Oct 1914 - 2 May 1915:       Attached to the C-in-C, 12th Army
2 May 1915 - 31 Mar 1917:       Attached to the C-in-C, 5th Army
31 Mar 1917 - 17 May 1917:      Commandant of Dvinsk
17 May 1917 - 1918:             Reserve officer, Moscow Military District


*Vice-Admiral* Pyotr Alekseyevich **Bezobrazov** (29 Jan 1845 - 17 Jul 1906)
12 Jul 1893 - 8 Aug 1897:       Commander, 9th Naval Depot
13 Apr 1897:                    Promoted to *Rear-Admiral*
8 Aug 1897 - 4 Oct 1898:        Head of Oil Applications, Fleet Vessels
4 Oct 1898 - 1901:              Chief of Staff, Port of Kronstadt

| | |
|---|---|
| 1901 - 1903: | Junior Flagman, Black Sea Naval Division |
| 1 Jan 1904: | Promoted to *Vice-Admiral* |
| 19 Apr 1904 - 27 Sep 1904: | Commander, 1st Squadron, Pacific Fleet |
| 27 Sep 1904 - 29 Nov 1904: | Senior Flagman, Baltic Fleet |
| 29 Nov 1904 - Nov 1905: | Acting Chief of the Main Naval Staff |

*General of Cavalry* Vladimir Mikhailovich **Bezobrazov** (11 Jan 1857 - 17 Sep 1932)
| | |
|---|---|
| 22 Jul 1900: | Promoted to *Major-General* |
| 22 Jul 1900 - 6 Apr 1904: | Commander, Guards Cavalry Regiment |
| 6 Apr 1904 - 6 Nov 1906: | Commander, 1st Brigade, 1st Guards Cavalry Division |
| 6 Nov 1906 - 5 Jan 1909: | Commandant of the Cavalry School |
| 22 Apr 1907: | Promoted to *Lieutenant-General* |
| 5 Jan 1909 - 29 Jan 1912: | Commander, 2nd Guards Cavalry Division |
| 29 Jan 1912 - 28 May 1915: | Commanding General, Guards Corps |
| 14 Apr 1913: | Promoted to *General of Cavalry* |
| 15 Dec 1914: | Promoted to *General-Adjutant* |
| 28 May 1915 - 26 Nov 1915: | Attached to the Supreme Commander-in-Chief |
| 26 Nov 1915 - 2 Jun 1916: | Commander, Guards Detachment |
| 2 Jun 1916 - 14 Aug 1916: | Commander of the Guards |
| 14 Aug 1916 - 11 Apr 1917: | Unassigned |
| 11 Apr 1917: | Retired |

*Major-General of the Fleet* Mikhail Mikhailovich **Bezpyatov** (30 Jul 1863 - 1928)
| | |
|---|---|
| 3 Aug 1909 - 1918: | Professor of Astronomy, Naval Cadet Corps |
| 14 Apr 1913: | Promoted to *Major-General of the Fleet* |

*General of Infantry* Dmitry Nikolayevich **Bezradetsky** (11 Feb 1853 - ?)
| | |
|---|---|
| 30 Dec 1897 - 18 Feb 1904: | Chief of Staff, II. Cavalry Corps |
| 16 Oct 1898: | Promoted to *Major-General* |
| 15 Jun 1902 - 8 Sep 1902: | Acting Commander, 1st Brigade, 8th Cavalry Division |
| 18 Feb 1904 - 28 Jan 1908: | Chief of Staff, Odessa Military District |
| 17 Apr 1905: | Promoted to *Lieutenant-General* |
| 28 Jan 1908 - 26 Jul 1914: | Commander, 15th Infantry Division |
| 26 Jul 1914 - 19 Nov 1914: | Commander, 57th Infantry Division |
| 19 Nov 1914: | Promoted to *General of Infantry* |
| 19 Nov 1914: | Retired |

*Major-General* Leonid Iosipovich **Bezradetsky** (6 Apr 1846 - 18 Apr 1905)
| | |
|---|---|
| 11 Dec 1895 - 1 Feb 1900: | Member of the Engineering Committee, Main Engineering Directorate |
| 6 Dec 1899: | Promoted to *Major-General* |
| 1 Feb 1900 - 18 Apr 1905: | Chairman of the Engineering Committee, Main Engineering Directorate |

*Lieutenant-General* Alexey Sergeyevich **Bezsonov** (4 Mar 1847 - ?)
| | |
|---|---|
| 23 Apr 1901: | Promoted to *Major-General* |
| 23 Apr 1901 - 19 Nov 1908: | Commander, 2nd Brigade, 11th Infantry Division |
| 19 Nov 1908 - 13 Mar 1909: | Transferred to the reserve |

13 Mar 1909: Promoted to *Lieutenant-General*
13 Mar 1909 - 1917: Honorary Trustee, Empress Maria Institutions

*Major-General* Dmitry Dmitrievich **Bezsonov** (10 Oct 1859 - ?)
29 May 1907 - 1913: Professor, Aleksandr Military Law Academy
18 Apr 1910: Promoted to *Major-General*

*Lieutenant-General* Vladimir Aleksandrovich **Bezsonov** (21 Jul 1842 - 24 Aug 1906)
1892 - 20 Jun 1904: Commander of Gendarmerie, Odessa
6 Dec 1901: Promoted to *Major-General*
20 Jun 1904 - Dec 1905: Commander of Gendarmerie, St. Petersburg
Dec 1905: Promoted to *Lieutenant-General*
Dec 1905: Retired

*Vice-Admiral* Viktor Aleksandrovich **Bezuar** (5 Nov 1841 - ?)
14 May 1896: Promoted to *Rear-Admiral*
1 Jul 1896 - 15 Mar 1899: Chief of Staff, Black Sea Fleet
15 Mar 1899 - 1900: Deputy Commander, Black Sea Naval Division
1900 - 19 Nov 1901: Chief of Mine Training, Black Sea
19 Nov 1901: Promoted to *Vice-Admiral*
19 Nov 1901: Retired

*Major-General* Mikhail Ilich **Bibikov** (4 Feb 1838 - 16 Feb 1912)
21 Sep 1887: Promoted to *Major-General*
21 Sep 1887 - 2 Jul 1891: Commander, 2nd Turkestan Line Brigade
2 Jul 1891 - 14 Feb 1894: Commander, 1st Brigade, 2nd Grenadier Division
14 Feb 1894 - 1899: Commander, 57th Reserve Infantry Brigade
1899 - 1900: Commander, 62nd Reserve Infantry Brigade

*Major-General* Nikolai Aleksandrovich **Bibikov** (2 Dec 1866 - ?)
1910: Promoted to *Major-General*

*General of Cavalry* Nikolai Valerianovich **Bibikov** (16 Aug 1842 - 6 Mar 1923)
4 Jun 1890 - 3 Oct 1893: General for Special Assignments, Warsaw Military District
30 Aug 1890: Promoted to *Major-General*
3 Oct 1893 - 16 Jun 1906: Mayor of Warsaw
6 Dec 1899: Promoted to *Lieutenant-General*
16 Jun 1906: Promoted to *General of Cavalry*
16 Jun 1906: Retired
18 Oct 1914 - 18 May 1917: Recalled; Honorary Trustee, Board of Trustees, Empress Maria Institutions
18 May 1917: Dismissed

*Lieutenant-General* Sergey Ilyich **Bibikov** (5 Jun 1851 - 7 May 1903)
25 Dec 1894: Promoted to *Major-General*
25 Dec 1894 - 21 Mar 1896: At the disposal of the Commander, Odessa Military District

| | |
|---|---|
| 21 Mar 1896 - 6 May 1898: | Commandant, Imperial Main Quarters |
| 6 May 1898 - 2 Mar 1899: | General à la suite |
| 2 Mar 1899 - 7 May 1901: | Commander, 2nd Brigade, 2nd Guards Cavalry Division |
| 7 May 1901 - 7 May 1903: | Commander, 10th Cavalry Division |
| 6 Dec 1901: | Promoted to *Lieutenant-General* |

*Lieutenant-General* Yevgeny Mikhailovich **Bibikov** (11 Aug 1840 - 27 Sep 1900)
| | |
|---|---|
| 30 Aug 1889: | Promoted to *Major-General* |
| 30 Aug 1899 - 8 Oct 1889: | At the disposal of Grand Duke Nikolai Nikolayevich |
| 8 Oct 1889 - 7 May 1891: | Commander, Battalion, Life Guards Reserve Regiment |
| 7 May 1891 - 14 Aug 1895: | Commander, Finland Life Guards Regiment |
| 14 Aug 1895 - 13 Sep 1899: | Commander, 2nd Brigade, 2nd Guards Infantry Division |
| 13 Sep 1899 - 27 Sep 1900: | Commander, 2nd Guards Infantry Division |
| 6 Dec 1899: | Promoted to *Lieutenant-General* |

*Lieutenant-General* Ignatiy Yakovlevich **Bibinov** (29 Jan 1852 - ?)
| | |
|---|---|
| 26 Mar 1904 - 2 Aug 1909: | Chief, Tsar Aleksandr II School |
| 2 May 1904: | Promoted to *Major-General* |
| 2 Aug 1909: | Promoted to *Lieutenant-General* |
| 2 Aug 1909: | Retired |

*General of Cavalry* Baron Aleksandr Aleksandrovich von **Bilderling** (23 Jun 1846 - 12 Jun 1912)
| | |
|---|---|
| 9 Feb 1878 - 22 May 1890: | Commandant, Nikolai Cavalry School |
| 1881: | Promoted to *Major-General* |
| 22 May 1890 - 2 Apr 1891: | Attached to the Main Department of Military Schools |
| 2 Apr 1891 - 7 Jan 1898: | Deputy Chief of the General Staff |
| 2 Apr 1891 - 14 Jul 1899: | Member, Military Research Committee |
| 30 Aug 1892: | Promoted to *Lieutenant-General* |
| 14 Jul 1899 - 4 Nov 1905: | Commanding General, XVII. Army Corps |
| 6 Dec 1901: | Promoted to *General of Cavalry* |
| 28 Jan 1905 - 30 Apr 1905: | Acting C-in-C, 3rd Manchurian Army |
| 14 Sep 1905 - 4 Nov 1905: | Acting C-in-C, 2nd Manchurian Army |
| 4 Nov 1905 - 12 Jun 1912: | Member of the Military Council |

*Lieutenant-General* Aleksandr Karlovich **Birger** (24 Oct 1847 - ?)
| | |
|---|---|
| 31 Jul 1895: | Promoted to *Major-General* |
| 31 Jul 1895 - 4 May 1903: | Chief of Staff, XIII. Army Corps |
| 4 May 1903 - 4 Jun 1905: | Commander, 41st Infantry Division |
| 6 Dec 1903: | Promoted to *Lieutenant-General* |
| 4 Jun 1905 - Nov 1905: | Attached to the C-in-C, 3rd Manchurian Army |

*Admiral* Aleksei Alekseyevich **Birilev** (16 Mar 1844 - 6 Feb 1915)
| | |
|---|---|
| 6 Dec 1894: | Promoted to *Rear-Admiral* |
| 1894 - 1900: | Chief of Naval Artillery Training, Baltic Fleet |
| 22 Jan 1900 - 1903: | Commander of Naval Units, Mediterranean |
| 6 Dec 1901: | Promoted to *Vice-Admiral* |
| 1903: | Commander of Coastal Defenses, Baltic Sea |

| | |
|---|---|
| 1903 - 9 Feb 1904: | Commander, Combined Training Squadron, Baltic Sea |
| 9 Feb 1904 - 10 May 1904: | Military Governor of Kronstadt |
| 10 May 1904 - 8 May 1905: | C-in-C, Baltic Sea Naval Forces |
| 8 May 1905 - 29 Jun 1905: | C-in-C, Pacific Fleet |
| 29 Jun 1905 - 11 Jan 1907: | Minister of the Navy, Member, Council of National Defense |
| 3 Nov 1905 - 6 Feb 1915: | Member of the State Council |
| 11 Jan 1907: | Promoted to *Admiral* |

*Lieutenant-General* Pavel Petrovich **Birk** (13 Apr 1836 - 15 Aug 1900)

| | |
|---|---|
| 23 Feb 1883 - 25 Aug 1886: | Member of Cossack Forces Committee, Main Cossack Directorate |
| 30 Aug 1884: | Promoted to *Major-General* |
| 25 Aug 1886 - 31 Jul 1899: | Chief of Staff, Orenburg Cossack Army |
| 31 Jul 1899: | Promoted to *Lieutenant-General* |
| 31 Jul 1899: | Retired |

*Major-General* Vladimir Nikolayevich **Birkin** (29 Jul 1851 - 28 Sep 1902)

| | |
|---|---|
| 30 Nov 1895 - 28 Sep 1902: | Commander of Engineers, Fortress Dvina |
| 9 Apr 1900: | Promoted to *Major-General* |

*Lieutenant-General* Lyudomir Karlovich **Biron** (1842 - 1910)

| | |
|---|---|
| 10 May 1905: | Promoted to *Major-General* |
| 10 May 1905 - 28 Dec 1905: | At the disposal of the Commander, Pacific Ocean Flotilla |
| 28 Dec 1905 - 1910: | Attached to the Ministry of Internal Affairs |
| 2 Mar 1910: | Promoted to *Lieutenant-General* |

*Major-General* Aleksandr Aleksandrovich **Birshert** (30 Jan 1856 - May 1910)

| | |
|---|---|
| 22 Apr 1896 - 1 Mar 1906: | Military Judge, Warsaw Military District Court |
| 1 Jan 1901: | Promoted to *Major-General* |
| 1 Mar 1906 - May 1910: | Military Judge, St. Petersburg Military District Court |

*Major-General* Ivan Alekseyevich **Biryukov** (22 Sep 1856 - 29 Sep 1919)

| | |
|---|---|
| 22 Oct 1908 - 23 Sep 1912: | Commander, 1st Astrakhan Cossack Regiment |
| 23 Sep 1912: | Promoted to *Major-General* |
| 23 Sep 1912: | Retired |
| 8 Feb 1913 - 3 Mar 1917: | Member, Astrakhan City Council |
| 3 Mar 1917 - 3 Oct 1917: | Acting Civil Governor, Astrakhan Province |
| 3 Oct 1917 - 25 Jan 1918: | Ataman, Astrakhan Cossack Army |

*Major-General* Nikolai Pavlovich **Biryukov** (3 Jul 1873 - 12 Jul 1919)

| | |
|---|---|
| 3 Mar 1915 - 1916: | Commander, 3rd Rifle Regiment |
| 12 Oct 1916: | Promoted to *Major-General* |
| 1916: | Commander, Brigade, 4th Rifle Division |
| 1917: | Commander, 2nd Siberian Rifle Division |

*Major-General* Vasily Viktorovich **Biskupsky** (27 Jun 1878 - 18 Jun 1945)
27 Dec 1914 - 15 Jan 1917: Commander, 1st Life Dragoon Regiment
7 Jun 1916: Promoted to *Major-General*
15 Jan 1917 - 16 May 1917: Commander, 1st Brigade, 3rd Cavalry Division
16 May 1917 - 1918: Commander, 3rd Cavalry Division

*Lieutenant-General* Baron Aleksandr Nikolayevich **Bistrom** (12 Jul 1849 - ?)
25 Sep 1895: Promoted to *Major-General*
25 Sep 1895 - 9 Aug 1897: Commander, 2nd Brigade, 14th Cavalry Division
9 Aug 1897 - 11 Mar 1899: Commander, His Majesty's Ulan Life Guards Regiment
11 Mar 1899 - 26 Jan 1904: Commander, Independent Guards Cavalry Brigade, Consolidated Cavalry Division
26 Jan 1904 - 8 Mar 1905: Transferred to the reserve
8 Mar 1905 - 29 Dec 1906: Commander, 3rd Cavalry Division
18 Feb 1904: Promoted to *Lieutenant-General*

*Lieutenant-General of the Admiralty* Baron Konrad Rikhardovich **Bistrom** (19 Jun 1838 - ?)
1889 - 1897: Captain, Port of Odessa
1893: Promoted to *Major-General of the Admiralty*
1897: Promoted to *Lieutenant-General of the Admiralty*
1897: Retired

*Major-General* Ivan Ivanovich **Bitner** (10 Feb 1846 - 10 Jan 1896)
22 Jan 1894 - 10 Jan 1896: Commander of Engineers, Fortress Novogeorgiyevsk
30 Aug 1894: Promoted to *Major-General*

*Lieutenant-General* Konstantin Yakovlevich **Bitsyutko** (26 Oct 1866 - 3 May 1916)
7 Mar 1913: Promoted to *Major-General*
7 Mar 1913 - 19 Nov 1915: Chief of Staff, I. Turkestan Army Corps
19 Nov 1915 - 3 May 1916: Commander, 3rd Caucasus Infantry Division
20 Jun 1916: Posthumously promoted to *Lieutenant-General*

*General of Infantry* Aleksandr Aleksandrovich **Blagoveshchensky** (29 Jul 1854 - 19 Mar 1918)
14 Apr 1899: Promoted to *Major-General*
14 Apr 1899 - 16 Sep 1899: Chief of Staff, I. Caucasus Army Corps
16 Sep 1899 - 27 Jan 1903: Chief of Communications, Kiev Military District
27 Jan 1903 - 11 Feb 1904: Quartermaster-General, Kiev Military District
11 Feb 1904 - 11 Aug 1904: Attached to the Manchurian Army
11 Aug 1904 - 27 Feb 1907: Attached to the C-in-C, Far East
21 Aug 1904: Promoted to *Lieutenant-General*
27 Feb 1907 - 1 Sep 1912: Commander, 2nd Infantry Division
1 Sep 1912 - 26 Aug 1914: Commanding General, VI. Army Corps
6 Dec 1912: Promoted to *General of Infantry*
26 Aug 1914 - Mar 1915: Unassigned
Mar 1915: Dismissed

*Major-General* Ignaty Pavlovich **Blavdzevich** (25 Jun 1849 - ?)
7 Jan 1910 - 1911: Deputy Chief of Engineers, Turkestan Military District
1911: Promoted to *Major-General*

*Lieutenant-General* Nikolai Andreyevich **Blazhovsky** (23 Jun 1854 - ?)
27 May 1906 - 15 Jun 1917: Commandant, Kiev Regional Arsenal
6 Dec 1906: Promoted to *Major-General*
14 Apr 1913: Promoted to *Lieutenant-General*
15 Jun 1917: Dismissed

*Lieutenant-General* Anton Stanislavovich **Bleshinsky** (25 Dec 1853 - 1932)
11 May 1909 - 7 Sep 1910: Commander, Brigade, 66th Infantry Division
22 May 1910: Promoted to *Major-General*
7 Sep 1910 - 25 Dec 1913: Commander, 2nd Brigade, 52nd Infantry Division
25 Dec 1913: Promoted to *Lieutenant-General*
25 Dec 1913: Retired

*Major-General* Pyotr Dmitriyevich **Blinov** (15 Jan 1869 - 28 Sep 1938)
1912 - 1915: Chief Engineer, Battleship Squadron, Baltic Fleet
18 Apr 1914: Promoted to *Major-General of Naval Engineers*
1915 - 1918: Attached to the Finnish Maritime Authority

*Lieutenant-General* Konstantin Aleksandrovich **Blok** (6 Feb 1833 - 17 Feb 1897)
1876 - 7 Aug 1883: Commander, 6th Uhlan Regiment
7 Aug 1883: Promoted to *Major-General*
7 Aug 1883 - 18 Aug 1884: Commander, 1st Brigade, 5th Cavalry Division
18 Aug 1884 - 20 Nov 1890: Commander, Life Guards Horse Regiment
20 Nov 1890 - 16 May 1892: Commander, 2nd Brigade, 1st Guards Cavalry Division
16 May 1892 - 17 Feb 1897: Member, Board of Trustees, Empress Maria Institutions
30 Aug 1893: Promoted to *Lieutenant-General*

*Major-General* Nikolai Sergeyevich **Blokhin** (4 Apr 1866 - ?)
19 Jan 1915: Promoted to *Major-General*
19 Jan 1915 - 4 Mar 1915: Commander, 1st Brigade, 16th Cavalry Division
4 Mar 1915 - 11 Dec 1915: Reserve officer, Kiev Military District
11 Dec 1915 - 19 Jul 1917: Special Purposes General, Moscow Military District
19 Jul 1917: Dismissed

*Major-General* Mikhail Ottovich von **Blom** (17 Sep 1856 - 7 Aug 1919)
19 Nov 1896 - 4 Jul 1900: Attached to the Ministry of War
6 Dec 1899: Promoted to *Major-General*
4 Jul 1900 - 11 Apr 1907: Senator, Imperial Finnish Senate,
Member of the Economic Department, Imperial Finnish Senate

*Lieutenant-General* Kaspar Nikolayevich **Blyumer** (1857 - 13 Sep 1941)
18 Feb 1907 - 21 Dec 1907: Commander, 5th East Siberian Rifle Artillery Brigade
31 May 1907: Promoted to *Major-General*

| | |
|---|---|
| 21 Dec 1907 - 30 Aug 1909: | Special Assignments General, Turkestan Military District |
| 30 Aug 1909 - 26 Jul 1910: | Commander, 35th Artillery Brigade |
| 26 Jul 1910 - 21 Jan 1913: | Inspector of Artillery, IV. Siberian Army Corps |
| 21 Jan 1913: | Promoted to *Lieutenant-General* |
| 21 Jan 1913: | Retired |

*Lieutenant-General* Anatoly Genrikhovich **Bo** (3 Apr 1845 - 6 Mar 1905)
| | |
|---|---|
| 10 Jun 1885 - 1898: | Military Judge, Kazan Military District |
| 30 Aug 1893: | Promoted to *Major-General* |
| 1898: | Promoted to *Lieutenant-General* |
| 1898: | Retired |

*Major-General* Fyodor Nikolayevich **Boborykin** (15 Aug 1841 - ?)
| | |
|---|---|
| 27 Dec 1887 - 21 May 1892: | Commander, 15th Dragoon Regiment |
| 21 May 1892: | Promoted to *Major-General* |
| 21 May 1892 - 7 Dec 1893: | Commander, Life Guards Cuirassier Regiment |
| 7 Dec 1893 - 1900: | At the disposal of the Commanding General, St. Petersburg Military District |

*Lieutenant-General* Eleazar Stepanovich **Bobrikov** (1 Aug 1843 - ?)
| | |
|---|---|
| 11 Oct 1893 - 1 Oct 1897: | Deputy Commander of Artillery, Amur Military District |
| 25 Dec 1893: | Promoted to *Major-General* |
| 1 Oct 1897 - 17 Jul 1900: | Commander, 45th Artillery Brigade |
| 17 Jul 1900 - 5 Aug 1905: | Commander of Artillery, XVII. Army Corps |
| 6 Dec 1901: | Promoted to *Lieutenant-General* |
| 5 Aug 1905 - Jul 1906: | Attached to Main Artillery Inspectorate |

*General of Infantry* Georgy Ivanovich **Bobrikov** (4 Aug 1840 - 26 Dec 1924)
| | |
|---|---|
| 2 Nov 1876 - 26 Jan 1880: | Attached to the Commander-in-Chief of the Army |
| 12 Apr 1878: | Promoted to *Major-General* |
| 26 Jan 1880 - 25 Feb 1881: | Attached to the General Staff |
| 25 Fev 1881 - 2 Nov 1885: | Member, Military Research Committee, General Staff |
| 2 Nov 1885 - 24 Aug 1898: | General for Special Assignments, St. Petersburg Military District |
| 30 Aug 1888: | Promoted to *Lieutenant-General* |
| 24 Aug 1898 - 15 Nov 1901: | Commander, 1st Guards Infantry Division |
| 15 Nov 1901 - 24 Feb 1902: | Attached to St. Petersburg Military District |
| 24 Feb 1902 - 1917: | Member, Committee for Wounded Veterans, Director, Izmailovskaya Military Almshouse |
| 14 Apr 1902: | Promoted to *General of Infantry* |

*General of Infantry* Nikolai Ivanovich **Bobrikov** (15 Jan 1839 - 17 Jun 1904)
| | |
|---|---|
| 14 Apr 1877 - 26 Feb 1884: | Deputy Chief of Staff, St. Petersburg Military District |
| 30 Aug 1878: | Promoted to *Major-General* |
| 26 Feb 1884 - 17 Aug 1898: | Chief of Staff, St. Petersburg Military District |
| 30 Aug 1884: | Promoted to *Lieutenant-General* |
| 6 Dec 1897: | Promoted to *General of Infantry* |

| | |
|---|---|
| 28 Mar 1898 - 17 Jun 1904: | Member of the Military Council, Member of the State Council |
| 17 Aug 1898: | Promoted to *General-Adjutant* |
| 17 Aug 1898 - 17 Jun 1904: | Governor-General of Finland, Commanding General, Finland Military District |

*Lieutenant-General* Count Georgy Aleksandrovich **Bobrinsky** (11 Jul 1863 - 7 Mar 1928)

| | |
|---|---|
| 26 Nov 1904: | Promoted to *Major-General* |
| 26 Nov 1904 - 11 Apr 1905: | General for Special Assignments to C-in-C of land and naval forces operating against Japan |
| 11 Apr 1905 - 28 Sep 1905: | Attached to the C-in-C, 1st Manchurian Army |
| 28 Sep 1905 - 26 May 1910: | Attached to the Ministry of War |
| 26 May 1910 - 8 Aug 1914: | At the disposal of the Minister of War |
| 6 Dec 1910: | Promoted to *Lieutenant-General* |
| 8 Aug 1914 - 4 Oct 1914: | At the disposal of the C-in-C, Southwestern Front |
| 4 Oct 1914 - 3 Apr 1916: | Governor-General of Galicia |
| 9 Apr 1915: | Promoted to *General-Adjutant* |
| 3 Apr 1916 - 7 Jul 1917: | At the disposal of the C-in-C, Southwestern Front |
| 7 Jul 1917: | Dismissed |

*Major-General* Boris Pavlovich **Bobrovsky** (7 Jan 1868 - Feb 1919)

| | |
|---|---|
| 3 Jul 1911: | Promoted to *Major-General* |
| 3 Jul 1911 - 5 Mar 1914: | Chief of Military Communications, Vilnius Military District |
| 5 Mar 1914 - 19 Jul 1914: | Chief of Military Communications, Warsaw Military District |
| 19 Jul 1914 - 15 Dec 1914: | Chief of Economics Section, 2nd Army |
| 15 Dec 1914 - 26 May 1915: | Reserve officer, Dvinsk Military District |
| 26 May 1915 - 29 Jul 1916: | Commander, 25th Replacement Infantry Brigade |
| 29 Jul 1916 - 1917: | Chief of Staff, Dvinsk Military District |

*General of Infantry* Nikolai Petrovich **Bobrovsky** (6 Jun 1855 - ?)

| | |
|---|---|
| 11 Mar 1903 - 25 Mar 1906: | Military Judge, Siberian Military District Court |
| 6 Apr 1903: | Promoted to *Major-General* |
| 25 Mar 1906 - 2 Aug 1906: | Military Judge, Warsaw Military District Court |
| 2 Aug 1906 - 1 Mar 1907: | Transferred to the reserve |
| 1 Mar 1907: | Retired |
| 11 Nov 1907 - 2 Jul 1908: | Recalled; Military Judge, Irkutsk Military District Court |
| 2 Jul 1908 - 16 Sep 1910: | Military Judge, Vilnius Military District Court |
| 16 Sep 1910 - 4 Aug 1911: | Military Judge, St. Petersburg Military District Court |
| 4 Aug 1911 - 18 Feb 1912: | Military Prosecutor, Kazan Military District Court |
| 18 Feb 1912 - 23 May 1915: | Military Prosecutor, Moscow Military District Court |
| 6 Dec 1912: | Promoted to *Lieutenant-General* |
| 23 May 1915 - 27 May 1917: | Chairman of the Military Court, Turkestan Military District |
| 27 May 1917: | Promoted to *General of Infantry* |
| 27 May 1917: | Dismissed |

*General of Infantry* Pavel Osipovich **Bobrovsky** (21 Mar 1832 - 3 Feb 1905)
| | |
|---|---|
| 10 Jun 1864 - 25 Dec 1875: | Special Assignments Officer, Inspectorate of Military Schools |
| 1 Jan 1872: | Promoted to *Major-General* |
| 25 Dec 1875 - 1 Jan 1897: | Head of the Military Legal Academy |
| 30 Aug 1881: | Promoted to *Lieutenant-General* |
| 14 May 1896: | Promoted to *General of Infantry* |
| 1 Jan 1897 - 3 Feb 1905: | Senator |

*Lieutenant-General* Vladimir Osipovich **Bobrovsky** (2 Jul 1840 - 4 Apr 1904)
| | |
|---|---|
| 9 Jan 1890: | Promoted to *Major-General* |
| 9 Jan 1890 - 16 Mar 1892: | Commander, 29th Artillery Brigade |
| 16 Mar 1892 - 16 Mar 1899: | Commander, 26th Artillery Brigade |
| 16 Mar 1899 - 1903: | Commander of Artillery, XII. Army Corps |
| 6 Dec 1899: | Promoted to *Lieutenant-General* |
| 1903: | Retired |

*Lieutenant-General* Aleksandr Fomich **Bobyansky** (4 Jun 1853 - 10 Dec 1931)
| | |
|---|---|
| 23 Aug 1892 - 1904: | Military Judge, St. Petersburg Military District Court |
| 6 Dec 1898: | Promoted to *Major-General* |
| 1904: | Promoted to *Lieutenant-General* |
| 1904: | Resigned |

*Lieutenant-General* Fyodor Nilovich **Bobylev** (4 Feb 1842 - ?)
| | |
|---|---|
| 17 May 1889 - 15 Dec 1894: | Commander, 31st Dragoon Regiment |
| 14 Nov 1894: | Promoted to *Major-General* |
| 15 Dec 1894 - 13 Oct 1900: | Commander, 1st Brigade, 14th Cavalry Division |
| 13 Oct 1900 - Dec 1905: | Commander, 14th Cavalry Division |
| 6 Dec 1900: | Promoted to *Lieutenant-General* |

*General of Cavalry* Nikolai Pavlovich **Bobyr** (14 Jan 1854 - Dec 1920)
| | |
|---|---|
| 27 Sep 1899 - 24 Jul 1900: | Chief of Staff, Fortress Kaunas |
| 6 Dec 1899: | Promoted to *Major-General* |
| 24 Jul 1900 - 12 May 1904: | Commandant of Fortress Osovets |
| 12 May 1904 - 17 Mar 1906: | Chief of Staff, Siberian Military District |
| 6 Dec 1905: | Promoted to *Lieutenant-General* |
| 17 Mar 1906 - 14 Feb 1907: | Chief of Staff, Omsk Military District |
| 14 Feb 1907 - 6 Aug 1915: | Commandant of Fortress Modlin |
| 6 Dec 1911: | Promoted to *General of Cavalry* |
| 6 Aug 1915 - 1918: | POW, Germany |

*Major-General of Naval Artillery* Semyon Osipovich **Bocharov** (24 May 1859 - 1930)
| | |
|---|---|
| 1 Feb 1898 - 1917: | Naval Artillery Inspector |
| 1915: | Promoted to *Major-General of Naval Artillery* |

*Major-General* Nikolai Andreyevich **Bochkovsky** (6 Dec 1859 - ?)
| | |
|---|---|
| ? - 1917: | Commander, Brigade, 15th Infantry Division |
| 22 Sep 1916: | Promoted to *Major-General* |

*Lieutenant-General* Baron Nikolai Andreyevich de **Bode** (28 Nov 1860 - 9 Nov 1924)
30 May 1912: Promoted to *Major-General*
30 May 1912 - 7 Oct 1914: Commander, St. Petersburg Life Guards Regiment
7 Oct 1914 - 12 May 1915: Commander, 1st Brigade, 3rd Guards Infantry Division
12 May 1915 - 1917: Commander, 57th Infantry Division
18 Jul 1916: Promoted to *Lieutenant-General*

*General of Cavalry* Konstantin Konstantinovich **Bodisko** (18 Feb 1831 - 2 Dec 1902)
7 May 1877: Promoted to *Major-General*
7 May 1877 - 28 Jun 1879: Commander, 2nd Brigade, 13th Cavalry Division
28 Jun 1879 - 10 Jul 1883: At the disposal of the Commander, Kharkov Military District
10 Jul 1883 - 4 Mar 1884: Commander, 10th Cavalry Division
4 Mar 1884 - 1 Sep 1894: Commander, 7th Cavalry Division
30 Aug 1886: Promoted to *Lieutenant-General*
1 Sep 1894 - 27 Feb 1896: Deputy Commanding General, Warsaw Military District
27 Feb 1896 - 23 Jan 1901: Commanding General, V. Army Corps
6 Dec 1898: Promoted to *General of Cavalry*
23 Jan 1901 - 2 Dec 1902: Member of the Military Council

*Major-General* Vladimir Konstantinovich **Bodisko** (20 Jun 1866 - 11 Nov 1941)
1914 - 14 Feb 1915: Commander, 72nd Artillery Brigade
14 Feb 1915 - 28 Apr 1917: Commander, 1st Siberian Rifle Artillery Brigade
27 Jun 1915: Promoted to *Major-General*
28 Apr 1917 - 1917: Inspector of Artillery, I. Siberian Army Corps

*Lieutenant-General* Vladimir Danilovich **Bodzento-Belyatsky** (7 Oct 1849 - 4 Nov 1910)
24 Feb 1901: Promoted to *Major-General*
24 Feb 1901 - 12 Jun 1906: Commander, 1st Artillery Brigade, 1st Infantry Division
12 Jun 1906 - 19 Jun 1908: Commander of Artillery, IV. Army Corps
22 Apr 1907: Promoted to *Lieutenant-General*
19 Jun 1908 - 4 Nov 1910: Inspector of Artillery, VII. Army Corps

*Lieutenant-General* Nikolai Iosifovich **Bogatko** (5 Dec 1864 - 30 Jul 1930)
16 Jun 1910 - 22 Mar 1916: Deputy Chief Quartermaster-General
6 Dec 1910: Promoted to *Major-General*
6 Dec 1914: Promoted to *Lieutenant-General*
22 Mar 1916 - 1917: Intendant-General, Ministry of War, Chief of the Main Intendant Directorate

*Major-General* Adam Ivanovich **Bogatsky** (12 Dec 1858 - 9 Sep 1914)
9 Jul 1910: Promoted to *Major-General*
9 Jul 1910 - 7 Apr 1911: Commander, 1st Brigade, 38th Infantry Division
7 Apr 1911 - 22 Aug 1914: Commander, 1st Brigade, 8th Infantry Division
22 Aug 1914 - 9 Sep 1914: At the disposal of the C-in-C, 2nd Army

*Major-General* Afrikan Petrovich **Bogayevsky** (27 Dec 1872 - 21 Oct 1934)
14 Jan 1915 - 4 Oct 1915: Commander, Life Guards Consolidated Cossack

| | Regiment |
|---|---|
| 22 Mar 1915: | Promoted to *Major-General* |
| 4 Oct 1915 - 7 Apr 1917: | Chief of Staff, Ataman of all Cossack Troops |
| 7 Apr 1917 - 19 Aug 1917: | Commander, 1st Trans-Baikal Cossack Division |
| 19 Aug 1917 - Oct 1917: | Commander, 1st Guards Cavalry Division |

*Lieutenant-General* Ivan Venediktovich **Bogayevsky** (14 Aug 1846 - 1918)
| | |
|---|---|
| 29 Apr 1895 - 27 Nov 1897: | Commander, 17th Infantry Regiment |
| 14 May 1896: | Promoted to *Major-General* |
| 27 Nov 1897 - 12 Jul 1900: | Commander, 1st Brigade, 28th Infantry Division |
| 12 Jul 1900 - 12 Jan 1904: | Commander, 1st Rifle Brigade |
| 12 Jan 1904 - 1 May 1910: | Commander, 16th Infantry Division |
| 28 Mar 1904: | Promoted to *Lieutenant-General* |
| 1 May 1910: | Retired |

*Major-General* Lev Alekseyevich **Bogayevsky** (21 Feb 1867 - 18 Jan 1919)
| | |
|---|---|
| 11 Oct 1914 - 10 Oct 1916: | Commander, 9th Artillery Brigade |
| 14 Nov 1914: | Promoted to *Major-General* |
| 10 Oct 1916 - 1917: | Inspector of Artillery, Grenadier Corps |

*General of Engineers* Nikolai Venediktovich **Bogayevsky** (6 Feb 1843 - 12 Sep 1912)
| | |
|---|---|
| 20 Sep 1882 - 9 Sep 1894: | Commander of Engineers, Odessa Military District |
| 8 Apr 1884: | Promoted to *Major-General* |
| 30 Aug 1894: | Promoted to *Lieutenant-General* |
| 9 Sep 1894 - 21 Jun 1899: | Commander, 34th Infantry Division |
| 21 Jun 1899 - 21 Mar 1906: | Commandant of Fortress Modlin |
| 6 Dec 1904: | Promoted to *General of Engineers* |
| 21 Mar 1906 - 12 Apr 1908: | Deputy Commanding General, Odessa Military District |
| 12 Apr 1908 - 12 Sep 1912: | Member of the Military Council |

*Lieutenant-General* Pavel Ivanovich **Bogdanov** (28 Dec 1845 - ?)
| | |
|---|---|
| 26 Nov 1886 - 17 Jan 1894: | Military Judge, Moscow Military District Court |
| 30 Aug 1892: | Promoted to *Major-General* |
| 17 Jan 1894 - 4 May 1897: | Military Prosecutor, Kazan Military District |
| 4 May 1897 - 7 Feb 1903: | Military Prosecutor, Warsaw Military District |
| 7 Feb 1903 - Sep 1905: | Chairman of the Military Tribunal, Kiev Military District |
| 6 Apr 1903: | Promoted to *Lieutenant-General* |

*General of Cavalry* Grigory Osipovich **Bogdanovich** (9 Jan 1858 - ?)
| | |
|---|---|
| 11 Oct 1898 - 9 Dec 1904: | Chief of Staff, Kuban Cossack Army |
| 14 Apr 1902: | Promoted to *Major-General* |
| 9 Dec 1904 - 2 Feb 1907: | Attached to the Warsaw Military District |
| 2 Feb 1907 - 1 Sep 1910: | Quartermaster-General, General Staff |
| 13 Apr 1908: | Promoted to *Lieutenant-General* |
| 1 Sep 1910 - Jun 1911: | Chairman of the Military Commission of the historical description of the Russian-Turkish war |
| Jun 1911 - 31 Dec 1911: | At the disposal of the Chief of General Staff |

31 Dec 1911: Promoted to *General of Cavalry*
31 Dec 1911: Retired

*Major-General* Iosif Ivanovich **Bogdanovich** (19 Mar 1862 - ?)
11 Feb 1914: Promoted to *Major-General*
11 Feb 1914 - 13 May 1916: Commander, 24th Artillery Brigade
13 May 1916 - 9 May 1917: Inspector of Artillery, XXIX. Army Corps

*Major-General* Sergey Aleksandrovich **Bogdanovich** (10 Jun 1852 - 12 Feb 1911)
11 Sep 1909: Promoted to *Major-General*
11 Sep 1909 - 12 Feb 1911: Commander, 1st Brigade, 9th Infantry Division

*Major-General* Sergey Ilyich **Bogdanovich** (16 Jul 1865 - ?)
12 Feb 1915 - 25 May 1915: Reserve officer, Dvinsk Military District
28 Mar 1915: Promoted to *Major-General*
25 May 1915 - 7 Apr 1917: Chief of Staff, III. Siberian Army Corps
7 Apr 1917 - 8 Jun 1917: Commander, 7th Siberian Rifle Division
8 Jun 1917 - 1917: Commander, 8th Infantry Division

*General of Infantry* Yevgeny Vasilievich **Bogdanovich** (26 Feb 1829 - 1 Sep 1914)
3 May 1865 - 15 Mar 1885: Special Assignments Officer, Minister of the Interior
16 Apr 1878: Promoted to *Major-General*
15 Mar 1885 - 18 May 1887: Transferred to the reserve
18 May 1887: Retired
31 Mar 1888 - 1 Sep 1914: Recalled with rank of *Privy Councillor*,
 Member, Council of Ministers, Ministry of the Interior
10 Apr 1891: Redesignated *Major-General*
1 Apr 1901: Promoted to *Lieutenant-General*
6 May 1908: Promoted to *General of Infantry*

*Major-General* Mikhail Andreyevich **Bogdanovsky** (1 Jun 1855 - ?)
Aug 1909 - 20 Oct 1915: Staff Officer, Main Engineering Directorate
6 Apr 1914: Promoted to *Major-General*
20 Oct 1915 - 1917: Reserve officer attached to the Commander of
 Engineers, Petrograd Military District

*Major-General* Dmitry Ivanovich **Boginsky** (24 Oct 1827 - ?)
7 Nov 1881 - 1898: Commander of Gendarmerie, Yekaterinoslav Province
6 Dec 1894: Promoted to *Major-General*

*Major-General* Vsevolod Petrovich **Boginsky** (2 Jan 1862 - 23 May 1933)
30 Nov 1912 - 1917: Intendant-General, Odessa Military District
6 Dec 1912: Promoted to *Major-General*

*General of Infantry* Andrey Andreyevich **Bogolyubov** (27 Nov 1841 - 27 Jan 1909)
24 Jul 1884 - 22 Dec 1894: Attached to the General Staff,
30 Aug 1885: Promoted to *Major-General*
30 Aug 1893: Promoted to *Lieutenant-General*

| | |
|---|---|
| 22 Dec 1894 - 5 Oct 1898: | At the disposal of the Minister of War |
| 5 Oct 1898 - 19 Mar 1901: | Commanding General, Trans-Caspian Region |
| 12 Jul 1899 - 19 Mar 1901: | Commanding General, II. Turkestan Army Corps |
| 19 Mar 1901 - 5 Jun 1902: | Commanding General, V. Army Corps |
| 5 Jun 1902 - 19 May 1906: | Deputy Commanding General, Warsaw Military District |
| 28 Mar 1904: | Promoted to *General of Infantry* |
| 19 May 1906: | Retired |

*Lieutenant-General* Ivan Andreyevich **Bogolyubov** (27 Feb 1831 - ?)

| | |
|---|---|
| 25 Jun 1875 - 1 Aug 1887: | Director, Orenburg Military School |
| 30 Aug 1885: | Promoted to *Major-General* |
| 1 Aug 1887 - 10 Aug 1891: | Director, 2nd Orenburg Cadet Corps |
| 10 Aug 1891 - 1901: | Director, Pskov Cadet Corps |
| 26 May 1899: | Promoted to *Lieutenant-General* |
| 1901: | Retired |

*Major-General of the Fleet* Nikolai Dmitriyevich **Bogolyubov** (12 Oct 1867 - ?)

| | |
|---|---|
| 3 May 1910 - ?: | Staff officer, 5th Class, Main Naval Staff |
| 6 Dec 1915: | Promoted to *Major-General of the Fleet* |
| ?: | Chairman of the Commission for the Establishment of Donations |

*Lieutenant-General* Fyodor Gerasimovich **Bogoslavsky** (2 Apr 1846 - ?)

| | |
|---|---|
| 24 Dec 1903 - 12 Oct 1908: | Deputy Quartermaster-General, Amur Military District |
| 1905: | Promoted to *Major-General* |
| 12 Oct 1908 - 2 Dec 1911: | Quartermaster-General, Kazan Military District |
| 2 Dec 1911: | Promoted to *Lieutenant-General* |
| 2 Dec 1911: | Retired |

*Major-General* Aleksandr Lukich **Bogushevich** (28 Sep 1832 - ?)

| | |
|---|---|
| 31 Oct 1881 - 5 Nov 1890: | Commander, 32nd Dragoon Regiment |
| 5 Nov 1890: | Promoted to *Major-General* |
| 5 Nov 1890 - Apr 1899: | Commander, 1st Brigade, 6th Cavalry Division |

*Major-General* Mikhail Yegorovich **Bogushevsky** (8 Nov 1854 - Jun 1936)

| | |
|---|---|
| 23 Oct 1910 - 1912: | Commander, 22nd Infantry Regiment |
| 1912: | Promoted to *Major-General* |
| 1912: | Retired |
| 2 Dec 1914 - 15 Feb 1915: | Recalled; Reserve officer, Kiev Military District |
| 15 Feb 1915 - 3 Jan 1916: | Commander, Brest-Litovsk Fortress Militia Regiment |
| 3 Jan 1916 - 1917: | Commander, 15th Militia Brigade |

*General of Infantry* Fyodor Kononovich **Bogutsky** (15 Jul 1850 - 8 Dec 1913)

| | |
|---|---|
| 9 Mar 1898: | Promoted to *Major-General* |
| 9 Mar 1898 - 11 Mar 1902: | Deputy Chief of Staff, Odessa Military District |
| 11 Mar 1902 - 7 Mar 1905: | Commandant of Fortress Kerch |
| 6 Dec 1904: | Promoted to *Lieutenant-General* |
| 7 Mar 1905 - 19 Jan 1906: | Commander, 70th Infantry Division |

19 Jan 1906 - 29 May 1907: Commander, 1st Infantry Division
29 May 1907 - 29 Dec 1908: Commandant of Fortress Libau
29 Dec 1908: Promoted to *General of Infantry*
29 Dec 1908: Retired

*Major-General of Naval Engineers* Konstantin Petrovich **Boklevsky** (24 Apr 1862 - 1 Jun 1928)
1902 - 1923: Dean of Shipbuilding Faculty, Polytechnic Institute
1914: Promoted to *Major-General of Naval Engineers*

*Major-General* Aleksandr Fedorovich **Bokov** (8 Jun 1860 - ?)
27 Feb 1909 - 26 Aug 1911: Commander, Volyn Borderguard Brigade
26 Aug 1911 - 1916: Commander, Kars Borderguard Brigade
14 Apr 1913: Promoted to *Major-General*

*Lieutenant-General* Frants-Martselian Vikentyevich **Bokshchanin** (16 Jan 1854 - ?)
6 Jul 1904: Promoted to *Major-General*
6 Jul 1904 - 29 Jan 1909: Commander, 2nd Brigade, 29th Infantry Division
29 Jan 1909 - 21 Jul 1910: Commander, 1st Siberian Replacement Infantry Brigade
21 Jul 1910 - 21 Dec 1910: Commander, 2nd Brigade, 15th Infantry Division
21 Dec 1910 - 9 Apr 1913: Commander, 1st Caucasus Rifle Brigade
9 Apr 1913: Promoted to *Lieutenant-General*
9 Apr 1913: Retired

*Major-General* Nikolai Ksenofontovich **Boldyrev** (23 Apr 1856 - ?)
15 Jan 1907: Promoted to *Major-General*
15 Jan 1907 - 21 May 1910: Commander, 2nd Brigade, 4th East Siberian Rifle Division
21 May 1910 - 19 Jul 1914: Commander, 1st Brigade, 1st Infantry Division
19 Jul 1914 - 8 Oct 1914: Commander, 56th Infantry Division
8 Oct 1914: Retired

*Lieutenant-General* Stepan Alekseyevich **Boldyrev** (26 Dec 1852 - 11 Feb 1923)
25 Jun 1904: Promoted to *Major-General*
25 Jun 1904 - Dec 1911: Commander, 2nd Brigade, 1st Don Cossack Division
Dec 1911: Promoted to *Lieutenant-General*
Dec 1911: Retired

*Lieutenant-General* Vasily Georgievich **Boldyrev** (5 Apr 1875 - 20 Aug 1933)
Aug 1914 - 8 Mar 1915: Chief of Staff, 2nd Guards Infantry Division
8 Mar 1915 - 29 Feb 1916: Commander, 30th Infantry Regiment
31 Aug 1915: Promoted to *Major-General*
29 Feb 1916 - 9 Aug 1916: Attached to the C-in-C, 4th Army
9 Aug 1916 - 19 Apr 1917: Quartermaster-General, Northern Front
19 Apr 1917 - 9 Sep 1917: Commanding General, XLIII. Army Corps
9 Apr 1917: Promoted to *Lieutenant-General*
9 Sep 1917 - 13 Nov 1917: C-in-C, 5th Army

*Lieutenant-General* Vasily Ksenofontovich **Boldyrev** (23 Apr 1850 - 8 Dec 1916)
14 Jul 1892 - 17 Mar 1900: Commander, Altai District
14 May 1896: Promoted to *Major-General*
17 Mar 1900 - 1907: Chief of Land & Factory Department, Imperial Government
9 Jan 1903 - 1907: Deputy Chief of Cabinet to the Tsar
17 Apr 1905: Promoted to *Lieutenant-General*
1907: Retired

*Major-General* Vladimir Aleksandrovich **Boldyrev** (15 Dec 1863 - ?)
9 Nov 1913 - 1917: Inspector of Classes, Technical Artillery College
6 Dec 1913: Promoted to *Major-General*

*Major-General* Aleksey Iosifovich **Bolkhovitinov** (11 Mar 1867 - 1943)
8 May 1916 - 27 Feb 1917: Commander, 19$^{th}$ Artillery Brigade
10 Jul 1916: Promoted to *Major-General*
27 Feb 1917 - 1917: Inspector of Artillery, XVI. Army Corps

*Lieutenant-General* Leonid Mitrofanovich **Bolkhovitinov** (5 Jan 1871 - 11 Jun 1925)
20 Feb 1912 - Jul 1914: Commander, 90$^{th}$ Infantry Regiment
21 Jun 1914: Promoted to *Major-General*
Jul 1914 - 2 Oct 1914: Quartermaster-General, Caucasus Military District
2 Oct 1914 - 31 Jan 1915: Quartermaster-General, Caucasus Army
31 Jan 1915 - 9 Jun 1917: Chief of Staff, Caucasus Army
9 Jun 1917 - 15 Jun 1917: Reserve officer, Petrograd Military District
15 Jun 1917 - 1918: Commanding General, I. Army Corps
23 Aug 1917: Promoted to *Lieutenant-General*

*Lieutenant-General* Aleksandr Nikolayevich **Bolotov** (27 Feb 1836 - 1906)
1 Nov 1899: Promoted to *Major-General*
1 Nov 1899 - 1903: Commander, Vladikavkaz Regional Brigade
1903: Promoted to *Lieutenant-General*
1903: Retired

*Major-General* Ivan Mikhailovich **Bolotov** (12 Sep 1868 - 1918)
9 Nov 1913: Promoted to *Major-General*
9 Nov 1913 - 22 Dec 1914: Chief of Staff, V. Siberian Army Corps
22 Dec 1914 - 31 Mar 1915: Reserve officer, Minsk Military District
31 Mar 1915 - 19 Mar 1916: Section Chief, General Staff
19 Mar 1916 - 15 Oct 1917: Commandant, Tashkent Military School
15 Oct 1917: Retired

*Major-General* Nikolai Andreyevich **Bolotov** (2 Nov 1863 - ?)
3 Jun 1903 - 1917: Chairman, Guards Economic Society
18 Apr 1910: Promoted to *Major-General*

*Lieutenant-General* Vladimir Andreyevich **Bolotov** (24 Aug 1865 - 20 May 1922)
11 Sep 1910 - 21 Jan 1914: Technical Engineer, Communications Section, General

| | |
|---|---|
| | Staff |
| 6 Dec 1910: | Promoted to *Major-General* |
| 21 Jan 1914 - 26 Feb 1915: | Chief of Technical Section, Main Technical Directorate |
| 26 Feb 1915 - 23 Aug 1915: | Chief of Communications Exploitation Section, Field Army |
| 23 Aug 1915 - 19 May 1917: | Chief of Technical Section, Main Technical Directorate |
| 2 Apr 1917: | Promoted to *Lieutenant-General* |
| 19 May 1917 - Oct 1917: | Member of the Engineering Committee, Main Technical Directorate |

*General of Infantry* Vladimir Vasilyevich **Bolotov** (1 Jan 1856 - 1938)
| | |
|---|---|
| 18 Apr 1901 - 1 Jun 1904: | Commander, 2nd Grenadier Regiment |
| 1 Jun 1904: | Promoted to *Major-General* |
| 1 Jun 1904 - 14 Mar 1906: | Commander, 1st Brigade, 72nd Infantry Division |
| 14 Mar 1906 - 17 Feb 1907: | Commander, 1st Brigade, 3rd Infantry Division |
| 17 Feb 1907 - 9 Jul 1910: | Commander, 59th Replacement Infantry Brigade |
| 9 Jul 1910 - 1 Apr 1917: | Commander, 47th Infantry Division |
| 17 Oct 1910: | Promoted to *Lieutenant-General* |
| 1 Apr 1917 - 10 Sep 1917: | Commanding General, XXV. Army Corps |
| 2 Apr 1917: | Promoted to *General of Infantry* |
| 10 Sep 1917 - Oct 1917: | Reserve officer, Kiev Military District |

*Major-General* Aleksandr Vladimirovich **Bolshev** (20 Jul 1869 - 19 Nov 1938)
| | |
|---|---|
| 28 Mar 1913 - 27 Aug 1916: | Director, Khabarovsk Cadet Corps |
| 14 Apr 1913: | Promoted to *Major-General* |
| 27 Aug 1916 - 1917: | Director, Pskov Cadet Corps |

*Major-General* Andrey Aleksandrovich **Bolshev** (8 Jul 1828 - 24 May 1904)
| | |
|---|---|
| 6 Apr 1879 - 3 May 1897: | Map Editor, Military Topographical Section, General Staff |
| 30 Aug 1893: | Promoted to *Major-General* |
| 3 May 1897 - 24 May 1904: | Chief of Cartography Office, Military Topographical Section, General Staff |

*Major-General* Fyodor Dmitriyevich **Boltenko** (17 Apr 1843 - 13 Oct 1918)
| | |
|---|---|
| 22 May 1912 - 10 Feb 1915: | Deputy Chief of Topographical Survey, St. Petersburg Province & Finland |
| 10 Feb 1915: | Promoted to *Major-General* |
| 10 Feb 1915: | Retired |

*Lieutenant-General* Ivan Grigoryevich **Boltenkov** (5 Jan 1827 - 28 Jun 1915)
| | |
|---|---|
| 7 Sep 1876 - 8 Jun 1889: | Commander, 20th Artillery Brigade |
| 16 Jul 1879: | Promoted to *Major-General* |
| 8 Jun 1889 - 1899: | Commander of Artillery, VII. Army Corps |
| 30 Aug 1889: | Promoted to *Lieutenant-General* |
| 1899: | Retired |

*Lieutenant-General* Nikolai Lvovich **Boltin** (21 Aug 1834 - ?)
| | |
|---|---|
| 30 Aug 1892: | Promoted to *Major-General* |
| 30 Aug 1892 - 24 Mar 1895: | Attached to the Inspectorate of Riflemen |
| 24 Mar 1895 - 18 Sep 1897: | Commander, 1st Brigade, 4th Infantry Division |
| 18 Sep 1897 - 7 Oct 1899: | Commander, 1st Brigade, 23rd Infantry Division |
| 7 Oct 1899: | Promoted to *Lieutenant-General* |
| 7 Oct 1899: | Retired |

*Lieutenant-General* Leonid Dmitriyevich **Bolychevtsov** (28 Oct 1848 - ?)
| | |
|---|---|
| 1 Jun 1889 - 6 Nov 1906: | Military Judge, Moscow Military District Court |
| 14 May 1896: | Promoted to *Major-General* |
| 6 Nov 1906 - 1908: | Military Judge, Vilnius Military District Court |
| 1908: | Promoted to *Lieutenant-General* |
| 1908: | Retired |

*Major-General* Aleksandr Mikhailovich **Bonch-Bogdanovsky** (13 Feb 1872 - ?)
| | |
|---|---|
| 27 Feb 1915 - 2 Sep 1916: | Commander, 220th Infantry Regiment |
| 16 Apr 1916: | Promoted to *Major-General* |
| 2 Sep 1916 - 19 Sep 1916: | Commander, Brigade, 51st Infantry Division |
| 19 Sep 1916 - 18 Apr 1917: | Commander, Brigade, 55th Infantry Division |
| 18 Apr 1917 - 1917: | Commander, 27th Infantry Division |

*Major-General* Iosif Mikhailovich **Bonch-Bogdanovsky** (7 Feb 1863 - 17 Aug 1909)
| | |
|---|---|
| 28 Nov 1908: | Promoted to *Major-General* |
| 28 Nov 1908 - 17 Aug 1909: | Commander, 1st Brigade, 9th Infantry Division |

*Major-General* Mikhail Dmitrievich **Bonch-Bruyevich** (24 Feb 1870 - 3 Aug 1956)
| | |
|---|---|
| 10 Sep 1914: | Promoted to *Major-General* |
| 10 Sep 1914 - 17 Sep 1914: | Quartermaster-General, 3rd Army |
| 17 Sep 1914 - 1 Apr 1915: | Quartermaster-General, Northwestern Front |
| 1 Apr 1915 - 20 Aug 1915: | At the disposal of the Supreme Commander-in-Chief |
| 20 Aug 1915 - 25 Feb 1916: | Chief of Staff, Northern Front |
| 25 Feb 1916 - 29 Aug 1917: | Attached to the C-in-C, Northern Front |
| Mar 1916: | Commandant, Pskov Garrison |
| 29 Aug 1917 - 9 Sep 1917: | C-in-C, Northern Front |
| 28 Nov 1917 - 1918: | Chief of Staff to the Supreme Commander-in-Chief |

*Lieutenant-General* Fyodor Aleksandrovich **Bonch-Osmolovsky** (1836 - 19 Sep 1900)
| | |
|---|---|
| 6 Dec 1897: | Promoted to *Major-General* |
| 6 Dec 1897 - Sep 1899: | Commander, West Siberian Line Brigade |
| Sep 1899: | Promoted to *Lieutenant-General* |
| Sep 1899: | Retired |

*Major-General* Nikolai Vasilyevich **Bonch-Osmolovsky** (6 Mar 1847 - ?)
| | |
|---|---|
| 19 Sep 1894 - Jul 1907: | Commander, 16th Sapper Battalion |
| 17 Jun 1906: | Promoted to *Major-General* |

*Lieutenant-General* Vasily Vasilyevich **Bonch-Osmolovsky** (19 Feb 1864 - ?)
| | |
|---|---|
| 1 May 1903 - 20 Sep 1910: | Section Chief, General Staff |
| 6 Dec 1908: | Promoted to *Major-General* |
| 20 Sep 1910 - 8 Jan 1914: | General for Assignments, General Staff |
| 8 Jan 1914 - 22 Apr 1914: | Chief of Assignment Section, General Staff |
| 22 Apr 1914 - Oct 1917: | Chief of Administration Section, General Staff |
| 6 Dec 1914: | Promoted to *Lieutenant-General* |

*General of Infantry* Aksel Robertovich **Bonsdorf** (9 Dec 1839 - 25 Jul 1919)
| | |
|---|---|
| 30 Mar 1884 - 11 Jan 1904: | Chief of Surveying, Finland & St. Petersburg |
| 30 Aug 1888: | Promoted to *Major-General* |
| 6 Dec 1900: | Promoted to *Lieutenant-General* |
| 11 Jan 1904 - 17 Apr 1913: | Chief of Triangulation, Western Border |
| 17 Apr 1913: | Promoted to *General of Infantry* |
| 17 Apr 1913: | Retired |

*General of Artillery* Georg Robertovich **Bonsdorf** (17 Apr 1844 - 26 Mar 1919)
| | |
|---|---|
| 1 Apr 1891 - 28 Nov 1896: | Commander of Artillery Polygon, Vilnius Military District |
| 30 Aug 1891: | Promoted to *Major-General* |
| 28 Nov 1896 - 10 Apr 1901: | Artillery Inspector, Kazan Military District |
| 6 Dec 1900: | Promoted to *Lieutenant-General* |
| 10 Apr 1901 - 26 Apr 1904: | Commander of Artillery, VIII. Army Corps |
| 26 Apr 1904 - 17 Dec 1908: | Commander of Artillery, Vilnius Military District |
| 17 Dec 1908: | Promoted to *General of Artillery* |
| 17 Dec 1908: | Retired |

*Major-General* Vladimir Georgiyevich von **Bool** (31 Mar 1836 - 8 Dec 1899)
| | |
|---|---|
| 22 Aug 1884 - 8 Dec 1899: | Inspector of Classes, Aleksandrov Military School |
| 30 Aug 1885: | Promoted to *Major-General* |

*Major-General* Nikolai Yevgenievich **Bordel von Bordelius** (22 Sep 1859 - 5 Apr 1910)
| | |
|---|---|
| 9 Apr 1902 - 13 Aug 1906: | Inspector of Classes, Vladikavkaz Cadet Corps |
| 1906: | Promoted to *Major-General* |
| 13 Aug 1906 - Jul 1908: | Director of the Yaroslavl Cadet Corps |
| Jul 1908: | Retired |

*Major-General* Sergey Yevgenievich **Bordel von Bordelius** (9 Jul 1871 - 1917)
| | |
|---|---|
| 2 Apr 1916 - 1917: | Deputy Section Chief, Main Artillery Directorate |
| 10 Apr 1916: | Promoted to *Major-General* |

*Lieutenant-General* Mikhail Matveyevich **Boreskov** (19 Apr 1829 - 17 Feb 1898)
| | |
|---|---|
| 16 Feb 1877: | Promoted to *Major-General* |
| 1880 - 8 Jun 1886: | Deputy Chief of Electrotechnical Section, Ministry of War |
| 8 Jun 1886 - 17 Feb 1898: | Chief of Electrotechnical Section, Ministry of War |
| 30 Aug 1886: | Promoted to *Lieutenant-General* |

*Major-General* Nikolai Fyodorovich **Borgenstrem** (26 Aug 1851 - ?)
10 Jul 1903 - 11 Jul 1905: Director-General of Customs Authority, Finland
1905: Promoted to *Major-General*
11 Jul 1905 - 27 Sep 1911: Governor of Abo-Berneborgsky
27 Sep 1911: Retired

*Major-General* Yegor Vasilyevich **Borisoglebsky** (13 Dec 1840 - ?)
14 Jan 1898: Promoted to *Major-General*
14 Jan 1898 - Aug 1899: Commander, 2$^{nd}$ Brigade, 19$^{th}$ Infantry Division

*Major-General* Nikolai Prokofyevich **Borisov** (19 Sep 1853 - 20 Dec 1937)
7 Feb 1904 - 1907: Commander, 89$^{th}$ Infantry Regiment
1907: Promoted to *Major-General*
1907: Retired
3 Aug 1915 - 1917: Recalled; Reserve officer, Minsk Military District

*Lieutenant-General of the Admiralty* Pavel Evgrafovich **Borisov** (24 Jan 1834 - 6 Aug 1903)
1889: Promoted to *Major-General of the Admiralty*
1889 - 1892: Chairman, Nikolayev Naval Court
1892 - 1896: Chairman, Kronstadt Naval Court
1896: Promoted to *Lieutenant-General of the Admiralty*
1896 - 6 Aug 1903: Member, Main Naval Tribunal

*Major-General* Vasily Nikolayevich **Borisov** (12 Dec 1857 - ?)
27 Dec 1915 - 1917: Commander, 81$^{st}$ Artillery Brigade
6 Dec 1916: Promoted to *Major-General*

*Major-General* Viktor Mikhailovich **Borisov** (20 Feb 1849 - ?)
7 Apr 1899 - Aug 1901: Commander, Railway Brigade
30 Aug 1899: Promoted to *Major-General*

*Lieutenant-General* Vyacheslav Yevstafyevich **Borisov** (24 Sep 1861 - 20 May 1941)
27 Feb 1907 - 24 Feb 1909: Second Chief Quartermaster, General Directorate of the General Staff
22 Apr 1907: Promoted to *Major-General*
24 Feb 1909 - 1910: Quartermaster-General, Vilnius Military District
1910: Retired
1914 - 28 Mar 1915: Recalled; Special Purposes General, Northwest Front
28 Mar 1915 - 24 Apr 1916: Special Purposes General, Western Front
6 Dec 1915: Promoted to *Lieutenant-General*
24 Apr 1916 - 20 May 1917: Special Purposes General, Chief of the General Staff
20 May 1917 - 13 Jun 1917: Special Purposes General, Commander-in-Chief of the Armed Forces
13 Jun 1917 - 22 Jun 1917: Reserve officer, Petrograd Military District
22 Jun 1917 - 15 Feb 1918: At the disposal of the Chief of the General Staff

*Major-General* Konstantin Konstantinovich **Bork** (10 Mar 1869 - ?)
21 May 1915: Promoted to *Major-General*

| | |
|---|---|
| 21 May 1915 - 22 Dec 1915: | Commander, 16th Siberian Rifle Regiment |
| 22 Dec 1915 - 8 Oct 1916: | Chief of Staff, 79th Infantry Division |
| 8 Oct 1916 - 1 Nov 1916: | Chief of Staff, II. Siberian Army Corps |
| 1 Nov 1916 - 13 Apr 1917: | Chief of Staff, II. Army Corps |
| 13 Apr 1917 - ?: | Commander, 115th Infantry Division |

*Lieutenant-General* Count Yuri Aleksandrovich von der **Borkh** (1836 - 6 Apr 1911)
| | |
|---|---|
| 28 Aug 1875: | Promoted to *Major-General* |
| 18 May 1878 - 5 Mar 1881: | Commander, 2nd Brigade, 39th Infantry Division |
| 5 Mar 1881 - 14 Jun 1883: | Commander, 1st Brigade, 19th Infantry Division |
| 14 Jun 1883 - 12 Oct 1895: | Commander, 21st Infantry Division |
| 6 May 1884: | Promoted to *Lieutenant-General* |
| 12 Oct 1895 - 1906: | At the disposal of the Commanding General, Caucasus Military District |

*Major-General* Vasily Grigorievich **Bornio** (1 Jan 1849 - ?)
| | |
|---|---|
| 5 Oct 1902 - 24 Oct 1904: | Commander, 3rd Reserve Artillery Brigade |
| 6 Apr 1903: | Promoted to *Major-General* |
| 24 Oct 1904 - 11 Mar 1906: | Commander, 60th Artillery Brigade |
| 11 Mar 1906 - 27 May 1907: | Commander, 8th Reserve Artillery Brigade |
| 27 May 1907 - 1907: | Acting Commander of Artillery, VI. Army Corps |

*Major-General* Aleksandr Arkadyevich **Borodayevsky** (1 Mar 1847 - ?)
| | |
|---|---|
| 25 Apr 1900 - 1907: | Special Assignments General, Warsaw Military District |
| 6 Dec 1900: | Promoted to *Major-General* |
| 1907: | Retired |

*Major-General* Matvey Illarionovich **Borodin** (16 Nov 1862 - ?)
| | |
|---|---|
| 1 Aug 1908 - 2 Feb 1917: | Director, Voronezh Cadet Corps |
| 10 Apr 1911: | Promoted to *Major-General* |
| 2 Feb 1917 - 2 May 1918: | Director, Aleksandr Cadet Corps |

*Major-General* Mikhail Nikanorovich **Borodin** (3 Nov 1868 - 1948)
| | |
|---|---|
| 16 Sep 1915 - 27 Mar 1917: | Commander, 1st Ural Cossack Regiment |
| 17 Jan 1917: | Promoted to *Major-General* |
| 27 Mar 1917 - Dec 1917: | Ataman, Ural Cossack Army |

*Major-General* Mikhail Pavlovich **Borodin** (29 Sep 1862 - ?)
| | |
|---|---|
| 8 Dec 1902 - 14 Aug 1910: | Inspector of Classes, Nizhny Novgorod Cadet Corps |
| 29 Mar 1909: | Promoted to *Major-General* |
| 14 Aug 1910 - 29 Jul 1918: | Director, Volsky Cadet Corps |

*Lieutenant-General* Vasily Nikolayevich **Borodin** (15 Jul 1833 - 8 Jul 1910)
| | |
|---|---|
| 12 Sep 1892: | Promoted to *Major-General* |
| 12 Sep 1892 - 9 Oct 1899: | Commander, 1st Brigade, 1st Infantry Division |
| 9 Oct 1899: | Promoted to *Lieutenant-General* |
| 9 Oct 1899: | Retired |

*Lieutenant-General* Mikhail Mikhailovich **Borodkin** (1 Sep 1852 - 1919)
| | |
|---|---|
| 24 Aug 1895 - 16 Aug 1901: | Military Judge, St. Petersburg Military District Court |
| 6 Dec 1899: | Promoted to *Major-General* |
| 16 Aug 1901 - 20 Jan 1906: | Attached to the Minister of War |
| 20 Jan 1906 - 24 Nov 1909: | Special Assignments General, Ministry of War |
| 6 Dec 1907: | Promoted to *Lieutenant-General* |
| 24 Nov 1909 - 25 Feb 1911: | Deputy Chief Military Prosecutor, Deputy Chief, Main Military Justice Directorate |
| 25 Feb 1911 - 21 May 1912: | Chief, Aleksandr Military Law Academy |
| 24 Apr 1916 - 1917: | Member of the State Council |

*General of Cavalry* Georgy Aleksandrovich **Borozdin** (26 Nov 1835 - ?)
| | |
|---|---|
| 9 Sep 1877 - 3 Feb 1878: | Commander, 1st Brigade, 12th Cavalry Division |
| 10 Sep 1877: | Promoted to *Major-General* |
| 3 Feb 1878 - 27 Oct 1883: | Commander, 1st Brigade, 1st Cavalry Division |
| 27 Oct 1883 - 30 Aug 1885: | Commander, 9th Cavalry Division |
| 30 Aug 1885 - 14 Nov 1894: | Commander, 8th Cavalry Division |
| 30 Aug 1886: | Promoted to *Lieutenant-General* |
| 14 Nov 1894 - 29 May 1899: | Commanding General, XV. Army Corps |
| 6 Dec 1898: | Promoted to *General of Cavalry* |
| 29 May 1899 - Sep 1905: | Member, Committee for Wounded Veterans |

*Major-General* Aleksandr Mikhailovich **Borukayev** (6 Jul 1850 - 30 Mar 1919)
| | |
|---|---|
| 5 Sep 1905 - 16 Aug 1908: | Commander, 10th Artillery Brigade |
| 31 May 1907: | Promoted to *Major-General* |

*Rear-Admiral* Fyodor Yemiliyevich **Bosse** (9 Mar 1861 - 1 Sep 1936)
| | |
|---|---|
| 26 Mar 1909 - 9 Aug 1916: | Attached to 2nd Baltic Naval Crew |
| 5 Oct 1915: | Promoted to *Major-General of the Fleet* |
| 9 Aug 1916: | Redesignated *Rear-Admiral* |
| 9 Aug 1916: | Retired |

*Vice-Admiral* Ivan Fyodorovich **Bostrem** (22 Dec 1857 - 2 Jan 1934)
| | |
|---|---|
| 1906 - 1907: | Commander, Training Detachment |
| 19 Aug 1906: | Promoted to *Rear-Admiral* |
| 1907 - 15 Feb 1909: | Deputy Minister of the Navy, Vice-Chairman, Board of Admiralty |
| 15 Feb 1909 - 9 Oct 1909: | Chief of Naval Forces of the Black Sea |
| 5 Sep 1909: | Promoted to *Vice-Admiral* |
| 9 Oct 1909 - 30 May 1911: | Commandant, Port of Sevastopol, Military Governor of Sevastopol |
| 30 May 1911 - 1911: | Chief of Naval Forces, Black Sea |
| 1911: | Resigned |

*Major-General* Adam Adamovich **Boyarovsky** (20 Jan 1850 - ?)
| | |
|---|---|
| 8 Apr 1909: | Promoted to *Major-General* |
| 8 Apr 1909 - 14 Jul 1910: | Commander, 2nd Brigade, 7th East Siberian Rifle Division |

14 Jul 1910: Retired

*Major-General* Boleslav Ioakimovich **Boyarsky** (23 Oct 1848 - ?)
12 May 1909: Promoted to *Major-General*
12 May 1909 - 16 May 1911: Commander, 1st Brigade, 19th Infantry Division

*Major-General* Sergey Nikolayevich **Boyarsky** (16 Sep 1858 - ?)
12 Feb 1916 - 1917: Commander, 30th Artillery Brigade
19 Nov 1916: Promoted to *Major-General*

*Major-General* Vladimir Aleksandrovich **Boyarsky** (1 Nov 1874 - 30 Aug 1915)
12 Aug 1895 - 30 Aug 1915: Officer, Life Guards Moscow Regiment
25 Jan 1916: Posthumously promoted to *Major-General*

*Major-General* Vsevolod Petrovich **Boychevsky** (18 Jan 1870 - ?)
27 Jul 1915 - 1917: Commander, 36th Sapper Battalion
28 Nov 1916: Promoted to *Major-General*

*Major-General* Viktor Viktorovich **Boye** (4 Mar 1861 - 9 Jul 1914)
27 Jan 1909 - 9 Jul 1914: Staff officer, Vologda Regional Brigade
7 Sep 1914: Posthumously promoted to *Major-General*

*Lieutenant-General* Vladimir Aleksandrovich **Boye** (8 Aug 1844 - ?)
16 Mar 1899: Promoted to *Major-General*
16 Mar 1899 - 2 May 1900: Commander, 40th Artillery Brigade
2 May 1900 - 20 Aug 1903: Deputy Commander of Artillery, Kiev Military District
20 Aug 1903 - Jun 1906: Commander of Artillery, Kiev Military District
17 Apr 1905: Promoted to *Lieutenant-General*

*Rear-Admiral* Roman Romanovich **Boyl** (4 Apr 1836 - 2 Feb 1901)
?: Promoted to *Rear-Admiral*

*Major-General* Aleksandr Ivanovich **Bozheryanov** (25 Jan 1838 - 4 May 1906)
31 Jan 1894: Promoted to *Major-General*
31 Jan 1894 - 16 Feb 1900: Commander, Life Guards Pavlovsky Regiment
16 Feb 1900: Retired

*Major-General* Aleksandr Vasilyevich **Bozheryanov** (24 Nov 1859 - ?)
13 Jan 1911: Promoted to *Major-General*
13 Jan 1911 - 17 Sep 1911: Commander, 1st Brigade, 3rd Grenadier Division
17 Sep 1911: Retired

*Major-General* Pyotr Mikhailovich von **Bradke** (9 Feb 1826 - 1904)
1 Feb 1865 - 1896: Commander of Gendarmerie, Simbirsk Province
28 Mar 1882: Promoted to *Major-General*

*Major-General* Viktor Aleksandrovich **Brakker** (30 Aug 1849 - ?)
31 Dec 1900 - 27 Sep 1901: Deputy Intendant, Amur Military District

| | |
|---|---|
| 1 Apr 1901: | Promoted to *Major-General* |
| 27 Sep 1901 - 20 Dec 1901: | At the disposal of the Commanding General, Amur Military District |
| 20 Dec 1901 - 7 Nov 1903: | Deputy Intendant, Turkestan Military District |
| 7 Nov 1903 - 1906: | Intendant, Turkestan Military District |

*Lieutenant-General* Nikolai Yefimovich von **Brandenburg** (8 Aug 1839 - 31 Aug 1903)
| | |
|---|---|
| 20 May 1872 - 31 Aug 1903: | Director of the Artillery Museum |
| 29 Jan 1878 - 31 Aug 1903: | Special Assignments Officer, Main Artillery Directorate |
| 19 Jan 1886: | Promoted to *Major-General* |
| 14 May 1896: | Promoted to *Lieutenant-General* |

*Major-General* Nikolai Aleksandrovich **Brandorf** (5 Jun 1833 - 15 Sep 1906)
| | |
|---|---|
| 4 Mar 1891 - 1900: | Deputy Intendant, Kiev Military District |
| 30 Aug 1892: | Promoted to *Major-General* |

*Major-General* Vasily Aleksandrovich **Brandorf** (8 Jan 1839 - ?)
| | |
|---|---|
| 17 Jul 1893: | Promoted to *Major-General* |
| 17 Jul 1893 - 21 Sep 1895: | Commander, 1st Brigade, 32nd Infantry Division |

*Major-General* Pyotr Aleksandrovich **Brandt** (12 Jun 1861 - ?)
| | |
|---|---|
| 7 Sep 1910 - 24 Feb 1916: | Intendant, IX. Army Corps |
| 14 Apr 1913: | Promoted to *Major-General* |
| 24 Feb 1916 - 1917: | Reserve officer, District Intendant Administration, Kiev Military District |

*Lieutenant-General* Vasily Nikolayevich **Bratanov** (29 Dec 1862 - ?)
| | |
|---|---|
| 14 Jul 1910: | Promoted to *Major-General* |
| 14 Jul 1910 - 25 Apr 1915: | Chief of Staff, III. Siberian Army Corps |
| 18 Sep 1914: | Promoted to *Lieutenant-General* |
| 25 Apr 1915 - 6 Apr 1917: | Commander, 7th Siberian Rifle Division |
| 6 Apr 1917 - Oct 1917: | Reserve officer, Minsk Military District |

*Major-General* Nikolai Matveyevich **Bratchikov** (26 Feb 1860 - ?)
| | |
|---|---|
| 24 Feb 1911: | Promoted to *Major-General* |
| 24 Feb 1911 - 28 Nov 1914: | Commander, 2nd Brigade, 11th Infantry Division |
| 28 Nov 1914 - 7 Apr 1916: | Commander, Militia Brigade |
| 7 Apr 1916 - 1917: | Commander, 117th Militia Brigade |

*Lieutenant-General* Ivan Nikolayevich **Bratkov** (13 Apr 1845 - 13 Jan 1912)
| | |
|---|---|
| 9 Nov 1904 - 13 Jan 1912: | Ataman, Caucasus Division, Kuban Cossack Army |
| 2 Apr 1906: | Promoted to *Major-General* |
| 1 Jan 1912: | Promoted to *Lieutenant-General* |

*Lieutenant-General* Nikolai-Pavel-Konstantin Emilievich **Bredov** (30 Oct 1873 - ?)
| | |
|---|---|
| 1915 - 20 Aug 1915: | Quartermaster-General, 11th Army |
| 5 Aug 1915: | Promoted to *Major-General* |
| 20 Aug 1915 - 8 Sep 1916: | Quartermaster-General, Northern Front |

| | |
|---|---|
| 8 Sep 1916 - 22 Apr 1917: | Chief of Staff, Kiev Military District |
| 22 Apr 1917 - 9 Sep 1917: | Commander, 6th Finnish Infantry Division |
| 9 Sep 1917 - 30 Sep 1917: | Commanding General, XXIV. Army Corps |
| 30 Sep 1917 - Apr 1918: | Commanding General, XXI. Army Corps |
| 12 Oct 1917: | Promoted to *Lieutenant-General* |

*Major-General* Vladimir Petrovich **Bresler** (24 Jun 1874 - ?)
| | |
|---|---|
| 2 Sep 1915 - 22 Dec 1916: | Commander, 129th Infantry Regiment |
| 2 Jun 1916: | Promoted to *Major-General* |
| 22 Dec 1916 - 19 Oct 1917: | Chief of Staff, 18th Infantry Division |
| 19 Oct 1917 - 1918: | Deputy Chief of Logistics, Southwestern Front |

*Major-General* Yegor Ivanovich von **Brevern** (1 Apr 1843 - ?)
| | |
|---|---|
| 14 Nov 1888: | Promoted to *Major-General* |
| 14 Nov 1888 - 12 May 1897: | Commander, 1st Brigade, 7th Cavalry Division |
| 12 May 1897 - 1898: | Commander, 6th Replacement Cavalry Brigade |

*Major-General* Petr Romanovich **Breyksh** (11 Aug 1853 - 1934)
| | |
|---|---|
| 19 Aug 1911 - 3 Sep 1912: | District Commander, Sterlitamak |
| 3 Sep 1912: | Promoted to *Major-General* |
| 3 Sep 1912: | Retired |
| 1914 - 8 Feb 1915: | Recalled; Commander, 16th Militia Brigade |
| 8 Feb 1915 - 8 May 1915: | Commander, Brigade, 24th Infantry Division |
| 8 May 1915 - 26 May 1917: | Commander, Brigade, 25th Infantry Division |
| 26 May 1917 - ?: | Commander, 189th Infantry Division |

*Lieutenant-General of the Fleet* Aleksandr Mikhailovich **Briger** (17 Feb 1861 - 20 May 1931)
| | |
|---|---|
| 10 Jul 1906 - 28 Feb 1917: | Inspector of Classes, Marine Corps |
| 18 Apr 1910: | Promoted to *Major-General of the Fleet* |
| 22 Mar 1915: | Promoted to *Lieutenant-General of the Fleet* |
| 28 Feb 1917 - 1919: | Director of the Marine Corps |

*Lieutenant-General* Andrey Aleksandrovich **Briks** (3 Mar 1858 - 1918)
| | |
|---|---|
| 4 Jan 1900 - 18 Feb 1914: | Inspector of Classes, Mikhailovsky Artillery Academy |
| 17 Apr 1905: | Promoted to *Major-General* |
| 18 Feb 1914 - Oct 1917: | Member of the Artillery Committee, Main Artillery Directorate |
| 6 Apr 1914: | Promoted to *Lieutenant-General* |
| 28 Nov 1915 - Oct 1917: | Chief of Section 4, Artillery Committee, Main Artillery Directorate |

*Major-General* Afanasy Vasilyevich **Brilevich** (5 Jul 1852 - ?)
| | |
|---|---|
| 23 Nov 1908: | Promoted to *Major-General* |
| 23 Nov 1908 - 13 May 1910: | Commander, 7th Artillery Brigade |

*General of Infantry* Aleksandr Vasilyevich **Brilevich** (23 Feb 1851 - ?)
| | |
|---|---|
| 24 Aug 1898: | Promoted to *Major-General* |

| | |
|---|---|
| 24 Aug 1898 - 9 Nov 1898: | General for Special Assignments, St. Petersburg Military District |
| 9 Nov 1898 - 4 Apr 1901: | Commander, Life Guards Grenadier Regiment |
| 4 Apr 1901 - 7 Nov 1904: | Commandant of the Infantry School |
| 7 Nov 1904 - 26 Oct 1905: | Commander, 13th Infantry Division |
| 6 Dec 1904: | Promoted to *Lieutenant-General* |
| 26 Oct 1905 - 22 Dec 1906: | Chief of Staff, St. Petersburg Military District |
| 22 Dec 1906 - 23 Nov 1907: | At the disposal of the Commanding General, St. Petersburg Military District |
| 23 Nov 1907 - 10 Aug 1910: | Deputy Commanding General, Irkutsk Military District |
| 10 Aug 1910 - 10 Mar 1911: | Commanding General, Irkutsk Military District, Ataman, Trans-Baikal Cossack Army |
| 6 Dec 1910: | Promoted to *General of Infantry* |
| 10 Mar 1911 - 1917: | Member of the Military Council |

*Lieutenant-General of Naval Artillery* Anton Frantsevich **Brink** (1 Dec 1851 - 30 May 1925)

| | |
|---|---|
| 1899 - 1 Sep 1907: | Deputy Inspector of Naval Artillery |
| 1 Apr 1901: | Promoted to *Major-General of Naval Artillery* |
| 1 Sep 1907 - 11 Oct 1911 : | Inspector of Naval Artillery |
| 27 Feb 1908 - 1913: | Member of the Artillery Committee, Main Artillery Directorate |
| 6 May 1909: | Promoted to *Lieutenant-General of Naval Artillery* |
| 11 Oct 1911 - 1913: | Chief of Artillery Section, Main Directorate of Shipbuilding |
| 1913: | Retired |

*General of Infantry* Baron Aleksandr-Pavel Fridrikhovich von der **Brinken** (28 Aug 1859 - 25 Mar 1917)

| | |
|---|---|
| 2 May 1904: | Promoted to *Major-General* |
| 2 May 1904 - 9 Nov 1904: | Attached to the Chief of Lines of Communication, Manchurian Army |
| 9 Nov 1904 - 12 Nov 1905: | Chief of Staff, I. Siberian Army Corps |
| 12 Nov 1905 - 12 Sep 1908: | Chief of Staff, I. Army Corps |
| 12 Sep 1908: | Promoted to *Lieutenant-General* |
| 12 Sep 1908 - 26 Aug 1912: | Chief of Staff, St. Petersburg Military District |
| 26 Aug 1912 - 25 Mar 1917: | Commanding General, XXII. Army Corps |
| 6 Dec 1914: | Promoted to *General of Infantry* |

*Lieutenant-General* Baron Leopold Fridrikhovich von der **Brinken** (8 Mar 1858 - 29 Aug 1925)

| | |
|---|---|
| 29 Mar 1907 - 30 May 1912: | Commander, Life Guards St. Petersburg Regiment |
| 31 May 1907: | Promoted to *Major-General* |
| 30 May 1912 - 3 Apr 1915: | Commander, 1st Brigade, 1st Guards Infantry Division |
| 3 Apr 1915 - 18 Apr 1917: | Commander, 28th Infantry Division |
| 8 May 1915: | Promoted to *Lieutenant-General* |
| 21 Sep 1917: | Retired |

*General of Infantry* Nikolai Petrovich **Brok** (10 Jan 1839 - 7 Feb 1919)
| | |
|---|---|
| 11 Mar 1875 - 27 Oct 1877: | Commander, Life Guards Moscow Regiment |
| 30 Aug 1875: | Promoted to *Major-General* |
| 27 Oct 1877 - 12 Dec 1880: | Commander, 1st Brigade, 2nd Guards Infantry Division |
| 12 Dec 1880 - 9 May 1884: | Member of the Tsar's retinue |
| 9 May 1884 - 19 Apr 1897: | Chief of Gendarmerie, Warsaw |
| 30 Aug 1885: | Promoted to *Lieutenant-General* |
| 19 Apr 1897 - 1 Jan 1900: | At the disposal of the Commanding General of the Gendarmerie |
| 1 Jan 1900 - 1917: | Honorary Trustee, Board of Trustees, Empress Maria Institutions |
| 9 Apr 1900: | Promoted to *General of Infantry* |

*Major-General* Anton Ferdinandovich **Brokhotsky** (19 Jun 1850 - ?)
| | |
|---|---|
| 31 Oct 1899 - 23 Oct 1904: | Commander, 8th Infantry Regiment |
| 23 Oct 1904: | Promoted to *Major-General* |
| 23 Oct 1904 - 21 Jun 1905: | Commander, 1st Brigade, 38th Infantry Division |
| 21 Jun 1905 - 1905: | At the disposal of the Chief of the General Staff |

*Major-General* Aleksandr Aleksandrovich **Broterus** (14 Nov 1838 - ?)
| | |
|---|---|
| 12 Dec 1884 - 21 Sep 1895: | Commander, 69th Infantry Regiment |
| 14 Nov 1894: | Promoted to *Major-General* |
| 21 Sep 1895 - 18 Oct 1896: | Commander, 1st Brigade, 32nd Infantry Division |
| 18 Oct 1896 - 23 Feb 1898: | Commander, 2nd Brigade, 2nd Infantry Division |
| 23 Feb 1898 - 23 Jul 1900: | Commander, Turkestan Rifle Brigade |
| 23 Jul 1900 - 8 Jul 1901: | Commander, 1st Turkestan Rifle Brigade |

*Major-General* Eduard Vilgelmovich **Brunneman** (9 Jul 1851 - ?)
| | |
|---|---|
| 11 Feb 1904 - 6 Dec 1908: | Commandant, Warsaw-St. Petersburg Railway Station |
| 6 Dec 1908: | Promoted to *Major-General* |
| 6 Dec 1908: | Retired |

*Major-General* Yevgeny Vilgelmovich **Brunneman** (23 Mar 1857 - ?)
| | |
|---|---|
| 24 Apr 1904 - 1906: | Commander, Verzhbolovsk Borderguard Brigade |
| 1906: | Promoted to *Major-General* |
| 1906: | Retired |
| 17 Oct 1915 - 21 Aug 1917: | Recalled; At the disposal of the Chief, Main Directorate for Remounts |
| 21 Aug 1917: | Retired |

*General of Cavalry* Aleksei Alekseyevich **Brusilov** (19 Aug 1853 - 17 Mar 1926)
| | |
|---|---|
| 10 Nov 1898 - 10 Feb 1902: | Assistant Commandant, Cavalry Officers School |
| 6 May 1900: | Promoted to *Major-General* |
| 10 Feb 1902 - 19 Apr 1906: | Commandant, Cavalry School |
| 19 Apr 1906 - 5 Jan 1909: | Commander, 2nd Guards Cavalry Division |
| 6 Dec 1906: | Promoted to *Lieutenant-General* |
| 5 Jan 1909 - 15 May 1912: | Commanding General, XIV. Army Corps |
| 15 May 1912 - 15 Aug 1913: | Deputy Commanding General, Warsaw Military District |

| | |
|---|---|
| 15 Aug 1913 - 19 Jul 1914: | Commanding General, XII. Army Corps |
| 6 Dec 1912: | Promoted to *General of Cavalry* |
| 19 Jul 1914 - 28 Jul 1914: | Commander, Proskurovskaya Group |
| 28 Jul 1914 - 17 Mar 1916: | C-in-C, 8th Army |
| 10 Apr 1915: | Promoted to *General-Adjutant* |
| 17 Mar 1916 - 21 May 1917: | C-in-C, Southwestern Front |
| 22 May 1917 - 19 Jul 1917: | Supreme Commander-in-Chief |
| 19 Jul 1917 - Oct 1917: | Military adviser to the government |

*Major-General* Boris Nikolayevich **Brusilov** (7 Aug 1861 - 6 Sep 1936)
| | |
|---|---|
| 1906 - 1 Sep 1914: | Commander, Avar District, Dagestan Region |
| 1 Sep 1914: | Promoted to *Major-General* |
| 1 Sep 1914: | Retired |

*Vice-Admiral* Lev Alekseyevich **Brusilov** (27 Feb 1857 - 22 Jul 1909)
| | |
|---|---|
| Jun 1906 - 14 Jul 1908: | Chief of the Naval General Staff |
| 1907: | Promoted to *Rear-Admiral* |
| 14 Jul 1908 - 1909: | Junior Flagman, Baltic Fleet |
| 1909: | Promoted to *Vice-Admiral* |
| 1909: | Retired |

*Major-General* Aleksandr Dmitriyevich **Brylkin** (4 Jul 1864 - ?)
| | |
|---|---|
| 10 Mar 1914 - 1917: | Military Judge, Odessa Military District Court |
| 22 Mar 1915: | Promoted to *Major-General* |
| 1917: | Chairman of the Military Court, XXXVI. Army Corps |

*Lieutenant-General of the Admiralty* Vladimir Nikolayevich **Brylkin** (4 Feb 1832 - 11 Mar 1899)
| | |
|---|---|
| 1886: | Promoted to *Rear-Admiral* |
| 1886 - 1887: | Junior Flagman |
| 1887 - 11 Mar 1899: | Commandant of Kronstadt |
| 1892: | Promoted to *Lieutenant-General of the Admiralty* |

*Major-General* Vladimir Vladimirovich **Bryukhov** (21 Nov 1861 - 24 Apr 1939)
| | |
|---|---|
| 4 Feb 1915 - 1917: | Commander, 70th Infantry Regiment |
| 1916: | Promoted to *Major-General* |
| 1917 - 28 Apr 1917: | Commander, Brigade, 180th Infantry Division |
| 28 Apr 1917 - 1918: | Commander, 180th Infantry Division |

*Lieutenant-General* Konstantin Fyodorovich von **Bryummer** (5 Dec 1856 - 11 Jul 1930)
| | |
|---|---|
| 4 Feb 1906 - 28 Jul 1914: | Staff Officer to Grand Duke Nikolai Mikhailovich |
| 6 Dec 1906: | Promoted to *Major-General* |
| 14 Apr 1913: | Promoted to *Lieutenant-General* |
| 28 Jul 1914 - 19 Apr 1917: | At the disposal of the C-in-C, Southwestern Front |
| 19 Apr 1917: | Retired |

*Major-General* Aleksandr Iosifovich **Brzhezitsky** (14 Feb 1860 - ?)
| | |
|---|---|
| 7 Jan 1911: | Promoted to *Major-General* |

| | |
|---|---|
| 7 Jan 1911 - 16 Jul 1912: | Special Purposes General to the Commanding General, Borderguard Corps |
| 16 Jul 1912 - 21 Sep 1914: | Commander, 4th Borderguard District |
| 21 Sep 1914 - 16 Oct 1914: | Special Purposes General, 3rd Army |
| 16 Oct 1914 - 1917: | Chief of Medical Section, 3rd Army |

*Lieutenant-General* Nikolai Aleksandrovich **Brzhozovsky** (20 Dec 1857 - ?)
| | |
|---|---|
| 20 Dec 1911: | Promoted to *Major-General* |
| 20 Dec 1911 - 4 Aug 1915: | Commander of Artillery, Fortress Osovets |
| 4 Aug 1915 - Jul 1916: | Commandant of Fortress Osovets |
| 6 Dec 1915: | Promoted to *Lieutenant-General* |
| Jul 1916 - 22 Apr 1917: | Commanding General, XLIV. Army Corps |

*Major-General* Yevgeny Vasilyevich **Brzhozovsky** (5 Mar 1859 - Nov 1915)
| | |
|---|---|
| 17 Jun 1905 - Nov 1915: | Commander, 5th Replacement Cavalry Regiment |
| 14 Apr 1913: | Promoted to *Major-General* |

*Rear-Admiral* Aleksandr Dmitrievich **Bubnov** (6 May 1883 - 2 Feb 1963)
| | |
|---|---|
| 30 Jul 1916 - 19 Dec 1917: | Chief of Naval Administration |
| 28 Jul 1917: | Promoted to *Rear-Admiral* |

*Major-General of Naval Engineers* Ivan Grigoryevich **Bubnov** (18 Jan 1872 - 13 Mar 1919)
| | |
|---|---|
| 18 Feb 1908 - 1914: | Chief of Naval Test Tank |
| 25 Mar 1912: | Promoted to *Major-General of Naval Engineers* |
| 1912 - 1917: | Consultant to Baltic Works, St. Petersburg |

*Vice-Admiral* Mikhail Vladimirovich **Bubnov** (6 Nov 1859 - ?)
| | |
|---|---|
| 27 Oct 1908 - 18 Apr 1911: | Chief of Warehouse Section, Main Shipbuilding Directorate |
| 14 May 1910: | Promoted to *Rear-Admiral* |
| 18 Apr 1911 - 25 May 1915: | Deputy Minister of the Navy |
| 14 Apr 1913: | Promoted to *Vice-Admiral* |
| 25 May 1915: | Retired |

*Lieutenant-General of the Fleet* Nikolai Livovich **Bubnov** (11 May 1854 - ?)
| | |
|---|---|
| 25 Sep 1899 - Jul 1911: | Director of the Naval Museum |
| 22 Apr 1907: | Promoted to *Major-General of the Admiralty* |
| 8 Apr 1913: | Redesignated *Major-General of the Fleet* |
| 26 Aug 1913: | Promoted to *Lieutenant-General of the Fleet* |

*Major-General of the Fleet* Pyotr Kapitonovich **Bubnov** (14 Aug 1857 - ?)
| | |
|---|---|
| 17 Sep 1888 - Jul 1913: | Training Officer, Marine Corps |
| 6 May 1910: | Promoted to *Major-General of the Admiralty* |
| 8 Apr 1913: | Redesignated *Major-General of the Fleet* |

*Major-General* Vladimir Ivanovich **Bubnov** (7 Jun 1851 - 6 Sep 1910)
| | |
|---|---|
| 9 Jun 1903: | Promoted to *Major-General* |
| 9 Jun 1903 - 14 Feb 1907: | Commander, 1st Brigade, 32nd Infantry Division |

14 Feb 1907 - 3 Oct 1907:     Commander, 1st Brigade, 42nd Infantry Division
3 Oct 1907 - 8 Aug 1908:      Commander, 1st Turkestan Rifle Brigade

*General of Artillery* Sergey Aleksandrovich **Budayevsky** (23 Mar 1851 - ?)
29 Jan 1896 - 4 Oct 1900:     Inspector of Classes, Nikolayev Cavalry School
14 May 1896:                  Promoted to *Major-General*
4 Oct 1900 - 5 Apr 1901:      Special Purposes General, Main Directorate for Military Schools
5 Apr 1901 - 30 Jun 1906:     Deputy Chief of Military Schools
28 Mar 1904:                  Promoted to *Lieutenant-General*
30 Jun 1906 - 3 May 1910:     Special Purposes General, Main Directorate for Military Schools
3 May 1910:                   Promoted to *General of Artillery*
3 May 1910 - 27 Jul 1911:     Transferred to the reserve
27 Jul 1911:                  Retired
28 Jul 1911 - 1917:           Attached to the Ministry of War
1914 - 1917:                  Ministry of War Representative to the Ministry of Education
1917:                         Retired

*Lieutenant-General* Baron Aleksei Pavlovich von **Budberg** (21 May 1869 - 15 Dec 1945)
31 Jul 1902 - 1 Mar 1913:     Chief of Staff, Fortress Vladivostok
6 Dec 1910:                   Promoted to *Major-General*
1 Mar 1913 - 15 Aug 1914:     Quartermaster-General, Amur Military District
15 Aug 1914 - 23 Dec 1914:    Quartermaster-General, 10th Army
23 Dec 1914 - 13 Feb 1915:    Chief of Staff, 10th Army
13 Feb 1915 - 19 Aug 1915:    Attached to the C-in-C, 1st Army
19 Aug 1915 - 21 Oct 1915:    Commander, 40th Infantry Division
21 Oct 1915 - 22 Apr 1917:    Commander, 70th Infantry Division
8 Mar 1916:                   Promoted to *Lieutenant-General*
22 Apr 1917 - Oct 1917:       Commanding General, XIV. Army Corps

*Major-General* Baron Anatoly Aleksandrovich **Budberg** (22 Feb 1857 - June 1918)
15 Apr 1905 - 15 May 1908:    Commander, 13th Hussar Regiment
15 May 1908:                  Promoted to *Major-General*
15 May 1908 - 29 Jun 1912:    Commander, 1st Brigade, 8th Cavalry Division
29 Jun 1912 - 18 Jul 1914:    Commander, 3rd Independent Cavalry Brigade
18 Jul 1914:                  Retired

*Major-General* Baron Andrey-Ebergard-Reyngold Romanovich **Budberg** (8 Dec 1851 - Oct 1918)
2 Feb 1895 - 6 Jun 1915:      Chief of the Moscow Metropolitan Police
6 Dec 1904:                   Promoted to *Major-General*
6 Jun 1915 - 24 Jul 1917:     Commander, 2nd Brigade, 4th Cavalry Division
24 Jul 1917:                  Dismissed

*Lieutenant-General* Baron Nikolai Aleksandrovich **Budberg** (4 Feb 1856 - 8 Nov 1921)
7 Jan 1904:                   Promoted to *Major-General*

| | |
|---|---|
| 7 Jan 1904 - 24 Feb 1907: | Commander, Life Guards Horse-Grenadier Regiment |
| 24 Feb 1907 - 19 Mar 1912: | Commander, 2nd Brigade, 1st Guards Cavalry Division |
| 19 Mar 1912 - 20 May 1917: | General à la suite |
| 20 May 1917: | Promoted to *Lieutenant-General* |
| 20 May 1917: | Dismissed |

*General of Artillery* Aleksandr Emmanuilovich **Budde** (9 Dec 1833 - 16 Jun 1915)

| | |
|---|---|
| 9 Dec 1888: | Promoted to *Major-General* |
| 9 Dec 1888 - 9 Jan 1890: | Commander, 17th Artillery Brigade |
| 9 Jan 1890 - 9 Aug 1896: | Commander, 9th Artillery Brigade |
| 9 Aug 1896 - 1 Jan 1898: | Commander of Artillery, XIV. Army Corps |
| 6 Dec 1897: | Promoted to *Lieutenant-General* |
| 1 Jan 1898 - 2 Sep 1902: | Commander of Artillery, XXI. Army Corps |
| 2 Sep 1902 - 16 Jun 1915 : | Member, Committee for Wounded Veterans |
| 6 Dec 1906: | Promoted to *General of Artillery* |

*General of Infantry* Viktor Emmanuilovich **Budde** (1 Mar 1836 - 2 Feb 1903)

| | |
|---|---|
| 10 Aug 1875 - 8 Nov 1878: | Commander, 46th Infantry Regiment |
| 3 Oct 1878: | Promoted to *Major-General* |
| 8 Nov 1878 - 13 Jul 1879: | Commander, 2nd Brigade, 30th Infantry Division |
| 13 Jul 1879 - 15 Oct 1885: | Commander, 1st Brigade, 12th Infantry Division |
| 15 Oct 1885 - 19 Feb 1890: | Commander, 2nd Brigade, 12th Infantry Division |
| 19 Feb 1890 - 18 Dec 1900: | Commander, 31st Infantry Division |
| 30 Aug 1890: | Promoted to *Lieutenant-General* |
| 18 Dec 1900: | Promoted to *General of Infantry* |
| 18 Dec 1900: | Retired |

*Major-General* Anton Romanovich **Budilovich** (11 Feb 1859 - 18 Nov 1914)

| | |
|---|---|
| Aug 1914 - 18 Nov 1914: | Commander, 298th Infantry Regiment |
| 1 Jun 1916: | Posthumously promoted to *Major-General* |

*Major-General* Vladimir Iosifovich **Budkevich** (29 Jul 1850 - ?)

| | |
|---|---|
| 14 Dec 1901 - 1907: | Commander, Odessa Borderguard Brigade |
| 28 Mar 1904: | Promoted to *Major-General* |

*Major-General* Pyotr Mikhaylovich **Budzilovich** (19 Jan 1863 - ?)

| | |
|---|---|
| 9 Apr 1916 - 1917: | Commander, 449th Infantry Regiment |
| 26 Aug 1916: | Promoted to *Major-General* |

*Lieutenant-General of Naval Engineers* Stanislav Konstantinovich **Budzynsky** (15 Dec 1848 - ?)

| | |
|---|---|
| 6 Dec 1897: | Promoted to *Major-General of Naval Engineers* |
| 15 Dec 1898 - ?: | Chief Inspector of Construction, Naval Technical Committee |
| 6 Dec 1904: | Promoted to *Lieutenant-General of Naval Engineers* |

*Major-General* Konstantin Aleksandrovich **Bukh** (11 Feb 1859 - ?)

| | |
|---|---|
| 17 Aug 1914 - 6 Nov 1916: | Commander, 1st Heavy Artillery Brigade |

25 Oct 1914: Promoted to *Major-General*
6 Nov 1916 - 1917: Commander, 14th Heavy Field Artillery Brigade

*Lieutenant-General* Mir Sayyid Muhammad Alim Khan **Bukharsky**, Emir of Bukhara (3 Jan 1880 - 5 May 1944)
4 Dec 1910 - 30 Aug 1920: Emir of Bukhara
13 May 1911: Promoted to *Major-General à la suite*
30 Dec 1915: Promoted to *Lieutenant-General à la suite*
30 Dec 1915: Promoted to *General-Adjutant*

*General of Cavalry* Seid-Abdul-Agad-Khan **Bukharsky**, Emir of Bukhara (26 Mar 1859 - 3 Jan 1911)
12 Nov 1885 - 4 Dec 1910: Emir of Bukhara
22 Apr 1895: Promoted to *Lieutenant-General*
1 Jan 1900: Promoted to *General of Cavalry*
1902: Promoted to *General-Adjutant*

*General of Infantry* Vladimir Yegorovich **Bukholts** (18 Jul 1850 - 7 Apr 1929)
14 Nov 1895: Promoted to *Major-General*
14 Nov 1895 - 2 Nov 1899: Chief of Staff, IV. Army Corps
2 Nov 1899 - 10 Dec 1902: Chief of Staff, XV. Army Corps
10 Dec 1902 - 18 Apr 1903: Commander, 4th Infantry Division
6 Apr 1903: Promoted to *Lieutenant-General*
18 Apr 1903 - 4 Nov 1905: Intendant, Moscow Military District
4 Nov 1905 - 4 Aug 1907: Deputy Quartermaster-General, Ministry of War
4 Aug 1907 - 3 Oct 1909: Chief of Intendant Training Courses
3 Oct 1909 - 1 Sep 1912: Commander, 31st Infantry Division
1 Sep 1912 - 21 Apr 1913: Commanding General, III. Siberian Army Corps
6 Dec 1912: Promoted to *General of Infantry*
21 Apr 1913 - 19 Jul 1914: Deputy Commanding General, Irkutsk Military District
19 Jul 1914 - 10 Nov 1914: Acting Commanding General, Kiev Military District
10 Nov 1914 - 7 Oct 1915: Commanding General, Irkutsk Military District
7 Oct 1915 - 1917: At the disposal of the C-in-C, Southwestern Front
1917 - 7 Jul 1917: Commanding General, Kiev Military District
7 Jul 1917: Retired

*Major-General of the Hydrographic Corps* Afanasy Mikhailovich **Bukhteyev** (24 Jan 1862 - 15 Jan 1940)
16 Apr 1912 - 1917: Deputy Chief of the Hydrographic Department, Ministry of the Navy
6 Dec 1912: Promoted to *Major-General of the Admiralty*
4 Feb 1913: Redesignated *Major-General of the Hydrographic Corps*

*Major-General* Ivan Vasilievich **Bukin** (3 Jan 1848 - ?)
5 Aug 1903: Promoted to *Major-General*
5 Aug 1903 - 2 May 1904: Commander, 31st Artillery Brigade
2 May 1904 - Dec 1905: Commander, 3rd Grenadier Artillery Brigade

*Major-General* Aleksandr Petrovich **Bukovsky** (11 Aug 1868 - 21 Apr 1944)
14 Dec 1913: Promoted to *Major-General*
14 Dec 1913 - 2 Feb 1916: Commander, Life Guards Jaeger Regiment
2 Feb 1916 - Aug 1916: Commander, Brigade, 3rd Guards Infantry Division
Aug 1916 - 9 Sep 1916: Commander, 1st Turkestan Rifle Division
9 Sep 1916 - 17 Jan 1917: Commander, Brigade, 3rd Guards Infantry Division
17 Jan 1917 - 19 Jun 1917: Commander, 38th Infantry Division
19 Jun 1917 - 30 Dec 1917: Transferred to the reserve, Petrograd Military District
30 Dec 1917: Dismissed

*Major-General* Nikolai Andrianovich **Bukretov** (6 Apr 1876 - 8 May 1930)
11 Oct 1915 - 29 Jul 1916: Commander, 90th Infantry Regiment
18 Feb 1916: Promoted to *Major-General*
29 Jul 1916 - 1917: Commander, 2nd Kuban Cossack Infantry Brigade

*Major-General* Nikolai Vladimirovich **Bukreyev** (5 Nov 1854 - ?)
30 Sep 1911 - 1917: Intendant, Fortress Brest-Litovsk
6 Dec 1911: Promoted to *Major-General*

*Major-General* Vladimir Arkhipovich **Bulakh** (3 Jun 1848 - ?)
18 Sep 1908 - 1911: Chief of Kremenchug Artillery Depot
6 Dec 1908: Promoted to *Major-General*

*General of Artillery* Nikolai Ilyich **Bulatov** (21 Jan 1857 - ?)
9 Feb 1905 - 23 Apr 1907: Commander, 16th Artillery Brigade
5 Mar 1905: Promoted to *Major-General*
23 Apr 1907 - 3 Jul 1908: Commander, 1st Grenadier Artillery Brigade
3 Jul 1908 - 2 Apr 1913: Inspector of Artillery, XIII. Army Corps
1 Oct 1908: Promoted to *Lieutenant-General*
2 Apr 1913 - 24 Jan 1914: Inspector of Artillery, VIII. Army Corps
24 Jan 1914 - 13 Nov 1914: Commander of Artillery, Irkutsk Military District
13 Nov 1914 - 17 Jun 1916: Commander, 3rd Infantry Division
17 Jun 1916 - 14 Aug 1916: At the disposal of the C-in-C, 8th Army
14 Aug 1916 - 2 Apr 1917: Commanding General, I. Army Corps
6 Dec 1916: Promoted to *General of Artillery*
2 Apr 1917 - 23 Jun 1917: Reserve officer, Kiev Military District
23 Jun 1917: Retired

*Major-General* Stepan Konstantinovich **Bulatovich** (13 Jul 1866 - ?)
15 Mar 1915 - 1917: Military Judge, Amur Military District Court
22 Mar 1915: Promoted to *Major-General*

*Major-General* Vasily Petrovich **Bulayev** (30 Jul 1832 - 19 Sep 1895)
2 Sep 1891: Promoted to *Major-General*
2 Sep 1891 - 19 Sep 1895: Commander, 30th Artillery Brigade

*Major-General* Dmitry Yakovlevich **Bulgakov** (24 Oct 1849 - Jul 1908)
7 Jul 1888 - Jul 1908: Commander, Kuban Cossack Battalion

16 Jan 1907:				Promoted to *Major-General*

*General of Artillery* Pavel Ilyich **Bulgakov** (3 Aug 1856 - 1940)
11 Nov 1902 - 15 Jul 1907:		Commander, 2nd Reserve Artillery Brigade
6 Apr 1903:				Promoted to *Major-General*
15 Jul 1907:				Promoted to *Lieutenant-General*
15 Jul 1907 - 28 Jul 1910:		Commander of Artillery, XIV. Army Corps
28 Jul 1910 - 12 Oct 1911:		Inspector of Artillery, XIV. Army Corps
12 Oct 1911 - 6 Dec 1914:		Commander, 25th Infantry Division
6 Dec 1914:				Promoted to *General of Artillery*
6 Dec 1914 - 22 Feb 1915:		Commanding General, XX. Army Corps
22 Feb 1915 - 3 Aug 1918:		POW, Germany

*Major-General* Nikolai Ivanovich **Bulkin** (30 Jan 1864 - 2 Nov 1913)
20 May 1910 - 2 Nov 1913:		Military Judge, Odessa Military District Court
6 Dec 1910:				Promoted to *Major-General*

*Lieutenant-General* Yevgeny-Filipp-Bernard Mikhailovich **Bulmering** (14 Nov 1834 - 4 Nov 1897)
22 May 1878:				Promoted to *Major-General*
22 May 1878 - 10 Aug 1878:		Commander, 1st Brigade, 40th Infantry Division
10 Aug 1878 - 12 Jul 1879:		At the disposal of the Commanding General, Warsaw Military District
12 Jul 1879 - 10 Dec 1882:		Commander of Engineers, Finland Military District
10 Dec 1882 - 28 Nov 1892:		Commandant of Fortress Kerch
30 Aug 1888:				Promoted to *Lieutenant-General*
28 Nov 1892 - 4 Nov 1897:		Member, Committee for Wounded Veterans

*Lieutenant-General* Vasily Aleksandrovich **Bunakov** (30 Dec 1839 - 1 Jan 1897)
8 Feb 1875 - 6 Jun 1878:		Chief of Staff, 2nd Guards Cavalry Division
1 Jan 1878:				Promoted to *Major-General*
6 Jun 1878 - 25 Oct 1878:		Unassigned
25 Oct 1878 - 7 Feb 1880:		At the disposal of the Commanding General, St. Petersburg Military District
7 Feb 1880 - 30 Aug 1881:		Chief of Staff, II. Army Corps
30 Aug 1881 - 12 Feb 1891:		Chief of Staff, Vilnius Military District
30 Aug 1886:				Promoted to *Lieutenant-General*
12 Feb 1891 - 1 Jan 1897:		Chief of the Main Cossack Directorate

*Lieutenant-General* Aleksey Nikolayevich **Bunin** (28 Jan 1858 - ?)
19 Jan 1909:				Promoted to *Major-General*
19 Jan 1909 - 22 Apr 1915:		Commander, 1st Brigade, 1st Siberian Rifle Division
22 Apr 1915 - 29 Oct 1915:		Commander, 4th Siberian Rifle Division
15 Aug 1915:				Promoted to *Lieutenant-General*
29 Oct 1915 - 7 Feb 1917:		Reserve officer, Petrograd Military District
7 Feb 1917 - 18 Apr 1917:		Commander, 16th Siberian Rifle Division
18 Apr 1917 - 9 Sep 1917:		Reserve officer, Petrograd Military District
9 Sep 1917:				Dismissed

*General of Infantry* Viktor Ivanovich **Bunin** (12 Oct 1840 - 5 Jan 1908)
| | |
|---|---|
| 3 Dec 1886 - 24 Dec 1889: | Intendant, Finland Military District |
| 30 Aug 1888: | Promoted to *Major-General* |
| 24 Dec 1889 - 3 Jan 1899: | Intendant, Vilnius Military District |
| 14 May 1896: | Promoted to *Lieutenant-General* |
| 3 Jan 1899 - 1906: | Deputy Intendant-General of the Army |
| 1906: | Promoted to *General of Infantry* |
| 1906: | Retired |

*Major-General* Vsevolod Viktorovich **Bunyakovsky** (5 Apr 1875 - ?)
| | |
|---|---|
| 1 Apr 1915 - 20 Nov 1915: | Commander, 225$^{th}$ Infantry Regiment |
| 9 Aug 1915: | Promoted to *Major-General* |
| 20 Nov 1915 - 3 Feb 1917: | Professor of Military Sciences, Aleksandr Military School |
| 3 Feb 1917 - Oct 1917: | Commandant of the Imperial Military Academy |

*Vice-Admiral* Pavel Stepanovich **Burachek** (24 Dec 1837 - ?)
| | |
|---|---|
| 1890: | Promoted to *Rear-Admiral* |
| 1890 - 1892: | Junior Flagman, Baltic Fleet |
| 1892 - 1893: | Commander, 2$^{nd}$ Division, Baltic Fleet |
| 1893 - 1894: | Commander, Artillery Training Detachment |
| 1894 - 1898: | Chairman, Naval Artillery Testing Commission |
| 5 Jan 1898: | Promoted to *Vice-Admiral* |
| 5 Jan 1898: | Retired |

*Major-General* Pyotr Alekseyevich **Burago** (21 Dec 1863 - ?)
| | |
|---|---|
| 25 Jul 1909 - 1917: | Chairman of the Remount Commission, Siberian Region |
| 6 Dec 1916: | Promoted to *Major-General* |

*Lieutenant-General* Nikolai Livovich **Burenin** (2 May 1851 - 1930)
| | |
|---|---|
| 9 Sep 1907: | Promoted to *Major-General* |
| 9 Sep 1907 - 20 Sep 1908: | Commander, St. Petersburg Arms & Ammunition Depot |
| 20 Sep 1908 - 1913: | Commander, Kursk Artillery Depot |
| 1913: | Promoted to *Lieutenant-General* |
| 1913: | Retired |

*Major-General* Vasily Vasilyevich **Burkhanovsky** (13 Nov 1867 - ?)
| | |
|---|---|
| 1 Dec 1912 - 3 Feb 1916: | Commander, 1$^{st}$ Battalion, 28$^{th}$ Artillery Brigade |
| 26 Aug 1915: | Promoted to *Major-General* |
| 3 Feb 1916 - 1917: | Commander, 127$^{th}$ Artillery Brigade |

*Major-General* Vladimir Konstantinovich **Burkovsky** (13 Mar 1863 - 20 Oct 1941)
| | |
|---|---|
| 7 Aug 1912: | Promoted to *Major-General* |
| 7 Aug 1912 - 15 Feb 1917: | Chief of Staff, Fortress Kaunas |
| 15 Feb 1917 - Oct 1917: | Commander, Erevan District |

*Rear-Admiral* Sergey Ivanovich **Burley** (15 Jan 1861 - 1920)
| | |
|---|---|
| 1912 - 9 Dec 1913: | Commandant, Port of Kerch |
| 6 Dec 1913: | Promoted to *Rear-Admiral* |
| 9 Dec 1913 - Apr 1917: | Mayor of Sevastopol |
| 1 Jan 1915 - Apr 1917: | Admiral for Special Assignments, Black Sea Fleet |

*Major-General* Andrey Vladimirovich **Burman** (2 May 1867 - 31 Jul 1918)
| | |
|---|---|
| 22 Jun 1912: | Promoted to *Major-General* |
| 22 Jun 1912 - 18 Dec 1913: | Commander, 9th Artillery Brigade |
| 18 Dec 1913 - 12 May 1916: | Commander, Life Guards 3rd Artillery Brigade |
| 12 May 1916 - 29 Sep 1916: | Inspector of Artillery, Grenadier Corps |
| 29 Sep 1916 - 7 Aug 1917: | Inspector of Artillery, 1st Guards Corps |

*Major-General* Georgy Vladimirovich **Burman** (4 Nov 1865 - 3 Feb 1922)
| | |
|---|---|
| 6 Sep 1908 - 30 Nov 1914: | Commander, Military Electro-Technical School |
| 31 Dec 1910: | Promoted to *Major-General* |
| 30 Nov 1914 - 22 Jul 1915: | Chief of Air Defense, Petrograd |
| 22 Jul 1915 - 8 May 1916: | Chief of Air Defense, Petrograd & Tsarskoye Selo |
| 8 May 1916 - 20 Mar 1917: | Chairman, Committee on Unit Stationing, Main Military Technical Directorate |
| 20 Mar 1917 - 31 Aug 1917: | Commander, Officer Electro-Technical School |
| 31 Aug 1917 - 1918: | Chief of Air Defense, Petrograd |

*General of Engineers* Voldemar Georgiyevich **Burman** (4 Nov 1832 - 16 Mar 1909)
| | |
|---|---|
| 5 May 1873: | Promoted to *Major-General* |
| 5 May 1873 - 1876: | Commander, 1st Sapper Brigade |
| 1876 - 3 Oct 1893: | Commander, 4th Sapper Brigade |
| 30 Aug 1885: | Promoted to *Lieutenant-General* |
| 1887 - 1891: | Chief of Fortress Construction, Privislinskom Territory |
| 3 Oct 1893 - 17 Jun 1899: | Commandant of Fortress Modlin |
| 6 Dec 1898: | Promoted to *General of Engineers* |
| 17 Jun 1899 - Sep 1905: | Member, Committee for Wounded Veterans |

*Lieutenant-General* Fyodor Adolfovich **Burmeyster** (8 Sep 1825 - 1897)
| | |
|---|---|
| 29 Mar 1874 - 17 Mar 1878: | Commander, 112th Infantry Regiment |
| 2 Mar 1878: | Promoted to *Major-General* |
| 17 Mar 1878 - 17 Nov 1885: | Commander, 1st Brigade, 28th Infantry Division |
| 17 Nov 1885 - 1897: | Commander, 11th Regional Brigade |
| 30 Aug 1888: | Promoted to *Lieutenant-General* |

*Lieutenant-General* Apollon Ivanovich **Burov** (30 Jul 1860 - ?)
| | |
|---|---|
| 27 Feb 1900 - 3 Jun 1910: | Chief of Staff of Troops, Semirechensk Region |
| 22 Apr 1907: | Promoted to *Major-General* |
| 3 Jun 1910 - 4 Jul 1913: | Commander, 2nd Brigade, 48th Infantry Division |
| 4 Jul 1913: | Promoted to *Lieutenant-General* |
| 4 Jul 1913: | Retired |
| 5 Aug 1914 - 14 Apr 1917: | Recalled; Commander, 1st Siberian Reserve Rifle Brigade |

14 Apr 1917 - Oct 1917: Reserve officer, Petrograd Military District

*Major-General* Pyotr Nikitich **Burov** (2 Oct 1872 - 2 Nov 1954)
1 Sep 1916 - 1917: Chief of Staff, 10th Infantry Division
3 Oct 1916: Promoted to *Major-General*
1917 - 20 Feb 1917: Chief of Staff, V. Army Corps
20 Feb 1917 - 5 Sep 1917: Commander, 178th Infantry Division
5 Sep 1917 - 23 Sep 1917: Commander, 129th Infantry Division
23 Sep 1917 - Nov 1917: Chief of Staff, Special Army

*Lieutenant-General* Ivan Karlovich von **Burzi** (21 Jun 1835 - 28 Oct 1899)
3 Mar 1877 - 14 Dec 1884: Commander, 8th Grenadier Regiment
14 Dec 1884: Promoted to *Major-General*
14 Dec 1884 - 5 Nov 1886: Deputy Chief of Staff, Kazan Military District
5 Nov 1886 - 1 Sep 1892: Chief of Staff, XV. Army Corps
1 Sep 1892 - 28 Oct 1899: Commandant of Bobruysk
14 Nov 1894: Promoted to *Lieutenant-General*

*General of Infantry* Alfons Ivanovich **Bush** (13 Sep 1842 - ?)
26 Dec 1892: Promoted to *Major-General*
26 Dec 1892 - 27 Apr 1900: Commander, 1st Brigade, 16th Infantry Division
27 Apr 1900 - 10 Jan 1904: Commander, 34th Infantry Division
6 Dec 1900: Promoted to *Lieutenant-General*
10 Jan 1904: Promoted to *General of Infantry*
10 Jan 1904: Retired

*Major-General* Ferdinand Yulyevich **Bush** (4 Sep 1866 - ?)
27 Nov 1915 - 2 Feb 1916: Commander, 1st Brigade, 8th Cavalry Division
2 Feb 1916 - 1917: Commander, 2nd Brigade, 8th Cavalry Division
17 Sep 1916: Promoted to *Major-General*

*Major-General* Ivan Danilovich **Buslavsky** (24 Jun 1846 - ?)
13 Nov 1902: Promoted to *Major-General*
13 Nov 1902 - 1 Jul 1906: Commander, 2nd Brigade, 21st Infantry Division

*Lieutenant-General* Konstantin Ivanovich **Bussov** (21 May 1855 - ?)
6 Jul 1907: Promoted to *Major-General*
6 Jul 1907 - 16 Jul 1913: Commander, 1st Brigade, 6th Infantry Division
16 Jul 1913: Promoted to *Lieutenant-General*
16 Jul 1913: Retired
2 Jan 1916 - 29 May 1916: Recalled; Commander, Brigade, 7th Infantry Division
29 May 1916 - 1917: Commander, 29th Reserve Brigade

*Major-General* Pyotr Fedotovich **Busygin** (6 Oct 1844 - ?)
22 Mar 1894 - 1905: Senior Artillery Inspector, Main Artillery Directorate
6 Dec 1903: Promoted to *Major-General*

*Major-General* Avgustin-Feofil Iosifovich **But-Gusainov** (7 Sep 1857 - ?)
21 Feb 1906 - 1908: Commander, 226th Reserve Infantry Regiment
1908: Promoted to *Major-General*

*Rear-Admiral* Aleksandr Grigoryevich **Butakov** (25 Jun 1861 - 1 Mar 1917)
6 Nov 1913 - 1 Mar 1917: Chief of Staff, Port of Kronstadt
6 Dec 1913: Promoted to *Rear-Admiral*

*General of Infantry* Aleksandr Mikhailovich **Butakov** (22 Jun 1851 - 7 Jul 1936)
18 Aug 1899: Promoted to *Major-General*
18 Aug 1899 - 7 Feb 1901: Commander, St. Petersburg Life Guards Regiment
22 Mar 1901 - 7 Dec 1904: Commander, 2nd Brigade, 3rd Guards Infantry Division
7 Dec 1904 - 30 Dec 1913: Commander, 7th Infantry Division
6 Dec 1906: Promoted to *Lieutenant-General*
30 Dec 1913: Promoted to *General of Infantry*
30 Dec 1913: Retired

*Rear-Admiral* Aleksey Grigoryevich **Butakov** (4 Sep 1862 - 1921)
28 Jul 1914: Promoted to *Rear-Admiral*
1914 - Sep 1916: Commandant, Port of Petrograd
Sep 1916 - 1917: Attached to the Minister of the Navy
1917: Retired

*Lieutenant-General* Mikhail Mikhailovich **Butchik** (2 Jul 1868 - 8 Apr 1922)
15 Apr 1915: Promoted to *Major-General*
15 Apr 1915 - 4 Dec 1915: Chief of Staff, XVII. Army Corps
4 Dec 1915 - 11 Mar 1917: Chief of Staff, XL. Army Corps
11 Mar 1917 - 9 Sep 1917: Commander, 6th Rifle Division
9 Sep 1917 - 22 Oct 1917: Commanding General, XXVIII. Army Corps
12 Oct 1917: Promoted to *Lieutenant-General*
22 Oct 1917 - 1918: Commanding General, XV. Army Corps

*Lieutenant-General* Semyon Ivanovich **Butenko** (30 Aug 1831 - 1 Jul 1896)
27 Jan 1883 - 15 Nov 1884: Commander, 87th Infantry Regiment
15 May 1883: Promoted to *Major-General*
15 Nov 1884 - 1 Jun 1888: Commander, 2nd Brigade, 9th Infantry Division
1 Jun 1888 - 4 Jun 1892: Commander, 2nd Brigade, 22nd Infantry Division
4 Jun 1892 - Jul 1895: Commander, 1st Brigade, 22nd Infantry Division
Jul 1895: Promoted to *Lieutenant-General*
Jul 1895: Retired

*Lieutenant-General* Ivan Andrianovich **Butkevich** (29 Aug 1840 - 1913)
9 Jul 1878 - 1913: Member of the Artillery Committee, Main Artillery Directorate
30 Aug 1888: Promoted to *Major-General*
6 Dec 1898: Promoted to *Lieutenant-General*

*Major-General* Fyodor Vasilyevich **Butkov** (8 Jun 1856 - Feb 1916)
| | |
|---|---|
| 25 Mar 1905 - 26 Apr 1913: | Commander, 9<sup>th</sup> Grenadier Regiment |
| 14 Apr 1913: | Promoted to *Major-General* |
| 26 Apr 1913 - 2 May 1913: | Commander, 1<sup>st</sup> Brigade, 39<sup>th</sup> Infantry Division |
| 2 May 1913 - 31 Jul 1915: | Commander, 1<sup>st</sup> Brigade, 10<sup>th</sup> Infantry Division |
| 31 Jul 1915 - Feb 1916: | Reserve officer, Dvinsk Military District |

*Major-General of Naval Engineers* Bronislav-Stanislav Fyodor Lvovich **Butler** (5 Oct 1866 - 1930)
| | |
|---|---|
| 21 Mar 1911 - 28 Sep 1915: | Chief Civil Engineer, Port of Sevastopol |
| 14 Apr 1913: | Promoted to *Major-General of Naval Engineers* |
| 28 Sep 1915 - 22 Aug 1917: | Chief Civil Engineer, Port of Petrograd |
| 22 Aug 1917 - Oct 1917: | Member of Port Commission, Main Shipbuilding Directorate |

*Lieutenant-General* Baron Ivan Reyngoldovich von **Butler** (28 Dec 1847 - 1921)
| | |
|---|---|
| 8 Dec 1892 - 29 Dec 1899: | Commander, 1<sup>st</sup> Caucasus Artillery Training Polygon |
| 6 Dec 1899: | Promoted to *Major-General* |
| 29 Dec 1899 - 14 Oct 1903: | Commander, 4<sup>th</sup> Reserve Artillery Brigade |
| 14 Oct 1903 - 1907: | Commander of Artillery, XI. Army Corps |
| 6 Dec 1906: | Promoted to *Lieutenant-General* |
| 1907: | Retired |

*Major-General* Mikhail Ilich **Butovich** (11 Sep 1829 - ?)
| | |
|---|---|
| 30 Jul 1888: | Promoted to *Major-General* |
| 30 Jul 1888 - Apr 1897: | Commander, 7<sup>th</sup> Artillery Brigade |

*Lieutenant-General* Vasily Vasilievich **Butovich** (5 Feb 1864 - ?)
| | |
|---|---|
| 18 Feb 1908 - 29 Jul 1909: | Commander, 3<sup>rd</sup> Grenadier Regiment |
| 29 Jul 1909: | Promoted to *Major-General* |
| 29 Jul 1909 - 20 Dec 1914: | Commander, Life Guards Grenadier Regiment |
| 20 Dec 1914 - 2 May 1915: | Reserve officer, Petrograd Military District |
| 2 May 1915 - 26 Jun 1915: | Reserve officer, 6<sup>th</sup> Army |
| 26 Jun 1915 - 7 Apr 1917: | Commander, 83<sup>rd</sup> Infantry Division |
| 10 Apr 1916: | Promoted to *Lieutenant-General* |
| 7 Apr 1917 - 10 Aug 1917: | Unassigned |
| 10 Aug 1917: | Retired |

*General of Infantry* Aleksey Dmitriyevich **Butovsky** (9 Jun 1838 - 25 Feb 1917)
| | |
|---|---|
| 9 Apr 1890 - 4 Mar 1910: | Special Purposes General, Main Directorate for Military Schools |
| 8 Oct 1891: | Promoted to *Major-General* |
| 4 Mar 1910 - 25 Feb 1917: | Special Purposes General, Inspector-General of Military Schools |
| 28 Mar 1904: | Promoted to *Lieutenant-General* |
| 1915: | Promoted to *General of Infantry* (with seniority of 16 Jun 1916) |

*General of Infantry* Nikolai Dmitrievich **Butovsky** (20 Jan 1850 - 25 Feb 1917)
| | |
|---|---|
| 10 Sep 1900: | Promoted to *Major-General* |
| 10 Sep 1900 - 22 Feb 1901: | Commander, 2nd Brigade, 27th Infantry Division |
| 22 Feb 1901 - 16 Jun 1904: | Commander, 2nd Brigade, 29th Infantry Division |
| 16 Jun 1904 - 22 Mar 1907: | Commander, 2nd Turkestan Reserve Brigade |
| 22 Mar 1907 - 21 Jul 1910: | Commander, 7th East Siberian Rifle Division |
| 22 Apr 1907: | Promoted to *Lieutenant-General* |
| 21 Jul 1910 - 25 Mar 1911: | Commander, 32nd Infantry Division |
| 25 Mar 1911: | Promoted to *General of Infantry* |
| 25 Mar 1911: | Retired |

*General of Infantry* Dmitry Sergeyevich **Buturlin** (3 Feb 1850 - 12 May 1920)
| | |
|---|---|
| 25 May 1895: | Promoted to *Major-General* |
| 25 May 1895 - 26 Feb 1898: | Special Assignments General, Vilnius Military District |
| 26 Feb 1898 - 4 Jun 1899: | Commander, 2nd Brigade, 27th Infantry Division |
| 4 Jun 1899 - 24 Oct 1899: | Commander, 1st Brigade, 3rd Grenadier Division |
| 24 Oct 1899 - 27 Sep 1903: | Commander, 61st Reserve Infantry Brigade |
| 27 Sep 1903 - 17 Feb 1907: | Commander, 26th Infantry Division |
| 6 Dec 1903: | Promoted to *Lieutenant-General* |
| 17 Feb 1907: | Promoted to *General of Infantry* |
| 17 Feb 1907: | Retired |

*General of Infantry* Sergey Sergeyevich **Buturlin** (18 Sep 1842 - 1920)
| | |
|---|---|
| 4 Oct 1884 - 12 Dec 1890: | Military Attaché, London |
| 30 Aug 1886: | Promoted to *Major-General* |
| 12 Dec 1890 - 22 Apr 1892: | Commander, 2nd Brigade, 26th Infantry Division |
| 22 Apr 1892 - 9 Jul 1898: | Special Assignments General, Moscow Military District |
| 9 Jul 1898: | Promoted to *Lieutenant-General* |
| 9 Jul 1898 - Jun 1906: | Commander, 2nd Grenadier Division |
| Jun 1906: | Promoted to *General of Infantry* |
| Jun 1905: | Retired |

*Major-General* Sergey Nikolayevich **Butyrkin** (4 Dec 1874 - Jun 1924)
| | |
|---|---|
| 21 Feb 1915 - 1917: | Commandant, Konstantinov Artillery School |
| 1916: | Promoted to *Major-General* (with seniority of 26 Mar 1917) |

*Lieutenant-General* Yevgeny Vladimirovich **Buyakovich** (8 Mar 1848 - ?)
| | |
|---|---|
| 11 Aug 1900 - 20 Aug 1903: | Commander, 9th Artillery Brigade |
| 1 Jan 1901: | Promoted to *Major-General* |
| 20 Aug 1903 - 9 Jul 1906: | Deputy Commander of Artillery, Kiev Military District |
| 9 Jul 1906 - 5 Feb 1908: | Commander of Artillery, Kiev Military District |
| 6 Dec 1907: | Promoted to *Lieutenant-General* |

*Major-General* Vladimir Ivanovich **Buymistrov** (11 Dec 1868 - ?)
| | |
|---|---|
| 31 Oct 1914 - 4 Mar 1917: | Chief of Staff, XVI. Army Corps |
| 16 Nov 1914: | Promoted to *Major-General* |
| 4 Mar 1917 - 12 Jul 1917: | Commander, 160th Infantry Division |

12 Jul 1917: Transferred to the reserve, Kiev Military District

*Lieutenant-General* Nestor Aloiziyevich **Buynitsky** (23 Jan 1863 - 4 Dec 1914)
11 Dec 1904 - 22 Jul 1910: Professor, Nikolayev Engineering Academy
6 Dec 1906: Promoted to *Major-General*
18 Mar 1909 - Oct 1914: Member of the Technical Committee, Main Military Technical Directorate
31 May 1913: Promoted to *Lieutenant-General*
Oct 1914 - 4 Dec 1914: Chief of Engineering Logistics, Northwestern Front

*Major-General* Rafail Vikentyevich **Buyvid** (24 Oct 1862 - ?)
14 Dec 1916 - 30 Apr 1917: Commander, Brigade, 137th Infantry Division
9 Feb 1917: Promoted to *Major-General*
30 Apr 1917 - 30 Sep 1917: Commander, 181st Infantry Division
30 Sep 1917: Transferred to the reserve, Minsk Military District

*Lieutenant-General of the Hydrographic Corps* Yevgeny Lyudvigovich **Byalokoz** (25 Jul 1861 - 1919)
14 Jan 1908 - 10 Apr 1916: Chief of Hydrographic Expedition, Baltic Sea
25 Mar 1912: Promoted to *Major-General of the Admiralty*
4 Feb 1913: Redesignated *Major-General of the Hydrographic Corps*
10 Apr 1916: Promoted to *Lieutenant-General of the Hydrographic Corps*
Feb 1917 - 1919: Chief of the Hydrographic Department, Ministry of the Navy

*Major-General* Ivan Yegorovich **Bychinsky** (19 Oct 1849 - 5 Dec 1919)
12 Jul 1908: Promoted to *Major-General*
12 Jul 1908 - 20 Jul 1910: Commander, 1st Brigade, 33rd Infantry Division
20 Jul 1910: Retired
22 Jun 1916 - 1917: Recalled; Commander, 44th Replacement Infantry Brigade

*Major-General* Aleksandr Mikhailovich **Bykov** (11 Apr 1858 - ?)
26 May 1911: Promoted to *Major-General*
26 May 1911 - 4 Nov 1911: Commander, 1st Brigade, 19th Infantry Division
4 Nov 1911 - 4 Jun 1913: Commander, 1st Brigade, 51st Infantry Division

*Lieutenant-General* Aleksandr Nikolayevich **Bykov** (1 Aug 1845 - ?)
4 Apr 1900: Promoted to *Major-General*
4 Apr 1900 - 16 Sep 1902: Commander, 2nd Brigade, 18th Infantry Division
16 Sep 1902 - 5 Feb 1904: Commander, 2nd Brigade, 16th Infantry Division
5 Feb 1904: Promoted to *Lieutenant-General*
5 Feb 1904: Retired

*Major-General* Leonid Nikolayevich **Bykov** (16 Apr 1865 - 1937)
28 Sep 1913 - 18 Dec 1914: Commander, 1st Brigade, 6th Siberian Rifle Division

22 Mar 1914: Promoted to *Major-General*
18 Dec 1914 - 1918: POW, Germany

*Major-General* Boleslav-Aurelian Boleslavovich **Bylchinsky** (14 Sep 1867 - 25 Jan 1918)
5 Apr 1915 - 1917: Inspector of Classes, Alekseyev Engineering College
6 Dec 1915: Promoted to *Major-General*

*Major-General* Pavel Boleslavovich **Bylchinsky** (26 Mar 1862 - ?)
11 Oct 1906 - 1912: Chief of Zhitomir Engineering Center
1912: Promoted to *Major-General*
1912: Retired
5 Aug 1915 - 1917: Recalled; Vice-Chairman, Commission for the Construction of Pipe-Manufacturing Plants

*Major-General* Faddey Sigizmundovich **Bylevsky** (21 Jul 1866 - 17 Jul 1939)
24 Dec 1907 - 1913: Attached to Life Guards St. Petersburg Regiment
1913: Promoted to *Major-General*
1913: Retired
1916 - 8 Feb 1917: Recalled; Commander, 26$^{th}$ Militia Brigade
8 Feb 1917 - 10 Apr 1917: Commander, Polish Rifle Division
10 Apr 1917 - 1918: Chairman of the Military Committee for the Formation of Polish Units

*Major-General* Semyon Petrovich **Bylim-Kolosovsky** (2 Feb 1857 - ?)
27 Sep 1913: Promoted to *Major-General*
27 Sep 1913 - 3 Aug 1914: Commander, 1$^{st}$ Brigade, 10$^{th}$ Siberian Rifle Division
3 Aug 1914 - 25 Jun 1916: Commander, 1$^{st}$ Brigade, 14$^{th}$ Siberian Rifle Division
25 Jun 1916 - 1917: Commander, 118$^{th}$ Infantry Division

*Major-General* Mikhail Ivanovich **Bylinsky** (8 Nov 1873 - 24 Jan 1917)
22 May 1916 - 24 Jan 1917: Commander, 150$^{th}$ Infantry Regiment
4 Apr 1917: Posthumously promoted to *Major-General*

*Major-General* Pavel Ilyich **Byrdin** (28 Jul 1847 - 18 Apr 1912)
31 Mar 1899 - 1907: Commander, Transbaikal Gendarmerie Branch, Siberian Railway
1907: Promoted to *Major-General*
1907: Retired

*Major-General* Sergey Dmitriyevich **Bystreyevsky** (21 Apr 1866 - 1926)
20 May 1905 - 10 Aug 1914: Inspector of Classes, 2$^{nd}$ Emperor Peter the Great Cadet Corps
31 May 1907: Promoted to *Major-General*
10 Aug 1914 - 13 Jul 1917: Director, 2$^{nd}$ Moscow Cadet Corps
13 Jul 1917 - 1918: Deputy Chief, Main Directorate for Military Schools

*Major-General* Pyotr Mikhailovich **Bystritsky** (19 Jun 1866 - ?)
20 May 1910 - 4 Jun 1912: Military Judge, Irkutsk Military District Court

6 Dec 1911: Promoted to *Major-General*
4 Jun 1912 - 1917: Military Judge, Kiev Military District Court

*Major-General* Aleksei Georgievich von **Byunting** (11 Feb 1866 - 6 Feb 1930)
4 Oct 1911 - 18 Aug 1912: Commander, Life Guards Hussar Regiment
18 Aug 1912 - 2 Dec 1914: Commander, 2nd Brigade, 15th Cavalry Division
30 Aug 1912: Promoted to *Major-General*
2 Dec 1914 - 29 Jul 1915: Commander, 2nd Brigade, 14th Cavalry Division
29 Jul 1915 - 12 Sep 1915: Commander, 15th Cavalry Division
12 Sep 1915 - 1917: Reserve officer, Kiev Military District

*Lieutenant-General of the Admiralty* Anton Pavlovich **Chabovsky** (1 Apr 1857 - ?)
14 Jan 1908 - Jul 1913: Commandant of the Machinery School, Black Sea Fleet
10 Apr 1911: Promoted to *Major-General of the Admiralty*
Jul 1913: Promoted to *Lieutenant -General of the Admiralty*
Jul 1913: Retired

*Rear-Admiral* Ivan Ivanovich **Chagin** (12 Nov 1860 - 12 Oct 1912)
7 Nov 1905 - 12 Oct 1912: Commander, Imperial Yacht "*Standart*"
29 Mar 1909: Promoted to *Rear-Admiral*

*General of Artillery* Nikolai Ivanovich **Chagin** (7 May 1831 - 13 Apr 1915)
18 May 1875 - 1903: Permanent Member of the Artillery Committee, Main Artillery Directorate
30 Aug 1875: Promoted to *Major-General*
30 Aug 1885: Promoted to *Lieutenant-General*
1903: Promoted to *General of Artillery*
1903: Retired

*Lieutenant-General* Vladimir Aleksandrovich **Chagin** (15 Aug 1862 - 25 Dec 1936)
9 Jul 1908: Promoted to *Major-General*
9 Jul 1908 - 19 Oct 1914: Chief of Staff, III. Army Corps
19 Oct 1914 - 4 Dec 1914: Chief of Staff, 2nd Army
4 Dec 1914 - 30 Oct 1915: Commander, 6th Siberian Rifle Division
28 Sep 1915: Promoted to *Lieutenant-General*
30 Oct 1915 - 10 Oct 1917: Commander, 41st Infantry Division
10 Oct 1917 - 1917: Reserve officer, Odessa Military District
1917 - 1918: Commanding General, XVI. Army Corps

*Lieutenant-General of Naval Engineers* Stepan Zakharovich **Chakhlin** (28 Nov 1862 - ?)
1909 - 1917: Deputy Chief of Mechanical Engineers, Black Sea Fleet
6 Dec 1911: Promoted to *Major-General of Naval Engineers*
10 Apr 1916: Promoted to *Lieutenant-General of Naval Engineers*

*Lieutenant-General* Ivan Nikolayevich **Chaleyev** (26 Jan 1826 - 20 May 1896)
17 Oct 1867 - 30 Dec 1890: Chief of Gendarmerie, Kostroma
5 Apr 1887: Promoted to *Major-General*
30 Dec 1890 - 20 Jul 1893: Chief of Gendarmerie, Tula

20 Jul 1893 - 20 May 1896: Chief of Gendarmerie, Ryazan
1896: Promoted to *Lieutenant-General*

*Major-General* Shaykhil-Islam-Mukhammed Gireyevich **Chanyshev** (23 Nov 1853 - ?)
15 Jan 1909: Promoted to *Major-General*
15 Jan 1909 - 7 Apr 1911: Commander, 1st Brigade, 8th Infantry Division

*Major-General* Pavel Moiseyevich **Chaplin** (1849 - Apr 1900)
Sep 1899 - Apr 1900: Commander, 17th Artillery Brigade
29 Dec 1899: Promoted to *Major-General*

*Major-General* Sergey Mikhailovich **Chaplin** (27 Sep 1864 - ?)
? - 1917: Section Chief, Main Artillery Directorate
6 Dec 1914: Promoted to *Major-General*

*Major-General* Viktor Viktorovich **Chaplin** (15 Mar 1862 - ?)
6 Jul 1910 - 7 May 1916: Commander, 1st Caucasus Rifle Regiment
31 Dec 1914: Promoted to *Major-General*
7 May 1916 - 10 Aug 1916: Reserve officer, Petrograd Military District
10 Aug 1916 - 10 Oct 1917: Commander, Brigade, 14th Siberian Rifle Division
10 Oct 1917 - 1918: Commander, 14th Siberian Rifle Division

*Major-General* Zenon Afanasyevich **Chaplinsky** (23 Jul 1858 - ?)
9 Mar 1914 - 23 Jun 1916: Commander, 8th Caucasus Rifle Regiment
23 Jun 1916 - 1917: Reserve officer, Caucasus Military District
25 Aug 1916: Promoted to *Major-General*

*Lieutenant-General* Aleksandr Ivanovich **Chaplygin** (13 Dec 1858 - ?)
14 Feb 1907 - 14 Oct 1911: Commander, 1st Life Grenadier Regiment
14 Oct 1911: Promoted to *Major-General*
14 Oct 1911 - 31 Dec 1913: Commander, 1st Brigade, 3rd Grenadier Division
31 Dec 1913 - 3 May 1914: Commander, 1st Brigade, 2nd Grenadier Division
3 May 1914 - 19 Nov 1915: Commander, 5th Turkestan Rifle Brigade
19 Nov 1915 - 25 Apr 1917: Commander, 5th Turkestan Rifle Division
8 Sep 1916: Promoted to *Lieutenant-General*
25 Apr 1917 - 12 Oct 1917: Commanding General, II. Turkestan Army Corps
12 Oct 1917 - 1918: Reserve officer, Caucasus Military District

*Major-General* Arseny Ivanovich **Chaplygin** (23 Mar 1860 - 16 Aug 1932)
25 Jul 1914 - 6 Aug 1917: Commander, 65th Artillery Brigade
28 Oct 1914: Promoted to *Major-General*
6 Aug 1917 - 1918: Inspector of Artillery, XXVI. Army Corps

*Major-General* Pyotr Vladimirovich **Charkovsky** (15 Apr 1845 - ?)
3 Jul 1888 - 1 Mar 1893: Chief of Military Staff, Kuban Cossack Army
30 Aug 1890: Promoted to *Major-General*
1 Mar 1893 - 12 Sep 1897: Commander, 1st Brigade, 2nd Caucasus Cossack Division

12 Sep 1897 - 2 Mar 1899: Commander, 4th Cavalry Division
2 Mar 1899 - 1899: Unassigned

*Major-General* Ivan Grigoryevich **Charnolussky** (29 Aug 1849 - ?)
29 May 1899 - 1905: Commander of Gendarmerie, Bessarabia
6 Dec 1903: Promoted to *Major-General*

*Major-General* Friedrich Wilhelm **Charpentier** (23 Nov 1849 - 25 May 1918)
13 Aug 1908 - 25 Sep 1910: Commander, 3rd Eastern Siberian Rifle Regiment
25 Sep 1910: Promoted to *Major-General*
25 Sep 1910: Retired

*Lieutenant-General* Klaas Gustav Robert Robertovich **Charpentier** (8 Nov 1858 - 18 Dec 1918)
24 Jan 1904 - 9 Jun 1907: Commander, Life Guards Grodno Hussar Regiment
6 Dec 1904: Promoted to *Major-General*
9 Jun 1907 - 22 Dec 1910: Commander, Independent Guards Cavalry Brigade
22 Dec 1910: Promoted to *Lieutenant-General*
22 Dec 1910 - 29 Dec 1915: Commander, Caucasus Cavalry Division
29 Dec 1915 - 1917: At the disposal of the C-in-C, Caucasus Army

*General of Artillery* Aleksandr Vasilyevich **Chartoriysky** (8 Sep 1855 - 1 Mar 1917)
23 Aug 1897 - 2 Oct 1902: Section Chief, Main Military Justice Directorate
9 Apr 1900: Promoted to *Major-General*
2 Oct 1902 - 3 Sep 1914: At the disposal of Grand Duke Mikhail Aleksandrovich
2 Apr 1906: Promoted to *Lieutenant-General*
3 Sep 1914 - 1 Mar 1917: Senator
6 Dec 1914: Promoted to *General of Artillery*

*Major-General* Nikolai Dmitriyevich **Chausov** (15 May 1860 - ?)
6 Nov 1912 - 1915: Commander, 31st Siberian Rifle Regiment
31 Dec 1914: Promoted to *Major-General*
1915 - 18 Jul 1915: Commander, Brigade, 8th Siberian Rifle Division
18 Jul 1915 - 7 Feb 1917: Chief of Staff, III. Army Corps
7 Feb 1917 - 28 Apr 1917: Commander, 171st Infantry Division
28 Apr 1917 - 1918: Reserve officer, Minsk Military District

*Major-General* Prince Archil Gulbatovich **Chavchavadze** (13 Mar 1841 - 27 Jun 1902)
2 Oct 1889 - 24 Dec 1896: Commander, 45th Dragoon Regiment
24 Dec 1896: Promoted to *Major-General*
24 Dec 1896 - 5 Jun 1902: Commander, 2nd Brigade, 9th Cavalry Division

*General of Cavalry* Prince Nikolai Zurabovich **Chavchavadze** (22 Oct 1830 - 9 Mar 1897)
10 Dec 1866 - 25 Oct 1876: Military Commander, Dagestan
30 Aug 1869: Promoted to *Major-General*
25 Oct 1876 - 3 Jun 1877: General à la suite
3 Jun 1877 - 7 Jul 1877: Commander, Caucasus-Turkestan Consolidated Cavalry Division

| | |
|---|---|
| 7 Jul 1877 - 1 Jul 1883: | Commander, Dagestan Region |
| 30 Aug 1881: | Promoted to *Lieutenant-General* |
| 1 Jul 1883 - 9 Mar 1896: | Military Governor of Dagestan |
| 9 Mar 1896 - 9 Mar 1897: | Member, Committee for Wounded Veterans |
| 14 May 1896: | Promoted to *General of Cavalry* |

*General of Cavalry* Prince Zakhar Gulbatovich **Chavchavadze** (5 Oct 1825 - 22 Oct 1905)

| | |
|---|---|
| 26 Nov 1871: | Promoted to *Major-General* |
| 26 Nov 1871 - 16 Mar 1878: | Commander, 2nd Brigade, Caucasus Cavalry Division |
| 19 Apr 1877: | Promoted to *Lieutenant-General* |
| 13 Jul 1877 - 16 Mar 1878: | Commander, Separate Cavalry Detachment |
| 16 Mar 1878 - 21 Jan 1879: | Commander, 2nd Consolidated Caucasus Cavalry Division |
| 21 Jan 1879 - 10 Apr 1883: | Commander, 1st Caucasus Cavalry Division |
| 10 Apr 1883 - 3 Nov 1885: | Commander, Caucasus Cavalry Division |
| 3 Nov 1885 - 16 Jan 1893: | Commanding General, I. Caucasus Army Corps |
| 30 Aug 1891: | Promoted to *General of Cavalry* |
| 16 Jan 1893 - 22 Oct 1905: | Member, Committee for Wounded Veterans |
| 1898: | Promoted to *General-Adjutant* |

*General of Infantry* Andrey Petrovich **Chaykovsky** (15 Aug 1841 - 1920)

| | |
|---|---|
| 27 Oct 1884 - 4 Dec 1895: | Commander, 98th Infantry Regiment |
| 14 Nov 1894: | Promoted to *Major-General* |
| 4 Dec 1895 - 6 Nov 1897: | Commander, 1st Brigade, 28th Infantry Division |
| 6 Nov 1897 - 4 Jul 1898: | Commander, Trans-Caspian Rifle Brigade |
| 4 Jul 1898 - 20 May 1901: | Military Governor, Ferghana Region |
| 6 Dec 1900: | Promoted to *Lieutenant-General* |
| 20 May 1901 - 12 Feb 1903: | Commander, 12th Infantry Division |
| 12 Feb 1903 - 20 Dec 1903: | Deputy Governor-General of Amur |
| 20 Dec 1903: | Promoted to *General of Infantry* |
| 20 Dec 1903: | Retired |

*General of Infantry* Mitrofan Petrovich **Chaykovsky** (7 Apr 1840 - 25 Mar 1903)

| | |
|---|---|
| 28 Mar 1879 - 24 Mar 1881: | Commander, 4th Grenadier Regiment |
| 23 Sep 1879: | Promoted to *Major-General* |
| 24 Mar 1881 - 2 Sep 1882: | Commander, 2nd Brigade, 39th Infantry Division |
| 2 Sep 1882 - 2 Aug 1884: | Commander, 1st Brigade, Caucasus Grenadier Division |
| 2 Aug 1884 - 22 Feb 1889: | Chief of Staff, VI. Army Corps |
| 22 Feb 1889 - 28 Nov 1889: | Deputy Chief of Staff, Kiev Military District |
| 28 Nov 1889 - 22 Jun 1891: | Commander, 2nd Rifle Brigade |
| 30 Aug 1890: | Promoted to *Lieutenant-General* |
| 22 Jun 1891 - 13 Jun 1899: | Commandant of Fortress Ivangorod |
| 13 Jun 1899 - 25 Mar 1903: | Commanding General, III. Army Corps |
| 6 Dec 1900: | Promoted to *General of Infantry* |

*Major-General* Nikolai Ivanovich **Chaykovsky** (30 Jul 1857 - ?)

| | |
|---|---|
| 22 Jan 1907 - 21 May 1912: | Commander, 6th Uhlan Regiment |
| 21 May 1912: | Promoted to *Major-General* |

21 May 1912 - 2 Aug 1914: Commander, 1st Brigade, 14th Cavalry Division
2 Aug 1914 - 11 Aug 1914: Commander, Brigade, 1st Kuban Cossack Division
11 Aug 1914 - 7 Sep 1914: Commander, Brigade, 2nd Kuban Cossack Division
7 Sep 1914 - 28 Jan 1915: Commander, 1st Brigade, 14th Cavalry Division
28 Jan 1915 - 29 Jul 1915: Commander, 5th Cavalry Division
29 Jul 1915 - 13 Mar 1916: Unassigned
13 Mar 1916 - 22 Apr 1917: Commander, 13th Cavalry Division
22 Apr 1917 - Oct 1917: Reserve officer, Kiev Military District

*Major-General* Porfiry Grigoryevich **Chebotarev** (25 Feb 1873 - 10 Feb 1920)
19 Jul 1914 - Aug 1915: Commander, 58th Artillery Brigade
18 Apr 1915: Promoted to *Major-General*
1915: Acting Commander, 58th Infantry Division
Aug 1915 - 1918: POW

*Lieutenant-General* Aleksandr Nestorovich **Chebykin** (6 Feb 1857 - 1920)
17 Nov 1907: Promoted to *Major-General*
17 Nov 1907 - 24 Sep 1913: Commander, Life Guards 3rd Rifle Regiment
24 Sep 1913 - 24 Dec 1913: Commander, 1st Brigade, 2nd Guards Infantry Division
24 Dec 1913 - 29 Jul 1914: General à la suite
29 Jul 1914 - 9 Jun 1916: Commander, Guards Replacement Infantry Brigade
10 Apr 1916: Promoted to *Lieutenant-General*
9 Jun 1916 - 9 Jan 1917: Commander of Guards and Reserve Battalions for the defense of Petrograd
9 Jan 1917 - 12 May 1917: Unassigned
12 May 1917: Retired

*Major-General* Vladimir Nikolayevich **Chebyshev** (18 Jan 1853 - ?)
23 Dec 1882 - 1907: Manager, Limarevsk State Horse Farm
28 Mar 1904: Promoted to *Major-General*
1907: Retired
8 Aug 1916 - 1917: Recalled; Reserve officer, Caucasus Military District

*Lieutenant-General* Sergey Mikhailovich **Chechurin** (26 Jul 1855 - 26 Aug 1914)
3 Feb 1903: Promoted to *Major-General*
3 Feb 1903 - 17 Jul 1906: Duty General, St. Petersburg Military District
17 Jul 1906 - 28 Mar 1910: Commander, St. Petersburg Regional Brigade
6 Dec 1909: Promoted to *Lieutenant-General*
28 Mar 1910: Retired

*Major-General* Mikhail Petrovich **Cheglov** (26 Sep 1876 - 4 Aug 1931)
22 Jan 1915 - 2 May 1916: Commander, 27th Infantry Regiment
8 Mar 1916: Promoted to *Major-General*
2 May 1916 - 31 Aug 1916: Chief of Staff, 27th Infantry Division
31 Aug 1916 - 1917: Chief of Staff, 55th Infantry Division
1917: Commander, 55th Infantry Division
1917 - 5 Sep 1917: Quartermaster-General, Special Army
5 Sep 1917 - 1918: Commander, 122nd Infantry Division

*Lieutenant-General* Kazimir Ivanovich **Chekhovich** (1 Mar 1847 - ?)
12 Nov 1893 - 30 Jan 1904: General for Assignments, Commanding General, Borderguard Corps
1 Apr 1901: Promoted to *Major-General*
30 Jan 1904 - 26 May 1906: Commander, 7th Borderguard District
26 May 1906 - 1909: Commander, 5th Borderguard District
6 Dec 1906: Promoted to *Lieutenant-General*

*Major-General* Antony-Foma Nikiforovich **Chekhovsky** (13 Jul 1859 - 1917)
29 Jun 1915 - 19 Oct 1916: Commander, 15th Finnish Rifle Regiment
22 Sep 1916: Promoted to *Major-General*
19 Oct 1916 - 1917: Deputy Commander, 42nd Replacement Infantry Brigade

*Lieutenant-General* Andrey Ivanovich **Chekmarev** (13 Dec 1844 - 23 Oct 1904)
22 Nov 1893: Promoted to *Major-General*
22 Nov 1893 - 28 Nov 1895: Commander, Life Guards 1st Rifle Battalion
28 Nov 1895 - 25 Apr 1900: Commander, Life Guards Chasseur Regiment
21 May 1898 - 25 Apr 1900: Commander, 2nd Brigade, 1st Guards Infantry Division
25 Apr 1900 - 18 Dec 1900: Commander, 1st Brigade, 1st Guards Infantry Division
18 Dec 1900 - 18 Apr 1903: Commander, 43rd Infantry Division
6 Dec 1901: Promoted to *Lieutenant-General*
18 Apr 1903 - 23 Oct 1904: Commander, 37th Infantry Division

*Major-General* Konstantin Ivanovich **Chekmarev** (10 May 1846 - ?)
23 Jul 1898: Promoted to *Major-General*
23 Jul 1898 - 16 Mar 1904: Commander, 2nd Brigade, 6th Infantry Division

*Lieutenant-General* Viktor Ivanovich **Chekmarev** (8 Apr 1861 - 14 Oct 1939)
21 Apr 1903 - 30 Jul 1906: Commander, 5th Grenadier Regiment
30 Jul 1906: Promoted to *Major-General*
30 Jul 1906 - 13 Dec 1909: Chief of Staff, Fortress Brest-Litovsk
13 Dec 1909 - 9 Aug 1917: Commandant of Fortress Ochakov
6 Dec 1912: Promoted to *Lieutenant-General*
9 Aug 1917 - 1918: Reserve officer, Kiev Military District

*Major-General* Ignaty Mikhailovich **Chekster** (25 Nov 1842 - 16 Sep 1914)
12 Apr 1882 - 1908: Attached to Military Topographical Corps
1908: Promoted to *Major-General*
1908: Retired

*Lieutenant-General* Prince Bedzina Otarovich **Chelokayev** (8 Sep 1829 - ?)
30 Aug 1893: Promoted to *Major-General*
30 Aug 1893 - 1901: Special Purposes General, Caucasus Military District
6 Dec 1901: Promoted to *Lieutenant-General*

*Lieutenant-General* Prince Grigory Paatovich **Chelokayev** (1 Jan 1846 - ?)
25 Sep 1901 - 20 Feb 1904: Commander, 1st Ivangorod Fortress Infantry Regiment
20 Feb 1904: Promoted to *Major-General*

20 Feb 1904:                    Retired
10 Sep 1908 - 10 Jul 1916:      Recalled; Attached to the Ministry of War
10 Jul 1916 - 10 Jun 1917:      Chief of 37th Rear Evacuation Point
10 Jun 1917:                    Promoted to *Lieutenant-General*
10 Jun 1917:                    Retired

*Major-General* Mikhail Mikhailovich **Chelyustkin** (4 Feb 1866 - 6 Jun 1935)
23 Sep 1912 - 27 Jul 1916:      Commander, 2nd Battalion, 42nd Artillery Brigade
22 May 1916:                    Promoted to *Major-General*
27 Jul 1916 - 4 Dec 1917:       Commander, 48th Artillery Brigade
25 Aug 1917 - 31 Aug 1917:      Acting Commander, 48th Infantry Division

*Lieutenant-General* Nikolai Mikhailovich **Chelyustkin** (23 Jan 1855 - ?)
22 Oct 1908:                    Promoted to *Major-General*
22 Oct 1908 - 27 Aug 1913:      Commander, 28th Artillery Brigade
27 Aug 1913 - 4 Dec 1915:       Inspector of Artillery, X. Army Corps
6 Dec 1914:                     Promoted to *Lieutenant-General*
4 Dec 1915 - 1918:              Reserve officer, Petrograd Military District

*General of Engineers* Aleksandr Yakovlevich **Chemerzin** (28 Jun 1830 - 25 Jan 1916)
30 Aug 1873:                    Promoted to *Major-General*
30 Aug 1873 - 20 Mar 1874:      Attached to the Inspector-General of Engineers
20 Mar 1874 - 5 Jun 1881:       Deputy Commander of Engineers, St. Petersburg Military District
5 Jun 1881 - 19 Oct 1887:       Commander of Engineers, Kharkov Military District
15 May 1883:                    Promoted to *Lieutenant-General*
19 Oct 1887 - 5 Nov 1890:       Commandant of Fortress Bender
5 Nov 1890 - 31 Aug 1892:       Commander, 2nd Infantry Division
31 Aug 1892 - 17 Jun 1899:      Commandant of Fortress Kaunas
14 May 1896:                    Promoted to *General of Engineers*
17 Jun 1899 - 25 Jan 1916:      Member, Committee for Wounded Veterans

*General of Infantry* Aleksey Yakovlevich **Chemerzin** (29 Jan 1825 - 24 Aug 1902)
1 Oct 1869:                     Promoted to *Major-General*
1 Oct 1869 - 1 Jul 1875:        Deputy Chief of Staff, Kazan Military District
1 Jul 1875 - 16 Aug 1880:       Chief of Staff, Kazan Military District
30 Aug 1879:                    Promoted to *Lieutenant-General*
16 Aug 1880 - 25 Feb 1887:      Commander, 33rd Infantry Division
25 Feb 1887 - 22 Jan 1890:      Commandant of Kiev
22 Jan 1890 - 12 Feb 1891:      Commanding General, XVI. Army Corps
12 Feb 1891 - 11 Mar 1895:      Deputy Commanding General, Vilnius Military District
30 Aug 1893:                    Promoted to *General of Infantry*
11 Mar 1895 - 24 Aug 1902:      Member of the Military Council

*Lieutenant-General* Aleksandr Ivanovich **Chepurnov** (2 Sep 1820 - ?)
26 Apr 1875:                    Promoted to *Major-General*
26 Apr 1875 - 22 Mar 1884:      At the disposal of the Commanding General, Finland Military District

| | |
|---|---|
| 22 Mar 1884 - 1902: | Commandant of Helsingfors |
| 21 Mar 1888: | Promoted to *Lieutenant-General* |
| 1902: | Retired |

*Lieutenant-General* Grigory Fyodorovich **Chepurnov** (20 Nov 1853 - ?)
| | |
|---|---|
| 16 Jan 1909: | Promoted to *Major-General* |
| 16 Jan 1909 - 27 Apr 1910: | Commander, 41st Artillery Brigade |
| 27 Apr 1910 - 20 Nov 1913: | Commander, 25th Artillery Brigade |
| 20 Nov 1913: | Promoted to *Lieutenant-General* |
| 20 Nov 1913: | Retired |
| 16 Jan 1914 - 6 Nov 1914: | Recalled; At the disposal of the Minister of War |
| 6 Nov 1914 - 9 Feb 1915: | Inspector of Artillery, XV. Army Corps |
| 9 Feb 1915 - 29 Jun 1915: | Unassigned |
| 29 Jun 1915 - 1 Oct 1916: | Inspector of Artillery, XXXIV. Army Corps |
| 1 Oct 1916 - 1918: | Reserve officer, Petrograd Military District |

*Major-General* Sergey Ivanovich **Cherdyntsev** (16 Sep 1862 - ?)
| | |
|---|---|
| 7 May 1913 - 14 Aug 1916: | Head of Business, Mikhailovsky Artillery Academy |
| 6 Dec 1913: | Promoted to *Major-General* |
| 14 Aug 1916 - 1918: | Inspector, Technical Artillery Institutions, Main Artillery Directorate |

*Lieutenant-General* Nikolai Vladimirovich **Cheremisinov** (20 Feb 1835 - May 1899)
| | |
|---|---|
| 2 Mar 1887 - 11 Dec 1888: | Commander, 1st Brigade, 3rd Grenadier Division |
| 20 Mar 1887: | Promoted to *Major-General* |
| 11 Dec 1888 - 19 Apr 1896: | Chief of Staff, XVI. Army Corps |
| 19 Apr 1896 - May 1899: | Commander, 29th Infantry Division |
| 14 May 1896: | Promoted to *Lieutenant-General* |

*Major-General* Vladimir Aleksandrovich **Cheremisinov** (15 Aug 1861 - ?)
| | |
|---|---|
| 1915 - 27 Jan 1917: | Commander, 4th Amur Border Cavalry Regiment |
| 26 Sep 1916: | Promoted to *Major-General* |
| 27 Jan 1917 - 21 Sep 1917: | Commander, 1st Brigade, Amur Cavalry Division |
| 21 Sep 1917 - 1918: | Reserve officer, Kiev Military District |

*Major-General* Vladimir Mikhailovich **Cheremisinov** (12 Jul 1875 - ?)
| | |
|---|---|
| 24 Oct 1915 - 30 May 1916: | Deputy Quartermaster-General, 7th Army |
| 30 May 1916 - 1916: | Quartermaster-General, 11th Army |
| 1916 - 10 Dec 1916: | Quartermaster-General, Danube Army |
| 6 Dec 1916: | Promoted to *Major-General* |
| 10 Dec 1916 - 16 Sep 1917: | Quartermaster-General, Romanian Front |
| 16 Sep 1917 - 1918: | Commandant of Fortress Sevastopol |

*General of Infantry* Vladimir Andreyevich **Cheremisov** (9 May 1871 - ?)
| | |
|---|---|
| Jun 1914 - 1915: | Commander, 120th Infantry Regiment |
| 1 Dec 1914: | Promoted to *Major-General* |
| 1915 - 6 Feb 1916: | Quartermaster-General, 5th Army |
| 6 Feb 1916 - 12 Jul 1916: | Commander, Consolidated Brigade, 32nd Infantry |

| | |
|---|---|
| | Division |
| 12 Jul 1916 - 31 Mar 1917: | Special Purposes General, 7th Army |
| 31 Mar 1917 - 12 Apr 1917: | Commander, 159th Infantry Division |
| 12 Apr 1917 - 18 Jul 1917: | Commanding General, XII. Army Corps |
| 29 Apr 1917: | Promoted to *Lieutenant-General* |
| 11 Jul 1917 - 25 Jul 1917: | Acting C-in-C, 8th Army |
| 18 Jul 1917 - 25 Jul 1917: | Acting C-in-C, Southwestern Front |
| 2 Aug 1917 - 11 Aug 1917: | Unassigned |
| 11 Aug 1917: | Promoted to *General of Infantry* |
| 11 Aug 1917 - 9 Sep 1917: | C-in-C, 9th Army |
| 9 Sep 1917 - 14 Nov 1917: | C-in-C, Northern Front |
| 14 Nov 1917: | Dismissed |

*Major-General* Dmitry Sergeyevich **Cherepakhin-Ivashchenko** (22 Oct 1852 - 1910)
| | |
|---|---|
| 21 Feb 1905 - 1910: | Commander, 51st Infantry Regiment |
| 6 Dec 1909: | Promoted to *Major-General* |

*Lieutenant-General* Afanasy Vasilyevich **Cherepanov** (10 Feb 1858 - ?)
| | |
|---|---|
| 10 Apr 1911: | Promoted to *Major-General* |
| 10 Apr 1911 - 12 May 1917: | Attached to Prince A. P. Oldenburg |
| 12 May 1917: | Promoted to *Lieutenant-General* |
| 12 May 1917: | Retired |

*Major-General* Aleksey Ivanovich **Cherepennikov** (28 Jun 1869 - 26 Oct 1937)
| | |
|---|---|
| 4 Nov 1911 - Feb 1915: | Commander, 8th Grenadier Regiment |
| 14 Jan 1915: | Promoted to *Major-General* |
| Feb 1915 - 31 May 1915: | Special Assignments General, 5th Army |
| 31 May 1915 - 5 Oct 1915: | Duty General, 5th Army |
| 5 Oct 1915 - 20 Apr 1916: | Duty General, 6th Army |
| 20 Apr 1916 - 20 Apr 1916: | Duty General, 12th Army |
| 20 Apr 1916 - 7 Apr 1917: | Chief of Staff, XXIII. Army Corps |
| 7 Apr 1917 - 1918: | Commander, 43rd Infantry Division |

*Lieutenant-General* Pyotr Aleksandrovich **Cherevin** (11 Oct 1837 - 19 Feb 1896)
| | |
|---|---|
| 24 May 1869 - 13 Aug 1878: | Commander of the Tsar's Convoy |
| 7 Oct 1877: | Promoted to *Major-General* |
| 13 Aug 1878 - 5 Oct 1878: | Unassigned |
| 5 Oct 1878 - 6 Aug 1880: | Deputy Chief of the Gendarmerie |
| Mar 1880 - 6 Aug 1880: | Acting Chief of the Gendarmerie |
| 6 Aug 1880 - 25 Dec 1881: | Deputy Minister of Internal Affairs |
| 25 Dec 1881 - 28 May 1894: | General à la suite |
| 1 Jan 1882: | Promoted to *General-Adjutant* |
| 30 Aug 1886: | Promoted to *Lieutenant-General* |
| 28 May 1894 - 19 Feb 1896: | Duty General to the Tsar |

*Major-General* Evfimy Makaryevich **Cherevko** (11 Mar 1841 - ?)
| | |
|---|---|
| 7 Mar 1900: | Promoted to *Major-General* |
| 7 Mar 1900 - 1904: | Commander, Orenburg Regional Brigade |

*Major-General* Vladimir Ivanovich **Cherkas** (4 Jul 1868 - ?)
24 Jun 1914 - 1917: Commander, 9th Sapper Battalion
22 Dec 1916: Promoted to *Major-General*

*Lieutenant-General* Petr Vladimirovich **Cherkasov** (24 Oct 1872 - ?)
2 Nov 1914 - 16 Mar 1916: Commander, 136th Infantry Regiment
6 Dec 1915: Promoted to *Major-General*
16 Mar 1916 - 19 Feb 1917: Chief of Staff, 113th Infantry Division
19 Feb 1917 - 12 Apr 1917: Chief of Staff, XLI. Army Corps
12 Apr 1917 - 22 Jul 1917: Commander, 19th Infantry Division
22 Jul 1917 - 7 Oct 1917: Commanding General, XII. Army Corps
23 Aug 1917: Promoted to *Lieutenant-General*
7 Oct 1917 - 1918: Reserve officer, Moscow Military District

*General of Cavalry* Vladimir Aleksandrovich **Cherkasov** (4 Feb 1842 - ?)
20 Jul 1893 - 6 Dec 1905: Commander of Gendarmerie, Vilnius Province
13 Apr 1897: Promoted to *Major-General*
6 Dec 1905: Promoted to *Lieutenant-General*
6 Dec 1905 - 11 Jan 1911: Commander of Gendarmerie, Moscow Province
11 Jan 1911: Promoted to *General of Cavalry*
11 Jan 1911: Retired

*General of Infantry* Pavel Platonovich **Cherkov** (1 Nov 1846 - ?)
31 Dec 1901 - 19 Oct 1907: Commander, 14th Grenadier Regiment
19 Oct 1907 - 22 Aug 1916: Commandant of Tiflis
6 Dec 1907: Promoted to *Major-General*
6 Dec 1913: Promoted to *Lieutenant-General*
22 Aug 1916: Retired
21 Dec 1916: Promoted to *General of Infantry*

*Major-General* Vladimir Aleksandrovich **Chermoyev** (23 Feb 1866 - ?)
8 Oct 1913 - 16 Sep 1915: Commander, 94th Infantry Regiment
23 Feb 1915: Promoted to *Major-General*
16 Sep 1915 - 7 Feb 1917: Commander, 1st Brigade, 67th Infantry Division
7 Feb 1917 - 6 Aug 1917: Commander, 170th Infantry Division
6 Aug 1917 - 1 Oct 1917: Reserve officer, Moscow Military District
1 Oct 1917 - 1918: Commander, 1st Grenadier Division

*Major-General* Vasily Leontyevich **Chernavin** (19 Jan 1848 - 1906)
26 Jan 1897 - 1903: Commander of Engineers, Fortress Kars
6 Dec 1899: Promoted to *Major-General*

*Lieutenant-General* Vsevolod Vladimirovich **Chernavin** (29 Jan 1859 - Aug 1938)
19 Mar 1904 - 19 Dec 1906: Commander, 7th Finnish Rifle Regiment
6 Dec 1906: Promoted to *Major-General*
19 Dec 1906 - 3 May 1910: Commander, Life Guards 4th Rifle Battalion
3 May 1910 - 19 Jul 1914: Commander, 2nd Brigade, 3rd Guards Infantry Division

| | |
|---|---|
| 19 Jul 1914 - 16 Sep 1914: | Commander, 58th Infantry Division |
| 16 Sep 1914 - 25 Aug 1917: | Commander, 3rd Guards Infantry Division |
| 30 Dec 1914: | Promoted to *Lieutenant-General* |
| 25 Aug 1917 - 1918: | Commanding General, II. Guards Corps |

*Major-General* Aleksandr Nikolayevich **Chernevsky** (9 Feb 1845 - ?)
| | |
|---|---|
| 4 Dec 1902 - 1906: | Deputy Military Governor of Samarkand |
| 6 Dec 1903: | Promoted to *Major-General* |

*Lieutenant-General* Vasily Ivanovich **Chernevsky** (7 Feb 1840 - ?)
| | |
|---|---|
| 14 Aug 1876 - 22 Mar 1892: | Military Judge, Warsaw Military District Court |
| 30 Aug 1886: | Promoted to *Major-General* |
| 22 Mar 1892 - 5 Apr 1899: | Military Judge, Odessa Military District Court |
| 5 Apr 1899 - 28 Mar 1908: | Military Judge, Kiev Military District Court |
| 28 Mar 1908 - 1914: | Military Judge, Vilnius Military District Court |
| 23 Oct 1910: | Promoted to *Lieutenant-General* |

*Lieutenant-General of Naval Shipbuilding* Pyotr Yevdokimovich **Chernigovsky** (15 Jan 1855 - 9 Jul 1910)
| | |
|---|---|
| Apr 1905 - 31 Dec 1907: | Deputy Chief Inspector of Naval Shipbuilding |
| 19 Mar 1907: | Promoted to *Major-General of Naval Shipbuilding* |
| 31 Dec 1907 - 6 Jul 1910: | Chief of Admiralty Shipyard |
| 6 Jul 1910: | Promoted to *Lieutenant-General of Naval Shipbuilding* |
| 6 Jul 1910: | Retired |

*Major-General* Georgy Prokofyevich **Chernik** (6 Jan 1864 - 12 Jan 1942)
| | |
|---|---|
| 21 Sep 1914 - 1915: | Reserve officer, Kiev Military District |
| 1915 - 1916: | Commander of Engineers, XVII. Army Corps |
| 10 Apr 1916: | Promoted to *Major-General* |
| 1916 - 11 Nov 1916: | Reserve officer, Kiev Military District |
| 11 Nov 1916 - 1918: | Commander of Engineers, 11th Army |

*Lieutenant-General* Prokofy Ivanovich **Chernik** (7 Jun 1831 - 11 Dec 1913)
| | |
|---|---|
| 25 Jan 1881 - 27 Nov 1886: | Inspector of Engineers, Caucasus Military District |
| 27 Feb 1883: | Promoted to *Major-General* |
| 27 Nov 1886 - 1903: | Deputy Commander of Engineers, Odessa Military District |
| 1903: | Promoted to *Lieutenant-General* |
| 1903: | Retired |

*Major-General* Vasily Ivanovich **Chernik** (7 Mar 1837 - ?)
| | |
|---|---|
| 31 May 1888 - 1897: | Ataman, Yeysk Division, Kuban Cossack Army |
| 6 May 1895: | Promoted to *Major-General* |

*Major-General* Porfiry Dmitriyevich **Chernoglazov** (7 Sep 1856 - 16 Apr 1939)
| | |
|---|---|
| 2 Nov 1914 - 17 Jun 1916: | Reserve officer, Kiev Military District |
| 22 Jan 1915: | Promoted to *Major-General* |
| 17 Jun 1916 - 1918: | Commander, 36th Replacement Infantry Brigade |

*Major-General* Grigory Ivanovich **Chernogubov** (25 Oct 1849 - ?)
8 Apr 1915 - 1917: Commander, 93rd State Militia Brigade
14 Sep 1915: Promoted to *Major-General*

*Lieutenant-General* Kondraty Stepanovich **Chernoknizhnikov** (9 Mar 1854 - ?)
6 Jan 1902 - 10 Feb 1909: General Staff Officer, Main Engineering Directorate
14 Apr 1902: Promoted to *Major-General*
10 Feb 1909: Promoted to *Lieutenant-General*
10 Feb 1909: Retired

*Major-General* Konstantin Ilich **Chernopyatov** (18 Jun 1866 - ?)
1915 - 11 Jan 1916: Commander, 1st Fortress Kronstadt Artillery Regiment
11 Jan 1916 - 23 Jan 1917: Commander, 12th Heavy Field Artillery Brigade
19 Oct 1916: Promoted to *Major-General*
23 Jan 1917 - 30 Apr 1917: Commander, 200th Artillery Brigade
30 Apr 1917 - Jul 1917: Inspector of Artillery, XLI. Army Corps

*Lieutenant-General* Bronislav Lyudvigovich **Chernota-de-Boyary-Boyarsky** (6 Oct 1853 - 25 Feb 1923)
22 Mar 1901 - 18 Jan 1907: Commander, 9th Dragoon Regiment
18 Jan 1907: Promoted to *Major-General*
18 Jan 1907 - 24 Aug 1907: Commander, 1st Brigade, 8th Cavalry Division
24 Aug 1907 - 9 Oct 1912: Commander, 2nd Brigade, 8th Cavalry Division
9 Oct 1912: Promoted to *Lieutenant-General*
9 Oct 1912: Retired
27 Aug 1913 - 1917: Recalled; Attached to the Ministry of the Imperial Court

*Major-General* Aleksandr Nikolayevich **Chernov** (3 Mar 1851 - ?)
21 Jan 1904 - 7 Jun 1906: Commander of Fortress Artillery, Vladivostok
11 Jun 1905: Promoted to *Major-General*
7 Jun 1906 - 1908: Attached to the Field Foot Artillery

*Major-General* Mikhail Mikhailovich **Chernov** (5 Nov 1865 - 1 Sep 1918)
3 Oct 1909 - 25 Dec 1915: Staff Officer, Main Artillery Directorate
6 Dec 1914: Promoted to *Major-General*
25 Dec 1914 - 1917: Vice-Chairman, Commission for the Construction of Nizhny Novgorod Factory

*Major-General* Nikolai Pavlovich **Chernov** (9 Apr 1867 - ?)
18 Jan 1914 - 23 Dec 1915: Commander, 132nd Infantry Regiment
23 Dec 1915: Promoted to *Major-General*
23 Dec 1915 - 31 Mar 1917: Commander, 2nd Brigade, 33rd Infantry Division
31 Mar 1917 - 6 May 1917: Reserve officer, Dvinsk Military District
6 May 1917 - 1918: Commander, Brigade, 166th Infantry Division

*Major-General* Diodor Nikolayevich **Chernoyarov** (9 Apr 1864 - 18 Jun 1929)
6 Sep 1902 - 20 Oct 1914: Company Commander, Corps of Pages

| | |
|---|---|
| 20 Oct 1914: | Promoted to *Major-General* |
| 20 Oct 1914: | Retired |
| 1914 - 1918: | Recalled; Commandant of Rostov-on-Don |

*Lieutenant-General* Fyodor Grigoryevich **Chernozubov** (14 Sep 1863 - 14 Nov 1919)
| | |
|---|---|
| 26 Dec 1908: | Promoted to *Major-General* |
| 26 Dec 1908 - 1 Apr 1915: | Chief of Staff, Terek Cossack Army |
| 1 Apr 1915 - 4 Jul 1916: | Commander, 4th Caucasus Cossack Division |
| 18 Jun 1915: | Promoted to *Lieutenant-General* |
| 4 Jul 1916 - 15 Feb 1917: | Commanding General, II. Caucasus Cavalry Corps |
| 15 Feb 1917 - 25 Apr 1917: | Commanding General, VII. Caucasus Army Corps |
| 25 Apr 1917 - 10 Oct 1917: | Reserve officer, Caucasus Military District |
| 10 Oct 1917 - 1918: | Commanding General, V. Caucasus Army Corps |

*Lieutenant-General* Mikhail Petrovich **Chernushevich** (11 Feb 1857 - ?)
| | |
|---|---|
| 9 Mar 1901 - 21 Feb 1912: | Commander, 24th (Crimean) Borderguard Brigade |
| 6 Dec 1904: | Promoted to *Major-General* |
| 21 Feb 1912 - 13 Nov 1915: | Special Assignments General to the Commanding General, Borderguard Corps |
| 14 Apr 1913: | Promoted to *Lieutenant-General* |
| 13 Nov 1915: | Retired |
| 2 Apr 1916 - Oct 1917: | Recalled; Reserve officer, Petrograd Military District |

*Major-General* Georgy Fyodorovich **Chernyavsky** (18 Aug 1860 - ?)
| | |
|---|---|
| 3 Aug 1912: | Promoted to *Major-General* |
| 3 Aug 1912 - 1917: | Commander of Engineers, Fortress Warsaw |

*Lieutenant-General* Ivan Seliverstovich **Chernyavsky** (12 Nov 1835 - 5 Nov 1904)
| | |
|---|---|
| 28 Nov 1872 - 21 Jan 1879: | At the disposal of the C-in-C, Caucasus Army |
| 2 Oct 1877: | Promoted to *Major-General* |
| 21 Jan 1879 - 13 Jun 1888: | Attached to the Caucasus Army |
| 25 Jun 1887: | Promoted to *Lieutenant-General* |
| 13 Jun 1888 - 27 Jan 1899: | Chief of the Military History Section, Caucasus Military District |
| 27 Jan 1899 - 24 Mar 1901: | At the disposal of the Main Artillery Directorate |
| 24 Mar 1901 - 5 Nov 1904: | At the disposal of the Chief of the General Staff |

*General of Artillery* Vasily Timofeyevich **Chernyavsky** (1 May 1850 - 8 Mar 1932)
| | |
|---|---|
| 1 Aug 1894 - 4 Oct 1903: | Commandant, Konstantinov Artillery School |
| 17 Dec 1894 - Nov 1917: | Member of the Artillery Committee, Main Artillery Directorate |
| 6 May 1897: | Promoted to *Major-General* |
| 4 Oct 1903 - 21 Jan 1913: | Commandant, Mikhailovsky Artillery Academy |
| 6 Dec 1905: | Promoted to *Lieutenant-General* |
| 21 Jan 1913 - Nov 1917: | Member of the Military Council |
| 14 Apr 1913: | Promoted to *General of Artillery* |

*Lieutenant-General* Mikhail Grigoryevich **Chernyayev** (22 Oct 1828 - 4 Aug 1898)
| | |
|---|---|
| 12 Jul 1864: | Promoted to *Major-General* |
| 5 Aug 1864 - 13 Feb 1865: | Attached to the Ministry of War |
| 13 Feb 1865 - 4 Jul 1866: | Military Governor, Turkestan Region |
| 4 Jul 1866 - 26 Jan 1874: | Transferred to the reserve |
| 26 Jan 1874 - 20 Jun 1875: | At the disposal of the Commanding General, Warsaw Military District |
| 20 Jun 1875 - 17 Apr 1877: | Transferred to the reserve |
| 17 Apr 1877 - 19 Mar 1880: | At the disposal of Grand Duke Mikhail Nikolayevich |
| 1880: | Promoted to *Lieutenant-General* |
| 19 Mar 1880 - 15 Dec 1881: | Transferred to the reserve |
| 15 Dec 1881 - 25 May 1882: | Attached to the General Staff |
| 25 May 1882 - 21 Feb 1884: | Governor-General of Turkestan, Commanding General Turkestan Military District |
| 21 Feb 1884 - 7 Apr 1886: | Member of the Military Council |
| 7 Apr 1886 - 8 May 1890: | Transferred to the reserve |
| 8 May 1890 - 4 Aug 1898: | Member of the Military Council |

*Lieutenant-General* Nikolai Grigoryevich **Chernyayev** (2 Oct 1838 - 1910)
| | |
|---|---|
| 11 Aug 1883 - 11 Nov 1896: | Commander, 66th Infantry Regiment |
| 14 May 1896: | Promoted to *Major-General* |
| 11 Nov 1896 - 5 Feb 1897: | Commander, 2nd Brigade, 8th Infantry Division |
| 5 Feb 1897 - 11 Oct 1900: | Commander, 1st Brigade, 24th Infantry Division |
| 11 Oct 1900: | Promoted to *Lieutenant-General* |
| 11 Oct 1900: | Retired |

*Major-General* Ivan Stepanovich **Chernyshev** (18 Jan 1844 - ?)
| | |
|---|---|
| 29 Jan 1901: | Promoted to *Major-General* |
| 29 Jan 1901 - 17 Feb 1904: | Commander, Caucasus Sapper Brigade |
| 17 Feb 1904: | Retired |

*Major-General of the Fleet* Vladimir Kuzmich **Chernyshev** (9 Dec 1866 - 16 Apr 1939)
| | |
|---|---|
| 1916: | Promoted to *Major-General of the Fleet* |
| 12 May 1916 - 1917: | Inspector of Classes, Marine Corps, Sevastopol |

*Major-General* Vladimir Vasilyevich **Chernyshev** (15 Jul 1869 - ?)
| | |
|---|---|
| 14 Sep 1906 - 1912: | Chairman of the Military Board, Ussuri Cossack Army |
| 6 Dec 1910: | Promoted to *Major-General* |

*Major-General* Konstantin Konstantinovich **Chernyy** (9 Feb 1871 - 21 Feb 1934)
| | |
|---|---|
| 23 Jan 1914 - 2 Feb 1916: | Commander, 1st Regiment, Kuban Cossack Army |
| 21 Jan 1916: | Promoted to *Major-General* |
| 2 Feb 1916 - 7 Dec 1916: | Chief of Staff, 16th Cavalry Division |
| 7 Dec 1916 - 9 Jan 1917: | Chief of Staff, I. Cavalry Corps |
| 9 Jan 1917 - 2 Sep 1917: | Quartermaster-General, 5th Army |
| 2 Sep 1917 - 29 Nov 1917: | Commander, 5th Caucasus Cossack Division |

*Major-General* Vladimir Yakovlevich **Chersky** (13 May 1844 - ?)

| | |
|---|---|
| 29 Mar 1900 - 3 Oct 1902: | Commander, 2nd Grenadier Artillery Brigade |
| 1 Jan 1901: | Promoted to *Major-General* |

*Major-General* Grigory Grigoryevich **Chertkov** (2 May 1872 - 20 Jun 1938)
| | |
|---|---|
| 23 Jun 1915 - 23 Aug 1916: | Commander, 12th Dragoon Regiment |
| 23 Aug 1916 - 14 Oct 1917: | Commander, 1st Brigade, 12th Cavalry Division |
| 26 Feb 1917: | Promoted to *Major-General* |
| 14 Oct 1917 - 1918: | Reserve officer, Kiev Military District |

*General of Cavalry* Mikhail Ivanovich **Chertkov** (2 Aug 1829 - 19 Oct 1905)
| | |
|---|---|
| 16 Oct 1860: | Promoted to *Major-General* |
| 16 Oct 1860 - 12 Apr 1861: | General à la suite |
| 12 Apr 1861 - 8 Jan 1864: | Military Governor of Voronezh |
| 8 Jan 1864 - 5 May 1866: | Military Governor of Volyn |
| 5 May 1866 - 5 Sep 1867: | Unassigned |
| 5 Sep 1867 - 2 Mar 1868: | Deputy Governor-General of Vilnius, Kovno, Grodno & Minsk |
| 2 Mar 1868: | Promoted to *Lieutenant-General* |
| 2 Mar 1868 - 14 Apr 1874: | Ataman, Don Cossack Army |
| 31 Jul 1869: | Promoted to *General-Adjutant* |
| 14 Apr 1874 - 13 Sep 1877: | Unassigned |
| 13 Sep 1877 - 13 Jan 1881: | Governor-General of Kiev, Podolsky & Volyn |
| 15 Sep 1878 - 13 Jan 1881: | Commanding General, Kiev Military District |
| 13 Jan 1881 - 24 Mar 1901: | Member of the State Council |
| 15 May 1883: | Promoted to *General of Cavalry* |
| 24 Mar 1901 - 17 Feb 1905: | Governor-General of Warsaw, Commanding General, Warsaw Military District |
| 17 Feb 1905 - 19 Oct 1905: | General à la suite |

*Major-General* Yaroslav Vyacheslavovich **Chervinka** (13 May 1848 - 9 Jan 1933)
| | |
|---|---|
| 28 Jul 1906 - 1 Dec 1908: | Commander, Czestochowa Borderguard Brigade |
| 1 Dec 1908: | Promoted to *Major-General* |
| 1 Dec 1908: | Retired |
| 14 Jun 1915 - Aug 1916: | Recalled; Special Assignments General, Kiev Military District |
| Aug 1916 - Mar 1917: | Attached to the High Command |
| Mar 1917 - 15 Oct 1917: | Chairman, Commission for Formation of Czechoslovak Units |
| 15 Oct 1917 - 1918: | Commander, Czechoslovak Replacement Rifle Brigade |

*Major-General* Konstantin Petrovich **Chervinov** (30 Apr 1854 - ?)
| | |
|---|---|
| 16 Jan 1909: | Promoted to *Major-General* |
| 16 Jan 1909 - 8 Jul 1913: | Commander, 4th Artillery Brigade |

*Lieutenant-General* Nikolai Petrovich **Chervinov** (12 Sep 1857 - ?)
| | |
|---|---|
| 14 Feb 1907: | Promoted to *Major-General* |
| 14 Feb 1907 - 19 Oct 1910: | Commander, Amur Sapper Brigade |
| 19 Oct 1910 - 29 Nov 1912: | Inspector of Field Engineers, Amur Military District |

1912: Promoted to *Lieutenant-General*
29 Nov 1912 - 1918: Inspector of Engineers, Amur Military District

*Lieutenant-General* Vladimir Petrovich **Chervinov** (12 Sep 1857 - Apr 1912)
1 Jun 1906: Promoted to *Major-General*
1 Jun 1906 - 6 Mar 1909: Commander, Caucasus Sapper Brigade
6 Mar 1909 - Apr 1912: Commandant of Fortress Kars
1910: Promoted to *Lieutenant-General*

*General of Cavalry* Sergey Prokofyevich **Chervonny** (15 Apr 1836 - 3 Dec 1907)
30 Aug 1881 - 15 Apr 1891: Commander, Life Guards Uhlan Regiment
24 Aug 1885 - 21 Sep 1885: Acting Commander, 1$^{st}$ Brigade, 2$^{nd}$ Guards Cavalry Division
30 Aug 1885: Promoted to *Major-General*
15 Apr 1891 - 8 Dec 1894: Commander, 2$^{nd}$ Brigade, 2$^{nd}$ Guards Cavalry Division
8 Dec 1894 - Dec 1905: Commandant of Peterhof
6 Dec 1895: Promoted to *Lieutenant-General*
Dec 1905: Promoted to *General of Cavalry*
Dec 1905: Retired

*Major-General* Aleksandr Vasilyevich **Cheryachukin** (18 Mar 1872 - 12 May 1944)
11 Dec 1913 - May 1915: Commander, 11$^{th}$ Don Cossack Regiment
May 1915 - 13 Jun 1915: Commander, 2$^{nd}$ Amur Cavalry Brigade
13 Jun 1915 - 26 Sep 1917: Chief of Staff, IV. Cavalry Corps
6 Dec 1915: Promoted to *Major-General*
26 Sep 1917 - 1918: Commander, 2$^{nd}$ Consolidated Cossack Division

*Major-General* Pyotr Vladimirovich **Chesnakov** (20 Jun 1875 - 20 Sep 1948)
15 Jan 1916 - 18 Jan 1917: Chief of Staff, 2$^{nd}$ Cavalry Division
3 Aug 1916: Promoted to *Major-General*
18 Jan 1917 - 21 Oct 1917: Chief of Staff, I. Cavalry Corps
21 Oct 1917 - 1918: Commander, 1$^{st}$ Cavalry Division

*Lieutenant-General* Nikolai Nikolayevich **Chetyrikin** (1 Aug 1850 - 1919)
4 Dec 1901: Promoted to *Major-General*
4 Dec 1901 - 27 Nov 1904: Commander, 2$^{nd}$ Brigade, 13$^{th}$ Infantry Division
27 Nov 1904 - 1 Aug 1905: Chief of the Sanatory Service, 3$^{rd}$ Manchurian Army
1 Aug 1905 - 27 Feb 1906: Commander, 41$^{st}$ Infantry Division
27 Feb 1906 - Jul 1906: Attached to the General Staff
Jul 1906: Promoted to *Lieutenant-General*
Jul 1906: Retired

*Major-General* Dmitry Yevgrafovich **Chevakinsky** (15 Aug 1861 - 17 Mar 1927)
7 Mar 1914 - 1916: Commander, 3$^{rd}$ Detachment, Amur Special Borderguard District
9 May 1914: Promoted to *Major-General*

*Major-General* Mikhail Mikhailovich **Chichagov** (23 Feb 1854 - 1900)
| | |
|---|---|
| 2 Jun 1895 - 1900: | Special Assignments General, Inspectorate-General of Cavalry |
| 14 May 1896: | Promoted to *Major-General* |

*Lieutenant-General* Nikolai Mikhailovich **Chichagov** (3 Sep 1852 - 17 Nov 1910)
| | |
|---|---|
| 6 May 1894: | Promoted to *Major-General* |
| 6 May 1894 - 3 Oct 1894: | General for Special Assignments, Odessa Military District |
| 3 Oct 1894 - 14 Jul 1897: | Deputy Chief of Staff, Odessa Military District |
| 14 Jul 1897 - 4 Jan 1899: | Chief of Staff, Amur Military District |
| 4 Jan 1899 - 9 Jan 1903: | Military Governor of the Maritime Region, Ataman, Ussuri Cossack Army |
| 15 Aug 1900: | Promoted to *Lieutenant-General* |
| 9 Jan 1903 - 17 Nov 1910: | Commanding General, Amur Military District Borderguard Corps |

*Major-General* Modest Grigoryevich **Chigir** (24 Oct 1863 - ?)
| | |
|---|---|
| 1 Aug 1908 - 1917: | Director of Polotsk Cadet Corps |
| 18 Apr 1910: | Promoted to *Major-General* |

*Lieutenant-General* Vladimir Nikolayevich **Chikalin** (17 Sep 1853 - ?)
| | |
|---|---|
| 4 Jun 1904 - 3 Sep 1904: | Commander, 58th Artillery Brigade |
| 3 Sep 1904 - 5 Jul 1910: | Commander, Caucasus Grenadier Artillery Brigade |
| 6 Dec 1906: | Promoted to *Major-General* |
| 5 Jul 1910 - 27 Mar 1917: | Inspector of Artillery, II. Caucasus Army Corps |
| 6 Dec 1910: | Promoted to *Lieutenant-General* |

*Admiral* Nikolai Matveyevich **Chikhachov** (17 Apr 1830 - 2 Jan 1917)
| | |
|---|---|
| 14 Mar 1862 - 20 Oct 1876: | Managing Director, Russian Society of Shipping and Trade |
| 15 Oct 1867: | Promoted to *Rear-Admiral* |
| 20 Oct 1876 - 20 Feb 1884: | Chief of Naval Defenses, Odessa |
| 1 Jan 1880: | Promoted to *Vice-Admiral* |
| 20 Feb 1884 - 14 May 1884: | Chief of the Naval General Staff |
| 14 May 1884 - 19 Jun 1885: | Commander, Baltic Sea Training Squadron |
| 19 Jun 1885 - 9 Jan 1888: A | dministrator, Ministry of the Navy |
| 9 Jan 1888 - 14 Sep 1888: | Commander, Baltic Sea Training Squadron |
| 14 Sep 1888 - 28 Nov 1888: | Administrator, Ministry of the Navy |
| 28 Nov 1888 - 13 Jul 1896: | Minister of the Navy |
| 1 Jan 1892: | Promoted to *Admiral* |
| 12 Aug 1893: | Promoted to *General-Adjutant* |
| 13 Jul 1896 - 2 Jan 1917: | Member of the State Council |

*Major-General* Vasily Dmitryevich **Chikov** (16 Oct 1842 - 20 Jan 1903)
| | |
|---|---|
| 1 Jan 1899 - 20 Jan 1903: | Ataman, Mozdoksky District, Terek Cossack Army |
| 6 May 1899: | Promoted to *Major-General* |

*Major-General* Vissarion Pavlovich **Chikovani** (13 Aug 1856 - ?)
| | |
|---|---|
| ? - 2 Jan 1914: | Attached to Life Grenadier Regiment |
| 2 Jan 1914: | Promoted to *Major-General* |
| 2 Jan 1914: | Retired |
| 10 Jul 1915 - Jan 1916: | Recalled; Commander, 2nd Caucasus State Militia Brigade |
| Jan 1916 - Jul 1916: | Attached to I. Caucasus Army Corps |
| Jul 1916 - 2 Aug 1916: | Commander, 1st Trans-Caucasus Rifle Brigade |
| 2 Aug 1916 - 1917: | Commander, Ossetia Foot Brigade |

*Major-General* Mikhail Gavrilovich **Chirikov** (1 Oct 1851 - 1908)
| | |
|---|---|
| 18 Feb 1901 - 4 Feb 1904: | Ataman, 2nd Military Division, Siberian Cossack Army |
| 6 May 1901: | Promoted to *Major-General* |
| 4 Feb 1904 - 21 Aug 1904: | Commander, 2nd Brigade, Siberian Cossack Division |
| 21 Aug 1904 - 1908: | Ataman, 2nd Military Division, Siberian Cossack Army |

*Lieutenant-General* Yevgeny Dmitriyevich **Chirkin** (5 Nov 1842 - ?)
| | |
|---|---|
| 30 Aug 1886: | Promoted to *Major-General* |
| 30 Mar 1887 - 19 Aug 1888: | Military Judge, St. Petersburg Military District Court |
| 19 Aug 1888 - 23 Nov 1889: | Military Prosecutor, Kiev Military District Court |
| 23 Nov 1889 - 22 Mar 1892: | Chairman of the Military Tribunal, Kazan Military District |
| 22 Mar 1892 - Dec 1897: | Chairman of the Military Tribunal, Vilnius Military District |
| 14 May 1896: | Promoted to *Lieutenant-General* |

*Major-General* Aleksandr Stepanovich **Chistyakov** (23 Aug 1855 - ?)
| | |
|---|---|
| 10 Aug 1910 - 1913: | Commander, 184th Infantry Regiment |
| 1913: | Promoted to *Major-General* |
| 1913: | Retired |
| 6 Nov 1914 - 20 Jun 1916: | Recalled; Chief of Sanitation Staff, 5th Army |
| 20 Jun 1916 - 1917: | Commander, 24th Replacement Infantry Brigade |

*Major-General* Ivan Dmitriyevich **Chistyakov** (27 Jul 1865 - 15 May 1939)
| | |
|---|---|
| 20 Apr 1916 - 29 Jan 1917: | Commander, Brigade, 38th Infantry Division |
| 16 Jul 1916: | Promoted to *Major-General* |
| 29 Jan 1917 - 25 Apr 1917: | Commander, 183rd Infantry Division |
| 25 Apr 1917 - 1917: | Reserve officer, Dvinsk Military District |
| 1917: | Commander, 7th Turkestan Rifle Division |

*Major-General* Mikhail Mikhailovich **Chistyakov** (12 Sep 1848 - ?)
| | |
|---|---|
| 20 Jul 1907: | Promoted to *Major-General* |
| 20 Jul 1907 - May 1910: | Commander, 8th East Siberian Rifle Artillery Brigade |

*Lieutenant-General* Pyotr Yegorovich **Chistyakov** (8 Jun 1855 - 1919)
| | |
|---|---|
| 25 Jul 1910 - 12 Jan 1914: | Deputy Chief of Troop Billeting, Moscow Military District |
| 6 Dec 1910: | Promoted to *Major-General* |

12 Jan 1914 - 1917: Chief of Troop Billeting, Moscow Military District
6 Dec 1916: Promoted to *Lieutenant-General*

*Lieutenant-General* Sergey Dmitriyevich **Chistyakov** (23 Sep 1860 - ?)
9 Mar 1899 - 3 Dec 1904: Attached to Nikolayev General Staff Academy
28 Mar 1904: Promoted to *Major-General*
3 Dec 1904 - 30 Jan 1909: Chief of Staff, XVIII. Army Corps
8 Jun 1906 - 8 Aug 1906: Acting Commander, Brigade, 23rd Infantry Division
30 Jan 1909 - 9 Oct 1912: Commander, 1st Brigade, 29th Infantry Division
9 Oct 1912 - 19 Jul 1914: Commander, 1st Brigade, 46th Infantry Division
19 Jul 1914 - 20 Apr 1915: Commander, 81st Infantry Division
Jan 1915: Promoted to *Lieutenant-General*
20 Apr 1915 - Feb 1916: Reserve officer, Kiev Military District
Feb 1916: Retired
27 Sep 1916 - 18 Feb 1917: Recalled; Reserve officer, Odessa Military District
18 Feb 1917 - 22 Apr 1917: Commander, 156th Infantry Division
22 Apr 1917 - 17 Nov 1917: Reserve officer, Kiev Military District

*Major-General* Konstantin Aleksandrovich **Chivadze** (20 May 1866 - ?)
26 Oct 1908 - Jul 1914: Military Judge, Vilnius Military District Court
6 Dec 1908: Promoted to *Major-General*
Jul 1914 - 20 Apr 1916: Military Judge, Dvinsk Military District Court
20 Apr 1916 - 1918: Military Prosecutor, Caucasus Military District

*Major-General* Aleksandr Stepanovich **Chizh** (22 Aug 1852 - 6 Jul 1909)
30 Sep 1904: Promoted to *Major-General*
30 Sep 1904 - 6 Jul 1909: Commander, 1st Brigade, 12th Infantry Division

*Major-General* Stepan Stepanovich **Chizh** (25 Aug 1856 - ?)
8 Jul 1913: Promoted to *Major-General*
8 Jul 1913 - 27 Sep 1914: Commander, 4th Artillery Brigade
27 Sep 1914: Retired
23 Jun 1916 - 1917: Recalled; Reserve officer, Dvinsk Military District

*Major-General* Nikolai Mikhailovich **Chizhev** (18 Nov 1846 - ?)
5 Jun 1903: Promoted to *Major-General*
5 Jun 1903 - 25 Aug 1906: Commander, 44th Artillery Brigade

*Major-General* Georgy Vladislavovich **Chizhevich** (5 Sep 1848 - ?)
17 May 1903: Promoted to *Major-General*
17 May 1903 - 9 Mar 1905: Commander, 1st Brigade, 31st Infantry Division
9 Mar 1905 - 9 Oct 1906: Attached to the General Staff
9 Oct 1906 - Jun 1908: Commander, 1st Brigade, 33rd Infantry Division

*Major-General* Leonid Vasilyevich **Chizhevsky** (1 Jan 1861 - 14 Apr 1929)
29 Jan 1913 - 1917: Commander, 1st Battalion, 3rd Artillery Brigade
19 Oct 1916: Promoted to *Major-General*

*Major-General* Nikolai Konstantinovich **Chizhevsky** (23 Jul 1861 - 19 Oct 1918)
4 Feb 1915 - 1918: Commander, 326th Infantry Regiment
20 Oct 1916: Promoted to *Major-General*

*Lieutenant-General* Aleksey Martyanovich **Chizhikov** (20 Mar 1858 - 25 Jun 1916)
21 Jul 1913 - 9 Aug 1915: Commander, 11th Turkestan Rifle Regiment
9 Aug 1915: Promoted to *Major-General*
9 Aug 1915 - 25 Jun 1916: Commander, 1st Brigade, 9th Infantry Division
27 Nov 1916: Posthumously promoted to *Lieutenant-General*

*Lieutenant-General* Nikolai Aleksandrovich **Chizhikov** (14 Mar 1850 - 27 Dec 1908)
28 Jan 1899 - 1906: Commander of Artillery, Fortress Kronstadt
9 Apr 1900: Promoted to *Major-General*
1906: Promoted to *Lieutenant-General*
1906: Retired

*Lieutenant-General* Mikhail Ivanovich **Chizhov** (11 Jan 1857 - ?)
11 Dec 1908: Promoted to *Major-General*
11 Dec 1908 - 7 Jan 1909: Commander, 1st Brigade, 45th Infantry Division
7 Jan 1909 - 19 Jul 1914: Commander, 2nd Brigade, 1st Infantry Division
19 Jul 1914 - 13 Oct 1914: Commander, 54th Infantry Division
13 Oct 1914 - 24 May 1915: Commander, 2nd Brigade, 29th Infantry Division
24 May 1915 - 17 Apr 1916: POW, Germany
23 Apr 1916 - 16 Jan 1917: Reserve officer, Minsk Military District
16 Jan 1917 - 2 Apr 1917: Commander, 16th Replacement Infantry Brigade
2 Apr 1917: Promoted to *Lieutenant-General*
2 Apr 1917 - Oct 1917: Inspector of Replacements, Western Front

*Major-General* Konstantin Assalovich **Chkoniya** (1 Dec 1849 - 1913)
22 Apr 1901 - 1913: Chief of Horse Breeding, Terek Cosasck Army
14 Apr 1913: Promoted to *Major-General*

*Lieutenant-General* Grigory Ivanovich **Choglokov** (4 Nov 1867 - 27 Jun 1921)
7 Jan 1909 - 25 Jan 1912: Commander, 1st Don Cossack Regiment
25 Jan 1912: Promoted to *Major-General*
25 Jan 1912 - 15 Aug 1914: Commander, 2nd Brigade, 2nd Cavalry Division
15 Aug 1914 - 20 May 1916: Commander, 1st Don Cossack Division
13 Jul 1915: Promoted to *Lieutenant-General*
20 May 1916 - 22 Apr 1917: Commander, 2nd Turkestan Cossack Division
22 Apr 1917 - Oct 1917: Commanding General, II. Caucasus Army Corps

*Lieutenant-General* Adolf Alekseyevich **Chudovsky** (26 Aug 1848 - ?)
7 Jul 1897: Promoted to *Major-General*
7 Jul 1897 - 1904: Commander, 3rd Sapper Brigade
28 Mar 1904: Promoted to *Lieutenant-General*

*Vice-Admiral* Grigory Pavlovich **Chukhnin** (23 Jan 1848 - 28 Jun 1906)
1 Jan 1896: Promoted to *Rear-Admiral*

| | |
|---|---|
| 1 Jan 1896 - 20 Oct 1896: | Junior Flagman, Pacific Squadron |
| 20 Oct 1896 - 1 Apr 1901: | Commander, Port of Vladivostok |
| 1 Apr 1901 - 1 Jul 1902: | Junior Flagman, Pacific Squadron |
| 1 Jul 1902 - 2 Apr 1904: | Commandant, Nikolayev Imperial Naval Academy, Director of the Sea Cadet Corps |
| 6 Apr 1903: | Promoted to *Vice-Admiral* |
| 2 Apr 1904 - 28 Jun 1906: | C-in-C, Black Sea Fleet |

*Major-General* Sergey Alekseyevich **Chuksanov** (21 Sep 1861 - 8 Dec 1920)
| | |
|---|---|
| 16 Nov 1913 - 16 Jan 1916: | Military Judge, Odessa Military District Court |
| 6 Dec 1913: | Promoted to *Major-General* |
| 16 Jan 1916 - 1917: | Military Judge, Moscow Military District Court |

*Major-General* Vasily Timofeyevich **Chumakov** (24 Aug 1861 - 17 Aug 1937)
| | |
|---|---|
| 25 Jul 1914 - 29 Apr 1917: | Commander, 13th Siberian Rifle Artillery Brigade |
| 27 Jun 1915: | Promoted to *Major-General* |
| 29 Apr 1917 - 1917: | Inspector of Artillery, XII. Army Corps |
| 1917 - 1918: | Commanding General, XII. Army Corps |

*General of Infantry* Aleksei Yevgrafovich **Churin** (7 Feb 1857 - 2 Apr 1916)
| | |
|---|---|
| 27 Apr 1899: | Promoted to *Major-General* |
| 27 Apr 1899 - 8 Jul 1902: | Special Purposes General, Vilnius Military District |
| 8 Jul 1902 - 13 Aug 1905: | Commander, 5th Rifle Brigade |
| 13 Aug 1905 - 1 Jul 1906: | Commander, 5th Rifle Division |
| 1 Jul 1906 - 19 Apr 1907: | Commander, 18th Infantry Division |
| 6 Dec 1906: | Promoted to *Lieutenant-General* |
| 19 Apr 1907 - 4 Feb 1909: | Chief of Staff, Warsaw Military District |
| 4 Feb 1909 - 22 Apr 1914: | Commanding General, XXI. Army Corps |
| 6 Dec 1912: | Promoted to *General of Infantry* |
| 22 Apr 1914 - 19 Jul 1914: | Deputy Commanding General, Vilnius Military District |
| 19 Jul 1914 - 30 Aug 1914: | Commanding General, Dvinsk Military District |
| 30 Aug 1914 - 14 Jan 1915: | Commanding General, II. Army Corps |
| 14 Jan 1915 - 8 Jun 1915: | C-in-C, 5th Army |
| 8 Jun 1915 - 20 Aug 1915: | C-in-C, 12th Army |
| 20 Aug 1915 - 7 Mar 1916: | C-in-C, 6th Army |
| 7 Mar 1916 - 2 Apr 1916: | Member of the Military Council |

*Major-General* Mikhail Fyodorovich **Dabich** (22 Nov 1868 - ?)
| | |
|---|---|
| 8 Dec 1914 - 1 Nov 1915: | Commander, Life Guards Horse-Grenadier Regiment |
| 11 Feb 1915: | Promoted to *Major-General* |
| 1 Nov 1915 - 19 Dec 1915: | Commander, 2nd Brigade, 1st Guards Cavalry Division |
| 19 Dec 1915 - 15 Feb 1917: | Reserve officer, Petrograd Military District |
| 15 Feb 1917 - Oct 1917: | Inspector of Cavalry, 8th Army |

*Vice-Admiral* Nikolai Dmitriyevich **Dabich** (23 Apr 1857 - ?)
| | |
|---|---|
| 5 Mar 1907: | Promoted to *Rear-Admiral* |
| 5 Mar 1907 - 20 Oct 1908: | Chief, Main Directorate of Procurement & Supply, Ministry of the Navy |

20 Oct 1908: Promoted to *Vice-Admiral*
20 Oct 1908: Retired

*Major-General* Aleksandr Dmitrievich **Dabovsky** (28 Aug 1868 - 23 Sep 1936)
16 Jan 1916 - 1917: Military Judge, Odessa Military District Court
10 Apr 1916: Promoted to *Major-General*
1917: Chairman of the Military Tribunal, Romanian Front

*Lieutenant-General* Prince Andrey Davidovich **Dadiani** (24 Oct 1850 - 12 Jun 1910)
?: Promoted to *Major-General*
?: Promoted to *Lieutenant-General*

*General of Infantry* Prince Grigori Levanovich **Dadiani** (6 Oct 1814 - 24 Dec 1901)
19 Jan 1854: Promoted to *Major-General*
12 Jan 1858 - 4 Mar 1859: Commander, 1st Brigade, Caucasus Grenadier Division
4 Mar 1859 - 25 Dec 1862: Special Assignments General, Caucasus Army
28 Jan 1860: Promoted to *Lieutenant-General*
25 Dec 1862 - 24 Dec 1901: Special Assignments General to the C-in-C of the Caucasus
11 Mar 1880: Promoted to *General-Adjutant*
15 May 1883: Promoted to *General of Infantry*

*Major-General* Timofey Mikhailovich **Dagayev** (13 Feb 1843 - ?)
3 Nov 1902: Promoted to *Major-General*
3 Nov 1902 - 1906: Commandant of Bobruysk

*Lieutenant-General* Aleksandr Aleksandrovich **Daller** (24 Dec 1839 - 12 Jul 1907)
14 Nov 1871 - 8 Sep 1884: Military Attaché, Berlin
6 May 1884: Promoted to *Major-General*
8 Sep 1884 - 5 Apr 1885: Attached to the Main Artillery Directorate
5 Apr 1885 - 12 Jul 1907: At the disposal of Grand Duke Vladimir Aleksandrovich
30 Aug 1894: Promoted to *Lieutenant-General*

*Rear-Admiral* Aleksandr Mikhailovich **Damozhirov** (? - ?)
?: Promoted to *Rear-Admiral*
1901 - 1902: Commandant of the Imperial Naval Academy, Director of the Marine Corps

*Major-General* Aleksandr-Genrikh Yulyevich **Damye** (13 Apr 1851 - ?)
14 Aug 1900 - Jul 1906: Director, Nizhny Novgorod Count Arakcheyev Cadet Corps
1 Apr 1901: Promoted to *Major-General*

*Lieutenant-General of the Fleet* Arseny Mikhailovich **Danchich** (20 Jan 1856 - 1921)
16 Jun 1903 - 1917: Inspector of Naval Training, Main Directorate of Merchant Shipping & Ports
13 Apr 1908: Promoted to *Major-General of the Admiralty*
8 Apr 1913: Redesignated *Major-General of the Fleet*

1913:                           Promoted to *Lieutenant-General of the Fleet*
1916:                           Member, Council of Ministry of Trade & Industry

*General of Infantry* Viktor Dezidierievich **Dandevil** (5 Oct 1826 - 8 Sep 1907)
8 Apr 1862 - 3 Jun 1865:       Ataman, Ural Cossack Army
17 Apr 1863:                   Promoted to *Major-General*
3 Jun 1865 - 14 Jun 1867:      Attached to the Ministry of Finance
14 Jun 1867 - 22 Sep 1871:     Chief of Staff, Turkestan Military District
22 Sep 1871 - 29 Mar 1872:     Commander of Independent Cossack Troops
29 Mar 1872 - 2 Dec 1872:      Acting Chief of the Main Department of Cossack Troops
2 Dec 1872:                    Retired
11 Jan 1877 - 17 Mar 1877:     Recalled; Chief of Russian Volunteers, Belgrade
17 Mar 1877 - 15 Aug 1877:     Commander, 2nd Brigade, 37th Infantry Division
15 Aug 1877 - 18 Oct 1877:     Commander, 1st Brigade, 3rd Infantry Division
18 Oct 1877 - 29 Dec 1877:     Commander, 2nd Brigade, 3rd Infantry Division
29 Dec 1877:                   Promoted to *Lieutenant-General*
29 Dec 1877 - 18 Jul 1887:     Commander, 3rd Guards Infantry Division
18 Jul 1887 - 9 Apr 1889:      Commanding General, V. Army Corps
9 Apr 1889 - 24 Nov 1890:      Commanding General, X. Army Corps
24 Nov 1890 - 3 Jan 1906:      Member of the Military Council
30 Aug 1891:                   Promoted to *General of Infantry*
3 Jan 1906:                    Retired

*Major-General* Zakhary Viktorovich **Dandevil** (29 Oct 1850 - ?)
13 Oct 1907:                   Promoted to *Major-General*
13 Oct 1907 - 1909:            Commander, 2nd Replacement Artillery Brigade

*Lieutenant-General* Konstantin Aleksandrovich **Danich** (14 Sep 1854 - ?)
20 Jan 1907:                   Promoted to *Major-General*
20 Jan 1907 - 29 Jun 1910:     Commander, 2nd Brigade, 2nd East Siberian Rifle Division
29 Jun 1910:                   Promoted to *Lieutenant-General*
29 Jun 1910:                   Retired

*Major-General* Aleksandr Arsenyevich **Danilchuk** (8 Mar 1849 - ?)
31 Dec 1904 - 28 Jun 1905:     Commander, 1st Brigade, 2nd Siberian Infantry Division
9 Mar 1905:                    Promoted to *Major-General*
28 Jun 1905 - 2 Jul 1906:      Commander, 2nd Brigade, 22nd Infantry Division

*Rear-Admiral* Aleksandr Aleksandrovich **Danilevsky** (27 Nov 1859 - ?)
1911 - 9 Dec 1911:             Chief of Staff, C-in-C of Naval Forces, Black Sea
6 Dec 1911:                    Promoted to *Rear-Admiral*
9 Dec 1911 - 23 Jun 1917:      Chairman, Commission for Oversight of Shipbuilding, Black Sea
23 Jun 1917 - 21 Dec 1917:     Reserve officer, Ministry of the Navy
21 Dec 1917:                   Dismissed

*Major-General* Fyodor Stepanovich **Danilevsky** (16 May 1862 - 1922)
6 Nov 1916 - 1918: Commander, Brigade, 3rd Caucasus Infantry Division
23 Dec 1916: Promoted to *Major-General*
Jan 1917: Acting Commander, 124th Infantry Division

*Lieutenant-General* Maksim Maksimovich **Danilevsky** (11 Nov 1851 - 1937)
22 Apr 1907 - 19 Aug 1907: Commander of Artillery, Fortress Warsaw
31 May 1907: Promoted to *Major-General*
19 Aug 1907 - 10 Jan 1908: Attached to the Commander of Artillery, Warsaw Military District
10 Jan 1908 - 18 Nov 1911: Commander of Artillery, Fortress Sveaborg
18 Nov 1911: Promoted to *Lieutenant-General*
18 Nov 1911: Retired
1915 - 1916: Recalled; Inspector of Medical Institutions, Chernigov Province
1916: Retired

*Rear-Admiral* Mikhail Aleksandrovich **Danilevsky** (8 Nov 1851 - ?)
1903: Promoted to *Rear-Admiral*
1903 - 1905: Chief of Staff, Black Sea Fleet
1905 - 24 Apr 1906: Commander, 1st Naval Division, Black Sea Fleet
24 Apr 1906: Retired

*Major-General* Nikolai Mikhailovich **Danilevsky** (10 Mar 1847 - ?)
1 Apr 1888 - 1911: Chief of Bureau, Nikolayev Engineering Academy
6 Dec 1903: Promoted to *Major-General*

*Major-General* Aleksandr Sergeyevich **Danilov** (12 Aug 1862 - ?)
17 Sep 1912 - 20 Nov 1915: Commander, 10th Uhlan Regiment
21 Jul 1915: Promoted to *Major-General*
20 Nov 1915 - 14 Aug 1916: Commander, 2nd Brigade, 11th Cavalry Division
14 Aug 1916 - 1917: Reserve officer, Kiev Military District

*Major-General* Aleksey Mikhailovich **Danilov** (12 Dec 1842 - ?)
22 Jun 1894 - 1906: Commander of Railway Gendarmerie, Vladkavkaz
6 Dec 1903: Promoted to *Major-General*

*General of Artillery* Aleksey Nikolayevich **Danilov** (7 Feb 1837 - 29 Jun 1916)
6 May 1882 - 12 Aug 1892: Commandant, Officers Artillery School
6 May 1884: Promoted to *Major-General*
12 Aug 1892 - 30 Mar 1900: Commander of Artillery, I. Army Corps
30 Aug 1894: Promoted to *Lieutenant-General*
30 Mar 1900 - 1 Sep 1912: Commandant of Tsarskoye Selo
6 May 1911: Promoted to *General of Artillery*
1 Sep 1912: Retired

*Lieutenant-General* Anton Vasilievich **Danilov** (3 Aug 1861 - ?)
4 Jun 1909: Promoted to *Major-General*

| | |
|---|---|
| 4 Jun 1909 - 13 Nov 1917: | Chief of Staff, Kronstadt Fortress |
| 6 Dec 1916: | Promoted to *Lieutenant-General* |
| 13 Nov 1917: | Retired |

*Major-General* Boris Fyodorovich **Danilov** (1 Sep 1869 - ?)

| | |
|---|---|
| 4 Mar 1908 - 1 Sep 1914: | Attached to the Borderguard Corps, Amur Military District |
| 1 Sep 1914: | Promoted to *Major-General* |
| 1 Sep 1914: | Retired |

*Major-General* Georgy Alekseyevich **Danilov** (22 Apr 1867 - ?)

| | |
|---|---|
| 14 May 1913: | Promoted to *Major-General* |
| 14 May 1913 - 11 Aug 1914: | Duty General, Turkestan Military District |
| 11 Aug 1914 - 8 Nov 1914: | Chief of Staff, II. Siberian Army Corps |
| 8 Nov 1914 - 26 Jun 1915: | Chief of Staff, XII. Army Corps |
| 26 Jun 1915 - 20 Jun 1916: | Reserve officer, Kiev Military District |
| 20 Jun 1916 - 29 Nov 1916: | Chief of Lines of Communication, 3$^{rd}$ Army |
| 29 Nov 1916 - 19 May 1917: | Commander, 130$^{th}$ Infantry Division |
| 17 Jul 1917 - Oct 1917: | Commander, 11$^{th}$ Siberian Rifle Division |

*General of Infantry* Mikhail Pavlovich **Danilov** (15 May 1825 - 17 Jan 1906)

| | |
|---|---|
| 1 Oct 1868: | Promoted to *Major-General* |
| 1 Oct 1868 - 1871: | Deputy Commander, 3$^{rd}$ Grenadier Division |
| 1871 - 22 Feb 1877: | Member, Committee for Troop Training |
| 22 Feb 1877 - 5 Jan 1884: | Commander, 3$^{rd}$ Grenadier Division |
| 16 Apr 1878: | Promoted to *Lieutenant-General* |
| 5 Jan 1884 - 19 Jan 1889: | Commander, 1$^{st}$ Guards Infantry Division |
| 19 Jan 1889 - 26 May 1896: | Commanding General, I. Army Corps |
| 30 Aug 1892: | Promoted to *General of Infantry* |
| 26 May 1896 - 3 Jun 1903: | Deputy Commanding General, Moscow Military District |
| 3 Jun 1903 - 17 Jan 1906: | Member of the Military Council |
| 1898: | Promoted to *General-Adjutant* |

*Major-General* Mikhail Pavlovich **Danilov** (16 Aug 1860 - ?)

| | |
|---|---|
| 4 Dec 1913: | Promoted to *Major-General* |
| 4 Dec 1913 - 1917: | Commander of Artillery, Fortress Kaunas |

*General of Infantry* Nikolai Aleksandrovich **Danilov** (13 Apr 1867 - 1 May 1934)

| | |
|---|---|
| 2 Jul 1905 - 20 Feb 1911: | Deputy Chief of Bureau, Ministry of War |
| 13 Apr 1908: | Promoted to *Major-General* |
| 20 Feb 1911 - 19 Jul 1914: | Chief of Bureau, Ministry of War |
| 10 Apr 1911: | Promoted to *Lieutenant-General* |
| 19 Jul 1914 - 13 Jun 1916: | Chief of Logistics, Northwestern Front |
| 23 Oct 1914: | Promoted to *General of Infantry* |
| 13 Jun 1916 - 12 Jul 1917: | Commanding General, X. Army Corps |
| 12 Jul 1917 - 20 Nov 1917: | C-in-C, 2$^{nd}$ Army |

*Major-General* Vasily Nikolayevich **Danilov** (3 Jan 1860 - ?)
22 Dec 1914 - 26 Mar 1917: Commander, 2nd Artillery Brigade
16 Feb 1915: Promoted to *Major-General*
26 Mar 1917 - 1917: Inspector of Artillery, IV. Army Corps

*General of Infantry* Vladimir Nikolayevich **Danilov** (27 Dec 1852 - 1 Nov 1914)
26 Mar 1903: Promoted to *Major-General*
26 Mar 1903 - 21 Sep 1904: General for Special Assignments, Amur Military District
21 Sep 1904 - 25 Nov 1905: Commander, 6th East Siberian Rifle Division
14 Feb 1905: Promoted to *Lieutenant-General*
25 Nov 1905 - 21 Jun 1906: Commander, 2nd Guards Infantry Division
1906: Promoted to *General-Adjutant*
21 Jun 1906 - 28 Jan 1912: Commanding General, Guards Corps
10 Apr 1911: Promoted to *General of Infantry*
28 Jan 1912 - 1 Nov 1914: Member, Committee on Wounded Veterans
1 Jan 1913 - 30 Aug 1914: Commandant of Fortress St. Petersburg
30 Aug 1914 - 1 Nov 1914: Commanding General, XXIII. Army Corps

*General of Infantry* Yuri Nikiforovitch **Danilov** (13 Apr 1866 - 3 Feb 1937)
18 Oct 1908 - 19 Jul 1914: Chief Quartermaster-General of the General Staff
29 Mar 1909: Promoted to *Major-General*
22 Dec 1910 - 19 Jul 1914: Chairman of the Fortress Commission, Main Directorate of the General Staff
14 Apr 1913: Promoted to *Lieutenant-General*
19 Jul 1914 - 30 Aug 1915: Quartermaster-General to the Supreme Commander-in-Chief
22 Oct 1914: Promoted to *General of Infantry*
30 Aug 1915 - 11 Aug 1916: Commanding General, XXV. Army Corps
11 Aug 1916 - 29 Apr 1917: Chief of Staff, Northern Front
29 Apr 1917 - 9 Sep 1917: C-in-C, 5th Army
9 Sep 1917: Transferred to the reserve

*General of Infantry* Grigory Grigoryevich **Danilovich** (17 Nov 1825 - 6 Apr 1906)
28 Jun 1866 - 28 Apr 1877: Director, 2nd St. Petersburg Military High School
28 Oct 1866: Promoted to *Major-General*
28 Apr 1877 - 25 Feb 1881: Member, Main Military Education Committee
1 Jan 1878: Promoted to *Lieutenant-General*
25 Feb 1881 - 20 Oct 1894: Tutor to Grand Dukes Nikolai and Georgy Aleksandrovich
1881: Promoted to *General-Adjutant*
30 Aug 1892: Promoted to *General of Infantry*
20 Oct 1894 - 6 Apr 1906: Member of the Tsar's retinue,
Honorary member, Mikhailovsky Artillery Academy

*Major-General* Nikolai Aleksandrovich **Danilovich** (17 Jul 1866 - 10 Jan 1936)
1914 - 17 Dec 1915: Commander, 2nd Battalion, 60th Artillery Brigade
6 Sep 1915: Promoted to *Major-General*

| | |
|---|---|
| 17 Dec 1915 - 13 Apr 1917: | Commander, 3rd Caucasus Rifle Artillery Brigade |
| 13 Apr 1917 - Oct 1917: | Inspector of Artillery, XXIX. Army Corps |

*Major-General* Sergey Aleksandrovich **Danilovich** (14 Nov 1857 - ?)
| | |
|---|---|
| 19 Aug 1904 - 28 Jun 1905: | At the disposal of the Chief of the General Staff |
| 1904: | Promoted to *Major-General* |
| 28 Jun 1905 - 9 Jan 1906: | Commander, 1st Brigade, 2nd Siberian Infantry Division |
| 9 Jan 1906 - 19 Jun 1906: | Commander, 2nd Brigade, 4th East Siberian Rifle Division |
| 19 Jun 1906 - Jul 1907: | Commander, 2nd Brigade, 9th East Siberian Rifle Division |

*Lieutenant-General* Anatoly Alekseyevich **Danilovsky** (7 May 1845 - 23 Apr 1917)
| | |
|---|---|
| 30 Oct 1893 - 27 Nov 1909: | Professor of drawing and shooting, General Staff Academy |
| 4 Oct 1894 - 9 Jul 1902: | Inspector of Classes, Corps of Pages |
| 6 Dec 1895: | Promoted to *Major-General* |
| 27 Nov 1909 - 23 Apr 1917: | Professor, Imperial Nikolayev Military Academy |
| 18 Apr 1910: | Promoted to *Lieutenant-General* |

*General of Artillery* Pyotr Alekseyevich **Danilovsky** (25 Dec 1842 - 1914)
| | |
|---|---|
| 30 Jan 1891 - 14 Jul 1894: | Section Chief, Main Artillery Directorate |
| 30 Aug 1891: | Promoted to *Major-General* |
| 14 Jul 1894 - 27 Feb 1897: | Commander of Artillery, Fortress St. Petersburg |
| 27 Feb 1897 - 10 Mar 1910: | Inspector of Technical Schools, Main Intendant Directorate, Member of the Artillery Committee, Main Artillery Directorate |
| 6 Dec 1900: | Promoted to *Lieutenant-General* |
| 10 Mar 1910: | Promoted to *General of Artillery* |
| 10 Mar 1910: | Retired |

*Lieutenant-General* Vladimir Eduardovich **Dankvart** (13 Feb 1857 - 26 Jan 1918)
| | |
|---|---|
| 19 Oct 1907 - 10 Aug 1914: | Director, 2nd Moscow Cadet Corps |
| 6 Dec 1908: | Promoted to *Major-General* |
| 10 Aug 1914: | Promoted to *Lieutenant-General* |
| 10 Aug 1914: | Retired |

*Lieutenant-General* Stepan Iosifovich **Danovsky** (16 Jan 1853 - ?)
| | |
|---|---|
| 19 Mar 1903 - 12 Aug 1907: | Commander, 84th Infantry Regiment |
| 31 May 1907: | Promoted to *Major-General* |
| 12 Aug 1907 - 16 Jan 1913: | Commander, 1st Brigade, 44th Infantry Division |
| 16 Jan 1913: | Promoted to *Lieutenant-General* |
| 16 Jan 1913: | Retired |
| 2 Aug 1914 - 1917: | Recalled; Commander, 2nd Replacement Infantry Brigade |

*Major-General* Aggey Aleksandrovich **Daronov** (16 Dec 1834 - ?)
14 May 1891 - 20 Feb 1904:   Intendant, Fortress Kaunas
6 Dec 1898:   Promoted to *Major-General*

*Lieutenant-General* Vladimir Ivanovich **Darovsky** (3 Apr 1856 - ?)
11 Aug 1900 - 23 Jun 1909:   Section Chief, Main Directorate for Military Schools
6 Dec 1906:   Promoted to *Major-General*
23 Jun 1909 - 3 Jan 1912:   Chief Secretary, Main Directorate for Military Schools
3 Jan 1912 - 14 Jun 1912:   Attached to the Chief of the General Staff
14 Jun 1912:   Promoted to *Lieutenant-General*
17 Jun 1912 - 2 Apr 1917:   Attached to the Ministry of War
2 Apr 1917:   Retired

*Major-General* Andrey Yakovlevich **Dashkov** (2 Oct 1850 - 18 Dec 1919)
? - 1899:   Attached to the Life Guards Cavalry Regiment
1899:   Promoted to *Major-General*
1899:   Retired

*Lieutenant-General* Dmitry Yakovlevich **Dashkov** (28 Jun 1853 - ?)
25 Dec 1897 - 25 Oct 1909:   Attached to Grand Duke Mikhail Alexandrovich
11 Aug 1904:   Promoted to *Major-General*
25 Oct 1909 - 21 Mar 1917:   General à la suite
1914 - 21 Mar 1917:   Chief Commissioner of the Red Cross, Northwestern Front
21 Mar 1917:   Promoted to *Lieutenant-General*
21 Mar 1917:   Retired

*Lieutenant-General of the Admiralty* Valerian Nikolayevich **Davidovich-Nashchinsky** (23 Jul 1857 - 1943)
1902 - 3 May 1911:   Senior Clerk, Main Naval Staff
18 Apr 1910:   Promoted to *Major-General of the Admiralty*
3 May 1911 - 25 Oct 1912:   Member of the Board, Baltic & Admiralty Shipyards
25 Oct 1912:   Promoted to *Lieutenant-General of the Admiralty*
25 Oct 1912:   Retired

*Major-General* Abdel-Aziz Abdulovich **Davletshin** (20 Jul 1861 - Feb 1920)
10 Sep 1910 - 1917:   Chief of Asian Section, General Staff
6 Dec 1913:   Promoted to *Major-General*

*Major-General* Antony Dmitrievich **Davydov** (7 Dec 1868 - ?)
28 Jan 1912 - 1917:   Chief of Military Topography, Amur Military District
6 Dec 1915:   Promoted to *Major-General*

*Lieutenant-General* Dmitry Alekseyevich **Davydov** (3 Aug 1856 - ?)
31 May 1912:   Promoted to *Major-General*
31 May 1912 - 25 Mar 1914:   Commander, 2$^{nd}$ Grenadier Artillery Brigade
25 Mar 1914 - 21 Feb 1916:   Commander of Artillery, Omsk Military District
21 Feb 1916 - 26 Sep 1916:   Commander, 101$^{st}$ Artillery Brigade

26 Sep 1916: Promoted to *Lieutenant-General*
26 Sep 1916 - 1917: Commander of Artillery, XLI. Army Corps
1917: Reserve officer, Kiev Military District

*Lieutenant-General* Fyodor Vasilyevich **Davydov** (11 Aug 1830 - ?)
11 Aug 1878 - 10 Mar 1895: Attached to the Inspectorate of Riflemen
30 Aug 1878: Promoted to *Major-General*
30 Aug 1890: Promoted to *Lieutenant-General*
10 Mar 1895 - 1900: Commander, St. Petersburg Regional Brigade

*Major-General* Grigory Alekseyevich **Davydov** (27 Aug 1871 - ?)
25 Aug 1908 - 1912: Commander, 3rd Horse Artillery Battalion
1912: Promoted to *Major-General*
1912: Retired
28 Sep 1915 - 8 Apr 1917: Recalled; Commander, 1st Brigade, 102nd Infantry Division
8 Apr 1917 - 1917: Commander, 28th Artillery Brigade

*Major-General* Ivan Nikolayevich **Davydov** (21 Jun 1850 - 21 Jun 1908)
5 Jun 1895 - 5 Jun 1906: Commander, Kherson Penal Battalion
2 Jul 1905: Promoted to *Major-General*
5 Jun 1906 - 21 Jun 1908: Commander, 2nd Brigade, 13th Infantry Division

*Lieutenant-General* Mikhail Pavlovich **Davydov** (26 Jul 1854 - ?)
29 Jan 1901: Promoted to *Major-General*
29 Jan 1901 - 16 Jun 1904: Commander, 1st Brigade, 16th Infantry Division
16 Jun 1904 - 28 Jun 1905: Commander, 47th Reserve Infantry Brigade
28 Jun 1905 - 5 Sep 1906: Commander, 47th Infantry Division
5 Sep 1906 - 8 Jun 1907: Commander, 34th Infantry Division
1907: Promoted to *Lieutenant-General*
1907: Retired

*Major-General* Nikolai Aleksandrovich **Davydov** (2 Dec 1860 - ?)
9 Feb 1906 - 15 Apr 1909: Special Assignments Officer, Inspectorate-General of Infantry
6 Dec 1908: Promoted to *Major-General*
15 Apr 1909 - 15 Jan 1910: Chief of Bureau, Inspectorate-General of Infantry
15 Jan 1910 - 1917: Special Assignments General, Inspectorate of Rifles

*Lieutenant-General of the Admiralty* Sergey Nikolayevich **Davydov** (7 Dec 1848 - ?)
1897 - 1904: Commander, 8th Naval Depot
1899: Promoted to *Major-General of the Admiralty*
1904 - 13 Mar 1906: Inspector of Machinery, Baltic Fleet
13 Mar 1906: Promoted to *Lieutenant-General of the Admiralty*
13 Mar 1906: Retired

*Lieutenant-General of the Admiralty* Vasily Alekseyevich **Davydov** (5 Mar 1842 - 5 Mar 1905)

27 Sep 1891 - 5 Mar 1905: Chief of Drill & Economics, Naval Cadet Corps
1898: Promoted to *Major-General of the Admiralty*
10 Mar 1903: Promoted to *Lieutenant-General of the Admiralty*

*Major-General* Yevgraf Savvich **Davydov** (10 Dec 1858 - ?)
16 Apr 1903 - 1906: Inspector of Classes, Siberian Cadet Corps
2 Apr 1906: Promoted to *Major-General*

*Major-General* Yakov Aleksandrovich **Davydovich** (29 Oct 1853 - ?)
2 Jul 1899 - 13 Jun 1905: Military Judge, Caucasus Military District Court
6 Dec 1901: Promoted to *Major-General*
13 Jun 1905 - 3 Dec 1907: Special Assignments General, Far East
3 Dec 1907 - 1917: Military Judge, Turkestan Military District Court

*Lieutenant-General* Sergey Evstafievich **Debesh** (28 Nov 1858 - 1 Feb 1915)
1 Jun 1904: Promoted to *Major-General*
1 Jun 1904 - 9 Mar 1906: Commander, 1st Brigade, 56th Infantry Division
9 Mar 1906 - 19 Nov 1906: Attached to the Commanding General, Amur Military District
19 Nov 1906 - 11 Oct 1908: Quartermaster-General, Amur Military District
11 Oct 1908: Promoted to *Lieutenant-General*
11 Oct 1908 - 29 Dec 1909: Chief of Staff, Amur Military District
29 Dec 1909 - 9 Apr 1910: At the disposal of the Chief of General Staff
9 Apr 1910 - 23 Jan 1913: Commander, 5th Siberian Rifle Division
23 Jan 1913: Retired
Jul 1914 - 11 Oct 1914: Commander, 2nd State Militia Brigade
11 Oct 1914 - 1 Feb 1915: Commanding General, II. Militia Corps

*Major-General* Yevgeny Pavlovich **Debil** (7 Dec 1846 - ?)
6 Feb 1897 - 1906: Commander of Gendarmerie, Tiflis Province
6 Dec 1901: Promoted to *Major-General*

*General of Infantry* Nikolai Pavlovich **Debogory-Mokriyevich** (9 Mar 1840 - ?)
24 Apr 1889 - 8 Dec 1894: Commander, 143rd Infantry Regiment
14 Nov 1894: Promoted to *Major-General*
8 Dec 1894 - 29 Jan 1901: Commander, 1st Brigade, 3rd Infantry Division
29 Jan 1901 - 1910: Commander, Yaroslavl Regional Brigade
6 Dec 1904: Promoted to *Lieutenant-General*
7 May 1910: Promoted to *General of Infantry*

*Lieutenant-General* Vasily Pavlovich **Debogory-Mokriyevich** (20 Nov 1849 - ?)
5 Mar 1895 - 14 Jan 1905: Commander, Dagestan Mounted Regiment
14 Jan 1905: Promoted to *Major-General*
14 Jan 1905 - 7 May 1910: Commander, 1st Brigade, 11th Cavalry Division
7 May 1910: Promoted to *Lieutenant-General*
7 May 1910: Retired

*Major-General* Eduard Leopoldovich **De-Bondi** (24 Nov 1849 - ?)
31 Aug 1915 - 1917: Reserve officer, Petrograd Military District
11 Jul 1916: Promoted to *Major-General*

*Major-General* Nikolai Aleksandrovich **De-Bryuks** (17 Mar 1848 - 17 May 1913)
26 Nov 1904: Promoted to *Major-General*
26 Nov 1904 - Dec 1906: Commander, 5$^{th}$ East Siberian Rifle Artillery Brigade
Dec 1906: Retired

*Major-General* Lev Nikolayevich **Dedintsev** (30 Dec 1870 - ?)
30 Nov 1915 - 1917: Commander, 5$^{th}$ Grenadier Regiment
27 Dec 1916: Promoted to *Major-General*
1917 - 26 Apr 1917: Commander, Brigade, 5$^{th}$ Grenadier Division
26 Apr 1917 - 1917: Commander, 23$^{rd}$ Replacement Infantry Brigade

*Major-General* Nikolai Georgiyevich **Dedintsev** (17 Dec 1867 - 1932)
1915 - 6 Apr 1916: Commander, Brigade, 44$^{th}$ Infantry Division
21 Jan 1916: Promoted to *Major-General*
6 Apr 1916 - Nov 1916: Reserve officer, Petrograd Military District
Nov 1916 - 1917: Commander, 174$^{th}$ Infantry Regiment

*Major-General* Mikhail Vladimirovich **Dedyulin** (2 Feb 1864 - Mar 1915)
16 Aug 1914 - Feb 1915: Commander, 236$^{th}$ Infantry Regiment
12 May 1915: Posthumously promoted to *Major-General*

*General of Cavalry* Vladimir Aleksandrovich **Dedyulin** (12 Jul 1858 - 26 Oct 1913)
21 Oct 1900 - 28 Oct 1903: Section Chief, Directorate of Military Communications
1 Jan 1901: Promoted to *Major-General*
28 Oct 1903 - 17 Jan 1905: Chief of Staff, Corps of Gendarmerie
17 Jan 1905 - 31 Dec 1905: Mayor of St. Petersburg
31 Dec 1905 - 3 Sep 1906: Commanding General, Corps of Gendarmerie
3 Sep 1906 - 26 Oct 1913: Commandant of the Imperial Palace
6 Dec 1906: Promoted to *Lieutenant-General*
1909: Promoted to *General-Adjutant*
6 Dec 1912: Promoted to *General of Cavalry*

*Major-General of the Hydrographic Corps* Ivan Ivanovich **Defabr** (4 Jun 1868 - 23 Feb 1918)
1 Dec 1911 - 23 Feb 1918: Director of Lighthouses & Navigation, Black Sea
10 Apr 1916: Promoted to *Major-General of the Hydrographic Corps*

*Major-General of the Fleet* Konstantin Ivanovich **Defabr** (18 Mar 1863 - 17 Apr 1933)
14 Jan 1908 - Oct 1915: Attached to the Admiralty Factory
14 Apr 1913: Promoted to *Major-General of the Fleet*
Oct 1915 - 1918: Chief of Artillery Section, Admiralty Factory

*Major-General* Konstantin Mikhailovich **Dekinleyn** (1 Jul 1847 - ?)
7 May 1903 - 2 May 1904: Commander, 19$^{th}$ Artillery Brigade

| | |
|---|---|
| 6 Dec 1903: | Promoted to *Major-General* |
| 2 May 1904 - 22 Feb 1905: | Commander, 31st Artillery Brigade |
| 22 Feb 1905 - 1905: | Attached to the Main Artillery Directorate |

*Admiral* Karl Karlovich **Delivron** (13 Oct 1838 - 1918)
| | |
|---|---|
| 9 Jun 1890 - 10 Jan 1892: | Commander, 2nd Naval Depot |
| 1 Jan 1891: | Promoted to *Rear-Admiral* |
| 10 Jan 1892 - 4 Feb 1894: | Commander, Mediterranean Naval Detachment |
| 4 Feb 1894 - 11 Apr 1894: | Chief of Artillery Training, Baltic Fleet |
| 11 Apr 1894 - 7 Nov 1894: | Junior Flagman, 2nd Naval Division |
| 7 Nov 1894 - 15 Aug 1895: | Inspector of Naval Artillery |
| 15 Aug 1895 - 1897: | Junior Flagman, Baltic Sea Training Squadron |
| 1897: | Promoted to *Vice-Admiral* |
| 1897 - 1903: | Commander, Port of St. Petersburg |
| 1903 - 28 Aug 1909: | Member, Board of Admiralty |
| 6 Dec 1906: | Promoted to *Admiral* |
| 28 Aug 1909: | Retired |

*Major-General* Pavel Petrovich **Dello** (10 Jun 1845 - ?)
| | |
|---|---|
| 12 Feb 1899 - 1902: | Commander of Gendarmerie, Yekaterinoslav Province |
| 1 Jan 1901: | Promoted to *Major-General* |

*Lieutenant-General* Pyotr Alekseyevich **Delsal** (11 Jun 1861 - ?)
| | |
|---|---|
| 5 Oct 1905 - 26 Aug 1910: | Commander, Life Guards 2nd Rifle Battalion |
| 6 Dec 1906: | Promoted to *Major-General* |
| 26 Aug 1910 - 19 Jan 1913: | Commander, Life Guards 2nd Tsarskoye Selo Rifle Regiment |
| 19 Jan 1913 - 13 Apr 1913: | Commander, 2nd Brigade, 2nd Guards Infantry Division |
| 13 Apr 1913 - 17 Feb 1915: | Commander, Guards Rifle Brigade |
| 6 Dec 1914: | Promoted to *Lieutenant-General* |
| 17 Feb 1915 - 16 Apr 1917: | Commander, Guards Rifle Division |

*Lieutenant-General* Vladimir Petrovich **Delsal** (8 Jul 1844 - 1908)
| | |
|---|---|
| 23 Dec 1898: | Promoted to *Major-General* |
| 23 Dec 1898 - 12 Feb 1903: | Commander, 15th Artillery Brigade |
| 12 Feb 1903 - 1906: | Commander of Artillery, XIV. Army Corps |
| 17 Apr 1905: | Promoted to *Lieutenant-General* |
| 1906: | Retired |

*Lieutenant-General* Baron Sergey Nikolayevich **Delvig** (4 Jul 1866 - 1944)
| | |
|---|---|
| 24 Jan 1909: | Promoted to *Major-General* |
| 24 Jan 1909 - 26 Jan 1914: | Commander, 24th Artillery Brigade |
| 26 Jan 1914 - 19 Apr 1915: | Inspector of Artillery, IX. Army Corps |
| 20 Jan 1915: | Promoted to *Lieutenant-General* |
| 19 Apr 1915 - 6 Aug 1915: | Commandant of Fortress Przemysl |
| 6 Aug 1915 - 20 Oct 1915: | At the disposal of the C-in-C, Southwestern Front |
| 20 Oct 1915 - 20 Apr 1916: | Commanding General, XL. Army Corps |
| 20 Apr 1916 - 1917: | Inspector of Artillery, Southwestern Front |

| | |
|---|---|
| 1917: | Retired |

*General of Infantry* Leonid Matveyevich **Dembovsky** (11 Jul 1838 - 1908)
| | |
|---|---|
| 19 Apr 1887 - 16 Apr 1890: | Commander, St. Petersburg Grenadier Regiment |
| 30 Aug 1887: | Promoted to *Major-General* |
| 16 Apr 1890 - 12 Feb 1897: | Commandant, 1st Pavlovsky Military College |
| 14 May 1896: | Promoted to *Lieutenant-General* |
| 12 Feb 1897 - 10 Jan 1902: | Commander, 24th Infantry Division |
| 10 Jan 1902 - 1 Jun 1904: | At the disposal of the Minister of War |
| 1 Jun 1904 - 5 May 1906: | Commanding General, V. Siberian Army Corps |
| 5 May 1906 - 18 Sep 1906: | At the disposal of the Minister of War |
| 18 Sep 1906 - 2 Apr 1907: | Commanding General, Consolidated Manchurian Army Corps |
| 30 Dec 1906 - 1908: | Member of the Military Council |
| 6 Jun 1907: | Promoted to *General of Infantry* |

*General of Cavalry* Konstantin Varfolomeyevich **Dembsky** (13 May 1847 - ?)
| | |
|---|---|
| 30 Nov 1892 - 26 May 1897: | Commander, 5th Life Dragoon Regiment |
| 26 May 1897: | Promoted to *Major-General* |
| 26 May 1897 - 2 Apr 1899: | Commander, 1st Brigade, 3rd Cavalry Division |
| 2 Apr 1899 - 21 Apr 1902: | Commander, Life Guards Cossack Regiment |
| 21 Apr 1902 - 7 Feb 1905: | Commander, 2nd Brigade, 1st Guards Cavalry Division |
| 7 Feb 1905: | Promoted to *Lieutenant-General* |
| 7 Feb 1905 - 18 Feb 1910: | Commander, 8th Cavalry Division |
| 18 Feb 1910: | Promoted to *General of Cavalry* |
| 18 Feb 1910: | Retired |
| 28 Aug 1912 - 1917: | Recalled; Trustee, Board of Trustees, Empress Maria Institutions |

*Major-General of the Fleet* Pyotr Vasilyevich **Demchenko** (19 Jul 1861 - ?)
| | |
|---|---|
| 17 Nov 1908 - 1912: | Deputy Captain, Port of Sevastopol |
| ?: | Promoted to *Major-General of the Fleet* |
| ?: | Member of the Supervisory Commission, Economic Committee, Black Sea Fleet |

*Major-General* Ivan Nikolayevich **Dementyev** (12 Oct 1858 - ?)
| | |
|---|---|
| 27 Feb 1902 - 20 Jul 1916: | Chief of Studies, Imperial Military Medical Academy |
| 20 Jul 1916: | Promoted to *Major-General* |
| 20 Jul 1916: | Retired |

*Lieutenant-General* Nikolai Petrovich **Demidov** (26 Aug 1865 - 13 Nov 1941)
| | |
|---|---|
| 30 May 1910: | Promoted to *Major-General* |
| 30 May 1910 - 25 Jul 1910: | Commander, 7th Artillery Brigade |
| 25 Jul 1910 - 13 Nov 1914: | Commander, Life Guards 1st Artillery Brigade |
| 13 Nov 1914 - 1917: | Chairman, Commission for Construction of Central Scientific-Technical Military Laboratory |
| 6 Dec 1916: | Promoted to *Lieutenant-General* |

*Major-General* Sergey Andreyevich **Demidov** (28 May 1848 - ?)
1 Feb 1898 - 1903: Commander, Siberian Gendarmerie District
10 Apr 1899: Promoted to *Major-General*

*Major-General* Mikhail Mikhailovich **Demidovsky** (26 Oct 1841 - 3 Oct 1908)
?: Promoted to *Major-General*

*Major-General* Ivan Sergeyevich **Demin** (30 Dec 1840 - ?)
13 Feb 1897: Promoted to *Major-General*
13 Feb 1897 - 16 Jun 1900: Director, 2nd Moscow Cadet Corps

*Major-General* Konstantin Mikhailovich **Demkov** (6 Sep 1858 - ?)
1914 - 1915: Commander, 310th Infantry Regiment
3 Apr 1915: Promoted to *Major-General*
1915 - 16 Jun 1916: Reserve officer, Kiev Military District
16 Jun 1916 - 1917: Commander, 6th Replacement Infantry Brigade

*Major-General* Sergey Petrovich **Demor** (25 Sep 1856 - Nov 1910)
1 Dec 1907: Promoted to *Major-General*
1 Dec 1907 - Nov 1910: Commander, 1st Brigade, 7th Cavalry Division

*General of Artillery* Nikolai Afanasievich **Demyanenkov** (6 Nov 1830 - 31 May 1907)
25 Nov 1865 - 31 May 1907: Member of the Artillery Committee, Main Artillery Directorate
2 Nov 1867 - 15 Oct 1891: Professor, Mikhailovsky Artillery Academy
30 Aug 1873: Promoted to *Major-General*
4 Sep 1881 - 8 Dec 1898: Commandant, Mikhailovsky Artillery Academy
26 Feb 1885: Promoted to *Lieutenant-General*
8 Dec 1898: Promoted to *General of Artillery*
8 Dec 1898 - 31 May 1907: Member of the Military Council

*Major-General* Mikhail Yegorovich **Demyanovich** (12 Jul 1833 - ?)
23 Oct 1893: Promoted to *Major-General*
23 Oct 1893 - 1898: Commander, 3rd Reserve Artillery Brigade

*Lieutenant-General* Viktor Nikolayevich **Demyanovich** (24 Aug 1841 - 1909)
24 Jan 1886 - 13 Nov 1900: Section Chief, General Staff
30 Aug 1890: Promoted to *Major-General*
13 Nov 1900 - 1907: Section Chief, Directorate of Militlary Communications
1907: Promoted to *Lieutenant-General*
1907: Retired

*Major-General* Aleksandr Aleksandrovich von **Den** (10 Jun 1867 - 21 Jan 1930)
17 Jun 1914: Promoted to *Major-General*
17 Jun 1914 - 1 Sep 1914: Commander, 36th Artillery Brigade
1 Sep 1914 - Aug 1918: POW, Germany

*General of Infantry* Voldemar Aleksandrovich von **Den** (20 Feb 1838 - 28 Dec 1900)
| | |
|---|---|
| 30 Aug 1878: | Promoted to *Major-General* |
| 30 Aug 1878 - 1882: | Governor of Stavropol |
| 1882 - 26 Jan 1889: | Governor of Vyborg |
| 30 Aug 1888: | Promoted to *Lieutenant-General* |
| 26 Jan 1889 - 30 Mar 1891: | Deputy Minister & Secretary of State, Finland |
| 30 Mar 1891 - 11 Jun 1898: | Minister & Secretary of State, Finland |
| 11 Jun 1898: | Promoted to *General of Infantry* |
| 11 Jun 1898: | Retired |

*Lieutenant-General* Anton Ivanovich **Denikin** (4 Dec 1872 - 7 Aug 1947)
| | |
|---|---|
| 21 Jun 1914: | Promoted to *Major-General* |
| 19 Jul 1914 - 19 Sep 1914: | Quartermaster-General, 8th Army |
| 19 Sep 1914 - 6 Aug 1915: | Commander, 4th Rifle Brigade |
| 6 Aug 1915 - 9 Sep 1916: | Commander, 4th Rifle Division |
| 11 May 1916: | Promoted to *Lieutenant-General* |
| 9 Sep 1916 - Feb 1917: | Commanding General, VIII. Army Corps |
| Feb 1917 - 5 Apr 1917: | Deputy Chief of Staff to the Supreme Commander-in-Chief |
| 5 Apr 1917 - 31 May 1917: | Chief of Staff to the Supreme Commander-in-Chief |
| 31 May 1917 - 2 Aug 1917: | C-in-C, Western Front |
| Jun 1917 - 2 Aug 1917: | Deputy Chief of Staff to the Supreme Commander-in-Chief |
| 2 Aug 1917 - 29 Aug 1917: | C-in-C, Southwestern Front |
| 29 Aug 1917: | Dismissed |

*Major-General* Ivan Nikolayevich **Denisov** (22 Feb 1864 - 7 Oct 1914)
| | |
|---|---|
| 14 Nov 1908 - 7 Oct 1914: | Military Judge, Vilnius Military District Court |
| 29 Mar 1909: | Promoted to *Major-General* |

*Lieutenant-General* Varlaam Aleksandrovich **Denisov** (14 Sep 1839 - 27 Dec 1904)
| | |
|---|---|
| 28 Jun 1877 - 29 May 1885: | Commander, 10th Don Cossack Regiment |
| 29 May 1885 - 23 Mar 1889: | Transferred to the reserve |
| 6 May 1887: | Promoted to *Major-General* |
| 23 Mar 1889 - 15 Jan 1901: | Commander, 1st Brigade, 2nd Consolidated Cossack Division |
| 15 Jan 1901: | Promoted to *Lieutenant-General* |
| 15 Jan 1901: | Retired |

*Major-General* Kasten Karlovich **De-Pont** (3 Feb 1849 - 1 Apr 1929)
| | |
|---|---|
| 22 Jan 1895 - 24 Jan 1897: | Commander, Life Guards 3rd Finnish Rifle Battalion |
| 14 May 1896: | Promoted to *Major-General* |
| 24 Jan 1897 - 31 Aug 1900: | Governor of Uusimaa |
| 31 Aug 1900: | Resigned |

*Lieutenant-General* Nikolai Aleksandrovich **Depp** (19 Jul 1837 - 6 Sep 1904)
| | |
|---|---|
| 2 May 1886 - 28 Feb 1891: | Commander of Engineers, Fortress St. Petersburg |
| 30 Aug 1886: | Promoted to *Major-General* |

28 Feb 1891 - 9 Oct 1894: Commander of Engineers, Kiev Military District
9 Oct 1894 - 6 Sep 1904: Commander of Engineers, Odessa Military District
14 May 1896: Promoted to *Lieutenant-General*

*Major-General* Mikhail Aleksandrovich **Deppish** (5 Feb 1861 - ?)
18 Jun 1906 - 29 Oct 1913: Company Commander, Orlov-Bakhtina Cadet Corps
29 Oct 1913: Promoted to *Major-General*
29 Oct 1913: Retired

*Major-General* Ivan Iosifovich **Derengovsky** (7 Apr 1868 - 15 Jun 1916)
3 Apr 1915 - 15 Jun 1916: Commander, 95th Infantry Regiment
24 Nov 1916: Posthumously promoted to *Major-General*

*Lieutenant-General* Pyotr Aleksandrovich **Derevitsky** (10 Dec 1857 - 4 Jan 1938)
26 Jul 1910: Promoted to *Major-General*
26 Jul 1910 - 19 Mar 1915: Commander, 33rd Artillery Brigade
19 Mar 1915 - 1917: Inspector of Artillery, XXXI. Army Corps
11 Sep 1915: Promoted to *Lieutenant-General*

*Lieutenant-General* Ivan Platonovich von **Derfelden** (18 Jun 1849 - 8 Mar 1913)
10 Apr 1893 - 8 Jan 1898: Special Assignments General, Inpsectorate-General of Cavalry
6 May 1897: Promoted to *Major-General*
8 Jan 1898 - 8 Mar 1913: Member, Main Horse Breeding Directorate
6 Dec 1912: Promoted to *Lieutenant-General*

*Major-General* Baron Khristofor Platonovich von **Derfelden** (1 Mar 1851 - 18 Dec 1909)
22 Feb 1901 - 14 Mar 1905: Commander, Life Guards Cuirassier Regiment
6 Dec 1901: Promoted to *Major-General*
14 Mar 1905 - 23 Feb 1907: Commander, 2nd Brigade, 1st Guards Cavalry Division
23 Feb 1907 - 18 Dec 1909: Member of the Tsar's retinue

*Lieutenant-General* Dmitry Mikhailovich **Dernov** (19 Sep 1862 - ?)
1 Jul 1905 - 21 Mar 1913: Chief of Communications, Warsaw Military District
13 Apr 1908: Promoted to *Major-General*
21 Mar 1913 - Aug 1914: Commander, 2nd Brigade, 8th Infantry Division
Aug 1914 - 10 May 1915: Chief of Communications Northwestern Front
10 May 1915 - 13 Jun 1916: At the disposal of the C-in-C, Western Front
30 Sep 1915: Promoted to *Lieutenant-General*
13 Jun 1916 - 25 Oct 1916: Commander, Brigade, 80th Infantry Division
25 Oct 1916 - 15 Apr 1917: Commander, 2nd Zaamursky Borderguard Infantry Division
15 Apr 1917 - 1918: Reserve officer, Kiev Military District

*Major-General* Aleksandr Oskarovich **De-Roberti** (10 Aug 1848 - ?)
12 Jun 1915 - 7 Apr 1916: Commander, State Militia Brigade
29 Jan 1916: Promoted to *Major-General*
7 Apr 1916 - 1917: Commander, 116th State Militia Brigade

*Lieutenant-General* Aleksandr Valentinovich **De-Roberti** (4 Apr 1851 - ?)
24 Aug 1907: Promoted to *Major-General*
24 Aug 1907 - 13 Jan 1910: Commander, 6th Artillery Brigade
13 Jan 1910: Retired
11 Nov 1914 - 29 Apr 1917: Recalled; Chief of the Sanatory Section, 2nd Army
29 Apr 1917: Promoted to *Lieutenant-General*
29 Apr 1917: Retired

*General of Infantry* Mikhail Yevseyevich **Deryugin** (25 Sep 1838 - 5 Oct 1906)
30 Aug 1891: Promoted to *Major-General*
30 Aug 1891 - 8 May 1899: Director, 2nd Orenburg Cadet Corps
8 May 1899 - 30 Jul 1906: Director, Odessa Cadet Corps
6 Apr 1903: Promoted to *Lieutenant-General*
30 Jul 1906: Promoted to *General of Infantry*
30 Jul 1906: Retired

*Lieutenant-General* Konstantin Nikolayevich **Desino** (4 Oct 1857 - 11 Feb 1940)
28 Oct 1899 - 9 Sep 1906: Military Attaché, China
6 Apr 1903: Promoted to *Major-General*
9 Sep 1906 - 3 Oct 1909: Attached to the General Directorate of the General Staff
16 May 1909 - 16 Sep 1909: Acting Commander, Brigade, 22nd Infantry Division
16 Sep 1909 - 1 May 1913: Chief of Staff, Grenadier Corps
1 May 1913 - 14 Dec 1914: Chief of Staff, IV. Army Corps
14 Dec 1914 - 21 Apr 1915: Reserve officer, Dvinsk Military District
21 Apr 1915: Promoted to *Lieutenant-General*
21 Apr 1915 - 5 Jun 1916: Commander, 71st Infantry Division
5 Jun 1916 - 1917: At the disposal of the Chief of the General Staff

*Lieutenant-General* Adam Yegorovich **De Struve** (30 May 1835 - 12 Sep 1898)
16 Nov 1879: Promoted to *Major-General*
16 Nov 1879 - 22 May 1892: Reserve officer, Corps of Engineers
22 May 1892 - 12 Sep 1898: Member of the Engineering Committee, Main Engineering Directorate
14 May 1896: Promoted to *Lieutenant-General*

*General of Cavalry* Daniil Fyodorovich **Devel** (13 Nov 1852 - 14 Feb 1933)
11 Aug 1891 - 25 Jan 1900: Commander, 43rd Dragoon Regiment
25 Jan 1900: Promoted to *Major-General*
25 Jan 1900 - 1 Dec 1901: Commander, 2nd Brigade, 7th Cavalry Division
1 Dec 1901 - 19 Jun 1905: Commander, 2nd Brigade, 1st Cavalry Division
19 Jun 1905 - 23 May 1907: Commander, 1st Brigade, 2nd Guards Cavalry Division
23 May 1907: Promoted to *Lieutenant-General*
23 May 1907 - 13 Nov 1913: Commander, 6th Cavalry Division
13 Nov 1913: Promoted to *General of Cavalry*
13 Nov 1913: Retired

*Lieutenant-General* Georgy Fyodorovich **Devel** (13 Apr 1836 - ?)
1 Jan 1898: Promoted to *Major-General*

1 Jan 1898 - 5 Dec 1900: Commander, 18th Artillery Brigade
5 Dec 1900: Promoted to *Lieutenant-General*
5 Dec 1900: Retired

*Major-General* Vladimir Petrovich **Devi** (3 Jul 1848 - ?)
25 Jan 1904: Promoted to *Major-General*
25 Jan 1904 - 14 Jan 1905: Commander, 1st Brigade, 8th Infantry Division
14 Jan 1905 - 21 May 1910: Commander, 1st Brigade, 1st Infantry Division

*Major-General of the Naval Legal Corps* Pyotr Vladimirovich **Devison** (6 Jan 1873 - 1956)
1903 - 1917: Member of the Naval Legal Service
6 Dec 1915: Promoted to *Major-General of the Naval Legal Corps*

*Lieutenant-General* Lev Vladimirovich **De-Vitt** (7 Mar 1861 - ?)
23 Dec 1902 - 31 Mar 1904: Commander, Life-Dragoon Regiment
31 Mar 1904: Promoted to *Major-General*
31 Mar 1904 - 21 Apr 1905: Commandant, Yelisavetgrad Cavalry School
21 Apr 1905 - 3 May 1910: Commandant, Nikolai Cavalry School
23 May 1909 - 8 Sep 1909: Acting Commander, 2nd Brigade, 9th Cavalry Division
18 Apr 1910: Promoted to *Lieutenant-General*
3 May 1910 - 22 Oct 1914: Commander, 11th Cavalry Division
22 Oct 1914 - 24 Jun 1915: Reserve officer, Kiev Military District
24 Jun 1915 - Aug 1915: Commander, 58th Infantry Division
Aug 1915 - 1918: POW, Germany

*General of Infantry* Vladimir Vladimirovich **De-Vitt** (15 Jan 1859 - ?)
19 Sep 1903 - 9 Mar 1905: Commander, 12th Infantry Regiment
6 Dec 1904: Promoted to *Major-General*
9 Mar 1905 - 18 Aug 1905: Commander, 1st Brigade, 3rd Infantry Division
18 Aug 1905 - 4 Aug 1906: Chief of Staff, II. Consolidated Rifle Corps
4 Aug 1906 - 11 May 1907: Chief of Staff, Fortress Modlin
11 May 1907 - 10 Aug 1910: Commander, Novogeorgievsk Fortress Infantry Brigade
10 Aug 1910 - 17 Feb 1913: Commander, 2nd Brigade, 28th Infantry Division
17 Feb 1913: Promoted to *Lieutenant-General*
17 Feb 1913 - 19 Dec 1915: Commander, 39th Infantry Division
19 Dec 1915 - Jun 1917: Commanding General, IV. Caucasus Army Corps
Jun 1917 - Oct 1917: Acting C-in-C, Caucasus Army
8 Sep 1917: Promoted to *General of Infantry*

*General of Cavalry* Konstantin Pavlovich **De-Vitte** (21 May 1846 - ?)
12 Aug 1892: Promoted to *Major-General*
12 Aug 1892 - 18 Feb 1899: Commander, 1st Brigade, 9th Cavalry Division
18 Feb 1899 - 26 Apr 1900: Commander, 12th Cavalry Division
6 Dec 1899: Promoted to *Lieutenant-General*
26 Apr 1900 - 16 Dec 1904: Commander, 9th Cavalry Division
16 Dec 1904 - 21 May 1908: Commanding General, IX. Army Corps
6 Dec 1907: Promoted to *General of Cavalry*
21 May 1908: Retired

*Major-General* Prince Aleksandr Logginovich **Devlet-Kildeyev** (1837 - ?)
| | |
|---|---|
| 11 Feb 1887 - 1900: | Commander of Gendarmerie, Pskov Province |
| 13 Apr 1897: | Promoted to *Major-General* |

*Major-General* Grigory Grigoryevich **Deyev** (24 Nov 1873 - ?)
| | |
|---|---|
| 24 Jul 1916 - 1917: | Chief of Staff, 6th Caucasus Rifle Division |
| 6 Dec 1916: | Promoted to *Major-General* |
| 1917 - 16 Dec 1917: | Chief of Posts & Telegraphs, Main Directorate of Military Communications |

*Major-General* Anatoly Mikhailovich **Didenko** (28 Jul 1874 - ?)
| | |
|---|---|
| 8 Oct 1916 - 20 Jun 1917: | Chief of Staff, 123rd Infantry Division |
| 6 Dec 1916: | Promoted to *Major-General* |
| 20 Jun 1917 - 1918: | Chief of Staff, VI. Caucasus Army Corps |

*Major-General* Vladimir Anatolyevich **Didkovsky** (7 Jan 1852 - ?)
| | |
|---|---|
| 6 Dec 1905 - 1914: | Section Chief, Intendant Department, St. Petersburg Military District |
| 1914: | Promoted to *Major-General* |
| 1914: | Retired |
| 19 Oct 1914 - 1917: | Recalled; Reserve officer, Petrograd Military District |

*Vice-Admiral* Richard Robertovich **Diker** (14 Aug 1847 - 1939)
| | |
|---|---|
| 1894 - 1898: | Captain, Battleship "*Sevastopol*" |
| 1896: | Promoted to *Rear-Admiral* |
| 1898 - 1900: | Chairman, Commission for Naval Artillery Testing |
| 1900 - 1902: | Commander, Mine Training Detachment, Baltic Fleet |
| 1902 - 1903: | Junior Flagman, Baltic Fleet |
| 1903 - 1904: | Chairman, Baltic Factory |
| 1904: | Promoted to *Vice-Admiral* |
| 1904: | Retired |

*Admiral* Ivan Mikhailovich **Dikov** (17 Jul 1833 - 30 Sep 1914)
| | |
|---|---|
| 6 Dec 1886 - 1890: | Inspector-General of Mines |
| 1 Jan 1888: | Promoted to *Rear-Admiral* |
| 1890 - 22 Aug 1891: | Deputy Commander, Black Sea Squadron |
| 22 Aug 1891 - 21 Dec 1892: | Deputy Chief of the Naval General Staff |
| 21 Dec 1892 - 6 Feb 1895: | Commander, Black Sea Naval Division |
| 1 Jan 1894: | Promoted to *Vice-Admiral* |
| 6 Feb 1895 - 1896: | Commander, Black Sea Training Squadron |
| 20 Jan 1897 - 1 Jan 1901: | Chairman, Naval Technical Committee |
| 15 Jul 1898 - 8 Jan 1909: | Member of the Admiralty Board |
| 6 Dec 1905: | Promoted to *Admiral* |
| 14 Jan 1906: | Promoted to *General-Adjutant* |
| 29 Dec 1906 - 30 Sep 1914: | Member of the Defense Council |
| 11 Jan 1907 - 8 Jan 1909: | Minister of the Navy |
| 8 Jan 1909: | Retired |

*Major-General* Nikolai Ivanovich **Dimich** (23 Nov 1854 - ?)
31 Jan 1912 - 3 Aug 1915: Chairman of the Remount Commission, Penza Region
25 Mar 1912: Promoted to *Major-General*
3 Aug 1915: Retired

*Major-General* Aleksandr Nikolayevich **Dirin** (10 Mar 1852 - ?)
25 Feb 1908: Promoted to *Major-General*
25 Feb 1908 - 28 Mar 1912: Commander, 43$^{rd}$ Artillery Brigade
28 Mar 1912: Retired

*Lieutenant-General* Baron Nikolai Aleksandrovich von **Disterlo** (25 Mar 1871 - ?)
10 May 1910 - 4 Nov 1914: Chief of Administration, Inspectorate-General of Cavalry
6 Dec 1912: Promoted to *Major-General*
4 Nov 1914 - 3 Nov 1915: Chief of Staff, II. Cavalry Corps
3 Nov 1915 - 1918: Commander, 11$^{th}$ Cavalry Division
15 Jun 1917: Promoted to *Lieutenant-General*

*Major-General* Baron Sergey Aleksandrovich von **Disterlo** (6 Sep 1872 - 3 Dec 1918)
28 Nov 1912 - Jul 1914: Military Judge, Warsaw Military District Court
14 Apr 1913: Promoted to *Major-General*
Jul 1914 - Oct 1917: Military Judge, Minsk Military District Court

*General of Artillery* Fyodor Karlovich **Diterikhs** (4 Aug 1831 - 31 Jan 1899)
8 Aug 1873 - 15 Feb 1878: Director, 3$^{rd}$ Siberian Military College
30 Aug 1873: Promoted to *Major-General*
15 Feb 1878 - 4 Nov 1894: Director, Corps of Pages
15 May 1883: Promoted to *Lieutenant-General*
4 Nov 1894 - 31 Jan 1899: Special Assignments General, Main Directorate for Military Schools
14 May 1896: Promoted to *General of Artillery*

*Lieutenant-General* Ivan Yakovlevich **Diterikhs** (25 Aug 1845 - ?)
12 Aug 1889 - 20 May 1894: Commander of Artillery, Fortress St. Petersburg, Commandant, Artillery Depot, St. Petersburg Military District
30 Aug 1890: Promoted to *Major-General*
20 May 1894 - 11 May 1901: Deputy Commanding General, Borderguard Corps
6 Dec 1899: Promoted to *Lieutenant-General*
11 May 1901 - 1 Jan 1903: Commander of Borderguards, Amur Military District
1 Jan 1903 - Jan 1913: Member of the Board of the Ministry of Finance

*Major-General* Mikhail Konstantinovich **Diterikhs** (5 Apr 1874 - 8 Oct 1937)
19 Mar 1915 - 28 May 1916: Quartermaster-General, Southwestern Front
28 May 1915: Promoted to *Major-General*
28 May 1916 - Oct 1916: Commander, 2$^{nd}$ Special Infantry Brigade
Oct 1916 - 18 Jul 1917: Commander, Joint Franco-Russian Division
18 Jul 1917 - 24 Aug 1917: Reserve officer, Petrograd Military District

| | |
|---|---|
| 24 Aug 1917 - 27 Aug 1917: | Chief of Staff, Special Army |
| 27 Aug 1917 - 31 Aug 1917: | Chief of Staff, III. Cavalry Corps |
| 10 Sep 1917 - 3 Nov 1917: | Quartermaster-General, Supreme Commander-in-Chief |
| 3 Nov 1917 - 8 Nov 1917: | Acting Chief of the Staff to the Supreme Commander-in-Chief |
| 8 Nov 1917 - Mar 1918: | At the disposal of the Chief of Staff, Caucasus Front |

*Major-General* Nikolai Nikolayevich **Diterikhs** (14 Apr 1857 - ?)
| | |
|---|---|
| 14 Jun 1904 - Jun 1910: | Commander, 33$^{rd}$ Artillery Brigade |
| 6 Dec 1905: | Promoted to *Major-General* |

*Rear-Admiral* Vladimir Konstantinovich **Diterikhs** (25 Nov 1860 - 1924)
| | |
|---|---|
| 7 May 1913 - 30 Apr 1917: | Chairman, Baltic Sea Shipbuilding Commission |
| 6 Apr 1914: | Promoted to *Rear-Admiral* |
| 30 Apr 1917 - 30 May 1917: | Reserve officer, Ministry of the Navy |
| 30 May 1917: | Retired |

*Major-General* Konstantin Mikhailovich **Dlotovsky** (23 May 1828 - ?)
| | |
|---|---|
| 16 Feb 1886: | Promoted to *Major-General* |
| 16 Feb 1886 - 31 Jan 1894: | Commander, 2$^{nd}$ Brigade, 33$^{rd}$ Infantry Division |
| 31 Jan 1894 - 1895: | Commander, 51$^{st}$ Reserve Infantry Brigade |

*Major-General* Viktor Mikhailovich **Dlotovsky** (30 Mar 1857 - ?)
| | |
|---|---|
| 15 Nov 1910 - 27 Aug 1914: | Commander, 2$^{nd}$ Battalion, 45$^{th}$ Artillery Brigade |
| 27 Aug 1914: | Promoted to *Major-General* |
| 27 Aug 1914: | Retired |
| 1915 - ?: | Recalled in the rank of *Colonel*, Commander, 2$^{nd}$ Battalion, 45$^{th}$ Artillery Brigade |

*Major-General* Mikhail Mikhailovich **Dlussky** (22 Oct 1853 - Dec 1941)
| | |
|---|---|
| 22 May 1910 - 31 Dec 1913: | Military Commander, Warsaw District |
| 14 Apr 1913: | Promoted to *Major-General* |
| 31 Dec 1913 - 29 Jul 1914: | Commander, Tambov Regional Brigade |
| 29 Jul 1914 - 1917: | Commander, Omsk Regional Brigade |

*Major-General* Pyotr Ivanovich **Dmitrevsky** (26 Jun 1869 - 2 Aug 1926)
| | |
|---|---|
| 28 May 1915: | Promoted to *Major-General* |
| 28 May 1915 - 17 Dec 1915: | Commander, Brigade, 29$^{th}$ Infantry Division |
| 17 Dec 1915 - 31 Aug 1916: | Chief of Staff, 55$^{th}$ Infantry Division |
| 31 Aug 1916 - 17 Jan 1917: | Chief of Staff, V. Army Corps |
| 17 Jan 1917 - 22 Aug 1917: | Chief of Staff, XLIV. Army Corps |
| 22 Aug 1917 - 30 Aug 1917: | Commander, Consolidated Border Infantry Division |
| 30 Aug 1917 - 2 Dec 1917: | Acting Commanding General, XLVI. Army Corps |
| 2 Dec 1917: | Resigned |

*Major-General* Yevgeny Nikolayevich **Dmitrevsky** (14 Apr 1870 - 1931)
| | |
|---|---|
| 8 Nov 1915 - 1917: | Deputy Chief of Sestroretsk Arms Factory |
| 6 Dec 1915: | Promoted to *Major-General* |

*Lieutenant-General* Avgust Aleksandrovich **Dmitriev** (24 Sep 1860 - 23 Sep 1919)
| | |
|---|---|
| 14 Dec 1901 - 20 Dec 1908: | Section Commander, Hotinsky Brigade, Borderguard Corps |
| 6 Dec 1906: | Promoted to *Major-General* |
| 20 Dec 1908 - 16 Jul 1912: | Commander, $2^{nd}$ District Section, Borderguard Corps |
| 16 Jul 1912 - 3 Jan 1914: | Deputy Commanding General, Borderguard Corps |
| 26 Feb 1913: | Promoted to *Lieutenant-General* |
| 3 Jan 1914 - 13 Nov 1915: | Commander of Borderguards, Amur Military District |
| 13 Nov 1915 - 1916: | Reserve officer, Kiev Military District |
| 1916 - 12 Aug 1916: | At the disposal of the C-in-C, $7^{th}$ Army |
| 12 Aug 1916 - 15 Apr 1917: | Commander, $4^{th}$ Infantry Division |
| 15 Apr 1917 - 25 Apr 1917: | Acting Commanding General, VI. Army Corps |

*Rear-Admiral* Apollon Apollonovich **Dmitriev** (5 Oct 1863 - 12 Sep 1914)
| | |
|---|---|
| 1911 - 10 Sep 1914: | Commander, Battleship *"Ioann Zlatoust"* |
| 10 Sep 1914: | Promoted to *Rear-Admiral* |
| 10 Sep 1914: | Retired |

*Major-General* Mikhail Andreyevich **Dmitriev** (19 Aug 1849 - 1911)
| | |
|---|---|
| 4 Mar 1910: | Promoted to *Major-General* |
| 4 Mar 1910 - 1911: | Commander, $3^{rd}$ Replacement Artillery Brigade |

*Major-General* Nikolai Alekseyevich **Dmitriev** (6 Dec 1862 - ?)
| | |
|---|---|
| 5 Apr 1915 - 10 Jun 1917: | Commander, $20^{th}$ Artillery Brigade |
| 8 Nov 1915: | Promoted to *Major-General* |
| 10 Jun 1917 - 1917: | Inspector of Artillery, II. Turkestan Army Corps |

*Major-General* Pyotr Gavrilovich **Dmitriev** (28 Feb 1860 - ?)
| | |
|---|---|
| 5 Jun 1910 - 1917: | Commander, $22^{nd}$ Sapper Battalion |
| 6 Dec 1915: | Promoted to *Major-General* |

*Major-General* Pyotr Nikolayevich **Dmitriev** (20 Dec 1871 - 20 Jun 1916)
| | |
|---|---|
| 1916 - 20 Jun 1916: | Commander, Battalion, $266^{th}$ Infantry Regiment |
| 12 Oct 1916: | Posthumously promoted to *Major-General* |

*Major-General of the Fleet* Vladimir Yevdokimovich **Dmitriev** (23 Jul 1860 - 21 May 1937)
| | |
|---|---|
| ? - 1917: | Senior Deputy Commander, Port of Sevastopol |
| ?: | Promoted to *Major-General of the Fleet* |

*Lieutenant-General* Nikolai Grigoryevich **Dmitriev-Baytsurov** (9 Nov 1848 - ?)
| | |
|---|---|
| 16 Mar 1902 - 6 Jul 1912: | Chief, Sestroresk Arms Factory |
| 6 Dec 1902: | Promoted to *Major-General* |
| 6 Dec 1910: | Promoted to *Lieutenant-General* |
| 6 Jul 1912: | Retired |

*Major-General* Iosif Konstantinovich **Dmitrov** (27 Feb 1844 - ?)
| | |
|---|---|
| 8 Aug 1892 - 22 Nov 1894: | Ataman, $2^{nd}$ Don District, Don Cossack Army |

| | |
|---|---|
| 6 May 1893: | Promoted to *Major-General* |
| 22 Nov 1894 - 19 Jun 1899: | Commander, Taganrog District, Don Cossack Army |
| 19 Jun 1899 - 1900: | Attached to the Don Cossack Army |

*General of Infantry* Viktor Ivanovich **Dmitrovsky** (15 Jan 1834 - 12 Apr 1902)
| | |
|---|---|
| 1 Nov 1876 - 24 Sep 1878: | Chief of Staff, VIII. Army Corps |
| 15 Jun 1877: | Promoted to *Major-General* |
| 24 Sep 1878 - 20 Mar 1880: | Transferred to the reserve |
| 20 Mar 1880 - 3 Nov 1886: | Commander, 2nd Rifle Brigade |
| 30 Aug 1886: | Promoted to *Lieutenant-General* |
| 3 Nov 1886 - 11 Oct 1892: | Commander, 17th Infantry Division |
| 11 Oct 1892 - 12 Apr 1902: | Member, Committee for Wounded Veterans |
| 28 Oct 1894 - 1 Jan 1898: | Commanding General, III. Army Corps |
| 1 Jan 1898 - 4 Aug 1899: | Commanding General, XX. Army Corps |
| 6 Dec 1898: | Promoted to *General of Infantry* |

*Major-General* Genrikh Kazimirovich **Dmokhovsky** (26 Jul 1847 - ?)
| | |
|---|---|
| 9 Jul 1899 - 1906: | Commander, Riga Borderguard Brigade |
| 14 Apr 1902: | Promoted to *Major-General* |
| 1906 - 1908: | Commander, 7th Border District |

*Major-General* Iosif Yustinovich **Doboshinsky** (15 Jul 1841 - ?)
| | |
|---|---|
| 16 May 1891 - 1900: | Director of Yaroslavl Military School |
| 30 Aug 1893: | Promoted to *Major-General* |

*Major-General* Nikolai Rafailovich **Doboshinsky** (11 Nov 1872 - 1913)
| | |
|---|---|
| 20 Jul 1910 - ?: | Section Chief, General Staff |
| 1912: | Promoted to *Major-General* |

*Major-General* Aleksandr Petrovich **Dobromyslov** (16 Jul 1836 - 17 Oct 1900)
| | |
|---|---|
| 27 Oct 1883 - 11 Mar 1892: | Commander, 13th Dragoon Regiment |
| 11 Mar 1892: | Promoted to *Major-General* |
| 11 Mar 1892 - 2 Oct 1895: | Commander, 2nd Brigade, 12th Cavalry Division |
| 2 Oct 1905 - 17 Oct 1900: | Commander, 8th Reserve Cavalry Brigade |

*Lieutenant-General* Sergey Alekseyevich **Dobronravov** (18 Jul 1857 - ?)
| | |
|---|---|
| 12 Feb 1904 - 21 Sep 1905: | Attached to the C-in-C, 1st Manchurian Army |
| 31 Jan 1905: | Promoted to *Major-General* |
| 21 Sep 1905 - 12 Jan 1907: | Inspector of Hospitals, 1st Manchurian Army |
| 12 Jan 1907 - 20 Sep 1908: | Commander, 1st Brigade, 6th East Siberian Rifle Division |
| 20 Sep 1908 - 18 Nov 1911: | Commander, 2nd Brigade, 21st Infantry Division |
| 18 Nov 1911 - 30 Nov 1913: | Commander, 1st Brigade, 52nd Infantry Division |
| 30 Nov 1913 - 30 Dec 1914: | Attached to the Minister of War |
| 30 Dec 1914 - 30 Sep 1917: | Reserve officer, Kiev Military District |
| 30 Sep 1917: | Promoted to *Lieutenant-General* |
| 30 Sep 1917: | Dismissed |

*Lieutenant-General* Sergey Konstantinovich **Dobrorolsky** (11 Oct 1867 - 1930)
| | |
|---|---|
| 6 Dec 1910: | Promoted to *Major-General* |
| 6 Dec 1910 - 9 Feb 1913: | Deputy Chief of Main Department for Mobilization, General Staff |
| 9 Feb 1913 - 8 Nov 1914: | Chief of Main Department for Mobilization, General Staff |
| 8 Nov 1914: | Promoted to *Lieutenant-General* |
| 8 Nov 1914 - 3 Jun 1915: | Chief of Staff, 3$^{rd}$ Army |
| 3 Jun 1915 - 17 Jul 1917: | Commander, 78$^{th}$ Infantry Division |
| 17 Jul 1917 - 12 Aug 1917: | Commanding General, XLIV. Army Corps |
| 12 Aug 1917 - 1918: | Commanding General, X. Army Corps |

*General of Infantry* Sergei Fyodorovich **Dobrotin** (24 Sep 1854 - ?)
| | |
|---|---|
| 31 Jan 1904 - 30 Jul 1905: | Commander, 12$^{th}$ Siberian Infantry Regiment |
| 25 Feb 1905: | Promoted to *Major-General* |
| 30 Jul 1905 - 30 May 1906: | At the disposal of the Commanding General, Kiev Military District |
| 30 May 1906 - 3 May 1914: | Commander, 3$^{rd}$ Rifle Brigade |
| 25 Feb 1909: | Promoted to *Lieutenant-General* |
| 3 May 1914 - 3 Apr 1915: | Commander, 44$^{th}$ Infantry Division |
| 3 Apr 1915 - 14 Sep 1915: | Commanding General, XXXIII. Army Corps |
| 14 Sep 1915 - 1917: | Inspector-General of Infantry |
| 6 Dec 1915: | Promoted to *General of Infantry* |

*Rear-Admiral* Leonid Fyodorovich **Dobrotvorsky** (13 Apr 1856 - 21 Oct 1915)
| | |
|---|---|
| 24 Jun 1904 - 17 Dec 1907: | Commander, Cruiser "Oleg" |
| 17 Dec 1907 - 14 Jul 1908: | Reserve officer, Ministry of the Navy |
| 14 Jul 1908: | Promoted to *Rear-Admiral* |
| 14 Jul 1908: | Retired |

*Lieutenant-General* Aleksandr Ivanovich **Dobrov** (12 Aug 1871 - ?)
| | |
|---|---|
| 10 Mar 1912: | Promoted to *Major-General* |
| 10 Mar 1912 - 20 Jun 1915: | Commander, 37$^{th}$ Artillery Brigade |
| 20 Jun 1915 - 3 Oct 1917: | Inspector of Artillery, XXXIX. Army Corps |
| 24 Nov 1916: | Promoted to *Lieutenant-General* |
| 3 Oct 1917: | Dismissed |

*Major-General* Aleksandr Mikhailovich **Dobrovolsky** (19 Dec 1863 - 1917)
| | |
|---|---|
| 11 Mar 1907 - 1917: | Professor, Aleksandr Military Law Academy |
| 22 Apr 1907: | Promoted to *Major-General* |

*Major-General* Ivan Adamovich **Dobrovolsky** (3 Oct 1864 - ?)
| | |
|---|---|
| 9 Aug 1913 - 1917: | Deputy Chief of Administration, Tsarskoye Selo Palace |
| 6 Dec 1915: | Promoted to *Major-General* |

*Rear-Admiral* Kirill Romanovich **Dobrovolsky** (6 Jun 1854 - 15 Feb 1907)
| | |
|---|---|
| 9 Sep 1902 - 27 Sep 1904: | Commander, 2$^{nd}$ Naval Depot |
| 24 Apr 1906: | Promoted to *Rear-Admiral* |

24 Apr 1906:                           Retired

*Lieutenant-General* Mikhail Mikhailovich **Dobrovolsky** (27 Sep 1860 - 13 Oct 1914)
1 Apr 1904 - 22 Dec 1905:          Commander, 2nd Brigade, 55th Infantry Division
1 Jun 1904:                        Promoted to *Major-General*
29 Nov 1904 - 12 Jan 1905:         Acting Chief of Communications, Far East
12 Jan 1905 - 9 Feb 1905:          Acting Chief of Logistics, Manchurian Army
9 Feb 1905 - 12 Oct 1905:          Acting Quartermaster-General for Logistics, Manchurian Army
22 Dec 1905 - 22 Nov 1906:         At the disposal of the Chief of Logistics, Manchurian Army
22 Nov 1906 - 13 Jul 1910:         Chief of Staff, XX. Army Corps
13 Jul 1910:                       Promoted to *Lieutenant-General*
13 Jul 1910 - 12 Oct 1911:         Commander, 3rd Siberian Rifle Division
12 Oct 1911 - 25 Aug 1914:         Commander, 34th Infantry Division
26 Aug 1914:                       Dismissed

*Lieutenant-General* Nikolai Vasilievich **Dobrovolsky** (24 Jan 1850 - ?)
10 Nov 1898 - 5 Sep 1905:          Commandant, Kursk Artillery Depot
6 Dec 1903:                        Promoted to *Major-General*
5 Sep 1905 - 1912:                 Deputy Commander of Artillery, Odessa Military District
1912:                              Promoted to *Lieutenant-General*
1912:                              Retired

*Lieutenant-General* Nikolai Vasilievich **Dobrovolsky** (24 Jan 1864 - 8 Jan 1917)
6 Dec 1908:                        Promoted to *Major-General*
6 Dec 1908 - 22 Mar 1911:          Commander, Life Guards Sapper Battalion
22 Mar 1911 - 29 Nov 1912:         Inspector of Field Engineers, St. Petersburg Military District
29 Nov 1912 - 8 Jan 1917:          Inspector of Engineers, St. Petersburg Military District
22 Mar 1915:                       Promoted to *Lieutenant-General*

*Major-General* Vladimir Ivanovich **Dobryakov** (4 May 1855 - 1915)
13 Jun 1884 - 1915:                Attached to the Gendarmerie Corps
6 Dec 1909:                        Promoted to *Major-General*

*Lieutenant-General* Aleksandr Fyodorovich **Dobryshin** (16 May 1871 - Feb 1942)
24 Dec 1911 - 19 Jan 1915:         Commander, 8th Finnish Infantry Regiment
31 Dec 1914:                       Promoted to *Major-General*
19 Jan 1915 - 9 Nov 1916:          Chief of Staff, XXVI. Army Corps
9 Nov 1916 - 15 Apr 1917:          Commander, Caucasus Grenadier Division
15 Apr 1917 - 23 Aug 1917:         Acting Chief of Staff, 10th Army
23 Aug 1917:                       Promoted to *Lieutenant-General*
23 Aug 1917 - 1918:                Commanding General, XXXVIII. Army Corps

*Lieutenant-General* Filipp Nikolayevich **Dobryshin** (8 Dec 1855 - 1920)
6 Dec 1903:                        Promoted to *Major-General*

| | |
|---|---|
| 6 Dec 1903 - 9 May 1914: | Chief of Communciations Department, General Staff |
| 6 Dec 1909: | Promoted to *Lieutenant-General* |
| 9 May 1914 - 19 Sep 1914: | Commander, 3rd Grenadier Division |
| 19 Sep 1914 - Oct 1914: | Reserve officer, Kiev Military District |
| Oct 1914 - 12 May 1915: | At the disposal of the Chief of Logistics, Southwestern Front |
| 12 May 1915 - 25 Mar 1917: | Chief of Staff, Kazan Military District |
| 25 Mar 1917 - 5 Dec 1917: | Reserve officer, Kazan Military District |
| 5 Dec 1917 - Jan 1918: | Reserve officer, Moscow Military District |
| Jan 1918: | Retired |

*Major-General* Vladimir Aleksandrovich **Dobrzhansky** (27 Feb 1867 - ?)

| | |
|---|---|
| 1915 - 22 Feb 1916: | Commander, 3rd Siberian Rifle Regiment |
| 18 Apr 1915: | Promoted to *Major-General* |
| 22 Feb 1916 - 7 Feb 1917: | Commander, Brigade, 31st Infantry Division |
| 7 Feb 1917 - 6 Aug 1917: | Commander, 169th Infantry Division |

*Lieutenant-General* Ksavery Antonovich **Dobrzhinsky** (1 Nov 1847 - ?)

| | |
|---|---|
| 1 Feb 1896 - 28 Feb 1901: | Attached to the Inspector of Riflemen |
| 14 May 1896: | Promoted to *Major-General* |
| 3 Feb 1897 - 1908: | Member of the Artillery Committee, Main Artillery Directorate |
| 28 Feb 1901 - 19 Apr 1904: | Commander, 3rd Rifle Brigade |
| 19 Apr 1904: | Promoted to *Lieutenant-General* |
| 19 Apr 1904 - Dec 1908: | Commander, 35th Infantry Division |

*Lieutenant-General* Valerian Petrovich **Dobuzhinsky** (24 Jun 1844 - 27 Jun 1921)

| | |
|---|---|
| 14 Feb 1899: | Promoted to *Major-General* |
| 14 Feb 1899 - 16 Mar 1899: | Commander, 40th Artillery Brigade |
| 16 Mar 1899 - 28 Mar 1903: | Commander, 43rd Artillery Brigade |
| 28 Mar 1903 - 13 Aug 1905: | Commander of Artillery, XIX. Army Corps |
| 17 Apr 1905: | Promoted to *Lieutenant-General* |
| 13 Aug 1905 - 24 Aug 1906: | Commander of Artillery, XV. Army Corps |
| 24 Aug 1906 - 1907: | Commander of Artillery, XIX. Army Corps |
| 1907: | Retired |
| 20 Jun 1915 - 5 Nov 1916: | Recalled; Deputy Commander of Artillery, Dvinsk Military District |
| 5 Nov 1916 - 1917: | Reserve officer, Dvinsk Military District |

*General of Cavalry* Dmitry Petrovich **Dokhturov** (30 Mar 1838 - 12 Mar 1905)

| | |
|---|---|
| 14 Sep 1877: | Promoted to *Major-General* |
| 14 Sep 1877 - 25 Sep 1877: | Commander, 1st Brigade, 33rd Infantry Division |
| 25 Sep 1877 - 21 Apr 1878: | Commander, 2nd Brigade, 33rd Infantry Division |
| 21 Apr 1878 - 18 Apr 1880: | Commander, 2nd Brigade, 16th Infantry Division |
| 18 Apr 1880 - 20 Nov 1884: | Commander, 2nd Brigade, 2nd Guards Cavalry Division |
| 20 Nov 1884 - 16 Jun 1886: | Commander, 2nd Guards Cavalry Division |
| 16 Jun 1886 - 14 Aug 1886: | At the disposal of the Minister of War |
| 14 Aug 1886 - 18 Sep 1892: | Commander, 12th Infantry Division |

| | |
|---|---|
| 30 Aug 1886: | Promoted to *Lieutenant-General* |
| 18 Sep 1892 - 17 Mar 1895: | Commander, 13th Infantry Division |
| 17 Mar 1895 - 30 Apr 1900: | Commanding General, XI. Army Corps |
| 6 Dec 1898: | Promoted to *General of Cavalry* |
| 30 Apr 1900 - 14 Apr 1901: | Deputy Commanding General, Odessa Military District |
| 14 Apr 1901 - 1904: | Member of the Military Council |
| 1904 - 1905: | Attached to the C-in-C, 2nd Manchurian Army |
| 1905 - 12 Mar 1905: | C-in-C-Designate, 3rd Manchurian Army |

*Major-General* Georgy Arkadiyevich **Dokuchayev** (14 Jan 1864 - ?)
| | |
|---|---|
| 1914 - 4 Jul 1916: | Commander, 5th Caucasus Rifle Regiment |
| 1916: | Promoted to *Major-General* |
| 4 Jul 1916 - 1918: | Commander, Brigade, 5th Caucasus Rifle Division |

*Lieutenant-General* Mitrofan Vladimirovich **Dolginsky** (16 Oct 1853 - ?)
| | |
|---|---|
| 28 Jan 1900 - 29 Aug 1902: | Military Judge, Amur Military District |
| 14 Apr 1902: | Promoted to *Major-General* |
| 29 Aug 1902 - 10 Jul 1909: | Retired |
| 10 Jul 1909 - 31 Oct 1912: | Recalled; Military Judge, Caucasus Military District |
| 31 Oct 1912 - 31 Dec 1914: | Military Judge, Amur Military District |
| 31 Dec 1914: | Promoted to *Lieutenant-General* |
| 31 Dec 1914: | Retired |

*Major-General of the Fleet* Prince Aleksandr Aleksandrovich **Dolgorukov** (10 Dec 1866 - Sep 1919)
| | |
|---|---|
| 1902 - 1908: | Naval Attaché, Germany |
| 1908 - 15 Apr 1911: | Attached to the Naval General Staff |
| 15 Apr 1911: | Retired |
| 1915 - 1917: | Recalled to duty |
| 1917: | Promoted to *Major-General of the Fleet* |

*Lieutenant-General* Prince Aleksandr Nikolayevich **Dolgorukov** (27 Dec 1872 - 17 Jan 1948)
| | |
|---|---|
| 17 Dec 1912: | Promoted to *Major-General* |
| 17 Dec 1912 - 13 Nov 1914: | Commander, Guards Cavalry Regiment |
| 10 Nov 1914 - 7 Jul 1915: | Commander, 3rd Don Cossack Division |
| 7 Jul 1915 - 11 Jan 1916: | Unassigned |
| 11 Jan 1916 - 19 Apr 1917: | Commander, 3rd Don Cossack Division |
| 19 Apr 1917 - 28 Aug 1917: | Commanding General, I. Cavalry Corps |
| 29 Apr 1917: | Promoted to *Lieutenant-General* |
| 9 Sep 1917 - Feb 1918: | Reserve officer, Petrograd Military District |

*Major-General of the Fleet* Nikolai Vasilyevich **Dolgorukov** (30 Nov 1849 - ?)
| | |
|---|---|
| 22 Jan 1901 - Jan 1909: | Senior Deputy Chief Inspector of Shipbuilding |
| 19 Mar 1907: | Promoted to *Major-General of the Fleet* |

*Major-General* Prince Vasily Aleksandrovich **Dolgorukov** (1 Aug 1868 - 10 Jul 1918)
| | |
|---|---|
| 16 Mar 1910 - 3 Mar 1912: | Commander, 3rd Dragoon Regiment |

| | |
|---|---|
| 3 Mar 1912 - 4 Feb 1914: | Commander, Life Guards Horse-Grenadier Regiment |
| 25 Mar 1912: | Promoted to *Major-General* |
| 4 Feb 1914 - 23 Jul 1914: | Commander, 1st Brigade, 1st Guards Cavalry Division |
| 23 Jul 1914 - Dec 1917: | Court Marshal to the Tsar |
| Dec 1917: | Retired |

*General of Infantry* Prince Nikolai Sergeyevich **Dolgoruky** (28 Apr 1840 - 28 Feb 1913)
| | |
|---|---|
| 8 Nov 1879 - 20 Apr 1886: | Attached to the Kaiser of Germany |
| 26 Feb 1882: | Promoted to *Major-General* |
| 20 Apr 1886 - 18 Nov 1889: | Envoy Extraordinary & Minister Plenipotentiary at the Persian Court |
| 18 Nov 1889 - 14 Oct 1905: | Attached to the Ministry of Foreign Affairs |
| 14 May 1896: | Promoted to *Lieutenant-General* |
| 1896: | Promoted to *General-Adjutant* |
| 14 Oct 1905 - 25 Jan 1909: | Deputy Commandant of the Imperial Main Headquarters |
| 6 Dec 1906: | Promoted to *General of Infantry* |
| 25 Jan 1909 - 6 May 1912: | Ambassador Extraordinary and Plenipotentiary to the King of Italy |
| 6 May 1912 - 28 Feb 1913: | Member of the State Council |

*Major-General* Prince Sergei Aleksandrovich **Dolgoruky** (15 May 1872 - 11 Nov 1933)
| | |
|---|---|
| 15 Jan 1915 - Mar 1917: | Attached to Tsarina Maria Feodorovna |
| 22 Mar 1915: | Promoted to *Major-General* |

*Lieutenant-General* Aleksandr Aleksandrovich **Dolgov** (28 Jan 1859 - 23 Aug 1930)
| | |
|---|---|
| 30 Sep 1904 - 25 Jan 1906: | Commander, 68th Artillery Brigade |
| 25 Jan 1906 - 1 Jul 1910: | Commander, 4th Reserve Artillery Brigade |
| 2 Apr 1906: | Promoted to *Major-General* |
| 1 Jul 1910: | Promoted to *Lieutenant-General* |
| 1 Jul 1910 - 27 Aug 1913: | Inspector of Artillery, X. Army Corps |
| 27 Aug 1913 - 23 Sep 1915: | Commander of Artillery, XXI. Army Corps |
| 23 Sep 1915 - 19 Feb 1917: | Inspector of Artillery, VII. Turkestan Army Corps |
| 19 Feb 1917 - Oct 1917: | Reserve officer, Kiev Military District |
| Oct 1917: | Retired |

*General of Infantry* Dmitry Aleksandrovich **Dolgov** (18 Jul 1860 - 23 Sep 1939)
| | |
|---|---|
| 14 Jul 1903 - 27 Nov 1905: | General Staff officer, Vilnius Military District |
| 6 Dec 1903: | Promoted to *Major-General* |
| 27 Nov 1905 - 28 Nov 1908: | Chief of Staff, XXI. Army Corps |
| 28 Nov 1908 - 3 Jul 1910: | Commander, 60th Replacement Infantry Brigade |
| 3 Jul 1910: | Promoted to *Lieutenant-General* |
| 3 Jul 1910 - 24 Jun 1915: | Commander, 46th Infantry Division |
| 24 Jun 1915 - 16 Nov 1915: | Commanding General, XIX. Army Corps |
| 16 Nov 1915 - 26 Jan 1916: | Reserve officer, Petrograd Military District |
| 26 Jan 1916 - 1 Mar 1916: | Commanding General, XXXVII. Army Corps |
| 20 Mar 1916 - Sep 1916: | Commanding General, VII. Siberian Army Corps |
| Sep 1916 - 22 Nov 1916: | Reserve officer, Kiev Military District |

| | |
|---|---|
| 22 Nov 1916 - 2 Dec 1916: | Reserve officer, Petrograd Military District |
| 2 Dec 1916 - 15 Jun 1917: | Reserve officer, Moscow Military District |
| 15 Jun 1917: | Promoted to *General of Infantry* |
| 15 Jun 1917: | Retired |

*General of Infantry* Pyotr Innokentyevich **Dolinsky** (19 Dec 1852 - ?)
| | |
|---|---|
| 15 Aug 1892 - 4 May 1897: | Military Judge, Turkestan Military District Court |
| 6 Dec 1895: | Promoted to *Major-General* |
| 4 May 1897 - 27 Feb 1898: | Military Prosecutor, Omsk Military District |
| 27 Feb 1898 - 1 Jan 1899: | Military Prosecutor, Turkestan Military District |
| 1 Jan 1899 - 1 Nov 1905: | Chairman of the Military Tribunal, Amur Military Tribunal |
| 6 Dec 1903: | Promoted to *Lieutenant-General* |
| 1 Nov 1905 - 25 Feb 1906: | Chairman of the Military Tribunal, Vilnius Military Tribunal |
| 25 Feb 1906 - 1 May 1908: | Chairman of the Military Tribunal, Turkestan Military Tribunal |
| 1 May 1908 - 10 Oct 1909: | Permanent Member, Supreme Military Tribunal |
| 10 Oct 1909 - 17 Jul 1911: | Chairman of the Supreme Military Tribunal |
| 17 Jul 1911: | Promoted to *General of Infantry* |
| 17 Jul 1911: | Retired |

*Major-General* Yemelyan Pavlovich **Dolinsky** (8 Aug 1853 - 1909)
| | |
|---|---|
| 6 Dec 1905: | Promoted to *Major-General* |
| 6 Dec 1905 - 1909: | Attached to Grand Duke Pavel Aleksandrovich |

*General of Artillery* Count Viktor Viktorovich **Dolivo-Dobrovolsky-Yevdokimov** (2 Jul 1861 - 1932)
| | |
|---|---|
| 22 Oct 1908: | Promoted to *Major-General* |
| 22 Oct 1908 - 12 Nov 1910: | Commander, 30th Artillery Brigade |
| 12 Nov 1910 - 18 Dec 1913: | Commander, Life Guards 3rd Artillery Brigade |
| 18 Dec 1913 - 16 Apr 1916: | Inspector of Artillery, III. Army Corps |
| 12 Dec 1914: | Promoted to *Lieutenant-General* |
| 16 Apr 1916 - 19 Apr 1917: | Inspector of Artillery, 12th Army |
| 24 May 1917: | Promoted to *General of Artillery* |
| 24 May 1917: | Dismissed |

*Major-General* Arseny Sergeyevich **Dolukhanov** (21 Jan 1863 - ?)
| | |
|---|---|
| 8 Apr 1906 - 26 Nov 1916: | Commander, 4th Sapper Battalion |
| 10 Apr 1916: | Promoted to *Major-General* |
| 26 Nov 1916 - Apr 1917: | Commander, Brigade, 104th Infantry Division |
| Apr 1917 - 1918: | Commander, 4th Engineering Regiment |

*Major-General* Pavel Matveyevich **Dolzhenkov** (4 Nov 1856 - ?)
| | |
|---|---|
| 26 Jun 1910 - 22 May 1915: | Commander, 4th Turkestan Rifle Regiment |
| 23 Mar 1915: | Promoted to *Major-General* |
| 22 May 1915 - 6 Mar 1917: | Commander, Brigade, 2nd Infantry Division |
| 6 Mar 1917 - 20 Sep 1917: | Commander, 161st Infantry Division |

*Major-General* Vladimir Matveyevich **Dolzhenkov** (20 Jan 1858 - ?)
23 Jan 1907 - 1911: Deputy Chief of Mikhailovsky Shostensky Gunpowder Factory
18 Apr 1910: Promoted to *Major-General*

*Lieutenant-General* Nikolai Ivanovich **Domaniyevsky** (10 May 1835 - ?)
1878: Promoted to *Major-General*
1878 - 1884: Member, Main Committee on Troop Training
1884 - 17 Jun 1888: Attached to the Main Intendant Directorate
17 Jun 1888 - 1899: Intendant, Turkestan Military District
30 Aug 1893: Promoted to *Lieutenant-General*

*General of Cavalry* Aleksey Ivanovich **Domantovich** (10 Mar 1846 - 1908)
31 Jul 1893: Promoted to *Major-General*
31 Jul 1893 - 23 Mar 1894: Commander, 1$^{st}$ Brigade, 1$^{st}$ Caucasus Cossack Division
23 Mar 1894 - 18 May 1898: Commander, 2$^{nd}$ Brigade, 2$^{nd}$ Consolidated Cossack Division
18 May 1898 - 28 Jul 1899: Commander, 1$^{st}$ Caucasus Cossack Division
28 Jul 1899 - 14 Sep 1904: Commander, 2$^{nd}$ Consolidated Cossack Division
6 Dec 1900: Promoted to *Lieutenant-General*
14 Sep 1904 - 1906: At the disposal of the Minister of War
1906: Promoted to *General of Cavalry*
1906: Retired

*Major-General* Adam Iordanovich **Dombrovsky** (22 Dec 1843 - Oct 1920)
1 Jun 1889 - 1 Oct 1894: Military Judge, Omsk Military District Court
30 Aug 1893: Promoted to *Major-General*
1 Oct 1894 - 1898: Military Judge, Turkestan Military District Court

*Lieutenant-General* Iosif Genrikhovich **Dombrovsky** (20 Mar 1846 - ?)
28 Dec 1907: Promoted to *Major-General*
28 Dec 1907 - 20 Mar 1913: Commander, Tiflis Local Brigade
20 Mar 1913: Promoted to *Lieutenant-General*
20 Mar 1913: Retired

*Lieutenant-General* Leonid Andreyevich **Dombrovsky** (8 Feb 1861 - ?)
21 Nov 1904 - 31 Jul 1906: Section Chief, Main Directorate of Military Justice
17 Apr 1905: Promoted to *Major-General*
31 Jul 1906 - 23 Feb 1907: Military Judge, Vilnius Military District Court
23 Feb 1907 - 19 Feb 1908: Military Judge, Kazan Military District Court
19 Feb 1908 - 18 Feb 1912: Military Judge, Moscow Military District Court
18 Feb 1912 - 31 Mar 1917: Chairman of the Court, Moscow Military District
25 Mar 1912: Promoted to *Lieutenant-General*
31 Mar 1917 - 13 Apr 1917: Member of the Supreme Military Tribunal
13 Apr 1917 - ?: Chairman of the Court, Moscow Military District

*Lieutenant-General* Pavel Kaetanovich **Dombrovsky** (26 Jun 1848 - ?)
2 Apr 1898 - 2 Feb 1902: Commander, 11$^{th}$ East Siberian Rifle Regiment

| | |
|---|---|
| 26 Feb 1901: | Promoted to *Major-General* |
| 2 Feb 1902 - 31 May 1903: | Commander, 1st Brigade, 32nd Infantry Division |
| 31 May 1903 - 15 Sep 1904: | Commander, 1st Brigade, 33rd Infantry Division |
| 15 Sep 1904 - 13 Aug 1905: | Commander, 1st Rifle Brigade |
| 13 Aug 1905 - 7 Oct 1906: | Commander, 1st Rifle Division |
| 7 Oct 1906 - 19 Nov 1908: | Commander, 40th Infantry Division |
| 22 Apr 1907: | Promoted to *Lieutenant-General* |
| 19 Nov 1908 - 1912: | Member, Moscow Military District Court |
| 1912 - 1917: | Chairman, Moscow Military District Court |

*Lieutenant-General* Vikenty Iordanovich **Dombrovsky** (9 Jul 1845 - 3 Sep 1914)

| | |
|---|---|
| 12 Apr 1884 - 1906: | Military Judge, Odessa Military District Court |
| 30 Aug 1891: | Promoted to *Major-General* |
| 1906: | Promoted to *Lieutenant-General* |
| 1906: | Retired |

*Major-General* Nikolai Fyodorovich **Domelunksen** (18 Jun 1868 - ?)

| | |
|---|---|
| 27 Jul 1910 - 3 Aug 1912: | Chief of Communications, Amur Military District |
| 6 Dec 1910: | Promoted to *Major-General* |
| 3 Aug 1912 - 26 Oct 1912: | Commander, 2nd Brigade, 4th Siberian Rifle Division |
| 26 Oct 1912 - 11 Sep 1914: | Commander, 1st Brigade, 49th Infantry Division |
| 11 Sep 1914: | Retired |

*General of Infantry* Mikhail Alekseyevich **Domontovich** (24 Nov 1830 - 8 Oct 1902)

| | |
|---|---|
| 16 May 1873 - 27 Nov 1876: | Inspector of Classes, Nikolai Cavalry School |
| 30 Aug 1875: | Promoted to *Major-General* |
| 27 Nov 1876 - 1 Jul 1877: | Head of Chancellery, C-in-C of the Danube Army |
| 1 Jul 1877 - 15 Feb 1878: | Governor of Tyrnova, Bulgaria |
| 15 Feb 1878 - 21 Apr 1878: | Special Purposes General, Main Directorate for Military Schools |
| 15 Feb 1878 - 31 Dec 1896: | Supernumerary Member, Military Training Committee |
| 21 Apr 1878 - 1 Jun 1879: | Director, Office of the Russian Imperial Commission, Bulgaria |
| 1 Jun 1879 - 8 Nov 1881: | Chief of Military Training Group, Persian Cossack Brigade |
| 30 Aug 1886: | Promoted to *Lieutenant-General* |
| 31 Dec 1896 - 8 Oct 1902: | Member of the Military Council |
| 5 Nov 1897 - 20 Aug 1900: | Chief of Codification Section, Military Council |
| 6 Dec 1898: | Promoted to *General of Infantry* |

*Lieutenant-General* Moisey Yakovlevich **Domoradsky** (28 Aug 1834 - Jan 1898)

| | |
|---|---|
| 16 Sep 1886 - Jan 1898: | Commandant of Fortress Ust-Dvinsk |
| 25 Dec 1886: | Promoted to *Major-General* |
| 14 May 1896: | Promoted to *Lieutenant-General* |

*Rear-Admiral* Aleksandr Mikhailovich **Domozhirov** (21 Jul 1850 - 25 Feb 1902)

| | |
|---|---|
| 1 Apr 1901: | Promoted to *Rear-Admiral* |
| 1 Apr 1901 - 25 Feb 1902: | Director of the Marine Corps, |

Commandant, Nikolayev Naval Academy

*Lieutenant-General* Fyodor Dmitryevich **Domozhirov** (14 Apr 1857 - Mar 1909)
7 Aug 1900: Promoted to *Major-General*
7 Aug 1900 - 29 Sep 1900: Commander, 4$^{th}$ Siberian Infantry Brigade
29 Sep 1900 - 8 Jan 1903: At the disposal of the Chief of the General Staff
8 Jan 1903 - 14 Jul 1907: Chief of Staff, XV. Army Corps
14 Jul 1907: Promoted to *Lieutenant-General*
14 Jul 1907 - Mar 1909: Commander, 34$^{th}$ Infantry Division

*Lieutenant-General* Pyotr Petrovich **Domozhirov** (9 Jul 1855 - 1921)
3 Aug 1900: Promoted to *Major-General*
3 Aug 1900 - 10 Jan 1905: Commander, Life Guards Volyn Regiment
10 Jan 1905 - 22 Feb 1907: Commander, 2$^{nd}$ Brigade, 3$^{rd}$ Guards Infantry Division
22 Feb 1907 - 9 Apr 1910: Commander, 9$^{th}$ Infantry Division
22 Apr 1907: Promoted to *Lieutenant-General*
9 Apr 1910: Retired

*Major-General* Pavel Aleksandrovich **Don** (28 Jun 1860 - 1920)
20 Mar 1906 - 2 Jul 1908: Judge, Vilnius Military District Court
2 Apr 1906: Promoted to *Major-General*
2 Jul 1908 - 1917: Judge, St. Petersburg Military District Court

*Major-General* Aleksandr Dmitriyevich **Donchenko** (12 Mar 1863 - ?)
23 Jun 1910 - 19 Oct 1916: Commander, 2$^{nd}$ Petrograd Troop Billeting District
14 Apr 1913: Promoted to *Major-General*
19 Oct 1916 - 1917: Inspector of Troop Billeting, Kazan Military District

*Major-General* Georgy Karlovich **Dorian** (24 Jul 1857 - 18 Jul 1933)
23 Dec 1911: Promoted to *Major-General*
23 Dec 1911 - 1917: Commander, Amur Railway Borderguard Brigade

*Major-General* Mikhail Antonovich **Dorman** (1 Nov 1868 - 6 Oct 1918)
6 Jan 1915: Promoted to *Major-General*
6 Jan 1915 - 29 Jan 1917: Chief of Staff, XXI. Army Corps
29 Jan 1917 - Jan 1918: Commander, 185$^{th}$ Infantry Division

*Major-General* Grigoriy Ivanovich **Dorodnitsky** (25 Jan 1857 - ?)
24 Apr 1906 - 1915: Deputy Ataman, Donetsk District, Don Cossack Army
1915: Promoted to *Major-General*
1915: Retired

*Lieutenant-General* Pavel Aleksandrovich **Dorogoy** (5 Nov 1851 - ?)
28 Apr 1892 - 28 Feb 1908: Military Judge, Kazan Military District Court
6 Dec 1898: Promoted to *Major-General*
28 Feb 1908 - 16 Mar 1913: Military Judge, Odessa Military District Court
16 Mar 1913: Promoted to *Lieutenant-General*
16 Mar 1913: Retired

*General of Infantry* Nikolai Fedotovich **Doroshevsky** (31 Jan 1855 - 1919)
| | |
|---|---|
| 16 Mar 1898 - 12 Dec 1905: | Military Prosecutor, Vilnius Military District |
| 18 Apr 1899: | Promoted to *Major-General* |
| 12 Dec 1905 - 23 May 1909: | Chairman of the Military Tribunal, Warsaw Military District |
| 6 Dec 1906: | Promoted to *Lieutenant-General* |
| 23 May 1909 - 1917: | Member, Supreme Military Tribunal |
| 22 Mar 1915: | Promoted to *General of Infantry* |

*Major-General* Veniamin Konstantinovich **Doroshin** (5 Oct 1862 - ?)
| | |
|---|---|
| 24 Jul 1912 - 24 Apr 1916: | Deputy Chief, Sestroretsk Arms Factory |
| 6 Dec 1912: | Promoted to *Major-General* |
| 24 Apr 1916 - 1917: | Chairman of Commission for Construction of Simbirsk Cartridge Factory |

*Lieutenant-General* Iosif Romanovich **Dovbor-Musnitsky** (25 Oct 1867 - 26 Oct 1937)
| | |
|---|---|
| 22 Nov 1914 - 3 Sep 1915: | Commander, 14$^{th}$ Siberian Rifle Regiment |
| 15 Aug 1915: | Promoted to *Major-General* |
| 3 Sep 1915 - 25 Feb 1916: | Special Assignments General, 1st Army |
| 25 Feb 1916 - 7 Nov 1916: | Commander, 123$^{rd}$ Infantry Division |
| 7 Nov 1916 - 17 Jan 1917: | Commander, 38$^{th}$ Infantry Division |
| 17 Jan 1917 - 28 Apr 1917: | Chief of Staff, 1$^{st}$ Army |
| 28 Apr 1917 - Aug 1917: | Commanding General, XXXVIII. Army Corps |
| 5 May 1917: | Promoted to *Lieutenant-General* |
| Aug 1917 - 23 Aug 1917: | Commissioner, Petrograd Military District |
| 23 Aug 1917 - Jan 1918: | Commanding General, Polish Corps |

*Lieutenant-General* Konstantin Romanovich **Dovbor-Musnitsky** (20 Apr 1857 - 1931)
| | |
|---|---|
| 5 Oct 1904: | Promoted to *Major-General* |
| 5 Oct 1904 -15 Mar 1907: | Commander, 1$^{st}$ Brigade, 1$^{st}$ East Siberian Rifle Division |
| Feb - Mar 1905: | Acting Commander, 1$^{st}$ East Siberian Rifle Division |
| 15 Mar 1907 - 21 Nov 1908: | Commander, 1$^{st}$ Brigade, 9$^{th}$ Infantry Division |
| 21 Nov 1908 - 19 Jul 1911: | Commander, 2$^{nd}$ Caucasus Rifle Brigade |
| 24 Jul 1911: | Promoted to *Lieutenant-General* |
| 24 Jul 1911: | Retired |
| 11 Sep 1914 - 22 Jan 1917: | Recalled; Commander, 14$^{th}$ Siberian Rifle Division |
| 22 Jan 1917 - 1918: | Reserve officer, Petrograd Military District |

*Major-General* Ivan Mikhailovich **Dovgilevich** (8 Nov 1842 - ?)
| | |
|---|---|
| 16 Mar 1899: | Promoted to *Major-General* |
| 16 Mar 1899 - 8 Nov 1902: | Commander, 32$^{nd}$ Artillery Brigade |
| 8 Nov 1902: | Retired |

*Major-General* Stefan Agatonovich **Dovgird** (15 Apr 1871 - ?)
| | |
|---|---|
| 22 Mar 1915: | Promoted to *Major-General* |
| 22 Mar 1915 - 4 Sep 1915: | Chief of Staff, IV. Caucasus Army Corps |
| 4 Sep 1915 - 9 Oct 1916: | Commander, Brigade, 40$^{th}$ Infantry Division |

23 Jul 1916 - 1 Aug 1916:        Chief of Staff, 59th Infantry Division
9 Oct 1916 - 23 Jun 1917:        Chief of Staff, Grenadier Corps
23 Jun 1917 - Oct 1917:          Commander, 2nd Grenadier Division

*Major-General* Daniil Vasilievich **Drachevsky** (29 Mar 1858 - 1918)
21 Dec 1905 - 9 Jan 1907:        Mayor of Rostov-on-Don
6 Dec 1906:                      Promoted to *Major-General*
9 Jan 1907 - 18 Jul 1914:        Mayor of St. Petersburg
18 Jul 1914 - 1915:              Unassigned
1915:                            Discharged

*Lieutenant-General* Lyudomir Iosifovich **Dragat** (1 Jan 1834 - ?)
21 May 1878 - 24 Sep 1881:       Military Commander, Lublin
21 Aug 1879:                     Promoted to *Major-General*
24 Sep 1881 - 22 Jul 1883:       Commander, 8th Regional Brigade
22 Jul 1883 - 26 Dec 1892:       Commander, 1st Brigade, 41st Infantry Division
26 Dec 1892 - 1900:              Commander, Minsk Regional Brigade
30 Aug 1894:                     Promoted to *Lieutenant-General*

*General of Cavalry* Abram Mikhailovich **Dragomirov** (21 Sep 1868 - 9 Dec 1955)
23 Feb 1910 - 24 May 1912:       Commander, 9th Hussar Regiment
21 May 1912:                     Promoted to *Major-General*
24 May 1912 - 7 Aug 1912:        Chief of Staff, Fortress Kaunas
7 Aug 1912 - 27 Nov 1912:        Commander, 2nd Brigade, 9th Cavalry Division
27 Nov 1912 - 12 Dec 1914:       Commander, 2nd Independent Cavalry Brigade
16 Aug 1914:                     Promoted to *Lieutenant-General*
12 Dec 1914 - 6 Apr 1915:        Commander, 16th Cavalry Division
6 Apr 1915 - 14 Aug 1916:        Commanding General, IX. Army Corps
13 Aug 1916:                     Promoted to *General of Cavalry*
14 Aug 1916 - 27 Apr 1917:       C-in-C, 5th Army
29 Apr 1917 - 13 May 1917:       C-in-C, Northern Front
1 Jun 1917:                      Retired

*General of Infantry* Mikhail Ivanovich **Dragomirov** (8 Nov 1830 - 15 Oct 1905)
17 Mar 1865 - 14 Feb 1869:       Member, Advisory Committee, General Staff
30 Aug 1868:                     Promoted to *Major-General*
14 Feb 1869 - 14 Mar 1873:       Chief of Staff, Kiev Military District
14 Mar 1873 - 1 Sep 1877:        Commander, 14th Infantry Division
1 Sep 1877:                      Promoted to *Lieutenant-General*
1 Sep 1877 - 1 Apr 1878:         Attached to the Commander-in-Chief of the Army
1 Apr 1878 - 13 Aug 1889:        Commandant of the General Staff Academy
15 Jun 1878:                     Promoted to *General-Adjutant*
13 Aug 1889 - 24 Dec 1903:       Commanding General, Kiev Military District
30 Aug 1891:                     Promoted to *General of Infantry*
24 Dec 1903 - 15 Oct 1905:       Member of the State Council

*Lieutenant-General* Vladimir Mikhailovich **Dragomirov** (7 Feb 1867 - 29 Jan 1928)
21 Jun 1906 - 9 Oct 1908:        Commander, Life Guards Preobrazhensky Regiment

| | |
|---|---|
| 31 May 1907: | Promoted to *Major-General* |
| 9 Oct 1908 - 3 Aug 1912: | Quartermaster-General, Kiev Military District |
| 3 Aug 1912 - 19 Jul 1914: | Chief of Staff, Kiev Military District |
| 14 Apr 1913: | Promoted to *Lieutenant-General* |
| 19 Jul 1914 - 4 Nov 1914: | Chief of Staff, 3rd Army |
| 4 Nov 1914 - 16 Dec 1914: | Commander, 2nd Guards Infantry Division |
| 16 Dec 1914 - 23 Mar 1915: | Commanding General, VIII. Army Corps |
| 23 Mar 1915 - 5 Aug 1915: | Chief of Staff, Southwestern Front |
| 5 Aug 1915 - 18 Aug 1915: | At the disposal of the Supreme Commander-in-Chief |
| 18 Aug 1915 - 9 Sep 1916: | Commanding General, VIII. Army Corps |
| 9 Sep 1916 - 8 Oct 1916: | Reserve officer, Kiev Military District |
| 8 Oct 1916 - 2 Apr 1917: | Commanding General, XVI. Army Corps |
| 2 Apr 1917 - 22 Aug 1917: | Reserve officer, Kiev Military District |
| 22 Aug 1917: | Retired |

*General of Infantry* Lyudvig Lyudvigovich **Drake** (31 Jan 1842 - 11 Jul 1916)
| | |
|---|---|
| 20 Jul 1892: | Promoted to *Major-General* |
| 20 Jul 1892 - 25 Sep 1892: | Deputy Chief of Staff, Vilnius Military District |
| 25 Sep 1892 - 6 Jul 1893: | Duty General, Vilnius Military District |
| 6 Jul 1893 - 16 Jan 1895: | Chief of Staff, XIII. Army Corps |
| 16 Jan 1895 - 20 Feb 1897: | General for Special Assignments, General Staff |
| 20 Feb 1897 - 5 Aug 1899: | Commandant, Pavlovsk Military School |
| 5 Aug 1899 - 16 Dec 1904: | Commander, 33rd Infantry Division |
| 6 Dec 1899: | Promoted to *Lieutenant-General* |
| 16 Dec 1904 - 2 Oct 1906: | Commanding General, XXI. Army Corps |
| 2 Oct 1906: | Promoted to *General of Infantry* |
| 2 Oct 1906: | Retired |

*Major-General* Vladimir Lyudvigovich **Drake** (8 Sep 1874 - 15 Oct 1933)
| | |
|---|---|
| 12 May 1916 - 23 Jan 1917: | Commander, 16th Artillery Brigade |
| 23 Jan 1917 - 28 Apr 1917: | Commander, Guards Rifle Artillery Brigade |
| 26 Feb 1917: | Promoted to *Major-General* |
| 28 Apr 1917 - 1918: | Inspector of Artillery, XLIX. Army Corps |

*Lieutenant-General* Mikhail Nikolayevich **Drashkovsky** (8 Nov 1851 - 1912)
| | |
|---|---|
| 6 Dec 1902: | Promoted to *Major-General* |
| 6 Dec 1902 - 1912: | Attached to Grand Duke Konstantin Konstantinovich |
| 29 Mar 1909: | Promoted to *Lieutenant-General* |

*Major-General* Aleksandr Aleksandrovich von **Drenteln** (19 Jan 1868 - 14 May 1925)
| | |
|---|---|
| 28 Nov 1915: | Promoted to *Major-General* |
| 28 Nov 1915 - 27 Apr 1917: | Commander, Life Guards Preobrazhensky Regiment |

*Major-General* Aleksey Lyudvigovich **Dreving** (21 Apr 1837 - ?)
| | |
|---|---|
| 24 Mar 1900: | Promoted to *Major-General* |
| 24 Mar 1900 - 28 Apr 1904: | Commander, Odessa Regional Brigade |

*Major-General* Pyotr Fyodorovich **Dreving** (10 Sep 1869 - 27 Aug 1914)
27 Apr 1913 - 27 Aug 1914:     Chief of Staff, 2nd Grenadier Division
18 Jan 1915:                   Posthumously promoted to *Major-General*

*Major-General* Nikolai Konstantinovich von **Dreyer** (25 Nov 1853 - 1911)
29 May 1908:                   Promoted to *Major-General*
29 May 1908 - 1911:            Chief, Kharabovsk Artillery Depot

*General of the Hydrographic Corps* Fyodor Kirillovich **Drizhenko** (22 Apr 1858 - 16 Apr 1922)
1905 - 8 Sep 1908:             Chief of Survey, White Sea
6 Dec 1906:                    Promoted to *Major-General of the Hydrographic Corps*
8 Sep 1908 - 24 Dec 1912:      Deputy Chief of the Hydrographic Department
17 Apr 1912:                   Promoted to *Lieutenant-General of the Hydrographic Corps*
24 Dec 1912 - 8 May 1917:      Chief of Survey, Murmansk Coast
8 May 1917:                    Promoted to *General of the Hydrographic Corps*
8 May 1917:                    Retired

*Major-General* Sergey Arkadyevich **Drobyazgin** (2 Jul 1868 - 1917)
9 Oct 1912 - 14 Jan 1916:      Commander, Crimean Cavalry Regiment
8 Jan 1916:                    Promoted to *Major-General*
14 Jan 1916 - 30 Apr 1917:     Commander, 2nd Brigade, Caucasus Native Cavalry Division
30 Apr 1917 - 1917:            Reserve officer, Kiev Military District

*Major-General* Aleksandr Ivanovich **Drozd-Bonyachevsky** (7 Aug 1859 - Sep 1918)
26 Jan 1909 - 23 Jun 1917:     Commandant of Gatchina
6 Dec 1912:                    Promoted to *Major-General*
23 Jun 1917:                   Dismissed

*Lieutenant-General* Nikolai Fyodorovich **Drozdov** (6 Aug 1862 - 29 Nov 1853)
29 May 1909 - 19 Dec 1913:     Senior Clerk, Artillery Committee, Main Artillery Directorate
6 Dec 1910:                    Promoted to *Major-General*
19 Dec 1913 - Oct 1917:        Member of the Artillery Committee, Main Artillery Directorate
7 Sep 1915 - Oct 1917:         Chief of Section 3, Technical Artillery Department, Main Artillery Directorate
30 Jul 1916:                   Promoted to *Lieutenant-General*

*Major-General* Iosif Mikhailovich **Drozdovich** (23 Nov 1844 - ?)
13 Sep 1890 - 1901:            Military Judge, Vilnius Military District Court
30 Aug 1891:                   Promoted to *Major-General*

*Major-General* Yemelyan Mikhailovich **Drozdovich** (30 Sep 1842 - ?)
29 Oct 1889:                   Promoted to *Major-General*
29 Oct 1889 - 28 Dec 1899:     Commander, 1st Brigade, 39th Infantry Division

28 Dec 1899 - 1905: Attached to the Caucasus Military District

*Major-General* Nikolai Pavlovich **Drozdovsky** (20 Nov 1859 - 25 Jan 1915)
31 Dec 1913 - 25 Jan 1915: Commander, Kursk Artillery Depot
?: Promoted to *Major-General*

*Major-General* Semyon Ivanovich **Drozdovsky** (22 Aug 1869 - ?)
5 Jul 1915 - 1916: Commander, 2$^{nd}$ Zaamursky Cavalry Brigade
14 Aug 1915: Promoted to *Major-General*
1916 - 12 Oct 1916: Commander, 1$^{st}$ Brigade, Zaamursky Cavalry Division
12 Oct 1916: Dismissed

*Major-General* Prince Sergey Aleksandrovich **Drutskoy** (31 Oct 1869 - ?)
25 Jan 1903 - 6 Dec 1916: Professor, Aleksandr Military Law Academy
14 Apr 1913: Promoted to *Major-General*
6 Dec 1916 - 1918: Military Judge, Moscow Military District Court

*Lieutenant-General* Konstantin Aleksandrovich **Druzhinin** (1 Apr 1842 - 18 Oct 1905)
7 Nov 1894: Promoted to *Major-General*
7 Nov 1894 - 14 Feb 1901: Deputy Chief of Staff, St. Petersburg Military District
14 Feb 1901 - 7 Jan 1903: At the disposal of the Commanding General, St. Petersburg Military District
7 Jan 1903: Promoted to *Lieutenant-General*
7 Jan 1903 - 18 Oct 1905: Commandant of Krasnoye Selo

*Major-General* Konstantin Ivanovich **Druzhinin** (8 Aug 1863 - 27 Aug 1914)
Sep 1906 - 3 Jun 1908: Chief of Staff, Ural Cossack Army
22 Apr 1907: Promoted to *Major-General*
3 Jun 1908: Retired
Jul 1914 - 27 Aug 1914: Recalled; Commander, 1$^{st}$ Brigade, 26$^{th}$ Infantry Division

*General of Artillery* Yakov Aleksandrovich **Druzhinin** (9 Dec 1830 - 12 Dec 1902)
8 Aug 1873 - 30 Sep 1878: Head of the preparatory boarding school, Nikolayev Cavalry School
30 Aug 1873: Promoted to *Major-General*
30 Sep 1878 - 15 Jan 1900: Director, Nikolayev Cadet Corps
30 Aug 1892: Promoted to *Lieutenant-General*
15 Jan 1900 - 6 Apr 1900: Attached to the Main Directorate for Military Schools
6 Apr 1900 - 12 Dec 1902: Trustee, Board of Trustees, Empress Maria Institutions
6 Dec 1902: Promoted to *General of Artillery*

*Lieutenant-General* Mikhail Nikolayevich **Dryagin** (1 Nov 1852 - ?)
24 Feb 1900 - 25 Jun 1903: Deputy Military Governor of Kutaisi
14 Apr 1902: Promoted to *Major-General*
25 Jun 1903 - 14 Jun 1905: Military Governor of Batumi Region
14 Jun 1905 - 1 Mar 1910: Attached to the Caucasus Military District
1 Mar 1910 - 11 Sep 1911: Transferred to the reserve

| | |
|---|---|
| 11 Sep 1911: | Promoted to *Lieutenant-General* |
| 11 Sep 1911: | Retired |
| 14 Nov 1914 - 1917: | Recalled; Reserve officer, Caucasus Military District |

*Admiral* Fyodor Vasilyevich **Dubasov** (21 Jun 1845 - 19 Jun 1912)
| | |
|---|---|
| 1892 - Aug 1897: | Naval Attaché, Berlin |
| 30 Aug 1893: | Promoted to *Rear-Admiral* |
| Aug 1897 - 6 Dec 1899: | Commander, Pacific Squadron |
| 15 Mar 1899: | Promoted to *Vice-Admiral* |
| 6 Dec 1899 - 1 Jan 1901: | Senior Flagman, 1st Naval Division |
| 1 Jan 1901 - 24 Nov 1905: | Chairman, Naval Technical Committee |
| 14 Mar 1905: | Promoted to *General-Adjutant* |
| 1905 - 1907: | Member, Council of Defense |
| 24 Nov 1905 - Jul 1906: | Governor-General of Moscow |
| Jul 1906 - 19 Jun 1912: | Member, Council of State |
| 6 Dec 1906: | Promoted to *Admiral* |

*General of Cavalry* Nikolai Vasilievich **Dubasov** (21 Nov 1850 - ?)
| | |
|---|---|
| 16 Jun 1900 - 14 Dec 1901: | Director, 2nd Moscow Cadet Corps |
| 1 Apr 1901: | Promoted to *Major-General* |
| 14 Dec 1901 - 20 Apr 1905: | Commandant of Pavlovsk Military School |
| 20 Apr 1905 - 12 May 1906: | Chief of Staff, Don Army |
| 12 May 1906 - 21 Feb 1909: | Quartermaster-General of the General Staff |
| 22 Apr 1907: | Promoted to *Lieutenant-General* |
| 21 Feb 1909 - 1 Jan 1910: | At the disposal of the Ministry of War |
| 1 Jan 1910 - 5 Dec 1913: | Military Governor of the Ural Region, Ataman of the Ural Cossack Army |
| 5 Dec 1913: | Promoted to *General of Cavalry* |
| 5 Dec 1913: | Retired |

*Lieutenant-General* Pavel Petrovich **Dubelt** (24 Jun 1827 - 27 Apr 1904)
| | |
|---|---|
| 31 Jul 1874 - 13 May 1886: | Commander, 100th Infantry Regiment |
| 15 May 1883: | Promoted to *Major-General* |
| 13 May 1886 - 11 Oct 1899: | Commander, 2nd Brigade, 14th Infantry Division |
| 11 Oct 1899: | Promoted to *Lieutenant-General* |
| 11 Oct 1899: | Retired |

*Lieutenant-General* Aleksandr Nikolayevich **Dubensky** (30 Aug 1850 - 29 Jan 1913)
| | |
|---|---|
| 12 May 1885 - 30 Aug 1890: | Adjutant to Grand Duke Mikhail Nikolayevich |
| 30 Aug 1890: | Promoted to *Major-General* |
| 30 Aug 1890 - 1 Apr 1896: | Transferred to the reserve |
| 1 Apr 1896 - 13 Nov 1896: | Commander, 1st Brigade, 11th Cavalry Division |
| 14 Nov 1896 - 29 May 1897: | Commander, 2nd Brigade, 4th Cavalry Division |
| 29 May 1897 - 2 Mar 1899: | Commander, Life Guards Grodno Hussar Regiment |
| 2 Mar 1899 - 17 May 1900: | Commander, 2nd Brigade, 1st Guards Cavalry Division |
| 17 May 1900 - 30 Jan 1902: | Commander, 1st Brigade, 2nd Guards Cavalry Division |
| 30 Jan 1902: | Promoted to *Lieutenant-General* |
| 30 Jan 1902 - 31 Mar 1905: | Commander, 2nd Cavalry Division |

31 Mar 1905 - 10 Feb 1907: Commander, 1st Guards Cavalry Division
10 Feb 1907: Retired

*Lieutenant-General* Dmitry Nikolayevich **Dubensky** (26 Oct 1857 - 5 Jul 1923)
1 Jan 1912: Promoted to *Major-General*
1 Jan 1912 - 24 Jan 1912: Unassigned
24 Jan 1912 - 15 Jun 1915: Attached to the Main Directorate for Horse Breeding
15 Jun 1915 - 1917: Council Member, Main Directorate for Horse Breeding
1916: Promoted to *Lieutenant-General*

*Major-General* Roman Ivanovich **Dubinin** (23 Jul 1861 - ?)
Dec 1914 - 10 Nov 1915: Chief of Staff, II. Army Corps
31 Dec 1914: Promoted to *Major-General*
10 Nov 1915 - 18 Feb 1917: Chief of Staff, XXXIV. Army Corps
18 Feb 1917 - 23 Jul 1917: Commander, 6th Grenadier Division
23 Jul 1917 - 1918: Reserve officer, Kiev Military District

*Lieutenant-General* Filipp-Stanislav Iosifovich **Dubissky** (23 Aug 1860 - 28 Sep 1919)
25 Mar 1914: Promoted to *Major-General*
25 Mar 1914 - 2 Apr 1916: Commander, 2nd Brigade, 39th Infantry Division
2 Apr 1916 - 16 Sep 1917: Commander, 5th Caucasus Rifle Division
16 Sep 1917 - 5 Nov 1917: Commanding General, I. Caucasus Army Corps
5 Nov 1917: Promoted to *Lieutenant-General*
5 Nov 1917: Dismissed

*Major-General* Kazimir Iosifovich **Dubitsky** (2 Aug 1858 - ?)
10 Jun 1902 - 4 Apr 1905: Inspector of Building Works, Port Arthur
4 Apr 1905: Promoted to *Major-General*
4 Apr 1905 - 1905: At the disposal of the Inspector-General of Naval Construction

*Major-General* Yakov Yevgenyevich **Duble** (28 Oct 1858 - 7 Jan 1916)
2 Jan 1906 - 26 Oct 1908: Military Judge, Vilnius Military District Court
2 Apr 1906: Promoted to *Major-General*
26 Oct 1908 - 7 Jan 1916: Military Judge, Moscow Military District Court

*Lieutenant-General* Ivan Semyonovich **Dublyansky** (9 Jan 1861 - 31 Oct 1932)
16 Jul 1910: Promoted to *Major-General*
16 Jul 1910 - 15 Jan 1914: Duty General, Amur Military District
15 Jan 1914 - 16 Aug 1914: Commander, Kharkov Regional Brigade
16 Aug 1914 - 8 Mar 1915: Duty General, Southwestern Front
8 Mar 1915 - 1917: Commander, Odessa Regional Brigade
6 Dec 1916: Promoted to *Lieutenant-General*

*Major-General* Aleksandr Grigoryevich **Dubnitsky** (1 Sep 1866 - Feb 1917)
1 Sep 1909 - 8 Feb 1915: Deputy Chief of Izhevsk Arms Factory
14 Apr 1913: Promoted to *Major-General*
8 Feb 1915 - Feb 1917: Chief of Izhevsk Arms Factory

Feb 1917: Chief of Pulitov Factory

*Major-General* Aleksandr Nikanorovich **Dubovsky** (25 Aug 1863 - ?)
1910 - Sep 1912: Reserve officer, St. Petersburg Military District
Sep 1912: Promoted to *Major-General*
Sep 1912: Retired
29 Jan 1915 - 6 May 1915: Recalled; Chief of Staff, 6$^{th}$ Militia Corps
6 May 1915 - 27 May 1916: Deputy Chief of Sanatory Service, Northwestern Front
27 May 1916 - 25 Jul 1916: Reserve officer, Kazan Military District
25 Jul 1916 - 18 Apr 1917: Reserve officer, Caucasus Military District
18 Apr 1917 - 13 Sep 1917: Chief of Staff, Caucasus Military District
13 Sep 1917 - 1918: Commandant of Fortress Mikhailov

*Major-General* Nikolai Ivanovich **Dubovsky** (9 May 1858 - 1902)
2 May 1900 - 1902: Ataman, Khopersky District, Don Cossack Army
1 Apr 1902: Promoted to *Major-General*

*Lieutenant-General of Naval Artillery* Kir Terentyevich **Dubrov** (18 Jan 1854 - ?)
11 Oct 1902 - 1911: Senior Deputy Chief Inspector of Naval Artillery
6 Dec 1904: Promoted to *Major-General of Naval Artillery*
19 Oct 1911 - 1913: Deputy Chief of Artillery Section, Main Shipbuilding Directorate
6 Dec 1911: Promoted to *Lieutenant-General of Naval Artillery*

*Major-General* Nikolai Mikhailovich **Dubrova** (6 Apr 1847 - ?)
16 Mar 1900: Promoted to *Major-General*
16 Mar 1900 - 17 Mar 1906: Commander, 2$^{nd}$ Brigade, 8$^{th}$ Infantry Division
17 Mar 1906 - 12 May 1910: Commander, 1$^{st}$ Brigade, 10$^{th}$ Infantry Division

*Lieutenant-General* Nikolai Fyodorovich **Dubrovin** (26 Nov 1837 - 25 Jun 1904)
17 Mar 1869 - 4 Nov 1882: Attached to the General Staff
30 Aug 1878: Promoted to *Major-General*
4 Nov 1882 - 25 Jun 1904 Member of the Military Academic Committee, General Staff
30 Aug 1888: Promoted to *Lieutenant-General*
4 Sep 1893 - 25 Jun 1904: Secretary, Imperial Academy of Sciences

*Major-General* Sergey Georgiyevich **Dubrovinsky** (20 Sep 1862 - ?)
21 Aug 1911: Promoted to *Major-General*
21 Aug 1911 - 1914: Duty General, Irkutsk Military District
1914 - 28 Dec 1914: Duty General, Odessa Military District
28 Dec 1914 - 13 Jul 1915: Duty General, Irkutsk Military District
13 Jul 1915 - 1918: Duty General, 7$^{th}$ Army

*Major-General* Sergey Platonovich **Dubrovsky** (20 Jun 1851 - 11 Aug 1919)
? - 1910: Commander, 238$^{th}$ Infantry Regiment
1910: Promoted to *Major-General*
1910: Retired

| | |
|---|---|
| 5 Oct 1914 - 12 Dec 1914: | Recalled; Commander, 18th Militia Brigade |
| 12 Dec 1914 - 7 Aug 1915: | Commander, 2nd Brigade, 114th Infantry Division |
| 7 Aug 1915 - 1917: | POW |

*Major-General* Vasily Ivanovich **Dubrovsky** (23 Jan 1868 - ?)
| | |
|---|---|
| 3 Apr 1913 - 1917: | Military Judge, Caucasus Military District Court |
| 14 Apr 1913: | Promoted to *Major-General* |

*Major-General* Vladimir Nikolayevich **Dubrovsky** (17 Mar 1851 - Aug 1910)
| | |
|---|---|
| 11 Apr 1906 - Aug 1910: | Intendant, IX. Army Corps |
| 19 Sep 1908: | Promoted to *Major-General* |

*Major-General* Aleksandr Yegorovich **Dubyago** (22 Aug 1843 - ?)
| | |
|---|---|
| 24 Oct 1899: | Promoted to *Major-General* |
| 24 Oct 1899 - 27 Aug 1903: | Commander, 1st Brigade, 1st Infantry Division |

*Major-General* Vitt Aleksandrovich **Dudin** (14 Jun 1855 - ?)
| | |
|---|---|
| 24 May 1910 - 14 Jun 1913: | Commander, 2nd Battalion, 13th Artillery Brigade |
| 14 Jun 1913: | Promoted to *Major-General* |
| 14 Jun 1913: | Retired |
| 12 Dec 1914 - 23 Dec 1916: | Recalled; Commander, 15th Artillery Brigade |
| 23 Dec 1916 - 22 Jan 1917: | Inspector of Artillery, I. Army Corps |

*Lieutenant-General* Vyacheslav Mikhailovich **Duditsky-Lishin** (2 Aug 1839 - ?)
| | |
|---|---|
| 13 Jun 1891: | Promoted to *Major-General* |
| 13 Jun 1891 - 11 Jan 1894: | Commander, 1st Brigade, 8th Infantry Division |
| 22 Jan 1894 - 13 Dec 1897: | Commander, 2nd Brigade, 10th Infantry Division |
| 6 Oct 1899 - 17 Oct 1902: | Commander, 39th Infantry Division |
| 6 Dec 1899: | Promoted to *Lieutenant-General* |

*Major-General* Yakov Gennadyevich **Dudyshkin** (19 Nov 1849 - 4 Dec 1906)
| | |
|---|---|
| 10 Jun 1904: | Promoted to *Major-General* |
| 10 Jun 1904 - 14 Jan 1905: | Commander, 1st Brigade, 34th Infantry Division |

*Major-General* Nikolai Yelpidiforovich **Dukhanin** (29 Nov 1864 - ?)
| | |
|---|---|
| 14 May 1914 - 1917: | Chief of Officer, Inspectorate-General of Engineering |
| 10 Apr 1916: | Promoted to *Major-General* |

*Major-General* Konstantin Lavrentyevich **Dukhonin** (19 Mar 1846 - 1901)
| | |
|---|---|
| 14 May 1898 - 1901: | Commander of Engineers, Fortress Brest-Litovsk |
| 6 Dec 1899: | Promoted to *Major-General* |

*Lieutenant-General* Mikhail Lavrentyevich **Dukhonin** (31 Aug 1837 - 17 Dec 1895)
| | |
|---|---|
| 10 Dec 1873 - 14 Feb 1878: | Commander, 55th Infantry Regiment |
| 5 Sep 1877: | Promoted to *Major-General* |
| 14 Feb 1878 - 7 Apr 1878: | Unassigned |
| 7 Apr 1878 - 10 Aug 1882: | Chief of Staff, IV. Army Corps |
| 10 Aug 1882 - 23 Apr 1885: | Deputy Chief of Staff, Warsaw Military District |

| | |
|---|---|
| 23 Apr 1885 - 15 Feb 1889: | Commandant of Vyborg |
| 30 Aug 1886: | Promoted to *Lieutenant-General* |
| 15 Feb 1889 - 16 Mar 1893: | Commander, 36th Infantry Division |
| 16 Mar 1893 - 17 Dec 1895: | Chief of Staff, Moscow Military District |
| 8 Mar 1895 - 30 Dec 1895: | Acting Commanding General, II. Army Corps |

*Lieutenant-General* Nikolai Nikolayevich **Dukhonin** (1 Dec 1876 - 20 Nov 1917)
| | |
|---|---|
| 8 Sep 1915 - 22 Dec 1915: | Attached to the C-in-C, Southwestern Front |
| 6 Dec 1915: | Promoted to *Major-General* |
| 22 Dec 1915 - 29 May 1916: | Quartermaster-General, Southwestern Front |
| 29 May 1916 - 8 Apr 1917: | Chief of Staff, Southwestern Front |
| 8 Apr 1917 - 9 Oct 1917: | Chief of Staff, Western Front |
| 4 Aug 1917: | Promoted to *Lieutenant-General* |
| 9 Oct 1917 - 1 Nov 1917: | Chief of Staff to the Supreme Commander-in-Chief |
| 2 Nov 1917 - 20 Nov 1917: | Supreme Commander-in-Chief |

*General of Infantry* Sergei Mikhailovich **Dukhovskoy** (7 Oct 1838 - 1 Mar 1901)
| | |
|---|---|
| 11 Nov 1876 - 7 Sep 1877: | Chief of Staff, Caucasus-Turkey Border Corps |
| 15 Jun 1877: | Promoted to *Major-General* |
| 7 Sep 1877 - 2 Jan 1878: | Attached to the C-in-C, Caucasus Army |
| 2 Jan 1878 - 4 Feb 1878: | Commander, Hnysskim Detachment |
| 17 Feb 1878 - 11 Oct 1878: | Acting Commandant of Erzurum, Acting Military Governor of Erzurum |
| 11 Oct 1878 - 20 May 1879: | Attached to the General Staff |
| 20 May 1879 - 9 Mar 1893: | Chief of Staff, Moscow Military District |
| 30 Aug 1886: | Promoted to *Lieutenant-General* |
| 9 Mar 1893 - 28 Mar 1898: | Commanding General, Amur Military District, Governor-General of Amur Region, Ataman, Amur Cossack Army |
| 28 Mar 1898 - 1 Jan 1901: | Commanding General, Turkestan Military District, Governor-General of Turkestan |
| 6 Dec 1898: | Promoted to *General of Infantry* |
| 1 Jan 1901: | Retired |

*Major-General* Daniil Grigoryevich **Dukmasov** (24 Dec 1848 - 25 Sep 1904)
| | |
|---|---|
| 31 Jul 1898: | Promoted to *Major-General* |
| 31 Jul 1898 - 21 Jul 1899: | Commander, 1st Brigade, 8th Cavalry Division |
| 21 Jul 1899 - 10 Dec 1903: | Commander, 2nd Brigade, 8th Cavalry Division |
| 10 Dec 1903 - 25 Sep 1904: | At the disposal of the Commanding General, Odessa Military District |

*General of Infantry* Pavel Grigoryevich **Dukmasov** (6 Nov 1838 - 15 Feb 1911)
| | |
|---|---|
| 30 Jun 1874 - 10 Oct 1875: | Special Assignments Officer, Odessa Military District |
| 8 Sep 1874: | Promoted to *Major-General* |
| 10 Oct 1875 - 1 Nov 1876: | Deputy Chief of Staff, Kiev Military District |
| 1 Nov 1876 - 20 Feb 1877: | Chief of Staff, XII. Army Corps |
| 20 Feb 1877 - 8 Sep 1877: | Deputy Chief of Staff, Kiev Military District |
| 8 Sep 1877 - 19 Oct 1886: | Chief of Staff, XIII. Army Corps |

| | |
|---|---|
| 19 Oct 1886: | Promoted to *Lieutenant-General* |
| 19 Oct 1886 - 21 Jul 1894: | Commander, 2nd Grenadier Division |
| 21 Jul 1894 - 17 Mar 1895: | Commanding General, XI. Army Corps |
| 17 Mar 1895 - 3 Jul 1900: | Commanding General, VII. Army Corps |
| 6 Dec 1898: | Promoted to *General of Infantry* |
| 3 Jul 1900 - 15 Feb 1911: | Member of the Military Council |
| 1906 - 15 Feb 1911: | Chairman, Supreme Military Tribunal |

*Major-General* Ignaty Ivanovich **Dumansky** (31 Jul 1829 - ?)

| | |
|---|---|
| 23 May 1877 - 7 Mar 1879: | Intendant, Caucasus Military District |
| 1878: | Promoted to *Major-General* |
| 7 Mar 1879 - 27 Jun 1880: | Unassigned |
| 27 Jun 1880 - 10 Mar 1881: | Chief Superintendant, Kuban-Stavropol Supply Depot |
| 10 Mar 1881 - 3 Jul 1881: | At the disposal of the Commanding General, Caucasus Military District |
| 3 Jul 1881 - 30 Jan 1896: | Deputy Intendant, Caucasus Military District |
| 30 Jan 1896 - 1898: | At the disposal of the General Staff |

*Major-General* Iosif Antonovich **Dumbadze** (3 Jan 1865 - ?)

| | |
|---|---|
| 13 Dec 1910 - 4 Feb 1912: | Commander, 2nd Vladivostok Fortress Artillery Regiment |
| 4 Feb 1912 - 1917: | Commander, 1st Vladivostok Fortress Artillery Brigade |
| 1913: | Promoted to *Major-General* |

*Major-General* Ivan Antonovich **Dumbadze** (19 Jan 1851 - Sep 1916)

| | |
|---|---|
| 26 May 1903 - 15 Oct 1907: | Commander, 16th Rifle Regiment |
| 31 May 1907: | Promoted to *Major-General* |
| 15 Oct 1907 - 10 Jul 1908: | Commander, 2nd Brigade, 34th Infantry Division |
| 10 Jul 1908 - 23 Jul 1912: | Commander, 2nd Brigade, 13th Infantry Division |
| 23 Jul 1912 - 1 Jul 1914: | At the disposal of the Minister of War |
| 1 Jul 1914 - Sep 1916: | Mayor of Yalta |

*Lieutenant-General* Nikolai Antonovich **Dumbadze** (10 Jul 1854 - 9 Mar 1927)

| | |
|---|---|
| 20 May 1904 - 3 Feb 1907: | Commander, 49th Infantry Regiment |
| 16 Aug 1906: | Promoted to *Major-General* |
| 3 Feb 1907 - 6 Jan 1911: | Commander, 1st Brigade, 3rd Grenadier Division |
| 6 Jan 1911 - 1912: | Commander, 1st Brigade. 31st Infantry Division |
| 1912: | Promoted to *Lieutenant-General* |
| 1912: | Retired |

*Major-General* Samson Antonovich **Dumbadze** (2 Feb 1866 - ?)

| | |
|---|---|
| 12 Jan 1914 - 1917: | Chief of Billeting, Omsk Military District |
| 22 Feb 1915: | Promoted to *Major-General* |
| 1917: | Commanding General, Omsk Military District |

*Major-General* Lev Trofimovich **Dumbrova** (21 Feb 1865 - 2 Dec 1916)

| | |
|---|---|
| 3 Apr 1915 - 5 Mar 1916: | Commander, 311th Infantry Regiment |
| 5 Jul 1915: | Promoted to *Major-General* |

5 Mar 1916 - 13 Apr 1916:     Chief of Staff, 28th Infantry Division
13 Apr 1916 - 2 Dec 1916:     Reserve officer, Petrograd Military District

*Major-General* Artur Romualdovich **Dunten** (29 Apr 1863 - ?)
23 Aug 1913:     Promoted to *Major-General*
23 Aug 1913:     Retired
26 Dec 1914 - 1916:     Recalled; Commandant of Smolensk
1916 - 22 Mar 1917:     Reserve officer, Dvinsk Military District
22 Mar 1917:     Dismissed

*Major-General* Konstantin Dmitriyevich **Duplitsky** (16 May 1863 - ?)
20 Nov 1911 - 1913:     Attached to 2nd Artillery Brigade
1913:     Promoted to *Major-General*
1913:     Retired

*Major-General* Karl Avgustovich **Durlyakher** (4 Aug 1857 - ?)
22 Sep 1910 - 26 May 1914:     Military Judge, Amur Military District Court
6 Dec 1910:     Promoted to *Major-General*
26 May 1914 - 10 May 1917:     Military Judge, Kazan Military District Court
10 May 1917:     Dismissed

*Lieutenant-General* Robert Avgustovich **Durlyakher** (6 Jan 1856 - 1937)
21 Nov 1903 - 1 Apr 1916:     Member of the Artillery Committee, Main Artillery Directorate
6 Dec 1903:     Promoted to *Major-General*
18 Apr 1910:     Promoted to *Lieutenant-General*
1 Apr 1916 - Oct 1917:     Chief of Section 7, Artillery Committee, Main Artillery Directorate

*General of Infantry* Pyotr Pavlovich **Durnovo** (6 Dec 1835 - 31 Dec 1918)
29 Nov 1866:     Promoted to *Major-General*
29 Nov 1866 - 17 Jun 1870:     Governor of Kharkov
17 Jun 1870 - 16 Dec 1872:     Attached to the Ministry of Internal Affairs
16 Dec 1872 - 14 Sep 1878:     Governor of Moscow
30 Aug 1876:     Promoted to *Lieutenant-General*
14 Sep 1878 - 14 Feb 1882:     Attached to the Ministry of Internal Affairs
14 Feb 1882 - 9 May 1884:     Chief of the Department of Imperial Estates
9 May 1884 - 11 Feb 1885:     Attached to the Ministry of Internal Affairs
11 Feb 1885 - 11 Aug 1904:     Attached to the Ministry of War
30 Aug 1890:     Promoted to *General of Infantry*
11 Aug 1904 - 25 Oct 1917:     Member of the State Council
30 Jul 1905:     Promoted to *General-Adjutant*
15 Jul 1905 - 24 Nov 1905:     Governor-General of Moscow

*Lieutenant-General* Sergey Sergeyevich **Durnovo** (28 Apr 1869 - 9 Jun 1939)
17 Oct 1910 - 15 Mar 1916:     Inspector of Classes, 1st Moscow Cadet Corps
6 Dec 1913:     Promoted to *Major-General*
15 Mar 1916 - 1917:     Director, Tiflis Cadet Corps

| | |
|---|---|
| 1917: | Promoted to *Lieutenant-General* |
| 1917: | Chief of Artillery Logistics, Caucasus Front |

*General of Infantry* Konstantin Nikolayevich **Durop** (6 May 1843 - 1911)
| | |
|---|---|
| 11 Apr 1888 - 26 Aug 1895: | Inspector of Classes, Pavlovsky Military School |
| 30 Aug 1888: | Promoted to *Major-General* |
| 26 Aug 1895 - 15 Jul 1900: | Director, 2nd Cadet Corps |
| 15 Jul 1900 - 1 May 1903: | Member of the Military Training Committee, General Staff |
| 6 Dec 1900: | Promoted to *Lieutenant-General* |
| 1 May 1903 - 1907: | Representative of the Ministry of War, Main Censorship Committee |
| 1907: | Promoted to *General of Infantry* |
| 1907: | Retired |

*Major-General* Nikolai Nikolayevich **Durov** (18 Dec 1862 - ?)
| | |
|---|---|
| 9 Oct 1908 - 21 May 1912: | Commander, 6th Dragoon Regiment |
| 21 May 1912: | Promoted to *Major-General* |
| 21 May 1912 - 12 Apr 1917: | Commander, 1st Brigade, 7th Cavalry Division |
| 12 Apr 1917 - 17 Jul 1917: | Commander, 7th Cavalry Division |
| 17 Jul 1917 - Oct 1917: | Reserve officer, Kiev Military District |

*General of Infantry* Aleksandr Aleksandrovich **Dushkevich** (20 Sep 1853 - 1918)
| | |
|---|---|
| 31 Jan 1904 - 24 Aug 1905: | Commander, 9th Siberian Infantry Regiment |
| 18 Jul 1905: | Promoted to *Major-General* |
| 24 Aug 1905 - 20 Dec 1905: | Acting Commander, 1st Brigade, 3rd Siberian Infantry Division |
| 20 Dec 1905 - 14 Jun 1908: | Deputy Commandant of Fortress St. Petersburg |
| 14 Jun 1908 - 8 Aug 1908: | Commander, 1st Turkestan Reserve Brigade |
| 8 Aug 1908 - 21 Jul 1910: | Commander, 1st Turkestan Rifle Brigade |
| 21 Jul 1910: | Promoted to *Lieutenant-General* |
| 21 Jul 1910 - 30 Jul 1912: | Commander, 7th Siberian Rifle Division |
| 30 Jul 1912 - 6 Oct 1914: | Commander, 22nd Infantry Division |
| 30 Aug 1914 - 13 Apr 1916: | Commanding General, I. Army Corps |
| 27 Sep 1915: | Promoted to *General of Infantry* |
| 13 Apr 1916 - 14 Feb 1917: | Reserve officer, Petrograd Military District |
| 14 Feb 1917 - Oct 1917: | Reserve officer, Dvinsk Military District |

*Lieutenant-General* Nikolai Ivanovich **Dutkin** (5 Dec 1846 - ?)
| | |
|---|---|
| 26 Aug 1887 - 5 Jan 1895: | Commander, 7th Don Cossack Regiment |
| 14 Nov 1894: | Promoted to *Major-General* |
| 5 Jan 1895 - 5 Jan 1900: | Commander, 2nd Brigade, 5th Cavalry Division |
| 5 Jan 1900: | Promoted to *Lieutenant-General* |

*Major-General* Ilya Petrovich **Dutov** (10 Jul 1851 - ?)
| | |
|---|---|
| 1 May 1904 - 18 Jul 1905: | Commander, 5th Orenburg Cossack Regiment |
| 18 Jul 1905 - 18 Nov 1905: | Acting Commander, 1st Brigade, 1st Turkestan Cossack Division |

| | |
|---|---|
| 18 Nov 1905 - 10 May 1906: | Commander, 5th Orenburg Cossack Regiment |
| 10 May 1906 - 9 May 1907: | Commander, 4th Orenburg Cossack Regiment |
| 9 May 1907: | Promoted to *Major-General* |
| 9 May 1907: | Retired |

*General of Infantry* Nikolai Ottovich **Duve** (19 Feb 1826 - 27 Jan 1902)

| | |
|---|---|
| 20 Jun 1873 - 12 Sep 1874: | Governor & Military Commander, Kalisz |
| 30 Aug 1873: | Promoted to *Major-General* |
| 12 Sep 1874 - 17 Oct 1881: | Governor & Military Commander, Siedlce |
| 17 Oct 1881 - 11 Dec 1881: | Unassigned |
| 11 Dec 1881 - 3 Apr 1883: | Attached to the Commanding General, Warsaw Military District |
| 3 Apr 1883 - 2 Aug 1884: | Commander, 2nd Brigade, 30th Infantry Division |
| 2 Aug 1884 - 12 Dec 1894: | Commander, 20th Infantry Division |
| 30 Aug 1884: | Promoted to *Lieutenant-General* |
| 12 Dec 1894: | Promoted to *General of Infantry* |
| 12 Dec 1894: | Retired |

*General of Artillery* Konstantin Ivanovich **Dvorzhitsky** (18 Oct 1847 - ?)

| | |
|---|---|
| 29 Dec 1899 - 3 Sep 1904: | Commander, 1st Reserve Artillery Brigade |
| 9 Apr 1900: | Promoted to *Major-General* |
| 3 Sep 1904 - 18 Oct 1910: | Commander of Artillery, XX. Army Corps |
| 6 Dec 1906: | Promoted to *Lieutenant-General* |
| 18 Oct 1910: | Promoted to *General of Artillery* |
| 18 Oct 1910: | Retired |

*Major-General of the Fleet* Aleksey Pavlovich **Dyachkov** (8 Mar 1867 - 10 Feb 1936)

| | |
|---|---|
| 4 Oct 1913 - 23 Jun 1917: | Vice-Chairman, Commission to oversee construction of ships in the Black Sea |
| 6 Dec 1915: | Promoted to *Major-General of the Fleet* |
| 23 Jun 1917 - Oct 1917: | Reserve officer, Ministry of the Navy |

*Major-General* Sergei Ivanovich **Dyadyusha** (26 Sep 1870 - 23 May 1933)

| | |
|---|---|
| 20 Jan 1916 - 11 Mar 1917: | Chief of Staff, 84th Infantry Division |
| 10 Apr 1916: | Promoted to *Major-General* |
| 11 Mar 1917 - 1 Feb 1918: | Chief of Staff, IV. Army Corps |
| 1 Feb 1918 - 27 Feb 1918: | Chief of Staff, 6th Army |
| 27 Feb 1918: | Dismissed |

*Lieutenant-General* Pavel Pavlovich **Dyagilev** (18 May 1848 - 20 Jul 1914)

| | |
|---|---|
| 7 Jun 1893 - 10 Apr 1895: | Commander, 74th Infantry Regiment |
| 14 Nov 1894: | Promoted to *Major-General* |
| 10 Apr 1895 - 4 Dec 1895: | Commander, 1st Brigade, 5th Infantry Division |
| 4 Dec 1895 - 18 Sep 1897: | Commander, 1st Brigade, 23rd Infantry Division |
| 18 Sep 1897 - 28 Apr 1904: | Commander, 2nd Brigade, 37th Infantry Division |
| 28 Apr 1904 - 1907: | Commander, Odessa Regional Brigade |
| 2 Apr 1906: | Promoted to *Lieutenant-General* |
| 1907: | Retired |

*Major-General* Mikhail Ardalonovich **Dyakov** (27 Nov 1863 - ?)
28 Feb 1908 - 26 Nov 1912: Military Judge, Warsaw Military District Court
13 Apr 1908: Promoted to *Major-General*
26 Nov 1912 - 1917: Military Prosecutor, Turkestan Military District Court

*Major-General* Nikolai Yakovlevich **Dyakov** (6 May 1854 - ?)
20 Jan 1906 - 17 Feb 1910: Commander, 2nd Don Cossack Regiment
17 Feb 1910: Promoted to *Major-General*
17 Feb 1910 - Jul 1911: Commander, 1st Brigade, 1st Don Cossack Division

*Major-General* Dmitry Ivanovich **Dykhov** (27 Dec 1864 - ?)
14 Feb 1914 - 13 May 1916: Deputy Chief of the Ordnance Factory
6 Apr 1914: Promoted to *Major-General*
13 May 1916 - 1917: Deputy Chief of the Petrograd Arsenal

*Major-General* Mikhail Petrovich **Dymsha** (4 Oct 1864 - 23 Jan 1916)
18 Mar 1909 - 31 Dec 1913: Special Assignments General, Inspectorate-General of Artillery
18 Apr 1910: Promoted to *Major-General*
31 Dec 1913 - 7 Sep 1915: Chief of Okhtenskaya Explosives Factory
7 Sep 1915 - 23 Jan 1916: Chief of Section 2, Main Artillery Directorate

*Major-General* Fyodor Vladimirovich **Dyubreyl-Eshappar** (5 Jun 1860 - Nov 1915)
30 Apr 1900 - 16 Jan 1913: Chief of the Court, Grand Duke Georgy Mikhailovich
6 Dec 1909: Promoted to *Major-General*
16 Jan 1913 - Nov 1915: Council Member, Ministry of the Imperial Court

*Lieutenant-General* Fyodor Aleksandrovich **Dyubyuk** (20 Nov 1843 - 30 Mar 1900)
17 Sep 1894 - 27 Sep 1896: Chief of Staff, XIX. Army Corps
14 Nov 1894: Promoted to *Major-General*
27 Sep 1896 - 28 May 1899: Commander, 1st Brigade, 3rd Grenadier Division
28 May 1899: Promoted to *Lieutenant-General*
28 May 1899: Retired

*Major-General* Mikhail Kapitonovich **Dyugaev** (11 Feb 1865 - ?)
1 Sep 1910 - 26 Apr 1913: Commander, 11th Grenadier Regiment
26 Apr 1913: Promoted to *Major-General*
26 Apr 1913 - 9 Apr 1914: General Staff officer, Caucasus Military District
9 Apr 1914 - 24 Mar 1917: Deputy Chief of General Administration for Biletting
24 Mar 1917 - 27 Jul 1917: Chief of Staff, XLIX. Army Corps
27 Jul 1917 - Oct 1917: Reserve officer, Kiev Military District

*General of the Fleet* Sergey Petrovich **Dyushen** (29 Jan 1857 - 1918)
2 Feb 1904 - 9 Mar 1909: Chief of Legislative Section, Naval General Staff
17 Apr 1905: Promoted to *Major-General of the Admiralty*
9 Mar 1909 - 18 Apr 1911: Chief of Main Directorate of Shipbuilding & Supply
6 Dec 1909: Promoted to *Lieutenant-General of the Admiralty*

| | |
|---|---|
| 18 Apr 1911 - 24 Dec 1914: | Member, Supreme Naval Tribunal |
| 8 Apr 1913: | Redesignated *Lieutenant-General of the Fleet* |
| 24 Dec 1914 - 31 Mar 1917: | Chairman, Supreme Naval Tribunal |
| 22 Mar 1915: | Promoted to *General of the Fleet* |
| 13 Apr 1917: | Retired |

*Lieutenant-General* Vyacheslav Aleksandrovich **Dyushen** (26 Dec 1847 - 3 Dec 1916)

| | |
|---|---|
| 14 Jul 1891 - 1911: | Member of the Artillery Committee, Main Artillery Directorate |
| 6 Dec 1895: | Promoted to *Major-General* |
| 6 Dec 1903: | Promoted to *Lieutenant-General* |
| 1911: | Retired |

*Major-General* Boris Vladimirovich **Dzerozhinsky** (8 Feb 1864 - 17 Feb 1915)

| | |
|---|---|
| 2 May 1913 - 17 Feb 1915: | Commander, 38th Siberian Rifle Regiment |
| 16 May 1915: | Posthumously promoted to *Major-General* |

*Major-General* Vyacheslav Andreyevich **Dzevanovsky** (20 Sep 1870 - Sep 1944)

| | |
|---|---|
| 27 Aug 1915 - 23 Dec 1915: | Commander, 1st Life Grenadier Regiment |
| 6 Dec 1915: | Promoted to *Major-General* |
| 23 Dec 1915 - 7 Apr 1916: | Chief of Communications, Odessa Military District |
| 7 Apr 1916 - 14 Oct 1916: | Chief of Communications, Northern Front |
| 14 Oct 1916 - 1917: | Chief of Communications, Southwestern Front |

*Major-General* Ivan Pavlovich **Dzhalyuk** (3 Jan 1863 - 2 Mar 1918)

| | |
|---|---|
| 19 Jul 1916 - 1917: | Commander, Brigade, 11th Infantry Division |
| 27 Dec 1916: | Promoted to *Major-General* |
| 1917 - 7 Sep 1917: | Commander, Brigade, 23rd Infantry Division |
| 7 Sep 1917 - ?: | Commander, 28th Replacement Infantry Brigade |

*General of Cavalry* Prince Ivan Makarovich **Dzhambakurian-Orbeliani** (22 Sep 1845 - 13 Nov 1919)

| | |
|---|---|
| 2 Nov 1892 - 7 Apr 1895: | General for Special Assignments, Caucasus Military District |
| 30 Aug 1893: | Promoted to *Major-General* |
| 7 Apr 1895 - 28 Feb 1896: | Commander, 2nd Brigade, Caucasus Cossack Division |
| 28 Feb 1896 - 8 Nov 1896: | Commander, Terek Cossack Brigade |
| 8 Nov 1896 - 24 Oct 1897: | Commander, 1st Brigade, Caucasus Cossack Division |
| 24 Oct 1897 - 15 Jan 1899: | Commander, 1st Brigade, 2nd Caucasus Cossack Division |
| 15 Jan 1899 - 18 Jul 1905: | Commander, 2nd Caucasus Cossack Division |
| 6 Dec 1900: | Promoted to *Lieutenant-General* |
| 18 Jul 1905 - 1 Aug 1905: | Commanding General, XXII. Army Corps |
| 1 Aug 1905 - 6 Jul 1906: | Commanding General, XVIII. Army Corps |
| 6 Jul 1906: | Promoted to *General of Cavalry* |
| 6 Jul 1906: | Retired |

*Major-General* Tarnel Konstantinovich **Dzhavrov** (10 May 1853 - 1910)
24 Jul 1907 - 1910:            Commander, 39th Artillery Park
1910:                          Promoted to *Major-General*

*Major-General* Ilya Fomich **Dzhayani** (5 Feb 1854 - 29 Jan 1916)
7 Jul 1909 - 5 Feb 1912:       Commander, 83rd Infantry Regiment
5 Feb 1912:                    Promoted to *Major-General*
5 Feb 1912:                    Retired
21 May 1915 - 29 Jan 1916:     Recalled; Reserve officer, Caucasus Military District

*Major-General* Dmitry Dmitriyevich **Dzheneyev** (19 Jan 1857 - 28 Mar 1929)
18 Apr 1916 - 3 May 1916:      Commander, Brigade, 19th Infantry Division
3 May 1916 - 5 May 1917:       Commander, Brigade, 13th Infantry Division
28 Aug 1916:                   Promoted to *Major-General*
5 May 1917 - 1917:             Commander, 13th Infantry Division

*Major-General* Mikhail Vasilyevich **Dzheneyev** (5 Sep 1838 - 1900)
19 Jan 1889 - 16 Jan 1890:     Commander, 1st Brigade, 21st Infantry Division
12 Feb 1889:                   Promoted to *Major-General*
16 Jan 1890 - 31 Jan 1894:     Commander, 2nd Brigade, Caucasus Grenadier Division
31 Jan 1894 - 1899:            Commander, 3rd Caucasus Reserve Infantry Brigade
1899 - 1900:                   Commander, 63rd Reserve Infantry Brigade

*Lieutenant-General* Gerbert Georgievich **Dzhonson** (13 Apr 1857 - 21 Jun 1919)
8 Feb 1911:                    Promoted to *Major-General*
8 Feb 1911 - 17 Feb 1913:      Chief of Staff, Semirechensk Region
17 Feb 1913 - 8 Feb 1915:      Commander, 1st Brigade, 25th Infantry Division
22 Jan 1915:                   Promoted to *Lieutenant-General*
8 Feb 1915 - 4 Apr 1915:       Commander, 27th Infantry Division
4 Apr 1915 - 1918:             POW, Germany

*Major-General* Stepan Stepanovich **Dzhunkovsky** (18 Aug 1868 - 20 Aug 1926)
13 Jan 1915 - 8 Oct 1916:      Commander, Life Guards Dragoon Regiment
14 Nov 1915:                   Promoted to *Major-General*
8 Oct 1916 - 1917:             Commander, 2nd Brigade, 1st Guards Cavalry Division
1917:                          Commander, Brigade, 16th Cavalry Division

*Lieutenant-General* Vladimir Fyodorovich **Dzhunkovsky** (7 Sep 1865 - 26 Feb 1938)
11 Nov 1905 - 25 Jan 1913:     Governor of Moscow
6 Dec 1908:                    Promoted to *Major-General*
25 Jan 1913 - 19 Aug 1915:     Deputy Minister of Internal Affairs,
                               Commanding General, Corps of Gendarmerie
19 Aug 1915 - 26 Dec 1915:     General à la suite
26 Dec 1915 - 29 Nov 1916:     Commander, Brigade, 8th Siberian Rifle Division
29 Nov 1916 - 10 Jan 1917:     Commander, 131st Infantry Division
10 Jan 1917 - 4 Oct 1917:      Commander, 15th Siberian Rifle Division
2 Apr 1917:                    Promoted to *Lieutenant-General*
4 Oct 1917 - Nov 1917:         Commanding General, III. Siberian Army Corps

Nov 1917 - 17 Dec 1917: Unassigned
17 Dec 1917: Retired

*Major-General* **Dzhura-Bek** (1 Jan 1839 - 25 Jan 1906)
6 Apr 1876 - 25 Jan 1906: Special Purposes Officer, Governor-General of Turkestan
6 May 1901: Promoted to *Major-General*

*General of Infantry* Aleksey Iosifovich **Dzichkanets** (29 May 1842 - ?)
7 May 1891: Promoted to *Major-General*
7 May 1891 - 31 May 1895: Commander, 6th Life Guards Reserve Infantry Regiment
31 May 1895 - 31 Nov 1899: Commander, Moscow Life Guards Infantry Regiment
31 Nov 1899 - 17 Feb 1900: Commander, 1st Brigade, 2nd Guards Infantry Division
17 Feb 1900: Promoted to *Lieutenant-General*
17 Feb 1900 - 17 Oct 1904: Commander, 29th Infantry Division
17 Oct 1904 - 22 Dec 1905: At the disposal of the C-in-C, 2nd Manchurian Army
22 Dec 1905 - 26 Feb 1907: Chief of the Medical Service, 2nd Manchurian Army
26 Feb 1907: Promoted to *General of Infantry*
26 Feb 1907: Retired
23 Jul 1915 - 1917: Recalled; Reserve officer, Dvinsk Military District

*Lieutenant-General* Boris Alekseyevich **Dzichkanets** (30 Sep 1866 - ?)
13 May 1910: Promoted to *Major-General*
13 May 1910 - 3 Apr 1915: Commander, 2nd Brigade, 1st Grenadier Division
3 Apr 1915 - 22 Apr 1917: Commander, 29th Infantry Division
17 Nov 1915: Promoted to *Lieutenant-General*
22 Apr 1917 - 2 Jun 1917: Reserve officer, Minsk Military District
2 Jun 1917 - 22 Oct 1917: Commanding General, L. Army Corps
22 Oct 1917 - 1918: Commanding General, III. Army Corps

*Major-General* Pyotr Aloizovich **Dzyubandovsky** (29 Jun 1834 - 1907)
1 Oct 1897: Promoted to *Major-General*
1 Oct 1897 - 1 Jan 1898: Commander, 47th Artillery Brigade
1 Jan 1898 - 29 Dec 1899: Commander, 44th Artillery Brigade
29 Dec 1899: Retired

*General of Infantry* Mikhail Isayevich **Ebelov** (12 Sep 1855 - 13 Jul 1919)
15 Jul 1900 - 18 Jun 1901: Chief of Communications, Amur Military District
31 Jul 1900: Promoted to *Major-General*
18 Jun 1901 - 7 Nov 1902: Chief of Communications, Caucasus Military District
7 Nov 1902 - 25 Oct 1906: Chief of Staff, XX. Army Corps
25 Oct 1906 - 26 Apr 1908: Commander, Trans-Baikal Region, C-in-C, Trans-Baikal Cossack Army
22 Apr 1907: Promoted to *Lieutenant-General*
26 Apr 1908 - 20 Mar 1909: Military Governor, Trans-Baikal Region, C-in-C, Trans-Baikal Cossack Army
20 Mar 1909 - 14 Sep 1911: Commander, 34th Infantry Division
14 Sep 1911 - 21 Apr 1913: Deputy Commanding General, Irkutsk Military District

| | |
|---|---|
| 14 Apr 1913: | Promoted to *General of Infantry* |
| 21 Apr 1913 - 19 Jul 1914: | Deputy Commanding General, Odessa Military District |
| 19 Jul 1914 - 9 Aug 1917: | Commanding General, Odessa Military District |
| 9 Aug 1917 - Oct 1917: | Reserve officer, Odessa Military District |

*Admiral* Andrei Avgustovich **Ebergardt** (9 Nov 1856 - 19 Apr 1919)
| | |
|---|---|
| 1906 - 1908: | Deputy Chief of the Main Naval Staff |
| 1907: | Promoted to *Rear-Admiral* |
| 1908 - 14 Jul 1908: | Commander, Baltic Naval Detachment |
| 14 Jul 1908 - 11 Oct 1911: | Chief of the Naval General Staff |
| 6 Dec 1909: | Promoted to *Vice-Admiral* |
| 11 Oct 1911 - 1914: | C-in-C of Naval Forces, Black Sea |
| 14 Apr 1913: | Promoted to *Admiral* |
| 1914 - 28 Jun 1916: | C-in-C, Black Sea Fleet |
| Jul 1916 - 1917: | Member of the State Council |
| 13 Dec 1917: | Dismissed |

*Major-General* Ivan Ivanovich **Efirov** (28 Oct 1862 - ?)
| | |
|---|---|
| 3 Feb 1911 - 1912: | Commander, 66$^{th}$ Infantry Regiment |
| 1912: | Promoted to *Major-General* |
| 1912: | Retired |
| 24 Jul 1914 - 31 Oct 1915: | Commander, 2$^{nd}$ Brigade, 33$^{rd}$ Infantry Division |
| 31 Oct 1915 - 25 Oct 1916: | Commander, 13$^{th}$ Siberian Rifle Division |
| 25 Oct 1916 - 31 Oct 1916: | Reserve officer, Kiev Military District |
| 31 Oct 1917 - 1917: | Reserve officer, Petrograd Military District |

*General of Artillery* Nikolai Fyodorovich **Egershtrom** (26 Aug 1831 - 1916)
| | |
|---|---|
| 28 Jan 1865 - 14 Mar 1877: | Professor, Mikhalovsky Artillery Academy |
| 20 Apr 1869: | Promoted to *Major-General* |
| 14 Mar 1877 - 28 Jul 1891: | Professor Emeritus, Mikhalovsky Artillery Academy |
| 30 Aug 1881: | Promoted to *Lieutenant-General* |
| 28 Jul 1891 - 1905: | Member of the Artillery Committee, Main Artillery Directorate |
| 14 May 1896: | Promoted to *General of Artillery* |
| 1905: | Retired |

*Lieutenant-General* Konstantin-Leopold-Fridrikh Konstantinovich **Egger** (22 Apr 1865 - 25 Jan 1946)
| | |
|---|---|
| 25 Jul 1914 - 22 Jan 1917: | Commander, 75$^{th}$ Artillery Brigade |
| 28 Oct 1914: | Promoted to *Major-General* |
| 22 Jan 1917 - 1918: | Inspector of Artillery, I. Army Corps |
| 1917: | Promoted to *Lieutenant-General* |

*Major-General* Viktor Viktorovich **Eggert** (7 Nov 1867 - ?)
| | |
|---|---|
| 3 Mar 1912: | Promoted to *Major-General* |
| 3 Mar 1912 - 22 Jan 1913: | Commander, 2$^{nd}$ Brigade, 45$^{th}$ Infantry Division |
| 22 Jan 1913 - 16 May 1914: | Quartermaster-General, Caucasus Military District |
| 16 May 1914 - 15 Aug 1914: | Quartermaster-General, General Staff |

| | |
|---|---|
| 15 Aug 1914 - 14 Dec 1914: | Duty General, 10th Army |
| 14 Dec 1914 - 17 Jul 1915: | Chief of Staff, III. Army Corps |
| 17 Jul 1915 - 25 Oct 1916: | Commander, 12th Siberian Rifle Division |
| 25 Oct 1916 - 29 Jan 1917: | Reserve officer, Petrograd Military District |
| 29 Jan 1917 - Oct 1917: | Commander, 186th Infantry Division |

*General of Infantry* Eduard Vladimirovich **Ekk** (11 Apr 1851 - 5 Apr 1937)
| | |
|---|---|
| 3 Dec 1897: | Promoted to *Major-General* |
| 3 Dec 1897 - 30 Apr 1900: | Chief of Staff, VII. Army Corps |
| 30 Apr 1900 - 20 May 1902: | Deputy Chief of Staff, Odessa Military District |
| 20 May 1902 - 23 Mar 1904: | Duty General, Odessa Military District |
| 23 Mar 1904 - 1 Jun 1904: | At the disposal of the Chief of the General Staff |
| 1 Jun 1904 - 3 Jun 1906: | Commander, 71st Infantry Division |
| 6 Dec 1904: | Promoted to *Lieutenant-General* |
| 3 Jun 1906 - 1 Oct 1907: | Commander, 8th Infantry Division |
| 1 Oct 1907 - 15 May 1912: | Commanding General, Grenadier Corps |
| 6 Dec 1910: | Promoted to *General of Infantry* |
| 15 May 1912 - 19 Oct 1916: | Commanding General, VII. Army Corps |
| 19 Oct 1916 - 2 Apr 1917: | Commanding General, XXIII. Army Corps |
| 2 Apr 1917 - Oct 1917: | Reserve officer, Kiev Military District |

*Major-General* Feofil Aleksandrovich **Ekkersdorf** (14 Jan 1862 - Nov 1914)
| | |
|---|---|
| 7 Apr 1911 - Nov 1914: | Commander, 163rd Infantry Regiment |
| 17 May 1916: | Posthumously promoted to *Major-General* |

*Major-General* Fyodor Karlovich von **Ekse** (15 Aug 1835 - ?)
| | |
|---|---|
| 19 Aug 1874 - 1896: | Commander of Railway Gendarmerie, Vilnius |
| 6 Dec 1894: | Promoted to *Major-General* |

*Major-General* Nikolai Aleksandrovich **Eksten** (24 Nov 1845 - ?)
| | |
|---|---|
| 17 Dec 1900: | Promoted to *Major-General* |
| 17 Dec 1900 - 17 Mar 1906: | Commander, 1st Brigade, 10th Infantry Division |

*Major-General* Fridrikh Ivanovich **Elliot** (28 Aug 1849 - ?)
| | |
|---|---|
| 18 Dec 1902: | Promoted to *Major-General* |
| 18 Dec 1902 - 16 Jun 1906: | Commander, 1st Brigade, 41st Infantry Division |

*General of Infantry* Aleksandr Veniaminovich **Ellis** (22 Jul 1825 - 21 Nov 1907)
| | |
|---|---|
| 13 Feb 1868 - 17 Apr 1876: | Commander, Life Guards Gatchina Regiment |
| 20 May 1868: | Promoted to *Major-General* |
| 17 Apr 1876 - 4 Mar 1877: | Commander, 2nd Brigade, 1st Guards Infantry Division |
| 4 Mar 1877 - 17 Dec 1883: | Commander, Guards Rifle Brigade |
| 16 Apr 1878: | Promoted to *Lieutenant-General* |
| 17 Dec 1883 - 1 Jan 1888: | Member of Artillery Advisory Committee, Main Artillery Directorate |
| 1 Jan 1888 - 9 Apr 1889: | Commanding General, VII. Army Corps |
| 9 Apr 1889 - 3 Jan 1906: | Member of the Military Council |
| 30 Aug 1892: | Promoted to *General of Infantry* |

23 Jan 1896 - 3 Jan 1906: Commandant of Fortress St. Petersburg
3 Jan 1906: Retired

*General of Infantry* Nikolai Veniaminovich **Ellis** (6 Jun 1829 - 28 Oct 1902)
17 Sep 1870 - 30 Aug 1875: Commander, 1st Life Grenadier Regiment
30 Aug 1875: Promoted to *Major-General*
30 Aug 1875 - 17 Apr 1876: Unassigned
17 Apr 1876 - 29 Dec 1877: Commander, Life Guards Izmaylov Regimnet
29 Dec 1877 - 19 Feb 1883: Commander, 1st Brigade, 3rd Grenadier Division
19 Feb 1883 - 4 Feb 1886: Commander, 1st Grenadier Division
30 Aug 1885: Promoted to *Lieutenant-General*
4 Feb 1886 - 9 Apr 1889: Unassigned
9 Apr 1889 - 3 Jun 1896: Commander, 40th Infantry Division
3 Jun 1896 - 26 Aug 1898: Commander, 41st Infantry Division
26 Aug 1898: Promoted to *General of Infantry*
26 Aug 1898: Retired

*Lieutenant-General* Fridrikh-Vilgelm-Voldemar Matveyevich **Elrikh** (17 Feb 1845 - 16 Dec 1916)
24 Jan 1886 - 13 Nov 1900: Clerk, Troop & Cargo Movement Section, General Staff
9 Apr 1900: Promoted to *Major-General*
13 Nov 1900 - 20 Jan 1902: Chief of Military Communications Section, General Staff
20 Jan 1902 - 18 Aug 1907: At the disposal of the Chief of the General Staff
18 Aug 1907 - 2 Dec 1916: Chief of the Joint Archives, General Staff
6 Dec 1913: Promoted to *Lieutenant-General*
2 Dec 1916: Dismissed

*Lieutenant-General* Karl-Feofil Matveyevich **Elrikh** (15 Jul 1846 - 1909)
8 Mar 1904: Promoted to *Major-General*
8 Mar 1904 - 1909: Commander, Warsaw Regional Brigade
1909: Promoted to *Lieutenant-General*

*Major-General* Vladimir Fyodorovich **Elsh** (15 Jul 1848 - ?)
28 Nov 1907: Promoted to *Major-General*
28 Nov 1907 - May 1910: Commander, 2nd Brigade, 5th East Siberian Rifle Division

*Major-General* Konstantin Ottovich **Elsner** (19 Sep 1853 - 6 Apr 1915)
2 Aug 1902 - 2 Jun 1906: Commander, 25th (Black Sea) Borderguard Brigade
2 Jun 1906 - 31 May 1912: Commander, Riga Borderguard Brigade
31 May 1907: Promoted to *Major-General*
31 May 1912: Retired

*Major-General* Nikolai Yevgenyevich **Elsner** (10 Jan 1859 - ?)
6 Dec 1905 - 1918: Section Chief, Main Intendant Directorate
25 Mar 1912: Promoted to *Major-General*

*Lieutenant-General* Yevgeny Feliksovich **Elsner** (12 Dec 1867 - 5 Jul 1930)
| | |
|---|---|
| 22 Sep 1910 - 25 Aug 1912: | Deputy Chief of Support & Service Troops, General Staff |
| 10 Apr 1911: | Promoted to *Major-General* |
| 25 Aug 1912 - 19 Jul 1914: | Deputy Chief of Troop Billeting, General Staff |
| 19 Jul 1914 - 23 Jul 1916: | Deputy Chief of Logistics, Southwestern Front |
| 1915: | Promoted to *Lieutenant-General* |
| 23 Jul 1916 - 30 Aug 1917: | Chief of Logistics, Southwestern Front |
| 30 Aug 1917: | Dismissed |

*Major-General* Fridrikh-Oskar Ivanovich **Enberg** (19 Jul 1859 - 12 Oct 1937)
| | |
|---|---|
| 12 Dec 1911: | Promoted to *Major-General* |
| 12 Dec 1911 - 4 Feb 1917: | Commander of Engineers, Fortress Sevastopol |
| 4 Feb 1917 - 1918: | Deputy Chief of Troop Billeting, Minsk Military District |

*Major-General* Mikhail Aleksandrovich **Enden** (22 Sep 1839 - 1901)
| | |
|---|---|
| 28 Oct 1895 - 1901: | Inspector of Classes, Pavlovsky Military School |
| 6 Dec 1895: | Promoted to *Major-General* |

*Lieutenant-General* Pyotr Petrovich von **Enden** (18 Nov 1838 - 28 Aug 1909)
| | |
|---|---|
| 18 May 1887 - 8 Oct 1889: | Commander, Life Guards 6$^{th}$ Reserve Infantry Regiment |
| 30 Aug 1888: | Promoted to *Major-General* |
| 8 Oct 1889 - 22 Nov 1893: | Commander, Life Guards Moscow Regiment |
| 22 Nov 1893 - 19 Jul 1895: | Commander, 1$^{st}$ Brigade, 2$^{nd}$ Guards Infantry Division |
| 19 Jul 1895 - 10 May 1897: | Commander, 2$^{nd}$ Brigade, 13$^{th}$ Infantry Division |
| 10 May 1897: | Promoted to *Lieutenant-General* |
| 10 May 1897: | Retired |

*Major-General* Konstantin Ivanovich **Engel** (29 Jan 1839 - ?)
| | |
|---|---|
| 26 May 1890 - 22 Jan 1896: | Commander, 151$^{st}$ Infantry Regiment |
| 14 Nov 1894: | Promoted to *Major-General* |
| 22 Jan 1896 - 7 Feb 1901: | Commander, 1$^{st}$ Brigade, 13$^{th}$ Infantry Division |

*Major-General* Viktor Nikolayevich von **Engel** (22 May 1874 - 27 Mar 1933)
| | |
|---|---|
| 14 Jun 1913 - 29 Dec 1914: | Chief of Staff, 16$^{th}$ Infantry Division |
| 29 Dec 1914 - 29 Feb 1916: | Commander, 101$^{st}$ Infantry Regiment |
| 6 Dec 1915: | Promoted to *Major-General* |
| 29 Feb 1916 - 19 Feb 1917: | Chief of Staff, 125$^{th}$ Infantry Division |
| Sep 1916: | Acting Commander, 125$^{th}$ Infantry Division |
| 19 Feb 1917 - 10 Oct 1917: | Chief of Staff, XVI. Army Corps |
| 10 Oct 1917 - 1918: | Commander, 47$^{th}$ Infantry Division |

*Lieutenant-General* Aleksandr Petrovich **Engelgardt** (15 Apr 1836 - Jul 1907)
| | |
|---|---|
| 5 Sep 1865 - 19 Jan 1886: | Attached to the Main Artillery Directorate |
| 1878: | Promoted to *Major-General* |
| 19 Jan 1886 - 4 Jan 1900: | Inspector of Artillery Acceptance |
| 30 Aug 1891: | Promoted to *Lieutenant-General* |

4 Jan 1900 - Jul 1907: Member of the Artillery Committee, Main Artillery Directorate

*Major-General* Vladimir Mikhailovich **Engelgardt** (28 Sep 1865 - ?)
8 Sep 1913 - 1917: Inspector of Classes, 2nd Moscow Cadet Corps
6 Dec 1916: Promoted to *Major-General*

*Major-General* Aleksandr Petrovich **Engelke** (15 Aug 1844 - ?)
26 Feb 1894: Promoted to *Major-General*
26 Feb 1894 - 4 Jun 1899: Commander, 25th Artillery Brigade

*Major-General* Aleksandr Petrovich **Engelke** (2 Aug 1863 - ?)
1 Jul 1908 - 18 Feb 1912: Deputy Section Chief, Main Military Justice Administration
18 Apr 1910: Promoted to *Major-General*
18 Feb 1912 - 1917: Military Judge, St. Petersburg Military District Court

*Lieutenant-General* Nikolai Petrovich **Engelke** (12 Oct 1850 - ?)
24 Oct 1899: Promoted to *Major-General*
24 Oct 1899 - 20 Apr 1903: Commander, 2nd Brigade, 9th Infantry Division
20 Apr 1903 - 28 Jun 1905: Commander, 46th Reserve Infantry Brigade
28 Jun 1905 - 29 Apr 1906: Commander, 46th Infantry Division
29 Apr 1906 - 1910: Commander, 46th Reserve Infantry Brigade
1910: Promoted to *Lieutenant-General*
1910: Retired

*Major-General* Andrey Aleksandrovich **Enin** (21 Nov 1853 - ?)
24 May 1905 - 1911: Commander, 2nd Battalion, 15th Artillery Brigade
1911: Promoted to *Major-General*
1911: Retired
15 Nov 1914 - 1917: Recalled; Commander, 8th Artillery Brigade

*General of Infantry* Karl Karlovich **Enkel** (10 Oct 1839 - 26 Feb 1921)
9 Apr 1881 - 22 Oct 1885: Ministry of War Representative to the Finnish Army
6 May 1884: Promoted to *Major-General*
22 Oct 1885 - 19 Aug 1903: Director of the Finland Cadet Corps
30 Aug 1894: Promoted to *Lieutenant-General*
19 Aug 1903: Promoted to *General of Infantry*
19 Aug 1903: Retired

*Major-General* Nikolai Gustavovich **Enkel** (20 Aug 1833 - ?)
7 Oct 1893: Promoted to *Major-General*
7 Oct 1893 - 20 Jul 1899: Commander, 4th Artillery Brigade

*Lieutenant-General* Otton Magnusovich **Enkel** (3 Dec 1830 - ?)
8 Oct 1889 - 21 Jul 1900: Commander, Vladikavkaz Military Hospital
4 Jun 1895: Promoted to *Major-General*
21 Jul 1900: Promoted to *Lieutenant-General*

21 Jul 1900: Retired

*Vice-Admiral* Oskar Adolfovich **Enquist** (28 Oct 1849 - 3 Mar 1912)
6 Sep 1900 - 9 Sep 1902: Commander, 9th Naval Depot
6 Dec 1901: Promoted to *Rear-Admiral*
9 Sep 1902 - 26 Apr 1904: Commandant, Port of Nikolaiev
26 Apr 1904 - 21 May 1905: Commander, 1st Cruiser Division, 2nd Pacific Squadron
21 May 1905 - Sep 1905: Interned in Manila
13 Mar 1906 - 10 Nov 1907: Junior Flagman, Baltic Fleet
10 Nov 1907: Promoted to *Vice-Admiral*
10 Nov 1907: Retired

*Lieutenant-General* Ivan Kondratyevich **Entel** (15 Dec 1842 - ?)
6 Mar 1909 - 8 Dec 1911: General for Special Assignments, Main Engineering Directorate
29 Mar 1909: Promoted to *Major-General*
8 Dec 1911: Promoted to *Lieutenant-General*
8 Dec 1911: Retired

*Major-General* Mikhail Vasilyevich **Envald** (1 Jan 1868 - 29 May 1928)
23 Feb 1913 - 17 Nov 1915: Commander, 200th Infantry Regiment
7 May 1915: Promoted to *Major-General*
17 Nov 1915 - 30 Apr 1917: Commander, Brigade, 50th Infantry Division
30 Apr 1917 - 1918: Commander, 50th Infantry Division

*Major-General* Yevgeny Vasilyevich **Envald** (26 Apr 1862 - 19 Dec 1925)
8 Mar 1904 - 23 Apr 1915: Commander, 124th Infantry Regiment
14 Nov 1914: Promoted to *Major-General*
23 Apr 1915 - 18 Apr 1917: Commander, Brigade, 42nd Infantry Division
18 Apr 1917 - 25 Aug 1917: Commander, 28th Infantry Division

*Major-General* Aleksei Nikolayevich **Erdeli** (1 Mar 1851 - ?)
1 May 1903 - 1908: Staff Officer, 5th Class, General Staff
6 Dec 1903: Promoted to *Major-General*

*Lieutenant-General* Ivan Georgievich **Erdeli** (15 Oct 1870 - 3 Jul 1939)
9 Jun 1907 - 15 May 1910: Commander, 8th Dragoon Regiment
15 May 1910: Promoted to *Major-General*
15 May 1910 - 6 Nov 1912: Commander, Life Guards Dragoon Regiment
6 Nov 1912 - 19 Jul 1914: Quartermaster-General, St. Petersburg Military District
19 Jul 1914 - 9 Aug 1914: Quartermaster-General, 6th Army
9 Aug 1914 - 18 Oct 1914: Quartermaster-General, 9th Army
18 Oct 1914 - 13 May 1915: Commander, 14th Cavalry Division
13 May 1915 - 23 Nov 1916: Commander, 2nd Guards Cavalry Division
15 May 1916: Promoted to *Lieutenant-General*
23 Nov 1916 - 6 Apr 1917: Commander, 64th Infantry Division
6 Apr 1917 - 30 May 1917: Commanding General, XVIII. Army Corps
30 May 1917 - 9 Jul 1917: C-in-C, 11th Army

| | |
|---|---|
| 12 Jul 1917 - 29 Aug 1917: | C-in-C, Special Army |
| 29 Aug 1917: | Dismissed |

*Major-General* Aleksandr-Otto-Paul Gustavovich **Erdman** (24 Aug 1851 - ?)
| | |
|---|---|
| 11 Jul 1904: | Promoted to *Major-General* |
| 16 Apr 1904 - 9 Jun 1906: | Commander, 1st Brigade, Orenburg Cossack Division |
| 9 Jun 1906 - 1906: | Attached to Kazan Military District |

*Lieutenant-General* Alfred-Yevgeny-Gustav Avgustovich **Erdman** (25 Nov 1861 - 30 Jul 1918)
| | |
|---|---|
| 20 Jun 1907 - 9 Sep 1910: | Intendant, Turkestan Military District |
| 9 Sep 1910 - 17 Aug 1914: | Intendant-General, Kiev Military District |
| 6 Dec 1910: | Promoted to *Major-General* |
| 17 Aug 1914 - 13 Mar 1917: | Intendant-General, Southwestern Front |
| 6 Dec 1916: | Promoted to *Lieutenant-General* |
| 13 Mar 1917: | Dismissed |

*Lieutenant-General* Prince Aleksandr Nikolayevich **Eristov** (5 Jul 1873 - 10 Feb 1955)
| | |
|---|---|
| 10 Nov 1914 - 7 May 1916: | Commander, Guards Cavalry Regiment |
| 22 Mar 1915: | Promoted to *Major-General* |
| 7 May 1916 - 14 May 1917: | Commander, 1st Brigade, 1st Guards Cavalry Division |
| 14 May 1917 - 6 Aug 1917: | Commander, 1st Guards Cavalry Division |
| 6 Aug 1917 - Oct 1917: | Commanding General, III. Caucasus Army Corps |
| 23 Aug 1917: | Promoted to *Lieutenant-General* |

*General of Cavalry* Prince David Evstafiyevich **Eristov** (2 Jul 1843 - 29 Jun 1910)
| | |
|---|---|
| 3 Nov 1886: | Promoted to *Major-General* |
| 3 Nov 1886 - 6 Nov 1891: | Commander, 2nd Brigade, 6th Cavalry Division |
| 6 Nov 1891 - 11 Jun 1895: | Commander, 2nd Brigade, 13th Cavalry Division |
| 11 Jun 1985 - 11 Jun 1901: | Commander, 5th Cavalry Division |
| 14 May 1896: | Promoted to *Lieutenant-General* |
| 11 Jun 1901 - 29 Jun 1910: | Member, Committee for Wounded Veterans |
| 6 Dec 1906: | Promoted to *General of Cavalry* |

*Lieutenant-General* Prince Nikolai Bogdanovich **Eristov** (1834 - 19 Apr 1912)
| | |
|---|---|
| 1 Jun 1883 - 4 Feb 1895: | Deputy Military Governor of Kutaisi |
| 6 May 1884: | Promoted to *Major-General* |
| 4 Feb 1895: | Promoted to *Lieutenant-General* |
| 4 Feb 1895: | Retired |

*Lieutenant-General* Aleksandr Emmanuilovich **Ertel** (16 May 1840 - 13 Feb 1907)
| | |
|---|---|
| 22 Jun 1896 - 15 Oct 1906: | Chief of St. Petersburg-Semenov-Aleksandrov Military Hospital |
| 6 Dec 1897: | Promoted to *Major-General* |
| 15 Oct 1906: | Promoted to *Lieutenant-General* |
| 15 Oct 1906: | Retired |

*Major-General* Mikhail Nilovich **Esaulov** (6 Nov 1853 - ?)
30 Apr 1900: Promoted to *Major-General*
30 Apr 1900 - 23 Jul 1901: Chief of Staff, VII. Army Corps
23 Jul 1901 - 25 Jan 1904: Commander, 1st Brigade, 8th Infantry Division

*Major-General* Nikolai Mikhailovich **Esmont** (10 Nov 1830 - ?)
15 Aug 1886: Promoted to *Major-General*
15 Aug 1886 - 1899: Commander, Artillery Depot, Warsaw Military District

*Admiral* Nikolai Ottovich von **Essen** (23 Dec 1860 - 20 May 1915)
2 Oct 1906 - 8 Dec 1907: Commander, 1st Mine Detachment, Baltic Fleet
5 Apr 1907: Promoted to *Rear-Admiral*
8 Dec 1907 - 24 Nov 1908: Commander, Mine Division, Baltic Fleet
24 Nov 1908 - 3 Dec 1909: Commander of Combined Squadrons, Baltic Sea
3 Dec 1909 - 30 May 1911: C-in-C of Naval Forces, Baltic Sea
18 Apr 1910: Promoted to *Vice-Admiral*
30 May 1911 - 14 May 1915: C-in-C, Baltic Fleet
14 Apr 1913: Promoted to *Admiral*

*Lieutenant-General* Pavel Yemelyanovich von **Essen** (3 Jan 1850 - ?)
23 Nov 1896: Promoted to *Major-General*
23 Nov 1896 - 12 Aug 1897: Special Assignments General, Odessa Military District
12 Aug 1897 - 14 Mar 1900: Deputy Chief of Staff, Odessa Military District
14 Mar 1900 - 30 Jan 1902: Chief of Staff, Siberian Military District
23 Nov 1901: Promoted to *Lieutenant-General*
30 Jan 1902 - 8 Aug 1906: Commander, 17th Infantry Division

*Major-General* Ivan Sevastyanovich von **Etter** (24 Jul 1863 - 12 Oct 1938)
14 Nov 1909 - 22 Nov 1913: Commander, 5th Grenadier Regiment
22 Nov 1913: Promoted to *Major-General*
22 Nov 1913 - 22 Aug 1915: Commander, Life Guards Semyonovsky Regiment
22 Aug 1915 - 15 Nov 1916: General à la suite
15 Nov 1916 - 1917: Commander, Brigade, 79th Infantry Division

*Lieutenant-General* Pavel Pavlovich von **Etter** (18 May 1840 - ?)
1 Dec 1880 - 1 Apr 1893: Commander, 1st Brigade, Caucasus Cossack Division
5 Dec 1880: Promoted to *Major-General*
1 Apr 1893 - 3 Dec 1894: Commander, 3rd Reserve Cavalry Brigade
30 Aug 1894: Promoted to *Lieutenant-General*
3 Dec 1894 - 19 Dec 1901: Commander, Guards Reserve Cavalry Brigade
19 Dec 1901 - 1905: Attached to St. Petersburg Military District

*Major-General* Otton Ottonovich von **Ettingen** (24 Nov 1866 - 11 Jan 1920)
6 Dec 1913: Promoted to *Major-General*
6 Dec 1913 - 1 Mar 1915: Commander of Engineers, Fortress Kiev
1 Mar 1915 - 1918: Engineer officer, 8th Army

*General of Infantry* Aleksey Yermolaevich **Evert** (20 Feb 1857 - 10 May 1926)
| | |
|---|---|
| 24 Dec 1900: | Promoted to *Major-General* |
| 24 Dec 1900 - 9 Apr 1901: | Chief of Staff, XI. Army Corps |
| 9 Apr 1901 - 11 Oct 1903: | Chief of Staff, XIV. Army Corps |
| 11 Oct 1903 - 28 Oct 1904: | Chief of Staff, V. Army Corps |
| 28 Oct 1904 - 24 Mar 1905: | Quartermaster-General, Land & Naval Forces against Japan |
| 24 Mar 1905: | Promoted to *Lieutenant-General* |
| 24 Mar 1905 - 18 Apr 1906: | Chief of Staff, 1st Manchurian Army |
| 18 Apr 1906 - 21 May 1908: | Chief of the General Staff |
| 21 May 1908 - 19 Jun 1912: | Commanding General, XIII. Army Corps |
| 10 Apr 1911: | Promoted to *General of Infantry* |
| 19 Jun 1912 - 10 Aug 1914: | Commanding General, Irkutsk Military District |
| 10 Aug 1914 - 22 Aug 1914: | C-in-C, 10th Army |
| 22 Aug 1914 - 20 Aug 1915: | C-in-C, 4th Army |
| 20 Aug 1915 - 11 Mar 1917: | C-in-C, Western Front |
| 23 Dec 1915: | Promoted to *General-Adjutant* |
| 22 Mar 1917: | Retired |

*Lieutenant-General* Apollon Yermolayevich **Evert** (25 Feb 1845 - ?)
| | |
|---|---|
| 30 Mar 1898: | Promoted to *Major-General* |
| 30 Mar 1898 - 23 Jun 1900: | Commander, 1st Transcaucasus Rifle Brigade |
| 23 Jun 1900 - 24 Oct 1902: | Commander, 6th Turkestan Rifle Brigade |
| 24 Oct 1902 - 10 Aug 1904: | Commander, 1st Finnish Rifle Brigade |
| 10 Aug 1904 - 8 Feb 1906: | Commander, 42nd Infantry Division |
| 6 Dec 1904: | Promoted to *Lieutenant-General* |
| 8 Feb 1906 - 4 May 1907: | Commander, 13th Infantry Division |

*Major-General* Nikolai Matveyevich **Eygel** (10 Mar 1871 - ?)
| | |
|---|---|
| 18 Mar 1915 - 29 May 1917: | Deputy Chief of Staff, Moscow Military District |
| 6 Dec 1915: | Promoted to *Major-General* |
| 29 May 1917: | Retired |

*Major-General of the Naval Legal Corps* Nikolai Frantsevich **Eykar** (18 Oct 1865 - 1942)
| | |
|---|---|
| 6 Jun 1905 - 1917: | Military Judge, Kronstadt Naval Court |
| 1 Nov 1911 - 1917: | Chairman of the Naval Court, Emperor Aleksandr III Port (Libau) |
| 6 Dec 1911: | Promoted to *Major-General of the Naval Legal Corps* |

*Major-General* Georgy Fyodorovich **Eykhe** (22 Oct 1863 - ?)
| | |
|---|---|
| 2 Jun 1903 - 6 Jul 1907: | Commander, 104th Infantry Regiment |
| 6 Jul 1907: | Promoted to *Major-General* |
| 6 Jul 1907 - 19 Jul 1914: | Commander, 1st Brigade, 16th Infantry Division |
| 19 Jul 1914 - 28 Oct 1914: | Commander, 65th Infantry Division |
| 28 Oct 1914 - 1918: | Reserve officer, Kiev Military District |

*General of Cavalry* Aleksandr Rudolfovich **Eykhgolts** (2 Feb 1854 - ?)
| | |
|---|---|
| 28 Apr 1899 - 23 Mar 1904: | Commander, 14th Dragoon Regiment |

| | |
|---|---|
| 23 Mar 1904: | Promoted to *Major-General* |
| 23 Mar 1904 - 13 Nov 1904: | Commander, 2nd Brigade, 13th Cavalry Division |
| 13 Nov 1904 - 5 May 1905: | Special Assignments General, 3rd Manchurian Army |
| 5 May 1905 - 18 Oct 1905: | At the disposal of the C-in-C, 2nd Manchurian Army |
| 18 Oct 1905 - 30 Jun 1906: | At the disposal of the Chief of the General Staff |
| 30 Jun 1906 - 15 Aug 1907: | Attached to the General Staff |
| 15 Aug 1907 - 22 Sep 1913: | Chief of Communications Section, General Staff |
| 18 Apr 1910: | Promoted to *Lieutenant-General* |
| 22 Sep 1913: | Promoted to *General of Cavalry* |
| 22 Sep 1913: | Retired |

*Major-General* Aleksandr Nikolayevich **Eyler** (16 Dec 1862 - 13 Apr 1921)

| | |
|---|---|
| 26 Sep 1912 - 11 Apr 1917: | Inspector of Posts & Telegraphs |
| 15 Aug 1913: | Promoted to *Major-General* |

*Major-General* Karl Ivanovich **Ezering** (28 Aug 1868 - 29 Sep 1934)

| | |
|---|---|
| 8 Feb 1916 - 22 Aug 1916: | Chief of Staff, 74th Infantry Division |
| 10 Apr 1916: | Promoted to *Major-General* |
| 22 Aug 1916 - 14 Mar 1917: | At the disposal of the Chief of the General Staff |
| 14 Mar 1917 - 1918: | Chief of Administration, General Staff |

*Major-General* Karl Semonovich **Fabian** (5 Sep 1840 - ?)

| | |
|---|---|
| 24 Sep 1886 - 2 Nov 1895: | Deputy Commander of Engineers, Turkestan Military District |
| 30 Aug 1891: | Promoted to *Major-General* |
| 2 Nov 1895 - 1896: | At the disposal of the Main Engineering Directorate |

*Major-General* Aleksey Aleksandrovich **Fabritsius** (15 Mar 1869 - 1938)

| | |
|---|---|
| 16 Aug 1914 - 1917: | Commander, 265th Infantry Regiment |
| 16 Jul 1916: | Promoted to *Major-General* |
| 1917: | Commander, Brigade, 67th Infantry Division |

*Lieutenant-General* Ivan Ivanovich **Fabritsius** (12 Jun 1851 - ?)

| | |
|---|---|
| 14 Dec 1894 - 15 Apr 1910: | Staff officer, Engineering Committee, Main Engineering Directorate |
| 6 Dec 1899: | Promoted to *Major-General* |
| 15 Apr 1910: | Promoted to *Lieutenant-General* |
| 15 Apr 1910: | Retired |

*Rear-Admiral* Semyon Semyonovich **Fabritsky** (14 Feb 1874 - 3 Feb 1941)

| | |
|---|---|
| Feb 1915 - 17 Oct 1916: | Commander, Moonsund Naval Defense Brigade |
| 28 Jun 1916: | Promoted to *Rear-Admiral* |
| 17 Oct 1916 - Apr 1917: | Commander, Separate Baltic Naval Division |
| Apr 1917 - 22 Jun 1917: | Reserve officer, Ministry of the Navy |
| 22 Jun 1917: | Retired |

*General of Infantry* Semyon Andreyevich **Faddeyev** (21 Jul 1835 - 14 Feb 1909)

| | |
|---|---|
| 20 Dec 1887: | Promoted to *Major-General* |

| | |
|---|---|
| 20 Dec 1887 - 22 Apr 1898: | Commandant of Fortress Kars |
| 14 May 1896: | Promoted to *Lieutenant-General* |
| 22 Apr 1898 - 7 Dec 1901: | Commander, 14th Infantry Division |
| 7 Dec 1901 - 27 Jun 1902: | Commanding General, VI. Army Corps |
| 27 Jun 1902 - 21 Sep 1906: | Commanding General, II. Caucasus Army Corps |
| 22 Jul 1906: | Promoted to *General of Infantry* |
| 21 Sep 1906 - 14 Feb 1909: | Attached to the Caucasus Military District |

*General of Artillery* Aleksandr Aleksandrovich **Fadeyev** (30 Mar 1811 - 3 Dec 1898)
| | |
|---|---|
| 19 May 1849 - 12 Feb 1857: | Chief of Okhtenskaya Explosives Factory |
| 25 Jun 1852: | Promoted to *Major-General* |
| 12 Feb 1857 - 11 Mar 1858: | Unassigned |
| 11 Mar 1858 - 13 Jul 1859: | Conference Member, Mikhailovsky Artillery School |
| 13 Jul 1859 - 16 Apr 1867: | Unassigned |
| 30 Aug 1862: | Promoted to *Lieutenant-General* |
| 16 Apr 1867 - 31 Dec 1883: | Member of the Artillery Committee, Main Artillery Directorate |
| 1 Jan 1879: | Promoted to *General of Artillery* |
| 31 Dec 1883 - 3 Dec 1898: | Member, Committee for Wounded Veterans |

*Lieutenant-General* Fyodor Petrovich **Falenberg** (25 Jul 1846 - ?)
| | |
|---|---|
| 22 Jun 1902 - 28 Mar 1903: | Commander, 28th Artillery Brigade |
| 3 Oct 1902: | Promoted to *Major-General* |
| 28 Mar 1903 - 18 Jan 1905: | Commander, 42nd Artillery Brigade |
| 18 Jan 1905 - 9 Jan 1914: | General for Special Assignments, Vilnius Military District |
| 9 Jan 1914: | Promoted to *Lieutenant-General* |
| 9 Jan 1914: | Retired |
| 7 Aug 1915 - Oct 1917: | Recalled; Reserve officer, Dvinsk Military District |
| 8 Apr 1917: | Retired |

*Major-General* Frants-Karl-Fridrikh Iosifovich von **Faler** (25 Apr 1865 - 3 Mar 1937)
| | |
|---|---|
| 16 Dec 1910 - Oct 1917: | Governor of Vyborg |
| 6 Dec 1912: | Promoted to *Major-General* |

*Major-General* Aleksandr Georgiyevich **Faleyev** (24 Jul 1875 - 14 Dec 1920)
| | |
|---|---|
| 24 Oct 1916 - 1918: | Chief of Lines of Communication Section, 8th Army |
| 6 Dec 1916: | Promoted to *Major-General* |

*Rear-Admiral* Georgy Petrovich **Falk** (5 Jan 1862 - 31 Jul 1919)
| | |
|---|---|
| 7 Dec 1908 - 1917: | Commander, Imperial Yacht "Aleksandria" |
| 6 Dec 1913: | Promoted to *Rear-Admiral* |

*Lieutenant-General* Ivan Amvrosiyevich **Falkovsky** (1 Aug 1854 - ?)
| | |
|---|---|
| 31 Mar 1905 - 29 May 1910: | Commander, 2nd Life Dragoon Regiment |
| 29 May 1910: | Promoted to *Major-General* |
| 29 May 1910 - 1 Aug 1913: | Commander, 2nd Brigade, 4th Cavalry Division |
| 1 Aug 1913: | Promoted to *Lieutenant-General* |

1 Aug 1913: Retired

*Major-General* Sergey Sergeyevich **Famintsyn** (13 Dec 1836 - ?)
30 Dec 1886 - 8 May 1887: Chief of Gendarmerie, Baku
5 Apr 1887: Promoted to *Major-General*
8 May 1887 - 23 Dec 1894: Chief of Gendarmerie, Warsaw Province
23 Dec 1894 - 1898: Chief of Gendarmerie, Kursk

*General of Artillery* Konstantin Petrovich **Fan-der-Flit** (19 Sep 1844 - Apr 1933)
30 Apr 1890 - 23 Feb 1893: Commander, Horse Artillery Brigade, Kuban Cossack Army
30 Aug 1890: Promoted to *Major-General*
23 Feb 1893 - 30 Jan 1895: Commander, 1st Grenadier Artillery Brigade
30 Jan 1895 - 29 Aug 1895: Unassigned
29 Aug 1895 - 5 Dec 1899: Commander, 37th Artillery Brigade
5 Dec 1899 - 30 Jun 1900: Commander of Artillery, XVII. Army Corps
1 Jan 1900: Promoted to *Lieutenant-General*
30 Jun 1900 - 17 Aug 1905: Commander of Artillery, I. Army Corps
17 Aug 1905 - 19 Apr 1906: Inspector of Artillery, 1st Manchurian Army
19 Apr 1906 - 24 Apr 1908: Commander of Artillery, Guards Corps
24 Apr 1908 - 9 Apr 1913: Deputy Commanding General, Odessa Military District
6 Dec 1908: Promoted to *General of Artillery*
9 Apr 1913 - 19 Jul 1914: Deputy Commanding General, St. Petersburg Military District
19 Jul 1914 - 21 Jun 1915: C-in-C, 6th Army
18 Nov 1914 - 14 Sep 1915: Commanding General, St. Petersburg Military District
22 Mar 1915: Promoted to *General-Adjutant*
21 Jun 1915 - 1917: Member of the State Council
1917: Retired

*Major-General* Ioasaf Lvovich **Fateyev** (21 Oct 1837 - ?)
16 Oct 1893 - 1904: Section Chief, Main Cossack Directorate
6 Dec 1899: Promoted to *Major-General*

*Major-General* Nikolai Afanasyevich **Faydysh** (8 Mar 1863 - ?)
5 Jul 1916 - 20 Oct 1916: Special Assignments General, Kazan Military District
26 Sep 1916: Promoted to *Major-General*
20 Oct 1916 - 1917: Commander, 13th Replacement Infantry Brigade
1917: Staff officer, Kazan Military District

*Major-General* Dmitry Dmitriyevich **Fedchenko** (18 Nov 1868 - 27 Aug 1914)
18 Dec 1913: Promoted to *Major-General*
18 Dec 1913 - 27 Aug 1914: Commander, 9th Artillery Brigade

*Major-General* Vasily Timofeyevich **Fedorenko** (27 Dec 1871 - 13 Jul 1919)
13 Apr 1916 - 18 May 1917: Chief of Staff, 28th Infantry Division
6 Dec 1916: Promoted to *Major-General*
18 May 1917 - 26 May 1917: Chief of Staff, XX. Army Corps

26 May 1917 - 1918: Commander, 137th Infantry Division

*Lieutenant-General* Aleksey Vasiliyevich **Fedorov** (4 Mar 1845 - ?)
11 Mar 1891 - 30 Jan 1897: Commander, 165th Infantry Regiment
14 May 1896: Promoted to *Major-General*
30 Jan 1897 - 6 Mar 1900: Commander, 1st Brigade, 38th Infantry Division
6 Mar 1900 - 17 May 1903: Commander, 59th Reserve Infantry Brigade
17 May 1903 - 6 Apr 1907: Commander, 4th Infantry Division
28 Mar 1904: Promoted to *Lieutenant-General*

*Major-General* Anatoly Semyonovich **Fedorov** (24 Jul 1871 - ?)
18 May 1915 - 26 Sep 1916: Commander, 38th Artillery Brigade
27 Jun 1915: Promoted to *Major-General*

*Major-General* Dmitry Yakovlevich **Fedorov** (21 Oct 1869 - 21 Jan 1953)
16 Jul 1910 - 6 Dec 1914: Commander, 18th Rifle Regiment
6 Dec 1914: Promoted to *Major-General*
6 Dec 1914 - 30 Sep 1917: Chief of Staff, II. Caucasus Army Corps
30 Sep 1917 - Oct 1917: Commander, 129th Infantry Division

*Major-General of the Fleet* Fyodor Ivanovich **Fedorov** (21 Oct 1867 - 1918)
1907 - 1917: Company Commander, Marine Corps
30 Jul 1915: Promoted to *Major-General of the Fleet*

*Major-General* Ivan Ivanovich **Fedorov** (9 Oct 1868 - ?)
28 Jul 1913 - 14 Mar 1916: Commander, 7th Railway Battalion
16 Sep 1915: Promoted to *Major-General*
14 Mar 1916 - 1918: Commander, 3rd Railway Brigade

*Major-General of Naval Artillery* Leonid Fyodorovich **Fedorov** (3 Aug 1865 - ?)
21 Jan 1913 - 1917: Deputy Chief of Artillery Section, Main Shipbuilding Directorate
6 May 1913: Promoted to *Major-General of Naval Artillery*

*Major-General* Mikhail Stepanovich **Fedorov** (8 Sep 1824 - ?)
28 Mar 1891 - 1894: Commander of Gendarmerie, Sedletsk Province
17 Apr 1894: Promoted to *Major-General*

*Major-General* Nikolai Ivanovich **Fedorov** (5 Nov 1864 - ?)
6 Jul 1910 - 3 Apr 1915: Commander, 1st Turkestan Rifle Regiment
22 Jan 1915: Promoted to *Major-General*
3 Apr 1915 - 1917: Commander, Brigade, 77th Infantry Division

*Lieutenant-General* Nikolai Nikolayevich **Fedorov** (1 Sep 1851 - Feb 1940)
18 Nov 1892 - 31 Dec 1913: Deputy Chief of Tula Imperial Arms Factory
29 Mar 1909: Promoted to *Major-General*
31 Dec 1913: Promoted to *Lieutenant-General*
31 Dec 1913: Retired

*General of Artillery* Nikolai Pavlovich **Fedorov** (6 Aug 1835 - 2 Mar 1912)
| | |
|---|---|
| 10 Mar 1867 - 25 Nov 1895: | Conference Member, Mikhailovsky Artillery Academy |
| 1 Jan 1878: | Promoted to *Major-General* |
| 30 Aug 1888: | Promoted to *Lieutenant-General* |
| 25 Nov 1895 - 24 Feb 1900: | Member of the Artillery Committee, Main Artillery Directorate |
| 24 Feb 1900: | Promoted to *General of Artillery* |
| 24 Feb 1900: | Retired |

*Major-General* Pavel Alekseyevich **Fedorov** (20 Dec 1859 - ?)
| | |
|---|---|
| 2 Apr 1916 - 1917: | Member, Section for the Control of Gunpowder & Ammunition Depots, Main Artillery Directorate |
| 10 Apr 1916: | Promoted to *Major-General* |

*Major-General* Pyotr Nikonovich **Fedorov** (7 Nov 1857 - ?)
| | |
|---|---|
| 25 Oct 1913: | Promoted to *Major-General* |
| 25 Oct 1913 - 12 May 1916: | Commander, 17$^{th}$ Artillery Brigade |
| 12 May 1916 - 1 Feb 1917: | Inspector of Artillery, VII. Siberian Army Corps |
| 1 Feb 1917 - 27 Feb 1917: | Unassigned |
| 27 Feb 1917 - 19 Sep 1917: | Inspector of Artillery, III. Caucasus Army Corps |
| 19 Sep 1917 - ?: | Reserve officer, Kiev Military District |

*Lieutenant-General* Pyotr Petrovich **Fedorov** (23 Oct 1847 - 1913)
| | |
|---|---|
| 1 Dec 1899: | Promoted to *Major-General* |
| 1 Dec 1899 - 23 Jul 1900: | Commander, Siberian Replacement Line Brigade |
| 23 Jul 1900 - 18 May 1902: | Commander, 8$^{th}$ Turkestan Rifle Brigade |
| 18 May 1902 - 19 Nov 1904: | Intendant, Odessa Military District |
| 19 Nov 1904 - 12 Jun 1906: | Intendant, 3$^{rd}$ Manchurian Army |
| 2 Apr 1906: | Promoted to *Lieutenant-General* |
| 12 Jun 1906 - Mar 1909: | Commander, 19$^{th}$ Infantry Division |

*Lieutenant-General* Semyon Ivanovich **Fedorov** (27 May 1855 - 6 Apr 1916)
| | |
|---|---|
| 11 Oct 1903: | Promoted to *Major-General* |
| 11 Oct 1903 - 22 Feb 1910: | Chief of Staff, XIV. Army Corps |
| 22 Feb 1910 - 19 Jul 1914: | General for Assignments, Inspector of Rifles |
| 3 Jul 1910: | Promoted to *Lieutenant-General* |
| 19 Jul 1914 - Feb 1915: | Commander, 53$^{rd}$ Infantry Division |
| Feb 1915 - 6 Apr 1916: | POW, Germany |

*Major-General* Stepan Alekseyevich **Fedorov** (28 Mar 1839 - ?)
| | |
|---|---|
| 14 Jan 1898: | Promoted to *Major-General* |
| 14 Jan 1898 - Jan 1902: | Commander, 2$^{nd}$ Brigade, 45$^{th}$ Infantry Division |

*Major-General* Viktor Ivanovich **Fedorov** (31 Jan 1860 - ?)
| | |
|---|---|
| 31 Dec 1913 - 1917: | Commander, Kharabovsk Artillery Depot |
| 22 Mar 1915: | Promoted to *Major-General* |

*Major-General* Vladimir Grigoryevich **Fedorov** (3 May 1874 - 19 Sep 1966)
22 Sep 1915 - 1918: Member, Artillery Committee Section, Main Artillery Directorate
10 Apr 1916: Promoted to *Major-General*

*Lieutenant-General* Yakov Dmitriyevich **Fedorov** (17 Nov 1840 - 13 Sep 1903)
2 May 1890: Promoted to *Major-General*
2 May 1890 - 10 Jun 1896: Chief of Staff, Transcaspian Region
10 Jun 1896 - 28 Aug 1897: Chief of Staff, Turkestan Military District
28 Aug 1897 - 2 Oct 1899: Military Governor of Samarkand
2 Oct 1899: Promoted to *Lieutenant-General*
2 Oct 1899: Retired

*Major-General* Aleksandr Ippolitovich **Fedotov** (26 May 1869 - Jun 1922)
31 Dec 1912 - 14 May 1915: Commander, 5$^{th}$ Uhlan Regiment
1 May 1915: Promoted to *Major-General*
14 May 1915 - 29 Apr 1917: Chief of Staff, XIX. Army Corps
29 Apr 1917 - 21 Aug 1917: Quartermaster-General, 2$^{nd}$ Army
21 Aug 1917 - 30 Dec 1917: Commander, 4$^{th}$ Cavalry Division

*Lieutenant-General* Aleksandr Petrovich **Fedotov** (23 Oct 1843 - ?)
6 Apr 1903 - 9 Nov 1910: Map Editor, Military Topographical Section, General Staff
13 Apr 1908: Promoted to *Major-General*
9 Nov 1910 - 31 May 1917: Chief of Kiev Military Topographical Survey
31 May 1917: Promoted to *Lieutenant-General*
31 May 1917: Retired

*General of Infantry* Ivan Ivanovich **Fedotov** (20 Feb 1855 - ?)
10 Jul 1903 - 8 Dec 1904: General Staff officer, Turkestan Military District
13 Aug 1903: Promoted to *Major-General*
8 Dec 1904 - 28 Jun 1905: Quartermaster-General, Turkestan Military District
28 Jun 1905 - 30 Jul 1906: Military Governor of Syr-Darya Region
30 Jul 1906 - 2 Jul 1910: Chief of Staff, II. Turkestan Army Corps
2 Jul 1910: Promoted to *Lieutenant-General*
2 Jul 1910 - 3 Apr 1915: Commander, 11$^{th}$ Infantry Division
3 Apr 1915 - 23 Jun 1917: Commanding General, XXXII. Army Corps
25 Aug 1916: Promoted to *General of Infantry*
22 May 1917 - 4 Jun 1917: Acting C-in-C, 11$^{th}$ Army
23 Jun 1917 - Oct 1917: Reserve officer, Kiev Military District

*Lieutenant-General* Ivan Semonovich **Fedotov** (10 Aug 1853 - ?)
15 Aug 1900 - 15 Mar 1910: Section Chief, Main Cossack Directorate
6 Dec 1904: Promoted to *Major-General*
15 Mar 1910 - 14 May 1913: Duty General, Moscow Military District
14 May 1913: Promoted to *Lieutenant-General*
14 May 1913: Retired

*Major-General* Mikhail Demyanovich **Fedotov** (16 Sep 1859 - 1911)
12 Nov 1907: Promoted to *Major-General*
12 Nov 1907 - 8 Jan 1909: Commander, 1st Brigade, 5th Infantry Division
8 Jan 1909 - Oct 1911: Commander, 1st Brigade, 42nd Infantry Division

*Lieutenant-General* Leonid Vasilyevich **Fedyay** (15 Aug 1859 - ?)
15 Jun 1907: Promoted to *Major-General*
15 Jun 1907 - 8 Feb 1914: Quartermaster-General, Turkestan Military District
8 Feb 1914 - 22 Oct 1914: Chief of Staff, XXV. Army Corps
22 Oct 1914 - 24 Oct 1915: Commander, Brigade, 61st Infantry Division
24 Oct 1915 - 18 Apr 1917: Commander, 31st Infantry Division
21 Oct 1916: Promoted to *Lieutenant-General*
18 Apr 1917 - Oct 1917: Reserve officer, Kiev Military District

*Major-General* Esper Aleksandrovich **Feldman** (23 Jul 1854 - 1913)
22 Dec 1906: Promoted to *Major-General*
22 Dec 1906 - 22 Dec 1910: Commander, Life Guards Uhlan Regiment
22 Dec 1910 - 18 Feb 1912: Commander, Independent Guards Cavalry Brigade
18 Feb 1912 - 1913: General à la suite

*General of Infantry* Fyodor Aleksandrovich **Feldman** (10 Dec 1835 - 2 Feb 1902)
23 May 1876 - 8 Oct 1881: Military Attaché, Vienna
1 Jan 1878: Promoted to *Major-General*
8 Oct 1881 - 10 Aug 1896: Head of Military Research Committee, General Staff
30 Aug 1888: Promoted to *Lieutenant-General*
10 Aug 1896 - 30 Jun 1900: Director of the Imperial Aleksandr Lyceum
10 Aug 1896 - 2 Feb 1902: Member, Military-Scientific Committee, General Staff
30 Jun 1900 - 2 Feb 1902: Trustee, Board of Trustees, Empress Maria Institutions
1 Apr 1901: Promoted to *General of Infantry*

*General of Infantry* Iogann-Nikolai Aleksandrovich **Feldman** (27 Dec 1831 - ?)
18 Jan 1874 - 20 Sep 1877: Commander, 130th Infantry Regiment
20 Sep 1877: Promoted to *Major-General*
20 Sep 1877 - 2 Mar 1878: Transferred to the reserve
2 Mar 1878 - 9 Feb 1879: Commander, 1st Brigade, 5th Reserve Infantry Division
9 Feb 1879 - 1 Aug 1879: Unassigned
1 Aug 1879 - 21 Mar 1888: Commander, 2nd Brigade, 18th Infantry Division
21 Mar 1888 - 29 Dec 1900: Commander, Poltava Local Brigade
30 Aug 1888. Promoted to *Lieutenant-General*
29 Dec 1900: Promoted to *General of Infantry*
29 Dec 1900: Retired

*Major-General* Voldemar Nikolayevich **Feldman** (13 Jul 1858 - 23 May 1928)
1911 - 21 Jul 1911: Commander, 15th Hussar Regiment
21 Jul 1911: Promoted to *Major-General*
21 Jul 1911: Retired
21 Oct 1914 - 25 May 1918: Recalled; Chief of Staff, III. State Militia Corps

*Major-General* Vladimir Konstantinovich **Feldt** (6 Jul 1860 - ?)
| | |
|---|---|
| 19 Feb 1909 - 24 Aug 1914: | Chief of Kovel-Vladimir Volyn Military Railway |
| 6 Dec 1909: | Promoted to *Major-General* |
| 24 Aug 1914 - 28 Mar 1915: | Chief of Military Communications Section, Operations Department, Southwestern Front |
| 28 Mar 1915 - 1917: | Reserve officer, Kiev Military District |

*Major-General* Aleksandr Rafailovich **Felitsyn** (1 Oct 1848 - ?)
| | |
|---|---|
| 24 Jul 1893 - 1909: | Commander, Moscow Gendarmerie Division |
| 30 Jul 1905: | Promoted to *Major-General* |

*Major-General of the Naval Legal Corps* Anatoly Antonovich **Felitsyn** (18 Oct 1868 - ?)
| | |
|---|---|
| 14 Sep 1909 - 13 May 1913: | Naval Prosecutor, Port of Kronstadt |
| 6 Dec 1909: | Promoted to *State Councillor (Naval Legal Official, $4^{th}$ Class)* |
| 13 May 1913 - ?: | Deputy Chief Naval Prosecutor |
| 9 Jun 1914: | Redesignated *Major-General of the Naval Legal Corps* |

*Rear-Admiral* Dimitri Gustavovich von **Felkerzam** (29 Apr 1846 - 11 May 1905)
| | |
|---|---|
| 6 Dec 1899: | Promoted to *Rear-Admiral* |
| 6 Dec 1899 - 7 Feb 1900: | Commandant, Naval Gunnery School |
| 7 Feb 1900 - 9 Sep 1902: | Chairman of the Naval Artillery Testing Commission |
| 9 Sep 1902 - 11 May 1904: | Chief of Training & Naval Artillery, Baltic Fleet |
| 10 May 1904 - 11 May 1905: | Commander, $2^{nd}$ Battleship Division, $2^{nd}$ Pacific Squadron |

*Major-General* Yeremy Yakovlevich **Fenster (Vrasky)** (5 Dec 1868 - 1 Apr 1944)
| | |
|---|---|
| 18 Apr 1914: | Promoted to *Major-General* |
| 18 Apr 1914 - 15 Dec 1917: | Commandant, Chuguevsky Military School |

*Vice-Admiral* Yevgeny Petrovich **Feodosyev** (3 Feb 1842 - 16 Jan 1914)
| | |
|---|---|
| 1897: | Promoted to *Rear-Admiral* |
| 1897 - 1899: | Senior Flagman, Black Sea Naval Division |
| 1899 - 1902: | Commander, Port of Sevastopol, Mayor of Sevastopol |
| 1902: | Promoted to *Vice-Admiral* |
| 1902: | Retired |

*Major-General* Count Nikolai Pavlovich **Fersen** (14 Jun 1858 - 3 Nov 1921)
| | |
|---|---|
| 13 Apr 1908: | Promoted to *Major-General* |
| 13 Apr 1908 - 14 Feb 1909: | Attached to Grand Duke Vladimir Aleksandrovich |
| 14 Feb 1909 - 16 Apr 1917: | General à la suite |
| 16 Apr 1917: | Dismissed |

*General of Infantry* Yevgeny Aleksandrovich **Fersman** (4 Mar 1855 - 1937)
| | |
|---|---|
| 29 May 1898 - 6 Apr 1903: | Commandant, Odessa Infantry Cadet School |
| 6 Apr 1903: | Promoted to *Major-General* |
| 22 Aug 1903 - 5 Jul 1905: | Director, $3^{rd}$ Moscow Cadet Corps |

| | |
|---|---|
| 5 Jul 1905 - 18 Nov 1908: | Commandant, Aleksandr Military School |
| 6 Dec 1907: | Promoted to *Lieutenant-General* |
| 18 Nov 1908 - 13 May 1914: | Commander, 40th Infantry Division |
| 13 May 1914: | Promoted to *General of Infantry* |
| 13 May 1914: | Retired |

*Vice-Admiral* Baron Vasili Nikolayevich **Ferzen** (14 May 1858 - 6 May 1937)
| | |
|---|---|
| 18 Apr 1910: | Promoted to *Rear-Admiral* |
| 18 Apr 1910 - 25 Oct 1911: | Commander, 2nd Destroyer Division, Baltic Fleet |
| 25 Oct 1911 - 14 Apr 1913: | Commander, Cruiser Squadron, Baltic Fleet |
| 14 Apr 1913: | Promoted to *Vice-Admiral* |
| 14 Apr 1913 - 20 Oct 1914: | Commander, Battleship Squadron, Baltic Fleet |
| 20 Oct 1914 - 13 Apr 1917: | Attached to the Naval General Staff |
| 13 Apr 1917: | Retired |

*Major-General* Yevgeny Viktorovich **Fetter** (12 Feb 1845 - 7 Dec 1902)
| | |
|---|---|
| 15 Feb 1900: | Promoted to *Major-General* |
| 15 Feb 1900 - 7 Dec 1902: | Commander, 1st Brigade, 41st Infantry Division |

*Major-General* Nikolai Fyodorovich **Fevralev** (14 Oct 1856 - ?)
| | |
|---|---|
| 5 Dec 1908: | Promoted to *Major-General* |
| 5 Dec 1908 - 1910: | Commander, 228th Reserve Infantry Regiment |

*Major-General* Aleksey Flegontovich **Fialkovsky** (23 Jan 1859 - ?)
| | |
|---|---|
| 25 Jun 1914 - 1917: | Commander, 12th Siberian Rifle Artillery Brigade |
| 8 Nov 1915: | Promoted to *Major-General* |

*Major-General* Nikolai Nikolayevich **Fialkovsky** (12 Aug 1859 - ?)
| | |
|---|---|
| 4 Jun 1911 - 1917: | Commander, 10th Horse Artillery Battalion |
| 27 Sep 1916: | Promoted to *Major-General* |

*Lieutenant-General* Afako Patsiyevich **Fidarov** (29 Aug 1859 - 1930)
| | |
|---|---|
| 12 Feb 1907 - 23 Jul 1910: | Commander, 1st Cossack Regiment, Kuban Cossack Army |
| 22 Jul 1910: | Promoted to *Major-General* |
| 23 Jul 1910 - 2 Aug 1913: | Commander, 2nd Brigade, 2nd Caucasus Cossack Division |
| 2 Aug 1913 - Dec 1917: | Commander, 1st Turkestan Cossack Division |
| 22 Jul 1916: | Promoted to *Lieutenant-General* |

*Lieutenant-General* Nikolai Mikhailovich **Filatov** (27 Sep 1862 - 24 Feb 1935)
| | |
|---|---|
| 6 Feb 1905 - 16 Dec 1914: | Commandant, Firearms Polygon, Rifle Officers School |
| 6 Dec 1909: | Promoted to *Major-General* |
| 16 Dec 1914 - 28 Nov 1915: | Member, 5th Section, Artillery Committee, Main Artillery Directorate |
| 28 Nov 1915 - 1918: | Chief of 5th Section, Artillery Committee, Main Artillery Directorate |
| 10 Apr 1916: | Promoted to *Lieutenant-General* |

*Lieutenant-General* Aleksandr Valerianovich **Filatyev** (23 Jan 1849 - ?)
| | |
|---|---|
| 15 Jan 1912: | Promoted to *Major-General* |
| 15 Jan 1912 - 15 Jan 1914: | Commander, Kharkov Regional Brigade |
| 15 Jan 1914: | Promoted to *Lieutenant-General* |
| 15 Jan 1914: | Retired |
| 11 Mar 1915: | Recalled with the rank of *Major-General* |
| 11 Mar 1915 - 1917: | Reserve officer, Kiev Military District |

*Lieutenant-General* Dmitry Vladimirovich **Filatyev** (3 Sep 1866 - 21 Sep 1932)
| | |
|---|---|
| 8 Feb 1912 - 24 Feb 1913: | Clerk, Office of the Ministry of War |
| 25 Mar 1912: | Promoted to *Major-General* |
| 24 Feb 1913 - Oct 1914: | Professor, Nikolayev Military Academy |
| Oct 1914 - 1 Jan 1916: | Deputy Chief of Logistics, Northwest Front |
| 1 Jan 1916 - 10 Jun 1916: | Deputy Chief of Logistics, Western Front |
| 10 Jun 1916 - 14 Jan 1917: | Deputy Chief, Office of the Ministry of War |
| 6 Dec 1916: | Promoted to *Lieutenant-General* |
| 14 Jan 1917 - Dec 1917: | Chief, Office of the Ministry of War |
| 10 May 1917 - Dec 1917: | Member of the Military Council |

*Major-General* Mikhail Nikolayevich **Filatyev** (2 Nov 1846 - ?)
| | |
|---|---|
| 3 May 1907 - 1912: | Commander of Gendarmerie, Don Region |
| 6 Dec 1907: | Promoted to *Major-General* |

*Lieutenant-General* Vasily Ivanovich **Filenkov** (1 Jan 1854 - ?)
| | |
|---|---|
| 2 Apr 1899 - 16 Aug 1906: | Ataman, Ust-Medveditskaya Division, Don Cossack Army |
| 6 Apr 1903: | Promoted to *Major-General* |
| 16 Aug 1906 - 19 Jun 1908: | Ataman, 2nd Division, Don Cossack Army |
| 19 Jun 1908 - 6 Jan 1913: | Commander, 1st Brigade, 2nd Consolidated Cossack Division |
| 6 Jan 1913: | Promoted to *Lieutenant-General* |
| 6 Jan 1913: | Retired |

*Major-General* Boris Petrovich **Filimonov** (24 Jul 1862 - ?)
| | |
|---|---|
| 23 Aug 1915 - 4 Jan 1917: | Commander, 269th Infantry Regiment |
| 19 Jul 1915: | Promoted to *Major-General* |
| 4 Jan 1917 - 30 Apr 1917: | Commander, Brigade, 113th Infantry Division |
| 30 Apr 1917 - 18 Dec 1917: | Commander, 23rd Infantry Division |

*Major-General* Fyodor Petrovich **Filimonov** (7 Jun 1862 - 14 Jan 1940)
| | |
|---|---|
| 27 Aug 1913 - 25 Aug 1916: | Commander, 2nd Brigade, 3rd Caucasus Cossack Division |
| 6 Apr 1914: | Promoted to *Major-General* |
| 25 Aug 1916 - 1918: | Commander, 4th Caucasus Cossack Division |

*Lieutenant-General* Nikolai Grigoryevich **Filimonov** (28 Nov 1866 - 7 Nov 1917)
| | |
|---|---|
| 1 Apr 1911: | Promoted to *Major-General* |
| 1 Apr 1911 - 18 Sep 1912: | Commander, 1st Brigade, 4th Infantry Division |

| | |
|---|---|
| 18 Sep 1912 - 18 Jan 1914: | Chief of Staff, Fortress Modlin |
| 18 Jan 1914 - 19 Jul 1914: | Chief of Fortress Section, General Staff |
| 19 Jul 1914 - 22 Oct 1914: | Quartermaster-General, 2nd Army |
| 22 Oct 1914 - 14 Dec 1914: | Commander, 1st Rifle Brigade |
| 14 Dec 1914 - 17 Oct 1915: | Chief of Staff, Fortress Brest-Litovsk |
| 17 Oct 1915 - 7 Nov 1917: | Commander, 25th Infantry Division |
| 22 Aug 1917: | Promoted to *Lieutenant-General* |

*Major-General* Semyon Vasilyevich **Filimonov** (24 May 1848 - ?)
| | |
|---|---|
| 12 Dec 1885 - 22 Jan 1902: | Section Chief, Main Artillery Directorate |
| 30 Aug 1899: | Promoted to *Major-General* |
| 22 Jan 1902 - 25 Apr 1905: | Deputy Commander of Artillery, Caucasus Military District |

*Major-General* Vasily Vasilyevich **Filimonov** (27 Mar 1847 - ?)
| | |
|---|---|
| 22 Jan 1902: | Promoted to *Major-General* |
| 22 Jan 1902 - 1906: | Commander, 1st Replacement Artillery Brigade |

*Major-General* Yakov Ivanovich **Filipov** (22 Oct 1842 - ?)
| | |
|---|---|
| 23 Mar 1909 - 1913: | Commandant of Warsaw District Arsenal |
| 6 Dec 1911: | Promoted to *Major-General* |

*Major-General* Ivan Ivanovich **Filippov** (7 Jul 1849 - ?)
| | |
|---|---|
| 6 Nov 1900 - 1911: | Military Commander, Vladikavkaz District |
| 1911: | Promoted to *Major-General* |
| 1911: | Retired |

*Major-General of the Admiralty* Pyotr Gavrilovich **Filippov** (3 Jun 1862 - 9 Apr 1942)
| | |
|---|---|
| 1898 - 1917: | Naval Artillery Inspector |
| 22 Mar 1915: | Promoted to *Major-General of the Admiralty* |

*Major-General* Pyotr Grigoryevich **Filippov** (29 Jun 1867 - ?)
| | |
|---|---|
| 4 Aug 1913 - 31 Aug 1916: | Commander, 1st Black Sea Regiment, Kuban Cossack Army |
| 12 Jul 1916: | Promoted to *Major-General* |
| 31 Aug 1916 - 1917: | Commander, 1st Brigade, 5th Caucasus Cossack Division |

*Lieutenant-General* Vladimir Nikolayevich **Filippov** (2 Nov 1838 - 12 May 1903)
| | |
|---|---|
| 11 Dec 1880 - 12 Sep 1886: | Military Attaché, Constantinople |
| 24 Mar 1885: | Promoted to *Major-General* |
| 12 Sep 1886 - 9 Nov 1889: | Commander, 1st Brigade, 13th Infantry Division |
| 9 Nov 1889 - 4 Feb 1891: | Deputy Chief of Staff, Odessa Military District |
| 4 Feb 1891 - 20 Mar 1895: | Commander, 4th Rifle Brigade |
| 1 Jan 1895: | Promoted to *Lieutenant-General* |
| 20 Mar 1895 - 28 Dec 1896: | Commander, 13th Infantry Division |
| 28 Dec 1896 - 3 May 1900: | Commander, 15th Infantry Division |
| 3 May 1900 - 12 May 1903: | Commanding General, XI. Army Corps |
| Aug 1900 - Sep 1901: | Commanding General, Amphibious Corps |

*General of Infantry* Nikolai Ivanovich **Filippovsky** (22 Dec 1848 - ?)
| | |
|---|---|
| 4 Aug 1905: | Promoted to *Major-General* |
| 4 Aug 1905 - 28 Mar 1910: | Commander, Archangel Regional Brigade |
| 28 Mar 1910 - 31 Dec 1913: | Commander, St. Petersburg Regional Brigade |
| 31 Dec 1910: | Promoted to *Lieutenant-General* |
| 31 Dec 1913: | Promoted to *General of Infantry* |
| 31 Dec 1913: | Retired |
| 16 Apr 1916 - 1918: | Reserve officer, Petrograd Military District |

*Major-General* Vladimir Fomich **Filonov** (10 Jan 1868 - 6 Apr 1946)
| | |
|---|---|
| 16 Jul 1916 - 1917: | Quartermaster-General, Caucasus Military District |
| 6 Dec 1916: | Promoted to *Major-General* |
| 1917 - 1918: | Quartermaster-General, Caucasus Front |

*Major-General* Sergey Dmitriyevich **Finikov** (28 Jun 1852 - ?)
| | |
|---|---|
| 6 Oct 1910 - 31 Dec 1913: | Deputy Chief of Mikhailovsky Shostensky Gunpowder Factory |
| 31 Dec 1914 - 15 Mar 1914: | Unassigned |
| 15 Mar 1914: | Retired |
| 15 Mar 1914: | Promoted to *Major-General* |

*Major-General* Baron Nikolai Aleksandrovich von **Firks** (11 Mar 1852 - ?)
| | |
|---|---|
| 8 Apr 1908: | Promoted to *Major-General* |
| 8 Apr 1908 - 13 Feb 1909: | Chief of Staff, Ural Cossack Army |
| 13 Feb 1909 - 5 Jul 1910: | Chief of Staff, XI. Army Corps |
| 5 Jul 1910: | Retired |

*Major-General* Aleksandr Dmitriyevich **Firsov** (13 Sep 1852 - 12 Jul 1907)
| | |
|---|---|
| 23 Aug 1905 - 25 Aug 1906: | Commander, 6th East Siberian Rifle Artillery Brigade |
| 17 May 1906: | Promoted to *Major-General* |
| 25 Aug 1906 - Jun 1907: | Commander, 44th Artillery Brigade |

*Major-General* Viktor Vasilyevich **Firsov** (3 Apr 1870 - 13 Feb 1941)
| | |
|---|---|
| 16 Feb 1916 - 19 Feb 1917: | Chief of Staff, 30th Infantry Division |
| 11 May 1916: | Promoted to *Major-General* |
| 19 Feb 1917 - 28 Aug 1917: | Chief of Staff, XXXIII. Army Corps |
| 28 Aug 1917 - 1918: | Commander, 2nd Amur Border Infantry Division |

*Major-General* Mikhail Georgiyevich **Fisenko** (25 Sep 1874 - ?)
| | |
|---|---|
| 4 Jul 1915 - 29 Feb 1916: | Commander, 1st Brigade, 1st Caucasus Cossack Division |
| 29 Feb 1916 - 17 Dec 1916: | Chief of Staff, Consolidated Kuban Cossack Division |
| 1916: | Promoted to *Major-General* |
| ?: | Acting Chief of Staff, Caucasus Cavalry Corps |
| 17 Dec 1916 - 5 Sep 1917: | Chief of Supply, I. Caucasus Cavalry Corps |
| 5 Sep 1917 - 1918: | Commander, 3rd Kuban Cossack Division |

*Major-General* Nikolai Ivanovich **Fisenko** (6 Feb 1861 - ?)
| | |
|---|---|
| 22 Jul 1910: | Promoted to *Major-General* |

| | |
|---|---|
| 22 Jul 1910 - 19 Jul 1914: | Commander, 1st Brigade, 3rd Caucasus Cossack Division |
| 19 Jul 1914 - 6 Nov 1914: | Commander, 2nd Kuban Cossack Division |
| 6 Nov 1914 - 13 Apr 1915: | Reserve officer, Kiev Military District |
| 13 Apr 1915 - 1918: | Commander, Independent Militia Cavalry Brigade |

*Lieutenant-General* Aleksandr Adamovich **Fisher** (26 Dec 1834 - 26 Jan 1908)
| | |
|---|---|
| 26 Feb 1872 - 7 Feb 1880: | Chief of Sub-Section, Main Artillery Directorate |
| 30 Aug 1878: | Promoted to *Major-General* |
| 7 Feb 1880 - 19 Jan 1886: | Inspector of Artillery Acceptance |
| 19 Jan 1886 - 26 Jan 1908: | Inspector of Regional Arsenals |
| 30 Aug 1888: | Promoted to *Lieutenant-General* |
| ? - 26 Jan 1908: | Member of the Artillery Committee, Main Artillery Directorate |

*Lieutenant-General* Vladimir Mikhailovich **Fisher** (15 Jul 1858 - ?)
| | |
|---|---|
| 10 Nov 1906 - 24 Oct 1908: | Military Judge, Moscow Military District Court |
| 22 Apr 1907: | Promoted to *Major-General* |
| 24 Oct 1908 - 31 May 1913: | Military Judge, Turkestan Military District Court |
| 31 May 1913: | Promoted to *Lieutenant-General* |
| 31 May 1913: | Retired |

*Lieutenant-General* Baron Yevgeny Emilyevich **Fitingof** (4 May 1854 - 1939)
| | |
|---|---|
| 14 May 1901: | Promoted to *Major-General* |
| 14 May 1901 - 18 Feb 1905: | Commander, Life Guards 4th Rifle Battalion |
| 18 Feb 1905 - 13 Nov 1907: | Commander, 1st Brigade, 2nd Guards Infantry Division |
| 13 Nov 1907: | Promoted to *Lieutenant-General* |
| 13 Nov 1907 - 17 Aug 1914: | Commander, 8th Infantry Division |
| 17 Aug 1914 - 1918: | POW |

*Major-General of the Admiralty* Baron Aleksandr Aleksandrovich von **Fitingof-Shel** (31 Aug 1857 - ?)
| | |
|---|---|
| 21 Jan 1908 - Mar 1913: | Commander, Revel Commercial Port |
| 6 Dec 1911: | Promoted to *Major-General of the Admiralty* |

*Major-General* Konstantin Aleksandrovich **Fleming** (21 Oct 1856 - ?)
| | |
|---|---|
| 14 Oct 1911 - 7 May 1913: | Commander, 48th Infantry Regiment |
| 14 Apr 1913: | Promoted to *Major-General* |
| 7 May 1913 - 1917: | Commander, 2nd Brigade, 9th Siberian Rifle Division |

*Major-General* Ivan Ivanovich **Flevitsky** (5 Sep 1852 - ?)
| | |
|---|---|
| 5 Apr 1910 - 1911: | Deputy Intendant, Kazan Military District |
| 18 Apr 1910: | Promoted to *Major-General* |

*Major-General* Aleksey Nikolayevich **Fleysher** (30 Mar 1844 - 9 May 1903)
| | |
|---|---|
| 27 Jan 1899 - 9 May 1903: | Ataman, Kizlyar Division, Terek Cossack Army |
| 6 Dec 1901: | Promoted to *Major-General* |

*Lieutenant-General* Nikolai Nikolayevich **Fleysher** (26 Nov 1846 - 11 Dec 1909)
| | |
|---|---|
| 1 Mar 1899: | Promoted to *Major-General* |
| 1 Mar 1899 - 16 Dec 1902: | Commander, 1st East Siberian Rifle Brigade |
| 16 Dec 1902: | Promoted to *Lieutenant-General* |
| 16 Dec 1902 - 10 Feb 1903: | At the disposal of the Chief of the General Staff |
| 10 Feb 1903 - 10 Aug 1904: | Commander, 20th Infantry Division |
| 10 Aug 1904 - 18 Aug 1905: | At the disposal of the Viceroy, Far East |
| 18 Aug 1905 - 5 May 1906: | Commanding General, Consolidated Rifle Corps |
| 5 May 1906 - 27 Dec 1906: | At the disposal of the Minister of War |
| 27 Dec 1906 - 30 Jul 1907: | Commanding General, III. Siberian Army Corps |

*General of Infantry* Rafail Nikolayevich **Fleysher** (19 Feb 1852 - 1 Oct 1916)
| | |
|---|---|
| 1 Dec 1902: | Promoted to *Major-General* |
| 1 Dec 1902 - 18 Jul 1905: | Commander, 2nd Brigade, 41st Infantry Division |
| 18 Jul 1905 - 19 Jul 1906: | Commander, Separate Sakhalin Reserve Brigade |
| 19 Jul 1906 - 27 Jan 1909: | Commander, 1st Siberian Replacement Infantry Brigade |
| 27 Jan 1909: | Promoted to *Lieutenant-General* |
| 27 Jan 1909 - 19 Feb 1914: | Commander, 27th Infantry Division |
| 19 Feb 1914: | Promoted to *General of Infantry* |
| 19 Feb 1914: | Retired |
| 1915 - 13 Mar 1916: | Recalled; Sanitary Inspector of the Army |
| 13 Mar 1916 - 11 Sep 1916: | Commander, 7th Turkestan Rifle Division |
| 11 Sep 1916 - 1 Oct 1916: | Special Assignments General, 2nd Army |

*General of Cavalry* Sergey Nikolayevich **Fleysher** (4 Feb 1856 - 27 Dec 1918)
| | |
|---|---|
| Nov 1900 - 16 Feb 1901: | Acting Commander, 1st Brigade, 2nd Caucasus Cossack Division |
| 16 Feb 1901 - 22 Jun 1910: | Commander, 2nd Brigade, 2nd Caucasus Cossack Division |
| 6 Dec 1901: | Promoted to *Major-General* |
| 5 Jul 1904 - 9 May 1904: | Acting Governor-General of Yelisavetpol Province |
| 24 Nov 1905 - 16 Jan 1906: | Acting Governor-General of Yelisavetpol Province |
| 16 Apr 1908 - 4 Jul 1909: | Acting Governor-General of Yelisavetpol Province |
| 22 Jun 1910: | Promoted to *Lieutenant-General* |
| 22 Jun 1910 - 16 Sep 1912: | Commander, 2nd Caucasus Cossack Division |
| 16 Sep 1912 - 22 Jul 1917: | Commander, Terek Region, Ataman, Terek Cossack Army |
| 22 Jul 1917: | Promoted to *General of Cavalry* |
| 22 Jul 1917: | Retired |

*General of Infantry* Vasily Yegorovich **Flug** (19 Mar 1860 - 3 Dec 1955)
| | |
|---|---|
| 22 Jan 1902 - 1 Jan 1904: | Chief of Staff, Kwantung Region |
| 27 Aug 1903: | Promoted to *Major-General* |
| 1 Jan 1904 - 29 Jan 1904: | Chief of Staff to Governor-General, Far East |
| 29 Jan 1904 - 27 Nov 1904: | Quartermaster-General to Governor-General, Far East |
| 27 Nov 1904 - 14 Jan 1905: | Attached to C-in-C of Armed Forces operating against Japan |
| 14 Jan 1905 - 21 Sep 1905: | Quartermaster-General, 2nd Manchurian Army |

| | |
|---|---|
| 21 Sep 1905 - 19 Nov 1909: | Military Governor of Primorye Region, Ataman of the Ussuri Cossack Army |
| 6 Dec 1908: | Promoted to *Lieutenant-General* |
| 19 Nov 1909 - 30 Jul 1912: | Commander, 37th Infantry Division |
| 30 Jul 1912 - 12 Jan 1913: | Commander, 2nd Guards Infantry Division |
| 12 Jan 1913 - 22 Aug 1914: | Deputy Commanding General, Turkestan Military District, Deputy Governor-General of Turkestan |
| 22 Aug 1914 - 23 Sep 1914: | C-in-C, 10th Army |
| 23 Sep 1914 - 14 Jan 1915: | At the disposal of the Supreme Commander-in-Chief |
| 14 Jan 1915 - 30 May 1917: | Commanding General, II. Army Corps |
| 6 Dec 1914: | Promoted to *General of Infantry* |
| 30 May 1917: | Transferred to the reserve |

*Major-General* Vladimir Timofeyevich **Fofanov** (23 Sep 1850 - ?)
| | |
|---|---|
| 16 Sep 1902: | Promoted to *Major-General* |
| 16 Sep 1902 - 29 May 1906: | Commander, 1st Brigade, 21st Infantry Division |
| 29 May 1906 - 1907: | Commander, 1st Turkestan Reserve Brigade |

*Lieutenant-General* Aleksandr Aleksandrovich **Fogel** (10 Jan 1868 - ?)
| | |
|---|---|
| 10 Mar 1912: | Promoted to *Major-General* |
| 10 Mar 1912 - 22 Dec 1915: | Commander, 46th Artillery Brigade |
| 22 Dec 1915 - 12 May 1916: | Inspector of Artillery, I. Turkestan Army Corps |
| 12 May 1916 - 1917: | Inspector of Artillery, XXV. Army Corps |
| 3 Jun 1917: | Promoted to *Lieutenant-General* |

*Major-General of the Fleet* Nikolai Fyodorovich **Fogel** (22 Aug 1874 - 11 May 1943)
| | |
|---|---|
| 1912 - 1917: | Chief of Section, Inspectorate-General of Aviation |
| 3 Nov 1914: | Promoted to *Major-General of the Fleet* |
| 1917: | Dismissed |

*Lieutenant-General* Aleksandr Viktorovich **Fok** (25 Sep 1843 - 2 Dec 1926)
| | |
|---|---|
| 17 Jul 1900: | Promoted to *Major-General* |
| 17 Jul 1900 - 22 Feb 1904: | Commander, 4th East Siberian Rifle Brigade |
| 22 Feb 1904 - 19 Aug 1906: | Commander, 4th East Siberian Rifle Division |
| 21 Aug 1904: | Promoted to *Lieutenant-General* |
| 19 Aug 1906 - 1908: | At the disposal of the General Staff |
| 1908: | Dismissed |

*Major-General* Aleksey Aleksandrovich **Fok** (17 Mar 1849 - ?)
| | |
|---|---|
| 17 Apr 1905: | Promoted to *Major-General* |
| 17 Apr 1905 - 8 Oct 1907: | Commander, 8th Turkestan Rifle Brigade |

*Major-General* Nikolai Aleksandrovich **Fok** (1 Oct 1859 - ?)
| | |
|---|---|
| 29 Jan 1913 - Jul 1916: | Commander, 2nd Battalion, 37th Artillery Brigade |
| 22 Mar 1915: | Promoted to *Major-General* |
| Jul 1916 - 1918: | Commander, 3rd Rifle Artillery Brigade |

*Lieutenant-General* Yakov Aleksandrovich **Fok** (17 Dec 1864 - 6 Apr 1916)
16 Apr 1904 - 2 Mar 1914:            Commandant, Chuguevsky Military School
6 Dec 1910:                          Promoted to *Major-General*
2 Mar 1914 - 1 Nov 1914:             Commander, 1st Brigade, 15th Infantry Division
1 Nov 1914 - 6 Aug 1915:             Commander, 3rd Rifle Brigade
6 Aug 1915 - 6 Apr 1916:             Commander, 3rd Rifle Division
6 May 1916:                          Posthumously promoted to *Lieutenant-General*

*Major-General* Nikolai Aleksandrovich von **Fokht** (11 Oct 1850 - ?)
13 May 1898:                         Promoted to *Major-General*
13 May 1898 - May 1905:              Commander, 2nd Brigade, 33rd Infantry Division

*Lieutenant-General* Mikhail Aleksandrovich **Folbaum** (22 Oct 1866 - 22 Oct 1916)
26 Jan 1907 - 20 Feb 1908:           Commander, 82nd Infantry Regiment
18 Oct 1907:                         Promoted to *Major-General*
20 Feb 1908 - 22 Nov 1908:           Mayor of Baku
22 Nov 1908 - 24 Oct 1914:           Military Governor of Semirechensk Region,
                                     Ataman, Semirechensk Cossack Army
14 Apr 1913:                         Promoted to *Lieutenant-General*
24 Oct 1914 - 29 Sep 1915:           Commander, 3rd Siberian Rifle Division
29 Sep 1915 - 22 Oct 1916:           Military Governor of Semirechensk Region,
                                     Ataman, Semirechensk Cossack Army

*Major-General* Vladimir Nikolayevich **Folimonov** (14 Jul 1861 - 6 Dec 1919)
10 Mar 1912:                         Promoted to *Major-General*
10 Mar 1912 - 31 Mar 1915:           Commander, 27th Artillery Brigade
31 Mar 1915 - 1918:                  POW

*Major-General* Sevastyan Raymundovich **Folk** (10 Jan 1859 - ?)
24 Apr 1915 - 23 Jun 1917:           Commander, 41st Infantry Regiment
25 Aug 1916:                         Promoted to *Major-General*
23 Jun 1917 - 6 Sep 1917:            Commander, 101st Infantry Division

*General of Cavalry* Leonid Petrovich **Fomin** (27 Jul 1846 - ?)
17 Sep 1894 - 4 Jul 1902:            Chief of Staff, I. Cavalry Corps
14 Nov 1894:                         Promoted to *Major-General*
4 Jul 1902 - 15 Jun 1907:            Commander, 7th Cavalry Division
6 Dec 1902:                          Promoted to *Lieutenant-General*
15 Jun 1907:                         Promoted to *General of Cavalry*
15 Jun 1907:                         Retired

*Major-General* Mikhail Nazarovich **Fomin** (18 Dec 1850 - ?)
1 Jun 1904:                          Promoted to *Major-General*
1 Jun 1904 - 1906:                   Commander, 2nd Brigade, 54th Infantry Division

*Major-General* Nikolai Pavlovich **Fomin** (11 Mar 1869 - 15 Sep 1934)
16 Nov 1915 - 1917:                  Special Assignments General, Ataman of the Don Cossacks

6 Dec 1915: Promoted to *Major-General*

*Major-General* Nikolai Ilich **Fonshteyn** (7 May 1878 - ?)
24 Dec 1914 - 6 Aug 1916: Commander, Heavy Artillery Regiment
6 Aug 1916 - 1918: Commander, 1st Replacement Heavy Artillery Brigade
6 Dec 1916: Promoted to *Major-General*

*Major-General of the Fleet* Vladimir Magnusovich **Forsel** (4 May 1860 - ?)
3 Sep 1914 - 1 Oct 1915: Commander, Port of Emperor Aleksandr III (Libau)
6 Dec 1914: Promoted to *Major-General of the Fleet*
1 Oct 1915 - 17 Mar 1917: Commander, Port of Archangelsk
17 Mar 1917: Dismissed

*Lieutenant-General* Baron Karl-Iogan-Gabriel Fyodorovich **Forseles** (11 Dec 1858 - ?)
10 May 1904: Promoted to *Major-General*
10 May 1904 - 15 Feb 1907: Special Assignments General, Vilnius Military District
15 Feb 1907 - 17 Nov 1912: Commander, 2nd Brigade, 43rd Infantry Division
1912: Promoted to *Lieutenant-General*
1912: Retired

*Major-General* Konstantin Aleksandrovich **Fortunatov** (11 Sep 1856 - ?)
3 Oct 1910 - 1917: Special Assignments General, General Staff
6 Dec 1910: Promoted to *Major-General*

*Major-General* Fyodor Erastovich **Fortvengler** (8 Feb 1862 - ?)
27 Sep 1912 - 1917: Deputy Governor of Petrokovsk
6 Dec 1912: Promoted to *Major-General*

*Major-General* Sergey Frantsevich **Foss** (3 Jul 1860 - 6 Dec 1927)
18 Jan 1909 - 2 Dec 1914: Commander, 15th Dragoon Regiment
2 Dec 1914 - 1915: Commander, 2nd Brigade, 15th Cavalry Division
31 Dec 1914: Promoted to *Major-General*
1915: Retired

*Rear-Admiral* Nikolai Dmitriyevich **Fotaki** (1856 - 1918)
23 Jun 1903 - 10 Apr 1906: Commander of Torpedo Boats, 29th Naval Depot
10 Apr 1906: Promoted to *Rear-Admiral*
10 Apr 1906: Retired

*Lieutenant-General* Ivan Aleksandrovich **Fotengauer** (6 Jan 1856 - ?)
20 May 1909: Promoted to *Major-General*
20 May 1909 - 18 Aug 1912: Commander, 2nd Brigade, 3rd Siberian Infantry Division
18 Aug 1912 - 1914: Commander, 2nd Brigade, 49th Infantry Division
1914: Promoted to *Lieutenant-General*
1914: Dismissed

*Major-General* Pyotr Petrovich **Fotiyev** (7 Dec 1862 - 1 Nov 1914)
Jul 1914 - 1 Nov 1914: Commander, 279th Infantry Regiment

19 Jul 1916: Posthumously promoted to *Major-General*

*Major-General* Yevgeny Vladimirovich von **Frankenshteyn** (23 Jan 1857 - ?)
24 Jul 1913 - 1917: Chief of Gendarmerie, Central Asian Railway
6 Dec 1914: Promoted to *Major-General*

*Major-General* Rafail Fomich **Frankovsky** (3 Nov 1849 - ?)
4 Jul 1901 - 1 Jun 1904: Commander, 6th Grenadier Regiment
1 Jun 1904: Promoted to *Major-General*
1 Jun 1904 - ?: Commander, 1st Brigade, 55th Infantry Division

*Major-General* Vladislav Ignatyevich **Frankovsky** (23 Nov 1858 - 30 Aug 1922)
28 Feb 1908 - 8 Sep 1913: Commander, 12th Uhlan Regiment
8 Sep 1913: Promoted to *Major-General*
8 Sep 1913 - 28 Feb 1916: Commander, 2nd Brigade, 12th Cavalry Division
28 Feb 1916: Dismissed

*Lieutenant-General* Karl Rudolf Ivanovich **Frants** (9 Mar 1846 - ?)
5 May 1889 - 9 Jul 1899: Commander, Czestochowa Borderguard Brigade
14 May 1896: Promoted to *Major-General*
9 Jul 1899 - 22 Jun 1901: At the disposal of the Commanding General of Borderguards
22 Jun 1901: Promoted to *Lieutenant-General*
22 Jun 1901: Retired

*Major-General of Naval Engineers* Aleksandr Ivanovich **Frantskevich** (25 Aug 1860 - 1919)
1908 - 1917: Attached to the Admiralty Shipyard
6 Dec 1913: Promoted to *Major-General of Naval Engineers*

*General of Infantry* Baron Lev Aleksandrovich **Frederiks** (18 Jan 1839 - 23 Sep 1914)
12 Oct 1876 - 29 Jul 1899: Military Attaché, Paris
30 Aug 1884: Promoted to *Major-General*
30 Aug 1894: Promoted to *Lieutenant-General*
1896: Promoted to *General-Adjutant*
29 Jul 1899 - 23 Sep 1914: Honorary Trustee, Board of Trustees, Empress Maria Institutions
6 Dec 1904: Promoted to *General of Infantry*

*General of Cavalry* Count Vladimir Borisovich **Frederiks** (16 Nov 1838 - 5 Jul 1927)
27 Jul 1875 - 14 Jul 1883: Commander, Life Guards Cavalry Regiment
1 Jan 1879: Promoted to *Major-General*
9 Jun 1881 - 16 Mar 1891: Commander, 1st Brigade, 1st Guards Cavalry Division
30 Aug 1891: Promoted to *Lieutenant-General*
16 Mar 1891 - 4 Dec 1893: Master of the Horse, Imperial Court
1 Dec 1893 - 6 May 1897: Deputy Minister of the Imperial Court
24 Mar 1896: Promoted to *General-Adjutant*
6 May 1897 - 28 Mar 1917: Minister of the Imperial Court

| | |
|---|---|
| 14 Jun 1898 - 2 Mar 1917: | Commander of the Imperial Headquarters |
| 6 Dec 1900: | Promoted to *General of Cavalry* |
| 4 Nov 1905 - 28 Mar 1917: | Member of the State Council |

*Major-General* Yuly Eduardovich **Freyberg** (7 Mar 1854 - ?)
| | |
|---|---|
| 4 May 1899 - 19 Jan 1906: | Commander of Gendarmerie, Finland |
| 6 Dec 1901: | Promoted to *Major-General* |
| 19 Jan 1906 - 8 Mar 1908: | Commander of Gendarmerie, St. Petersburg |
| 8 Mar 1908 - 11 Jun 1913: | Commander of Moscow Railway Gendarmerie |
| 11 Jun 1913 - 1917: | Commander of Railway Gendarmerie, Finland |

*Lieutenant-General* Ivan Lyudvigovich **Freyer** (14 Apr 1836 - ?)
| | |
|---|---|
| 19 Feb 1881 - 1 Jul 1883: | Deputy Chief of Administration, Cossack Forces |
| 15 May 1883: | Promoted to *Major-General* |
| 1 Jul 1883 - 3 Jun 1888: | Deputy Military Governor of Dagestan |
| 3 Jun 1888 - 31 Jan 1894: | Commander, 1st Brigade, 38th Infantry Division |
| 31 Jan 1894 - 1896: | Commander, 4th Caucasus Reserve Infantry Brigade |
| 14 May 1896: | Promoted to *Lieutenant-General* |

*General of Infantry* Aleksandr Vasilyevich **Freygang** (21 Feb 1821 - 28 Jul 1896)
| | |
|---|---|
| 22 Jul 1861: | Promoted to *Major-General* |
| 6 Oct 1861 - 19 Dec 1864: | Director, 2nd Moscow Cadet Corps |
| 19 Dec 1864 - 27 Nov 1867: | Chairman of the Military Justice Commission, Kiev Military Command |
| 27 Nov 1867 - 25 Feb 1869: | Commandant of Krasnoselsk |
| 25 Feb 1869 - 28 Jul 1896: | Commandant of Peterhof, Chief of Peterhof Military Hospital |
| 30 Aug 1874: | Promoted to *Lieutenant-General* |
| 30 Aug 1888: | Promoted to *General of Infantry* |

*Lieutenant-General* Aleksandr Konstantinovich **Freyman** (21 Oct 1862 - ?)
| | |
|---|---|
| 1 May 1903 - 15 Oct 1906: | Section Chief, General Staff |
| 6 Dec 1905: | Promoted to *Major-General* |
| 15 Oct 1906 - 24 Feb 1909: | Clerk of the Mobilization Section, General Staff |
| 15 Feb 1907 - 1 May 1907: | Acting Commander, 2nd Brigade, 37th Infantry Division |
| 24 Feb 1909 - 27 Mar 1915: | Chief of Staff, XVIII. Army Corps |
| 27 Mar 1915 - 2 Jun 1915: | Commander, 37th Infantry Division |
| 8 May 1915: | Promoted to *Lieutenant-General* |
| 2 Jun 1915 - 21 Feb 1916: | Reserve officer, Minsk Military District |
| 21 Feb 1916 - 1 Nov 1916: | Commander, 115th Infantry Division |
| 1 Nov 1916 - 25 May 1917: | Reserve officer, Kiev Military District |
| 25 May 1917 - 1918: | Special Assignments General, Chief of Logistics, Northern Front |

*Lieutenant-General* Eduard Rudolfovich von **Freyman** (1 Dec 1855 - 25 Dec 1920)
| | |
|---|---|
| 10 Jun 1908: | Promoted to *Major-General* |
| 10 Jun 1908 - 2 Aug 1914: | Commander, 2nd Brigade, 23rd Infantry Division |
| 2 Aug 1914 - 16 Nov 1914: | Commander, Brigade, 67th Infantry Division |

16 Nov 1914: Promoted to *Lieutenant-General*
16 Nov 1914: Retired

*Major-General* Karl Vladimirovich von **Freyman** (21 Oct 1861 - 20 Nov 1920)
8 Mar 1913 - 2 Oct 1915: Commander, 85th Infantry Regiment
1915: Promoted to *Major-General*
2 Oct 1915 - 11 Mar 1917: Commander, Brigade, 111th Infantry Division
11 Mar 1917 - Oct 1917: Commander, 192nd Infantry Division

*General of Infantry* Aleksandr Aleksandrovich **Freze** (17 Jun 1840 - 1918)
3 Dec 1878: Promoted to *Major-General*
3 Dec 1878 - 17 Aug 1880: Attached to St. Petersburg Military District
17 Aug 1880 - 4 May 1887: Commander, Life Guards Chasseur Regiment
4 May 1887 - 4 Dec 1888: Chief of Staff, II. Caucasus Army Corps
4 Dec 1888 - 17 Apr 1889: Attached to Caucasus Military District
17 Apr 1889 - 2 Feb 1891: Chief of Staff, Caucasus Army Corps
2 Feb 1891 - 16 Nov 1895: Governor of Erivan
30 Aug 1894: Promoted to *Lieutenant-General*
16 Nov 1895 - 24 May 1896: Governor of Vilnius
24 May 1896 - 4 Feb 1897: Deputy Commanding General, Gendarmerie Corps
4 Feb 1897 - 12 Oct 1904: Deputy C-in-C of the Caucasus,
Deputy Commanding General, Caucasus Military District
6 Dec 1903: Promoted to *General of Infantry*
12 Oct 1904 - 19 Dec 1905: Commanding General, Vilnius Military District,
Governor-General of Vilnius, Kaunas & Grodno
19 Dec 1905 - 14 Dec 1917: Member of the State Council
14 Dec 1917: Retired

*Major-General* Ivan Nikolayevich **Frezer** (10 Apr 1846 - ?)
15 Feb 1900: Promoted to *Major-General*
15 Feb 1900 - 12 Apr 1906: Commander, 2nd Brigade, 28th Infantry Division

*Lieutenant-General* Aleksey Yakovlevich **Fride** (8 Mar 1838 - 9 Jul 1896)
4 Sep 1879: Promoted to *Major-General*
4 Sep 1879 - 16 Apr 1880: Deputy Commander, Syr Darya Region
16 Apr 1880 - 29 May 1882: Chief of the Military Office, Commanding General, Turkestan Military District
29 May 1882 - 21 May 1887: Military Governor of Semirechensk,
Ataman, Semirechensk Cossack Army
21 May 1887 - 9 Jul 1896: Governor of Yaroslavl
30 Aug 1894: Promoted to *Lieutenant-General*

*General of Artillery* Vasily Yakovlevich **Fride** (1 Jan 1840 - 1912)
17 Aug 1884 - 2 Apr 1888: Commander of Artillery, Amur Military District
30 Aug 1887: Promoted to *Major-General*
2 Apr 1888 - 17 May 1895: Commander, 33rd Artillery Brigade
17 May 1895 - 16 Nov 1896: Commander of Artillery, XII. Army Corps

14 May 1896: Promoted to *Lieutenant-General*
16 Nov 1896 - 1 Jan 1903: Commander of Artillery, XVIII. Army Corps
1 Jan 1903: Promoted to *General of Artillery*
1 Jan 1903: Retired

*Major-General* Oskar Fyodorovich **Fridlyander** (30 Mar 1842 - ?)
10 Apr 1897 - 1902: Commander of Artillery, Fortress St. Petersburg, Commandant, St. Petersburg Military District Artillery Depot
9 Apr 1900: Promoted to *Major-General*

*Major-General* Fyodor Aleksandrovich **Fridrikhs** (29 Jul 1837 - ?)
6 Apr 1871 - 16 May 1894: Chief of Warsaw Railway Gendarmerie
5 Apr 1887: Promoted to *Major-General*
16 May 1894 - 1898: Chief of Gendarmerie, Finland

*Major-General* Lev Lvovich **Friman** (18 Nov 1856 - ?)
17 Aug 1907 - 1 Oct 1914: Deputy Chief of Troop Billeting, St. Petersburg Military District
29 Mar 1909: Promoted to *Major-General*
1 Oct 1914 - 1918: Reserve officer, Petrograd Military District

*Lieutenant-General* Matvey Nikolayevich **Frish** (22 Apr 1850 - ?)
2 May 1904: Promoted to *Major-General*
2 May 1904 - 9 Mar 1905: Commander, 2$^{nd}$ Brigade, 22$^{nd}$ Infantry Division
9 Mar 1905 - 7 Jun 1905: Attached to the General Staff
7 Jun 1905 - 13 May 1910: Commander, 2$^{nd}$ Brigade, 1$^{st}$ Grenadier Division
13 May 1910: Promoted to *Lieutenant-General*
13 May 1910: Retired

*Lieutenant-General* Mikhail Mikhailovich **Frolov** (29 Oct 1853 - ?)
19 Jul 1907: Promoted to *Major-General*
19 Jul 1907 - 11 Jan 1913: Commander, 20$^{th}$ Artillery Brigade
11 Jan 1913 - 19 Feb 1917: Inspector of Artillery, XI. Army Corps
19 Jul 1913: Promoted to *Lieutenant-General*

*Lieutenant-General* Nikolai Aleksandrovich **Frolov** (7 Nov 1846 - ?)
14 May 1898 - 20 Jan 1904: Chief of Kremenchug Artillery Depot
1 Jan 1901: Promoted to *Major-General*
20 Jan 1904 - 1906: Deputy Commander of Artillery, Amur Military District
1906: Retired
1 Apr 1915 - 1917: Reserve officer, Kiev Military District
9 Dec 1916: Promoted to *Lieutenant-General*

*General of Infantry* Pyotr Aleksandrovich **Frolov** (4 Oct 1852 - ?)
26 Jan 1893 - 31 Jan 1898: General Staff Officer, Kiev Military District
30 Aug 1894: Promoted to *Major-General*
31 Jan 1898 - 1 May 1903: Deputy Chief of the General Staff

| | |
|---|---|
| 6 Dec 1900: | Promoted to *Lieutenant-General* |
| 1 May 1903 - 11 Mar 1904: | Duty General, General Staff |
| 11 Mar 1904 - 28 Jun 1905: | Chief of the General Staff |
| 28 Jun 1905 - 9 May 1917: | Member of the Military Council |
| 6 Dec 1907: | Promoted to *General of Infantry* |
| 4 Feb 1916 - 6 Mar 1917: | Deputy Minister of War |
| 9 May 1917 - Oct 1917: | Chief of Logistics, Northern Front |

*Lieutenant-General* Pyotr Petrovich **Frolov** (12 Dec 1847 - 19 May 1911)
| | |
|---|---|
| 11 Sep 1900 - 14 May 1904: | Inspector of Classes, 2nd Cadet Corps |
| 6 Dec 1903: | Promoted to *Major-General* |
| 14 May 1904 - 17 Jun 1909: | Inspector of Classes, 1st Cadet Corps |
| 17 Jun 1909: | Promoted to *Lieutenant-General* |
| 17 Jun 1909: | Retired |

*Major-General* Ivan Pavlovich **Fromandier** (22 Feb 1832 - ?)
| | |
|---|---|
| 14 Apr 1875 - 1 Jan 1883: | Commander, 60th Infantry Regiment |
| 1 Jan 1883: | Promoted to *Major-General* |
| 1 Jan 1883 - 1 Jan 1885: | Transferred to the reserve |
| 1 Jan 1885 - 20 Jun 1888: | Commander, Western Siberian Line Brigade |
| 20 Jun 1888 - 5 Aug 1896: | Commander, 2nd Brigade, 39th Infantry Division |
| 5 Aug 1896 - 10 Aug 1898: | Commander, 1st Brigade, 21st Infantry Division |

*Major-General* Sergey Leonidovich **Fufayevsky** (16 Jan 1867 - 30 Apr 1924)
| | |
|---|---|
| 1 Aug 1911: | Promoted to *Major-General* |
| 1 Aug 1911 - 7 May 1915: | Commander, 38th Artillery Brigade |
| 7 May 1915 - 20 Sep 1915: | Inspector of Artillery, XXXVII. Army Corps |
| 20 Sep 1915 - 1918: | Reserve officer, Petrograd Military District |

*Major-General* Lev Eduardovich **Fuks** (22 Dec 1875 - 26 Sep 1916)
| | |
|---|---|
| 11 Jul 1915 - 26 Sep 1916: | Chief of Staff, 9th Cavalry Division |
| 21 Dec 1916: | Posthumously promoted to *Major-General* |

*General of Infantry* Ivan Aleksandrovich **Fullon** (23 Jul 1844 - 1920)
| | |
|---|---|
| 5 May 1890 - 8 Jun 1899: | Commander, Life Guards St. Petersburg Regiment |
| 30 Aug 1890: | Promoted to *Major-General* |
| 12 Oct 1895 - 8 Jun 1899: | Commander, 2nd Brigade, 3rd Guards Infantry Division |
| 8 Jun 1899 - 5 Aug 1899: | Commander, 39th Infantry Division |
| 5 Aug 1899 - 9 Mar 1900: | Commander, 4th Infantry Division |
| 6 Dec 1899: | Promoted to *Lieutenant-General* |
| 9 Mar 1900 - 12 Feb 1904: | Deputy Governor-General of Warsaw |
| 12 Feb 1904 - 11 Jan 1905: | Mayor of St. Petersburg |
| 1904: | Promoted to *General-Adjutant* |
| 1 Jun 1905 - 7 Aug 1911: | Commanding General, XI. Army Corps |
| 6 Dec 1907: | Promoted to *General of Infantry* |
| 7 Aug 1911 - 23 Oct 1914: | Reserve status |
| 23 Oct 1914 - 20 May 1917: | Chief of Petrograd Military Hospital |
| 20 May 1917: | Retired |

*Major-General* Baron Maksimilian Vilgelmovich von **Funk** (25 Jan 1846 - ?)
13 Oct 1900: Promoted to *Major-General*
13 Oct 1900 - Dec 1905: Commander, 2nd Brigade, 26th Infantry Division

*Major-General* Pyotr Ilich **Furs** (12 Jul 1857 - ?)
19 Mar 1908 - 14 Jul 1917: Chief of St. Petersburg Railway Gendarmerie
22 Mar 1915: Promoted to *Major-General*
14 Jul 1917: Dismissed

*Major-General* Valerian Kazimirovich **Furs-Zhirkevich** (5 Jun 1846 - ?)
22 Feb 1904: Promoted to *Major-General*
22 Feb 1904 - 25 Aug 1905: Commander, 1st Brigade, 8th East Siberian Rifle Division
25 Aug 1905 - 1906: At the disposal of the C-in-C of Forces operating against Japan

*Lieutenant-General* Dmitry Semyonovich **Fursov** (12 May 1843 - ?)
21 Jun 1894: Promoted to *Major-General*
21 Jun 1894 - 13 Sep 1899: Commander, 1st Brigade, 41st Infantry Division
13 Sep 1899 - 29 Mar 1903: Commander, 58th Replacement Infantry Brigade
29 Mar 1903: Promoted to *Lieutenant-General*
29 Mar 1903 - 18 Jun 1905: Commander, 12th Infantry Division

*Major-General* Sergey Yanushevich **Gaas** (13 Dec 1863 - ?)
8 Oct 1916 - 1917: Commander, 108th Artillery Brigade
20 Oct 1916: Promoted to *Major-General*

*Lieutenant-General* Vladimir Aleksandrovich **Gaaz de Gryunenvald** (24 Jul 1852 - ?)
31 Oct 1907: Promoted to *Major-General*
31 Oct 1907 - 1 Aug 1910: Commander, 5th Reserve Artillery Brigade
1 Aug 1910 - 24 Jul 1912: Commander, 47th Artillery Brigade
24 Jul 1912: Promoted to *Lieutenant-General*
24 Jul 1912: Retired

*Major-General* Prangistan Andreyevich **Gabayev** (5 Oct 1853 - 1 Jan 1928)
21 Oct 1915 - 1917: Commander, 301st Infantry Regiment
1917: Promoted to *Major-General*
15 Oct 1917 - 1918: Commander, 4th Special Infantry Division

*Lieutenant-General* Vasily Davidovich **Gabayev** (30 Mar 1853 - 17 Mar 1933)
19 Feb 1908 - 30 Mar 1913: Commander, 1st Brigade, Caucasus Grenadier Division
28 Nov 1908: Promoted to *Major-General*
30 Mar 1913: Promoted to *Lieutenant-General*
30 Mar 1913: Retired
3 Sep 1914 - 5 Jul 1915: Recalled; Commander, 3rd Caucasus Rifle Brigade
5 Jul 1915 - 31 Aug 1916: Commander, Caucasus Grenadier Division
31 Aug 1916 - 1917: Commandant of Tbilisi

*Major-General* Nikolai Ivanovich **Gabbin** (20 May 1864 - ?)
| | |
|---|---|
| 6 Dec 1907 - 15 Apr 1916: | Chief Engineer, Syrdarya Region |
| 6 Dec 1915: | Promoted to *Major-General* |
| 15 Apr 1916 - 1917: | Chairman, Commission for Cotton Mill Construction |

*Lieutenant-General* Martyn-Stanislav Feliksovich **Gabrialovich** (18 Nov 1852 - ?)
| | |
|---|---|
| 1 Jul 1889 - 7 Dec 1905: | Military Judge, Siberian Military District Court |
| 1 Jan 1901: | Promoted to *Major-General* |
| 7 Dec 1905 - Jul 1908: | Military Judge, Caucasus Military District Court |
| 2 Oct 1908: | Promoted to *Lieutenant-General* |
| 2 Oct 1908: | Retired |

*Vice-Admiral* Leonard-Lyudvig Fyodorovich **Gadd** (5 May 1827 - 22 Jun 1895)
| | |
|---|---|
| 6 Nov 1872 - 26 Jun 1887: | Chief of Izhora Admiralty Factories |
| 15 May 1883: | Promoted to *Rear-Admiral* |
| 26 Jun 1887: | Promoted to *Vice-Admiral* |
| 26 Jun 1887: | Retired |
| 12 Jul 1887: | Recalled with the rank of *Privy Councillor* |
| 12 Jul 1887 - 4 May 1892: | Member of the Board, Obukhov Steel Factory |
| 4 May 1892 - 1893: | Manager of Pension Fund, Ministry of the Navy |
| 1893 - 22 Jun 1895: | Chairman of the Board, Obukhov Steel Factory |

*Lieutenant-General of the Admiralty* Otto Fyodorovich **Gadd** (5 Mar 1831 - 7 Jun 1898)
| | |
|---|---|
| 6 Oct 1895 - 10 Jan 1894: | Director of Lighthouses & Pilotage, Helsingfors |
| 13 Jan 1886: | Promoted to *Major-General of the Admiralty* |
| 9 Apr 1893: | Promoted to *Lieutenant-General of the Admiralty* |
| 10 Jan 1894 - 7 Jun 1898: | Senator, Imperial Finnish Senate |

*Major-General* Guidon Nikolayevich **Gadolin** (16 Jul 1851 - 12 Apr 1932)
| | |
|---|---|
| 3 Feb 1895 - 20 Mar 1902: | Commander, 2$^{nd}$ Finnish Rifle Battalion |
| 20 Mar 1902 - 3 Nov 1906: | Transferred to the reserve |
| 3 Nov 1906: | Promoted to *Major-General* |
| 3 Nov 1906: | Retired |

*Major-General* Vladimir Sergeyevich **Gadon** (17 Jan 1860 - 17 Sep 1937)
| | |
|---|---|
| 1903: | Promoted to *Major-General* |
| 29 Apr 1903 - 21 Oct 1904: | Attached to Grand Duke Sergey Aleksandrovich |
| 21 Oct 1904 - 21 Jun 1906: | Commander, Preobrazhensky Life Guards Regiment |
| 21 Jun 1906: | Retired |
| 30 May 1912 - 10 Jul 1916: | Recalled; General à la suite |
| Aug 1914 - May 1917: | General for Special Assignments with the Red Cross |
| May 1917: | Retired |

*Major-General* Fyodor-Karl Ivanovich **Gafferberg** (16 Dec 1860 - 11 Jun 1916)
| | |
|---|---|
| 9 Oct 1915 - 11 Jun 1916: | Commander, 212$^{th}$ Infantry Regiment |
| 13 Jan 1917: | Posthumously promoted to *Major-General* |

*Major-General* Prince Aleksandr Petrovich **Gagarin** (16 Aug 1857 - 21 Feb 1903)
11 Aug 1896 - 1 Jun 1902: Commander, Life Guards Hussar Regiment
9 Apr 1900: Promoted to *Major-General*
1 Jun 1902 - 21 Feb 1903: Attached to the Guards Cavalry

*Major-General* Prince Aleksandr Vasilievich **Gagarin** (9 Oct 1866 - 1917)
24 Feb 1914 - 1 Oct 1915: Commander, 9th Uhlan Regiment
12 May 1915: Promoted to *Major-General*
1 Oct 1915 - 28 Aug 1917: Commander, 3rd Brigade, Caucasus Native Cavalry Division
28 Aug 1917 - 2 Sep 1917: Commander, 1st Caucasus Native Cavalry Division
2 Sep 1917 - 1917: Reserve officer, Petrograd Military District

*Lieutenant-General* Prince Nikolai Nikolayevich **Gagarin** (20 Aug 1859 - 1918)
6 Dec 1905: Promoted to *Major-General*
6 Dec 1905 - 14 Apr 1913: Attached to the Ministry of War
14 Apr 1913: Promoted to *Lieutenant-General*
14 Apr 1913 -1914: At the disposal of the Minister of War
1914 - 28 Aug 1915: At the disposal of the Military Governor of Galicia
28 Aug 1915 - 23 Oct 1917: General for Special Assignments, General Directorate of State Horse Breeding

*Rear-Admiral* Grigory Fyodorovich **Gagman** (26 May 1858 - ?)
6 Dec 1908 - 8 Jul 1913: Commander, 2nd Group, 1st Mine Division
8 Jul 1913: Promoted to *Rear-Admiral*
8 Jul 1913: Retired

*Major-General* Nikolai Dmitriyevich **Gaibov** (19 Apr 1864 - 20 Oct 1915)
13 Mar 1909 - 15 Aug 1915: Deputy Military Commander, Terek Region, Ataman, Terek Cossack Army
6 Dec 1913: Promoted to *Major-General*
15 Aug 1915: Retired

*General of Artillery* Valerian Mikhailovich **Gaitenov** (12 Feb 1855 - ?)
28 May 1905 - 2 Jul 1905: Commander, 10th East Siberian Rifle Artillery Brigade
2 Jul 1905 - 23 Nov 1908: Commander, 3rd Artillery Brigade
23 Nov 1905: Promoted to *Major-General*
23 Nov 1908 - 6 Feb 1910: Commander of Artillery, XI. Army Corps
26 Nov 1908: Promoted to *Lieutenant-General*
6 Feb 1910 - 24 Jul 1910: Commander of Artillery, Grenadier Corps
24 Jul 1910 - 31 Dec 1913: Inspector of Artillery, Grenadier Corps
31 Dec 1913 - 5 Oct 1914: Chief of Officers Artillery Schools
5 Oct 1914 - 23 Apr 1915: Inspector of Artillery, Grenadier Corps
23 Apr 1915 - 10 May 1915: Commander, 42nd Infantry Division
10 May 1915 - 29 Mar 1916: Inspector of Artillery, Grenadier Corps
29 Mar 1916 - 1917: Inspector of Artillery, Northern Front
6 Dec 1916: Promoted to *General of Artillery*

*General of Artillery* Vladimir Ignatyevich **Gakhovich** (6 Dec 1842 - 11 Aug 1916)
| | |
|---|---|
| 5 Jun 1892: | Promoted to *Major-General* |
| 5 Jun 1892 - 30 Nov 1892: | Chief, St. Petersburg Cartridge Factory |
| 30 Nov 1892 - 21 Jun 1901: | Chief, St. Petersburg Pipe Tool Factory |
| 21 Jun 1901 - 1910: | Chief, Nikolayev Rocket Factory |
| 29 Mar 1909: | Promoted to *Lieutenant-General* |
| 1910 - 7 Jan 1912: | Transferred to the reserve |
| 7 Jan 1912: | Promoted to *General of Artillery* |
| 7 Jan 1912: | Retired |

*General of Artillery* Dmitry Ivanovich **Galakhov** (1 Jan 1845 - ?)
| | |
|---|---|
| 19 Apr 1890 - 8 Jan 1898: | Chief of Mobilization Section, Main Artillery Directorate |
| 30 Aug 1890: | Promoted to *Major-General* |
| 8 Jan 1898 - 21 Jun 1912: | Deputy Chief of the Main Artillery Directorate |
| 6 Dec 1899: | Promoted to *Lieutenant-General* |
| 16 Nov 1904 - 21 Jun 1912: | Member of the Fortress Committee |
| 21 Jun 1912: | Promoted to *General of Artillery* |
| 21 Jun 1912: | Retired |

*Lieutenant-General* Gavriil Aristarkhovich **Galakhov** (14 Jan 1826 - 1899)
| | |
|---|---|
| 2 Nov 1888: | Promoted to *Major-General* |
| 2 Nov 1888 - 14 Jun 1898: | Commander, 1st Brigade, 11th Infantry Division |
| 14 Jun 1898: | Promoted to *Lieutenant-General* |
| 14 Jun 1898: | Retired |

*Rear-Admiral* Valerian Ivanovich **Galanin** (18 Oct 1866 - 23 Mar 1915)
| | |
|---|---|
| 7 Dec 1911 - 23 Mar 1915: | Commander, Battleship "*Yevstafy*" |
| 25 Mar 1915: | Posthumously promoted to *Rear-Admiral* |

*Lieutenant-General* Anatoly Mikhailovich von **Galberg** (19 Nov 1854 - ?)
| | |
|---|---|
| 12 Mar 1907 - 9 Feb 1914: | Commander, 116th Infantry Regiment |
| 26 Jan 1914: | Promoted to *Major-General* |
| 9 Feb 1914 - 29 Jul 1914: | Commander, 2nd Brigade, 40th Infantry Division |
| 29 Jul 1914 - 1917: | Commander, Brigade, 76th Infantry Division |
| 1917 - 19 Jun 1917: | Reserve officer, Dvinsk Military District |
| 19 Jun 1917: | Promoted to *Lieutenant-General* |
| 19 Jun 1917: | Dismissed |

*Major-General* Adrian Petrovich **Galdin** (28 Aug 1845 - 28 Apr 1922)
| | |
|---|---|
| 15 Jul 1906 - 22 May 1910: | Attached to Don Cossack Regiments |
| 22 May 1910: | Promoted to *Major-General* |
| 22 May 1910: | Retired |
| 22 Oct 1914 - 24 Mar 1917: | Recalled; Commander, 34th Don Cossack Regiment |
| 24 Mar 1917 - 1917: | Unassigned |

*Major-General* Pavel Andreyevich **Galenkovsky** (28 Mar 1861 - ?)
| | |
|---|---|
| 2 Dec 1912 - 16 Aug 1917: | Military Commander, Polotsk District |

1 Jul 1915: Promoted to *Major-General*
16 Aug 1917: Dismissed

*Lieutenant-General* Viktor Petrovich **Galfter** (20 Oct 1868 - 16 Mar 1951)
22 Jan 1915 - 25 May 1917: Commander, Moscow Life Guards Regiment
10 Jul 1916: Promoted to *Major-General*
25 May 1917 - 1917: Commander, 10th Infantry Division
1917: Promoted to *Lieutenant-General*
1917: Commanding General, X. Army Corps

*Lieutenant-General* Nikolai Kaetanovich **Galitsinsky** (21 Sep 1840 - ?)
11 Oct 1883 - 6 Feb 1892: Military Judge, Vilnius Military District Court
30 Aug 1890: Promoted to *Major-General*
6 Feb 1892 - 5 Mar 1897: Military Prosecutor, Vilnius Military District Court
5 Mar 1897: Promoted to *Lieutenant-General*
5 Mar 1897: Retired

*Lieutenant-General* Aleksandr Semyonovich **Galkin** (23 Aug 1855 - 1920)
20 May 1896 - 27 Feb 1903: Commander, Amu-Darya District
14 Apr 1902: Promoted to *Major-General*
27 Feb 1903 - 27 Jun 1903: General Staff officer, Turkestan Military District
27 Jun 1903 - 2 Jan 1908: Military Governor of Semipalatinsk Region
2 Jan 1908 - 1 Feb 1911: Military Governor of Samarkand Region
13 Apr 1908: Promoted to *Lieutenant-General*
1 Feb 1911 - 1917: Military Governor of Syr-Darya Region

*Lieutenant-General* Aleksei Semyonovich **Galkin** (21 Sep 1866 - 3 Mar 1942)
13 May 1910: Promoted to *Major-General*
13 May 1910 - 22 Aug 1914: Duty General, Warsaw Military District
22 Aug 1914 - 1917: Duty General, Western Front
6 Dec 1915: Promoted to *Lieutenant-General*

*Major-General* Mikhail Sergeyevich **Galkin** (21 Dec 1866 - 15 Jan 1920)
23 Dec 1914 - 16 Feb 1916: Commander, 71st Infantry Regiment
28 Jan 1916: Promoted to *Major-General*
16 Feb 1916 - Jul 1916: Chief of Staff, 10th Infantry Division
Jul 1916 - 10 Nov 1916: Chief of Staff, 20th Infantry Division
10 Nov 1916 - 1917: Chief of Staff, XLVII. Army Corps

*General of Cavalry* Aleksandr Aleksandrovich **Gall** (16 Mar 1831 - 22 Feb 1904)
17 Apr 1866 - 14 Nov 1876: Attached to Grand Duke Nikolai Nikolayevich
30 Aug 1867: Promoted to *Major-General*
14 Nov 1876 - 15 Jun 1878: Special Assignments General to the C-in-C, Operations Army
20 Oct 1877: Promoted to *Lieutenant-General*
15 Jun 1878 - 6 Mar 1880: Attached to the Commanding General, St. Petersburg Military District
6 Mar 1880 - 12 May 1881: Special Assignments General, St. Petersburg Military

| | |
|---|---|
| | District |
| 12 May 1881: | Promoted to *General-Adjutant* |
| 12 May 1881 - 22 Feb 1904: | Member of the Tsar's retinue |
| 30 Aug 1891: | Promoted to *General of Cavalry* |

*Major-General* Aleksandr Aleksandrovich **Gall** (6 Aug 1860 - 1920)
| | |
|---|---|
| 2 Apr 1906: | Promoted to *Major-General* |
| 2 Apr 1906 - 1908: | At the disposal of Grand Duke Nikolai Nikolayevich |
| 1908: | Retired |

*Major-General* Vladislav Frantsevich **Galle** (28 Oct 1862 - ?)
| | |
|---|---|
| 24 Oct 1903 - 15 Nov 1916: | Chief of Police, St. Petersburg |
| 6 Dec 1912: | Promoted to *Major-General* |
| 15 Nov 1916 - 31 May 1917: | Chief of Police, Warsaw |
| 31 May 1917: | Dismissed |

*Lieutenant-General* Karl Ferdinandovich **Galler** (29 Mar 1845 - ?)
| | |
|---|---|
| 26 Jun 1902 - 31 Oct 1907: | Commander of Engineers, Mikhailov Fortress |
| 26 Nov 1902: | Promoted to *Major-General* |
| 31 Oct 1907 - 12 Jun 1910: | Deputy Commander of Engineers, Turkestan Military District |
| 12 Jun 1910: | Promoted to *Lieutenant-General* |
| 12 Jun 1910: | Retired |

*General of Engineers* Mikhail Ferdinandovich **Galler** (19 Oct 1841 - ?)
| | |
|---|---|
| 6 Mar 1898 - 28 Jun 1904: | Inspector of Engineering Works, Caucasus Military District |
| 6 Dec 1899: | Promoted to *Major-General* |
| 28 Jun 1904 - 23 Jun 1905: | Deputy Commander of Engineers, Vilnius Military District |
| 23 Jun 1905 - 27 Jun 1910: | Commander of Engineers, Odessa Military District |
| 6 Dec 1906: | Promoted to *Lieutenant-General* |
| 27 Jun 1910: | Promoted to *General of Engineers* |
| 27 Jun 1910: | Retired |

*Major-General* Nikolai Nikolayevich von **Galler** (21 Nov 1834 - Dec 1900)
| | |
|---|---|
| 22 Mar 1893 - Dec 1900: | Commander of Gendarmerie, Radom Province |
| 6 May 1898: | Promoted to *Major-General* |

*Major-General* Adolf Eduardovich **Galnbek** (3 Sep 1864 - ?)
| | |
|---|---|
| 21 Dec 1916: | Promoted to *Major-General* |
| 21 Dec 1916 - 1917: | Commander, Brigade, 2nd Zaamursky Borderguard Infantry Division |

*Major-General* Aleksandr Aleksandrovich **Gamburtsev** (9 Aug 1866 - ?)
| | |
|---|---|
| 15 Apr 1913 - 1915: | Commander, 13th Rifle Regiment |
| 1 May 1915: | Promoted to *Major-General* |
| 1915 - 22 Jun 1916: | Unassigned (wounded) |

| | |
|---|---|
| 22 Jun 1916 - 22 Apr 1917: | Commander, 41st Replacement Infantry Brigade |
| 22 Apr 1917 - 1918: | Commander, 64th Infantry Division |

*Major-General* Ivan Spiridonovich **Gamchenko** (29 Oct 1864 - ?)
| | |
|---|---|
| 4 Mar 1915 - 1917: | Commander, 39th Artillery Brigade |
| 24 Mar 1916: | Promoted to *Major-General* |

*Major-General* Mikhail Grigoryevich **Gamrat-Kurek** (24 Sep 1868 - ?)
| | |
|---|---|
| 12 Sep 1912 - 1917: | Section Chief, General Staff |
| 6 Dec 1916: | Promoted to *Major-General* |

*Major-General* Sergey Lvovich **Gamzagurdi** (21 Jul 1862 - ?)
| | |
|---|---|
| 22 Dec 1913 - 4 Jul 1916: | Commander, 6th Hussar Regiment |
| 22 May 1916: | Promoted to *Major-General* |
| 4 Jul 1916 - 1918: | Commander, 2nd Brigade, 15th Cavalry Division |

*Major-General* Georgy Nikolayevich **Gamzagurdy** (23 Aug 1866 - ?)
| | |
|---|---|
| 19 Nov 1910 - 17 Dec 1915: | Commander, 6th Pontoon Battalion |
| 6 Dec 1915: | Promoted to *Major-General* |
| 17 Dec 1915 - 1918: | At the disposal of the C-in-C, Southwestern Front |

*General of Infantry* Aleksandr Fyodorovich **Gan** (7 Jul 1809 - 7 Mar 1895)
| | |
|---|---|
| 16 Jun 1850 - 9 Mar 1859: | Commander, 35th Infantry Regiment |
| 26 Aug 1857: | Promoted to *Major-General* |
| 9 Mar 1859 - 22 Apr 1859: | Deputy Division Commander, IV. Army Corps |
| 22 Apr 1859 - 18 Apr 1860: | Deputy Commander, 9th Infantry Division |
| 18 Apr 1860 - 16 Apr 1861: | Attached to the C-in-C, 1st Army |
| 16 Apr 1861 - 29 Jun 1862: | Duty General, 1st Army |
| 29 Jun 1862 - 6 Jul 1862: | Chief of Staff, III. Army Corps |
| 6 Jul 1862 - 11 Aug 1865: | Chief of Staff, Kiev Military District |
| 26 Dec 1863: | Promoted to *Lieutenant-General* |
| 11 Aug 1865 - 19 Jan 1866: | Unassigned |
| 19 Jan 1866 - 21 Feb 1867: | Commander, 23rd Infantry Division |
| 21 Feb 1867 - 28 Mar 1875: | Regional Commander, Moscow Military District |
| 28 Mar 1875 - 19 Feb 1877: | Commander, 17th Infantry Division |
| 19 Feb 1877 - 15 Sep 1877: | Commanding General, XIII. Army Corps |
| 15 Sep 1877 - 17 Mar 1887: | Member, Committee for Wounded Veterans |
| 16 Apr 1878: | Promoted to *General of Infantry* |
| 16 Apr 1878 - 7 Mar 1895: | Member of the Military Council |
| 4 Jan 1885 - 17 Mar 1887: | Director, Nikolaev Chesmenskaya Almshouses |

*General of Infantry* Baron Dmitry Karlovich **Gan** (23 Aug 1830 - 2 Feb 1907)
| | |
|---|---|
| 27 Sep 1863 - 17 Apr 1874: | Deputy Inspector, Special Borderguard Corps |
| 16 Apr 1872: | Promoted to *Major-General* |
| 17 Apr 1874 - 12 Feb 1893: | Inspector, Special Borderguard Corps |
| 28 Mar 1882: | Promoted to *Lieutenant-General* |
| 12 Feb 1893 - Jul 1906: | Member of the Board, Ministry of Finance |
| 13 Jun 1898: | Promoted to *General of Infantry* |

*Lieutenant-General* Eduard Fridrikhovich **Gan** (21 Jan 1835 - ?)
| | |
|---|---|
| 20 Apr 1880 - 14 May 1884: | Commander, 5th Life Dragoon Regiment |
| 14 May 1884: | Promoted to *Major-General* |
| 14 May 1884 - 22 Jun 1886: | Transferred to the reserve |
| 22 Jun 1886 - 1902: | Commander, 4th Replacement Cavalry Brigade |
| 14 May 1896: | Promoted to *Lieutenant-General* |

*Lieutenant-General* Ivan Konstantinovich **Gandurin** (4 Jul 1866 - Dec 1946)
| | |
|---|---|
| 13 Jun 1906 - 15 Jul 1910: | Commandant of Fortress Mykolayiv |
| 15 Jul 1910: | Promoted to *Major-General* |
| 15 Jul 1910 - 26 Oct 1912: | Commander, 1st Brigade, 49th Infantry Division |
| 26 Oct 1912 - 29 Jul 1914: | Commander, 1st Brigade, 29th Infantry Division |
| 29 Jul 1914 - 25 Mar 1915: | Commander, Brigade, 81st Infantry Division |
| 25 Mar 1915 - 3 Jul 1915: | Commander, 2nd State Militia Division |
| 13 Jun 1915: | Promoted to *Lieutenant-General* |
| 3 Jul 1915 - 20 Oct 1915: | Commander, 102nd Infantry Division |
| 20 Oct 1915 - 31 Mar 1917: | Commanding General, II. Siberian Army Corps |
| 31 Mar 1917: | Retired |

*Lieutenant-General* Aleksandr Pavlovich von **Ganenfeldt (Karsakov)** (20 May 1854 - ?)
| | |
|---|---|
| 1 Jun 1904: | Promoted to *Major-General* |
| 1 Jun 1904 - 18 Jul 1905: | Commander, 2nd Brigade, 78th Infantry Division |
| 18 Jul 1905 - 26 Feb 1907: | Unassigned |
| 26 Feb 1907 - 15 Jul 1910: | Commander, 2nd Turkestan Rifle Brigade |
| 15 Jul 1910 - 1 Oct 1911: | Reserve officer, St. Petersburg Military District |
| 1 Oct 1911: | Retired |
| 27 Dec 1911: | Promoted to *Lieutenant-General* |
| 1914 - 9 Jun 1915: | Recalled; Commander, 108th Militia Brigade |
| 9 Jun 1915 - Aug 1915: | Reserve officer, 6th Army |
| Aug 1915 - 1917: | Reserve officer, Petrograd Military District |

*Lieutenant-General* Mikhail Pavlovich **Ganenfeldt** (27 Jul 1858 - ?)
| | |
|---|---|
| 8 Oct 1901 - 15 Dec 1904: | Commander, 3rd Grenadier Regiment |
| 15 Dec 1904: | Promoted to *Major-General* |
| 15 Dec 1904 - 15 Apr 1907: | Commander, Life Guards Grenadier Regiment |
| 15 Apr 1907 - 1914: | At the disposal of the Commanding General, St. Petersburg Military District |
| 6 Dec 1913: | Promoted to *Lieutenant-General* |
| 1914 - 6 Jun 1915: | Commander, Militia Corps |
| 6 Jun 1915 - 9 Mar 1917: | Commander, 110th Infantry Division |

*Major-General* Vladimir Pavlovich **Ganenfeldt** (6 May 1864 - 3 Sep 1914)
| | |
|---|---|
| 8 Aug 1911 - 30 Aug 1914: | Commander, 6th Rifle Regiment |
| 21 Jul 1915: | Posthumously promoted to *Major-General* |

*General of Infantry* Nikolai Stepanovich **Ganetsky** (24 Nov 1815 - 20 Apr 1904)
| | |
|---|---|
| 3 Oct 1853 - 14 May 1860: | Commander, 70th Infantry Regiment |
| 26 Aug 1856: | Promoted to *Major-General* |

23 Sep 1860 - 6 Jul 1862: Deputy Commander, Reserve Division, I. Army Corps
6 Jul 1862 - 15 Aug 1863: Deputy Commander, 3rd Grenadier Division
15 Aug 1863 - 13 Sep 1863: Commander, 28th Infantry Division
30 Aug 1863: Promoted to *Lieutenant-General*
31 Oct 1863 - 19 Feb 1877: Commander, 3rd Grenadier Division
19 Feb 1877 - 7 Sep 1878: Commanding General, VII. Army Corps
16 Apr 1878: Promoted to *General of Infantry*
7 Sep 1878 - 10 May 1882: Commanding General, VIII. Army Corps
10 May 1882 - 13 Mar 1886: Commanding General, Grenadier Corps
13 Mar 1886 - 11 Feb 1895: Commanding General, Vilnius Military District
11 Feb 1895 - 20 Apr 1904: Member of the State Council

*Major-General* Dmitry Ivanovich **Gangardt** (13 Jan 1841 - ?)
18 Aug 1895 - 1906: Commander, 27th Erivan Borderguard Brigade
6 Apr 1903: Promoted to *Major-General*

*Major-General* Ivan Ivanovich **Gangardt** (26 Sep 1844 - ?)
1891 - 1906: Commander of Gendarmerie, Shlisselburg
6 Dec 1901: Promoted to *Major-General*
1906: Retired

*Lieutenant-General* Vladimir Fedorovich **Ganskau** (25 Apr 1862 - Jan 1939)
20 Dec 1911 - 27 Jul 1915: Commander, 152nd Infantry Regiment
2 Nov 1914: Promoted to *Major-General*
27 Jul 1915 - 1917: Special Assignments General, 3rd Army
1917 - 15 Jun 1917: Reserve officer, Minsk Military District
15 Jun 1917: Promoted to *Lieutenant-General*
15 Jun 1917: Dismissed

*Major-General* Prince Aleksey Gavrilovich **Gantimurov** (16 Mar 1859 - ?)
2 Oct 1912: Promoted to *Major-General*
2 Oct 1912 - 7 Jan 1916: Commander, 2nd Siberian Rifle Artillery Brigade
7 Jan 1916 - 1917: Inspector of Artillery, XLIV. Army Corps

*Major-General* Konstantin Danilovich **Gapanovich** (20 May 1855 - ?)
30 Jun 1902: Promoted to *Major-General*
30 Jun 1902 - Jul 1907: Chief of Military Communications, Moscow Military District

*Lieutenant-General* Leonty Vasilyevich **Gaponov** (8 Oct 1846 - ?)
3 Aug 1887 - 1 Feb 1895: Commander, Non-Commissioned Officers Training Battalion
30 Aug 1893: Promoted to *Major-General*
1 Feb 1895 - 22 Feb 1901: Commandant, Infantry Officers School
22 Feb 1901 - 10 Feb 1903: Commander, 20th Infantry Division
1 Apr 1901: Promoted to *Lieutenant-General*
10 Feb 1903 - 1 Jun 1905: Commander, 3rd Grenadier Division
1 Jun 1905 - 4 Oct 1906: Commanding General, XIX. Army Corps

*Major-General* Mikhail Matveyevich **Garanin** (3 Nov 1855 - 1913)
21 Aug 1906 - 4 Jul 1913: Commander, 80th Infantry Regiment
4 Jul 1913: Promoted to *Major-General*

*Lieutenant-General* Yakov Aleksandrovich **Gardenin** (25 Jul 1838 - 1902)
11 Dec 1882 - 14 Dec 1884: Commander, Pavlogradsky Life Dragoon Regiment
20 Oct 1884: Promoted to *Major-General*
20 Oct 1884 - 10 Aug 1885: Commander, 2nd Brigade, 9th Cavalry Division
10 Aug 1885 - 10 Apr 1896: Commander, 2nd Brigade, 1st Cavalry Division
10 Apr 1896 - 10 Dec 1901: Commander, 7th Reserve Cavalry Brigade
14 May 1896: Promoted to *Lieutenant-General*
10 Dec 1901 - 1902: At the disposal of the Commanding General, Moscow Military District

*Lieutenant-General* Yevgeny Georgiyevich **Garf** (27 Sep 1854 - 26 Mar 1911)
30 Jan 1893 - 20 Sep 1901: Section Chief, General Staff
6 Dec 1899: Promoted to *Major-General*
20 Sep 1901 - 30 Jan 1907: Deputy Chief, Directorate-General of Cossack Troops, Ministry of War
2 Apr 1906: Promoted to *Lieutenant-General*
30 Jan 1907 - 3 Mar 1910: Chief, Main Directorate of Cossack Troops, Ministry of War
3 Mar 1910 - 26 Mar 1911: Chief of the Chancellery, Ministry of War
20 Feb 1911 - 26 Mar 1911: Member of the Military Council

*Lieutenant-General* Aleksandr Leontievich **Garnak** (22 Jun 1850 - 1 May 1910)
26 Jul 1894 - 23 Aug 1897: Commander, 9th Dragoon Regiment
23 Aug 1897: Promoted to *Major-General*
23 Aug 1897 - 2 Jul 1898: Commander, 2nd Brigade, 14th Cavalry Division
2 Jul 1898 - 6 Dec 1906: Chief of Staff, XVI. Army Corps
6 Dec 1906: Promoted to *Lieutenant-General*
6 Dec 1906 - 1 May 1910: Commander, 4th Cavalry Division

*Major-General* Iustin Ignatyevich **Garnishevsky** (6 Jul 1852 - ?)
1909 - 1910: Commander, 129th Infantry Regiment
1910: Promoted to *Major-General*

*Major-General* Pyotr-Pavel Iosifovich **Garnovsky** (29 Jun 1836 - ?)
19 Apr 1892: Promoted to *Major-General*
19 Apr 1892 - 26 May 1893: Commander, 1st Brigade, 25th Infantry Division
26 May 1893 - 30 Sep 1897: Commander, 2nd Brigade, 24th Infantry Division
30 Sep 1897 - 1899: Commander, 55th Reserve Infantry Brigade

*Major-General* Boris Georgiyevich **Gartman** (19 Jun 1878 - 29 Apr 1950)
3 Oct 1914 - 23 Apr 1917: Commander, Life Guards Cavalry Regiment
25 Mar 1915: Promoted to *Major-General*
23 Apr 1917 - 1918: Commander, Kurdistan Detachment, Independent Cavalry Corps

*Major-General* Yevgeny Yulyevich **Gartman** (20 Jan 1857 - ?)
8 Oct 1906 - 1915:		Commander, 5th Siberian Sapper Battalion
1915:				Promoted to *Major-General*
1915:				Dismissed

*Major-General* Lev Fedorovich **Gartung** (6 Jan 1868 - ?)
4 Jun 1910:			Promoted to *Major-General*
4 Jun 1910 - 17 Aug 1914:	Commander, 2nd Artillery Brigade
17 Aug 1914 - 1918:		POW

*Major-General* Aleksandr Genrikhovich **Gartvig** (15 Mar 1843 - ?)
24 Jul 1898 - 1904:		Commandant, Dvinsk Artillery Depot
1 Apr 1901:			Promoted to *Major-General*

*Lieutenant-General* Aliar-Bek Mekhtiyevich **Gashimbekov** (8 Mar 1856 - ?)
26 May 1908 - 14 Jul 1913:	Deputy Military Governor of Kars
6 Dec 1908:			Promoted to *Major-General*
14 Jul 1913:			Promoted to *Lieutenant-General*
14 Jul 1913:			Retired
21 Jun 1916 - 1917:		Recalled at the rank of *Major-General*;
				Commander, 3rd Caucasus Convoy Brigade

*Major-General* Yustinian Leopoldovich **Gasparini** (22 Nov 1864 - May 1911)
13 Jun 1907:			Promoted to *Major-General*
13 Jun 1907 - 7 Jul 1910:	Commander, 42nd Artillery Brigade

*Lieutenant-General* Pavel Yegorovich von **Gastfer** (31 Mar 1854 - 1918)
1 Jan 1895 - 1913:		Staff Officer (5th Class), Main Horsebreeding
				Directorate
2 Apr 1906:			Promoted to *Major-General*
1913:				Promoted to *Lieutenant-General*
1913:				Retired

*Lieutenant-General* Vilgelm Karlovich **Gauger** (3 Jul 1847 - 23 Mar 1937)
9 Dec 1892 - 20 Mar 1900:	Commander, 1st St. Petersburg Engineering Detachment
22 Mar 1898:			Promoted to *Major-General*
20 Mar 1900 - 1907:		Attached to the Main Engineering Directorate
1907:				Promoted to *Lieutenant-General*
1907:				Retired

*Vice-Admiral* Nikolai Aleksandrovich **Gaupt** (3 Dec 1846 - 24 Mar 1909)
27 Sep 1900 - 1 Apr 1901:	Commander, 20th Naval Depot
1 Jan 1901:			Promoted to *Rear-Admiral*
1 Apr 1901 - 27 Sep 1904:	Commander, Port of Vladivostok
27 Sep 1904 - 20 Nov 1906:	Junior Flagman, Baltic Fleet
20 Nov 1906:			Promoted to *Vice-Admiral*
20 Nov 1906:			Retired

*Major-General* Vladislav-Antony Teofilovich **Gaurilkevich** (10 Apr 1850 - ?)
25 Nov 1908: Promoted to *Major-General*
25 Nov 1908 - 15 Jun 1910: Commander, 2nd Brigade, 11th Infantry Division
15 Jun 1910: Retired

*General of Artillery* Iosif Karlovich **Gausman** (10 Feb 1852 - ?)
19 Dec 1882 - 2 Feb 1911: Chief of the Commission on Troop Billetting
14 May 1896: Promoted to *Major-General*
6 Dec 1902: Promoted to *Lieutenant-General*
2 Feb 1911 - 25 Aug 1912: Chairman of the Main Committee on Troop Billetting
10 Apr 1911: Promoted to *General of Artillery*
25 Aug 1912 - 1917: Chief of Main Directorate for Troop Billetting

*Lieutenant-General* Aleksandr Nilovich **Gavrilov** (27 May 1855 - 27 Sep 1926)
4 Jan 1906 - 16 Nov 1912: Chief of St. Petersburg-Nikolayev Military Hospital
31 May 1906: Promoted to *Major-General*
16 Nov 1912 - 1 May 1913: Reserve officer, St. Petersburg Military District
1 May 1913 - 1917: Commander, Minsk Local Brigade
6 Dec 1913: Promoted to *Lieutenant-General*

*Lieutenant-General* Aleksandr Petrovich **Gavrilov** (26 Aug 1855 - ?)
11 Dec 1908: Promoted to *Major-General*
11 Dec 1908 - 31 Mar 1912: Commander, 1st Brigade, 41st Infantry Division
31 Mar 1912 - 19 Jul 1914: Commander, 1st Brigade, 31st Infantry Division
19 Jul 1914 - 3 Jun 1917: Commander, 69th Infantry Division
12 Dec 1914: Promoted to *Lieutenant-General*
3 Jun 1917 - Oct 1917: Reserve officer, Minsk Military District

*Major-General* Feliks Aleksandrovich **Gavrilov** (17 May 1853 - ?)
24 Jul 1908 - 1913: Commander, 2nd Sapper Battalion
1913: Retired
10 Jul 1915: Recalled; Promoted to *Major-General*
16 Nov 1915 - 23 Dec 1915: Reserve officer, Petrograd Military District
23 Dec 1915 - 1917: Reserve officer, Minsk Military District

*Lieutenant-General* Nikolai Ivanovich **Gavrilov** (13 Apr 1857 - ?)
1 Jun 1904 - 29 Sep 1907: Commander, 15th Grenadier Regiment
31 May 1907: Promoted to *Major-General*
29 Sep 1907 - 3 Feb 1910: Commander, 2nd Brigade, Caucasus Grenadier Division
3 Feb 1910 - 19 Jul 1914: Commander, 1st Brigade, 21st Infantry Division
19 Jul 1914 - 22 Apr 1917: Commander, 79th Infantry Division
23 Mar 1915: Promoted to *Lieutenant-General*

*Major-General* Sergey Ivanovich **Gavrilov** (21 Aug 1866 - ?)
10 Mar 1914: Promoted to *Major-General*
10 Mar 1914 - 8 Nov 1914: Chief of Staff, Orenburg Cossack Army
8 Nov 1914 - 19 Apr 1915: Staff officer, 11th Army
19 Apr 1915 - 17 Dec 1915: Chief of Staff, Fortress Przemysl

17 Dec 1915 - 11 Mar 1916: Commander, Black Sea Infantry Brigade
11 Mar 1916 - 29 May 1917: Commander, 100th Infantry Division
29 May 1917 - 30 Jul 1917: Reserve officer, Kiev Military District
30 Jul 1917 - 1918: Reserve officer, Odessa Military District

*Major-General* Sergey Pavlovich **Gavrilov** (14 Sep 1850 - ?)
28 Mar 1906 - 1913: District Commander, Nizhny Novgorod
14 Apr 1913: Promoted to *Major-General*

*Lieutenant-General* Vasily Timofeyevich **Gavrilov** (6 Mar 1867 - ?)
19 Jul 1911: Promoted to *Major-General*
19 Jul 1911 - 25 Oct 1913: Commander, 17th Artillery Brigade
25 Oct 1913: Retired
3 Aug 1914 - 13 Mar 1915: Recalled; Commander, 10th Artillery Brigade
13 Mar 1915 - 18 Apr 1916: Commander, 10th Infantry Division
9 Apr 1915: Promoted to *Lieutenant-General*
18 Apr 1916 - 14 Aug 1916: Commanding General, I. Army Corps
14 Aug 1916 - 1917: Commanding General, XXX. Army Corps

*Major-General* Viktor Ivanovich **Gavrilov** (10 Nov 1862 - 25 Jan 1918)
15 Jul 1914: Promoted to *Major-General*
15 Jul 1914 - 3 Feb 1917: Commandant, 2nd Kiev Military School
3 Feb 1917 - 4 Sep 1917: Commander, 3rd Brigade, Grenadier Division
4 Sep 1917 - 25 Jan 1918: Commander, 34th Infantry Division

*Major-General* Dmitry Grigorovich **Gavrishev** (11 Feb 1855 - ?)
31 May 1912: Promoted to *Major-General*
31 May 1912 - 23 Apr 1915: Commander, 10th Siberian Rifle Artillery Brigade
23 Apr 1915 - 27 May 1917: Inspector of Artillery, IV. Siberian Army Corps

*Major-General* Viktor Kaetanovich **Gavronsky** (20 Apr 1863 - 11 Aug 1946)
14 Mar 1916 - 1917: Commander, 7th Railway Brigade
6 Dec 1916: Promoted to *Major-General*

*Major-General* Ivan Savvateyevich **Gavryushin** (26 Sep 1858 - ?)
22 Oct 1912 - 5 Aug 1916: Ataman, 3rd Military Division, Ural Cossack Army
5 Aug 1916: Promoted to *Major-General*
5 Aug 1916: Retired

*Major-General* Ivan Aleksandrovich **Gazenkampf** (6 Jan 1846 - ?)
16 Mar 1900: Promoted to *Major-General*
16 Mar 1900 - 21 Jun 1905: Commander, 2nd Brigade, 38th Infantry Division

*General of Infantry* Mikhail Aleksandrovich **Gazenkampf** (13 Oct 1843 - 4 Apr 1913)
11 Sep 1880 - 9 Jun 1891: Professor, General Staff Academy
6 May 1884: Promoted to *Major-General*
9 Jun 1891 - 31 Aug 1891: Commander, Moscow Life Guards Regiment
31 Aug 1891 - 4 Nov 1895: Quartermaster-General, St. Petersburg Military District

| | |
|---|---|
| 14 Nov 1894: | Promoted to *Lieutenant-General* |
| 4 Nov 1895 - 9 Sep 1903: | Governor of Astrakhan, Ataman, Astrakhan Cossack Army |
| 9 Sep 1903 - 4 Apr 1913: | Member of the Military Council |
| 26 Oct 1905 - 4 Apr 1913: | Deputy Commanding General, St. Petersburg Military District |
| 6 Dec 1905: | Promoted to *General of Infantry* |

*Major-General* Dmitry Danilovich **Gedeonov** (8 Nov 1854 - 11 Sep 1908)
| | |
|---|---|
| 21 Sep 1900 - 11 Sep 1908: | Chief of Military Topographical Section, Turkestan Military District |
| 1 Apr 1901: | Promoted to *Major-General* |

*Major-General* Gedeon Petrovich **Gedeonov** (14 Mar 1852 - ?)
| | |
|---|---|
| 4 Aug 1907: | Promoted to *Major-General* |
| 4 Aug 1907 - 1908: | Commander, Poltava Regional Brigade |

*General of Infantry* Ivan Mikhailovich **Gedeonov** (6 Jan 1816 - 20 Jan 1907)
| | |
|---|---|
| 7 Apr 1857: | Promoted to *Major-General* |
| 7 Apr 1857 - 11 Dec 1862: | Deputy Director, Land Survey Corps |
| 11 Dec 1862 - 16 May 1870: | Director, Land Survey Corps |
| 30 Aug 1864: | Promoted to *Lieutenant-General* |
| 1 Jan 1865 - 20 Jan 1907: | Senator |
| 28 Mar 1882: | Promoted to *General of Infantry* |

*Lieutenant-General* Mikhail Danilovich **Gedeonov** (24 Oct 1858 - ?)
| | |
|---|---|
| 2 Apr 1902 - 22 Jul 1912: | Deputy Commandant of Kiev Arsenal |
| 29 Mar 1909: | Promoted to *Major-General* |
| 22 Jul 1912 - 31 Dec 1913: | Chief of Sestroresk Arms Factory |
| 31 Dec 1913 - 1917: | Commandant of St. Petersburg Arsenal |
| 16 Jan 1914 - 1917: | Member of the Artillery Committee, Main Artillery Directorate |
| 10 Apr 1916: | Promoted to *Lieutenant-General* |

*Major-General* Prince Aleksandr Konstantinovich **Gedevanov** (16 Feb 1870 - ?)
| | |
|---|---|
| 29 Dec 1914 - 14 Aug 1917: | Commander, 203$^{rd}$ Infantry Regiment |
| 21 Dec 1916: | Promoted to *Major-General* |
| 14 Aug 1917 - 1918: | Commander, 51$^{st}$ Infantry Division |

*Lieutenant-General* Viktor Aleksandrovich **Gedlund** (25 May 1853 - 4 Jul 1922)
| | |
|---|---|
| 29 Oct 1899 - 3 Feb 1903: | Commander, Life Guards 3$^{rd}$ Finnish Rifle Battalion |
| 1 Apr 1901: | Promoted to *Major-General* |
| 3 Feb 1903 - 9 Jun 1903: | Attached to St. Petersburg Military District |
| 9 Jun 1903 - 10 Jan 1905: | Commander, Lifeguards Kexholm Regiment |
| 10 Jan 1905 - 10 Oct 1909: | Commander, 1$^{st}$ Brigade, 3$^{rd}$ Guards Infantry Division |
| 10 Oct 1909 - 1917: | Senator; Member of the Economic Department, Finnish Senate |
| 6 Dec 1909: | Promoted to *Lieutenant-General* |

*Major-General* Prince Mikhail Mikhailovich **Gedroyts** (18 Jul 1856 - 21 Oct 1931)
7 Jul 1908 - 1917: Military Commander, Vyazemsky District
6 Dec 1914: Promoted to *Major-General*

*Lieutenant-General* Andrey Konstantinovich **Gek** (15 Sep 1838 - 11 Jun 1908)
4 May 1892: Promoted to *Major-General*
4 May 1892 - 15 Sep 1900: Commander, 2nd Brigade, 26th Infantry Division
15 Sep 1900: Promoted to *Lieutenant-General*
15 Sep 1900: Retired

*Major-General* Aleksandr Ivanovich **Gekkel** (3 Jul 1845 - 1908)
30 Aug 1894: Promoted to *Major-General*
30 Aug 1894 - 1908: At the disposal of the Main Engineering Directorate

*Major-General* Vladimir Andreyevich **Geldt** (7 Feb 1872 - Jan 1916)
20 Aug 1914 - Jan 1916: Chief of Engineer Sub-Section, Etape Section, 9th Army
1915: Promoted to *Major-General*

*Lieutenant-General* Pavel Oskarovich **Gelfreykh** (19 Aug 1862 - 18 Apr 1921)
18 Feb 1909 - 28 Mar 1910: Secretary of the Artillery Committee, Main Artillery Directorate
29 Mar 1909: Promoted to *Major-General*
28 Mar 1910 - Oct 1917: Member of the Artillery Committee, Main Artillery Directorate
10 Apr 1916: Promoted to *Lieutenant-General*

*Lieutenant-General* Nikolai Pavlovich von **Gelmersen** (26 May 1842 - 22 Apr 1908)
25 Sep 1889: Promoted to *Major-General*
25 Sep 1889 - 31 Aug 1894: Attached to Grand Duke Sergey Mikhailovich
31 Aug 1894 - 22 Apr 1908: Attached to Grand Duke Mikhail Nikolayevich
6 May 1900: Promoted to *Lieutenant-General*

*Lieutenant-General* Vasily Pavlovich von **Gelmersen** (26 Feb 1840 - ?)
3 Mar 1879 - 23 Jan 1886: Military Judge, Kharkov Military District Court
15 Oct 1884: Promoted to *Major-General*
23 Jan 1886 - 8 Mar 1886: Transferred to the reserve
8 Mar 1886 - 8 Dec 1892: Military Judge, Vilnius Military District Court
8 Dec 1892 - 1896: Military Judge, St. Petersburg Military District Court
1896: Promoted to *Lieutenant-General*
1896: Retired

*Lieutenant-General* Nikolai Fyodorovich **Gelmgolts** (18 Mar 1856 - 24 Dec 1937)
25 Mar 1904: Promoted to *Major-General*
25 Mar 1904 - 30 Sep 1906: Chief of Staff, Warsaw Fortified District
30 Sep 1906 - 27 Dec 1908: Commandant of Fortress Osovets
27 Dec 1908: Promoted to *Lieutenant-General*
27 Dec 1908: Retired
8 Nov 1914 - 1917: Recalled; Reserve officer, Kiev Military District

*Lieutenant-General* Pyotr Varfolomeyevich **Gembitsky** (27 May 1864 - 11 Sep 1921)
25 Aug 1915 - 19 Jul 1916: Reserve officer, Kiev Military District
12 Jul 1916: Promoted to *Major-General*
19 Jul 1916 - 12 May 1917: Deputy Commander, 31st Replacement Infantry Brigade
12 May 1917 - 27 Oct 1917: Reserve officer, Kazan Military District
27 Oct 1917: Promoted to *Lieutenant-General*
27 Oct 1917: Dismissed

*Lieutenant-General* Karl Fyodorovich **Gemmelman** (31 Oct 1832 - ?)
9 Sep 1872 - 22 Nov 1888: Commander, Simferopol Engineering Detachment
5 May 1886: Promoted to *Major-General*
22 Nov 1888 - 1898: Commander of Engineers, Amur Military District
14 May 1896: Promoted to *Lieutenant-General*

*Lieutenant-General* Count Dmitry Aleksandrovich **Gendrikov** (24 Apr 1831 - 1898)
15 Jul 1882 - 4 Nov 1896: Special Assignments General, Corps of Gendarmerie
13 Apr 1886: Promoted to *Major-General*
4 Nov 1896: Promoted to *Lieutenant-General*
4 Nov 1896: Retired

*Lieutenant-General* Ivan Adamovich **Genik** (6 Jan 1854 - 12 Jul 1919)
16 Jun 1910: Promoted to *Major-General*
16 Jun 1910 - 18 Nov 1911: Commander, 1st Brigade, 52nd Infantry Division
18 Nov 1911 - 6 Jan 1914: Commander, 2nd Brigade, 21st Infantry Division
6 Jan 1914: Promoted to *Lieutenant-General*
6 Jan 1914: Retired
22 Aug 1914: Recalled with rank of *Major-General*
22 Aug 1914 - 21 Aug 1915: Commander, 3rd Kuban Light Infantry Brigade
21 Aug 1915 - 12 Sep 1915: Reserve officer, Kiev Military District
12 Sep 1915 - 1917: Commander, 15th Replacement Infantry Brigade

*Lieutenant-General* Nikolai Ivanovich **Genishta** (19 Jan 1865 - 27 Mar 1932)
16 Apr 1904 - 8 Dec 1908: Commandant, Kazan Infantry Cadet School
6 Dec 1908: Promoted to *Major-General*
8 Dec 1908 - Aug 1917: Commandant, Aleksandr Military School
22 Mar 1915: Promoted to *Lieutenant-General*
Aug 1917: Dismissed

*Lieutenant-General* Oskar Aleksandrovich von **Gennings** (11 May 1855 - ?)
25 Nov 1899 - 23 Jan 1906: Commander, 2nd Rifle Regiment
18 Jan 1905: Promoted to *Major-General*
23 Jan 1906 - 31 Dec 1913: Commander, 2nd Brigade, 40th Infantry Division
31 Dec 1913: Promoted to *Lieutenant-General*
31 Dec 1913 - 4 Dec 1914: Commander, 6th Siberian Rifle Division
4 Dec 1914 - 14 May 1915: Reserve officer, Minsk Military District
14 May 1915: Retired

*Major-General* Eduard Eduardovich **Genritsi** (22 Jul 1870 - 3 Nov 1929)
11 Mar 1916 - 3 Jun 1917: Commander, Life Guards Grodno Hussar Regiment
6 Dec 1916: Promoted to *Major-General*

*Admiral* **George V**, King of the United Kingdom and the British Dominions, Emperor of India (3 Jun 1865 - 20 Jan 1936)
21 Jul 1909: Promoted to *Admiral*

*Major-General* Sergey Andreyevich **Geppener** (28 Jul 1863 - 1937)
10 Aug 1908 - 30 Oct 1916: Deputy Military Governor of Syr-Darya Region
6 Dec 1913: Promoted to *Major-General*
30 Oct 1916: Dismissed

*Major-General* Arkady Konstantinovich **Gerandli** (26 Jan 1862 - 25 Jun 1933)
6 Dec 1907 - 12 Apr 1917: Chief of Section 1, Military Technical Directorate
6 Dec 1913: Promoted to *Major-General*
12 Apr 1917 - Oct 1917: Deputy Chief of Administration, Military Technical Directorate

*Lieutenant-General* Andrey Frantsevich **Gerardi** (14 Sep 1843 - ?)
13 Aug 1898 - 18 Jan 1902: Deputy Commander of Artillery, Caucasus Military District
6 Dec 1899: Promoted to *Major-General*
18 Jan 1902 - 27 Sep 1906: Artillery Inspector, Siberian Military District
27 Sep 1906 - Jun 1907: Commander of Artillery, XIV. Army Corps
6 Dec 1906: Promoted to *Lieutenant-General*

*Vice-Admiral* Aleksandr Mikhailovich **Gerasimov** (14 Nov 1861 - 11 Mar 1931)
28 Aug 1909 - 29 Apr 1913: Commander, Artillery Training Detachment, Baltic Fleet
6 Dec 1911: Promoted to *Rear-Admiral*
29 Apr 1913: Promoted to *Vice-Admiral*
29 Apr 1913 - 1917: Commander, Peter the Great Naval Fortress
1914 - 1917: Governor-General of Estonia & Livonia

*Lieutenant-General* Aleksandr Vasilievich **Gerasimov** (7 Nov 1861 - 2 Jan 1944)
3 Feb 1905 - 25 Sep 1909: Head of the Office for the Protection of Public Safety & Order, St. Petersburg
5 Oct 1907: Promoted to *Major-General*
25 Sep 1909 - 22 Jan 1914: General of Gendarmerie, Ministry of Internal Affairs
22 Jan 1914: Promoted to *Lieutenant-General*
22 Jan 1914: Retired

*Major-General* Nikolai Vasilyevich **Gerasimov** (22 Apr 1867 - ?)
26 Oct 1908 - 11 Sep 1912: Commander, 2$^{nd}$ Kronstadt Fortress Artillery Regiment
11 Sep 1912 - 19 Nov 1912: Commander of Artillery, Fortress Novogeorgiyevsk
19 Nov 1912: Promoted to *Major-General*
19 Nov 1912 - 1917: Commander, Kronstadt Fortress Artillery Brigade

*Major-General* Yevgeny Mikhailovich **Gerasimov** (7 Oct 1873 - 15 Mar 1949)
16 Sep 1915 - 20 Oct 1916: Commander, 17th Turkestan Rifle Regiment
23 Jul 1916: Promoted to *Major-General*
20 Oct 1916 - 11 May 1917: Chief of Staff, 5th Caucasus Cossack Division
11 May 1917 - Dec 1917: Quartermaster-General, Caucasus Army

*Major-General of the Fleet* Nikolai Karlovich **Gerbikh** (5 Sep 1868 - ?)
Jun 1913 - 1917: Chief of Ship Construction, Baltic Sea
6 Dec 1916: Promoted to *Major-General of the Fleet*

*Major-General* Eduard Eduardovich von **Gering** (6 Aug 1872 - 23 Mar 1943)
14 Jul 1906 - 11 Apr 1916: City Manager of Pavlovsk
6 Dec 1911: Promoted to *Major-General*
11 Apr 1916 - 24 Dec 1916: Reserve officer, Kiev Military District
24 Dec 1916 - 12 Aug 1917: Commander, 6th Caucasus Rifle Artillery Brigade
12 Aug 1917 - ?: Commander, 13th Artillery Brigade

*Major-General* Eduard Pavlovich von **Gering** (29 Apr 1838 - ?)
11 Oct 1889: Promoted to *Major-General*
11 Oct 1889 - 9 Feb 1897: Commander, Caucasus Grenadier Artillery Brigade

*Admiral* Fyodor Alekseyevich **Gerken** (2 Mar 1835 - 20 Dec 1906)
1886: Promoted to *Rear-Admiral*
1886 - 1888: Chief of Staff, Port of Kronstadt
1888 - 1890: Detachment Commander, Baltic Training Squadron
1890 - 1892: Detachment Commander, Naval Corps
1892: Promoted to *Vice-Admiral*
1893 - 1895: Commander, Baltic Training Squadron
1896 - 20 Dec 1906: Member, Committee for Wounded Veterans
1904: Promoted to *Admiral*

*Major-General* Nikolai-Konstantin Karlovich **Gerle** (16 Dec 1868 - ?)
22 Jan 1912 - 5 Feb 1914: Clerk of the Technical Committee, Main Military Technical Directorate
6 Dec 1913: Promoted to *Major-General*
5 Feb 1914 - Oct 1917: Member, Economic Commission, Main Military Technical Directorate
30 Aug 1914 - Oct 1917: Clerk of the Technical Committee, Main Military Technical Directorate

*Lieutenant-General* Eduard Karlovich **Germonius** (6 May 1864 - 5 Oct 1938)
3 Mar 1898 - 21 Jul 1909: Deputy Chief of Izhevsk Arms Factory
29 Mar 1909: Promoted to *Major-General*
21 Jul 1909 - 14 Dec 1911: Chairman, Samara Pipe Factory Construction Commission
14 Dec 1911 - 15 Jun 1914: Chief of Samara Pipe Factory
15 Jun 1914 - 1916: Chief of Artillery Acceptance
10 Apr 1916: Promoted to *Lieutenant-General*

1916 - 1918:	Chairman, Russian Government Committee in London

*General of Infantry* Konstantin Karlovich **Gernet** (27 Nov 1844 - ?)
15 Jun 1891 - 22 Dec 1913:	Chief of Gatchina Palace Administration
30 Aug 1891:	Promoted to *Major-General*
14 Apr 1902:	Promoted to *Lieutenant-General*
22 Dec 1913:	Promoted to *General of Infantry*
22 Dec 1913:	Retired

*General of Infantry* Aleksandr Alekseyevich **Gerngross** (4 Aug 1851 - 17 Mar 1925)
14 Aug 1897 - 11 May 1901:	Chief of Security Forces
1900:	Commandant of Harbin Garrison
13 Jul 1900:	Promoted to *Major-General*
11 May 1901 - 6 Jan 1902:	Deputy Commander of Borderguards, Amur Military District
6 Jan 1902 - 16 Dec 1902:	At the disposal of the Chief of the General Staff
16 Dec 1902 - 22 Feb 1904:	Commander, 1st East Siberian Rifle Brigade
22 Feb 1904 - 23 May 1905:	Commander, 1st East Siberian Rifle Division
1 Jun 1904:	Promoted to *Lieutenant-General*
23 May 1905 - 7 Jun 1910:	Commanding General, I. Siberian Army Corps
7 Jun 1910 - 20 Jan 1913:	Commanding General, XXIV. Army Corps
6 Dec 1910:	Promoted to *General of Infantry*
20 Jan 1913 - 15 Aug 1914:	Member of the Military Council
15 Aug 1914 - 28 Dec 1916:	Commanding General, XXVI. Army Corps
28 Dec 1916 - 1917:	Member of the Military Council

*Lieutenant-General* Yevgeny Aleksandrovich **Gerngross** (10 Feb 1855 - 15 May 1912)
2 Sep 1896 - 6 Mar 1901:	Commander, 35th Dragoon Regiment
6 Mar 1901:	Promoted to *Major-General*
6 Mar 1901 - 25 Mar 1901:	Attached to the Inspector-General of Cavalry
25 Mar 1901 - 24 Jun 1904:	Commander, Life Guards Regiment
24 Jun 1904 - 2 Jan 1907:	Chief of Staff, Guards Corps
2 Jan 1907 - 19 Sep 1909:	Attached to the Imperial Court
22 Apr 1907:	Promoted to *Lieutenant-General*
19 Sep 1909 - 22 Feb 1911:	Chief of the General Directorate of the General Staff
22 Feb 1911 - 15 May 1912:	At the disposal of the Minister of War

*General of Infantry* Dmitry Konstantinovich **Gershelman** (11 Sep 1859 - 22 Jul 1913)
1 May 1897 - 28 Mar 1904:	Section Chief, General Staff
1904:	Promoted to *Major-General*
28 Mar 1904 - 31 Jul 1905:	Attached to the General Staff
31 Jul 1905 - 27 Oct 1906:	Section Chief, General Staff
27 Oct 1906 - 14 Oct 1907:	Deputy Duty General, General Staff
14 Oct 1907 - 22 Jul 1913:	Chief of Staff, Separate Corps of Gendarmes
31 Dec 1910:	Promoted to *Lieutenant-General*
1913:	Posthumously promoted to *General of Infantry*

*General of Cavalry* Fyodor Konstantinovich **Gershelman** (1 Jan 1853 - ?)
5 May 1893 - 19 Jul 1898:        Chief of Staff, Kuban Cossack Army
14 Apr 1895:                     Promoted to *Major-General*
19 Jul 1898 - 22 Apr 1901:       Military Governor of Kutaisi
22 Apr 1901:                     Promoted to *Lieutenant-General*
22 Apr 1901 - 2 Sep 1905:        Chief of Staff, Warsaw Military District
2 Sep 1905 - 15 May 1912:        Deputy Commanding General, Warsaw Military District
13 Apr 1908:                     Promoted to *General of Cavalry*
15 May 1912 - 1917:              Member of the Military Council

*Lieutenant-General* German Fyodorovich **Gershelman** (20 Feb 1854 - ?)
30 Jun 1907:                     Promoted to *Major-General*
30 Jun 1907 - 17 Aug 1913:       Commander, 2nd Brigade, 5th Infantry Division
17 Aug 1913:                     Promoted to *Lieutenant-General*
17 Aug 1913:                     Retired

*Lieutenant-General* Ivan Romanovich **Gershelman** (20 Dec 1854 - ?)
24 Jun 1902:                     Promoted to *Major-General*
24 Jun 1902 - 3 Oct 1909:        Chief of Staff, Grenadier Corps
3 Oct 1909:                      Promoted to *Lieutenant-General*
3 Oct 1909 - 24 May 1910:        Commander, 51st Replacement Infantry Brigade
24 May 1910 - 5 Sep 1914:        Commander, 45th Infantry Division
9 Sep 1914:                      Retired

*General of Infantry* Konstantin Ivanovich **Gershelman** (2 Dec 1825 - 16 Nov 1898)
11 Aug 1864 - 7 Feb 1876:        Deputy Chief of Staff, St. Petersburg Military District
15 Sep 1864:                     Promoted to *Major-General*
30 Aug 1873:                     Promoted to *Lieutenant-General*
7 Feb 1876 - 1 Nov 1876:         Member of the Tsar's retinue
17 Apr 1876:                     Promoted to *General-Adjutant*
1 Nov 1876 - 29 Dec 1877:        Commander, 24th Infantry Division
29 Dec 1877 - 30 May 1878:       At the disposal of the C-in-C of the Field Army
30 May 1878 - 11 Sep 1880:       At the disposal of the Commanding General, St.
                                 Petersburg Military District
11 Sep 1880 - 7 Dec 1894:        Attached to St. Petersburg Military District
7 Dec 1894 - 16 Nov 1898:        Member of the Tsar's retinue
14 May 1896:                     Promoted to *General of Infantry*

*Major-General* Konstantin Vladimirovich **Gershelman** (26 Feb 1849 - 6 May 1901)
18 Jan 1900:                     Promoted to *Major-General*
18 Jan 1900 - 6 May 1901:        Commander, 1st Brigade, 39th Infantry Division

*General of Infantry* Sergey Konstantinovich **Gershelman** (25 Jul 1854 - 17 Nov 1910)
29 Jan 1898:                     Promoted to *Major-General*
29 Jan 1898 - 20 Jan 1903:       Chief of Staff, II. Army Corps
20 Jan 1903 - 2 May 1904:        Chief of Staff, Siberian Military District
2 May 1904 - 17 Jan 1906:        Commander, 9th Infantry Division
5 Jul 1904:                      Promoted to *Lieutenant-General*

2 May 1904 - 17 Jan 1906:        Commanding General, X. Army Corps
17 Jan 1906 - 17 Mar 1909:       Commanding General, Moscow Military District
5 Jul 1906 - 17 Mar 1909:        Governor-General of Moscow
17 Mar 1909 - 17 Nov 1910:       Commanding General, Vilnius Military District
17 Nov 1910:                     Promoted to *General of Infantry*

*Major-General* Baron Aleksandr Mikhailovich **Gert** (4 May 1851 - ?)
14 Feb 1896 - 1910:              Section Chief, Main Artillery Directorate
4 Jan 1900 - 1910:               Member of the Artillery Committee, Main Artillery Directorate
9 Apr 1900:                      Promoted to *Major-General*

*Major-General* Konstantin Ivanovich **Gertik** (11 Jun 1822 - ?)
24 Feb 1879 - 1894:              General Staff Officer V. Class, General Staff
30 Aug 1882:                     Promoted to *Major-General*

*Major-General* Fyodor Vilyamovich **Gertrig** (24 Nov 1867 - ?)
24 Jul 1914 - 1917:              Commander of Engineers, Fortress Osovets
10 Apr 1916:                     Promoted to *Major-General*

*Lieutenant-General* Aleksandr Kuzmich **Gertso-Vinogradsky** (18 Apr 1840 - ?)
6 Jul 1878 - 26 Jan 1887:        Commander of Artillery, Fortress Kerch
6 May 1884:                      Promoted to *Major-General*
26 Jan 1887 - 4 Nov 1894:        Deputy Commander of Artillery, Odessa Military District
4 Nov 1894 - 3 Feb 1903:         Commander of Artillery, Warsaw Military District
14 Nov 1894:                     Promoted to *Lieutenant-General*
3 Feb 1903 - 1905:               Member, Committee for Wounded Veterans

*Lieutenant-General* Yakov Kuzmich **Gertso-Vinogradsky** (2 Jun 1838 - 7 Aug 1904)
16 Oct 1892 - 28 Jul 1899:       Deputy Intendant, Kazan Military District
21 Dec 1894:                     Promoted to *Major-General*
28 Jul 1899 - 1901:              Deputy Intendant, St. Petersburg Military District
1901:                            Promoted to *Lieutenant-General*
1901:                            Retired

*Major-General* Konstantin Andreyevich **Gertsog** (3 Feb 1837 - 26 Nov 1897)
10 Apr 1880 - 1894:              Commander of Tiflis Railway Gendarmerie
17 Apr 1894:                     Promoted to *Major-General*

*Lieutenant-General* Aleksandr Antonovich **Gertsyk** (31 Aug 1857 - 31 Jan 1916)
23 Jun 1906 - 10 Aug 1908:       Commander, Pavlovsky Life Guards Regiment
6 Dec 1906:                      Promoted to *Major-General*
10 Aug 1908 - 19 Jul 1914:       Commander, 2$^{nd}$ Brigade, 1$^{st}$ Guards Infantry Division
19 Jul 1914 - 16 Jan 1915:       Commander, 80$^{th}$ Infantry Division
16 Jan 1915:                     Promoted to *Lieutenant-General*
16 Jan 1915 - 3 Jul 1915:        Commander, 1$^{st}$ Guards Infantry Division
3 Jul 1915 - 31 Jan 1916:        Reserve officer, Petrograd Military District

*Lieutenant-General* Aleksandr Vladimirovich **Gerua** (24 Mar 1870 - ?)
14 Sep 1912 - 4 Feb 1914: Commander, 7th Finnish Rifle Regiment
4 Feb 1914: Promoted to *Major-General*
4 Feb 1914 - 25 Jan 1915: Commander, Volyn Life Guards Regiment
25 Jan 1915 - 1915: Quartermaster-General, 5th Army
1915 - 10 Oct 1915: Quartermaster-General, 12th Army
10 Oct 1915 - 31 Oct 1916: Commander, 38th Infantry Division
31 Oct 1916 - 7 Jul 1917: Chief of Staff, 2nd Army
7 Jul 1917: Promoted to *Lieutenant-General*
7 Jul 1917 - 1917: Commanding General, XVIII. Army Corps

*Major-General* Boris Vladimirovich **Gerua** (3 Mar 1876 - Mar 1942)
19 May 1915 - 14 Jul 1916: Commander, Izmailovo Life Guards Regiment
7 Jul 1916: Promoted to *Major-General*
14 Jul 1916 - 2 Dec 1916: Quartermaster-General of the Guard
2 Dec 1916 - 1 May 1917: Quartermaster-General, Special Army
1 May 1917 - 31 Aug 1917: Chief of Staff, 11th Army

*Major-General* Vladimir Aleksandrovich **Gerua** (18 Jun 1839 - 21 Dec 1904)
20 Jun 1900: Promoted to *Major-General*
20 Jun 1900 - 21 Dec 1904: Commander, Minsk Local Brigade

*Major-General* Ivan Ivanovich **Geshtovt** (24 Mar 1866 - 1943)
16 Nov 1911 - 25 Aug 1915: Commander, 11th Rifle Regiment
1 May 1915: Promoted to *Major-General*
25 Aug 1915 - 12 Apr 1917: Commander, Brigade, 1st Finnish Rifle Division
12 Apr 1917 - 20 May 1917: Commander, 4th Finnish Rifle Division

*Major-General* Aleksandr Davidovich **Gesket** (4 Jan 1862 - 3 Jul 1937)
1 Feb 1910 - 1917: Chief of Privislensky Railways
25 Mar 1912: Promoted to *Major-General*

*Major-General* Sergey Davidovich **Gesket** (18 Jun 1859 - ?)
14 Mar 1905 - Dec 1907: Military Governor of Samarkand
17 Apr 1905: Promoted to *Major-General*

*Lieutenant-General* Pyotr Pavlovich **Gesse** (18 Feb 1846 - 14 Jul 1905)
30 Aug 1888: Promoted to *Major-General*
30 Aug 1888 - 21 Mar 1896: Commandant of the Imperial Apartments
21 Mar 1896 - 14 Jul 1905: Commandant of the Royal Palace
14 May 1896: Promoted to *Lieutenant-General*
14 May 1896: Promoted to *General-Adjutant*

*Vice-Admiral* Fyodor Yegoryevich **Gessen** (5 Apr 1841 - 7 Mar 1902)
28 Mar 1893: Promoted to *Rear-Admiral*
28 Mar 1893 - 3 Jan 1894: Junior Flagman, Baltic Fleet
3 Jan 1894 - 25 Aug 1894: Port Captain, Nikolaev
25 Aug 1894 - 26 Jan 1898: Port Captain, Kronstadt

| | |
|---|---|
| 26 Jan 1898 - 9 Apr 1901: | Commander, 1st Naval Division, Baltic Fleet |
| 9 Apr 1901: | Promoted to *Vice-Admiral* |
| 9 Apr 1901: | Retired |

*Lieutenant-General* Demyan Yefimovich **Getmanov** (1 Nov 1849 - 1 Jul 1910)

| | |
|---|---|
| 27 Jul 1892 - 19 Nov 1904: | Ataman, Caucasus Division, Kuban Cossack Army |
| 6 May 1901: | Promoted to *Major-General* |
| 19 Nov 1904 - 1907: | Ataman, Batalpashinsk Division, Kuban Cossack Army |
| 1907: | Promoted to *Lieutenant-General* |
| 1907: | Retired |

*Lieutenant-General* Dmitry Nikolayevich **Gets** (21 Dec 1833 - 25 Apr 1900)

| | |
|---|---|
| 4 Feb 1886: | Promoted to *Major-General* |
| 4 Feb 1886 - 23 Dec 1889: | Commander, 2nd Brigade, 5th Infantry Division |
| 23 Dec 1889 - 17 Oct 1890: | Chief of Staff, X. Army Corps |
| 17 Oct 1890 - 3 Mar 1892: | Chief of Staff, Omsk Military District |
| 3 Mar 1892 - 1 Dec 1892: | At the disposal of the Chief of the General Staff |
| 1 Dec 1892 - 18 Jan 1896: | Commander, 46th Reserve Infantry Brigade |
| 18 Jan 1896 - 18 Aug 1898: | Commander, 27th Infantry Division |
| 14 May 1896: | Promoted to *Lieutenant-General* |
| 18 Aug 1898 - 25 Apr 1900: | Commander, 3rd Grenadier Division |

*Vice-Admiral* Count Aleksandr Fyodorovich **Geyden** (22 Apr 1859 - 15 Aug 1919)

| | |
|---|---|
| 21 Aug 1906 - 13 Apr 1908: | Chief of the Naval Chancellery |
| 13 Apr 1908: | Promoted to *Rear-Admiral* |
| 13 Apr 1908 - 1916: | Admiral à la suite |
| 1913: | Promoted to *Vice-Admiral* |
| 24 Dec 1914 - 1917: | Deputy Chief of the Naval General Staff |
| 1916 - 1917: | Member of the Admiralty Board |

*General of Infantry* Count Fyodor Logginovich **Geyden** (15 Sep 1821 - 18 Aug 1900)

| | |
|---|---|
| 18 Dec 1854 - 17 May 1856: | Chief of Staff, Baltic Corps |
| 17 Apr 1855: | Promoted to *Major-General* |
| 17 May 1856 - 8 Sep 1856: | Chief of Staff, I. Army Corps |
| 8 Sep 1856 - 6 Jun 1861: | Chief of Staff, Independent Grenadier Corps |
| 6 Jun 1861 - 1 Jan 1866: | Duty General, General Staff |
| 30 Aug 1861: | Promoted to *Lieutenant-General* |
| 30 Aug 1862: | Promoted to *General-Adjutant* |
| 1 Jan 1866 - 22 May 1881: | Chief of the General Staff |
| 17 Apr 1870: | Promoted to *General of Infantry* |
| 22 May 1881 - 1897: | Governor-General of Finland, Commanding General, Finland Military District |
| 22 May 1881 - 18 Aug 1900: | Member of the State Council |

*Lieutenant-General* Count Nikolai Fyodorovich **Geyden** (17 Jan 1856 - 28 Feb 1919)

| | |
|---|---|
| 21 May 1893 - 5 May 1908: | Director of Special Office, Ministry of War |
| 6 Dec 1899: | Promoted to *Major-General* |

| | |
|---|---|
| 20 Nov 1899 - 5 May 1908: | General for Special Assignments for the Minister of War |
| 6 Dec 1906: | Promoted to *Lieutenant-General* |
| 5 May 1908: | Retired |
| 17 May 1908 - 1917: | Recalled; Attached to the Ministry of War, Honorary Trustee, Empress Maria Institutions |

*Lieutenant-General* Nikolai Pavlovich **Geyer** (5 Nov 1857 - ?)
| | |
|---|---|
| 7 Jun 1907: | Promoted to *Major-General* |
| 7 Jun 1907 - 17 Oct 1910: | Commander, 6th Sapper Brigade |
| 17 Oct 1910 - 27 Apr 1911: | Inspector of Field Engineers, Moscow Military District |
| 27 Apr 1911 - 29 Nov 1912: | Inspector of Field Engineers, Odessa Military District |
| 29 Nov 1912 - 1917: | Inspector of Engineering Troops, Odessa Military District |
| 7 Jun 1913: | Promoted to *Lieutenant-General* |

*Major-General* Baron Aleksandr-Karl-Eduard Aleksandrovich von **Geyking** (22 Oct 1855 - 26 Jul 1930)
| | |
|---|---|
| 2 Aug 1905 - 25 Nov 1913: | Commander, 54th Infantry Regiment |
| 21 Jan 1912: | Promoted to *Major-General* |
| 25 Nov 1913: | Retired |

*Major-General* Baron Andrey Karlovich von **Geyking** (30 Nov 1864 - 1945)
| | |
|---|---|
| 23 Feb 1913 - 1918: | Commander, 22nd Borderguard Brigade |
| 6 Dec 1916: | Promoted to *Major-General* |

*Major-General* Mikhail Konstantinovich **Geyshtor** (8 Nov 1851 - ?)
| | |
|---|---|
| 29 Jun 1900: | Promoted to *Major-General* |
| 29 Jun 1900 - 12 Sep 1906: | Attached to Main Directorate of Appanages |
| 12 Sep 1906 - 1917: | Director, Gatchina Orphan Institute |

*General of Infantry* Platon Aleksandrovich **Geysman** (20 Feb 1853 - 27 Jan 1919)
| | |
|---|---|
| 15 Dec 1894 - 16 Jun 1902: | Ordinary Professor, General Staff Academy |
| 9 Apr 1900: | Promoted to *Major-General* |
| 5 Jul 1901 - 8 Sep 1901: | Acting Commander, 2nd Brigade, 37th Infantry Division |
| 16 Jun 1902 - 15 Jan 1907: | Emeritus Professor, General Staff Academy |
| 15 Jan 1907 - 31 Mar 1911: | Commander, 44th Infantry Division |
| 22 Apr 1907: | Promoted to *Lieutenant-General* |
| 31 Mar 1911 - 13 Oct 1914: | Commanding General, XVI. Army Corps |
| 14 Apr 1913: | Promoted to *General of Infantry* |
| 13 Oct 1914 - 1 Jan 1915: | Reserve officer, Kiev Military District |
| 1 Jan 1915 - 6 Jan 1915: | Member of the Military Council |
| 6 Jan 1915 - 8 Aug 1915: | Commanding General, Kazan Military District |
| 8 Aug 1915 - 1917: | Member of the Military Council |

*Major-General* Aleksei Grigorievich **Giber von Greyfenfels** (17 Feb 1869 - ?)
| | |
|---|---|
| 1916 - 8 Dec 1916: | Chairman, Government Commission on Artillery Supply, London |

| | |
|---|---|
| 18 Aug 1916: | Promoted to *Major-General* |
| 8 Dec 1916 - 30 Sep 1917: | Chief of Staff, 1st Siberian Rifle Division |
| 30 Sep 1917 - 15 Feb 1919: | Reserve officer, Minsk Military District |

*Lieutenant-General* Viktor Ivanovich **Giber von Greyfenfels** (14 May 1863 - ?)

| | |
|---|---|
| 2 Apr 1911 - 28 Sep 1915: | Deputy Chief of St. Petersburg Pipe Plant |
| 10 Apr 1911: | Promoted to *Major-General* |
| 28 Sep 1915 - 1917: | Chief of Sestroretsk Arms Factory |
| 2 Apr 1917: | Promoted to *Lieutenant-General* |
| 1917 - 1918: | Attached to the Chairman, Russian Government Committee in London |

*Major-General* Nikolai Petrovich **Gibner** (3 Jan 1858 - 1922)

| | |
|---|---|
| 14 Aug 1906 - 1907: | Military Judge, Irkutsk Military District Court |
| 6 Dec 1906: | Promoted to *Major-General* |
| 1907: | Retired |

*Lieutenant-General* Konstantin Lukich **Gilchevsky** (5 Mar 1857 - ?)

| | |
|---|---|
| 19 Mar 1908 - 3 Sep 1908: | Commander, 2nd Brigade, 21st Infantry Division |
| 3 Sep 1908 - 3 Apr 1913: | Commander, 1st Brigade, 39th Infantry Division |
| 28 Nov 1908: | Promoted to *Major-General* |
| 3 Apr 1913 - 19 Jul 1914: | Commander, 1st Brigade, Caucasus Grenadier Division |
| 19 Jul 1914 - 9 Nov 1914: | Commander, 83rd Infantry Division |
| 9 Nov 1914 - 25 Mar 1915: | Reserve officer, Kiev Military District |
| 25 Mar 1915 - 3 Jul 1915: | Commander, 1st State Militia Division |
| 3 Jul 1915 - 6 Apr 1917: | Commander, 101st Infantry Division |
| 12 Jul 1916: | Promoted to *Lieutenant-General* |
| 6 Apr 1917 - Apr 1917: | Commanding General, XI. Army Corps |

*Lieutenant-General* Leopold Fyodorovich **Gilferding** (18 Sep 1855 - ?)

| | |
|---|---|
| 12 Nov 1910: | Promoted to *Major-General* |
| 12 Nov 1910 - 19 Nov 1914: | Commander, 30th Artillery Brigade |
| 19 Nov 1914 - 15 Jan 1915: | Reserve officer, Dvinsk Military District |
| 15 Jan 1915 - 28 May 1915: | Commander, 30th Artillery Brigade |
| 28 May 1915 - 28 Aug 1915: | Reserve officer, Dvinsk Military District |
| 28 Aug 1915: | Promoted to *Lieutenant-General* |
| 28 Aug 1915: | Retired |

*General of Artillery* Eduard Vikentyevich **Gilkhen** (26 Sep 1831 - ?)

| | |
|---|---|
| 12 Apr 1870 - 1 Aug 1877: | Commander, 31st Artillery Brigade |
| 30 Aug 1875: | Promoted to *Major-General* |
| 1 Aug 1877 - 28 Apr 1878: | Commander of Artillery, IX. Army Corps |
| 28 Apr 1878 - 16 Jan 1882: | Unassigned |
| 16 Jan 1882 - 2 Dec 1883: | Deputy Commander of Artillery, Kiev Military District |
| 2 Dec 1883 - 14 Nov 1888: | Commander of Artillery, XV. Army Corps |
| 30 Aug 1885: | Promoted to *Lieutenant-General* |
| 14 Nov 1888 - 20 Oct 1899: | Commander of Artillery, XVII. Army Corps |
| 20 Oct 1899 - 1905: | Member, Committee for Wounded Veterans |

9 Apr 1900:                          Promoted to *General of Artillery*

*Lieutenant-General* Aleksandr Fyodorovich von **Gillenshmidt** (1 Oct 1867 - 17 Dec 1942)
16 Aug 1908:                         Promoted to *Major-General*
16 Aug 1908 - 30 May 1910:           Commander, 23rd Artillery Brigade
30 May 1910 - 21 Mar 1913:           Commander, Life Guards 2nd Artillery Brigade
21 Mar 1913:                         Promoted to *Lieutenant-General*
21 Mar 1913:                         Retired
15 Aug 1914 - 29 Dec 1915:           Recalled; Inspector of Artillery, XXVI. Army Corps
29 Dec 1915 - 23 Aug 1917:           Inspector of Artillery, II. Guards Corps

*Lieutenant-General* Yakov Fyodorovich von **Gillenshmidt** (21 Oct 1870 - Apr 1918)
7 Jul 1906 - 21 May 1912:            Commander, 17th Dragoon Regiment
21 May 1912:                         Promoted to *Major-General*
21 May 1912 - 8 Jun 1912:            Commander, 1st Brigade, Caucasus Cavalry Division
8 Jun 1912 - 25 Mar 1914:            Commander, Life Guards Cuirassier Regiment
25 Mar 1914 - 29 Sep 1914:           Commander, Life Guards Horse Artillery
29 Sep 1914 - 11 Oct 1914:           Commander, 3rd Don Cossack Division
11 Oct 1914 - 13 May 1915:           Commander, 2nd Guards Cavalry Division
13 May 1915 - Jan 1918:              Commanding General, IV. Cavalry Corps
7 May 1916:                          Promoted to *Lieutenant-General*

*Admiral* Yakov Apollonovich **Giltebrandt** (20 Apr 1842 - 1915)
5 Apr 1892:                          Promoted to *Rear-Admiral*
1892 - 1894:                         Chief of Staff, Black Sea Fleet
1894 - 1895:                         Deputy C-in-C, Baltic Fleet
1895 - 1896:                         Commander of Training & Artillery, Baltic Fleet
1896 - Dec 1898:                     Deputy Chief of the Naval General Staff
6 Dec 1898:                          Promoted to *Vice-Admiral*
1899 - 1900:                         Commander, Pacific Squadron
1901 - 1902:                         Commander, Black Sea Training Squadron
1903 - 1907:                         Chief of the Hydrographic Office, Ministry of the Navy
1907 - 1909:                         Member, Board of Admiralty
1909:                                Promoted to *Admiral*

*Lieutenant-General* Bronislav-Lyudvig Leonardovich **Gineyko** (14 Aug 1857 - ?)
12 Mar 1906 - 4 Mar 1910:            Military Judge, Turkestan Military District
2 Apr 1906:                          Promoted to *Major-General*
4 Mar 1910 - 10 May 1910:            Military Judge, Odessa Military District
10 May 1910 - 18 Feb 1912:           Military Judge, St. Petersburg Military District
18 Feb 1912 - 3 Jul 1914:            Military Prosecutor, Kazan Military District
14 Apr 1913:                         Promoted to *Lieutenant-General*
3 Jul 1914 - 25 Oct 1916:            Chairman of the Military Court, Irkutsk Military District
25 Oct 1916 - 31 Mar 1917:           Chairman of the Military Court, Minsk Military District
31 Mar 1917 - 1918:                  Member, Supreme Military Tribunal

*Lieutenant-General* Aleksandr Ivanovich **Gippius** (27 Sep 1855 - ?)
7 Nov 1906 - 26 Jan 1907:            Deputy Military Governor of Samarkand

| | |
|---|---|
| 6 Dec 1906: | Promoted to *Major-General* |
| 26 Jan 1907 - 8 Mar 1911: | Deputy Military Governor of Ferghana |
| 8 Mar 1911 - Jul 1916: | Military Governor of Ferghana |
| 6 Dec 1912: | Promoted to *Lieutenant-General* |
| Jul 1916 - 25 Feb 1917: | Reserve officer, Caucasus Military District |
| 25 Feb 1917: | Dismissed |

*General of Artillery* Vladimir Ivanovich **Gippius** (18 Jun 1847 - 1918)
| | |
|---|---|
| 16 Mar 1899: | Promoted to *Major-General* |
| 16 Mar 1899 - 29 Dec 1899: | Commander, 26th Artillery Brigade |
| 29 Dec 1899 - 6 Jan 1903: | Commander, Life Guards 3rd Artillery Brigade |
| 6 Jan 1903 - 12 Feb 1903: | Acting Commander of Artillery, XIV. Army Corps |
| 12 Feb 1903 - 11 Mar 1906: | Commander of Artillery, Grenadier Corps |
| 17 Apr 1905: | Promoted to *Lieutenant-General* |
| 11 Mar 1906 - 24 Jun 1910: | Commander of Artillery, VIII. Army Corps |
| 24 Jun 1910: | Promoted to *General of Artillery* |
| 24 Jun 1910: | Retired |

*Major-General* Aleksandr Fyodorovich **Girgas** (11 Aug 1840 - ?)
| | |
|---|---|
| ? - 11 Feb 1909: | Senior Inspector, Main Intendant Directorate |
| 13 Apr 1908: | Promoted to *Major-General* |
| 11 Feb 1909 - 1910: | Inspector of Workshops, Kazan |

*Major-General* Vasily Platonovich **Girman** (1 Feb 1853 - ?)
| | |
|---|---|
| 6 Oct 1904 - 1909: | Section Chief, General Staff |
| 6 Dec 1905: | Promoted to *Major-General* |

*Major-General of the Fleet* Aleksandr Konstantinovich **Girs** (8 Nov 1859 - 1 Mar 1917)
| | |
|---|---|
| 3 Jan 1911 - 3 Nov 1913: | Commander, 2nd Baltic Naval Depot |
| 25 Mar 1912: | Promoted to *Major-General of the Admiralty* |
| 8 Apr 1913: | Redesignated *Major-General of the Fleet* |
| 3 Nov 1913 - 1 Mar 1917: | Commander, 1st Baltic Naval Depot |

*Vice-Admiral* Fyodor Aleksandrovich **Girs** (30 Jul 1835 - 3 Jun 1906)
| | |
|---|---|
| 1885 - 1890: | Captain, Imperial Yacht "Derzhava" |
| 1888: | Promoted to *Rear-Admiral* |
| 1890 - 1896: | Commander, Training Squadron, Baltic Sea |
| 1892: | Promoted to *Vice-Admiral* |
| 1896 - 3 Jun 1906: | Member, Committee for Wounded Veterans |

*Vice-Admiral* Vladimir Konstantinovich **Girs** (9 Jun 1861 - 31 Aug 1918)
| | |
|---|---|
| 28 Sep 1909 - 29 Apr 1913: | Commandant, Reval Naval Base |
| 6 Dec 1910: | Promoted to *Rear-Admiral* |
| 29 Apr 1913: | Promoted to *Vice-Admiral* |
| 29 Apr 1913 - 27 Jun 1916: | Chief of Artillery Section, Main Directorate of Shipbuilding |
| 27 Jun 1916 - 15 Dec 1917: | Chief of Main Directorate of Shipbuilding, Member of the Admiralty Board |

15 Dec 1917: Retired

*Major-General* Vladimir Viktorovich **Girsh** (3 Apr 1873 - 19 Jul 1916)
1915 - 19 Jul 1916: Commander, 1st Battalion, Life Guards 1st Artillery Brigade
8 Oct 1916: Posthumously promoted to *Major-General*

*Major-General* Konstantin Grigorievich **Girshfeld** (17 Dec 1870 - 25 Aug 1917)
13 Apr 1916 - 31 Jul 1917: Commander, 1st Brigade, 53rd Infantry Division
5 Sep 1916: Promoted to *Major-General*
31 Jul 1917 - 23 Aug 1917: Commander, 192nd Infantry Division
23 Aug 1917 - 25 Aug 1917: Commander, 111th Infantry Division

*Lieutenant-General* Vasily Andreyevich **Girshfeld** (30 Jan 1865 - 1930)
3 Aug 1910: Promoted to *Major-General*
3 Aug 1910 - 17 Jan 1913: Commander of Engineers, Fortress Osovets
17 Jan 1913 - 1915: Commander of Engineers, Fortress Modlin
1915 - 21 Apr 1916: Special Assignments General, Western Front
21 Apr 1916 - 1917: Commander of Engineers, Western Front
6 Dec 1916: Promoted to *Lieutenant-General*

*Major-General* Georgy Georgievich **Gisser** (3 Jan 1872 - ?)
23 Aug 1914 - 10 Nov 1915: Commander, 197th Infantry Regiment
5 Oct 1915: Promoted to *Major-General*
10 Nov 1915 - 1 Nov 1916: Chief of Staff, II. Army Corps
1 Nov 1916 - 22 Jun 1917: Quartermaster-General, 11th Army
22 Jun 1917 - 15 Sep 1917: Deputy Quartermaster-General, General Staff

*Major-General* Pyotr Dmitriyevich **Gladkov** (3 Mar 1870 - ?)
12 May 1916 - 1917: Commander, 22nd Artillery Brigade
6 Dec 1916: Promoted to *Major-General*

*Major-General* Stepan Vasilyevich **Gladky** (7 Jan 1870 - ?)
16 Nov 1908 - 14 Aug 1912: Inspector of Horse Artillery Train
6 Dec 1911: Promoted to *Major-General*
14 Aug 1912 - 1917: Special Purposes General, Army Remount Directorate

*Lieutenant-General* Gavriil Fyodorovich **Gladyshev** (25 Mar 1849 - 1917)
27 May 1900 - 5 Dec 1910: Commander, 17th Sapper Battalion
8 Oct 1905: Promoted to *Major-General*
5 Dec 1910: Promoted to *Lieutenant-General*
5 Dec 1910: Retired
1914 - 1917: Recalled; Commander, 20th Engineer Battalion, 5th Army

*General of Infantry* Pyotr Ivanovich **Gladyshev** (25 Nov 1850 - ?)
16 Apr 1887 - 11 Mar 1900: Chief of Military Topography, Amur Military District
6 Dec 1898: Promoted to *Major-General*

| | |
|---|---|
| 11 Mar 1900 - 21 Sep 1904: | Chief of Topographic Survey, Southwestern Border |
| 21 Sep 1904 - 1 Jun 1907: | Chief of Topographic Survey, Manchuria |
| 6 Dec 1906: | Promoted to *Lieutenant-General* |
| 1 Jun 1907 - 6 Jun 1917: | Chief of Topographic Survey, Southwestern Border |
| 6 Jun 1917: | Promoted to *General of Infantry* |
| 6 Jun 1917: | Retired |

*Major-General* Adrian Sergeyevich **Glagolev** (14 Nov 1861 - 14 Dec 1921)
| | |
|---|---|
| 29 Jul 1906 - 7 Oct 1916: | Commander, 1st Caucasus Sapper Battalion |
| 6 Dec 1915: | Promoted to *Major-General* |
| 7 Oct 1916 - 1917: | Commander, Brigade, 7th Caucasus Rifle Division |

*Lieutenant-General* Pavel Fyodorovich **Glagolev** (15 Jan 1849 - ?)
| | |
|---|---|
| 4 Jul 1904: | Promoted to *Major-General* |
| 4 Jul 1904 - 4 Jun 1910: | Commander, 5th Sapper Brigade |
| 4 Jun 1910: | Promoted to *Lieutenant-General* |
| 4 Jun 1910: | Retired |

*Lieutenant-General* Aleksandr Stepanovich **Glasko** (18 May 1844 - 1920)
| | |
|---|---|
| 31 Oct 1899: | Promoted to *Major-General* |
| 31 Oct 1899 - 14 Jul 1905: | Commander, 2nd Brigade, 35th Infantry Division |
| 14 Jul 1905 - 27 Apr 1906: | Attached to the General Staff |
| 27 Apr 1906 - 18 Dec 1908: | Commander, Perm Regional Brigade |
| 6 Dec 1907: | Promoted to *Lieutenant-General* |
| 18 Dec 1908: | Retired |
| 15 Sep 1914 - Feb 1917: | Recalled; Commander, 10th Replacement Infantry Brigade |
| Feb 1917 - 1917: | Commandant, Ryazan Garrison |

*Major-General* Genrikh Aleksandrovich **Glasko** (17 Feb 1861 - ?)
| | |
|---|---|
| 1914 - 17 Aug 1915: | Commander, 12th Sapper Battalion |
| 16 May 1915: | Promoted to *Major-General* |
| 17 Aug 1915 - 1917: | Commander of Engineers, VII. Army Corps |

*Major-General* Nikolai Fyodorovich **Glavatsky** (28 Sep 1841 - ?)
| | |
|---|---|
| 19 Dec 1882 - 13 Mar 1885: | Commander, 16th Dragoon Regiment |
| 13 Mar 1885: | Promoted to *Major-General* |
| 13 Mar 1885 - Nov 1896: | Commander, 1st Brigade, 10th Cavalry Division |

*Major-General* Georgy Aleksandrovich von **Glazenap** (22 Sep 1849 - ?)
| | |
|---|---|
| 3 Oct 1902: | Promoted to *Major-General* |
| 3 Oct 1902 - 20 May 1906: | Commander, 2nd Grenadier Artillery Brigade |
| Oct 1908 - 16 Dec 1908: | Commander of Artillery, XIX. Army Corps |

*General of Infantry* Vladimir Gavrilovich **Glazov** (12 Sep 1848 - 1918)
| | |
|---|---|
| 17 Feb 1891 - 22 Nov 1893: | Commander, 1st Life Guards Infantry Battalion |
| 30 Aug 1891: | Promoted to *Major-General* |
| 22 Nov 1893 - 31 May 1895: | Commander, Moscow Life Guards Regiment |

| | |
|---|---|
| 31 May 1895 - 18 Aug 1899: | Chief of Staff, Guards Corps |
| 18 Aug 1899 - 2 Jul 1901: | Chief of Staff, Finland Military District |
| 6 Dec 1899: | Promoted to *Lieutenant-General* |
| 2 Jul 1901 - 10 Apr 1904: | Commandant, Nikolai Military Academy |
| 10 Apr 1904 - 18 Oct 1905: | Minister of Education |
| 18 Oct 1905 - 26 Oct 1905: | Attached to the Ministry of War |
| 26 Oct 1905 - 3 Apr 1909: | Deputy Commanding General, Moscow Military District |
| 24 Apr 1906 - 3 Apr 1909: | Commanding General, XVII. Army Corps |
| 6 Dec 1907: | Promoted to *General of Infantry* |
| 3 Apr 1909 - 1917: | Member of the Military Council |

*Major-General of Naval Engineers* Nikolai Konstantinovich **Glazyrin** (? - ?)
| | |
|---|---|
| ?: | Promoted to *Major-General of Naval Engineers* |
| 1894 - Oct 1895: | Chief Inspector of Shipbuilding |

*General of Infantry* Nikolai Ivanovich **Glebov** (5 Dec 1848 - ?)
| | |
|---|---|
| 31 Oct 1899: | Promoted to *Major-General* |
| 31 Oct 1899 - 18 Jul 1905: | Commander, 1st Brigade, 14th Infantry Division |
| 18 Jul 1905 - 19 Mar 1906: | Commander, 3rd Rifle Division |
| 19 Mar 1906 - 5 Dec 1911: | Commander, 20th Infantry Division |
| 6 Dec 1906: | Promoted to *Lieutenant-General* |
| 5 Dec 1911: | Promoted to *General of Infantry* |
| 5 Dec 1911: | Retired |

*Major-General* Pyotr Grigoryevich **Glebov** (16 Dec 1847 - ?)
| | |
|---|---|
| 12 Nov 1903 - 1906: | Commandant of Helsingfors |
| 6 Dec 1904: | Promoted to *Major-General* |

*Major-General* Pyotr Genrikhovich **Glindeman** (28 Jan 1854 - 25 Sep 1915)
| | |
|---|---|
| 22 Mar 1915: | Promoted to *Major-General* |
| 22 Mar 1915 - 25 Sep 1915: | Chief of Archives, Main Intendant Directorate |

*Lieutenant-General of the Admiralty* Pavel Konstantinovich **Glinka** (12 Jan 1844 - 1902)
| | |
|---|---|
| 1887 - 1896: | Judge, Kronstadt Naval Court |
| 1895: | Promoted to *Major-General of the Admiralty* |
| 1896 - 5 Mar 1901: | Chairman, Sevastopol Naval District Court |
| 5 Mar 1901: | Promoted to *Lieutenant-General of the Admiralty* |
| 5 Mar 1901: | Retired |

*General of Infantry* Boris Grigoryevich **Glinka-Mavrin** (1810 - 13 Mar 1895)
| | |
|---|---|
| 17 Aug 1849 - 15 Jan 1850: | Chief of Staff, IV. Army Corps |
| 26 Aug 1849: | Promoted to *Major-General* |
| 15 Jan 1850 - 28 Sep 1854: | Chief of Staff, St. Petersburg Military District |
| 28 Sep 1854 - 17 Jul 1856: | Chief of Staff, Guards Reserve Corps |
| 26 Aug 1856: | Promoted to *General-Adjutant* |
| 26 Aug 1856 - 12 Sep 1856: | Deputy Inspector of Riflemen |
| 12 Sep 1856 - 21 Feb 1867: | Chief of Staff, Inspector of Riflemen |

| | |
|---|---|
| 30 Aug 1857: | Promoted to *Lieutenant-General* |
| 21 Feb 1867 - 16 Apr 1872: | Commanding General, Kazan Military District |
| 20 Apr 1869: | Promoted to *General of Infantry* |
| 16 Apr 1872 - 13 Mar 1895: | Member of the Military Council |

*Major-General* Antony Viktorovich **Glinsky** (14 May 1847 - 1918)

| | |
|---|---|
| 7 May 1901 - 1905: | Commandant, Simbirsk Garrison |
| 1905: | Promoted to *Major-General* |
| 1905: | Retired |
| 1 Jun 1916 - 24 Jul 1917: | Recalled; Commander, 214th Reserve Infantry Regiment |
| 24 Jul 1917: | Retired |

*Lieutenant-General* Iosif Aloizovich **Glinsky** (2 Mar 1848 - ?)

| | |
|---|---|
| 31 Mar 1903: | Promoted to *Major-General* |
| 31 Mar 1903 - 20 Feb 1910: | Commander, 1st Brigade, 35th Infantry Division |
| 20 Feb 1910: | Promoted to *Lieutenant-General* |
| 20 Feb 1910: | Retired |

*Lieutenant-General* Nikolai Sergeyevich **Glinsky** (14 Nov 1858 - ?)

| | |
|---|---|
| 9 Mar 1901 - 26 Apr 1905: | At the disposal of the Commander, Kwantung Area |
| 6 Dec 1903: | Promoted to *Major-General* |
| 26 Apr 1905 - 13 Nov 1906: | Chief of Logistics, Manchurian Army |
| 13 Nov 1906 - 4 Jun 1910: | Chief of Staff, Fortress Warsaw |
| 27 May 1908 - 31 Aug 1908: | Commander, Brigade, 38th Infantry Division |
| 4 Jun 1910: | Promoted to *Lieutenant-General* |
| 4 Jun 1910 - 31 Dec 1913: | Chief of Staff, Turkestan Military District |
| 31 Dec 1913 - 27 Mar 1915: | Commander, 14th Infantry Division |
| 18 Apr 1915 - 1918: | Inspector of Militias, Southwest Front |

*Major-General* Pavel Vasilyevich **Glinsky** (16 Jan 1851 - ?)

| | |
|---|---|
| 4 Jul 1897 - 30 May 1910: | Intendant, VII. Army Corps |
| 6 Dec 1906: | Promoted to *Major-General* |

*Major-General* Pyotr Fyodorovich **Glinsky** (16 Aug 1848 - ?)

| | |
|---|---|
| 21 Aug 1892 - 1901: | Military Judge, Vilnius Military District Court |
| 6 Dec 1895: | Promoted to *Major-General* |

*Major-General* Sergey Sergeyevich **Glinsky** (13 Jun 1852 - ?)

| | |
|---|---|
| 13 Aug 1905: | Promoted to *Major-General* |
| 13 Aug 1905 - 1906: | Commander of Artillery, Fortress St. Petersburg, Commandant, St. Petersburg Artillery Depot |

*Major-General* Aleksandr Vasilyevich **Globa** (13 Oct 1857 - ?)

| | |
|---|---|
| 11 Oct 1913 - 19 Apr 1915: | Commander, 67th Infantry Regiment |
| 2 Nov 1914: | Promoted to *Major-General* |
| 19 Apr 1915 - 15 Mar 1917: | Commander, Brigade, 4th Siberian Rifle Division |
| 15 Mar 1917 - 1917: | Commander, 76th Infantry Division |

*Major-General* Mikhail Aleksandrovich **Globa** (8 May 1850 - 5 Feb 1908)
14 Jul 1902 - 1906: Attached to the General Staff
26 Nov 1904: Promoted to *Major-General*
1906: Retired

*Lieutenant-General* Pyotr Petrovich **Globa** (17 Jul 1855 - ?)
12 Jun 1901 - 1912: Commander of Gendarmerie, Ryazan Province
13 Apr 1908: Promoted to *Major-General*
1912: Promoted to *Lieutenant-General*
1912: Retired

*Major-General* Konstantin Ivanovich **Globachev** (24 Apr 1870 - 1 Dec 1941)
11 Feb 1915 - 1 Mar 1917: Chief, Department of Public Safety & Order, Petrograd
1 Jan 1916: Promoted to *Major-General*

*Major-General* Nikolai Ivanovich **Globachev** (28 Mar 1869 - 20 Apr 1947)
11 Jul 1910 - 15 May 1915: Commander, 6$^{th}$ Infantry Regiment
11 May 1915: Promoted to *Major-General*
15 May 1915 - 20 Aug 1915: Chief of Staff, Fortress Modlin
20 Aug 1915 - 1918: POW, Germany

*Lieutenant-General* Pyotr Timofeyevich **Glovatsky** (5 Oct 1834 - ?)
24 Mar 1891: Promoted to *Major-General*
24 Mar 1891 - 4 May 1894: Special Assignments General, Kiev Military District
4 May 1894 - 29 Apr 1900: Commander, Kiev Regional Brigade
29 Apr 1900: Promoted to *Lieutenant-General*
29 Apr 1900: Retired

*General of Infantry* Aleksandr Ivanovich **Glukhovsky** (22 Oct 1838 - 1912)
30 Aug 1878: Promoted to *Major-General*
30 Aug 1878 - 30 Aug 1888: Attached to the Chief of the General Staff
30 Aug 1888: Promoted to *Lieutenant-General*
30 Aug 1888 - 1 Jan 1909: Member, Military Academic Committee, General Staff
1 Jan 1909 - 13 Jan 1911: Attached to the Ministry of War
13 Jan 1911: Promoted to *General of Infantry*
13 Jan 1911: Retired

*Major-General* Konstantin Adamovich **Glukhovsky** (28 Nov 1847 - ?)
19 Dec 1899 - 1917: Chief of Chesmensky Invalid Home
14 Apr 1913: Promoted to *Major-General*

*Lieutenant-General* Nikolai Galaktionovich **Glushanovsky** (7 May 1853 - ?)
21 Sep 1905 - 1912: Chief of Amu Darya Department, Turkestan Military District
2 Apr 1906: Promoted to *Major-General*
1912: Promoted to *Lieutenant-General*
1912: Retired

*Major-General* Vladislav-Aleksandr Eduardovich **Glyass** (21 Nov 1864 - 9 Nov 1918)
31 May 1916 - 15 Feb 1917: Commander, Brigade, 24th Infantry Division
22 Oct 1916: Promoted to *Major-General*
15 Feb 1917 - Jan 1918: Commander, 24th Infantry Division

*Lieutenant-General* Dmitry Ivanovich **Gnida** (21 Sep 1859 - ?)
25 Mar 1904 - 22 Dec 1905: Commander, 20th East Siberian Rifle Regiment
4 Jan 1905: Promoted to *Major-General*
22 Dec 1905 - 17 Jun 1906: At the disposal of the Chief of Logistics, Manchurian Army
17 Jun 1906 - 28 Jun 1906: General Staff officer, Far East
28 Jun 1906 - 3 Sep 1907: Deputy Chief of Staff, Omsk Military District
3 Sep 1907 - 5 Jul 1910: Commander, 3rd Siberian Replacement Infantry Brigade
5 Jul 1910: Promoted to *Lieutenant-General*
5 Jul 1910: Retired
1915 - 30 Oct 1915: Recalled; Commander, Brigade, 68th Infantry Division
30 Oct 1915 - 17 Mar 1917: Commander, 43rd Infantry Division
17 Mar 1917 - 1918: Reserve officer, Petrograd Military District

*Lieutenant-General* Ignaty Iosifovich **Gnoinsky** (29 Jun 1859 - ?)
12 Jun 1905 - 3 May 1916: Commander of Gendarmerie, Vilnius Military District
6 Dec 1909: Promoted to *Major-General*
3 May 1916: Promoted to *Lieutenant-General*
3 May 1916: Retired

*Lieutenant-General* Leonid Nikolayevich **Gobyato** (6 Feb 1875 - 21 May 1915)
26 Jul 1914 - Jan 1915: Commander, 2nd Battalion, 35th Artillery Brigade
14 Nov 1914: Promoted to *Major-General*
Jan 1915 - 31 Mar 1915: Commander, 32nd Artillery Brigade
31 Mar 1915 - 21 May 1915: Commander, 35th Artillery Brigade
8 Nov 1915: Posthumously promoted to *Lieutenant-General*

*Lieutenant-General* Leonard Kaetanovich **Godlevsky** (6 Nov 1832 - ?)
15 Apr 1899: Promoted to *Major-General*
15 Apr 1899 - 1907: Special Assignments General, Kazan Military District
6 Dec 1906: Promoted to *Lieutenant-General*

*General of Artillery* Dmitry Antonovich **Gofman** (1 Jun 1828 - 7 Jan 1907)
18 Jun 1885: Promoted to *Major-General*
18 Jun 1885 - 7 Oct 1893: Commander, 4th Artillery Brigade
7 Oct 1893 - 19 Mar 1901: Commander of Artillery, VIII. Army Corps
14 Nov 1894: Promoted to *Lieutenant-General*
19 Mar 1901 - 7 Jan 1907: Member, Committee for Wounded Veterans
6 Dec 1906: Promoted to *General of Artillery*

*Major-General* Genrikh Ernestovich **Gofman** (16 Jul 1850 - ?)
17 Feb 1902: Promoted to *Major-General*
17 Feb 1902 - 1907: Commander, 5th Reserve Artillery Brigade

*Major-General* Vladimir Emiliyevich **Gofman** (23 Jan 1858 - 9 Jun 1929)
| | |
|---|---|
| ? - 1914: | Chief of Gendarmerie, Volyn Province |
| 1914: | Promoted to *Major-General* |
| 1914: | Retired |
| 4 Aug 1914 - 9 Mar 1916: | Recalled; Commandant, HQ Office, C-in-C, Southwestern Front |
| 9 Mar 1916 - 1917: | Reserve officer, Petrograd Military District |

*Major-General* Ivan Almaskhanovich **Gogoberidze** (11 Jan 1858 - 2 Aug 1916)
| | |
|---|---|
| 3 Apr 1915 - 2 Aug 1916: | Commander, 3rd Siberian Rifle Artillery Brigade |
| 22 Jul 1915: | Promoted to *Major-General* |

*Lieutenant-General* Mikhail Grigoryevich **Golembatovsky** (30 Aug 1852 - 9 Oct 1907)
| | |
|---|---|
| 12 Oct 1902: | Promoted to *Major-General* |
| 12 Oct 1902 - 2 Jun 1904: | Commander, 2nd Brigade, 34th Infantry Division |
| 2 Jun 1904 - 11 Aug 1906: | Commander, 2nd Brigade, 15th Infantry Division |
| 11 Aug 1906 - Nov 1906: | Commander, 54th Replacement Infantry Brigade |
| 14 Nov 1906: | Promoted to *Lieutenant-General* |
| 14 Nov 1906: | Retired |

*Major-General* Iosif Ivanovich **Golembiovsky** (1869 - 1912)
| | |
|---|---|
| 27 May 1907 - 1912: | Commander, 1st Telegraph Regiment |
| 1912: | Promoted to *Major-General* |

*Major-General* Count Aleksandr Vasilyevich **Golenishchev-Kutuzov** (19 Mar 1846 - 23 Aug 1897)
| | |
|---|---|
| 20 Apr 1886 - 14 Mar 1892: | Attached to the Kaiser of Germany |
| 30 Aug 1887: | Promoted to *Major-General* |
| 14 Mar 1892 - 7 Jun 1893: | Court Marshal to the Tsar |
| 7 Jun 1893 - 23 Aug 1897: | Member of the Tsar's retinue |
| 1896: | Promoted to *General-Adjutant* |

*Major-General* Fyodor Ilich **Golenkin** (24 Jan 1871 - 8 Aug 1936)
| | |
|---|---|
| 6 Dec 1916: | Promoted to *Major-General* |
| 6 Dec 1916 - Jan 1918: | Director of Operations, 2nd Rear Area District, Northern Front |

*Major-General* Konstantin Konstantinovich **Goleyevsky** (23 Apr 1850 - ?)
| | |
|---|---|
| 14 May 1898 - 13 Jun 1905: | Deputy Commander of Engineers, Warsaw Military District |
| 3 Jul 1898: | Promoted to *Major-General* |
| 13 Jun 1905 - Dec 1905: | Commander of Engineers, Vilnius Military District |

*Major-General* Maksimilian Nikolayevich **Goleyevsky** (19 Oct 1862 - 18 Jun 1931)
| | |
|---|---|
| 27 Nov 1908 - 1917: | Commandant, Odessa Military School |
| 1 Sep 1910: | Promoted to *Major-General* |

*General of Artillery* Andrey Andreyevich **Golitsyn** (25 Nov 1865 - ?)
| | |
|---|---|
| 3 Sep 1904 - 23 Apr 1910: | Commander, 1$^{st}$ Reserve Artillery Brigade |
| 2 Apr 1906: | Promoted to *Major-General* |
| 23 Apr 1910: | Promoted to *Lieutenant-General* |
| 23 Apr 1910 - 31 Jul 1910: | Commander of Artillery, XXI. Army Corps |
| 31 Jul 1910 - 20 Aug 1913: | Inspector of Artillery, XXI. Army Corps |
| 20 Aug 1913 - 30 Aug 1914: | Commander of Artillery, Kiev Military District |
| 30 Aug 1914 - 1917: | Chief of Artillery Logistics, Southwestern Front |
| 6 Dec 1916: | Promoted to *General of Artillery* |

*General of Cavalry* Prince Dmitry Borisovich **Golitsyn** (5 Nov 1851 - 29 Mar 1920)
| | |
|---|---|
| 17 Nov 1889 - Mar 1917: | Chief of the Imperial Hunt to the Tsar |
| 30 Aug 1891: | Promoted to *Major-General* |
| 6 Dec 1899: | Promoted to *Lieutenant-General* |
| 1901: | Promoted to *General-Adjutant* |
| 6 Dec 1912: | Promoted to *General of Cavalry* |
| 25 May 1913 - 1917: | Member of the Board, Main Department of State Breeding |

*General of Infantry* Prince Grigory Sergeyevich **Golitsyn** (20 Dec 1838 - 28 Mar 1907)
| | |
|---|---|
| 16 Apr 1872 - 30 Aug 1876: | Commander, Finland Life Guards Regiment |
| 30 Aug 1873: | Promoted to *Major-General* |
| 30 Aug 1876 - 5 Jan 1885: | Military Governor of the Ural Region, Ataman, Ural Cossack Army |
| Sep 1880: | Acting Governor-General of Orenburg, Acting Commanding General, Orenburg Military District |
| 26 Feb 1883: | Promoted to *Lieutenant-General* |
| 5 Jan 1885 - 1 Jan 1893: | Appointed to the Senate |
| 1 Jan 1893 - 12 Dec 1896: | Member of the State Council |
| 14 May 1896: | Promoted to *General of Infantry* |
| 12 Dec 1896 - 1 Jan 1905: | Commanding General, Caucasus Military District, Ataman, Caucasus Cossack Army |
| 2 Mar 1897: | Promoted to *General-Adjutant* |

*General of Cavalry* Prince Mikhail Mikhailovich **Golitsyn** (13 Jun 1840 - 1918)
| | |
|---|---|
| 2 Dec 1891: | Promoted to *Major-General* |
| 2 Dec 1891 - 31 Jan 1900: | Special Assignments General to the Governor-General of Moscow |
| 2 Jul 1901 - 24 Mar 1909: | Court Chamberlain to Grand Duke Vladimir Alexandrovich |
| 6 Dec 1900: | Promoted to *Lieutenant-General* |
| 24 Mar 1909 - 1917: | Court Chamberlain to Grand Duchess Maria Pavlovna |
| 6 Dec 1912: | Promoted to *General of Cavalry* |

*Major-General* Vladimir Alekseyevich **Golitsyn** (22 Apr 1865 - ?)
| | |
|---|---|
| 6 Dec 1912: | Promoted to *Major-General* |
| 6 Dec 1912 - 31 May 1913: | Commander of Engineers, Fortress Mikhailov |

| | |
|---|---|
| 31 May 1913 - 16 Jun 1914: | Commander of Engineers, Fortress Brest-Litovsk |
| 16 Jun 1914 - 22 Jul 1915: | Commander of Engineers, Fortress Mikhailov |
| 22 Jul 1915 - 13 Sep 1916: | Deputy Inspector of Engineers, Caucasus Military District |
| 13 Sep 1916 - 27 Apr 1917: | Reserve officer, Caucasus Military District |
| 27 Apr 1917 - 8 Sep 1917: | Commander of Engineers, Caucasus Army |
| 8 Sep 1917 - 1918: | Commander of Engineers, Caucasus Front |

*Major-General* Aleksandr Nikolayevich **Golitsynsky** (30 Aug 1864 - 2 Feb 1931)

| | |
|---|---|
| 28 Mar 1911 - Oct 1915: | Commander, 62$^{nd}$ Infantry Regiment |
| 30 Jul 1915: | Promoted to *Major-General* |
| Oct 1915 - 4 Jan 1916: | Commander, Brigade, 74$^{th}$ Infantry Division |
| 4 Jan 1916 - 24 Jan 1916: | Reserve officer, Kiev Military District |
| 24 Jan 1916 - 1917: | Special Purposes General, Moscow Military District |
| 1917 - 8 Oct 1917: | Commandant of Moscow |
| 8 Oct 1917: | Dismissed |

*Lieutenant-General* Oskar Eduardovich **Golmblat** (14 Aug 1843 - ?)

| | |
|---|---|
| 11 Oct 1883 - 5 Jul 1888: | Military Prosecutor, Ministry of War |
| 30 Aug 1887: | Promoted to *Major-General* |
| 5 Jul 1888 - 22 Oct 1892: | Deputy Chief Prosecutor, Ministry of War, Deputy Chief of the Main Military Justice Directorate |
| 22 Oct 1892 - 22 Aug 1894: | At the disposal of the Minister of War |
| 22 Aug 1894 - 1898: | Chairman of the Military Tribunal, Caucasus Military District |
| 25 Nov 1897: | Promoted to *Lieutenant-General* |

*Lieutenant-General* Nikolai Gustavovich **Golmdorf** (17 Oct 1842 - ?)

| | |
|---|---|
| 15 Oct 1895: | Promoted to *Major-General* |
| 15 Oct 1895 - 1 Apr 1896: | Commander, 30$^{th}$ Artillery Brigade |
| 1 Apr 1896 - 9 Apr 1901: | Commander, 22$^{nd}$ Artillery Brigade |
| 9 Apr 1901 - 7 Dec 1905: | Commander of Artillery, II. Army Corps |
| 6 Dec 1903: | Promoted to *Lieutenant-General* |

*General of Infantry* Vladimir Petrovich **Golokhvastov** (8 Aug 1833 - 24 Nov 1905)

| | |
|---|---|
| 8 May 1885: | Promoted to *Major-General* |
| 8 May 1885 - 27 Mar 1886: | Commander, 2$^{nd}$ Brigade, 11$^{th}$ Infantry Division |
| 27 Mar 1886 - 2 Nov 1892: | Commander, 1$^{st}$ Brigade, 31$^{st}$ Infantry Division |
| 2 Nov 1892 - 9 Jan 1900: | Commander, 6$^{th}$ Infantry Division |
| 14 Nov 1894: | Promoted to *Lieutenant-General* |
| 9 Jan 1900: | Promoted to *General of Infantry* |
| 9 Jan 1900: | Retired |

*Major-General* Vasily Ivanovich **Goloshchapov** (20 Feb 1865 - Oct 1918)

| | |
|---|---|
| 6 Jun 1914 - 27 Aug 1914: | Commander, 2nd Brigade, 2nd Consolidated Cossack Division |
| 28 Aug 1914 - 29 Mar 1916: | Commander, Brigade, 1$^{st}$ Terek Cossack Division |
| 10 Mar 1915: | Promoted to *Major-General* |

29 Mar 1916 - 1917: Commander, Terek Cossack Division

*Major-General* Vladimir Nikolayevich **Goloshchapov** (1 Jun 1849 - ?)
14 Mar 1895 - 19 May 1898: Commander, 21st Dragoon Regiment
19 May 1898: Promoted to *Major-General*
19 May 1898 - 1 Jan 1907: Commander, 1st Brigade, Caucasus Cavalry Division

*Major-General* Vsevolod Petrovich **Golosov** (26 Aug 1858 - 1913)
1 Dec 1903 - 20 Nov 1907: Commander, 7th Grenadier Regiment
20 Nov 1907 - Dec 1908: Deputy Chief of Staff, Omsk Military District
6 Dec 1907: Promoted to *Major-General*
Dec 1908: Retired

*Lieutenant-General of the Fleet* Dmitry Andreyevich **Golov** (3 Feb 1861 - ?)
18 May 1909 - 19 Oct 1911: Deputy Chief of Naval Mechanical Engineers
6 Dec 1910: Promoted to *Major-General of the Fleet*
19 Oct 1911 - 21 Jul 1914: Deputy Chief of Mechanical Section, Main Shipbuilding Directorate
21 Jul 1914 - 29 Feb 1916: Attached to Baltic Fleet
29 Feb 1916: Promoted to *Lieutenant-General of the Fleet*
29 Feb 1916: Retired

*Lieutenant-General* Aleksei Dmitrievich **Golovachev** (21 Oct 1858 - ?)
22 Apr 1907 - 3 Jul 1908: Commander, 23rd Artillery Brigade
31 May 1907: Promoted to *Major-General*
3 Jul 1908 - 25 Jul 1910: Commander, Life Guards 1st Artillery Brigade
25 Jul 1910 - 22 Apr 1917: Inspector of Artillery, XXII. Army Corps
30 Jul 1911: Promoted to *Lieutenant-General*

*Major-General* Sergey Aleksandrovich **Golovan** (20 Sep 1872 - 8 Aug 1927)
13 Sep 1914 - 1917: Military Attaché, Switzerland
6 Dec 1915: Promoted to *Major-General*

*General of Infantry* Nikolai Mikhailovich **Golovin** (28 Apr 1836 - 20 Dec 1911)
23 Aug 1878 - 9 Jul 1887: Deputy Chief of Troop Movements (Railroads & Waterways), General Staff
30 Aug 1880: Promoted to *Major-General*
6 Oct 1884 - 7 May 1892: Alternate Board Member, Military Department, Ministry of Railways
9 Jul 1887 - 7 Dec 1898: Chief of Troop Movements Department, General Staff
7 Dec 1889 - 7 Dec 1898: Member, Military Technical Department Council, Ministry of Railways
30 Aug 1894: Promoted to *Lieutenant-General*
7 Dec 1898 - 3 Jan 1906: Member of the Military Council
6 Dec 1904: Promoted to *General of Infantry*
3 Jan 1906: Retired

*Lieutenant-General* Nikolai Nikolayevich **Golovin** (4 Dec 1875 - 10 Jan 1944)
| | |
|---|---|
| 3 Nov 1914 - 24 Oct 1915: | Quartermaster-General, 9th Army |
| 29 Jan 1915: | Promoted to *Major-General* |
| 24 Oct 1915 - 17 Apr 1917: | Chief of Staff, 7th Army |
| 17 Apr 1917 - 15 Oct 1917: | Deputy Chief of Staff, Romanian Front |
| 16 Aug 1917: | Promoted to *Lieutenant-General* |
| 15 Oct 1917 - 1918: | At the disposal of the Supreme Commander-in-Chief |

*Major-General of the Admiralty* Ivan Petrovich **Golovkin** (7 Sep 1865 - ?)
| | |
|---|---|
| 1 Jan 1907 - 1916: | Senior Clerk, 5th Class, Main Naval Staff |
| 14 Apr 1913: | Promoted to *Major-General of the Admiralty* |
| 1916 - 1917: | Special Assignments General, Ministry of the Navy |
| 1917: | Retired |

*Major-General* Timofey Davidovich **Golovkov** (19 Jan 1848 - ?)
| | |
|---|---|
| 21 Jun 1899: | Promoted to *Major-General* |
| 21 Jun 1899 - 1903: | Deputy Military Governor of Kars Province |

*Major-General* Konstantin Aleksandrovich **Goltgoyer** (4 Jan 1865 - 20 Mar 1933)
| | |
|---|---|
| 28 Jun 1910: | Promoted to *Major-General* |
| 28 Jun 1910 - 25 Aug 1910: | Commander, Life Guards 4th Rifle Battalion |
| 25 Aug 1910 - 22 Apr 1915: | Commander, Life Guards 4th Rifle Regiment |
| 22 Apr 1915 - 21 Aug 1916: | Commander, 1st Brigade, 1st Guards Infantry Division |
| 21 Aug 1916 - 9 Apr 1917: | Commander, 2nd Guards Infantry Division |

*Major-General* Sergey Aleksandrovich **Goltgoyer** (29 Dec 1866 - 15 Feb 1930)
| | |
|---|---|
| 4 Aug 1911 - 1917: | Inspector of Students, Imperial Law School |
| 6 Dec 1915: | Promoted to *Major-General* |

*Major-General* Aleksandr Aleksandrovich **Golub** (8 Aug 1839 - ?)
| | |
|---|---|
| 10 Jun 1879 - 1896: | Military Judge, Vilnius Military District Court |
| 30 Aug 1889: | Promoted to *Major-General* |

*Lieutenant-General* Fyodor Fyodorovich **Golubev** (1 Nov 1835 - 19 Nov 1901)
| | |
|---|---|
| Oct 1880 - 24 Aug 1884: | Commander, Infantry Regiment |
| 1881: | Promoted to *Major-General* |
| 24 Aug 1884 - 16 Apr 1889: | Commander, 2nd Brigade, 30th Infantry Division |
| 16 Apr 1889 - 30 Nov 1892: | Commander, 2nd brigade, 3rd Grenadier Division |
| 30 Nov 1892 - 17 Dec 1897: | Commander, 5th Infantry Division |
| 30 Aug 1894: | Promoted to *Lieutenant-General* |
| 17 Dec 1897: | Retired |

*Major-General* Nikolai Grigoryevich **Golubev** (19 Aug 1862 - 1914)
| | |
|---|---|
| 3 Jan 1913 - 1914: | Military Judge, Warsaw Military District Court |
| 14 Apr 1913: | Promoted to *Major-General* |

*Major-General* Yevgeny Petrovich **Golubkov** (12 Aug 1852 - ?)
| | |
|---|---|
| 3 Jul 1902: | Promoted to *Major-General* |

3 Jul 1902 - Sep 1907:          Commander, 1st Brigade, 1st Cavalry Division
Sep 1907:                       Retired

*Major-General* Vladimir Mikhailovich **Golubov** (2 Feb 1848 - 3 Aug 1911)
27 Dec 1902 - 1 Dec 1908:       Commander, Skulyany Borderguard Brigade
1 Dec 1908:                     Promoted to *Major-General*
1 Dec 1908:                     Retired

*Major-General of Naval Artillery* Vladimir Lvovich **Golubtsov** (18 Mar 1865 - ?)
26 Nov 1912 - 1917:             Commander of Naval Artillery, Port of Kronstadt
14 Apr 1913:                    Promoted to *Major-General of Naval Artillery*

*Major-General* Pavel Vasilyevich **Golubyatnikov** (14 Jan 1855 - ?)
4 Aug 1898 - 26 Nov 1912:       Deputy Commander of Engineers, Irkutsk Military
                                District
10 Apr 1911:                    Promoted to *Major-General*
26 Nov 1912 - 26 Oct 1915:      Deputy Chief of Troop Billeting, Kiev Military District
26 Oct 1915 - 1917:             Chief of Troop Billeting, Kiev Military District

*Major-General* Andrey Yuryevich **Goncharenko** (27 Aug 1856 - 18 Jan 1920)
1 Jan 1899 - 26 Nov 1910:       Section Chief, Main Artillery Directorate
31 May 1907:                    Promoted to *Major-General*
26 Nov 1910 - 6 Apr 1912:       Transferred to the reserve
6 Apr 1912 - 20 Dec 1916:       Deputy Commander of Artillery, Odessa Military
                                District
20 Dec 1916 - 1917:             Commander of Artillery, Odessa Military District

*Lieutenant-General* Mikhail Ivanovich **Goncharenko** (5 Nov 1861 - Oct 1917)
3 Jul 1906:                     Promoted to *Major-General*
3 Jul 1906 - 1 Dec 1908:        Chief of Staff, Orenburg Cossack Army
1 Dec 1908 - 1917:              Special Purposes General, Directorate-General of
                                Military Schools
6 Dec 1912:                     Promoted to *Lieutenant-General*

*Major-General* Fyodor Osipovich **Goncharov** (17 Feb 1830 - ?)
12 Oct 1885:                    Promoted to *Major-General*
12 Oct 1885 - 26 Jan 1886:      Commander, 2nd Brigade, 5th Infantry Division
26 Jan 1886 - 2 May 1894:       Commander, 2nd Brigade, 36th Infantry Division
2 May 1894 - 9 Oct 1899:        Commander, 1st Brigade, 36th Infantry Division

*General of Infantry* Stepan Osipovich **Goncharov** (28 Mar 1831 - 8 Jun 1912)
18 Dec 1874 - 19 Dec 1884:      Chief of Staff, Kharkov Military District
30 Aug 1878:                    Promoted to *Major-General*
19 Dec 1884 - 18 Jul 1887:      At the disposal of the Chief of the General Staff
18 Jul 1887 - 16 Mar 1893:      Commandant of Fortress Sveaborg
30 Aug 1888:                    Promoted to *Lieutenant-General*
16 Mar 1893 - 27 Nov 1898:      Deputy Commanding General, Finland Military District,
                                Deputy Governor-General of Finland

| | |
|---|---|
| 31 Jan 1897 - 12 Oct 1898: | Acting Governor-General of Finland |
| 27 Nov 1898 - 8 Jun 1912: | Member of the Military Council |
| 9 Apr 1900: | Promoted to *General of Infantry* |

*Major-General* Maksimilian Mikhailovich **Goraysky** (12 Oct 1857 - ?)
| | |
|---|---|
| 11 Oct 1908 - 12 Jul 1916: | Commander, 9th Siberian Rifle Regiment |
| 12 Jul 1916: | Promoted to *Major-General* |
| 12 Jul 1916 - 26 Sep 1916: | Reserve officer, Petrograd Military District |
| 26 Sep 1916: | Dismissed |

*Lieutenant-General* Aleksandr Yevstafyevich **Gorbachevich** (2 Aug 1866 - ?)
| | |
|---|---|
| 23 Nov 1909: | Promoted to *Major-General* |
| 23 Nov 1909 - 25 Jul 1910: | Commander, 37th Artillery Brigade |
| 25 Jul 1910 - 21 Feb 1915: | Commander, 7th Artillery Brigade |
| 21 Feb 1915 - 29 Apr 1917: | Commander of Artillery, V. Army Corps |
| 6 Dec 1915: | Promoted to *Lieutenant-General* |

*Major-General* Nikolai Aleksandrovich **Gorbatovsky** (7 Oct 1841 - ?)
| | |
|---|---|
| 20 Nov 1898: | Promoted to *Major-General* |
| 20 Nov 1898 - 2 Feb 1902: | Commander, 2nd Brigade, 40th Infantry Division |

*General of Infantry* Vladimir Nikolayevich **Gorbatovsky** (26 May 1851 - 30 Jul 1924)
| | |
|---|---|
| 22 Feb 1904: | Promoted to *Major-General* |
| 22 Feb 1904 - 22 Mar 1905: | Commander, 1st Brigade, 7th East Siberian Rifle Division |
| 22 Mar 1905 - 30 Apr 1905: | Commander, 2nd Brigade, 1st Grenadier Division |
| 30 Apr 1905 - 8 May 1909: | Commandant, Alekseyev Military School |
| 6 Dec 1908: | Promoted to *Lieutenant-General* |
| 8 May 1909 - 9 May 1914: | Commander, 3rd Grenadier Division |
| 9 May 1914 - 12 Jun 1915: | Commanding General, XIX. Army Corps |
| 18 Aug 1914: | Promoted to *General of Infantry* |
| 12 Jun 1915 - 20 Aug 1915: | C-in-C, 13th Army |
| 20 Aug 1915 - 20 Mar 1916: | C-in-C, 12th Army |
| 20 Mar 1916 - 12 Dec 1916: | C-in-C, 6th Army |
| 12 Dec 1916 - 1 Apr 1917: | C-in-C, 10th Army |
| 1 Apr 1917: | Transferred to the reserve |

*Major-General* Nikolai Matveyevich **Gorbenkov** (5 May 1838 - 27 Dec 1906)
| | |
|---|---|
| 12 Feb 1889 - 3 Feb 1894: | Deputy Commander of Engineers, Moscow Military District |
| 30 Aug 1889: | Promoted to *Major-General* |
| 3 Feb 1894 - 18 Mar 1897: | Deputy Commander of Engineers, Warsaw Military District |
| 18 Mar 1897 - 1900: | Commandant of Dvinsk |
| 1900: | Retired |

*Major-General* Nikolai Nikolayevich **Gorbunov** (8 Oct 1865 - 27 Aug 1914)
| | |
|---|---|
| Jan 1906 - 27 Aug 1914: | Company Commander, Life Guards Grenadier |

| | Regiment |
|---|---|
| 26 Jun 1916: | Posthumously promoted to *Major-General* |

*Lieutenant-General* Aleksandr Nikolayevich **Gorchakov** (19 Feb 1856 - ?)
| | |
|---|---|
| 18 Jun 1904: | Promoted to *Major-General* |
| 18 Jun 1904 - 9 Feb 1914: | Commander, 2nd Brigade, Caucasus Cavalry Division |
| 9 Feb 1914: | Promoted to *Lieutenant-General* |
| 9 Feb 1914: | Retired |

*General of Infantry* Prince Nikolai Pavlovich **Gorchakov** (9 Mar 1831 - 2 Sep 1918)
| | |
|---|---|
| 29 Nov 1879: | Promoted to *Major-General* |
| 29 Nov 1879 - 9 Feb 1894: | Special Assignments General, Odessa Military District |
| 1887 - 1888: | Chief of Odessa Military Hospital |
| 9 Feb 1894 - 20 Oct 1899: | Commander, 53rd Reserve Infantry Brigade |
| 14 May 1896: | Promoted to *Lieutenant-General* |
| 20 Oct 1899: | Promoted to *General of Infantry* |
| 20 Oct 1899: | Retired |

*Major-General* Ivan Ivanovich **Gordeyev** (4 Jan 1855 - ?)
| | |
|---|---|
| 29 Oct 1912: | Promoted to *Major-General* |
| 29 Oct 1912 - 27 Jan 1913: | Commander, 2nd Brigade, 4th Siberian Rifle Division |
| 27 Jan 1913 - 5 Sep 1914: | Commander, 2nd Brigade, 45th Infantry Division |
| 5 Sep 1914: | Retired |
| 9 Apr 1916 - 1917: | Recalled; Special Purposes General, Kazan Military District |

*Major-General* Fyodor Ivanovich **Gorelov** (11 Aug 1867 - 11 Jun 1931)
| | |
|---|---|
| 1914 - 12 May 1916: | Commander, 70th Artillery Brigade |
| 3 Mar 1915: | Promoted to *Major-General* |
| 12 May 1916 - 18 Jun 1917: | Inspector of Artillery, XIV. Army Corps |
| 18 Jun 1917 - 9 Oct 1917: | Commander of Artillery, Don Army |

*Major-General* Konstantin Georgievich **Gorelov** (3 Nov 1854 - ?)
| | |
|---|---|
| 25 Jan 1911 - 1914: | Deputy Commander, 19th Artillery Brigade |
| 1914: | Retired |
| 29 Mar 1915 - 25 Sep 1916: | Recalled; Reserve officer, Kiev Military District |
| 29 Mar 1915: | Promoted to *Major-General* |
| 25 Sep 1916 - 1917: | Commander, 64th Artillery Brigade |

*Lieutenant-General* Mikhail Georgiyevich **Gorelov** (12 Jul 1859 - ?)
| | |
|---|---|
| 9 Aug 1908 - 19 Feb 1914: | Commander, 10th Grenadier Regiment |
| 19 Feb 1914: | Promoted to *Major-General* |
| 19 Feb 1914 - 17 Oct 1915: | Commander, 2nd Brigade, 14th Infantry Division |
| 17 Oct 1915 - 19 Jun 1916: | Commander, 36th Infantry Division |
| 19 Jun 1916 - 23 Aug 1916: | Reserve officer, Dvinsk Military District |
| 23 Aug 1916 - 21 Aug 1917: | Commander, Vyborg Fortress Infantry Brigade |
| 21 Aug 1917: | Promoted to *Lieutenant-General* |
| 21 Aug 1917: | Dismissed |

*General of Infantry* Aleksandr Dmitrievich **Goremykin** (16 Jan 1832 - 8 Jun 1904)
| | |
|---|---|
| 1 Jan 1866 - 5 Oct 1869: | Governor of Kamenetz-Podolsk Prison |
| 30 Aug 1869: | Promoted to *Major-General* |
| 1 Nov 1869 - 31 Aug 1876: | Chief of Staff, Odessa Military District |
| 31 Aug 1876 - 9 Apr 1889: | Commander, 15th Infantry Division |
| 30 Aug 1879: | Promoted to *Lieutenant-General* |
| 9 Apr 1889 - 26 May 1889: | Commanding General, VIII. Army Corps |
| 26 May 1889 - 9 Apr 1900: | Commanding General, Irkutsk Military District, Governor-General of Irkutsk |
| 30 Aug 1893: | Promoted to *General of Infantry* |
| 9 Apr 1900 - 8 Jun 1904: | Member of the State Council |

*Major-General* Konstantin Yefimovich **Goretsky** (3 Dec 1870 - 5 Mar 1947)
| | |
|---|---|
| 26 Oct 1911 - 1918: | Deputy Chief Intendant, Ministry of War |
| 1912: | Promoted to *Major-General* |

*Lieutenant-General* Tarasy Grigoryevich **Gorkovenko** (5 Jul 1859 - ?)
| | |
|---|---|
| 16 Jan 1914: | Promoted to *Major-General* |
| 16 Jan 1914 - 1916: | Commandant of Moscow |
| 1916 - 2 Apr 1917: | Reserve officer, Moscow Military District |
| 2 Apr 1917: | Promoted to *Lieutenant-General* |
| 2 Apr 1917: | Retired |

*Major-General* Nikolai Ivanovich **Gorlyavil** (26 Oct 1850 - 1910)
| | |
|---|---|
| 9 Aug 1908 - 1910: | At the disposal of the Main Engineering Directorate |
| 1909: | Promoted to *Major-General* |

*Major-General* Fyodor Dmitriyevich **Gornostayev** (4 Jan 1869 - ?)
| | |
|---|---|
| 1915 - 25 Feb 1916: | Commander, 8th Siberian Rifle Regiment |
| 24 May 1915: | Promoted to *Major-General* |
| 25 Feb 1916 - 1917: | Commander, Brigade, 123rd Infantry Division |

*Major-General* Mikhail Petrovich **Gorokh** (5 Aug 1856 - 1913)
| | |
|---|---|
| 9 Nov 1894 - 1913: | Attached to the Caucasus Military District |
| 1913: | Promoted to *Major-General* |

*Major-General* Aleksandr Nikolayevich **Gorsky** (30 Jan 1865 - ?)
| | |
|---|---|
| 28 Mar 1914 - 9 Dec 1914: | Commander, 17th Infantry Regiment |
| 9 Dec 1914: | Promoted to *Major-General* |
| 9 Dec 1914: | Retired |
| 13 Jun 1916 - 1 May 1917: | Recalled; Commander, 161st Reserve Infantry Regiment |
| 1 May 1917 - 2 Sep 1917: | Reserve officer, Petrograd Military District |
| 2 Sep 1917 - 1918: | Commander, 14th Replacement Infantry Brigade |

*Major-General* Iosif Ivanovich **Gorsky** (24 Feb 1850 - 1905)
| | |
|---|---|
| 11 May 1901: | Promoted to *Major-General* |
| 11 May 1901 - 28 Jun 1901: | Commander, 1st Brigade, 5th Infantry Division |
| 28 Jun 1901 - 30 Nov 1904: | Commander, 2nd Brigade, 7th Infantry Division |

30 Nov 1904 - Jun 1905: Commander, 1ˢᵗ Caucasus Rifle Brigade

*Lieutenant-General* Dmitry Andreyevich **Goryachev** (2 Jun 1853 - ?)
10 Jan 1908: Promoted to *Major-General*
10 Jan 1908 - 2 Feb 1913: Commander, 5ᵗʰ Siberian Rifle Artillery Brigade
2 Feb 1913 - 23 Apr 1915: Inspector of Artillery, IV. Siberian Army Corps
1913: Promoted to *Lieutenant-General*
23 Apr 1915 - 12 Sep 1915: Reserve officer, Dvinsk Military District
12 Sep 1915: Retired

*General of Cavalry* Aleksei Alekseyevich **Goryaynov** (15 Apr 1840 - 7 Oct 1917)
12 Oct 1885: Promoted to *Major-General*
12 Oct 1885 - 2 Jan 1890: Attached to the Ministry of War
2 Jan 1890 - 9 Jun 1895: Governor of Penza
9 Jun 1895 - 1914: Member, Council of Ministry of Internal Affairs
9 Jun 1895 - 1917: Honorary Trustee, Board of Trustees, Empress Maria Institutions
6 Dec 1895: Promoted to *Lieutenant-General*
16 Jun 1909: Promoted to *General of Cavalry*

*Major-General* Feofil Nikolayevich **Gotovsky** (6 Feb 1845 - ?)
20 Apr 1893 - 24 Apr 1895: Commander, 42ⁿᵈ Dragoon Regiment
24 Apr 1895: Promoted to *Major-General*
24 Apr 1895 - Dec 1899: Commander, 2ⁿᵈ Brigade, 6ᵗʰ Cavalry Division

*Major-General* Vladimir Yurevich **Gotsky-Danilovich** (4 Dec 1842 - ?)
13 Apr 1899: Promoted to *Major-General*
13 Apr 1899 - 18 Aug 1899: Commander, 2ⁿᵈ East Siberian Artillery Brigade
18 Aug 1899 - Nov 1902: Commander, 21ˢᵗ Artillery Brigade
Nov 1902: Retired

*Lieutenant-General* Nikolai Ivanovich **Govorov** (29 Jun 1853 - ?)
24 Feb 1902: Promoted to *Major-General*
24 Feb 1902 - 7 Apr 1903: At the disposal of the Commanding General, Moscow Military District
7 Apr 1903 - 5 Jul 1904: Commander, 1ˢᵗ Brigade, 36ᵗʰ Infantry Division
5 Jul 1904 - 2 Jul 1908: Commander, 1ˢᵗ Brigade, 1ˢᵗ Grenadier Division
2 Jul 1908 - 13 Oct 1908: Commander, 24ᵗʰ Infantry Division
1908: Promoted to *Lieutenant-General*
1908: Retired

*Major-General* Yevgeny Vasilyevich **Govorov** (21 Jan 1867 - 20 Jun 1916)
16 Sep 1915 - 20 Jun 1916: Commander, 183ʳᵈ Infantry Regiment
23 Jul 1916: Posthumously promoted to *Major-General*

*Lieutenant-General* Aleksandr Nikolayevich **Govorukha-Otrok** (25 Aug 1829 - ?)
1 Sep 1865 - 5 Mar 1881: Chief of Fortress Section, Main Artillery Directorate
30 Aug 1878: Promoted to *Major-General*

| | |
|---|---|
| 5 Mar 1881 - 1898: | Member of the Artillery Committee, Main Artillery Directorate |
| 30 Aug 1888: | Promoted to *Lieutenant-General* |

*Major-General* Ivan Iosifovich **Goylevich** (16 Dec 1855 - ?)
| | |
|---|---|
| 21 Jan 1905: | Promoted to *Major-General* |
| 21 Jan 1905 - 11 Apr 1905: | Special Assignments General, 1st Manchurian Army |
| 11 Apr 1905 - 1907: | Special Assignments General to the C-in-C of Forces fighting against Japan |

*Lieutenant-General* Count Mikhail Nikolayevich von **Grabbe** (18 Jul 1868 - 23 Jul 1942)
| | |
|---|---|
| 22 Sep 1911 - 14 Jan 1915: | Commander, Consolidated Life Guards Cossack Regiment |
| 8 Nov 1912: | Promoted to *Major-General* |
| 14 Jan 1915 - 24 Jan 1915: | Commander, 3rd Brigade, 1st Guards Cavalry Division |
| 24 Jan 1915 - 6 May 1916: | Commander, 4th Don Cossack Division |
| 6 May 1916: | Promoted to *Lieutenant-General* |
| 6 May 1916 - 22 Mar 1917: | Ataman, Don Cossack Army |
| 22 Mar 1917 - 31 May 1917: | Reserve officer, Odessa Military District |
| 31 May 1917: | Retired |

*Major-General* Count Aleksandr Nikolayevich **Grabbe-Nikitin** (12 Dec 1864 - 5 Jul 1947)
| | |
|---|---|
| 2 Jan 1914: | Promoted to *Major-General* |
| 2 Jan 1914 - 22 Mar 1917: | Commander, Tsar's Personal Retinue |
| 22 Mar 1917: | Retired |

*Major-General* Andrey Pavlovich **Gradov** (12 Jun 1866 - Oct 1935)
| | |
|---|---|
| 1914 - 5 Apr 1915: | Chairman of the Economic Construction Commission for the Construction of the 2nd Engineering School |
| 22 Mar 1915: | Promoted to *Major-General* |
| 5 Apr 1915 - 1917: | Commandant, 2nd Engineering School |

*General of Artillery* Nikolai Genrikhovich **Graff** (25 Dec 1826 - 19 Oct 1904)
| | |
|---|---|
| 16 Oct 1873 - 29 Mar 1878: | Commander, 28th Artillery Brigade |
| 30 Aug 1874: | Promoted to *Major-General* |
| 29 Mar 1878 - 1 Dec 1882: | Deputy Commander of Artillery, Odessa Military District |
| 1 Dec 1882 - 12 Jan 1886: | Commander of Artillery, IX. Army Corps |
| 15 May 1883: | Promoted to *Lieutenant-General* |
| 12 Jan 1886 - 22 Apr 1888: | Transferred to the reserve |
| 22 Apr 1888 - 8 May 1895: | Commander of Artillery, XIV. Army Corps |
| 8 May 1895: | Promoted to *General of Artillery* |
| 8 May 1895: | Retired |

*Vice-Admiral* Konstantin Aleksandrovich **Grammatchikov** (6 Aug 1856 - ?)
| | |
|---|---|
| 6 Dec 1908: | Promoted to *Rear-Admiral* |
| 6 Dec 1908 - 1909: | Junior Flagman, Baltic Fleet |
| 1909 - 30 May 1911: | Chief of Staff, Pacific Fleet |

30 May 1911 - Jul 1911: Commander, Siberian Flotilla
1911: Retired
1912: Promoted to *Vice-Admiral*

*Lieutenant-General* Aleksandr Alekseyevich **Gramotin** (6 Aug 1850 - ?)
2 Nov 1905: Promoted to *Major-General*
2 Nov 1905 - 22 May 1910: Commander, 1st Brigade, 2nd Caucasus Cossack Division
22 May 1910: Promoted to *Lieutenant-General*
22 May 1910: Retired
2 Apr 1916 - 1917: Recalled; Reserve officer, Caucasus Military District

*Major-General* Aleksandr Aleksandrovich **Grannikov** (28 Aug 1858 - 12 Aug 1914)
7 Jun 1910 - 12 Aug 1914: Commander, 109th Infantry Regiment
3 Feb 1915: Posthumously promoted to *Major-General*

*Major-General* Diodor Petrovich **Granovsky** (19 Nov 1862 - ?)
28 May 1908 - 3 Apr 1913: Military Judge, Caucasus Military District Court
29 Mar 1909: Promoted to *Major-General*
3 Apr 1913 - 10 Oct 1917: Military Judge, Moscow Military District Court
10 Oct 1917: Dismissed

*Lieutenant-General* Konstantin Vladimirovich **Grave** (6 Jan 1831 - Jan 1900)
15 Sep 1873 - 31 Oct 1877: Commander, 120th Infantry Regiment
16 Aug 1877: Promoted to *Major-General*
31 Oct 1877 - 4 Dec 1879: Transferred to the reserve
4 Dec 1879 - 24 Sep 1881: Military Commander, Novgorod Province
24 Sep 1881 - 22 Apr 1890: Commander, 2nd Regional Brigade
30 Aug 1886: Promoted to *Lieutenant-General*
22 Apr 1890 - Jan 1900: Commander, 19th Regional Brigade

*Lieutenant-General* Aleksandr Andreyevich **Grebenshchikov** (15 Nov 1858 - ?)
1 Jul 1906 - 17 Oct 1910: Section Chief, General Staff
6 Dec 1909: Promoted to *Major-General*
17 Oct 1910 - 4 Sep 1912: Section Chief, Main Intendant Directorate
4 Sep 1912 - 19 Mar 1914: Section Chief, Main Directorate for Troop Billeting
19 Mar 1914 - 1917: Special Purposes General, Main Directorate for Troop Billeting
10 Apr 1916: Promoted to *Lieutenant-General*

*General of Infantry* Yakov Aleksandrovich **Grebenshchikov** (18 Mar 1837 - 10 Mar 1907)
11 Aug 1885 - 4 Feb 1891: Commander, Kexholm Grenadier Regiment
30 Aug 1885: Promoted to *Major-General*
19 Apr 1887 - 4 Feb 1891: Commander, 1st Brigade, 3rd Guards Infantry Division
4 Feb 1891 - 15 Sep 1895: Commander, 2nd Brigade, 3rd Guards Infantry Division
15 Sep 1895 - 21 Feb 1896: Commander, 32nd Infantry Division
6 Dec 1895: Promoted to *Lieutenant-General*
21 Feb 1896 - 26 Jul 1899: Commander, 4th Infantry Division

26 Jul 1899 - 5 Mar 1904: Commandant of Fortress Kaunas
5 Mar 1904 - 10 Mar 1907: Member of the Military Council
7 Oct 1904 - 10 Jan 1907: Chairman, Main Committee on Fortresses
2 Apr 1906: Promoted to *General of Infantry*

*Major-General* Konstantin Emilyevich **Grebner** (25 Nov 1863 - ?)
23 Feb 1913 - 23 Apr 1915: Commander, 65$^{th}$ Infantry Regiment
2 Nov 1914: Promoted to *Major-General*
23 Apr 1915 - 1917: Commander, Brigade, 11$^{th}$ Siberian Rifle Division

*Major-General* Aleksandr Andreyevich **Grechko** (30 Aug 1862 - Jan 1919)
28 Feb 1908 - 1917: Military Judge, Kiev Military District Court
13 Apr 1908: Promoted to *Major-General*
1917: Chairman of the Military Tribunal, 8$^{th}$ Army

*Major-General* Nikolai Nikolayevich **Gredyakin** (26 Jan 1852 - ?)
15 Mar 1898 - 21 Nov 1899: Military Prosecutor, Omsk Military District
6 Dec 1898: Promoted to *Major-General*
21 Nov 1899 - 1906: Military Prosecutor, Siberian Military District

*General of Infantry* Viktor Konstantinovich **Grek** (11 Mar 1849 - ?)
15 Feb 1900: Promoted to *Major-General*
15 Feb 1900 - 26 Aug 1903: Commander, 2$^{nd}$ Brigade, 10$^{th}$ Infantry Division
26 Aug 1903 - 25 Jan 1905: Commander, 4$^{th}$ Turkestan Rifle Brigade
25 Jan 1905 - 16 May 1905: Commander, 33$^{rd}$ Infantry Division
16 May 1905 - 11 Mar 1912: Commander, 38$^{th}$ Infantry Division
6 Dec 1906: Promoted to *Lieutenant-General*
11 Mar 1912: Promoted to *General of Infantry*

*Major-General* Vladimir Konstantinovich **Grek** (31 Dec 1850 - ?)
11 Mar 1906 - 1908: Commander, 1$^{st}$ Battalion, 3$^{rd}$ Reserve Artillery Brigade
1908: Retired
15 Sep 1915: Promoted to *Major-General*
13 Jun 1916 - 6 Aug 1917: Recalled; Reserve officer, Kiev Military District
6 Aug 1917: Retired

*General of Cavalry* Aleksandr Matveyevich **Grekov** (1 Aug 1839 - 20 Feb 1917)
7 Jul 1882 - 10 Apr 1888: Vice-Chairman of Public Assistance, Don Military Region
6 May 1885: Promoted to *Major-General*
10 Apr 1888 - 2 Jun 1893: Committee Member, Main Directorate of Cossack Affaris
2 Jun 1893 - 1 Jan 1903: Deputy Military Ataman, Don Cossack Army
14 May 1896: Promoted to *Lieutenant-General*
1 Jan 1903 - 4 Aug 1910: Senior Deputy Military Ataman, Don Cossack Army
4 Aug 1910: Promoted to *General of Cavalry*
4 Aug 1910: Retired

*Major-General* Aleksandr Mitrofanovich **Grekov** (17 Mar 1877 - 13 Jul 1968)
1915 - Jun 1917: Commander, Life Guards, Cossack Regiment
10 Apr 1916: Promoted to *Major-General*

*Major-General* Aleksei Danilovich **Grekov** (15 Mar 1859 - ?)
24 Nov 1916 - 1917: Commandant, Tiflis Artillery Depot
6 Dec 1916: Promoted to *Major-General*

*Major-General* Aleksei Kirillovich **Grekov** (6 Feb 1873 - 6 Oct 1918)
21 May 1915 - 21 Aug 1915: Commander, 1st Brigade, 4th Don Cossack Division
25 May 1915: Promoted to *Major-General*
Jun 1915: Acting Commander, 4th Don Cossack Division
21 Aug 1915 - Dec 1917: Commander, 1st Cavalry Division

*Major-General* Ivan Erastovich **Grekov** (28 Jan 1830 - ?)
1 Jul 1887 - 8 Aug 1892: Ataman, 2nd Don Division, Don Cossack Army
6 May 1890: Promoted to *Major-General*
8 Aug 1892 - 1899: Ataman, Cherkassy Division, Don Cossack Army

*Major-General* Matvey Matveyevich **Grekov** (30 May 1838 - ?)
1 Jul 1887 - 1897: Ataman, Donetsk Division, Don Cossack Army
6 May 1892: Promoted to *Major-General*

*General of Cavalry* Mitrofan Ilyich **Grekov** (11 May 1842 - 1915)
19 Dec 1886 - 9 Dec 1893: Commander, Ataman Life Guards Regiment
24 Apr 1888: Promoted to *Major-General*
5 Apr 1893 - 9 Dec 1893: Commander, 3rd Brigade, 1st Guards Cavalry Division
9 Dec 1893 - 20 Aug 1898: Commander, 1st Don Cossack Division
20 Aug 1898 - 14 Jul 1900: Attached to the Don Cossack Army
14 Jul 1900 - 18 Feb 1901: Commander, 1st Brigade, Siberian Cossack Division
18 Feb 1901 - 7 Feb 1904: Attached to the Don Cossack Army
7 Feb 1904 - 25 Mar 1905: Commander, 2nd Brigade, Transbaikal Cossack Division
25 Nov 1904: Promoted to *Lieutenant-General*
25 Mar 1905 - 1908: Reserve officer, Don Cossack Army
1908: Retired
1913: Promoted to *General of Cavalry*

*Major-General* Porfiry Petrovich **Grekov** (19 Jan 1844 - ?)
14 Oct 1891: Promoted to *Major-General*
14 Oct 1891 - Jan 1895: Commander, 2nd Brigade, 5th Cavalry Division

*Major-General* Pyotr Ivanovich **Grekov** (29 Jan 1863 - Jan 1951)
11 Sep 1914: Promoted to *Major-General*
11 Sep 1914 - 6 Oct 1914: Commander, Brigade, 5th Cossack Division
6 Oct 1914 - 13 Jun 1916: Commander, 2nd Brigade, 1st Don Cossack Division
13 Jun 1916 - 1917: Commander, 1st Don Cossack Division

*Major-General* Pyotr Petrovich **Grekov** (30 Mar 1857 - ?)
20 Jan 1900 - 7 Dec 1904: Commander, 11th Don Cossack Cavalry Regiment
7 Dec 1904: Promoted to *Major-General*
7 Dec 1904 - 20 Jan 1906: Commander, 1st Brigade, 1st Don Cossack Division
20 Jan 1906 - 19 Jun 1908: Commander, 1st Brigade, 2nd Consolidated Cossack Division

*General of Cavalry* Vladimir Pavlovich **Grekov** (18 Jul 1852 - ?)
26 Jan 1900: Promoted to *Major-General*
26 Jan 1900 - 16 Apr 1904: Commander, 2nd Brigade, 5th Cavalry Division
16 Apr 1904 - 9 Jul 1906: Commander, Orenburg Cossack Division
24 Aug 1905: Promoted to *Lieutenant-General*
1 Aug 1906 - 18 Jul 1913: Commander, 1st Turkestan Cossack Division
18 Jul 1913: Promoted to *General of Cavalry*
18 Jul 1913: Retired

*Major-General* Khristian Petrovich **Grenkvist** (14 Jan 1854 - 1 Aug 1904)
10 Aug 1900 - 11 Aug 1902: Commander, 1st Turkestan Artillery Brigade
5 Feb 1901: Promoted to *Major-General*
11 Aug 1902 - 3 Mar 1904: Commander, 8th Artillery Brigade

*General of Infantry* Nikolai Apollonovich **Gresser** (14 Aug 1827 - 3 Apr 1903)
15 May 1883: Promoted to *Major-General*
15 May 1883 - 17 Mar 1884: Transferred to the reserve
17 Mar 1884 - 31 Aug 1884: Deputy Commander of Regional Forces, Caucasus Military District
31 Aug 1884 - 1899: Commander, 23rd (Vladikavkaz) Regional Brigade
30 Aug 1894: Promoted to *Lieutenant-General*
1899: Promoted to *General of Infantry*
1899: Retired

*Vice-Admiral* Nikolai Romanovich **Greve** (26 Mar 1853 - 30 May 1913)
7 Oct 1902 - 27 Aug 1904: Commandant of Port Arthur
6 Dec 1902: Promoted to *Rear-Admiral*
27 Aug 1904 - 1906: Commandant, Port of Vladivostok
1906 - 26 Mar 1907: Commandant, Port of St. Petersburg
26 Mar 1907 - 19 Nov 1907: Commander, Naval Detachment, Baltic Fleet
19 Nov 1907: Promoted to *Vice-Admiral*
19 Nov 1907: Retired

*Major-General* Lyudvig Khristianovich **Greyfan** (4 Oct 1860 - 9 Aug 1931)
18 May 1910 - 1914: Chief of Section 8, Main Intendant Directorate
6 Dec 1910: Promoted to *Major-General*

*Major-General* Aleksandr Bogdanovich **Greym** (29 Aug 1855 - ?)
3 Jun 1901 - 29 Dec 1905: Military Judge, Siberian Military District Court
6 Apr 1903: Promoted to *Major-General*
29 Dec 1905 - 18 Mar 1906: Military Judge, St. Petersburg Military District Court

| | |
|---|---|
| 18 Mar 1906 - 1908: | Deputy Chief of the Main Military Justice Directorate |
| 27 Dec 1906 - 15 Jan 1907: | Acting Chief of the Main Military Justice Directorate |

*Lieutenant-General* Konstantin Nikolayevich **Gribsky** (8 Sep 1845 - ?)
| | |
|---|---|
| 21 Jan 1891: | Promoted to *Major-General* |
| 21 Jan 1891 - 25 Sep 1892: | Chief of Staff, Fortress Brest-Litovsk |
| 25 Sep 1892 - 20 Jul 1895: | Chief of Staff, XV. Army Corps |
| 25 Jul 1895 - 2 Jul 1897: | Chief of Staff, Amur Military District |
| 2 Jul 1897 - 21 Feb 1902: | Military Governor, Amur Region, Ataman, Amur Cossack Army |
| 6 Dec 1899: | Promoted to *Lieutenant-General* |
| 21 Feb 1902 - 25 Apr 1903: | At the disposal of the Chief of the General Staff |
| 25 Apr 1903 - 21 May 1905: | Commander, 11$^{th}$ Infantry Division |
| 21 May 1905 - 18 Mar 1906: | Commanding General, VI. Army Corps |
| 18 Mar 1906: | Retired |

*Lieutenant-General* Ilya Petrovich **Gribunin** (12 Jul 1854 - ?)
| | |
|---|---|
| 5 Jun 1903 - 2 Jul 1905: | Commander, 3$^{rd}$ Artillery Brigade |
| 6 Dec 1903: | Promoted to *Major-General* |
| 2 Jul 1905 - 5 Aug 1905: | Unassigned |
| 5 Aug 1905 - 20 Jun 1906: | Attached to the Main Artillery Directorate |
| 20 Jun 1906 - 16 Jan 1909: | Commander, 13$^{th}$ Artillery Brigade |
| 16 Jan 1909 - 28 Sep 1912: | Artillery Inspector, Kazan Military District |
| 28 Sep 1912: | Promoted to *Lieutenant-General* |
| 28 Sep 1912 - 27 Jun 1913: | Inspector of Artillery, XXIII. Army Corps |
| 27 Jun 1913: | Retired |

*Major-General* Mikhail Gordeyevich **Griff** (6 Sep 1852 - 10 Sep 1916)
| | |
|---|---|
| 10 Apr 1907 - 1910: | Commander, 2$^{nd}$ Fortress Battalion |
| 1910: | Promoted to *Major-General* |
| 1910: | Retired |
| 7 Apr 1916 - 10 Sep 1916: | Recalled; Commander, 40$^{th}$ Militia Brigade |

*Major-General* Appolon Appolonovich **Grigorenko** (23 Nov 1864 - 1937)
| | |
|---|---|
| 28 Oct 1906 - 1912: | Chief of Engineers, Fortress Sevastopol |
| 1912: | Promoted to *Major-General* |
| 1912: | Retired |

*Rear-Admiral* Nikolai Mitrofanovich **Grigorov** (11 Jan 1873 - 14 Feb 1944)
| | |
|---|---|
| 3 Jun 1915: | Promoted to *Rear-Admiral* |
| 3 Jun 1915 - 15 Mar 1917: | Chief of Staff, C-in-C, Baltic Fleet |
| 15 Mar 1917 - 15 Sep 1917: | Reserve officer, Ministry of the Navy |
| 15 Sep 1917 - 18 Nov 1917: | Chief of Freight Traffic, Baltic Sea |
| 18 Nov 1917: | Dismissed |

*Lieutenant-General* Vasily Vasilievich **Grigorov** (25 Apr 1860 - 1911)
| | |
|---|---|
| 1 Apr 1902 - 8 Mar 1911: | Director, 2$^{nd}$ Orenburg Cadet Corps |
| 14 Apr 1902: | Promoted to *Major-General* |

13 Apr 1908: Promoted to *Lieutenant-General*
8 Mar 1911 - 1911: Military Governor of Samarkand Region

*Major-General* Andrey Lvovich **Grigorovich** (17 Aug 1852 - ?)
30 Nov 1904 - 25 Jul 1910: Commander, 38th Artillery Brigade
6 Dec 1906: Promoted to *Major-General*
25 Jul 1910 - 1912: Inspector of Artillery, VI. Army Corps

*Admiral* Ivan Konstantinovich **Grigorovich** (26 Jan 1853 - 3 Mar 1930)
28 Mar 1904: Promoted to *Rear-Admiral*
28 Mar 1904 - Jan 1905: Commandant of Port Arthur
Jan 1905 - 28 Dec 1906: Chief of Staff, Black Sea Fleet
28 Dec 1906 - 1 Oct 1908: Commander, Port of Emperor Aleksander III (Libau)
1 Oct 1908 - 9 Feb 1909: Military Governor of Kronstadt
9 Feb 1909 - 19 Mar 1911: Deputy Minister of the Navy
29 Mar 1909: Promoted to *Vice-Admiral*
19 Mar 1911 - 28 Feb 1917: Minister of the Navy
27 Sep 1911: Promoted to *Admiral*
Dec 1912: Promoted to *General-Adjutant*
28 Feb 1917: Retired

*Lieutenant-General* Karl-Ignaty Yulianovich **Grigorovich** (4 Nov 1846 - ?)
3 Oct 1907: Promoted to *Major-General*
3 Oct 1907 - 4 Nov 1913: Commander, Moscow Regional Brigade
4 Nov 1913: Promoted to *Lieutenant-General*
4 Nov 1913: Retired

*Major-General* Aleksandr Yevgrafovich **Grigoryev** (13 Feb 1836 - ?)
1 Jun 1889 - 1894: Military Judge, Omsk Military District Court
30 Aug 1890: Promoted to *Major-General*

*Lieutenant-General* Apollon Gavrilovich **Grigoryev** (22 Jan 1847 - 17 Aug 1916)
27 Mar 1902 - 10 Nov 1905: Special Assignments General, Odessa Military District
1903: Promoted to *Major-General*
10 Nov 1905 - 2 Dec 1907: Mayor of Odessa
2 Dec 1907: Promoted to *Lieutenant-General*
2 Dec 1907: Retired

*Lieutenant-General* Dmitry Petrovich **Grigoryev** (25 Oct 1827 - 21 Feb 1896)
25 Mar 1877 - 13 Oct 1878: Commander, 12th Artillery Brigade
12 Oct 1877: Promoted to *Major-General*
13 Oct 1878 - 21 Jun 1879: Deputy Commander of Artillery, Field Army
21 Jun 1879 - 28 Jun 1880: Chief of Artillery Section, Commission for Demobilization of the Field Army
28 Jun 1880 - 26 Dec 1883: Deputy Commander of Artillery, Warsaw Military District
26 Dec 1883 - 15 Feb 1892: Deputy Chief of the Main Artillery Directorate
30 Aug 1886: Promoted to *Lieutenant-General*

| | |
|---|---|
| 15 Feb 1892 - 21 Feb 1896: | Member, Committee for Wounded Veterans |

*General of Artillery* Fyodor Alekseyevich **Grigoryev** (8 Mar 1850 - Jun 1926)
| | |
|---|---|
| 29 Nov 1901 - 8 Jan 1905: | Director, Mikhailov-Voronezh Cadet Corps |
| 14 Apr 1902: | Promoted to *Major-General* |
| 8 Jan 1905 - 9 Sep 1917: | Director, 1st Cadet Corps |
| 13 Apr 1908: | Promoted to *Lieutenant-General* |
| 9 Sep 1917: | Promoted to *General of Artillery* |
| 9 Sep 1917: | Retired |

*Major-General* Georgy Aleksandrovich **Grigoryev** (22 Apr 1851 - ?)
| | |
|---|---|
| 22 Apr 1907 - 9 Sep 1907: | Commander, 9th East Siberian Rifle Artillery Brigade |
| 31 May 1907: | Promoted to *Major-General* |

*Major-General* Grigory Vasilyevich **Grigoryev** (23 Jan 1864 - 10 Oct 1919)
| | |
|---|---|
| 31 Oct 1908 - 1912: | Military Judge, Omsk Military District Court |
| 6 Dec 1909: | Promoted to *Major-General* |
| 1912: | Retired |

*Major-General* Konstantin Andreyevich **Grigoryev** (1848 - 1902)
| | |
|---|---|
| 6 Dec 1901: | Promoted to *Major-General* |
| 1901 - 1902: | Commander, Kiev Artillery Arsenal |

*Lieutenant-General* Mikhail Mikhaylovich **Grigoryev** (5 Nov 1865 - Apr 1912)
| | |
|---|---|
| 27 May 1902 - 3 Jun 1910: | Section Chief, Main Department of Cossack Troops |
| 6 Dec 1906: | Promoted to *Major-General* |
| 3 Jun 1910 - Apr 1912: | Commander, 1st Brigade, 46th Infantry Division |
| Apr 1912: | Promoted to *Lieutenant-General* |

*Major-General of the Fleet* Vasily Fyodorovich **Grigoryev** (30 Dec 1868 - ?)
| | |
|---|---|
| 19 Oct 1911 - ?: | Attached to the Main Naval Staff |
| 22 Mar 1915: | Promoted to *Major-General of the Fleet* |

*General of Cavalry* Vladimir Nikolayevich **Grigoryev** (14 Jul 1851 - ?)
| | |
|---|---|
| 7 Aug 1900: | Promoted to *Major-General* |
| 7 Aug 1900 - 31 Aug 1905: | Chief of Staff, Fortress Warsaw |
| 31 Aug 1905 - 11 Mar 1907: | Commandant of Fortress Ochakov |
| 6 Dec 1906: | Promoted to *Lieutenant-General* |
| 11 Mar 1907 - 7 Mar 1909: | Commandant of Fortress Sevastopol |
| 7 Mar 1909 - 4 Aug 1915: | Commandant of Fortress Kaunas |
| 6 Dec 1912: | Promoted to *General of Cavalry* |
| Sep 1915: | Dismissed from the Army |

*Major-General* Nikolai Vasilyevich **Grinevich** (5 Aug 1861 - ?)
| | |
|---|---|
| 13 Aug 1906 - 1917: | Section Chief, Main Directorate for Military Schools |
| 6 Dec 1910: | Promoted to *Major-General* |

*General of Cavalry* Artur-Otto-Morits Aleksandrovich von **Grinvald** (12 Mar 1847 - 13 Jun 1922)
| | |
|---|---|
| 3 Feb 1892: | Promoted to *Major-General* |
| 3 Feb 1892 - 11 Aug 1896: | Commander, Guards Cavalry Regiment |
| 11 Aug 1896 - 12 Jun 1897: | Commander, 1st Brigade, 1st Guards Cavalry Division |
| 12 Jun 1897 - 19 Apr 1917: | Equerry to the Court of the Tsar |
| 6 Dec 1899: | Promoted to *Lieutenant-General* |
| 25 Feb 1901 - 19 Apr 1917: | Member of the Board, Main Directorate of State Horse Breeding |
| 1904: | Promoted to *General-Adjutant* |
| 6 Dec 1912: | Promoted to *General of Cavalry* |
| 19 Apr 1917: | Retired |

*Major-General* Yevgeny Eduardovich **Gripenberg** (26 Aug 1859 - ?)
| | |
|---|---|
| 22 Apr 1907 - 29 May 1910: | Commander, 2nd Artillery Brigade |
| 31 May 1907: | Promoted to *Major-General* |

*Lieutenant-General* Aksel Sevastyanovich **Grippenberg** (1 Mar 1833 - 12 Jun 1918)
| | |
|---|---|
| 5 May 1873 - 5 Dec 1884: | Commander, 147th Infantry Regiment |
| 15 May 1883: | Promoted to *Major-General* |
| 5 Dec 1884 - 24 Apr 1886: | Commander, 1st Brigade, 7th Infantry Division |
| 24 Apr 1886 - 10 Feb 1889: | Governor of Oulu |
| 10 Feb 1889 - Dec 1899: | Governor of Vyborg |
| 30 Aug 1893: | Promoted to *Lieutenant-General* |
| Dec 1899: | Resigned |

*General of Infantry* Oskar-Ferdinand Kazimirovich von **Grippenberg** (1 Jan 1838 - 25 Dec 1915)
| | |
|---|---|
| 25 Oct 1877 - 1 Jan 1883: | Commander, Moscow Life Guards Regiment |
| 21 Nov 1877: | Promoted to *Major-General* |
| 1 Jan 1883 - 20 Jan 1888: | Commander, Life Guards Regiment |
| 20 Jan 1888 - 11 Sep 1889: | Commander, 1st Brigade, 1st Guards Infantry Division |
| 11 Sep 1889 - 7 Apr 1897: | Commander, Guards Rifle Brigade |
| 30 Aug 1890: | Promoted to *Lieutenant-General* |
| 7 Apr 1897 - 12 May 1898: | Commander, 1st Guards Infantry Division |
| 12 May 1898 - 3 Jan 1906: | Member, Committee for Wounded Veterans |
| 3 May 1900 - 7 Dec 1901: | Commanding General, VI. Army Corps |
| 6 Dec 1900: | Promoted to *General of Infantry* |
| 7 Dec 1901 - 10 Nov 1902: | Deputy Commanding General, Vilnius Military District |
| 10 Nov 1902 - 11 Sep 1904: | Commanding General, Vilnius Military District |
| 30 Jul 1904: | Promoted to *General-Adjutant* |
| 11 Sep 1904 - 12 Mar 1905: | C-in-C, 2nd Manchurian Army |
| 25 Apr 1905 - 25 Dec 1915: | Member of the State Council |
| 15 Jun 1905 - 23 Mar 1906: | Inspector-General of Infantry |

*Major-General* Aleksei Samoylovich **Grishinsky** (17 Apr 1872 - ?)
| | |
|---|---|
| 2 Jun 1915: | Promoted to *Major-General* |
| 2 Jun 1915 - 28 Jan 1916: | Special Purposes General, 4th Army |

| | |
|---|---|
| 28 Jan 1916 - 1 Jul 1916: | Commander, Life Guards Grenadier Regiment |
| 6 Jul 1916 - 25 Apr 1917: | Chief of Staff, II. Guards Corps |
| 25 Apr 1917 - 29 Apr 1917: | Commander, 7th Infantry Division |
| 29 Apr 1917 - 29 Aug 1917: | Commander, Guards Rifle Division |
| 29 Aug 1917 - Nov 1917: | Chief of Staff, 7th Army |

*Major-General* Konstantin Nikolayevich **Grishkov** (16 May 1861 - 1913)
| | |
|---|---|
| 1 Aug 1908: | Promoted to *Major-General* |
| 1 Aug 1908 - 1913: | Director, Khabarovsk Count Muravyov-Amursky Cadet Corps |

*Lieutenant-General* Mikhail Petrovich **Grishkov** (15 Oct 1847 - ?)
| | |
|---|---|
| 10 Feb 1902: | Promoted to *Major-General* |
| 10 Feb 1902 - 8 Apr 1906: | Section Chief, Main Directorate for Military Schools |
| 8 Apr 1906 - 1917: | Special Purposes General, Main Directorate for Military Schools |
| 13 Apr 1908: | Promoted to *Lieutenant-General* |

*General of Infantry* Nikolai Ivanovich **Grodekov** (22 Sep 1843 - 12 Dec 1913)
| | |
|---|---|
| 30 May 1876 - 19 Apr 1883: | At the disposal of the Commanding General, Turkestan Military District |
| 6 Jul 1880: | Promoted to *Major-General* |
| 19 Apr 1883 - 2 Jun 1883: | Reserve officer, Turkestan Military District |
| 2 Jun 1883 - 12 Jun 1893: | Military Governor of Syrdarya Region |
| 30 Aug 1890: | Promoted to *Lieutenant-General* |
| 12 Jun 1893 - 12 Oct 1893: | At the disposal of the Minister of War |
| 12 Oct 1893 - 28 Mar 1898: | Deputy Commanding General, Amur Military District, Deputy Governor-General of Amur |
| 28 Mar 1898 - 30 Aug 1902: | Commanding General, Amur Military District, Governor-General of Amur, Ataman, Amur Cossack Army |
| 6 Dec 1900: | Promoted to *General of Infantry* |
| 30 Aug 1902 - 12 Dec 1913: | Member of the State Council |
| 18 Jun 1905 - 3 Feb 1906: | Permanent Member of the Council of State for Defence |
| 3 Feb 1906 - 22 Sep 1906: | C-in-C, Far East |
| 15 Dec 1906 - 8 Mar 1908: | Commanding General, Turkestan Military District, Governor-General of Turkestan, Ataman, Semirecheskogo Cossack Army |

*General of Infantry* Vladimir Ivanovich **Grodekov** (6 Jan 1838 - 25 Apr 1910)
| | |
|---|---|
| 30 Aug 1882: | Promoted to *Major-General* |
| 13 Jan 1886 - 23 May 1894: | Chairman of the Military Tribunal, Kazan Military District |
| 30 Aug 1892: | Promoted to *Lieutenant-General* |
| 23 May 1894 - 1905: | Member of the Supreme Military Tribunal |
| 6 Dec 1903: | Promoted to *General of Infantry* |
| 1905: | Retired |

*Major-General* Georgy Dmitriyevich **Grodsky** (19 Jun 1871 - 1943)
7 Sep 1912 - Oct 1917: Professor, Mikhailovsky Artillery Academy
6 Dec 1913: Promoted to *Major-General*

*Major-General* Gustav-Leon Konstantinovich **Grodzinksy** (9 Apr 1841 - ?)
21 Jul 1899: Promoted to *Major-General*
21 Jul 1899 - 1901: Chief of Kiev Military Hospital

*Lieutenant-General* Mikhail Mikhailovich **Gromyko** (29 Jul 1847 - ?)
31 Oct 1897 - 1909: Commander of Gendarmerie, Smolensk
6 Apr 1903: Promoted to *Major-General*
1909: Promoted to *Lieutenant-General*
1909: Retired

*Major-General* Bronislav Lyudvigovich **Grombchevsky** (15 Jan 1855 - 27 Feb 1926)
26 Aug 1899 - 28 Sep 1903: Civilian Commissioner, Kwantung
1903: Promoted to *Major-General*
28 Sep 1903 - 1906: Commander, Astrakhan Cossack Troops, Governor of Astrakhan
1906: Retired

*Lieutenant-General* Vladimir Bogdanovich **Grosman** (6 May 1836 - 1 Dec 1903)
8 Mar 1893: Promoted to *Major-General*
8 Mar 1893 - 13 Oct 1898: Attached to the Kuban Cossack Army
13 Oct 1898 - Sep 1899: Commander, Kuban Cossack Horse Artillery Brigade
Sep 1899: Promoted to *Lieutenant-General*
Sep 1899: Retired

*Lieutenant-General of the Fleet* Fyodor Khristoforovich **Gross** (9 Feb 1855 - 1919)
8 Jan 1899 - 10 Nov 1908: Flagman Engineer-Mechanic of the Fleet
17 Apr 1905: Promoted to *Major-General of the Fleet*
10 Nov 1908 - 21 Oct 1911: Chairman, Obukhov & Izhorsk Admiralty Steel Plants
18 Apr 1910: Promoted to *Lieutenant-General of the Fleet*
21 Oct 1911 - 1915: Chairman, Baltic & Admiralty Shipyards
1915 - 1917: Chief Inspector of Factories, Ministry of the Navy

*Major-General* Richard Robertovich **Grossman** (6 Apr 1866 - ?)
Apr 1915 - Dec 1917: Commander, 8th Zaamursky Border Infantry Regiment
30 Jan 1917: Promoted to *Major-General*
Dec 1917: Dismissed

*Major-General* Aleksandr Konstantinovich **Grossul-Tolstoy** (25 Oct 1866 - ?)
1916 - 1917: Commander, Sapper Battalion
22 Dec 1916: Promoted to *Major-General*

*Major-General* Aleksandr-Yevgeny Yulyevich von **Grot** (29 Aug 1865 - ?)
18 Jul 1911 - 1917: Senior Artillery Inspector, Main Directorate of Artillery
14 Apr 1913: Promoted to *Major-General*

*Major-General* Pavel Pavlovich **Groten** (18 Sep 1870 - 27 Dec 1962)
| | |
|---|---|
| 14 Nov 1915 - 7 Feb 1917: | Commander, Life Guards Cavalry Grenadier Regiment |
| 10 Apr 1916: | Promoted to *Major-General* |
| 7 Feb 1917 - 9 Jun 1917: | Commandant of Aleksandr Palace |
| 9 Jun 1917 - ?: | Reserve officer, Kiev Military District |

*Lieutenant-General* Aleksandr Aleksandrovich **Grotengelm** (24 May 1831 - 1903)
| | |
|---|---|
| 23 Feb 1877 - 16 Mar 1887: | Commander, Amu Darya Sector |
| 1882: | Promoted to *Major-General* |
| 16 Mar 1887 - 22 Aug 1890: | Commander, 1st Brigade, 8th Infantry Division |
| 22 Aug 1890 - 1894: | Commandant of Fortress Ochakov |
| 30 Aug 1893: | Promoted to *Lieutenant-General* |
| 1894: | Retired |

*Lieutenant-General* Yevgeny Iosifovich **Grozmani** (27 Jan 1849 - 9 Feb 1928)
| | |
|---|---|
| 25 Apr 1900: | Promoted to *Major-General* |
| 25 Apr 1900 - 9 Feb 1901: | Commander, 2nd Brigade, 11th Infantry Division |
| 9 Feb 1901 - 25 Jan 1907: | Commander, 1st Brigade, 42nd Infantry Division |
| 25 Jan 1907 - 10 Sep 1907: | Commander, 8th East Siberian Rifle Division |
| 22 Apr 1907: | Promoted to *Lieutenant-General* |
| 10 Sep 1907: | Retired |

*Major-General* Pompey Mikhailovich **Grudnev** (7 Jul 1864 - 17 Feb 1918)
| | |
|---|---|
| 21 Sep 1912 - 1917: | Ataman, Khoper District |
| 6 Dec 1916: | Promoted to *Major-General* |

*Lieutenant-General* Aleksandr Valerianovich **Gruel** (14 Oct 1856 - ?)
| | |
|---|---|
| 29 Mar 1907 - 9 Dec 1910: | Commander of Engineers, Fortress Libau |
| 6 Dec 1907: | Promoted to *Major-General* |
| 9 Dec 1910 - 14 Jun 1912: | Deputy Commander of Engineers, Warsaw Military District |
| 14 Jun 1912 - 22 Oct 1912: | Commander of Engineers, Odessa Military District |
| 22 Oct 1912 - 1917: | Chief of Troop Billeting, Odessa Military District |
| 6 Dec 1913: | Promoted to *Lieutenant-General* |

*Lieutenant-General* Mikhail Vladimirovich **Grulev** (20 Aug 1857 - 17 Sep 1943)
| | |
|---|---|
| 30 May 1904 - 3 Oct 1906: | Commander, 11th Infantry Regiment |
| 19 Feb 1905: | Promoted to *Major-General* |
| 3 Oct 1906 - 29 Dec 1909: | Member, Military Commission of the history of the Russian-Japanese War |
| 29 Dec 1909 - 1912: | Chief of Staff, Fortress Brest-Litovsk |
| 1912: | Promoted to *Lieutenant-General* |
| 1912: | Retired |

*Major-General* Vilgelm-Eduard-Nikolai Lvovich von **Grumbkov** (5 Oct 1848 - ?)
| | |
|---|---|
| 31 Jan 1897 - 1903: | Commander of Gendarmerie, Olonets |
| 14 Apr 1902: | Promoted to *Major-General* |

*Major-General* Mikhail Yefimovich **Grumm-Grzhimaylo** (2 Jun 1861 - 8 May 1921)
12 May 1907 - Dec 1908:     Commander, 41st Artillery Brigade
31 May 1907:                Promoted to *Major-General*
Dec 1908:                   Retired
21 Jun 1915 - 17 Dec 1915:  Recalled; Inspector of Artillery, XLIII. Army Corps
17 Dec 1915 - 1917:         Reserve officer, Petrograd Military District

*General of Artillery* Pyotr Moiseyevich **Grumm-Grzhimaylo** (4 Feb 1824 - 11 Sep 1897)
2 Dec 1863 - 13 Jan 1877:   Commander, 25th Artillery Brigade
20 May 1868:                Promoted to *Major-General*
13 Jan 1877 - 25 Jan 1879:  Deputy Commander of Artillery, Kharkov Military District
25 Jan 1879 - 22 Sep 1884:  Commander of Artillery, X. Army Corps
30 Aug 1879:                Promoted to *Lieutenant-General*
22 Sep 1884 - May 1896:     Commandant of Fortress Dvinsk
May 1896:                   Promoted to *General of Artillery*
May 1896:                   Retired

*Major-General* Aleksandr Fyodorovich **Grushetsky** (17 Oct 1854 - ?)
25 Nov 1903 - 19 Sep 1914:  Chairman, Remount Commission for Eastern Regions
10 Apr 1911:                Promoted to *Major-General*
19 Sep 1914 - 1917:         Board Member, Main Directorate of Horse Breeding

*Lieutenant-General* Pyotr Dmitriyevich **Gruyev** (3 Jul 1855 - ?)
6 Mar 1902 - 9 Oct 1908:    Section Chief, General Staff
31 May 1907:                Promoted to *Major-General*
9 Oct 1908 - 6 Jun 1911:    Commander, Orenburg Regional Brigade
6 Jun 1911:                 Promoted to *Lieutenant-General*
6 Jun 1911:                 Retied

*Major-General* Mikhail Grigorievich **Gruzevich-Nechay** (9 Jan 1865 - 30 Jul 1920)
10 Apr 1913 - 1 Jan 1917:   Commander, 24th Sapper Battalion
1 Jan 1917:                 Promoted to *Major-General*
1 Jan 1917 - 1918:          Corps Engineer, XXIV. Army Corps

*Major-General* Nikolai Grigorievich **Gruzevich-Nechay** (14 Sep 1857 - 15 Oct 1933)
6 Nov 1915 - 1 Feb 1917:    Commander, 1st Zaamursky Artillery Brigade
12 Jul 1916:                Promoted to *Major-General*
1 Feb 1917 - 1917:          Commander, 9th Siberian Rifle Artillery Brigade

*Major-General* Illarion Ivanovich **Gruzintsev** (15 Sep 1853 - ?)
6 Oct 1914 - 29 Jan 1917:   Commander, 1st Brigade, 6th Infantry Division
26 Sep 1915:                Promoted to *Major-General*
29 Jan 1917 - 18 Apr 1917:  Commander, 181st Infantry Division

*Major-General* Fyodor Fyodorovich **Gryaznov** (13 May 1855 - 16 Jan 1906)
22 Mar 1899 - 1 Dec 1903:   Commander, Life Guards Grodno Hussar Regiment
6 Dec 1899:                 Promoted to *Major-General*

| | |
|---|---|
| 1 Dec 1903 - 3 Apr 1905: | Commandant, Nikolayev Cavalry School |
| 3 Apr 1905 - 16 Jan 1906: | Chief of Staff, Caucasus Military District |

*Lieutenant-General* Nikolai Pavlovich **Gryaznov** (20 Jun 1851 - ?)
| | |
|---|---|
| 10 Jul 1900 - 21 May 1905: | Commander, 15th East Siberian Rifle Regiment |
| 22 Oct 1904: | Promoted to *Major-General* |
| 21 May 1905 - 15 Dec 1908: | Commander, 1st Brigade, 8th Infantry Division |
| 15 Dec 1908 - 1 Jun 1910: | Commander, 7th Turkestan Rifle Brigade |
| 1 Jun 1910: | Promoted to *Lieutenant-General* |
| 1 Jun 1910: | Retired |

*Major-General* Sergey Pavlovich **Gryaznov** (21 Jul 1856 - ?)
| | |
|---|---|
| 2 Feb 1914 - 25 Jun 1916: | Deputy Chief of Biletting, Odessa Military District |
| 6 Apr 1914: | Promoted to *Major-General* |
| 25 Jun 1916 - 1917: | Reserve officer, Odessa Military District |

*Major-General* Aleksandr Fyodorovich **Gryzov** (10 Jun 1852 - ?)
| | |
|---|---|
| 25 Jul 1906 - 1908: | Commander, Kiev Artillery Depot |
| 22 Apr 1907: | Promoted to *Major-General* |

*Major-General* Mikhail Felitsianovich **Grzhibovsky** (11 May 1859 - ?)
| | |
|---|---|
| 13 Oct 1914 - 28 Sep 1916: | Commander, 112th Infantry Regiment |
| 6 Dec 1915: | Promoted to *Major-General* |
| 28 Sep 1916 - 7 Apr 1917: | Commander, Brigade, 51st Infantry Division |
| 7 Apr 1917 - 14 Aug 1917: | Commander, 51st Infantry Division |

*Major-General* Vikenty Venediktovich **Gubarzhevsky** (11 Nov 1852 - ?)
| | |
|---|---|
| 11 Sep 1904 - 1912: | Commander, 20th Turkestan Rifle Battalion |
| 1912: | Promoted to *Major-General* |
| 1912: | Retired |
| 1914 - 1915: | Recalled; Commander, 1st Reserve Infantry Battalion |
| 1915 - 6 May 1915: | Commander, Militia Brigade |
| 6 May 1915 - 1917: | Commander, Brigade, 110th Infantry Division |

*Lieutenant-General* Konstantin Petrovich **Guber** (24 Jul 1854 - 16 Feb 1916)
| | |
|---|---|
| 6 Apr 1903: | Promoted to *Major-General* |
| 6 Apr 1903 - 28 Apr 1904: | Intendant, Amur Military District |
| 28 Apr 1904 - 29 Jul 1905: | Intendant, 1st Manchurian Army |
| 29 Jul 1905 - 14 Feb 1907: | Chief Field Quartermaster |
| 14 Feb 1907 - 10 Jan 1908: | At the disposal of the Intendant-General, Ministry of War |
| 10 Jan 1908 - 10 Apr 1911: | Deputy Intendant-General of the Army |
| 10 Apr 1911: | Promoted to *Lieutenant-General* |
| 10 Apr 1911: | Retired |
| 6 Mar 1915 - 16 Feb 1916: | Recalled; Chief of Medical Staff, 5th Army |

*Lieutenant-General* Aleksey Petrovich **Gudim** (20 Oct 1849 - 1912)
| | |
|---|---|
| 6 Aug 1894 - 1912: | Inspector of Prisoner Escorts, Eastern Siberia |

6 Dec 1905:                           Promoted to *Major-General*
1912:                                   Promoted to *Lieutenant-General*

*General of Infantry* Pavel Konstantinovich **Gudim-Levkovich** (29 Jun 1842 - 24 Oct 1907)
30 Aug 1885:                 Promoted to *Major-General*
30 Aug 1885 - 7 May 1891:    Deputy Chief of Staff, St. Petersburg Military District
7 May 1891 - 27 May 1893:    Deputy Chief, Department of Principalities
27 May 1893 - 1 Jan 1900:     Chief of the Tsar's Cabinet
2 Apr 1895:                  Promoted to *Lieutenant-General*
1 Jan 1900 - 24 Oct 1907:     Member of the State Council
6 Dec 1906:                 Promoted to *General of Infantry*

*Major-General* Vladimir Zakharovich **Gudima** (6 Jan 1862 - ?)
24 Nov 1908 - 3 Sep 1913:     Commander, 94th Infantry Regiment
20 Jul 1913:                 Promoted to *Major-General*
3 Sep 1913 - 1 Aug 1914:      Commander, 1st Brigade, 30th Infantry Division
1 Aug 1914 - 3 Jul 1916:       Commander, Brigade, 59th Infantry Division
3 Jul 1916 - 2 Nov 1916:       Commander, 5th Special Infantry Brigade
2 Nov 1916 - 27 Jan 1917:     Commander, 2nd Special Infantry Division
27 Jan 1917 - 20 May 1917:   Commander, 3rd Special Infantry Division

*Major-General* Aleksandr Mikhailovich **Gudzansky** (29 Mar 1858 - ?)
12 Jul 1908 - 1913:            Chief of Artillery Administration, Turkestan Military District
9 Jul 1913:                  Promoted to *Major-General*

*Lieutenant-General* Karl Yegorovich **Guk** (19 May 1847 - 1910)
15 Nov 1885 - 14 Jun 1899:   Inspector of Classes, Mikhailovsky Artillery Academy
6 Dec 1895:                 Promoted to *Major-General*
14 Jun 1899 - 9 Jan 1906:     Member of the Artillery Committee, Main Artillery Directorate
6 Dec 1903:                 Promoted to *Lieutenant-General*
9 Jan 1906 - 1907:            Conference Member, Mikhailovsky Artillery Academy
1907:                            Retired

*Lieutenant-General* Viktor Nikolayevich **Gukov** (28 Oct 1846 - ?)
8 Dec 1895 - 18 Jun 1904:    Commander of Engineers, Fortress Kiev
6 Dec 1898:                 Promoted to *Major-General*
18 Jun 1904 - 1906:           Commandant of Fortress Osovets
6 Dec 1904:                 Promoted to *Lieutenant-General*

*Major-General* Yakov Nikolayevich **Gukov** (15 Oct 1850 - ?)
14 Jul 1897 - 25 Apr 1901:    Commander, 10th Grenadier Regiment
25 Apr 1901:                Promoted to *Major-General*
25 Apr 1901 - 14 Mar 1905:   Commander, 2nd Brigade, 1st Grenadier Division
14 Mar 1905 - 24 Apr 1906:   Deputy Chief of Staff, Siberian Military District
24 Apr 1906 - 1906:          Commander, 61st Reserve Infantry Brigade

*Lieutenant-General* Arseny Anatolievich **Gulevich** (14 Feb 1866 - 12 Apr 1947)
| | |
|---|---|
| 21 Jun 1905 - 9 Oct 1908: | Chief of Office of the Council of National Defense |
| 13 Apr 1908: | Promoted to *Major-General* |
| 9 Oct 1908 - 26 Aug 1912: | Commander, Preobrazhensky Life Guards Regiment |
| 26 Aug 1912 - 19 Jul 1914: | Chief of Staff, St. Petersburg Military District |
| 6 Apr 1914: | Promoted to *Lieutenant-General* |
| 19 Jul 1914 - 9 Aug 1914: | Chief of Staff, 6$^{th}$ Army |
| 9 Aug 1914 - 2 Feb 1915: | Chief of Staff, 9$^{th}$ Army |
| 2 Feb 1915 - 21 Sep 1915: | Chief of Staff, Northern Front |
| 21 Sep 1915 - 20 Mar 1916: | At the disposal of the C-in-C, Northern Front |
| 20 Mar 1916 - 19 Apr 1917: | Commanding General, XLII. Army Corps |
| 19 Apr 1917 - 9 Sep 1917: | Commanding General, XXI. Army Corps |
| 9 Sep 1917 - 1918: | Reserve officer, Petrograd Military District |

*Major-General of the Hydrographic Corps* Leonid Orestovich **Gulkevich** (15 Feb 1865 - 13 Jul 1919)
| | |
|---|---|
| 1909 - 1917: | Commander of Nikolayev Pilots, Black Sea Fleet |
| 22 Mar 1915: | Promoted to *Major-General of the Hydrographic Corps* |

*Lieutenant-General* Nikolai Nikolayevich **Gulkovsky** (9 Oct 1849 - ?)
| | |
|---|---|
| 12 Jun 1897: | Promoted to *Major-General* |
| 12 Jun 1897 - 11 Apr 1905: | Commander, 2$^{nd}$ Brigade, 4$^{th}$ Cavalry Division |
| 11 Apr 1905 - 8 Mar 1907: | Commander, 2$^{nd}$ Cavalry Division |
| 6 Dec 1905: | Promoted to *Lieutenant-General* |

*Lieutenant-General of the Admiralty* Erast Yevgenyevich **Gulyayev** (17 Oct 1846 - 1919)
| | |
|---|---|
| 1896 - 1904: | Assistant Chief Inspector of Shipbuilding |
| ?: | Promoted to *Major-General of the Admiralty* |
| 1904 - 1908: | Member of the Board, Baltic Shipbuilding & Mechanical Factory |
| 1908: | Promoted to *Lieutenant-General of the Admiralty* |
| 1908: | Retired |

*Major-General* Vasily Mitrofanovich **Gulyayev** (22 Mar 1833 - ?)
| | |
|---|---|
| 9 Nov 1892: | Promoted to *Major-General* |
| 9 Nov 1892 - 30 Dec 1897: | Commander, 1$^{st}$ Brigade, 31$^{st}$ Infantry Division |

*Lieutenant-General* Ivan Emelyanovich **Gulyga** (26 Aug 1859 - 2 Jun 1934)
| | |
|---|---|
| 28 Mar 1912 - 30 Jul 1914: | Ataman, Caucasus Department of the Kuban Cossack Army |
| 6 Dec 1912: | Promoted to *Major-General* |
| 30 Jul 1914 - 2 Mar 1915: | Commander, 2$^{nd}$ Kuban Cossack Infantry Brigade |
| 2 Mar 1915 - 10 Jan 1917: | Commander, 1$^{st}$ Kuban Cossack Infantry Brigade |
| 10 Jan 1917 - Feb 1918: | Commanding General, Kuban-Terek Cossack Infantry Corps |
| 1 Oct 1917: | Promoted to *Lieutenant-General* |

*Major-General* Konstantin Nikolayevich **Gunnius** (9 Aug 1840 - ?)
31 May 1888 - 19 Oct 1895:	Ataman, Maikop Division, Kuban Cossack Army
6 May 1893:	Promoted to *Major-General*
19 Oct 1895 - 27 Jan 1896:	Commander, Terek Cossack Brigade
27 Jan 1896 - 1898:	Deputy Commander, Terek Region,
	Ataman, Terek Cossack Army

*Lieutenant-General* David Konstantinovich **Guntsadze** (8 Sep 1861 - 1922)
25 Feb 1912 - 13 Oct 1914:	Commander, 97th Infantry Regiment
5 Oct 1914:	Promoted to *Major-General*
13 Oct 1914 - 28 Aug 1915:	Commander, Brigade, 67th Infantry Division
28 Aug 1915 - 9 Sep 1917:	Commander, 53rd Infantry Division
9 Sep 1917 - 22 Nov 1912:	Commanding General, XLIII. Army Corps
12 Oct 1917:	Promoted to *Lieutenant-General*
22 Nov 1917 - 29 Dec 1917:	Acting C-in-C, 12th Army
29 Dec 1917 - Apr 1918:	Attached to the 12th Army

*General of Infantry* Aleksandr Vikentyevich **Gurchin** (26 Feb 1833 - 15 Sep 1902)
3 Dec 1876 - 9 Feb 1886:	Commander, Caucasus Rifle Brigade
12 Jun 1877:	Promoted to *Major-General*
1880 - 1882:	Inspector of Riflemen
9 Feb 1886 - 17 Sep 1894:	Commander, 38th Infantry Division
30 Aug 1886:	Promoted to *Lieutenant-General*
17 Sep 1894 - 24 Oct 1900:	Commanding General, XIX. Army Corps
6 Dec 1898:	Promoted to *General of Infantry*
24 Oct 1900 - 15 Sep 1902:	Member of the Military Council
13 Sep 1901 - 15 Sep 1902:	Commanding General, Vilnius Military District

*Major-General* Aleksandr Pavlovich **Gurkovsky** (15 Mar 1852 - 25 Jan 1905)
4 Dec 1902:	Promoted to *Major-General*
4 Dec 1902 - 25 Jan 1905:	Commander, 21st Artillery Brigade

*Lieutenant-General* Aleksei Pavlovich **Gurkovsky** (18 Mar 1850 - 10 Jan 1909)
29 Jun 1900:	Promoted to *Major-General*
29 Jun 1900 - 10 Mar 1904:	At the disposal of Grand Duke Sergei Alexandrovich
10 Mar 1904 - 10 Jan 1909:	Commandant of Moscow
6 Dec 1906:	Promoted to *Lieutenant-General*

*General of Infantry* Genrikh-Gelmut-Georgy Stepanovich **Guro** (19 Sep 1835 - 25 May 1907)
13 Mar 1885 - 14 Jun 1896:	Chief of St. Petersburg Semenovsky Aleksandrovsky
	Military Hospital
30 Aug 1885:	Promoted to *Major-General*
14 Jun 1896 - Sep 1905:	Special Assignments General, St. Petersburg Military
	District
6 Dec 1897:	Promoted to *Lieutenant-General*
Sep 1905:	Promoted to *General of Infantry*
Sep 1905:	Retired

*General of Infantry* Aleksandr Mikhailovich **Gursky** (3 Aug 1856 - ?)
22 Mar 1898 - 9 Jan 1906: Military Judge, Warsaw Military District Court
6 Dec 1900: Promoted to *Major-General*
9 Jan 1906 - 23 Aug 1906: Military Prosecutor, Kiev Military District
23 Aug 1906 - 16 Oct 1909: Deputy Chief Military Prosecutor, Supreme Military Tribunal
22 Apr 1907: Promoted to *Lieutenant-General*
3 Nov 1907 - 16 Oct 1909: Chief of the Military Justice Administration
16 Oct 1909 - 31 Mar 1917: Member, Supreme Military Tribunal
6 Dec 1915: Promoted to *General of Infantry*
31 Mar 1917 - 1918: Chairman of the Supreme Military Tribunal

*Major-General* Ivan Ignatyevich **Gursky** (18 Jul 1856 - Apr 1913)
29 Dec 1910: Promoted to *Major-General*
29 Dec 1910 - Apr 1913: Commander, $1^{st}$ Brigade, $27^{th}$ Infantry Division

*Major-General* Petr Mikhailovich **Gursky** (27 Jun 1862 - ?)
1 Jun 1915 - 1917: Section Chief, General Staff
6 Dec 1916: Promoted to *Major-General*

*Major-General* Aleksey Matveyevich **Gurtikh** (10 Mar 1862 - ?)
25 Oct 1915 - 1917: Commander, $327^{th}$ Infantry Regiment
20 Oct 1916: Promoted to *Major-General*

*Major-General* Mikhail Vasilyevich **Gurzhin** (2 Nov 1868 - ?)
22 Jun 1913 - 10 Jul 1916: Commander, $2^{nd}$ Battalion, $13^{th}$ Artillery Brigade
12 Feb 1916: Promoted to *Major-General*
10 Jul 1916 - 1917: Commander, $62^{nd}$ Artillery Brigade

*General of Infantry* Yepifany Arsenievich **Gusakov** (12 May 1850 - 14 Mar 1916)
6 Oct 1899: Promoted to *Major-General*
6 Oct 1899 - 23 Jun 1902: Commandant of Fortress Zegrze
23 Jun 1902 - 6 Feb 1907: Commandant of Fortress Ivangorod
6 Dec 1906: Promoted to *Lieutenant-General*
6 Feb 1907 - 31 Dec 1910: Commandant of Fortress Kronstadt
31 Dec 1910 - 26 Aug 1911: At the disposal of the Minister of War
26 Aug 1911: Promoted to *General of Infantry*
26 Aug 1911: Retired

*Major-General* Vladimir Nikolayevich **Gusakovsky** (11 Feb 1869 - 8 Sep 1923)
30 Mar 1915 - 1917: Commander, $13^{th}$ Caucasus Rifle Regiment
26 Feb 1917: Promoted to *Major-General*

*Major-General* Georgy Ivanovich **Gusev** (23 Apr 1860 - ?)
31 Oct 1903 - 1911: Chairman of the Remount Commission, Astrakhan
1911: Promoted to *Major-General*
1911: Retired
1914 - 4 Aug 1916: Recalled; Attached to the Militia

4 Aug 1916 - 1917: Special Purposes General, Odessa Military District

*Lieutenant-General* Vladimir Yakovlevich **Gusev** (2 Jun 1858 - 5 Jan 1926)
23 Nov 1908: Promoted to *Major-General*
23 Nov 1908 - 25 Jul 1910: Commander, 2nd East Siberian Rifle Artillery Brigade
25 Jul 1910 - 24 Jan 1914: Commander, 34th Artillery Brigade
24 Jan 1914 - 21 Oct 1915: Inspector of Artillery, VIII. Army Corps
22 Dec 1914: Promoted to *Lieutenant-General*
21 Oct 1915 - 1917: Reserve officer, Kiev Military District

*Lieutenant-General* Pyotr Lukich **Guslavsky** (29 Jun 1863 - ?)
26 May 1910: Promoted to *Major-General*
26 May 1910 - 6 Oct 1910: Deputy Chief of Staff, Kazan Military District
6 Oct 1910 - 27 Aug 1913: Quartermaster-General, Kazan Military District
27 Aug 1913 - 21 Jul 1917: Commander, 1st Brigade, 2nd Consolidated Cossack Division
17 Oct 1916: Promoted to *Lieutenant-General*
21 Jul 1917 - ?: Reserve officer, Kiev Military District

*Major-General* Aleksandr Andreyevich **Gust** (6 Jan 1838 - ?)
8 Sep 1884 - 1894: Commander of Artillery, Fortress Ochakov
30 Aug 1887: Promoted to *Major-General*

*Admiral* King **Gustaf V**, King of Sweden (16 Jun 1858 - 29 Oct 1950)
20 Apr 1908: Promoted to *Admiral*

*Lieutenant-General* Karl-Nikolai Karlovich **Gut** (11 Dec 1837 - 28 Sep 1925)
6 Dec 1901: Promoted to *Major-General*
6 Dec 1901 - 16 Dec 1906: Attached to the Chief of the General Staff
16 Dec 1906 - 20 Sep 1910: Treasurer, General Staff
20 Sep 1910: Promoted to *Lieutenant-General*
20 Sep 1910: Retired

*Major-General* Aleksandr Yevgenyevich **Gutor** (11 May 1866 - ?)
7 Dec 1911 - 12 Dec 1914: Commander, 139th Infantry Regiment
12 Dec 1914: Promoted to *Major-General*
12 Dec 1914: Retired

*Lieutenant-General* Aleksei Yevgenyevich **Gutor** (30 Aug 1868 - 13 Aug 1938)
4 Nov 1910: Promoted to *Major-General*
4 Nov 1910 - 6 Mar 1913: Commander, Moscow Life Guards Regiment
6 Mar 1913 - 19 Jul 1914: Chief of Staff, Kazan Military District
19 Jul 1914 - 1 Apr 1915: Chief of Staff, 4th Army
31 Dec 1914: Promoted to *Lieutenant-General*
1 Apr 1915 - 6 Mar 1916: Commander, 34th Infantry Division
6 Mar 1916 - 15 Apr 1917: Commanding General, VI. Army Corps
15 Apr 1917 - 22 May 1917: C-in-C, 11th Army
22 May 1917 - 10 Jul 1917: C-in-C, Southwestern Front

10 Jul 1917 - Oct 1917: Unassigned

*Major-General* Mikhail Dmitriyevich **Gutor** (2 Aug 1859 - ?)
5 Nov 1905 - 6 Nov 1914: Attached to Caucasus Military District
14 Apr 1913: Promoted to *Major-General*
6 Nov 1914 - 26 Oct 1917: Reserve officer, Caucasus Military District
26 Oct 1917: Dismissed

*Lieutenant-General* Yevgeny Simonovich **Gutor** (27 May 1843 - ?)
18 Mar 1897: Promoted to *Major-General*
18 Mar 1897 - May 1905: Director of Polotsk Cadet Corps
1905: Promoted to *Lieutenant-General*
1905: Retired

*Major-General* Iosif-Martin Romualdovich **Gvozdetsky** (25 Jul 1864 - ?)
14 Aug 1912 - 9 Dec 1915: Inspector of Troop Billeting, Turkestan Military District
14 Apr 1913: Promoted to *Major-General*
9 Dec 1915 - 1917: Inspector of Troop Billeting, Kazan Military District

*Major-General* Eduard-Khristofor Matveyevich von **Gyubbenet** (19 Aug 1836 - ?)
31 Dec 1898: Promoted to *Major-General*
31 Dec 1898 - 19 Dec 1901: Commander, 5th Replacement Cavalry Brigade
19 Dec 1901 - 1904: At the disposal of the Commanding General, Kiev Military District

*General of Infantry* Oskar Yakovlevich von **Gyubbenet** (29 Mar 1835 - 7 May 1906)
7 Jan 1877 - 6 Jul 1881: Section Chief, General Staff
30 Aug 1878: Promoted to *Major-General*
6 Jul 1881 - 25 Jan 1898: Business Manager, Mobilization Committee, General Staff
30 Aug 1888: Promoted to *Lieutenant-General*
25 Jan 1898 - 7 Dec 1898: At the disposal of the Minister of War
7 Dec 1898 - 3 Jan 1906: Member of the Military Council
9 Apr 1900: Promoted to *General of Infantry*
3 Jan 1906: Retired

*General of Cavalry* Franz Ferdinand Carl Ludwig Joseph Maria von **Habsburg**, Erzherzog von Österreich (18 Dec 1863 - 28 Jun 1914)
7 Nov 1892: Promoted to *Major-General*
?: Promoted to *General of Cavalry*
?: Honorary Colonel, 26th Dragoon Regiment

*Lieutenant-General* Ludwig Viktor Joseph Anton von **Habsburg**, Erzherzog von Österreich (15 May 1842 - 18 Jan 1919)
?: Promoted to *Lieutenant-General*
?: Honorary Colonel, 39th Infantry Regiment

*General-Field Marshal* Carol I von **Hohenzollern-Sigmaringen**, King of Romania (20 Apr 1839 - 10 Oct 1914)
15 Mar 1881 - 10 Oct 1914: King of Romania
17 Sep 1912: Promoted to *General-Field Marshal*

*Major-General* Magomet Chanka **Ibragimov** (2 Jul 1863 - ?)
19 Sep 1915 - 29 May 1917: Commander, 306th Infantry Regiment
19 Feb 1917: Promoted to *Major-General*
29 May 1917 - 1918: Commander, 177th Infantry Division

*Major-General* Boris Genrikhovich **Igelstrom** (29 Jul 1866 - 10 Jun 1935)
4 Feb 1909 - 30 Aug 1914: Special Assignments General, Warsaw Military District
6 Dec 1910: Promoted to *Major-General*
30 Aug 1914 - 5 Oct 1915: Special Assignments General, Northwest Front
5 Oct 1915 - 1917: Special Assignments General, Western Front
1917: Inspector of Horses, Western Front

*General of Infantry* Genrikh Gustavovich **Igelstrom** (10 Jan 1825 - 11 Feb 1899)
3 May 1867 - 29 Jun 1872: Commander, Caucasus Operational Brigade
30 Aug 1870: Promoted to *Major-General*
29 Jun 1872 - 30 Aug 1873: General à la suite
30 Aug 1873 - 21 Mar 1881: Commander, 2nd Brigade, 25th Infantry Division
21 Mar 1881 - 30 Aug 1881: General à la suite
30 Aug 1881: Promoted to *Lieutenant-General*
30 Aug 1881 - 24 Oct 1890: Commander, 10th Infantry Division
24 Oct 1890 - 3 Jul 1894: Commanding General, XIII. Army Corps
3 Jul 1894 - 11 Feb 1899: Member, Committee for Wounded Veterans
6 Dec 1895: Promoted to *General of Infantry*

*Lieutenant-General* Vladimir Yevgrafovich **Ignatovich** (29 Nov 1864 - 6 Feb 1931)
28 May 1908 - 4 Jun 1912: Military Judge, Kiev Military District Court
6 Dec 1908: Promoted to *Major-General*
4 Jun 1912 - 15 Mar 1917: Deputy Chief Military Prosecutor,
 Deputy Chief of Military Justice Administration
6 Dec 1914: Promoted to *Lieutenant-General*
15 Mar 1917: Dismissed

*General of Cavalry* Count Aleksey Pavlovich **Ignatyev** (22 May 1842 - 9 Dec 1906)
18 Dec 1873 - 11 Jan 1881: Commander, Guards Cavalry Regiment
30 Aug 1875: Promoted to *Major-General*
1 Jan 1876 - 11 Jan 1881: Member, Main Committee on Troop Training
11 Jan 1881 - 10 Oct 1884: Chief of Staff, Guards Corps
4 Jan 1885 - 13 May 1889: Commanding General, Irkutsk Military District,
 Governor-General of Eastern Siberia
30 Aug 1886: Promoted to *Lieutenant-General*
13 May 1889 - 12 Aug 1889: Deputy Minister of Internal Affairs
12 Aug 1889 - 7 Dec 1897: Governor-General, Southwestern Region
7 Dec 1897 - 9 Dec 1906: Member of the State Council

6 Dec 1898: Promoted to *General of Cavalry*
1904: Promoted to *General-Adjutant*

*Major-General* Fyodor Mikhailovich **Ignatyev** (31 Mar 1862 - ?)
26 Nov 1910 - 1916: Commander, 1st (St. Petersburg) Borderguard Brigade
1915: Promoted to *Major-General*

*Major-General* Ignaty Petrovich **Ignatyev** (29 Dec 1865 - 1933)
Aug 1914 - 18 May 1917: Commander, 257th Infantry Regiment
12 Jul 1916: Promoted to *Major-General*
18 May 1917 - 8 Jun 1917: Commander, 103rd Infantry Division
8 Jun 1917 - 1918: Commander, 2nd Infantry Division

*Lieutenant-General* Ivan Ivanovich **Ignatyev** (25 Jun 1861 - ?)
6 Mar 1902 - 23 Jan 1906: Military Judge, Amur Military District Court
28 Mar 1904: Promoted to *Major-General*
23 Jan 1906 - 24 Oct 1908: Military Prosecutor, Amur Military District
24 Oct 1908 - 8 Apr 1917: Chairman of the Military Tribunal, Caucasus Military District
18 Apr 1910: Promoted to *Lieutenant-General*
8 Apr 1917: Retired

*Major-General* Count Leonid Nikolayevich **Ignatyev** (14 Mar 1865 - 22 Oct 1943)
25 Mar 1913 - 17 Oct 1915: At the disposal of the Minister of War
6 Dec 1913: Promoted to *Major-General*
17 Oct 1915 - Oct 1917: At the disposal of Commander of Army Remounts

*Lieutenant-General* Lev Ivanovich **Ignatyev** (18 Feb 1848 - ?)
13 Aug 1898: Promoted to *Major-General*
13 Aug 1898 - 25 Jun 1905: Commander, 6th Sapper Brigade
17 Apr 1905: Promoted to *Lieutenant-General*
25 Jun 1905 - 4 Jul 1906: Commander, 11th Infantry Division
4 Jul 1906 - 29 Dec 1908: Commander, 2nd Grenadier Division

*Major-General* Count Nikolai Nikolayevich **Ignatyev** (9 Aug 1872 - 20 Feb 1962)
7 Dec 1914 - 28 Nov 1915: Commander, Life Guards Preobrazhensky Regiment
22 Mar 1915: Promoted to *Major-General*
28 Nov 1915 - 17 May 1916: Chief of Staff, Guards Detachment
17 May 1916 - 21 Aug 1916: Acting Chief of Staff of the Guards
21 Aug 1916 - 16 Apr 1917: Commander, 1st Brigade, 1st Guards Infantry Division
16 Apr 1917 - 29 Apr 1917: Commander, Guards Rifle Division
29 Apr 1917 - 31 Jul 1917: Commander, 1st Guards Infantry Division
31 Jul 1917 - Oct 1917: Reserve officer, Kiev Military District

*General of Infantry* Count Nikolai Pavlovich **Ignatyev** (17 Jan 1832 - 20 Jun 1908)
17 May 1859 - 21 Aug 1861: Authorized Representative in China
4 Oct 1860: Promoted to *Major-General*
8 Dec 1860: Promoted to *General-Adjutant*

| | |
|---|---|
| 21 Aug 1861 - 14 Jul 1864: | Director of Asian Department, Ministry of Foreign Affairs |
| 14 Jul 1864 - 25 Mar 1867: | Envoy to the Ottoman Court |
| 30 Aug 1865: | Promoted to *Lieutenant-General* |
| 25 Mar 1867 - 6 Jul 1879: | Ambassador Extraordinary and Plenipotentiary to the Ottoman Empire |
| 16 Apr 1878: | Promoted to *General of Infantry* |
| 6 Jul 1879 - 1 Jan 1881: | Governor-General of Nizhny Novgorod |
| 25 Mar 1881 - 4 May 1881: | Minister of State Property |
| 4 May 1881 - 30 May 1882: | Minister of Internal Affairs |
| 30 May 1882 - 20 Jun 1908: | Member of the State Council |

*Major-General* Nikolai Petrovich **Ignatyev** (27 Dec 1844 - ?)
| | |
|---|---|
| 4 Mar 1898: | Promoted to *Major-General* |
| 4 Mar 1898 - 28 Nov 1898: | Commander, 1st Brigade, 4th Infantry Division |
| 28 Nov 1898 - 23 Jun 1899: | Commander, 2nd Brigade, 4th Infantry Division |
| 23 Jun 1899 - 20 Jun 1900: | Commander, 1st Brigade, 22nd Infantry Division |
| 20 Jun 1900 - 1 Jun 1904: | Commander, 55th Reserve Infantry Brigade |
| 1 Jun 1904 - 2 Aug 1904: | Commander, 55th Infantry Division |
| 2 Aug 1904 - 1904: | At the disposal of the Commanding General, Moscow Military District |

*Major-General* Pyotr Makarovich **Ignatyev** (31 Jan 1859 - ?)
| | |
|---|---|
| 6 Apr 1907 - 23 May 1917: | Chairman of Remount Commission, Odessa Region |
| 10 Apr 1911: | Promoted to *Major-General* |
| 23 May 1917: | Dismissed |

*General of Engineers* Nikolai Ivanovich **Ikornikov** (23 Sep 1826 - 1911)
| | |
|---|---|
| 21 Apr 1877 - 1895: | Conference Member, Nikolayev Engineering Academy |
| 1 Jan 1878: | Promoted to *Major-General* |
| 30 Aug 1888: | Promoted to *Lieutenant-General* |
| 1895: | Promoted to *General of Engineers* |
| 1895: | Retired |

*Major-General* Baron Aleksandr Georgiyevich **Ikskul von Gildebandt** (16 Sep 1856 - ?)
| | |
|---|---|
| 15 Mar 1904: | Promoted to *Major-General* |
| 15 Mar 1904 - 9 Oct 1905: | Chief of Lines of Communication, 1st Manchurian Army |
| 9 Oct 1905 - 23 Jul 1906: | Chief of Communications, 1st Manchurian Army |
| 23 Jul 1906 - 9 Jul 1908: | Chief of Staff, III. Army Corps |
| 9 Jul 1908: | Retired |

*Major-General of Fleet Navigators* Ivan Ivanovich **Ilin** (6 Dec 1858 - ?)
| | |
|---|---|
| 1909 - 1914: | Chief of Navigation, Black Sea Naval Forces |
| 6 May 1912: | Promoted to *Major-General of Fleet Navigators* |

*Major-General* Ivan Vasilyevich **Ilin** (26 Feb 1860 - 30 Mar 1940)
| | |
|---|---|
| 12 Jun 1906 - 1917: | Intendant, XVII. Army Corps |
| 14 Apr 1913: | Promoted to *Major-General* |

*Major-General* Nikolai Fyodorovich **Ilin** (6 Mar 1844 - ?)
| | |
|---|---|
| 22 Mar 1878 - 30 Aug 1885: | Commander, 7th Uhlan Regiment |
| 5 Jul 1885: | Promoted to *Major-General* |
| 30 Aug 1885 - 10 Apr 1886: | Transferred to the reserve |
| 10 Apr 1886 - 13 Jul 1890: | Commander, 2nd Brigade, 2nd Cavalry Division |
| 13 Jul 1890 - 7 Jun 1895: | Commander, 1st Brigade, 2nd Cavalry Division |
| 7 Jun 1895 - 28 Jun 1904: | Transferred to the reserve |
| 28 Jun 1904 - 24 Nov 1904: | Recalled; At the disposal of the C-in-C, Far East |
| 24 Nov 1904 - 28 Jan 1905: | Transferred to the reserve |
| 28 Jan 1905 - 24 Sep 1905: | Attached to the General Staff |
| 24 Sep 1905 - 1907: | At the disposal of the Chief of the General Staff |

*Major-General of Naval Engineers* Nikolai Ivanovich **Ilin** (17 Nov 1864 - ?)
| | |
|---|---|
| 9 Mar 1909 - 19 Oct 1911: | Senior Deputy Inspector of Mechanics |
| 10 Apr 1911: | Promoted to *Major-General of Naval Engineers* |
| 19 Oct 1911 - 1917: | Deputy Chief of Mechanical Section, Main Shipbuilding Directorate |

*Major-General* Pyotr Nikolayevich **Ilinsky** (12 Jan 1861 - ?)
| | |
|---|---|
| 1 Mar 1913 - 5 Jun 1915: | Commander, 78th Infantry Regiment |
| 1915: | Promoted to *Major-General* |

*Major-General* Sergey Petrovich **Ilinsky** (27 Jun 1867 - ?)
| | |
|---|---|
| 17 Feb 1911 - 16 Jul 1913: | Chief of Military Science Archives & Library, Main General Staff Directorate |
| 10 Apr 1911: | Promoted to *Major-General* |
| 16 Jul 1913 - 15 Aug 1914: | Commander, 1st Brigade, 6th Infantry Division |
| 15 Aug 1914 - 1918: | POW |

*Lieutenant-General* Viktor Fyodorovich **Ilinsky** (27 Oct 1842 - ?)
| | |
|---|---|
| 8 Jun 1892: | Promoted to *Major-General* |
| 8 Jun 1892 - 9 Mar 1896: | Chief of Staff, VII. Army Corps |
| 9 Mar 1896 - 1 Feb 1899: | Commander, 1st East Siberian Rifle Brigade |
| 1 Feb 1899 - 5 Dec 1900: | Commander, 57th Reserve Infantry Brigade |
| 5 Dec 1900 - 16 May 1905: | Commander, 38th Infantry Division |
| 5 Dec 1900: | Promoted to *Lieutenant-General* |
| 16 May 1905 - Sep 1905: | Commander, 60th Infantry Division |

*Lieutenant-General* Nikolai Andreyevich **Ilkevich** (17 Jun 1868 - 1 Dec 1932)
| | |
|---|---|
| 5 Aug 1912: | Promoted to *Major-General* |
| 5 Aug 1912 - 24 Jun 1915: | Commander, 3rd Grenadier Artillery Brigade |
| 24 Jun 1915 - 6 Apr 1917: | Commander, 46th Infantry Division |
| 10 Oct 1915: | Promoted to *Lieutenant-General* |
| 6 Apr 1917 - Jul 1917: | Commanding General, I. Guards Corps |
| Jul 1917 - 7 Oct 1917: | Reserve officer, Kiev Military District |
| 7 Oct 1917 - 1918: | Inspector of Artillery, Special Army |

*Lieutenant-General* Valerian-Stanislav Yakovlevich **Illyashevich** (19 Nov 1822 - 10 Nov 1907)
20 Dec 1868 - 10 Nov 1907:     Conference Member, Nikolayev Engineering Academy
30 Aug 1876:     Promoted to *Major-General*
30 Aug 1887:     Promoted to *Lieutenant-General*

*Major-General* Yevgeny Valerianovich **Illyashevich** (2 Oct 1864 - ?)
7 Dec 1910 - 21 Jan 1915:     Commander, 5th Dragoon Regiment
14 Apr 1913:     Promoted to *Major-General*
21 Jan 1915 - 11 Apr 1917:     Duty General, Irkutsk Military District
11 Apr 1917:     Retired

*General of Infantry* Iakinf Ivanovich **Illyustrov** (10 Jul 1845 - ?)
15 Feb 1898 - 4 Feb 1902:     Military Prosecutor, Kazan Military District Court
6 Dec 1898:     Promoted to *Major-General*
4 Feb 1902 - 9 Jan 1906:     Military Prosecutor, Kiev Military District Court
6 Dec 1905:     Promoted to *Lieutenant-General*
9 Jan 1906 - 3 May 1908:     Chairman, Moscow Military District Court
3 May 1908 - 4 Aug 1911:     Member, Supreme Military Tribunal
4 Aug 1911 - 3 May 1912:     Chairman, Supreme Military Tribunal
3 May 1912:     Promoted to *General of Infantry*
3 May 1912:     Retired

*Major-General* Ivan Vasilyevich **Ilovaysky** (3 Mar 1840 - ?)
10 Apr 1885:     Promoted to *Major-General*
10 Apr 1885 - 26 Feb 1886:     Commander, 1st Brigade, 1st Don Cossack Division
26 Feb 1886 - 13 Apr 1889:     Commander, Life Guards Cossack Regiment
13 Apr 1889 - 26 Nov 1890:     Unassigned
26 Nov 1890 - 7 Nov 1895:     Commander, 2nd Brigade, 3rd Cavalry Division
7 Nov 1895 - 3 Feb 1900:     Attached to the Don Cossack Army

*Lieutenant-General* Nikolai Petrovich **Ilovaysky** (2 Nov 1844 - 24 Jan 1912)
9 Mar 1900:     Promoted to *Major-General*
9 Mar 1900 - 25 Nov 1904:     Commander, 1st Brigade, 1st Don Cossack Division
25 Nov 1904:     Promoted to *Lieutenant-General*
25 Nov 1904:     Retired

*Major-General* Aleksandr Nikolayevich **Ilyashenko** (9 Aug 1865 - ?)
17 Jul 1915 - 20 Nov 1916:     Commander, 5th Rifle Regiment
26 Sep 1916:     Promoted to *Major-General*
20 Nov 1916 - 18 Apr 1917:     Commander, Brigade, 35th Infantry Division
18 Apr 1917 - 1917:     Commander, 35th Infantry Division

*General of Infantry* Prince Aleksandr Konstantinovich **Imeretinsky** (24 Dec 1837 - 17 Nov 1900)
10 Jun 1867 - 12 Dec 1869:     Adjutant to the Tsar
30 Aug 1869:     Promoted to *Major-General à la suite*
12 Dec 1869 - 30 Aug 1873:     Deputy Chief of Staff, Warsaw Military District

| | |
|---|---|
| 30 Aug 1873 - 28 Jun 1875: | Chief of Staff, Warsaw Military District |
| 7 Jun 1876 - 8 Oct 1876: | Assistant Inspector of Infantry Battalions |
| 8 Oct 1876- 3 Aug 1877: | Attached to the Military Headquarters of the Tsar |
| 3 Aug 1877 - 2 Oct 1877: | Commander, 2nd Infantry Division |
| 1 Sep 1877: | Promoted to *Lieutenant-General* |
| 2 Oct 1877 - 16 Apr 1878: | ember of the Tsar's retinue |
| 16 Apr 1878: | Appointed *General-Adjutant* |
| 16 Apr 1878 - 17 Apr 1879: | Chief of Staff, Operations Army |
| 2 Jun 1879 - 13 Mar 1881: | Chief of Staff of the Guards & St. Petersburg Military District |
| 13 Mar 1881 - 1 Jan 1892: | Chief of the Military Justice Directorate, Chief Military Prosecutor |
| 30 Aug 1891: | Promoted to *General of Infantry* |
| 1 Jan 1892 - 1 Jan 1897: | Member of the State Council |
| 1 Jan 1897 - 17 Nov 1900: | Commanding General, Warsaw Military District, Governor-General of Warsaw |

*Major-General* Yevgeny Semyonovich **Imnadze** (4 Dec 1875 - ?)

| | |
|---|---|
| 24 Nov 1916 - 1917: | Chief of Staff, 14th Sibirian Rifle Division |
| 6 Dec 1916: | Promoted to *Major-General* |

*Lieutenant-General* Nikolai Timofeyevich **Indutny** (10 Sep 1847 - ?)

| | |
|---|---|
| 2 May 1895 - 20 Jan 1900: | Commandant of Kiev Arsenal |
| 14 May 1896: | Promoted to *Major-General* |
| 20 Jan 1900 - 1913: | Commandant of St. Petersburg Regional Arsenal |
| 29 Mar 1909: | Promoted to *Lieutenant-General* |

*Major-General* Mikhail Aleksandrovich **Inostrantsev** (26 Jul 1872 - 5 Dec 1938)

| | |
|---|---|
| 9 Oct 1915 - 15 Mar 1916: | Commander, Brigade, 38th Infantry Division |
| 21 Oct 1915: | Promoted to *Major-General* |
| 15 Mar 1916 - 1917: | Special Assignments General, Main Directorate for Military Schools |

*Lieutenant-General* Adam-Feofil-Konstantin Adamovich **Iokher** (2 Nov 1833 - 19 Nov 1900)

| | |
|---|---|
| 16 Dec 1878 - 19 Nov 1900: | Conference Member, Nikolayev Engineering Academy |
| 30 Aug 1880: | Promoted to *Major-General* |
| 30 Aug 1890: | Promoted to *Lieutenant-General* |

*Major-General* Mikhail Lyudvigovich **Iolshin** (4 Jul 1825 - ?)

| | |
|---|---|
| 5 Jul 1891: | Promoted to *Major-General* |
| 5 Jul 1891 - 1894: | Commander, 2nd Turkestan Line Brigade |

*Major-General* Nikolai Mikhailovich **Iolshin** (12 Jul 1860 - ?)

| | |
|---|---|
| 19 Apr 1906 - 30 Dec 1910: | Attached to 2nd Life Guards Dragoon Regiment |
| 30 Dec 1910: | Promoted to *Major-General* |
| 30 Dec 1910: | Retired |
| 7 Feb 1915 - 28 Jul 1916: | Recalled; Reserve officer, Kiev Military District |

28 Jul 1916 - 1917: Reserve officer, Petrograd Military District

*Lieutenant-General* Leonid Dmitriyevich **Ionov** (10 May 1848 - ?)
13 Oct 1893 - 2 Nov 1905: Commander, Guards Field Gendarmerie Squadron
2 Nov 1905: Promoted to *Major-General*
2 Nov 1905 - 1 Jan 1910: Commandant of Krasnoye Selo
1 Jan 1910: Promoted to *Lieutenant-General*
1 Jan 1910: Retired

*General of Infantry* Mikhail Yefremovich **Ionov** (12 Mar 1846 - 16 Jan 1924)
17 Apr 1894: Promoted to *Major-General*
17 Apr 1894 - 9 May 1894: At the disposal of the Commanding General, Turkestan Military District
9 May 1894 - 25 Jan 1897: Commander, 4th Turkestan Line Brigade
25 Jan 1897 - 24 Oct 1899: Commander, Turkestan Line Brigade
24 Oct 1899 - 19 Jun 1907: Military Governor of Semirechensk, Ataman, Semirechensk Cossack Army
11 Jun 1901: Promoted to *Lieutenant-General*
19 Jun 1907 - 1907: At the disposal of the Minister of War
1907: Promoted to *General of Infantry*
1907: Retired

*Major-General* Vladimir Yefremovich **Ionov** (14 Aug 1850 - 20 Nov 1905)
15 Jun 1891 - 20 Nov 1905: Chief of Court Administration, Tsarskoye Selo
14 May 1896: Promoted to *Major-General*

*Major-General* Aleksandr Fridrikhovich **Iordan** (22 Jul 1864 - ?)
25 Jul 1914 - 27 Feb 1917: Commander, 74th Artillery Brigade
23 Nov 1915: Promoted to *Major-General*
27 Feb 1917 - 30 Apr 1917: Inspector of Artillery, XLI. Army Corps
30 Apr 1917 - 1917: Inspector of Artillery, 7th Army

*Lieutenant-General* Feliks Dominikovich **Iozefovich** (20 Nov 1857 - 1921)
7 May 1905 - 20 Aug 1907: Commander, 152nd Infantry Regiment
20 Aug 1907: Promoted to *Major-General*
20 Aug 1907 - 10 May 1910: Deputy Chief of Staff, Kazan Military District
10 May 1910 - 19 Jul 1914: Commander, 1st Brigade, 26th Infantry Division
19 Jul 1914 - 8 Oct 1914: Commander, 76th Infantry Division
8 Oct 1914 - 31 Mar 1915: Commander, 56th Infantry Division
13 Mar 1915 - 26 May 1915: Unassigned
26 May 1915 - 13 Jun 1916: Commander, 24th Replacement Infantry Brigade
13 Jun 1916 - 14 Nov 1916: Commander, 3rd Caucasus Rifle Division
14 Nov 1916 - 2 Apr 1917: Reserve officer, Petrograd Military District
2 Apr 1917: Promoted to *Lieutenant-General*
2 Apr 1917 - 1918: Inspector of Reserves & Militias, Front
1918: Retired

*Lieutenant-General* Aleksandr Ivanovich **Ipatovich-Goransky** (30 Dec 1863 - ?)
16 Feb 1905 - 7 Mar 1915: Professor, Nikolayev Engineering Academy
29 Mar 1909: Promoted to *Major-General*
7 Mar 1915 - 29 Apr 1915: Commander of Engineers, 11$^{th}$ Army
29 Apr 1915 - 1 May 1915: Commander of Engineers, Fortress Przemysl
1 May 1915 - 2 Apr 1917: Commander of Engineers, 11$^{th}$ Army
2 Apr 1917: Promoted to *Lieutenant-General*
2 Apr 1917 - Oct 1917: Commander of Engineers, Turkestan Military District

*Lieutenant-General* Vladimir Nikolayevich **Ipatyev** (9 Nov 1867 - 29 Nov 1952)
7 Jun 1910 - 2 May 1916: Supernumerary Member, Technical & Construction Committee, Ministry of Internal Affairs
6 Dec 1910: Promoted to *Major-General*
2 May 1916 - 1917: Chairman, Committee on Chemicals, Explosives, Incendiaries & Gas, Main Artillery Directorate
1917: Promoted to *Lieutenant-General*

*Admiral* Aleksandr Aleksandrovich **Iretskoy** (22 Nov 1848 - ?)
1899 - Dec 1901: Commander, 10$^{th}$ Naval Depot
6 Dec 1901: Promoted to *Rear-Admiral*
1902 - 28 Dec 1906: Commander, Port of Emperor Aleksander III (Libau)
28 Dec 1906 - 1 Sep 1909: Director of Lighthouses & Navigation, Baltic Sea, Commander, Port of Revel
6 Dec 1908: Promoted to *Lieutenant-General of the Admiralty*
1 Sep 1909 - 17 May 1913: Member, Supreme Naval Tribunal
1912: Redesignated *Vice-Admiral*
17 May 1913: Promoted to *Admiral*
17 May 1913: Retired

*General of Artillery* Vladimir Aleksandrovich von **Irman** (1916: Irmanov) (18 Oct 1852 - 27 Sep 1931)
18 Feb 1904 - 7 Mar 1906: Commander, 4$^{th}$ East Siberian Rifle Artillery Brigade
13 Jul 1904: Promoted to *Major-General*
7 Mar 1906 - 11 May 1912: Commandant of Fortress Vladivostok
13 Jul 1908: Promoted to *Lieutenant-General*
Jun 1910 - 11 May 1912: Commanding General, IV. Siberian Army Corps
11 May 1912 - 8 Jun 1917: Commanding General, III. Caucasus Army Corps
6 Dec 1914: Promoted to *General of Artillery*
8 Jun 1917 - Oct 1917: Reserve officer, Caucasus Military District

*Major-General* Mikhail-Iogann Semyonovich von **Irtel** (18 May 1869 - ?)
1 Sep 1906 - 17 Sep 1916: Inspector of Classes, Siberian Cadet Corps
6 Dec 1912: Promoted to *Major-General*
17 Sep 1916 - 1917: Reserve officer, Petrograd Military District

*Lieutenant-General of the Fleet* Andrey Ivanovich **Isakov** (22 May 1865 - 29 Sep 1940)
26 Dec 1905 - 1917: Chief Construction Engineer, Port of Vladivostok
6 Dec 1911: Promoted to *Major-General of the Admiralty*

1917: Promoted to *Lieutenant-General of the Fleet*

*Major-General* Nikolai Sergeyevich **Isakov** (12 Oct 1829 - 19 Nov 1898)
24 Dec 1890: Promoted to *Major-General*
24 Dec 1890 - 19 Nov 1898: Commander, 15th Artillery Brigade

*Major-General* Iosif Lukich **Isarlov** (3 Jul 1862 - ?)
29 May 1910 - 2 Apr 1914: Commander, 8th Dragoon Regiment
2 Apr 1914: Promoted to *Major-General*
2 Apr 1914 - 20 Aug 1916: Commander, 2nd Brigade, Caucasus Cavalry Division
20 Aug 1916 - 1917: Reserve officer, Kiev Military District

*Lieutenant-General* Ivan Georgiyevich **Isayev** (13 Feb 1861 - 17 Jun 1917)
18 Jun 1905 - 18 Dec 1908: Inspector of Works, Engineering Department, Turkestan Military District
6 Dec 1906: Promoted to *Major-General*
18 Dec 1908 - 16 Nov 1911: Commander of Engineers, Fortress Sevastopol
16 Nov 1911 - 9 Apr 1914: Deputy Commander of Engineers, Vilnius Military District
9 Apr 1914 - 1914: Chief of Troop Billeting, Irkutsk Military District
1914 - 17 Jun 1917: Chief of Troop Billeting, Dvinsk Military District
6 Dec 1914: Promoted to *Lieutenant-General*

*Major-General* Prince Pyotr Aleksandrovich **Ishcheyev** (5 May 1846 - ?)
1901: Promoted to *Major-General*

*Lieutenant-General* Yevgeny Andreyevich **Iskritsky** (3 Aug 1874 - 1949)
4 Nov 1914 - 22 Aug 1915: Commander, Life Guards Pavlovsky Regiment
22 Mar 1915: Promoted to *Major-General*
22 Aug 1915 - 29 Feb 1916: Attached to the Chief of Staff to the Supreme Commander-in-Chief
29 Feb 1916 - 7 Feb 1917: Chief of Staff, IX. Army Corps
7 Feb 1917 - 5 May 1917: Commander, 168th Infantry Division
5 May 1917 - 3 Jul 1917: Attached to the Guards Corps
3 Jul 1917: Promoted to *Lieutenant-General*
3 Jul 1917 - 1918: Commanding General, I. Siberian Army Corps

*Lieutenant-General* Konstantin Konstantinovich **Istomin** (4 Sep 1853 - ?)
18 Feb 1904 - Mar 1917: Deputy Chief of Administration, Moscow Palace
22 Apr 1907: Promoted to *Major-General*
6 Dec 1914: Promoted to *Lieutenant-General*

*Lieutenant-General* Nikolai Mikhailovich **Istomin** (9 May 1855 - ?)
7 Nov 1904: Promoted to *Major-General*
7 Nov 1904 - 28 Jul 1905: Commander, 2nd Brigade, 1st Siberian Infantry Division
6 Jul 1905 - 6 Aug 1905: Acting Chief of Communications, C-in-C, Far East
28 Jul 1905 - 16 Feb 1906: Chief of Lines of Communication, Far East
20 Dec 1905 - 16 Feb 1906: Acting Chief of Communications, C-in-C, Far East

16 Feb 1906 - 1 May 1913: Chief of Staff, IV. Army Corps
1 May 1913: Promoted to *Lieutenant-General*
1 May 1913 - 15 Mar 1915: Commander, 20th Infantry Division
15 Mar 1915 - 2 Apr 1916: Commanding General, V. Caucasus Army Corps
2 Apr 1916 - 6 Apr 1917: Commanding General, XLVI. Army Corps
6 Apr 1917 - 23 Oct 1917: Reserve officer, Minsk Military District
23 Oct 1917: Retired

*Major-General* Nikolai Nikolayevich **Iuon** (13 Dec 1867 - ?)
1916 - 10 Nov 1916: Chief of Staff, 105th Infantry Division
10 Apr 1916: Promoted to *Major-General*
10 Nov 1916 - 8 May 1917: Chief of Staff, II. Siberian Army Corps
8 May 1917 - 30 Sep 1917: Commander, 4th Siberian Rifle Division
30 Sep 1917 - 1918: Reserve officer, Petrograd Military District

*Major-General* Ksenofont Nikolayevich **Ivanenko** (15 Jan 1856 - ?)
23 Sep 1912: Promoted to *Major-General*
23 Sep 1912 - 12 Dec 1914: Commander, 15th Artillery Brigade
12 Dec 1914: Retired
5 Feb 1916 - 1917: Recalled; Reserve officer, Odessa Military District

*Major-General* Vladimir Nikolayevich **Ivanenko** (2 Aug 1857 - ?)
18 May 1896 - 12 Mar 1902: Military Judge, Caucasus Military District Court
6 Dec 1900: Promoted to *Major-General*
12 Mar 1902 - 6 Nov 1906: Military Judge, Moscow Military District Court
6 Nov 1906 - 1 Nov 1907: Military Judge, Warsaw Military District Court
1 Nov 1907 - 1908: Military Judge, Kazan Military District Court

*Lieutenant-General* Aleksandr Yakovlevich **Ivanitsky** (22 Jan 1840 - 4 Aug 1903)
22 Jan 1892 - 14 Jan 1898: Commander, 52nd Infantry Regiment
14 May 1896: Promoted to *Major-General*
14 Jan 1898 - 22 Jan 1901: Commander, 1st Brigade, 44th Infantry Division
22 Jan 1901: Promoted to *Lieutenant-General*
22 Jan 1901: Retired

*Major-General* Pyotr Stepanovich **Ivankov** (3 Oct 1851 - ?)
1916: Promoted to *Major-General*

*Major-General* Aleksandr Georgiyevich **Ivanov** (9 Dec 1863 - Feb 1918)
1 Apr 1912 - 8 Apr 1915: Intendant, Vilnius Military District
6 Dec 1912: Promoted to *Major-General*
8 Apr 1915 - 1917: Commander, 92nd Militia Brigade

*Major-General* Aleksandr Ilich **Ivanov** (15 Aug 1844 - 1916)
2 Mar 1904 - 18 Apr 1904: Chief of Gendarmerie, Perm Province
28 Mar 1904: Promoted to *Major-General*
18 Apr 1904 - 1916: Attached to the St. Petersburg Gendarmerie

*Major-General* Aleksandr Mikhailovich **Ivanov** (11 Mar 1872 - ?)
11 Jun 1912 - 17 May 1915: Commander, 64th Infantry Regiment
3 Apr 1915: Promoted to *Major-General*
17 May 1915 - 25 May 1915: Acting Chief of Staff, 5th Army
25 May 1915 - 29 Jan 1917: Chief of Staff, XXVII. Army Corps
29 Jan 1917 - 31 Jan 1918: Commander, 187th Infantry Division
31 Jan 1918: Dismissed

*Lieutenant-General* Aleksandr Nikolayevich **Ivanov** (27 Aug 1855 - 11 Nov 1917)
22 Apr 1907: Promoted to *Major-General*
22 Apr 1907 - 23 Feb 1910: Commandant of Vilnius
23 Feb 1910 - 22 Jun 1912: Commander, 2nd Brigade, 3rd Cavalry Division
22 Jun 1912: Promoted to *Lieutenant-General*
22 Jun 1912: Retired

*Lieutenant-General* Aleksandr Petrovich **Ivanov** (2 Nov 1837 - 16 Jun 1905)
2 Jan 1878 - 3 Nov 1896: Sub-Section Chief, General Staff
30 Aug 1886: Promoted to *Major-General*
3 Nov 1896 - 1 Mar 1903: Attached to the General Staff
1 Mar 1903 - 16 Jun 1905: Member, General Staff Committee
6 Dec 1903: Promoted to *Lieutenant-General*

*Major-General* Aleksey Yulianovich **Ivanov** (22 Feb 1862 - ?)
? - 18 Jan 1916: Commander, 210th Infantry Regiment
23 Dec 1915: Promoted to *Major-General*
18 Jan 1916 - 1917: Commander, Brigade, 108th Infantry Division
1917 - 22 Apr 1917: Commander, 180th Infantry Division
22 Apr 1917 - ?: Commander, 107th Infantry Division

*Major-General* Fyodor Fedorovich **Ivanov** (28 Apr 1873 - ?)
1915 - 1917: Commander, 131st Infantry Regiment
29 Jul 1916: Promoted to *Major-General*

*Major-General* Fyodor Matveyevich **Ivanov** (6 Feb 1866 - ?)
13 May 1914 - 7 Apr 1916: Commander, 114th Infantry Regiment
30 Jul 1915: Promoted to *Major-General*
7 Apr 1916 - 29 Jan 1917: Commander, 1st Brigade, 45th Infantry Division
29 Jan 1917 - Mar 1917: Commander, 180th Infantry Division

*Major-General* Fyodor Mikhailovich **Ivanov** (16 Feb 1852 - 1930)
5 Nov 1906 - 1908: Commander, 1st East Siberian Siege Artillery Regiment
1908: Promoted to *Major-General*
1908: Retired
1914 - 1917: Recalled; Commander, 721st Foot Militia Squad

*Vice-Admiral* Fyodor Nikolayevich **Ivanov** (9 Sep 1860 - 1934)
6 Oct 1912 - 19 Jan 1915: Member, Committee on Organization of Coastal Defense

| | |
|---|---|
| 7 May 1913 - 19 Jan 1915: | Commander, 1st Baltic Naval Depot |
| 1914: | Promoted to *Rear-Admiral* |
| 19 Jan 1915: | Promoted to *Vice-Admiral* |
| 19 Jan 1915: | Retired |

*Major-General* Gavriil Gavriilovich **Ivanov** (10 Mar 1864 - ?)
| | |
|---|---|
| 31 Oct 1906 - 4 May 1916: | Commander, 19th Sapper Battalion |
| 11 Feb 1915: | Promoted to *Major-General* |
| 4 May 1916 - 25 Apr 1917: | Commander of Engineers, 6th Army |
| 25 Apr 1917 - 1918: | Reserve officer, Petrograd Military District |

*Lieutenant-General* Grigory Ivanovich **Ivanov** (17 Sep 1841 - 1899)
| | |
|---|---|
| 22 Jun 1882 - 15 Jun 1887: | Chief of Asia Section, General Staff |
| 30 Aug 1886: | Promoted to *Major-General* |
| 15 Jun 1887 - 1899: | Military Governor, Semirechensk Province |
| 14 May 1896: | Promoted to *Lieutenant-General* |

*Major-General* Isaaky Petrovich **Ivanov** (21 Jan 1860 - ?)
| | |
|---|---|
| 24 Jun 1906 - 1908: | Military Judge, Odessa Military District Court |
| 6 Dec 1906: | Promoted to *Major-General* |

*Major-General* Ivan Ivanovich **Ivanov** (27 Nov 1837 - Nov 1902)
| | |
|---|---|
| 25 Aug 1898 - Nov 1902: | Commander of Gendarmerie, Warsaw |
| 6 Dec 1901: | Promoted to *Major-General* |

*Lieutenant-General* Ivan Vasilyevich **Ivanov** (13 Apr 1843 - ?)
| | |
|---|---|
| 21 Mar 1894 - 26 Jun 1902: | Commander of Engineers, Fortress Sveaborg |
| 1 Jan 1895: | Promoted to *Major-General* |
| 26 Jun 1902 - 13 Jun 1910: | Deputy Commander of Engineers, Moscow Military District |
| 13 Jun 1910: | Promoted to *Lieutenant-General* |
| 13 Jun 1910: | Retired |

*Major-General* Ivan Vasilyevich **Ivanov** (19 Dec 1868 - ?)
| | |
|---|---|
| 1914 - 17 Sep 1916: | Commander, 6th Rifle Regiment |
| 3 Feb 1915: | Promoted to *Major-General* |
| 17 Sep 1916 - 13 Apr 1917: | Commander, Brigade, 4th Rifle Division |
| 13 Apr 1917 - 1918: | Commander, 2nd Rifle Division |

*Major-General* Konstantin Tikhonovich **Ivanov** (13 May 1861 - ?)
| | |
|---|---|
| 4 Sep 1912 - 1917: | Clerk, Committee for Unit Barracks, Main Directorate for Troop Billeting |
| 6 Dec 1916: | Promoted to *Major-General* |

*Lieutenant-General* Leonid Mikhailovich **Ivanov** (18 Dec 1845 - ?)
| | |
|---|---|
| 30 Aug 1887 - 16 Mar 1898: | Section Chief, Main Engineering Directorate |
| 14 May 1896: | Promoted to *Major-General* |
| 16 Mar 1898 - 1908: | Chief of Electro-Technical Department, Main |

| | Engineering Directorate |
|---|---|
| 2 Apr 1906: | Promoted to *Lieutenant-General* |

*Major-General* Mikhail Mikhailovich **Ivanov** (22 Sep 1861 - 6 Nov 1935)
| | |
|---|---|
| 18 Jan 1916 - 1917: | Commander, Brigade, 121st Infantry Division |
| 1 Mar 1916: | Promoted to *Major-General* |

*Lieutenant-General* Mikhail Nikitich **Ivanov** (24 Oct 1852 - 1914)
| | |
|---|---|
| 14 May 1901: | Promoted to *Major-General* |
| 14 May 1901 - 9 Nov 1904: | Chief of Staff, I. Siberian Army Corps |
| 9 Nov 1904 - 13 Jun 1905: | At the disposal of the Chief of Communications, 1st Manchurian Army |
| 13 Jun 1905 - 3 Feb 1906: | Attached to the General Staff |
| 3 Feb 1906 - 28 Nov 1908: | Commander, 60th Replacement Infantry Brigade |
| 28 Nov 1908: | Promoted to *Lieutenant-General* |
| 28 Nov 1908 - 6 Feb 1914: | Commander, 30th Infantry Division |

*Major-General* Mikhail Onufriyevich **Ivanov** (17 Dec 1866 - 14 Apr 1938)
| | |
|---|---|
| 16 Aug 1914 - 23 Dec 1916: | Commander, 48th Siberian Rifle Regiment |
| 20 Jul 1916: | Promoted to *Major-General* |
| 23 Dec 1916 - Feb 1917: | Reserve officer, Kiev Military District |
| Feb 1917: | Transferred to the Ukrainian armed forces |

*Lieutenant-General* Nikolai Aleksandrovich **Ivanov** (26 Jan 1842 - 18 May 1904)
| | |
|---|---|
| 12 Jan 1876 - 6 Jan 1877: | At the disposal of the Governor-General of Turkestan |
| 4 Apr 1876: | Promoted to *Major-General* |
| 6 Jan 1877 - Sep 1883: | Commander of Zaryavshansky District |
| Sep 1883 - 18 Jan 1889: | Military Governor of Ferghana Region |
| 18 Jan 1889: | Retired |
| 28 May 1898 - 3 Jul 1899: | At the disposal of the Minister of War |
| 10 Aug 1898: | Promoted to *Lieutenant-General* |
| 3 Jul 1899 - 23 Jan 1901: | Recalled; Deputy Commanding General, Turkestan Military District, Deputy Governor-General of Turkestan |
| 23 Jan 1901 - 18 May 1904: | Commanding General, Turkestan Military District, Governor-General of Turkestan |

*Major-General* Nikolai Aleksandrovich **Ivanov** (1 Dec 1855 - ?)
| | |
|---|---|
| 15 Feb 1913: | Promoted to *Major-General* |
| 15 Feb 1913 - 1915: | Commander, 5th Siberian Rifle Artillery Brigade |

*Major-General* Nikolai Alekseyevich **Ivanov** (24 May 1862 - ?)
| | |
|---|---|
| ? - 6 Aug 1916: | Commander, 191st Infantry Regiment |
| 6 Aug 1916: | Promoted to *Major-General* |
| 6 Aug 1916: | Retired |

*Major-General* Nikolai Davydovich **Ivanov** (26 Nov 1835 - ?)
| | |
|---|---|
| 1 Oct 1897: | Promoted to *Major-General* |

1 Oct 1897 - 29 Dec 1899: Commander, 27th Artillery Brigade

*Major-General* Nikolai Dmitriyevich **Ivanov** (17 Oct 1827 - ?)
25 Oct 1889: Promoted to *Major-General*
25 Oct 1889 - 6 Apr 1895: Commander, 1st Brigade, 5th Infantry Division

*Lieutenant-General* Nikolai Fyodorovich **Ivanov** (9 Jul 1839 - ?)
19 Dec 1882 - 10 Jan 1885: Commander, Life Guards Dragoon Regiment
15 May 1883: Promoted to *Major-General*
10 Jan 1885 - 22 Oct 1889: Commander, 3rd Brigade, 2nd Guards Cavalry Division
22 Oct 1889 - 7 Nov 1894: Commander, Guards Cavalry Reserve Brigade
7 Nov 1894 - 1900: Special Assignments General, Moscow Military District
6 Dec 1894: Promoted to *Lieutenant-General*

*General of Artillery* Nikolai Iudovich **Ivanov** (22 Jul 1851 - 11 Feb 1919)
11 Apr 1890 - 14 Dec 1899: Commander of Artillery, Fortress Kronstadt
30 Aug 1894: Promoted to *Major-General*
14 Dec 1899 - 22 Apr 1904: Attached to the Master-General of Ordnance
14 Aug 1900 - 1 Jan 1901: Commander of Artillery, Mobile Corps
6 Dec 1901: Promoted to *Lieutenant-General*
22 Apr 1904 - 15 Sep 1905: Attached to 1st Manchurian Army
15 Sep 1905 - 19 Dec 1905: Commanding General, III. Siberian Army Corps
19 Dec 1905 - 6 Nov 1906: Commanding General, I. Army Corps
6 Nov 1906 - 20 Apr 1907: Governor-General of Kronstadt
31 Dec 1906 - 2 Dec 1908: Member, Council of National Defense
20 Apr 1907 - 2 Dec 1908: Commandant of Kronstadt
1907: Promoted to *General-Adjutant*
13 Apr 1908: Promoted to *General of Artillery*
2 Dec 1908 - 19 Jul 1914: Commanding General, Kiev Military District
19 Jul 1914 - 17 Mar 1916: C-in-C, Southwestern Front
17 Mar 1916 - 27 Feb 1917: Military Advisor to the Tsar
27 Feb 1917 - 2 Mar 1917: Commanding General, Petrograd Military District

*Lieutenant-General* Nikolai Maksimovich **Ivanov** (19 Nov 1859 - 1 Mar 1935)
14 Jul 1910: Promoted to *Major-General*
14 Jul 1910 - 14 Jan 1914: Commander, 2nd Brigade, 7th Siberian Rifle Division
14 Jan 1914 - 1 Jul 1915: Commander, 2nd Brigade, 21st Infantry Division
26 Sep 1914: Promoted to *Lieutenant-General*
1 Jul 1915 - Jul 1917: Commander, 52nd Infantry Division
Jul 1917 - 6 Aug 1917: Commanding General, III. Caucasus Army Corps

*Lieutenant-General* Nikolai Martinovich **Ivanov** (25 Apr 1838 - ?)
2 Oct 1892: Promoted to *Major-General*
2 Oct 1892 - 7 Apr 1898: Commander, 2nd Brigade, 15th Infantry Division
7 Apr 1898 - 14 Mar 1900: Commander, 52nd Reserve Infantry Brigade
14 Mar 1900 - 19 May 1900: Commander, 4th Rifle Brigade
19 May 1900 - 6 Aug 1905: Commander, 15th Infantry Division
6 Dec 1900: Promoted to *Lieutenant-General*

6 Aug 1905 - 1906: Chief of Sanatory Department, Naval & Army High Command

*Vice-Admiral* Nikolai Mikhailovich **Ivanov** (4 Dec 1856 - ?)
24 Jul 1908: Promoted to *Rear-Admiral*
24 Jul 1908 - 1911: Chief of Staff, Port of Kronstadt
1911: Promoted to *Vice-Admiral*

*Major-General of Naval Artillery* Nikolai Nikolayevich **Ivanov** (30 Mar 1855 - ?)
1 Jul 1899 - 19 Oct 1911: Deputy Chief Inspector of Naval Artillery
6 Dec 1907: Promoted to *Major-General of Naval Artillery*
19 Oct 1911 - Mar 1913: Deputy Chief of Artillery Section, Main Shipbuilding Directorate

*Major-General of the Fleet* Nikolai Nikolayevich **Ivanov** (4 May 1864 - ?)
11 Jan 1903 - 1912: Chief Engineer, Cruiser "Kagul"
1912: Promoted to *Major-General of the Fleet*
1912: Retired

*Major-General* Nikolai Petrovich **Ivanov** (19 Sep 1863 - ?)
1915 - 25 Jul 1915: Commander, 5th Siberian Rifle Artillery Brigade
30 Apr 1915: Promoted to *Major-General*
25 Jul 1915 - 4 Nov 1916: Commander, 71st Artillery Brigade
4 Nov 1916 - 1917: Inspector of Artillery XLVI. Army Corps

*Major-General* Nikolai Yakovlevich **Ivanov** (13 Oct 1858 - ?)
16 Jul 1910: Promoted to *Major-General*
16 Jul 1910 - 8 Dec 1911: Commander, 2nd Brigade, 2nd Siberian Rifle Division
8 Dec 1911 - 3 May 1913: Commander, 2nd Brigade, 3rd Infantry Division

*Major-General* Pavel Maksimovich **Ivanov** (20 Feb 1855 - ?)
18 Jun 1891 - 1905: Chief of the Warsaw Palace Administration
14 May 1896: Promoted to *Major-General*

*Major-General* Pyotr Aleksandrovich **Ivanov** (28 Jun 1849 - ?)
29 Jan 1900 - 1906: Commander of Artillery, Fortress Brest-Litovsk
6 Apr 1903: Promoted to *Major-General*

*Major-General* Pyotr Ivanovich **Ivanov** (22 Sep 1868 - 20 May 1937)
2 Apr 1914 - 8 May 1916: Commander, 14th Finnish Rifle Regiment
16 Dec 1915: Promoted to *Major-General*
8 May 1916 - 1917: Commander, Brigade, 117th Infantry Division

*Rear-Admiral* Sergey Aleksandrovich **Ivanov** (9 Jun 1870 - 1918)
1914 - 1917: Captain, Cruiser "*Askold*"
1917: Promoted to *Rear-Admiral*

*Major-General of the Hydrographic Corps* Vasiliy Dmitriyevich **Ivanov** (24 Apr 1862 - ?)
| | |
|---|---|
| 1911 - 1917: | Head of Nautical Charts & Books Depot, Main Hydrographic Department |
| 30 Jul 1915: | Promoted to *Major-General of the Hydrographic Corps* |

*Major-General of the Admiralty* Vasily Maksimovich **Ivanov** (31 Dec 1851 - ?)
| | |
|---|---|
| 1 Jul 1900 - 1909: | Deputy Chief of Facilities, Main Directorate of Shipbuilding & Equipment |
| 17 Apr 1905: | Promoted to *Major-General of the Admiralty* |

*Lieutenant-General* Vasily Vasilyevich **Ivanov** (3 Mar 1852 - ?)
| | |
|---|---|
| 28 Jun 1902 - 24 Jan 1909: | Commander of Engineers, Fortress Sveaborg |
| 6 Dec 1902: | Promoted to *Major-General* |
| 24 Jan 1909 - 1 Sep 1911: | Deputy Commander of Engineers, St. Petersburg Military District |
| 1 Sep 1911: | Promoted to *Lieutenant-General* |
| 1 Sep 1911: | Retired |

*Lieutenant-General* Viktor Mikhailovich **Ivanov** (8 Sep 1846 - 25 Sep 1919)
| | |
|---|---|
| 16 Apr 1901 - 1909: | Professor, Nikolayev General Staff Academy |
| 27 Jun 1901: | Promoted to *Major-General* |
| 1909: | Promoted to *Lieutenant-General* |
| 1909: | Retired |

*Lieutenant-General* Vladimir Andreyevich **Ivanov** (26 Nov 1849 - ?)
| | |
|---|---|
| 9 Sep 1894 - 4 Jun 1898: | Military Judge, St. Petersburg Military District Court |
| 24 Apr 1898: | Promoted to *Major-General* |
| 4 Jun 1898 - 14 Oct 1905: | Military Prosecutor, Moscow Military District |
| 6 Dec 1904: | Promoted to *Lieutenant-General* |
| 14 Oct 1905 - 1906: | Chairman of the Military Tribunal, Kazan Military District |

*Lieutenant-General* Vladimir Apollonovich **Ivanov** (28 Apr 1837 - ?)
| | |
|---|---|
| 31 Jul 1889: | Promoted to *Major-General* |
| 31 Jul 1889 - 7 Feb 1894: | Commander, 1st Brigade, 2nd Infantry Division |
| 7 Feb 1894 - 1899: | Commander, 50th Reserve Infantry Brigade |
| 1899 - 11 Jan 1900: | Commander, 54th Reserve Infantry Brigade |
| 11 Jan 1900: | Promoted to *Lieutenant-General* |
| 11 Jan 1900: | Retired |

*Major-General* Vladimir Stepanovich **Ivanov** (25 Jun 1870 - ?)
| | |
|---|---|
| 26 Apr 1913 - 22 Oct 1915: | Commander, 19th Rifle Regiment |
| 5 Oct 1915: | Promoted to *Major-General* |
| 22 Oct 1915 - 26 Apr 1916: | Commander, 5th Rifle Division |
| 26 Apr 1916 - 24 May 1916: | Unassigned |
| 24 May 1916 - 1917: | Duty General, 6th Army |
| 1917: | Quartermaster-General, 6th Army |

*Major-General* Vladimir Vasilyevich **Ivanov** (8 Feb 1857 - ?)
| | |
|---|---|
| 19 Jan 1914: | Promoted to *Major-General* |
| 19 Jan 1914 - 10 Oct 1916: | Commander, 25th Artillery Brigade |
| 10 Oct 1916 - 1917: | Inspector of Artillery, XXXVIII. Army Corps |

*Lieutenant-General* Vladimir Zakharovich **Ivanov** (26 Oct 1848 - ?)
| | |
|---|---|
| 29 Dec 1899 - 24 Feb 1901: | Commander, 16th Artillery Brigade |
| 1 Jan 1901: | Promoted to *Major-General* |
| 24 Feb 1901 - 21 Apr 1908: | Deputy Commander of Artillery, Vilnius Military District |
| 21 Apr 1908: | Promoted to *Lieutenant-General* |
| 21 Apr 1908: | Retired |

*Major-General of the Admiralty* Yakov Maksimovich **Ivanov** (19 Oct 1860 - ?)
| | |
|---|---|
| 25 Mar 1912: | Promoted to *Major-General of Naval Navigators* |
| 26 Nov 1912 - 1913: | Commandant, Commercial Port of Taganrog |
| 29 Apr 1913: | Redesignated *Major-General of the Admiralty* |
| 1913 - 1917: | Commandant, Commercial Port of Rostov-on-Don |

*General of Cavalry* Nikolai Fyodorovich **Ivanov-Lutsevin** (9 Jul 1839 - 29 Jan 1929)
| | |
|---|---|
| 19 Dec 1882 - 10 Jan 1885: | Commander, Life Guards Dragoon Regiment |
| 15 May 1883: | Promoted to *Major-General* |
| 6 May 1883 - 4 Jul 1883: | Acting Commander, 2nd Brigade, 2nd Guards Cavalry Division |
| 15 May 1884 - 24 May 1884: | Acting Commander, 2nd Brigade, 2nd Guards Cavalry Division |
| 10 Jun 1884 - 21 Jul 1884: | Acting Commander, 2nd Brigade, 2nd Guards Cavalry Division |
| 10 Jan 1885 - 22 Oct 1889: | Commander, 3rd Brigade, 2nd Guards Cavalry Division |
| 22 Oct 1889 - 7 Nov 1894: | Commander, Guards Reserve Cavalry Brigade |
| 30 Dec 1889 - 11 Jan 1890: | Acting Commandant of Tver Garrison |
| 7 Nov 1894 - 18 Sep 1906: | General for Special Assignments, Moscow Military District |
| 6 Dec 1894: | Promoted to *Lieutenant-General* |
| 18 Sep 1906 - 1917: | Honorary Trustee, Board of Trustees, Empress Maria Institutions |
| 25 Jul 1908: | Promoted to *General of Cavalry* |
| 19 Mar 1914: | Promoted to *General-Adjutant* |

*Major-General* Rudolf Khristoforovich **Ivanovich** (1 Oct 1852 - 1920)
| | |
|---|---|
| 1 Aug 1910: | Promoted to *Major-General* |
| 1 Aug 1910 - 2 Oct 1912: | Commander, 11th Siberian Rifle Artillery Brigade |
| 2 Oct 1912: | Retired |

*Rear-Admiral* Viktor Yakovlevich **Ivanovsky** (27 Mar 1862 - 23 Mar 1924)
| | |
|---|---|
| 1909 - 1913: | Chief of Training, Mine Division, Baltic Fleet |
| 1913 - 1917: | Attached to the Baltic Fleet |
| 15 Jun 1915: | Promoted to *Rear-Admiral* |

*Major-General* Vilgelm Kaetanovich **Ivanovsky** (1844 - ?)
1 Jan 1900: Promoted to *Major-General*
1 Jan 1900 - 27 Feb 1900: Commander, 2$^{nd}$ Grenadier Artillery Brigade
27 Feb 1900: Retired

*Major-General* Vladimir Gavrilovich **Ivanovsky** (30 Dec 1848 - ?)
13 Aug 1905 - 15 Apr 1910: Commander, 5$^{th}$ Artillery Brigade
6 Dec 1906: Promoted to *Major-General*

*Major-General of the Admiralty* Yuri Konstantinovich **Ivanovsky** (11 Jan 1852 - 13 Aug 1906)
1893 - 13 Aug 1906: Chief of Baltic Sea Survey
1903: Promoted to *Major-General of the Admiralty*

*Major-General* Vasily Polikarpovich **Ivashchenko** (18 Jul 1862 - ?)
30 May 1910 - 1917: Intendant, VII. Army Corps
6 Dec 1916: Promoted to *Major-General*
1917: Special Assignments General, Romanian Front

*Lieutenant-General* Vladimir Porfiryevich **Ivashchenko** (29 Nov 1859 - ?)
7 Aug 1903 - 21 Jul 1909: Deputy Chief of Okhtenskaya Explosives Factory
29 Mar 1909: Promoted to *Major-General*
21 Jul 1909 - 14 Dec 1911: Chairman, Commission for Construction of Samara Explosives Factory
14 Dec 1911 - 30 Apr 1915: Chief of Sergeyev Samara Explosives Factory
30 Apr 1915: Promoted to *Lieutenant-General*
30 Apr 1915: Retired

*Lieutenant-General* Sergey Vasilyevich **Ivashentsov** (13 Sep 1857 - 4 Nov 1921)
17 Oct 1903: Promoted to *Major-General*
17 Oct 1903 - 24 Oct 1904: Commander, 27$^{th}$ Artillery Brigade
24 Oct 1904 - 14 Nov 1907: Commander, 2$^{nd}$ Life Guards Artillery Brigade
14 Nov 1907: Promoted to *Lieutenant-General*
14 Nov 1907 - 23 Nov 1908: Commander of Artillery, XI. Army Corps
23 Nov 1908: Retired

*Lieutenant-General* Andrey Vasilyevich **Ivashintsov** (24 Dec 1869 - 25 Mar 1921)
13 May 1910: Promoted to *Major-General*
13 May 1910 - 30 May 1910: Commander, 7$^{th}$ Artillery Brigade
30 May 1910 - 18 Oct 1913: Commander, 23$^{rd}$ Artillery Brigade
18 Oct 1913 - 8 Sep 1914: Commander of Artillery, Don Cossack Army
8 Sep 1914 - 1917: Inspector of Artillery, VI. Siberian Army Corps
15 Jun 1915: Promoted to *Lieutenant-General*

*Lieutenant-General* Nikolai Vasilyevich **Ivashintsov** (22 Jul 1872 - 1933)
29 Nov 1912: Promoted to *Major-General*
29 Nov 1912 - 12 May 1916: Commander, 22$^{nd}$ Artillery Brigade
28 Nov 1916: Promoted to *Lieutenant-General*

| | |
|---|---|
| 12 May 1916 - 5 Jan 1917: | Inspector of Artillery, I. Army Corps |
| 5 Jan 1917 - 1 Feb 1917: | Reserve officer, Petrograd Military District |
| 1 Feb 1917 - 1917: | Inspector of Artillery, VII. Siberian Army Corps |

*Vice-Admiral* Vasily Fyodorovich **Ivashintsov** (1 Jan 1839 - 3 Aug 1899)
| | |
|---|---|
| 1893: | Promoted to *Rear-Admiral* |
| 1893 - ?: | Junior Flagman, Black Sea Fleet |
| ? - 1896: | Junior Flagman, Baltic Fleet |
| 1896 - 4 Jan 1899: | Director of Lighthouses & Navigation, Baltic Sea |
| 4 Jan 1899: | Promoted to *Vice-Admiral* |
| 4 Jan 1899: | Retired |

*Major-General* Anatoly Viktorovich **Ivashkevich** (9 Feb 1863 - 12 Mar 1940)
| | |
|---|---|
| 14 Mar 1916 - 1917: | Commander, 5th Railway Brigade |
| 6 Dec 1916: | Promoted to *Major-General* |

*Major-General* Vyacheslav Vitalyevich **Ivashkevich** (17 Aug 1871 - 25 Nov 1922)
| | |
|---|---|
| 16 Aug 1914 - 9 Nov 1915: | Commander, 54th Siberian Rifle Regiment |
| 30 Jul 1915: | Promoted to *Major-General* |
| 9 Nov 1915 - 3 Jun 1917: | Commander, Brigade, 3rd Siberian Rifle Division |
| 3 Jun 1917 - 19 Sep 1917: | Commander, Finnish Consolidated Border Division |

*Lieutenant-General* Vladimir Nikolayevich **Ivashkin** (7 May 1839 - 14 Jul 1903)
| | |
|---|---|
| 1 Mar 1878 - 2 Feb 1885: | Commander, 4th Hussar Regiment |
| 2 Feb 1885: | Promoted to *Major-General* |
| 2 Feb 1885 - 15 Oct 1886: | Commander, 2nd Brigade, 6th Cavalry Division |
| 15 Oct 1886 - 19 Nov 1889: | Chief of Staff XIV. Army Corps |
| 19 Nov 1889 - 25 Nov 1891: | Chief of Staff, Grenadier Corps |
| 25 Nov 1891 - 19 Jan 1897: | Chief of Staff, XVII. Army Corps |
| 19 Jan 1897 - 2 Jul 1902: | Commander, Caucasus Cavalry Division |
| 6 Dec 1897: | Promoted to *Lieutenant-General* |

*General of Engineers* Dmitry Petrovich **Ivkov** (17 Jul 1849 - 25 Oct 1916)
| | |
|---|---|
| 21 Jun 1898 - 29 Jun 1910: | Chief of Section 5, Main Engineering Directorate |
| 6 Apr 1903: | Promoted to *Major-General* |
| 29 Jun 1910 - 28 Mar 1914: | Deputy Chief of the Main Engineering Directorate |
| 6 Dec 1910: | Promoted to *Lieutenant-General* |
| 28 Mar 1914 - 1915: | Chief of Administration, Main Military Technical Directorate |
| 1915: | Promoted to *General of Engineers* |
| 1915: | Retired |

*Lieutenant-General of the Fleet* Nikolai Avenirovich **Ivkov** (9 Oct 1858 - 1 Feb 1917)
| | |
|---|---|
| 6 Dec 1911: | Promoted to *Major-General of the Admiralty* |
| 6 Dec 1911 - 1 Feb 1917: | Commandant of the Machinery School, Baltic Fleet |
| 8 Apr 1913: | Redesignated *Major-General of the Fleet* |
| 30 Jan 1917: | Promoted to *Lieutenant-General of the Fleet* |

*Lieutenant-General* Nikolai Petrovich **Ivkov** (22 Jun 1852 - 27 Dec 1908)
| | |
|---|---|
| 15 Jan 1902: | Promoted to *Major-General* |
| 15 Jan 1902 - 22 Jun 1904: | Commander, Life Guards Sapper Battalion |
| 22 Jun 1904 - 17 Jul 1905: | Commander, 3rd Sapper Brigade |
| 17 Jul 1906 - 7 Dec 1906: | Commander, 6th Sapper Brigade |
| 7 Dec 1906: | Promoted to *Lieutenant-General* |
| 7 Dec 1906: | Retired |

*Lieutenant-General* Aleksandr Aleksandrovich **Izbyshev** (12 Jul 1837 - 23 Mar 1903)
| | |
|---|---|
| 7 May 1879 - 12 Aug 1893: | Ataman, 3rd Military Division, Orenburg Military District |
| 6 May 1889: | Promoted to *Major-General* |
| 12 Aug 1893 - 1901: | Member, Orenburg Cossack Army Committee |
| 10 Feb 1900: | Promoted to *Lieutenant-General* |

*Major-General* Vladimir Nikolayevich **Izergin** (31 May 1864 - ?)
| | |
|---|---|
| 2 Sep 1906 - 10 Feb 1916: | Commander, Ust-Dvinsk Fortress Artillery Battalion |
| 5 Oct 1915: | Promoted to *Major-General* |
| 10 Feb 1916 - 1917: | Commander, 4th Siege Artillery Regiment |

*Major-General* Khodzhi-Akhmet Iskhakovich **Izhbulatov** (16 Mar 1851 - 1921)
| | |
|---|---|
| 1908: | Promoted to *Major-General* |
| 1908: | Retired |
| 9 Jul 1915 - 27 Jul 1915: | Recalled; Attached to Kazan Military District |
| 27 Jul 1915 - 9 Feb 1916: | Commander, 146th Reserve Infantry Battalion |
| 18 Apr 1916 - 1917: | Commander, 152nd Reserve Infantry Regiment |

*Major-General* Mikhail Vikentyevich **Izhitsky** (11 Jan 1865 - ?)
| | |
|---|---|
| 7 Apr 1908 - 16 Jul 1915: | Commander, 30th Siberian Rifle Regiment |
| 15 Feb 1915: | Promoted to *Major-General* |
| 16 Jul 1915 - 1917: | Reserve officer, Dvinsk Military District |

*Major-General* Fyodor Nikolayevich **Izmaylov** (6 Aug 1852 - 1911)
| | |
|---|---|
| 5 Mar 1898 - 1911: | Attached to Grand Duke Dmitry Konstantinovich |
| 1 Jun 1907: | Promoted to *Major-General* |

*Lieutenant-General* Adolf Vikentyevich **Izmaylovich** (10 Apr 1845 - ?)
| | |
|---|---|
| 22 Dec 1890 - 14 Aug 1896: | Commander, 2nd Artillery Training Polygon, Caucasus Military District |
| 30 Aug 1893: | Promoted to *Major-General* |
| 14 Aug 1896 - 20 Jul 1899: | Artillery Inspector, Trans-Caspian Province |
| 20 Jul 1899 - 17 Feb 1900: | Commander, 2nd Turkestan Artillery Brigade |
| 17 Feb 1900 - 9 May 1906: | Commander of Artillery, IV. Army Corps |
| 6 Dec 1901: | Promoted to *Lieutenant-General* |

*Major-General* Pyotr Ivanovich **Izmestyev** (10 Sep 1873 - 31 Mar 1925)
| | |
|---|---|
| 1915 - Jun 1915: | Commander, 297th Infantry Regiment |
| 20 Apr 1915: | Promoted to *Major-General* |

Jun 1915 - 29 Jan 1917: Chief of Lines of Communication Section, 12th Army
29 Jan 1917 - 1918: Commander, 20th Siberian Rifle Division

*Major-General* Aleksandr Nikolayevich **Izvekov** (8 Aug 1839 - ?)
16 Jun 1885: Promoted to *Major-General*
16 Jun 1885 - 25 Apr 1890: Reserve officer, Corps of Engineers
25 Apr 1890 - 13 May 1894: Special Assignments General, Omsk Military District
13 May 1894 - 1895: Attached to the Main Engineering Directorate

*Lieutenant-General of the Admiralty* Nikolai Nilovich **Izvekov** (26 Jun 1842 - ?)
1894: Promoted to *Major-General of the Admiralty*
1894 - 1896: Prosecutor, Kronstadt Naval Court
1896 - 1904: Chief Naval Prosecutor, Ministry of the Navy
1902: Promoted to *Lieutenant-General of the Admiralty*
1904 - 1906: Member, Supreme Naval Tribunal

*General of Infantry* Konstantin Yakovlevich **Kabakov** (20 Jan 1840 - ?)
5 Jan 1900: Promoted to *Major-General*
5 Jan 1900 - 5 Feb 1906: Special Assignments General, Inspectorate of Rifles
5 Feb 1906 - 24 Dec 1909: Special Assignments General, Inspectorate-General of Infantry
29 Mar 1909: Promoted to *Lieutenant-General*
24 Dec 1909 - 14 Sep 1915: Inspector of Riflemen
14 Sep 1915: Promoted to *General of Infantry*
14 Sep 1915: Retired

*Lieutenant-General* Klavdy Yegorovich **Kabalevsky** (18 Mar 1844 - ?)
29 Mar 1895: Promoted to *Major-General*
29 Mar 1895 - 24 Oct 1906: Chief of Lugansk Cartridge Factory
24 Oct 1906: Promoted to *Lieutenant-General*
24 Oct 1906: Retired

*Major-General* Andrey Nikolayevich **Kacharovsky** (1 May 1861 - ?)
17 Aug 1914 - 25 Aug 1916: Commander, 3rd Heavy Artillery Brigade
23 Nov 1915: Promoted to *Major-General*
25 Aug 1916 - 19 Oct 1916: Commander of Artillery, Fortress Mikhailov
19 Oct 1916 - 1917: Commander of Artillery, Fortress Sevastopol
1917 - 20 May 1917: Reserve officer, Odessa Military District
20 May 1917: Dismissed

*Major-General* Pavel Ivanovich **Kachin** (11 Jan 1867 - 30 Sep 1914)
1913 - 30 Sep 1914: Attached to 1st Siberian Rifle Regiment
6 Jun 1915: Posthumously promoted to *Major-General*

*Major-General* Anton Viktorovich **Kachinsky** (26 Jul 1874 - 4 Mar 1925)
23 May 1915 - 28 Aug 1917: Commander, 55th Artillery Brigade
18 Aug 1916: Promoted to *Major-General*
28 Aug 1917 - 1918: Inspector of Artillery, I. Polish Rifle Corps

*Lieutenant-General* Nikolai Semyonovich **Kachura** (25 Jul 1851 - ?)
| | |
|---|---|
| 16 Aug 1901: | Promoted to *Major-General* |
| 16 Aug 1901 - 24 Apr 1906: | Commander, 1st Brigade, 19th Infantry Division |
| 24 Apr 1906 - 15 Aug 1910: | Commander, 62nd Reserve Infantry Brigade |
| 3 Oct 1909: | Promoted to *Lieutenant-General* |
| 15 Aug 1910 - 14 Oct 1911: | Transferred to the reserve |
| 14 Oct 1911: | Retired |
| 27 Sep 1914 - 1917: | Recalled; Commander, 12th Replacement Infantry Brigade |

*Major-General* Aleksandr Nazarovich **Kadilov** (13 Aug 1836 - ?)
| | |
|---|---|
| 25 Mar 1897: | Promoted to *Major-General* |
| 25 Mar 1897 - 23 Jul 1900: | Commander, Trans-Caspian Regional Brigade |
| 23 Jul 1900 - 1901: | Commander, 2nd Turkestan Reserve Brigade |

*Major-General* Dmitry Petrovich **Kadomsky** (21 Oct 1868 - 1935)
| | |
|---|---|
| 17 Jul 1907 - 8 Oct 1913: | Commander, 167th Infantry Regiment |
| 14 Apr 1913: | Promoted to *Major-General* |
| 8 Oct 1913 - 5 Dec 1913: | Commander, 1st Brigade, 5th Infantry Division |
| 5 Dec 1913 - 1 Aug 1914: | Chief of Office to the Governor-General of Finland |
| 1 Aug 1914 - 13 Jan 1915: | Commander, 2nd Brigade, 3rd Grenadier Division |
| 13 Jan 1915 - 1 Apr 1915: | Reserve officer, Dvinsk Military District |
| 1 Apr 1915 - 8 Feb 1916: | Commander, 76th Militia Brigade |
| 8 Feb 1916 - 17 Dec 1916: | Chief of Staff, 126th Infantry Division |
| 17 Dec 1916 - 7 Jul 1917: | Chief of Staff, XV. Army Corps |
| 7 Jul 1917 - 10 Oct 1917: | Commander, 6th Infantry Division |
| 10 Oct 1917 - 17 Mar 1918: | Reserve officer, Kiev Military District |

*Major-General* Andrey Fyodorovich **Kadoshnikov** (15 Oct 1876 - ?)
| | |
|---|---|
| 2 Dec 1916 - 3 Jan 1917: | Reserve officer, Moscow Military District |
| 12 Dec 1916: | Promoted to *Major-General* |
| 3 Jan 1917 - 28 Apr 1917: | Chief of Staff, 3rd Infantry Division |
| 28 Apr 1917 - 6 Aug 1917: | Commander, 156th Infantry Division |
| 6 Aug 1917 - 30 Sep 1917: | Unassigned |
| 30 Sep 1917 - 1918: | Commander, 77th Infantry Division |

*Major-General* Aleksandr Petrovich **Kaffka** (5 Sep 1869 - Jan 1917)
| | |
|---|---|
| 26 Jul 1915 - Jan 1917: | Chief of Office, Commanding General, Caucasus Military District |
| 8 Dec 1916: | Promoted to *Major-General* |

*Lieutenant-General* Ivan Vasilyevich **Kakhanov** (17 Mar 1845 - ?)
| | |
|---|---|
| 2 Jan 1893: | Promoted to *Major-General* |
| 2 Jan 1893 - 24 Oct 1896: | Commander, 16th Artillery Brigade |
| 24 Oct 1896 - 5 Dec 1899: | Commander, 1st Reserve Artillery Brigade |
| 5 Dec 1899 - 28 Sep 1904: | Commander of Artillery, XVI. Army Corps |
| 1 Apr 1901: | Promoted to *Lieutenant-General* |
| 28 Sep 1904 - 1906: | Inspector of Artillery, 2nd Manchurian Army |

*General of Cavalry* Semyon Vasilievich **Kakhanov** (2 Apr 1842 - 14 Aug 1908)

| | |
|---|---|
| 8 Jan 1877 - 1 Dec 1878: | Chief of Siege Artillery, Caucasus-Turets Border Corps |
| 8 Nov 1877: | Promoted to *Major-General* |
| 1 Dec 1878 - 2 Feb 1879: | Unassigned |
| 2 Feb 1879 - 25 Mar 1880: | Commander, 38th Artillery Brigade |
| 25 Mar 1880 - 20 Dec 1884: | Commander, 2nd Brigade, 38th Infantry Division |
| 20 Dec 1884 - 16 Jan 1890: | Commander, 2nd Brigade, Caucasus Grenadier Division |
| 16 Jan 1890 - 10 Feb 1890: | Commander, 31st Infantry Division |
| 10 Feb 1890 - 2 Jul 1899: | Commander, Terek Region, Ataman, Terek Cossack Army |
| 30 Aug 1890: | Promoted to *Lieutenant-General* |
| 2 Jul 1899 - 1 Mar 1901: | Commanding General, I. Turkestan Army Corps |
| 6 Dec 1900: | Promoted to *General of Cavalry* |
| 1 Mar 1901 - 22 Oct 1904: | Commanding General, XX. Army Corps |
| 22 Oct 1904 - 27 Aug 1905: | Commanding General, Odessa Military District |

*Lieutenant-General* Vasily Apollonovich **Kakhanov** (1 Jan 1830 - 28 Dec 1901)

| | |
|---|---|
| 18 Nov 1869 - 22 Feb 1876: | Commander, 10th Dragoon Regiment |
| 22 Feb 1876: | Promoted to *Major-General* |
| 22 Feb 1876 - 4 Jun 1883: | Commander, 2nd Brigade, 14th Cavalry Division |
| 4 Jun 1883 - 19 Feb 1890: | Commander, 6th Cavalry Division |
| 30 Aug 1886: | Promoted to *Lieutenant-General* |
| 19 Feb 1890 - 21 Jul 1891: | At the disposal of the Inspector-General of Cavalry |
| 21 Jul 1891 - 7 Jun 1895: | Attached to the Ministry of War |
| 7 Jun 1895 - 28 Dec 1901: | At the disposal of the Minister of War |

*Lieutenant-General* Yevgeny Nikolayevich **Kakurin** (15 Mar 1846 - ?)

| | |
|---|---|
| 19 Oct 1888 - 27 Jan 1892: | Chief of Staff, Trans-Baikal Region |
| 30 Aug 1890: | Promoted to *Major-General* |
| 17 Jan 1892 - 24 Mar 1894: | Deputy Chief of Staff, Amur Military District |
| 24 Mar 1894 - 2 Jul 1897: | Deputy Chief of Staff, Kazan Military District |
| 2 Jul 1897 - 17 Feb 1900: | Commander, 59th Replacement Infantry Brigade |
| 17 Feb 1900: | Promoted to *Lieutenant-General* |
| 17 Feb 1900 - 4 Jul 1901: | Commander, 11th Infantry Division |
| 4 Jul 1901 - 23 Dec 1904: | Commander, 5th Infantry Division |
| 23 Dec 1904 - 3 Oct 1906: | Commanding General, XIV. Army Corps |

*Lieutenant-General* Arkady Ivanovich **Kalachev** (31 Jul 1821 - ?)

| | |
|---|---|
| 15 Jan 1863 - 3 Feb 1869: | Commander, 16th Artillery Brigade |
| 30 Aug 1866: | Promoted to *Major-General* |
| 3 Feb 1869 - 4 Nov 1876: | Deputy Commander of Artillery, Vilnius Military District |
| 4 Nov 1876 - 6 Nov 1877: | Commander of Artillery, IX. Army Corps |
| 21 Aug 1877: | Promoted to *Lieutenant-General* |
| 6 Nov 1877 - 12 Sep 1878: | Unassigned |
| 12 Sep 1878 - 29 Jan 1879: | Commander of Artillery, Occupation Forces, Bulgaria |
| 29 Jan 1879 - 1 Feb 1895: | Commander of Artillery, Vilnius Military District |

*Major-General* Nikolai Khristoforovich **Kalachev** (8 Feb 1866 - 1942)
| | |
|---|---|
| 29 Jan 1913: | Promoted to *Major-General* |
| 29 Jan 1913 - 23 May 1914: | Chief of Staff, XI. Army Corps |
| 23 May 1914 - 12 Nov 1914: | Chief of Staff, XII. Army Corps |
| 12 Nov 1914 - Nov 1917: | Commandant, Kiev Military School |

*Major-General* Stepan Gerasimovich **Kalantarov** (16 Aug 1855 - 9 Jul 1926)
| | |
|---|---|
| 9 Apr 1911 - 23 Sep 1914: | Commandant of Vilnius |
| 6 Dec 1911: | Promoted to *Major-General* |
| 23 Sep 1914 - 1 Nov 1916: | Commandant of Vitebsk |
| 1 Nov 1916 - 1918: | Deputy Commandant of Petrograd |
| Jul 1918: | Retired |

*Major-General* Leonid Petrovich **Kalashnikov** (23 Sep 1851 - ?)
| | |
|---|---|
| 28 Jun 1901 - 23 Jun 1917: | Chief, Kiev Military Paramedic School |
| 14 Apr 1913: | Promoted to *Major-General* |
| 23 Jun 1917: | Dismissed |

*Major-General* Nikolai Konstantinovich **Kalchenko** (27 Jul 1854 - ?)
| | |
|---|---|
| 11 Dec 1894 - 1906: | Company Commander, Petrov-Poltava Cadet Corps |
| 1906: | Promoted to *Major-General* |
| 1906: | Retired |
| 1915 - 11 Oct 1916: | Recalled; Commander of Rakovets Line of Communications Base |
| 11 Oct 1916 - 23 Jul 1917: | Reserve officer, Kiev Military District |

*General of Cavalry* Aleksei Maksimovich **Kaledin** (12 Oct 1861 - 29 Jan 1918)
| | |
|---|---|
| 26 Aug 1906 - 2 Jun 1910: | Deputy Chief of Staff, Don Army |
| 31 May 1907: | Promoted to *Major-General* |
| 2 Jun 1910 - 6 Dec 1912: | Commander, $2^{nd}$ Brigade, $11^{th}$ Cavalry Division |
| 6 Dec 1912 - 18 Jun 1915: | Commander, $12^{th}$ Cavalry Division |
| 31 May 1913: | Promoted to *Lieutenant-General* |
| 18 Jun 1915 - 5 Jul 1915: | Commanding General, XLI. Army Corps |
| 5 Jul 1915 - 20 Mar 1916: | Commanding General, XII. Army Corps |
| 20 Mar 1916 - 29 Apr 1917: | C-in-C, $8^{th}$ Army |
| 10 Jun 1916: | Promoted to *General of Cavalry* |
| 29 Apr 1917 - 19 Jun 1917: | Member of the Military Council |
| 19 Jun 1917 - 29 Jan 1918: | Military Ataman of the Don Cossacks |

*Major-General* Vasily Maksimovich **Kaledin** (5 Oct 1859 - 3 Jun 1919)
| | |
|---|---|
| 30 May 1911 - 27 Apr 1915: | Commander, $12^{th}$ Don Cossack Regiment |
| 14 Nov 1914: | Promoted to *Major-General* |
| 27 Apr 1915 - 3 Jun 1916: | Commander, $2^{nd}$ Brigade, $3^{rd}$ Don Cossack Division |
| 3 Jun 1916 - Oct 1917: | Commander, $4^{th}$ Don Cossack Division |

*Major-General* Ivan Ivanovich **Kaliks** (15 Feb 1860 - ?)
| | |
|---|---|
| 16 Jul 1910: | Promoted to *Major-General* |
| 16 Jul 1910 - 12 Feb 1915: | Commander, $1^{st}$ Railway Brigade |

12 Feb 1915 - 14 Mar 1916:     Commander, Consolidated State Militia Brigade, Dvinsk Military District
14 Mar 1916 - 1917:     Commander, 1st Railway Brigade

*Major-General* Nikolai Dmitriyevich **Kalin** (21 Oct 1859 - ?)
28 Feb 1908 - 1917:     Military Judge, Kazan Military District Court
13 Apr 1908:     Promoted to *Major-General*

*Lieutenant-General* Vladimir Dmitriyevich **Kalin** (2 Jan 1857 - 1924)
1 Aug 1910:     Promoted to *Major-General*
1 Aug 1910 - 21 Feb 1915:     Commander, 39th Artillery Brigade
12 Nov 1914:     Promoted to *Lieutenant-General*
21 Feb 1915 - 10 Jun 1917:     Inspector of Artillery, II. Turkestan Army Corps
10 Jun 1917 - Oct 1917:     Reserve officer, Kiev Military District

*Major-General* Konstantin Ivanovich **Kalinin** (12 Sep 1859 - 3 Oct 1916)
16 Dec 1905 - 3 Oct 1916:     Chief of Gendarmerie, Kazan Province
10 Apr 1916:     Promoted to *Major-General*

*Major-General* Mikhail Yevdokimovich **Kalinin** (28 May 1868 - ?)
11 Apr 1916 - 1917:     Deputy Duty General, General Staff
6 Dec 1916:     Promoted to *Major-General*

*Major-General* Nikolai Matveyevich **Kalinin** (6 Dec 1836 - ?)
14 Jul 1888 - 8 Aug 1892:     Ataman, Cherkassy Division, Don Cossack Army
6 May 1890:     Promoted to *Major-General*
8 Aug 1892 - 22 Jan 1894:     Unassigned
22 Jan 1894 - 24 Jan 1900:     Commander, 1st Brigade, 1st Don Cossack Division

*Major-General* Anatoly Apollonovich **Kalinovsky** (25 May 1865 - ?)
Sep 1916 - 1917:     Commander, Brigade, 67th Infantry Division
12 Dec 1916:     Promoted to *Major-General*

*Lieutenant-General* Aleksandr Iosifovich **Kalishevsky** (12 Apr 1856 - 1918)
16 Jun 1900 - 13 Aug 1906:     Director of Yaroslavl Cadet Corps
1 Apr 1901:     Promoted to *Major-General*
13 Aug 1906 - 20 Jan 1917:     Director of Tsar Aleksandr II Cadet Corps
22 Apr 1907:     Promoted to *Lieutenant-General*
20 Jan 1917:     Dismissed

*Lieutenant-General* Anatoly Iosifovich **Kalishevsky** (28 Mar 1870 - 1 Apr 1937)
21 Jul 1915 - 10 Aug 1916:     Reserve officer, 6th Army
11 Oct 1915:     Promoted to *Major-General*
10 Aug 1916 - 3 Jan 1917:     Chief of Staff, 3rd Turkestan Rifle Division
3 Jan 1917 - Feb 1917:     Attached to the Chief of the General Staff
Feb 1917:     Chief of POW Transport Section, General Staff
18 Feb 1917 - 16 Mar 1917:     Chief of Staff, III. Caucasus Army Corps
13 Apr 1917 - Jan 1918:     Chief of POW Transport Section, General Staff

1917: Promoted to *Lieutenant-General*
Jan 1918: Dismissed

*Major-General* Fyodor Iosifovich **Kalishevsky** (1 Oct 1852 - 29 Jun 1903)
19 May 1893 - 10 Mar 1899: Commandant, Caucasus Siege Artillery Park
6 Dec 1898: Promoted to *Major-General*
10 Mar 1899 - 29 Jun 1903: Commandant, Odessa Fortress Artillery Depot

*Major-General* Sergey Iosifovich **Kalishevsky** (17 Jul 1860 - 3 Dec 1908)
30 Aug 1900 - 7 Mar 1906: Military Judge, Siberian Military District Court
6 Apr 1903: Promoted to *Major-General*
7 Mar 1906 - 14 Aug 1906: Military Prosecutor, Siberian Military District
14 Aug 1906 - 19 Sep 1906: Military Prosecutor, Omsk Military District
19 Sep 1906 - 3 Dec 1908: Military Prosecutor, Odessa Military District

*Major-General* Nikolai Tarasovich **Kalita** (23 Sep 1845 - 1916)
8 Apr 1909 - 31 Dec 1913: Commandant, Fortress Warsaw Artillery Depot
6 Dec 1909: Promoted to *Major-General*
31 Dec 1913: Retired

*General of Cavalry* Pyotr Petrovich **Kalitin** (30 Oct 1853 - 7 Jun 1927)
26 Nov 1902: Promoted to *Major-General*
26 Nov 1902 - 28 May 1903: Attached to the Chief of the General Staff
28 May 1903 - 8 Aug 1906: Commander, 2$^{nd}$ Brigade, 2$^{nd}$ Consolidated Cossack Division
8 Aug 1906 - 10 Jul 1907: Commander, Ussuri Mounted Brigade
10 Jul 1907 - 22 Sep 1909: Commander, Trans-Baikal Cossack Brigade
23 Sep 1908: Promoted to *Lieutenant-General*
22 Sep 1909 - 4 Feb 1915: Commander, Siberian Cossack Brigade
4 Feb 1915 - 12 Mar 1917: Commanding General, I. Caucasus Army Corps
22 Mar 1915: Promoted to *General of Cavalry*
12 Mar 1917 - Oct 1917: Member, Committee on Wounded Veterans

*Major-General* Vilgelm-Aleksandr Aleksandrovich **Kalmeyer** (28 Feb 1866 - 2 Aug 1943)
27 Oct 1914 - 8 Nov 1916: Commander, 7$^{th}$ Uhlan Regiment
2 Jun 1916: Promoted to *Major-General*
8 Nov 1916 - 1917: Commander, 1$^{st}$ Brigade, Amur Cavalry Division

*Lieutenant-General* Nikolai Aleksandrovich **Kalmykov** (28 Oct 1833 - 7 Jan 1904)
1 Jul 1886 - 1895: Military Judge, Turkestan Military District Court
30 Aug 1886: Promoted to *Major-General*
1895: Promoted to *Lieutenant-General*
1895: Retired

*Lieutenant-General* Emmanuil Khristianovich **Kalnin** (28 Feb 1855 - ?)
20 Aug 1899 - 19 Nov 1904: Military Attaché, Constantinople
6 Dec 1902: Promoted to *Major-General*
19 Nov 1904 - 1913: Quartermaster-General, Odessa Military District

1913: Promoted to *Lieutenant-General*
1913: Retired

*Lieutenant-General* Mikhail Nikolayevich **Kalnitsky** (6 Nov 1870 - 30 Jun 1961)
3 May 1914 - 13 May 1915: Commander, 14th Grenadier Regiment
31 Dec 1914: Promoted to *Major-General*
13 May 1915 - 21 Jun 1915: Reserve officer, Dvinsk Military District
21 Jun 1915 - 4 May 1916: Chief of Staff, VII. Siberian Army Corps
4 May 1916 - 10 Nov 1916: Chief of Staff, V. Caucasus Army Corps
10 Nov 1916 - 16 Sep 1917: Commander, 123rd Infantry Division
1917: Promoted to *Lieutenant-General*
16 Sep 1917 - 1918: Chief of Staff, Caucasus Military District

*Major-General* Nikolai Ivanovich **Kalugin** (5 Apr 1864 - ?)
7 Apr 1908 - Oct 1917: Staff Officer for Assignments (5th Class), General Staff
14 Apr 1913: Promoted to *Major-General*

*Major-General* Andrey Andreyevich **Kalyuzhny** (6 Aug 1860 - 16 Aug 1914)
27 Sep 1913: Promoted to *Major-General*
27 Sep 1913 - 16 Aug 1914: Commander, 2nd Brigade, 36th Infantry Division

*Major-General* Aleksandr Ivanovich **Kamberg** (10 Feb 1856 - ?)
10 Dec 1908 - 13 Feb 1914: Commander, 29th Siberian Rifle Regiment
13 Feb 1914: Promoted to *Major-General*
13 Feb 1914: Retired
4 Nov 1914 - 12 Dec 1914: Recalled; Commander, 1st Brigade, 36th Infantry Division
12 Dec 1914 - 2 Jan 1915: Acting Commander, 36th Infantry Division
2 Jan 1915 - 11 Jan 1915: Commander, 2nd Brigade, 6th Infantry Division
11 Jan 1915 - 1917: Commander, 1st Brigade, 10th Siberian Rifle Division
4 Oct 1917 - 24 Dec 1917: Commander, 28th Replacement Infantry Brigade

*Lieutenant-General* Dmitry Alekseyevich **Kamenetsky** (15 Nov 1849 - ?)
22 Jan 1894: Promoted to *Major-General*
24 Jan 1894 - 31 Jul 1895: Chief of Staff, IV. Army Corps
31 Jul 1895 - 20 Oct 1899: Chief of Staff, Fortress Kaunas
20 Oct 1899 - 30 Jan 1902: Commander, 53rd Reserve Infantry Brigade
30 Jan 1902 - 25 Nov 1906: Commander, 28th Infantry Division
14 Apr 1902: Promoted to *Lieutenant-General*

*Lieutenant-General* Konstantin Iosifovich **Kamenev** (26 Apr 1858 - ?)
5 Feb 1902 - 4 Nov 1910: Section Chief, Main Artillery Directorate
1904: Promoted to *Major-General*
4 Nov 1910 - 2 May 1916: Deputy Chief of Section 2, Main Artillery Directorate
2 May 1916 - Oct 1917: Chief of Section 3, Main Artillery Directorate
6 Dec 1916: Promoted to *Lieutenant-General*

*Lieutenant-General* Konstantin Mikhailovich **Kamenev** (21 May 1855 - ?)
28 Oct 1909 - 12 Mar 1910: Chief of the Imperial Court Stables
6 Dec 1909: Promoted to *Major-General*
12 Mar 1910 - 9 Aug 1913: General for Special Assignments to the Minister of the Imperial Court
9 Aug 1913 - 26 Sep 1914: Deputy Chief of the Warsaw Palace Administration
26 Sep 1914 - 1917: Chief of the Warsaw Palace Administration
10 Apr 1916: Promoted to *Lieutenant-General*

*Major-General* Nikolai Mikhailovich **Kamenev** (5 Oct 1862 - ?)
10 Apr 1911 - Oct 1917: Special Assignments General, Ministry of War
6 Dec 1911: Promoted to *Major-General*

*Lieutenant-General* Nikolai Nikolayevich **Kamenev** (18 Nov 1848 - ?)
11 Jul 1909 - 31 Dec 1913: Commandant, Dvinsk Artillery Depot
6 Dec 1909: Promoted to *Major-General*
31 Dec 1913: Promoted to *Lieutenant-General*
31 Dec 1913: Retired

*Major-General* Ivan Ivanovich **Kamennov** (26 Mar 1856 - ?)
12 Jul 1911: Promoted to *Major-General*
12 Jul 1911 - 11 Sep 1913: Commander, 1st Brigade, 1st Don Cossack Division
11 Sep 1913: Retired

*Lieutenant-General* Pavel Aleksandrovich **Kamenogradsky** (1 Sep 1838 - 20 Jun 1902)
2 Feb 1878 - 20 Dec 1892: Commander, 128th Infantry Regiment
11 Dec 1892: Promoted to *Major-General*
20 Dec 1892 - 20 Oct 1899: Commander, 2nd Brigade, 11th Infantry Division
20 Oct 1899 - 1901: Commander, Saratov Regional Brigade
1901: Promoted to *Lieutenant-General*
1901: Retired

*Lieutenant-General* Aleksey Semyonovich **Kamensky** (11 Jul 1844 - ?)
24 Oct 1899: Promoted to *Major-General*
24 Oct 1899 - 16 Jul 1904: Commander, 1st Brigade, 37th Infantry Division
1904: Promoted to *Lieutenant-General*
1904: Retired

*Major-General* Bogdan Iosifovich **Kamensky** (1855 - May 1910)
27 Nov 1907 - 1910: Commander, 4th Reserve Cavalry Regiment
1910: Promoted to *Major-General*

*Major-General* Mikhail Pavlovich **Kamensky** (18 Jan 1874 - Oct 1937)
23 Sep 1915 - 11 Jan 1918: Chief of Logistics Section, General Staff
6 Dec 1915: Promoted to *Major-General*
6 Jun 1916 - 11 Jan 1918: Member, Technical Committee for Air Force Administration

*Major-General* Nikolai Semyonovich **Kamensky** (9 Oct 1846 - 14 Nov 1904)
7 Mar 1901: Promoted to *Major-General*
7 Mar 1901 - 20 May 1902: Deputy Chief of Staff, Moscow Military District
20 May 1902 - 14 Nov 1904: Duty General, Moscow Military District

*Major-General* Pavel Yevgenyevich **Kamensky** (31 Oct 1863 - ?)
22 Jul 1913 - 1917: Military Judge, Irkutsk Military District Court
22 Mar 1915: Promoted to *Major-General*

*Major-General* Count Sergey Nikolayevich **Kamensky** (13 Mar 1868 - 1 Feb 1951)
28 Oct 1915 - 19 Feb 1917: Chief of Staff, XVIII. Army Corps
1916: Promoted to *Major-General*
19 Feb 1917 - 12 Apr 1917: Chief of Staff, XXII. Army Corps
12 Apr 1917 - 25 Aug 1917: Commander, 47th Infantry Division
25 Aug 1917 - Oct 1917: Chief of Staff, 7th Army

*General of Cavalry* Yevgeny Semyonovich **Kamensky** (21 Jan 1848 - 16 May 1917)
1 Oct 1893 - 17 Jan 1896: Commander, 2nd Dragoon Regiment
17 Jan 1896 - 28 Jul 1899: Deputy Intendant, St. Petersburg Military District
14 May 1896: Promoted to *Major-General*
28 Jul 1899 - 6 Oct 1903: Intendant, Turkestan Military District
6 Apr 1903: Promoted to *Lieutenant-General*
6 Oct 1903 - 30 Sep 1904: At the disposal of the Intendant-General
30 Sep 1904 - 23 Jun 1905: Intendant, Kiev Military District
23 Jun 1905 - 23 Feb 1908: At the disposal of the Intendant-General
23 Feb 1908 - 1909: Deputy Intendant-General, Ministry of War
1909: Promoted to *General of Cavalry*
1909: Retired

*Major-General* Anatoly Frantsevich **Kaminsky** (4 Jul 1859 - 1912)
5 Jun 1907 - 1912: Military Judge, Warsaw Military District Court
6 Dec 1907: Promoted to *Major-General*

*Lieutenant-General* Stanislav Klementyevich **Kaminsky** (12 Nov 1841 - 12 Feb 1899)
4 May 1880 - 18 Jun 1885: Member of the Artillery Committee, Main Artillery Directorate
15 May 1883: Promoted to *Major-General*
18 Jun 1885 - 12 Feb 1899: Inspector of Gunpowder Factories
30 Aug 1893: Promoted to *Lieutenant-General*

*Major-General* Aleksandr Aleksandrovich **Kamkov** (1 Jan 1868 - ?)
7 Jun 1912 - 1917: Military Judge, Amur Military District Court
14 Apr 1913: Promoted to *Major-General*

*Major-General* Dmitry Ivanovich **Kanabeyev** (22 Oct 1856 - ?)
7 Apr 1902 - 1905: Military Judge, Vilnius Military District Court
14 Apr 1902: Promoted to *Major-General*

*Major-General* Ivan Yakovlevich **Kanevsky** (11 Jan 1845 - ?)
29 Dec 1899 - 22 Jan 1902: Commander, 39th Artillery Brigade
6 Dec 1900: Promoted to *Major-General*
22 Jan 1902 - May 1905: Deputy Chief of Artillery, Odessa Military District

*Admiral* Vasily Aleksandrovich **Kanin** (11 Jun 1862 - 17 Jun 1927)
6 Dec 1913: Promoted to *Rear-Admiral*
6 Dec 1913 - 14 May 1915: Commander of Minelayers, Baltic Fleet
1915 - 14 May 1915: Chief of Mine Defenses, Baltic Sea
9 Feb 1915: Promoted to *Vice-Admiral*
14 May 1915 - 6 Aug 1916: C-in-C, Baltic Fleet
10 Apr 1916: Promoted to *Admiral*
6 Aug 1916 - 4 Apr 1917: Member, Council of State
4 Apr 1917 - 14 Jun 1917: Deputy Minister of the Navy
14 Jun 1917 - 13 Dec 1917: Member, Board of Admiralty
13 Dec 1917: Dismissed

*General of Artillery* Sergey Stepanovich **Kanishchev** (5 May 1836 - 21 Apr 1905)
14 Jul 1879 - 12 Aug 1892: Commander of Artillery, Don Cossack Army
26 Feb 1881: Promoted to *Major-General*
30 Aug 1891: Promoted to *Lieutenant-General*
12 Aug 1892 - 8 Mar 1893: Commander of Artillery, Moscow Military District
8 Mar 1893 - 19 Jan 1901: Commander of Artillery, Guards Corps
19 Jan 1901 - 21 Apr 1905: Member, Committee for Wounded Veterans
6 Dec 1902: Promoted to *General of Artillery*

*Major-General* Vasily Nikityevich **Kankrov** (10 Jan 1846 - ?)
19 Sep 1902 - 12 Jul 1908: Military Commander, Murom District
12 Jul 1908: Promoted to *Major-General*
12 Jul 1908: Retired
1915 - 1 Jun 1916: Recalled; Commander, Replacement Infantry Battalion
1 Jun 1916 - 1917: Commander, 203rd Replacement Infantry Regiment

*Lieutenant-General* Ioann-Filipp-Vilgelm Aleksandrovich **Kannabikh** (15 Dec 1847 - ?)
28 Jan 1903: Promoted to *Major-General*
28 Jan 1903 - 10 May 1910: Commander, 1st Brigade, 26th Infantry Division
10 May 1910: Promoted to *Lieutenant-General*
10 May 1910: Retired

*Lieutenant-General* Aleksey Tikhonovich **Kanshin** (13 Mar 1846 - 19 Dec 1905)
14 May 1894 - 30 Nov 1892: Commander, Life Dragoon Kurland Regiment
30 Nov 1892: Promoted to *Major-General*
30 Nov 1892 - 2 Mar 1894: Commander, 1st Brigade, 15th Cavalry Division
2 Mar 1894 - Jul 1902: Commander, 1st Brigade, 1st Cavalry Division
Jul 1902: Promoted to *Lieutenant-General*
Jul 1902: Retired

*Lieutenant-General* Pyotr Pavlovich **Kanshin** (4 Jul 1868 - ?)
28 Jun 1912 - 30 Mar 1915: Commander, 6th Uhlan Regiment
13 Aug 1914: Promoted to *Major-General*
30 Mar 1915 - 22 Oct 1915: Commander, 1st Brigade, 15th Cavalry Division
22 Oct 1915 - 22 Jan 1917: Commander, 4th Independent Cavalry Brigade
22 Jan 1917 - 27 Aug 1917: Commander, 17th Cavalry Division
11 Oct 1917 - 1918: Reserve officer, Petrograd Military District
19 Nov 1917: Promoted to *Lieutenant-General*

*Major-General* Viktor Pavlovich **Kanshin** (28 Oct 1863 - ?)
5 May 1907 - 1917: Inspector of Classes, Sumy Cadet Corps
6 Dec 1913: Promoted to *Major-General*

*Lieutenant-General* Prince Mikhail Mikhailovich **Kantakuzen** (13 Oct 1858 - 17 Sep 1927)
16 Aug 1908: Promoted to *Major-General*
16 Aug 1908 - 23 Nov 1909: Commander, 9th Artillery Brigade
23 Nov 1909 - 27 Jun 1913: Commander, 3rd Artillery Brigade
27 Jun 1913 - 22 Apr 1917: Inspector of Artillery, XXIII. Army Corps
Jan 1915: Promoted to *Lieutenant-General*

*Lieutenant-General* Prince Mikhail Alekseyevich **Kantakuzin** (23 Jan 1840 - 16 Dec 1894)
6 Apr 1878 - 18 Jun 1878: Commander of Gendarmerie, Southern Turkestan
1 Jun 1878: Promoted to *Major-General*
18 Jun 1878 - 4 Jan 1880: Deputy Chief of Staff, Field Army
4 Jan 1880 - 27 May 1882: Attached to the General Staff
27 May 1882 - 27 Jul 1882: Deputy Chief of Staff, Warsaw Military District
27 Jul 1882 - 29 Jan 1884: Chief of Staff, Corps of Gendarmerie
29 Jan 1884 - 10 Sep 1885: Unassigned
10 Sep 1885 - 2 Dec 1885: Attached to the Imperial Diplomatic Agency, Bulgaria
2 Dec 1885 - 1 Jul 1887: At the disposal of the Minister of War
1 Jul 1887 - 17 Mar 1891: Chief of Staff, XIII. Army Corps
17 Mar 1891 - 18 Oct 1881: Chief of Staff, Finland Military District
18 Oct 1881 - 1 Feb 1892: At the disposal of the Chief of the General Staff
1 Feb 1892 - 16 Dec 1894: Military Attaché, Athens
30 Aug 1893: Promoted to *Lieutenant-General*

*Major-General* Prince Mikhail Mikhailovich **Kantakuzin**, Count Speransky (29 Apr 1875 - 25 Mar 1955)
29 Jul 1915 - 1917: Commander, Life Guards Cuirassier Regiment
21 Nov 1915: Promoted to *Major-General*
1917 - Apr 1917: Commander, 2nd Brigade, 1st Guards Cavalry Division
Apr 1917 - 1917: Reserve officer, Guards Cavalry

*Major-General* Pavel Grigoryevich **Kantserov** (3 Jun 1866 - ?)
15 Nov 1915 - 12 May 1917: Commander, 283rd Infantry Regiment
13 Jan 1917: Promoted to *Major-General*
12 May 1917 - 1918: Commander, 71st Infantry Division

*Major-General* Leonid Petrovich **Kapitsa** (2 Sep 1864 - 1919)
29 Sep 1913 - 1917: Senior Inspector of Engineers, Main Military Technical Directorate
10 Apr 1916: Promoted to *Major-General*

*Rear-Admiral* Count Aleksey Pavlovich **Kapnist** (17 May 1871 - 31 Oct 1918)
1914 - Jan 1916: Deputy Chief of the Naval General Staff
Jan 1916 - Jul 1916: Officer for Assignments, Supreme Commander-in-Chief
Jul 1916 - 27 Jul 1917: Commander, White Sea-Murmansk Region
1917: Promoted to *Rear-Admiral*
27 Jul 1917 - 15 Nov 1917: Acting Chief of the Naval General Staff, Deputy Minister of the Navy

*Major-General* Amir Tchoban-Bek-Umtsyev **Kara-Kaytagsky** (1836 - 1914)
26 Jan 1907: Promoted to *Major-General*
26 Jan 1907 - 1914: Attached to the Caucasus Military District

*Major-General* Nikolai Andreyevich **Karabashev** (11 Aug 1858 - ?)
9 Nov 1911 - 16 Mar 1916: Commander, 188th Infantry Regiment
13 Nov 1915: Promoted to *Major-General*
16 Mar 1916 - 1917: Commander, Brigade, 3rd Turkestan Rifle Division

*Major-General* Ivan Rafailovich **Karachan** (5 Jan 1868 - 18 Jul 1942)
1 Jul 1910 - 1917: Inspector of Technical Institutions, Quartermaster-General's Office
6 Dec 1910: Promoted to *Major-General*

*Lieutenant-General* Pyotr Petrovich **Karachan** (14 Apr 1868 - 30 Oct 1917)
26 Oct 1912 - 21 Oct 1916: Commandant, Mikhailov Artillery School
6 Dec 1912: Promoted to *Major-General*
12 Oct 1916 - 4 Feb 1917: Inspector of Artillery, XVII. Army Corps
4 Feb 1917 - 15 Jun 1917: Inspector of Artillery, 11th Army
2 Apr 1917: Promoted to *Lieutenant-General*
15 Jun 1917 - Oct 1917: Reserve officer, Odessa Military District

*Major-General* Vladimir Sergeyevich **Karachev** (20 Jul 1850 - ?)
14 Dec 1901 - 14 Nov 1906: Ministry of War Representative, Amur Military District Council
6 Dec 1903: Promoted to *Major-General*
14 Nov 1906 - 1908: Attached to the Ministry of War

*Major-General* Grigory Ivanovich **Karachun** (28 Nov 1858 - ?)
7 Jan 1911 - 1917: Commander, 5th Borderguard Brigade
14 Apr 1913: Promoted to *Major-General*

*Major-General* Prince Arseny Aleksandrovich **Karageorgiyevich** (4 Apr 1859 - 19 Oct 1938)
28 Oct 1914 - 1 Jan 1916: Commander, 2nd Brigade, 2nd Cavalry Division

| | |
|---|---|
| 6 Dec 1914: | Promoted to *Major-General* |
| 1 Jan 1916 - 8 Apr 1916: | Reserve officer, Kiev Military District |
| 8 Apr 1916 - 1917: | Reserve officer, Petrograd Military District |

*Major-General* Aleksandr Aleksandrovich **Karandeyev** (20 May 1850 - 1895)
| | |
|---|---|
| 15 Nov 1887 - 1895: | Special Assignments Officer, 5th Class, Government-General of Warsaw |
| 30 Aug 1893: | Promoted to *Major-General* |

*Major-General* Valerian Aleksandrovich **Karandeyev** (1 Jan 1854 - 1916)
| | |
|---|---|
| 5 Jun 1902: | Promoted to *Major-General* |
| 5 Jun 1902 - 3 Jul 1903: | Commander, 2nd Brigade, 7th Cavalry Division |
| 3 Jul 1903 - 1 Dec 1907: | Commander, 1st Brigade, 7th Cavalry Division |

*Major-General* Konstantin Adamovich **Karangozov** (18 Feb 1852 - 23 Jul 1907)
| | |
|---|---|
| 26 Nov 1903 - 16 Dec 1903: | Commander, 22nd Dragoon Regiment |
| 16 Dec 1903: | Promoted to *Major-General* |
| 16 Dec 1903 - 23 Jul 1907: | Commander, 2nd Brigade, 8th Cavalry Division |
| 1905: | Acting Military Commander, Odessa |
| 1905: | Acting Governor-General of Odessa |

*General of Infantry* Ivan Aleksandrovich **Karass** (28 Feb 1838 - 1910)
| | |
|---|---|
| 9 Mar 1885: | Promoted to *Major-General* |
| 9 Mar 1885 - 16 Sep 1885: | General for Special Assignments, Kazan Military District |
| 16 Sep 1885 - 12 Mar 1886: | Commander, 2nd Brigade, 20th Infantry Division |
| 12 Mar 1886 - 12 Feb 1893: | Commander, 1st Brigade, 20th Infantry Division |
| 12 Feb 1893 - 14 Aug 1895: | Commander, Commander, 2nd Caucasus Replacement Infantry Brigade |
| 14 Aug 1895 - 11 Aug 1900: | Commander, 12th Infantry Division |
| 6 Dec 1895: | Promoted to *Lieutenant-General* |
| 11 Aug 1900 - 9 Sep 1900: | Commanding General, VII. Army Corps |
| 9 Sep 1900 - 8 Nov 1904: | Commanding General, XII. Army Corps |
| 8 Nov 1904 - 7 Dec 1905: | Deputy Commanding General, Kiev Military District |
| Oct 1905: | Acting Commanding General, Kiev Military District |
| 6 Dec 1905: | Promoted to *General of Infantry* |
| 7 Dec 1905 - 24 Sep 1907: | Commanding General, Kazan Military District |
| 24 Sep 1907: | Retired |

*Major-General* Ippolit Ivanovich **Karateyev** (27 Jan 1848 - ?)
| | |
|---|---|
| 16 Dec 1894 - 1907: | Commander of Gendarmerie, Plotsk Province |
| 6 Dec 1903: | Promoted to *Major-General* |

*Major-General* Login Aleksandrovich **Karaulshchikov** (29 Sep 1866 - ?)
| | |
|---|---|
| 27 Nov 1915 - 20 Jan 1918: | Inspector of Engineers, Kazan Military District |
| 6 Dec 1915: | Promoted to *Major-General* |
| 20 Jan 1918: | Dismissed |

*Major-General* Viktor Ignatyevich **Kardashevsky** (23 Dec 1840 - ?)
19 Jul 1896: Promoted to *Major-General*
28 Dec 1896 - Dec 1901: Commander, 2nd Brigade, 2nd Cavalry Division

*Lieutenant-General* Mikhail Grigoryevich **Kardinalovsky** (3 May 1868 - 26 Jan 1917)
12 Nov 1910: Promoted to *Major-General*
12 Nov 1910 - 20 Jun 1915: Commander, 52nd Artillery Brigade
20 Jun 1915 - 28 Sep 1916: Inspector of Artillery, XXXVIII. Army Corps
30 Aug 1915: Promoted to *Lieutenant-General*
28 Sep 1916 - 26 Jan 1917: Inspector of Artillery, 11th Army

*Lieutenant-General* Pyotr Mikhailovich **Kardinalovsky** (13 Oct 1841 - 5 Sep 1912)
1 Oct 1878 - 21 Mar 1907: Military Judge, Odessa Military District Court
30 Aug 1888: Promoted to *Major-General*
21 Mar 1907: Promoted to *Lieutenant-General*
21 Mar 1907: Retired

*Lieutenant-General* Nikolai Nikolayevich **Karepov** (3 Jan 1860 - 13 Aug 1926)
15 Jan 1909: Promoted to *Major-General*
15 Jan 1909 - 4 Nov 1914: Commander, 1st Brigade, 40th Infantry Division
4 Nov 1914 - 1917: Commander, 30th Infantry Division
28 Feb 1915: Promoted to *Lieutenant-General*

*Major-General* Pyotr Nikolayevich **Kareyev** (1 Feb 1863 - ?)
24 Nov 1908 - 4 Nov 1914: Commander, 6th Finnish Infantry Regiment
27 Aug 1914: Promoted to *Major-General*
4 Nov 1914 - 2 Dec 1914: Commander, 1st Brigade, 1st Infantry Division
2 Dec 1914 - 2 Jan 1915: Acting Commander, 1st Infantry Division
2 Jan 1915 - 30 Jan 1916: Commander, 36th Independent Infantry Brigade
30 Jan 1916 - 22 Jun 1916: Reserve officer, Petrograd Military District
22 Jun 1916 - Mar 1917: Commander, 32nd Replacement Infantry Brigade
Mar 1917 - 3 Aug 1917: Commandant of Chelyabinsk Garrison

*General of Cavalry* Sergey Alekseyevich **Kareyev** (29 Jun 1846 - ?)
29 May 1891 - 25 Jan 1900: Commander, 10th Dragoon Regiment
25 Jan 1900: Promoted to *Major-General*
25 Jan 1900 - 19 Feb 1904: Commander, 2nd Brigade, 6th Cavalry Division
19 Feb 1904 - 6 Nov 1906: Commander, 1st Independent Cavalry Brigade
6 Nov 1906 - 30 Apr 1910: Commander, 2nd Replacement Cavalry Brigade
22 Apr 1907: Promoted to *Lieutenant-General*
30 Apr 1910: Promoted to *General of Cavalry*
30 Apr 1910: Retired

*Major-General* Aleksandr Nikolayevich **Kargalskov** (8 Oct 1860 - ?)
31 Dec 1913 - ?: Commander, 13th Don Cossack Regiment
? - 12 Jul 1916: Reserve officer, Kiev Military District
12 Jul 1916: Promoted to *Major-General*
12 Jul 1916: Retired

*General of Cavalry* Adam Solomonovich **Karganov** (15 Aug 1846 - 1918)
24 Feb 1891 - 28 Apr 1899: Commander, 22nd Dragoon Regiment
28 Apr 1899: Promoted to *Major-General*
28 Apr 1899 - 3 Feb 1904: Commander, 1st Brigade, 3rd Cavalry Division
3 Feb 1904 - 10 Jan 1905: Commander, 11th Cavalry Division
10 Jan 1905 - 21 May 1908: Commander, 9th Cavalry Division
17 Apr 1905: Promoted to *Lieutenant-General*
21 May 1908 - 15 Aug 1913: Commanding General, XII. Army Corps
10 Aug 1911: Promoted to *General of Cavalry*
15 Aug 1913: Retired

*Major-General* Konstantin-Karl-Eduard Fyodorovich **Karger** (17 Mar 1849 - ?)
30 Jun 1903 - 3 Mar 1906: Commander of Engineers, Fortress Osovets
6 Dec 1903: Promoted to *Major-General*
3 Mar 1906 - 27 Nov 1908: Deputy Commander of Engineers, Warsaw Military District

*Major-General* Aleksandr Lvovich **Karlevich** (13 Jul 1851 - ?)
12 Nov 1907: Promoted to *Major-General*
12 Nov 1907 - 11 Dec 1908: Commander, 1st Brigade, 45th Infantry Division

*Major-General* Vyacheslav Aleksandrovich **Karlikov** (15 Nov 1871 - 17 Oct 1937)
2 Mar 1915 - 2 Mar 1916: Commander, Brigade, 48th Infantry Division
5 Jun 1915: Promoted to *Major-General*
23 Apr 1915 - 1 May 1915: Acting Commander, 48th Infantry Division
12 May 1915 - 19 May 1915: Acting Commander, 48th Infantry Division
2 Jul 1915 - 8 Sep 1915: Acting Commander, 48th Infantry Division
2 Mar 1916 - 29 Jul 1916: Chief of Staff, 3rd Grenadier Division
29 Jul 1916 - 20 May 1917: Chief of Staff, XXV. Army Corps
20 May 1917 - 21 Sep 1917: Commander, 125th Infantry Division

*Major-General* Ferdinand-Aleksandr-Vladimir Aleksandrovich **Karlstedt** (14 May 1857 - ?)
8 May 1912: Promoted to *Major-General*
8 May 1912 - 10 May 1915: Commander, 1st Brigade, 4th Siberian Rifle Division
10 May 1915 - 1917: Reserve officer, Kiev Military District

*General of Infantry* Nikolai Nikolayevich **Karmalin** (25 May 1824 - 23 Jul 1900)
23 Jan 1859 - 5 Oct 1862: Chief of Staff, III. Army Corps
30 Aug 1861: Promoted to *Major-General*
5 Oct 1862 - 4 Sep 1865: At the disposal of the C-in-C, Caucasus Army
4 Sep 1865 - 8 May 1869: Military Commander, North Dagestan
8 May 1869 - 14 Jun 1873: Military Governor of Erivan
30 Aug 1869: Promoted to *Lieutenant-General*
14 Jun 1873 - 23 Jan 1882: Commander, Kuban Region, Ataman, Kuban Cossack Army
23 Jan 1882 - 23 Jul 1900: Member of the Military Council
15 May 1883: Promoted to *General of Infantry*

*Major-General* Valerian Vasilyevich **Karmin** (25 Mar 1844 - ?)
13 Oct 1898:                        Promoted to *Major-General*
13 Oct 1898 - 18 Jan 1902:          Commander, 1st Replacement Artillery Brigade
18 Jan 1902 - 1904:                 Commander of Artillery, X. Army Corps

*Major-General* Yuri Kharitonovich **Karnakovsky** (6 Apr 1852 - ?)
9 Feb 1899 - 1906:                  Commander of Railway Gendarmerie, Warsaw
6 Dec 1904:                         Promoted to *Major-General*

*Major-General* Mikhail Mikhailovich **Karnaukhov** (1 Nov 1867 - 1918)
1915 - 28 Sep 1915:                 Commander, Brigade, 14th Infantry Division
3 Apr 1915:                         Promoted to *Major-General*
28 Sep 1915 - Apr 1916:             Chief of Staff, XLI. Army Corps
Apr 1916 - 20 Jun 1916:             Unassigned
20 Jun 1916 - 14 Aug 1917:          Chief of Supply, Caucasus Army
14 Aug 1917 - 17 Oct 1917:          Commander, 39th Infantry Division
17 Oct 1917 - 1918:                 Reserve officer, Caucasus Military District

*Major-General* Aleksandr Alekseyevich **Karneyev** (22 Aug 1860 - 7 Dec 1940)
Dec 1915 - 1917:                    Commander, 2nd Brigade, 14th Cavalry Division
24 Jul 1916:                        Promoted to *Major-General*

*Major-General* Aleksandr Stanislavovich **Karnitsky** (30 Jan 1867 - 12 Oct 1942)
30 Apr 1910 - 15 Jun 1917:          Commander, 2nd Cavalry Regiment, Amur Military
                                    District Borderguard Corps
26 Mar 1916:                        Promoted to *Major-General*
15 Jun 1917 - 25 Aug 1917:          Commander, 1st Amur Cavalry Brigade
25 Aug 1917 - 1918:                 Commander, Caucasus Cavalry Division

*Major-General* Iosif Ivanovich **Karolinsky** (3 Apr 1858 - 1913)
18 Jul 1911 - 1913:                 Commandant of Tiflis Railway Station
1913:                               Promoted to *Major-General*

*Lieutenant-General* Aleksandr Fyodorovich **Karpov** (27 Aug 1842 - ?)
13 Aug 1890 - 15 Jul 1891:          Chief of Staff, XI. Army Corps
30 Aug 1890:                        Promoted to *Major-General*
15 Jul 1891 - Sep 1901:             Military Governor of Semipalatinsk Region
6 Dec 1899:                         Promoted to *Lieutenant-General*
28 Jul 1900 - 14 Apr 1901:          Acting Commanding General, Siberian Military District
23 Oct 1901:                        Retired

*Major-General* Anany Petrovich **Karpov** (30 Mar 1839 - ?)
15 May 1883:                        Promoted to *Major-General*
15 May 1883 - 1898:                 Attached to the Don Cossack Army

*Lieutenant-General* Ivan Vladimirovich **Karpov** (29 Mar 1851 - ?)
11 Apr 1905:                        Promoted to *Major-General*
11 Apr 1905 - 1 Apr 1911:           Commander, 1st Brigade, 4th Infantry Division

1 Apr 1911: Promoted to *Lieutenant-General*
1 Apr 1911: Retired

*Lieutenant-General* Nikolai Aleksandrovich **Karpov** (4 Nov 1843 - ?)
5 Sep 1888 - 3 Mar 1891: Commandant, Artillery Training Polygon, Kiev Military District
30 Aug 1889: Promoted to *Major-General*
3 Mar 1891 - 20 Apr 1898: Commander of Artillery, Fortress Warsaw
20 Apr 1898 - 14 Feb 1899: Commander of Artillery, Caucasus Army Corps
6 Dec 1898: Promoted to *Lieutenant-General*
14 Feb 1899 - 4 Mar 1903: Commander of Artillery, Caucasus Military District
4 Mar 1903 - 21 Mar 1906: Commander of Artillery, Warsaw Military District
21 Mar 1906 - 1907: Commandant of Fortress Modlin

*Major-General* Pyotr Petrovich **Karpov** (28 Jun 1866 - 13 Sep 1918)
1915 - 21 Nov 1915: Commander, 183$^{rd}$ Infantry Regiment
1 May 1915: Promoted to *Major-General*
21 Nov 1915 - 29 Nov 1916: Commander, Brigade, 46$^{th}$ Infantry Division
29 Nov 1916 - 4 May 1917: Commander, 129$^{th}$ Infantry Division

*Major-General* Vladimir Aleksandrovich **Karpov** (7 Jun 1872 - 25 Sep 1915)
Apr 1915 - 25 Sep 1915: Commander, 68$^{th}$ Infantry Regiment
17 Dec 1915: Posthumously promoted to *Major-General*

*Lieutenant-General* Vladimir Kirillovich **Karpov** (19 Apr 1864 - ?)
9 Jul 1908: Promoted to *Major-General*
9 Jul 1908 - 5 Oct 1914: Chief of Communications, Caucasus Military District
20 Oct 1914 - 2 Apr 1917: Chief of Communications, Caucasus Army
2 Apr 1917: Promoted to *Lieutenant-General*
2 Apr 1917 - 12 Aug 1917: Commander, Consolidated Caucasus Infantry Division
12 Aug 1917 - 12 Jan 1918: Chief of Logistics, VII. Caucasus Army Corps

*Major-General* Yanuary Fedorovich **Karpov** (19 Apr 1861 - ?)
11 Jul 1907 - 23 Jul 1911: Commander of Artillery, Fortress Novogeorgiyevsk
6 Dec 1908: Promoted to *Major-General*
23 Jul 1911: Retired
17 Nov 1915 - 1917: Recalled; Commander, 4$^{th}$ Border Infantry Regiment

*Major-General* Zosim Aleksandrovich **Karpov** (17 Apr 1858 - ?)
11 Jan 1916 - 1917: Commander, 111$^{th}$ Artillery Brigade
6 Dec 1916: Promoted to *Major-General*

*Lieutenant-General* Ivan Aleksandrovich **Karpovich** (31 Aug 1867 - 1938)
12 Nov 1910: Promoted to *Major-General*
12 Nov 1910 - 29 Nov 1912: Commander, 51$^{st}$ Artillery Brigade
29 Nov 1912 - 7 May 1915: Commander, Caucasus Grenadier Artillery Brigade
7 May 1915 - Oct 1917: Inspector of Artillery, XXXV. Army Corps
14 Jul 1916: Promoted to *Lieutenant-General*

*Major-General* Mikhail Aleksandrovich **Karpovich** (11 Sep 1857 - ?)
5 Jan 1911 - 1917: Commander, 8th Sapper Battalion
15 Jun 1915: Promoted to *Major-General*

*Major-General* Arkady Ivanovich **Kartamyshev** (23 Nov 1838 - Oct 1900)
3 May 1895: Promoted to *Major-General*
3 May 1895 - Oct 1900: Commander, 12th Artillery Brigade

*Major-General* Konstantin Stepanovich **Kartashev** (17 Sep 1855 - 2 May 1909)
23 Jul 1904 - 2 May 1909: Commander of Engineer Depot, Fortress Kiev
6 Dec 1904: Promoted to *Major-General*

*Major-General* Semyon Grigoryevich **Kartashev** (1 Feb 1856 - ?)
28 Nov 1915 - 1917: Commander, 22nd Replacement Infantry Brigade
30 Nov 1916: Promoted to *Major-General*
1917 - 20 May 1917: Reserve officer, Kiev Military District
20 May 1917: Dismissed

*Major-General* Vasily Trofimovich **Kartashev** (19 Feb 1852 - ?)
24 Feb 1900 - 4 Sep 1907: Commander, 23rd Dragoon Regiment
4 Sep 1907: Promoted to *Major-General*
4 Sep 1907 - 15 May 1908: Commander, 1st Brigade, 8th Cavalry Division

*Major-General* Grigory Ivanovich **Kartashevsky** (3 Oct 1851 - ?)
28 Sep 1907: Promoted to *Major-General*
28 Sep 1907 - 17 Oct 1910: Commander, 1st Brigade, 1st Cavalry Division

*Major-General* Viktor Ivanovich **Kartikovsky** (22 Aug 1848 - ?)
3 May 1906 - 1909: Commandant, Dvinsk Artillery Depot
6 Dec 1906: Promoted to *Major-General*

*Lieutenant-General* Pyotr Aleksandrovich **Kartsev** (24 Mar 1852 - 1919)
23 Oct 1900: Promoted to *Major-General*
23 Oct 1900 - 20 Nov 1904: General for Special Assignments, Caucasus Military District
20 Nov 1904 - 16 Jun 1906: Commander, Consolidated Caucasus Cossack Division
2 Jan 1906: Promoted to *Lieutenant-General*
16 Jun 1906 - 1907: Commanding General, II. Turkestan Army Corps
1907: Retired

*Vice-Admiral* Viktor Andreyevich **Kartsov** (31 Jan 1868 - 2 May 1936)
1913 - 28 Feb 1917: Commandant of the Imperial Naval Academy, Director of the Marine Corps
3 Aug 1914: Promoted to *Rear-Admiral*
6 Feb 1916: Promoted to *Vice-Admiral*
28 Feb 1917: Dismissed

*Lieutenant-General* Vladimir Aleksandrovich **Kartsov** (15 Jul 1860 - 15 Oct 1938)
14 Oct 1904 - 14 Mar 1905: Attached to the C-in-C, 1st Manchurian Army
14 Mar 1905 - 21 May 1905: Unassigned
17 Apr 1905: Promoted to *Major-General*
21 May 1905 - 4 Sep 1905: Chief of Staff, Trans-Baikal Region
4 Sep 1905 - 22 Jun 1907: Chief of Staff, II. Caucasus Army Corps
22 Jun 1907 - 14 Jun 1910: Commander, 1st Brigade, Caucasus Cavalry Division
14 Jun 1910: Promoted to *Lieutenant-General*
14 Jun 1910: Retired
11 Aug 1914 - 18 Oct 1915: Recalled; Commander, 1st Brigade, Kuban Cossack Division
18 Oct 1915: Retired

*Lieutenant-General* Yevgeny Petrovich **Kartsov** (1 Feb 1861 - 24 Apr 1917)
28 Mar 1913: Promoted to *Major-General*
28 Mar 1913 - 19 Nov 1914: Deputy Chief of Staff, Omsk Military District
19 Nov 1914 - 24 Dec 1914: Chief of Staff, XIII. Army Corps
24 Dec 1914 - 11 Nov 1915: Commander, 1st Rifle Brigade
11 Nov 1915 - 24 Apr 1917: Commander, 4th Siberian Rifle Division
20 May 1917: Posthumously promoted to *Lieutenant-General*

*Major-General* Yevgeny Feofilovich **Karvovsky** (16 Feb 1861 - ?)
4 Jul 1912 - 1917: Military Judge, Irkutsk Military District Court
14 Apr 1913: Promoted to *Major-General*

*Major-General* Vladimir Gavrilovich **Karzin** (13 Apr 1856 - Nov 1916)
31 Dec 1913 - Nov 1916: Commander, Tiflis Artillery Depot
6 Dec 1914: Promoted to *Major-General*

*Major-General* Nikolai Petrovich **Kasatkin** (4 May 1856 - ?)
11 Aug 1906 - 1913: Commander, Moscow-Archangel Railway Gendarmerie
6 Dec 1912: Promoted to *Major-General*

*Major-General* Arseny Feofanovich **Kashchenko** (12 Mar 1842 - ?)
9 Jun 1891: Promoted to *Major-General*
9 Jun 1891 - Dec 1898: Chief of Staff, XII. Army Corps

*Vice-Admiral* Aleksandr Parmenovich **Kasherininov** (10 Apr 1843 - 21 Dec 1920)
6 Sep 1896 - 3 Jul 1900: Commander, 9th Naval Depot
5 Jan 1898: Promoted to *Rear-Admiral*
3 Jul 1900 - 1 Jan 1901: Commander, Consolidated Detachment of Naval Depots, St. Petersburg
1 Jan 1901 - 13 Mar 1903: Junior Flagman, Pacific Fleet
13 Mar 1903: Promoted to *Vice-Admiral*
13 Mar 1903: Retired

*Lieutenant-General* Vladimir Mikhailovich **Kasherininov** (18 May 1850 - ?)
29 Dec 1894 - 13 Mar 1900: Commander, 92nd Infantry Regiment

| | |
|---|---|
| 13 Mar 1900: | Promoted to *Major-General* |
| 13 Mar 1900 - 26 Jul 1902: | Commander, Life Guards Reserve Regiment |
| 26 Jul 1902 - 8 Nov 1903: | Commander, Life Guards Rifle Regiment |
| 8 Nov 1903 - 7 Jun 1908: | Commander, Guards Rifle Brigade |
| 6 Dec 1906: | Promoted to *Lieutenant-General* |
| 7 Jun 1908 - 29 Dec 1908: | Commanding General, XIV. Army Corps |
| 29 Dec 1908: | Retired |
| 9 Dec 1912 - 1917: | Recalled; Honorary Trustee, Board of Trustees, Tsarina Maria Institutions |

*Major-General* Aleksey Petrovich **Kashperov** (27 Feb 1847 - ?)

| | |
|---|---|
| 15 Feb 1900: | Promoted to *Major-General* |
| 15 Feb 1900 - 23 Apr 1901: | Commander, 1st Brigade, 8th Infantry Division |

*General of Infantry* Nikolai Aleksandrovich **Kashtalinsky** (6 May 1849 - 21 Mar 1917)

| | |
|---|---|
| 22 Aug 1890 - 25 Nov 1900: | Manager, Murghab Imperial Estates |
| 6 Dec 1899: | Promoted to *Major-General* |
| 25 Nov 1900: | Retired |
| 11 Feb 1902 - 21 May 1903: | Recalled; Commander, 1st Brigade, 33rd Infantry Division |
| 21 May 1903 - 22 Feb 1904: | Commander, 3rd East Siberian Rifle Brigade |
| 22 Feb 1904 - 4 Jul 1906: | Commander, 3rd East Siberian Rifle Division |
| 4 Jul 1904: | Promoted to *Lieutenant-General* |
| 4 Jul 1906 - 27 Dec 1906: | Attached to the General Staff |
| 27 Dec 1906 - 22 Nov 1908: | Commanding General, IV. Army Corps |
| 22 Nov 1908: | Promoted to *General of Infantry* |
| 22 Nov 1908: | Retired |
| 26 Sep 1914 - 6 Oct 1915: | Recalled; Commanding General, XXVIII. Army Corps |
| 6 Oct 1915 - 20 Apr 1916: | Reserve officer, Kiev Military District |
| 20 Apr 1916 - 13 Nov 1916: | Commanding General, XL. Army Corps |
| 13 Nov 1916 - 21 Mar 1917: | Member, Committee for Wounded Veterans |

*Rear-Admiral* Mitrofan Ivanovich **Kaskov** (9 Feb 1867 - 15 Nov 1917)

| | |
|---|---|
| 25 Jan 1916: | Promoted to *Rear-Admiral* |
| 25 Jan 1916 - 3 Apr 1917: | Chief of Staff, Black Sea Fleet |
| 3 Apr 1917 - 15 Nov 1917: | Reserve officer, Black Sea Fleet |

*Major-General* Boris Nikolayevich **Kastalsky** (13 Feb 1868 - 21 Jan 1943)

| | |
|---|---|
| 8 Aug 1914 - 1917: | Commander of Engineers, I. Turkestan Army Corps |
| 10 Apr 1916: | Promoted to *Major-General* |

*Major-General* Eduard Renatovich **Kastellaz** (6 Sep 1855 - ?)

| | |
|---|---|
| 1 Jul 1903 - 19 Jun 1905: | Commander, 6th Rifle Regiment |
| 19 Jun 1905: | Promoted to *Major-General* |
| 19 Jun 1905 - 31 Dec 1906: | Commander, 1st Brigade, 2nd Rifle Division |
| 31 Dec 1906 - 11 Apr 1907: | Commander, 2nd Brigade, 9th Infantry Division |

*Major-General* Sergey Yevgenyevich **Kastorsky** (2 Oct 1843 - ?)
29 Dec 1899 - 17 Oct 1903:    Commander, 27th Artillery Brigade
1 Jan 1901:    Promoted to *Major-General*

*Lieutenant-General* Georgy Yefremovich **Katanayev** (22 Apr 1848 - 18 Dec 1921)
19 May 1889 - 1907:    Chairman, Military Economics Board, Siberian Cossack Army
8 Jul 1900:    Promoted to *Major-General*
6 Dec 1906:    Promoted to *Lieutenant-General*
1907:    Retired

*Major-General* Konstantin Vasilyevich **Katayev** (28 Mar 1861 - ?)
22 Nov 1914 - 14 Aug 1916:    Commander, 226th Infantry Regiment
24 Jul 1916:    Promoted to *Major-General*
14 Aug 1916 - 20 Dec 1916:    Reserve officer, Minsk Military District
20 Dec 1916 - 1917:    Commander, Brigade, 46th Infantry Division

*Major-General* Prince Pavel Mikhailovich **Katkov-Shalikov** (21 Jun 1859 - 26 Aug 1930)
10 Apr 1911:    Promoted to *Major-General*
10 Apr 1911 - Jan 1915:    Attached to the Minister of Internal Affairs
Jan 1915 - 1 Oct 1915:    Commander, State Militia Brigade
17 Oct 1915 - Jul 1916:    Reserve officer, Petrograd Military District
Jul 1916 - 1917:    Commander, Brigade, 2nd Finnish Rifle Division

*Major-General* Eduard-Orest Gustavovich **Katlubay** (13 Oct 1861 - ?)
1915 - 25 Feb 1916:    Commander, 413th Infantry Regiment
27 Nov 1915:    Promoted to *Major-General*
25 Feb 1916 - 9 May 1917:    Commander, Brigade, 69th Infantry Division
9 May 1917 - 21 Oct 1917:    Commander, 2nd Caucasus Grenadier Division
21 Oct 1917:    Dismissed

*General of Engineers* Mikhail Petrovich von **Kaufman** (2 Nov 1822 - 7 Jan 1902)
30 Mar 1860 - 28 Oct 1866:    Commandant, Nikolayev Engineering Academy
17 Apr 1863:    Promoted to *Major-General*
28 Oct 1866:    Promoted to *Lieutenant-General*
28 Oct 1866 - 30 Mar 1867:    Intendant-General
30 Mar 1867 - 21 Jun 1879:    Chief of Main Intendant Directorate
25 Nov 1869:    Promoted to *General Adjutant*
21 Jun 1879 - 16 Mar 1882:    Deputy Inspector-General of Engineers
16 Apr 1878:    Promoted to *General of Engineers*
16 Mar 1882 - 7 Jan 1902:    Member of the State Council

*General of Cavalry* Aleksey Mikhailovich von **Kaufman-Turkestansky** (15 Nov 1861 - 25 Jul 1934)
9 Jun 1907:    Promoted to *Major-General*
9 Jun 1907 - 10 Apr 1911:    Commander, Life Guards Grodno Hussar Regiment
10 Apr 1911 - 19 Jul 1914:    General à la suite
19 Jul 1914 - 18 Apr 1917:    Commander, Ural Cossack Division

| | |
|---|---|
| 30 Jan 1915: | Promoted to *Lieutenant-General* |
| 30 Jul 1917: | Promoted to *General of Cavalry* |
| 30 Jul 1917: | Retired |

*General of Cavalry* Baron Aleksandr Vasiliyevich von **Kaulbars** (11 May 1844 - 25 Jan 1929)

| | |
|---|---|
| 1 Jan 1880: | Promoted to *Major-General* |
| 1 Jan 1880 - 31 May 1882: | Commander, 1st Brigade, 14th Cavalry Division |
| 31 May 1882 - 23 Jul 1891: | Commander, 1st Brigade, 1st Cavalry Division |
| 23 Jul 1891 - 28 Nov 1897: | Commander, 15th Cavalry Division |
| 30 Aug 1894: | Promoted to *Lieutenant-General* |
| 28 Nov 1897 - 31 Jul 1900: | Commanding General, II. Cavalry Corps |
| 31 Jul 1900 - 14 Apr 1901: | Commanding General, II. Siberian Army Corps |
| 14 Apr 1901 - 1 Jan 1904: | Deputy Commanding General, Odessa Military District |
| 6 Dec 1901: | Promoted to *General of Cavalry* |
| 1 Jan 1904 - 22 Oct 1904: | Commanding General, Odessa Military District |
| 22 Oct 1904 - 13 Mar 1905: | C-in-C, 3rd Manchurian Army |
| 13 Mar 1905 - 27 Aug 1905: | C-in-C, 2nd Manchurian Army |
| 27 Aug 1905 - 23 Dec 1909: | Commanding General, Odessa Military District |
| 23 Dec 1909 - 23 Dec 1915: | Member of the Military Council |
| 6 Oct 1914 - 21 Oct 1915: | Chief of Aviation, Northwestern Front |
| 23 Dec 1915: | Retired |

*General of Infantry* Baron Nikolai Vasiliyevich von **Kaulbars** (22 May 1842 - 20 Nov 1905)

| | |
|---|---|
| 18 Oct 1881 - 17 Dec 1886: | Military Attaché, Austria |
| 30 Aug 1885: | Promoted to *Major-General* |
| 17 Dec 1886 - 5 Dec 1889: | At the disposal of the Commanding General, St. Petersburg Military District |
| 5 Dec 1889 - 28 Oct 1891: | Chief of Staff, VI. Army Corps |
| 28 Oct 1891 - 24 Dec 1898: | Chief of Staff, Finland Military District |
| 14 Nov 1894: | Promoted to *Lieutenant-General* |
| 24 Dec 1898 - 1905: | Member of the Military Scientific Committee, General Staff |
| 1905: | Promoted to *General of Infantry* |
| 1905: | Retired |

*Major-General of the Fleet* Baron Yevgraf Romanovich von **Kaulbars** (17 Nov 1862 - 1920)

| | |
|---|---|
| 1 Jan 1908 - 1915: | Member of the Board, Baltic & Admiralty Shipyards |
| 6 Dec 1911: | Promoted to *Major-General of the Admiralty* |
| 8 Apr 1913: | Redesignated *Major-General of the Fleet* |
| 1915 - 1916: | Chief of Workers & Civilian Employees Office, Ministry of the Navy |

*Major-General* Yevgeny Fyodorovich **Kayander** (31 Mar 1861 - ?)

| | |
|---|---|
| 7 Aug 1909 - 31 Dec 1913: | Commander, 8th Hussar Regiment |
| 31 Dec 1913: | Promoted to *Major-General* |

31 Dec 1913 - 13 Feb 1918: Commander, 1st Brigade, 4th Cavalry Division
1915 - 1918: On occasion, Acting Commander, 4th Cavalry Division
13 Feb 1918: Dismissed

*Major-General* Andrei Aleksandrovich **Kaygorodov** (23 Aug 1858 - 1920)
31 Dec 1913 - 10 Nov 1917: Commandant, Dvinsk Artillery Depot
6 Dec 1914: Promoted to *Major-General*
10 Nov 1917 - 1918: Commandant, Moscow Artillery Depot

*General of Infantry* Mikhail Nikiforovich **Kaygorodov** (25 Oct 1853 - Oct 1918)
25 Feb 1901 - 7 May 1905: Governor of Nyuland
25 Dec 1901: Promoted to *Major-General*
7 May 1905 - 13 Jan 1906: Governor of Irkutsk
13 Jan 1906 - 18 Mar 1906: Attached to the Ministry of Internal Affairs
18 Mar 1906 - 5 May 1906: Attached to the General Staff
5 May 1906 - 9 Nov 1907: Commander, 2nd Brigade, 2nd Grenadier Division
9 Nov 1907: Promoted to *Lieutenant-General*
9 Nov 1907 - 23 Aug 1913: Commander, 26th Infantry Division
23 Aug 1913 - 1915: Commandant of Fortress Grodno
6 Dec 1913: Promoted to *General of Infantry*
1915 - 10 Jul 1916: Unassigned
10 Jul 1916 - 1917: Reserve officer, Minsk Military District

*Lieutenant-General* Nestor Nikiforovich **Kaygorodov** (14 Nov 1840 - 1916)
1 May 1886 - 19 Sep 1891: Commander of Artillery, Fortress Sevastopol
19 Sep 1891: Promoted to *Major-General*
19 Sep 1891 - 2 Feb 1900: Commander of Artillery, Fortress Sveaborg
2 Feb 1900 - 3 Apr 1903: Commandant of Fortress Vyborg
6 Dec 1900: Promoted to *Lieutenant-General*
3 Apr 1903 - 7 Nov 1905: Commandant of Fortress Sveaborg
7 Nov 1905 - Jul 1906: At the disposal of the Main Artillery Directorate
Jul 1906: Dismissed

*Major-General* Andrey Alexeyevich **Kayunchin** (1 Nov 1839 - ?)
6 May 1894: Promoted to *Major-General*
6 May 1894 - 1895: Attached to Don Cossack Army

*Lieutenant-General* Ignaty Fyodorovich **Kazakevich** (17 Nov 1849 - ?)
20 Apr 1903: Promoted to *Major-General*
20 Apr 1903 - 8 Nov 1904: Commander, 1st Brigade, 6th Infantry Division
8 Nov 1904 - 4 Sep 1906: Commander, 1st Brigade, 27th Infantry Division
4 Sep 1906 - 5 May 1910: Commander, 61st Replacement Infantry Brigade
5 May 1910: Promoted to *Lieutenant-General*
5 May 1910: Retired

*Major-General* Yevgeny Mikhailovich **Kazakevich** (29 Apr 1869 - 1931)
4 Apr 1915 - 10 Apr 1916: Aide-de-Camp to the Tsar
25 Mar 1916: Promoted to *Major-General*

10 Apr 1916 - 1917: Reserve officer, Petrograd Military District
1917: Commander, Infantry Division

*Major-General* Matvey Ivanovich **Kazakov** (22 Dec 1858 - ?)
19 Mar 1910 - Feb 1917: Commander, St. Petersburg Gendarmerie Battalion
18 Apr 1910: Promoted to *Major-General*
Feb 1917: Dismissed

*Major-General* Boris Ilyich **Kazanovich** (10 Jul 1871 - 2 Jun 1943)
22 Mar 1916 - 5 May 1917: Chief of Staff, 6$^{th}$ Siberian Rifle Division
6 Dec 1916: Promoted to *Major-General*
5 May 1917 - Oct 1917: Commander, 6$^{th}$ Siberian Rifle Division

*General of Infantry* Pavel Petrovich **Kazansky** (2 Dec 1834 - ?)
7 May 1878 - 6 Nov 1889: Chief of Staff, Odessa Military District
30 Aug 1878: Promoted to *Major-General*
6 Nov 1889 - 2 Jun 1894: Chief of Staff, Kazan Military District
30 Aug 1890: Promoted to *Lieutenant-General*
2 Jun 1894 - 9 Jan 1900: Commander, 9$^{th}$ Infantry Division
9 Jan 1900: Promoted to *General of Infantry*
9 Jan 1900: Retired

*Lieutenant-General* Grigory Kuzmich **Kazantsev** (10 Jan 1833 - 21 Dec 1907)
29 Nov 1893: Promoted to *Major-General*
29 Nov 1893 - 31 Oct 1899: Commander, 19$^{th}$ Artillery Brigade
31 Oct 1899: Promoted to *Lieutenant-General*
31 Oct 1899: Retired

*Lieutenant-General* Georgy Nikolayevich **Kazbek** (3 Nov 1840 - ?)
29 Oct 1892: Promoted to *Major-General*
29 Oct 1892 - 27 Mar 1897: Chief of Staff, Fortress Warsaw
27 Mar 1897 - 3 Jul 1899: Quartermaster-General, Warsaw Military District
3 Jul 1899 - 23 Jun 1902: Commandant of Fortress Ivangorod
6 Dec 1900: Promoted to *Lieutenant-General*
23 Jun 1902 - 25 Jan 1905: Commandant of Fortress Warsaw
25 Jan 1905 - 7 Mar 1906: Commandant of Fortress Vladivostok
7 Mar 1906 - 14 Dec 1906: At the disposal of the C-in-C, Far East
14 Dec 1906 - Jul 1907: Attached to the General Staff

*Major-General* Ivan Nikolayevich **Kazbek** (11 Jun 1860 - Feb 1944)
12 May 1916 - 1917: Commander, Caucasus Grenadier Artillery Brigade
13 Sep 1916: Promoted to *Major-General*

*Rear-Admiral* Aleksandr Ilich **Kazi** (1 Dec 1841 - 1918)
1894 - 1896: Commander, 14$^{th}$ Naval Depot
1896: Promoted to *Rear-Admiral*
1896: Retired

*Major-General of the Fleet* Sergey Ilich **Kazi** (24 Sep 1844 - 29 May 1917)
1 Jan 1911: Promoted to *Major-General of the Admiralty*
8 Apr 1913: Redesignated *Major-General of the Fleet*
1914 - ?: Attached to the Borderguard Corps

*Major-General* Dmitriy Nilovich **Kazin** (6 Jul 1851 - 1913)
12 Nov 1907: Promoted to *Major-General*
12 Nov 1907 - 1909: Commander, 2nd Brigade, 3rd East Siberian Rifle Division
1909: Retired

*Major-General* Platon Petrovich **Kazmin** (17 Nov 1857 - ?)
12 May 1913 - 1917: Chairman of the Remount Commission, Vladimir Region
6 Dec 1913: Promoted to *Major-General*

*Lieutenant-General* Nikolai Vladimirovich **Kaznacheyev** (22 Aug 1857 - ?)
29 Nov 1905 - 13 Sep 1906: Military Judge, Kiev Military District Court
6 Dec 1905: Promoted to *Major-General*
13 Sep 1906 - 31 Dec 1912: Military Prosecutor, Warsaw Military District
6 Dec 1912: Promoted to *Lieutenant-General*
31 Dec 1912 - 4 Dec 1917: Chairman of the Military Tribunal, Kazan Military District
4 Dec 1917: Discharged

*Admiral* Nikolai Ivanovich **Kaznakov** (5 Nov 1834 - 1 Jul 1906)
30 Aug 1880 - 24 May 1883: Director of Chancellery, Ministry of the Navy
30 Aug 1882: Promoted to *Rear-Admiral*
24 May 1883 - 20 Feb 1884: Director, Department of Inspections, Ministry of the Navy
20 Feb 1884 - 16 Jun 1886: Commander, Naval Detachment in Greek Waters
10 Oct 1886 - 5 Jan 1891: Chief Inspector of Naval Artillery
1 Jan 1889: Promoted to *Vice-Admiral*
5 Jan 1891 - 27 Sep 1891: Commander, Baltic Sea Training Squadron
27 Sep 1891 - 30 Aug 1893: Senior Flagman, Baltic Fleet
1893: Commander, Atlantic Ocean Squadron
30 Aug 1893 - 6 Dec 1899: Military Governor of Kronstadt, Commander, Port of Kronstadt
6 Dec 1899 - 1 Jul 1906: Member, Board of Admiralty
6 Dec 1901: Promoted to *Admiral*
13 Aug 1902: Promoted to *General-Adjutant*

*General of Infantry* Nikolai Nikolayevich **Kaznakov** (12 Jan 1856 - 15 Apr 1929)
15 Apr 1905: Promoted to *Major-General*
15 Apr 1905 - 28 Aug 1907: Commander, 2nd Brigade, 5th Cavalry Division
28 Aug 1907 - 4 Feb 1910: Commander, 1st Brigade, 5th Cavalry Division
4 Feb 1910 - 23 Dec 1910: At the disposal of the Commanding General, St. Petersburg Military District

| | |
|---|---|
| 23 Dec 1910: | Promoted to *Lieutenant-General* |
| 23 Dec 1910 - 30 Mar 1916: | Commander, 1st Guards Cavalry Division |
| 30 Mar 1916 - 10 Apr 1917: | Commanding General, XII. Army Corps |
| 15 Jan 1917: | Promoted to *General of Infantry* |
| 10 Apr 1917 - Oct 1917: | Reserve officer, Kiev Military District |

*Major-General* Vladimir Ivanovich **Kedrin** (12 Jul 1866 - ?)
| | |
|---|---|
| 12 Jun 1908 - 1917: | Commandant, Kazan Military School |
| 18 Apr 1910: | Promoted to *Major-General* |

*Rear-Admiral* Mikhail Aleksandrovich **Kedrov** (1 Sep 1878 - 29 Oct 1945)
| | |
|---|---|
| 28 Jun 1916: | Promoted to *Rear-Admiral* |
| 28 Jun 1916 - Mar 1917: | Commander, Mine Division, Baltic Fleet |
| Mar 1917 - Jun 1917: | Deputy Minister of the Navy |
| Apr 1917 - Jun 1917: | Chief of the Naval General Staff |
| Jun 1917 - Oct 1917: | At the disposal of the Minister of the Navy |

*Major-General* Vonifaty Aleksandrovich **Kedrov** (11 May 1854 - 16 Oct 1905)
| | |
|---|---|
| 6 Nov 1902: | Promoted to *Major-General* |
| 6 Nov 1902 - 21 Jul 1905: | Commander, 1st Brigade, 17th Infantry Division |

*Major-General* Aleksandr Adolfovich **Kegel** (2 Jul 1873 - 1915)
| | |
|---|---|
| ? - 1915: | Attached to 14th East Siberian Rifle Regiment |
| 5 Oct 1915: | Posthumously promoted to *Major-General* |

*Major-General* Prince Nikolai Aleksandrovich **Kekuatov** (3 May 1869 - 3 Mar 1922)
| | |
|---|---|
| 1 Jan 1916 - 28 Aug 1917: | Commander, 1st Brigade, 1st Trans-Baikal Cossack Division |
| 16 Oct 1916: | Promoted to *Major-General* |
| 28 Aug 1917 - 1918: | Commander, 1st Trans-Baikal Cossack Division |

*Lieutenant-General* Anatoly Ignatyevich **Kelchevsky** (7 May 1855 - ?)
| | |
|---|---|
| 21 Dec 1902 - 30 Aug 1913: | Inspector of Classes, Moscow Alekseyev Military School |
| 6 Dec 1904: | Promoted to *Major-General* |
| 30 Aug 1913: | Promoted to *Lieutenant-General* |
| 30 Aug 1913: | Retired |

*Lieutenant-General* Anatoly Kipriyanovich **Kelchevsky** (19 Jan 1869 - 1 Apr 1923)
| | |
|---|---|
| 1 Jun 1915: | Promoted to *Major-General* |
| 1915 - 2 Nov 1915: | Attached to the C-in-C, 9th Army |
| 2 Nov 1915 - 15 Apr 1917: | Quartermaster-General, 9th Army |
| 15 Apr 1917 - 9 Sep 1917: | Chief of Staff, 9th Army |
| 9 Sep 1917: | Promoted to *Lieutenant-General* |
| 9 Sep 1917 - Nov 1917: | C-in-C, 9th Army |

*Major-General* Count Artur Arturovich **Keller** (13 May 1868 - 5 Jul 1915)
| | |
|---|---|
| 23 Sep 1912 - 5 Mar 1915: | Commander, 1st Astrakhan Cossack Regiment |

31 Jan 1915: Promoted to *Major-General*
5 Mar 1915 - 7 May 1915: Commander, Brigade, 4th Don Cossack Division
7 May 1915 - 2 Jul 1915: Reserve officer, Dvinsk Military District
2 Jul 1915 - 5 Jul 1915: Duty General, 6th Army

*General of Cavalry* Count Fyodor Arturovich **Keller** (12 Oct 1857 - 21 Dec 1918)
6 Nov 1906 - 15 May 1910: Commander, Life Guards Dragoon Regiment
31 May 1907: Promoted to *Major-General*
14 Jun 1910 - 25 Feb 1912: Commander, 1st Brigade, Caucasus Cavalry Division
25 Feb 1912 - 3 Apr 1915: Commander, 10th Cavalry Division
31 May 1913: Promoted to *Lieutenant-General*
3 Apr 1915 - 7 Apr 1917: Commanding General, III. Cavalry Corps
15 Jan 1917: Promoted to *General of Cavalry*
7 Apr 1917 - 1918: Reserve officer, Kiev Military District

*Lieutenant-General* Count Fyodor Eduardovich **Keller** (3 Aug 1850 - 18 Jul 1904)
30 Dec 1883 - 7 Sep 1887: Commander, Life Guards 4th Rifle Battalion
7 Sep 1887 - 4 Nov 1894: Transferred to the reserve
1890: Promoted to *Major-General*
4 Nov 1894 - 20 Apr 1900: Director, Corps of Pages
6 Dec 1899: Promoted to *Lieutenant-General*
20 Apr 1900 - 7 Mar 1904: Governor of Yekaterinoslav
7 Mar 1904 - Mar 1904: At the disposal of the Minister of War
Mar 1904 - 18 Jul 1904: Commanding General, II. East Siberian Army Corps

*Major-General* Karl-Yulius-Vilgelm-Eduard Genrikhovich **Keller** (20 Oct 1830 - ?)
19 Nov 1891: Promoted to *Major-General*
19 Nov 1891 - 11 Oct 1899: Commander, 2nd Brigade, 5th Infantry Division

*Major-General* Baron Boris Borisovich **Kene** (27 Apr 1846 - ?)
7 Feb 1901: Promoted to *Major-General*
7 Feb 1901 - 4 Jun 1901: Commander, 2nd Brigade, 14th Infantry Division

*General of Artillery* Pavel Yegorovich **Keppen** (19 Dec 1846 - 5 Aug 1911)
23 Apr 1888: Promoted to *Major-General*
23 Apr 1888 - 20 Feb 1892: Court Marshal to Grand Duke Konstantin Nikolayevich
20 Feb 1892 - 5 Aug 1911: Court Marshal to Grand Duchess Alexandra Iosifovna
23 Apr 1898: Promoted to *Lieutenant-General*
6 Dec 1910: Promoted to *General of Artillery*

*Vice-Admiral* Ludvig Bernhardovich **Kerber** (19 Apr 1863 - 9 Apr 1919)
7 May 1913 - 12 Feb 1915: Chief of Staff, Baltic Fleet
1913: Promoted to *Rear-Admiral*
24 Dec 1914: Promoted to *Vice-Admiral*
12 Feb 1915 - 10 Nov 1916: Member, Board of Admiralty
10 Nov 1916 - 7 Mar 1917: C-in-C, Northern Fleet
7 Mar 1917 - 3 Dec 1917: Unassigned
3 Dec 1917: Dismissed

*Lieutenant-General* Aleksandr Eduardovich **Kern** (12 Nov 1856 - ?)
| | |
|---|---|
| 19 Aug 1903 - 12 Jul 1913: | Member of the Artillery Committee, Main Artillery Directorate |
| 6 Dec 1906: | Promoted to *Major-General* |
| 30 Apr 1913: | Promoted to *Lieutenant-General* |
| 12 Jul 1913: | Retired |
| 16 May 1914 - Oct 1917: | Recalled; Attached to the Ministry of War |

*Major-General* Alfred Fyodorovich **Kern** (25 Sep 1859 - 30 Nov 1924)
| | |
|---|---|
| 27 Jan 1909 - 1915: | Commander, 3$^{rd}$ Replacement Cavalry Regiment |
| 14 Apr 1913: | Promoted to *Major-General* |
| 1915 - 18 May 1917: | Commander, 3$^{rd}$ Replacement Cavalry Brigade |
| 18 May 1917: | Dismissed |

*Major-General* Konstantin Iskrovich **Kesyakov** (14 Jul 1839 - 3 Mar 1900)
| | |
|---|---|
| 28 Apr 1899: | Promoted to *Major-General* |
| 28 Apr 1899 - 6 Sep 1899: | Commander, 2$^{nd}$ Brigade, 39$^{th}$ Infantry Division |
| 6 Sep 1899 - 3 Mar 1900: | Commander, 1$^{st}$ Brigade, 26$^{th}$ Infantry Division |

*Major-General* Georgy Aleksandrovich **Ketkhudov** (24 Oct 1868 - ?)
| | |
|---|---|
| 10 Nov 1915 - 1917: | Commandant of Helsingfors |
| 6 Dec 1916: | Promoted to *Major-General* |

*Lieutenant-General of the Naval Legal Corps* Yuly Ernestovich **Ketrits** (20 Mar 1862 - 15 Dec 1917)
| | |
|---|---|
| 7 Aug 1906 - 28 Nov 1911: | Military Judge, Sevastopol Naval Court |
| 6 Dec 1909: | Promoted to *Major-General of the Naval Legal Corps* |
| 28 Nov 1911 - 24 Dec 1914: | Procurator, Sevastopol Naval Court |
| 6 Apr 1914: | Promoted to *Lieutenant-General of the Naval Legal Corps* |
| 24 Dec 1914 - 1917: | Chairman of the Naval Court, Sevastopol |

*Rear-Admiral* Vladislav Ksaveryevich **Kevnarsky** (13 Mar 1856 - ?)
| | |
|---|---|
| ?: | Promoted to *Rear-Admiral* |

*Lieutenant-General* Sergey Semyonovich **Khabalov** (21 Apr 1858 - 1924)
| | |
|---|---|
| 2 Oct 1903 - 27 Apr 1905: | Commandant, Moscow Military School |
| 6 Dec 1904: | Promoted to *Major-General* |
| 27 Apr 1905 - 24 Jan 1914: | Commandant, Pavlovsk Military School |
| 6 Dec 1910: | Promoted to *Lieutenant-General* |
| 24 Jan 1914 - 13 Jun 1916: | Military Governor of the Ural Region, Ataman, Ural Cossack Army |
| 13 Jun 1916 - 27 Feb 1917: | Commanding General, Petrograd Military District |
| 27 Feb 1917 - 11 Nov 1917: | Reserve officer, Petrograd Military District |
| 11 Nov 1917: | Retired |

*Major-General* Mikhail Fedorovich **Khabarov** (8 Sep 1857 - 27 Dec 1924)
| | |
|---|---|
| 9 Jan 1909 - 20 Aug 1915: | Commander, 10$^{th}$ Borderguard Brigade |

14 Apr 1913:                   Promoted to *Major-General*
20 Aug 1915 - 1918:            POW

*Major-General* Gugo Gustavovich von **Khakevits** (4 Sep 1849 - ?)
24 Oct 1902 - 14 Dec 1907:     Commander, 6th Turkestan Rifle Brigade
17 Apr 1905:                   Promoted to *Major-General*

*Major-General* Vladimir Fedorovich **Khaldeyev** (30 Mar 1869 - ?)
27 Nov 1910 - 1917:            Sub-Section Chief, Main Military-Technical Directorate
6 Dec 1916:                    Promoted to *Major-General*

*Lieutenant-General* Nikolai Aleksandrovich **Khamin** (13 Apr 1864 - ?)
22 May 1909:                   Promoted to *Major-General*
22 May 1909 - 28 Sep 1917:     Commandant, Alexeyev Military School
6 Dec 1915:                    Promoted to *Lieutenant-General*
28 Sep 1917 - 1918:            Chief of Main Directorate for Military Schools

*Major-General* Pavel Georgiyevich **Khandakov** (16 Jun 1861 - ?)
27 Dec 1914 - 1917:            Commander, 2nd Brigade, 3rd Cavalry Division
31 May 1915:                   Promoted to *Major-General*

*Major-General* Aleksandr Pavlovich **Khanukov** (18 Dec 1867 - 4 Dec 1943)
22 Nov 1913 - 1915:            Commander, 131st Infantry Regiment
6 Jun 1915:                    Promoted to *Major-General*
1915 - 13 Nov 1915:            Commander, Brigade, 31st Infantry Division
13 Nov 1915 - 20 Apr 1916:     Chief of Staff, XXIII. Army Corps
20 Apr 1916 - 18 Feb 1917:     Chief of Staff, XLI. Army Corps
18 Feb 1917 - 20 Jul 1917:     Commander, 5th Amur Border Infantry Division
20 Jul 1917 - 1918:            Reserve officer, Kiev Military District

*Major-General* Nikolai Leonidovich **Khanykov** (29 Jan 1862 - 29 Aug 1916)
28 Feb 1908 - 29 Aug 1916:     Military Judge, Odessa Military District Court
13 Apr 1908:                   Promoted to *Major-General*

*Lieutenant-General* Mikhail Vasilyevich **Khanzhin** (17 Oct 1871 - 20 Dec 1961)
9 Aug 1910 - 19 Feb 1914:      Commander, Battalion, 44th Artillery Brigade
3 Feb 1914:                    Promoted to *Major-General*
19 Feb 1914 - 31 Jul 1915:     Commander, 19th Artillery Brigade
31 Jul 1915 - 18 Apr 1916:     Commander, 12th Infantry Division
18 Apr 1916 - 19 Dec 1916:     Inspector of Artillery, 8th Army
25 Aug 1916:                   Promoted to *Lieutenant-General*
19 Dec 1916 - 14 Apr 1917:     Inspector of Artillery, Romanian Front
14 Apr 1917 - Oct 1917:        Inspector-General of Field Artillery, Supreme High Command

*Major-General* Viktor Vasilyevich **Kharchenko** (18 Dec 1853 - ?)
14 Mar 1916 - 1918:            Chief of Evacuation Points, Penza District
9 Jun 1916:                    Promoted to *Major-General*

*Major-General* Ivan Nikolayevich **Kharin** (1 May 1860 - 6 Jun 1923)
11 Mar 1911 - 21 Mar 1914:   Attached to the General Staff
21 Mar 1914:                 Promoted to *Major-General*
21 Mar 1914:                 Retired
23 Mar 1914 - Oct 1917:      At the disposal of the Chief of the General Staff

*Lieutenant-General* Pavel Petrovich **Kharinsky** (24 Jun 1845 - ?)
5 Apr 1883 - 20 Nov 1897:    Section Chief, Main Artillery Directorate
30 Aug 1893:                 Promoted to *Major-General*
20 Nov 1897 - 11 Nov 1910:   Deputy Chief of the Main Artillery Directorate
1 Apr 1901:                  Promoted to *Lieutenant-General*
11 Nov 1910:                 Transferred to the reserve

*Major-General* Filipp Kazimirovich **Kharkevich** (9 Nov 1859 - ?)
1914 - 29 Jul 1916:          Attached to 62$^{nd}$ Infantry Regiment
29 Jul 1916:                 Promoted to *Major-General*
29 Jul 1916:                 Retired

*Lieutenant-General* Vladimir Ivanovich **Kharkevich** (29 Sep 1856 - 13 Aug 1906)
26 Aug 1892 - 16 Feb 1904:   Chief of Communications, Vilnius Military District
30 Aug 1900:                 Promoted to *Major-General*
16 Feb 1904 - 16 Apr 1904:   At the disposal of the C-in-C, Manchurian Army
16 Apr 1904 - 28 Oct 1904:   Quartermaster-General, Manchurian Army
20 Aug 1904:                 Promoted to *Lieutenant-General*
28 Oct 1904 - 17 Mar 1905:   Chief of the Field Staff, Manchurian Army
17 Mar 1905 - 13 Aug 1906:   Chief of Staff, High Command of Armed Forces, Far East

*Major-General* Viktor Viktorovich **Kharlamov** (1 Dec 1869 - 14 Dec 1933)
1915:                        Commander, 10$^{th}$ Rifle Regiment
31 May 1915:                 Promoted to *Major-General*
1915 - 11 Mar 1916:          Reserve officer, Kiev Military District
11 Mar 1916 - 1917:          Commander, Brigade, 100$^{th}$ Infantry Division
1917 - 1918:                 Commander, 12$^{th}$ Siberian Rifle Division

*Major-General* Eduard Oskarovich **Kharten** (12 May 1860 - ?)
9 Apr 1914 - 1 Sep 1916:     Commander, 16$^{th}$ Dragoon Regiment
1 Sep 1916 - 1918:           Commander, 2$^{nd}$ Brigade, Caucasus Cavalry Division
22 Sep 1916:                 Promoted to *Major-General*

*Major-General* Fyodor Viktorovich **Khartulari** (30 Dec 1868 - Dec 1916)
12 May 1915 - Dec 1916:      Deputy Chief of Izhevsk Arms Factory
6 Dec 1915:                  Promoted to *Major-General*

*Major-General* Konstantin Konstantinovich **Khartulari** (22 Jan 1844 - ?)
11 Feb 1897 - 1900:          Chief of Gendarmerie, Vitebsk Province
5 Apr 1898:                  Promoted to *Major-General*

*Major-General* Mikhail Viktorovich **Khartulari** (15 Oct 1867 - Nov 1916)
30 Sep 1906 - 14 Jan 1914: Commander, 2nd Grenadier Regiment
14 Jan 1914: Promoted to *Major-General*
14 Jan 1914 - 12 Mar 1915: Commander, 1st Brigade, 3rd Grenadier Division
12 Mar 1915: Retired
1915 - 16 Jul 1916: Recalled; Chief of Vladimir District Evacuation Point
16 Jul 1916 - 13 Nov 1916: Special Assignments General, Moscow Military District
13 Nov 1916 - Nov 1916: Reserve officer, Minsk Military District

*Major-General* Viktor Viktorovich **Khartulari** (7 Sep 1865 - 5 Sep 1928)
30 Mar 1911 - 12 Oct 1914: Chief of Control Section, Main Artillery Directorate
14 Apr 1913: Promoted to *Major-General*
12 Oct 1914 - 1918: Deputy Chief of Economic Department, Main Artillery Directorate

*Major-General* Iakinf Apollinariyevich **Kharzhevsky** (3 Jan 1861 - ?)
9 Jan 1916 - 1918: Commander, 37th Replacement Infantry Brigade
6 Dec 1916: Promoted to *Major-General*

*Lieutenant-General* Andrey Vladimirovich **Khaskin** (2 Dec 1862 - ?)
28 Sep 1906 - 17 Nov 1907: Deputy Intendant, Irkutsk Military District
22 Apr 1907: Promoted to *Major-General*
17 Nov 1907 - 5 May 1910: Intendant, Irkutsk Military District
5 May 1910 - 20 Aug 1913: Transferred to the reserve
20 Aug 1913: Promoted to *Lieutenant-General*
20 Aug 1913: Retired

*Major-General* Aleksandr Sergeyevich **Khatov** (3 Mar 1852 - ?)
10 Dec 1905 - 1907: Commander of Artillery, Fortress Kars
1906: Promoted to *Major-General*

*Major-General* Sergey Sergeyevich **Khatov** (31 May 1858 - ?)
17 Feb 1897 - 7 Feb 1904: Commander, 9th Rifle Regiment
4 Feb 1904: Promoted to *Major-General*
7 Feb 1904 - 13 Dec 1906: Commander, 7th Turkestan Rifle Brigade

*Major-General* Semyon Yegorovich **Khaynovsky** (21 Jul 1844 - ?)
23 Nov 1895 - 8 Mar 1901: Deputy Commander of Engineers, Turkestan Military District
14 May 1896: Promoted to *Major-General*
8 Mar 1901 - 1901: Special Assignments General, Main Engineering Directorate

*Major-General* Ivan Ivanovich **Khazov** (23 Oct 1861 - ?)
Jul 1914 - 25 Dec 1915: Commander, 240th Infantry Regiment
17 Nov 1915: Promoted to *Major-General*
25 Dec 1915 - 1918: Commander, 1st Brigade, Caucasus Rifle Division

*Major-General* Baron Yalmar Fyodorovich von **Khellens** (13 Jun 1869 - 24 May 1953)
1915 - 7 Apr 1916: Commander, 4th Infantry Regiment
7 Apr 1916 - 10 Oct 1917: Commander, Brigade, 12th Siberian Rifle Division
15 Jun 1916: Promoted to *Major-General*
10 Oct 1917 - 1918: Commander, 108th Infantry Division

*General of Cavalry* Pavel Lyudvigovich **Khelmitsky** (15 Jul 1855 - 28 Jul 1918)
3 May 1904: Promoted to *Major-General*
3 May 1904 - 5 Jul 1910: Commander, Trans-Caspian Cossack Brigade
21 Jan 1909: Promoted to *Lieutenant-General*
5 Jul 1910 - 16 Apr 1917: Commander, 3rd Caucasus Cossack Division
Dec 1914 - ?: Simultaneously, Commanding General, Consolidated Cavalry Corps, Southwestern Front
16 Apr 1917 - 29 Jul 1917: Reserve officer, Kiev Military District
29 Jul 1917: Promoted to *General of Cavalry*
29 Jul 1917: Retired

*Major-General* Nikolai Vladimirovich **Khenrikson** (5 Dec 1871 - 9 Dec 1941)
23 Nov 1915 - 19 Apr 1917: Special Assignments General, Northern Front
6 Dec 1916: Promoted to *Major-General*
19 Apr 1917 - 7 Oct 1917: Commander, 109th Infantry Division
7 Oct 1917 - 15 Mar 1918: Commander of Land Forces subordinate to the C-in-C, Baltic Fleet

*Major-General* Magis Karlovich **Kheykel** (16 Oct 1838 - ?)
10 May 1888 - 5 Jan 1895: Commander, 110th Infantry Regiment
14 Nov 1894: Promoted to *Major-General*
5 Jan 1895 - 24 Oct 1900: Commander, 1st Brigade, 10th Infantry Division

*Major-General* Grigory Grigoryevich **Khilchenko** (8 Aug 1867 - ?)
22 Jan 1912 - 4 Apr 1915: Commander, 25th Siberian Rifle Regiment
31 Dec 1914: Promoted to *Major-General*
4 Apr 1915 - 1917: Commander, 1st Brigade, 5th Siberian Rifle Division

*Lieutenant-General* Vasily Aleksandrovich **Khimets** (24 Jan 1861 - 1919)
12 Apr 1902 - 7 Jan 1909: Deputy Commandant, Officers Cavalry School
31 May 1907: Promoted to *Major-General*
7 Jan 1909 - 15 Aug 1914: Commandant, Officers Cavalry School
14 Apr 1913: Promoted to *Lieutenant-General*
15 Aug 1914 - 4 Jul 1915: Commander, 4th Independent Cavalry Brigade
4 Jul 1915 - 1918: Chief of Army Remount Directorate

*General of Artillery* Prince Georgy Spiridonovich **Khimshiyev** (14 Jun 1836 - 16 Jul 1917)
12 Oct 1892: Promoted to *Major-General*
12 Oct 1892 - 30 Jan 1893: Commander, 6th Artillery Brigade
30 Jan 1893 - 9 Feb 1897: Commander, 39th Artillery Brigade
9 Feb 1897 - 13 Apr 1899: Commander, Caucasus Grenadier Artillery Brigade
13 Apr 1899 - 5 Mar 1905: Commander of Artillery, I. Caucasus Army Corps

6 Dec 1900: Promoted to *Lieutenant-General*
5 Mar 1905 - 16 Jul 1917: Member, Committee for Wounded Veterans
13 Apr 1908: Promoted to *General of Artillery*

*Major-General* Favst Fyodorovich **Khinevich-Vaskovsky** (3 Aug 1841 - ?)
6 May 1901 - 1904: Deputy Intendant, Kiev Military District
6 Dec 1901: Promoted to *Major-General*

*Lieutenant-General* Aleksandr Mikhailovich **Khitrovo** (3 Jul 1845 - 17 Jul 1911)
13 Oct 1898: Promoted to *Major-General*
13 Oct 1898 - 29 Dec 1899: Commander, 3rd Replacement Artillery Brigade
29 Dec 1899 - 18 Jan 1902: Commander, 36th Artillery Brigade
18 Jan 1902 - 1908: Commander of Artillery, XIII. Army Corps
6 Dec 1904: Promoted to *Lieutenant-General*
1908: Retired

*Major-General* Fyodor Konstantinovich **Khitrovo** (15 Feb 1869 - 13 Aug 1914)
31 Dec 1913: Promoted to *Major-General*
31 Dec 1913 - 13 Aug 1914: Commander, 2nd Brigade, 31st Infantry Division

*General of Artillery* Nikolai Mikhailovich **Khitrovo** (10 Aug 1844 - 17 Nov 1909)
8 Mar 1893: Promoted to *Major-General*
8 Mar 1893 - 13 Oct 1898: Commander, 5th Reserve Artillery Brigade
13 Oct 1898 - 5 Dec 1899: Commander, 2nd Reserve Artillery Brigade
5 Dec 1899 - 18 Jan 1902: Commander of Artillery, X. Army Corps
1 Apr 1901: Promoted to *Lieutenant-General*
18 Jan 1902 - 7 Aug 1903: Commander of Artillery, Kiev Military District
7 Aug 1903 - 18 Mar 1906: Commander of Artillery, Guards Corps
18 Mar 1906 - 17 Nov 1909: Commanding General, VI. Army Corps
6 Dec 1908: Promoted to *General of Artillery*

*Major-General* Vladimir Mikhailovich **Khitrovo** (22 May 1861 - ?)
14 Nov 1904 - 11 Feb 1908: Commander, 12th Uhlan Regiment
11 Feb 1908: Promoted to *Major-General*
11 Feb 1908 - 19 Jul 1914: Commander, 2nd Brigade, 10th Cavalry Division
19 Jul 1914 - 18 Dec 1914: Commander, 4th Don Cossack Division
18 Dec 1914 - 25 Jan 1915: Reserve officer, Dvinsk Military District
25 Jan 1915 - 21 Mar 1917: Commander, 2nd Brigade, 2nd Kuban Cossack Division
21 Mar 1917 - 1918: Chief of Staff, XXXVII. Army Corps

*Major-General* Serene Khan Seid-Asfendiar-Bogadur-Khan **Khivinsky** (1 Jan 1873 - Sep 1918)
30 Jul 1910: Promoted to *Major-General*
30 Jul 1910 - 1917: General à la suite
16 Aug 1910 - Sep 1918: Khan of Khiva

*General of Cavalry* Serene Khan Seid Mohammed Rahim Bogadur Khan **Khivinsky** (1845 - 16 Aug 1910)

| | |
|---|---|
| 10 Sep 1864 - 16 Aug 1910: | Khan of Khiva |
| ?: | Promoted to *Major-General* |
| 14 May 1896: | Promoted to *Lieutenant-General* |
| 29 Jan 1904: | Promoted to *General of Cavalry* |

*General of Engineers* Konstantin Dmitriyevich **Khlebnikov** (12 Sep 1822 - 1908)
| | |
|---|---|
| 25 Mar 1866 - 18 Mar 1869: | Governor of Kielce |
| 30 Aug 1867: | Promoted to *Major-General* |
| 18 Mar 1869 - 8 Aug 1869: | Unassigned |
| 8 Aug 1869 - 26 Jan 1874: | Special Assignments General, Warsaw Military District |
| 26 Jan 1874 - 14 Jul 1883: | Transferred to the reserve |
| 30 Aug 1882: | Promoted to *Lieutenant-General* |
| 14 Jul 1883 - 3 May 1893: | Commandant of Fortress Modlin |
| 3 May 1893 - 3 Jan 1906: | Member of the Military Council |
| 14 May 1896: | Promoted to *General of Engineers* |
| 3 Jan 1906: | Retired |

*Major-General* Pyotr Vasilyevich **Khlebnikov** (15 Jan 1864 - 24 Jan 1918)
| | |
|---|---|
| 8 Sep 1914 - 23 Dec 1916: | Commander, 2$^{nd}$ Orenburg Cossack Regiment |
| 22 Oct 1916: | Promoted to *Major-General* |
| 23 Dec 1916 - Apr 1917: | Commander, 1$^{st}$ Brigade, Orenburg Cossack Division |
| Apr 1917 - Jan 1918: | Commander, 1$^{st}$ Brigade, 1$^{st}$ Orenburg Cossack Division |

*General of Artillery* Vladimir Nikolayevich **Khlebnikov** (25 Jul 1836 - 9 Feb 1915)
| | |
|---|---|
| 19 Oct 1877 - 24 Dec 1885: | Commander, 15$^{th}$ Dragoon Regiment |
| 1884: | Promoted to *Major-General* |
| 24 Dec 1885 - 23 Oct 1893: | Commander, 3$^{rd}$ Reserve Artillery Brigade |
| 23 Oct 1893 - 14 Feb 1899: | Commander of Artillery, VI. Army Corps |
| 14 Nov 1894: | Promoted to *Lieutenant-General* |
| 14 Feb 1899 - 28 Feb 1901: | Commander of Artillery, Moscow Military District |
| 28 Feb 1901 - 9 Feb 1915: | Honorary Trustee, Board of Trustees, Empress Maria Institutions |
| 29 Jan 1906: | Promoted to *General of Artillery* |

*Major-General of Naval Engineers* Fyodor Konstantinovich **Khlestov** (9 Nov 1860 - ?)
| | |
|---|---|
| 15 Dec 1908 - 1917: | Chief Mechanical Engineer, Port of Kronstadt |
| 29 Mar 1909: | Promoted to *Major-General of Naval Engineers* |

*Major-General* Mikhail Ivanovich **Khlynovsky** (14 Sep 1859 - 1910)
| | |
|---|---|
| 30 Jul 1904 - 1 Mar 1905: | Deputy Chief of Staff, Siberian Military District |
| 6 Dec 1904: | Promoted to *Major-General* |
| 1 Mar 1905 - 12 Jun 1906: | Chief of Sanitation & Evacuation Service, Siberian Military District |
| 12 Jun 1906 - 1910: | Commander, Nerchinsk District |

*Major-General of the Fleet* Sergey Leonidovich **Khmelev** (16 Mar 1869 - ?)
| | |
|---|---|
| 1912 - 1916: | Commander, Siberian Naval Depot |
| 10 Apr 1916: | Promoted to *Major-General of the Fleet* |

*Major-General* Ivan Dmitriyevich **Khodnev** (1 Jan 1847 - ?)
31 Oct 1899 - 11 Sep 1903: Commander, 11th Grenadier Regiment
11 Sep 1903: Promoted to *Major-General*
11 Sep 1903 - 14 Jan 1905: Commander, 1st Brigade, 1st Infantry Division
14 Jan 1905 - 28 Mar 1907: Commander, 1st Brigade, 2nd Grenadier Division
28 Mar 1907: Retired

*General of Infantry* Nikolai Aleksandrovich **Khodorovich** (6 Dec 1857 - 21 Jul 1936)
22 Nov 1904 - 16 May 1905: Chief of Lines of Communication, 3rd Manchurian Army
17 Feb 1905: Promoted to *Major-General*
16 May 1905 - 7 Sep 1906: Chief of Communications, 3rd Manchurian Army
7 Sep 1906 - 1 Jun 1911: Chief of Communications, Kiev Military District
1 Jun 1911: Promoted to *Lieutenant-General*
1 Jun 1911 - 19 Jul 1914: Chief of Staff, Omsk Military District
19 Jul 1914 - 23 Jul 1915: Chief of Staff, Kiev Military District
23 Jul 1915 - 8 Apr 1916: Deputy Commanding General, Kiev Military District
8 Apr 1916 - Oct 1917: Commanding General, Kiev Military District
24 Oct 1917: Promoted to *General of Infantry*
Oct 1917 - 1918: Reserve officer, Petrograd Military District

*Major-General* Gidayat-Ulla-Mirbidalev **Khodzha** (6 Dec 1849 - ?)
14 May 1900 - 7 Sep 1913: Military Commander, Samarkand
7 Sep 1913: Promoted to *Major-General*
7 Sep 1913: Retired
28 Feb 1915 - ?: Recalled; Special Assignments General, Turkestan Military District

*Lieutenant-General* Prince Tarkhan Agamalovich **Khodzhamisanov** (28 May 1825 - 1909)
30 Aug 1875: Promoted to *Major-General*
30 Aug 1875 - 1896: Attached to the Caucasus Military District
30 Aug 1887: Promoted to *Lieutenant-General*
1896: Retired

*Major-General* Kazimir Aleksandrovich **Khodzinsky** (? - ?)
?: Promoted to *Major-General*

*Major-General* Konstantin Nikolayevich **Khogondokov** (14 Sep 1871 - 2 Dec 1958)
1 Sep 1914 - 17 Feb 1915: Commander, 3rd Brigade, Caucasus Native Cavalry Division
17 Feb 1915 - 18 Jul 1915: Chief of Staff to General Adjutant Mishchenko
18 Jul 1915 - Oct 1915: Chief of Staff, II. Cavalry Corps
Oct 1915 - 30 Nov 1915: Commander, 2nd Brigade, Caucasus Native Cavalry Brigade
22 Oct 1915: Promoted to *Major-General*
30 Nov 1915 - 20 Jan 1916: Chief of Staff, II. Cavalry Corps
20 Jan 1916 - 31 May 1917: Military Governor of Amur Region,

| | Ataman, Amur Cossack Army |
|---|---|
| 31 May 1917 - 20 Oct 1917: | Commanding General, Amur Military District, Ataman, Amur & Ussuri Cossack Army |
| 20 Oct 1917 - Dec 1917: | Reserve officer, Caucasus Military District |

*Major-General* Ivan Alekseyevich **Kholmsen** (28 Sep 1865 - 19 Mar 1941)
| | |
|---|---|
| 28 Oct 1906 - 14 Jan 1913: | Military Attaché, Turkey |
| 6 Dec 1910: | Promoted to *Major-General* |
| 14 Jan 1913 - 29 Jul 1914: | Commander, 1st Brigade, 1st Grenadier Division |
| 29 Jul 1914 - Feb 1915: | Commander, 1st Brigade, 53rd Infantry Division |
| Feb 1915 - Apr 1917: | POW, Germany |

*Lieutenant-General* Nikolai Aleksandrovich **Kholmsky** (13 Apr 1843 - ?)
| | |
|---|---|
| 12 Aug 1893 - 2 Jul 1903: | Ataman, 3rd Military Division, Orenburg Cossack Army |
| 6 May 1898: | Promoted to *Major-General* |
| 2 Jul 1903: | Promoted to *Lieutenant-General* |
| 2 Jul 1903: | Retired |

*Lieutenant-General* Ivan Ivanovich **Kholodovsky** (4 Sep 1848 - ?)
| | |
|---|---|
| 4 Apr 1901: | Promoted to *Major-General* |
| 4 Apr 1901 - 4 Feb 1906: | Special Assignments General, Inspectorate of Rifles |
| 19 Apr 1901 - 11 Nov 1907: | Member of the Artillery Committee, Main Artillery Directorate |
| 4 Feb 1906 - 11 Nov 1907: | Special Assignments General, Inspectorate-General of Infantry |
| 11 Nov 1907: | Promoted to *Lieutenant-General* |
| 11 Nov 1907 - 24 Nov 1908: | Commander, 29th Infantry Division |

*General of Artillery* Nikolai Ivanovich **Kholodovsky** (14 Apr 1851 - 15 May 1933)
| | |
|---|---|
| 5 Aug 1900 - 29 Jan 1903: | Commander of Artillery, Kwantung Region |
| 26 Feb 1901: | Promoted to *Major-General* |
| 29 Jan 1903 - 20 Jan 1904: | Deputy Commander of Artillery, Amur Military District |
| 20 Jan 1904 - 29 Feb 1904: | At the disposal of the Main Artillery Directorate |
| 29 Feb 1904 - 18 Aug 1905: | General for Special Assignments, C-in-C, Far East |
| 18 Aug 1905 - 18 Apr 1907: | Commander of Siege Artillery, Manchurian Army |
| 18 Apr 1907 - 20 Dec 1916: | Commander of Artillery, Odessa Military District |
| 22 Apr 1907: | Promoted to *Lieutenant-General* |
| 6 Dec 1915: | Promoted to *General of Artillery* |
| 20 Dec 1916 - Oct 1917: | Commander of Artillery Logistics, Romanian Front |

*General of Engineers* Konstantin Fyodorovich **Kholostov** (26 Aug 1849 - ?)
| | |
|---|---|
| 23 Dec 1899 - 16 Nov 1908: | Engineer Inspector, Omsk Military District |
| 6 Dec 1901: | Promoted to *Major-General* |
| 16 Nov 1908 - Jul 1912: | Commander of Engineers, Kiev Military District |
| 29 Mar 1909: | Promoted to *Lieutenant-General* |
| 8 Aug 1912: | Promoted to *General of Engineers* |
| 8 Aug 1912: | Retired |

*Lieutenant-General* Ivan Vasilyevich **Kholshchevnikov** (17 May 1852 - 10 Jan 1927)
| | |
|---|---|
| 25 Mar 1899: | Promoted to *Major-General* |
| 25 Mar 1899 - 17 Jul 1899: | Chief of Staff, Transcaspian Region |
| 17 Jul 1899 - 7 Aug 1901: | Chief of Staff, II. Turkestan Army Corps |
| 7 Aug 1901 - 5 Jul 1904: | Chief of Staff, Amur Military District |
| 18 Jun 1904: | Promoted to *Lieutenant-General* |
| 5 Jul 1904 - 1 Mar 1906: | Military Governor of Trans-Baikal Region, Ataman, Trans-Baikal Cossack Army |
| 1 Mar 1906 - Jul 1906: | Attached to the Ministry of War |
| Jul 1906 - Jan 1907: | Imprisoned |
| Jan 1907 - Jul 1907: | Unassigned |
| Jul 1907: | Discharged |

*General of Infantry* Ivan Mikhailovich **Kholyavko** (31 Mar 1858 - 24 Nov 1916)
| | |
|---|---|
| 15 May 1900 - 3 Dec 1902: | Military Judge, St. Petersburg Military District Court |
| 1 Apr 1901: | Promoted to *Major-General* |
| 3 Dec 1902 - 25 Feb 1906: | Military Prosecutor, Siberian Military District |
| 25 Feb 1906 - 14 Aug 1906: | Chairman of the Military Tribunal, Siberian Military District |
| 14 Aug 1906 - 27 Feb 1916: | Chairman of the Military Tribunal, Omsk Military District |
| 22 Apr 1907: | Promoted to *Lieutenant-General* |
| 27 Feb 1916: | Promoted to *General of Infantry* |
| 27 Feb 1916: | Retired |

*Vice-Admiral* Aleksandr Aleksandrovich **Khomenko** (25 Mar 1867 - 12 Nov 1939)
| | |
|---|---|
| 20 Sep 1911 - 1915: | Captain, Port of Kronstadt |
| 5 Oct 1912: | Promoted to *Rear-Admiral* |
| 1915 - 1917: | Commander, Transport Flotilla, Black Sea |
| 10 Apr 1916: | Promoted to *Vice-Admiral* |
| 23 Aug 1916 - 1917: | Commander of Freight Traffic, Black Sea & Azov Sea |

*Vice-Admiral* Anatoly Iliodorovich **Khomutov** (16 Oct 1857 - 1918)
| | |
|---|---|
| 10 Nov 1908 - Jan 1914: | Commander, Port of St. Petersburg |
| 6 Dec 1909: | Promoted to *Rear-Admiral* |
| 1915: | Promoted to *Vice-Admiral* |

*Major-General* Aleksandr Vasilyevich **Khomyakov** (25 Jan 1857 - ?)
| | |
|---|---|
| 23 Jan 1914: | Promoted to *Major-General* |
| 23 Jan 1914 - 1 May 1916: | Commander, 16$^{th}$ Artillery Brigade |
| 1 May 1916 - 25 Aug 1916: | Reserve officer, Kiev Military District |
| 25 Aug 1916: | Dismissed |

*Major-General* Mikhail Petrovich **Khondakov** (17 Sep 1834 - ?)
| | |
|---|---|
| 24 Dec 1890: | Promoted to *Major-General* |
| 24 Dec 1890 - 1899: | Commander, 1$^{st}$ Reserve Artillery Brigade |

*Lieutenant-General* Martsely Stanislavovich **Khonsky** (16 Jan 1851 - ?)
| | |
|---|---|
| 8 Aug 1906 - 6 Jun 1913: | Military Judge, Warsaw Military District Court |
| 6 Dec 1906: | Promoted to *Major-General* |
| 6 Jun 1913: | Promoted to *Lieutenant-General* |
| 6 Jun 1913: | Retired |

*Lieutenant-General* Iosif Zakharovich **Khoranov** (1842 - 1935)
| | |
|---|---|
| 5 Aug 1904 - 15 Oct 1906: | At the disposal of the C-in-C, Manchurian Army |
| 31 Jan 1905: | Promoted to *Major-General* |
| 15 Oct 1906 - 6 Mar 1916: | Attached to the Caucasus Military District |
| 6 Mar 1916 - 28 Apr 1916: | Reserve officer, Kiev Military District |
| 28 Apr 1916 - Jun 1917: | Commander, 1st Brigade, 1st Terek Cossack Division |
| Jun 1917 - 1917: | Acting Commander, 1st Terek Cossack Division |
| 1917 - 28 Aug 1917: | Reserve officer, Kiev Military District |
| 23 Aug 1917: | Promoted to *Lieutenant-General* |
| 28 Aug 1917 - 1918: | Commander, 2nd Caucasus Native Cavalry Division |

*Major-General* Vasily Mikhailovich **Khoromansky** (22 Feb 1860 - ?)
| | |
|---|---|
| 24 Oct 1908 - 1918: | Military Judge, Caucasus Military District Court |
| 6 Dec 1909: | Promoted to *Major-General* |

*Major-General* Ivan Pavlovich **Khoroshkhin** (14 Jun 1850 - Jul 1908)
| | |
|---|---|
| 16 Dec 1906 - Jul 1908: | Ataman, 2nd Military Division, Ural Cossack Army |
| 22 Apr 1907: | Promoted to *Major-General* |

*Lieutenant-General* Mikhail Pavlovich **Khoroshkhin** (20 May 1844 - 17 Dec 1898)
| | |
|---|---|
| 26 Nov 1881 - 22 Feb 1888: | Section Chief, Main Cossack Directorate |
| 30 Aug 1886: | Promoted to *Major-General* |
| 22 Feb 1888 - 16 May 1893: | Military Governor, Transbaikal Region |
| 16 May 1893 - 9 Jul 1893: | At the disposal of the Minister of War |
| 9 Jul 1893 - 3 Jun 1896: | Chief of Staff, Turkestan Military District |
| 14 May 1896: | Promoted to *Lieutenant-General* |
| 3 Jun 1896 - 17 Dec 1898: | Commander, 40th Infantry Division |

*Major-General* Aleksandr Aleksandrovich **Khorunzhenkov** (27 Mar 1847 - ?)
| | |
|---|---|
| 3 Apr 1898 - 2 Feb 1902: | Commander, 1st East Siberian Rifle Regiment |
| 26 Feb 1901: | Promoted to *Major-General* |
| 2 Feb 1902 - 16 Apr 1906: | Commander, 2nd Brigade, 45th Infantry Division |

*Lieutenant-General* Dmitry Leonidovich **Khorvat** (13 Jul 1859 - 16 May 1937)
| | |
|---|---|
| 13 Nov 1902 - 27 Apr 1918: | Chief of the Chinese Eastern Railway |
| 1904: | Promoted to *Major-General* |
| 6 Dec 1911: | Promoted to *Lieutenant-General* |

*Lieutenant-General* Aleksandr Ivanovich **Khotyaintsov** (9 Nov 1832 - 19 Nov 1896)
| | |
|---|---|
| 25 Jun 1885 - 19 Nov 1896: | Director, 3rd Moscow Cadet Corps |
| 30 Aug 1885: | Promoted to *Major-General* |
| 1896: | Promoted to *Lieutenant-General* |

*Major-General* Sergey Aleksandrovich **Khotyaintsev** (17 Aug 1867 - 1911)
20 May 1905 - 1911: Chief of Section 2, Military Communications, General Staff
13 Apr 1908: Promoted to *Major-General*

*Major-General* Aleksandr Ivanovich von der **Khoven** (22 Mar 1843 - 1901)
14 Aug 1898: Promoted to *Major-General*
14 Aug 1898 - 1901: Special Assignments General, Main Artillery Directorate

*Lieutenant-General* Baron Nikolai Yegorovich von der **Khoven** (2 Nov 1836 - 11 Oct 1900)
2 Jul 1878 - 8 Aug 1888: Commander, 9th Grenadier Regiment
8 Aug 1888: Promoted to *Major-General*
8 Aug 1888 - 31 Jul 1889: Commander, 2nd Brigade, 19th Infantry Division
31 Jul 1889 - 7 Feb 1894: Commander, 2nd Brigade, 9th Infantry Division
7 Feb 1894 - 23 Jun 1897: Commander, 59th Reserve Infantry Brigade
23 Jun 1897 - 11 Oct 1900: Commander, 19th Infantry Division
6 Dec 1898: Promoted to *Lieutenant-General*

*Rear-Admiral* Aleksandr Nikolayevich **Khrabrostin** (1851 - 29 Feb 1908)
27 Sep 1900 - ?: Commander, 7th Naval Depot
?: Promoted to *Rear-Admiral*

*Major-General* Nikolai Mikhailovich **Khrabrov** (16 Nov 1869 - 1940)
13 Nov 1904 - 1917: Senior Artillery Inspector, Main Artillery Directorate
14 Apr 1913: Promoted to *Major-General*

*Major-General of the Admiralty* Georgy Nikolayevich **Khreptovich** (7 Apr 1856 - ?)
5 Feb 1907 - 14 Oct 1909: Senior Deputy Commander, Port of Emperor Aleksandr III (Libau)
24 Oct 1909 - 26 Apr 1910: Attached to Libau Naval Sub-Depot
26 Apr 1910: Promoted to *Major-General of the Admiralty*
26 Apr 1910: Retired

*Major-General* Boris Rostislavovich **Khreshchatitsky** (11 Jul 1881 - 22 Jul 1940)
6 Aug 1914 - 9 Sep 1916: Commander, 52nd Don Cossack Regiment
18 May 1916: Promoted to *Major-General*
9 Sep 1916 - 22 Oct 1917: Commander, 2nd Brigade, 1st Don Cossack Division

*General of Cavalry* Rostislav Aleksandrovich **Khreshchatitsky** (30 Mar 1841 - 20 Jan 1906)
26 Mar 1881 - 7 May 1884: Commander, 2nd Brigade, 6th Cavalry Division
30 Aug 1882: Promoted to *Major-General*
7 May 1884 - 6 Oct 1888: Commander, 2nd Brigade, 10th Cavalry Division
6 Oct 1888 - 7 Mar 1891: Commander, Taganrog District
7 Mar 1891 - 17 Apr 1891: Unassigned
17 Apr 1891 - 10 Mar 1893: Commander, 3rd Brigade, 1st Guards Cavalry Division
10 Mar 1893 - 13 Jun 1899: Commander, 2nd Consolidated Cossack Division

30 Aug 1893: Promoted to *Lieutenant-General*
13 Jun 1899 - 14 Nov 1904: Commanding General, XIV. Army Corps
28 Mar 1904: Promoted to *General of Cavalry*
14 Nov 1904 - 8 Nov 1905: Commanding General, Amur Military District, Governor-General of Amur Region

*Lieutenant-General* Grigory Grigoryevich **Khristiani** (1 Apr 1863 - 1922)
31 Oct 1903 - 3 Nov 1904: Professor, Nikolayev General Staff Academy
28 Mar 1904: Promoted to *Major-General*
3 Nov 1904 - 10 May 1905: Sub-Section Chief, General Staff
10 May 1905 - 1918: Professor, Nikolayev General Staff Academy
6 Dec 1913: Promoted to *Lieutenant-General*

*Lieutenant-General* Vasily Vasiliyevich **Khristiani** (7 May 1841 - 22 Jan 1902)
5 Oct 1887: Promoted to *Major-General*
5 Oct 1887 - 31 Aug 1894: Commander, 4th Turkestan Line Brigade
31 Aug 1894 - 28 Dec 1896: Commander, 45th Reserve Infantry Brigade
14 May 1896: Promoted to *Lieutenant-General*
28 Dec 1896 - 22 Jan 1902: Commander, 13th Infantry Division

*Major-General* Pavel Afanasyevich **Khristich** (24 Oct 1835 - ?)
11 Sep 1871 - 1899: Professor, Nikolayev Cavalry School
28 Jan 1888 - 1899: Member of the Artillery Committee, Main Artillery Directorate
14 May 1896: Promoted to *Major-General*
1899: Retired

*Lieutenant-General* Anatoly Vladimirovich **Khrostitsky** (21 Jul 1867 - 5 Mar 1919)
29 Dec 1909 - 19 Nov 1914: Commander, 127th Infantry Regiment
14 Nov 1914: Promoted to *Major-General*
19 Nov 1914 - 26 Aug 1916: Chief of Staff, Grenadier Corps
26 Aug 1916 - 31 Jul 1917: Commander, 67th Infantry Division
31 Jul 1917 - 1918: Commanding General, Grenadier Corps
23 Aug 1917: Promoted to *Lieutenant-General*

*Major-General* Aleksandr Stepanovich **Khrulev** (1849 - ?)
? - 25 Apr 1900: Special Assignments General, Warsaw Military District
6 Dec 1899: Promoted to *Major-General*

*General of Cavalry* Nikolai Stepanovich **Khrulev** (9 Sep 1841 - 1912)
10 Aug 1886 - 4 May 1892: Commander, Life Guards Cuirassier Regiment
24 Apr 1888: Promoted to *Major-General*
4 May 1892 - 24 Nov 1894: Commander, 3rd Brigade, 2nd Guards Cavalry Division
24 Nov 1894 - 28 Nov 1897: Commander, 8th Cavalry Division
14 May 1896: Promoted to *Lieutenant-General*
28 Nov 1897 - 18 Feb 1904: Commander, Consolidated Cavalry Division
18 Feb 1904 - 1907: Transferred to the reserve
1907: Promoted to *General of Cavalry*

1907: Retired

*Major-General* Aleksandr Vadimovich **Khrushchev** (22 Mar 1854 - ?)
28 May 1903 - 1911: Deputy Chief of Okhtenskaya Explosives Factory
29 Mar 1909: Promoted to *Major-General*

*Major-General* Vasily Konstantinovich **Khrushchev** (2 Jul 1850 - ?)
18 Jun 1911 - 1913: Commander, Khabarovsk Artillery Depot
6 Dec 1911: Promoted to *Major-General*

*Major-General* Pavel Pavlovich **Khrzhanovsky** (18 Jun 1846 - ?)
3 Feb 1885 - 16 May 1894: Military Judge, Caucasus Military District Court
30 Aug 1892: Promoted to *Major-General*
16 May 1894 - 1 May 1898: Military Judge, Amur Military District Court
1 May 1898 - 29 Aug 1900: Military Judge, Turkestan Military District Court
29 Aug 1900 - May 1901: Military Judge, Kazan Military District Court

*Lieutenant-General* Vladimir Korneyevich **Khudyakov** (10 Jan 1832 - 8 Oct 1908)
26 Mar 1887 - 30 Mar 1894: Commander, 2$^{nd}$ Grenadier Regiment
30 Mar 1894: Promoted to *Major-General*
30 Mar 1894 - 27 May 1896: Commander, 1$^{st}$ Turkestan Line Brigade
27 May 1896 - 29 Feb 1900: Commander, 4$^{th}$ Rifle Brigade
29 Feb 1900: Promoted to *Lieutenant-General*
29 Feb 1900: Retired

*Major-General* Iosif Nikolayevich **Khuramovich** (4 Jan 1865 - 27 Sep 1914)
31 Mar 1912 - 27 Sep 1914: Commander, 14$^{th}$ Siberian Rifle Regiment
30 Dec 1914: Posthumously promoted to *Major-General*

*Major-General* Vladimir Dmitriyevich **Khvastunov** (18 Jul 1862 - ?)
6 Jul 1913 - 1918: Military Commander, Izyaslav District
12 May 1915: Promoted to *Major-General*

*Major-General* Nikolai Semyonovich **Khvatov** (31 Jan 1872 - ?)
10 Oct 1914 - 1917: Chief of the Drafting Section, Main Artillery Directorate
6 Dec 1915: Promoted to *Major-General*

*Lieutenant-General* Aleksandr Mikhailovich **Khvostov** (21 Jan 1867 - ?)
23 Jun 1913: Promoted to *Major-General*
23 Jun 1913 - 29 Jul 1914: Commander, 2$^{nd}$ Brigade, 32$^{nd}$ Infantry Division
29 Jul 1914 - 22 Oct 1915: Commander, 1$^{st}$ Brigade, 69$^{th}$ Infantry Division
22 Oct 1915 - 13 Nov 1915: Reserve officer, Dvinsk Military District
13 Nov 1915 - 3 Dec 1915: Chief of Staff, XXXVIII. Army Corps
3 Dec 1915 - 22 Jan 1916: Commander, 62$^{nd}$ Infantry Division
22 Jan 1916 - 6 Apr 1917: Commander, 112$^{th}$ Infantry Division
6 Apr 1917 - 16 Apr 1917: Reserve officer, Minsk Military District
16 Apr 1917 - 28 Jan 1918: Chief of Staff, Minsk Military District
1 Jul 1917: Promoted to *Lieutenant-General*

*Major-General* Leonty Leontyevich **Kibort** (11 Feb 1855 - ?)
17 Sep 1907 - 21 Dec 1912: Commander, 113th Infantry Regiment
?: Acting Commander, 1st Brigade, 29th Infantry Division
21 Dec 1912: Promoted to *Major-General*
21 Dec 1912: Retired

*Lieutenant-General* Aleksandr Petrovich **Kicheyev** (18 Mar 1840 - 15 Feb 1910)
4 Aug 1888 - 22 Oct 1892: Director, 3rd Moscow Cadet Corps
30 Aug 1890: Promoted to *Major-General*
22 Oct 1892 - 16 Nov 1899: Director, Siberian Cadet Corps
16 Nov 1899 - 1902: Director, Tiflis Cadet Corps
1902: Promoted to *Lieutenant-General*
1902: Retired

*Major-General of Naval Engineers* Pyotr Ivanovich **Kigel** (15 Apr 1865 - ?)
8 Sep 1908 - 1915: Chief of Baltic Factories
6 Dec 1911: Promoted to *Major-General of Naval Engineers*
1915 - 1917: Engineer for Manufacturing Plants, Ministry of the Navy

*Major-General* Prince Pavel Andreyevich **Kildishev** (15 Jan 1847 - ?)
27 Aug 1890 - 14 Mar 1896: Commander, 14th Grenadier Regiment
14 Nov 1894: Promoted to *Major-General*
14 Mar 1896 - 23 Feb 1897: Commander, 2nd Brigade, 18th Infantry Division
23 Feb 1897 - 22 Nov 1900: Commander, 2nd East Siberian Rifle Brigade

*Major-General* Nikolai Aleksandrovich **Kilenin** (21 Dec 1860 - 18 Jun 1926)
3 Apr 1916 - 7 Aug 1917: Commander, Brigade, 103rd Infantry Division
12 Oct 1916: Promoted to *Major-General*
7 Aug 1917: Dismissed

*General of Cavalry* Aleksandr Alekseyevich **Kireyev** (26 Oct 1833 - 13 Jul 1910)
9 Sep 1877: Promoted to *Major-General*
9 Sep 1877 - 1 Mar 1892: Adjutant to Grand Duke Konstantin Nikolayevich
30 Aug 1888: Promoted to *Lieutenant-General*
1 Mar 1892 - 13 Jul 1910: Attached to Grand Duke Aleksandr Iosifovich
26 Jun 1907: Promoted to *General of Cavalry*

*Lieutenant-General* Ivan Petrovich **Kireyev** (28 Feb 1838 - ?)
6 Feb 1888 - 1893: Deputy Governor, Turgay Region
30 Aug 1890: Promoted to *Major-General*
1893: Retired
1897 - 6 Jul 1900: Recalled; Governor of Yelisavetpol
6 Jul 1900: Promoted to *Lieutenant-General*
6 Jul 1900: Retired

*General of Infantry* Nikolai Vladimirovich **Kirilin** (11 Sep 1855 - 1917)
13 Jul 1894 - 11 Nov 1905: Chief of Office, Main Military Legal Directorate

| | |
|---|---|
| 6 Dec 1901: | Promoted to *Major-General* |
| 11 Nov 1905 - 16 Jun 1908: | Military Judge, St. Petersburg Military District Court |
| 16 Jun 1908 - 25 Feb 1911: | Commandant, Military Law Academy |
| 6 Dec 1908: | Promoted to *Lieutenant-General* |
| 25 Feb 1911 - 22 Apr 1917: | Chairman of the Military Tribunal, St. Petersburg Military District |
| 22 Apr 1917: | Promoted to *General of Infantry* |
| 22 Apr 1917: | Retired |

*Major-General* Nikolai Vasilyevich **Kirillov** (8 May 1867 - 21 Sep 1914)
| | |
|---|---|
| 30 Sep 1912 - 21 Sep 1914: | Commander, 4$^{th}$ Hussar Regiment |
| 11 Feb 1915: | Posthumously promoted to *Major-General* |

*Major-General* Mikhail Alekseyevich **Kirilov** (4 Jul 1843 - ?)
| | |
|---|---|
| 29 Dec 1899: | Promoted to *Major-General* |
| 29 Dec 1899 - 1903: | Commander, 3$^{rd}$ Replacement Artillery Brigade |

*Major-General* Mitrofan Andreyevich **Kirilov** (22 Nov 1844 - ?)
| | |
|---|---|
| 15 May 1898 - 13 Mar 1904: | Chief of St. Petersburg Fire Brigade |
| 6 Dec 1903: | Promoted to *Major-General* |

*Major-General* Fyodor Aleksandrovich **Kirkhgof** (5 Jan 1859 - ?)
| | |
|---|---|
| 10 Jan 1909 - Oct 1917: | Chief of Bureau, General Staff |
| 6 Dec 1913: | Promoted to *Major-General* |

*Major-General* Mikhail Vasilyevich **Kirkin** (2 Oct 1848 - ?)
| | |
|---|---|
| 14 Apr 1900 - 28 Oct 1906: | Commander, 74$^{th}$ Infantry Regiment |
| 28 Oct 1906: | Promoted to *Major-General* |
| 28 Oct 1906: | Retired |
| 19 Dec 1915 - 22 Apr 1917: | Recalled; Staff officer, 3$^{rd}$ Army |
| 22 Apr 1917: | Dismissed |

*General of Engineers* Konstantin Lvovich **Kirpichev** (26 Jul 1844 - 30 Mar 1910)
| | |
|---|---|
| 3 Dec 1886 - 21 Mar 1891: | Professor, Nikolayev Engineering Academy |
| 30 Aug 1890: | Promoted to *Major-General* |
| 21 Mar 1891 - 6 Mar 1903: | Deputy Chief of Main Engineering Directorate |
| 6 Dec 1899: | Promoted to *Lieutenant-General* |
| 6 Mar 1903 - 1909: | Member, Engineering Committee of the Chief Engineer's Office |
| 1909: | Promoted to *General of Engineers* |
| 1909: | Retired |

*General of Engineers* Nil Lvovich **Kirpichev** (2 Nov 1850 - 1927)
| | |
|---|---|
| 23 Jul 1890 - 10 Aug 1904: | Professor, Nikolayev Engineering Academy |
| 5 Sep 1894 - 1918: | Member of the Engineering Committee, Main Engineering Directorate |
| 6 Dec 1895: | Promoted to *Major-General* |
| 2 Apr 1906: | Promoted to *Lieutenant-General* |

| | |
|---|---|
| 1911 - 1914: | Chairman of the Aeronautical Committee, Main Engineering Directorate |
| 1914 - 25 Jan 1917: | Member of the Engineering Committee, Main Military Technical Directorate |
| 25 Jan 1917 - 1918: | Administrator, Engineering Committee, Main Military Technical Directorate |
| 2 Apr 1917: | Promoted to *General of Engineers* |

*Major-General* Sergey Antonovich **Kirpotenko** (14 Jun 1875 - ?)
| | |
|---|---|
| 10 Apr 1916 - 11 May 1917: | Chief of Staff, 20$^{th}$ Infantry Division |
| 19 Oct 1916: | Promoted to *Major-General* |
| 11 May 1917 - 14 Jul 1917: | Chief of Staff, XXIII. Army Corps |
| 14 Jul 1917 - 22 Sep 1917: | Commander, 20$^{th}$ Infantry Division |
| 22 Sep 1917 - 1918: | Chief of Staff, 11$^{th}$ Army |

*Lieutenant-General* Dmitry Yefimovich **Kirsanov** (20 Nov 1845 - ?)
| | |
|---|---|
| 28 Feb 1898 - 22 Oct 1911: | Commander of Gendarmerie, Voronezh Railway |
| 6 Dec 1902: | Promoted to *Major-General* |
| 22 Oct 1911: | Promoted to *Lieutenant-General* |
| 22 Oct 1911: | Retired |

*Rear-Admiral* Nikolai Gerasimovich **Kirsanov** (1845 - 25 Dec 1907)
| | |
|---|---|
| ?: | Promoted to *Rear-Admiral* |

*Lieutenant-General* Nikolai Yefimovich **Kirsanov** (1 Dec 1837 - ?)
| | |
|---|---|
| 23 Aug 1890 - 17 Dec 1890: | Deputy Chief of Staff, Warsaw Military District |
| 30 Aug 1890: | Promoted to *Major-General* |
| 17 Dec 1890 - 22 Dec 1894: | Chief of Staff, Fortress Novogeorgiyevsk |
| 22 Dec 1894 - 9 Dec 1898: | Commander, 1$^{st}$ Caucasus Reserve Infantry Brigade |
| 9 Dec 1898: | Promoted to *Lieutenant-General* |
| 9 Dec 1898: | Retired |

*Major-General* Yevgeny Yulyevich **Kirshfeld** (27 Sep 1864 - ?)
| | |
|---|---|
| 25 Jul 1911 - 27 Jan 1912: | Deputy Intendant, Turkestan Military District |
| 1912: | Promoted to *Major-General* |
| 25 Jul 1912 - 1915: | Intendant, St. Petersburg Military District |
| 1915 - 5 Jul 1916: | Intendant, Northern Front |
| 5 Jul 1916 - 1917: | Chief of Intendant Service, Petrograd Military District |
| 1917 - 7 Jun 1917: | Reserve officer, Petrograd Military District |
| 7 Jun 1917: | Dismissed |

*Major-General* Ivan Ivanovich **Kiselev** (30 Jan 1855 - ?)
| | |
|---|---|
| 28 Jun 1910 - 1912: | Commander, 35$^{th}$ Siberian Rifle Regiment |
| 1912: | Promoted to *Major-General* |
| 1912: | Retired |
| 23 Jan 1915 - 1917: | Recalled; Reserve officer, Engineering Service, Dvinsk Military District |

*Major-General* Leonid Petrovich **Kiselev** (4 Feb 1859 - 1930)
28 Mar 1906 - 19 Feb 1912: Commander, 18th Hussar Regiment
19 Feb 1912: Promoted to *Major-General*
19 Feb 1912 - 5 Feb 1915: Commander, Ussuri Mounted Brigade
5 Feb 1915 - 2 Jan 1916: Commander, 8th Cavalry Division
2 Jan 1916 - 1917: Reserve officer, Minsk Military District

*Major-General* Pyotr Trifonovich **Kiselev** (21 Dec 1843 - ?)
12 May 1899 - 1903: Commander of Artillery, Fortress Novogeorgiyevsk
1 Jan 1901: Promoted to *Major-General*

*Lieutenant-General* Nikolai Mikhailovich **Kiselevsky** (6 Jan 1866 - 21 Jul 1939)
11 Feb 1908: Promoted to *Major-General*
11 Feb 1908 - 24 Dec 1913: Commander, Izmailovo Life Guards Regiment
24 Dec 1913 - 4 Nov 1914: Commander, 1st Brigade, 2nd Guards Infantry Division
4 Nov 1914 - 23 Aug 1916: Commander, 3rd Grenadier Division
30 Sep 1915: Promoted to *Lieutenant-General*
23 Aug 1916 - 9 Apr 1917: Commanding General, IX. Army Corps
9 Apr 1917 - 12 Jul 1917: C-in-C, 10th Army
12 Jul 1917: Transferred to the reserve

*Major-General* Valerian Aleksandrovich **Kishinets** (19 Jul 1845 - ?)
24 Oct 1899: Promoted to *Major-General*
24 Oct 1899 - 29 Mar 1906: Commander, 2nd Brigade, 32nd Infantry Division

*Lieutenant-General* Stepan Iosifovich **Kishmishev** (10 Jun 1833 - ?)
8 Nov 1877: Promoted to *Major-General*
16 Jan 1879 - 1 Feb 1885: At the disposal of the Commanding General, Caucasus Military District
1 Feb 1885 - 22 Dec 1887: Attached to Caucasus Military District
22 Dec 1887 - 1897: Commander, 24th (Tiflis) Regional Brigade
30 Aug 1888: Promoted to *Lieutenant-General*

*Lieutenant-General* Orest Mikhailovich **Kislinsky** (27 Sep 1836 - ?)
30 Aug 1880 - 18 Dec 1888: Commander, 4th Grenadier Regiment
18 Dec 1888: Promoted to *Major-General*
18 Dec 1888 - 17 Sep 1896: Commander, 1st Brigade, 3rd Grenadier Division
17 Sep 1896 - 10 Jan 1898: Commander, 5th Rifle Brigade
10 Jan 1898 - 8 Jan 1902: Commander, 28th Infantry Division
5 Apr 1898: Promoted to *Lieutenant-General*

*Major-General* Andrey Vladimirovich **Kislyakov** (22 Apr 1865 - 8 Feb 1915)
29 Jul 1914 - 8 Feb 1915: Commander, 53rd Artillery Brigade
6 Feb 1915 - 8 Feb 1915: Commander of Artillery, XX. Army Corps
27 Sep 1915: Posthumously promoted to *Major-General*

*Major-General* Vladimir Nikolayevich **Kislyakov** (13 Oct 1875 - 1919)
1914 - 17 Oct 1915: Chief of Lines of Communication, Army

| | |
|---|---|
| 5 Aug 1915: | Promoted to *Major-General* |
| 17 Oct 1915 - 1917: | Chief of Communications, Western Front |
| 1917 - Aug 1917: | Deputy Minister of Communications, Theater of Operations |
| Aug 1917: | Dismissed |

*Lieutenant-General* Gavriil Petrovich **Kisnemsky** (19 Mar 1853 - ?)
| | |
|---|---|
| 20 Sep 1908 - 24 Nov 1916: | Chief of Mikhailov Shostka Gunpowder Factory |
| 6 Dec 1908: | Promoted to *Major-General* |
| 6 Dec 1914: | Promoted to *Lieutenant-General* |
| 24 Nov 1916 - 1918: | Member of the Artillery Committee, Main Artillery Directorate |

*Major-General* Yevgeny Rudolfovich **Kister** (27 Oct 1856 - May 1912)
| | |
|---|---|
| 1 Aug 1910: | Promoted to *Major-General* |
| 1 Aug 1910 - May 1912: | Commander, $10^{th}$ Siberian Rifle Artillery Brigade |

*Lieutenant-General* Mikhail Dmitriyevich **Kitchenko** (30 Aug 1857 - 7 Aug 1931)
| | |
|---|---|
| 28 May 1904 - 13 Mar 1909: | Commander, Erivan Borderguard Brigade |
| 6 Dec 1908: | Promoted to *Major-General* |
| 13 Mar 1909 - 30 Mar 1911: | Commander, $3^{rd}$ Borderguard District |
| 30 Mar 1911 - 1915: | Commander, $5^{th}$ Borderguard District |
| 1915 - 7 Sep 1915: | Commander, Brigade, $71^{st}$ Infantry Division |
| 7 Sep 1915 - 4 May 1917: | Commander, $80^{th}$ Infantry Division |
| 27 Nov 1915: | Promoted to *Lieutenant-General* |
| 4 May 1917: | Dismissed |

*Rear-Admiral* Aleksandr Pavlovich **Kitkin** (7 Apr 1859 - 14 Sep 1914)
| | |
|---|---|
| 1910 - 10 Dec 1912: | Member, Kronstadt Naval Court |
| 10 Dec 1912: | Promoted to *Rear-Admiral* |
| 10 Dec 1912: | Retired |

*Major-General* Karl-Eduard Karlovich **Kivekäs** (6 Dec 1866 - 19 Feb 1940)
| | |
|---|---|
| 11 May 1916 - 19 Oct 1917: | Commander, $113^{th}$ Artillery Brigade |
| 21 Dec 1916: | Promoted to *Major-General* |
| 19 Oct 1917 - 3 Apr 1918: | Commander, $113^{th}$ Infantry Division |

*Lieutenant-General* Mikhail Ivanovich **Kiyanovsky** (9 Oct 1867 - 5 Jul 1917)
| | |
|---|---|
| 15 Oct 1907 - 27 May 1911: | Commander, $16^{th}$ Rifle Regiment |
| 9 Feb 1910: | Promoted to *Major-General* |
| 27 May 1911 - 30 Nov 1912: | Chief of Communications, Odessa Military District |
| 30 Nov 1912 - 19 Jul 1914: | Chief of Communications, Moscow Military District |
| 19 Jul 1914 - 18 Jan 1915: | Chief of Logistics, $5^{th}$ Army |
| 18 Jan 1915 - 4 Oct 1915: | Chief of Logistics, $12^{th}$ Army |
| 4 Oct 1915 - 14 Dec 1916: | Deputy Chief of Logistics, Northern Front |
| 10 Apr 1916: | Promoted to *Lieutenant-General* |
| 14 Dec 1916 - 12 Apr 1917: | Chief of Logistics, Rumanian Front |
| 12 Apr 1917 - 5 Jul 1917: | Chief of Logistics, Western Front |

*Lieutenant-General* Andrei Ivanovich **Kiyashko** (30 Nov 1857 - 13 Dec 1917)
2 Feb 1907 - 23 Dec 1907: Ataman, Maikop District, Kuban Cossack Army
31 May 1907: Promoted to *Major-General*
23 Dec 1907 - 28 Mar 1912: Chief of Staff, Kuban Cossack Army
28 Mar 1912 - 21 Jan 1917: Military Governor, Trans-Baikal Region,
 Ataman, Trans-Baikal Cossack Army
14 Apr 1913: Promoted to *Lieutenant-General*
21 Jan 1917 - 18 Feb 1917: Reserve officer, Kazan Military District
18 Feb 1917 - Mar 1917: Reserve officer, Caucasus Military District
Mar 1917 - 13 Dec 1917: Commanding General, Turkestan Military District

*Lieutenant-General* Dmitry Petrovich **Kladishchev** (26 Feb 1838 - 7 Nov 1903)
6 May 1884: Promoted to *Major-General*
6 May 1884 - 27 Feb 1886: Transferred to the reserve
27 Feb 1886 - 16 Feb 1893: Governor of Ryazan
16 Feb 1893 - 12 May 1898: Council Member, Ministry of Internal Affairs
14 May 1896: Promoted to *Lieutenant-General*
12 May 1898 - 7 Nov 1903: Senator

*Major-General of the Admiralty* Nikolai Lavrentyevich **Klado** (1 Nov 1862 - 10 Jul 1919)
21 Aug 1910 - May 1917: Ordinary Professor, Naval Academy
25 Mar 1912: Promoted to *Major-General of the Admiralty*
May 1917 - 10 Jul 1919: Commandant of the Naval Academy

*Major-General of the Admiralty* Ivan Petrovich **Klapye de Kolong** (22 Feb 1839 - 13 May 1901)
1878 - 1898: Chief, Kronstadt Compass Observatory
1893: Promoted to *Major-General of the Admiralty*
1895 - 1898: Conference Member, Naval Academy
1898 - 13 May 1901: Deputy Chief, Main Hydrographic Directorate

*General of Infantry* Pavel Fyodorovich **Klauz** (24 Aug 1846 - ?)
5 Jan 1898: Promoted to *Major-General*
5 Jan 1898 - 31 Aug 1900: Chief of Staff, XIX. Army Corps
31 Aug 1900 - 2 May 1904: Commander, 47th Replacement Infantry Brigade
2 May 1904 - 11 Apr 1909: Commander, 6th Infantry Division
6 Dec 1904: Promoted to *Lieutenant-General*
11 Apr 1909 - 20 Feb 1911: Commanding General, XV. Army Corps
20 Feb 1911: Promoted to *General of Infantry*
20 Feb 1911: Retired

*Lieutenant-General* Nikolai Karlovich **Klaver** (26 Nov 1847 - ?)
28 Jun 1895: Promoted to *Major-General*
28 Jun 1895 - 20 Jan 1901: Commander, 2nd Brigade, 13th Cavalry Division
20 Jan 1901 - 10 Nov 1903: Chairman of the Remount Commission, Don Steppe
10 Nov 1903 - 19 May 1906: Commander, 2nd Replacement Cavalry Brigade
12 May 1904: Promoted to *Lieutenant-General*
19 May 1906 - 10 Mar 1907: Commander, 3rd Reserve Cavalry Brigade

| | |
|---|---|
| 10 Mar 1907: | Dismissed |
| 24 Jun 1908 - 23 Aug 1916: | Recalled; General for Special Assignments, Main Directorate of Horse Breeding |
| 23 Aug 1916 - 1917: | Member of the Board, Main Directorate of Horse Breeding |

*Major-General* Artur-Oskar Napoleonovich **Klembovsky** (2 Mar 1862 - Dec 1920)
| | |
|---|---|
| 28 Mar 1914 - 16 Nov 1914: | Commander, 57$^{th}$ State Militia Brigade |
| 5 Oct 1914: | Promoted to *Major-General* |
| 16 Nov 1914 - 13 Apr 1915: | Commander, Brigade, 67$^{th}$ Infantry Division |
| 13 Apr 1915 - 27 Jul 1915: | Commander, 2$^{nd}$ State Militia Division |
| 27 Jul 1915 - 20 May 1917: | Transferred to the reserve |
| 20 May 1917: | Retired |

*General of Infantry* Vladislav Napoleonovich **Klembovsky** (28 Jun 1860 - 19 Jul 1921)
| | |
|---|---|
| 21 Oct 1904: | Promoted to *Major-General* |
| 21 Oct 1904 - 4 Feb 1906: | Chief of Staff, IV. Army Corps |
| 4 Feb 1906 - 29 Jun 1912: | Chief of Staff, X. Army Corps |
| 29 Jun 1912: | Promoted to *Lieutenant-General* |
| 29 Jun 1912 - 13 Oct 1914: | Commander, 9$^{th}$ Infantry Division |
| 13 Oct 1914 - 13 Dec 1915: | Commanding General, XVI. Army Corps |
| 17 Sep 1915: | Promoted to *General of Infantry* |
| 13 Dec 1915 - 6 Dec 1915: | Chief of Staff, Southwestern Front |
| 6 Dec 1915 - 30 Jan 1916: | C-in-C, 5$^{th}$ Army |
| 30 Jan 1916 - 19 Oct 1916: | Chief of Staff, Southwestern Front |
| 19 Oct 1916 - 20 Dec 1916: | C-in-C, 11$^{th}$ Army |
| 20 Dec 1916 - 11 Mar 1917: | Deputy Chief of Staff to the Supreme Commander-in-Chief |
| 11 Mar 1917 - 5 Apr 1917: | Chief of Staff to the Supreme Commander-in-Chief |
| 28 Mar 1917 - 31 May 1917: | Member of the Military Council |
| 13 May 1917 - 9 Sep 1917: | C-in-C, Northern Front |
| 9 Sep 1917 - Oct 1917: | Member of the Military Council |

*Lieutenant-General* Vladimir Nikolayevich **Klevezal** (29 Sep 1835 - ?)
| | |
|---|---|
| 17 Aug 1878 - 14 Feb 1888: | Commander, 6$^{th}$ Grenadier Regiment |
| 14 Feb 1888: | Promoted to *Major-General* |
| 14 Feb 1888 - 23 Jun 1897: | Commander, 1$^{st}$ Brigade, 34$^{th}$ Infantry Division |
| 1889: | Acting Commander, 34$^{th}$ Infantry Division |
| 23 Jun 1897 - 24 Oct 1899: | Commander, 61$^{st}$ Reserve Infantry Brigade |
| 24 Oct 1899: | Promoted to *Lieutenant-General* |
| 24 Oct 1889: | Retired |

*Major-General* Vladimir Robertovich **Klevezal** (1 Jul 1856 - ?)
| | |
|---|---|
| 6 Dec 1906 - 7 Apr 1913: | At the disposal of Grand Duke Mikhail Alexandrovich |
| 6 Dec 1912: | Promoted to *Major-General* |
| 7 Apr 1913 - 31 Mar 1915: | Attached to the Ministry of War |
| 31 Mar 1915 - Jul 1916: | At the disposal of Grand Duke Mikhail Alexandrovich |
| Jul 1916 - 1917: | Attached to the C-in-C, 12$^{th}$ Army |

*Major-General* Kazimir-Aleksandr Ivanovich **Kley** (2 Mar 1854 - ?)
3 Nov 1904:                     Promoted to *Major-General*
3 Nov 1904 - 18 Jul 1905:       Commander, 1st Brigade, 25th Infantry Division
18 Jul 1905 - 1906:             Attached to 25th Infantry Division

*General of Cavalry* Nikolai Vasilyevich **Kleygels** (25 Nov 1850 - 20 Jul 1916)
13 Feb 1888 - 6 Dec 1895:       Chief of Police, Warsaw
30 Aug 1892:                    Promoted to *Major-General*
6 Dec 1895 - 24 Dec 1903:       Mayor of St. Petersburg
6 Dec 1899:                     Promoted to *Lieutenant-General*
24 Dec 1903:                    Promoted to *General-Adjutant*
24 Dec 1903 - 19 Oct 1905:      Governor-General of Kiev, Podolia & Volhynia,
                                Commanding General, Kiev Military District
19 Oct 1905 - 20 Jul 1916:      General à la suite
18 Apr 1910:                    Promoted to *General of Cavalry*

*Major-General* Vladimir Vasilyevich **Kleygels** (12 Sep 1844 - ?)
14 Mar 1900 - 1904:             Commander of Engineers, Fortress St. Petersburg
9 Apr 1900:                     Promoted to *Major-General*

*Lieutenant-General* Ivan Yulyevich **Kleynenberg** (10 Nov 1861 - ?)
7 Jul 1910 - 19 Apr 1915:       Commander, 42nd Artillery Brigade
23 Mar 1912:                    Promoted to *Major-General*
19 Apr 1915 - 16 Apr 1916:      Inspector of Artillery, IX. Army Corps
16 Apr 1916 - 1917:             Inspector of Artillery, 3rd Army
24 Jul 1916:                    Promoted to *Lieutenant-General*

*Major-General* Yevgeny Yulyevich **Kleynenberg** (28 Aug 1864 - 5 Feb 1922)
25 Jul 1914 - 29 Mar 1917:      Commander, 56th Artillery Brigade
12 Jan 1916:                    Promoted to *Major-General*
29 Mar 1917 - Oct 1917:         Reserve officer, Petrograd Military District

*Major-General* Ignaty Florianovich **Klimashevsky** (18 Dec 1858 - ?)
28 Feb 1908 - 27 Feb 1909:      Military Judge, Omsk Military District Court
13 Apr 1908:                    Promoted to *Major-General*
27 Feb 1909 - 1917:             Military Judge, Turkestan Military District Court

*Lieutenant-General* Konstantin Vasilyevich **Klimenko** (20 Sep 1832 - 11 Nov 1900)
7 Mar 1883 - 8 Jun 1889:        Commander of Engineers, Fortress Kerch
30 Aug 1888:                    Promoted to *Major-General*
8 Jun 1889 - 8 Nov 1893:        Commander of Engineers, Fortress Modlin
8 Nov 1893 - 29 Jul 1896:       Commander of Engineers, Turkestan Military District.
29 Jul 1896 - 18 Mar 1897:      Commandant of the Engineer Depot, Fortress Dvinsk
18 Mar 1897 - 11 Nov 1900:      Commander of Engineers, Warsaw Military District
6 Dec 1898:                     Promoted to *Lieutenant-General*

*Major-General* Aleksey Pankratyevich **Klimov** (11 Mar 1841 - ?)
2 Jul 1898 - 1905:              Commander of Artillery, Fortress Kaunas

6 Dec 1898: Promoted to *Major-General*

*Major-General* Feliks Antonovich **Klimovich** (20 Oct 1838 - ?)
29 Apr 1895 - 13 May 1897: Commander, 124th Infantry Regiment
14 May 1896: Promoted to *Major-General*
13 May 1897 - 4 Dec 1901: Commander, 2nd Brigade, 13th Infantry Division

*Lieutenant-General* Yevgeny Konstantinovich **Klimovich** (24 Jan 1871 - 5 Jun 1930)
26 Dec 1909 - 16 Nov 1914: Mayor of Kerch-Yenikale
14 Apr 1913: Promoted to *Major-General*
16 Nov 1914 - Jun 1915: Mayor of Rostov-on-Don
Jun 1915 - 14 Feb 1916: Mayor of Moscow
14 Feb 1916 - 15 Sep 1916: Director of the Police Department
1916: Promoted to *Lieutenant-General*
15 Sep 1916: Transferred to the reserve

*Major-General* Pavel Petrovich **Klimovsky** (7 Sep 1864 - ?)
6 Jul 1910 - 10 Jul 1916: Commander, 39th Siberian Rifle Regiment
14 Aug 1915: Promoted to *Major-General*
12 Jul 1916 - 10 Apr 1917: Commander, 2nd Brigade, 10th Siberian Rifle Division
10 Apr 1917 - Oct 1917: Commander, 26th Infantry Division

*Major-General* Mikhail Mikhailovich **Klingenberg** (3 May 1861 - 23 Dec 1939)
8 Sep 1910 - 15 Sep 1911: Special Assignments General, Main Administration for Military Schools
6 Dec 1910: Promoted to *Major-General*
15 Sep 1911 - 1917: Director, Pyotrovsky Poltava Cadet Corps

*Major-General* Ipaty Ivanovich **Klochenko** (27 Dec 1859 - ?)
25 Jul 1914 - 2 Sep 1916: Commander, 73rd Artillery Brigade
25 Mar 1916: Promoted to *Major-General*
2 Sep 1916 - 1917: Reserve officer, Minsk Military District

*Lieutenant-General* Pyotr Ivanovich **Klochenko** (5 Oct 1850 - ?)
20 Apr 1903: Promoted to *Major-General*
20 Apr 1903 - 6 Oct 1910: Commander, 2nd Brigade, 24th Infantry Division
6 Oct 1910: Promoted to *Lieutenant-General*
6 Oct 1910: Retired

*Major-General of Naval Artillery* Mikhail Vlasyevich **Klochkov** (1 Nov 1861 - 5 Nov 1936)
1912 - 1 Jan 1915: Board member, Baltic Shipbuilding, Mechanical & Admiralty Shipyard
6 Dec 1913: Promoted to *Major-General of Naval Artillery*
1 Jan 1915 - 1917: Member of the Economic Committee, Ministry of the Navy Admiralty Shipyard

*General of Infantry* Eduard Karlovich von **Klodt** (7 Feb 1855 - 23 Nov 1919)
24 Dec 1903: Promoted to *Major-General*

| | |
|---|---|
| 24 Dec 1903 - 6 Jun 1904: | Attached to Amur Military District. |
| 6 Jun 1904 - 9 May 1906: | Attached to the Governor-General, Far East |
| 9 May 1906 - 29 Nov 1908: | Commander, 47th Reserve Infantry Brigade |
| 29 Nov 1908: | Promoted to *Lieutenant-General* |
| 29 Nov 1908 - 7 Aug 1914: | Commander, 8th East Siberian Rifle Division |
| 8 Aug 1914 - 11 Sep 1914: | Commander, 14th Siberian Rifle Division |
| 11 Sep 1914: | Promoted to *General of Infantry* |
| 11 Sep 1914: | Retired |

*Major-General* Baron Pavel Adolfovich **Klodt von Yurgensburg** (14 Dec 1867 - 26 Feb 1938)

| | |
|---|---|
| 15 Mar 1915 - 1 Jun 1917: | Commander, Life Guards Finland Regiment |
| 12 Apr 1915: | Promoted to *Major-General* |

*Major-General* Pyotr Nikolayevich **Klokachev** (6 Oct 1863 - Apr 1917)

| | |
|---|---|
| 7 Apr 1907 - Apr 1917: | Professor, Nikolayev Engineering Academy |
| 13 Apr 1908: | Promoted to *Major-General* |
| 24 Sep 1909 - 20 Feb 1914: | Member of the Technical Committee, Main Military Technical Directorate |

*Lieutenant-General* Nikolai Iosifovich **Klunnikov** (2 Oct 1858 - 9 Dec 1917)

| | |
|---|---|
| 9 Oct 1899 - 29 Oct 1912: | Chief of Taganrog District, Don Cossack Army |
| 29 Mar 1909: | Promoted to *Major-General* |
| 29 Oct 1912: | Promoted to *Lieutenant-General* |
| 29 Oct 1912: | Retired |

*Major-General* Pyotr Pavlovich **Klushin** (23 Nov 1852 - 1908)

| | |
|---|---|
| 31 May 1893 - 1908: | Attached to the Caucasus Military District |
| 25 Mar 1894: | Promoted to *Major-General* |

*Lieutenant-General* Mitrofan Yakovlevich **Klykov** (17 Oct 1847 - 1918)

| | |
|---|---|
| 13 Jan 1902 - 16 Dec 1905: | Chief of Gendarmerie, Vilnius Province |
| 6 Dec 1904: | Promoted to *Major-General* |
| 16 Dec 1905 - 12 Dec 1914: | Chief of Gendarmerie, St. Petersburg |
| 14 Apr 1913: | Promoted to *Lieutenant-General* |
| 12 Dec 1914 - Feb 1917: | Deputy Governor-General of Warsaw |

*Lieutenant-General* Sergey Ivanovich **Klyucharev** (28 Feb 1835 - ?)

| | |
|---|---|
| 30 May 1878 - 25 Apr 1890: | Commander, 10th Grenadier Regiment |
| 25 Apr 1890: | Promoted to *Major-General* |
| 25 Apr 1890 - 21 Oct 1891: | Commander, 2nd Brigade, 4th Infantry Division |
| 21 Oct 1891 - 23 Jul 1894: | Commander, 1st Brigade, 4th Infantry Division |
| 23 Jul 1894 - 4 Sep 1896: | Commander, 1st Brigade, 6th Infantry Division |
| 4 Sep 1896 - 1 Jan 1898: | Commander, 47th Reserve Infantry Brigade |
| 1 Jan 1898 - 28 Feb 1900: | Commander, 44th Infantry Division |
| 6 Dec 1899: | Promoted to *Lieutenant-General* |

*Major-General* Iosif Ignatyevich **Klyuchevsky** (19 Mar 1841 - ?)
15 Jan 1882 - 22 Apr 1893:     Commander, Caucasus District Artillery Park
30 Aug 1891:     Promoted to *Major-General*
22 Apr 1893 - 1894:     Commander of Artillery, Fortress Mikhailov

*Major-General* Aleksandr Frantsevich **Klyuki von Klugenau** (4 Jul 1842 - ?)
26 Feb 1894:     Promoted to *Major-General*
26 Feb 1894 - Feb 1896:     Commander, 2$^{nd}$ Brigade, 2$^{nd}$ Caucasus Cossack Division

*Rear-Admiral* Yevgeny Vladislavovich **Klyupfel** (31 Jan 1860 - 16 Mar 1934)
6 Dec 1913:     Promoted to *Rear-Admiral*
6 Dec 1913 - 5 Mar 1917:     Director of Lighthouses & Navigation, Caspian Sea, Commandant, Port of Baku
5 Mar 1917 - 10 Sep 1917:     Unassigned
10 Sep 1917 - 6 Oct 1917:     Reserve officer, Ministry of the Navy
6 Oct 1917:     Dismissed

*Lieutenant-General* Nikolai Alekseyevich **Klyuyev** (5 May 1859 - 29 Dec 1921)
2 Mar 1902 - 3 Sep 1904:     Commander, 182$^{nd}$ Reserve Infantry Regiment
2 Sep 1904:     Promoted to *Major-General*
3 Sep 1904 - 10 Jan 1905:     Attached to Warsaw Military District
10 Jan 1905 - 4 Feb 1909:     Commander, Life Guards Volyn Regiment
4 Feb 1909:     Promoted to *Lieutenant-General*
4 Feb 1909 - 15 Aug 1913:     Chief of Staff, Warsaw Military District
15 Aug 1913 - 19 Jul 1914:     Commanding General, I. Caucasus Army Corps
19 Jul 1914 - 17 Aug 1914:     Commanding General, XIII. Army Corps
17 Aug 1914 - 1918:     POW, Germany

*Major-General* Baron Andrei Romanovich von **Knorring** (28 Sep 1862 - 29 Mar 1918)
6 Dec 1909:     Promoted to *Major-General*
6 Dec 1909 - 10 Jun 1914:     General for Special Assignments, Ministry of War
10 Jun 1914 - 6 Mar 1916:     General for Special Assignments, Governor-General of Galicia
6 Mar 1916 - 29 Mar 1918:     Reserve officer, Kiev Military District

*Major-General* Nikolai Gustavovich **Knorring** (9 Dec 1827 - ?)
1 Jan 1887 - 1894:     Clerk of the Main Sanatory Committee
30 Aug 1892:     Promoted to *Major-General*

*Lieutenant-General* Baron Vladimir Romanovich von **Knorring** (9 Sep 1861 - 20 Oct 1938)
4 May 1909 - 1917:     Master of the Horse, Court of Grand Duchess Maria Pavlovna
18 Apr 1910:     Promoted to *Major-General*
10 Apr 1916:     Promoted to *Lieutenant-General*

*Admiral* Mikhail Valerianovich **Knyazev** (9 Nov 1856 - 14 Feb 1933)
1906 - 1907:     Commander, Mine Detachment, Baltic Fleet

5 Oct 1907: Promoted to *Rear-Admiral*
1907 - 14 Jul 1908: Chief of Staff, Port of Kronstadt
14 Jul 1908 - 18 Apr 1911: Deputy Chief of the Main Naval Staff
18 Apr 1911 - 17 Sep 1913: Chief of the Main Naval Staff
6 Dec 1911: Promoted to *Vice-Admiral*
17 Sep 1913 - 29 Sep 1917: Chairman of the Board, Volunteer Fleet
29 Sep 1917: Promoted to *Admiral*
29 Sep 1917: Retired

*Major-General* Dmitry Maksimovich **Knyazhevich** (21 Jun 1874 - 1918)
24 Dec 1913 - 9 Aug 1915: Commander, Life Guards Uhlan Regiment
20 Jan 1915: Promoted to *Major-General*
9 Aug 1915 - 30 Aug 1915: Commander, 2$^{nd}$ Brigade, 1$^{st}$ Guards Cavalry Division
30 Aug 1915 - 19 Dec 1915: Commander, 2$^{nd}$ Brigade, 2$^{nd}$ Guards Cavalry Division
10 Dec 1915 - 18 Apr 1917: Commander, 1$^{st}$ Brigade, 2$^{nd}$ Guards Cavalry Division
18 Apr 1917 - Oct 1917: Commander, 2$^{nd}$ Cavalry Division

*Major-General* Fyodor Iosifovich **Knyazhevich** (24 Mar 1861 - 1918)
1 May 1910: Promoted to *Major-General*
1 May 1910 - 3 Feb 1915: Special Assignments General, St. Petersburg Military District
3 Feb 1915 - Oct 1917: Special Assignments General, 6$^{th}$ Army

*Major-General* Nikolai Antonovich **Knyazhevich** (19 Jan 1871 - 4 Mar 1950)
11 Sep 1908 - 9 Oct 1912: Commander, Crimean Cavalry Regiment
23 Apr 1912: Promoted to *Major-General*
9 Oct 1912 - 14 Nov 1914: Commander, 2$^{nd}$ Brigade, 8$^{th}$ Cavalry Division
14 Nov 1914 - 11 Jan 1917: Governor of Tauride
11 Jan 1917 - Oct 1917: Mayor of Odessa

*Lieutenant-General* Aleksandr Pavlovich **Kobelev** (2 Aug 1838 - 14 Oct 1897)
15 Oct 1870 - 4 Feb 1879: Commander, 4$^{th}$ Sapper Battalion
7 Dec 1878: Promoted to *Major-General*
4 Feb 1879 - 15 Mar 1889: Commander, 3$^{rd}$ Sapper Brigade
15 Mar 1889 - 24 Jan 1895: Member of the Engineering Committee, Main Engineering Directorate
30 Aug 1889: Promoted to *Lieutenant-General*
24 Jan 1895 - 14 Oct 1897: Chief of Engineers

*Major-General* Aleksandr Iosifovich **Kobiyev** (18 Apr 1857 - ?)
7 Jun 1909 - 1913: Deputy Chief of Izhevsk Arms Factory
6 Dec 1910: Promoted to *Major-General*

*Major-General* Mikhail Andreyevich **Kobiyev** (29 Jun 1862 - 21 Dec 1931)
1915 - 1917: Commander, 1$^{st}$ Brigade, Caucasus Native Cavalry Division
20 Oct 1916: Promoted to *Major-General*

*Major-General* Boleslav Konstantinovich **Kobordo** (4 Aug 1831 - ?)
26 Feb 1894: Promoted to *Major-General*
26 Feb 1894 - 21 Dec 1896: Commander, 2nd Brigade, 9th Infantry Division

*Lieutenant-General* Yevgraf Nikolayevich **Kobozev** (10 Dec 1851 - 10 Oct 1912)
14 Apr 1900 - 12 Jun 1906: Commander, 17th Artillery Brigade
1 Jan 1901: Promoted to *Major-General*
12 Jun 1906 - 24 Aug 1906: Commander of Artillery, XIX. Army Corps
24 Aug 1906 - 10 Oct 1912: Commander of Artillery, XV. Army Corps
22 Apr 1907: Promoted to *Lieutenant-General*

*Major-General* Konstantin Nikolayevich **Kobylinsky** (12 Nov 1836 - ?)
5 Apr 1895 - 1899: Commander, 1st East Siberian Line Brigade
14 May 1896: Promoted to *Major-General*

*Lieutenant-General* Stepan Osipovich **Kobylinsky** (26 Dec 1827 - ?)
14 Aug 1877 - 22 Oct 1878: Commander, 3rd Reserve Artillery Brigade
22 Oct 1878 - 7 Sep 1889: Commander, 26th Artillery Brigade
30 Aug 1879: Promoted to *Major-General*
7 Sep 1889: Promoted to *Lieutenant-General*
7 Sep 1889 - 2 May 1890: Commander of Artillery, XII. Army Corps
2 May 1890 - 30 Nov 1892: Commander of Artillery, XI. Army Corps
30 Nov 1892 - 1899: Commander of Artillery, IX. Army Corps

*Lieutenant-General* Nikolai Mikhailovich **Kochanovsky** (17 Nov 1847 - ?)
16 Jun 1902 - 1908: Member of the Artillery Advisory Committee, Main Artillery Directorate
6 Dec 1903: Promoted to *Major-General*
6 Dec 1903 - 4 Feb 1906: Attached to the Inspector-General of Rifle Troops
4 Feb 1906 - 15 Jan 1910: Attached to the Inspector-General of Infantry
15 Jan 1910 - 20 Jun 1913: Attached to the Inspector-General of Rifle Troops
20 Jun 1913: Promoted to *Lieutenant-General*
20 Jun 1913: Retired

*Major-General* Pavel Fortunatovich **Kochengin** (15 Dec 1858 - ?)
9 Jul 1910 - 21 Aug 1915: Commander, 3rd Caucasus Rifle Regiment
1 May 1915: Promoted to *Major-General*
21 Aug 1915 - 10 Aug 1916: Commander, Brigade, 51st Infantry Division
10 Aug 1916 - 7 Oct 1917: Commander, 6th Siberian Replacement Rifle Brigade
7 Oct 1917 - 1917: Commander, 111th Infantry Division

*Major-General* Mikhail Vasilyevich **Kochergin** (27 Jun 1869 - ?)
24 Oct 1910 - 1914: Section Chief, Main Directorate of the General Staff
1914: Retired
20 May 1915 - 1917: Recalled; Attached to the Sanatory Department, High Command
10 Apr 1916: Promoted to *Major-General*

*Major-General* Grigory Ivanovich **Kochkonogov** (16 Nov 1857 - ?)
26 Aug 1906 - 16 Nov 1913:    Commander, 11th Don Cossack Regiment
16 Nov 1913:                  Promoted to *Major-General*

*Major-General* Aleksandr Vasilyevich **Kochnev** (23 Feb 1862 - ?)
? - 31 Jul 1916:              Commander, 27th Siberian Replacement Rifle Battalion
31 Jul 1916:                  Promoted to *Major-General*
31 Jul 1916:                  Retired

*Lieutenant-General* Prince Viktor Sergeyevich **Kochubey** (11 Oct 1860 - 4 Dec 1923)
14 Dec 1899:                  Promoted to *Major-General*
14 Dec 1899 - 19 Apr 1917:    Chief of Department of Appanages
1909:                         Promoted to *General-Adjutant*
10 Apr 1911:                  Promoted to *Lieutenant-General*
19 Apr 1917:                  Dismissed

*Lieutenant-General* Sheikh Il-Islam Abdul-Vaganovich **Kochurov** (30 Nov 1850 - Jan 1918)
17 Nov 1905 - 30 Jan 1906:    Commander, 1st Brigade, 1st Turkestan Cossack Division
30 Jan 1906 - 4 May 1910:     Commander, 2nd Brigade, 1st Turkestan Cossack Division
6 Dec 1906:                   Promoted to *Major-General*
4 May 1910:                   Promoted to *Lieutenant-General*
4 May 1910:                   Retired

*Major-General* Ivan Iosifovich **Kognovitsky** (27 Dec 1839 - Oct 1916)
6 Dec 1911:                   Promoted to *Major-General*
6 Dec 1911 - Oct 1916:        General for Special Assignments, Governor-General of the Caucasus

*Major-General* Vladimir Matveyevich von **Kokh** (28 Feb 1863 - ?)
11 Aug 1905 - 10 Aug 1908:    Inspector of Classes, Tashkent Cadet Corps
13 Apr 1908:                  Promoted to *Major-General*
10 Aug 1908 - 1917:           Director, Tashkent Cadet Corps

*General of Artillery* Ivan Semyonovich **Kokhanov** (12 Jul 1825 - 25 Feb 1909)
23 Jan 1864 - 7 Dec 1866:     Commander, 3rd Guards Artillery Brigade
30 Aug 1865:                  Promoted to *Major-General*
7 Dec 1866 - 1 Jan 1867:      Unassigned
1 Jan 1867 - 14 Jan 1884:     Governor of Petrokovsk
30 Aug 1876:                  Promoted to *Lieutenant-General*
14 Jan 1884 - 6 Sep 1884:     Deputy Governor-General of Vilnius, Kovno & Grodno
6 Sep 1884 - 1 Jan 1893:      Governor-General of Vilnius, Kovno & Grodno
30 Aug 1890:                  Promoted to *General of Artillery*
1 Jan 1893 - 25 Feb 1909:     Member of the State Council

*General of Artillery* Nikolai Vasilyevich **Kokhanov** (18 Jan 1854 - ?)
28 Mar 1903 - 12 Feb 1908:    Commander, 43rd Artillery Brigade

| | |
|---|---|
| 6 Dec 1903: | Promoted to *Major-General* |
| 12 Feb 1908: | Promoted to *Lieutenant-General* |
| 12 Feb 1908 - 25 Jul 1910: | Commander of Artillery, VI. Army Corps |
| 25 Jul 1910 - 16 Apr 1916: | Inspector of Artillery, XXV. Army Corps |
| 16 Apr 1916 - 1917: | Inspector of Artillery, 4th Army |
| 1917: | Promoted to *General of Artillery* |
| 1917: | Retired |

*Lieutenant-General* Pyotr Andreyevich **Kokhno** (24 Jul 1850 - ?)
| | |
|---|---|
| 5 Apr 1904 - 24 Jan 1909: | Commander, 11th Artillery Brigade |
| 6 Dec 1904: | Promoted to *Major-General* |
| 24 Jan 1909: | Promoted to *Lieutenant-General* |
| 24 Jan 1909 - 23 Apr 1910: | Commander of Artillery, IX. Army Corps |
| 23 Apr 1910: | Retired |

*Major-General* Leonid Andreyevich **Kokin** (29 Dec 1837 - ?)
| | |
|---|---|
| 14 Jan 1898: | Promoted to *Major-General* |
| 14 Jan 1898 - 14 Jan 1900: | Commander, 1st Brigade, 8th Infantry Division |

*Major-General* Grigory Mikhailovich **Kokorev** (23 Jan 1859 - ?)
| | |
|---|---|
| 29 Jul 1910 - ?: | Commander, 3rd (Arensburg) Borderguard Brigade |
| 1913: | Promoted to *Major-General* |

*Lieutenant-General* Mikhail Ivanovich **Kokorin** (29 Aug 1839 - 13 Apr 1906)
| | |
|---|---|
| 28 May 1885: | Promoted to *Major-General* |
| 28 May 1885 - 28 Jan 1891: | Commander of Artillery, Fortress Sveaborg |
| 28 Jan 1891 - 6 Dec 1895: | Deputy Commander of Artillery, Kiev Military District |
| 6 Dec 1895: | Promoted to *Lieutenant-General* |
| 6 Dec 1895 - 13 Apr 1906: | Commander of Artillery, Odessa Military District |

*Lieutenant-General* Pyotr Ivanovich **Kokunko** (10 Jun 1851 - 10 Jun 1939)
| | |
|---|---|
| 22 Jun 1910 - 25 Sep 1916: | Ataman, Yeisk Division, Kuban Region |
| 6 Dec 1910: | Promoted to *Major-General* |
| 25 Sep 1916: | Promoted to *Lieutenant-General* |
| 25 Sep 1916: | Dismissed |

*Lieutenant-General* Sergey Antonovich **Kolbe** (3 Oct 1840 - ?)
| | |
|---|---|
| 15 Jun 1884 - 16 Jan 1896: | Head of the Regulations Committee, General Staff |
| 30 Aug 1886: | Promoted to *Major-General* |
| 16 Jan 1896 - 1902: | Deputy Chief Intendant, Ministry of War |
| 14 May 1896: | Promoted to *Lieutenant-General* |

*Major-General* Vladimir Nikitich **Kolbe** (15 Jun 1862 - ?)
| | |
|---|---|
| 6 Feb 1913: | Promoted to *Major-General* |
| 6 Feb 1913 - 1915: | Commander, 2nd Brigade, 4th Siberian Rifle Division |
| 1915 - 4 Apr 1916: | Commander, Brigade, 12th Siberian Rifle Division |
| 4 Apr 1916 - 1917: | Commander, Brigade, 107th Infantry Division |

*Admiral* Aleksandr Vasilievich **Kolchak** (16 Nov 1874 - 7 Feb 1920)
Sep 1915 - Jun 1916:        Commander of Naval Forces, Gulf of Riga
10 Apr 1916:                Promoted to *Rear-Admiral*
28 Jun 1916 - 7 Jun 1917:   C-in-C, Black Sea Fleet
Aug 1916:                   Promoted to *Vice-Admiral*
18 Nov 1918:                Promoted to *Admiral*
18 Nov 1918 - 4 Jan 1920:   Supreme Ruler and Commander-in-Chief of all Russian Land and Sea Forces

*Major-General* Nikolai Ivanovich **Kolchigin** (27 Jul 1855 - ?)
9 Dec 1914 - 1917:          Reserve officer, Kiev Military District
9 Sep 1915:                 Promoted to *Major-General*

*Lieutenant-General* Konstantin Konstantinovich **Kolen** (25 May 1863 - 9 Jun 1925)
19 Sep 1910 - 3 Apr 1915:   Commander, 164$^{th}$ Infantry Regiment
31 Dec 1914:                Promoted to *Major-General*
3 Apr 1915 - 25 May 1917:   Commander, 1$^{st}$ Brigade, 33$^{rd}$ Infantry Division
25 May 1917 - 1917:         Commander, 18$^{th}$ Siberian Rifle Division
1917:                       Promoted to *Lieutenant-General*

*Major-General* Konstantin Konstantinovich von **Kolen** (9 Sep 1864 - 18 Jun 1915)
28 May 1907 - 10 Nov 1911:  Commander, 4$^{th}$ Grenadier Regiment
10 Nov 1911:                Promoted to *Major-General*
10 Nov 1911 - 22 Dec 1914:  Chief of Staff, II. Army Corps
22 Dec 1914 - 18 Jun 1915:  Reserve officer, Dvinsk Military District

*Major-General* Vilgelm Ivanovich **Kolenius** (28 May 1843 - ?)
17 Feb 1900 - 1903:         Commander, 6$^{th}$ Reserve Artillery Brigade
1 Jan 1901:                 Promoted to *Major-General*

*Lieutenant-General* Aleksandr Ivanovich **Kolenkin** (20 Jul 1851 - ?)
9 Feb 1901 - 20 Jun 1901:   Commander, Life Guards 2$^{nd}$ Artillery Brigade
1 Apr 1901:                 Promoted to *Major-General*
20 Jun 1901 - 16 Jul 1912:  Deputy Commanding General, Borderguard Corps
22 Apr 1907:                Promoted to *Lieutenant-General*

*Lieutenant-General* Yevgeny Vasilyevich **Kolenko** (31 Jan 1846 - ?)
30 May 1900:                Promoted to *Major-General*
30 May 1900 - 31 Jul 1900:  Chief of Staff, South Ussuri Department Troops
31 Jul 1900 - 10 Sep 1902:  Chief of Staff, II. Siberian Army Corps
1901 - 1902:                Chief of Staff, Mancuhrian Expeditionary Force
10 Sep 1902 - 7 Jan 1904:   Commander, 1$^{st}$ Brigade, 30$^{th}$ Infantry Division
7 Jan 1904 - 1 Jun 1907:    Commandant of Fortress Kars
6 Dec 1906:                 Promoted to *Lieutenant-General*
1 Jun 1907:                 Retired

*Major-General* Ivan Nikiforovich **Kolesnikov** (7 Sep 1860 - Jan 1920)
8 Feb 1916 - 26 Sep 1917:   Commander, 2$^{nd}$ Brigade, 5$^{th}$ Caucasus Cossack

|  |  |
|---|---|
| | Division |
| 22 Oct 1916: | Promoted to *Major-General* |
| 26 Sep 1917 - Dec 1917: | Commander, 1st Kuban Cossack Division |

*Major-General* Pyotr Nikolayevich **Kolesnikov** (24 Jun 1848 - Nov 1901)
| | |
|---|---|
| 26 Jul 1891 - 25 Apr 1896: | Commander, 47th Dragoon Regiment |
| 25 Apr 1896: | Promoted to *Major-General* |
| 25 Apr 1896 - Nov 1901: | Commander, 2nd Brigade, 1st Cavalry Division |

*Major-General* Vladimir Lyudvigovich **Kollontay** (9 Jul 1867 - 1917)
| | |
|---|---|
| 13 May 1900 - Apr 1915: | Professor, Nikolayev Engineering Academy |
| 14 Apr 1913: | Promoted to *Major-General* |
| Apr 1915 - 20 May 1916: | Commander of Lines of Communication, 3rd Army |
| 20 May 1916 - 1917: | Commander of Engineering Logistics, Northern Front |

*Major-General* Nikolai Klavdiyevich **Kolmakov** (16 Nov 1858 - ?)
| | |
|---|---|
| 24 Nov 1913 - 20 May 1917: | Deputy Military Commander, Trans-Caspian Region |
| 22 Mar 1915: | Promoted to *Major-General* |
| 20 May 1917: | Dismissed |

*Major-General* Mikhail Viktorovich **Kolobov** (11 Oct 1868 - 8 Apr 1944)
| | |
|---|---|
| 12 Sep 1914 - 1917: | Commander, 2nd Amur Railway Brigade |
| 6 Dec 1914: | Promoted to *Major-General* |

*Major-General* Nikolai Aleksandrovich **Kolobov** (11 Nov 1858 - ?)
| | |
|---|---|
| 11 Mar 1911 - 1917: | Chairman of the Remount Commission, Orenburg Region |
| 6 Dec 1911: | Promoted to *Major-General* |

*Major-General* Fyodor Aleksandrovich **Kolodeyev** (8 Feb 1872 - 1920)
| | |
|---|---|
| 11 Oct 1914 - 20 Dec 1916: | Commander, 2nd Mountain Horse Artillery Battalion |
| 22 Sep 1916: | Promoted to *Major-General* |
| 20 Dec 1916 - 9 May 1917: | Commander, 14th Artillery Brigade |
| 9 May 1917 - 1918: | Inspector of Artillery, VIII. Army Corps |

*General of the Admiralty* Aleksandr Aleksandrovich **Kolokoltsov** (18 Sep 1833 - 1 Oct 1904)
| | |
|---|---|
| Nov 1864 - Apr 1894: | Head of the Obukhov Steel Plant, St. Petersburg |
| 1882: | Promoted to *Rear-Admiral* |
| 1892: | Promoted to *Lieutenant-General of the Admiralty* |
| Apr 1894 - 1 Oct 1904: | Member of the Admiralty Board |
| 1898: | Promoted to *General of the Admiralty* |

*Lieutenant-General* Konstantin Vasilyevich **Kolokoltsov** (20 Dec 1854 - 8 Dec 1927)
| | |
|---|---|
| 4 Jun 1904 - 16 Jan 1909: | Commander, 34th Artillery Brigade |
| 2 Apr 1905: | Promoted to *Major-General* |
| 16 Jan 1909 - 26 Jul 1910: | Commander of Artillery, XIX. Army Corps |
| 6 Dec 1909: | Promoted to *Lieutenant-General* |

26 Jul 1910 - 14 Apr 1916:    Inspector of Artillery, XIX. Army Corps
14 Apr 1916 - 14 May 1917:    Inspector of Artillery, Petrograd Military District
14 May 1917:    Dismissed

*Major-General* Nikolai Petrovich **Kolomensky** (7 Mar 1874 - 30 Dec 1928)
10 Nov 1916 - 30 Apr 1917:    Chief of Staff, 1st Finland Rifle Division
11 Nov 1916:    Promoted to *Major-General*
30 Apr 1917 - 18 Nov 1917:    Commander, 155th Infantry Division
18 Nov 1917 - 1918:    Commander, 1st Czechoslovak Rifle Division

*Vice-Admiral* Nikolai Nikolayevich **Kolomeytsov** (16 Jul 1867 - 6 Oct 1944)
6 Dec 1913:    Promoted to *Rear-Admiral*
12 May 1914 - 24 Dec 1914:    Commander, Cruiser Brigade, Baltic Fleet
24 Dec 1914 - 16 Sep 1915:    Reserve officer, Ministry of the Navy
16 Sep 1915 - 31 Mar 1917:    Commander, Chudskoy Flotilla
31 Mar 1917 - 6 Oct 1917:    Reserve officer, Ministry of the Navy
6 Oct 1917:    Promoted to *Vice-Admiral*
6 Oct 1917:    Retired

*Major-General* Andrey Pavlovich **Kolomiyts** (6 Aug 1846 - ?)
4 Apr 1901:    Promoted to *Major-General*
4 Apr 1901 - 1904:    Chief of Kiev Military Hospital

*Major-General* Dmitry Dmitriyevich **Kolomnin** (21 Dec 1851 - ?)
15 Jan 1898 - 4 Feb 1904:    Commander, 15th Dragoon Regiment
4 Feb 1904:    Promoted to *Major-General*
4 Feb 1904 - 3 May 1908:    Commander, 1st Brigade, 3rd Cavalry Division

*Major-General* Emil Vilgelmovich **Kolonius** (26 Jun 1840 - ?)
16 Aug 1870 - 1904:    Inspector of Classes, Finnish Cadet Corps
30 Aug 1884:    Promoted to *Major-General*

*General of Engineers* Aleksandr Nikolayevich **Kolosov** (29 Sep 1851 - ?)
11 Feb 1903 - 11 Dec 1908:    Commander of Engineers, Fortress Sevastopol
6 Apr 1903:    Promoted to *Major-General*
11 Dec 1908 - 22 Oct 1912:    Deputy Commander of Engineers, Kiev Military District
22 Oct 1912 - 4 Oct 1915:    Chief of Troop Billeting, Kiev Military District
6 Dec 1912:    Promoted to *Lieutenant-General*
4 Oct 1915:    Promoted to *General of Engineers*
4 Oct 1915:    Retired

*Major-General* Dmitry Pavlovich **Kolosovsky** (14 Nov 1862 - 5 Jun 1930)
2 Jul 1912:    Promoted to *Major-General*
2 Jul 1912 - 1914:    Chief of Construction, Fortress Grodno
1914 - 3 May 1916:    Commander of Engineers, Fortress Grodno
3 May 1916 - 1917:    Commander of Engineers, Caucasus Army

*Major-General* Viktor Firsovich **Kolovertnov** (22 Mar 1853 - ?)
1 Jun 1903 - 1908:				Senior Board Member, Ural Cossack Army
22 Apr 1907:				Promoted to *Major-General*

*Lieutenant-General* Aleksandr Aleksandrovich **Kolpakov** (16 Aug 1845 - ?)
18 Feb 1895 - 29 Jan 1901:		Deputy Chief of Staff, Moscow Military District
15 Mar 1895:				Promoted to *Major-General*
29 Jan 1901 - 1907:			Commander, Moscow Regional Brigade
6 Dec 1905:				Promoted to *Lieutenant-General*

*Major-General* Aleksandr Aleksandrovich **Kolpakov** (26 Feb 1871 - 23 Feb 1920)
18 Dec 1912 - 1 Oct 1915:		Chief of Communications, Amur Military District
14 Apr 1913:				Promoted to *Major-General*
1 Oct 1915 - 7 Apr 1916:		Chief of Communications, Northern Front
7 Apr 1916 - 20 Dec 1916:		Chief of Communications, Odessa Military District
20 Dec 1916 - 1917:			Chief of Communications, Romanian Front

*Lieutenant-General* Sergey Nikolayevich **Kolpakov** (6 Jul 1860 - ?)
22 Jul 1911:				Promoted to *Major-General*
22 Jul 1911 - 15 Apr 1915:		Commander, 12th Artillery Brigade
15 Apr 1915 - 29 Apr 1917:		Inspector of Artillery, XXXII. Army Corps
5 Aug 1916:				Promoted to *Lieutenant-General*

*General of Infantry* Gerasim Alekseyevich **Kolpakovsky** (4 Jan 1819 - 23 Apr 1896)
19 Jun 1858 - 21 Dec 1864:		Commander, Alatavskogo District
24 Oct 1862:				Promoted to *Major-General*
21 Dec 1864 - 14 Jul 1867:		Commander, Semipalatinsk Region
14 Jul 1867 - 28 May 1882:		Military Governor, Semirechensk Region
28 Mar 1871:				Promoted to *Lieutenant-General*
28 May 1882 - 24 Oct 1889:		Governor-General of the Steppes,
					Commanding General, Omsk Military District
30 Aug 1885:				Promoted to *General of Infantry*
24 Oct 1889 - 23 Apr 1896:		Member of the Military Council

*Lieutenant-General* Ivan Vasilyevich **Kolpikov** (24 Mar 1855 - ?)
26 Mar 1904 - 6 Apr 1907:		Commander, 41st Infantry Regiment
6 Dec 1906:				Promoted to *Major-General*
6 Apr 1907 - 29 Nov 1911:		Commander, 1st Brigade, 2nd Infantry Division
29 Nov 1911 - 12 Mar 1916:		Commander, 2nd Turkestan Rifle Brigade
30 Sep 1915:				Promoted to *Lieutenant-General*
12 Mar 1916 - 26 Feb 1917:		Commander, 2nd Turkestan Rifle Division
4 Sep 1917:				Dismissed

*Lieutenant-General* Mikhail Petrovich **Kolpychev** (16 Oct 1851 - ?)
31 Jan 1908 - 31 Dec 1913:		General for Special Assignments, Kazan Military District
13 Apr 1908:				Promoted to *Major-General*
31 Dec 1913:				Promoted to *Lieutenant-General*

| | |
|---|---|
| 31 Dec 1913: | Retired |
| 1914 - 22 Jul 1915: | Recalled; Chief of Sanatory Service, 4th Army |
| 22 Jul 1915: | Retired |

*Major-General* Viktor Brunovich **Kolshmidt** (22 Jul 1862 - ?)
| | |
|---|---|
| 13 Jan 1911: | Promoted to *Major-General* |
| 13 Jan 1911 - 21 Jun 1915: | Commander, 2nd Brigade, 17th Infantry Division |
| 1914: | Acting Commander, 17th Infantry Division |
| 21 Jun 1915 - 20 Aug 1915: | Commander, 63rd Infantry Division |
| 20 Aug 1915 - 24 Jun 1918: | POW |

*Lieutenant-General of the Admiralty* Mitrofan Yegorovich **Koltovskoy** (29 Jan 1836 - 2 Dec 1896)
| | |
|---|---|
| 14 Sep 1885 - 22 Nov 1896: | Mayor of Kerch-Yenikalsky |
| 1887: | Promoted to *Rear-Admiral* |
| 1895: | Promoted to *Lieutenant-General of the Admiralty* |

*Lieutenant-General of the Fleet* Aleksandr Leontyevich **Kolyankovsky** (3 Sep 1857 - ?)
| | |
|---|---|
| 14 Jan 1908 - Jul 1913: | Board member, Obhukov Steel & Izhora Factories |
| 6 Dec 1910: | Promoted to *Major-General of the Admiralty* |
| 8 Apr 1913: | Redesignated *Major-General of the Fleet* |
| 23 Sep 1913: | Promoted to *Lieutenant-General of the Fleet* |

*Lieutenant-General* Eduard Arkadyevich **Kolyankovsky** (13 Oct 1857 - ?)
| | |
|---|---|
| 3 Feb 1905: | Promoted to *Major-General* |
| 3 Feb 1905 - 25 Jul 1906: | Deputy Inspector of Engineers, 3rd Manchurian Army |
| Jun 1905 - Aug 1905: | Acting Commander, Infantry Brigade |
| 25 Jul 1906 - 6 Feb 1914: | Commander, 1st Brigade, 17th Infantry Division |
| 6 Feb 1914: | Promoted to *Lieutenant-General* |
| 6 Feb 1914 - 3 Oct 1914: | Commander, 30th Infantry Division |
| 3 Oct 1914 - 21 Dec 1914: | Reserve officer, Minsk Military District |
| 21 Dec 1914 - 5 Jul 1915: | Commander, 8th Infantry Division |
| 5 Jul 1915 - 19 Nov 1915: | Commander, 3rd Caucasus Rifle Brigade |
| 19 Nov 1915 - 1 Jan 1916: | Reserve officer, Dvinsk Military District |
| 1 Jan 1916 - 18 Apr 1917: | Commander, 120th Infantry Division |
| 18 Apr 1917 - 29 Jun 1917: | Reserve officer, Dvinsk Military District |
| 29 Jun 1917: | Dismissed |

*Major-General* Vladimir Arkadyevich **Kolyankovsky** (27 Dec 1854 - ?)
| | |
|---|---|
| 3 Feb 1905: | Promoted to *Major-General* |
| 3 Feb 1905 - 1905: | Deputy Inspector of Engineers, 3rd Manchurian Army |

*Lieutenant-General* Aleksey Mikhailovich **Kolyubakin** (22 Jun 1851 - 13 May 1917)
| | |
|---|---|
| 29 Jul 1899: | Promoted to *Major-General* |
| 29 Jul 1899 - 20 Jan 1903: | Duty General, Turkestan Military District |
| 20 Jan 1903 - 16 Aug 1905: | Military Governor of Primorye |
| 16 Aug 1905 - 29 Nov 1908: | Military Governor of Terek Region |
| 2 Apr 1906: | Promoted to *Lieutenant-General* |

29 Nov 1908 - 27 Feb 1916: Attached to Caucasus Military District
27 Feb 1916 - 19 Oct 1916: Reserve officer, Caucasus Military District
19 Oct 1916 - 13 May 1917: Inspector of Militia Units, Caucasus Army

*Lieutenant-General* Boris Mikhailovich **Kolyubakin** (12 Jun 1853 - 1924)
27 Jul 1898 - 1917: Professor, Nikolayev General Staff Academy
14 Apr 1902: Promoted to *Major-General*
6 Dec 1909: Promoted to *Lieutenant-General*

*Major-General* Vladimir Nikolayevich **Kolyubakin** (28 Aug 1873 - 16 Jul 1944)
1915 - 17 Dec 1915: Special Assignments General, ? Army
13 Nov 1915: Promoted to *Major-General*
17 Dec 1915 - 8 Feb 1917: Chief of Line of Communications Section, 7$^{th}$ Army
8 Feb 1917 - 1917: Chief of Communications, Western Front

*Vice-Admiral* Pavel Vasilyevich **Kolyupanov** (10 Jan 1857 - 13 Jan 1913)
2 Aug 1910: Promoted to *Rear-Admiral*
2 Aug 1910 - 13 Jan 1913: Commander, Port of Vladivostok
12 Jan 1913: Promoted to *Vice-Admiral*

*Major-General* Pyotr Nikolayevich **Kolzakov** (27 Jul 1861 - 22 Feb 1937)
21 Mar 1914 - 8 Oct 1915: Commander, 1$^{st}$ Amur Mounted Borderguard Regiment
8 Oct 1915 - 1917: Commander, 2$^{nd}$ Brigade, 7$^{th}$ Cavalry Division
23 Dec 1915: Promoted to *Major-General*

*General of Infantry* Aleksandr Vissarionovich **Komarov** (24 Aug 1830 - 27 Sep 1904)
21 May 1868: Promoted to *Major-General*
21 May 1868 - 4 Oct 1877: Mayor of Derbent,
 Military Commander, Southern Dagestan
4 Oct 1877: Promoted to *Lieutenant-General*
4 Oct 1877 - 22 Mar 1883: Chief of Caucasus Mountains Management
 Administration
22 Mar 1883 - 27 Mar 1890: Commander, Transcaspian Region
27 Mar 1890 - 30 Aug 1891: At the disposal of the Minister of War
30 Aug 1891 - 12 Mar 1896: Transferred to the reserve
12 Mar 1896: Promoted to *General of Infantry*
12 Mar 1896 - 27 Sep 1904: Member, Committee for Wounded Veterans

*General of Infantry* Dmitry Narkizovich **Komarov** (21 Feb 1839 - 1919)
29 Apr 1891: Promoted to *Major-General*
29 Apr 1891 - 2 Jun 1900: Commander, Life Guards Volyn Regiment
2 Jun 1900 - 1913: Commandant of Warsaw
6 Dec 1900: Promoted to *Lieutenant-General*
26 Jun 1907: Promoted to *General of Infantry*
1913: Retired

*General of Infantry* Konstantin Vissarionovich **Komarov** (5 Oct 1832 - 18 Dec 1912)
6 Mar 1868 - 28 Jul 1877: Commander, 152$^{nd}$ Infantry Regiment

| | |
|---|---|
| 16 Jul 1877: | Promoted to *Major-General* |
| 28 Jul 1877 - 18 Feb 1878: | Attached to the C-in-C, Caucasus Army |
| 18 Feb 1878 - 15 Nov 1878: | Commander, 2nd Brigade, 38th Infantry Division |
| 15 Nov 1878 - 4 Apr 1881: | Military Governor of Batum Region |
| 4 Apr 1881 - 7 Apr 1883: | Attached to the C-in-C, Caucasus Army |
| 7 Apr 1883 - 11 Aug 1883: | Commander, Turkestan Infantry Brigade |
| 11 Aug 1883 - 22 Jun 1891: | Commandant of Fortress Ivangorod |
| 30 Aug 1886: | Promoted to *Lieutenant-General* |
| 22 Jun 1891 - 7 Dec 1898: | Commandant of Fortress Warsaw |
| 1896 - 1897: | Member, Commission for the Revision of Regulations on Fortresses |
| 1897 - 1898: | Member, Commission for Training Programs in Large Garrisons |
| 6 Dec 1898: | Promoted to *General of Infantry* |
| 7 Dec 1898 - 8 Apr 1902: | Deputy Commanding General, Warsaw Military District |
| 8 Apr 1902 - 18 Dec 1912: | Member of the Military Council |
| 24 Nov 1907 - 18 Dec 1912: | Commandant of Fortress St. Petersburg |
| 1910: | Promoted to *General-Adjutant* |

*Major-General* Nikolai Aleksandrovich **Komarov** (19 Apr 1857 - ?)

| | |
|---|---|
| 3 Mar 1904: | Promoted to *Major-General* |
| 3 Mar 1904 - 1906: | Deputy Chief of Staff, Siberian Military District |

*General of Infantry* Nikolai Nikolayevich **Komarov** (24 Nov 1855 - ?)

| | |
|---|---|
| 17 Apr 1904: | Promoted to *Major-General* |
| 17 Apr 1904 - 7 Jun 1912: | Chief of Staff, VII. Army Corps |
| 30 May 1912: | Promoted to *Lieutenant-General* |
| 7 Jun 1912 - 26 Aug 1914: | Commander, 4th Infantry Division |
| 30 Aug 1914 - 17 Jan 1915: | Reserve officer, Minsk Military District |
| 17 Jan 1915: | Promoted to *General of Infantry* |
| 17 Jan 1915: | Retired |

*Major-General* Nikolai Varfolomeyevich **Komarov** (28 Apr 1853 - ?)

| | |
|---|---|
| 16 Jul 1910 - 4 Apr 1917: | Military Commander, Kazan Region |
| 26 Feb 1915: | Promoted to *Major-General* |
| 4 Apr 1917 - 1917: | Reserve officer, Kazan Military District |

*Major-General* Pyotr Dmitriyevich **Komarov** (25 Feb 1870 - 4 Aug 1914)

| | |
|---|---|
| 23 Mar 1913 - 4 Aug 1914: | Commander, 105th Infantry Regiment |
| 3 Feb 1915: | Posthumously promoted to *Major-General* |

*Lieutenant-General* Vladimir Aleksandrovich **Komarov** (27 Sep 1861 - 1918)

| | |
|---|---|
| 3 Sep 1907: | Promoted to *Major-General* |
| 3 Sep 1907 - 13 Aug 1914: | Commander, His Imperial Majesty's Consolidated Infantry Regiment |
| 13 Aug 1914 - 1917: | Chief of the Petrograd Palace Administration |
| 6 Dec 1914: | Promoted to *Lieutenant-General* |

*General of Infantry* Count Dmitry Yegorovich **Komarovsky** (1 Jun 1837 - 9 Mar 1901)
17 Apr 1870 - 29 Dec 1877: Commander, 10th Infantry Regiment
17 Apr 1877: Promoted to *Major-General*
29 Dec 1877 - 28 Jan 1889: Commander, 2nd Brigade, 3rd Infantry Division
28 Jan 1889 - 17 Jan 1890: Commander, 2nd Brigade, 10th Infantry Division
17 Jan 1890 - 29 Sep 1890: Commander, 7th Infantry Division
30 Aug 1890: Promoted to *Lieutenant-General*
29 Sep 1890 - 9 Aug 1894: Commander, 8th Infantry Division
9 Aug 1894 - 2 Apr 1898: Commander, 3rd Guards Infantry Division
2 Apr 1898 - 1 Oct 1899: Commanding General, IV. Army Corps
1 Oct 1899 - 9 Mar 1901: Commanding General, XV. Army Corps
6 Dec 1900: Promoted to *General of Infantry*

*Major-General* Mikhail Stepanovich **Komissarov** (6 Sep 1870 - 20 Oct 1933)
1915 - Jan 1916: Deputy Chief of Police, St. Petersburg
1 Jan 1916: Promoted to *Major-General*
Jan 1916 - 20 Feb 1916: At the disposal of the Minister of the Interior
20 Feb 1916 - 4 Aug 1916: Mayor of Rostov-on-Don
4 Aug 1916: Retired

*Major-General* Nikolai Nikolayevich **Komstadius** (7 Aug 1866 - 11 Oct 1917)
26 Oct 1905 - 29 Mar 1908: Commander, Life Guards Cuirassier Regiment
6 Dec 1906: Promoted to *Major-General*
29 Mar 1908 - 13 Dec 1911: At the disposal of the Commanding General, St. Petersburg Military District
13 Dec 1911 - 14 Nov 1912: Commander, 2nd Brigade, 2nd Guards Cavalry Division
14 Nov 1912 - 1917: General à la suite

*Major-General* Pavel Nikiforovich **Komyansky** (31 Aug 1858 - ?)
21 Aug 1915 - 1917: Commander, 3rd Kuban Light Infantry Brigade
18 Jan 1916: Promoted to *Major-General*

*Lieutenant-General* Daniil Albertovich **Konarzhevsky** (9 Jul 1831 - ?)
27 Mar 1874 - 17 Apr 1879: Commander, 121st Infantry Regiment
17 Apr 1879: Promoted to *Major-General*
17 Apr 1879 - 22 Nov 1880: Unassigned
22 Nov 1880 - 19 Apr 1887: Commander, St. Petersburg Grenadier Regiment
19 Apr 1887 - 24 Dec 1890: Commander, 2nd Brigade, 3rd Guards Infantry Division
24 Dec 1890 - 9 Apr 1898: Commander, 14th Infantry Division
30 Aug 1891: Promoted to *Lieutenant-General*

*General of Engineers* Genrikh Albertovich **Konarzhevsky** (22 Mar 1833 - 3 Oct 1906)
30 Aug 1873: Promoted to *Major-General*
29 Feb 1876 - 23 Dec 1896: Commander of Engineers, St. Petersburg Military District
30 Aug 1882: Promoted to *Lieutenant-General*
23 Dec 1896 - 3 Aug 1898: At the disposal of the Minister of War
1 Jan 1897: Promoted to *General of Engineers*

3 Aug 1898 - 3 Jan 1906:  Member, Committee for Wounded Veterans
3 Jan 1906:  Retired

*Lieutenant-General* Nikolai Platonovich **Konchakovsky** (24 Dec 1854 - ?)
5 Apr 1906:  Promoted to *Major-General*
5 Apr 1906 - 1 Aug 1907:  Commander, Tiflis Regional Brigade
1 Aug 1907 - 8 Aug 1914:  Commander, Vladikavkaz Regional Brigade
6 Apr 1914:  Promoted to *Lieutenant-General*
8 Aug 1914 - 12 Sep 1915:  Commander, 15th Replacement Infantry Brigade
12 Sep 1915 - 30 Sep 1917:  Commander, Vladikavkaz Regional Brigade
30 Sep 1917:  Dismissed

*Major-General* Valentin Ilich **Kondakov** (18 Sep 1850 - ?)
2 May 1886 - 1907:  Ataman, 1st Division, Astrakhan Cossack Army
2 Apr 1906:  Promoted to *Major-General*

*Major-General of the Fleet* Nikolai Yegorovich **Kondoguri** (18 Jan 1866 - ?)
8 Dec 1908 - 12 Jun 1917:  Commandant, Astrabad Naval Station
10 Apr 1916:  Promoted to *Major-General of the Fleet*
12 Jun 1917:  Dismissed

*Lieutenant-General* Roman Isidorovich **Kondratenko** (30 Sep 1857 - 2 Dec 1904)
23 Jun 1901:  Promoted to *Major-General*
23 Jun 1901 - 8 Nov 1903:  Duty General, Amur Military District
8 Nov 1903 - 10 Feb 1904:  Commander, 7th East Siberian Rifle Brigade
10 Feb 1904 - 2 Dec 1904:  Commander, 7th East Siberian Rifle Division
Dec 1904:  Posthumously promoted to *Lieutenant-General*

*General of Infantry* Kiprian Antonovich **Kondratovich** (28 Apr 1859 - 31 Oct 1932)
7 Feb 1901:  Promoted to *Major-General*
7 Feb 1901 - 11 Jul 1902:  Commander, 2nd Brigade, 36th Infantry Division
11 Jul 1902 - 24 Dec 1903:  Attached to the C-in-C, Kwantung Area
24 Dec 1903 - 31 Jan 1904:  At the disposal of the C-in-C, Far East
31 Jan 1904 - 22 Feb 1904:  Commander, 9th East Siberian Rifle Brigade
22 Feb 1904 - 4 Jul 1906:  Commander, 9th East Siberian Rifle Division
20 Aug 1904:  Promoted to *Lieutenant-General*
4 Jul 1906 - 2 Jan 1907:  Attached to the General Staff
2 Jan 1907 - 25 Jan 1907:  Commanding General, II. Army Corps
25 Jan 1907 - 1 Jan 1910:  Deputy Commanding General, Turkestan Military District,
  Deputy Governor-General of Turkestan
1 Jan 1910 - 15 Aug 1913:  Commanding General, I. Caucasus Army Corps
6 Dec 1910:  Promoted to *General of Infantry*
15 Aug 1913 - 30 Aug 1914:  Commanding General, XXIII. Army Corps
30 Aug 1914 - 14 Dec 1914:  Reserve officer, Minsk Military District
14 Dec 1914:  Retired
25 Nov 1915 - 8 May 1917:  Recalled; Reserve officer, Minsk Military District
8 May 1917 - Oct 1917:  Commander, 78th Infantry Division

*Major-General* Luka Lukich **Kondratovich** (17 Oct 1866 - ?)
| | |
|---|---|
| 9 Apr 1913: | Promoted to *Major-General* |
| 9 Apr 1913 - 22 Dec 1914: | Chief of Staff, Semirechensk Region |
| 22 Dec 1914 - 2 Nov 1915: | Chief of Staff, XXIII. Army Corps |
| 2 Nov 1915 - 5 Mar 1916: | Commander, 1st Independent Infantry Brigade |
| 5 Mar 1916 - 18 May 1917: | Commander, 1st Infantry Division |
| 18 May 1917 - 1917: | Reserve officer, Dvinsk Military District |

*Lieutenant-General* Kondraty Kallistratovich **Kondratsky** (5 Apr 1849 - ?)
| | |
|---|---|
| 14 Jun 1899 - 22 Jun 1902: | Commander, 3rd Grenadier Artillery Brigade |
| 1 Jan 1900: | Promoted to *Major-General* |
| 22 Jun 1902 - 26 Apr 1904: | Commander, 5th Artillery Brigade |
| 26 Apr 1904 - Sep 1905: | Commander of Artillery, VIII. Army Corps |
| Sep 1905: | Promoted to *Lieutenant-General* |
| Sep 1905: | Retired |

*Lieutenant-General* Nikolai Grigoryevich **Kondratyev** (4 Dec 1859 - 1911)
| | |
|---|---|
| 4 Jul 1902 - 17 May 1907: | Chief of Communications, St. Petersburg Military District |
| 1903: | Promoted to *Major-General* |
| 17 May 1907 - 14 Apr 1908: | Member, Committee for Military Education |
| 14 Apr 1908 - 14 Mar 1909: | Quartermaster-General, General Staff |
| 17 Apr 1909: | Promoted to *Lieutenant-General* |
| 14 Mar 1909 - Feb 1911: | Chief of the General Staff |

*Major-General* Kronid Pavlovich **Kondyrev** (6 Jun 1842 - ?)
| | |
|---|---|
| 31 Oct 1899: | Promoted to *Major-General* |
| 31 Oct 1899 - 26 Jun 1902: | Commander, 1st Brigade, 29th Infantry Division |

*Lieutenant-General* Pyotr Konstantinovich **Kondzerovsky** (22 Jun 1869 - 16 Aug 1929)
| | |
|---|---|
| 2 Dec 1908 - 19 Jul 1914: | Duty General, General Staff |
| 29 Mar 1909: | Promoted to *Major-General* |
| 19 Jul 1914 - 2 Apr 1917: | Duty General, Supreme Commander-in-Chief |
| 22 Oct 1914: | Promoted to *Lieutenant-General* |
| 2 Apr 1917 - 21 May 1918: | Member of the Military Council |

*Major-General* Mikhail Yegorovich **Konevsky** (5 Nov 1854 - ?)
| | |
|---|---|
| 1 Dec 1906 - 1908: | Mayor of Baku |
| 6 Dec 1906: | Promoted to *Major-General* |

*Major-General* Pyotr Dmitriyevich **Konevtsov** (27 Nov 1856 - ?)
| | |
|---|---|
| 6 Feb 1906 - 1917: | Chief of Railway Gendarmerie, Kharkov |
| 6 Dec 1916 | Promoted to *Major-General* |

*Major-General* Aleksandr Yakovlevich **Konisky** (5 Sep 1835 - ?)
| | |
|---|---|
| 12 Apr 1879 - 1904: | Military Judge, Kiev Military District Court |
| 30 Aug 1882: | Promoted to *Major-General* |

*Major-General* Zakhary Semyonovich **Kononenko** (6 Sep 1867 - Jan 1920)
5 Jul 1916 - 1917: Intendant, Northern Front
6 Dec 1916 Promoted to *Major-General*

*Lieutenant-General* Kuzma Spiridonovich **Kononov** (9 Oct 1827 - 13 Aug 1902)
11 Oct 1879 - 1897: Commander of Gendarmerie, Novgorod Province
6 Dec 1894: Promoted to *Major-General*
1897: Promoted to *Lieutenant-General*
1897: Retired

*Lieutenant-General* Nikolai Kuzmich **Kononov** (2 Dec 1859 - ?)
16 May 1895 - 9 Apr 1903: Commandant, Tver Cavalry Cadet School
6 Dec 1902: Promoted to *Major-General*
9 Apr 1903 - 9 Nov 1904: Duty General, Warsaw Military District
9 Nov 1904 - 27 Sep 1906: Duty General, 3rd Manchurian Army
27 Sep 1906 - 17 Nov 1906: Quartermaster-General, General Staff
17 Nov 1906 - 8 Mar 1917: Chief of Staff, Borderguard Corps
6 Dec 1907: Promoted to *Lieutenant-General*
8 Mar 1917: Retired

*Major-General* Iosif Kazimirovich **Kononovich** (13 May 1863 - 15 Dec 1921)
18 Nov 1910 - 24 Jan 1915: Commander, 138th Infantry Regiment
14 Nov 1914: Promoted to *Major-General*
24 Jan 1915 - 24 Jun 1915: Commander, 2nd Brigade, 75th Infantry Division
24 Jun 1915 - 29 Oct 1916: Commander, Life Guards Lithuanian Regiment
29 Oct 1916 - 7 Apr 1917: Commander, 1st Brigade, Guards Rifle Division
7 Apr 1917 - 31 Nov 1917: Commander, 83rd Infantry Division
31 Nov 1917 - 1918: Reserve officer, Kiev Military District

*Major-General* Kazimir Iosifovich **Kononovich** (10 Mar 1823 - 28 Jun 1897)
20 Aug 1876 - 31 Jul 1877: Unassigned
30 Aug 1876: Promoted to *Major-General*
31 Jul 1877 - Jan 1897: Commander, 1st Brigade, 24th Infantry Division
Jan 1897: Retired

*Major-General* Nikolai Kazimirovich **Kononovich** (27 Apr 1859 - 3 Mar 1929)
3 Sep 1908 - 1917: Military Commander, Bezhetsky District
14 Jan 1915: Promoted to *Major-General*
1917: Commander, Kharkov Regional Brigade

*General of Infantry* Pyotr Vikentyevich **Kononovich-Gorbatsky** (15 Aug 1842 - ?)
1 Nov 1887 - 18 Apr 1891: Chief of Staff, Fortress Kovno
30 Aug 1888: Promoted to *Major-General*
18 Apr 1891 - 16 May 1891: Chief of Staff, XII. Army Corps
16 May 1891 - 14 Jul 1894: Commandant, 2nd Konstantinovsky Military School
14 Jul 1894 - 30 Oct 1896: Chief of Staff, Kiev Military District
14 May 1896: Promoted to *Lieutenant-General*
30 Oct 1896 - 13 May 1899: Commander, 33rd Infantry Division

| | |
|---|---|
| 13 May 1899 - 18 Jan 1900: | Commander, 29th Infantry Division |
| 18 Jan 1900 - 4 Feb 1903: | Deputy Chief, Main Directorate for Military Schools |
| 4 Feb 1903 - 16 Dec 1904: | Commanding General, XXI. Army Corps |
| 16 Dec 1904 - 3 Jan 1906: | Member of the Military Council |
| 3 Jan 1906: | Promoted to *General of Infantry* |
| 3 Jan 1906: | Retired |

*Major-General* Pyotr Mikhailovich **Konopchansky** (16 Mar 1867 - ?)

| | |
|---|---|
| 17 Aug 1914 - 23 Aug 1916: | Commander, 5th Heavy Artillery Brigade |
| 24 May 1915: | Promoted to *Major-General* |
| 23 Aug 1916 - 2 Sep 1916: | Commander, 110th Artillery Brigade |
| 2 Sep 1916 - 1 Feb 1917: | Commander, 73rd Artillery Brigade |
| 1 Feb 1917 - 24 Jun 1917: | Inspector of Artillery, XLVIII. Army Corps |
| 24 Jun 1917 - 1917: | Inspector of Artillery, XIII. Army Corps |

*Lieutenant-General* Fyodor Yakovlevich **Konoplyansky** (16 Oct 1829 - ?)

| | |
|---|---|
| 2 Mar 1878: | Promoted to *Major-General* |
| 2 Mar 1878 - 29 Oct 1878: | Commander, 1st Brigade, 7th Reserve Infantry Brigade |
| 29 Oct 1878 - 19 Oct 1883: | Commander, 2nd Brigade, 4th Infantry Division |
| 19 Oct 1883 - 30 Jun 1893: | Commander, 2nd Brigade, 40th Infantry Division |
| 30 Jun 1893 - 1901: | Commander, Yaroslav Regional Brigade |
| 30 Aug 1894: | Promoted to *Lieutenant-General* |

*Major-General* Leonid Vasilyevich **Konovalov** (21 Jul 1859 - ?)

| | |
|---|---|
| 1916 - 21 Oct 1916: | Commander of Engineers, I. Caucasus Army Corps |
| 30 Jul 1916: | Promoted to *Major-General* |
| 21 Oct 1916 - 1917: | Deputy Chief of Troop Billeting, Kiev Military District |

*Lieutenant-General* Nikolai Vasilyevich **Konovalov** (24 Jul 1850 - ?)

| | |
|---|---|
| 26 Jul 1902 - 1909: | Engineer Officer, Finland Military District |
| 6 Dec 1904: | Promoted to *Major-General* |
| 1909: | Promoted to *Lieutenant-General* |
| 1909: | Retired |

*Lieutenant-General* Vladimir Georgiyevich **Konradi** (2 Jul 1851 - ?)

| | |
|---|---|
| 23 Aug 1905 - 17 Jun 1906: | Commander, 9th East Siberian Artillery Brigade |
| 17 Jun 1906: | Promoted to *Major-General* |
| 17 Jun 1906 - 4 Nov 1906: | Commander, 9th East Siberian Rifle Artillery Brigade |
| 4 Nov 1906 - 20 Jul 1911: | Commander, 12th Artillery Brigade |
| 20 Jul 1911: | Promoted to *Lieutenant-General* |
| 20 Jul 1911: | Retired |

*Major-General* Konstantin Vasilyevich **Konstantinov** (22 Feb 1854 - ?)

| | |
|---|---|
| 1 Jun 1904 - 1905: | Commander, 218th Infantry Regiment |
| 1905: | Promoted to *Major-General* |
| 1905: | Retired |
| 15 Nov 1916 - 1917: | Recalled; Chief of Evacuation Points, Simbirsk Region |

*Major-General* Nikolai Aleksandrovich **Konstantinov** (8 Nov 1859 - 23 May 1917)
8 Mar 1907 - 20 May 1910: Commander, 1st Battalion, 3rd East Siberian Rifle Artillery Brigade
20 May 1910: Promoted to *Major-General*
20 May 1910: Retired
5 Oct 1914 - ?: Recalled; Commander, 29th Militia Brigade
? - 18 Sep 1916: Commander, 114th Militia Brigade
18 Sep 1916 - 23 May 1917: Commander, 78th Militia Brigade

*Major-General* Vyacheslav Aleksandrovich **Konstantinov** (5 Mar 1870 - 17 Sep 1937)
17 Oct 1912 - 6 Jan 1915: Commander, 16th Uhlan Regiment
2 Nov 1914: Promoted to *Major-General*
6 Jan 1915 - 1917: Commander, 2nd Brigade, 16th Cavalry Division
1917 - Oct 1917: Commander, 13th Cavalry Division
Oct 1917: Dismissed

*Lieutenant-General* Aleksandr Petrovich **Konstantinovich** (26 Aug 1832 - 12 Sep 1903)
23 Apr 1870 - 10 Oct 1878: Chief of Artillery Section, Orenburg Military District
19 Feb 1877: Promoted to *Major-General*
10 Oct 1878 - 30 Jul 1883: Military Commander of Turgai
30 Jul 1883 - 6 Jul 1899: Governor of Bessarabia
30 Aug 1889: Promoted to *Lieutenant-General*
6 Jul 1899 - 12 Sep 1903: Member of the Council, Ministry of Internal Affairs

*Major-General of Naval Navigators* Ivan Ivanovich **Konyushkov** (13 Jan 1865 - 8 Aug 1919)
1903 - 14 Apr 1913: Chief Navigator, Imperial Yacht "Standart"
14 Apr 1913: Promoted to *Major-General of Naval Navigators*
14 Apr 1913: Retired

*Major-General* Nikolai Nikolayevich **Kopachev** (1 Aug 1860 - ?)
1 Jul 1913 - 24 Jun 1915: Commander, 18th Dragoon Regiment
3 Jul 1915: Promoted to *Major-General*
21 Aug 1915 - 1917: Commander, 1st Brigade, Caucasus Cavalry Division

*Lieutenant-General* Nikolai Vasilyevich **Kopansky** (24 Jul 1832 - ?)
13 May 1886: Promoted to *Major-General*
13 May 1886 - 22 Jun 1892: Commander, 2nd Eastern Siberian Rifle Brigade
22 Jun 1892 - 14 Jun 1895: Military Commander, Southern Ussuri Sector
9 Jun 1895: Promoted to *Lieutenant-General*
14 Jun 1895 - 4 Jul 1901: Commander, 16th Infantry Division

*Major-General* Nikolai Vasilyevich **Kopansky** (26 Sep 1869 - ?)
22 Apr 1916 - 1917: Vice-Chairman, Commission for the Construction of a Cartridge Plant
6 Dec 1916: Promoted to *Major-General*

*Major-General* Ivan Grigoryevich **Kopestynsky** (13 Nov 1869 - ?)
| | |
|---|---|
| 9 Apr 1914: | Promoted to *Major-General* |
| 9 Apr 1914 - 19 Nov 1914: | Commander, 2nd Grenadier Artillery Brigade |
| 19 Nov 1914 - 13 Feb 1915: | Unassigned |
| 13 Feb 1915 - 12 May 1916: | Commander, 6th Artillery Brigade |
| 12 May 1916 - 14 May 1918: | Inspector of Artillery, XXXVI. Army Corps |

*Major-General* Pavel Samsonovich **Kopeykin** (27 Feb 1856 - 11 Nov 1918)
| | |
|---|---|
| 16 Jul 1898 - 1906: | Chairman of the Military Board, Ussuri Cossack Army |
| 1906: | Promoted to *Major-General* |
| 1906: | Retired |

*Major-General of the Admiralty* Dmitry Mikhailovich **Koptev** (9 Mar 1855 - 17 Feb 1909)
| | |
|---|---|
| 25 Sep 1906 - 17 Feb 1909: | Chief of Riflemen, Naval Corps |
| 22 Apr 1907: | Promoted to *Major-General of the Admiralty* |

*Lieutenant-General* Nikolai Arkadyevich **Koptev** (18 Jan 1848 - ?)
| | |
|---|---|
| 24 Dec 1879 - 11 Jun 1897: | Commander, Chuguyevsk Artillery Training Polygon, Kiev Military District |
| 6 Dec 1895: | Promoted to *Major-General* |
| 11 Jun 1897 - 14 Jun 1899: | Commander, 38th Artillery Brigade |
| 14 Jun 1899 - 11 Aug 1900: | Commander, 25th Artillery Brigade |
| 11 Aug 1900 - 5 Oct 1902: | Commander of Artillery, I. Siberian Army Corps |
| 5 Oct 1902 - 17 Dec 1908: | Commander of Artillery, XXI. Army Corps |
| 6 Dec 1903: | Promoted to *Lieutenant-General* |

*Lieutenant-General* Pyotr Stepanovich **Koptev** (18 Jul 1841 - 1909)
| | |
|---|---|
| 11 Apr 1901 - 12 Jul 1905: | Ministry of War Representative, Turkestan Military District Council |
| 6 Dec 1901: | Promoted to *Major-General* |
| 12 Jul 1905 - 1909: | Ministry of War Representative, Warsaw Military District Council |
| 6 Dec 1907: | Promoted to *Lieutenant-General* |

*Major-General* Nikolai Kirillovich **Kopylov** (1853 - ?)
| | |
|---|---|
| 10 Aug 1906 - 1913: | Intendant, XIV. Army Corps |
| 1913: | Promoted to *Major-General* |
| 1913: | Retired |

*Vice-Admiral* Nikolai Vasilyevich **Kopytov** (5 Jul 1833 - 9 Feb 1901)
| | |
|---|---|
| 23 Mar 1882: | Promoted to *Rear-Admiral* |
| 23 Mar 1882 - 1884: | Commander, Pacific Naval Detachment |
| 1884 - 1885: | Junior Flagman, Baltic Fleet |
| 1885 - 1 Jan 1888: | Commander, Squadron, Baltic Fleet |
| 1 Jan 1888: | Promoted to *Vice-Admiral* |
| 1 Jan 1888 - 1 Jan 1891: | Senior Flagman, Baltic Fleet |
| 1 Jan 1891 - 1898: | C-in-C, Black Sea & Caspian Sea Fleet |
| 1898: | Promoted to *General-Adjutant* |

1898 - 9 Feb 1901: Member, Board of Admiralty

*Major-General* Yulian Yulianovich **Kopytynsky** (5 Feb 1864 - ?)
26 Jun 1910 - 4 Feb 1915: Commander, 93rd Infantry Regiment
18 Sep 1913: Promoted to *Major-General*
4 Feb 1915 - 1917: Reserve officer, Dvinsk Military District

*General of Cavalry* Yevgeny Zakharovich **Korbut** (27 Jul 1849 - ?)
30 May 1895 - 7 May 1901: Commander, 48th Dragoon Regiment
7 May 1901: Promoted to *Major-General*
7 May 1901 - 30 Apr 1910: Commander, 2nd Brigade, 12th Cavalry Division
30 Apr 1910: Promoted to *Lieutenant-General*
30 Apr 1910 - 31 Dec 1913: Commander, 2nd Replacement Cavalry Brigade
31 Dec 1913: Promoted to *General of Cavalry*
31 Dec 1913: Retired

*Lieutenant-General* Pavel Alekseyevich **Kordyukov** (19 Oct 1862 - 9 May 1930)
1 Oct 1904 - 10 Mar 1912: Commander, 148th Infantry Regiment
22 Dec 1911: Promoted to *Major-General*
10 Mar 1912 - 1 Jul 1915: Commander, 1st Brigade, 23rd Infantry Division
1 Jul 1915 - 22 Apr 1917: Commander, 23rd Infantry Division
1 Oct 1915: Promoted to *Lieutenant-General*
31 Jul 1917 - 1918: Commander, 83rd Infantry Division

*Major-General* Kazimir Yevstafyevich **Korevitsky** (4 Mar 1852 - ?)
8 Mar 1901 - 7 Apr 1903: Inspector of Works, Turkestan Military District
6 Dec 1901: Promoted to *Major-General*
7 Apr 1903 - 1907: Deputy Commander of Engineers, Turkestan Military District

*Major-General* Albert Iosifovich **Korevo** (28 Feb 1854 - 12 Mar 1916)
31 Mar 1905 - 12 Mar 1916: Chairman of the Remount Commission, Caucasus Region
6 Dec 1911: Promoted to *Major-General*

*Lieutenant-General* Pyotr Simforianovich **Koreyvo** (25 Nov 1856 - 9 Oct 1923)
20 Aug 1901 - 19 Nov 1904: Military Judge, Odessa Military District Court
6 Dec 1901: Promoted to *Major-General*
19 Nov 1904 - 1905: Chief of Military Justice, 3rd Manchurian Army
1905 - 19 Feb 1908: Military Judge, Odessa Military District Court
19 Feb 1908 - 4 Aug 1911: Military Procurator, Kazan Military District
13 Apr 1908: Promoted to *Lieutenant-General*
4 Aug 1911 - 9 Mar 1912: Chairman of the Military Tribunal, Turkestan Military District
9 Mar 1912 - 1917: Chairman of the Military Tribunal, Odessa Military District

*Lieutenant-General* Vitold-Cheslav Simforianovich **Koreyvo** (18 Aug 1859 - 29 Nov 1938)
7 Nov 1901 - 22 May 1904: Military Judge, Moscow Military District Court
6 Dec 1901: Promoted to *Major-General*
22 May 1904 - 29 Nov 1904: Chief of the Military Justice Section, 1st Manchurian Army
29 Nov 1904 - 11 Mar 1906: Chief of Military Justice, Land & Naval Forces operating against Japan
11 Mar 1906 - 3 May 1907: Military Prosecutor, St. Petersburg Military District
3 May 1907 - 25 Feb 1911: Chairman of the Military Tribunal, St. Petersburg Military District
6 Dec 1907: Promoted to *Lieutenant-General*
25 Feb 1911 - Oct 1917: Deputy Chief Military Prosecutor, Chief of the Military Justice Administration

*Major-General* Baron Aleksandr Karlovich **Korf** (8 Jan 1841 - ?)
26 Nov 1891 - 14 Apr 1894: Commander, 35th Dragoon Regiment
14 Apr 1894: Promoted to *Major-General*
14 Apr 1894 - Jun 1896: Commander, 1st Brigade, 15th Cavalry Division

*Major-General* Baron Nikolai Andreyevich **Korf** (27 Sep 1866 - 14 Oct 1924)
1915 - 1 Apr 1916: Commander, Brigade, 65th Infantry Division
17 Mar 1915: Promoted to *Major-General*
1 Apr 1916 - 30 Apr 1917: Reserve officer, Dvinsk Military District
30 Apr 1917 - 5 Jun 1917: Commander, 40th Infantry Division

*Major-General* Baron Sesil Arturovich von **Korf** (12 Dec 1867 - 9 Aug 1934)
7 Dec 1910 - 27 May 1915: Commander, 5th Hussar Regiment
27 May 1915: Promoted to *Major-General*
27 May 1915 - 1917: Commander, 1st Brigade, 6th Cavalry Division

*Major-General* Grigory Gavrilovich **Korganov** (3 Dec 1844 - 14 Jun 1914)
16 Sep 1899 - 16 Mar 1906: Attached to the Main Artillery Directorate
15 Mar 1906: Promoted to *Major-General*
16 Mar 1906 - 1908: At the disposal of the Main Artillery Directorate
1908: Retired

*Major-General* Georgy Petrovich **Korkashvili** (23 Jan 1865 - Oct 1916)
5 Sep 1907 - 9 Feb 1910: Commander of Artillery, Fortress Kerch
6 Dec 1909: Promoted to *Major-General*
9 Feb 1910 - 16 Jun 1910: Commander of Artillery, Fortress Vyborg
16 Jun 1910 - Oct 1916: Commander of Artillery, Fortress Sevastopol

*General of Infantry* Vladimir Petrovich **Korneyev** (28 Dec 1854 - ?)
22 Feb 1901: Promoted to *Major-General*
22 Feb 1901 - 2 Aug 1901: Commander, 2nd Brigade, 27th Infantry Division
2 Aug 1901 - 11 Oct 1904: Chief of Staff, IV. Army Corps
11 Oct 1904 - 8 Mar 1907: Commander, 66th Replacement Infantry Brigade
8 Mar 1907 - 31 Jan 1913: Commander, 39th Infantry Division

| | |
|---|---|
| 22 Apr 1907: | Promoted to *Lieutenant-General* |
| 31 Jan 1913 - 24 Apr 1913: | Commander, Caucasus Grenadier Division |
| 24 Apr 1913 - 7 Aug 1914: | Commanding General, III. Siberian Army Corps |
| 6 Dec 1913: | Promoted to *General of Infantry* |
| 7 Aug 1914 - 7 Oct 1915: | Deputy Commanding General, Irkutsk Military District |
| 7 Oct 1915 - 20 Mar 1916: | Attached to the Ministry of War |
| 20 Mar 1916 - 10 Aug 1917: | Deputy Commanding General, Irkutsk Military District |
| 10 Aug 1917 - Oct 1917: | Reserve officer, Caucasus Military District |

*Major-General* Konstantin Andreyevich **Kornilov** (13 May 1862 - ?)

| | |
|---|---|
| 26 Jun 1907 - 14 Mar 1916: | Commander, 4th Railway Battalion |
| 6 Dec 1915: | Promoted to *Major-General* |
| 14 Mar 1916 - 1917: | Commander, 6th Railway Brigade |

*General of Infantry* Lavr Georgievich **Kornilov** (18 Aug 1870 - 13 Apr 1918)

| | |
|---|---|
| 3 Jun 1911 - 4 Jul 1913: | Commander, 2nd Amur District |
| 26 Dec 1911: | Promoted to *Major-General* |
| 4 Jul 1913 - 24 Aug 1914: | Commander, 1st Brigade, 9th Siberian Rifle Division |
| 24 Aug 1914 - 11 Sep 1914: | Acting Commander, 48th Infantry Division |
| 26 Aug 1914: | Promoted to *Lieutenant-General* |
| 11 Sep 1914 - 30 Dec 1914: | Commander, 1st Brigade, 49th Infantry Division |
| 30 Dec 1914 - 12 May 1915: | Commander, 48th Infantry Division |
| 12 May 1915 - Jul 1916: | Prisoner of war, Austria |
| 13 Sep 1916 - 2 Mar 1917: | Commanding General, XXV. Army Corps |
| 2 Mar 1917 - 29 Apr 1917: | Commanding General, Petrograd Military District |
| 29 Apr 1917 - 7 Jul 1917: | C-in-C, 8th Army |
| 27 Jun 1917: | Promoted to *General of Infantry* |
| 7 Jul 1917 - 18 Jul 1917: | C-in-C, Southwestern Front |
| 19 Jul 1917 - 27 Aug 1917: | Supreme Commander-in-Chief |
| 29 Aug 1917: | Dismissed |

*Major-General of the Fleet* Nikolai Aleksandrovich **Kornilov** (31 Dec 1865 - ?)

| | |
|---|---|
| 1915 - 1917: | Commandant, Petrograd Joint Schools for Seagoing Engineers & Merchant Fleet |
| 6 Dec 1915: | Promoted to *Major-General of the Fleet* |

*Major-General* Aleksandr Ivanovich **Kornilovich** (6 Mar 1839 - ?)

| | |
|---|---|
| 11 Jun 1878 - 24 Aug 1888: | Commander of Artillery Training Polygon, Kiev Military District |
| 30 Aug 1885: | Promoted to *Major-General* |
| 24 Aug 1888 - 9 Sep 1895: | Commander, 34th Artillery Brigade |

*Major-General* Konstantin Petrovich **Kornilovich** (4 Dec 1844 - ?)

| | |
|---|---|
| 17 Nov 1879 - 1 Dec 1892: | Military Judge, Caucasus Military District Court |
| 30 Aug 1889: | Promoted to *Major-General* |
| 1 Dec 1892 - 1897: | Military Judge, Turkestan Military District Court |

*Lieutenant-General* Aleksandr Fyodorovich **Korobka** (14 Feb 1845 - 5 Oct 1906)
13 Jun 1894: Promoted to *Major-General*
13 Jun 1894 - 29 Jul 1899: Commander, 2nd Brigade, 36th Infantry Division
29 Jul 1899 - 23 Jul 1900: Commander, 2nd Turkestan Line Brigade
23 Jul 1900 - 1 Jul 1903: Commander, 2nd Turkestan Rifle Brigade
1 Jul 1903 - 1903: Commander, 2nd Turkestan Rifle Division
1903: Promoted to *Lieutenant-General*
1903: Retired

*General of Artillery* Mikhail Nikolayevich **Korobkov** (12 Oct 1842 - 2 Jun 1914)
19 Sep 1891: Promoted to *Major-General*
19 Sep 1891 - 26 Jul 1893: Commandant of Bryansk Regional Arsenal
26 Jul 1893 - 26 Jan 1900: Commandant of St. Petersburg Regional Arsenal
26 Jan 1900 - 1914: Inspector of Artillery Acceptance, Main Artillery Directorate
6 Dec 1900: Promoted to *Lieutenant-General*
1914 - 2 Jun 1914: Chief of Technical Acceptance, Main Artillery Directorate
1914: Promoted to *General of Artillery*

*General of Artillery* Aleksey Petrovich **Korochentsev** (9 Mar 1832 - 9 Jan 1904)
15 May 1883: Promoted to *Major-General*
15 May 1883 - 13 Oct 1886: Commander, Ataman Life Guards Regiment
13 Oct 1886 - 10 Mar 1893: Commander, 2nd Consolidated Cossack Division
10 Mar 1893 - 1899: Commander of Artillery, Don Cossack Army
30 Aug 1893: Promoted to *Lieutenant-General*
1899 - 1900: Ataman, Don Cossack Army
19 Nov 1899: Promoted to *General of Artillery*

*Lieutenant-General* Vasily Petrovich **Korochentsov** (9 Jul 1844 - ?)
11 May 1889: Promoted to *Major-General*
11 May 1889 - 4 Feb 1893: Commander, Life Guards Cossack Regiment
4 Feb 1893 - 6 Aug 1894: Unassigned
6 Aug 1894 - 1 Mar 1895: Commander, 2nd Brigade, 7th Cavalry Division
1 Mar 1895 - 3 Feb 1900: Commander, 2nd Brigade, 10th Cavalry Division
3 Feb 1900: Dismissed from the service
25 Jun 1903 - 3 Mar 1910: Reinstated; Attached to the General Staff
3 Mar 1910: Promoted to *Lieutenant-General*
3 Mar 1910: Retired

*Lieutenant-General* Prokofy Grigoryevich **Korolenko** (8 Jul 1820 - 29 Apr 1910)
Aug 1869 - 20 May 1873: Commander, 8th Infantry Battalion, Black Sea Army
17 Apr 1871: Promoted to *Major-General*
20 May 1873 - 29 Apr 1910: Attached to the Kuban Cossack Army
6 Oct 1888: Promoted to *Lieutenant-General*

*Lieutenant-General* Mikhail Efimovich **Korolev** (4 Jan 1841 - ?)
1 Jul 1882 - 1 Feb 1898: Section Chief, Main Cossack Directorate

30 Aug 1887: Promoted to *Major-General*
1 Feb 1898 - 1906: Deputy Chief of the Main Cossack Directorate
6 Dec 1898: Promoted to *Lieutenant-General*

*Vice-Admiral* Nikolai Semyonovich **Korolev** (18 Jun 1849 - 28 Jun 1911)
5 Apr 1902 - 9 Sep 1902: Junior Flagman, Pacific Squadron
14 Apr 1902: Promoted to *Rear-Admiral*
9 Sep 1902 - 1 Aug 1905: Director of Lighthouses & Navigation, Caspian Sea
1 Aug 1905 - 31 Oct 1905: Commander, Emperor Aleksandr III Port (Libau)
31 Oct 1905: Promoted to *Vice-Admiral*
31 Oct 1905: Retired

*Lieutenant-General* Aleksey Lvovich **Korolkov** (27 Jan 1859 - 1931)
8 Mar 1901 - 20 Jul 1917: Professor, Mikhailovsky Artillery Academy
17 Apr 1905: Promoted to *Major-General*
6 Apr 1914: Promoted to *Lieutenant-General*
20 Jul 1917: Dismissed

*Major-General* Fyodor Ivanovich **Korolkov** (11 Sep 1876 - Dec 1920)
5 Feb 1916 - 3 Jan 1917: Commander, 48th Infantry Regiment
12 Oct 1916: Promoted to *Major-General*
3 Jan 1917 - 23 Jul 1917: Special Assignments General, 6th Army
23 Jul 1917 - Oct 1917: Commander, 61st Infantry Division

*Lieutenant-General* Georgy Karpovich **Korolkov** (4 Feb 1863 - 1936)
28 Mar 1913: Promoted to *Major-General*
28 Mar 1913 - 14 Dec 1914: Chief of Staff, Fortress Vladivostok
14 Dec 1914 - 11 Mar 1917: Chief of Staff, IV. Siberian Army Corps
11 Mar 1917 - 18 May 1917: Commander, 21st Siberian Rifle Division
18 May 1917 - 7 Sep 1917: Commanding General, IV. Siberian Army Corps
20 May 1917: Promoted to *Lieutenant-General*
7 Sep 1917 - 1918: Reserve officer, Moscow Military District

*General of Infantry* Nikolai Ivanovich **Korolkov** (28 Dec 1837 - 13 Feb 1906)
7 Jan 1878 - 24 Dec 1884: Officer for Special Assignments, Turkestan Military District
30 Aug 1882: Promoted to *Major-General*
24 Dec 1884 - 26 Sep 1887: Commander, 4th Turkestan Line Brigade
26 Sep 1887 - 30 Jun 1893: Governor of Ferghana Region
30 Aug 1892: Promoted to *Lieutenant-General*
30 Jun 1893 - 11 May 1905: Governor of Syr-Darya Region
1898: Acting Governor-General of Turkestan
11 May 1905 - 3 Jan 1906: Member of the Military Council
3 Jan 1906: Promoted to *General of Infantry*
3 Jan 1906: Retired

*Major-General* Yaroslav Ivanovich **Korolkov** (2 Sep 1843 - 2 Jul 1933)
20 Dec 1899 - 1902: Commander, 1st East Siberian Artillery Brigade

1 Jan 1901: Promoted to *Major-General*
1902: Retired

*Lieutenant-General* Izmail Vladimirovich **Korostovets** (1 Aug 1863 - 17 Mar 1933)
11 Jul 1907 - 1917: Governor of Estonia
6 Dec 1910: Promoted to *Major-General*
6 Dec 1916: Promoted to *Lieutenant-General*

*Lieutenant-General* Konstantin Vladimirovich **Korostovets** (3 May 1857 - ?)
20 Jul 1899 - 12 May 1912: Attached to the Ministry of War
28 Mar 1904: Promoted to *Major-General*
12 May 1912: Promoted to *Lieutenant-General*
12 May 1912: Retired

*Lieutenant-General* Nikolai Nikolayevich **Korotkevich** (24 Nov 1859 - ?)
4 Mar 1904 - 14 Aug 1905: Commander, 56th Infantry Regiment
21 Feb 1905: Promoted to *Major-General*
14 Aug 1905 - 12 Dec 1905: Commander, 2nd Brigade, 31st Infantry Division
12 Dec 1905 - 17 Oct 1910: Commander, 2nd Brigade, 30th Infantry Division
17 Oct 1910 - 13 May 1914: Commander, 1st Finnish Rifle Brigade
13 May 1914: Promoted to *Lieutenant-General*
13 May 1914 - 8 May 1915: Commander, 40th Infantry Division
8 May 1915 - 1917: Commanding General, XXXVI. Army Corps

*Lieutenant-General* Pyotr Nikolayevich **Korovin** (13 Jun 1854 - Sep 1913)
5 Nov 1908 - Sep 1913: Commander, 1st Brigade, 6th Siberian Rifle Division
15 Jan 1909: Promoted to *Major-General*
Sep 1913: Promoted to *Lieutenant-General*

*Lieutenant-General of the Fleet* Nikolai Georgiyevich **Korsakevich** (9 May 1857 - ?)
6 Dec 1907: Promoted to *Major-General of the Admiralty*
31 Dec 1907 - ?: Senior Deputy Chief Inspector of Naval Construction
1914: Promoted to *Lieutenant-General of the Fleet*

*Major-General* Vladimir Nikitich **Korsakov** (20 Dec 1846 - 12 Oct 1900)
6 Dec 1897: Promoted to *Major-General*
6 Dec 1897 - 12 Oct 1900: General for Special Assignments, Ministry of War

*Major-General* Nikolai Vasilyevich **Korshunov** (12 Jun 1844 - ?)
14 Aug 1896 - 14 Feb 1901: Commander, 2nd Grenadier Regiment
14 Feb 1901: Promoted to *Major-General*
14 Feb 1901 - May 1904: Commander, 1st Brigade, 1st Grenadier Division

*Major-General* Florentin Dmitriyevich **Korsun** (5 Jan 1863 - 3 Jul 1933)
3 Feb 1916 - 1917: Commander, 105th Artillery Brigade
15 Feb 1916: Promoted to *Major-General*

*Major-General* Georgy Ivanovich **Kortatstsi** (10 Aug 1866 - 29 Dec 1932)
26 Aug 1910 - 30 Dec 1914: Commander, 133rd Infantry Regiment
2 Nov 1914: Promoted to *Major-General*
30 Dec 1914 - 21 Mar 1915: Reserve officer, Kiev Military District
21 Mar 1915 - 1917: Duty General, Southwestern Front
1917 - 14 Jun 1917: Duty General, High Command

*Lieutenant-General* Aleksandr Nikolayevich **Korulsky** (21 Aug 1863 - ?)
10 Jun 1906 - 22 Feb 1911: Clerk, Office of the Ministry of War
18 Apr 1910: Promoted to *Major-General*
22 Feb 1911 - Aug 1914: Director of Legislative Affairs, Office of the Ministry of War
Aug 1914 - 7 Jan 1915: General for Assignments, Northwestern Front
7 Jan 1915 - Jun 1916: Director of Legislative Affairs, Office of the Ministry of War
22 Mar 1915: Promoted to *Lieutenant-General*
Jun 1916 - 7 Sep 1916: Chief, Office of the Ministry of War
7 Sep 1916 - Jan 1917: Reserve officer, Petrograd Military District
Jan 1917 - 12 May 1917: Military Governor of Syr-Darya Region
12 May 1917 - Feb 1918: Reserve officer, Petrograd Military District

*Major-General* Pyotr Aleksandrovich **Korvin-Piotrovsky** (29 Dec 1855 - ?)
16 Sep 1902: Promoted to *Major-General*
16 Sep 1902 - 14 Nov 1906: Commander, 2nd Brigade, 1st Infantry Division

*Lieutenant-General* Nikolai Alekseyevich **Kosach** (13 Dec 1844 - 13 Jun 1906)
21 Aug 1892 - 13 Jun 1906: Deputy Governor of St. Petersburg
30 Aug 1894: Promoted to *Major-General*
Jun 1906: Promoted to *Lieutenant-General*

*Lieutenant-General* Vladimir Andreyevich **Kosagovsky** (14 Jan 1857 - 12 Sep 1918)
7 May 1894 - 1903: Attached to the Commanding General, Caucasus Military District
6 May 1900: Promoted to *Major-General*
1903 - Apr 1904: Attached to the General Staff
Apr 1904 - Jul 1904: Commander, Lyaokheyskim Detachment
Jul 1904 - Aug 1904: Commander, Siberian Cossack Division
Aug 1904 - Apr 1905: Commander, Lyaokheyskim Detachment
Apr 1905 - 5 Dec 1905: Commander, Amur Cossack Brigade
5 Dec 1905 - 16 Jun 1906: Acting Commanding General, II. Turkestan Army Corps, Acting Military Commander, Trans-Caspian Region
1906: Promoted to *Lieutenant-General*
Jun 1906: Retired

*Major-General* Aleksandr Petrovich **Koshelev** (3 Jan 1857 - ?)
19 Jan 1904 - 28 Mar 1908: Military Judge, Vilnius Military District Court
28 Mar 1904: Promoted to *Major-General*
28 Mar 1908 - 22 Apr 1917: Military Judge, Moscow Military District Court

22 Apr 1917:                        Dismissed

*Lieutenant-General* Pavel Yefimovich **Koshlich** (20 Aug 1861 - ?)
9 Aug 1905 - 1915:                  Inspector of Classes, Odessa Cadet Corps
6 Dec 1910:                         Promoted to *Major-General*
1915 - 12 May 1917:                 Director, Odessa Cadet Corps
12 May 1917:                        Promoted to *Lieutenant-General*
12 May 1917:                        Dismissed

*Major-General* Iosif Fedotovich **Kosinsky** (4 Apr 1848 - ?)
1 Mar 1905:                         Promoted to *Major-General*
1 Mar 1905 - Jun 1907:              Commander, 31st Artillery Brigade

*Major-General* Vladimir Andreyevich **Kosogovsky** (14 Jan 1857 - 1918)
7 Mar 1894 - 1903:                  At the disposal of the Commanding General, Caucasus
                                    Military District,
                                    Commander, Persian Cossack Brigade
7 Jul 1900:                         Promoted to *Major-General*
1904 - 1905:                        Commander, Liaohe Group, Manchuria
1905:                               Acting Commander, Siberian Cossack Division
1905:                               Commander, Consolidated Amur Cossack Brigade
1905 - 1908:                        Commander, Transcaspian Region

*Lieutenant-General* Vasily Ivanovich **Kosov** (6 Mar 1860 - ?)
2 Nov 1902 - 4 Oct 1905:            Commander, 8th Dragoon Regiment
4 Aug 1905:                         Promoted to *Major-General*
4 Oct 1905 - 18 Aug 1908:           Commander, 2nd Brigade, 1st Cavalry Division
18 Aug 1908 - 23 Jan 1910:          Duty General, Moscow Military District
23 Jan 1910 - 1912:                 Military Governor, Transbaikal Region,
                                    Ataman, Transbaikal Cossack Army
6 Dec 1911:                         Promoted to *Lieutenant-General*

*Lieutenant-General* Aleksandr Ignatyevich **Kossovich** (7 Mar 1841 - ?)
1 Nov 1885 - 7 May 1893:            Commander, 141st Infantry Regiment
16 Mar 1893:                        Promoted to *Major-General*
7 May 1893 - 29 Jan 1901:           Commander, 1st Brigade, 1st Grenadier Division
29 Jan 1901 - 7 Mar 1904:           Commander, 36th Infantry Division
1 Apr 1901:                         Promoted to *Lieutenant-General*

*Rear-Admiral* Iosif Vasilyevich **Kossovich** (8 Sep 1855 - 1928)
24 Aug 1906 - 30 Apr 1907:          Commander, 6th, 9th, 15th Naval Depots
14 Sep 1906 - 25 Sep 1906:          Acting Commander, Port of Emperor Aleksandr III
                                    (Libau)
30 Apr 1907:                        Promoted to *Rear-Admiral*
30 Apr 1907:                        Retired

*Lieutenant-General* Lev Ignatyevich **Kossovich** (16 Mar 1848 - ?)
6 Sep 1899:                         Promoted to *Major-General*

| | |
|---|---|
| 6 Sep 1899 - 26 Jun 1902: | Commander, 2nd Brigade, 19th Infantry Division |
| 26 Jun 1902 - 31 Jan 1904: | Commander, 3rd Siberian Reserve Infantry Brigade |
| 31 Jan 1904 - 19 Feb 1905: | Commander, 3rd Siberian Infantry Division |
| 19 Feb 1905 - 22 Nov 1906: | Commandant, Kiev Military School |
| 22 Nov 1906 - 22 Feb 1907: | Commander, 9th Infantry Division |
| 6 Dec 1906: | Promoted to *Lieutenant-General* |
| 22 Feb 1907: | Retired |

*General of Artillery* Apostol Spiridonovich **Kostanda** (12 Dec 1817 - 23 Nov 1898)

| | |
|---|---|
| 30 Aug 1858: | Promoted to *Major-General* |
| 30 Aug 1858 - 24 Dec 1863: | Attached to the Master-General of Ordnance |
| 24 Dec 1863 - 5 Jun 1864: | Commander, 8th Infantry Division |
| 5 Jun 1864 - 30 Aug 1864: | Unassigned |
| 30 Aug 1864: | Promoted to *Lieutenant-General* |
| 30 Aug 1864 - 6 Nov 1869: | Commander, 5th infantry Division |
| 6 Nov 1869 - 14 Jun 1872: | Commander, 2nd Grenadier Division |
| 14 Jun 1872 - 29 Jan 1879: | Commander of Artillery, Warsaw Military District |
| 29 Jun 1874: | Promoted to *General-Adjutant* |
| 16 Apr 1878: | Promoted to *General of Artillery* |
| 29 Jan 1879 - 1 Mar 1880: | Commander of Artillery, St. Petersburg Military District |
| 1 Mar 1880 - 30 Aug 1888: | Deputy Commanding General, St. Petersburg Military District |
| 30 Aug 1888 - 26 May 1896: | Commanding General, Moscow Military District |
| 28 Feb 1891 - 5 May 1891: | Acting Governor-General of Moscow |
| 26 May 1896 - 23 Nov 1898: | Member of the State Council |

*Major-General* Nikolai Fyodorovich **Kostenetsky** (24 May 1835 - ?)

| | |
|---|---|
| 17 Sep 1882 - 19 Jul 1886: | Commander of Artillery, Fortress Terek-Dagestan |
| 30 Aug 1885: | Promoted to *Major-General* |
| 19 Jul 1886 - 1898: | Deputy Commander of Artillery, Caucasus Military District |

*Major-General* Aleksandr Ivanovich **Kostenko** (23 Jan 1862 - ?)

| | |
|---|---|
| 24 Dec 1914 - 6 May 1917: | Commander, 17th Uhlan Regiment |
| 16 Apr 1916: | Promoted to *Major-General* |
| 6 May 1917 - 1917: | Commander, 1st Brigade, 16th Cavalry Division |

*Lieutenant-General* Mikhail Ivanovich **Kostenko** (1 Nov 1855 - ?)

| | |
|---|---|
| 6 Mar 1902 - 18 Apr 1906: | Military Judge, Amur Military District Court |
| 6 Apr 1903: | Promoted to *Major-General* |
| ?: | Chairman, Fortress Port Arthur Military Court |
| 18 Apr 1906 - 28 May 1908: | Military Judge, Kiev Military District Court |
| 28 May 1908 - 28 May 1909: | Military Prosecutor, Caucasus Military District Court |
| 28 May 1909 - 1912: | Military Prosecutor, Kiev Military District Court |
| 6 Dec 1909: | Promoted to *Lieutenant-General* |

*Major-General* Ivan Matveyevich **Kostin** (27 Aug 1855 - ?)

| | |
|---|---|
| 25 Jul 1906 - 21 Feb 1915: | Regional Military Commander, Don Cossack Army |

6 Dec 1911: Promoted to *Major-General*
21 Feb 1915 - 1917: Commander, 1st Don Cossack Brigade

*Major-General* Konstantin Mikhailovich **Kostin**
? - 13 Dec 1909: Commander, 9th Don Cossack Regiment
13 Dec 1909: Promoted to *Major-General*
13 Dec 1909: Retired

*Lieutenant-General* Vladimir Ivanovich **Kostin** (14 Dec 1837 - 26 Mar 1899)
7 Oct 1890 - 5 May 1894: Military Judge, Warsaw Military District Court
30 Aug 1892: Promoted to *Major-General*
5 May 1894 - 26 Mar 1899: Military Judge, Moscow Military District Court
1899: Promoted to *Lieutenant-General*

*Major-General* Tikhon Dmitriyevich **Kostitsyn** (24 Feb 1874 - ?)
8 Jun 1915 - 1917: Deputy Intendant, Caucasus Military District
6 Dec 1916: Promoted to *Major-General*

*Major-General* Dmitry Koronatovich **Kostomarov** (15 Oct 1857 - 10 Feb 1920)
11 Jan 1909 - 20 Jan 1917: Commander of Engineers, Fortress Kars
29 Mar 1909: Promoted to *Major-General*
20 Jan 1917 - Oct 1917: Reserve officer, Petrograd Military District

*Major-General* Matvey Petrovich **Kostromin** (15 Jan 1863 - 22 Jun 1916)
1915 - 22 Jun 1916: Commander, 87th Infantry Regiment
21 Oct 1916: Posthumously promoted to *Major-General*

*Major-General* Dmitry Yevstafyevich **Kostrov** (29 May 1871 - 29 Apr 1911)
26 Oct 1908 - 29 Apr 1911: Commander, 4th Vladivostok Fortress Artillery Regiment
1911: Promoted to *Major-General*

*Major-General* Semyon Adamovich **Kostsesha-Statkovsky** (5 Mar 1854 - ?)
12 Aug 1912 - 19 Dec 1915: Member of the Steering Committee for Fortress Osovets, Ministry of War
6 Dec 1912: Promoted to *Major-General*
19 Dec 1915 - 1917: Reserve officer, Petrograd Military District

*Lieutenant-General* Nikolai Pavlovich **Kostylev** (10 Oct 1852 - ?)
13 Jun 1907: Promoted to *Major-General*
13 Jun 1907 - 18 Feb 1912: Commander, 44th Artillery Brigade
18 Feb 1912 - 22 Apr 1917: Inspector of Artillery, 2nd Siberian Army Corps
13 Jun 1913: Promoted to *Lieutenant-General*
22 Apr 1917: Dismissed

*General of Artillery* Pyotr Zakharovich **Kostyrko** (23 Aug 1843 - 25 Dec 1913)
4 May 1880 - 14 Jan 1891: Chief of Arsenal Department, Main Artillery Directorate
30 Aug 1889: Promoted to *Major-General*

| | |
|---|---|
| 14 Jan 1891 - 25 Dec 1913: | Member of the Artillery Committee, Main Artillery Directorate |
| 6 Dec 1897: | Promoted to *Lieutenant-General* |
| 1898 - 1904 (occasionally): | Acting Deputy Master-General of Ordnance |
| 1900 - 12 Dec 1904: | Chairman, Commission for Field Artillery |
| 12 Dec 1904 - 25 Dec 1913: | Member of the Military Council |
| 6 Dec 1906: | Promoted to *General of Artillery* |

*Lieutenant-General* Pyotr Ivanovich **Kosyakin** (4 Oct 1842 - 23 Aug 1918)

| | |
|---|---|
| 2 Apr 1899: | Promoted to *Major-General* |
| 2 Apr 1899 - 18 Jun 1899: | Commander, 1st Brigade, 2nd Caucasus Cossack Division |
| 18 Jun 1899 - 20 Jan 1907: | Ataman, Maikop Division, Kuban Region |
| 20 Jan 1907 - 2 Dec 1916: | Deputy Commander, Kuban Region, Ataman, Kuban Cossack Army |
| 2 Dec 1916: | Promoted to *Lieutenant-General* |
| 2 Dec 1916: | Dismissed |

*General of Infantry* Andrei Ivanovich **Kosych** (1 Oct 1833 - 15 Mar 1917)

| | |
|---|---|
| 27 Jul 1875: | Promoted to *Major-General* |
| 27 Jul 1875 - 24 Aug 1875: | Commander, 2nd Brigade, 9th Cavalry Division |
| 24 Aug 1875 - 31 Aug 1876: | Commander, 2nd Brigade, 8th Cavalry Division |
| 31 Aug 1878 - 20 Feb 1877: | Deputy Chief of Staff, Odessa Military District |
| 20 Feb 1877 - 25 Sep 1879: | Chief of Staff, XII. Army Corps |
| 25 Sep 1879 - 30 Aug 1881: | Commander, 7th Cavalry Division |
| 30 Aug 1881 - 30 May 1887: | Chief of Staff, Kiev Military District |
| 6 May 1884: | Promoted to *Lieutenant-General* |
| 30 May 1887 - 11 Dec 1891: | Governor of Saratov |
| 11 Dec 1891 - 8 Mar 1895: | Commanding General, IV. Army Corps |
| 8 Mar 1895 - 15 Sep 1901: | Deputy Commanding General, Kiev Military District |
| 6 Dec 1897: | Promoted to *General of Infantry* |
| 14 Jul 1900 - 19 Jul 1900: | Acting Commanding General, Kiev Military District |
| 5 May 1901 - 12 May 1901: | Acting Commanding General, Kiev Military District |
| 26 May 1901 - 26 Jul 1901: | Acting Commanding General, Kiev Military District |
| 15 Sep 1901 - 21 Oct 1905: | Commanding General, Kazan Military District |
| 21 Oct 1905 - 15 Mar 1917: | Member, Council of State |

*Major-General* Aleksandr Ivanovich **Kotelnikov** (22 Feb 1858 - ?)

| | |
|---|---|
| 10 Aug 1904 - 1914: | Commander, 1st Field Gendarmerie Squadron |
| 1914: | Promoted to *Major-General* |
| 1914: | Retired |

*Major-General* Aleksandr Fridrikhovich von **Koten** (27 Mar 1867 - 1920)

| | |
|---|---|
| 4 Jan 1910 - 13 Mar 1917: | Senator, Imperial Finnish Senate |
| 6 Dec 1912: | Promoted to *Major-General* |
| 13 Mar 1917: | Dismissed |

*Major-General* Baron Gustav-Aksel Ferdinandovich von **Koten** (5 Jul 1843 - 25 Jun 1906)
12 Dec 1888 - 8 Mar 1895: Commander, 65$^{th}$ Infantry Regiment
14 Nov 1894: Promoted to *Major-General*
8 Mar 1895 - 13 Dec 1898: Commander, Lithuanian Life Guards Regiment
13 Dec 1898 - 8 Jan 1900: Governor of Vaasa Province
8 Jan 1900 - 25 Jun 1906: Governor of Tavastehus

*Major-General* Mikhail Fridrikhovich von **Koten** (29 Sep 1870 - 4 Mar 1917)
29 Dec 1909 - 1914: Chief of Police, St. Petersburg
1914: Promoted to *Major-General*
1914 - 4 Mar 1917: Chief of Staff, Fortress Kronstadt

*Major-General* Ivan Ivanovich **Kotikov** (21 Jun 1865 - ?)
26 Mar 1910 - 23 Nov 1915: Commander, 32$^{nd}$ Siberian Rifle Regiment
15 Feb 1915: Promoted to *Major-General*
23 Nov 1915 - 1917: Reserve officer, Minsk Military District

*Lieutenant-General* Andrey Panteleymonovich **Kotovsky** (13 Oct 1857 - ?)
28 Nov 1909 - 30 Jul 1910: Commander, 2$^{nd}$ Replacement Artillery Brigade
30 Jul 1910 - 26 Mar 1915: Commander, 49$^{th}$ Artillery Brigade
2 Aug 1910: Promoted to *Major-General*
26 Mar 1915 - 1917: Inspector of Artillery, V. Caucasus Army Corps
6 Dec 1916: Promoted to *Lieutenant-General*

*Major-General* Otto Ryurikovich **Kotsebue** (19 Sep 1860 - 1 Jun 1936)
6 Dec 1911: Promoted to *Major-General*
6 Dec 1911 - 4 Jun 1917: Master of the Horse, Grand Duke Pyotr Nikolayevich
4 Jun 1917: Dismissed

*Lieutenant-General* Pavel Aristovich von **Kotsebue** (8 Jun 1865 - 1947)
28 Oct 1914: Promoted to *Major-General*
28 Oct 1914 - 11 Nov 1915: Chief of Staff, XXIX. Army Corps
11 Nov 1915 - 27 Jan 1916: Commander, 1$^{st}$ Rifle Brigade
17 Jan 1916 - 14 May 1917: Commander, 1$^{st}$ Rifle Division
14 May 1917 - 1918: Commanding General, XLVII. Army Corps
20 May 1917: Promoted to *Lieutenant-General*

*Major-General* Pavel Avgustovich **Kotsebue** (17 Feb 1845 - ?)
4 Jul 1890: Promoted to *Major-General*
4 Jul 1890 - 13 Sep 1895: Commander, 1$^{st}$ Brigade, 12$^{th}$ Infantry Division

*General of Cavalry* Count Fyodor Karlovich **Kotsebue-Pillar von Pilkhau** (5 Jul 1848 - 7 Aug 1911)
20 Dec 1898: Promoted to *Major-General*
20 Dec 1898 - 1 Apr 1904: Ataman, Terek Cossack Army,
 Senior Deputy Chief, Terek Region
1 Apr 1904 - 21 Dec 1905: Mayor, Rostov-on-Don
17 Apr 1905: Promoted to *Lieutenant-General*

| | |
|---|---|
| 21 Dec 1905 - 9 Aug 1910: | Attached to the Ministry of the Interior |
| 9 Aug 1910: | Promoted to *General of Cavalry* |
| 9 Aug 1910: | Retired |

*Lieutenant-General* Vladimir Ivanovich **Kotsurik** (2 Jun 1854 - ?)

| | |
|---|---|
| 18 Jun 1904: | Promoted to *Major-General* |
| 18 Jun 1904 - 29 Jan 1913: | Commander, 1st Brigade, 15th Cavalry Division |
| 29 Jan 1913: | Promoted to *Lieutenant-General* |
| 29 Jan 1913: | Retired |
| 1916 - 1917: | Recalled; Commander, 52nd Militia Brigade |
| 1917: | Commanding General, V. Militia Corps |

*Lieutenant-General* Yevgeny Yakovlevich **Kotyuzhinsky** (5 Jan 1859 - ?)

| | |
|---|---|
| 24 Jul 1906 - 4 Dec 1912: | Commander, 52nd Infantry Regiment |
| 29 Oct 1911: | Promoted to *Major-General* |
| ?: | Acting Commander, 2nd Brigade, 13th Infantry Division |
| 4 Dec 1912: | Retired |
| 25 Jul 1914 - 25 Aug 1915: | Recalled; Commander, Brigade, 34th Infantry Division |
| 25 Aug 1915 - 21 Jan 1916: | Commander, 125th Infantry Division |
| 21 Jan 1916 - 14 Sep 1916: | Reserve officer, Kiev Military District |
| 14 Sep 1916 - 27 Sep 1916: | Reserve officer, Odessa Military District |
| 27 Sep 1916 - 25 Apr 1917: | Chairman, Commission for Requisitioning of Goods, Odessa Customs Department |
| 25 Apr 1917 - 7 Aug 1917: | Chairman, Commission for Verification of Officers |
| 7 Aug 1917: | Promoted to *Lieutenant-General* |
| 7 Aug 1917 - ?: | Commander, 193rd Infantry Division |

*Lieutenant-General* Aleksandr Nikolayevich **Kovalenko** (30 Aug 1856 - ?)

| | |
|---|---|
| 8 Jan 1908: | Promoted to *Major-General* |
| 8 Jan 1908 - 17 Oct 1910: | Commander, 2nd Sapper Brigade |
| 17 Oct 1910 - 29 Nov 1912: | Inspector of Field Engineers, Vilnius Military District |
| 29 Nov 1912 - Aug 1914: | Inspector of Engineers, Vilnius Military District |
| 1913: | Promoted to *Lieutenant-General* |
| Aug 1914 - 21 Jan 1915: | Deputy Chief of Engineering Logistics, Northwestern Front |
| 21 Jan 1915 - 1916: | Chief of Engineering Logistics, Northwestern Front |
| 1916 - 1917: | Chief of Engineering Logistics, Western Front |

*Major-General* Viktor Semyonovich **Kovalev** (4 Nov 1844 - ?)

| | |
|---|---|
| 17 Dec 1897: | Promoted to *Major-General* |
| 17 Dec 1897 - 3 May 1904: | Commander, Trans-Caspian Cossack Brigade |

*Major-General* Anatoly Gektorovich **Kovalevsky** (16 Sep 1861 - ?)

| | |
|---|---|
| 30 Aug 1910 - 13 May 1914: | Commander, 7th Pontoon Battalion |
| 13 May 1914: | Promoted to *Major-General* |
| 13 May 1914: | Retired |
| 25 May 1915 - 18 Jul 1915: | Recalled; Reserve officer, Petrograd Military District |
| 18 Jul 1915 - 28 May 1917: | Commandant, Ust-Izhora Engineer Ensign Training |

| | School |
|---|---|
| 28 May 1917: | Dismissed |

*Major-General* Dmitry Ivanovich **Kovalevsky** (26 Oct 1833 - 9 Mar 1906)
| 16 Oct 1889: | Promoted to *Major-General* |
|---|---|
| 16 Oct 1889 - 24 Nov 1895: | Commander, 1st Brigade, 23rd Infantry Division |
| 24 Nov 1895: | Retired |

*Major-General* Konstantin Afanasyevich **Kovalevsky** (1853 - 1908)
| 5 Sep 1903 - 1908: | Commander of Gendarmerie, Kiev Province |
|---|---|
| 6 Dec 1907: | Promoted to *Major-General* |

*Major-General* Nikolai Aleksandrovich **Kovalevsky** (19 May 1861 - ?)
| 31 Dec 1913 - 1917: | Deputy Chief of Kiev Arsenal |
|---|---|
| 6 Dec 1916: | Promoted to *Major-General* |

*Lieutenant-General* Vladimir Aleksandrovich **Kovalevsky** (9 Jul 1852 - 1913)
| 4 Sep 1896 - 26 Mar 1901: | Commander, 15th Dragoon Regiment |
|---|---|
| 26 Mar 1901: | Promoted to *Major-General* |
| 26 Mar 1901 - Sep 1907: | Commander, 1st Brigade, 6th Cavalry Division |
| 1907: | Promoted to *Lieutenant-General* |

*Lieutenant-General* Nikolai Aleksandrovich **Kovalkov** (30 Sep 1851 - ?)
| 21 Jun 1900: | Promoted to *Major-General* |
|---|---|
| 21 Jun 1900 - 1 Nov 1900: | Commander, 2nd Brigade, 12th Cavalry Division |
| 1 Nov 1900 - Oct 1907: | Commander, 1st Brigade, 14th Cavalry Division |
| Oct 1907: | Promoted to *Lieutenant-General* |
| Oct 1907: | Retired |
| 22 Apr 1914 - 1917: | Recalled; At the disposal of the Commanding General, Warsaw Military District |

*Major-General* Grigory Yakovlevich **Kovalsky** (1 Apr 1865 - ?)
| 23 Sep 1916 - 1917: | Deputy Commander, 4th Siberian Replacement Rifle Brigade |
|---|---|
| 29 Oct 1916: | Promoted to *Major-General* |

*Lieutenant-General* Aleksandr Matveyevich **Kovanko** (4 Mar 1856 - 20 Apr 1919)
| 30 Dec 1905 - 4 Aug 1910: | Commandant, Aviation Training Park |
|---|---|
| 6 Dec 1906: | Promoted to *Major-General* |
| 4 Aug 1910 - 1917. | Commandant, Aviation School |
| 14 Apr 1913: | Promoted to *Lieutenant-General* |

*Major-General* Nikolai Aleksandrovich **Kovanko** (8 May 1844 - ?)
| 9 Apr 1901 - 27 Nov 1904: | Commander, 45th Artillery Brigade |
|---|---|
| 6 Dec 1901: | Promoted to *Major-General* |

*General of Infantry* Eduard Avrelianovich **Koversky** (17 Mar 1837 - 30 Jan 1916)
| 5 Apr 1881 - 2 May 1894: | Chief, Geodetic Sub-Section, Military Topographical |
|---|---|

|  |  |
|---|---|
| | Section, General Staff |
| 15 May 1883: | Promoted to *Major-General* |
| 2 May 1894 - 11 Jan 1904: | Chief of Surveying, Western Border Region, Member, Military Scientific Committee, General Staff |
| 6 Dec 1895: | Promoted to *Lieutenant-General* |
| 11 Jan 1904 - 30 Jan 1916: | Chief of Topographical Survey, St. Petersburg Province & Finland |
| 1916: | Posthumously promoted to *General of Infantry* |

*Major-General of the Fleet* Lyudvig Andreyevich **Kovessky** (5 Aug 1870 - 27 Oct 1944)

| | |
|---|---|
| 1 Jan 1915 - 1917: | Chief of General Affairs Division, Main Shipbuilding Directorate |
| 9 Feb 1915 - 1917: | Member, Board of Shipbuilding |
| 22 Mar 1915: | Promoted to *Major-General of the Fleet* |

*Major-General* Sergey Ivanovich **Kovsharov** (22 Oct 1856 - Aug 1920)

| | |
|---|---|
| 12 Oct 1914 - 1917: | Section Chief, Main Artillery Directorate |
| 6 Dec 1916: | Promoted to *Major-General* |

*General of Infantry* Aleksei Gavrilovich **Kovtoradze** (15 Jul 1821 - 2 Aug 1907)

| | |
|---|---|
| 24 Nov 1871 - 8 Nov 1877: | Commander, 154$^{th}$ Infantry Regiment |
| 8 Nov 1877: | Promoted to *Major-General* |
| 8 Nov 1877 - 26 Dec 1877: | At the disposal of the C-in-C, Caucasus Army |
| 26 Dec 1877 - 22 May 1878: | Commander, 2$^{nd}$ Brigade, 39$^{th}$ Infantry Division |
| 22 May 1878 - 8 Oct 1889: | Commander, 1$^{st}$ Brigade, 39$^{th}$ Infantry Division |
| 8 Oct 1889 - 23 May 1894: | Commander, 9$^{th}$ Infantry Division |
| 30 Aug 1890: | Promoted to *Lieutenant-General* |
| 23 May 1894 - 2 Aug 1907: | Member, Committee for Wounded Veterans |
| 6 Dec 1900: | Promoted to *General of Infantry* |

*Major-General* Yakov Ivanovich **Kovtunovich** (6 Oct 1850 - ?)

| | |
|---|---|
| 22 Jan 1902: | Promoted to *Major-General* |
| 22 Jan 1902 - 7 Jun 1906: | Commander, 39$^{th}$ Artillery Brigade |

*Major-General* Khristo Neykovich **Koychev** (20 Jan 1863 - 3 Oct 1917)

| | |
|---|---|
| 27 Sep 1913: | Promoted to *Major-General* |
| 27 Sep 1913 - 10 Apr 1915: | Commander, 2$^{nd}$ Brigade, 48$^{th}$ Infantry Division |
| 10 Apr 1915 - 20 Jul 1915: | Commander, 1$^{st}$ Brigade, 9$^{th}$ Infantry Division |
| 20 Jul 1915 - 9 Aug 1916: | Reserve officer, Minsk Military District |
| 9 Aug 1916 - 7 Feb 1917: | Chief of Staff, 8$^{th}$ Siberian Rifle Division |
| 7 Feb 1917 - 3 Oct 1917: | Commander, 17$^{th}$ Siberian Rifle Division |

*Major-General* Nikolai-Konstantin Seliverstovich **Koyshevsky** (2 May 1854 - ?)

| | |
|---|---|
| 7 Dec 1904: | Promoted to *Major-General* |
| 7 Dec 1904 - 12 Apr 1906: | Commander, Brigade, 60$^{th}$ Infantry Division |
| 12 Apr 1906 - 30 Jun 1907: | Commander, 2$^{nd}$ Brigade, 28$^{th}$ Infantry Division |

*Major-General* Stepan Pavlovich **Kozakovich** (3 Aug 1854 - 17 Jun 1907)
22 Feb 1896 - 17 Jun 1907: Senior Artillery Acceptance Inspector, Main Artillery Directorate
6 Dec 1905: Promoted to *Major-General*

*Lieutenant-General* Yevgeny Nikolayevich **Kozelkin** (30 Oct 1860 - ?)
18 Jan 1906 - 19 Jul 1914: Military Judge, Warsaw Military District Court
2 Apr 1906: Promoted to *Major-General*
19 Jul 1914 - 23 Jun 1917: Military Judge, Minsk Military District Court
23 Jun 1917: Promoted to *Lieutenant-General*
23 Jun 1917: Retired

*General of Infantry* Aleksandr Fyodorovich **Kozen** (15 Nov 1833 - 14 Jun 1916)
24 Feb 1877 - 15 May 1885: Chief of Staff, III. Army Corps
1 Jan 1878: Promoted to *Major-General*
15 May 1885 - 6 Jun 1890: Commander, 2$^{nd}$ Brigade, 29$^{th}$ Infantry Division
6 Jun 1890 - 2 Nov 1892: Commander, 6$^{th}$ Infantry Division
30 Aug 1890: Promoted to *Lieutenant-General*
2 Nov 1892 - 23 Mar 1898: Commander, 17$^{th}$ Infantry Division
23 Mar 1898 - 14 Jun 1916: Honorary Trustee, Board of Trustees, Empress Maria Institutions
1 Apr 1901: Promoted to *General of Infantry*

*Lieutenant-General* Dmitry Dmitriyevich **Kozhukhov** (8 Sep 1831 - ?)
17 Jun 1871 - 7 Oct 1884: Commander, 57$^{th}$ Infantry Regiment
15 May 1883: Promoted to *Major-General*
7 Oct 1884 - 26 Nov 1884: Commander, 2$^{nd}$ Brigade, 16$^{th}$ Infantry Division
26 Nov 1884 - 9 Feb 1886: Commander, 2$^{nd}$ Brigade, 33$^{rd}$ Infantry Division
9 Feb 1886 - Sep 1901: Commander, 8$^{th}$ (Warsaw) Local Brigade
30 Aug 1894: Promoted to *Lieutenant-General*

*Major-General* Artur-Leon Voytsekhovich **Kozhukhovsky** (9 Feb 1834 - ?)
16 Mar 1892: Promoted to *Major-General*
16 Mar 1892 - 1987: Commander, 2$^{nd}$ Reserve Artillery Brigade

*Major-General* Yevgeny Maksimovich **Kozintsov** (15 Apr 1848 - ?)
3 May 1907 - 1909: Commander of Gendarmerie, Baku Province
13 Apr 1908: Promoted to *Major-General*
1909: Retired

*Major-General* Vladimir Albinovich **Kozitsky** (6 Apr 1857 - 1914)
? - 1914: Attached to 8$^{th}$ Grenadier Regiment
1914: Promoted to *Major-General*

*General of Cavalry* Aleksandr Aleksandrovich **Kozlov** (8 Apr 1837 - 29 Nov 1924)
2 Apr 1873 - 26 Jul 1878: Deputy Mayor of St. Petersburg
1 Jan 1878: Promoted to *Major-General*
26 Jul 1878 - 14 Oct 1878: Attached to the Ministry of Internal Affairs

| | |
|---|---|
| 14 Oct 1878 - 13 Aug 1881: | Chief of Police, Moscow |
| 13 Aug 1881 - 26 Jul 1882: | Chief of Police, St. Petersburg |
| 26 Mar 1882 - 26 Jul 1882: | Acting Chief of Staff, Special Corps of Gendarmes |
| 26 Jul 1882 - 17 Jan 1887: | Chief of Police, Moscow |
| 30 May 1883: | Promoted to *Lieutenant-General* |
| 17 Jan 1887 - Mar 1917: | Honorary Trustee, Board of Empress Maria Imperial Institutions |
| 22 Jul 1896: | Promoted to *General of Cavalry* |
| 14 Apr 1905 - 15 Jul 1905: | Governor-General of Moscow |
| 1905: | Promoted to *General-Adjutant* |

*Major-General* Aleksandr Khristoforovich **Kozlov** (18 Mar 1856 - ?)
| | |
|---|---|
| 7 Oct 1910 - 1912: | Commander, 1st Battalion, 25th Artillery Brigade |
| 1912: | Promoted to *Major-General* |
| 1912: | Retired |
| 15 Jun 1916 - 1917: | Recalled; Commander, 53rd Park Artillery Brigade |

*Major-General* Ivan Ivanovich **Kozlov** (14 Oct 1866 - ?)
| | |
|---|---|
| 31 Jul 1910: | Promoted to *Major-General* |
| 31 Jul 1910 - 29 Oct 1913: | Chief of Staff, V. Siberian Army Corps |
| 29 Oct 1913 - 31 Dec 1913: | Commander, 2nd Brigade, 16th Infantry Division |
| 31 Dec 1913 - 1915: | General for Special Assignments, Kazan Military District |
| 1915 - 7 Aug 1915: | General for Special Assignments, ? Army |
| 7 Aug 1915 - 16 Dec 1917: | Deputy Chief of Staff, Kazan Military District |

*Major-General* Nikolai Aleksandrovich **Kozlov** (7 Mar 1851 - ?)
| | |
|---|---|
| 11 Sep 1903 - 28 Jun 1904: | Member of the Technical Committee, Main Intendant Directorate |
| 6 Dec 1903: | Promoted to *Major-General* |
| 28 Jun 1904 - 1907: | At the disposal of the Intendant, 1st Manchurian Army |

*Major-General* Nikolai Khristoforovich **Kozlov** (13 Nov 1860 - ?)
| | |
|---|---|
| 28 May 1909 - 4 Jun 1912: | Military Judge, Kazan Military District Court |
| 6 Dec 1909: | Promoted to *Major-General* |
| 4 Jun 1912 - 1917: | Military Judge, Moscow Military District Court |

*Major-General* Pyotr Kuzmich **Kozlov** (3 Oct 1863 - 26 Sep 1935)
| | |
|---|---|
| 1916 - 1917: | Commandant of Jassy |
| 6 Dec 1916: | Promoted to *Major-General* |
| 1917: | Commandant of Tarnopol |

*Major-General* Sergey Vladimirovich **Kozlov** (29 Jul 1853 - 16 Jul 1906)
| | |
|---|---|
| 22 Apr 1900 - 18 Feb 1904: | Staff officer for Special Assignments, Chief of the General Staff |
| 6 Apr 1903: | Promoted to *Major-General* |
| 18 Feb 1904 - 19 Nov 1904: | General for Special Assignments, Viceroy for the Far East |

19 Nov 1904 - 16 Jul 1906: At the disposal of the Chief of the General Staff

*Lieutenant-General* Vladimir Apollonovich **Kozlov** (21 Mar 1856 - 14 Jan 1931)
15 Jun 1907: Promoted to *Major-General*
15 Jun 1907 - 13 Apr 1913: Commander, Life Guards Finland Regiment
13 Apr 1913 - 19 Jul 1914: Commander, 2nd Brigade, 2nd Guards Infantry Division
19 Jul 1914 - 15 Apr 1917: Commander, 84th Infantry Division
14 May 1915: Promoted to *Lieutenant-General*
15 Apr 1917 - 1917: Reserve officer, Odessa Military District
1917: Commanding General, Army Corps

*Major-General* Aleksandr Nikolayevich **Kozlovsky** (5 Aug 1864 - 7 Mar 1940)
2 Oct 1912: Promoted to *Major-General*
2 Oct 1912 - 13 May 1916: Commander, 11th Siberian Rifle Artillery Brigade
13 May 1916 - 10 Oct 1916: Inspector of Artillery, I. Turkestan Army Corps
10 Oct 1916 - 29 Apr 1917: Inspector of Artillery, XXXIV. Army Corps

*Major-General* David Yevstafyevich **Kozlovsky** (24 Jul 1870 - 12 Aug 1949)
2 Oct 1910 - 1917: Clerk, Main Directorate of the General Staff
6 Dec 1913: Promoted to *Major-General*

*Lieutenant-General* Ignaty Antonovich **Kozlovsky** (8 Oct 1838 - ?)
26 Feb 1894: Promoted to *Major-General*
26 Feb 1894 - 24 Nov 1899: Commander, 1st Brigade, Caucasus Grenadier Division
24 Nov 1899 - 17 Dec 1900: Commander, 2nd Brigade, Caucasus Grenadier Division
24 Oct 1900: Promoted to *Lieutenant-General*

*Major-General* Mikhail Aleksandrovich **Kozlovsky** (16 Jan 1840 - ?)
9 Dec 1890 - 3 Dec 1897: Commander, 25th Dragoon Regiment
3 Dec 1897: Promoted to *Major-General*
3 Dec 1897 - 26 Mar 1901: Commander, 1st Brigade, 10th Cavalry Division

*Major-General* Mikhail Kornilovich **Kozlovsky** (7 Jul 1851 - ?)
19 Jul 1901: Promoted to *Major-General*
19 Jul 1901 - 11 Nov 1902: Commander, 2nd Reserve Artillery Brigade
11 Nov 1902 - 29 Apr 1907: Commander, 32nd Artillery Brigade

*General of Cavalry* Pavel Aleksandrovich **Kozlovsky** (19 Jul 1845 - ?)
17 Jun 1896: Promoted to *Major-General*
1 / Jun 1896 - 19 May 1898: Commander, 1st Brigade, Caucasus Cavalry Division
19 May 1898 - 11 Jun 1901: Commander, 1st Independent Cavalry Brigade
11 Jun 1901 - 2 Jul 1907: Commander, 5th Cavalry Division
6 Dec 1902: Promoted to *Lieutenant-General*
2 Jul 1907 - 19 Jul 1912: Commanding General, I. Turkestan Army Corps
6 Dec 1908: Promoted to *General of Cavalry*
19 Jul 1912: Retired

*Lieutenant-General* Stepan Stanislavovich **Kozlovsky** (31 Aug 1858 - ?)
14 Feb 1904 - 23 Sep 1911:     Chief of Military Topographical Section, Amur Military District
2 Apr 1906:     Promoted to *Major-General*
23 Sep 1911 - 1917:     Chief of Military Survey, Northwest Frontier Region
14 Sep 1917:     Promoted to *Lieutenant-General*

*Major-General* Prince Yuri Ivanovich **Kozlovsky** (11 Oct 1853 - ?)
26 Jun 1907 - 31 Jul 1912:     Deputy Intendant, St. Petersburg Military District
25 Mar 1912:     Promoted to *Major-General*

*Major-General* Aleksandr Nikolayevich **Kozulin** (24 Feb 1855 - ?)
14 Jun 1911 - 1917:     Military Commander, Melitopol District
28 May 1915:     Promoted to *Major-General*

*Major-General* Andrey Mikhailovich **Kozyev** (10 Oct 1866 - ?)
1915 - 5 Jul 1915:     Commander, 34th Infantry Regiment
5 Jul 1915 - 20 Dec 1916:     Reserve officer, Minsk Military District
21 Jul 1915:     Promoted to *Major-General*
20 Dec 1916:     Dismissed

*Major-General of Naval Engineers* Pavel Andreyevich **Kraats** (17 Jan 1863 - 30 Jun 1926)
26 Oct 1909 - 1915:     Member of the Finnish Senate
6 Dec 1913:     Promoted to *Major-General of Naval Engineers*
1915:     Acting Head of Expedition Section, Department of Trade & Industry

*Vice-Admiral* Yevgeny Karlovich **Kraft** (22 Jul 1861 - ?)
6 Dec 1911:     Promoted to *Rear-Admiral*
6 Dec 1911 - 7 May 1913:     Chief of Staff, C-in-C of the Baltic Fleet
7 May 1913 - 1914:     Commander of Naval Artillery, Baltic Fleet
1914:     Promoted to *Vice-Admiral*
1914:     Retired

*Major-General* Pyotr Pavlovich **Kramarenko** (25 Jun 1873 - 16 Sep 1944)
25 Jun 1915 - 25 Aug 1917:     Commander, 223rd Infantry Regiment
10 Apr 1916:     Promoted to *Major-General*
25 Aug 1917 - 17 Sep 1917:     Commander, Brigade, 153rd Infantry Division
17 Sep 1917 - 3 Oct 1917:     Commander, 153rd Infantry Division

*Major-General* Nikolai Ivanovich **Kramarev** (28 Apr 1867 - 16 Feb 1940)
22 Aug 1912 - 3 Nov 1915:     Special Assignments General, Main Directorate for State Horse Breeding
6 Dec 1913:     Promoted to *Major-General*
3 Nov 1915 - 1917:     Council Member, Main Directorate for State Horse Breeding

*Lieutenant-General* Yevgeny Yevgenyevich **Krants** (6 Oct 1847 - ?)
28 Dec 1902 - 5 Jul 1910: Chief of Military Signals Section, General Staff
17 Apr 1905: Promoted to *Major-General*
5 Jul 1910: Promoted to *Lieutenant-General*
5 Jul 1910: Retired

*Major-General* Nikolai Ivanovich **Krasilnikov** (10 Nov 1852 - ?)
2 Dec 1906 - 1908: Commander, 225th Reserve Infantry Regiment
31 May 1907: Promoted to *Major-General*

*Major-General* Nikolai Ksenofontovich **Krasilnikov** (18 Nov 1845 - 13 Jan 1910)
19 Jul 1907: Promoted to *Major-General*
19 Jul 1907 - 13 Jan 1910: Commander, Omsk Regional Brigade

*Lieutenant-General* Vladimir Aleksandrovich **Krasilnikov** (11 Jul 1852 - 16 Jul 1920)
10 Sep 1906 - 1 Feb 1908: Commander, Finnish Artillery Regiment
6 Dec 1906: Promoted to *Major-General*
1 Feb 1908 - 23 Apr 1910: Commander, Finnish Artillery Brigade
23 Apr 1910 - 25 Jul 1910: Commander, 1st Reserve Artillery Brigade
25 Jul 1910 - 18 Feb 1912: Commander, 50th Artillery Brigade
18 Feb 1912 - 11 Jul 1914: Inspector of Artillery, XVI. Army Corps
1912: Promoted to *Lieutenant-General*
11 Jul 1914: Retired
21 Jul 1914 - 16 Feb 1917: Recalled; Inspector of Artillery, XVI. Army Corps

*Major-General* Aleksandr Vasilyevich **Krasnopevtsev** (26 Jun 1857 - ?)
28 Feb 1915 - 29 Jul 1916: Commander, 2nd Kuban Cossack Infantry Brigade
3 Apr 1915: Promoted to *Major-General*
29 Jul 1916 - 11 Jan 1917: Reserve officer, Caucasus Military District
11 Jan 1917 - 20 May 1917: Commander, 10th Turkestan Rifle Division

*Major-General* Apollon Petrovich **Krasnov** (15 Jan 1858 - ?)
1 Dec 1908 - Dec 1908: Commander, Arensburg Borderguard Brigade
6 Dec 1908: Promoted to *Major-General*

*Major-General* Pyotr Nikolayevich **Krasnov** (10 Sep 1869 - 17 Jan 1947)
Nov 1914: Promoted to *Major-General*
Nov 1914 - May 1915: Commander, 1st Brigade, 1st Cossack Division
May 1915 - 10 Sep 1915: Commander, 3rd Brigade, Caucasus Native Cavalry Division
7 Jul 1915 - 11 Jul 1915: Acting Commander, 3rd Don Cossack Division
10 Sep 1915 - 4 May 1917: Commander, 2nd Consolidated Cossack Division
4 May 1917 - Jun 1917: Unassigned
Jun 1917 - Sep 1917: Commander, 1st Kuban Cossack Division
Sep 1917 - 28 Oct 1917: Commanding General, III. Cavalry Division

*Major-General* Aleksandr Apollinariyevich **Krasovsky** (27 Dec 1865 - ?)
17 Apr 1908 - 30 Aug 1912: Commander, 4th Hussar Regiment

| | |
|---|---|
| 30 Aug 1912: | Promoted to *Major-General* |
| 30 Aug 1912 - 27 Nov 1915: | Commander, 1st Brigade, 8th Cavalry Division |
| 27 Nov 1915 - 2 Jan 1916: | Unassigned |
| 2 Jan 1916 - 16 Apr 1917: | Commander, 8th Cavalry Division |
| 24 May 1917: | Dismissed |

*Lieutenant-General* Bronislav Ivanovich **Krasovsky** (13 Nov 1862 - ?)
| | |
|---|---|
| 29 Jan 1905 - 6 Dec 1907: | Commander, 11th Dragoon Regiment |
| 6 Dec 1907: | Promoted to *Major-General* |
| 6 Dec 1907 - 31 Dec 1913: | Commander, 1st Brigade, 4th Cavalry Division |
| 31 Dec 1913: | Promoted to *Lieutenant-General* |
| 31 Dec 1913: | Retired |

*Major-General* Mikhail Antonovich **Krasovsky** (29 Sep 1848 - ?)
| | |
|---|---|
| 20 Jul 1893 - 1905: | Commander, Moscow Railway Gendarmerie |
| 1 Jan 1901: | Promoted to *Major-General* |

*Lieutenant-General* Rostislav Vladimirovich **Krasovsky** (11 Jul 1841 - 12 Jan 1909)
| | |
|---|---|
| 25 Jan 1885 - 13 Sep 1894: | Commander of Engineers, Fortress Osovets |
| 30 Aug 1890: | Promoted to *Major-General* |
| 13 Sep 1894 - 7 Jan 1897: | Commander of Engineers, Finland Military District |
| 7 Jan 1897 - 17 Jan 1900: | Commander of Engineers, St. Petersburg Military District |
| 17 Jan 1900 - 12 Jan 1909: | Member of the Engineering Committee, Main Engineering Directorate |
| 6 Dec 1900: | Promoted to *Lieutenant-General* |

*Major-General* Vladimir Antonovich **Krasovsky** (2 Nov 1839 - ?)
| | |
|---|---|
| 13 Jun 1894: | Promoted to *Major-General* |
| 13 Jun 1894 - 6 Feb 1896: | Commander, 2nd Brigade, 17th Infantry Division |
| 6 Feb 1896 - 11 Feb 1902: | Commander, 1st Brigade, 33rd Infantry Division |

*Major-General* Aleksandr Aleksandrovich **Krasyuk** (4 Jun 1850 - ?)
| | |
|---|---|
| 22 Apr 1907 - 27 Feb 1908: | Commander, 4th Artillery Brigade |
| 31 May 1907: | Promoted to *Major-General* |

*General of Infantry* Nikolai Fridrikhovich **Krauze** (10 Aug 1853 - ?)
| | |
|---|---|
| 22 Feb 1904: | Promoted to *Major-General* |
| 22 Feb 1904 - 30 Jan 1906: | Commander, 1st Brigade, 9th East Siberian Rifle Division |
| 30 Jan 1906 - 13 Dec 1908: | Commander, 2nd Brigade, 26th Infantry Division |
| 13 Dec 1908: | Promoted to *Lieutenant-General* |
| 13 Dec 1908 - 22 Apr 1915: | Commander, 4th East Siberian Rifle Division |
| 22 Apr 1915 - 3 Nov 1915: | Reserve officer, Dvinsk Military District |
| 3 Nov 1915: | Promoted to *General of Infantry* |
| 3 Nov 1915: | Retired |

*Lieutenant-General* Konstantin Stanislavovich **Krayevsky** (13 Jan 1826 - ?)
| | |
|---|---|
| 30 Oct 1867 - 9 Nov 1874: | Commander, 3rd Uhlan Regiment |
| 30 Aug 1874: | Promoted to *Major-General* |
| 9 Nov 1874 - 27 Jul 1875: | Unassigned |
| 27 Jul 1875 - 12 Apr 1880: | Commander, 2nd Brigade, 3rd Cavalry Division |
| 12 Apr 1880 - Nov 1894: | Commander, 3rd Cavalry Division |
| 15 May 1883: | Promoted to *Lieutenant-General* |

*Lieutenant-General* Mikhail Mikhailovich **Krayevsky** (2 Sep 1854 - ?)
| | |
|---|---|
| 2 Mar 1904 - 25 Mar 1905: | Commander, 6th Artillery Brigade |
| 6 Dec 1904: | Promoted to *Major-General* |
| 25 Mar 1905 - 19 May 1906: | Deputy Inspector of Artillery, 1st Manchurian Army |
| 19 May 1906 - 7 Jun 1906: | Commandant of Fortress Ust-Dvinsk |
| 7 Jun 1906 - 16 Oct 1908: | Attached to the Inspector-General of Artillery |
| 16 Oct 1908 - 10 May 1915: | Commander of Artillery, St. Petersburg Military District |
| 6 Dec 1908: | Promoted to *Lieutenant-General* |
| 12 Dec 1909 - 15 Jul 1914: | Member of the Artillery Committee, Main Artillery Directorate |
| 10 May 1915 - 1917: | Chief of Artillery Logistics, Northern Front |

*General of Infantry* Sergey Fyodorovich **Krekhovetsky-Yushchenko** (22 Sep 1857 - ?)
| | |
|---|---|
| 7 Apr 1902 - 23 Aug 1906: | Military Judge, Kiev Military District Court |
| 14 Apr 1902: | Promoted to *Major-General* |
| 23 Aug 1906 - 28 May 1909: | Military Prosecutor, Kiev Military District |
| 13 Apr 1908: | Promoted to *Lieutenant-General* |
| 28 May 1909 - 4 Jun 1912: | Chairman of the Military Tribunal, Warsaw Military District |
| 4 Jun 1912 - 31 Mar 1917: | Member, Supreme Military Tribunal |
| 6 Dec 1916: | Promoted to *General of Infantry* |
| 13 Mar 1917: | Retired |

*Major-General* Leonid Nikolayevich **Kremenetsky** (1 May 1862 - ?)
| | |
|---|---|
| 1913 - 1917: | Chief of Gendarmerie, Penza Region |
| 6 Dec 1916: | Promoted to *Major-General* |

*Admiral* Oskar Karlovich von **Kremer** (19 May 1829 - 1910)
| | |
|---|---|
| 18 Feb 1874 - 8 Mar 1876: | Captain, Port of Kronstadt |
| 1 Jan 1875: | Promoted to *Rear-Admiral* |
| 8 Mar 1876 - 11 Nov 1878: | Junior Flagman, Baltic Fleet |
| 11 Nov 1878 - 26 Apr 1882: | Commander, Naval Detachment in Greek Waters |
| 26 Apr 1882 - 1 Jan 1886: | Flag Captain to the Tsar |
| 1 Jan 1886: | Promoted to *Vice-Admiral* |
| 1 Jan 1886 - 28 Nov 1888: | Chairman of the Naval Technical Committee |
| 26 Feb 1886: | Promoted to *General-Adjutant* |
| 28 Nov 1888 - 14 May 1896: | Chief of the Main Naval Staff |
| 21 Aug 1896: | Promoted to *Admiral* |
| 14 May 1896 - 1910: | Member of the State Council |

*Major-General* Vilgelm Robertovich von **Kremer** (2 Aug 1836 - 25 Apr 1926)
13 Dec 1891: Promoted to *Major-General*
13 Dec 1891 - 1903: Commander, Abo-Berneborg Province

*Major-General* Mikhail Ivanovich **Kremkov** (8 Nov 1864 - ?)
28 May 1908 - 1917: Military Judge, Kazan Military District Court
6 Dec 1908: Promoted to *Major-General*

*Major-General* Aleksandr Konstantinovich **Krenke** (15 Jun 1863 - ?)
21 Feb 1912 - 1915: Commander, 12$^{th}$ Borderguard Brigade
14 Apr 1913: Promoted to *Major-General*
1915 - 1917: Commander, Brigade, Consolidated Borderguard Division
1917: Commander, 100$^{th}$ Infantry Division

*Lieutenant-General* Leonid Vladimirovich **Krestovsky** (16 Apr 1853 - ?)
9 Aug 1902 - 1 Dec 1908: Commander, Velyun Borderguard Brigade
6 Dec 1906: Promoted to *Major-General*
1 Dec 1908 - 16 Jul 1912: Commander, 4$^{th}$ Borderguard District
16 Jul 1912 - Oct 1917: Commander, 2$^{nd}$ Borderguard District
14 Apr 1913: Promoted to *Lieutenant-General*

*Major-General* Nikolai Nikolayevich **Krestyanov** (4 Dec 1862 - ?)
2 Feb 1914 - 29 Jul 1917: Chief of Administration, Gatchina Palace
6 Dec 1915: Promoted to *Major-General*
29 Jul 1917: Dismissed

*Lieutenant-General* Konstantin Ilich **Krichinsky** (25 Oct 1847 - ?)
22 Feb 1904: Promoted to *Major-General*
22 Feb 1904 - 29 Mar 1906: Commander, 2$^{nd}$ Brigade, 6$^{th}$ East Siberian Rifle Division
29 Mar 1906 - 28 Feb 1907: Commander, 2$^{nd}$ Brigade, 32$^{nd}$ Infantry Division
28 Feb 1907: Promoted to *Lieutenant-General*
28 Feb 1907: Retired

*Major-General* Baron Fyodor Nikolayevich von **Kridener** (6 Oct 1841 - ?)
14 Jun 1883 - 23 Sep 1891: Commander, 14$^{th}$ Dragoon Regiment
21 Sep 1891 - 11 Sep 1895: Commander, 2$^{nd}$ Brigade, 14$^{th}$ Cavalry Division
23 Sep 1891: Promoted to *Major-General*
11 Sep 1895 - 15 Sep 1895: At the disposal of the Commanding General, Vilnius Military District
15 Sep 1895 - May 1898: Commander, 1$^{st}$ Independent Cavalry Brigade

*Vice-Admiral* Aleksandr Khristianovich **Kriger** (17 Nov 1848 - 24 Apr 1917)
1896: Promoted to *Rear-Admiral*
31 Jan 1896 - 1896: Commander of naval units, Mediterranean
1896 - 1901: Commandant of the Imperial Naval Academy, Director of the Marine Corps

| | |
|---|---|
| 1901 - 1903: | Commander, Mediterranean Naval Detachment |
| 1903 - 9 Apr 1904: | Commander, Training Squadron, Black Sea Fleet |
| 6 Dec 1903: | Promoted to *Vice-Admiral* |
| 9 Apr 1904 - 1 Aug 1905: | Commander, Black Sea Squadron |
| 1 Jun 1905 - 1 Aug 1905: | Acting C-in-C, Black Sea Fleet |
| 1 Aug 1905: | Dismissed |

*Lieutenant-General* Morits-Eduard Fyodorovich **Kriger** (11 Jan 1861 - ?)
| | |
|---|---|
| 13 Feb 1906 - 14 Aug 1906: | Military Judge, Siberian Military District Court |
| 2 Apr 1906: | Promoted to *Major-General* |
| 14 Aug 1906 - 31 Oct 1908: | Military Judge, Omsk Military District Court |
| 31 Oct 1908 - 14 Nov 1908: | Military Judge, Amur Military District Court |
| 14 Nov 1908 - 1912: | Military Judge, Irkutsk Military District Court |
| 1912: | Promoted to *Lieutenant-General* |
| 1912: | Retired |

*Major-General* Oskar-Gustav-Aleksandr Filippovich **Kriger** (21 Jun 1870 - 26 Mar 1920)
| | |
|---|---|
| 30 Jan 1916 - Jan 1917: | Chief of Staff, 22$^{nd}$ Infantry Division |
| 10 Apr 1916: | Promoted to *Major-General* |
| Jan 1917 - 3 Sep 1917: | Chief of Staff, 104$^{th}$ Infantry Division |
| 3 Sep 1917: | Dismissed |

*Major-General* Konstantin Stepanovich **Krinitsky** (13 Oct 1822 - ?)
| | |
|---|---|
| 1 Feb 1885 - 1907: | Attached to the Caucasus Military District |
| 30 Aug 1889: | Promoted to *Major-General* |

*Major-General* Nikolai Ivanovich **Krinitsky** (20 Nov 1857 - ?)
| | |
|---|---|
| 28 Jul 1905: | Promoted to *Major-General* |
| 28 Jul 1905 - 24 Nov 1908: | Commander, 2$^{nd}$ Brigade, 41$^{st}$ Infantry Division |

*Rear-Admiral* Yevgeny Ivanovich **Krinitsky** (24 Sep 1863 - 1930)
| | |
|---|---|
| 1912 - 23 Mar 1915: | Commander, Cruiser "Hercules" |
| 24 Dec 1914: | Promoted to *Rear-Admiral* |
| 23 Mar 1915 - Oct 1918: | Attached to Sveaborg Flotilla |

*Major-General* Yevgeny Konstantinovich **Krinitsky** (20 Jul 1871 - 3 Nov 1914)
| | |
|---|---|
| 11 Sep 1914 - 3 Nov 1914: | Chief of Staff, 13$^{th}$ Siberian Rifle Division |
| 26 Feb 1915: | Posthumously promoted to *Major-General* |

*Lieutenant-General* Vladimir Mikhailovich **Krishtafovich** (4 Feb 1857 - ?)
| | |
|---|---|
| 10 Jan 1908 - 6 Jun 1911: | Commander of Artillery, Fortress Ivangorod |
| 27 Jul 1908: | Promoted to *Major-General* |
| 6 Jun 1911 - 1915: | Commander of Artillery, Fortress Vladivostok |
| 27 Jul 1912: | Promoted to *Lieutenant-General* |
| 1915 - 16 Apr 1916: | Commander of Artillery, Fortress Grodno |
| 16 Apr 1916 - 9 Sep 1917: | Inspector of Artillery, 9$^{th}$ Army |

*Lieutenant-General* Pavel Nikolayevich **Kritsky** (7 Jul 1857 - 12 Sep 1927)
| | |
|---|---|
| 2 Feb 1907 - 1 Apr 1910: | Chief of Office for Japanese War Claims, Ministry of War |
| 13 Apr 1908: | Promoted to *Major-General* |
| 1 Apr 1910 - 21 Feb 1916: | Commander, Vologda Regional Brigade |
| 6 Apr 1914: | Promoted to *Lieutenant-General* |
| 21 Feb 1916 - 1917: | Commander, Perm Regional Brigade |

*Major-General* Nikolai Nikolayevich **Krivitsky** (24 Oct 1866 - 1947)
| | |
|---|---|
| 28 Jan 1916 - 2 Aug 1916: | Commander, Life Guards 3$^{rd}$ Rifle Regiment |
| 10 Apr 1916: | Promoted to *Major-General* |
| 2 Aug 1916 - 1917: | Reserve officer, Petrograd Military District |

*Major-General* Grigory Grigoryevich **Krivoshein** (21 Jan 1868 - 29 Jul 1945)
| | |
|---|---|
| 1 Jan 1907 - 7 Feb 1913: | Associate Professor, Nikolayev Engineering Academy |
| 25 Mar 1912: | Promoted to *Major-General* |
| 7 Feb 1913 - 1918: | Tenured Professor, Nikolayev Engineering Academy |
| 16 Jul 1913 - 6 Jan 1915: | Professor, St. Petersburg Institute of Technology |

*Major-General* Andrey Nikolayevich **Krivosheyev** (1854 - 1911)
| | |
|---|---|
| 19 Jul 1906 - 1911: | Commander, 125$^{th}$ Infantry Regiment |
| 1911: | Promoted to *Major-General* |

*Major-General* Anatoly Rafailovich **Krizhanovsky** (7 Jun 1843 - 17 Jan 1904)
| | |
|---|---|
| 21 Jan 1894 - 7 Jul 1897: | Commander, 2$^{nd}$ Brigade, 34$^{th}$ Infantry Division |
| 31 Jan 1894: | Promoted to *Major-General* |
| 7 Jul 1897 - 18 Jun 1903: | Commander, 1$^{st}$ Brigade, 34$^{th}$ Infantry Division |
| 18 Jun 1903: | Retired |

*Major-General* Iosif Iosifovich **Krizhevich** (2 Apr 1853 - ?)
| | |
|---|---|
| 14 Jan 1908 - 2 Apr 1913: | Duty General, Caucasus Military District |
| 31 Dec 1910: | Promoted to *Major-General* |
| 2 Apr 1913: | Retired |
| 12 Feb 1915 - 1917: | Recalled; Commandant of Erivan |

*Lieutenant-General* Vasily Mikhailovich **Krokhalev** (2 Jan 1852 - ?)
| | |
|---|---|
| 12 Jul 1895 - 9 Nov 1913: | Commandant, Pyrotechnic Artillery School |
| 1 Apr 1901: | Promoted to *Major-General* |
| 9 Nov 1913 - 1914: | Attached to the Light Artillery Polygon |
| 1914: | Promoted to *Lieutenant-General* |

*General of Infantry* Aleksey Alekseyevich **Kronman** (25 Nov 1834 - ?)
| | |
|---|---|
| 28 Oct 1876 - 4 Oct 1879: | Deputy Chief of Staff, Kazan Military District |
| 30 Aug 1878: | Promoted to *Major-General* |
| 4 Oct 1879 - 5 Jun 1891: | Commander, 2$^{nd}$ Brigade, 32$^{nd}$ Infantry Division |
| 5 Jun 1891 - 6 Jun 1897: | Commander, 42$^{nd}$ Reserve Infantry Brigade |
| 30 Aug 1891: | Promoted to *Lieutenant-General* |
| 6 Jun 1897: | Promoted to *General of Infantry* |

6 Jun 1897: Retired

*Major-General* Prince Dmitry Alekseyevich **Kropotkin** (18 Mar 1867 - ?)
8 Jun 1910 - 24 May 1913: Commander, 61st Infantry Regiment
14 Apr 1913: Promoted to *Major-General*
24 May 1913 - 25 Apr 1915: Commander, 1st Brigade, 3rd Siberian Rifle Division
25 Apr 1915 - 15 Mar 1916: Chief of Staff, XXXV. Army Corps
15 Mar 1916 - 29 Nov 1916: Chief of Staff, XX. Army Corps
29 Nov 1916 - 30 Apr 1917: Commander, 133rd Infantry Division
30 Apr 1917 - 1918: Reserve officer, Minsk Military District

*Lieutenant-General of the Admiralty* Apollon Semyonovich **Krotkov** (1848 - 1917)
?: Promoted to *Major-General of the Admiralty*
1905: Inspector-General of Naval Artillery
?: Promoted to *Lieutenant-General of the Admiralty*
1908: Retired

*Major-General of the Fleet* Georgy Fomich **Kroun** (3 Sep 1858 - Apr 1939)
6 Dec 1911: Promoted to *Major-General of the Admiralty*
9 Jan 1912 - Jan 1914: Senior Deputy Commander, Port of St. Petersburg
8 Apr 1913: Redesignated *Major-General of the Fleet*

*General of Infantry* Konstantin Faddeyevich **Krshivitsky** (26 Sep 1840 - 21 Feb 1910)
18 Apr 1890: Promoted to *Major-General*
18 Apr 1890 - 10 Jul 1891: Chief of Staff, VII. Army Corps
10 Jul 1891 - 10 Feb 1895: Chief of Staff, Deputy Commanding General, Warsaw Military District
10 Feb 1895 - 6 Sep 1899: Commander, 56th Replacement Infantry Brigade
6 Sep 1899 - 23 Jan 1902: Commander, 35th Infantry Division
6 Dec 1899: Promoted to *Lieutenant-General*
23 Jan 1902 - 6 Feb 1903: Commander, 1st Grenadier Division
6 Feb 1903 - 1 Dec 1904: Commandant of Fortress Libau
1 Dec 1904 - 19 Dec 1905: Deputy Commanding General, Vilnius Military District
19 Dec 1905 - 13 Mar 1909: Commanding General, Vilnius Military District, Governor-General of Vilnius, Kaunas & Grodno
6 Dec 1906: Promoted to *General of Infantry*
13 Mar 1909 - 21 Feb 1910: Member of the State Council, Member of the Military Council

*Lieutenant-General* Nikolai Faddeyevich **Krshivitsky** (17 May 1838 - ?)
13 Jan 1890 - 10 Feb 1891: Special Assignments General, Vilnius Military District
18 Apr 1890: Promoted to *Major-General*
10 Feb 1891 - Sep 1896: Commander, 5th Rifle Brigade
Sep 1896: Promoted to *Lieutenant-General*
Sep 1896: Retired

*Major-General* Pavel Faddeyevich **Krshivitsky** (19 Apr 1843 - 1900)
11 Jan 1900 - 1900: At the disposal of the Commanding General, Amur

| | Military District |
|---|---|
| 9 Apr 1900: | Promoted to *Major-General* |

*Major-General* Viktor Platonovich von **Krug** (9 Dec 1864 - 9 Feb 1919)
| | |
|---|---|
| 4 Dec 1907 - 17 Sep 1912: | Commander, 4th Uhlan Regiment |
| 17 Sep 1912: | Promoted to *Major-General* |
| 17 Sep 1912 - 7 Jan 1916: | Commander, 1st Brigade, 13th Cavalry Division |
| 7 Jan 1916 - 1917: | Reserve officer, Petrograd Military District |

*Major-General* Vasily Aleksandrovich **Kruglevsky** (21 Apr 1866 - ?)
| | |
|---|---|
| 24 Dec 1913: | Promoted to *Major-General* |
| 24 Dec 1913 - Feb 1915: | Commander, Life Guards Izmailovsky Regiment |
| Feb 1915 - 19 Dec 1915: | Reserve officer, Dvinsk Military District |
| 19 Dec 1915 - 8 Oct 1916: | Commander, 2nd Brigade, 1st Guards Cavalry Division |
| 8 Oct 1916 - 6 Apr 1917: | Unassigned |
| 6 Apr 1917 - 1917: | Commander, 3rd Siberian Rifle Division |

*Lieutenant-General* Matvey Yegorovich **Krupensky** (15 Jun 1859 - ?)
| | |
|---|---|
| 6 Nov 1904: | Promoted to *Major-General* |
| 6 Nov 1904 - 26 Mar 1917: | Attached to Grand Duke Nikolai Nikolayevich |
| 14 Mar 1913: | Promoted to *Lieutenant-General* |
| 26 Mar 1917: | Dismissed |

*Lieutenant-General* Nikolai Konstantinovich **Krushevsky** (24 Apr 1852 - 16 Jul 1916)
| | |
|---|---|
| 4 Jan 1906 - 31 Dec 1913: | General for Special Assignments, Odessa Military District |
| 6 Dec 1906: | Promoted to *Major-General* |
| 31 Dec 1913: | Promoted to *Lieutenant-General* |
| 31 Dec 1913: | Retired |

*Major-General* Anton Yevgrafovich **Kruten** (7 Dec 1861 - ?)
| | |
|---|---|
| 15 May 1912 - 30 Aug 1915: | Commander, 17th Turkestan Rifle Regiment |
| 29 Jun 1915: | Promoted to *Major-General* |
| 30 Aug 1915 - 16 Sep 1917: | Commander, 4th Kuban Light Infantry Brigade |
| 16 Sep 1917 - ?: | Commander, 5th Caucasus Rifle Division |

*Major-General* Nikolai Yevgrafovich **Kruten** (7 May 1858 - ?)
| | |
|---|---|
| 1915 - 13 Nov 1916: | Staff Officer, Intendant Department, Southwestern Front |
| 13 Nov 1916: | Promoted to *Major-General* |
| 13 Nov 1916: | Retired |

*Major-General* Nikolai Aleksandrovich **Krutikov** (30 Jan 1871 - 1920)
| | |
|---|---|
| 6 Dec 1907 - 24 Jan 1916: | Commander, 6th Battery, Life Guards 1st Artillery Brigade |
| 17 Sep 1915: | Promoted to *Major-General* |
| 24 Jan 1916 - 1917: | Commander, 51st Artillery Brigade |

*Major-General* Yevgeny Borisovich **Kruze** (15 Feb 1861 - ?)
16 May 1913 - 1917: Chairman of the Military Board, Ussuri Cossack Army
6 Dec 1915: Promoted to *Major-General*

*Lieutenant-General* Aksel-Fridrikh-Karl-Pankraty Fridrikhovich von **Kruzenshtern** (27 Dec 1851 - 10 May 1913)
2 Jun 1901: Promoted to *Major-General*
2 Jun 1901 - 7 Jun 1907: Commander, 2nd Brigade, 3rd Grenadier Division
7 Jun 1907 - 10 Jun 1908: Commander, 2nd Brigade, 23rd Infantry Division
10 Jun 1908: Promoted to *Lieutenant-General*
10 Jun 1908: Retired

*Major-General* Aleksey-Ebert Karlovich von **Kruzenshtern** (7 Jan 1850 - ?)
22 Mar 1901 - 15 Jan 1905: Commander, 40th Dragoon Regiment
15 Jan 1905: Promoted to *Major-General*
15 Jan 1905 - Jul 1908: Commander, 1st Brigade, 13th Cavalry Division

*General of Infantry* Nikolai Fyodorovich von **Kruzenshtern** (7 Feb 1854 - 5 Apr 1940)
24 Oct 1900 - 10 Mar 1902: Commander, 11th Dragoon Regiment
10 Mar 1902: Promoted to *Major-General*
10 Mar 1902 - 3 Feb 1904: Commander, 1st Brigade, 4th Cavalry Division
3 Feb 1904 - 16 Feb 1906: Commander, Life Guards Uhlan Regiment
16 Feb 1906 - 10 Feb 1907: Commander, 2nd Brigade, 2nd Guards Cavalry Division
10 Feb 1907 - 23 Dec 1910: Commander, 1st Guards Cavalry Division
31 May 1907: Promoted to *Lieutenant-General*
23 Dec 1910 - 4 Oct 1916: Commanding General, XVIII. Army Corps
14 Apr 1913: Promoted to *General of Infantry*
4 Oct 1916 - 1917: Member of the Military Council

*General of the Fleet* Aleksey Nikolayevich **Krylov** (3 Aug 1863 - 26 Oct 1945)
21 Jan 1908 - 21 Aug 1910: Chief Inspector of Shipbuilding
8 Sep 1908: Promoted to *Major-General of the Admiralty*
21 Aug 1910 - 6 Dec 1911: Professor, Nikolayev Naval Academy
6 Dec 1911: Promoted to *Lieutenant-General of the Admiralty*
6 Dec 1911 - 1916: General for Special Assignments, Ministry of the Navy
8 Apr 1913: Redesignated *Lieutenant-General of the Fleet*
6 Dec 1916: Promoted to *General of the Fleet*
1916 - 1919: Director, Main Physical Observatory, Chief of the Main Military Meteorological Administration

*Lieutenant-General* Dmitry Dmitriyevich **Krylov** (20 Feb 1853 - Feb 1919)
1 Jun 1904 - 1 Mar 1906: Commander of Artillery, Fortress Sevastopol
6 Dec 1904: Promoted to *Major-General*
1 Mar 1906 - 28 Jun 1907: Commander of Artillery, Fortress Libau
28 Jun 1907: Retired
18 May 1908 - 9 Feb 1910: Recalled; Deputy Commander of Artillery, Amur Military District

9 Feb 1910: Promoted to *Lieutenant-General*
9 Feb 1910 - 1917: Commander of Artillery, Amur Military District

*Lieutenant-General* Ivan Aleksandrovich **Krylov** (26 Nov 1864 - ?)
22 Jan 1911 - Oct 1917: Member of the Artillery Committee, Main Artillery Directorate
10 Apr 1911: Promoted to *Major-General*
3 Aug 1914 - Oct 1917: Deputy Chief of Central Scientific-Technical Laboratory, Ministry of War
6 Dec 1916: Promoted to *Lieutenant-General*

*General of Infantry* Konstantin Aleksandrovich **Krylov** (26 May 1860 - 30 Mar 1930)
12 Jan 1904 - 14 Dec 1906: Commander, 130th Infantry Regiment
12 Sep 1906: Promoted to *Major-General*
14 Dec 1906 - 22 Oct 1914: Commandant of Kiev Military School
6 Dec 1910: Promoted to *Lieutenant-General*
22 Oct 1914 - 23 Sep 1915: Commander, 35th Infantry Division
23 Sep 1915 - 8 Jun 1917: Commanding General, XXXIII. Army Corps
15 Jan 1917: Promoted to *General of Infantry*
8 Jun 1917 - Oct 1917: Reserve officer, Kiev Military District

*Lieutenant-General* Nikolai Sergeyevich **Krylov** (5 May 1849 - ?)
9 Apr 1900: Promoted to *Major-General*
9 Apr 1900 - 11 Mar 1901: At the disposal of the Commanding General, St. Petersburg Military District
11 Mar 1901 - 25 Nov 1905: Commandant of St. Petersburg
25 Nov 1905 - 1906: Attached to the Ministry of War
1906: Promoted to *Lieutenant-General*
1906: Retired

*Major-General* Pavel Yevstafyevich **Krylov** (7 Jan 1861 - ?)
27 May 1906 - 18 Jan 1916: Clerk, Office of the Ministry of War
6 Dec 1911: Promoted to *Major-General*
18 Jan 1916 - Oct 1917: Ministry of War Representative, Odessa Military District Council

*Lieutenant-General* Aleksandr Mikhailovich **Krymov** (23 Oct 1871 - 31 Aug 1917)
7 Sep 1914 - 27 Mar 1915: Commander, Brigade, 2nd Kuban Cossack Division
6 Dec 1914: Promoted to *Major-General*
27 Mar 1915 - 18 Dec 1915: Commander, Ussuri Mounted Brigade
18 Dec 1915 - 7 Apr 1917: Commander, Ussuri Cavalry Division
7 Apr 1917 - 24 Aug 1917: Commanding General, III. Cavalry Corps
29 Apr 1917: Promoted to *Lieutenant-General*
24 Aug 1917 - 31 Aug 1917: C-in-C, Petrograd Independent Army

*Major-General* Aleksandr Ivanovich **Kryuger** (17 Sep 1862 - ?)
14 Jul 1906 - 26 May 1910: Section Chief, Main Directorate of Cossack Troops
13 Apr 1908: Promoted to *Major-General*

26 May 1910 - 29 Aug 1914:        Duty General, Vilnius Military District
29 Aug 1914 - 1918:                Duty General, 1st Army

*General of Infantry* Grigory Vasilyevich **Kryukov** (14 Jun 1837 - 28 Sep 1917)
7 Apr 1886:                         Promoted to *Major-General*
7 Apr 1886 - 18 Sep 1890:          General for Special Assignments, Moscow Military District
18 Sep 1890 - 9 Oct 1894:          Commander, 2nd Brigade, 1st Grenadier Division
9 Oct 1894 - 24 Oct 1900:          Commander, 38th Infantry Division
14 May 1896:                        Promoted to *Lieutenant-General*
24 Oct 1900 - 29 Nov 1903:         Commanding General, XIX. Army Corps
29 Nov 1903 - 28 Sep 1917:         Member, Committee for Wounded Veterans
6 Dec 1906:                         Promoted to *General of Infantry*

*General of Engineers* Nikolai Aleksandrovich **Kryukov** (11 May 1850 - 29 Oct 1915)
3 Feb 1900 - 10 May 1906:          Inspector of Classes, Nikolayev Engineering Academy
25 Feb 1900:                        Promoted to *Major-General*
10 May 1906 - 1914:                Commandant, Nikolayev Engineering Academy
6 Dec 1906:                         Promoted to *Lieutenant-General*
1914 - Oct 1914:                    At the disposal of the Minister of War
Oct 1914 - 29 Oct 1915:            Member of the Military Council
22 Mar 1915:                        Promoted to *General of Engineers*

*Major-General* Prokofy Ilich **Kryukov** (8 Jun 1824 - ?)
16 Dec 1876 - 1894:                Attached to Kuban Cossack Army
15 May 1883:                        Promoted to *Major-General*

*Lieutenant-General* Dmitry Viktorovich **Kryzhanovsky** (8 Dec 1846 - 21 Aug 1906)
27 Jan 1893 - 25 Jan 1900:         Commander, 12th Dragoon Regiment
25 Jan 1900:                        Promoted to *Major-General*
25 Jan 1900 - 10 Jan 1905:         Commander, 1st Brigade, 13th Cavalry Division
10 Jan 1905 - 21 Aug 1906:         Commander, 11th Cavalry Division
11 Jan 1906:                        Promoted to *Lieutenant-General*

*Major-General* Nikolai Nikolayevich **Kryzhanovsky** (14 Oct 1849 - ?)
13 May 1894 - 26 May 1897:         Commander, 24th Dragoon Regiment
26 May 1897:                        Promoted to *Major-General*
26 May 1897 - 15 Mar 1904:         Commander, Ussuri Mounted Brigade
15 Mar 1904 - 1905:                 At the disposal of the Chief of the General Staff

*Major-General* Nikolai Nikolayevich **Kryzhanovsky** (27 Oct 1867 - ?)
9 Aug 1905 - 1917:                  Senior Artillery Inspector, Main Artillery Directorate
14 Apr 1913:                        Promoted to *Major-General*

*General of Artillery* Pavel Andreyevich **Kryzhanovsky** (4 Oct 1831 - 22 Jun 1911)
10 Jul 1865 - 3 May 1878:          Inspector of Classes, 1st Pavlovsk Military School
1 Jan 1878:                         Promoted to *Major-General*
3 May 1878 - 10 Oct 1881:          Attached to the Main Artillery Directorate

| | |
|---|---|
| 10 Oct 1881 - 4 Mar 1887: | Commander of Artillery, Fortress Vyborg |
| 4 Mar 1887 - 2 Jan 1890: | Inspector of Fortress Artillery |
| 30 Aug 1888: | Promoted to *Lieutenant-General* |
| 2 Jan 1890 - 26 Aug 1897: | Deputy Chief of the Main Artillery Directorate |
| 26 Aug 1897 - 22 Jun 1911: | Member of the Military Council |
| 9 Apr 1900: | Promoted to *General of Artillery* |

*Major-General* Nikolai Nikolayevich **Krzheminsky** (8 May 1867 - 3 Apr 1931)

| | |
|---|---|
| 27 Nov 1915 - Jan 1917: | Commander, 9th Siberian Rifle Regiment |
| 22 Sep 1916: | Promoted to *Major-General* |
| Jan 1917 - 29 Apr 1917: | Chief of Staff, 18th Siberian Rifle Division |
| 29 Apr 1917 - 1918: | Chief of Staff, VI. Siberian Army Corps |

*General of Infantry* Yakov Stepanovich **Krzhivoblotsky** (29 Jul 1832 - 21 Apr 1900)

| | |
|---|---|
| 20 Feb 1870 - 1876: | Deputy Chief of Staff, Odessa Military District |
| 16 Apr 1872: | Promoted to *Major-General* |
| 1876 - 27 Jul 1882: | Chief of Staff, Odessa Military District |
| 30 Aug 1881: | Promoted to *Lieutenant-General* |
| 27 Jul 1882 - 20 Dec 1890: | Commander, 14th Infantry Division |
| 20 Dec 1890 - 14 Nov 1894: | Commanding General, XIV. Army Corps |
| 14 Nov 1894 - 7 Dec 1898: | Deputy Commanding General, Warsaw Military District |
| 6 Dec 1895: | Promoted to *General of Infantry* |
| 7 Dec 1898 - 21 Apr 1900: | Member of the Military Council |

*Lieutenant-General* Ivan Vasilyevich **Kubarovsky** (28 Jul 1853 - ?)

| | |
|---|---|
| 16 Jan 1909: | Promoted to *Major-General* |
| 16 Jan 1909 - 28 Jul 1913: | Commander, 1st Grenadier Artillery Brigade |
| 28 Jul 1913: | Promoted to *Lieutenant-General* |
| 28 Jul 1913: | Retired |

*Major-General* Aleksandr Aleksandrovich **Kubasov** (4 Jun 1864 - ?)

| | |
|---|---|
| ? - 28 Jan 1916: | Deputy Chief of Tula Arms Factory |
| 6 Dec 1915: | Promoted to *Major-General* |
| 28 Jan 1916 - 1917: | Vice-Chairman, Commission for the Construction of an Arms Factory |

*Lieutenant-General* Yuly-Nikolai Maksimilianovich von **Kube** (20 May 1854 - 17 Apr 1917)

| | |
|---|---|
| 26 Jun 1902 - 11 May 1908: | Commander, 6th Hussar Regiment |
| 11 May 1908: | Promoted to *Major-General* |
| 11 May 1908 - 20 May 1913: | Commander, 1st Brigade, 6th Cavalry Division |
| 20 May 1913: | Promoted to *Lieutenant-General* |
| 20 May 1913: | Retired |
| 15 Nov 1914 - 17 Apr 1917: | Recalled; Special Assignments General, Main Directorate of State Horse Breeding |

*General of Infantry* Pyotr Sofronovich **Kublitsky** (16 Jan 1845 - 19 Aug 1905)

| | |
|---|---|
| 1 Oct 1879 - 3 May 1898: | Professor, Nikolai General Staff Academy |

| | |
|---|---|
| 30 Aug 1890: | Promoted to *Major-General* |
| 3 May 1898 - 22 Feb 1901: | Member, Military Academic Committee of the General Staff |
| 6 Dec 1899: | Promoted to *Lieutenant-General* |
| 22 Feb 1901 - 8 Mar 1903: | Commander, 31$^{st}$ Infantry Division |
| 8 Mar 1903 - 8 Aug 1905: | At the disposal of the Minister of War |
| 8 Aug 1905: | Promoted to *General of Infantry* |
| 8 Aug 1905: | Retired |

*Lieutenant-General* Frants Feliksovich **Kublitsky-Piotukh** (29 Jan 1860 - 27 Jan 1920)
| | |
|---|---|
| 12 Feb 1911: | Promoted to *Major-General* |
| 12 Feb 1911 - 15 Aug 1911: | Commander, 1$^{st}$ Brigade, 9$^{th}$ Infantry Division |
| 15 Aug 1911 - 4 Nov 1914: | Commander, 2$^{nd}$ Brigade, 37$^{th}$ Infantry Division |
| 4 Nov 1914 - 21 Aug 1915: | Commander, Brigade, 74$^{th}$ Infantry Division |
| 21 Aug 1915 - 15 Apr 1917: | Commander, 2$^{nd}$ Finnish Rifle Division |
| 22 Sep 1916: | Promoted to *Lieutenant-General* |
| 15 Apr 1917 - 29 Apr 1917: | Reserve officer, Kiev Military District |
| 29 Apr 1917 - 1917: | Commander, 22$^{nd}$ Replacement Infantry Brigade |

*Lieutenant-General* Lev Iosifovich **Kublitsky-Piottukh** (15 Dec 1849 - 9 Jan 1907)
| | |
|---|---|
| 9 Apr 1900: | Promoted to *Major-General* |
| 9 Apr 1900 - 2 Jun 1905: | Director, Sumy Cadet Corps |
| 2 Jun 1905 - 9 Jan 1907: | Director, Vladimir (Kiev) Cadet Corps |
| 6 Dec 1906: | Promoted to *Lieutenant-General* |

*Major-General* Mikhail Ivanovich **Kucherov** (1854 - 7 Nov 1909)
| | |
|---|---|
| ? - 7 Nov 1909: | Chief of Workshops, St. Petersburg Armory |
| 1909: | Promoted to *Major-General* |

*Lieutenant-General* Ignaty Karlovich **Kuchevsky** (28 Aug 1848 - ?)
| | |
|---|---|
| 4 Mar 1907 - 31 Dec 1913: | Inspector of Engineering Works, Caucasus Military District |
| 6 Dec 1911: | Promoted to *Major-General* |
| 31 Dec 1913: | Promoted to *Lieutenant-General* |
| 31 Dec 1913: | Retired |
| 31 Dec 1914 - 1917: | Recalled; Reserve officer, Caucasus Military District |

*Major-General* Dmitry Aleksandrovich **Kuchin** (17 Oct 1854 - ?)
| | |
|---|---|
| 28 Mar 1912: | Promoted to *Major-General* |
| 28 Mar 1912 - 3 Jul 1915: | Commander, 18$^{th}$ Artillery Brigade |
| 3 Jul 1915 - 1 Oct 1916: | Inspector of Artillery, XXVIII. Army Corps |
| 1 Oct 1916 - Oct 1917: | Reserve officer, Kiev Military District |

*Major-General* Nikolai Petrovich **Kuchin** (24 Apr 1860 - ?)
| | |
|---|---|
| 5 Jul 1910: | Promoted to *Major-General* |
| 5 Jul 1910 - 31 Mar 1912: | Commander, 1$^{st}$ Brigade, 11$^{th}$ Siberian Rifle Division |
| 31 Mar 1912 - 1 Oct 1912: | Commander, 1$^{st}$ Brigade, 41$^{st}$ Infantry Division |
| 1 Oct 1912: | Retired |

5 Oct 1914 - 28 Sep 1915:    Recalled; Commander, 34th Militia Brigade
28 Sep 1915 - 18 Feb 1917:   Commander, 2nd Brigade, 102nd Infantry Division
18 Feb 1917 - 6 Apr 1917:    Commander, 154th Infantry Division
6 Apr 1917 - Oct 1917:       Reserve officer, Kiev Military District

*Major-General* Antony-Lyutsian Antonovich **Kuchinsky** (5 Jan 1860 - ?)
1 Dec 1912 - 1917:           Inspector of Works, Troop Billeting Department, Caucasus Military District
14 Apr 1913:                 Promoted to *Major-General*

*Major-General* Vladimir Vladimirovich **Kuchkel** (13 Feb 1865 - 30 Jun 1916)
18 Jun 1913 - 25 Jun 1916:   Commander, 3rd Amur Border Infantry Regiment
2 Jun 1916:                  Promoted to *Major-General*
25 Jun 1916 - 30 Jun 1916:   Commander, Brigade, 118th Infantry Division

*Major-General* Stanislav-Iosif-Martselly Romualdovich **Kuchkovsky** (26 Apr 1865 - May 1915)
1914 - May 1915:             Commander, 31st Siberian Rifle Regiment
19 May 1916:                 Posthumously promoted to *Major-General*

*Major-General* Koronat Ivanovich **Kuchuk** (16 Aug 1855 - ?)
10 Aug 1910 - 2 Jan 1913:    Commander, 19th Siberian Rifle Regiment
2 Jan 1913:                  Promoted to *Major-General*
2 Jan 1913:                  Retired
21 Jan 1915 - 1 Apr 1915:    Recalled; Reserve officer, Kiev Military District
1 Apr 1915 - 1917:           Commander, 81st State Militia Brigade

*Major-General* Stepan Onufriyevich **Kudlenko** (1 Jan 1869 - 7 Dec 1914)
1914 - 7 Dec 1914:           Commander, 203rd Infantry Regiment
25 May 1915:                 Posthumously promoted to *Major-General*

*Major-General* Vladimir Sergeyevich **Kudrev** (27 Jul 1860 - ?)
25 Jan 1915 - 1917:          Commander, 22nd Siberian Rifle Regiment
21 Dec 1916:                 Promoted to *Major-General*

*Major-General* Ivan Ivanovich **Kudryavtsev** (21 Jan 1853 - ?)
11 Jul 1902:                 Promoted to *Major-General*
11 Jul 1902 - 12 Aug 1907:   Commander, 2nd Brigade, 36th Infantry Division

*Major-General* Nikolai Dmitriyevich **Kudryavtsev** (7 Jul 1859 - 1920)
20 Aug 1915 - 24 Oct 1917:   Deputy Chief of Izhevsk Arms Factory
6 Dec 1915:                  Promoted to *Major-General*
24 Oct 1917:                 Dismissed

*Lieutenant-General* Nikolai Trifonovich **Kudryayev** (26 Oct 1845 - ?)
18 Feb 1891 - 5 Dec 1899:    Chief of Brest-Litovsk Military Hospital
30 Aug 1892:                 Promoted to *Major-General*
5 Dec 1899 - 3 Oct 1902:     Deputy Commander of Artillery, Warsaw Military

| | District |
|---|---|
| 3 Oct 1902 - 1906: | Commander of Artillery, Odessa Military District |
| 6 Dec 1902: | Promoted to *Lieutenant-General* |

*General of Infantry* Ivan Ksaveryevich **Kukel** (23 Jan 1838 - 1912)
| | |
|---|---|
| 26 Jul 1889: | Promoted to *Major-General* |
| 26 Jul 1889 - 19 May 1892: | Deputy Chief of Staff, Vilnius Military District |
| 19 May 1892 - 11 Jun 1895: | Chief of Staff, Amur Military District |
| 11 Jun 1895 - 29 Jul 1899: | Commander, Kharkov Regional Brigade |
| 29 Jul 1899 - 7 Oct 1904: | Commander, Vilnius Regional Brigade |
| 6 Dec 1900: | Promoted to *Lieutenant-General* |
| 7 Oct 1904 - 22 Dec 1905: | Chief of Sanatory Unit, 2$^{nd}$ Manchurian Army |
| 22 Dec 1905 - 17 Jun 1906: | At the disposal of the C-in-C, Manchurian Army |
| 17 Jun 1906 - Jan 1907: | Chief of Sanatory Troops, Rear Areas, Far East |
| Jan 1907: | Promoted to *General of Infantry* |
| Jan 1907: | Retired |

*Lieutenant-General* Aleksandr Yakovlevich **Kukharenko** (9 Apr 1836 - 1 Dec 1914)
| | |
|---|---|
| 23 Sep 1897 - 2 Apr 1910: | Ataman, Yeisky District of Kuban Region |
| 28 Mar 1904: | Promoted to *Major-General* |
| 2 Apr 1910: | Promoted to *Lieutenant-General* |
| 2 Apr 1910: | Retired |

*Major-General* Vladimir Aleksandrovich **Kukharsky** (16 Jul 1859 - 23 Jan 1916)
| | |
|---|---|
| 5 Mar 1910: | Promoted to *Major-General* |
| 5 Mar 1910 - 31 Oct 1911: | Chief of Engineers, Fortress Vladivostok |
| 31 Oct 1911 - 29 Nov 1912: | Deputy Chief of Engineers, St. Petersburg Military District |
| 29 Nov 1912 - 23 Jan 1916: | Deputy Inspector of Engineers, St. Petersburg Military District |

*Major-General* Vasily Vasilyevich **Kukuran** (28 Jan 1851 - 19 Jul 1908)
| | |
|---|---|
| 18 Dec 1904 - 25 Sep 1907: | Commander, 23$^{rd}$ East Siberian Rifle Regiment |
| 15 May 1907: | Promoted to *Major-General* |
| 25 Sep 1907 - 19 Jul 1908: | Commander, 1$^{st}$ Brigade, 39$^{th}$ Infantry Division |

*Major-General* Nikolai Ivanovich **Kulakov** (4 Jun 1848 - 20 Nov 1909)
| | |
|---|---|
| 4 Jan 1901 - 20 Nov 1909: | Staff Officer, VI. Class, Main Directorate of Horse Breeding |
| 1909: | Promoted to *Major-General* |

*Lieutenant-General* Pavel Pavlovich **Kulberg** (30 Dec 1843 - 9 Feb 1909)
| | |
|---|---|
| 4 Dec 1892 - 9 Feb 1909: | Chief of the Topography Department, Caucasus Military District |
| 30 Aug 1894: | Promoted to *Major-General* |
| 6 Dec 1902: | Promoted to *Lieutenant-General* |

*Lieutenant-General* Aleksandr Parfentyevich **Kulebyakin** (29 May 1870 - ?)
| | |
|---|---|
| 4 Jun 1915 - Jul 1916: | Commander, 2nd Brigade, 4th Caucasus Cossack Division |
| 6 Dec 1915: | Promoted to *Major-General* |
| Jul 1916 - 1917: | Commander, 2nd Caucasus Cossack Division |
| 1917: | Promoted to *Lieutenant-General* |
| 1917 - Nov 1917: | Acting Commanding General, IV. Caucasus Army Corps |

*Major-General* Stepan Ivanovich **Kuleshin** (31 Oct 1870 - 1918)
| | |
|---|---|
| 23 Jun 1915 - 5 Sep 1916: | Commander, 173rd Infantry Regiment |
| 2 Jun 1916: | Promoted to *Major-General* |
| 5 Sep 1916 - 12 Jul 1917: | Chief of Staff, 44th Infantry Division |
| 12 Jul 1917 - 22 Oct 1917: | Commander, 44th Infantry Division |
| 22 Oct 1917 - 1918: | Commanding General, XXVIII. Army Corps |

*General of Cavalry* Aleksey Petrovich **Kulgachev** (5 Nov 1825 - 19 Mar 1904)
| | |
|---|---|
| 12 Jan 1867 - 1873: | Chief of Military Horse Farm |
| 21 May 1870: | Promoted to *Major-General* |
| 1873 - 27 Jul 1875: | Member, Committee on Troop Training |
| 27 Jul 1875 - 7 May 1877: | Commander, 2nd Brigade, 13th Cavalry Division |
| 7 May 1877 - 2 Feb 1878: | Commander, 3rd Don Cossack Division |
| 2 Feb 1878 - 25 Dec 1882: | Commander, 13th Cavalry Division |
| 30 Aug 1880: | Promoted to *Lieutenant-General* |
| 25 Dec 1882 - 26 Sep 1884: | Chairman, Commission for Economic Management, Don Cossack Region |
| 26 Sep 1884 - 28 May 1889: | Commander, 14th Cavalry Division |
| 28 May 1889 - 3 May 1900: | Commanding General, VI. Army Corps |
| 30 Aug 1894: | Promoted to *General of Cavalry* |
| 3 May 1900 - 19 Mar 1904: | Member of the Military Council |

*Major-General* Aleksandr Nikanorovich **Kulikovsky** (22 Apr 1851 - ?)
| | |
|---|---|
| 16 Jan 1911 - 1917: | At the disposal of the Chief of the Army Remount Directorate |
| 6 Dec 1912: | Promoted to *Major-General* |

*Major-General* Ilya Yakovlevich **Kulnev** (18 Dec 1856 - 26 Mar 1910)
| | |
|---|---|
| 12 Jul 1908: | Promoted to *Major-General* |
| 12 Jul 1908 - 21 Dec 1908: | Commander, 1st Brigade, 1st Grenadier Division |
| 21 Dec 1908 - 26 Mar 1910: | Commander, Semenov Life Guards Regiment |

*General of Artillery* Fyodor Lavrentevich **Kulstrem** (13 Sep 1825 - 11 Feb 1906)
| | |
|---|---|
| 6 Dec 1867 - 17 Nov 1884: | Commander, Caucasus Grenadier Artillery Brigade |
| 13 Jun 1877: | Promoted to *Major-General* |
| 17 Nov 1884 - 1885: | Commander of Artillery, X. Army Corps |
| 1885 - 14 Nov 1888: | Commander of Artillery, II. Caucasus Army Corps |
| 30 Aug 1886: | Promoted to *Lieutenant-General* |
| 14 Nov 1888 - 5 Sep 1893: | Commander of Artillery, XVI. Army Corps |

5 Sep 1893 - 11 Feb 1906:  Member, Committee for Wounded Veterans
6 Dec 1898:  Promoted to *General of Artillery*

*Lieutenant-General of the Fleet* Sergey Karlovich **Kulstrem** (23 Mar 1859 - 3 Jun 1913)
2 Mar 1909 - 3 Jun 1913:  Mayor of Sevastopol
6 Dec 1909:  Promoted to *Major-General of the Admiralty*
8 Apr 1913:  Redesignated *Major-General of the Fleet*
1913:  Promoted to *Lieutenant-General of the Fleet*

*Major-General* Viktor Stepanovich **Kultashev** (5 Nov 1846 - ?)
16 Feb 1900 - 19 Oct 1907:  Military Commander of Serpukhov
19 Oct 1907:  Promoted to *Major-General*
19 Oct 1907:  Retired
28 Sep 1915 - 1917:  Recalled; Commander, Tambov District Evacuation Points

*Major-General* Sergey Nikolayevich **Kulzhinsky** (18 Jun 1869 - 1938)
3 Sep 1914 - 12 Jul 1915:  Commander, 12$^{th}$ Hussary Regiment
12 Jul 1915 - Feb 1916:  Reserve officer, 6$^{th}$ Army
Feb 1916 - 12 Jul 1916:  Chief of Staff, 4$^{th}$ Cavalry Division
12 Jul 1916:  Promoted to *Major-General*
12 Jul 1916 - 7 Feb 1917:  Chief of Staff, III. Cavalry Corps
7 Feb 1917 - 1918:  Special Assignments General, 8$^{th}$ Army

*Major-General* Georgy Nikolayevich **Kumani** (29 Feb 1864 - 31 Dec 1936)
12 Sep 1915 - 1917:  Chief of Okhtenskaya Explosives Factory
6 Dec 1915:  Promoted to *Major-General*

*General of Artillery* Aleksandr Vladimirovich **Kun** (17 Feb 1846 - 19 Nov 1916)
4 Oct 1892 - 12 Jul 1915:  Chief of Tula Arms Factory
30 Aug 1893:  Promoted to *Major-General*
29 Mar 1909:  Promoted to *Lieutenant-General*
12 Jul 1915:  Promoted to *General of Artillery*
12 Jul 1915:  Retired
31 Jul 1915 - 19 Nov 1916:  Recalled; Attached to the Ministry of War

*Lieutenant-General* Yefim Fedorovich **Kunakov** (20 Jan 1859 - ?)
14 Jan 1912:  Promoted to *Major-General*
14 Jan 1912 - 18 Dec 1913:  Commander, 2$^{nd}$ Brigade, 1$^{st}$ Don Cossack Division
18 Dec 1913 - 15 Feb 1915:  Commander, 1$^{st}$ Brigade, 1$^{st}$ Don Cossack Division
15 Feb 1915 - 24 Mar 1917:  Commander, 1$^{st}$ Brigade, 3$^{rd}$ Don Cossack Division
8 Sep 1916:  Promoted to *Lieutenant-General*
24 Mar 1917 - 1917:  Commander, 7$^{th}$ Don Cossack Division

*Lieutenant-General* Nikolai Mikhailovich **Kunayev** (16 Jan 1857 - 13 Dec 1914)
19 Aug 1905 - 2 Sep 1912:  Deputy Commander of Engineers, Warsaw Military District
6 Dec 1905:  Promoted to *Major-General*

2 Sep 1912: Promoted to *Lieutenant-General*
2 Sep 1912: Retired

*Lieutenant-General* Aleksandr Petrovich **Kunitsky** (11 Aug 1840 - 16 Jan 1904)
28 Mar 1893: Promoted to *Major-General*
28 Mar 1893 - 1 Jul 1899: Deputy Inspector of the Borderguard
1 Jul 1899 - 16 Jan 1904: Commander, 7th Borderguard District
1 Apr 1901: Promoted to *Lieutenant-General*

*Major-General* Nikolai Nikolayevich **Kupchinsky** (4 Dec 1870 - ?)
29 Nov 1916 - 1917: Commander, Brigade, 134th Infantry Division
19 Feb 1917: Promoted to *Major-General*
1917 - 1918: Director, Poltava Cadet Corps

*Major-General of the Fleet* Aleksandr Andreyevich **Kupreyanov** (11 Jul 1853 - ?)
9 Oct 1906 - 1909: Senior Deputy Captain, Port of Kronstadt
6 May 1907: Promoted to *Major-General of the Fleet*

*Major-General* Dmitry Aleksandrovich **Kupriyanov** (8 Sep 1872 - 1928)
14 Jan 1900 - 1918: Professor, Mikhailovsky Artillery Academy
1916 - 1918: Deputy Director of Physics Department & Electrotechnical Laboratory, Mikhailovsky Artillery Academy
6 Dec 1916: Promoted to *Major-General*

*Major-General* Nikolai Aleksandrovich **Kupriyanov** (18 Feb 1855 - 1911)
27 Jul 1898 - 1911: Staff Officer, Moscow Military District
1911: Promoted to *Major-General*

*Admiral* Yakov Ivanovich **Kupriyanov** (4 Jan 1836 - 15 Aug 1906)
1882: Promoted to *Rear-Admiral*
1882 - 1883: Commander of Artillery Training Detachment
1883 - 1885: Chairman, Commission for Naval Artillery Testing
1885 - 1889: Junior Flagman, Baltic Fleet
1889 - 1891: Commander of Artillery Training Detachment
1891: Promoted to *Vice-Admiral*
1891 - 15 Aug 1906: Member, Supreme Naval Tribunal
?: Promoted to *Admiral*

*Lieutenant-General* Nikolai Ivanovich **Kurakin** (20 Jan 1851 - ?)
27 Jun 1906 - 4 Nov 1906: Commander, 12th Artillery Brigade
4 Nov 1906 - 24 May 1910: Commander, 3rd Grenadier Artillery Brigade
31 May 1907: Promoted to *Major-General*
24 May 1910 - 16 Jan 1914: Inspector of Artillery, III. Siberian Army Corps
31 May 1913: Promoted to *Lieutenant-General*

*Lieutenant-General* Aleksandr Sergeyevich **Kurbatov** (28 Jul 1836 - 1908)
10 Jul 1883 - 10 Aug 1891: Director, Pskov Cadet Corps

30 Aug 1883: Promoted to *Major-General*
10 Aug 1891 - 1895: Director, 2nd Cadet Corps
1895: Promoted to *Lieutenant-General*
1895: Retired

*Major-General* Aleksey Aleksandrovich **Kurbatov** (22 Jun 1868 - 13 Jul 1935)
12 Jul 1912 - 1916: Commander, 72nd Infantry Regiment
8 Jan 1916: Promoted to *Major-General*
1916 - 5 Jun 1917: Commander, Brigade, 40th Infantry Division
5 Jun 1917 - 1918: Commander, 40th Infantry Division

*Major-General* Stepan Osipovich **Kurch** (31 May 1850 - 11 Jan 1906)
25 Jul 1888 - 18 Sep 1897: Commander, 19th Infantry Regiment
14 May 1896: Promoted to *Major-General*
18 Sep 1897 - 4 Mar 1898: Commander, 1st Brigade, 4th Infantry Division
4 Mar 1898 - 31 Oct 1899: Commander, 2nd Brigade, 2nd Infantry Division
31 Oct 1899 - 14 Apr 1900: Commander, 2nd Brigade, 5th Infantry Division
14 Apr 1900 - 2 Feb 1905: Commander, 50th Reserve Infantry Brigade
2 Feb 1905 - 11 Jan 1906: Commander, Minsk Regional Brigade

*Major-General* Aleksandr Pavlovich **Kurdyumov** (18 Apr 1867 - 20 Sep 1926)
3 Aug 1914 - 1916: Section Chief, Central Scientific-Technical Laboratory, Ministry of War
6 Dec 1914: Promoted to *Major-General*
1916 - 1917: Chief of Department for the Construction of Aluminium Smelters in Russia

*General of Infantry* Konstantin Osipovich **Kurganovich** (6 Mar 1851 - ?)
18 Dec 1900: Promoted to *Major-General*
18 Dec 1900 - 31 Dec 1901: Commander, 1st Brigade, 24th Infantry Division
31 Dec 1901 - 30 Apr 1907: Commander, 2nd Finnish Rifle Brigade
30 Apr 1907 - Jul 1909: Commander, 37th Infantry Division
31 May 1907: Promoted to *Lieutenant-General*
Jul 1909: Promoted to *General of Infantry*
Jul 1909: Retired
1914 - 1917: Recalled; Commanding General, VI. Militia Corps

*Major-General* Ivan Petrovich **Kurguyev** (7 May 1868 - 1927)
27 Feb 1913 - 8 Oct 1916: Deputy Chief, Mikhailov Shostka Gunpowder Factory
14 Apr 1913: Promoted to *Major-General*
8 Oct 1916 - 1917: Chairman of the Commission for the Construction of the 5th Gunpowder Factory

*Major-General* Pyotr Fyodorovich **Kurilov** (21 Jun 1833 - ?)
15 Apr 1885: Promoted to *Major-General*
15 Apr 1885 - 5 Jun 1886: Transferred to the reserve
5 Jun 1886 - 1897: Commander, Tashkent Military Hospital

*General of Infantry* Pavel Grigoriyevich **Kurlov** (5 Jan 1860 - 20 Jun 1923)
| | |
|---|---|
| Apr 1903 - 16 May 1905: | Deputy Governor of Kursk |
| 1905: | Promoted to *State Councillor* |
| 16 May 1905 - 15 Jul 1906: | Governor of Minsk |
| 8 Dec 1906 - 7 Feb 1907: | Member of the Council, Ministry of Internal Affairs |
| 14 Apr 1907 - Aug 1907: | Deputy Director of the Police Department |
| Aug 1907 - 24 Mar 1909: | Chief of Prison Administration, Ministry of Justice |
| 24 Mar 1909 - 14 Oct 1911: | Deputy Minister of Internal Affairs, Commanding General, Corps of Gendarmerie |
| 24 Mar 1909: | Redesignated *Major-General* |
| 30 Jun 1910: | Promoted to *Lieutenant-General* |
| 14 Oct 1911: | Retired |
| 10 Aug 1914 - 30 Sep 1914: | Recalled; Attached to the Chief of Logistics, Northwestern Front |
| 30 Sep 1914 - 3 Aug 1915: | Deputy Commanding General, Dvinsk Military District |
| 3 Aug 1915 - 3 Nov 1915: | Reserve officer, Dvinsk Military District |
| 3 Nov 1915 - 16 Oct 1916: | Reserve officer, Petrograd Military District |
| 16 Oct 1916 - 23 Oct 1916: | Attached to the Ministry of Internal Affairs |
| 23 Oct 1916 - 5 Jan 1917: | Deputy Minister of Internal Affairs, Chief of the Police Department |
| 5 Jan 1917: | Promoted to *General of Infantry* |
| 5 Jan 1917: | Dismissed |

*Major-General* Ivan Aleksandrovich **Kurochkin** (24 May 1867 - 3 Feb 1914)
| | |
|---|---|
| 7 Feb 1913 - 24 Jun 1913: | Military Judge, Caucasus Military District Court |
| 14 Apr 1913: | Promoted to *Major-General* |
| 24 Jun 1913 - 3 Feb 1914: | Military Judge, Odessa Military District Court |

*General of Infantry* Aleksei Nikolayevich **Kuropatkin** (17 Mar 1848 - 16 Jan 1925)
| | |
|---|---|
| 22 Jan 1882 - 16 Mar 1883: | Commander, Turkestan Infantry Brigade |
| 29 Jan 1882: | Promoted to *Major-General* |
| 16 Mar 1883 - 27 Mar 1890: | Attached to the General Staff |
| 27 Mar 1890: | Promoted to *Lieutenant-General* |
| 27 Mar 1890 - 1 Jan 1898: | Commanding General, Trans-Caspian Region, Chief of the Transcaucasus Military Railway |
| 1 Jan 1898 - 1 Jul 1898: | Deputy Minister of War |
| 1 Jul 1898 - 7 Feb 1904: | Minister of War, Chairman of the Military Council |
| 6 Dec 1900: | Promoted to *General of Infantry* |
| 1902: | Promoted to *General-Adjutant* |
| 7 Feb 1904 - 13 Oct 1904: | C-in-C, Manchurian Army |
| 13 Oct 1904 - 3 Mar 1905: | C-in-C, Far East |
| 3 Mar 1905 - 3 Feb 1906: | C-in-C, 1st Manchurian Army |
| 3 Feb 1906 - 1907: | Member of the State Council |
| 1907: | Retired |
| 12 Sep 1915 - 30 Jan 1916: | Recalled; Commanding General, Grenadier Corps |
| 30 Jan 1916 - 6 Feb 1916: | C-in-C, 5th Army |
| 6 Feb 1916 - 22 Jul 1916: | C-in-C, Northern Front |

22 Jul 1916 - Feb 1917: Governor-General of Turkestan,
Commanding General, Turkestan Military District
Feb 1917: Dismissed

*Vice-Admiral* Aleksandr Parfenovich **Kurosh** (30 Mar 1862 - Aug 1918)
1911 - 17 Aug 1915: Commander, 2nd Mine Division, Baltic Fleet
6 Dec 1912: Promoted to *Rear-Admiral*
17 Aug 1915 - 23 Jan 1917: Commander, 2nd Cruiser Brigade, Baltic Fleet
30 Jul 1916: Promoted to *Vice-Admiral*
23 Jan 1917 - 2 Mar 1917: Commandant of Fortress Kronstadt
2 Mar 1917 - 3 Sep 1917: Unassigned
3 Sep 1917 - 7 Dec 1917: Reserve officer, Ministry of the Navy
7 Dec 1917: Dismissed

*Major-General* Mikhail Vasilyevich **Kuroyedov** (4 Apr 1858 - Dec 1915)
22 Mar 1914 - Dec 1915: Chief of Gendarmerie, Orlovsk
22 Mar 1915: Promoted to *Major-General*

*General of Infantry* Viktor Magnusovich **Kursel** (25 Dec 1836 - ?)
12 Dec 1884: Promoted to *Major-General*
12 Dec 1884 - 1 Jul 1888: Commander, 1st East Siberian Rifle Brigade
1 Jul 1888 - 19 Jun 1892: Commander, South Ussuri Sector
19 Jun 1892 - 1 Dec 1892: At the disposal of the Chief of the General Staff
1 Dec 1892 - 19 Aug 1894: Commander, 45th Reserve Infantry Brigade
19 Aug 1894 - 29 Feb 1900: Commander, 8th Infantry Division
14 Nov 1894: Promoted to *Lieutenant-General*
29 Feb 1900: Promoted to *General of Infantry*
29 Feb 1900: Retired

*Major-General* Iosaf Pavlovich **Kusakov** (20 Jul 1848 - ?)
30 Nov 1904 - 11 Apr 1908: Commander, 19th Artillery Brigade
6 Dec 1906: Promoted to *Major-General*

*Major-General* Vladimir Andreyevich **Kusakov** (1 Aug 1854 - ?)
12 May 1898 - 1910: Commander, 1st Battalion, 7th Grenadier Regiment
1910: Promoted to *Major-General*
1910: Retired
1 Jun 1916 - 1917: Recalled; Commander 102nd Train Battalion

*Lieutenant-General* Aleksey Yefimovich **Kushakevich** (3 Feb 1865 - 19 Apr 1932)
31 Jan 1915: Promoted to *Major-General*
31 Jan 1915 - 7 Apr 1917: Commander, Life Guards Volyn Regiment
7 Apr 1917 - 4 Jun 1917: Commander, 1st Turkestan Rifle Division
4 Jun 1917: Promoted to *Lieutenant-General*
4 Jun 1917 - Dec 1917: Commanding General, I. Turkestan Army Corps
Dec 1917: Acting C-in-C, Special Army

*Major-General* Roman-Antony Lyudvigovich **Kushelevsky** (20 Feb 1867 - ?)
4 Sep 1915 - 1 Aug 1916: Commander, 33rd Siberian Rifle Regiment
6 Dec 1915: Promoted to *Major-General*
1 Aug 1916 - 1917: Reserve officer, Minsk Military District

*Major-General* Yevgeny Sergeyevich **Kushkovsky** (31 Jul 1840 - ?)
3 Mar 1890: Promoted to *Major-General*
3 Mar 1890 - 1897: Chief of Bureau, Court of Grand Duke Pavel Aleksandrovich

*Lieutenant-General* Ivan Ivanovich **Kushnerev** (16 Oct 1835 - ?)
11 Nov 1887: Promoted to *Major-General*
11 Nov 1887 - 6 Jul 1888: Chief of Engineers, Kharkov Military District
6 Jul 1888 - 9 Oct 1894: Chief of Engineers, Kazan Military District
9 Oct 1894 - Jul 1906: Chief of Engineers, Kiev Military District
14 May 1896: Promoted to *Lieutenant-General*

*Major-General* Pavel Mikhailovich **Kusonsky** (15 Jan 1866 - ?)
14 May 1915 - Oct 1917: Deputy Chief of Military Communications, General Staff
6 Dec 1915: Promoted to *Major-General*

*Major-General* Aleksandr Aleksandrovich **Kusov** (9 Jul 1850 - ?)
1 Jun 1904: Promoted to *Major-General*
1 Jun 1904 - 19 Jun 1905: Commander, 2nd Brigade, 72nd Infantry Division
19 Jun 1905 - 30 Sep 1906: Attached to the General Staff
30 Sep 1906 - 21 Aug 1908: Commander, 2nd Brigade, 8th East Siberian Rifle Division

*Lieutenant-General* Inal Tegoyevich **Kusov** (18 May 1847 - ?)
3 Nov 1900: Promoted to *Major-General*
3 Nov 1900 - 11 Jun 1906: Commander, 1st Brigade, 1st Caucasus Cossack Division
11 Jun 1906 - Oct 1908: Commander, 1st Caucasus Cossack Division
6 Dec 1906: Promoted to *Lieutenant-General*

*Major-General* Pyotr Ivanovich **Kussaba-Valenich** (4 Sep 1865 - 1915)
? - 1915: Attached to 12th Infantry Regiment
5 Oct 1915: Posthumously promoted to *Major-General*

*Lieutenant-General* Kirill Petrovich **Kutateladze** (22 Feb 1861 - 1929)
15 Sep 1910 - 5 Jan 1916: Special Assignments General, Inspectorate-General of Artillery
6 Dec 1910: Promoted to *Major-General*
5 Jan 1916 - Oct 1917: Special Assignments General, Inspectorate of Field Artillery, High Command
6 Dec 1916: Promoted to *Lieutenant-General*

*General of Infantry* Count Pavel Ippolitovich **Kutaysov** (24 Dec 1837 - 11 Jul 1911)
27 Apr 1871 - 27 Jul 1882: Military Attaché, London
14 May 1873: Promoted to *Major-General*
27 Jul 1882 - 1 Apr 1884: Chief of Gendarmerie, Warsaw District
1 Apr 1884 - 9 Nov 1896: Member of the Board, Ministry of Internal Affairs
30 Aug 1888: Promoted to *Lieutenant-General*
9 Nov 1896 - 24 May 1903: Member of the Senate
9 Apr 1900: Promoted to *General of Infantry*
24 May 1903 - 15 Nov 1905: Governor-General of Irkutsk
11 Aug 1904 - 11 Jul 1911: Member of the State Council

*Lieutenant-General* Nikolai Ivanovich **Kutepov** (1 Jan 1851 - 23 Dec 1907)
5 Sep 1885 - Jul 1906: Chief of Economic Section of the Imperial Hunt
9 Apr 1900: Promoted to *Major-General*
Jul 1906: Promoted to *Lieutenant-General*
Jul 1906: Retired

*Major-General* Sergey Ivanovich **Kutepov** (15 Nov 1853 - 16 Sep 1905)
31 Oct 1899 - 6 Oct 1901: Commander, 147$^{th}$ Infantry Regiment
6 Oct 1901: Promoted to *Major-General*
6 Oct 1901 - 16 Sep 1905: Commander, Life Guards 2$^{nd}$ Rifle Battalion

*Lieutenant-General of the Admiralty* Nikolai Yevlampiyevich **Kuteynikov** (9 Mar 1845 - 25 Apr 1906)
1892 - 1895: Deputy Chief Inspector of Shipbuilding
1895: Promoted to *Major-General of the Admiralty*
1895 - Sep 1905: Chief Inspector of Shipbuilding,
Chief of Shipbuilding Department, Naval Technical Committee
1904: Promoted to *Lieutenant-General of the Admiralty*
Sep 1905: Retired

*General of Infantry* Nikolai Borisovich **Kutnevich** (11 Dec 1837 - 5 Nov 1915)
8 Jun 1894: Promoted to *Major-General*
8 Jun 1894 - 11 Aug 1899: General for Special Assignments, Kiev Military District
11 Aug 1899 - 13 Apr 1900: Commander, 3$^{rd}$ Rifle Brigade
13 Apr 1900 - 23 Oct 1904: Commander, 44$^{th}$ Infantry Division
6 Dec 1900: Promoted to *Lieutenant-General*
23 Oct 1904 - 12 Sep 1905: Commander, 22$^{nd}$ Infantry Division
12 Sep 1905 - 23 Jan 1906: Commanding General, Consolidated Rifle Corps
23 Jan 1906: Promoted to *General of Infantry*
23 Jan 1906: Retired

*Lieutenant-General* Yury Sergeyevich **Kuvyazev** (8 Apr 1846 - ?)
2 Jul 1898 - 25 Apr 1901: Commander of Artillery, Fortress Kars
6 Dec 1899: Promoted to *Major-General*
25 Apr 1901 - 28 Mar 1906: Commander of Artillery, Fortress Kaunas
28 Mar 1906 - 16 Jan 1909: Artillery Inspector, Kazan Military District

16 Jan 1909: Promoted to *Lieutenant-General*
16 Jan 1909 - 19 Feb 1911: Commander of Artillery, Vilnius Military District

*Major-General* Nikolai Nikolayevich **Kuzichev** (12 Jan 1853 - ?)
11 Aug 1899: Promoted to *Major-General*
11 Aug 1899 - 1902: Chief of Staff, XX. Army Corps

*Vice-Admiral* Konstantin Pavlovich **Kuzmich** (16 May 1846 - 1 May 1906)
5 Apr 1898: Promoted to *Rear-Admiral*
5 Apr 1898 - 1901: Chief of Staff, Black Sea Fleet
1901 - 20 Oct 1903: Junior Flagman, Pacific Squadron
20 Oct 1903 - 1 May 1906: Commandant, Port of St. Petersburg
5 Oct 1904: Promoted to *Vice-Admiral*

*Major-General* Konstantin Gerasimovich **Kuzmin** (2 May 1845 - ?)
29 Dec 1899: Promoted to *Major-General*
29 Dec 1899 - 11 Mar 1904: Commander, 2nd Replacement Artillery Brigade
11 Mar 1904 - 11 Feb 1905: Commander of Artillery, X. Army Corps
11 Feb 1905 - Sep 1905: Attached to the Main Artillery Directorate
Sep 1905: Retired

*Major-General* Vladimir Dmitriyevich **Kuzmin-Karavayev** (28 Aug 1859 - 17 Feb 1927)
5 Feb 1895 - 1905: Professor, Military Law Academy
1 Apr 1901: Promoted to *Major-General*

*Lieutenant-General* Aglay Dmitriyevich **Kuzmin-Korovayev** (23 May 1864 - 1918)
1 Jul 1906 - 17 Oct 1910: Quartermaster-General, Irkutsk Military District
6 Dec 1906: Promoted to *Major-General*
17 Oct 1910 - 18 Jul 1914: Commander, 1st Brigade, 5th Cavalry Division
18 Jul 1914: Promoted to *Lieutenant-General*
18 Jul 1914 - 15 Aug 1914: Commander, 1st Don Cossack Division
15 Aug 1914 - 3 Aug 1915: Reserve officer, Kiev Military District
3 Aug 1915 - 18 Apr 1917: Commander, 1st Kuban Cossack Division
18 Apr 1917 - 17 Aug 1917: Reserve officer, Minsk Military District
17 Aug 1917: Retired

*Lieutenant-General* Aleksandr Nikolayevich **Kuzmin-Korovayev** (7 Nov 1862 - 13 Feb 1923)
24 Nov 1901 - 6 Jul 1907: Military Attaché, Brussels and The Hague
6 Dec 1906: Promoted to *Major-General*
6 Jul 1907 - 3 Feb 1910: Commander, 1st Brigade, 21st Infantry Division
3 Feb 1910 - 7 Dec 1912: Commander, 2nd Brigade, Caucasus Grenadier Division
7 Dec 1912 - 11 Nov 1914: Chief of Staff, II. Caucasus Army Corps
11 Nov 1914 - 31 Dec 1916: Commander, 76th Infantry Division
8 May 1915: Promoted to *Lieutenant-General*
31 Dec 1916 - 14 May 1917: Commanding General, XXVII. Army Corps
14 May 1917 - 11 Oct 1917: Reserve officer, Dvinsk Military District
11 Oct 1917 - 1918: Reserve officer, Caucasus Military District

*Major-General* Boris Aleksandrovich **Kuzmin-Korovayev** (4 Jan 1857 - 10 May 1920)
3 Oct 1906 - 30 Aug 1912: Commander, 10th Uhlan Regiment
30 Aug 1912: Promoted to *Major-General*
30 Aug 1912 - 8 Sep 1913: Commander, 2nd Brigade, 12th Cavalry Division
8 Sep 1913 - 17 Jun 1916: Commander, 1st Brigade, 12th Cavalry Division
17 Jun 1916 - 1917: Reserve officer, Kiev Military District

*General of Artillery* Dmitry Dmitrievich **Kuzmin-Korovayev** (5 Dec 1856 - 19 Jan 1950)
29 Dec 1899 - 12 Jun 1904: Commander, Guards Horse Artillery Brigade
9 Apr 1900: Promoted to *Major-General*
12 Jun 1904 - 25 Feb 1905: Commander of Artillery, Don Army
25 Feb 1905 - 13 Feb 1909: Deputy Master-General of Ordnance
25 Feb 1905 - 24 May 1915: Chief of the Main Artillery Directorate
2 Apr 1906: Promoted to *Lieutenant-General*
6 Dec 1912: Promoted to *General of Artillery*
24 May 1915 - 1917: Member of the Military Council

*Major-General* Konstantin Konstantinovich **Kuzmin-Korovayev** (28 May 1861 - ?)
14 Jun 1912 - 28 Feb 1916: Commander, 9th Dragoon Regiment
21 Jan 1916: Promoted to *Major-General*
28 Feb 1916 - 13 Apr 1917: Commander, 1st Brigade, 9th Cavalry Division
13 Apr 1917 - Oct 1917: Reserve officer, Kiev Military District

*Major-General* Konstantin Georgiyevich **Kuzminsky** (21 May 1843 - ?)
29 Dec 1899: Promoted to *Major-General*
29 Dec 1899 - 5 Aug 1903: Commander, 31st Artillery Brigade

*Major-General* Ivan Alekseyevich **Kuznetsov** (23 Dec 1869 - ?)
15 Nov 1914 - 1 Dec 1916: Commandant, Rifle Regiment Officer School
1 Dec 1916: Promoted to *Major-General*
1 Dec 1916 - 1917: Commander, Brigade, 128th Infantry Division

*Major-General* Konstantin Nikolayevich **Kuznetsov** (18 Nov 1862 - 3 Oct 1915)
1915 - 3 Oct 1915: Commander, 1st Regiment, Trans-Baikal Cossack Army
10 Mar 1916: Posthumously promoted to *Major-General*

*Lieutenant-General* Nikolai Ivanovich **Kuznetsov** (25 Sep 1834 - 20 Apr 1905)
27 Jul 1880 - 24 Mar 1885: Ministry of War Representative, Caucasus Military District Council
30 Aug 1880: Promoted to *Major-General*
24 Mar 1885 - 1 Jan 1889: Ministry of War Representative, Kharkov Military District Council
1 Jan 1889 - 20 Apr 1905: Ministry of War Representative, Warsaw Military District Council
14 May 1896: Promoted to *Lieutenant-General*

*Major-General* Nikolai Mikhailovich **Kuznetsov** (6 May 1858 - ?)
10 Dec 1909: Promoted to *Major-General*

10 Dec 1909 - 22 Jun 1912: Commander, 9th Artillery Brigade

*Lieutenant-General* Polikarp Alekseyevich **Kuznetsov** (25 Feb 1860 - ?)
18 Aug 1905: Promoted to *Major-General*
18 Aug 1905 - 13 Jan 1906: Commander, 1st Brigade, 3rd Infantry Division
13 Jan 1906 - 29 Jan 1907: Commander, 1st Brigade, 15th Infantry Division
29 Jan 1907 - 21 Jul 1910: Commander, 2nd Brigade, 15th Infantry Division
21 Jul 1910 - 6 Oct 1914: Chief of Staff, VIII. Army Corps
6 Oct 1914 - 24 Oct 1915: Commander, 31st Infantry Division
Jan 1915: Promoted to *Lieutenant-General*
24 Oct 1915 - 26 Jan 1916: Commanding General, XXXVII. Army Corps
26 Jan 1916 - 9 Sep 1917: Commanding General, XIII. Army Corps
9 Sep 1917 - 1918: Reserve officer, Petrograd Military District

*Major-General* Sergey Alekseyevich **Kuznetsov** (8 Jan 1872 - 23 Sep 1919)
26 Jul 1915 - 5 May 1916: Commander, Life Guards Kexholmsky Regiment
11 Aug 1915: Promoted to *Major-General*
5 May 1916 - 11 Mar 1917: Chief of Staff, 3rd Guards Infantry Division
11 Mar 1917 - 7 Apr 1917: Chief of Staff, XXIV. Army Corps
7 Apr 1917 - 1918: Commander, 73rd Infantry Division

*Lieutenant-General* Vavila Alekseyevich **Kuznetsov** (4 Sep 1829 - ?)
24 Mar 1880 - 20 Aug 1882: Attached to the Ministry of Internal Affairs
30 Aug 1880: Promoted to *Major-General*
20 Aug 1882 - 10 Jan 1886: Attached to the Ministry of the Imperial Court
10 Jan 1886 - 1905: Chief of Administration, Moscow Imperial Court
17 Apr 1894: Promoted to *Lieutenant-General*

*Major-General* Mikhail Fyodorovich **Kuzovlev** (31 May 1870 - ?)
28 Mar 1913 - 2 Jan 1917: Military Judge, Amur Military District Court
14 Apr 1913: Promoted to *Major-General*
2 Jan 1917: Dismissed

*Major-General* Nikolai Matveyevich **Kuzubov** (9 Apr 1856 - ?)
18 Jul 1904 - 1907: Commander of Gendarmerie, Odessa
6 Dec 1906: Promoted to *Major-General*

*Major-General* Aleksandr Nikolayevich **Kuzyayevsky** (7 Aug 1836 - 1900)
23 Mar 1888: Promoted to *Major-General*
23 Mar 1888 - 4 Feb 1891: Commander, 2nd Brigade, 8th Infantry Division
4 Feb 1891 - 9 Jun 1891: Commander, 1st Brigade, 8th Infantry Division
9 Jun 1891 - 1897: Commander, 43rd Reserve Infantry Brigade
1897: Retired

*Major-General* Viktor Viktorovich **Kvadri** (16 Jul 1861 - 24 Mar 1908)
6 Dec 1904: Promoted to *Major-General*
6 Dec 1904 - 24 Mar 1908: At the disposal of the Commandant, Imperial Main Headquarters

*Lieutenant-General* Vladimir Viktorovich **Kvadri** (11 Jan 1859 - ?)
20 Jul 1906 - 1917: Director, Nikolayev Cadet Corps
6 Dec 1906: Promoted to *Major-General*
6 Dec 1913: Promoted to *Lieutenant-General*
1917: Director of the Pedagogical Museum, Main Directorate for Military Schools

*Major-General* Vasily Alekseyevich **Kvanchkhadze** (2 Feb 1858 - ?)
31 Dec 1913: Promoted to *Major-General*
31 Dec 1913 - 3 Jul 1916: Commander, 2nd Brigade, 52nd Infantry Division
3 Jul 1916 - 1917: Commander, 39th Replacement Infantry Brigade

*General of Infantry* Konstantin Petrovich **Kvashnin-Samarin** (24 Jul 1848 - ?)
12 Dec 1903: Promoted to *Major-General*
12 Dec 1903 - 31 Dec 1913: Commander, Smolensk Local Brigade
6 Dec 1908: Promoted to *Lieutenant-General*
31 Dec 1913: Promoted to *General of Infantry*
31 Dec 1913: Retired

*Major-General* Nikolai Petrovich **Kvashnin-Samarin** (6 May 1845 - 1920)
15 Jun 1891 - 1906: Deputy Chief of Administration, Peterhof Palace
11 Aug 1904: Promoted to *Major-General*

*Major-General* Sergey Petrovich **Kvashnin-Samarin** (6 Jun 1853 - ?)
23 Jan 1896 - 26 Mar 1910: Intendant, XV. Army Corps
6 Dec 1908: Promoted to *Major-General*
26 Mar 1910 - Jun 1913: Deputy Intendant, Warsaw Military District
Jun 1913: Retired

*Lieutenant-General* Mikhail Fyodorovich **Kvetsinsky** (3 Jan 1866 - 31 Mar 1923)
6 Jul 1910: Promoted to *Major-General*
6 Jul 1910 - 8 Jan 1915: Chief of Staff, III. Caucasus Army Corps
8 Jan 1915 - 8 Feb 1915: Commander, 21st Infantry Division
8 Feb 1915 - 21 Sep 1915: Chief of Staff, 2nd Army
28 Feb 1915: Promoted to *Lieutenant-General*
21 Sep 1915 - 3 Apr 1917: Chief of Staff, Western front
3 Apr 1917 - 11 Aug 1917: C-in-C, 3rd Army
11 Aug 1917 - 30 Oct 1917: Commanding General, Kiev Military District

*General of Cavalry* Erast Ksenofontovich **Kvitnitsky** (30 Dec 1843 - 3 Oct 1907)
17 Oct 1891: Promoted to *Major-General*
17 Oct 1891 - 17 Jun 1899: Commander, 2nd Brigade, 8th Cavalry Division
17 Jun 1899 - 14 Jan 1907: Commander, 15th Cavalry Division
6 Dec 1899: Promoted to *Lieutenant-General*
14 Jan 1907: Promoted to *General of Cavalry*
14 Jan 1907: Retired

*Major-General* Boris Iosifovich **Kvitsinsky** (15 Jan 1868 - 22 Jun 1934)
2 Feb 1916 - 10 Apr 1917: Commander, Life Guards Chasseur Regiment
10 Apr 1916: Promoted to *Major-General*

*General of Infantry* Iosif-Ignatiy Onufriyevich **Kvitsinsky** (21 May 1831 - Jul 1908)
13 Jan 1883: Promoted to *Major-General*
13 Jan 1883 - 8 Oct 1889: Commander, Life Guards Moscow Regiment
8 Oct 1889 - 12 Nov 1893: Commander, 1st Brigade, 2nd Guards Infantry Division
12 Nov 1893 - 2 Aug 1894: Commander, 36th Infantry Division
30 Aug 1894: Promoted to *Lieutenant-General*
2 Aug 1894 - 31 May 1898: Commander, 2nd Grenadier Division
31 May 1898 - Jul 1908: Honorary Trustee, Board of Trustees, Empress Maria Institutions
6 Dec 1904: Promoted to *General of Infantry*

*Major-General* Mikhail Stanislavovich **Kvitsinsky** (16 Oct 1845 - ?)
18 Dec 1900: Promoted to *Major-General*
18 Dec 1900 - 28 Nov 1901: Commander, 8th Replacement Cavalry Brigade
28 Nov 1901 - 19 May 1906: Commander, 3rd Replacement Cavalry Brigade
19 May 1906 - 1906: Commander, 2nd Replacement Cavalry Brigade

*Major-General* Nikolai Ilich **Kvyatkovsky** (15 Feb 1849 - ?)
21 Apr 1903 - 28 Jul 1906: Commander, 35th Infantry Regiment
25 Feb 1905: Promoted to *Major-General*
28 Jul 1906 - Sep 1908: Commander, 1st Brigade, 9th East Siberian Rifle Division

*General of Engineers* Tsezar Antonovich **Kyui** (7 Jan 1836 - 26 Mar 1918)
8 Apr 1880 - 1917: Professor, Nikolaev Military Engineering Academy
30 Aug 1885: Promoted to *Major-General*
14 May 1896: Promoted to *Lieutenant-General*
22 Jun 1906: Promoted to *General of Engineers*

*Lieutenant-General* Georgy Lvovich **Kyuster** (3 Jun 1851 - ?)
14 Mar 1906 - 10 Jul 1910: Commander of Engineers, Fortress Osovets
2 Apr 1906: Promoted to *Major-General*
10 Jul 1910 - 29 Sep 1911: Deputy Commander of Engineers, Vilnius Military District
29 Sep 1911: Promoted to *Lieutenant-General*
29 Sep 1911: Retired

*Major-General* Khrisanf Gavrilovich **Labutin** (19 Mar 1851 - ?)
1 Feb 1886 - 1906: Military Judge, Kiev Military District Court
30 Aug 1894: Promoted to *Major-General*

*General of Infantry* Nikolai Aleksandrovich **Lachinov** (4 Jan 1834 - ?)
3 Jul 1872 - 4 Oct 1893: Deputy Chief Editor, "Military Collection" and "Russian Invalid"

30 Aug 1882: Promoted to *Major-General*
4 Oct 1893 - 3 Aug 1899: Chief Editor, "Military Collection" and "Russian Invalid"
30 Aug 1894: Promoted to *Lieutenant-General*
3 Aug 1899 - 1906: Member, Military Research Committee, General Staff, At the disposal of the Minister of War
1906: Promoted to *General of Infantry*
1906: Retired

*Major-General* Pavel Ivanovich **Lachinov** (15 Mar 1859 - ?)
1 Aug 1905 - 1909: Inspector of Classes, Aleksandr Military School
6 Dec 1908: Promoted to *Major-General*
1909: Retired

*Major-General* Gavriil Mikhailovich **Ladyzhensky** (13 Nov 1865 - 6 Jan 1945)
May 1907 - 19 Sep 1907: Commander, Dragoon Cavalry Regiment
19 Sep 1907: Promoted to *Major-General*
19 Sep 1907: Retired
10 Sep 1914 - 21 Feb 1915: Recalled; Reserve officer, Minsk Military District
21 Feb 1915 - 20 May 1915: Commander, 1$^{st}$ Brigade, 3$^{rd}$ Cavalry Division
20 May 1915 - 25 Jun 1915: Chief of Staff, 62$^{nd}$ Infantry Division
25 Jun 1915 - 20 Dec 1916: Reserve officer, Dvinsk Military District
20 Dec 1916 - 17 Mar 1917: Chief of Staff, 62$^{nd}$ Infantry Division
17 Mar 1917 - 5 May 1917: Chief of Staff, III. Caucasus Army Corps
5 May 1917 - 3 Sep 1917: Chief of Staff, II. Cavalry Corps
3 Sep 1917 - 12 Apr 1918: Reserve officer, Kiev Military District
12 Apr 1918: Discharged

*Major-General* Pavel Pavlovich **Lagunov** (3 Jun 1862 - ?)
25 Jul 1914: Promoted to *Major-General*
25 Jul 1914 - 3 Apr 1915: Commander, 3$^{rd}$ Siberian Rifle Artillery Brigade
3 Apr 1915 - 1918: POW, Germany

*Major-General* Pyotr Pavlovich **Lagunov** (28 Jun 1858 - 9 Sep 1915)
16 Jan 1908 - 9 Sep 1915: Ataman, Maikop District, Kuban Region
22 Mar 1915: Promoted to *Major-General*

*Major-General* Vladimir Nilovich **Lakhtionov** (1 Jun 1872 - 9 Jun 1929)
Jan 1915 - 17 Nov 1915: Commander, Artillery Brigade
23 Apr 1915: Promoted to *Major-General*
17 Nov 1915 - 28 Dec 1915: Reserve officer, Dvinsk Military District
28 Dec 1915 - 21 Nov 1916: Commander, 4$^{th}$ Siberian Rifle Artillery Brigade
21 Nov 1916 - 15 Jun 1917: Inspector of Artillery, XXXIII. Army Corps
15 Jun 1917 - Oct 1917: Inspector of Artillery, 8$^{th}$ Army

*General of Artillery* Matvey Stepanovich **Lalayev** (12 Sep 1828 - 28 Oct 1912)
2 Jan 1865 - 19 Jan 1877: Attached to the Directorate-General of Military Schools
1 Jan 1872: Promoted to *Major-General*

| | |
|---|---|
| 19 Jan 1877 - Jan 1906: | Special Assignments General, Directorate-General of Military Schools |
| 30 Aug 1882: | Promoted to *Lieutenant-General* |
| 14 May 1896: | Promoted to *General of Artillery* |
| Jan 1906: | Retired |

*Major-General* Aleksandr Bogdanovich **Lampe** (24 Dec 1850 - 1913)
| | |
|---|---|
| 3 Sep 1901 - 1913: | Commander of Finnish Railway Gendarmerie |
| 13 Apr 1908: | Promoted to *Major-General* |

*Lieutenant-General* Count Konstantin Nikolayevich **Lamzdorf-Galagan** (24 Dec 1841 - 1900)
| | |
|---|---|
| 30 Apr 1877: | Promoted to *Major-General* |
| 30 Apr 1877 - 1900: | Staff Officer to the Tsar |
| 30 Aug 1886: | Promoted to *Lieutenant-General* |

*Major-General of the Admiralty* Gavriil Konstantinovich **Lanevsky-Volk** (17 Apr 1854 - ?)
| | |
|---|---|
| 9 Apr 1900 - Jul 1911: | Director of Lighthouses & Navigation, Black Sea & Sea of Azov |
| 22 Apr 1907: | Promoted to *Major-General of the Admiralty* |

*Lieutenant-General* Viktor-Genrikh Ivanovich **Lang** (5 Aug 1848 - ?)
| | |
|---|---|
| 19 Jul 1900 - 17 Jul 1904: | Deputy Intendant, Vilnius Military District |
| 1904: | Promoted to *Major-General* |
| 17 Jul 1904 - 24 Jul 1905: | Intendant, 2$^{nd}$ Manchurian Army |
| 24 Jul 1905 - 1 Sep 1908: | Intendant, Omsk Military District |
| 1 Sep 1908 - 5 May 1910: | Intendant, Warsaw Military District |
| 5 May 1910 - 17 Jun 1912: | Attached to the Intendant-General of the Army |
| 17 Jun 1912: | Promoted to *Lieutenant-General* |
| 17 Jun 1912: | Retired |

*Major-General of the Fleet* Karl Khristianovich **Lange** (12 Feb 1860 - 24 Feb 1918)
| | |
|---|---|
| 10 Jan 1911 - 1913: | Chief Engineer, Port of Nikolayev |
| 1913: | Promoted to *Major-General of the Fleet* |
| 1913: | Retired |

*General of Artillery* Pavel Karlovich **Lange** (13 Jul 1846 - ?)
| | |
|---|---|
| 1 Jan 1893: | Promoted to *Major-General* |
| 1 Jan 1893 - 3 Jan 1896: | Attached to the Master-General of Ordnance |
| 3 Jan 1896 - 5 Dec 1899: | Commander, Life Guards Horse Artillery |
| 5 Dec 1899 - 18 Mar 1906: | Commander of Artillery, VII. Army Corps |
| 6 Dec 1900: | Promoted to *Lieutenant-General* |
| 18 Mar 1906 - 21 May 1908: | Commanding General, XIII. Army Corps |
| 21 May 1908: | Promoted to *General of Artillery* |
| 21 May 1908: | Retired |

*Major-General* Vladimir Vladimirovich von **Lange** (2 Aug 1860 - ?)
| | |
|---|---|
| 1914 - 23 Dec 1915: | Commander, 46$^{th}$ Siberian Rifle Regiment |

| 23 Dec 1915 - 26 Nov 1916: | Reserve officer, Odessa Military District |
| 26 Nov 1916: | Promoted to *Major-General* |
| 26 Nov 1916: | Dismissed |

*Major-General* Nikolai Fyodorovich **Langensheld** (26 Aug 1855 - 1907)
| 25 Oct 1905 - 1907: | Member of the Artillery Committee, Main Artillery Directorate |
| 27 Mar 1906: | Promoted to *Major-General* |

*General of Infantry* Baron Karl-Fridrikh-Avgust Fyodorovich **Langhoff** (2 Feb 1856 - 18 Nov 1929)
| 13 Sep 1899 - 20 Oct 1904: | Commander, Life Guards Semyonov Regiment |
| 6 Dec 1900: | Promoted to *Major-General* |
| 20 Oct 1904 - 6 Feb 1906: | Commander, 1st Brigade, 1st Guards Infantry Division |
| 6 Feb 1906 - 8 Apr 1913: | Minister-Secretary of State of the Grand Duchy of Finland |
| 6 Dec 1906: | Promoted to *Lieutenant-General* |
| 8 Apr 1913: | Promoted to *General of Infantry* |
| 8 Apr 1913: | Retired |

*Lieutenant-General* Pavel Aleksandrovich **Lansere** (14 Nov 1845 - 29 May 1900)
| 12 Nov 1892 - 1899: | Deputy Chief of Engineers, Warsaw Military District |
| 30 Aug 1894: | Promoted to *Major-General* |
| 1899: | Promoted to *Lieutenant-General* |
| 1899: | Retired |

*Lieutenant-General* Aleksandr Aleksandrovich **Larionov** (23 Nov 1835 - ?)
| 9 Dec 1885 - 30 Nov 1895: | Commander, 102nd Infantry Regiment |
| 14 Nov 1894: | Promoted to *Major-General* |
| 30 Nov 1895 - 4 Mar 1896: | Commander, 1st Brigade, 9th Infantry Division |
| 4 Mar 1896 - 2 May 1896: | Commander, 1st Brigade, 5th Infantry Division |
| 2 May 1896 - 6 Jul 1900: | Commander, 2nd Brigade, 25th Infantry Division |
| 6 Jul 1900: | Promoted to *Lieutenant-General* |
| 6 Jul 1900: | Retired |

*Lieutenant-General of the Fleet* Aleksandr Vladimirovich **Larionov** (26 May 1860 - 19 Dec 1925)
| 19 Oct 1911 - 1917: | Senior Clerk, Main Naval Staff |
| 25 Mar 1912: | Promoted to *Major-General of the Admiralty* |
| 1917: | Promoted to *Lieutenant-General of the Fleet* |
| 1917: | Retired |

*Lieutenant-General* Dmitry Ivanovich **Larionov** (26 Oct 1836 - ?)
| 18 Mar 1878 - 21 Mar 1888: | Commander, 113th Infantry Regiment |
| 14 Feb 1888: | Promoted to *Major-General* |
| 21 Mar 1888 - 14 Mar 1896: | Commander, 2nd Brigade, 18th Infantry Division |
| 14 Mar 1896 - 11 Jan 1900: | Commander, 2nd Brigade, 23rd Infantry Division |
| 11 Jan 1900: | Promoted to *Lieutenant-General* |

11 Jan 1900: Retired

*Major-General* Nikolai Stepanovich **Larionov** (18 Jul 1859 - 22 May 1922)
11 Oct 1913 - 2 Jul 1915: Commander, 43rd Infantry Regiment
2 Jul 1915 - 1917: Commander, Brigade, 4th Finnish Rifle Division
10 Oct 1915: Promoted to *Major-General*

*Lieutenant-General* Yakov Mikhailovich **Larionov** (4 Oct 1858 - ?)
26 May 1911: Promoted to *Major-General*
26 May 1911 - 9 Nov 1913: Chief of Staff, I. Siberian Army Corps
9 Nov 1913 - 10 Nov 1914: Commander, 2nd Brigade, 26th Infantry Division
10 Nov 1914 - 17 Jan 1915: Sick leave
17 Jan 1915 - 27 Apr 1915: Reserve officer, Dvinsk Military District
27 Apr 1915 - 20 Jul 1915: Reserve officer, Vilnius Military District
20 Jul 1915 - 11 Sep 1916: Commander, 2nd Brigade, 1st Siberian Rifle Division
11 Sep 1916 - 14 Aug 1917: Commander, 7th Turkestan Rifle Division
14 Aug 1917 - 1918: Reserve officer, Minsk Military District
18 Sep 1917: Promoted to *Lieutenant-General*

*Major-General* Nikandr Arkadyevich **Lashchilin** (29 Sep 1865 - ?)
4 Jun 1910 - 11 Sep 1913: Commander, 10th Don Cossack Regiment
14 Apr 1913: Promoted to *Major-General*
11 Sep 1913 - 9 Nov 1913: Commander, 1st Brigade, 1st Don Cossack Division
9 Nov 1913 - 7 Dec 1915: Chief of Staff, Fortress Grodno
7 Dec 1915 - 8 Oct 1916: Chief of Staff, XXIX. Army Corps
8 Oct 1916 - 8 Jun 1917: Chief of Staff, I. Turkestan Army Corps
8 Jun 1917 - ?: Commander, 3rd Don Cossack Division

*Lieutenant-General* Aleksandr Grigoryevich **Lashkarev** (23 Nov 1823 - 29 Nov 1898)
5 Aug 1855 - 17 Sep 1860: Member of the Commission for Troop Development
17 Apr 1860: Promoted to *Major-General*
17 Sep 1860 - 22 Apr 1865: Military Governor of Perm
22 Apr 1865 - 29 Nov 1898: Council Member, Ministry of Internal Affairs
16 Apr 1867: Promoted to *Lieutenant-General*

*General of Infantry* Nikolai Alekseyevich **Lashkevich** (6 Jun 1856 - ?)
6 Dec 1899: Promoted to *Major-General*
6 Dec 1899 - 17 May 1900: Attached to the General Staff
17 May 1900 - 17 Jun 1901: Commander, Brigade, 37th Infantry Division
17 Jun 1901 - 1 May 1903: Attached to the General Staff
1 May 1903 - 10 Feb 1904: Chief of Control Section, General Staff
10 Feb 1904 - 8 Nov 1904: Chief of Staff, I. Army Corps
8 Nov 1904 - 27 Dec 1906: Commander, 8th East Siberian Rifle Division
6 Dec 1906: Promoted to *Lieutenant-General*
27 Dec 1906 - 23 Apr 1913: Commander, 36th Infantry Division
23 Apr 1913 - 31 Mar 1915: Commander, 28th Infantry Division
31 Mar 1915 - 22 Oct 1915: Reserve officer, Dvinsk Military District
22 Oct 1915 - 1917: Commander, 2nd Siberian Reserve Rifle Brigade

| | |
|---|---|
| 1917 - 2 Oct 1917: | Reserve officer, Petrograd Military District |
| 2 Oct 1917: | Promoted to *General of Infantry* |
| 2 Oct 1917: | Retired |

*Lieutenant-General* Fyodor Pavlovich **Laskovsky** (10 Apr 1843 - 1905)

| | |
|---|---|
| 30 Aug 1886: | Promoted to *Major-General* |
| 1 Sep 1886 - 17 Sep 1889: | Attached to the Inspector-General of Engineers |
| 17 Sep 1889 - 29 Sep 1894: | Commander, Life Guards Sapper Battalion |
| 29 Sep 1894 - 4 Jul 1898: | Commander, 6th Sapper Brigade |
| 14 May 1896: | Promoted to *Lieutenant-General* |
| 4 Jul 1898 - 16 Jan 1902: | Commander, 1st Grenadier Division |
| 16 Jan 1902 - 15 Apr 1904: | Commanding General, XVIII. Army Corps |
| 15 Apr 1904 - 1905: | Deputy Commanding General, Warsaw Military District |

*Lieutenant-General* Selvin Severinovich **Lassky** (29 Oct 1849 - ?)

| | |
|---|---|
| 2 May 1902 - 4 Jan 1905: | Commander, 21st Eastern Siberian Rifle Regiment |
| 4 Jan 1905: | Promoted to *Major-General* |
| 9 Mar 1905 - 14 Jul 1905: | Commander, 1st Brigade, 6th East Siberian Rifle Division |
| 14 Jul 1905 - 5 Aug 1905: | Unassigned |
| 5 Aug 1905 - 2 Jul 1908: | Commander, 1st Brigade, 3rd East Siberian Rifle Division |
| 2 Jul 1908 - 31 Dec 1910: | Commander, 2nd Finnish Rifle Brigade |
| 31 Dec 1910: | Promoted to *Lieutenant-General* |
| 31 Dec 1910: | Retired |
| 6 Jun 1915 - 16 Mar 1916: | Recalled; Commander, 108th Infantry Division |
| 16 Mar 1916 - 7 Sep 1916: | Reserve officer, Petrograd Military District |
| 7 Sep 1916 - 1917: | Commander, 40th Replacement Infantry Brigade |

*Major-General* Pyotr Platonovich **Lastochkin** (15 Jun 1846 - ?)

| | |
|---|---|
| 22 May 1902: | Promoted to *Major-General* |
| 22 May 1902 - Dec 1907: | Commander, 1st Brigade, 43rd Infantry Division |

*Major-General* Vladimir Guryevich **Lastochkin** (18 Feb 1871 - 1920)

| | |
|---|---|
| 7 Jan 1915 - 3 Jun 1917: | Chief of Staff, I. Caucasus Army Corps |
| 22 Mar 1915: | Promoted to *Major-General* |
| 3 Jun 1917 - 19 Jun 1917: | Commander, 4th Caucasus Rifle Division |
| 19 Jun 1917 - Oct 1917: | Reserve officer, Caucasus Military District |

*Major-General* Mikhail Sergeyevich **Laterner** (31 Aug 1857 - ?)

| | |
|---|---|
| 29 Dec 1905 - 19 Apr 1906: | Military Judge, Siberian Military District Court |
| 2 Apr 1906: | Promoted to *Major-General* |
| 19 Apr 1906 - 2 Jun 1911: | Military Judge, Amur Military District Court |
| 2 Jun 1911: | Retired |

*Lieutenant-General* Iosif-Karl Onufriyevich de **Latour** (20 May 1853 - ?)

| | |
|---|---|
| 4 Mar 1906: | Promoted to *Major-General* |
| 4 Mar 1906 - 8 Aug 1908: | Director, Orenburg Neplyuev Cadet Corps |

8 Aug 1908 - 21 Oct 1911: Director, Yaroslavl Cadet Corps
21 Oct 1911: Promoted to *Lieutenant-General*
21 Oct 1911: Retired

*General of Infantry* Vladimir Andreyevich de **Latour de Berngardt** (8 Mar 1836 - 11 Mar 1914)
21 Apr 1875 - 16 Apr 1883: Commandant, Artillery Proving Grounds, St. Petersburg Military District
8 Nov 1877: Promoted to *Major-General*
16 Apr 1883 - 2 May 1887: Commander, 24th Artillery Brigade
2 May 1887 - 9 Dec 1888: Commander of Artillery, II. Army Corps
30 Aug 1887: Promoted to *Lieutenant-General*
9 Dec 1888 - 7 Aug 1892: Commander of Artillery, I. Army Corps
7 Aug 1892 - 27 Sep 1897: Commander, 22nd Infantry Division
27 Sep 1897 - 18 Dec 1902: Commandant of Fortress Brest-Litovsk
6 Dec 1899: Promoted to *General of Infantry*
18 Dec 1902 - 11 Mar 1914: Member, Committee for Wounded Veterans

*General of Cavalry* Mikhail Vasilyevich von der **Launits** (23 Apr 1843 - 4 Oct 1911)
27 Jul 1875 - 1 Aug 1879: Commander, 7th Hussar Regiment
14 Jan 1878: Promoted to *Major-General*
1 Aug 1879 - 26 Oct 1886: Chief of Staff, XV. Army Corps
26 Oct 1886 - 14 Jun 1887: Chief of Staff, XIII. Army Corps
14 Jun 1887 - 1 Sep 1888: Chief of Staff, Kiev Military District
30 Aug 1888: Promoted to *Lieutenant-General*
1 Sep 1888 - 18 Feb 1897: Commander, 1st Cavalry Division
18 Feb 1897: Retired
19 Dec 1898 - 25 Sep 1901: Recalled; Reserve status
2 Feb 1901: Promoted to *General of Cavalry*
25 Sep 1901 - 3 Jan 1906: Member, Committee for Wounded Veterans
1 Jan 1903 - 17 Oct 1904: Deputy Commanding General, Vilnius Military District
17 Oct 1904 - 1 Nov 1905: At the disposal of the C-in-C, 2nd Manchurian Army
3 Jan 1906 - 27 Feb 1906: At the disposal of the C-in-C of Forces operating against Japan
27 Feb 1906 - 19 Jan 1907: Attached to the Ministry of War
19 Jan 1907 - 4 Oct 1911: Member, Committee for Wounded Veterans

*Major-General* Vladimir Fyodorovich von der **Launits** (10 Aug 1855 - 21 Dec 1906)
31 Dec 1905: Promoted to *Major-General*
31 Dec 1905 - 21 Dec 1906: Mayor of St. Petersburg

*Lieutenant-General* Vladimir Aleksandrovich **Lavdovsky** (19 Mar 1864 - 14 Sep 1932)
26 Jun 1912 - 23 Oct 1915: Commander, 59th Infantry Regiment
23 Aug 1914: Promoted to *Major-General*
23 Oct 1915 - 25 Sep 1915: Commander, Brigade, 15th Infantry Division
25 Sep 1915 - 23 Oct 1915: Chief of Staff, XVIII. Army Corps
23 Oct 1915 - Mar 1916: Commander, Brigade, 15th Infantry Division
Mar 1916 - 15 May 1916: Chief of Staff, XLV. Army Corps

| | |
|---|---|
| 15 May 1916 - 25 Sep 1916: | Chief of Staff, VIII. Army Corps |
| 25 Sep 1916 - 15 Apr 1917: | Commander, 50$^{th}$ Infantry Division |
| 15 Apr 1917 - 28 Apr 1917: | Commander, 2$^{nd}$ Infantry Division |
| 28 Apr 1917 - Jan 1918: | Commanding General, VII. Siberian Army Corps |
| 5 May 1917: | Promoted to *Lieutenant-General* |

*Lieutenant-General* Anton Dmitriyevich **Lavrentyev** (4 Aug 1861 - 23 Oct 1940)
| | |
|---|---|
| 18 Jul 1905 - 12 May 1910: | Commander, 1$^{st}$ Brigade, 25$^{th}$ Infantry Division |
| 6 Dec 1905: | Promoted to *Major-General* |
| 12 May 1910 - 19 Jul 1914: | Commander, 1$^{st}$ Brigade, 13$^{th}$ Infantry Division |
| 19 Jul 1914 - 26 Aug 1914: | Commander, 62$^{nd}$ Infantry Division |
| 26 Aug 1914 - 21 Apr 1915: | Commander, 71$^{st}$ Infantry Division |
| Jan 1915: | Promoted to *Lieutenant-General* |
| 1 May 1915 - 7 Aug 1915: | Reserve officer, Kiev Military District |
| 7 Aug 1915 - 28 Jun 1917: | Commander, 13$^{th}$ Replacement Infantry Brigade |
| 28 Jun 1917 - Oct 1917: | Reserve officer, Kazan Military District |

*Vice-Admiral* Ivan Mikhailovich **Lavrov** (28 Mar 1840 - ?)
| | |
|---|---|
| 1890 - 24 Jun 1896: | Mayor of Sevastopol |
| 1891: | Promoted to *Rear-Admiral* |
| 24 Jun 1896 - 1897: | Junior Flagman, Black Sea Fleet |
| 1897: | Promoted to *Vice-Admiral* |
| 1897 - 1899: | Commander, Training Squadron, Black Sea Fleet |
| 1899 - ?: | Commandant of Fortress Kronstadt |

*Major-General* Konstantin Vasilyevich **Lavrov** (15 May 1861 - ?)
| | |
|---|---|
| 21 Aug 1901 - 1917: | Commissioner for the Russian Frontier with Persia |
| 6 Dec 1912: | Promoted to *Major-General* |

*Lieutenant-General* Nikolai Nilovich **Lavrov** (9 Aug 1841 - ?)
| | |
|---|---|
| 16 Mar 1892: | Promoted to *Major-General* |
| 16 Mar 1892 - 5 Jan 1898: | Chief of Staff, II. Army Corps |
| 5 Jan 1898 - 20 Oct 1899: | Chief of Staff, III. Army Corps |
| 20 Oct 1899 - 10 Aug 1904: | Commander, 30$^{th}$ Infantry Division |
| 6 Dec 1899: | Promoted to *Lieutenant-General* |

*General of Cavalry* Stepan Nilovich **Lavrov** (31 Dec 1842 - 1918)
| | |
|---|---|
| 21 Jan 1892 - 8 May 1899: | Commandant, Kiev Military School |
| 1 Jan 1895: | Promoted to *Major-General* |
| 8 May 1899 - 1 Aug 1908: | Director, Suvorov Cadet Corps |
| 6 Apr 1903: | Promoted to *Lieutenant-General* |
| 1 Aug 1908 - 4 Mar 1910: | General for Special Assignments, Main Directorate for Military Schools |
| 4 Mar 1910 - 18 Sep 1917: | General for Special Assignments, Inspectorate-General of Military Schools |
| 18 Sep 1917: | Promoted to *General of Cavalry* |
| 18 Sep 1917: | Retired |

*Lieutenant-General of the Fleet* Vasily Mikhailovich **Lavrov** (28 Dec 1841 - 10 Oct 1903)
| | |
|---|---|
| 1895 - 5 Jun 1896: | Chairman, Baltic Shipbuilding & Mechanical Plant |
| 1895: | Promoted to *Rear-Admiral* |
| 5 Jun 1896 - 10 Oct 1903: | Commander, Port of St. Petersburg |
| 1 Jan 1902: | Promoted to *Lieutenant-General of the Fleet* |

*Major-General* Vasily Nikolayevich **Lavrov** (7 Mar 1865 - ?)
| | |
|---|---|
| 1 May 1910 - 1915: | Commander, 45th Infantry Regiment |
| 1914: | Promoted to *Major-General* |

*Major-General* Yevgraf Yevgrafovich **Lavrov** (28 May 1861 - ?)
| | |
|---|---|
| 20 Sep 1903 - 5 Dec 1910: | Commander, 5th Dragoon Regiment |
| 5 Dec 1910: | Promoted to *Major-General* |
| 5 Dec 1910 - 5 May 1912: | Commander, 1st Brigade, 7th Cavalry Division |
| 5 May 1912: | Retired |

*Lieutenant-General* Georgy Mikhailovich von **Layming** (14 Apr 1865 - 3 Jan 1958)
| | |
|---|---|
| 13 Apr 1908 - 23 Oct 1911: | At the disposal of the Chief, Main Directorate for Military Schools |
| 13 Apr 1908: | Promoted to *Major-General* |
| 23 Oct 1911 - 1917: | Special Assignments General, Directorate-General of Military Schools |
| 1912: | Promoted to *Lieutenant-General* |

*Major-General* Mikhail Aleksandrovich von **Layming** (15 Dec 1856 - ?)
| | |
|---|---|
| 13 Oct 1914: | Promoted to *Major-General* |
| 13 Oct 1914 - 1917: | Commander of Land Artillery, Peter the Great Imperial Maritime Fortress |

*General of Infantry* Pavel Aleksandrovich von **Layming** (5 Nov 1852 - 1918)
| | |
|---|---|
| 25 Dec 1896 - 25 Jun 1901: | Commandant, Moscow Military School |
| 6 Dec 1897: | Promoted to *Major-General* |
| 25 Jun 1901 - 15 Sep 1903: | Commandant, Aleksandrov Military School |
| 15 Sep 1903 - 2 Aug 1904: | Commander, 2nd Infantry Division |
| 2 Aug 1904 - 10 Apr 1906: | Commander, 55th Infantry Division |
| 1 Oct 1904: | Promoted to *Lieutenant-General* |
| 10 Apr 1906 - 30 May 1906: | Attached to the General Staff |
| 30 May 1906 - 7 Jul 1907: | Commanding General, X. Army Corps |
| 7 Jul 1907 - 23 Feb 1908: | At the disposal of the Minister of War |
| 23 Feb 1908 - 4 Mar 1910: | Deputy Chief, Main Administration for Military Schools |
| 4 Mar 1910 - 16 Mar 1916: | Special Assignments General, Inspectorate-General of Military Schools |
| 26 Nov 1914: | Promoted to *General of Infantry* |
| 16 Mar 1916 - 5 Apr 1917: | Commanding General, XLV. Army Corps |
| 5 Apr 1917 - Oct 1917: | Reserve officer, Petrograd Military District |

*General of Artillery* Vladimir Aleksandrovich von **Layming** (7 Jul 1854 - 7 Feb 1919)
| | |
|---|---|
| 3 Jul 1901 - 17 Feb 1905: | Commander of Artillery, Fortress Osovets |

| | |
|---|---|
| 6 Dec 1903: | Promoted to *Major-General* |
| 17 Feb 1905 - 7 Nov 1905: | Attached to the Main Artillery Directorate |
| 29 Mar 1905 - 20 Oct 1905: | Acting Inspector of Artillery, Fortress Vladivostok |
| 7 Nov 1905 - 19 Nov 1913: | Commandant of Fortress Sveaborg |
| 6 Dec 1908: | Promoted to *Lieutenant-General* |
| 19 Nov 1913 - 1 Sep 1916: | Commandant of Fortress Brest-Litovsk |
| 6 Dec 1914: | Promoted to *General of Artillery* |
| 1 Sep 1916 - 1917: | Reserve officer, Minsk Military District |

*Major-General* Aleksandr Ivanovich **Lazarev** (6 May 1858 - 29 Jan 1913)
| | |
|---|---|
| 14 Apr 1910 - 29 Jan 1913: | Attached to the Military Governor of the Caucasus |
| 6 Dec 1910: | Promoted to *Major-General* |

*Rear-Admiral* Andrey Maksimovich **Lazarev** (20 Jan 1865 - 20 Feb 1924)
| | |
|---|---|
| 1909 - 7 May 1913: | Commander, Battleship "Emperor Aleksandr II" |
| 29 Mar 1913: | Promoted to *Rear-Admiral* |
| 7 May 1913 - 1917: | Member, Commission for Acceptance of Mine Vessels |

*Major-General* Mikhail Mikhailovich **Lazarev** (11 Sep 1870 - 12 Jul 1928)
| | |
|---|---|
| 1908 - 1911: | Attached to Life Guards Cuirassier Regiment |
| 1911: | Promoted to *Major-General* |
| 1911: | Retired |
| 2 Oct 1915 - 14 Apr 1917: | Recalled; Commander, 3$^{rd}$ Baltic Cavalry Regiment |

*Lieutenant-General* Nikolai Ivanovich **Lazarev** (19 Aug 1856 - 8 Jan 1924)
| | |
|---|---|
| 10 Jan 1901 - 5 May 1913: | Ataman, 1$^{st}$ Don District, Don Cossack Army |
| 31 May 1907: | Promoted to *Major-General* |
| 5 May 1913: | Promoted to *Lieutenant-General* |
| 5 May 1913: | Retired |

*Major-General* Nikolai Stepanovich **Lazarev** (26 Nov 1835 - ?)
| | |
|---|---|
| 5 Sep 1894: | Promoted to *Major-General* |
| 5 Sep 1894 - 29 Oct 1899: | Commander, 2$^{nd}$ Artillery Brigade |

*General of Infantry* Pyotr Stepanovich **Lazarev** (2 Jun 1839 - ?)
| | |
|---|---|
| 19 Jun 1877 - 28 Jun 1881: | Deputy Chief of Staff, Caucasus Military District |
| 1878: | Promoted to *Major-General* |
| 28 Jun 1881 - 27 Feb 1886: | Military Governor of Amur Region, Ataman, Amur Cossack Army |
| 27 Feb 1886 - 24 Nov 1886: | Transferred to the reserve |
| 24 Nov 1886 - 1 Feb 1888: | Commander, 2$^{nd}$ Brigade, 35$^{th}$ Infantry Division |
| 1 Feb 1888 - 3 Nov 1893: | Commandant of Fortress Osovets |
| 3 Nov 1893 - 28 May 1895: | Commander, 16$^{th}$ Infantry Division |
| 30 Aug 1894: | Promoted to *Lieutenant-General* |
| 28 May 1895 - 1 Jan 1903: | Commandant of Fortress Libau |
| 1 Jan 1903 - Sep 1905: | Commandant of Fortress Brest-Litovsk |
| 6 Dec 1904: | Promoted to *General of Infantry* |

*Lieutenant-General* Vladimir Petrovich **Lazarev** (5 Feb 1865 - 19 Jun 1916)
15 May 1908 - 3 Jun 1914:     Commander, 13th Hussar Regiment
14 Apr 1913:                  Promoted to *Major-General*
3 Jun 1914 - 19 Jun 1916:     Chief of Staff, VII. Army Corps
19 Nov 1916:                  Posthumously promoted to *Lieutenant-General*

*General of Infantry* Pavel Nikolayevich **Lazarev-Stanishchev** (17 Nov 1856 - 17 Sep 1920)
4 Feb 1903 - 30 Jun 1917:     Director, Emperor Alexander III Don Cadet Corps
6 Dec 1906:                   Promoted to *Major-General*
6 Dec 1913:                   Promoted to *Lieutenant-General*
30 Jun 1917:                  Promoted to *General of Infantry*
30 Jun 1917:                  Retired

*Major-General* Yuri Sergeyevich **Lazarevich** (2 Sep 1863 - ?)
13 Oct 1910 - 1917:           Chief of Section, General Staff
6 Dec 1913:                   Promoted to *Major-General*

*Lieutenant-General* Pyotr Timofeyevich **Lazovsky** (21 Dec 1842 - 1910)
5 Aug 1894 - Jul 1906:        Commander, Tomaszów Borderguard Brigade
14 Apr 1902:                  Promoted to *Major-General*
Jul 1906 - 1 Dec 1908:        Commander, 7th Borderguard District
1 Dec 1908:                   Promoted to *Lieutenant-General*
1 Dec 1908:                   Retired

*General of Infantry* Aleksandr Nikolayevich **Lebedev** (2 Oct 1853 - ?)
27 Nov 1899 - 12 Jul 1902:    Chief of Staff, Fortress Brest-Litovsk
6 Dec 1899:                   Promoted to *Major-General*
12 Jul 1902 - 28 Dec 1904:    Commandant of Fortress Zegrze
28 Dec 1904 - 4 Jul 1906:     Commander, 77th Infantry Division
4 Jul 1906 - 3 May 1910:      Commander, 9th East Siberian Rifle Division
22 Apr 1907:                  Promoted to *Lieutenant-General*
3 May 1910:                   Promoted to *General of Infantry*
3 May 1910:                   Retired

*Lieutenant-General* Ivan Grigoryevich **Lebedev** (2 Sep 1855 - ?)
1900 - 15 Apr 1917:           Deputy Chief of the Kuban Region,
                              Ataman, Kuban Cossack Army
6 Dec 1906:                   Promoted to *Major-General*
15 Apr 1917:                  Promoted to *Lieutenant-General*
15 Apr 1917:                  Retired

*Major-General* Nikolai Nikolayevich **Lebedev** (15 Oct 1840 - ?)
1 Jul 1886 - 15 Aug 1892:     Military Judge, Turkestan Military District Court
30 Aug 1889:                  Promoted to *Major-General*
15 Aug 1892 - 1894:           Military Judge, Omsk Military District Court

*Major-General* Pavel Pavlovich **Lebedev** (21 Apr 1872 - 2 Jul 1933)
10 Sep 1915 - 17 Apr 1917:    Quartermaster-General, Western Front

6 Dec 1915: Promoted to *Major-General*
17 Apr 1917 - Apr 1918: Chief of Staff, 3rd Army

*Major-General* Sergey Pavlovich **Lebedev** (13 Jun 1865 - ?)
19 Apr 1911 - 27 Nov 1914: Special Assignments General, Inspectorate-General of Engineers
6 Dec 1911: Promoted to *Major-General*
27 Nov 1914 - 23 Apr 1916: Reserve officer, Kiev Military District
23 Apr 1916 - 1917: Commander of Engineers, 3rd Army

*General of Infantry* Timofey Aleksandrovich **Lebedev** (10 Jun 1837 - 1911)
7 Oct 1891: Promoted to *Major-General*
7 Oct 1891 - 8 Mar 1898: Chief of Moscow Military Hospital
8 Mar 1898 - 31 Oct 1899: Attached to the Commander, Moscow Regional Brigade
321 Oct 1899 - May 1904: Commander, Arkhangelsk Regional Brigade
1 Apr 1901: Promoted to *Lieutenant-General*
May 1904: Promoted to *General of Infantry*
May 1904: Retired

*Major-General* Vladimir Timofeyevich **Lebedev** (6 Mar 1867 - 27 Aug 1916)
21 Mar 1915 - 27 Aug 1916: Commander, 162nd Infantry Regiment
21 Oct 1916: Posthumously promoted to *Major-General*

*Lieutenant-General* Yevgeny Nikolayevich **Lebedev** (21 Jan 1859 - ?)
1 May 1906 - 30 Sep 1912: Intendant-General, XXI. Army Corps
31 May 1907: Promoted to *Major-General*
30 Sep 1912: Promoted to *Lieutenant-General*
30 Sep 1912: Retired

*Major-General* Fyodor Dmitriyevich **Lebedevich-Drayevsky** (19 Dec 1866 - 20 Jun 1926)
16 Aug 1914 - 25 Feb 1916: Commander, 253rd Infantry Regiment
21 May 1915: Promoted to *Major-General*
25 Feb 1916 - 7 Apr 1917: Commander, Brigade, 112th Infantry Division
7 Apr 1917 - 1918: Commander, 112th Infantry Division

*Major-General* Aleksandr Yakovlevich **Lebedinets** (17 Sep 1850 - ?)
5 Oct 1902: Promoted to *Major-General*
5 Oct 1902 - 28 Oct 1906: Commander, 4th Artillery Brigade

*Major-General* Yevgeny Vasilievich **Lebedinsky** (24 Dec 1873 - ?)
5 Mar 1915 - 3 Jul 1916: Commander, 81st Infantry Regiment
11 Mar 1916: Promoted to *Major-General*
13 Jul 1916 - Jan 1917: Commander, 6th Special Infantry Brigade
29 Jan 1917 - 30 Jun 1917: Commander, 4th Special Infantry Division
30 Jun 1917 - 13 Aug 1917: Chief of Staff, VII. Caucasus Army Corps
13 Aug 1917 - 5 Oct 1917: Duty General, Caucasus Front
5 Oct 1917 - 28 Dec 1917: Chief of Staff, Caucasus Front
28 Dec 1917 - May 1918: Acting C-in-C, Caucasus Front

*Major-General* Aleksandr Pavlovich **Lebedintsev** (18 Aug 1845 - ?)
| | |
|---|---|
| 10 Mar 1907 - 13 Jun 1910: | Military Commander, Tomsk District |
| 13 Jun 1910: | Promoted to *Major-General* |
| 13 Jun 1910: | Retired |
| 5 Feb 1915 - 1917: | Recalled; Commander, 68th Battalion |

*Major-General* Nikolai Georgyevich **Lebov** (8 Jul 1852 - ?)
| | |
|---|---|
| 6 Jul 1904 - 1909: | Military Commander, Kozlovsky District |
| 1909: | Promoted to *Major-General* |
| 1909: | Retired |
| 4 May 1916 - 17 Sep 1917: | Recalled; Reserve officer, Kiev Military District |
| 17 Sep 1917: | Dismissed |

*Major-General* Yevgeny Yasonovich **Lebov** (11 Mar 1857 - ?)
| | |
|---|---|
| 11 Jan 1916 - 1918: | Commander, 104th Artillery Brigade |
| 23 Jan 1917: | Promoted to *Major-General* |

*General of Infantry* Platon Alekseyevich **Lechitsky** (18 Mar 1856 - 18 Feb 1923)
| | |
|---|---|
| 3 Nov 1902 - 12 May 1905: | Commander, 24th East Siberian Rifle Regiment |
| 14 Feb 1905: | Promoted to *Major-General* |
| 14 Jul 1905 - 10 Mar 1906: | Commander, 1st Brigade, 6th East Siberian Rifle Division |
| 10 Mar 1906 - 21 Jun 1906: | Commander, 6th East Siberian Rifle Division |
| 21 Jun 1906 - 26 Aug 1908: | Commander, 1st Guards Infantry Division |
| 26 Aug 1908 - 3 Dec 1910: | Commanding General, XVIII. Army Corps |
| 31 Dec 1908: | Promoted to *Lieutenant-General* |
| 3 Dec 1910 - 9 Aug 1914: | Commanding General, Amur Military District, Ataman of Amur & Ussuri Cossacks |
| 14 Apr 1913: | Promoted to *General of Infantry* |
| 9 Aug 1914 - 18 Apr 1917: | C-in-C, 9th Army |
| 18 Apr 1917: | Retired |

*Major-General* Vasily Fyodorovich **Legat** (30 Jan 1853 - ?)
| | |
|---|---|
| 10 Apr 1907 - 5 Jul 1913: | Chief of Siverskoye Section, Northwest Railway Gendarmerie |
| 5 Jul 1913: | Promoted to *Major-General* |
| 5 Jul 1913: | Retired |

*Major-General* Mikhail Vasilyevich **Lekarev** (5 Nov 1869 - ?)
| | |
|---|---|
| 3 Feb 1915 - 18 Feb 1917: | Commander, 3rd Don Cossack Artillery Regiment |
| 8 Oct 1916: | Promoted to *Major-General* |
| 18 Feb 1917 - 28 Apr 1917: | Commander, 45th Artillery Brigade |
| 28 Apr 1917 - Oct 1917: | Inspector of Artillery, XXVII. Army Corps |

*Major-General* Aleksandr Karlovich **Lelong** (11 Jan 1859 - 28 Jul 1911)
| | |
|---|---|
| 16 Jul 1906 - 28 Jul 1911: | Director, St. Petersburg Military Paramedic School |
| 1911: | Promoted to *Major-General* |

*Major-General* Aleksandr Yakovlevich **Lelyevr** (20 Jul 1862 - ?)
17 Nov 1911 - 31 Oct 1916: Deputy Commander, 17th Borderguard Brigade
31 Oct 1916: Promoted to *Major-General*
31 Oct 1916: Retired

*Major-General* Mikhail Nikolayevich **Leman** (8 Nov 1845 - 18 Jun 1895)
4 Oct 1884 - 18 Jun 1895: Military Judge, St. Petersburg Military District Court
30 Aug 1891: Promoted to *Major-General*

*Major-General* Ivan Yefimovich **Lenchovsky** (10 Oct 1855 - ?)
8 Jul 1911: Promoted to *Major-General*
8 Jul 1911 - 1913: Commander of Artillery, Fortress Kars

*General of Infantry* Nikolai Petrovich **Lenevich** (24 Dec 1838 - 10 Apr 1908)
15 Oct 1885 - 10 Jul 1895: Commander, 2nd Transcaucasus Rifle Brigade
30 Aug 1891: Promoted to *Major-General*
10 Jul 1895 - 18 Jun 1900: Commander, South Ussuri District
6 Dec 1899: Promoted to *Lieutenant-General*
18 Jun 1900 - 31 Jul 1900: Commanding General, Siberian Army Corps
31 Jul 1900 - 2 Oct 1903: Commanding General, I. Siberian Army Corps
2 Oct 1903 - 22 Oct 1904: Commanding General, Amur Military District, Ataman, Amur Cossack Army
30 Jan 1904 - 23 Mar 1904: Acting C-in-C, Manchurian Army
21 Aug 1904: Promoted to *General of Infantry*
22 Oct 1904 - 3 Mar 1905: C-in-C, 1st Manchurian Army
1905: Promoted to *General-Adjutant*
3 Mar 1905 - 3 Feb 1906: C-in-C, Far East
3 Feb 1906 - 10 Apr 1908: Unassigned

*Major-General* Nikolai Vsevolodovich **Lenin** (12 Dec 1861 - ?)
20 Nov 1909 - 1917: Inspector of Classes, Vladimir-Kiev Cadet Corps
6 Dec 1909: Promoted to *Major-General*

*Lieutenant-General* Eduard Ivanovich **Lents** (14 Dec 1837 - ?)
16 Jul 1896: Promoted to *Major-General*
16 Jul 1896 - 11 Jan 1900: Commander, 2nd Brigade, 20th Infantry Division
11 Jan 1900: Promoted to *Lieutenant-General*

*General of Infantry* Mikhail Khristoforovich **Leo** (19 May 1826 - 11 Jan 1904)
17 Jan 1879: Promoted to *Major-General*
17 Jan 1879 - 10 Sep 1879: Transferred to the reserve
10 Sep 1879 - 10 Nov 1886: Commander, 1st Brigade, 30th Infantry Division
10 Nov 1886 - 2 Jun 1900: Commander, 1st Rifle Brigade
30 Aug 1887: Promoted to *Lieutenant-General*
2 Jun 1900: Promoted to *General of Infantry*
2 Jun 1900: Retired

*Lieutenant-General* Nikolai Nikolayevich **Leo** (22 Mar 1862 - ?)
| | |
|---|---|
| 1 May 1903 - 15 Jun 1907: | Section Chief, General Staff |
| 6 Dec 1905: | Promoted to *Major-General* |
| 15 Jun 1907 - 23 Dec 1911: | Commander, $2^{nd}$ Brigade, $2^{nd}$ Cavalry Division |
| 23 Dec 1911 - 25 Aug 1915: | Commander, $1^{st}$ Brigade, $1^{st}$ Cavalry Division |
| 25 Aug 1915 - Feb 1917: | Commander, $2^{nd}$ Brigade, $1^{st}$ Cavalry Division |
| Feb 1917 - 1918: | General for Horse Inspection, Northern Front |
| 1917: | Promoted to *Lieutenant-General* |

*General of Cavalry* Stepan Stepanovich **Leonov** (27 Dec 1834 - 4 Nov 1899)
| | |
|---|---|
| 2 Jan 1870 - 12 Oct 1876: | Commander, $18^{th}$ Dragoon Regiment |
| 12 Oct 1876: | Promoted to *Major-General* |
| 12 Oct 1876 - 21 Jan 1879: | Commander, $1^{st}$ Brigade, $8^{th}$ Cavalry Division |
| 21 Jan 1879 - 18 Aug 1883: | Commander, Caucasus Replacement Cavalry Brigade |
| 18 Aug 1883 - 18 Feb 1884: | Commandant of Stavropol Garrison |
| 18 Feb 1884 - 29 Mar 1884: | Commander, Caucasus Replacement Cavalry Brigade |
| 29 Mar 1884 - 20 Dec 1892: | Commander, $2^{nd}$ Caucasus Cossack Division |
| 30 Aug 1886: | Promoted to *Lieutenant-General* |
| 20 Dec 1892 - 14 Jul 1899: | Commanding General, XVII. Army Corps |
| 6 Dec 1898: | Promoted to *General of Cavalry* |
| 14 Jul 1899 - 4 Nov 1899: | Member, Committee for Wounded Veterans |

*Major-General* Sergey Gavrilovich **Leontovich** (24 May 1862 - ?)
| | |
|---|---|
| 17 Apr 1910: | Promoted to *Major-General* |
| 17 Apr 1910 - 6 Mar 1911: | Chief of Staff, XIV. Army Corps |
| 6 Mar 1911 - 3 Sep 1913: | Commander, $1^{st}$ Brigade, $30^{th}$ Infantry Division |
| 3 Sep 1913: | Retired |

*Lieutenant-General* Yevgeny Aleksandrovich **Leontovich** (1 Dec 1862 - 1937)
| | |
|---|---|
| 11 Sep 1906 - 11 Sep 1908: | Commander, $16^{th}$ Dragoon Regiment |
| 11 Sep 1908: | Promoted to *Major-General* |
| 11 Sep 1908 - 20 Aug 1914: | Commander, $1^{st}$ Brigade, $2^{nd}$ Cavalry Division |
| 20 Aug 1914 - 9 Sep 1914: | Acting Commander, $1^{st}$ Cavalry Division |
| 9 Sep 1914 - 13 Apr 1917: | Commander, $3^{rd}$ Cavalry Division |
| 6 Dec 1914: | Promoted to *Lieutenant-General* |
| 1916: | Acting Commanding General, VI. Cavalry Corps |
| 13 Apr 1917 - Oct 1917: | Reserve officer, Odessa Military District |

*Major-General* Ivan Mikhailovich **Leontovsky** (8 Jan 1864 - ?)
| | |
|---|---|
| 22 Jun 1914 - 14 Dec 1916: | Battalion Commander, Sergiev Artillery School |
| 6 Dec 1914: | Promoted to *Major-General* |
| 14 Dec 1916 - 3 Oct 1917: | Commandant, Mikailovsk Artillery School |
| 3 Oct 1917 - 1918: | Reserve officer, Petrograd Military District |

*Lieutenant-General* Konstantin Kharitonovich **Leontyev** (25 Apr 1857 - ?)
| | |
|---|---|
| 24 Sep 1901 - 25 Jul 1912: | Commander of Gendarmerie, Moscow |
| 13 Apr 1908: | Promoted to *Major-General* |
| 25 Jul 1912: | Promoted to *Lieutenant-General* |

25 Jul 1912: Retired

*Major-General* Maksim Nikolayevich **Leontyev** (26 Aug 1871 - 9 Jun 1948)
8 Mar 1913 - 20 Nov 1914: Military Attaché, Turkey
14 Apr 1913: Promoted to *Major-General*
20 Nov 1914 - 3 Jul 1916: Quartermaster-General, General Staff
3 Jul 1916 - 18 Jul 1917: Commander, 4th Special Infantry Brigade
18 Jul 1917 - Oct 1917: At the disposal of the Chief of the General Staff

*Lieutenant-General* Vladimir Georgiyevich **Leontyev** (12 Jul 1866 - ?)
22 Mar 1911: Promoted to *Major-General*
22 Mar 1911 - 1 May 1913: Chief of Staff, XIV. Army Corps
1 May 1913 - Aug 1914: Quartermaster-General, Warsaw Military District
Aug 1914 - 17 Sep 1914: Quartermaster-General, Northwestern Front
17 Sep 1914 - 25 Aug 1915: Special Assignments General, 2nd Army
25 Aug 1915 - 30 Sep 1917: Commander, 77th Infantry Division
10 Apr 1916: Promoted to *Lieutenant-General*
30 Sep 1917 - 1918: Reserve officer, Kiev Military District

*Lieutenant-General* Konstantin Ivanovich **Leopold** (28 May 1853 - ?)
2 Dec 1909 - 20 Mar 1914: Member of the Technical Committee, Main Military Technical Directorate
6 Dec 1909: Promoted to *Major-General*
20 Mar 1914 - 11 Apr 1917: Member of the Public Commission on Billeting, Main Directorate for Troop Billeting
10 Apr 1916: Promoted to *Lieutenant-General*
11 Apr 1917: Dismissed

*General of Cavalry* Archduke **Leopold** Ludwig Maria Franz Julius Eustorgius Gerhard von Österreich (6 Jun 1823 - 24 May 1898)
?: Honorary Colonel-in-Chief, 25th Dragoon Regiment

*Major-General* Ivan Fomich **Lepik** (22 Apr 1859 - ?)
1914 - Dec 1915: Commander, 318th Infantry Regiment
10 Oct 1915: Promoted to *Major-General*
Dec 1915 - 17 May 1916: Commander, 1st Brigade, 105th Infantry Division
17 May 1916 - 6 Aug 1916: Reserve officer, Kiev Military District
6 Aug 1916: Retired

*Lieutenant-General* Mikhail Varlamovich **Lepilin** (20 May 1853 - ?)
16 Apr 1903 - 11 Sep 1912: Inspector of Classes, 2nd Orenburg Cadet Corps
22 Apr 1906: Promoted to *Major-General*
11 Sep 1912: Promoted to *Lieutenant-General*
11 Sep 1912: Retired

*Major-General* Vladimir Andreyevich **Lerkam** (20 Apr 1859 - ?)
31 Mar 1912 - 23 Jul 1916: Commander, 2nd Battalion, 34th Artillery Brigade
31 Aug 1915: Promoted to *Major-General*

23 Jul 1916 - 23 Aug 1916: Commander, 35th Artillery Brigade

*General of Cavalry* Aleksandr Mikhailovich **Lermantov** (27 Feb 1838 - 26 Dec 1906)
23 Apr 1872 - 23 Feb 1878: Commander, 13th Dragoon Regiment
1878: Promoted to *Major-General*
23 Feb 1878 - 22 Jul 1878: Commander, 2nd Brigade, 9th Cavalry Division
22 Jul 1878 - 6 Nov 1881: Commander, 2nd Brigade, 1st Cavalry Division
6 Nov 1881 - 14 Jul 1883: Commander, Life Guards Cuirassier Regiment
14 Jul 1883 - 19 Jul 1886: Commander, 2nd Brigade, 1st Guards Cavalry Division
19 Jul 1886 - 23 Jul 1896: Commander, 12th Cavalry Division
30 Aug 1886: Promoted to *Lieutenant-General*
23 Jul 1896 - 2 Nov 1902: Commanding General, I. Cavalry Corps
6 Dec 1898: Promoted to *General of Cavalry*
2 Nov 1902 - 26 Dec 1906: Member of the Military Council

*General of Infantry* Dmitry Dmitriyevich **Lermantov** (13 Feb 1839 - 23 Jun 1909)
9 Sep 1878 - 28 May 1893: Section Chief, Main Directorate for Military Schools
30 Aug 1889: Promoted to *Major-General*
28 May 1893 - 9 Oct 1903: Chief of Bureau, Main Directorate for Military Schools
9 Oct 1903 - 8 Apr 1906: Special Assignments General, Main Directorate for Military Schools
6 Dec 1903: Promoted to *Lieutenant-General*
8 Apr 1906 - 1909: At the disposal of the Chief of Main Directorate for Military Schools
1909: Promoted to *General of Infantry*

*Lieutenant-General* Mikhail Aleksandrovich **Lermontov** (15 Jan 1859 - ?)
7 Jul 1906 - 8 Jul 1917: Chief of Administration, Peterhof Palace
13 Apr 1908: Promoted to *Major-General*
1913: Promoted to *Lieutenant-General*
8 Jul 1917: Retired

*Lieutenant-General* Nikolai Mikhailovich **Lesenevich** (23 Sep 1853 - ?)
5 Oct 1902: Promoted to *Major-General*
5 Oct 1902 - 12 May 1907: Commander, 1st Turkestan Artillery Brigade
12 May 1907 - 3 Oct 1908: Commander of Artillery, II. Army Corps
30 Jul 1907: Promoted to *Lieutenant-General*

*General of Infantry* Leonid Vilhelmovich **Lesh** (9 Jan 1862 - 28 Sep 1934)
7 Sep 1905: Promoted to *Major-General*
7 Sep 1905 - 24 May 1906: Commander, 2nd Brigade, 1st East Siberian Rifle Division
24 May 1906 - 27 Jun 1906: Commander, 1st Brigade, 9th East Siberian Rifle Division
27 Jun 1906 - 30 Apr 1907: Commander, 2nd Brigade, 23rd Infantry Division
30 Apr 1907 - 19 Jun 1908: Commander, 2nd Finnish Rifle Brigade
19 Jun 1908 - 3 May 1910: Commander, Guards Rifle Brigade
6 Dec 1909: Promoted to *Lieutenant-General*

| | |
|---|---|
| 3 May 1910 - 30 Jul 1912: | Commander, 2nd Guards Infantry Division |
| 30 Jul 1912 - 15 Jan 1913: | Commanding General, I. Turkestan Army Corps |
| 15 Jan 1913 - 3 Feb 1915: | Commanding General, II. Turkestan Army Corps, Commander, Trans-Caspian Region |
| 19 Jul 1914 - 3 Jun 1915: | Commanding General, XII. Army Corps |
| 22 Jan 1915: | Promoted to *General of Infantry* |
| 3 Jun 1915 - 3 Apr 1917: | C-in-C, 3$^{rd}$ Army |
| 3 Apr 1917: | Transferred to the reserve |

*Rear-Admiral* Pyotr Nikolayevich **Leskov** (11 Feb 1864 - 20 Dec 1937)
| | |
|---|---|
| 28 Jul 1914: | Promoted to *Rear-Admiral* |
| 28 Jul 1914 - Aug 1915: | Commander, 2$^{nd}$ Cruiser Brigade, Baltic Fleet |
| Aug 1915 - Oct 1917: | Chief of Coastal Defenses, Peter the Great Naval Fortress |

*Lieutenant-General* Aleksandr Aleksandrovich **Lesli** (16 Apr 1845 - 17 Mar 1900)
| | |
|---|---|
| 3 Feb 1878 - 23 Mar 1884: | Commander, 9$^{th}$ Hussar Regiment |
| 23 Mar 1884: | Promoted to *Major-General* |
| 23 Mar 1884 - 18 Mar 1896: | Commander, 1$^{st}$ Brigade, 11$^{th}$ Cavalry Division |
| 18 Mar 1896 - 17 Mar 1900: | Commander, 9$^{th}$ Cavalry Division |
| 14 May 1896: | Promoted to *Lieutenant-General* |

*Major-General* Dmitry Nikolayevich **Lesli** (29 May 1837 - ?)
| | |
|---|---|
| 11 Jun 1888 - 1896: | Commander, Trans-Siberian Line Brigade |
| 11 Jul 1888: | Promoted to *Major-General* |

*Major-General* Konstantin Petrovich **Lesli** (26 Apr 1849 - 9 Apr 1914)
| | |
|---|---|
| 29 May 1891 - 22 Aug 1897: | Military Judge, Odessa Military District |
| 30 Aug 1893: | Promoted to *Major-General* |
| 2 Aug 1897 - 1905: | Military Judge, Moscow Military District |

*Major-General* Iosif Vikentyevich **Lesnevsky** (14 Sep 1867 - 3 Oct 1921)
| | |
|---|---|
| 6 Feb 1913 - 3 Feb 1915: | Commander, 82$^{nd}$ Infantry Regiment |
| 31 Dec 1914: | Promoted to *Major-General* |
| 3 Feb 1915 - 7 Apr 1917: | Commander, Brigade, 2$^{nd}$ Grenadier Division |
| 7 Apr 1917 - 23 Sep 1917: | Commander, 8$^{th}$ Siberian Rifle Division |

*Lieutenant-General* Ivan Martynovich **Lesovoy** (22 Nov 1835 - ?)
| | |
|---|---|
| 10 Nov 1879 - 28 Oct 1883: | Transferred to the reserve |
| 21 Apr 1881: | Promoted to *Major-General* |
| 28 Oct 1883 - 12 Jul 1885: | Unassigned |
| 12 Jul 1885 - 30 Jan 1893: | Commander, 39$^{th}$ Artillery Brigade |
| 30 Jan 1893 - 5 Dec 1899: | Commander of Artillery, XI. Army Corps |
| 30 Aug 1893: | Promoted to *Lieutenant-General* |

*Major-General* Nikolai Nikolayevich Duke of **Leuchtenberg**, Prince de Beauharnais (5 Oct 1868 - 2 Mar 1928)
| | |
|---|---|
| 12 Jun 1915 - 28 Oct 1916: | Commander, 12$^{th}$ Turkestan Rifle Regiment |

| | |
|---|---|
| 28 Oct 1916 - 1918: | Attached to the Guards Corps |
| 22 Mar 1917: | Promoted to *Major-General* |

*General of Infantry* Illarion Mikhailovich **Levachev** (29 Oct 1837 - 1 Oct 1901)
| | |
|---|---|
| 30 Aug 1883: | Promoted to *Major-General* |
| 30 Aug 1883 - 16 May 1891: | Director, Don Cadet Corps |
| 16 May 1891 - 25 Jun 1901: | Commandant, 3rd Aleksandrov Military School |
| 30 Aug 1894: | Promoted to *Lieutenant-General* |
| 25 Jun 1901: | Promoted to *General of Infantry* |
| 25 Jun 1901: | Retired |

*Major-General* Vasily Illarionovich **Levachev** (8 Aug 1871 - 28 Dec 1914)
| | |
|---|---|
| 23 Sep 1912 - 19 Nov 1914: | Commander, Grenadier Mortar Artillery Battalion |
| 19 Nov 1914 - 28 Dec 1914: | Commander, 2nd Grenadier Artillery Brigade |
| Jan 1915: | Posthumously promoted to *Major-General* |

*Major-General* Ivan Mikhailovich **Levandovsky** (13 Nov 1860 - 29 Sep 1925)
| | |
|---|---|
| 26 Jul 1910 - 27 Jun 1916: | Commander, 1st Horse Artillery Battalion |
| 22 Sep 1915: | Promoted to *Major-General* |
| 27 Jun 1916 - Oct 1917: | Commander, 17th Artillery Brigade |

*Major-General* Vladimir Antonovich **Levandovsky** (26 Apr 1873 - Jul 1946)
| | |
|---|---|
| 30 Dec 1915: | Promoted to *Major-General* |
| 30 Dec 1915 - 21 Oct 1916: | Commander, 3rd Zabaikalskaya Cossack Brigade |
| 21 Oct 1916 - 23 Oct 1917: | Commander, Siberian Cossack Brigade |
| 23 Oct 1917 - Jul 1918: | Quartermaster-General, Caucasus Front |

*General of Artillery* Aleksandr Aleksandrovich **Levanevsky** (8 Nov 1842 - 10 Dec 1921)
| | |
|---|---|
| 16 Apr 1887 - 11 Jan 1895: | Commander of Artillery, Fortess Kerch |
| 30 Aug 1888: | Promoted to *Major-General* |
| 11 Jan 1895 - 21 Apr 1899: | Deputy Commander of Artillery, Odessa Military District |
| 21 Apr 1899: | Promoted to *Lieutenant-General* |
| 21 Apr 1899 - 30 Sep 1904: | Commander of Artillery, Finland Military District |
| 30 Sep 1904 - 3 Sep 1905: | Commander of Artillery, St. Petersburg Military District |
| 3 Dec 1905: | Promoted to *General of Artillery* |
| 3 Dec 1905: | Retired |

*Lieutenant-General* Aleksandr Aleksandrovich **Levashev** (28 Jul 1857 - 5 Apr 1936)
| | |
|---|---|
| 31 Oct 1905 - 21 Nov 1906: | At the disposal of the Commanding General of the Gendarmerie |
| 6 Dec 1906: | Promoted to *Major-General* |
| 21 Nov 1906 - 7 Feb 1915: | Special Assignments General, Ministry of Internal Affairs |
| 31 May 1913: | Promoted to *Lieutenant-General* |
| 7 Feb 1915 - 1917: | Reserve officer, Kiev Military District |

*Major-General* Nikolai Konstantinovich **Levashev** (3 Dec 1856 - 15 Aug 1915)
18 Sep 1897 - 11 Mar 1906: Military Judge, Caucasus Military District Court
6 Dec 1900: Promoted to *Major-General*
11 Mar 1906 - 1908: Military Judge, Moscow Military District Court

*Lieutenant-General* Nikolai Nikolayevich **Levashev** (5 Jul 1848 - 17 Jun 1907)
14 Aug 1892 - 22 Dec 1898: Chief of Railway Department, Trans-Caspian Region
30 Aug 1894: Promoted to *Major-General*
22 Dec 1898 - 21 Oct 1900: Chief of Transport Section, General Staff
25 Feb 1899 - 17 Jun 1907: Chief of Military Communications
6 Dec 1900: Promoted to *Lieutenant-General*

*General of Artillery* Count Vladimir Vasilyevich **Levashev** (30 Nov 1834 - 26 May 1896)
8 Nov 1866: Promoted to *Major-General*
8 Nov 1866 - 16 Apr 1867: Attached to the Viceroy of the Caucasus
16 Apr 1867 - 28 Sep 1874: Military Governor of Kutaisi
28 Sep 1874 - 11 Aug 1876: Member of the Tsar's retinue
11 Aug 1876 - 14 Sep 1878: Mayor of Odessa
14 Sep 1878 - 26 May 1896: Attached to the Ministry of War
30 Aug 1880: Promoted to *Lieutenant-General*
30 Aug 1880: Promoted to *General of Artillery*

*Major-General* Aleksandr Porfiryevich **Levengof** (17 Apr 1859 - Jul 1917)
1 Dec 1904 - 9 Aug 1907: Commander, 1st Regiment, Zabaikalskaya Cossack Army
9 Aug 1907: Promoted to *Major-General*
9 Aug 1907: Retired
21 Jan 1915 - 1917: Recalled; Reserve officer, Dvinsk Military District
1917 - Jul 1917: Military Commander, Bayburt District

*Major-General* Ivan-Aleksandr Fyodorovich **Levental** (26 Sep 1846 - 20 Dec 1899)
24 Oct 1899: Promoted to *Major-General*
24 Oct 1899 - 20 Dec 1899: Commander, 1st Brigade, 4th Infantry Division

*General of Infantry* Mikhail Yulyevich **Levestam** (23 Jan 1847 - 1906)
7 Aug 1900: Promoted to *Major-General*
7 Aug 1900 - 31 Jan 1904: Commander, 2nd Siberian Infantry Brigade
31 Jan 1904 - 27 Nov 1906: Commander, 2nd Siberian Infantry Division
4 Mar 1905: Promoted to *Lieutenant-General*
27 Nov 1906: Promoted to *General of Infantry*
27 Nov 1906: Retired

*Major-General* Yuri Yulyevich **Levestam** (23 May 1849 - 12 May 1911)
26 Aug 1896 - 12 May 1911: Duty Staff Officer, Poltava Local Brigade
1911: Promoted to *Major-General*

*Lieutenant-General* Nikolai-Faustin Matveyevich **Levinsky** (15 Dec 1849 - ?)
1 Jul 1903 - 7 Mar 1908: Intendant, I, Cavalry Corps

| | |
|---|---|
| 2 Apr 1906: | Promoted to *Major-General* |
| 7 Mar 1908 - 17 Dec 1911: | Intendant-General, II. Turkestan Army Corps |
| 17 Dec 1911: | Promoted to *Lieutenant-General* |
| 17 Dec 1911: | Retired |

*Major-General* Anton Ivanovich **Levitsky** (30 Aug 1849 - ?)
| | |
|---|---|
| 15 Feb 1905 - 1912: | Chief of Gendarmerie, Nizhny Novgorod |
| 1906: | Promoted to *Major-General* |

*Lieutenant-General* Georgy Aleksandrovich **Levitsky** (6 Sep 1857 - 23 Feb 1920)
| | |
|---|---|
| 20 May 1905 - 20 Feb 1909: | Commander, 65th Infantry Regiment |
| 14 Jul 1907: | Promoted to *Major-General* |
| 20 Feb 1909 - 20 May 1909: | Commander, 1st Brigade, Amur District, Borderguard Corps |
| 20 May 1909 - 5 Aug 1911: | Commander, 2nd Brigade, Amur District, Borderguard Corps |
| 5 Aug 1911 - 20 Aug 1913: | Commander, 2nd Brigade, 36th Infantry Division |
| 20 Aug 1913 - 19 Jul 1914: | Commander, 1st Brigade, 36th Infantry Division |
| 19 Jul 1914 - 8 Oct 1915: | Commander, 73rd Infantry Division |
| 19 May 1915: | Promoted to *Lieutenant-General* |
| 8 Oct 1915 - 7 Jan 1916: | Reserve officer, Dvinsk Military District |
| 7 Jan 1916 - 11 Mar 1917: | Commander, 126th Infantry Division |
| 11 Mar 1917: | Retired |

*Major-General* Konstantin Antonovich **Levitsky** (20 May 1858 - 14 Jul 1917)
| | |
|---|---|
| 13 Oct 1916 - 14 Jul 1917: | Commander, 1st Turkestan Rifle Artillery Brigade |
| 6 Dec 1916: | Promoted to *Major-General* |

*Major-General* Nikolai Aleksandrovich **Levitsky** (2 Mar 1859 - ?)
| | |
|---|---|
| 17 May 1906 - 1908: | Commander, 20th Eastern Siberian Rifle Regiment |
| 1908: | Promoted to *Major-General* |
| 1908: | Retired |
| Aug 1914 - 6 Jan 1915: | Recalled; Commander, 174th Reserve Infantry Regiment |
| 6 Jan 1915 - 1917: | Commander, 20th Replacement Infantry Brigade |
| ?: | Acting Commander, 65th Infantry Division |

*Major-General* Nikolai Petrovich **Levitsky** (26 Dec 1846 - ?)
| | |
|---|---|
| 7 Sep 1904: | Promoted to *Major-General* |
| 7 Sep 1904 - 31 Oct 1906: | At the disposal of the C-in-C, 1st Manchurian Army |
| 31 Oct 1906 - Jul 1908: | Commander, Orenburg Local Brigade |

*Lieutenant-General* Nikolai Vasilyevich **Levitsky** (28 Nov 1836 - ?)
| | |
|---|---|
| 9 Jun 1885: | Promoted to *Major-General* |
| 9 Jun 1885 - 20 Mar 1889: | Chief of Staff, Irkutsk Military District |
| 20 Mar 1889 - 8 Jan 1892: | Deputy Chief of Staff, Moscow Military District |
| 8 Jan 1892 - 31 Jul 1896: | Chief Inspector of Prisoner Transport, General Staff |
| 14 Nov 1894: | Promoted to *Lieutenant-General* |
| 31 Jul 1896: | Retired |

*Rear-Admiral* Pavel Pavlovich **Levitsky** (3 Oct 1859 - 31 Jul 1938)
17 Jun 1907 - 25 Mar 1912: Commander, Submarine Detachment, Baltic Fleet
25 Mar 1912: Promoted to *Rear-Admiral*
25 Mar 1912 - 23 Mar 1915: Commander, Submarine Brigade, Baltic Fleet
23 Mar 1915 - 18 Jan 1916: Attached to the Ministry of the Navy
18 Jan 1916 - Oct 1917: Head of Submarine Construction, Baltic Fleet

*Major-General* Vasily Nikolayevich **Levitsky** (24 Jun 1858 - 16 Feb 1911)
2 Dec 1904 - 21 Aug 1906: Commander, 80$^{th}$ Infantry Regiment
27 Feb 1906: Promoted to *Major-General*
21 Aug 1906 - 27 Oct 1906: Commander, 2$^{nd}$ Brigade, 21$^{st}$ Infantry Division
27 Oct 1906 - 16 Feb 1911: Commander, 63$^{rd}$ Replacement Infantry Brigade

*Major-General* Yevgeny-Vilgelm-Karl Aleksandrovich von **Leviz of Menar** (13 Sep 1839 - ?)
29 Sep 1897 - 1907: Commander, 3$^{rd}$ (Arensburg) Borderguard Brigade
6 Apr 1903: Promoted to *Major-General*

*Major-General* Dmitry Fyodorovich **Levshin** (19 May 1876 - 4 Mar 1947)
11 Jul 1915 - 8 May 1917: Commander, Life Guards Hussar Regiment
6 Nov 1915: Promoted to *Major-General*
8 May 1917 - Oct 1917: Special Assignments General to the Chief of Logistics, Southwestern Front

*Major-General* Ernest Lavrentyevich **Levstrem (Löfström)** (31 May 1865 - 5 Jan 1937)
30 Sep 1914 - 7 Feb 1917: Commander, 1$^{st}$ Life Guards Rifle Regiment
18 Dec 1914: Promoted to *Major-General*
7 Feb 1917 - 5 Sep 1917: Commander, Brigade, 3$^{rd}$ Infantry Division
5 Sep 1917 - 1917: Commander, Guards Rifle Division

*Major-General* Georgy-Verner Gustavovich **Leydenius** (2 Sep 1837 - 5 Oct 1914)
14 Jan 1898: Promoted to *Major-General*
14 Jan 1898 - 14 Jan 1900: Commander, 2$^{nd}$ Brigade, 44$^{th}$ Infantry Division
14 Jan 1900: Retired

*General of Infantry* Genrikh Antonovich **Leyer** (4 Apr 1829 - 16 Apr 1904)
1865 - 19 Jan 1877: Inspector of Classes, 2$^{nd}$ Konstantinov Military School
28 Mar 1871: Promoted to *Major-General*
19 Jan 1877 - 13 Aug 1889: General for Special Assignments, Directorate-General of Military Schools
1881 - 13 Aug 1889: Member, Committee on Military Training
30 Aug 1882: Promoted to *Lieutenant-General*
13 Aug 1889 - 17 Aug 1898: Commandant of the General Staff Academy
6 May 1896: Promoted to *General of Infantry*
6 May 1896 - 16 Apr 1904: Member of the Military Council

*General of Infantry* Stepan Andreyevich **Leykht** (1 Jan 1831 - 8 Dec 1907)
1 Aug 1867 - 1 May 1874: Military Judge, Caucasus Military District Court

| | |
|---|---|
| 10 Oct 1870: | Promoted to *Major-General* |
| 1 May 1874 - ?: | Chairman of the Military Tribunal, Caucasus Military District |
| ? - 19 Jan 1880: | Chairman of the Military Tribunal, Kharkov Military District |
| 19 Jan 1880 - 27 May 1884: | Chairman of the Military Tribunal, St. Petersburg Military District |
| 30 Aug 1881: | Promoted to *Lieutenant-General* |
| 27 May 1884 - 7 Apr 1890: | Member of the Supreme Military Tribunal |
| 7 Apr 1890 - 1905: | Chairman of the Supreme Military Tribunal |
| 6 Dec 1895: | Promoted to *General of Infantry* |
| 1905: | Retired |

*Major-General* Yevgeny Frantsevich **Leytner** (24 Sep 1853 - ?)

| | |
|---|---|
| 12 Jan 1911: | Promoted to *Major-General* |
| 12 Jan 1911 - 24 Sep 1913: | Commander of Engineers, Fortress St. Petersburg |
| 24 Sep 1913: | Retired |

*Major-General* Ernest-Vilgelm Karlovich von **Lezedov** (16 Jun 1850 - ?)

| | |
|---|---|
| 16 Nov 1904: | Promoted to *Major-General* |
| 16 Nov 1904 - Dec 1907: | Commander, 2$^{nd}$ Sapper Brigade |

*Lieutenant-General* Karl-Nikolai Karlovich von **Lezedov** (4 Jul 1852 - ?)

| | |
|---|---|
| 10 Sep 1906 - 11 Jun 1908: | Commander, 4$^{th}$ Mortar Artillery Battalion |
| 11 Jun 1908: | Promoted to *Major-General* |
| 11 Jun 1908 - 4 Jul 1912: | Commander, 3$^{rd}$ East Siberian Rifle Artillery Brigade |
| 4 Jul 1912: | Promoted to *Lieutenant-General* |
| 4 Jul 1912: | Retired |
| 6 Nov 1914 - 9 Feb 1915: | Recalled; Commander, 6$^{th}$ Artillery Brigade |
| 9 Feb 1915 - 18 Apr 1917: | Inspector of Artillery, XV. Army Corps |
| 18 Apr 1917 - 20 May 1917: | Reserve officer, Dvinsk Military District |
| 20 May 1917: | Retired |

*Major-General* Ivan Aleksandrovich **Liders** (31 Dec 1859 - ?)

| | |
|---|---|
| 9 May 1912: | Promoted to *Major-General* |
| 9 May 1912 - 29 Nov 1912: | Commander of Engineers, Fortress Mikhailovsk |
| 29 Nov 1912 - 28 Jun 1914: | Deputy Inspector of Engineers, Vilnius Military District |
| 28 Jun 1914 - 2 Sep 1915: | Commander of Engineers, Fortress Brest-Litovsk |
| 2 Sep 1915 - 1917: | Inspector of Engineers, Dvinsk Military District |

*Major-General* Orest Orestovich **Liders** (3 Jun 1866 - 15 Jun 1952)

| | |
|---|---|
| 14 Mar 1916 - 1918: | Commander, 4$^{th}$ Railway Brigade |
| 6 Dec 1916: | Promoted to *Major-General* |

*General of Artillery* Count Fyodor Aleksandrovich **Liders-Veymarn** (12 Dec 1859 - 7 Nov 1927)

| | |
|---|---|
| 17 Apr 1905: | Promoted to *Major-General* |
| 17 Apr 1905 - 11 Dec 1908: | At the disposal of the Minister of War |

11 Dec 1908 - 11 Nov 1909: Special Assignments General (5th Class), Ministry of War
11 Nov 1909 - 7 Sep 1917: Special Assignments General (4th Class), Ministry of War
10 Apr 1911: Promoted to *Lieutenant-General*
7 Sep 1917: Promoted to *General of Artillery*
7 Sep 1917: Retired

*Major-General* Aleksandr Nikiforovich **Likhachev** (16 Apr 1857 - ?)
12 Aug 1898 - 1903: Chief of Police, Warsaw
6 Dec 1901: Promoted to *Major-General*

*Major-General* Dmitry Fyodorovich **Likhachev** (26 Oct 1853 - 1908)
21 Feb 1906 - 1908: Chief of Engineers, Fortress Kars
2 Apr 1906: Promoted to *Major-General*

*Lieutenant-General* Gavriil Aleksandrovich **Likhachev** (25 Mar 1856 - 15 Jul 1924)
24 Mar 1910 - Nov 1915: Commander, 51st Infantry Regiment
2 Oct 1914: Promoted to *Major-General*
Nov 1915 - 1 May 1916: Commander, Brigade, 13th Infantry Division
1 May 1916 - 21 Oct 1916: Commander, Saratov Infantry Brigade
21 Oct 1916: Promoted to *Lieutenant-General*
21 Oct 1916 - 1917: Commander, 122nd Infantry Division
1917: Commander, 1st Guards Infantry Division

*Major-General* Pyotr Aleksandrovich **Likhachev** (22 Oct 1862 - ?)
8 Mar 1896 - Oct 1917: Professor, Nikolayev Engineering Academy
6 Dec 1912: Promoted to *Major-General*

*Lieutenant-General* Nikolai Zinovyevich **Likhtansky** (12 Sep 1833 - ?)
10 Mar 1881 - 30 Jul 1891: Commander, 43rd Dragoon Regiment
30 Jul 1891: Promoted to *Major-General*
30 Jul 1891 - 1 Dec 1899: Commander, 1st Brigade, 13th Cavalry Division
1 Dec 1899 - 5 Aug 1900: At the disposal of the Inspector of Remounts
5 Aug 1900 - 1906: Chairman of the Remount Commission, Yelisavetgrad Region
15 Jan 1904: Promoted to *Lieutenant-General*

*Major-General* Viktor Zinovyevich **Likhtansky** (3 Aug 1839 - ?)
6 Oct 1886 - 1905: Chief of the Moscow Fire Brigade
6 Dec 1903: Promoted to *Major-General*

*Major-General* Semyon Nikolayevich **Lileyev** (21 Dec 1861 - 16 Aug 1916)
6 Dec 1911: Promoted to *Major-General*
6 Dec 1911 - 17 May 1915: Intendant, Kazan Military District
17 May 1915 - 12 Apr 1916: Special Assignments General, Southwestern Front
12 Apr 1916 - 16 Aug 1916: Reserve officer, Petrograd Military District

*Major-General* Egmont Karlovich von **Liliyenfeld** (2 Apr 1845 - ?)
29 Jun 1890 - 1895: Military Judge, Moscow Military District Court
30 Aug 1894: Promoted to *Major-General*

*Lieutenant-General* Genrikh Gustavovich **Liliyental** (21 Nov 1857 - ?)
12 Feb 1905: Promoted to *Major-General*
12 Feb 1905 - 13 Feb 1913: Chief of Staff, I. Turkestan Army Corps
13 Feb 1913: Promoted to *Lieutenant-General*
13 Feb 1913 - 24 Jan 1915: Commander, 5$^{th}$ Siberian Rifle Division
24 Jan 1915 - 12 Jul 1915: Unassigned
12 Jul 1915 - 20 Aug 1915: Commander, 114$^{th}$ Infantry Division
20 Aug 1915 - 1918: POW

*Vice-Admiral* Vladimir Aleksandrovich **Lilye** (16 Dec 1855 - 1925)
1906: Promoted to *Rear-Admiral*
1906 - 1908: Commander, Mine Division, Baltic Fleet
1908 - 26 Apr 1910: Chief Inspector of Mines
18 Apr 1910: Promoted to *Vice-Admiral*
26 Apr 1910 - Jul 1911: Chairman, Naval Technical Committee
 Member, Committee on Coastal Defenses
5 Nov 1911: Retired

*Major-General* Pavel Matveyevich **Limantov** (6 Nov 1833 - ?)
21 Jul 1885: Promoted to *Major-General*
21 Jul 1885 - 1 Apr 1896: Commander, 22$^{nd}$ Artillery Brigade

*Lieutenant-General* Konstantin Khristoforovich **Limarenko** (20 Apr 1852 - ?)
12 Jul 1896 - 28 Jun 1905: At the disposal of the Ataman, Don Cossack Army
17 Apr 1905: Promoted to *Major-General*
28 Jun 1905 - 12 Apr 1911: Commander of Engineers, Fortress Warsaw
1909: Acting Commander, Brigade, 17$^{th}$ Infantry Division
12 Apr 1911 - 22 Oct 1912: Commander of Engineers, Vilnius Military District
6 Dec 1911: Promoted to *Lieutenant-General*
22 Oct 1912 - 20 Mar 1914: Chief of Troop Billeting, Vilnius Military District
20 Mar 1914 - 1917: Member of Barracks Committee, Main Directorate of Troop Billeting

*Major-General* Konstantin Pavlovich **Linda** (11 Mar 1868 - 17 Aug 1914)
22 Apr 1914 - 17 Aug 1914: Commander, 20$^{th}$ Infantry Regiment
22 Jul 1915: Posthumously promoted to *Major-General*

*Lieutenant-General of Naval Engineers* Aleksandr Yakovlevich **Lindebek** (31 Jan 1841 - 10 Feb 1908)
1893 - 1904: Chief Mechanical Engineer, Port of Kronstadt
14 Sep 1899: Promoted to *Major-General of Naval Engineers*
1904 - Feb 1905: Chief Mechanical Engineer, Pacific Fleet
Feb 1905 - 1906: At the disposal of the Naval Technical Committee
1906 - 4 Sep 1906: Chief Mechanical Engineer, Baltic Fleet

4 Sep 1906: Promoted to *Lieutenant-General of Naval Engineers*
4 Sep 1906: Retired

*Lieutenant-General* Aleksandr Karlovich **Lindeberg** (9 Mar 1860 - 2 Mar 1931)
19 Jul 1902 - 12 Jun 1906: Inspector of Classes, Corps of Pages
1906: Promoted to *Major-General*
12 Jun 1906 - 1917: Director, 2nd Emperor Peter the Great Cadet Corps
6 Dec 1913: Promoted to *Lieutenant-General*

*Lieutenant-General of the Fleet* Vilgelm Mikhailovich **Linden** (5 Mar 1843 - 30 Oct 1937)
1892 - 1906: Inspector of the Volunteer Navy
?: Promoted to *Major-General of the Fleet*
1906: Promoted to *Lieutenant-General of the Fleet*
1906: Retired

*Major-General* Leonid Yevgenyevich **Lindenbaum** (2 Apr 1868 - 27 Jan 1938)
1914 - 24 Jan 1916: Commander, 289th Infantry Regiment
24 Jul 1915: Promoted to *Major-General*
24 Jan 1916 - 12 Oct 1916: Commander, Brigade, 3rd Caucasus Rifle Division
12 Oct 1916 - 1917: Commandant of Fortress Kars

*Major-General* Mikhail Vladimirovich **Lindeström** (21 Apr 1854 - 1930)
24 Nov 1908: Promoted to *Major-General*
24 Nov 1908 - 16 Jun 1912: Commander, 1st Brigade, 5th Siberian Rifle Division
16 Jun 1912: Retired
26 Feb 1916 - 1917: Recalled; Attached to the Ministry of War

*Vice-Admiral* Vladimir Vladimirovich von **Lindeström** (1850 - Jun 1917)
22 Sep 1902 - 13 Nov 1905: Commander, 20th Naval Depot
19 Feb 1903: Promoted to *Rear-Admiral*
13 Nov 1905 - 4 Oct 1907: Commander, Port of Libau
4 Oct 1907 - 29 Jun 1908: Junior Flagman, Baltic Fleet
29 Jun 1908: Promoted to *Vice-Admiral*
29 Jun 1908: Retired

*Lieutenant-General* Nikolai Aleksandrovich **Linevich** (26 Jun 1855 - 22 Aug 1909)
22 May 1899 - 1 Apr 1902: Director, 2nd Orenburg Cadet Corps
1 Apr 1901: Promoted to *Major-General*
1 Apr 1902 - 30 Jul 1906: Director, Vladikavkaz Cadet Corps
30 Jul 1906 - 9 Oct 1907: General for Special Purposes, Main Training Directorate
9 Oct 1907: Promoted to *Lieutenant-General*
9 Oct 1907: Retired

*Major-General* Vasily Aleksandrovich **Linevich** (16 Feb 1860 - ?)
11 Feb 1915 - 11 Jan 1916: Commander, 5th Artillery Brigade
11 Jan 1916 - 1917: Commander, Border Artillery Brigade
5 Feb 1916: Promoted to *Major-General*

*Major-General* Aleksandr Ivanovich **Linitsky** (15 Nov 1871 - 1931)
17 Oct 1915 - 2 Feb 1916: Commander, 1st Brigade, 16th Cavalry Division
2 Feb 1916 - 30 Oct 1916: Chief of Staff, 7th Cavalry Division
9 Jul 1916: Promoted to *Major-General*
30 Oct 1916 - 1918: Chief of Staff, Caucasus Cavalry Corps

*Lieutenant-General* Aleksandr Vasilyevich **Liperovsky** (4 Dec 1843 - ?)
5 Aug 1888 - 9 Aug 1905: Inspector of Classes, Petrovsky Poltava Cadet Corps
6 Dec 1903: Promoted to *Major-General*
9 Aug 1905 - 1907: Inspector of Classes, 3rd Moscow Cadet Corps
1907: Promoted to *Lieutenant-General*
1907: Retired

*Major-General* Ivan Ivanovich **Lipinsky** (27 Mar 1866 - 13 Jun 1916)
6 Feb 1916 - 13 Jun 1916: Commander, 1st Battalion, 126th Artillery Brigade
26 Sep 1916: Posthumously promoted to *Major-General*

*Lieutenant-General* Vasily Iosifovich **Lipinsky** (3 Nov 1835 - 20 Dec 1902)
25 May 1878 - 15 May 1880: Deputy Chief of Staff, East Siberian Military District
30 Aug 1879: Promoted to *Major-General*
15 May 1880 - 27 May 1882: Attached to the Chief of the General Staff
27 May 1882 - 31 Dec 1892: Commander, 2nd Brigade, 2nd Grenadier Division
31 Dec 1892 - 29 Feb 1900: Commander, 10th (Odessa) Regional Brigade
30 Aug 1893: Promoted to *Lieutenant-General*
29 Feb 1900: Retired

*Major-General* Aleksandr Ksenofontovich **Lipkin** (14 Oct 1862 - ?)
25 Jul 1914 - 1917: Commander, 57th Artillery Brigade
21 Aug 1915: Promoted to *Major-General*

*Major-General* Maksim Ksenofontovich **Lipkin** (8 Feb 1864 - ?)
2 Jun 1908 - 10 Mar 1916: Military Judge, Caucasus Military District Court
6 Dec 1909: Promoted to *Major-General*
10 Mar 1916 - 1917: Military Judge, Minsk Military District Court

*Major-General* Mitrofan Florianovich **Lipnitsky** (1 Nov 1851 - ?)
28 May 1903 - 1907: Chief of Okhtenskaya Explosives Factory
6 Dec 1903: Promoted to *Major-General*

*Lieutenant-General* Aleksandr Fyodorovich **Lipsky** (20 Aug 1835 - ?)
28 Jun 1889 - 8 Feb 1891: Deputy Intendant, Kiev Military District
30 Aug 1890: Promoted to *Major-General*
8 Feb 1891 - 1904: Intendant, Kiev Military District
6 Dec 1899: Promoted to *Lieutenant-General*

*Major-General* Alfons Iosifovich **Lipsky** (12 May 1854 - ?)
1907 - 1909: Commander, 275th Reserve Battalion, 52nd Replacement Infantry Brigade

1909: Promoted to *Major-General*
1909: Retired
7 May 1915 - 1 Jun 1916: Recalled; Commander, 216th Replacement Battalion
1 Jun 1916 - 1917: Reserve officer, Minsk Military District

*Major-General* Osip Ignatyevich **Lipsky** (19 Jul 1850 - ?)
28 Nov 1901 - 16 Dec 1908: Commander, 4th Replacement Cavalry Regiment
16 Dec 1908 - 17 Feb 1914: Transferred to the reserve
17 Feb 1914: Promoted to *Major-General*
17 Feb 1914 - 1917: Attached to the Ministry of the Imperial Court

*Major-General* Andrey Kononovich **Lisenko** (29 Aug 1868 - 26 Nov 1925)
20 Aug 1914 - Oct 1917: Duty General, 9th Army
10 Apr 1916: Promoted to *Major-General*

*Lieutenant-General* Erast Mikhailovich **Lisenko** (18 Jun 1861 - 1926)
30 Sep 1905 - 19 Mar 1911: Clerk, Office of the Ministry of War
6 Dec 1910: Promoted to *Major-General*
19 Mar 1911 - Jan 1917: Director of Codification, Office of the Ministry of War
22 Mar 1915: Promoted to *Lieutenant-General*
Jan 1917 - Apr 1917: Deputy Chief, Office of the Ministry of War

*Major-General* Mikhail Mikhailovich **Lisenko** (12 Dec 1864 - ?)
10 Dec 1912 - 1917: Ministry of War Representative, Engineering Department, Fortress Sevastopol
6 Dec 1915: Promoted to *Major-General*

*Major-General* Pavel Mikhailovich **Lisevich** (29 Aug 1846 - ?)
19 May 1900: Promoted to *Major-General*
19 May 1900 - 16 Jan 1901: Commander, 1st Brigade, 16th Infantry Division
16 Jan 1901 - 1906: Commander, 57th Reserve Infantry Brigade

*Lieutenant-General* Vsevolod Aleksandrovich **Lishev** (25 Aug 1850 - 26 Jul 1912)
13 Feb 1897 - 17 Nov 1901: Commander of Engineers, Fortress Kronstadt
11 Jul 1897: Promoted to *Major-General*
17 Nov 1901 - 16 Dec 1904: Commander of Engineers, Fortress Brest-Litovsk
6 Dec 1904: Promoted to *Lieutenant-General*
16 Dec 1904 - 1906: Inspector of Engineers, 3rd Manchurian Army
1906 - 1907: Attached to the Main Engineering Directorate
1907: Retired

*Lieutenant-General* Nikolai Petrovich **Lishin** (31 Mar 1839 - 3 Jan 1906)
12 Jun 1877 - 15 May 1883: Attached to the Chief of the General Staff
15 May 1883: Promoted to *Major-General*
15 May 1883 - 23 Jan 1884: Transferred to the reserve
23 Jan 1884 - 3 Jan 1906: Attached to the Ministry of War
13 Mar 1886 - 3 Jan 1906: Member, Commission for Benefits Distribution
14 May 1896: Promoted to *Lieutenant-General*

*Major-General* Sergey Grigoryevich **Lishin** (7 Jul 1863 - ?)
| | |
|---|---|
| 4 Sep 1911 - 3 Jan 1914: | Commander, 6th Replacement Cavalry Regiment |
| 3 Jan 1914: | Promoted to *Major-General* |
| 3 Jan 1914 - 1917: | Commander, Guards Replacement Cavalry Regiment |

*Major-General* Vladimir Grigoryevich **Lishin** (2 Dec 1857 - ?)
| | |
|---|---|
| 30 Jul 1906 - 1917: | Inspector of Classes, Yelisavetgrad Cavalry School |
| 25 Mar 1912: | Promoted to *Major-General* |
| 1915 - 1917: | Acting Commandant, Yelisavetgrad Cavalry School |

*Major-General* Aleksey Ivanovich **Lishkin** (6 Jul 1843 - 15 Jun 1899)
| | |
|---|---|
| 17 Feb 1896 - 15 Jun 1899: | Commander of Engineers, Fortress Novogeorgiyevsk |
| 6 Dec 1897: | Promoted to *Major-General* |

*Lieutenant-General* Leonid Ivanovich **Lishkin** (25 Mar 1847 - ?)
| | |
|---|---|
| 9 Aug 1905 - 12 Sep 1910: | Inspector of Classes, Petrovsky Poltava Cadet Corps |
| 6 Dec 1906: | Promoted to *Major-General* |
| 12 Sep 1910: | Promoted to *Lieutenant-General* |
| 12 Sep 1910: | Retired |

*Major-General* Mikhail Iordanovich **Lisovsky** (7 Aug 1841 - 1903)
| | |
|---|---|
| 8 Jun 1886 - 20 Mar 1895: | Deputy Chief of the Electro-Technical Section, Corps of Engineers |
| 30 Aug 1889: | Promoted to *Major-General* |
| 20 Mar 1895 - 1903: | Attached to the Main Engineering Directorate |

*Lieutenant-General* Nikolai Yakovlevich **Lisovsky** (2 Dec 1856 - 7 Dec 1919)
| | |
|---|---|
| 31 Jan 1904 - 5 Oct 1904: | Commander, 33rd East Siberian Rifle Regiment |
| 2 Jun 1904: | Promoted to *Major-General* |
| 5 Oct 1904 - 29 Jul 1905: | Commander, 2nd Brigade, 54th Infantry Division |
| 29 Jul 1905 - 16 Nov 1911: | Chief of Staff, II. Siberian Army Corps |
| 16 Nov 1911: | Promoted to *Lieutenant-General* |
| 16 Nov 1911 - 28 Apr 1915: | Commander, 10th Siberian Rifle Division |
| 28 Apr 1915 - 8 May 1915: | Commanding General, XXXVI. Army Corps |
| 8 May 1915 - 3 Jun 1915: | Commanding General, II. Siberian Army Corps |
| 3 Jun 1915 - 16 Sep 1915: | Commanding General, XXXVII. Army Corps |
| 16 Sep 1915 - 15 Apr 1917: | Commanding General, XXIX. Army Corps |
| 15 Apr 1917 - 1918: | Reserve officer, Odessa Military District |

*Lieutenant-General* Valerian Yakovlevich **Lisovsky** (15 Oct 1852 - 2 Jan 1906)
| | |
|---|---|
| 25 Jan 1898 - 24 Mar 1899: | Chief of Staff, Caucasus Army Corps |
| 19 Jul 1898: | Promoted to *Major-General* |
| 24 Mar 1899 - 22 May 1902: | Quartermaster-General, Caucasus Military District |
| 22 May 1902 - 1 Jun 1904: | Commander, 2nd Turkestan Reserve Brigade |
| 1 Jun 1904 - 2 Jan 1906: | Commander, 78th Infantry Division |
| 6 Dec 1904: | Promoted to *Lieutenant-General* |

*Major-General* Anton Eduardovich **Listovsky** (17 Mar 1865 - 13 Sep 1927)
31 Oct 1916 - 25 Apr 1917:      Commander, Brigade, 17th Infantry Division
31 Dec 1916:                    Promoted to *Major-General*
25 Apr 1917 - 1917:             Commander, 138th Infantry Division
1917:                           Commanding General, XXXVII. Army Corps

*Lieutenant-General* Mikhail Grigoryevich **Lisunov** (11 Jan 1842 - ?)
1 Jul 1887 - 1 Feb 1898:        Commander of Artillery, Fortress Kaunas
30 Aug 1889:                    Promoted to *Major-General*
1 Feb 1898 - 9 Feb 1901:        Deputy Commander of Artillery, Vilnius Military District
9 Feb 1901:                     Promoted to *Lieutenant-General*
9 Feb 1901 - 15 Mar 1904:       Commander of Artillery, Vilnius Military District
15 Mar 1904 - 1906:             Commandant of Fortress Kaunas

*Major-General* Pavel Grigoryevich **Lisunov** (29 Jun 1843 - ?)
29 Dec 1899 - 11 Aug 1902:      Commander, 8th Artillery Brigade
9 Apr 1900:                     Promoted to *Major-General*

*Major-General* Yevgeny Valerianovich **Litvinenko** (20 Feb 1859 - 25 Oct 1916)
9 Jul 1899 - 9 Feb 1901:        Commander, Czestochowa Borderguard Brigade
9 Feb 1901 - 29 Jul 1910:       Commander, 2nd Revel Borderguard Brigade
6 Dec 1908:                     Promoted to *Major-General*
29 Jul 1910 - 2 Aug 1914:       Commander, 23rd (Odessa) Borderguard Brigade
2 Aug 1914 - 16 Jun 1916:       Commander, 6th Replacement Infantry Brigade
16 Jun 1916 - 25 Oct 1916:      Unassigned

*General of Cavalry* Aleksandr Ivanovich **Litvinov** (22 Aug 1853 - 1932)
23 Jun 1899:                    Promoted to *Major-General*
23 Jun 1899 - 20 Sep 1900:      Special Purposes General, Don Army
20 Sep 1900 - 9 Nov 1904:       Chief of Communications, Warsaw Military District
9 Nov 1904 - 9 Oct 1906:        Chief of Staff, Vilnius Military District
6 Dec 1905:                     Promoted to *Lieutenant-General*
9 Oct 1906 - 9 Mar 1911:        Commander, 1st Cavalry Division
9 Mar 1911 - 17 Nov 1914:       Commanding General, V. Army Corps
6 Dec 1911:                     Promoted to *General of Cavalry*
17 Nov 1914 - 2 Apr 1917:       C-in-C, 1st Army
2 Apr 1917:                     Retired

*Major-General* Aleksandr Vladimirovich **Litvinov** (27 Mar 1860 - 1926)
13 Mar 1904 - 18 Oct 1917:      Chief of St. Petersburg Fire Brigade
6 Dec 1916:                     Promoted to *Major-General*
18 Oct 1917:                    Dismissed

*Lieutenant-General* Aleksey Pavlovich **Litvinov** (1 Mar 1840 - 28 Mar 1918)
9 Aug 1894:                     Promoted to *Major-General*
9 Aug 1894 - 30 Dec 1896:       Commander, 13th Artillery Brigade
30 Dec 1896 - 5 Dec 1899:       Commander, 23rd Artillery Brigade

| | |
|---|---|
| 5 Dec 1899 - 1 Mar 1903: | Commander of Artillery, XIX. Army Corps |
| 14 Apr 1902: | Promoted to *Lieutenant-General* |
| 1 Mar 1903: | Retired |

*Major-General* Nikolai Mikhailovich **Litvinov** (30 Apr 1846 - 15 Dec 1906)
| | |
|---|---|
| 20 Jan 1901 - 27 Nov 1904: | Chairman of the Remount Commission, Astrakhan and North Caucasus |
| 6 Dec 1901: | Promoted to *Major-General* |
| 27 Nov 1904 - Nov 1906: | Attached to the Minister of the Interior |
| Nov 1906 - 15 Dec 1906: | Governor of Omsk Province |

*Admiral* Vladimir Ivanovich **Litvinov** (5 May 1857 - Aug 1919)
| | |
|---|---|
| 1906 - 1908: | Commander, Port of Sveaborg |
| 1907: | Promoted to *Rear-Admiral* |
| 1908 - 1910: | Commander, Baltic Naval Detachment |
| 1910 - 14 Mar 1911: | Commander, 1st Reserve Division, Baltic Fleet |
| 14 Mar 1911: | Promoted to *Vice-Admiral* |
| 14 Mar 1911 - 1917: | Member, Board of Admiralty |
| 10 Apr 1916: | Promoted to *Admiral* |

*Major-General* Georgy Vladimirovich **Livadin** (7 Jan 1867 - 1934)
| | |
|---|---|
| 18 Nov 1913 - 1 Apr 1918: | Deputy Intendant, Omsk Military District |
| 10 Apr 1916: | Promoted to *Major-General* |

*Vice-Admiral* Prince Aleksandr Aleksandrovich **Liven** (7 Jul 1860 - 23 Feb 1914)
| | |
|---|---|
| 24 Nov 1908 - 11 Oct 1911: | Commander, 1st Mine Division, Baltic Fleet |
| 6 Dec 1909: | Promoted to *Rear-Admiral* |
| 11 Oct 1911 - 23 Feb 1914: | Chief of the Naval General Staff |
| 25 Mar 1912: | Promoted to *Vice-Admiral* |

*Major-General* Nikolai Denisovich **Liventsev** (29 Apr 1870 - ?)
| | |
|---|---|
| 29 Jan 1911 - 14 Jan 1915: | Commander, 160th Infantry Regiment |
| 14 Jan 1915: | Promoted to *Major-General* |
| 14 Jan 1915 - 11 Oct 1915: | Chief of Staff, V. Army Corps |
| 1 Dec 1915 - 2 Dec 1916: | Chief of Staff, XXVIII. Army Corps |
| 2 Dec 1916 - 20 May 1917: | Commander, 137th Infantry Division |
| 6 Aug 1917 - 1918: | Commander, 168th Infantry Division |

*Lieutenant-General* Aleksandr-Vladimir Aleksandrovich von **Lizarkh-Kenigk** (4 Mar 1846 - 18 Nov 1904)
| | |
|---|---|
| 31 May 1895 | Promoted to *Major-General* |
| 31 May 1895 - 3 Jan 1897: | Commander, Staff Battalion, Life Guards Rifle Regiment |
| 3 Jan 1897 - 16 Feb 1900: | Commander, Life Guards Rifle Regiment |
| 16 Feb 1900 - 4 Mar 1903: | Commander, 2nd Brigade, 2nd Guards Infantry Division |
| 4 Mar 1903: | Promoted to *Lieutenant-General* |
| 4 Mar 1903 - 8 Apr 1904: | Commander, 6th Infantry Division |
| 8 Apr 1904 - 18 Nov 1904: | Member, Committee for Wounded Veterans |

*Lieutenant-General* Valerian Lukich **Lobachevsky** (1 Aug 1859 - ?)
21 Dec 1902 - 12 Jul 1905:     Director, Orlovsky Bakhtin Cadet Corps
1904:                          Promoted to *Major-General*
12 Jul 1905 - 1917:            Director, 3$^{rd}$ Moscow Cadet Corps
6 Dec 1913:                    Promoted to *Lieutenant-General*

*Major-General* Vladimir Vladimirovich **Lobachevsky** (7 Feb 1869 - 1922)
27 May 1913 - 23 Mar 1915:     Chief of Staff, 1$^{st}$ Caucasus Rifle Brigade
23 Mar 1915 - 17 Dec 1915:     Commander, 2$^{nd}$ Caucasus Rifle Regiment
27 Sep 1915:                   Promoted to *Major-General*
17 Dec 1915 - 18 Jul 1916:     Chief of Staff, 20$^{th}$ Infantry Division
18 Jul 1916 - 14 May 1917:     Chief of Staff, VI. Caucasus Army Corps
14 May 1917 - 10 Jul 1917:     Commander, 5$^{th}$ Turkestan Rifle Division
10 Jul 1917 - Oct 1917:        Reserve officer, Caucasus Military District

*Major-General* Aleksey Frantsevich **Lobanovsky** (13 Mar 1854 - ?)
11 Dec 1908 - 2 Nov 1911:      Commander, 4$^{th}$ Finnish Rifle Regiment
1911:                          Promoted to *Major-General*
2 Nov 1911 - 1917:             Commandant of Helsingfors

*Lieutenant-General* Lev Lvovich **Lobko** (1 Jun 1838 - 10 Sep 1907)
28 Jul 1881 - 10 Dec 1891:     General Staff Officer, General Staff
30 Aug 1882:                   Promoted to *Major-General*
10 Dec 1891 - 1906:            Member of the Military Training Committee, General Staff
                               Military Censor, St. Petersburg Military District
30 Aug 1893:                   Promoted to *Lieutenant-General*
1906:                          Retired

*General of Infantry* Pavel Lvovich **Lobko** (1 Jun 1838 - 25 Nov 1905)
5 Jun 1868 - 19 Feb 1881:      Clerk, Chancellery of the Ministry of War
3 Nov 1870 - 15 Apr 1883:      Professor, General Staff Academy
26 Feb 1878:                   Promoted to *Major-General*
18 Aug 1881 - 4 Jan 1884:      Chief of Military Research Committee, General Staff, Deputy Chief of Chancellery, Ministry of War
4 Jan 1884 - 30 Jun 1898:      Chief of Chancellery, Ministry of War
1 Jan 1889:                    Promoted to *Lieutenant-General*
1 Jan 1898 - 25 Nov 1905:      Member of the State Council
6 Dec 1899 - 26 Oct 1905:      State Comptroller
9 Apr 1900:                    Promoted to *General of Infantry*
26 Oct 1905:                   Promoted to *General-Adjutant*

*Major-General* Aleksandr Zakharovich **Lobko-Lobanovsky** (11 Mar 1857 - ?)
22 Aug 1910 - 1914:            Attached to 13$^{th}$ Artillery Brigade
1914:                          Promoted to *Major-General*
1914:                          Retired

*Major-General* Aleksandr Dmitriyevich **Lobkov** (2 Apr 1864 - ?)
12 Sep 1915 - 1917: Deputy Chief of Okhtenskaya Explosives Factory
6 Dec 1915: Promoted to *Major-General*

*Major-General* Nikolai Georgyevich **Lobov** (3 Oct 1842 - 1915)
1 Jan 1900: Promoted to *Major-General*
1 Jan 1900 - Sep 1902: Commander, Orenburg Cossack Horse Artillery Brigade
Sep 1902: Retired

*Major-General* Aleksandr Matveyevich **Loginov** (23 Nov 1857 - 1932)
16 Jul 1912: Promoted to *Major-General*
16 Jul 1912 - 16 Mar 1914: Commander, 2$^{nd}$ Brigade, 1$^{st}$ Turkestan Cossack Division
16 Mar 1914 - 1917: Commander, 1$^{st}$ Brigade, 1$^{st}$ Turkestan Cossack Division

*General of Infantry* Pyotr Petrovich **Loginov** (24 Apr 1842 - 6 Feb 1910)
14 Nov 1888 - 9 Nov 1898: Commander, Life Guards Grenadier Regiment
30 Aug 1889: Promoted to *Major-General*
2 Nov 1895 - 24 Nov 1899: Commander, 1$^{st}$ Brigade, 2$^{nd}$ Guards Infantry Division
24 Nov 1899: Retired
11 Nov 1904: Recalled; Promoted to *Lieutenant-General*
11 Nov 1904 - 3 Jan 1906: At the disposal of the C-in-C, 2$^{nd}$ Manchurian Army
3 Jan 1906 - 15 Dec 1906: At the disposal of the Chief of the General Staff
15 Dec 1906 - 28 Nov 1907: At the disposal of the Inspector-General of Infantry
28 Nov 1907 - 6 Feb 1910: Special Assignments General to the Inspector-General of Infantry
1910: Promoted to *General of Infantry*

*Major-General* Dmitry Nikolayevich **Logofet** (19 Mar 1865 - 1922)
Sep 1915 - Nov 1915: Commander, 7$^{th}$ Borderguard Brigade
Nov 1915 - 1917: Commander, 6$^{th}$ Border Cavalry Regiment
6 Dec 1916: Promoted to *Major-General*
1917 - Dec 1917: Director of Construction Works, Western Front

*Lieutenant-General* Aleksandr Petrovich **Logvinov** (9 Mar 1852 - 29 Jul 1916)
20 Nov 1904: Promoted to *Major-General*
20 Nov 1904 - 19 Jul 1906: Commander, 1$^{st}$ Brigade, Consolidated Caucasus Cossack Division
19 Jul 1906 - 15 Mar 1911: Commander, 1$^{st}$ Brigade, 1$^{st}$ Caucasus Cossack Division
15 Mar 1911: Promoted to *Lieutenant-General*
15 Mar 1911: Retired
17 Mar 1915 - 29 Jul 1916: Recalled; Commander, Consolidated Kuban Cossack Division

*Lieutenant-General* Nikolai Aleksandrovich **Lokhvitsky** (7 Oct 1867 - 5 Nov 1933)
30 May 1912 - 3 Apr 1915: Commander, 95$^{th}$ Infantry Regiment
11 Feb 1915: Promoted to *Major-General*
3 Apr 1915 - 8 May 1915: Commander, Brigade, 25$^{th}$ Infantry Division

| | |
|---|---|
| 8 May 1915 - 21 Jan 1916: | Commander, Brigade, 24th Infantry Division |
| 21 Jan 1916 - Jun 1917: | Commander, 1st Special Infantry Brigade |
| Jun 1917 - 1918: | Commander, Special Infantry Division |
| 1917: | Promoted to *Lieutenant-General* |

*General of Cavalry* Asinkrit Asinkritovich **Lomachevsky** (6 Apr 1848 - 1921)

| | |
|---|---|
| 25 Apr 1885 - 20 Apr 1895: | Deputy Governor of Orenburg |
| 30 Aug 1893: | Promoted to *Major-General* |
| 20 Apr 1895 - 30 Jan 1900: | Governor of Tomsk |
| 30 Jan 1900 - 14 Jan 1908: | Governor of Turgay Region |
| 6 Dec 1901: | Promoted to *Lieutenant-General* |
| 14 Jan 1908: | Promoted to *General of Cavalry* |
| 14 Jan 1908: | Retired |

*General of Infantry* Nikolai Pavlovich **Lomakin** (31 Jan 1830 - 14 Feb 1902)

| | |
|---|---|
| 26 May 1871 - 4 Apr 1874: | Commander, Mangyshlak Group, Aleksandrovsk Fortress |
| 22 Jul 1873: | Promoted to *Major-General* |
| 2 May 1874 - 14 Jan 1881: | Commander, Transcaspian Military Sector |
| 14 Jan 1881 - 31 Aug 1884: | Military Commander, Tiflis Province |
| 31 Aug 1884 - 22 Dec 1887: | Commander, 24th Regional Brigade |
| 30 Aug 1886: | Promoted to *Lieutenant-General* |
| 22 Dec 1887 - 16 Jun 1897: | Commander, 19th Infantry Division |
| 16 Jun 1897: | Promoted to *General of Infantry* |
| 16 Jun 1897: | Retired |

*Major-General of the Admiralty* Vladimir Petrovich **Loman** (9 Dec 1853 - 1 Mar 1912)

| | |
|---|---|
| 1900 - 28 Aug 1906: | Senior Deputy Commander, Port of Vladivostok |
| 28 Aug 1906: | Promoted to *Major-General of the Admiralty* |
| 28 Aug 1906: | Dismissed |

*Admiral* Nikolai Nikolayevich **Lomen** (28 May 1843 - Apr 1909)

| | |
|---|---|
| 3 Jun 1893 - 1905: | Adjutant & Flag Captain to the Tsar |
| 30 Aug 1893: | Promoted to *Rear-Admiral* |
| 1 Apr 1901: | Promoted to *Vice-Admiral* |
| 6 May 1901: | Promoted to *General-Adjutant* |
| 1906 - 1909: | Attached to the Tsar |
| 24 Dec 1907 - 29 Mar 1909: | Member, Council of State Defense |
| 29 Mar 1909: | Promoted to *Admiral* |

*Major-General* Konstantin Vladislavovich **Lomikovsky** (17 Sep 1868 - ?)

| | |
|---|---|
| 25 Jul 1914 - 29 Sep 1916: | Commander, 69th Artillery Brigade |
| 14 Nov 1914: | Promoted to *Major-General* |
| 29 Sep 1916 - 10 Jun 1917: | Inspector of Artillery, VI. Caucasus Army Corps |
| 10 Jun 1917 - 17 Dec 1917: | Reserve officer, Petrograd Military District |
| 17 Dec 1917: | Retired |

*Lieutenant-General* Pyotr Nikolayevich **Lomnovsky** (24 Nov 1871 - 2 Mar 1956)
| | |
|---|---|
| 21 Aug 1912: | Promoted to *Major-General* |
| 21 Aug 1912 - 19 Jul 1914: | Quartermaster-General, Kiev Military District |
| 19 Jul 1914 - 17 Jul 1915: | Chief of Staff, 8$^{th}$ Army |
| 17 Jul 1915 - 7 Apr 1917: | Commander, 15$^{th}$ Infantry Division |
| 21 Oct 1916: | Promoted to *Lieutenant-General* |
| 7 Apr 1917 - 12 Jul 1917: | Commanding General, VIII. Army Corps |
| 12 Jul 1917 - 9 Sep 1917: | C-in-C, 10$^{th}$ Army |
| 31 Jul 1917 - 5 Aug 1917: | Acting C-in-C, Western Front |
| 9 Sep 1917: | Transferred to the reserve |

*Major-General* Pavel Stepanovich **Lomshakov** (21 Feb 1859 - 15 Feb 1937)
| | |
|---|---|
| 27 Jun 1906 - 1907: | Military Judge, Moscow Military District Court |
| 6 Dec 1906: | Promoted to *Major-General* |
| 1907: | Retired |

*Lieutenant-General* Lyudvig Yustinovich **Lontkevich** (20 Oct 1840 - ?)
| | |
|---|---|
| 22 Jan 1892 - 9 Aug 1896: | Commander, Mountain Artillery Regiment |
| 14 May 1896: | Promoted to *Major-General* |
| 9 Aug 1896 - 11 Aug 1900: | Commander, 9$^{th}$ Artillery Brigade |
| 11 Aug 1900 - 1903: | Commander of Artillery, II. Siberian Army Corps |
| 6 Aug 1902: | Promoted to *Lieutenant-General* |

*Lieutenant-General* Aleksandr Nikolayevich **Lopatin** (17 Jun 1850 - ?)
| | |
|---|---|
| 27 Jan 1909: | Promoted to *Major-General* |
| 27 Jan 1909 - 17 Jun 1914: | Commander, Perm Regional Brigade |
| 17 Jun 1914: | Promoted to *Lieutenant-General* |
| 17 Jun 1914: | Retired |
| 28 Mar 1915 - 1917: | Recalled; Chief of 1$^{st}$ Moscow Administrative Evacuation Points |

*Major-General* Aleksey Ivanovich **Lopatin** (31 May 1862 - ?)
| | |
|---|---|
| 26 Jan 1906 - 31 Jul 1906: | Military Judge, Vilnius Military District Court |
| 2 Apr 1906: | Promoted to *Major-General* |
| 31 Jul 1906 - 14 Feb 1909: | Military Judge, Odessa Military District Court |
| 14 Feb 1909 - 1917: | Military Judge, Moscow Military District Court |

*Major-General of Naval Engineers* Nikolai Ivanovich **Lopatin** (28 Apr 1865 - 19 Oct 1929)
| | |
|---|---|
| 1915: | Promoted to *Major-General of Naval Engineers* |
| 1915 - 1917: | Vice-Chairman, Commission for Ship Testing |

*Major-General* Sergey Aleksandrovich **Lopatin** (11 Jun 1858 - ?)
| | |
|---|---|
| 13 Sep 1906 - 1910: | Duty General, Irkutsk Military District |
| 6 Dec 1907: | Promoted to *Major-General* |
| 1910: | Retired |
| 12 Sep 1915 - 1917: | Recalled; Commander, 1$^{st}$ Transcaucasus Replacement Infantry Brigade |

*Major-General* Dmitry Aleksandrovich **Lopukhin** (25 Mar 1865 - 23 Nov 1914)
20 Apr 1911 - 4 Feb 1914: Commander, 9th Uhlan Regiment
4 Feb 1914: Promoted to *Major-General*
4 Feb 1914 - 23 Nov 1914: Commander, Life Guards Horse-Grenadier Regiment
Aug 1914 - 23 Nov 1914: Commander, 1st Brigade, 2nd Guards Cavalry Division

*General of Infantry* Nikolai Yakovlevich **Lopushansky** (6 Dec 1852 - 1917)
14 Apr 1902: Promoted to *Major-General*
14 Apr 1902 - 1 Jan 1903: Special Assignments General, Kiev Military District
1 Jan 1903 - 1 May 1903: Deputy Chief of the General Staff
1 May 1903 - 25 Jun 1905: First Quartermaster-General, General Staff
25 Jun 1905 - 3 Feb 1906: Quartermaster-General, General Staff
3 Feb 1906 - 10 Jul 1908: Commander, 51st Reserve Infantry Brigade
10 Jul 1908: Promoted to *Lieutenant-General*
10 Jul 1908 - 13 Mar 1915: Commander, 10th Infantry Division
13 Mar 1915: Promoted to *General of Infantry*
13 Mar 1915: Retired
12 Jul 1915 - 13 Apr 1917: Recalled; Commander, 124th Infantry Division
16 Jun 1917 - 1917: Reserve officer, Kiev Military District

*Major-General of the Fleet* Aleksandr Nikolayevich **Losev** (7 Apr 1865 - ?)
1906 - 1917: Professor, Marine Corps
6 Dec 1913: Promoted to *Major-General of the Fleet*

*Major-General* Nikolai Ivanovich **Losev** (5 Apr 1851 - ?)
30 Dec 1904 - 1907: Commander of Gendarmerie, Chinese Eastern Railway
6 Dec 1906: Promoted to *Major-General*

*Lieutenant-General* Yakov Nikolayevich **Losev** (8 Oct 1838 - 1914)
26 Oct 1894 - 13 Mar 1897: Deputy Intendant, Turkestan Military District
6 Dec 1895: Promoted to *Major-General*
13 Mar 1897 - 6 Jul 1899: Intendant, Trans-Caspian Region
6 Jul 1899 - 1902: Intendant, Siberian Military District
1902: Promoted to *Lieutenant-General*
1902: Retired

*Vice-Admiral* Mikhail Fyodorovich **Loshchinsky** (5 Nov 1849 - 11 Jan 1917)
1900 - 1903: Commandant, Port of Sevastopol
1901: Promoted to *Rear-Admiral*
1903 - 28 Jan 1904: Junior Flagman, Baltic Fleet
28 Jan 1904 - 14 Mar 1904: Deputy Commandant of Port Arthur
14 Mar 1904 - 24 Aug 1904: Junior Flagman, Pacific Squadron
24 Aug 1904 - Jan 1905: Commander of Naval Defenses, Port Arthur
1905 - 1906: Member of Naval Commissions
1906 - 20 Oct 1908: Inspector-General of Mines
20 Oct 1908: Promoted to *Vice-Admiral*
20 Oct 1908: Retired

*Lieutenant-General* Iosif Semyonovich **Loshunov** (5 Apr 1856 - ?)
14 Oct 1911: Promoted to *Major-General*
14 Oct 1911 - 13 Oct 1914: Commander, 1st Brigade, 9th Infantry Division
13 Oct 1914: Promoted to *Lieutenant-General*
13 Oct 1914 - 28 Apr 1917: Commander, 9th Infantry Division
28 Apr 1917 - Oct 1917: Reserve officer, Minsk Military District

*Major-General* Mikhail Petrovich **Losyev** (1 Sep 1864 - 1919)
1914 - 5 Jul 1915: Commander, 312th Infantry Regiment
19 Apr 1915: Promoted to *Major-General*
5 Jul 1915 - 6 Mar 1917: Commander, 2nd Brigade, 78th Infantry Division
6 Mar 1917 - 14 May 1917: Commander, 179th Infantry Division
14 May 1917 - 1917: Commander, 80th Infantry Division

*Major-General* Grigory Petrovich **Loven** (30 Jan 1864 - ?)
14 Feb 1913 - 1917: Council member, Yelizabetpol Province
6 Dec 1916: Promoted to *Major-General*

*Lieutenant-General* Sergey Petrovich **Lovtsov** (28 Aug 1862 - ?)
7 Jul 1906: Promoted to *Major-General*
7 Jul 1906 - 20 Sep 1908: Commander, 2nd Brigade, 22nd Infantry Division
20 Sep 1908 - 27 Sep 1914: Chief of Staff, I. Army Corps
27 Sep 1914: Promoted to *Lieutenant-General*
27 Sep 1914: Retired

*Major-General* Nikolai Nikolayevich **Lovyagin** (3 Sep 1849 - 10 Jan 1914)
16 Feb 1907 - 24 Mar 1908: Chief of Gendarmerie, Tomsk Region
24 Mar 1908: Promoted to *Major-General*
24 Mar 1908: Retired

*Major-General* Aleksey Antonovich **Luchkovsky** (15 Mar 1853 - 28 May 1913)
5 Apr 1902 - 20 Aug 1905: Commander, 1st East Siberian Rifle Artillery Brigade
3 Oct 1902: Promoted to *Major-General*
20 Aug 1905 - 1906: At the disposal of the Main Artillery Directorate

*Major-General* Nikolai Pavlovich **Luchov** (2 Jul 1869 - 20 Apr 1934)
9 Dec 1915 - 19 Apr 1917: Commander, 1st Brigade, 5th Cavalry Division
10 Apr 1916: Promoted to *Major-General*
19 Apr 1917 - 24 Jun 1917: Commander, 14th Cavalry Division

*Major-General* Aleksandr Ivanovich **Luganin** (1 Jul 1851 - 17 Jan 1905)
11 Sep 1903: Promoted to *Major-General*
11 Sep 1903 - 17 Jan 1905: Commander, 2nd Brigade, 25th Infantry Division

*Lieutenant-General* Ivan Andreyevich **Luizov** (11 Jun 1844 - ?)
20 Nov 1899: Promoted to *Major-General*
20 Nov 1899 - 12 Jun 1904: Commander, 2nd Brigade, 1st Don Cossack Division
12 Jun 1904: Promoted to *Lieutenant-General*

12 Jun 1904: Retired

*Lieutenant-General* Anatoly Nikolayevich **Lukashev** (11 Sep 1857 - May 1917)
27 May 1906 - May 1917: Deputy Commandant of Bryansk Regional Arsenal
29 Mar 1909: Promoted to *Major-General*
2 Jun 1917: Posthumously promoted to *Lieutenant-General*

*Major-General* Nikolai Ivanovich **Lukashev** (3 Dec 1838 - ?)
11 Mar 1888 - 1899: Subsection Chief, Main Directorate for Cossack Forces
30 Aug 1893: Promoted to *Major-General*

*Lieutenant-General* Nikolai Yevgenyevich **Lukashev** (15 Apr 1849 - 1913)
13 Dec 1900 - 1 Jul 1905: Intendant, Kwantung Region
3 Oct 1902: Promoted to *Major-General*
1 Jul 1905 - 25 Nov 1905: At the disposal of the C-in-C, 2nd Manchurian Army
25 Nov 1905 - 1906: At the disposal of the Main Intendant Directorate
1906: Promoted to *Lieutenant-General*
1906: Retired

*Lieutenant-General* Yevdokim Yevgenyevich **Lukashev** (16 Jul 1850 - 7 Jan 1910)
26 May 1903 - 22 Jun 1904: Special Assignments Officer 5th Class, Office of the Intendant-General
6 Dec 1903: Promoted to *Major-General*
22 Jun 1904 - 1905: At the disposal of the Minister of War
1905: Promoted to *Lieutenant-General*
1905: Retired

*Major-General* Sergey Vladimirovich **Lukashevich** (6 Oct 1868 - 6 Jan 1935)
23 Nov 1911 - 3 Feb 1916: Commander, 2nd Battalion, 15th Artillery Brigade
11 Aug 1915: Promoted to *Major-General*
3 Feb 1916 - Oct 1917: Commander, 102nd Artillery Brigade

*Major-General* Ivan Yevgrafovich **Lukin** (30 Dec 1857 - ?)
25 Jul 1914 - 1917: Commander, 78th Artillery Brigade
3 Mar 1916: Promoted to *Major-General*

*Major-General* Nikolai Nikolayevich **Lukin** (27 Jul 1839 - ?)
3 Mar 1890: Promoted to *Major-General*
3 Mar 1890 - 1898: Special Assignments General, Kazan Military District

*Major-General* Stepan Petrovich **Lukin** (6 Nov 1859 - 2 Dec 1924)
29 Sep 1916 - 1917: Commander, Turkestan Consolidated Rifle Artillery Brigade
19 Oct 1916: Promoted to *Major-General*

*Lieutenant-General* Valentin Yevgrafovich **Lukin** (13 Apr 1863 - 1 Dec 1919)
13 May 1910: Promoted to *Major-General*
13 May 1910 - 16 Jun 1914: Commander, 2nd Brigade, 5th Siberian Rifle Division

| | |
|---|---|
| 16 Jun 1914: | Retired |
| 1915 - 30 Dec 1915: | Recalled; Chief of Staff, ? Militia Corps |
| 30 Dec 1915 - 18 Feb 1917: | Commander, Brigade, 20th Infantry Division |
| 18 Feb 1917 - 1918: | Commander, 165th Infantry Division |
| 23 Oct 1917: | Promoted to *Lieutenant-General* |

*Rear-Admiral* Veniamin Konstaninovich **Lukin** (26 Aug 1866 - 11 Apr 1928)
| | |
|---|---|
| 1916: | Promoted to *Rear-Admiral* |
| 1916 - 1917: | Commander, 2nd Battleship Brigade, Black Sea Fleet |
| 7 Jun 1917 - 18 Jul 1917: | Acting C-in-C, Black Sea Fleet |

*General of Artillery* Vsevolod Vsevolodovich **Luknitsky** (25 May 1845 - 14 Aug 1917)
| | |
|---|---|
| 15 May 1885 - 14 Aug 1917: | Chief of Kazan Gunpowder Factory |
| 30 Aug 1893: | Promoted to *Major-General* |
| 29 Mar 1909: | Promoted to *Lieutenant-General* |
| 1917: | Posthumously promoted to *General of Artillery* |

*Lieutenant-General* Aleksandr Sergeyevich **Lukomsky** (10 Jul 1868 - 25 Jan 1939)
| | |
|---|---|
| 3 Jan 1909 - 23 Jan 1913: | Chief of Mobilization Section, General Staff |
| 31 Dec 1910: | Promoted to *Major-General* |
| 23 Jan 1913 - 1914: | Deputy Chief of Bureau, Ministry of War |
| 1914 - 2 Apr 1916: | Chief of Bureau, Ministry of War |
| 8 Nov 1914: | Promoted to *Lieutenant-General* |
| 8 Aug 1915 - 2 Apr 1916: | Deputy Minister of War |
| 2 Apr 1916 - 14 Oct 1916: | Commander, 32nd Infantry Division |
| 14 Oct 1916 - 21 Oct 1916: | Chief of Staff, 10th Army |
| 21 Oct 1916 - 2 Apr 1917: | Quartermaster-General, GHQ |
| 2 Apr 1917 - 2 Jun 1917: | Commanding General, I. Army Corps |
| 2 Jun 1917 - 30 Aug 1917: | Chief of Staff to the Supreme Commander-in-Chief |
| 30 Aug 1917: | Dismissed |

*Lieutenant-General* Pyotr Viktorovich **Lukoshkov** (17 Dec 1840 - 1 Jan 1902)
| | |
|---|---|
| 29 Jan 1883 - 1 Jan 1902: | Commandant of Gatchina |
| 30 Aug 1891: | Promoted to *Major-General* |
| 6 Dec 1899: | Promoted to *Lieutenant-General* |

*Major-General* Ivan Vasilyevich **Lukyanov** (18 Apr 1867 - ?)
| | |
|---|---|
| 1915 - 11 Jan 1916: | Commander, 1st Siege Artillery Brigade |
| 11 Jan 1916 - 4 May 1917: | Commander, 6th Field Heavy Artillery Brigade |
| 12 Jan 1916: | Promoted to *Major-General* |
| 4 May 1917 - 5 Jun 1917: | Inspector of Artillery, XXIII. Army Corps |

*Lieutenant-General* Nikolai Ivanovich **Lukyanov** (11 Nov 1861 - 15 Jun 1937)
| | |
|---|---|
| 1 May 1903 - 21 Jul 1907: | Section Chief, General Staff |
| 1905: | Promoted to *Major-General* |
| 21 Jul 1907 - 3 May 1918: | Chief Inspector of Prisoner Transport, General Staff |
| 31 May 1913: | Promoted to *Lieutenant-General* |

*Major-General* Edgar Yuryevich **Lundberg** (6 Aug 1860 - ?)
5 Sep 1909 - 1917: Inspector of Classes, 1st Cadet Corps
6 Dec 1909: Promoted to *Major-General*

*Lieutenant-General* Yalmar-Leopold Ioganovich **Lundgren** (29 Jun 1854 - 10 May 1938)
11 Jul 1907 - 1916: Chief of Kremenchug Railway Gendarmerie
14 Apr 1913: Promoted to *Major-General*
1916: Promoted to *Lieutenant-General*
1916: Retired

*Major-General* Polikarp-Genrikh Osipovich **Lunkevich** (26 Jan 1852 - ?)
1 Jun 1904: Promoted to *Major-General*
1 Jun 1904 - 1906: Commander, 1st Brigade, 68th Infantry Division

*Major-General* Pyotr Ivanovich **Lunkevich** (14 Apr 1842 - ?)
1 May 1886 - 1898: Special Assignments Officer, Main State Horsebreeding Directorate
6 May 1897: Promoted to *Major-General*

*Major-General* Mikhail Vasilyevich **Lurye** (3 Jan 1865 - 4 Jun 1916)
Dec 1915 - 4 Jun 1916: Commander, 128th Infantry Regiment
16 Jul 1916: Posthumously promoted to *Major-General*

*Major-General* Mikhail Mikhaylovich **Lushkov** (24 Mar 1852 - 1909)
25 Oct 1905 - 1909: Chairman of the Economic Committee, Pipe Plant
1909: Promoted to *Major-General*

*Major-General* Nikolai Aleksandrovich **Lutsky** (30 Jul 1843 - ?)
1 Jul 1889 - 23 Jun 1901: Military Judge, Caucasus Military District Court
6 Dec 1898: Promoted to *Major-General*
23 Jun 1901 - 1903: Military Judge, Vilnius Military District Court

*Major-General* Nikolai Aleksandrovich von **Luttsau** (20 Nov 1853 - ?)
13 Jul 1900 - 1905: Governor of Yelisavetpol
6 Dec 1903: Promoted to *Major-General*

*General of Infantry* Pyotr Fomich **Luzanov** (4 Apr 1848 - ?)
25 Nov 1886 - 29 Oct 1892: Chief of Chancellery, Main Military Court Administration
30 Aug 1891: Promoted to *Major-General*
29 Oct 1892 - 28 Nov 1905: Deputy Chief Military Prosecutor, Deputy Chief of the Main Military Court Administration
6 Dec 1899: Promoted to *Lieutenant-General*
28 Nov 1905 - 1917: Senator
18 Apr 1910: Promoted to *General of Infantry*

*Lieutenant-General* Ivan Nikolayevich **Lvov** (24 Jun 1857 - Apr 1925)
17 Apr 1905: Promoted to *Major-General*

17 Apr 1905 - 14 Jan 1906:    Section Chief, General Staff
14 Jan 1906 - 20 May 1906:    Attached to the General Staff
20 May 1906 - Oct 1917:       Commandant of Fortress Dvinsk
10 Apr 1911:                  Promoted to *Lieutenant-General*

*Major-General* Leonid Ivanovich **Lvov** (3 Aug 1873 - ?)
1 Jun 1916 - 1917:            Commandant, Warsaw District Arsenal
6 Dec 1916:                   Promoted to *Major-General*

*Rear-Admiral* Lev Ivanovich **Lvov** (11 Feb 1838 - 10 Jul 1900)
?:                            Promoted to *Rear-Admiral*

*Rear-Admiral* Nikolai Georgiyevich **Lvov** (22 May 1869 - 23 Feb 1918)
11 Aug 1914:                  Promoted to *Rear-Admiral*
1914 - 1917:                  Commander, Black Sea Transport Flotilla

*Major-General* Nikolai Nikolayevich **Lvov** (8 Aug 1846 - ?)
4 Nov 1897 - 1 Aug 1914:      Chief of Gendarmerie, Moscow-Kamyshin Railway
1906:                         Promoted to *Major-General*
1 Aug 1914 - 18 May 1917:     Chief of Gendarmerie, Northwest Railway
18 May 1917:                  Dismissed

*Major-General* Nikolai Vladimirovich **Lvov** (3 May 1868 - 8 Jul 1933)
21 Apr 1900 - 10 Apr 1916:    Chief of Workshops, St. Peterburg Arms Factory
6 Dec 1915:                   Promoted to *Major-General*
10 Apr 1916 - 13 May 1916:    Deputy Chief of Section 1, Technical Artillery
                              Department, Main Artillery Directorate
13 May 1916 - 1917:           Deputy Chief, Petrograd Arms Factory

*Major-General* Vladimir Semonovich **Lvov** (6 Aug 1854 - 8 Dec 1926)
4 Dec 1910 - 1912:            Deputy Commander, 23$^{rd}$ Artillery Brigade
1912:                         Promoted to *Major-General*
1912:                         Retired

*Lieutenant-General* Vladimir Platonovich **Lyakhov** (20 Jun 1869 - 30 Apr 1920)
13 May 1912:                  Promoted to *Major-General*
13 May 1912 - 21 Jan 1915:    Chief of Staff, Kuban Cossack Army
21 Jan 1915 - 22 May 1916:    Commandant of Fortress Mikhail
22 May 1916 - 12 Mar 1917:    Commander, 39$^{th}$ Infantry Division
26 Aug 1916:                  Promoted to *Lieutenant-General*
12 Mar 1917 - Oct 1917:       Commanding General, I. Caucasus Army Corps

*Lieutenant-General* Vladimir Andreyevich **Lyakhovich** (31 Mar 1860 - 7 Jun 1941)
20 Nov 1904 - 21 Nov 1907:    Commander, 22$^{nd}$ Artillery Brigade
6 Dec 1906:                   Promoted to *Major-General*
21 Nov 1907 - 14 Nov 1909:    Commander, 2$^{nd}$ Life Guards Artillery Brigade
14 Nov 1909 - 11 Nov 1910:    Deputy Section Chief, Main Artillery Directorate
6 Dec 1910:                   Promoted to *Lieutenant-General*

| | |
|---|---|
| 11 Nov 1910 - 28 Sep 1914: | Section Chief, Main Artillery Directorate |
| 28 Sep 1914 - 6 Sep 1915: | Chief of Administrative Department, Main Artillery Directorate |
| 6 Sep 1915 - 25 Feb 1917: | Deputy Chief of Accounting & Procurement, Main Artillery Directorate |
| 25 Feb 1917 - 6 Mar 1917: | Deputy Minister of War-Designate |
| 6 Mar 1917 - 2 Dec 1917: | Chief of the Main Artillery Directorate |

*Lieutenant-General* Mikhail Alekseyevich **Lyalin** (23 Mar 1839 - 1915)
| | |
|---|---|
| 26 Jan 1888: | Promoted to *Major-General* |
| 26 Jan 1888 - 2 Jul 1897: | Director, Konstantinov Mechanical Institute |
| 2 Jul 1897: | Promoted to *Lieutenant-General* |
| 2 Jul 1897: | Retired |

*Lieutenant-General* Nikolai Yevseyevich **Lyalin** (20 Sep 1839 - 17 Dec 1896)
| | |
|---|---|
| 14 Nov 1894 - 17 Dec 1896: | Section Chief, Main Engineering Directorate |
| 30 Aug 1889: | Promoted to *Major-General* |
| 1896: | Promoted to *Lieutenant-General* |

*Major-General* Aleksandr Yakovlevich **Lyapunov** (27 Mar 1839 - 6 Nov 1895)
| | |
|---|---|
| 8 Jun 1892: | Promoted to *Major-General* |
| 8 Jun 1892 - 16 Feb 1894: | Commander, 1$^{st}$ Brigade, 40$^{th}$ Infantry Division |
| 16 Feb 1894 - 6 Nov 1895: | Commander, 1$^{st}$ Brigade, 2$^{nd}$ Grenadier Division |

*Major-General* Ivan Nikolayevich **Lyapunov** (13 Jun 1849 - ?)
| | |
|---|---|
| 3 Sep 1904 - 13 Mar 1906: | Commander, 52$^{nd}$ Artillery Brigade |
| 13 Mar 1906 - 22 Oct 1908: | Commander, 30$^{th}$ Artillery Brigade |
| 6 Dec 1906: | Promoted to *Major-General* |

*Lieutenant-General* Mikhail Nikolayevich **Lyapunov** (18 Feb 1848 - 19 Feb 1909)
| | |
|---|---|
| 27 Jun 1887 - 17 Oct 1893: | Military Prosecutor, Kazan Military District |
| 30 Aug 1892: | Promoted to *Major-General* |
| 17 Oct 1893 - 8 May 1898: | Military Prosecutor, Moscow Military District |
| 8 May 1898 - 31 Jan 1906: | Military Governor of Sakhalin |
| 6 Dec 1901: | Promoted to *Lieutenant-General* |
| 31 Jan 1906 - 19 Sep 1908: | Attached to the Military Legal Service, General Staff |
| 19 Sep 1908: | Retired |

*Major-General* Nikolai Nikolayevich **Lyapunov** (9 Nov 1846 - ?)
| | |
|---|---|
| 16 Mar 1899 - 3 Mar 1904: | Commander, 1$^{st}$ Life Guards Artillery Brigade |
| 6 Dec 1899: | Promoted to *Major-General* |

*Major-General* Sergey Nikolayevich **Lyapunov** (5 Oct 1850 - ?)
| | |
|---|---|
| 17 Feb 1900 - 1905: | Commander, 13$^{th}$ Artillery Brigade |
| 1 Jan 1901: | Promoted to *Major-General* |

*Major-General* Vadim Nikolayevich **Lyapunov** (17 Nov 1867 - Aug 1920)
| | |
|---|---|
| 22 Nov 1911 - 1917: | Chairman of the Kazan Intendant Selection Committee |

22 Mar 1915: Promoted to *Major-General*

*Major-General* Nikolai Mikhaylovich **Lyashenko** (20 Apr 1851 - ?)
27 Apr 1910: Promoted to *Major-General*
27 Apr 1910 - 27 Apr 1912: Commander, 41st Artillery Brigade

*Major-General* Iosif Vikentyevich **Lyaskovsky** (16 May 1835 - ?)
11 Oct 1893: Promoted to *Major-General*
11 Oct 1893 - 20 Dec 1899: Commander, 1st East Siberian Artillery Brigade

*Major-General* Stepan-Lyudvig Yulianovich **Lyatur** (2 Aug 1862 - 9 Nov 1923)
1 Mar 1915 - 13 Nov 1915: Commander, 246th Infantry Regiment
13 Jul 1915: Promoted to *Major-General*
13 Nov 1915 - Jul 1916: Commander, Brigade, 65th Infantry Division
Jul 1916 - 22 May 1917: Commander, Brigade, 73rd Infantry Division
22 May 1917 - Dec 1917: Commander, 60th Infantry Division

*Major-General* Yulian-Rokh Antonovich **Lyavdansky** (14 Aug 1846 - ?)
18 Mar 1906 - 1912: Inspector of Engineering Works, Caucasus Military District
22 Apr 1907: Promoted to *Major-General*

*Major-General* Aleksandr Sergeyevich **Lykoshin** (29 Aug 1867 - ?)
18 Feb 1912 - 1917: Section Chief, Main Directorate of Military Justice
25 Mar 1912: Promoted to *Major-General*
10 Jul 1915 - 1917: Professor, Aleksandrov Military Law Academy

*Major-General* Aleksey Ivanovich **Lykoshin** (17 Aug 1857 - ?)
1 Mar 1892 - 1905: Deputy Military Prosecutor, Kiev Military District
1905: Promoted to *Major-General*
1905: Retired
18 Dec 1914 - 13 Aug 1915: Recalled; Military Judge, Military Government of Galicia
13 Aug 1915 - 1917: Reserve officer, Petrograd Military District
1915 - 1916: Chairman of the Military Tribunal, XLIII. Army Corps
1916 - 1917: Military Judge, 12th Army Court

*Major-General* Nil Sergeyevich **Lykoshin** (20 Oct 1860 - 1922)
13 Mar 1912 - 22 Apr 1914: Commander, Amu-Darya Sector
6 Dec 1913: Promoted to *Major-General*
22 Apr 1914 - Jan 1917: Military Governor of Samarkand
Jan 1917: Retired

*Major-General* Mikhail Mikhailovich **Lysakovsky** (8 Aug 1858 - ?)
23 Apr 1916 - 1917: Commander, 486th Infantry Regiment
6 Jan 1917: Promoted to *Major-General*
1917: Reserve officer, Kiev Military District

*Major-General* Vasily Vasilyevich **Lysenko** (22 Dec 1836 - May 1899)
3 Mar 1894: Promoted to *Major-General*
3 Mar 1894 - May 1899: Commander, 41st Artillery Brigade

*Lieutenant-General* Mikhail Anzelmovich **Lyshchinsky** (5 Mar 1857 - ?)
22 Apr 1907: Promoted to *Major-General*
22 Apr 1907 - 18 Aug 1912: Commander, 2nd Brigade, 15th Cavalry Division
18 Aug 1912: Promoted to *Lieutenant-General*
18 Aug 1912: Retired

*Lieutenant-General* Aleksandr Adolfovich **Lyuba** (28 Jul 1851 - ?)
7 Jan 1894 - 12 Jul 1900: Deputy Intendant, Vilnius Military District
6 Dec 1899: Promoted to *Major-General*
12 Jul 1900 - 13 Apr 1902: Intendant, Odessa Military District
13 Apr 1902 - 1907: Intendant, Warsaw Military District
2 Apr 1906: Promoted to *Lieutenant-General*

*Major-General* Konstantin Andreyevich **Lyubarsky** (5 Sep 1854 - 30 Jun 1925)
12 May 1907 - 7 Nov 1909: Commander, Life Guards Moscow Regiment
30 Jun 1907: Promoted to *Major-General*
7 Nov 1909 - Aug 1914: Commander, 1st Brigade, 3rd Guards Infantry Division
Aug 1914 - 1917: POW

*Lieutenant-General* Gavriil Pavlovich **Lyubavin** (13 Jul 1850 - ?)
5 Jan 1904: Promoted to *Major-General*
5 Jan 1904 - Feb 1905: Commander, 2nd Brigade, Trans-Baikal Cossack Division
Feb 1905 - Sep 1905: Commander, 1st Brigade, Ural-Trans Baikal Consolidated Cossack Division
Sep 1905 - Jun 1906: Commander, Trans-Baikal Cossack Division
Jun 1906 - 1908: Attached to Warsaw Military District
1908: Promoted to *Lieutenant-General*
1908: Retired

*Lieutenant-General* Modest Dmitriyevich **Lyubavsky** (11 Dec 1848 - ?)
28 Feb 1880 - 9 Nov 1892: Deputy Military Prosecutor, Caucasus Military District Court
30 Aug 1889: Promoted to *Major-General*
9 Nov 1892 - 9 Feb 1898: Military Prosecutor, Turkestan Military District Court
9 Feb 1898 - 1906: Chairman of the Military Tribunal, Turkestan Military District
6 Dec 1899: Promoted to *Lieutenant-General*

*Major-General* Pavel Nikolayevich **Lyubavsky** (24 Apr 1857 - ?)
11 Dec 1914 - 24 Feb 1915: Commander, 190th Infantry Regiment
24 Feb 1915 - 14 May 1915: Reserve officer, Kiev Military District
14 May 1915: Promoted to *Major-General*
14 May 1915: Dismissed

*Major-General* Ilya Alekseyevich **Lyubimov** (20 Jul 1863 - 21 Feb 1937)
| | |
|---|---|
| 19 Jan 1904 - 1912: | Staff Officer for Assignments, Main Directorate for Military Schools |
| 1912: | Promoted to *Major-General* |
| 1912 - 1914: | Transferred to the reserve |
| 1914 - Feb 1917: | At the disposal of Prince A. P. Oldenburg |
| Feb 1917 - 2 Jul 1917: | Reserve officer, Petrogard Military District |
| 2 Jul 1917: | Dismissed |

*Lieutenant-General of the Admiralty* Lev Alekseyevich **Lyubimov** (24 Dec 1845 - 25 Jan 1906)
| | |
|---|---|
| ?: | Promoted to *Major-General of the Admiralty* |
| Apr 1902: | Promoted to *Lieutenant-General of the Admiralty* |
| Apr 1902 - 1906: | Chief, Main Directorate of Shipbuilding |
| 1906: | Retired |

*Vice-Admiral* Pavel Yakovlevich **Lyubimov** (24 Sep 1862 - 20 Mar 1931)
| | |
|---|---|
| 7 May 1913 - 16 Jul 1917: | Commandant, Port of Revel |
| 6 Dec 1913: | Promoted to *Rear-Admiral* |
| 6 Dec 1916: | Promoted to *Vice-Admiral* |
| 16 Jul 1917 - Oct 1917: | Reserve officer, Ministry of the Navy |

*Rear-Admiral* Vladimir Aleksandrovich **Lyubinsky** (15 Jul 1873 - ?)
| | |
|---|---|
| 7 Dec 1915 - 26 Apr 1917: | Chief of Staff, Emperor Peter the Great Naval Fortress |
| 6 Dec 1916: | Promoted to *Rear-Admiral* |
| 26 Apr 1917 - 21 Oct 1917: | Reserve officer, Ministry of the Navy |
| 21 Oct 1917: | Dismissed |

*Major-General* Yakov Yakovlevich **Lyubitsky** (21 Apr 1860 - 1918)
| | |
|---|---|
| 8 May 1915 - 11 May 1915: | Commander, Brigade, 8th Siberian Rifle Division |
| 11 May 1915: | Promoted to *Major-General* |
| 11 May 1915 - 8 Sep 1915: | Commander, 1st Brigade, 1st Siberian Rifle Division |
| 8 Sep 1915 - 10 Sep 1915: | Attached to XXXV. Army Corps |
| 10 Sep 1915 - 28 Oct 1915: | Acting Commander, 55th Infantry Division |
| 28 Oct 1915 - 7 Feb 1917: | Commander, 1st Brigade, 1st Siberian Rifle Division |
| 7 Feb 1917 - 29 May 1917: | Commander, 177th Infantry Division |
| 29 May 1917 - 30 Jun 1917: | Reserve officer, Kiev Military District |
| 30 Jun 1917: | Retired |

*Lieutenant-General* Pavel Petrovich **Lyubomirov** (21 Jun 1858 - Nov 1941)
| | |
|---|---|
| 16 Apr 1902 - 3 Nov 1904: | Commander, 11th Dragoon Regiment |
| 3 Nov 1904: | Promoted to *Major-General* |
| 3 Nov 1904 - 1 May 1910: | Chief of Staff, V. Army Corps |
| 1 May 1910: | Promoted to *Lieutenant-General* |
| 1 May 1910 - 29 Jul 1915: | Commander, 15th Cavalry Division |
| 25 Aug 1915 - 1918: | Reserve officer, Petrograd Military District |
| 4 Feb 1916 - 1917: | Head of Petrograd Military Censorship Committee |

*General of Infantry* Yulian Viktorovich **Lyubovitsky** (15 Oct 1836 - 16 Feb 1908)
12 Oct 1877: Promoted to *Major-General*
12 Oct 1877 - 14 Nov 1888: Commander, Life Guards Grenadier Regiment
1881 - 1888: Commander, 1st Brigade, 2nd Guards Infantry Division
30 Aug 1888: Promoted to *Lieutenant-General*
14 Nov 1888 - 10 Mar 1895: Commander, St. Petersburg Local Brigade
10 Mar 1895 - 7 Jan 1897: Commander, 2nd Guards Infantry Division
7 Jan 1897 - 6 Dec 1904: Commanding General, IX. Army Corps
6 Dec 1899: Promoted to *General of Infantry*
6 Dec 1904 - 16 Feb 1908: Member of the State Council

*Lieutenant-General* Prince Lyudovik Karlovich **Lyudovik-Napoleon** (4 Sep 1865 - 14 Oct 1934)
6 Mar 1897 - 2 Jul 1902: Commander, Life Guards Uhlan Regiment
9 Apr 1900: Promoted to *Major-General*
2 Jul 1902 - 3 Mar 1906: Commander, Caucasus Cavalry Division
3 Mar 1906 - 1914: Reserve officer, Guards Cavalry
23 Apr 1906: Promoted to *Lieutenant-General*
1914 - 1917: Representative to the Italian Army High Command

*Lieutenant-General* Yalmar Fyodorovich **Lyundekvist** (20 Dec 1842 - 1917)
1 Oct 1891 - 17 Nov 1896: Commander, 33rd Infantry Regiment
26 May 1896: Promoted to *Major-General*
17 Nov 1896 - 24 Jun 1898: Deputy Chief of Staff, Irkutsk Military District
24 Jun 1898 - 1907: Commander, Omsk Regional Brigade
6 Dec 1905: Promoted to *Lieutenant-General*

*Lieutenant-General* Sergey Nikolayevich **Lyupov** (7 Oct 1870 - 19 Nov 1945)
7 Dec 1913 - 23 Jul 1915: Commander, 182nd Infantry Regiment
3 Apr 1915: Promoted to *Major-General*
23 Jul 1915 - 25 Aug 1915: Commander, Brigade, 17th Infantry Division
25 Aug 1915 - 15 Mar 1916: Chief of Staff, XX. Army Corps
15 Mar 1916 - 23 Jul 1916: Reserve officer, Dvinsk Military District
23 Jul 1916 - 7 Mar 1917: Commander, 104th Infantry Division
16 Jan 1917: Promoted to *Lieutenant-General*
7 Mar 1917 - 7 Jul 1917: Attached to the General Staff
7 Jul 1917 - 9 Sep 1917: Commanding General, XLIX. Army Corps
9 Sep 1917 - 29 Oct 1917: Reserve officer, Kiev Military District
29 Oct 1917 - 1918: Commanding General, XXV. Army Corps

*Major-General* Nikolai Fyodorovich **Lyustrov** (9 Sep 1854 - ?)
1904 - 9 Sep 1912: Attached to 10th Grenadier Regiment
9 Sep 1912: Promoted to *Major-General*
9 Sep 1912: Retired
1 Jun 1916 - 1917: Recalled; Commander, 192nd Replacement Infantry Regiment

*Lieutenant-General* Vasily Mikhailovich **Lyutenskov** (16 Oct 1847 - 10 Apr 1913)
1 Jun 1883 - 24 Aug 1906:         Deputy Chief of Staff, Don Cossack Army
6 May 1892:                       Promoted to *Major-General*
24 Aug 1906:                      Promoted to *Lieutenant-General*
24 Aug 1906:                      Retired

*Lieutenant-General* Robert-Adolf Karlovich **Lyuter** (14 Sep 1861 - ?)
24 Jul 1905 - 1917:               Director, Orlovsky Bakhtin Cadet Corps
6 Dec 1906:                       Promoted to *Major-General*
6 Dec 1913:                       Promoted to *Lieutenant-General*

*Major-General of the Fleet* Vilgelm Aleksandrovich **Lyuter** (6 Mar 1876 - 1940)
1914 - 23 Jun 1917:               Senior Deputy Chief of Shipbuilding Section, Main Shipbuilding Directorate
30 Jul 1915:                      Promoted to *Major-General of the Fleet*

*Major-General* Aleksey Fyodorovich **Lyutse** (30 Jan 1846 - ?)
2 Oct 1892 - 24 Sep 1898:         Commander, 164th Infantry Regiment
4 Jul 1898:                       Promoted to *Major-General*
24 Sep 1898 - 30 Oct 1904:        Commander, 1st Brigade, 25th Infantry Division
30 Oct 1904:                      Promoted to *Lieutenant-General*
30 Oct 1904:                      Retired

*Major-General* Bernard Karlovich **Lyuttsau** (14 Aug 1834 - ?)
16 Dec 1891 - 1894:               Deputy Commander of Engineers, Kiev Military District
15 Mar 1892:                      Promoted to *Major-General*
1894:                             Retired

*Major-General* Aleksandr Ivanovich **Maas** (7 May 1860 - ?)
10 Apr 1911:                      Promoted to *Major-General*
10 Apr 1911 - 16 Apr 1911:        At the disposal of the Commanding General of the Gendarmerie
16 Apr 1911 - 26 Sep 1913:        Senior Staff Adjutant, Gendarmerie Corps
26 Sep 1913 - 1917:               Chief of Moscow-Kiev Railway Gendarmerie

*Major-General* Nikolai Ivanovich **Machugovsky** (9 Nov 1865 - 16 Aug 1914)
12 Nov 1904 - 9 Jul 1910:         Commander, 8th Infantry Regiment
9 Mar 1908:                       Promoted to *Major-General*
9 Jul 1910 - 29 Jan 1913:         Chief of Staff, XI. Army Corps
29 Jan 1913 - 16 Aug 1914:        Chief of Staff, XV. Army Corps

*Lieutenant-General* Aleksandr Semyonovich **Madritov** (26 Aug 1868 - 1918)
20 Aug 1913:                      Promoted to *Major-General*
20 Aug 1913 - 3 Apr 1915:         Commander, 1st Brigade, 5th Siberian Rifle Division
Nov 1914:                         Acting Commander, 5th Siberian Rifle Division
3 Apr 1915 - 26 Apr 1916:         Commander, 56th Infantry Division
22 Jul 1915:                      Promoted to *Lieutenant-General*

| | |
|---|---|
| 26 Apr 1916 - 29 Aug 1916: | Reserve officer, Petrograd Military District |
| 29 Aug 1916 - Jan 1917: | Deputy Governor of Syr-Darya Region |
| Jan 1917 - 9 Jun 1917: | Military Governor of Semirechensk |
| 9 Jun 1917 - 1918: | Reserve officer, Petrograd Military District |

*Major-General* Aleksey Fyodorovich **Makalinsky** (7 Sep 1860 - 3 Jul 1939)
| | |
|---|---|
| 28 May 1916 - 5 Nov 1916: | Commander, 1$^{st}$ Battalion, 1$^{st}$ Amur Artillery Brigade |
| 13 Sep 1916: | Promoted to *Major-General* |
| 5 Nov 1916 - 1917: | Reserve officer, Kiev Military District |

*Lieutenant-General* Ilya Sakvarelovich **Makarashvili** (1 Dec 1854 - ?)
| | |
|---|---|
| 4 Jun 1904 - 30 Sep 1904: | Commander, 67$^{th}$ Artillery Brigade |
| 30 Sep 1904 - Jul 1910: | Commander, 2$^{nd}$ Turkestan Artillery Brigade |
| 6 Dec 1906: | Promoted to *Major-General* |
| Jul 1910 - 15 Oct 1910: | Commander, 52$^{nd}$ Artillery Brigade |
| 15 Oct 1910: | Promoted to *Lieutenant-General* |
| 15 Oct 1910: | Retired |

*Lieutenant-General* Aleksandr Sergeyevich **Makarenko** (25 Jun 1861 - 8 May 1932)
| | |
|---|---|
| 25 Dec 1902 - 30 Apr 1908: | Section Chief, Main Military Justice Directorate |
| 13 Apr 1908: | Promoted to *Major-General* |
| 30 Apr 1908 - 12 Mar 1911: | Deputy Chief, Main Military Justice Directorate, Deputy Chief Military Prosecutor |
| 12 Mar 1911 - 27 Feb 1917: | Chief of the Main Military Justice Directorate, Chief Military Prosecutor |
| 10 Apr 1911: | Promoted to *Lieutenant-General* |
| 27 Feb 1917: | Retired |

*Lieutenant-General* Ivan Ivanovich **Makarevich** (20 Jul 1847 - ?)
| | |
|---|---|
| 3 Jun 1899: | Promoted to *Major-General* |
| 3 Jun 1899 - 3 Mar 1904: | Deputy Chief of Staff, Siberian Military District |
| 3 Mar 1904 - 12 Jan 1906: | At the disposal of the Chief of the General Staff |
| 12 Jan 1906 - Jun 1907: | Commander, Kazan Regional Brigade |
| 6 Dec 1906: | Promoted to *Lieutenant-General* |

*General of Infantry* Apollon Nikolayevich **Makarov** (5 Jan 1840 - 27 Apr 1917)
| | |
|---|---|
| 17 May 1878 - 10 Aug 1891: | Director, 2$^{nd}$ Cadet Corps |
| 30 Aug 1886: | Promoted to *Major-General* |
| 10 Aug 1891 - 1906: | Director, Pedagogical Museum of Military Schools |
| 14 May 1896: | Promoted to *Lieutenant-General* |
| 1906: | Promoted to *General of Infantry* |
| 1906: | Retired |

*Major-General* Mikhail Lvovich **Makarov** (30 Sep 1856 - ?)
| | |
|---|---|
| 9 Jun 1910 - 22 Oct 1915: | Commander, 2$^{nd}$ Battalion, 32$^{nd}$ Artillery Brigade |
| 28 Nov 1914: | Promoted to *Major-General* |
| 22 Oct 1915 - 1917: | Commander, 82$^{nd}$ Artillery Brigade |

*Major-General* Nikolai Arkadyevich **Makarov** (24 Aug 1844 - ?)
| | |
|---|---|
| 21 Apr 1899 - Aug 1904: | Commander, Caucasus Grenadier Artillery Brigade |
| 6 Dec 1899: | Promoted to *Major-General* |
| Aug 1904: | Retired |

*Vice-Admiral* Stepan Osipovich **Makarov** (27 Dec 1848 - 31 Mar 1904)
| | |
|---|---|
| 1 Jan 1890: | Promoted to *Rear-Admiral* |
| 1 Jan 1890 - 8 Oct 1891: | Junior Flagman, Baltic Sea |
| 8 Oct 1891 - 7 Nov 1894: | Inspector-General of Naval Artillery |
| 7 Nov 1894 - 1895: | Commander, Mediterranean Squadron |
| 1895 - 1896: | Commander, Pacific Squadron |
| 1896: | Commander, Baltic Training Squadron |
| 1896: | Promoted to *Vice-Admiral* |
| 20 Aug 1896 - 6 Dec 1899: | Commander, 1st Squadron, Baltic Fleet |
| 6 Dec 1899 - 24 Feb 1904: | Military Governor of Kronstadt, Commandant, Port of Kronstadt |
| 24 Feb 1904 - 31 Mar 1904: | C-in-C, Pacific Fleet |

*Major-General of the Admiralty* Yevgeny Andreyevich **Makarov** (13 Mar 1844 - 9 Feb 1909)
| | |
|---|---|
| 1 Jan 1898 - 9 Feb 1909: | Chief of Naval Section, Borderguard Corps |
| 6 Dec 1898: | Promoted to *Major-General of the Admiralty* |

*Major-General* Prince Avel Gavrilovich **Makayev** (6 Jun 1860 - 1920)
| | |
|---|---|
| 9 Nov 1914 - 7 Dec 1916: | Commander, 16th Grenadier Regiment |
| 18 Jan 1916: | Promoted to *Major-General* |
| 7 Dec 1916 - 26 Apr 1917: | Commander, Brigade, Caucasus Grenadier Division |
| 26 Apr 1917 - 1918: | Commander, Brigade, 1st Caucasus Grenadier Division |

*Major-General* Prince Ilya Zakharovich **Makayev** (4 Dec 1857 - ?)
| | |
|---|---|
| 14 Jan 1914: | Promoted to *Major-General* |
| 14 Jan 1914 - 29 Jul 1914: | Commander, 2nd Brigade, 6th Infantry Division |
| 29 Jul 1914 - 23 Sep 1917: | Commander, 1st Brigade, 56th Infantry Division |
| 23 Sep 1917 - Oct 1917: | Commander, 8th Siberian Rifle Division |

*Lieutenant-General of Naval Engineers* Ivan-Alfred Georgiyevich **Mak-Donald** (1850 - 29 Jun 1906)
| | |
|---|---|
| 19 Jan 1890 - 29 Jun 1906: | Chief of Construction, Emperor Aleksandr III (Libau) Military Port |
| 1893: | Promoted to *Major-General of Naval Engineers* |
| ?: | Promoted to *Lieutenant-General of Naval Engineers* |

*General of Infantry* Konstantin Konstantinovich **Makedonsky** (27 Jun 1838 - ?)
| | |
|---|---|
| 26 Oct 1878 - 1 Jun 1889: | Military Judge, Moscow Military District Court |
| 30 Aug 1888: | Promoted to *Major-General* |
| 1 Jun 1889 - 31 Oct 1892: | Military Prosecutor, Omsk Military District |
| 31 Oct 1892 - 9 Feb 1898: | Chairman, Turkestan Military District Court |
| 9 Feb 1898 - 22 Sep 1905: | Chairman, Caucasus Military District Court |

6 Dec 1898: Promoted to *Lieutenant-General*
22 Sep 1905: Promoted to *General of Infantry*
22 Sep 1905: Retired

*Major-General* Mikhail Pavlovich **Makedonsky** (31 Aug 1854 - ?)
3 Feb 1902 - 1902: Military Judge, Kazan Military District Court
14 Apr 1902: Promoted to *Major-General*

*Lieutenant-General* Mikhail Petrovich **Makeyev** (11 Jan 1840 - ?)
1 Jun 1892: Promoted to *Major-General*
1 Jun 1892 - 1 Oct 1892: Commander, 2nd Brigade, 2nd Infantry Division
19 Oct 1892 - 18 Oct 1896: Chief of Staff, Fortress Brest-Litovsk
18 Oct 1896 - 2 Jun 1898: Chief of Staff, Fortress Modlin
2 Jun 1898 - 1903: Commandant of Fortress Ochakov
6 Dec 1899: Promoted to *Lieutenant-General*

*Lieutenant-General* Mikhail Vladimirovich **Makeyev** (3 Mar 1873 - Apr 1925)
25 Jun 1907 - 26 Oct 1908: Commander, 1st Vladivostok Fortress Artillery Brigade
26 Oct 1908 - 9 Feb 1910: Commander, Kronstadt Fortress Artillery Brigade
6 Dec 1908: Promoted to *Major-General*
9 Feb 1910 - 11 Dec 1913: Deputy Commander of Artillery, Amur Military District
11 Dec 1913 - 11 Jun 1916: Inspector of Artillery, V. Siberian Army Corps
6 Dec 1914: Promoted to *Lieutenant-General*
11 Jun 1916 - Oct 1917: Inspector of Artillery, Caucasus Army

*Lieutenant-General* Vasily Vasilyevich **Makeyev** (22 Sep 1852 - 1925)
25 Jan 1906 - 7 Dec 1916: Ataman, Donetsk Region, Don Cossack Army
1906: Promoted to *Major-General*
7 Dec 1916: Promoted to *Lieutenant-General*
7 Dec 1916: Dismissed

*Lieutenant-General* Vladimir Petrovich **Makeyev** (16 Feb 1836 - 14 Oct 1900)
22 Jun 1892: Promoted to *Major-General*
22 Jun 1892 - 25 Jan 1896: Commander, 1st East Siberian Rifle Brigade
25 Jan 1896 - 1 Jan 1898: Commander, 46th Replacement Infantry Brigade
1 Jan 1898 - 14 Oct 1900: Commander, 43rd Infantry Division
8 Dec 1899: Promoted to *Lieutenant-General*

*Major-General* Boris Aleksandrovich **Makhatadze** (20 Jan 1865 - ?)
20 May 1909: Promoted to *Major-General*
20 May 1909 - May 1912: Commander, 1st Brigade, 4th Siberian Rifle Division

*Major-General* Pavel Petrovich **Makhayev** (24 Dec 1848 - ?)
2 Jul 1897 - 2 Sep 1903: Military Commander, Malmyzhsky District
2 Sep 1903: Promoted to *Major-General*
2 Sep 1903: Retired
28 Sep 1914 - 1917: Recalled; Chief of 2nd Moscow Evacuation Point

*Major-General* Pyotr Nikolayevich **Makhayev** (9 Oct 1855 - 20 Sep 1915)
| | |
|---|---|
| 19 Sep 1910 - 1913: | Commander, 100th Infantry Regiment |
| 1913: | Promoted to *Major-General* |
| 1913: | Retired |
| 14 Nov 1914 - 1915: | Recalled; Commander, 100th Infantry Regiment |
| 1915 - 29 Jun 1915: | Reserve officer, Dvinsk Military District |
| 29 Jun 1915 - 3 Aug 1915: | Deputy Chief of Lines of Communication, 4th Army |
| 3 Aug 1915 - 20 Sep 1915: | Chief of Sanatory Section, 4th Army |

*Major-General* Nikolai Pavlovich **Makhlayuk** (24 Jul 1865 - 1913)
| | |
|---|---|
| 9 Mar 1911 - 1913: | Chief of Staff, Caucasus Grenadier Division |
| 1913: | Promoted to *Major-General* |

*General of Infantry* Nikolai Antonovich **Makhotin** (4 Dec 1830 - 28 Jun 1903)
| | |
|---|---|
| 21 Jul 1866 - 13 Apr 1876: | Deputy Chief of Staff, St. Petersburg Military District |
| 30 Aug 1868: | Promoted to *Major-General* |
| 13 Apr 1876 - 1 May 1879: | Chief of Staff, Moscow Military District |
| 1 May 1879 - 4 Jul 1881: | Deputy Chief of the General Staff |
| 20 Apr 1880: | Promoted to *Lieutenant-General* |
| 4 Jul 1881 - 26 May 1899: | Chief of Military Schools, Chief of the Main Directorate for Military Schools |
| 30 Aug 1894: | Promoted to *General of Infantry* |
| 26 May 1899 - 28 Jun 1903: | Member of the State Council |

*Major-General* Mikhail Mikhailovich **Makhov** (26 Aug 1872 - 23 Sep 1919)
| | |
|---|---|
| 16 Apr 1914 - 18 May 1915: | Commander, 15th Hussar Regiment |
| 18 May 1915 - 24 Jun 1915: | Commander, 1st Brigade, 14th Cavalry Division |
| 27 May 1915: | Promoted to *Major-General* |
| 24 Jun 1915 - 29 Feb 1916: | Commander, 1st Brigade, 2nd Cavalry Division |
| 29 Feb 1916 - 1917: | Chief of Staff, 4th Don Cossack Division |
| 1917 - 15 Apr 1917: | Commander, Brigade, 2nd Cavalry Division |
| 15 Apr 1917 - 1918: | Chief of Staff, 5th Cavalry Division |

*General of Engineers* Kaetan Vlasovich **Makhovich** (7 Aug 1843 - 1927)
| | |
|---|---|
| 7 Nov 1891 - 11 Feb 1903: | Commander of Engineers, Fortress Sevastopol |
| 6 Dec 1897: | Promoted to *Major-General* |
| 11 Feb 1903 - 7 Aug 1906: | Deputy Commander of Engineers, Odessa Military District |
| 7 Aug 1906 - 5 Nov 1910: | Commander of Engineers, Warsaw Military District |
| 22 Apr 1907: | Promoted to *Lieutenant-General* |
| 5 Nov 1910: | Promoted to *General of Engineers* |
| 5 Nov 1910: | Retired |

*Major-General* Dmitry Mikhailovich **Makhovka** (15 Sep 1861 - ?)
| | |
|---|---|
| 28 Sep 1912 - 1914: | Commander, 35th Siberian Rifle Regiment |
| 1914: | Promoted to *Major-General* |
| 1914: | Retired |
| 16 Jan 1916 - 1917: | Recalled; Commander, Brigade, 120th Infantry Division |

1917: Commander, 120th Infantry Division

*Lieutenant-General* Aleksandr Fyodorovich **Makkaveyev** (23 Jun 1835 - ?)
21 Aug 1886 - 7 Nov 1894: Inspector of Classes, 2nd Konstantinov Military School
30 Aug 1888: Promoted to *Major-General*
7 Nov 1894 - 9 Sep 1896: Attached to the Main Directorate for Military Schools
9 Sep 1896: Promoted to *Lieutenant-General*
9 Sep 1896: Retired

*Lieutenant-General* Aleksandr Konstantinovich **Maklakov** (15 Feb 1838 - Nov 1910)
15 Aug 1888 - 7 Jun 1890: Commander, 9th Grenadier Regiment
7 Jun 1890: Promoted to *Major-General*
7 Jun 1890 - 7 Dec 1896: Commander, 2nd Brigade, 29th Infantry Division
7 Dec 1896 - 1900: Commander, 64th Reserve Infantry Brigade
1900: Retired
15 Feb 1910: Promoted to *Lieutenant-General*

*Lieutenant-General* Georgy Konstantinovich **Maklakov** (26 Apr 1834 - 12 Oct 1896)
29 Dec 1877: Promoted to *Major-General*
29 Dec 1877 - 12 Feb 1890: Commander, Life Guards Izmaylov Regiment
12 Feb 1890 - 12 Oct 1896: Commander, 24th Infantry Division
30 Aug 1890: Promoted to *Lieutenant-General*

*Lieutenant-General* Aleksandr Andreyevich **Maksheyev** (8 May 1851 - ?)
23 Oct 1904 - 6 Dec 1906: Commander, 75th Artillery Brigade
6 Dec 1906: Promoted to *Major-General*
6 Dec 1906 - 11 Apr 1908: Commander, 4th East Siberian Artillery Brigade
11 Apr 1908 - 8 May 1911: Commander, 19th Artillery Brigade
8 May 1911: Promoted to *Lieutenant-General*
8 May 1911: Retired

*General of Infantry* Fyodor Andreyevich **Maksheyev** (21 Jan 1855 - 5 Aug 1932)
22 Sep 1893 - 1910: Professor, Nikolayev General Staff Academy
9 Apr 1900: Promoted to *Major-General*
17 Nov 1904 - 1910: Chief Editor, "Military Collection"
6 Dec 1906: Promoted to *Lieutenant-General*
1910: Promoted to *General of Infantry*
1910: Resigned

*Major-General* Ivan Aleksandrovich **Maksheyev** (23 Sep 1858 - 19 Jun 1930)
1915 - 1917: Commander, 76th Artillery Brigade
12 Jul 1916: Promoted to *Major-General*

*Major-General* Nikolai Alekseyevich **Maksheyev** (7 Jul 1860 - ?)
16 Jul 1910 - 1914: Commander, Simbirsk District
1914: Promoted to *Major-General*

*General of Artillery* Zakhary Andreyevich **Maksheyev** (25 Mar 1858 - 1 Mar 1935)
15 Jan 1900 - 13 Aug 1906:     Director of the Aleksandr Cadet Corps
1 Apr 1901:                    Promoted to *Major-General*
13 Aug 1906 - 2 Apr 1917:      Director, Pedagogical Museum of Military Schools
22 Apr 1907:                   Promoted to *Lieutenant-General*
2 Apr 1917 - 30 Aug 1917:      Chief, Main Directorate for Military Schools
30 Aug 1917 - 28 Sep 1917:     Unassigned
28 Sep 1917:                   Promoted to *General of Artillery*
28 Sep 1917:                   Retired

*Major-General* Iov Samoylovich **Maksimenko** (6 May 1853 - 5 Feb 1909)
6 Dec 1906:                    Promoted to *Major-General*
6 Dec 1906 - 5 Feb 1909:       Chief of Lugansk Cartridge Factory

*Lieutenant-General* Aleksandr Aleksandrovich **Maksimov** (29 Jun 1829 - 22 Sep 1905)
25 Feb 1887:                   Promoted to *Major-General*
25 Feb 1887 - 3 May 1895:      Commander, 12$^{th}$ Artillery Brigade
3 May 1895:                    Promoted to *Lieutenant-General*
3 May 1895:                    Retired

*Vice-Admiral* Andrei Semyonovich **Maksimov** (10 Jul 1866 - 30 Mar 1951)
1913 - 1914:                   Commander, Cruiser Brigade, Baltic Fleet
1914:                          Promoted to *Rear-Admiral*
21 Jul 1914 - 1915:            Commander, 2$^{nd}$ Battleship Brigade, Baltic Fleet
1915 - 8 Mar 1917:             Commander of Mine Defenses, Baltic Sea
10 Apr 1916:                   Promoted to *Vice-Admiral*
8 Mar 1917 - 2 Jun 1917:       C-in-C, Baltic Fleet
6 Sep 1917 - 18 Nov 1917:      Chief of Naval Staff to the Supreme Commander-in-Chief

*Lieutenant-General* Ivan Ivanovich **Maksimov** (27 Dec 1839 - ?)
7 Nov 1886:                    Promoted to *Major-General*
7 Nov 1886 - 8 Oct 1889:       Special Assignments General, Vilnius Military District
8 Oct 1889 - 12 Apr 1892:      Commander, 1$^{st}$ Brigade, 25$^{th}$ Infantry Division
12 Apr 1892 - 20 Feb 1896:     Commander, 2$^{nd}$ Brigade, 23$^{rd}$ Infantry Division
20 Feb 1896 - 10 Jan 1898:     Commander, 28$^{th}$ Infantry Division
14 May 1896:                   Promoted to *Lieutenant-General*
10 Jan 1898 - 12 Jun 1898:     Commander, 26$^{th}$ Infantry Division

*Major-General* Pavel Florovich **Maksimov** (24 Mar 1860 - ?)
25 Jul 1914 - 1917:            Commander, 59$^{th}$ Artillery Brigade
8 Oct 1915:                    Promoted to *Major-General*

*Lieutenant-General of the Fleet* Vasily Vasilyevich **Maksimov** (20 Mar 1851 - ?)
4 Oct 1904 - 1 Jan 1908:       Inspector of Shipbuilding
19 Mar 1907:                   Promoted to *Major-General of the Fleet*
1 Jan 1908 - Jan 1914:         Member of the Board, Baltic & Admiralty Shipyard
6 Dec 1911:                    Promoted to *Lieutenant-General of the Fleet*

*Major-General* Anatoly Aleksandrovich **Maksimovich** (1 Nov 1849 - 3 Jan 1919)
| | |
|---|---|
| 22 Feb 1904: | Promoted to *Major-General* |
| 22 Feb 1904 - 9 Mar 1905: | Commander, 2nd Brigade, 1st East Siberian Rifle Division |
| 9 Mar 1905 - 1906: | Attached to the General Staff |
| 1906: | Retired |

*General of Cavalry* Konstantin Klavdyevich **Maksimovich** (14 May 1849 - 1921)
| | |
|---|---|
| 6 Dec 1888 - 28 Nov 1892: | Commander, Life Guards Horse - Grenadier Regiment |
| 9 Apr 1889: | Promoted to *Major-General* |
| 28 Nov 1892 - 24 Feb 1893: | Commander, 1st Brigade, 2nd Guards Cavalry Division |
| 24 Feb 1893 - 23 Feb 1899: | Military Governor of the Ural Region, Ataman, Ural Cossack Army |
| 6 Dec 1897: | Promoted to *Lieutenant-General* |
| 23 Feb 1899 - 19 Feb 1905: | Ataman, Don Cossack Army |
| 1904: | Promoted to *General-Adjutant* |
| 19 Feb 1905 - 15 Aug 1905: | Military Governor of Warsaw, Commanding General, Warsaw Military District |
| 15 Aug 1905 - 18 Dec 1915: | General à la suite |
| 6 Dec 1906: | Promoted to *General of Cavalry* |
| 18 Dec 1915 - Feb 1917: | Deputy Commander of the Imperial Main Headquarters |

*Major-General* Pavel Semyonovich **Maksimovich** (16 Dec 1866 - ?)
| | |
|---|---|
| 9 Dec 1912 - 26 Jun 1915: | Commander, 12th Turkestan Rifle Regiment |
| 26 Jun 1915: | Promoted to *Major-General* |
| 26 Jun 1915 - 8 Jul 1915: | Chief of Staff, XLI. Army Corps |
| 8 Jul 1915 - 4 May 1917: | Chief of Staff, V. Siberian Army Corps |
| 14 May 1917 - 1918: | Commander, 8th Turkestan Rifle Division |

*General of Infantry* Vasily Nikolayevich **Maksimovich** (1 Jan 1832 - ?)
| | |
|---|---|
| 14 Dec 1869 - 17 Oct 1881: | Military Commander, Volyn Region |
| 30 Aug 1875: | Promoted to *Major-General* |
| 17 Oct 1881 - 1 Aug 1882: | Unassigned |
| 1 Aug 1882 - 14 Jun 1884: | Chief of Staff, East Siberian Military District |
| 14 Jun 1884 - 9 Jun 1885: | Chief of Staff, Irkutsk Military District |
| 9 Jun 1885 - 18 Nov 1892: | Commander, 5th Infantry Division |
| 30 Aug 1885: | Promoted to *Lieutenant-General* |
| 18 Nov 1892 - 1 Jan 1898: | Commanding General, II. Army Corps |
| 1 Jan 1898 - 29 May 1899: | Commanding General, III. Army Corps |
| 6 Dec 1898: | Promoted to *General of Infantry* |
| 29 May 1899 - 3 Jan 1906: | Member, Committee for Wounded Veterans |
| 3 Jan 1906: | Retired |

*Major-General* Nikolai Romanovich **Maksimovich-Romanov** (21 Sep 1849 - ?)
| | |
|---|---|
| 9 Dec 1905 - 14 Mar 1910: | Commander, 2nd Battalion, 117th Infantry Regiment |
| 14 Mar 1910: | Promoted to *Major-General* |
| 14 Mar 1910: | Retired |

1915 - 4 Apr 1916: Recalled; Commandant of Lublin
4 Apr 1916 - 1917: Commandant of Bobruisk

*General of Infantry* Mikhail Semyonovich **Maksimovsky** (6 Sep 1832 - 18 Jan 1917)
13 May 1873: Promoted to *Major-General*
13 May 1873 - 18 Jan 1878: Attached to the General Staff
18 Jan 1878 - 1 Jul 1879: Director, Gatchina Orphan Institute
1 Jul 1879 - 28 Dec 1884: Trustee, Kharkov School District
30 Aug 1882: Promoted to *Lieutenant-General*
28 Dec 1884 - 20 Jul 1885: Attached to St. Petersburg Military District
20 Jul 1885 - 29 Sep 1889: Commander, 9th Infantry Division
29 Sep 1889 - 1 Feb 1905: Attached to the Ministry of War
14 May 1896: Promoted to *General of Infantry*
1 Feb 1905 - 1906: Member of the Military Council
1906: Retired

*Major-General* Nikolai Nikolayevich **Maksimovsky** (22 Aug 1862 - 10 Jul 1938)
27 May 1910 - 29 May 1913: Commander, 10th Hussar Regiment
14 Apr 1913: Promoted to *Major-General*
29 May 1913 - 4 May 1915: Commander, 1st Brigade, 6th Cavalry Division
4 May 1915 - 1917: Special Assignments General, Minsk Military District

*General of Infantry* Nikolai Nikolayevich **Malakhov** (6 May 1827 - 4 Apr 1908)
4 Nov 1864 - 30 May 1871: Commandant, Vilnius Cadet School
28 Mar 1871: Promoted to *Major-General*
3 Aug 1871 - 12 Sep 1874: Deputy Commander, 14th Infantry Division, Commander, 1st Brigade, 14th Infantry Division
12 Sep 1874 - 1 Oct 1874: Commander, 1st Brigade, 27th Infantry Division
1 Oct 1874 - 14 Mar 1879: Commander, 1st Brigade, 26th Infantry Division
14 Mar 1879 - 20 Jan 1888: Commander, 26th Infantry Division
12 Apr 1881: Promoted to *Lieutenant-General*
20 Jan 1888 - 11 Aug 1889: Commander, 1st Guards Infantry Division
11 Aug 1889 - 19 Jun 1904: Commanding General, Grenadier Corps
12 Jun 1895: Promoted to *General of Infantry*
3 Jun 1903 - 16 Feb 1905: Deputy Commanding General, Moscow Military District
16 Feb 1905 - 17 Jan 1906: Commanding General, Moscow Military District
17 Jan 1906 - 4 Apr 1908: At the disposal of the Minister of War

*General of Cavalry* Yakov Dmitriyevich **Malama** (4 Nov 1841 - Jan 1913)
17 Jul 1885 - 1 Jun 1888: Chief of Staff, Kuban Cossack Army
20 Jul 1885 - 1 Oct 1885: Commander, 1st Brigade, Caucasus Cavalry Division
6 May 1887: Promoted to *Major-General*
1 Jun 1888 - 7 Feb 1890: Deputy Governor of the Kuban Region, Deputy Ataman, Kuban Cossack Army
7 Feb 1890 - 21 Feb 1892: Chief of Staff, Kiev Military District
21 Feb 1892 - 26 Oct 1904: Governor of the Kuban Region, Ataman, Kuban Cossack Army

| | |
|---|---|
| 14 May 1896: | Promoted to *Lieutenant-General* |
| 26 Oct 1904 - 24 May 1905: | Deputy C-in-C of the Caucasus, Deputy Commanding General, Caucasus Military District |
| 24 May 1905 - 30 Dec 1906: | Deputy Military Governor of the Caucasus |
| 6 Dec 1906: | Promoted to *General of Cavalry* |
| 30 Dec 1906 - Jan 1913: | Member of the Military Council |

*Major-General* Aleksandr Leonidovich **Malashkin** (19 Jan 1867 - ?)
| | |
|---|---|
| 30 May 1915 - 1917: | Military Judge, Amur Military District Court |
| 6 Dec 1915: | Promoted to *Major-General* |

*Lieutenant-General* Leonid Gerasimovich **Maleyev** (8 Aug 1845 - ?)
| | |
|---|---|
| 29 Jan 1900 - 7 Oct 1910: | Section Chief, Main Engineering Directorate |
| 6 Apr 1903: | Promoted to *Major-General* |
| 7 Oct 1910: | Promoted to *Lieutenant-General* |
| 7 Oct 1910: | Retired |

*Major-General* Nikolai Andreyevich **Malinin** (26 Aug 1848 - ?)
| | |
|---|---|
| 12 Jan 1899 - 1903: | Commander of Gendarmerie, Tambov Province |
| 6 Dec 1902: | Promoted to *Major-General* |

*Lieutenant-General* Vladimir Ivanovich **Malinka** (24 Mar 1858 - 7 Jul 1917)
| | |
|---|---|
| 12 Aug 1902 - 5 May 1906: | Commander, $8^{th}$ Grenadier Regiment |
| 5 May 1906: | Promoted to *Major-General* |
| 5 May 1906 - 28 Nov 1907: | Chief of Staff, Kuban Cossack Army |
| 28 Nov 1907 - 30 Jan 1915: | Commander, $2^{nd}$ Brigade, $2^{nd}$ Grenadier Division |
| 30 Jan 1915 - 10 Feb 1915: | Reserve officer, Kiev Military District |
| 10 Feb 1915: | Promoted to *Lieutenant-General* |
| 10 Feb 1915: | Dismissed |

*Major-General* Ivan Fyodorovich **Malinko** (5 May 1861 - Mar 1917)
| | |
|---|---|
| 3 Nov 1916 - Mar 1917: | Special Assignments General, Moscow Military District |
| 13 Mar 1917: | Posthumously promoted to *Major-General* |

*Major-General* Aleksandr Mikhailovich **Malinovsky** (9 Apr 1857 - 4 Oct 1914)
| | |
|---|---|
| 27 Mar 1909: | Promoted to *Major-General* |
| 27 Mar 1909 - Sep 1914: | Commander, Life Guards Kexholm Regiment |
| Sep 1914 - 4 Oct 1914: | POW |

*Major-General* Vladislav-Yulian Vikentyevich **Malishevsky** (13 Feb 1856 - ?)
| | |
|---|---|
| 1 Jun 1907: | Promoted to *Major-General* |
| 1 Jun 1907 - 19 Oct 1910: | Commander, Turkestan Sapper Brigade |
| 19 Oct 1910 - 1912: | Engineer Officer, Turkestan Military District |

*Lieutenant-General* Vasily Vasilyevich **Malkov-Panin** (25 Jul 1859 - 1948)
| | |
|---|---|
| 4 Aug 1909 - 1916: | General for Assignments, Inspectorate-General of Engineers |

6 Dec 1909: Promoted to *Major-General*
6 Dec 1916: Promoted to *Lieutenant-General*
1916 - 1917: Chief of Engineering Works, 1st Rear Area District, Northwestern Front

*Major-General* Aleksandr Nikolayevich **Malkovsky** (12 Feb 1858 - ?)
23 Jun 1912 - 1 Apr 1915: Commander, 3rd Mortar Artillery Battalion
25 Oct 1914: Promoted to *Major-General*
1 Apr 1915 - 1915: Acting Commander, 59th Artillery Brigade
1915 - 6 Nov 1916: Commander, 53rd Artillery Brigade
6 Nov 1916 - 1917: Inspector of Artillery, III. Siberian Army Corps

*Lieutenant-General* Mikhail Grigoryevich **Malkovsky** (20 Sep 1852 - 18 Oct 1933)
10 Jul 1907 - 3 Oct 1908: Commander, 36th Artillery Brigade
29 Jul 1907: Promoted to *Major-General*
3 Oct 1908 - 11 Jan 1913: Deputy Commander of Artillery, Caucasus Military District
11 Jan 1913 - 6 Nov 1914: Inspector of Artillery, XV. Army Corps
10 Jul 1913: Promoted to *Lieutenant-General*
6 Nov 1914 - 1918: POW

*Major-General* Nikolai Nikolayevich **Malkovsky** (2 Apr 1865 - ?)
9 Mar 1914 - 25 Jul 1915: Battalion Commander, 67th Artillery Brigade
5 Mar 1915: Promoted to *Major-General*
25 Jul 1915 - 28 Apr 1917: Commander, 67th Artillery Brigade
28 Apr 1917 - 1918: Inspector of Artillery, XXXVIII. Army Corps

*Major-General* Vilgelm Fridrikhovich **Mallio** (12 Sep 1856 - ?)
30 Aug 1913: Promoted to *Major-General*
30 Aug 1913 - 9 Aug 1914: Commander, 28th Artillery Brigade
9 Aug 1914 - 27 Feb 1915: Unassigned
27 Feb 1915 - 9 Sep 1917: Commander, 6th Siberian Rifle Artillery Brigade
9 Sep 1917: Dismissed

*Major-General* Vilgelm Vilgelmovich **Malm** (5 Oct 1857 - 8 Nov 1926)
11 Jun 1910: Promoted to *Major-General*
11 Jun 1910 - 29 Jul 1914: Commander, 1st Brigade, 50th Infantry Division
29 Jul 1914 - 19 Apr 1915: Commander, Brigade, 68th Infantry Division
19 Apr 1915 - 1918: POW, Germany

*Major-General* Safar-Bey Tausultanovich **Malsagov** (25 Jul 1868 - 1944)
25 Jan 1915 - 10 Dec 1916: Commander, 1st Dagestan Cavalry Regiment
31 Oct 1915: Promoted to *Major-General*
10 Dec 1916 - 1918: Commander, 1st Brigade, 3rd Caucasus Cossack Division

*Major-General* Nikolai Petrovich **Maltsev** (24 Apr 1863 - 1921)
26 Nov 1910 - 17 Apr 1917: Ataman, 1st Military Division, Orenburg Cossack Army
6 Dec 1912: Promoted to *Major-General*

20 Mar 1917 - 27 Apr 1917:   Deputy Ataman, Orenburg Cossack Army
27 Apr 1917 - 1918:          Ataman, Orenburg Cossack Army

*Major-General* Aleksandr Pavlovich **Maltsov** (10 Apr 1848 - 7 Nov 1899)
22 Jan 1894:                 Promoted to *Major-General*
22 Jan 1894 - 25 Feb 1898:   Deputy Chief of Staff, Irkutsk Military District
25 Feb 1898 - 7 Nov 1899:    Staff Officer, General Staff

*Major-General of the Admiralty* Aleksey Dmitriyevich **Maltsov** (? - ?)
?:                           Promoted to *Major-General of the Admiralty*
1905:                        Chief of Procurement Section, Main Shipbuilding Directorate

*General of Infantry* Ivan Sergeyevich **Maltsov** (1 Feb 1847 - Dec 1920)
12 Feb 1890 - 17 Feb 1891:   Commander, Life Guards Lithuanian Regiment
30 Aug 1890:                 Promoted to *Major-General*
17 Feb 1891 - 24 Nov 1894:   Commander, Life Guards Chasseurs Regiment
24 Nov 1894 - 2 Sep 1899:    Commander, 1$^{st}$ Brigade, 1$^{st}$ Guards Infantry Division
2 Sep 1899 - 15 Nov 1901:    Attached to St. Petersburg Military District
15 Nov 1901:                 Promoted to *Lieutenant-General*
15 Nov 1901 - 16 Mar 1903:   Commander, 37$^{th}$ Infantry Division
16 Mar 1903 - 1905:          Attached to St. Petersburg Military District
1905:                        Promoted to *General of Infantry*
1905:                        Retired

*Major-General* Sergey Sergeyevich **Maltsov** (10 Jul 1845 - 1908)
9 Jul 1897 - 1908:           Attached to the Ministry of War
17 Apr 1905:                 Promoted to *Major-General*

*Lieutenant-General* Nikolai Petrovich **Malykhin** (9 Aug 1846 - 19 Nov 1910)
18 May 1899 - 1907:          Chief of Gendarmerie, Central Asia Railroad
9 Apr 1900:                  Promoted to *Major-General*
1907:                        Promoted to *Lieutenant-General*
1907:                        Retired

*Lieutenant-General* Vladimir Petrovich **Malykhin** (3 Apr 1850 - 1920)
20 Aug 1899 - 1907:          Commander, 4$^{th}$ Sapper Brigade
9 Apr 1900:                  Promoted to *Major-General*
6 Dec 1906:                  Promoted to *Lieutenant-General*
1907:                        Retired

*Major-General* Maksimilian Emilianovich **Malyshchitsky** (30 Sep 1858 - ?)
31 Mar 1912 - 21 Nov 1916:   Commander, 2$^{nd}$ Battalion, 6$^{th}$ Siberian Rifle Artillery Brigade
8 Oct 1916:                  Promoted to *Major-General*
21 Nov 1916 - 1917:          Commander, 4$^{th}$ Siberian Rifle Artillery Brigade
1917:                        Commander, 6$^{th}$ Siberian Rifle Artillery Brigade

*Lieutenant-General* Ivan Grigoryevich **Malyuga** (13 Nov 1853 - 1933)
14 Mar 1900 - 1909:		Professor, Academy of Engineering
6 Dec 1901:			Promoted to *Major-General*
1909:				Promoted to *Lieutenant-General*
1909:				Retired

*Major-General* Prince Aleksandr Ivanovich **Mamatov** (28 Nov 1856 - ?)
10 Dec 1910 - 1914:		Commander, 13th Borderguard Brigade
1914:				Retired
1914 - 20 Aug 1915:		Commander, Brigade, 119th Infantry Division
16 May 1915:			Promoted to *Major-General*
20 Aug 1915 - 1918:		POW

*Major-General* Konstantin Iosifovich **Mamatsev** (26 Jan 1849 - ?)
9 Sep 1907:			Promoted to *Major-General*
9 Sep 1907 - 6 Nov 1908:	Commander, 9th East Siberian Rifle Artillery Brigade

*Major-General* Leon Konstantinovich **Mamatsev** (2 Mar 1863 - 18 Jan 1916)
20 Dec 1912 - 18 Jan 1916:	Commander, 3rd Turkestan Rifle Artillery Battalion
20 Aug 1916:			Posthumously promoted to *Major-General*

*General of Artillery* Vladimir Petrovich **Mamontov** (19 Sep 1866 - 28 Aug 1916)
18 May 1910:			Promoted to *Major-General*
18 May 1910 - 25 Jul 1910:	Commander, 2nd Reserve Artillery Brigade
25 Jul 1910 - 7 Aug 1913:	Commander, 26th Artillery Brigade
7 Aug 1913 - 1 Oct 1914:	Commander, 1st Grenadier Artillery Brigade
1 Oct 1914 - 17 May 1915:	Inspector of Artillery, XXVIII. Army Corps
1915:				Acting Inspector of Artillery, 11th Army
16 May 1915:			Promoted to *Lieutenant-General*
17 May 1915 - 18 Apr 1916:	Commander, 60th Infantry Division
18 Apr 1916 - 28 Aug 1916:	Inspector of Artillery, 5th Army
28 Nov 1916:			Posthumously promoted to *General of Artillery*

*Lieutenant-General* Mikhail Mikhailovich **Manakin** (9 Feb 1862 - 17 Jun 1932)
23 Feb 1907 - 2 Jul 1910:	Consul, Qiqihar (China)
13 Apr 1908:			Promoted to *Major-General*
3 Jul 1910 - 28 Feb 1911:	Commander, 1st Brigade, 10th Siberian Rifle Division
28 Feb 1911 - 3 Jan 1914:	Military Governor of the Maritime Region,
				Ataman, Ussuri Cossack Army
3 Jan 1914 - 17 May 1917:	Chief of Asia Section, General Staff
6 Apr 1914:			Promoted to *Lieutenant-General*
17 May 1917:			Retired

*Major-General* Aleksey Akimovich **Mandryka** (10 Mar 1861 - 1 Feb 1909)
24 Jul 1905 - 1 Feb 1909:	Commander, 1st Battalion, 36th Artillery Brigade
1909:				Posthumously promoted to *Major-General*

*Lieutenant-General* Georgy Akimovich **Mandryka** (10 Apr 1869 - 6 May 1937)
| | |
|---|---|
| 1915 - 15 Dec 1915: | Chief of Staff, 16th Infantry Division |
| 5 Oct 1915: | Promoted to *Major-General* |
| 15 Dec 1915 - 20 May 1916: | Chief of Staff, 104th Infantry Division |
| 20 May 1916 - 23 Jul 1917: | Chief of Staff, 56th Infantry Division |
| 20 Jun 1917: | Promoted to *Lieutenant-General* |
| 23 Jul 1917 - 1917: | Commander, 16th Infantry Division |
| 1917 - 29 Nov 1917: | Commanding General, VI. Army Corps |

*Lieutenant-General* Ivan Akimovich **Mandryka** (22 Sep 1858 - 1934)
| | |
|---|---|
| 16 Jul 1904: | Promoted to *Major-General* |
| 16 Jul 1904 - 2 Apr 1910: | Commander, 1st Brigade, 37th Infantry Division |
| 2 Apr 1910: | Promoted to *Lieutenant-General* |
| 2 Apr 1910: | Retired |
| Nov 1914 - ?: | Recalled; Commanding General, VIII. Militia Corps |
| ? - 1918: | Commanding General, Amur Military District |

*Lieutenant-General* Aleksey Grigoryevich **Mandrykin** (12 Feb 1837 - 7 Oct 1913)
| | |
|---|---|
| 7 Feb 1890: | Promoted to *Major-General* |
| 7 Feb 1890 - 17 Nov 1890: | Commander, 2nd Brigade, 3rd Cavalry Division |
| 17 Nov 1890 - 29 Jan 1893: | Ataman, Khoper District, Don Cossack Army |
| 29 Jan 1893 - 22 Nov 1894: | Ataman, Taganrog District, Don Cossack Army |
| 22 Nov 1894 - 30 Nov 1902: | Ataman, Rostov District, Don Cossack Army |
| 30 Nov 1902: | Promoted to *Lieutenant-General* |
| 30 Nov 1902: | Retired |

*Major-General* Mikhail Georgiyevich **Mandryko** (27 Oct 1859 - 20 Aug 1915)
| | |
|---|---|
| 11 May 1907 - 1912: | Commander, 41st Dragoon Regiment |
| 1912: | Promoted to *Major-General* |
| 1912: | Retired |
| 5 Oct 1914 - 20 Jul 1915: | Recalled; Commander, 38th State Militia Brigade |
| 20 Jul 1915 - 20 Aug 1915: | Commander, 1st Brigade, 105th Infantry Division |

*Major-General* Vladimir Grigoryevich **Mandryko** (15 Feb 1851 - ?)
| | |
|---|---|
| 6 May 1897 - 9 Jul 1903: | Commander, 12th Dragoon Regiment |
| 9 Jul 1903: | Promoted to *Major-General* |
| 9 Jul 1903 - 3 Oct 1907: | Commander, 2nd Brigade, 7th Cavalry Division |

*Major-General of the Naval Legal Corps* Vitaly Aleksandrovich **Manevsky** (20 Nov 1867 - ?)
| | |
|---|---|
| 7 Aug 1906 - ?: | Military Judge, Kronstadt Naval Court |
| 6 Dec 1912: | Promoted to *Major-General of the Naval Legal Corps* |

*General of Artillery* Aleksei Alekseyevich **Manikovsky** (13 Mar 1865 - Jan 1920)
| | |
|---|---|
| 25 Sep 1906 - 23 Mar 1914: | Commander of Artillery, Fortress Kronstadt |
| 31 May 1907: | Promoted to *Major-General* |
| 30 Jul 1911: | Promoted to *Lieutenant-General* |
| 23 Mar 1914 - 24 May 1915: | Commandant of Fortress Kronstadt |

| | |
|---|---|
| 24 May 1915 - 6 Mar 1917: | Chief of Main Artillery Administration |
| 6 Dec 1916: | Promoted to *General of Artillery* |
| 6 Mar 1917 - 25 Oct 1917: | Deputy Minister of War |

*Lieutenant-General* Aleksandr Vasilyevich **Mankovsky** (20 Oct 1854 - ?)
| | |
|---|---|
| 25 Aug 1906 - 1912: | Commander of Artillery, Fortress Mikhailovsk |
| 6 Dec 1906: | Promoted to *Major-General* |
| 1912: | Promoted to *Lieutenant-General* |
| 1912: | Retired |

*Admiral* Nikolai Stepanovich **Mankovsky** (10 Jan 1859 - 1919)
| | |
|---|---|
| 21 Aug 1909: | Promoted to *Rear-Admiral* |
| 1909 - 1910: | Commander, Independent Naval Detachment |
| 1910 - 28 Mar 1911: | Commander, Baltic Naval Detachment |
| 28 Mar 1911 - 11 Mar 1913: | Commander, Battleship Brigade, Baltic Fleet |
| 25 Mar 1912: | Promoted to *Vice-Admiral* |
| 11 Mar 1913 - Oct 1917: | Commandant, Port of Sevastopol |
| 1916: | Promoted to *Admiral* |

*Lieutenant-General* Baron Karl-Gustav-Emil Karlovich **Mannerheim** (4 Jun 1867 - 28 Jan 1951)
| | |
|---|---|
| 1 Jan 1911 - 24 Dec 1913: | Commander, Life Guards Uhlan Regiment |
| 19 Feb 1911: | Promoted to *Major-General* |
| 24 Dec 1913 - 24 Jun 1915: | Commander, Independent Guards Cavalry Brigade |
| 24 Jun 1915 - 31 May 1917: | Commander, 12$^{th}$ Cavalry Division |
| 25 Apr 1917: | Promoted to *Lieutenant-General* |
| 31 May 1917 - 9 Sep 1917: | Commanding General, VI. Cavalry Corps |

*Major-General* Pyotr Ivanovich **Mansvetov** (26 Aug 1864 - ?)
| | |
|---|---|
| 17 Mar 1913 - 1917: | Military Judge, Turkestan Military District Court |
| 14 Apr 1913: | Promoted to *Major-General* |

**Manteyfel-Tsege**: see **Tsege von Manteyfel**

*Lieutenant-General* Aleksandr Ivanovich **Manykin-Nevstruyev** (12 Jul 1834 - 27 Dec 1894)
| | |
|---|---|
| 23 Dec 1872 - 24 Feb 1877: | Chief of Staff, 3$^{rd}$ Infantry Division |
| 1875: | Promoted to *Major-General* |
| 24 Feb 1877 - 16 Oct 1889: | Chief of Staff, Grenadier Corps |
| 16 Oct 1889 - 6 Nov 1889: | Chief of Staff, Kazan Military District |
| 6 Nov 1889 - 30 Jul 1894: | Chief of Staff, Odessa Military District |
| 30 Aug 1890: | Promoted to *Lieutenant-General* |
| 30 Jul 1894 - 27 Dec 1894: | Commander, 3$^{rd}$ Grenadier Division |

*General of Cavalry* Konstantin Nikolayevich **Manzey** (22 May 1821 - 4 Jan 1905)
| | |
|---|---|
| 5 Oct 1862 - 16 Apr 1869: | Commander, Life Guards Horse Grenadier Regiment |
| 17 Apr 1863: | Promoted to *Major-General* |
| 16 Apr 1869 - 27 Jul 1875: | Commander, 4$^{th}$ Cavalry Division |

| | |
|---|---|
| 28 Mar 1871: | Promoted to *Lieutenant-General* |
| 15 Feb 1875: | Promoted to *General-Adjutant* |
| 27 Jul 1875 - 2 Mar 1878: | Commander, 7th Cavalry Division |
| 2 Mar 1878 - 9 Apr 1889: | Commanding General, XIII. Army Corps |
| 30 Aug 1885: | Promoted to *General of Cavalry* |
| 9 Apr 1889 - 11 Aug 1889: | Commanding General, Grenadier Corps |
| 11 Aug 1889 - 29 Mar 1897: | Commanding General, Guards Corps |
| 29 Mar 1897 - 4 Jan 1905: | General à la suite |

*Major-General* Mitrofan Konstantinovich **Marchenko** (3 Sep 1866 - 7 Jul 1932)
| | |
|---|---|
| 2 Sep 1910 - 26 Oct 1912: | Commander, 19th Dragoon Regiment |
| 26 Oct 1912: | Promoted to *Major-General* |
| 26 Oct 1912 - 20 Mar 1917: | Commandant, Nikolayev Cavalry School |
| 20 Mar 1917: | Dismissed |

*Major-General* Nikolai Pavlovich **Marchenko** (31 Jul 1865 - ?)
| | |
|---|---|
| 19 Sep 1916 - 1917: | Commander, Brigade, 1st Grenadier Division |
| 6 Dec 1916: | Promoted to *Major-General* |

*Major-General* Aleksandr Yakovlevich **Mardanov** (25 Oct 1852 - ?)
| | |
|---|---|
| 22 Feb 1904: | Promoted to *Major-General* |
| 22 Feb 1904 - 18 Jun 1905: | Commander, 1st Brigade, 3rd East Siberian Rifle Division |
| 18 Jun 1905 - 4 Nov 1906: | Quartermaster-General, Amur Military District |
| 4 Nov 1906 - 3 Feb 1907: | Commander, 1st Brigade, 3rd Grenadier Division |
| 3 Feb 1907 - 1907: | Commander, 3rd Siberian Replacement Infantry Brigade |
| 1907: | Transferred to the reserve |

*Major-General* Malakhy Kvadzhiyevich **Marganiya** (29 Dec 1859 - ?)
| | |
|---|---|
| 14 Aug 1913: | Promoted to *Major-General* |
| 14 Aug 1913 - 4 Jun 1915: | Commander, 2nd Brigade, 2nd Caucasus Cossack Division |
| 4 Jun 1915 - 30 Oct 1916: | Commander, 1st Brigade, 3rd Caucasus Cossack Division |
| 30 Oct 1916 - 1917: | Reserve officer, Caucasus Military District |

*Major-General* Anton Ignatyevich **Markevich** (10 Jan 1860 - ?)
| | |
|---|---|
| 19 Jun 1898 - 8 Oct 1914: | Senior Clerk, Artillery Committee, Main Artillery Administration |
| 6 Dec 1908: | Promoted to *Major-General* |
| 8 Oct 1914 - Oct 1917: | Head of Technical Office, Main Artillery Administration |

*Major-General* Ignaty Ignatyevich **Markevich** (7 Jan 1850 - 1910)
| | |
|---|---|
| 13 Jul 1888 - 1910: | Military Judge, Kiev Military District Court |
| 30 Aug 1894: | Promoted to *Major-General* |

*Major-General* Mitrofan Ivanovich **Markevich** (28 May 1851 - ?)
| | |
|---|---|
| 3 Jan 1904: | Promoted to *Major-General* |
| 3 Jan 1904 - 1909: | Commander of Artillery, Fortress Novogeorgievsk |

*Major-General* Pyotr Ivanovich **Markevich** (25 Nov 1842 - 6 Jul 1901)
4 Mar 1891 - 30 Jan 1896: Deputy Intendant, Warsaw Military District
30 Aug 1893: Promoted to *Major-General*
30 Jan 1896 - 3 Jan 1899: Deputy Intendant, Caucasus Military District
3 Jan 1899 - 6 Jul 1901: Intendant, Finland Military District

*Major-General* Andrey Nikolayevich **Markgrafsky** (17 Aug 1849 - 20 Jul 1907)
9 Feb 1897 - 7 Dec 1905: Chief of Bureau, Deputy Governor-General of Warsaw
6 Dec 1904: Promoted to *Major-General*
7 Dec 1905 - 20 Jul 1907: Deputy Chief of Police, Warsaw

*Lieutenant-General* Pavel Anisimovich **Markodeyev** (5 Mar 1878 - ?)
3 Nov 1915 - Jan 1917: Commander, 12th Finnish Rifle Regiment
22 Sep 1916: Promoted to *Major-General*
Jan 1917 - 29 Apr 1917: Chief of Staff, 5th Finnish Rifle Division
29 Apr 1917 - 12 May 1917: Chief of Staff, XXII. Army Corps
12 May 1917: Promoted to *Lieutenant-General*
12 May 1917 - 9 Sep 1917: Commander, 3rd Finnish Rifle Division
9 Sep 1917 - 1918: Commanding General, VI. Army Corps

*Major-General* Aleksandr Dmitriyevich **Markov** (15 Jun 1861 - ?)
24 Mar 1910 - 1914: Commander, 118th Infantry Regiment
1914: Retired
2 May 1915: Promoted to *Major-General*
6 May 1915 - 1917: Recalled; Commander, 154th Replacement Infantry Battalion

*Lieutenant-General* Ivan Luppovich **Markov** (30 Jul 1845 - ?)
25 Apr 1896 - 12 Oct 1912: Ataman, 3rd District, Ural Cossack Army
17 Apr 1905: Promoted to *Major-General*
12 Oct 1912: Promoted to *Lieutenant-General*
12 Oct 1912: Retired

*Major-General* Mikhail Illarionovich **Markov** (9 Feb 1843 - 25 Jan 1899)
31 Aug 1881 - 10 Feb 1891: Commander, 1st Dragoon Regiment
10 Feb 1891: Promoted to *Major-General*
10 Feb 1891 - 30 Dec 1897: Chief of Staff, Caucasus Army Corps
30 Dec 1897 - 25 Jan 1899: Commander, 8th Cavalry Division

*Major-General* Mikhail Pavlovich **Markov** (15 Jan 1860 - ?)
27 Jun 1911 - 31 Dec 1913: Military Commander, Moscow
14 Apr 1913: Promoted to *Major-General*
31 Dec 1913 - 1917: Commander, Yaroslavl Local Brigade

*Major-General* Pyotr Alekseyevich **Markov** (24 Dec 1861 - ?)
6 Nov 1915 - 1917: Commander, 4th Rifle Artillery Brigade
26 Sep 1916: Promoted to *Major-General*

*General of Infantry* Sergey Dmitriyevich **Markov** (19 Jun 1862 - ?)
| | |
|---|---|
| 9 Mar 1905: | Promoted to *Major-General* |
| 9 Mar 1905 - 14 Jun 1905: | Commander, 2nd Brigade, 22nd Infantry Division |
| 14 Jun 1905 - 21 Sep 1905: | Chief of Staff, X. Army Corps |
| 21 Sep 1905 - 19 May 1907: | Quartemaster-General, Turkestan Military District |
| 19 May 1907 - 16 Jun 1910: | Member, Main Fortress Committee |
| 16 Jun 1910 - 21 Apr 1911: | Chief of Staff, XXV. Army Corps |
| 21 Apr 1911: | Promoted to *Lieutenant-General* |
| 21 Apr 1911 - 5 Mar 1914: | Chief of Staff, Irkutsk Military District |
| 5 Mar 1914 - 11 Aug 1914: | Commander, 1st Siberian Rifle Division |
| 11 Aug 1914 - 6 Oct 1914: | Chief of Staff, 10th Army |
| 6 Oct 1914 - 11 Dec 1914: | Commander, 22nd Infantry Division |
| 11 Dec 1914 - 9 Sep 1917: | Reserve officer, Dvinsk Military District |
| 9 Sep 1917: | Promoted to *General of Infantry* |
| 9 Sep 1917: | Retired |

*Lieutenant-General* Sergey Leonidovich **Markov** (7 Jul 1878 - 25 Jun 1918)
| | |
|---|---|
| 22 Sep 1915 - 20 Apr 1916: | Commander, 13th Rifle Regiment |
| 6 Dec 1915: | Promoted to *Major-General* |
| 20 Apr 1916 - 1 Jan 1917: | Chief of Staff, 2nd Caucasus Cossack Division |
| 1 Jan 1917 - 15 Apr 1917: | Special Assignments General, 10th Army |
| 15 Apr 1917 - 12 May 1917: | Commander, 10th Infantry Division |
| 12 May 1917 - 10 Jun 1917: | Second Quartermaster-General to the Supreme Commander-in-Chief |
| 10 Jun 1917 - 4 Aug 1917: | Chief of Staff, Western Front |
| 4 Aug 1917 - 29 Aug 1917: | Chief of Staff, Southwestern Front |
| 16 Aug 1917: | Promoted to *Lieutenant-General* |
| 29 Aug 1917: | Discharged |

*Lieutenant-General* Vasily Yevgenyevich **Markov** (7 Oct 1864 - 1 Mar 1935)
| | |
|---|---|
| 13 May 1910: | Promoted to *Major-General* |
| 13 May 1910 - 21 Apr 1915: | Commander, 1st Brigade, 10th Cavalry Division |
| 8 Aug 1914: | Promoted to *Lieutenant-General* |
| 21 Apr 1915 - 1917: | Commander, 10th Cavalry Division |

*Lieutenant-General* Viktor Georgiyevich **Markov** (20 Nov 1854 - 10 Jun 1917)
| | |
|---|---|
| 19 Nov 1908: | Promoted to *Major-General* |
| 19 Nov 1908 - 9 Sep 1910: | Commander of Engineers, Fortress Brest-Litovsk |
| 9 Sep 1910 - 22 Oct 1912: | Commander of Engineers, St. Petersburg Military District |
| 22 Oct 1912 - 10 Jun 1917: | Chief of Troop Billeting, St. Petersburg Military District |
| 6 Dec 1914: | Promoted to *Lieutenant-General* |

*Lieutenant-General* Vladimir Ivanovich **Markov** (26 Jul 1859 - Aug 1919)
| | |
|---|---|
| 16 Aug 1899 - 1 May 1903: | Deputy Chief Editor, "Military Digest" |
| 6 Apr 1903: | Promoted to *Major-General* |
| 1 May 1903 - 3 Jan 1909: | Chief of Mobilization Section, General Staff |
| 9 May 1908 - 9 Sep 1908: | Commander, Brigade, 2nd Guards Infantry Division |

| | |
|---|---|
| 3 Jan 1909 - 10 Jun 1909: | Chief of Staff, XVII. Army Corps |
| 10 Jun 1909 - 2 Nov 1909: | Military Governor of the Trans-Baikal Region, Ataman, Trans-Baikal Cossack Army |
| 2 Nov 1909 - 10 Apr 1913: | Senator & Vice-Chairman of the Economic Department, Finnish Senate |
| 1909: | Promoted to *Lieutenant-General* |
| 10 Apr 1913 - 1917: | Minister of State of the Grand Duchy of Finland |

*General of Infantry* Vasily Ivanovich **Markozov** (1 Jan 1838 - 26 Mar 1908)
| | |
|---|---|
| 31 Oct 1878: | Promoted to *Major-General* |
| 31 Oct 1878 - 27 Jul 1879: | Inspector of Hospitals, Field Army |
| 27 Jul 1879 - 29 Apr 1880: | Unassigned |
| 29 Apr 1880 - 21 Oct 1881: | At the disposal of the Commanding General, Kiev Military District |
| 21 Oct 1881 - 18 Apr 1891: | Chief of Staff, XII. Army Corps |
| 18 Apr 1891 - 5 Oct 1892: | Commander, 2nd Brigade, 6th Infantry Division |
| 5 Oct 1892 - 28 Feb 1897: | Commander, 2nd Infantry Division |
| 30 Aug 1893: | Promoted to *Lieutenant-General* |
| 28 Feb 1897: | Promoted to *General of Infantry* |
| 28 Feb 1897: | Retired |

*Lieutenant-General* Nikandr Aleksandrovich **Marks** (24 Sep 1861 - 29 Mar 1921)
| | |
|---|---|
| 23 Apr 1904 - 21 Jul 1914: | Ministry of War Representative, Moscow Military District Council |
| 31 May 1906: | Promoted to *Major-General* |
| 31 May 1913: | Promoted to *Lieutenant-General* |
| 21 Jul 1914: | Retired |
| 13 Jan 1916 - 4 Sep 1917: | Recalled; Chief of Staff, Odessa Military District |
| 4 Sep 1917 - 10 Sep 1917: | Reserve officer, Odessa Military District |
| 10 Sep 1917 - Oct 1917: | Chief of Staff, Odessa Military District |

*Major-General* Pavel Antonovich **Marsov-Tishevsky** (13 Jan 1856 - ?)
| | |
|---|---|
| 26 Jun 1910 - 13 Jan 1914: | Commander, 43rd Siberian Rifle Regiment |
| 13 Jan 1914: | Promoted to *Major-General* |
| 13 Jan 1914: | Retired |
| 29 Aug 1914 - 20 May 1917: | Commander, 4th Siberian Replacement Rifle Brigade |
| 20 May 1917: | Dismissed |

*Lieutenant-General* Aleksandr Grigoryevich **Martos** (8 Jun 1861 - ?)
| | |
|---|---|
| 1 Aug 1908 - 10 Aug 1912: | Inspector of Classes, Suvorov Cadet Corps |
| 6 Dec 1908: | Promoted to *Major-General* |
| 10 Aug 1912 - 28 Jan 1913: | Instructor, Suvorov Cadet Corps |
| 28 Jan 1913: | Promoted to *Lieutenant-General* |
| 28 Jan 1913: | Retired |

*General of Infantry* Nikolai Nikolayevich **Martos** (20 Nov 1858 - 14 Oct 1933)
| | |
|---|---|
| 2 Jul 1901: | Promoted to *Major-General* |
| 2 Jul 1901 - 21 Mar 1902: | General for Special Assignments, Odessa Military |

| | |
|---|---|
| | District |
| 21 Mar 1902 - 20 May 1902: | Deputy Chief of Staff, Odessa Military District |
| 20 May 1902 - 17 Oct 1904: | Quartermaster-General, Odessa Military District |
| 17 Oct 1904 - 16 Feb 1905: | Attached to the C-in-C, 2nd Manchurian Army |
| 16 Feb 1905 - 6 Aug 1905: | Chief of Staff, VIII. Army Corps |
| 6 Aug 1905 - 29 Dec 1907: | Commander, 15th Infantry Division |
| 31 May 1907: | Promoted to *Lieutenant-General* |
| 29 Dec 1907 - 23 Dec 1910: | Deputy Governor of the Amur Region, Deputy Commanding General, Amur Military District, Ataman, Amur & Ussuri Cossack Armies |
| 23 Dec 1910 - 28 Feb 1911: | Deputy Commanding General, Vilnius Military District |
| 28 Feb 1911 - 16 Aug 1914: | Commanding General, XV. Army Corps |
| 14 Apr 1913: | Promoted to *General of Infantry* |
| 16 Aug 1914 - 1918: | POW, Germany |

*Major-General* Leonid Mikhailovich **Marts** (26 May 1870 - 24 Aug 1916)
| | |
|---|---|
| 1894 - 24 Aug 1916: | Attached to 92nd Infantry Regiment |
| 31 Dec 1916: | Posthumously promoted to *Major-General* |

*General of Infantry* Fyodor Vladimirovich **Martson** (16 Sep 1853 - 3 Oct 1916)
| | |
|---|---|
| 23 Feb 1894 - 16 Aug 1899: | Chief of Communications, Kiev Military District |
| 6 May 1897: | Promoted to *Major-General* |
| 16 Aug 1899 - 30 Oct 1904: | Quartermaster-General, Warsaw Military District |
| 30 Oct 1904: | Promoted to *Lieutenant-General* |
| 30 Oct 1904 - 26 Feb 1906: | Chief of Field Staff, 3rd Manchurian Army |
| 26 Feb 1906 - 30 Jun 1907: | Commander, 42nd Infantry Division |
| 30 Jun 1907 - 11 Apr 1909: | Commanding General, XV. Army Corps |
| 11 Apr 1909 - 23 Nov 1910: | Deputy Commanding General, Vilnius Military District |
| 23 Nov 1910 - 17 Jan 1913: | Commanding General, Vilnius Military District |
| 6 Dec 1910: | Promoted to *General of Infantry* |
| 17 Jan 1913 - 4 Oct 1914: | Member of the Military Council |
| 4 Oct 1914 - 22 Jul 1916: | Acting Governor-General of Turkestan, Acting Commanding General, Turkestan Military District, Acting Ataman, Semirechensk Cossack Army |
| 22 Jul 1916 - 3 Oct 1916: | Member of the Military Council |

*Major-General* Leonty Vladimirovich **Martson** (12 Sep 1855 - 15 Aug 1904)
| | |
|---|---|
| 20 Apr 1903: | Promoted to *Major-General* |
| 20 Apr 1903 - 15 Aug 1904: | Commander, 2nd Brigade, 9th Infantry Division |

*Major-General* Anton Antonovich **Martusevich** (25 Feb 1863 - 9 Sep 1944)
| | |
|---|---|
| 25 Jul 1914 - 9 Mar 1917: | Commander, 14th Siberian Rifle Artillery Brigade |
| 22 Oct 1915: | Promoted to *Major-General* |
| 9 Mar 1917 - 1918: | Commander, 110th Infantry Division |

*Major-General* Vasily Georgiyevich **Martyanov** (24 Dec 1855 - ?)
| | |
|---|---|
| 19 Feb 1909 - 7 Sep 1913: | Deputy Chief of Lugansk Cartridge Factory |

10 Apr 1911: Promoted to *Major-General*

*Rear-Admiral* Aleksandr Fomich **Martyn** (? - ?)
?: Promoted to *Rear-Admiral*

*Lieutenant-General* Aleksandr Vladimirovich **Martynov** (27 May 1859 - ?)
29 Nov 1912: Promoted to *Major-General*
29 Nov 1912 - 9 Jan 1916: Commander, 51st Artillery Brigade
9 Jan 1916 - 6 Aug 1917: Inspector of Artillery, XXVI. Army Corps
9 Feb 1917: Promoted to *Lieutenant-General*
6 Aug 1917 - 7 Sep 1917: Commanding General, XXVI. Army Corps

*Lieutenant-General* Anatoly Ivanovich **Martynov** (22 Jan 1869 - 1942)
24 Oct 1910 - 30 Aug 1913: Commander, 3rd Hussar Regiment
14 Apr 1913: Promoted to *Major-General*
30 Aug 1913 - 6 Jun 1915: Commander, 2nd Brigade, 4th Cavalry Division
6 Jun 1915 - 15 Sep 1915: Reserve officer, Dvinsk Military District
15 Sep 1915 - 18 Nov 1916: Reserve officer, Petrograd Military District
18 Nov 1916 - 8 Dec 1916: Chief of Staff, I. Cavalry Corps
8 Dec 1916 - 1918: Commander, 15th Cavalry Division
1917: Promoted to *Lieutenant-General*

*General of Cavalry* Andrey Dmitriyevich **Martynov** (27 Jun 1838 - 17 May 1913)
31 Aug 1875 - 29 Apr 1883: Commander, Life Guards Ataman Regiment
26 Feb 1878: Promoted to *Major-General*
29 Apr 1883 - 23 Nov 1894: Chief of Staff, Don Cossack Army
30 Aug 1888: Promoted to *Lieutenant-General*
23 Nov 1894 - 25 Jan 1906: Attached to the Minister of War
6 Dec 1904: Promoted to *General of Cavalry*
25 Jan 1906 - 17 May 1913: At the disposal of the Don Cossack Army

*Major-General* Mikhail Vasilyevich **Martynov** (5 Sep 1850 - ?)
26 Nov 1901: Promoted to *Major-General*
26 Nov 1901 - 4 Jan 1902: At the disposal of the Chief of the General Staff
4 Jan 1902 - 20 Nov 1904: Commander, 1st Brigade, Caucasus Grenadier Division
20 Nov 1904 - 13 May 1906: Commander, 2nd Kuban Cossack Infantry Brigade
13 May 1906 - 1907: Commander, 1st Kuban Cossack Infantry Brigade

*Major-General* Nikolai Nikolayevich **Martynov** (4 May 1845 - Jan 1899)
26 May 1897: Promoted to *Major-General*
26 May 1897 - Jan 1899: Commander, 32nd Artillery Brigade

*Lieutenant-General* Nikolai Patrikeyevich **Martynov** (15 Jul 1853 - ?)
23 Feb 1904: Promoted to *Major-General*
23 Feb 1904 - 17 Jul 1912: Commander, 2nd Brigade, 14th Cavalry Division
17 Jul 1912: Promoted to *Lieutenant-General*
17 Jul 1912: Retired

*Lieutenant-General* Patrikey Vasilyevich **Martynov** (12 May 1828 - 28 May 1899)
27 Sep 1866 - 1 Feb 1898: Member, Committee for Revision of Cossack Regulations
6 May 1885: Promoted to *Major-General*
1 Feb 1898 - 1899: Attached to the Ural Cossack Army
1899: Promoted to *Lieutenant-General*

*Major-General* Vasily Patrikeyevich **Martynov** (20 Aug 1863 - Dec 1919)
24 Aug 1916 - 1917: Ataman, 1$^{st}$ Military Division, Ural Cossack Army
6 Dec 1916: Promoted to *Major-General*

*Lieutenant-General* Vladimir Gerasimovich **Martynov** (2 May 1841 - 1913)
23 Oct 1893 - 20 Feb 1902: Commander of Artillery, Fortress Sevastopol
14 May 1896: Promoted to *Major-General*
20 Feb 1902: Promoted to *Lieutenant-General*
20 Feb 1902: Retired

*Major-General* Yevgeny Denisovich **Martynov** (21 Jan 1850 - 3 Apr 1930)
14 May 1905 - 8 Jun 1915: Ataman, 1$^{st}$ Military Division, Ural Cossack Army
10 Apr 1911: Promoted to *Major-General*
26 Jul 1917 - 1917: Recalled; Reserve officer, Petrograd Military District

*Lieutenant-General* Yevgeny Ivanovich **Martynov** (22 Sep 1864 - 11 Dec 1937)
4 Jan 1905: Promoted to *Major-General*
4 Jan 1905 - 25 Oct 1905: Chief of Staff, III. Siberian Army Corps
25 Oct 1905 - 26 Jun 1906: At the disposal of the General Staff
26 Jun 1906 - 3 Apr 1908: Attached to the General Staff
3 Apr 1908 - 7 Dec 1910: Commander, 1$^{st}$ Rifle Brigade
7 Dec 1910: Promoted to *Lieutenant-General*
7 Dec 1910 - 19 Feb 1913: Commander of Borderguards, Amur Military District
19 Feb 1913 - 13 Apr 1913: Commander, 35$^{th}$ Infantry Division
13 Apr 1913: Dismissed
20 Jul 1914 - 10 Aug 1914: Recalled; At the disposal of the Chief of Staff, Southwestern Front
10 Aug 1914 - Feb 1918: POW

*Major-General* Zakhary Aleksandrovich **Martynov** (24 Sep 1861 - 1 Jul 1944)
16 Aug 1914 - Jul 1916: Commander, 256$^{th}$ Infantry Regiment
21 Aug 1915: Promoted to *Major-General*
Jul 1916 - 1917: Commander, Brigade, 118$^{th}$ Infantry Division
1917: Commander, 118$^{th}$ Infantry Division

*Major-General* Ilya Silvestrovich **Martynyuk** (21 Jul 1869 - ?)
28 Nov 1914 - 25 Dec 1916: Commander, 44$^{th}$ Infantry Regiment
25 Aug 1916: Promoted to *Major-General*
25 Dec 1916 - 15 Aug 1917: Commander, Brigade, 1$^{st}$ Amur Borderguard Infantry Division
15 Aug 1917 - 1918: Commander, 159$^{th}$ Infantry Division

*General of Artillery* Vladimir Konstantinovich **Martyushev** (18 Jun 1836 - 12 Sep 1905)
| | |
|---|---|
| 30 Jan 1885: | Promoted to *Major-General* |
| 30 Jan 1885 - 1 Feb 1895: | Commander, 3rd Life Guards Artillery Brigade |
| 1 Feb 1895 - 9 Feb 1901: | Commander of Artillery, Vilnius Military District |
| 2 Apr 1895: | Promoted to *Lieutenant-General* |
| 9 Feb 1901: | Promoted to *General of Artillery* |
| 9 Feb 1901: | Retired |

*Major-General* Vladimir Vladimirovich **Marushevsky** (12 Jul 1874 - 24 Feb 1951)
| | |
|---|---|
| 23 Jun 1915 - 3 Jul 1916: | Commander, 7th Finnish Rifle Regiment |
| 1916: | Promoted to *Major-General* |
| 3 Jul 1916 - 3 Jul 1917: | Commander, 3rd Special Infantry Brigade, France |
| 3 Jul 1917 - 26 Sep 1917: | Reserve officer, Petrograd Military District |
| 26 Sep 1917 - 23 Nov 1917: | Chief of the General Directorate of the General Staff |
| 23 Nov 1917: | Dismissed |

*Lieutenant-General* Nikolai Fyodorovich **Maryanov** (2 Apr 1842 - ?)
| | |
|---|---|
| 19 Aug 1892: | Promoted to *Major-General* |
| 19 Aug 1892 - 4 Dec 1900: | Commander, Caucasus Sapper Brigade |
| 4 Dec 1900 - 5 Apr 1905: | Commander, 19th Infantry Division |
| 6 Dec 1900: | Promoted to *Lieutenant-General* |
| 5 Apr 1905 - Sep 1905: | Commandant of Fortress Kerch |

*Lieutenant-General* Vasily Ivanovich **Masalitinov** (12 Feb 1861 - 17 Aug 1933)
| | |
|---|---|
| 21 Jul 1907: | Promoted to *Major-General* |
| 21 Jul 1907 - 18 May 1910: | Commander, 2nd Reserve Artillery Brigade |
| 18 May 1910 - 2 Apr 1913: | Commander, 10th Artillery Brigade |
| 2 Apr 1913 - Aug 1914: | Inspector of Artillery, XIII. Army Corps |
| 21 Jul 1913: | Promoted to *Lieutenant-General* |
| Aug 1914 - 1918: | POW |

*Lieutenant-General* Pavel Gavrilovich **Masalov** (29 Jun 1852 - ?)
| | |
|---|---|
| 17 Mar 1899: | Promoted to *Major-General* |
| 17 Mar 1899 - 18 Dec 1900: | Chief of Staff, XI. Army Corps |
| 18 Dec 1900 - 4 Oct 1904: | Commander, 66th Reserve Infantry Brigade |
| 4 Oct 1904 - 6 Jun 1906: | Commander, 69th Infantry Division |
| 17 Apr 1905: | Promoted to *Lieutenant-General* |
| 6 Jun 1906 - 26 Oct 1907: | Commander, 14th Infantry Division |

*General of Artillery* Prince Vladimir Nikolayevich **Masalsky** (31 Oct 1860 - 10 Apr 1940)
| | |
|---|---|
| 4 Jun 1904 - 25 Sep 1904: | Commander, 73rd Artillery Brigade |
| 25 Sep 1904 - 24 Jan 1909: | Commander, Life Guards Horse Artillery Brigade |
| 6 Dec 1905: | Promoted to *Major-General* |
| 24 Jan 1909 - 6 Feb 1910: | Commander of Artillery, Grenadier Corps |
| 6 Dec 1909: | Promoted to *Lieutenant-General* |
| 6 Feb 1910 - 24 Jul 1910: | Commander of Artillery, I. Army Corps |
| 24 Oct 1910 - 18 Oct 1913: | Inspector of Artillery, I. Army Corps |
| 18 Oct 1913: | Promoted to *General of Artillery* |

| | |
|---|---|
| 18 Oct 1913: | Retired |
| 24 Jul 1914 - 16 Apr 1916: | Recalled; Inspector of Artillery, I. Army Corps |
| 16 Apr 1916 - 22 Apr 1917: | Inspector of Artillery, 7th Army |
| 22 Apr 1917 - 24 Mar 1918: | Inspector of Artillery, Romanian Front |

*Lieutenant-General* Pyotr Aleksandrovich **Mashin** (13 Dec 1851 - ?)
| | |
|---|---|
| 20 Jun 1897 - 18 Aug 1899: | Chief of Staff, Terek Cossack Army |
| 6 May 1899: | Promoted to *Major-General* |
| 18 Aug 1899 - 1 Dec 1903: | Commandant, Nikolayev Cavalry School |
| 1 Dec 1903 - 3 Feb 1904: | At the disposal of the Chief of the General Staff |
| 3 Feb 1904 - 14 Aug 1907: | Commander, 10th Cavalry Division |
| 6 Dec 1906: | Promoted to *Lieutenant-General* |
| 14 Aug 1907: | Retired |

*General of Infantry* Nikolai Alekseyevich **Maslakovets** (9 May 1833 - 7 Feb 1908)
| | |
|---|---|
| 16 Sep 1875 - 12 Aug 1884: | Deputy Chairman of the Don Cossack Regional Board |
| 26 Feb 1878: | Promoted to *Major-General* |
| 12 Aug 1884 - 21 Jan 1892: | Governor of Orenburg, Ataman, Orenburg Cossack Army |
| 21 Jan 1892 - 18 May 1894: | Transferred to the reserve |
| 27 Dec 1893: | Promoted to *Lieutenant-General* |
| 18 May 1894 - 8 Jan 1906: | At the disposal of the Minister of War |
| 8 Jan 1906: | Promoted to *General of Infantry* |
| 8 Jan 1906: | Retired |

*General of Engineers* Aleksey Nikolayevich **Maslov** (7 Sep 1852 - 1922)
| | |
|---|---|
| 9 Oct 1887 - 9 Oct 1910: | Professor, Nikolayev Engineering College |
| 12 Jun 1898 - 1917: | Conference Member, Nikolayev Engineering Academy |
| 1 Jan 1901: | Promoted to *Major-General* |
| 6 Dec 1908: | Promoted to *Lieutenant-General* |
| 1917 - 27 Jul 1917: | Attached to the Minister of War |
| 27 Jul 1917: | Promoted to *General of Engineers* |
| 27 Jul 1917: | Dismissed |

*General of Infantry* Ignaty Petrovich **Maslov** (3 May 1840 - ?)
| | |
|---|---|
| 20 Jan 1883 - 25 Oct 1884: | Attached to St. Petersburg Military District |
| 6 May 1884: | Promoted to *Major-General* |
| 25 Oct 1884 - 11 Mar 1892: | Chief of Staff, II. Army Corps |
| 11 Mar 1892 - 24 Apr 1895: | Chief of Staff, Omsk Military District |
| 30 Aug 1894: | Promoted to *Lieutenant-General* |
| 24 Apr 1895 - 1 Oct 1899: | Commander, 30th Infantry Division |
| 1 Oct 1899 - 5 Dec 1906: | Commanding General, IV. Army Corps |
| 6 Dec 1904: | Promoted to *General of Infantry* |
| 5 Dec 1906 - 1907: | At the disposal of the Minster of War |

*Lieutenant-General* Mikhail Nikolayevich **Maslov** (6 Nov 1850 - ?)
| | |
|---|---|
| 25 Mar 1904: | Promoted to *Major-General* |
| 25 Mar 1904 - 2 Jan 1905: | Commander, 1st Brigade, 1st Siberian Infantry Division |

| | |
|---|---|
| 2 Jan 1905 - 24 Jul 1906: | Commander, Siberian Independent Infantry Brigade |
| 24 Jul 1906 - 23 Jul 1910: | Commander, 3rd Turkestan Rifle Brigade |
| 23 Jul 1910 - 14 Sep 1911: | Transferred to the reserve |
| 14 Sep 1911: | Promoted to *Lieutenant-General* |
| 14 Sep 1911: | Retired |
| 1 Oct 1914 - 24 Mar 1915: | Recalled; Commander, 3rd Turkestan Rifle Brigade |
| 24 Mar 1915 - 12 Jul 1915: | Unassigned |
| 12 Jul 1915 - 22 Apr 1917: | Commander, 111th Infantry Division |

*Major-General* Mikhail Yevgenyevich **Maslov** (7 May 1867 - 18 Apr 1936)
| | |
|---|---|
| 22 Aug 1915 - 10 Mar 1917: | Commander, Life Guards Uhlan Regiment |
| 23 Apr 1916: | Promoted to *Major-General* |
| 10 Mar 1917 - 1917: | Commander, 2nd Brigade, 2nd Guards Cavalry Division |

*General of Infantry* Nikolai Nikolayevich **Maslov** (1 Aug 1846 - Oct 1912)
| | |
|---|---|
| 6 Feb 1882 - 4 Jan 1892: | Military Prosecutor, St. Petersburg Military District |
| 24 Apr 1888: | Promoted to *Major-General* |
| 4 Jan 1892 - 14 Aug 1905: | Chief Military Prosecutor of the Army, Chief of the Main Military Justice Directorate |
| 6 May 1895: | Promoted to *Lieutenant-General* |
| 14 Aug 1905 - Oct 1912: | Member of the State Council |
| 6 Dec 1906: | Promoted to *General of Infantry* |

*Major-General* Dmitry Fyodorovich **Maslovsky** (20 Sep 1848 - 3 Nov 1894)
| | |
|---|---|
| 13 May 1891 - 3 Nov 1894: | Professor, Nikolayev General Staff Academy |
| 1890 - 3 Nov 1894: | Chief of the History Department, Nikolayev General Staff Academy |
| 30 Aug 1891: | Promoted to *Major-General* |
| 18 Nov 1893 - 3 Nov 1894: | Member of the Military Education Committee, General Staff |

*Major-General* Georgy Nikolayevich **Maslyanikov** (23 Mar 1868 - 27 Oct 1940)
| | |
|---|---|
| 30 Mar 1915 - 1917: | Commander, 16th Caucasus Rifle Regiment |
| 5 Aug 1916: | Promoted to *Major-General* |
| 1917 - Jun 1917: | Commander, Brigade, 127th Infantry Division |
| Jun 1917 - 1918: | Duty General, Caucasus Army |

*Major-General* Anton Pavlovich **Maslyanyy** (17 Jan 1865 - ?)
| | |
|---|---|
| 15 Jan 1915 - 18 Nov 1917: | Deputy Duty General, Western Front |
| 19 Apr 1916: | Promoted to *Major-General* |
| 18 Nov 1917 - 1918: | Duty General, Southwestern Front |

*Major-General* Aleksey Ivanovich **Matafanov** (4 Mar 1867 - 2 Jan 1945)
| | |
|---|---|
| 16 Jun 1916 - 1917: | Commander, 47th Militia Brigade |
| 6 Dec 1916: | Promoted to *Major-General* |
| 1917: | Military Commander, Kiev District |

*Lieutenant-General* Nikolai Ivanovich **Matafanov** (4 Mar 1865 - 1917)
2 Jun 1911 - 16 Jan 1914: Deputy Commandant of St. Petersburg Arsenal
6 Dec 1911: Promoted to *Major-General*
16 Jan 1914 - 13 Mar 1916: Member of the Artillery Committee, Main Artillery Directorate
13 Mar 1916 - 1917: Chief of Petrograd Gun Factory
1917: Posthumously promoted to *Lieutenant-General*

*Major-General of the Admiralty* Khristo Mateyevich **Mateyev** (20 Jul 1863 - ?)
6 Apr 1909 - ?: Chief Construction Engineer, Port of St. Petersburg
18 Apr 1910: Promoted to *Major-General of the Admiralty*

*Lieutenant-General* Emmanuil Aleksandrovich **Matias** (28 Jan 1841 - 2 Sep 1897)
8 Feb 1884 - 7 Feb 1890: Commander of Artillery, Fortress Kronstadt
26 Feb 1886: Promoted to *Major-General*
7 Feb 1890 - 10 Dec 1892: Inspector of Fortress Artillery
10 Dec 1892 - 2 Sep 1897: Deputy Chief of the Main Artillery Directorate
14 May 1896: Promoted to *Lieutenant-General*

*Major-General* Mikhail Felitsianovich **Matkovsky** (12 Jul 1868 - 7 Jul 1931)
17 Jan 1909 - 17 May 1911: Commander, 12th Grenadier Regiment
17 May 1911: Promoted to *Major-General*
17 May 1911: Retired

*Major-General* Adam Adolfovich **Matseyevsky** (10 Jul 1858 - 8 Nov 1915)
9 Feb 1915 - 8 Nov 1915: Commander, 119th Infantry Regiment
5 Oct 1915: Promoted to *Major-General*

*General of Infantry* Yevgeny Osipovich **Matsiyevsky** (13 Jan 1845 - 1910)
16 Mar 1893: Promoted to *Major-General*
16 Mar 1893 - 27 May 1893: Commander, 2nd Brigade, 17th Infantry Division
27 May 1893 - 10 Apr 1901: Military Governor, Trans-Baikal Region, Ataman, Trans-Baikal Cossack Army
30 Sep 1900: Promoted to *Lieutenant-General*
10 Apr 1901 - 14 Nov 1904: Deputy Governor-General of Turkestan, Deputy Commanding General, Turkestan Military District
14 Nov 1904 - 31 Aug 1906: Commanding General, I. Turkestan Army Corps
31 Aug 1906 - 1907: Deputy Governor-General of Turkestan, Deputy Commanding General, Turkestan Military District
1907: Promoted to *General of Infantry*
1907: Retired

*Major-General of Naval Navigators* Andrey Stanislavovich **Matskevich** (8 May 1862 - 1917)
22 Mar 1915: Promoted to *Major-General of Naval Navigators*
22 Mar 1915 - 14 Mar 1917: Navigation Officer, Imperial Yacht "Aleksandria"

14 Mar 1917 - 1917:                     Reserve officer, Ministry of the Navy

*Vice-Admiral* Nikolai Aleksandrovich **Matusevich** (1 Jan 1852 - 23 Jan 1912)
29 Mar 1904:                            Promoted to *Rear-Admiral*
1 Apr 1904 - 5 Apr 1904:                Chief of Staff, 1st Pacific Squadron
5 Apr 1904 - 28 Jul 1904:               Junior Flagman, 1st Pacific Squadron
28 Jul 1904 - 22 Dec 1905:              Unassigned
22 Dec 1905 - 30 Jul 1907:              Commander, Training Squadron, Black Sea Fleet
30 Jul 1907 - 12 Dec 1907:              Junior Flagman, Baltic Fleet
12 Dec 1907 - 7 Jul 1908:               Commandant, Port of Vladivostok
1 Jul 1908 - 29 Mar 1909:               C-in-C of Naval Forces, Pacific
29 Mar 1909:                            Promoted to *Vice-Admiral*
29 Mar 1909 - 23 Jan 1912:              Member, Board of Admiralty

*Major-General of the Fleet* Vasily Aleksandrovich **Matusevich** (1 Jan 1863 - 20 Feb 1923)
30 Aug 1916:                            Promoted to *Major-General of the Fleet*

*Major-General* Aleksandr Grigoryevich **Matveyenko** (22 Dec 1844 - ?)
24 Oct 1899:                            Promoted to *Major-General*
24 Oct 1899 - 3 Jun 1903:               Commander, 1st Brigade, 3rd Grenadier Division

*Lieutenant-General* Mikhail Lvovich **Matveyev** (15 Dec 1864 - ?)
10 Aug 1910:                            Promoted to *Major-General*
10 Aug 1910 - 23 Jul 1912:              Commander, 2nd Brigade, 4th Siberian Rifle Division
23 Jul 1912 - 29 Jul 1914:              Commander, 2nd Brigade, 9th Infantry Division
29 Jul 1914 - 17 Oct 1914:              Acting Commander, 60th Infantry Division
17 Oct 1914 - 24 Jan 1915:              Reserve officer, Kiev Military District
24 Jan 1915 - 3 Feb 1915:               Commander, Brigade, 49th Infantry Division
3 Feb 1915 - 7 Jun 1915:                Commander, 2nd Brigade, 78th Infantry Division
7 Jun 1915 - 17 Jul 1915:               Commander, 37th Infantry Division
17 Jul 1915 - 1 Sep 1915:               Reserve officer, Kiev Military District
1 Sep 1915 - 10 Jun 1917 :              Commander, 3rd Replacement Infantry Brigade
1916:                                   Promoted to *Lieutenant-General*
10 Jun 1917:                            Retired

*Lieutenant-General* Pavel Pavlovich **Matveyev** (20 Jul 1837 - ?)
6 Apr 1884 - 20 Apr 1893:               Deputy Chief of Staff, Turkestan Military District
30 Aug 1888:                            Promoted to *Major-General*
20 Apr 1893 - 26 Mar 1898:              Commander, 3rd Turkestan Line Brigade
26 Mar 1898 - 11 Feb 1900:              Commander, 11th Infantry Division
6 Dec 1898:                             Promoted to *Lieutenant-General*

*Major-General* Aleksandr Gavrilovich **Matyunin** (24 Jul 1860 - ?)
13 Sep 1900 - 20 Oct 1915:              Senior Artillery Inspector, Main Artillery Directorate
6 Dec 1908:                             Promoted to *Major-General*
20 Oct 1915 - Oct 1917:                 Deputy Chief of Artillery Acceptance, Main Artillery Directorate

*Lieutenant-General* Nikolai Ivanovich **Mau** (14 Feb 1844 - ?)
| | |
|---|---|
| 31 Jul 1895: | Promoted to *Major-General* |
| 31 Jul 1895 - 24 Oct 1899: | Chief of Staff, XV. Army Corps |
| 24 Oct 1899 - 3 Apr 1903: | Commander, 46th Reserve Infantry Brigade |
| 3 Apr 1903 - 9 Mar 1905: | Commander, 31st Infantry Division |
| 6 Dec 1903: | Promoted to *Lieutenant-General* |
| 9 Mar 1905 - 9 May 1905: | Attached to the General Staff |
| 9 May 1905 - Sep 1905: | Commander, Kharkov Regional Brigade |

*General of Infantry* Aleksey Alekseyevich **Mavrin** (19 May 1854 - ?)
| | |
|---|---|
| 19 Mar 1898 - 10 Apr 1902: | Duty General, Kiev Military District |
| 6 Dec 1898: | Promoted to *Major-General* |
| 10 Apr 1902 - 27 Jan 1903: | Quartermaster-General, Kiev Military District |
| 27 Jan 1903 - 21 May 1908: | Chief of Staff, Kiev Military District |
| 6 Dec 1904: | Promoted to *Lieutenant-General* |
| 21 May 1908 - 22 Oct 1912: | Commanding General, IX. Army Corps |
| 6 Dec 1910: | Promoted to *General of Infantry* |
| 22 Oct 1912 - 3 Jan 1915: | Member of the Military Council |
| 19 Jul 1914 - 24 Sep 1914: | Acting Commanding General, Kazan Military District |
| 18 Oct 1914 - 3 Jan 1915: | Acting Commanding General, Kazan Military District |
| 3 Jan 1915 - 23 Jul 1916: | Chief of Logistics, Southwestern Front |
| 23 Jul 1916 - 20 Mar 1917: | Member of the Military Council |
| 20 Mar 1917: | Retired |

*Major-General* Valerian Aleksandrovich **Mavrin** (23 May 1837 - 23 Jan 1904)
| | |
|---|---|
| 29 Jul 1897 - 23 Jan 1904: | Commander of Gendarmerie, Kharkov Province |
| 6 Dec 1903: | Promoted to *Major-General* |

*Major-General* Fyodor Bogdanovich **May** (18 Dec 1864 - 1943)
| | |
|---|---|
| 23 Nov 1915 - 1917: | Commander, 1st Battalion, 35th Artillery Brigade |
| 12 Dec 1916: | Promoted to *Major-General* |

*Major-General* Vladimir Zenonovich **May-Mayevsky** (15 Sep 1867 - 30 Nov 1920)
| | |
|---|---|
| 28 Nov 1914: | Promoted to *Major-General* |
| 28 Nov 1914 - 17 Dec 1915: | Commander, 2nd Brigade, 11th Infantry Division |
| 17 Dec 1915 - 8 Oct 1916: | Special Assignments General, 11th Army |
| 8 Oct 1916 - 18 Apr 1917: | Commander, 35th Infantry Division |
| 18 Apr 1917 - 8 Jul 1917: | Commander, 4th Infantry Division |
| 8 Jul 1917 - 1918: | Commanding General, I. Guards Corps |

*Major-General* Andrey Onisimovich **Mayboroda** (19 Aug 1855 - ?)
| | |
|---|---|
| 22 Jul 1910: | Promoted to *Major-General* |
| 22 Jul 1910 - 26 Jun 1913: | Commander, 2nd Brigade, 3rd Caucasus Cossack Division |
| 26 Jun 1913: | Retired |

*Major-General* Baron Ignaty Nikolayevich von **Maydel** (20 Dec 1874 - 23 Dec 1930)
| | |
|---|---|
| 22 Jul 1914 - 25 Oct 1915: | Commander, 2nd Battalion, 10th Artillery Brigade |

| | |
|---|---|
| 16 Jul 1915: | Promoted to *Major-General* |
| 25 Oct 1915 - 19 Jan 1916: | Commander, 26th Artillery Brigade |
| 19 Jan 1916 - 22 Mar 1917: | Attached to the Inspector-General of Artillery |
| 22 Mar 1917 - 29 May 1917: | Inspector of Artillery, XXIV. Army Corps |
| 29 May 1917 - 28 Sep 1917: | Inspector of Artillery, Special Army |
| 28 Sep 1917 - Oct 1917: | Inspector of Artillery, Western Front |

*Major-General* Baron Khristofor Germanovich von **Maydel** (13 Mar 1834 - ?)
| | |
|---|---|
| 16 Mar 1892: | Promoted to *Major-General* |
| 16 Mar 1892 - Sep 1899: | Commander, 17th Artillery Brigade |

*Major-General* Baron Roman Karlovich von **Maydel** (5 Aug 1859 - 1931)
| | |
|---|---|
| ? - 1907: | Attached to Life Guards Semenov Regiment |
| 1907: | Promoted to *Major-General* |
| 1907: | Retired |

*Major-General* Baron Vladimir Nikolayevich von **Maydel** (1 Apr 1864 - ?)
| | |
|---|---|
| 5 Oct 1910: | Promoted to *Major-General* |
| 5 Oct 1910 - 9 Nov 1913: | Commandant, Tver Cavalry School |
| 9 Nov 1913 - 11 Oct 1914: | Commander, 2nd Brigade, 3rd Cavalry Division |
| 11 Oct 1914 - 5 Dec 1914: | Commander, 1st Independent Cavalry Brigade |
| 5 Dec 1914 - 21 Aug 1915: | Commander, 1st Cavalry Division |
| 21 Aug 1915 - 16 Oct 1916: | Reserve officer, Dvinsk Military District |
| 16 Oct 1916 - 1918: | At the disposal of the Chief of the General Staff |

*Major-General of the Fleet* Aleksandr Aleksandrovich **Mayer** (5 May 1858 - ?)
| | |
|---|---|
| 1 Sep 1914 - 1917: | Attached to 2nd Baltic Naval Depot |
| 1915: | Promoted to *Major-General of the Fleet* |

*General of Engineers* Leonty Leontyevich **Mayer** (13 Sep 1839 - 30 Jan 1910)
| | |
|---|---|
| 16 Dec 1886 - 8 Jan 1892: | Member, Administrative Commission on Defensive Structures |
| 5 Apr 1887: | Promoted to *Major-General* |
| 8 Jan 1892 - 20 Nov 1895: | Member of the Engineering Committee, Main Engineering Directorate |
| 20 Nov 1895: | Promoted to *Lieutenant-General* |
| 20 Nov 1895: | Retired |
| 9 Nov 1898 - 22 Mar 1905: | Recalled; Deputy Chief, Main Engineering Directorate |
| Nov 1904 - 22 Mar 1905: | Member, Main Artillery Committee |
| 22 Mar 1905 - 3 Jan 1906: | Member of the Military Council |
| 3 Jan 1906: | Promoted to *General of Engineers* |
| 3 Jan 1906: | Retired |

*Major-General* Vilgelm-Fridrikh Vilgelmovich **Mayer** (4 Dec 1842 - 7 Feb 1909)
| | |
|---|---|
| 23 Feb 1896 - 7 Feb 1909: | Commandant of Moscow Railway Station |
| 1908: | Promoted to *Major-General* |

*Major-General* Vladimir Teofilovich **Mayevsky** (1857 - ?)
23 Jun 1916 - 1917: Special Assignments General, Caucasus Army
9 Nov 1916: Promoted to *Major-General*

*Major-General* Ivan Ivanovich **Mazan** (11 Nov 1837 - ?)
31 May 1888 - 1897: Ataman, Yekaterinodar Division, Kuban Cossack Army
14 Apr 1895: Promoted to *Major-General*

*Major-General* Arkady Viktorovich **Mazaraki** (4 Jan 1863 - ?)
31 Jul 1910 - 2 Jul 1915: Commander, 9th Finnish Rifle Regiment
2 Jul 1915: Promoted to *Major-General*
2 Jul 1915 - 1917: Commander, Brigade, 3rd Finnish Rifle Division

*General of Artillery* Mikhail Karlovich **Mazing** (6 Nov 1836 - 7 May 1911)
5 Mar 1886: Promoted to *Major-General*
5 Mar 1886 - 3 Mar 1891: Chief of Artillery, Trans-Caspian Region
3 Mar 1891 - 27 Sep 1895: Commander, 3rd Artillery Brigade
27 Sep 1895 - 19 Dec 1901: Commander of Artillery, XIII. Army Corps
14 May 1896: Promoted to *Lieutenant-General*
19 Dec 1901 - 7 May 1911: Member, Committee for Wounded Veterans
6 Dec 1906: Promoted to *General of Artillery*

*Major-General of the Fleet* Georgy Nikolayevich **Mazurov** (18 May 1867 - 1918)
1914 - Mar 1915: Commander, 2nd Battalion, 2nd Naval Depot
19 Jan 1915: Promoted to *Major-General of the Fleet*
Mar 1915 - 11 Sep 1916: Commander, Naval Special Purposes Regiment
11 Sep 1916 - Oct 1917: Commander, Naval Special Purposes Brigade

*Major-General* Feliks Vikentyevich **Mazurovsky** (6 Aug 1854 - Jul 1915)
14 Sep 1906 - 1910: Commander, 11th Grenadier Regiment
1910: Promoted to *Major-General*
1910: Retired
2 May 1915 - Jul 1915: Recalled; Chief of Evacuation Points, Tambov District

*Major-General* Mikhail Nikitich **Mazyukevich** (29 Jan 1829 - ?)
28 Oct 1891: Promoted to *Major-General*
28 Oct 1891 - 28 Nov 1898: Commander, 2nd Brigade, 4th Infantry Division
28 Nov 1898 - 9 Oct 1899: Commander, 1st Brigade, 4th Infantry Division

*Major-General* Prince Zakhary Aslanovich **Mdivani** (5 Sep 1867 - 18 Apr 1933)
31 May 1912 - 7 Apr 1915: Commander, 13th Grenadier Regiment
18 Jan 1915: Promoted to *Major-General*
7 Apr 1915 - 18 Jul 1915: Attached to the C-in-C, Caucasus Army
18 Jul 1915 - 20 Mar 1917: Chief of Staff, IV. Caucasus Army Corps
20 Mar 1917 - 11 Aug 1917: Commander, 39th Infantry Division
11 Aug 1917 - Sep 1917: Acting Commanding General, Caucasus Military District

*Major-General* Yevgraf Ivanovich **Mechnikov** (21 Sep 1825 - ?)
12 Feb 1898 - 1902: Special Assignments General, Main Directorate for Army Remounts
5 Apr 1898: Promoted to *Major-General*

*Major-General* Georgy Georgyevich Duke of **Mecklenburg-Strelitsky** (25 May 1859 - 5 Dec 1909)
14 Dec 1902: Promoted to *Major-General*
14 Dec 1902 - 6 Nov 1906: Commander, Life Guards Dragoon Regiment
6 Nov 1906 - 12 Nov 1907: Commander, 1$^{st}$ Brigade, 1$^{st}$ Guards Cavalry Division
12 Nov 1907 - 5 Dec 1909: At the disposal of the Commanding General, St. Petersburg Military District

*Lieutenant-General* Mikhail Georgyevich Duke of **Mecklenburg-Strelitsky** (5 Jun 1863 - 6 Dec 1934)
3 Mar 1904: Promoted to *Major-General*
3 Mar 1904 - 2 Jul 1908: Commander, Life Guards 1$^{st}$ Artillery Brigade
2 Jul 1908: Promoted to *Lieutenant-General*
2 Jul 1908 - 23 Jan 1910: Commander of Artillery, I. Army Corps
23 Jan 1910 - 5 Aug 1914: At the disposal of the Minister of War
5 Aug 1914 - 27 Dec 1914: At the disposal of the Commanding General, Guards Corps
27 Dec 1914 - 29 Dec 1915: Inspector of Artillery, Guards Corps
1 Dec 1915: Promoted to *General-Adjutant*
29 Dec 1915 - 24 May 1916: At the disposal of the Commanding General, Guards Corps
24 May 1916 - 19 Aug 1916: Inspector of Guards Artillery
19 Aug 1916 - 2 Mar 1917: General à la suite
31 Mar 1917: Retired

*Lieutenant-General* Baron Georgy Petrovich von **Medem** (8 Mar 1849 - 19 Jan 1911)
26 Mar 1903: Promoted to *Major-General*
26 Mar 1903 - 16 Jul 1905: Deputy Chief of Staff of the Gendarmerie
16 Jul 1905 -7 Jan 1906: Mayor of Moscow
7 Jan 1906: Promoted to *Lieutenant-General*
7 Jan 1906 - 17 Sep 1906: Attached to the Independent Corps of Gendarmerie
17 Sep 1906 - 19 Jan 1911: At the disposal of the Ministry of Internal Affairs

*Lieutenant-General* Baron Nikolai Nikolayevich **Medem** (25 Jun 1834 - 7 Sep 1899)
24 Oct 1866 - 1 Jan 1892: Governor of Warsaw
21 Sep 1868: Promoted to *Major-General*
30 Aug 1881: Promoted to *Lieutenant-General*
1 Jan 1892 - 18 Mar 1895: Deputy Governor-General of Warsaw
18 Mar 1895 - 7 Sep 1899: Senator

*Major-General* Aleksandr Arnoldovich **Meder** (4 Jun 1867 - ?)
14 Dec 1914 - 17 Dec 1915: Commander, 22$^{nd}$ Infantry Regiment
24 May 1915: Promoted to *Major-General*

17 Dec 1915 - 15 Apr 1917: Commander, Brigade, 61st Infantry Division
15 Apr 1917 - 1918: Commander, 3rd Caucasus Rifle Division

*Lieutenant-General* Pyotr Vladimirovich **Meder** (16 Aug 1856 - 1919)
9 Jun 1907 - 1918: Commandant of Kiev
13 Apr 1908: Promoted to *Major-General*
6 Apr 1914: Promoted to *Lieutenant-General*

*Major-General* Vladimir Arnoldovich **Meder** (4 Sep 1873 - 7 Aug 1914)
6 Apr 1914 - 7 Aug 1914: Attached to 115th Infantry Regiment
13 Jul 1915: Posthumously promoted to *Major-General*

*General of Cavalry* Viktor Yulianovich **Medinsky** (3 Dec 1837 - 8 Aug 1908)
28 Jan 1881 - 9 Jan 1896: Deputy Military Governor of Fergana Region
15 May 1883: Promoted to *Major-General*
9 Jan 1896 - 17 Oct 1899: Deputy Military Governor of Samarkand
17 Oct 1899 - 12 Mar 1905: Military Governor of Samarkand
6 Dec 1900: Promoted to *Lieutenant-General*
12 Mar 1905: Promoted to *General of Cavalry*
12 Mar 1905: Retired

*Lieutenant-General* Aleksandr Ardalionovich **Medvedev** (30 Jan 1858 - 7 Dec 1915)
19 May 1898 - 12 Jul 1906: Inspector of Classes, Neplyuev Orenburg Cadet Corps
6 Dec 1905: Promoted to *Major-General*
12 Jul 1906 - 7 Dec 1915: Director, 1st Siberian Cadet Corps
6 Dec 1911: Promoted to *Major-General*

*Lieutenant-General* Aleksandr Ivanovich **Medvedev** (22 Jul 1853 - ?)
8 Oct 1911 - 30 Sep 1914: Professor, Nikolayev Imperial Military Academy
6 Dec 1911: Promoted to *Major-General*
30 Sep 1914 - Jul 1916: Chief of Staff, Dvinsk Military District
Jul 1916 - 29 Apr 1917: Deputy Chief of Logistics, Western Front
29 Apr 1917 - 1918: Professor, Nikolaev Military Academy
21 Nov 1917: Promoted to *Lieutenant-General*

*Lieutenant-General* Nikolai Aleksandrovich **Medvedev** (17 Aug 1854 - ?)
24 Feb 1902 - 30 Oct 1906: Commander, 29th Dragoon Regiment
3 Oct 1906: Promoted to *Major-General*
30 Oct 1906 - 4 Jul 1907: Commander, 2nd Brigade, 4th Cavalry Division
4 Jul 1907 - 28 Feb 1911: Attached to the Main Intendant Directorate
28 Feb 1911: Promoted to *Lieutenant-General*
28 Feb 1911: Retired

*Major-General* Nikolai Afanasyevich **Medzvetsky** (4 Feb 1868 - 10 Sep 1929)
27 Apr 1911 - 1917: Commandant, Military Topographical School
14 Apr 1913: Promoted to *Major-General*
31 May 1917 - 24 Nov 1917: Chief, Kiev Military Topographical Survey

*General of Artillery* Samed-Bek-Sadyk-Bek-ogly **Mekhmandarov** (16 Oct 1855 - 12 Feb 1931)
| | |
|---|---|
| 18 Feb 1904 - 12 Jun 1906: | Commander, 7th East Siberian Rifle Artillery Battalion |
| 13 Jul 1904: | Promoted to *Major-General* |
| 12 Jun 1906 - 15 Jul 1907: | Commander, 7th East Siberian Rifle Artillery Brigade |
| 15 Jul 1907 - 24 May 1910: | Commander of Artillery, III. Siberian Army Corps |
| 13 Jul 1908: | Promoted to *Lieutenant-General* |
| 24 May 1910 - 31 Jul 1910: | Commander of Artillery, I. Caucasus Army Corps |
| 31 Jul 1910 - 31 Dec 1913: | Inspector of Artillery, I. Caucasus Army Corps |
| 31 Dec 1913 - 11 Dec 1914: | Commander, 21st Infantry Division |
| 11 Dec 1914 - 18 Apr 1917: | Commanding General, II. Caucasus Army Corps |
| 22 Mar 1915: | Promoted to *General of Artillery* |
| 18 Apr 1917 - 7 Aug 1917: | Reserve officer, Minsk Military District |
| 7 Aug 1917 - Oct 1917: | Member, Committee for Wounded Veterans |

*Major-General* Karl Karlovich **Melan** (4 Sep 1839 - ?)
| | |
|---|---|
| 16 Aug 1880 - 29 Jul 1891: | Intendant-General, Finland Military Commissariat |
| 15 May 1883: | Promoted to *Major-General* |
| 29 Jul 1891 - 1894: | Senator, Imperial Finnish Senate, Commander of the Finnish Militia |

*Lieutenant-General* Mikhail Erastovich **Melgunov** (18 Oct 1869 - 24 Jan 1926)
| | |
|---|---|
| 28 Mar 1913 - Jan 1915: | Commander, 165th Infantry Regiment |
| 28 Oct 1914: | Promoted to *Major-General* |
| Jan 1915 - 15 Apr 1915: | Commander, Brigade, 42nd Infantry Division |
| 15 Apr 1915 - 18 Oct 1915: | Chief of Staff, XXXIII. Army Corps |
| 18 Oct 1915 - 27 Jan 1916: | At the disposal of the C-in-C, Southwestern Front |
| 27 Jan 1916 - 13 Mar 1917: | Special Assignments General, Southwestern Front |
| 13 Mar 1917 - 16 May 1917: | Commander, 1st Amur Border Infantry Division |
| 29 Apr 1917: | Promoted to *Lieutenant-General* |
| 16 May 1917 - 7 Aug 1917: | Commanding General, XLI. Army Corps |
| 7 Aug 1917 - 22 Oct 1917: | Unassigned |
| 22 Oct 1917 - 1917: | Chief of Staff, 8th Army |

*Major-General* Sergey Modestovich **Melgunov** (13 Dec 1868 - ?)
| | |
|---|---|
| 14 Jun 1916 - 1917: | Commandant of Odessa |
| 6 Dec 1916: | Promoted to *Major-General* |

*Major-General* Isaak Osipovich **Melik-Gaykazov** (18 Dec 1838 - ?)
| | |
|---|---|
| 23 Aug 1895: | Promoted to *Major-General* |
| 23 Aug 1895 - 13 Apr 1899: | Commander, 2nd East Siberian Artillery Brigade |

*Major-General* Nikolai Medzhlumovich **Melik-Shakh-Nazarov** (13 Apr 1851 - ?)
| | |
|---|---|
| 14 Nov 1906 - 1910: | Commander, 2nd Battalion, 21st Artillery Brigade |
| 1910: | Attached to staff of Caucasus Military District |
| 1910: | Promoted to *Major-General* |
| 1910: | Retired |
| 11 Mar 1915 - 1917: | Recalled; Reserve officer, Caucasus Military District |

*Major-General* Prince Nikolai Levanovich **Melikov** (12 Jan 1867 - 30 Oct 1924)
27 Mar 1915 - 5 Feb 1917: Commander, 20th (Finland) Dragoon Regiment
28 Aug 1916: Promoted to *Major-General*

*Major-General* Prince Petr Levanovich **Melikov** (21 Sep 1862 - 11 Jul 1934)
6 Dec 1909: Promoted to *Major-General*
6 Dec 1909 - 1917: Special Assignments General, Governor-General of Warsaw

*Major-General of the Admiralty* Aleksandr Petrovich **Meller** (16 Oct 1865 - ?)
12 Nov 1907 - 25 Oct 1912: Chief, Obukhov Factory
27 Feb 1908 - 25 Oct 1912: Member of the Artillery Committee, Main Artillery Directorate
6 Dec 1909: Promoted to *Major-General of the Admiralty*
25 Oct 1912: Retired

*Major-General* Konstantin Aleksandrovich **Meller** (20 Aug 1868 - 7 Feb 1949)
1915 - 17 Oct 1915: Commander, 12th Finnish Rifle Regiment
19 Jul 1915: Promoted to *Major-General*
17 Oct 1915 - 22 Apr 1917: Commander, Brigade, 14th Infantry Division
22 Apr 1917 - 1917: Reserve officer, Odessa Military District
1917: Commanding General, VIII. Army Corps

*General of Infantry* Baron Aleksandr Nikolayevich **Meller-Zakomelsky** (1 Nov 1844 - 15 Apr 1928)
8 Jun 1880 - 15 May 1883: At the disposal of the Governor-General of Odessa
15 May 1883 - 10 May 1889: Transferred to the reserve
1883: Promoted to *Major-General*
10 May 1889 - 12 Feb 1890: Commander, 2nd Brigade, 17th Infantry Division
12 Feb 1890 - Jan 1894: Commander, 2nd Brigade, 10th Infantry Division
Jan 1894 - 10 Jun 1898: Commander, 47th Replacement Infantry Brigade
10 Jun 1898 - 16 Jun 1901: Commander, 10th Infantry Division
6 Dec 1898: Promoted to *Lieutenant-General*
16 Jun 1901 - 10 Feb 1904: Commander, 3rd Guards Infantry Division
10 Feb 1904 - 5 Jul 1906: Commanding General, VII. Army Corps
5 Jul 1906 - 28 Aug 1906: At the disposal of the Minister of War
28 Aug 1906 - 17 Oct 1906: Commanding General, V. Army Corps
17 Oct 1906 - 12 Jul 1909: Governor-General of the Baltic Region
6 Dec 1906: Promoted to *General of Infantry*
12 Jul 1909 - 1917: Member of the State Council
Feb 1915 - 1917: Inspector of Medical Institutions, Petrograd
1917: Retired

*Major-General* Baron Sergey Nikolayevich **Meller-Zakomelsky** (5 Oct 1848 - 19 Dec 1899)
21 Dec 1893: Promoted to *Major-General*
21 Dec 1893 - 11 Aug 1899: Commander, 2nd Brigade, 35th Infantry Division
11 Aug 1899 - 19 Dec 1899: Commander, 60th Reserve Infantry Brigade

*Major-General* Dmitry Antonovich **Melnikov** (26 Oct 1871 - ?)
27 Oct 1916 - 29 Jan 1918:    Chief of Staff, 49th Infantry Division
6 Dec 1916:                   Promoted to *Major-General*

*Major-General* Iliodor Ivanovich **Melnikov** (13 Nov 1866 - 25 Feb 1927)
23 Jul 1912 - 14 Mar 1916:    Commander, 204th Infantry Regiment
21 May 1915:                  Promoted to *Major-General*
14 Mar 1916 - 1917:           Commander, 14th Replacement Infantry Brigade

*Lieutenant-General* Pyotr Ivanovich **Melnikov** (23 Sep 1855 - Oct 1913)
15 Jan 1909:                  Promoted to *Major-General*
15 Jan 1909 - 19 Jan 1912:    Commander, 2nd Brigade, 38th Infantry Division
19 Jan 1912 - Oct 1913:       Commander, 6th Turkestan Rifle Brigade
1913:                         Promoted to *Lieutenant-General*

*Major-General* Konstantin Yevgenyevich **Melnitsky** (7 Mar 1848 - ?)
28 Mar 1895 - 1903:           Military Judge, Kazan Military District Court
6 Dec 1897:                   Promoted to *Major-General*

*Major-General* Pyotr Dmitriyevich **Melnitsky** (14 Jun 1852 - 22 Dec 1912)
21 Nov 1907:                  Promoted to *Major-General*
21 Nov 1907 - 15 Apr 1910:    Commander, 25th Artillery Brigade
15 Apr 1910:                  Retired

*Major-General* Yury Dmitriyevich **Melnitsky** (23 Sep 1853 - 1899)
5 Jul 1893:                   Promoted to *Major-General*
5 Jul 1893 - 6 Mar 1897:      Duty General, Vilnius Military District
6 Mar 1897 - 1899:            Chief of Staff, XVII. Army Corps

*Lieutenant-General* Aleksey Seliverstovich **Melyanin** (28 Jan 1845 - ?)
3 Nov 1890 - 14 Sep 1900:     Ataman, 1st Military Division, Orenburg Cossack Army
6 May 1894:                   Promoted to *Major-General*
14 Sep 1900 - 13 Oct 1904:    Commander, 1st Brigade, 1st Turkestan Cossack Division
13 Oct 1904 - Oct 1906:       Commander, 2nd Consolidated Cossack Division
6 Dec 1904:                   Promoted to *Lieutenant-General*

*Lieutenant-General* Aleksandr Aleksandrovich **Menchukov** (22 Apr 1852 - ?)
25 May 1905:                  Promoted to *Major-General*
25 May 1905 - 10 Mar 1912:    Commander, 1st Brigade, 23rd Infantry Division
10 Mar 1912:                  Promoted to *Lieutenant-General*
10 Mar 1912:                  Retired

*Major-General* Gennady Konstantinovich **Mende** (26 Dec 1863 - ?)
27 May 1909 - 1913:           Commander, 17th Siberian Rifle Regiment
1913:                         Promoted to *Major-General*

*Major-General* Mikhail Konstantinovich **Mende** (16 Aug 1861 - ?)
26 Jun 1908 - 10 Mar 1916:    Section Chief, Main Military Justice Directorate

14 Apr 1913: Promoted to *Major-General*
10 Mar 1916 - 1917: Military Judge, Petrograd Military District Court

*Lieutenant-General* Eduard Eduardovich **Mendt** (7 Dec 1844 - 7 Feb 1908)
26 Feb 1894: Promoted to *Major-General*
26 Feb 1894 - 30 Jan 1901: Commander, 1st Brigade, 18th Infantry Division
30 Jan 1901: Promoted to *Lieutenant-General*
30 Jan 1901: Retired

*Lieutenant-General* Count Georgy Fyodorovich **Mengden** (26 Dec 1836 - 8 Nov 1902)
21 Jan 1876: Promoted to *Major-General*
21 Jan 1876 - 28 Jan 1883: Commander, 2nd Brigade, 1st Guards Cavalry Division
28 Jan 1883 - 16 Mar 1886: General á la suite
16 Mar 1886 - 27 Jul 1891: Commander, 1st Brigade, 2nd Guards Cavalry Division
27 Jul 1891 - 20 Mar 1895: Commander, 14th Cavalry Division
30 Aug 1891: Promoted to *Lieutenant-General*
20 Mar 1895 - 8 Nov 1902: At the disposal of the Minister of War

*Lieutenant-General* Count Georgy Georgyevich **Mengden** (10 Oct 1861 - 1 Mar 1917)
18 Apr 1905 - 20 Nov 1908: Chief of Household, Grand Duchess Yelizaveta Fyodorovna
6 May 1908: Promoted to *Major-General*
20 Nov 1908 - 1 Jan 1912: Commander, Guards Cavalry Regiment
22 Apr 1910 - 30 Apr 1910: Acting Commander, 1st Brigade, 1st Guards Cavalry Division
1 Jan 1912 - 14 Nov 1912: General à la suite
14 Nov 1912 - 11 Oct 1914: Commander, 2nd Brigade, 2nd Guards Cavalry Division
11 Oct 1914 - 1 Mar 1917: At the disposal of the C-in-C, Western Front
6 Dec 1916: Promoted to *Lieutenant-General*

*Major-General* Iosif Boleslavovich-Ivanovich **Menitsky** (9 Jul 1864 - 1934)
14 Dec 1914: Promoted to *Major-General*
14 Dec 1914 - 11 Mar 1917: Chief of Staff, IV. Army Corps
11 Mar 1917 - 7 Jul 1917: Commander, 163rd Infantry Division
7 Jul 1917 - 16 Nov 1917: Commander, 3rd Rifle Division
16 Nov 1917 - 1918: Commanding General, IV. Army Corps

*Lieutenant-General* Dmitry Petrovich **Menshov** (17 Nov 1855 - 4 Jan 1918)
7 Oct 1908 - 17 Jun 1915: Commandant, Kiev Artillery Depot
6 Dec 1908: Promoted to *Major-General*
17 Jun 1915 - 1917: Deputy Chief of Artillery Logistics, Southwestern Front
6 Dec 1916: Promoted to *Lieutenant-General*

*Lieutenant-General* Dmitry Vasiliyevich **Merchansky** (24 Oct 1833 - ?)
8 May 1874 - 1905: Special Purposes Officer to the Governor-General of Moscow
6 May 1884: Promoted to *Major-General*
6 Dec 1897: Promoted to *Lieutenant-General*

*Major-General* Nikolai Ivanovich **Merchansky** (13 May 1845 - ?)
16 Jun 1906:                          Promoted to *Major-General*
16 Jun 1906 - 1907:                   At the disposal of the Chief of the General Staff

*Major-General* Aleksandr Petrovich **Merder** (20 Jul 1859 - ?)
10 Feb 1907 - 1908:                   Staff Officer (5th Class), Intendant-General
22 Apr 1907:                          Promoted to *Major-General*

*General of Cavalry* Pyotr Karlovich **Merder** (13 Apr 1819 - 6 Dec 1894)
31 Dec 1859 - 13 Nov 1860:            Inspector, Central Horse Breeding District
17 Apr 1860:                          Promoted to *Major-General*
13 Nov 1860 - 20 Apr 1869:            Inspector, 1st Horse Breeding District
16 Apr 1866:                          Promoted to *General-Adjutant*
28 Oct 1866:                          Promoted to *Lieutenant-General*
20 Apr 1869 - 30 Jul 1881:            Council Member, Main Directorate for Horse Breeding
16 Apr 1878:                          Promoted to *General of Cavalry*
30 Jul 1881 - 6 Dec 1894:             General à la suite

*Major-General* Dmitry Aleksandrovich **Merkazin** (1849 - 24 Apr 1900)
1894 - 15 Feb 1900:                   Commander, 121st Infantry Regiment
15 Feb 1900:                          Promoted to *Major-General*
15 Feb 1900 - 24 Apr 1900:            Commander, 1st Brigade, 19th Infantry Division

*Lieutenant-General* Vladimir Dmitriyevich **Merkazin** (27 Jun 1834 - 25 Jun 1903)
15 Dec 1887 - 20 Jun 1893:            Ataman, 3rd Military Division, Transbaikal Cossack
                                      Army
6 May 1888:                           Promoted to *Major-General*
20 Jun 1893 - 20 Nov 1894:            Military Commander of Sakhalin
20 Nov 1894 - May 1898:               Military Governor of Sakhalin,
                                      Commander, Sakhalin Regional Forces
May 1898:                             Promoted to *Lieutenant-General*
May 1898:                             Retired

*General of Cavalry* Nikolai Ivanovich **Merkling** (6 Oct 1838 - 18 Apr 1907)
10 Dec 1886:                          Promoted to *Major-General*
10 Dec 1886 - 17 Dec 1896:            Commander, 2nd Brigade, 9th Cavalry Division
17 Dec 1896 - 19 Dec 1901:            Commander, 1st Replacement Cavalry Brigade
6 Dec 1900:                           Promoted to *Lieutenant-General*
19 Dec 1901 - 1903:                   At the disposal of the Commanding General, Kazan
                                      Military District
1903:                                 Promoted to *General of Cavalry*
1903:                                 Retired

*Lieutenant-General* Innokenty Stepanovich **Merkushev** (14 Dec 1846 - ?)
22 Jul 1904 - 18 Sep 1907:            General for Special Assignments, Turkestan Military
                                      District
1905:                                 Promoted to *Major-General*
18 Sep 1907 - 19 May 1910:            Commandant of Fortress Kushkinsk

19 May 1910: Promoted to *Lieutenant-General*
19 May 1910: Retired

*Major-General* Mikhail Ivanovich **Merro** (26 Sep 1863 - ?)
17 Sep 1901 - 23 Aug 1913: Inspector of Classes, Tver Cavalry School
6 Dec 1912: Promoted to *Major-General*
23 Aug 1913 - 12 Jul 1915: Director, Simbirsk Cadet Corps
12 Jul 1915 - 7 Feb 1917: Commander, Brigade, 75th Infantry Division
7 Feb 1917 - 1918: Commander, 172nd Infantry Division

*Major-General* Baron Ivan Vladimirovich von **Mersheydt-Gillessem** (26 Sep 1861 - ?)
23 Mar 1909 - 19 Aug 1915: Commandant, Tiflis Artillery Arsenal
6 Dec 1911: Promoted to *Major-General*
19 Aug 1915 - 1917: Chairman, Commission for the Construction of a Pipe Plant

*Major-General* Konstantin Aleksandrovich **Mertsedin** (16 May 1855 - ?)
22 May 1910: Promoted to *Major-General*
22 May 1910 - 7 Sep 1910: Commander, Brigade, 65th Infantry Division
7 Sep 1910 - 4 Nov 1911: Commander, 1st Brigade, 51st Infantry Division
4 Nov 1911 - 6 Mar 1913: Commander, 1st Brigade, 19th Infantry Division

*General of Infantry* Grigory Vasilyevich **Meshcherinov** (22 Jan 1827 - 26 Aug 1901)
8 Sep 1856 - 20 Dec 1862: Chief of Staff, V. Army Corps
23 Apr 1861: Promoted to *Major-General*
20 Dec 1862 - 1 Jan 1866: Deputy Department Director, General Staff
1 Jan 1866 - 19 Feb 1881: Deputy Chief of the General Staff
20 May 1868: Promoted to *Lieutenant-General*
26 Dec 1876: Promoted to *General-Adjutant*
19 Feb 1881 - 25 May 1882: Commanding General, West Siberian Military District, Governor-General of Western Siberia, Ataman, Siberian Cossack Army
25 May 1882 - 26 Aug 1901: Commanding General, Kazan Military District
15 May 1883: Promoted to *General of Infantry*

*Major-General* Pavel Grigoryevich **Meshcherinov** (6 Sep 1867 - ?)
1 Sep 1915: Promoted to *Major-General*
1 Sep 1915 - 26 May 1917: Commander, 8th Siberian Rifle Artillery Brigade
26 May 1917 - 1918: Inspector of Artillery, XLII. Army Corps

*General of Infantry* Nikolai Fyodorovich **Meshetich** (2 May 1850 - 1910)
17 Mar 1891 - 14 Aug 1895: Commander, 2nd Life Guards Rifle Battalion
30 Aug 1891: Promoted to *Major-General*
14 Aug 1895 - 6 Sep 1899: Commander, Finland Life Guards Regiment
6 Sep 1899 - 20 Oct 1900: Chief of Staff, Guards Corps
20 Oct 1900: Promoted to *Lieutenant-General*
20 Oct 1900 - 7 Jun 1904: Commander, 2nd Guards Infantry Division
7 Jun 1904 - 26 Oct 1905: Chief of Staff of the Guards,

| | Chief of Staff, St. Petersburg Military District |
|---|---|
| 26 Oct 1905 - 18 Mar 1906: | At the disposal of the Commanding General, St. Petersburg Military District |
| 18 Mar 1906 - 21 May 1908: | Commanding General, XII. Army Corps |
| 13 Apr 1908: | Promoted to *General of Infantry* |
| 21 May 1908 - 21 Dec 1908: | Commanding General, XVI. Army Corps |
| 24 Dec 1908 - 1910: | Honorary Trustee, Board of Trustees of Empress Maria Institutions |

*Major-General* Dmitry Vasilyevich **Messarosh** (10 Feb 1836 - ?)
| 12 Jun 1891: | Promoted to *Major-General* |
|---|---|
| 12 Jun 1891 - Oct 1899: | Commander, 2$^{nd}$ Brigade, 32$^{nd}$ Infantry Division |

*Vice-Admiral* Vladimir Pavlovich **Messer** (21 Dec 1840 - 1904)
| 1892: | Promoted to *Rear-Admiral* |
|---|---|
| 1894 - 1895: | Detachment Commander, Naval Cadet Corps |
| 1896 - 1897: | Detachment Commander, Baltic Sea |
| 1898: | Promoted to *Vice-Admiral* |
| 1899 - Dec 1901: | Commander, Baltic Training Squadron |
| Dec 1901 - 1904: | Member, Main Naval Tribunal |

*Major-General* Aleksandr Yakovlevich **Messner** (8 Feb 1874 - 9 Dec 1919)
| 6 Mar 1915 - 21 Jul 1916: | Commander, 8$^{th}$ Grenadier Regiment |
|---|---|
| 21 Jul 1916 - 21 Aug 1916: | Chief of Staff, 45$^{th}$ Infantry Division |
| 21 Aug 1916 - 20 Dec 1916: | Deputy Chief of Communications, Caucasus Army |
| 8 Oct 1916: | Promoted to *Major-General* |
| 20 Dec 1916 - 21 Mar 1917: | Deputy Chief of Communications, Romanian Front |
| 21 Mar 1917 - 1918: | Chief of Communications, Western Front |

*Lieutenant-General* Fyodor Fyodorovich **Mets** (24 Jan 1842 - ?)
| 1 Mar 1902 - 1912: | Chief of the Moscow-Brest Railway |
|---|---|
| 6 Dec 1904: | Promoted to *Major-General* |
| 1912: | Promoted to *Lieutenant-General* |
| 1912: | Retired |

*General of Infantry* Mikhail Troyanovich von **Meves** (19 Dec 1835 - 12 Mar 1905)
| 2 Oct 1873 - 1 Jun 1878: | Commander, 66$^{th}$ Infantry Regiment |
|---|---|
| 14 Jan 1878: | Promoted to *Major-General* |
| 1 Jun 1878 - 19 Jun 1886: | Chief of Staff, XIV. Army Corps |
| 19 Jun 1886 - 18 Jan 1895: | Commander, 15$^{th}$ Regional Brigade |
| 30 Aug 1888: | Promoted to *Lieutenant-General* |
| 18 Jan 1895 - 3 Jun 1898: | Commander, 3$^{rd}$ Grenadier Division |
| 3 Jun 1898 - 25 Jan 1900: | At the disposal of the Minister of War |
| 25 Jan 1900 - 1 Jan 1903: | Member, Committee for Troop Mobilization |
| 1 Jan 1903 - 12 Mar 1905: | Member of the Military Council |
| 6 Apr 1903: | Promoted to *General of Infantry* |

*Lieutenant-General* Richard Troyanovich von **Meves** (3 Mar 1839 - 1901)
| | |
|---|---|
| 18 May 1884 - 10 Jan 1894: | Commander, Life Guards Pavlovsky Regiment |
| 30 Aug 1884: | Promoted to *Major-General* |
| 30 Mar 1893 - 10 Jan 1894: | Commander, 2nd Brigade, 2nd Guards Infantry Division |
| 10 Jan 1894 - 15 Jan 1897: | Commander, 23rd Infantry Division |
| 30 Aug 1894: | Promoted to *Lieutenant-General* |
| 15 Jan 1897 - 4 Aug 1899: | Commander, 2nd Guards Infantry Division |
| 4 Aug 1899 - 22 Feb 1901: | Commanding General, XX. Army Corps |

*Lieutenant-General* Georgy Konstantinovich **Meybaum** (9 Aug 1850 - ?)
| | |
|---|---|
| 29 Dec 1899 - 14 Oct 1903: | Commander, 24th Artillery Brigade |
| 9 Apr 1900: | Promoted to *Major-General* |
| 14 Oct 1903 - 27 May 1907: | Commander of Artillery, VI. Army Corps |
| 6 Dec 1906: | Promoted to *Lieutenant-General* |

*Lieutenant-General* Baron Aleksandr Yegorovich **Meyendorf** (27 Aug 1848 - 18 Feb 1907)
| | |
|---|---|
| 6 May 1893 - 12 Jun 1906: | Commander of the Tsar's Escort |
| 1 Apr 1901: | Promoted to *Major-General* |
| 12 Jun 1906: | Promoted to *Lieutenant-General* |
| 12 Jun 1906: | Promoted to *General-Adjutant* |
| 12 Jun 1906 - 18 Feb 1907: | Member of the Tsar's retinue |

*General of Cavalry* Baron Feofil Yegorovich **Meyendorf** (4 Aug 1838 - 18 Oct 1919)
| | |
|---|---|
| 6 Nov 1874 - 18 Dec 1877: | Commander, Life Guards Hussar Regiment |
| 12 Oct 1877: | Promoted to *Major-General* |
| 18 Dec 1877 - 6 May 1884: | General à la suite |
| 8 Jul 1883 - 11 Jul 1883: | Acting Commander, 2nd Brigade, 2nd Guards Cavalry Division |
| 20 Aug 1883 - 30 Aug 1883: | Acting Commander, 2nd Brigade, 2nd Guards Cavalry Division |
| 13 Sep 1883 - 29 Sep 1883: | Acting Commander, 2nd Brigade, 2nd Guards Cavalry Division |
| 6 May 1884 - 19 Apr 1892: | Commander, 2nd Cavalry Division |
| 30 Aug 1886: | Promoted to *Lieutenant-General* |
| 19 Apr 1892 - 14 Jun 1896: | Special Assignments General, St. Petersburg Military District |
| 14 Jun 1896 - 19 Dec 1905: | Commanding General, I. Army Corps |
| 6 Dec 1898: | Promoted to *General of Cavalry* |
| 1902: | Promoted to *General-Adjutant* |
| 19 Dec 1905 - Mar 1917: | General à la suite |

*Lieutenant-General* Baron Fyodor Yegorovich **Meyendorf** (3 Sep 1842 - 4 Oct 1911)
| | |
|---|---|
| 9 Apr 1895 - 6 May 1898: | Chief of Chancellery, Imperial Main Quarters |
| 14 May 1896: | Promoted to *Major-General* |
| 6 May 1898 - 2 Aug 1902: | Commandant, Imperial Main Quarters |
| 2 Aug 1902 - 4 Oct 1911: | Trustee, St. Petersburg Board of the Empress Maria Institutions |
| 17 Apr 1905: | Promoted to *Lieutenant-General* |

*General of Cavalry* Baron Nikolai Yegorovich **Meyendorf** (11 Jun 1835 - 12 Jan 1906)
17 Oct 1877: Promoted to *Major-General*
17 Oct 1877 - 10 Aug 1885: Commander, 1st Brigade, 4th Cavalry Division
10 Aug 1885 - 24 Nov 1886: Commander, 2nd Brigade, 9th Cavalry Division
24 Nov 1886 - 25 Apr 1897: Commander, 13th Cavalry Division
30 Aug 1887: Promoted to *Lieutenant-General*
25 Apr 1897 - 6 Jan 1902: At the disposal of the Minister of War
6 Jan 1902: Promoted to *General of Cavalry*
6 Jan 1902: Retired

*Major-General* Eduard Eduardovich **Meyer** (7 Oct 1838 - ?)
1 Jan 1900 - 1906: Special Assignments General, Main Horsebreeding Directorate
9 Apr 1900: Promoted to *Major-General*

*Major-General* Georgy Yakovlevich **Meyer** (4 Feb 1850 - 7 Mar 1905)
3 Jun 1903: Promoted to *Major-General*
3 Jun 1903 - 7 Mar 1905: Commander, 1st Brigade, 3rd Grenadier Division

*General of Infantry* Lev Lavrentyevich **Meyer** (1 Dec 1831 - 1903)
17 Nov 1876 - 27 Sep 1881: Deputy Chief of Staff, Orenburg Military District
1 Jan 1878: Promoted to *Major-General*
27 Sep 1881 - 13 Jan 1883: Attending Nikolayev General Staff Academy
13 Jan 1883 - 26 Jan 1885: Chief of Staff, Transcaspian Military Region
26 Jan 1885 - 14 Oct 1890: Chief of Staff, V. Army Corps
30 Aug 1890: Promoted to *Lieutenant-General*
14 Oct 1890 - 1901: Special Assignments General, Warsaw Military District
1901: Promoted to *General of Infantry*
1901: Retired

*Lieutenant-General* Pyotr Petrovich **Meyer** (10 Oct 1860 - 4 Dec 1925)
9 May 1905 - 15 Aug 1916: Chief of Police, Warsaw
6 Dec 1909: Promoted to *Major-General*
15 Aug 1916 - 11 Jul 1917: Mayor of Rostov-on-Don
11 Jul 1917: Promoted to *Lieutenant-General*
11 Jul 1917: Retired

*Major-General* Nikolai Adolfovich **Meynander** (28 Dec 1833 - ?)
2 May 1890: Promoted to *Major-General*
2 May 1890 - 12 Oct 1890: Commander, 15th Artillery Brigade
12 Oct 1890 - 1 Oct 1897: Commander, 27th Artillery Brigade
1 Oct 1897 - 1 Jan 1898: Commander, 46th Artillery Brigade
1 Jan 1898 - 2 Mar 1899: Commander, 43rd Artillery Brigade

*Major-General* Valter Valterovich **Meynard** (8 Apr 1860 - 1918)
20 May 1905: Promoted to *Major-General*
20 May 1905 - 20 Apr 1906: Commander, 2nd Brigade, 4th Cavalry Division
20 Apr 1906 - 1 Nov 1906: Commandant, Officers Cavalry School

1 Nov 1906: Retired

*Lieutenant-General* Viktor Polidorovich **Meyshtovich** (31 Jan 1847 - ?)
2 Apr 1904 - 23 Jan 1906: Deputy Intendant, Moscow Military District
6 Dec 1904: Promoted to *Major-General*
23 Jan 1906 - 4 Oct 1908: Intendant, Kazan Military District
4 Oct 1908 - 25 Mar 1910: Intendant, Omsk Military District
25 Mar 1910: Promoted to *Lieutenant-General*
25 Mar 1910: Retired

*Lieutenant-General* Viktor Voldemarovich **Meysner** (15 Nov 1859 - 2 Sep 1928)
26 Jul 1910: Promoted to *Major-General*
26 Jul 1910 - 31 Mar 1915: Commander, 35th Artillery Brigade
31 Mar 1915 - 14 Nov 1916: Inspector of Artillery, XXXIII. Army Corps
26 Apr 1915: Promoted to *Lieutenant-General*
14 Nov 1916 - 24 May 1917: Reserve officer, Petrograd Military District
24 May 1917: Dismissed

*Major-General* Yevgeny-Frants-Karl Vladimirovich **Meysner** (26 Nov 1852 - ?)
25 Sep 1901: Promoted to *Major-General*
25 Sep 1901 - May 1904: Commander, Railway Brigade

*Lieutenant-General* Aleksandr Reyngoldovich **Meyster** (2 Nov 1857 - ?)
18 Feb 1904 - 25 May 1905: Commander, 6th East Siberian Artillery Brigade
25 May 1905 - 14 Jan 1906: At the disposal of the Main Artillery Directorate
14 Jan 1906 - 16 Oct 1906: Commander, 3rd Grenadier Artillery Brigade
16 Oct 1906 - 4 Jul 1907: Unassigned
4 Jul 1907: Promoted to *Major-General*
4 Jul 1907 - 16 Feb 1911: Available for general assignment
16 Feb 1911 - 6 Jan 1913: Commander, 45th Artillery Brigade
6 Jan 1913 - 14 Feb 1915: Inspector of Artillery, VI. Army Corps
4 Jul 1913: Promoted to *Lieutenant-General*
14 Feb 1915 - 10 Jun 1917: Reserve officer, Dvinsk Military District
10 Jun 1917: Dismissed

*Major-General* Aleksandr Vladimirovich **Mezentsov** (14 Mar 1863 - ?)
1915 - 1917: Chief of Gendarmerie, Poltava Province
6 Dec 1916: Promoted to *Major-General*

*Major-General* Mikhail Ivanovich **Mezentsov** (6 Sep 1849 - ?)
25 Mar 1904: Promoted to *Major-General*
25 Mar 1904 - 14 Apr 1906: Commander, 2nd Brigade, 6th Cavalry Division
14 Apr 1906 - 29 May 1910: Commander, 3rd Independent Cavalry Brigade

*Major-General* Mikhail Petrovich **Mezentsov** (4 Mar 1860 - ?)
2 Oct 1900 - 20 Mar 1903: Chief of Staff, 1st Guards Infantry Division
20 Mar 1903: Promoted to *Major-General*
20 Mar 1903 - 1 May 1903: At the disposal of the Chief of the General Staff

1 May 1903 - 1904: Section Chief, General Staff

*General of Infantry* Pyotr Ivanovich **Mezentsov** (24 Aug 1824 - 15 Dec 1897)
1 May 1864 - 29 Dec 1871: Director, 2nd Moscow Cadet Corps
27 Mar 1866: Promoted to *Major-General*
29 Dec 1871 - 15 Feb 1878: Director, Corps of Pages
1 Jan 1878: Promoted to *Lieutenant-General*
15 Feb 1878 - 15 Dec 1897: Member, Military Education Committee, General Staff
30 Aug 1892: Promoted to *General of Infantry*

*Major-General* Sergey Nikolayevich **Mezentsov** (26 Dec 1847 - 21 May 1911)
30 Apr 1890 - 5 Mar 1893: Chief of Staff, South Ussuri Sector
30 Aug 1891: Promoted to *Major-General*
5 Mar 1893 - 1896: Chief of Staff, Independent Corps of Gendarmerie
1896: Resigned

*Major-General* Sergey Petrovich **Mezentsov** (8 Jan 1866 - 22 Oct 1937)
6 Dec 1907: Promoted to *Major-General*
6 Dec 1907 - 3 Jan 1910: At the disposal of the Master-General of Ordnance
3 Jan 1910 - 1917: General à la suite

*Major-General* Vladimir Petrovich **Mezentsov** (4 Mar 1858 - ?)
14 Oct 1903: Promoted to *Major-General*
14 Oct 1903 - 4 Jun 1904: Commander, 4th Reserve Artillery Brigade
4 Jun 1904 - 30 Sep 1904: Commander, 68th Artillery Brigade
30 Sep 1904 - 27 Jun 1906: Commander, 58th Artillery Brigade
27 Jun 1906 - 21 Nov 1907: Commander, 1st Artillery Brigade
21 Nov 1907: Retired
1915 - 1917: Recalled; Chief, 40th Logistical Evacuation Point

*Major-General* Pyotr Kasparovich **Mezhak** (18 Feb 1858 - 5 Sep 1941)
2 Apr 1910 - Dec 1915: Commander, 2nd Infantry Regiment
6 Jul 1915: Promoted to *Major-General*
Dec 1915- Feb 1916: Commander, 2nd Amur Borderguard Infantry Regiment
Feb 1916 - 24 Oct 1917: Commander, 1st Brigade, 1st Amur Borderguard Infantry Division
24 Oct 1917: Dismissed

*Lieutenant-General* Avessalom-Avel Ivanovich **Mgebrov** (20 Dec 1845 - ?)
5 Aug 1903 - 20 Feb 1914: Chief of Communications Sub-Section, General Staff
6 Dec 1903: Promoted to *Major-General*
20 Feb 1914 - 1917: Special Assignments General, Main Military-Technical Directorate
6 Apr 1914: Promoted to *Lieutenant-General*

*Lieutenant-General* Prince Aleksandr Platonovich **Mikeladze** (15 Oct 1867 - 20 Jan 1928)
12 May 1911 - 10 Jul 1915: Commander of Gendarmerie, Radom
6 Dec 1912: Promoted to *Major-General*

10 Jul 1915: Promoted to *Lieutenant-General*
10 Jul 1915: Retired

*Lieutenant-General* Prince Almaskhan Otiyevich **Mikeladze** (15 Oct 1834 - 20 Jan 1915)
6 May 1890: Promoted to *Major-General*
6 May 1890 - 30 Jun 1893: Attached to Caucasus Military District
30 Jun 1893 - 20 Jul 1895: Commander, 2nd Brigade, 40th Infantry Division
20 Jul 1895: Promoted to *Lieutenant-General*
20 Jul 1895: Retired

*Major-General* Prince Dmitry Otiyevich **Mikeladze** (26 Oct 1837 - 13 Jan 1910)
16 Mar 1906: Promoted to *Major-General*
16 Mar 1906 - 1908: Commandant of Fortress Abbas-Tuman
1908: Retired

*Major-General* Prince Konstantin Almkhaspovich **Mikeladze** (15 Oct 1866 - 1914)
3 Sep 1914 - 1914: Commander, 11th Caucasus Rifle Regiment
1914: Promoted to *Major-General*

*Major-General* Prince Vyacheslav Artemyevich **Mikeladze** (8 Mar 1875 - 1951)
8 Feb 1916 - 1917: Commander, 2nd Rifle Artillery Brigade
8 Oct 1916: Promoted to *Major-General*
1917 - 1918: Inspector of Artillery, XL. Army Corps

*Major-General* Nikolai Ivanovich **Mikhael** (14 Nov 1842 - ?)
24 Oct 1899: Promoted to *Major-General*
24 Oct 1899 - 22 Nov 1902: Commander, 2nd Brigade, 41st Infantry Division

*Major-General* Ivan Andreyevich **Mikhaelis** (11 May 1874 - 24 Jan 1917)
1915 - 19 Nov 1915: Commander, 15th Siberian Rifle Regiment
21 May 1915: Promoted to *Major-General*
19 Nov 1915 - 22 Dec 1915: Commander, Brigade, 108th Infantry Division
22 Dec 1915 - 3 Apr 1916: Chief of Staff, 121st Infantry Division
3 Apr 1916 - 18 Sep 1916: Chief of Staff, 115th Infantry Division
18 Sep 1916 - 24 Jan 1917: Chief of Staff, XXXV. Army Corps

*Major-General* Aleksandr Arkadyevich **Mikhailov** (10 Mar 1867 - 27 Sep 1915)
12 Oct 1905 - 10 Oct 1914: Senior Clerk, Artillery Committee, Main Artillery Directorate
14 Apr 1913: Promoted to *Major-General*
10 Oct 1914 - 26 Mar 1915: Clerk, Technical Department, Main Artillery Directorate
26 Mar 1915 - 27 Sep 1915: Member of the Artillery Committee, Main Artillery Directorate

*Major-General* Aleksandr Nikolayevich **Mikhailov** (28 Jul 1858 - 1917)
16 Aug 1914 - 1917: Commander, 300th Infantry Regiment
16 Jan 1917: Promoted to *Major-General*

*Major-General* Aleksandr Pavlovich **Mikhailov** (23 Aug 1868 - ?)
| | |
|---|---|
| 31 Dec 1913 - 3 Aug 1917: | Commandant, Khabarovsk Arsenal |
| 6 Apr 1914: | Promoted to *Major-General* |
| 3 Aug 1917 - 1918: | Commandant, Kiev Arsenal |

*Lieutenant-General* Dmitry Ivanovich **Mikhailov** (14 Mar 1831 - ?)
| | |
|---|---|
| 30 Aug 1885: | Promoted to *Major-General* |
| 30 Aug 1885 - 4 Nov 1894: | Commander, 11$^{th}$ Artillery Brigade |
| 4 Nov 1894 - 5 Dec 1899: | Commander of Artillery, XIX. Army Corps |
| 14 Nov 1894: | Promoted to *Lieutenant-General* |

*Major-General* Dmitry Mikhailovich **Mikhailov** (20 Oct 1872 - 9 Nov 1939)
| | |
|---|---|
| 28 Jan 1916 - 1 May 1917: | Chief of Staff, 108$^{th}$ Infantry Division |
| 6 Dec 1916: | Promoted to *Major-General* |
| 1 May 1917 - Nov 1917: | Chief of Staff, XLI. Army Corps |

*Major-General* Fyodor Nikolayevich **Mikhailov** (14 Sep 1858 - ?)
| | |
|---|---|
| 26 Oct 1907 - 19 Nov 1913: | Commander, 2$^{nd}$ Orenburg Cossack Regiment |
| 19 Nov 1913: | Promoted to *Major-General* |
| 19 Nov 1913 - 31 Jan 1915: | Commander, 2$^{nd}$ Brigade, 5$^{th}$ Cavalry Division |
| 31 Jan 1915 - 29 Aug 1915: | Reserve officer, Dvinsk Military District |
| 29 Aug 1915 - 14 Feb 1916: | Reserve officer, Caucasus Military District |
| 14 Feb 1916: | Retired |

*Lieutenant-General* Gavriil Gavrilovich **Mikhailov** (16 Oct 1837 - ?)
| | |
|---|---|
| 1 Aug 1888: | Promoted to *Major-General* |
| 1 Aug 1888 - 1 Feb 1895: | Commander, 37$^{th}$ Artillery Brigade |
| 1 Feb 1895 - 16 Nov 1896: | Commander, Life Guards 3$^{rd}$ Artillery Brigade |
| 16 Nov 1896 - 1898: | Commander of Artillery, XII. Army Corps |
| 1898: | Promoted to *Lieutenant-General* |
| 1898: | Retired |

*Major-General* Ivan Aleksandrovich **Mikhailov** (13 Nov 1864 - ?)
| | |
|---|---|
| 2 Feb 1905 - 12 Jun 1910: | Commander, 1$^{st}$ Infantry Regiment |
| 12 Jun 1910: | Promoted to *Major-General* |
| 12 Jun 1910 - 8 Jun 1913: | Commander, 1$^{st}$ Brigade, 47$^{th}$ Infantry Division |

*General of the Admiralty* Konstantin Ivanovich **Mikhailov** (1838 - 1918)
| | |
|---|---|
| 1891 - 1898: | Deputy Chief of the Hydrographic Department, Ministry of the Navy |
| 1 Jan 1892: | Promoted to *Major-General of the Admiralty* |
| 5 Apr 1898: | Promoted to *Lieutenant-General of the Admiralty* |
| 1898 - 8 Sep 1903: | Chief of the Hydrographic Department, Ministry of the Navy |
| 8 Sep 1903 - 1909: | Member, Main Naval Tribunal |
| 1909: | Promoted to *General of the Admiralty* |
| 1909: | Retired |

*Lieutenant-General* Leonid Kondratyevich **Mikhailov** (8 Jan 1834 - 2 Mar 1898)
8 Jul 1879 - 3 Dec 1883: At the disposal of the Governor-General of Odessa
15 May 1883: Promoted to *Major-General*
3 Dec 1883 - 2 Aug 1884: Chief of Staff, VI. Army Corps
2 Aug 1884 - 31 Mar 1890: Chief of Staff, VII. Army Corps
31 Mar 1890 - 9 Feb 1894: Chief of Staff, VIII. Army Corps
9 Feb 1894 - 2 Mar 1898: Commander, 52nd Reserve Infantry Brigade
14 May 1896: Promoted to *Lieutenant-General*

*Major-General* Mikhail Panteleymonovich **Mikhailov** (1 Nov 1857 - ?)
23 Jun 1914: Promoted to *Major-General*
23 Jun 1914 - 11 Dec 1916: Commander, 1st Brigade, 18th Infantry Division
11 Dec 1916 - 25 Apr 1917: Commander, 138th Infantry Division
25 Apr 1917 - 19 Dec 1917: Reserve officer, Dvinsk Military District
19 Dec 1917 - 1918: Reserve officer, Odessa Military District

*Major-General* Mikhail Vasilyevich **Mikhailov** (1 Nov 1840 - ?)
2 Jul 1898: Promoted to *Major-General*
2 Jul 1898 - 1 Nov 1901: Commander, 1st Brigade, 11th Infantry Division

*Major-General* Mily Kondratyevich **Mikhailov** (4 Sep 1843 - ?)
18 Jul 1900: Promoted to *Major-General*
18 Jul 1900 - 11 Sep 1903: Commander, 2nd Brigade, 25th Infantry Division

*Lieutenant-General* Nikolai Aleksandrovich **Mikhailov** (27 Oct 1855 - ?)
13 May 1910: Promoted to *Major-General*
13 May 1910 - 14 Feb 1915: Commander, 1st Siberian Rifle Artillery Brigade
14 Feb 1915 - 15 Feb 1917: Inspector of Artillery, VI. Army Corps
10 Apr 1916: Promoted to *Lieutenant-General*
15 Feb 1917 - 25 Sep 1917: Reserve officer, Petrograd Military District
25 Sep 1917: Retired

*Lieutenant-General* Nikolai Grigoryevich **Mikhailov** (2 Nov 1848 - ?)
12 Aug 1897: Promoted to *Major-General*
12 Aug 1897 - 16 Mar 1904: Deputy Chief of Staff, Kazan Military District
16 Mar 1904 - 3 Jun 1906: Commander, 8th Infantry Division
6 Dec 1904: Promoted to *Lieutenant-General*

*Lieutenant-General* Nikolai Ivanovich **Mikhailov** (25 Nov 1851 - 20 Oct 1917)
20 Jun 1900: Promoted to *Major-General*
20 Jun 1900 - 22 Aug 1903: Special Assignments General, Kiev Military District
22 Aug 1903 - 29 Mar 1906: Special Assignments General, Caucasus Military District
29 Mar 1906 - 3 Feb 1908: Ataman, Kuban Cossack Army
6 Dec 1906: Promoted to *Lieutenant-General*
3 Feb 1908 - 24 Oct 1908: At the disposal of the Ataman, Caucasus Cossack Army
24 Oct 1908 - Nov 1912: Commander, 1st Caucasus Cossack Division
Nov 1912: Retired

*Major-General* Nikolai Ivanovich **Mikhailov** (29 Apr 1859 - 20 Jun 1916)
29 Oct 1915 - 20 Jun 1916: Commander, 165th Infantry Regiment
29 Jul 1916: Posthumously promoted to *Major-General*

*Major-General* Timofey Vasilyevich **Mikhailov** (28 May 1872 - 16 Feb 1962)
28 Nov 1915 - 1917: Commander, Life Guards Ataman Regiment
Nov 1916: Promoted to *Major-General*
1917 - Oct 1917: Commander, Guards Cossack Brigade

*Major-General* Vadim Sergeyevich **Mikhailov** (26 Apr 1875 - 29 Oct 1929)
1916 - 4 May 1916: Chief of Okhta Explosives Factory
10 Apr 1916: Promoted to *Major-General*
4 May 1916 - 1917: Chief of Section 2, Technical Artillery Department, Main Artillery Directorate

*Lieutenant-General* Ivan Mechislavovich **Mikhailovsky** (6 Jan 1863 - ?)
24 Jan 1902 - 1914: Artillery Inspector, Main Artillery Directorate
29 Mar 1909: Promoted to *Major-General*
22 Nov 1913: Promoted to *Lieutenant-General*
1914 - ?: Senior Inspector of Artillery, Main Artillery Directorate

*Major-General* Ivan Petrovich **Mikhailovsky** (1 Jun 1874 - ?)
23 Aug 1916 - 7 Aug 1917: Commander, 35th Artillery Brigade
6 Dec 1916: Promoted to *Major-General*
7 Aug 1917 - 3 Oct 1917: Inspector of Artillery, I. Guards Corps

*Major-General* Valerian-Yegor-Onufriy Nikolayevich **Mikhailovsky** (26 Jul 1866 - 2 Sep 1913)
5 Jan 1895 - 2 Sep 1913: Chief of Artillery Workshop, St. Petersburg Weapons Factory
12 Jan 1912 - 2 Sep 1913: Member of the Artillery Committee, Main Artillery Directorate
1913: Promoted to *Major-General*

*Lieutenant-General* Yevgeny Mikhailovich **Mikhelis de Genig** (16 Dec 1863 - 14 Sep 1939)
16 Nov 1908: Promoted to *Major-General*
16 Nov 1908 - 2 Apr 1910: Quartermaster-General, Amur Military District
2 Apr 1910 - 23 Jul 1911: Commander, 2nd Brigade, 41st Infantry Division
23 Jul 1911 - 13 Aug 1914: Commander, 2nd Brigade, 18th Infantry Division
13 Aug 1914 - 21 Feb 1915: Commandant of Fortress Ivangorod
21 Feb 1915 - 5 May 1917: Commander, 13th Infantry Division
6 Dec 1915: Promoted to *Lieutenant-General*
5 May 1917 - Dec 1917: Commanding General, XXIX. Army Corps

*Lieutenant-General* Aleksandr Aleksandrovich **Mikhelson** (14 Dec 1864 - ?)
20 Jan 1906 - 30 Dec 1910: Military Attaché, Germany
18 Apr 1910: Promoted to *Major-General*

| | |
|---|---|
| 30 Dec 1910 - 6 Mar 1913: | Commander, 1st Brigade, 22nd Infantry Division |
| 6 Mar 1913 - 22 Jan 1915: | Commander, Life Guards Moscow Regiment |
| 22 Jan 1915 - 11 Aug 1916: | Special Assignments General, Chief of the General Staff |
| 11 Aug 1916 - 25 May 1917: | At the disposal of the Head of Chancellery, Ministry of War |
| 25 May 1917 - Oct 1917: | Director-General for Overseas Supplies |
| 24 Aug 1917: | Promoted to *Lieutenant-General* |

*Major-General* Aleksandr Dmitriyevich **Mikheyev** (16 Mar 1829 - ?)

| | |
|---|---|
| 18 Feb 1889: | Promoted to *Major-General* |
| 18 Feb 1889 - 20 Jul 1889: | Commander, 1st Brigade, 2nd Infantry Division |
| 20 Jul 1889 - Dec 1894: | Commander, 1st Brigade, 10th Infantry Division |

*Lieutenant-General* Aleksandr Stepanovich **Mikheyev** (1 Sep 1853 - 17 Dec 1914)

| | |
|---|---|
| 29 Dec 1899 - 4 Mar 1903: | Commander, 34th Artillery Brigade |
| 9 Apr 1900: | Promoted to *Major-General* |
| 4 Mar 1903 - 26 Apr 1904: | Inspector of Artillery, Amur Military District |
| 26 Apr 1904 - 17 Aug 1905: | Inspector of Artillery, 1st Manchurian Army |
| 13 Jul 1905: | Promoted to *Lieutenant-General* |
| 17 Aug 1905 - 21 Feb 1906: | Chief Inspector of Artillery, Far East High Command |
| 21 Feb 1906 - 3 Mar 1908: | Commander of Artillery, Caucasus Military District |
| 3 Mar 1908 - 7 Dec 1908: | Commander, Caucasus Grenadier Division |
| 7 Dec 1908 - 13 Sep 1912: | Commander, Terek Region, Ataman, Terek Cossack Army |
| 13 Sep 1912 - 17 Dec 1914: | Attached to the Department of Heraldry, Senate |

*Lieutenant-General* Mikhail Grigoryevich **Mikheyev** (7 Nov 1861 - 30 Dec 1938)

| | |
|---|---|
| 6 Dec 1907: | Promoted to *Major-General* |
| 6 Dec 1907 - 17 Jul 1912: | Chief of Staff, Fortress Modlin |
| 17 Jul 1912 - 19 Jul 1914: | Commander, 2nd Brigade, 14th Cavalry Division |
| 19 Jul 1914 - 31 Dec 1916: | Commander, Orenburg Cossack Division |
| 30 Jan 1915: | Promoted to *Lieutenant-General* |
| 31 Dec 1916 - 21 Feb 1917: | Reserve officer, Kiev Military District |
| 21 Feb 1917: | Retired |

*Major-General* Sergey Petrovich **Mikheyev** (5 Jul 1869 - ?)

| | |
|---|---|
| 29 May 1916 - 8 Sep 1916: | Commander, 161st Infantry Regiment |
| 9 Jul 1916: | Promoted to *Major-General* |
| 8 Sep 1916 - 27 Dec 1916: | Chief of Staff, 52nd Infantry Division |
| 27 Dec 1916 - Feb 1917: | Commandant, Infantry Junior Officer Training School, Petrograd Military District |
| Feb 1917 - 1 Aug 1917: | Commandant, Irkutsk Military School |
| 1 Aug 1917 - 1918: | Commandant, Aleksandr Military School |

*Lieutenant-General* Aleksandr Petrovich **Mikhnevich** (30 Aug 1853 - 1912)

| | |
|---|---|
| 12 Mar 1900 - 30 Jul 1906: | Inspector of Classes, Tsar Aleksandr II Cadet Corps |
| 11 Jul 1904: | Promoted to *Major-General* |
| 30 Jul 1906 - 1910: | General for Special Assignments, Main Directorate for |

| | |
|---|---|
| 1910: | Military Schools<br>Promoted to *Lieutenant-General* |
| 1910 - 1911: | Transferred to the reserve |
| 1911 - 1912: | Member, Teaching Committee, Main Directorate for Military Schools |

*General of Infantry* Nikolai Petrovich **Mikhnevich** (7 Oct 1849 - 8 Feb 1927)
| | |
|---|---|
| 20 Oct 1893 - 16 Jun 1902: | Professor, General Staff Academy |
| 6 Dec 1898: | Promoted to *Major-General* |
| 1901 - 14 Apr 1904: | Commander, Brigade, 23$^{rd}$ Infantry Division |
| 14 Apr 1904 - 10 Jan 1907: | Commandant, General Staff Academy |
| 6 Dec 1904: | Promoted to *Lieutenant-General* |
| 10 Jan 1907 - 24 Jun 1908: | Commander, 24$^{th}$ Infantry Division |
| 24 Jun 1908 - 30 Apr 1910: | Commander, 2$^{nd}$ Guards Infantry Division |
| 30 Apr 1910 - 7 Mar 1911: | Commanding General, V. Army Corps |
| 6 Dec 1910: | Promoted to *General of Infantry* |
| 7 Mar 1911 - 2 Apr 1917: | Chief of the General Staff |
| 24 Mar 1917 - 2 Apr 1917: | Member of the Military Council |
| 2 Apr 1917: | Retired |

*Lieutenant-General* Sergey Dmitriyevich **Mikhno** (26 Jan 1854 - 15 Feb 1919)
| | |
|---|---|
| 7 Dec 1904: | Promoted to *Major-General* |
| 7 Dec 1904 - 11 Aug 1906: | Commander, Brigade, 77$^{th}$ Infantry Division |
| 11 Aug 1906 - 28 Mar 1907: | Commander, 2$^{nd}$ Brigade, 3$^{rd}$ Infantry Division |
| 28 Mar 1907 - 31 Dec 1913: | Commander, 1$^{st}$ Brigade, 2$^{nd}$ Grenadier Division |
| 31 Dec 1913: | Promoted to *Lieutenant-General* |
| 31 Dec 1913 - 29 May 1916: | Commander, 7$^{th}$ Infantry Division |
| 29 May 1916 - 1917: | Reserve officer, Petrograd Military District |
| 1917: | Retired |

*Major-General* Nikolai Lyudvigovich **Mikhonsky** (10 May 1862 - 4 Oct 1930)
| | |
|---|---|
| 1 May 1916 - 1917: | Commander, Brigade, 2$^{nd}$ Turkestan Cossack Division |
| 22 Sep 1916: | Promoted to *Major-General* |

*Major-General of Naval Engineers* Aleksandr Aleksandrovich **Mikkov** (7 May 1852 - ?)
| | |
|---|---|
| 18 Feb 1899 - 1909: | Chief Engineer, Imperial Yacht "Polar Star" |
| 6 Dec 1908: | Promoted to *Major-General of Naval Engineers* |

*Major-General* Aleksandr Mikhailovich **Miklashevsky** (1 Oct 1850 - 19 Sep 1901)
| | |
|---|---|
| 15 Oct 1898 - 19 Sep 1901: | Chief of Aeronautical Section, Electrotechnical Division, Engineering Department |
| 6 Dec 1898: | Promoted to *Major-General* |

*Major-General* Nikolai-Amvrosy Yulianovich **Mikuchevsky** (7 Dec 1855 - ?)
| | |
|---|---|
| 10 Aug 1910 - 1912: | Commander, 180$^{th}$ Infantry Regiment |
| 1912: | Retired |
| 28 Oct 1914: | Promoted to *Major-General* |
| 8 Nov 1914 - 1917: | Recalled; Special Assignments General, Moscow |

Military District

*Lieutenant-General* Iosif Aleksandrovich **Mikulin** (4 Nov 1863 - 26 May 1916)
2 Nov 1908: Promoted to *Major-General*
2 Nov 1908 - 6 Nov 1912: Quartermaster-General, St. Petersburg Military District
6 Nov 1912 - 3 Jan 1915: Commander, 2nd Brigade, 13th Infantry Division
3 Jan 1915 - 25 Oct 1915: Reserve officer, Kiev Military District
25 Oct 1915 - 26 May 1916: Commander, 102nd Infantry Division
9 Jul 1916: Posthumously promoted to *Lieutenant-General*

*Major-General* Grigory Nikitich **Milashevich** (14 Dec 1855 - 23 Feb 1918)
20 Nov 1904: Promoted to *Major-General*
20 Nov 1904 - 31 Aug 1906: Commander, 2nd Brigade, Consolidated Caucasus Cossack Division
31 Aug 1906 - 18 Jul 1907: Commander, 2nd Brigade, 2nd Consolidated Cossack Division
18 Jul 1907: Retired

*Lieutenant-General* Gavriil Georgyevich **Mileant** (24 Mar 1864 - 11 May 1936)
31 Oct 1905 - 18 Jun 1907: Chief of Administration for the Return of Troops from the Far East
6 Dec 1906: Promoted to *Major-General*
18 Jun 1907 - 7 May 1913: Chief of Communications, St. Petersburg Military District
7 May 1913 - 20 Jul 1914: Chief of Staff, Vilnius Military District
31 May 1913: Promoted to *Lieutenant-General*
20 Jul 1914 - 30 Aug 1914: Chief of Staff, 1st Army
30 Aug 1914 - 6 Sep 1914: Unassigned
6 Sep 1914 - 29 Sep 1915: Commander, 4th Infantry Division
29 Sep 1915 - 15 Mar 1917: Chief, Main Military Technical Directorate
15 Mar 1917 - 2 Apr 1917: Reserve officer, Petrograd Military District
2 Apr 1917 - 3 Apr 1917: Reserve officer, Kiev Military District
3 Apr 1917 - 10 Dec 1917: Commanding General, V. Army Corps
10 Dec 1917: Dismissed

*Lieutenant-General* Aleksandr Pavlovich **Milkov** (5 Oct 1854 - ?)
2 Jan 1906 - 27 Nov 1906: Military Judge, Warsaw Military District Court
2 Apr 1906: Promoted to *Major-General*
27 Nov 1906 - 4 Aug 1911: Military Judge, Moscow Military District Court
4 Aug 1911 - 10 Mar 1916: Military Judge, St. Petersburg Military District Court
10 Mar 1916 - 10 May 1917: President, Omsk Military District Court
10 Apr 1916: Promoted to *Lieutenant-General*
10 May 1917: Dismissed

*Major-General* Aleksandr Karlovich **Miller** (27 Jul 1829 - ?)
20 Nov 1886: Promoted to *Major-General*
20 Nov 1886 - 24 Oct 1899: Commander, 1st Brigade, 30th Infantry Division

*Lieutenant-General* Anatoly Ivanovich **Miller** (4 Jun 1860 - ?)
6 Oct 1911: Promoted to *Major-General*
6 Oct 1911 - 18 Dec 1912: Commander of Engineers, Fortress Kiev Depot
18 Dec 1912 - 9 Jul 1915: Deputy Inspector of Engineers, Amur Military District
9 Jul 1915 - 1917: Inspector of Engineers, Minsk Military District
24 Oct 1917: Promoted to *Lieutenant-General*

*Major-General* Fyodor Ivanovich **Miller** (10 Sep 1846 - ?)
20 Jul 1893 - 1904: Chief of Gendarmerie, Tula Province
5 Apr 1898: Promoted to *Major-General*

*Major-General* Iulian Ivanovich **Miller** (21 Jun 1861 - ?)
10 Apr 1909 - 31 May 1912: Commander, 11$^{th}$ Borderguard Brigade
6 Dec 1911: Promoted to *Major-General*
31 May 1912 - 1917: Commander, 25$^{th}$ Borderguard Brigade

*Lieutenant-General* Pavel Logginovich **Miller** (6 Nov 1857 - 29 Jan 1942)
6 Jul 1910 - 13 Jul 1917: Deputy Chief of Administration, Peterhof Palace
6 Dec 1910: Promoted to *Major-General*
13 Jul 1917: Promoted to *Lieutenant-General*
13 Jul 1917: Dismissed
1917: Recalled; Commandant, Aleksandr Military School

*Major-General* Valerian Ivanovich **Miller** (25 Apr 1842 - ?)
18 Sep 1890 - 1906: Chief of St. Petersburg Military Nurses School
6 Dec 1901: Promoted to *Major-General*

*Lieutenant-General* Yevgeny-Lyudvig Karlovich **Miller** (25 Sep 1867 - 11 May 1939)
19 Aug 1909 - 3 May 1910: Quartermaster-General, General Staff
6 Dec 1909: Promoted to *Major-General*
3 May 1910 - 6 Oct 1912: Commandant, Nikolai Cavalry School
6 Oct 1912 - 19 Jul 1914: Chief of Staff, Moscow Military District
19 Jul 1914 - 14 Jan 1915: Chief of Staff, 5$^{th}$ Army
31 Dec 1914: Promoted to *Lieutenant-General*
14 Jan 1915 - 18 Jan 1915: Chief of Staff, 12$^{th}$ Army
18 Jan 1915 - Sep 1916: Chief of Staff, 5$^{th}$ Army
Sep 1916 - 7 Apr 1917: Commanding General, XXVI. Army Corps
7 Apr 1917 - 6 Aug 1917: Unassigned
6 Aug 1917 - Oct 1917: Representative of the Supreme Commander-in-Chief, Italian Army HQ

*Major-General* Yevgeny Aleksandrovich **Milodanovich** (19 Feb 1866 - ?)
1 May 1913: Promoted to *Major-General*
1 May 1913 - 3 Aug 1915: Chief of Staff, XIV. Army Corps
3 Aug 1915 - 19 Sep 1917: Commander, 5$^{th}$ Siberian Rifle Division
19 Sep 1917 - Oct 1917: Reserve officer, Dvinsk Military District

*Lieutenant-General* Count Grigory Aleksandrovich **Miloradovich** (24 Sep 1839 - 13 Aug 1905)
| | |
|---|---|
| 1 Jan 1878: | Promoted to *Major-General* |
| 1 Jan 1878 - 13 Aug 1905: | General à la suite |
| 30 Aug 1888: | Promoted to *Lieutenant-General* |
| 5 Feb 1898 - 13 Aug 1905: | Member, Ministry of Agriculture Council |
| August 1904 - 13 Aug 1905: | Senator |

*Lieutenant-General* Nikolai Emmanuilovich **Miloradovich** (15 Jul 1847 - 6 Apr 1917)
| | |
|---|---|
| 3 Mar 1891 - 18 Aug 1897: | Commander, 44$^{th}$ Infantry Regiment |
| 14 May 1896: | Promoted to *Major-General* |
| 18 Aug 1897 - 30 Mar 1900: | Commander, 2$^{nd}$ Brigade, 3$^{rd}$ Infantry Division |
| 30 Mar 1900 - 2 Sep 1904: | Commander, 52$^{nd}$ Replacement Infantry Brigade |
| 2 Sep 1904 - 29 Jan 1907: | Commander, 52$^{nd}$ Infantry Division |
| 6 Dec 1904: | Promoted to *Lieutenant-General* |
| 29 Jan 1907: | Retired |

*Major-General* Grigory Nikitich **Miloshevich** (1855 - ?)
| | |
|---|---|
| ? - 1908: | Attached to Kuban Cossack Army |
| 1908: | Promoted to *Major-General* |
| 1908: | Retired |

*Major-General* Leonid Ivanovich **Milostanov** (25 May 1871 - ?)
| | |
|---|---|
| 26 Jun 1916 - 1917: | Commander, 40$^{th}$ Artillery Brigade |
| 26 Aug 1916: | Promoted to *Major-General* |

*Major-General* Dmitry Yakovlevich **Milovich** (8 Feb 1870 - ?)
| | |
|---|---|
| 13 May 1915: | Promoted to *Major-General* |
| 28 May 1915 - 18 Jan 1916: | Commander, 30$^{th}$ Artillery Brigade |
| 18 Jan 1916 - 3 Feb 1917: | Commander, 14$^{th}$ Dragoon Regiment |

*Lieutenant-General* Fyodor Alekseyevich **Milovzorov** (8 Jan 1853 - ?)
| | |
|---|---|
| 10 Jan 1900 - 20 Mar 1911: | Section Chief, Main Artillery Directorate |
| 6 Dec 1906: | Promoted to *Major-General* |
| 20 Mar 1911 - 31 Dec 1913: | Deputy Commander of Artillery, Warsaw Military District |
| 31 Dec 1913: | Promoted to *Lieutenant-General* |
| 31 Dec 1913: | Retired |

*Lieutenant-General* Count Aleksey Dmitriyevich **Milyutin** (11 Nov 1845 - 20 Jan 1904)
| | |
|---|---|
| 23 May 1886 - 28 Apr 1892: | Vice-Governor of Kharkov |
| 21 Apr 1891: | Promoted to *Major-General* |
| 28 Apr 1892 - 15 Jun 1892: | Reserve officer, Field Horse Artillery |
| 15 Jun 1892 - Oct 1902: | Governor of Kursk |
| 1 Apr 1901: | Promoted to *Lieutenant-General* |
| Oct 1902: | Retired |

*General-Field Marshal* Count Dmitry Alekseyevich **Milyutin** (28 Jun 1816 - 25 Jan 1912)
26 Oct 1848 - 15 Oct 1856: General for Special Assignments, Minister of War
17 Apr 1855: Promoted to *Major-General*
15 Oct 1856 - 30 Aug 1860: Chief of Staff, Caucasus Army
30 Aug 1858: Promoted to *Lieutenant-General*
6 Aug 1859: Promoted to *General-Adjutant*
30 Aug 1860 - 10 Nov 1861: Deputy Minister of War
10 Nov 1861 - 22 May 1881: Minister of War
27 Mar 1866: Promoted to *General of Infantry*
22 May 1881 - 25 Jan 1912: Adjutant-General to the Tsar, Member of the State Council
16 Aug 1898: Promoted to *General-Field Marshal*

*Major-General* Georgy Aleksandrovich **Min** (9 Dec 1855 - 13 Aug 1906)
5 Dec 1904 - 13 Aug 1906: Commander, Semenov Life Guards Regiment
7 Jan 1906: Promoted to *Major-General à la suite*

*Major-General* Andrey Alekseyevich **Minchenko** (3 Oct 1855 - ?)
23 Jan 1908 - 1914: Commander, 24th Infantry Regiment
1914: Retired
25 Aug 1915: Promoted to *Major-General*
25 Aug 1915 - 1917: Recalled; Reserve officer, Kiev Military District

*Major-General* Dmitry Mikhailovich **Minervin** (24 Oct 1865 - 1915)
17 Jan 1911 - 1915: Senior Adjutant, Omsk Military District
9 Mar 1915: Posthumously promoted to *Major-General*

*Lieutenant-General* Iosif Feliksovich **Mingin** (12 Oct 1855 - 29 Oct 1931)
4 Sep 1903 - 13 Aug 1905: Commander, 41st Artillery Brigade
6 Dec 1903: Promoted to *Major-General*
13 Aug 1905 - 9 Nov 1905: Attached to the C-in-C, Far East
9 Nov 1905 - 21 Jun 1906: Commander of Artillery, I. Consolidated Rifle Corps
21 Jun 1906 - 13 Oct 1907: Commander, Life Guards 3rd Artillery Brigade
13 Oct 1907 - 21 Nov 1907: Inspector of Artillery, XIII. Army Corps
21 Nov 1907 - 25 Jul 1910: Commander of Artillery, V. Army Corps
6 Dec 1907: Promoted to *Lieutenant-General*
25 Jul 1910 - 20 Sep 1912: Inspector of Artillery, XXIII. Army Corps
20 Sep 1912 - 17 Aug 1914: Commander, 2nd Infantry Division
17 Aug 1914 - 1918: POW

*Lieutenant-General* Sergey Petrovich **Minin** (5 Jul 1858 - ?)
30 Jul 1903 - 15 Apr 1905: Military Judge, Warsaw Military District Court
6 Dec 1903: Promoted to *Major-General*
15 Apr 1905 - 10 Mar 1907: Military Judge, Kiev Military District Court
10 Mar 1907 - 14 Feb 1909: Military Judge, Moscow Military District Court
14 Feb 1909 - 1912: Military Judge, Odessa Military District Court
1912: Promoted to *Lieutenant-General*
1912: Retired

*Lieutenant-General* Viktor Nikolayevich **Minut** (17 Aug 1868 - 2 Jan 1934)
13 Oct 1910 - 12 Mar 1911: Section Chief, General Staff
6 Dec 1910: Promoted to *Major-General*
12 Mar 1911 - 19 Jul 1914: Chairman, Committee on Troop Billeting
19 Jul 1914 - 16 Apr 1916: Chief of Staff, Minsk Military District
5 Jan 1915: Promoted to *Lieutenant-General*
16 Apr 1916 - 6 Dec 1916: Chief of Staff, 6$^{th}$ Army
6 Dec 1916 - 11 Apr 1917: Chief of Staff, 10$^{th}$ Army
11 Apr 1917 - 9 May 1917: Chief of the General Staff
9 May 1917 - 14 Jun 1917: Duty General, Supreme Commander-in-Chief
14 Jun 1917 - 12 Jul 1917: Commanding General, Minsk Military District
12 Jul 1917 - 7 Dec 1917: Chief of Logistics, Western Front
7 Dec 1917 - 1918: Reserve officer, Petrograd Military District

*Major-General* Aleksandr Andreyevich **Mionchinsky** (13 Mar 1854 - ?)
5 Nov 1906 - 9 Feb 1910: Commander of Artillery, Fortress Vyborg
9 Feb 1910: Promoted to *Major-General*
9 Feb 1910 - 19 Dec 1912: Commander, Kronstadt Fortress Artillery Brigade

*Lieutenant-General* Ivan Andreyevich **Mionchinsky** (12 Nov 1855 - ?)
17 Dec 1906 - 19 Aug 1907: Attached (without assignment) to the Field Artillery
22 Apr 1907: Promoted to *Major-General*
19 Aug 1907 - 22 Sep 1910: Commander of Artillery, Fortress Warsaw
22 Sep 1910 - 1917: Commandant of Fortress Ust-Dvina
14 Apr 1913: Promoted to *Lieutenant-General*

*Lieutenant-General* Timofey Andreyevich **Mionchinsky** (23 Feb 1858 - 8 Jan 1916)
23 May 1907 - 1914: Deputy Chief of Kazan Gunpowder Factory
29 Mar 1909: Promoted to *Major-General*
1914 - 1915: Chairman of Commission for the Construction of Tambov Gunpowder Factory
1915: Promoted to *Lieutenant-General*
1915: Dismissed

*Major-General* Khodzha-Gidayat-Ulla **Mirbadalev** (6 Dec 1849 - ?)
14 May 1900 - 7 Sep 1913: Military Commander of Samarkand
7 Sep 1913: Promoted to *Major-General*
7 Sep 1913: Retired

*Major-General* Nikolai Nikolayevich von **Mirbakh** (16 May 1868 - 13 Apr 1915)
12 Jun 1910 - 13 Apr 1915: Commander, 11$^{th}$ Hussar Regiment
14 Nov 1914: Promoted to *Major-General*

*Major-General* Petr Nikolayevich **Mirolyubsky** (26 Jul 1861 - ?)
4 Dec 1914 - 6 Sep 1916: Commander, 2$^{nd}$ Heavy Artillery Brigade
22 Jan 1915: Promoted to *Major-General*
6 Sep 1916 - 1918: Commander of Artillery, Fortress Kars

*Lieutenant-General* Semyon Tarasovich **Miroshnichenko** (1833 - 1902)
| | |
|---|---|
| 17 Jun 1883 - 1899: | Chief of Military Topographical Section, Omsk Military District |
| 30 Aug 1893: | Promoted to *Major-General* |
| 1899: | Promoted to *Lieutenant-General* |
| 1899: | Retired |

*Major-General* Vasily Vasilyevich **Mirovich** (27 Feb 1865 - 26 Aug 1945)
| | |
|---|---|
| 31 Mar 1915 - 4 Dec 1915: | Commander, 32$^{nd}$ Artillery Brigade |
| 3 Jul 1915: | Promoted to *Major-General* |
| 4 Dec 1915 - 1917: | Commander, 3$^{rd}$ Finnish Rifle Artillery Brigade |
| 1917 - 1918: | Inspector of Artillery, XXII. Army Corps |
| 25 Mar 1917 - 31 Mar 1917: | Acting Commanding General, XXII. Army Corps |

*Lieutenant-General* Nikolai Nikolayevich **Mishchenko** (14 Nov 1838 - ?)
| | |
|---|---|
| 2 Dec 1881 - 6 Dec 1895: | Commander of Artillery, Fortress Kars |
| 30 Aug 1888: | Promoted to *Major-General* |
| 6 Dec 1895 - 15 Dec 1898: | Deputy Commander of Artillery, Kiev Military District |
| 15 Dec 1898: | Promoted to *Lieutenant-General* |
| 15 Dec 1898 - 1902: | Commander of Artillery, Kiev Military District |

*General of Artillery* Pavel Ivanovich **Mishchenko** (22 Jan 1853 - 1918)
| | |
|---|---|
| 2 Jun 1901: | Promoted to *Major-General* |
| 2 Jun 1901 - 9 Mar 1902: | Commander, 1$^{st}$ Brigade, 39$^{th}$ Infantry Division |
| 9 Mar 1902 - 23 Mar 1903: | At the disposal of the Commanding General, Kwantung District |
| 23 Mar 1903 - 17 Feb 1905: | Commander, Trans-Baikal Independent Cossack Brigade |
| 22 Oct 1904: | Promoted to *Lieutenant-General* |
| 22 Oct 1904: | Promoted to *General-Adjutant* |
| 17 Feb 1905 - 30 Aug 1905: | Commander, Separate Cossack Division |
| 30 Aug 1905 - 9 Nov 1905: | At the disposal of the C-in-C, Far East |
| 9 Nov 1905 - 5 May 1906: | Commanding General, Consolidated Cavalry Corps |
| 5 May 1906 - 21 Sep 1906: | At the disposal of the Minister of War |
| 21 Sep 1906 - 2 May 1908: | Commanding General, II. Caucasus Army Corps |
| 2 May 1908 - 17 Mar 1909: | Governor-General of Turkestan, Commanding General, Turkestan Military District, Ataman, Semirechensk Cossack Army |
| 17 Mar 1909 - 23 Dec 1910: | Attached to the Trans-Baikal Cossack Army |
| 23 Dec 1910 - 25 Feb 1911: | At the disposal of the Commanding General, Caucasus Military District |
| 12 Jan 1911: | Promoted to *General of Artillery* |
| 25 Feb 1911 - 23 Sep 1912: | Ataman, Don Cossack Army |
| 23 Sep 1912 - 10 Aug 1914: | Attached to the Caucasus Military District |
| 10 Aug 1914 - 23 Feb 1915: | Deputy Commanding General, II. Caucasus Army Corps |
| 19 Mar 1915 - 16 Apr 1917: | Commanding General, XXXI. Army Corps |
| 16 Apr 1917: | Retired |

*Lieutenant-General* Vasily Vasilyevich **Mishchenko** (4 Mar 1854 - ?)
23 Aug 1902 - 1910: Ataman, Temryuk Section, Kuban Region
6 Dec 1906: Promoted to *Major-General*
1910 - 21 Dec 1914: Ataman, Taman Section, Kuban Region
21 Dec 1914: Promoted to *Lieutenant-General*
21 Dec 1914: Retired

*Major-General* Yakov Petrovich **Mishin** (5 Feb 1843 - ?)
30 Mar 1902 - 1905: Commandant, Kiev Regional Arsenal
6 Apr 1903: Promoted to *Major-General*

*Major-General* Avgust Ernestovich **Misin** (21 Dec 1863 - 8 Jul 1940)
1915 - 8 Feb 1916: Commander, Brigade, 49th Infantry Division
8 Feb 1916 - 24 Oct 1916: Commander, Brigade, 79th Infantry Division
1 Mar 1916: Promoted to *Major-General*
24 Oct 1916 - 1917: Commander, 1st Latvian Rifle Brigade
1917 - 20 May 1917: Commander, Latvian Rifle Division
20 May 1917 - 12 Sep 1917: Commander, 3rd Special Infantry Division

*Major-General* Vladimir Petrovich **Mitkevich-Volchassky** (14 Oct 1846 - 1913)
9 Sep 1905 - 1906: Chief of Advanced Artillery Reserve, Manchurian Army
17 May 1906: Promoted to *Major-General*
1906: Retired

*Major-General* Vyacheslav Kupriyanovich **Mitkevich-Zheltok** (20 Oct 1857 - 1 Nov 1910)
10 Dec 1899 - 16 Mar 1906: Chief of Staff, Terek Cossack Army
6 Apr 1903: Promoted to *Major-General*
16 Mar 1906 - 1906: Commander, 63rd Reserve Infantry Brigade
1906: Retired

*Major-General* Nikolai Antonovich **Mitkevich-Zholtok** (9 Nov 1866 - ?)
25 Aug 1908 - 20 Apr 1916: Chief of the Moscow Metropolitan Police
30 Aug 1912: Promoted to *Major-General*
20 Apr 1916 - 1917: Chief of 7th Main Evacuation Points

*General of Infantry* Valerian Sergeyevich **Mitrofanov** (8 Mar 1837 - 25 Nov 1914)
27 Jun 1881 - 11 Jun 1888: Military Judge, Kazan Military District
15 May 1883: Promoted to *Major-General*
11 Jun 1888 - 23 Nov 1889: Military Judge, Warsaw Military District
23 Nov 1889 - 25 Nov 1892: Military Prosecutor, Warsaw Military District
25 Nov 1892 - 21 Nov 1899: Chairman, Omsk Military District Court
30 Aug 1893: Promoted to *Lieutenant-General*
21 Nov 1899 - 22 Aug 1901: Chairman, Siberian Military District Court
22 Aug 1901 - 9 Oct 1905: Chairman, Vilnius Military District Court
9 Oct 1905 - 10 Dec 1905: Member, Supreme Military Tribunal
6 Dec 1905: Promoted to *General of Infantry*
10 Dec 1905 - 8 Oct 1909: Chairman of the Supreme Military Tribunal
8 Oct 1909: Retired

*Lieutenant-General* Pavel Nikolayevich **Mitropolsky** (17 May 1855 - ?)
| | |
|---|---|
| 19 Feb 1893 - 12 Oct 1906: | Military Judge, Vilnius Military District Court |
| 6 Dec 1899: | Promoted to *Major-General* |
| 12 Oct 1906 - 13 Feb 1907: | Military Prosecutor, Turkestan Military District |
| 13 Feb 1907 - 14 Oct 1908: | Chairman of the Military Tribunal, Irkutsk Military District |
| 22 Apr 1907: | Promoted to *Lieutenant-General* |
| 14 Oct 1908: | Retired |
| 25 Jul 1916 - 5 May 1917: | Recalled; Reserve officer, Petrograd Military District |
| 5 May 1917: | Dismissed |

*Lieutenant-General* Vladimir Frantsevich **Mitselovsky** (19 Sep 1851 - ?)
| | |
|---|---|
| 12 Dec 1903 - 1909: | Commander of Engineers, Fortress Novogeorgiyevsk |
| 28 Mar 1904: | Promoted to *Major-General* |
| 1909: | Promoted to *Lieutenant-General* |
| 1909: | Retired |

*Lieutenant-General* Zakhary Vasilyevich **Mitskevich** (15 Nov 1859 - 15 Jun 1930)
| | |
|---|---|
| 4 Sep 1902 - 4 Aug 1911: | Inspector of Pupils, Imperial Law College |
| 6 Dec 1910: | Promoted to *Major-General* |
| 4 Aug 1911 - 1917: | Director of the Imperial Law College |
| 1917: | Promoted to *Lieutenant-General* |

*Major-General of the Admiralty* Aleksandr Ilich **Miturich** (26 Dec 1852 - ?)
| | |
|---|---|
| 21 Oct 1895 - 1913: | Instructor, Emperor Nikolai I Naval Engineering School |
| 6 Dec 1910: | Promoted to *Major-General of the Admiralty* |

*Rear-Admiral* Nikolai Ilich **Miturich** (13 Jan 1855 - 1920)
| | |
|---|---|
| 8 Aug 1905 - 21 Apr 1908: | Commander, 3rd Naval Depot |
| 21 Apr 1908: | Promoted to *Rear-Admiral* |
| 21 Apr 1908: | Retired |

*Major-General* Nikolai Illarionovich **Mochalov** (27 Apr 1863 - ?)
| | |
|---|---|
| 1 Mar 1908 - 29 Jun 1915: | Commander of Gendarmerie, Arkhangelsk |
| 6 Dec 1912: | Promoted to *Major-General* |
| 29 Jun 1915 - 3 Oct 1916: | Commander of Gendarmerie, Perm Province |
| 3 Oct 1916: | Dismissed |

*Major-General* Ozv Alfredovich **Modl** (1 Aug 1848 - ?)
| | |
|---|---|
| 3 Apr 1898 - 2 Feb 1902: | Commander, 2nd East Siberian Rifle Regiment |
| 15 Oct 1901: | Promoted to *Major-General* |
| 2 Feb 1902 - 28 Jul 1905: | Commander, 2nd Brigade, 40th Infantry Division |
| 28 Jul 1905 - 1906: | Commander, 10th East Siberian Rifle Division |

*Lieutenant-General* Pavel Alfredovich **Modl** (25 Jun 1853 - ?)
| | |
|---|---|
| 11 Apr 1905 - 26 Mar 1910: | Deputy Intendant, Warsaw Military District |
| 6 Dec 1906: | Promoted to *Major-General* |
| 26 Mar 1910 - 24 Aug 1913: | Intendant, XV. Army Corps |

24 Aug 1913: Promoted to *Lieutenant-General*
24 Aug 1913: Retired

*Major-General* Karl Andreyevich **Modrakh** (4 Jan 1840 - 11 Jan 1903)
15 Feb 1894 - 11 Jan 1903: Conference Member, Nikolayev Engineering Academy
6 Dec 1895: Promoted to *Major-General*

*Lieutenant-General of Naval Engineers* Aleksandr Ivanovich **Moiseyev** (20 Oct 1868 - 1918)
2 Aug 1910 - 1917: Chief of Admiralty Shipyards
10 Apr 1911: Promoted to *Major-General of Naval Engineers*
22 Mar 1915: Promoted to *Lieutenant-General of Naval Engineers*

*Major-General* Dmitry Yefimovich **Moiseyev** (19 Sep 1854 - ?)
1908 - 1909: Deputy Commander, 13th Life-Grenadier Regiment
1909: Promoted to *Major-General*
1909: Retired
1915 - 21 Jun 1916: Recalled; Reserve officer, Caucasus Military District
21 Jun 1916 - 1917: Commander, 4th Caucasus Brigade

*Major-General* Nikolai Alekseyevich **Moiseyev** (25 Nov 1852 - ?)
4 May 1897 - 1905: Military Judge, St. Petersburg Military District Court
6 Dec 1900: Promoted to *Major-General*

*Major-General* Nikolai Nikitich **Moiseyev** (23 Dec 1863 - ?)
25 Oct 1911 - 30 Apr 1915: Chief of Kharkov Section, Main Directorate of Troop Billeting
22 Mar 1915: Promoted to *Major-General*
30 Apr 1915 - 1917: Member of the Unit Barracks Committee, Main Directorate of Troop Billeting

*Lieutenant-General* Grigory Grigoryevich **Mokasey-Shibinsky** (30 Jan 1854 - 1918)
2 Aug 1902 - 1 Dec 1908: Commander, St. Petersburg Borderguard Brigade
6 May 1906: Promoted to *Major-General*
1 Dec 1908 - 3 Jan 1914: Commander, 1st Borderguard District
14 Apr 1913: Promoted to *Lieutenant-General*
3 Jan 1914 - Mar 1917: Deputy Commanding General, Borderguard Corps
Mar 1917 - Mar 1918: Commanding General, Borderguard Corps

*Major-General* Vasily Illarionovich **Mokhlin** (24 Feb 1862 - 15 Jul 1917)
21 Aug 1901 - 24 Nov 1915: Company Commander, 2nd Orenburg Cadet Corps
24 Nov 1915: Promoted to *Major-General*
24 Nov 1915: Retired

*Major-General* Valentin Fyodorovich **Mokhov** (14 Oct 1851 - 10 Apr 1910)
5 May 1909: Promoted to *Major-General*
5 May 1909 - 10 Apr 1910: Commander, 1st East Siberian Rifle Artillery Brigade

*Major-General* Adam-Vikenty Felitsian Aleksandrovich **Mokrzhetsky** (15 Jul 1856 - 6 Apr 1921)
30 Mar 1912 - 3 Feb 1915: Commander, 40th Infantry Regiment
2 Nov 1914: Promoted to *Major-General*
3 Feb 1915 - 8 Apr 1915: Reserve officer, Minsk Military District
8 Apr 1915 - 1917: Commander, 91st State Militia Brigade

*Lieutenant-General* Stepan Sigizmundovich **Mokulsky** (6 Feb 1860 - ?)
28 Feb 1908 - 31 Oct 1912: Military Judge, Kiev Military District Court
13 Apr 1908: Promoted to *Major-General*
31 Oct 1912 - 4 Oct 1914: Military Prosecutor, Caucasus Military District
4 Oct 1914 - 8 Apr 1917: Chief of Military Justice, Caucasus Army
6 Dec 1916: Promoted to *Lieutenant-General*
8 Apr 1917: Retired

*Rear-Admiral* Mikhail Pavlovich **Molas** (1852 - 31 Mar 1904)
1904: Promoted to *Rear-Admiral*
30 Jan 1904 - 24 Feb 1904: Commander, Cruiser Group, Pacific Fleet
24 Feb 1904 - 31 Mar 1904: Chief of Staff, C-in-C Pacific Fleet

*Vice-Admiral* Pyotr Pavlovich **Molas** (10 Jan 1847 - ?)
Nov 1898 - Jan 1900: Commander, Cruiser "Avrora"
1899: Promoted to *Rear-Admiral*
1903: Commander, Mediterranean Naval Detachment
1907: Promoted to *Vice-Admiral*
1907 - 1908: Attached to the Ministry of the Navy

*Major-General* Semyon Yegorovich **Molchanov** (1 Feb 1857 - 17 Jun 1919)
7 Jul 1908 - 14 Jan 1915: Commander, 122nd Infantry Regiment
11 Dec 1914: Promoted to *Major-General*
14 Jan 1915 - 3 Feb 1915: Commander, 2nd Brigade, 78th Infantry Division
3 Feb 1915 - 28 Apr 1915: Commander, 1st Brigade, 49th Infantry Division
28 Apr 1915 - 8 May 1915: Acting Commander, 48th Infantry Division
8 May 1915 - 25 Jun 1915: Acting Commander, 49th Infantry Division
25 Jun 1915 - 10 Mar 1917: Commander, 1st Brigade, 49th Infantry Division
10 Mar 1917 - 23 May 1917: Commander, 52nd Replacement Infantry Brigade
23 May 1917 - 27 Aug 1917: Commander, 84th Infantry Division

*Lieutenant-General* Vasily Yakovlevich **Molchanov** (28 Feb 1843 - 1913)
3 Mar 1894 - 13 Aug 1896: Deputy Commander of Engineers, Vilnius Military District
30 Aug 1894: Promoted to *Major-General*
13 Aug 1896 - Jan 1909: Deputy Commander of Engineers, St. Petersburg Military District
Jan 1909: Promoted to *Lieutenant-General*
Jan 1909: Retired

*Major-General* Nikolai Petrovich **Moller** (1 Aug 1840 - 9 May 1901)
7 May 1895 - 9 May 1901: Chancellery Clerk, Ministry of War
6 Dec 1895: Promoted to *Major-General*

*Lieutenant-General* Pyotr Petrovich **Mollerius** (2 Mar 1844 - 1913)
24 Feb 1901: Promoted to *Major-General*
24 Feb 1901 - 1904: Commander, Caucasus Reserve Artillery Brigade
1904: Promoted to *Lieutenant-General*

*Major-General of Naval Artillery* Mstislav Yegorovich **Monakhov** (27 May 1866 - ?)
1 Feb 1898 - 1917: Naval Artillery Inspector
6 Dec 1915: Promoted to *Major-General of Naval Artillery*

*Lieutenant-General* Nikolai Avgustovich **Monkevits** (22 Nov 1869 - Nov 1926)
22 Oct 1910 - 6 Jul 1914: First Deputy Quartermaster-General, General Staff
10 Apr 1911: Promoted to *Major-General*
6 Jul 1914 - 20 Nov 1914: uartermaster-General, General Staff
20 Nov 1914 - 5 Jun 1916: Chief of Staff, XXX. Army Corps
5 Jun 1916 - 25 Sep 1916: Commander, 71st Infantry Division
25 Sep 1916 - 25 Oct 1916: Chief of Staff, XLVII. Army Corps
19 Oct 1916: Promoted to *Lieutenant-General*
25 Oct 1916 - 12 May 1917: Commander, 71st Infantry Division
12 May 1917 - Oct 1917: Chief of Staff, 4th Army

*Major-General* Aleksandr Vladimirovich **Monomakhov** (31 Jul 1865 - 11 Sep 1919)
17 Jun 1908 - 23 Mar 1914: Commander, 13th Dragoon Regiment
23 Mar 1914: Promoted to *Major-General*
23 Mar 1914 - 9 May 1917: Commander, 1st Brigade, 11th Cavalry Division
9 May 1917 - 22 May 1917: Commander, Amur Cavalry Division
22 May 1917 - Oct 1917: Commander, 8th Cavalry Division

*Major-General* Vladimir Grigoryevich **Mooro** (1855 - 1933)
28 Oct 1906 - Apr 1914: Member, Main Technical Committee, Amur Military District
6 Dec 1913: Promoted to *Major-General*
Apr 1914: Retired

*Lieutenant-General* Pyotr Viktorovich **Moralevsky** (12 Jun 1857 - ?)
28 Jan 1906 - 21 Nov 1908: Director, Volsky Military School
22 Apr 1907: Promoted to *Major-General*
21 Nov 1908 - 14 Aug 1910: Director, Volsky Cadet Corps
14 Aug 1910: Promoted to *Lieutenant-General*
14 Aug 1910: Retired

*Lieutenant-General* Aleksandr Kuzmich **Moravsky** (23 Nov 1841 - ?)
30 Aug 1882 - 30 May 1888: Military Prosecutor, Warsaw Military District Court
30 Aug 1887: Promoted to *Major-General*
30 May 1888 - 21 Apr 1890: Military Prosecutor, Moscow Military District Court

| | |
|---|---|
| 21 Apr 1890 - 17 Jan 1903: | Chairman of the Military Tribunal, Kiev Military District |
| 6 Dec 1897: | Promoted to *Lieutenant-General* |
| 17 Jan 1903 - 1903: | At the disposal of the Main Military Justice Directorate |

*Major-General* Anton Lvovich **Moravsky** (27 May 1833 - ?)
| | |
|---|---|
| 7 Oct 1893: | Promoted to *Major-General* |
| 7 Oct 1893 - 11 Jun 1897: | Commander, 38th Artillery Brigade |

*Major-General of the Hydrographic Corps* Konstantin Pavlovich **Mordovin** (1 Aug 1870 - 3 Oct 1914)
| | |
|---|---|
| 16 Jan 1912 - 3 Oct 1914: | Chief of the Geodesic Section, Main Hydrographic Directorate |
| 1914: | Promoted to *Major-General of the Hydrographic Corps* |

*Lieutenant-General* Nikolai Viktorovich **Mordvinov** (5 Aug 1843 - 12 Jan 1915)
| | |
|---|---|
| 1 Jul 1886 - 1 Oct 1894: | Military Judge, Turkestan Military District Court |
| 30 Aug 1890: | Promoted to *Major-General* |
| 1 Oct 1894 - 1905: | Military Judge, Odessa Military District Court |
| 1905: | Promoted to *Lieutenant-General* |
| 1905: | Retired |

*Major-General* Vladimir Nikolayevich **Mordvinov** (9 Jul 1856 - ?)
| | |
|---|---|
| 21 Mar 1898 - 1906: | Deputy Military Prosecutor, St. Petersburg Military District |
| 1906: | Promoted to *Major-General* |
| 1906: | Retired |
| 14 Apr 1916 - 1917: | Recalled; Head of the Army & Navy Officers Assembly |

*Major-General* Mikhail Karlovich **Morel** (25 Oct 1839 - 4 Dec 1904)
| | |
|---|---|
| 27 Jan 1880 - 4 Dec 1904: | Senior Artillery Inspector, Main Artillery Directorate |
| 6 Dec 1903: | Promoted to *Major-General* |

*Major-General of the Fleet* Vladimir Aleksandrovich von **Morenshild** (27 Jul 1854 - ?)
| | |
|---|---|
| 19 Sep 1906 - 2 Mar 1909: | Mayor of Sevastopol |
| 6 Dec 1907: | Promoted to *Major-General of the Fleet* |

*Major-General* Vasily Alekseyevich **Morev** (22 Jan 1853 - ?)
| | |
|---|---|
| 17 Sep 1892 - 1902: | Military Judge, Moscow Military District Court |
| 1 Jan 1901: | Promoted to *Major-General* |

*Major-General* Baron Fyodor Fyodorovich **Morgenshtiyern** (14 Jun 1843 - ?)
| | |
|---|---|
| 2 Nov 1887 - 16 Mar 1899: | Military Commander, Novograd-Volynsky |
| 1899: | Promoted to *Major-General* |
| 16 Mar 1899 - 12 Mar 1905: | Transferred to the reserve |
| 12 Mar 1905 - 2 Dec 1906: | Chairman, Irkutsk Internal Evacuation Commission |
| 2 Dec 1906 - 1907: | Attached to the General Staff |

*General of Cavalry* Nikolai Mikhailovich **Morgoli** (20 Nov 1843 - 24 Dec 1916)
| | |
|---|---|
| 24 Mar 1889 - 9 Jul 1899: | Commander, Riga Borderguard Brigade |
| 5 Apr 1892: | Promoted to *Major-General* |
| 9 Jul 1899 - 1 Dec 1908: | Commander, 2$^{nd}$ Borderguard District |
| 9 Apr 1900: | Promoted to *Lieutenant-General* |
| 20 Dec 1908: | Promoted to *General of Cavalry* |
| 20 Dec 1908: | Retired |

*Lieutenant-General* Aleksandr Arnoldovich **Morits** (22 Aug 1861 - 18 Aug 1936)
| | |
|---|---|
| 21 Apr 1905 - 8 Jan 1907: | Commandant, Yelizavetgrad Cavalry School |
| 2 Apr 1906: | Promoted to *Major-General* |
| 8 Jan 1907 - 25 Feb 1912: | Chief of Staff, Guards Corps |
| 25 Feb 1912: | Promoted to *Lieutenant-General* |
| 25 Feb 1912 - 28 Jan 1915: | Commander, 5$^{th}$ Cavalry Division |
| 28 Jan 1915 - 19 Apr 1916: | Chief of Staff, Omsk Military District |
| 19 Apr 1916 - 1917: | Chief of Staff, Minsk Military District |
| 1917: | Commander, 2$^{nd}$ Guards Cavalry Division |
| 1917: | At the disposal of the C-in-C, Romanian Front |

*Major-General* Aleksandr Dormidontovich **Morozov** (6 Jan 1860 - ?)
| | |
|---|---|
| 31 Aug 1913 - 12 May 1916: | Commander, 3$^{rd}$ Caucasus Mortar Artillery Battalion |
| 23 Nov 1915: | Promoted to *Major-General* |
| 12 May 1916 - 1917: | Commander, 84$^{th}$ Artillery Brigade |

*Major-General* Dormidont Stepanovich **Morozov** (19 Sep 1833 - ?)
| | |
|---|---|
| 20 May 1879 - 20 Feb 1883: | Military Commander of Elisavetpol |
| 20 Feb 1883 - 4 Apr 1884: | Transferred to the reserve |
| 4 Apr 1884: | Promoted to *Major-General* |
| 4 Apr 1884: | Retired |
| 4 Jun 1888 - 27 Feb 1893: | Recalled; Ataman, Kizlyar Division, Terek Cossack Army |
| 27 Feb 1893 - 1894: | Ataman, Sunzhen Division, Terek Cossack Army |

*Major-General* Faddey Andreyevich **Morozov** (9 Aug 1850 - ?)
| | |
|---|---|
| 3 Aug 1900: | Promoted to *Major-General* |
| 3 Aug 1900 - 31 Jan 1904: | Commander, 1$^{st}$ Siberian Reserve Infantry Brigade |
| 31 Jan 1904 - 1905: | Commander, 1$^{st}$ Siberian Infantry Division |

*Major-General of the Hydrographic Corps* Nikolai Vasilyevich **Morozov** (9 Nov 1862 - 2 Mar 1925)
| | |
|---|---|
| 1911 - Jan 1913: | Chief of Cartographic Section, Main Hydrographic Department |
| Jan 1913: | Promoted to *Major-General of the Hydrographic Corps* |
| Jan 1913: | Retired |

*Major-General* Stepan Stepanovich **Morozov** (16 Dec 1847 - ?)
| | |
|---|---|
| 14 Dec 1904 - 7 Aug 1906: | Headquarters Commandant, 2$^{nd}$ Manchurian Army |
| 12 Feb 1905: | Promoted to *Major-General* |

7 Aug 1906 - 8 Jan 1909: Commander, 1st Brigade, 28th Infantry Division

*Major-General* Dydan-Stanislav Mikhailovich **Morzhitsky** (13 Nov 1855 - ?)
6 Sep 1908: Promoted to *Major-General*
6 Sep 1908 - 12 Jun 1912: Commander, 2nd Brigade, 1st East Siberian Rifle Division
12 Jun 1912 - 12 Mar 1916: Commander, 1st Turkestan Rifle Brigade
12 Mar 1916 - Aug 1916: Commander, 1st Turkestan Rifle Division
Aug 1916 - 21 Sep 1916: Reserve officer, Minsk Military District
21 Sep 1916 - 1917: Commander, 7th Siberian Replacement Rifle Brigade

*Major-General* Boleslav Yakovlevich **Moshchinsky** (14 Jan 1855 - ?)
13 Jul 1912 - 1917: Deputy Chief of Troop Billeting, Irkutsk Military District
6 Dec 1912: Promoted to *Major-General*

*Lieutenant-General* Valentin Aleksandrovich **Moshkov** (25 Mar 1852 - 19 Nov 1922)
12 Jun 1888 - 19 Sep 1913: Senior Artillery Acceptance Inspector, Main Artillery Directorate
6 Dec 1905: Promoted to *Major-General*
19 Sep 1913: Promoted to *Lieutenant-General*
19 Sep 1913: Retired

*Lieutenant-General* Vladimir Aleksandrovich **Moshnin** (14 Feb 1863 - 13 Oct 1928)
21 Oct 1903 - 11 Feb 1909: Commander, 14th Hussar Regiment
11 Feb 1909: Promoted to *Major-General*
11 Feb 1909 - 27 Nov 1912: Commander, 1st Brigade, 9th Cavalry Division
27 Nov 1912 - 26 Feb 1917: Commander, 2nd Brigade, 9th Cavalry Division
17 Aug 1916: Promoted to *Lieutenant-General*
26 Feb 1917 - 16 Apr 1917: Commander, 6th Cavalry Division
16 Apr 1917 - 1918: Reserve officer, Kiev Military District

*Major-General* Sergey Mikhailovich **Moskvin** (20 Apr 1868 - Jan 1915)
2 Apr 1913 - Jan 1915: Commander, 17th Siberian Rifle Regiment
6 May 1915: Posthumously promoted to *Major-General*

*Lieutenant-General* Aleksandr Aleksandrovich **Mosolov** (19 Feb 1854 - 1 Oct 1939)
17 Mar 1900 - 1917: Chief of Chancellery, Ministry of the Imperial Court
6 Dec 1902: Promoted to *Major-General*
6 Dec 1908: Promoted to *Lieutenant-General*

*Major-General* Sergey Ivanovich **Mossin** (23 Apr 1849 - 26 Jan 1902)
17 Dec 1894 - 26 Jan 1902: Chief of Sestroretsky Arms Factory, Member of the Artillery Committee, Main Artillery Directorate
9 Apr 1900: Promoted to *Major-General*

*Lieutenant-General* Ivan Gavrilovich **Motorny** (31 Mar 1849 - ?)
26 May 1903 - 12 May 1910:   Commander, 5th Turkestan Rifle Brigade
17 Apr 1905:                 Promoted to *Major-General*
12 May 1910:                 Promoted to *Lieutenant-General*
12 May 1910:                 Retired

*Major-General* Viktor Nikolayevich **Mozgalevsky** (11 Nov 1847 - ?)
11 Oct 1904:                 Promoted to *Major-General*
11 Oct 1904 - 17 Mar 1906:   Commander, 1st Brigade, 48th Infantry Division
17 Mar 1906 - 23 Dec 1906:   Commander, 2nd Brigade, 8th Infantry Division

*Major-General* Aleksandr Kalinnikovich **Mozhay-Mozharovsky** (15 Aug 1855 - ?)
6 Sep 1912 - 1917:           Commandant, Irkutsk Artillery Depot
6 Dec 1912:                  Promoted to *Major-General*
1917:                        Commander of Artillery, Irkutsk Military District

*Major-General* Konstantin Konstantinovich **Mozhay-Mozharovsky** (17 May 1857 - 11 Jan 1921)
1 Mar 1915 - 1917:           Commandant, Kursk Artillery Depot
6 Dec 1915:                  Promoted to *Major-General*

*Lieutenant-General* Ignaty Feliksovich **Mrochkevich** (21 Jan 1825 - ?)
17 Feb 1868 - 26 Jan 1878:   Commander, 110th Infantry Regiment
26 Jan 1878:                 Promoted to *Major-General*
26 Jan 1878 - 2 Mar 1878:    Unassigned
2 Mar 1878 - 19 Nov 1878:    Commander, 1st Brigade, 6th Reserve Infantry Division
19 Nov 1878 - 14 Mar 1879:   At the disposal of the Commanding General, Vilnius Military District
14 Mar 1879 - 7 May 1892:    Commander, 1st Brigade, 26th Infantry Division
7 May 1892 - 1899:           Commander, Saratov Regional Brigade
30 Aug 1892:                 Promoted to *Lieutenant-General*

*General of Artillery* Iosif Ivanovich **Mrozovsky** (14 Dec 1857 - 16 Sep 1934)
6 Apr 1902 - 5 Jan 1904:     Commander, 2nd Battalion, 5th Artillery Brigade
11 Nov 1903:                 Promoted to *Major-General*
5 Jan 1904 - 18 Feb 1904:    Commander, 18th Artillery Brigade
18 Feb 1904 - 23 Aug 1905:   Commander, 9th East Siberian Rifle Artillery Brigade
23 Aug 1905 - 7 Feb 1906:    Commander of Artillery, I. Army Corps
7 Feb 1906 - 26 Aug 1908:    Commander of Artillery, St. Petersburg Military District
6 Dec 1907:                  Promoted to *Lieutenant-General*
26 Aug 1908 - 21 May 1912:   Commander, 1st Guards Infantry Division
21 May 1912 - 2 Sep 1915:    Commanding General, Grenadier Corps
14 Apr 1913:                 Promoted to *General of Infantry*
26 Jan 1914:                 Redesignated *General of Artillery*
2 Sep 1915 - 10 Mar 1917:    Commanding General, Moscow Military District
10 Mar 1917:                 Retired

*Major-General* Ivan Viktorovich **Mudrov** (2 Jul 1851 - ?)
24 Jul 1907 - 1911:                Commander of Artillery, Fortress Kars
6 Dec 1908:                        Promoted to *Major-General*
1911:                              Retired

*Major-General* Matvey Mikhailovich **Mudry** (9 Aug 1855 - Jul 1916)
15 May 1904 - 3 Oct 1907:          Commander, 259th Reserve Infantry Regiment
3 Oct 1907:                        Promoted to *Major-General*
3 Oct 1907:                        Retired
9 Jan 1915 - 30 Aug 1915:          Recalled; Commander, 4th Kuban Cossack Infantry Brigade
30 Aug 1915 - Jul 1916:            Reserve officer, Caucasus Military District

*Lieutenant-General* Vladimir Nikolayevich **Mufel** (26 Jan 1847 - ?)
7 Feb 1901:                        Promoted to *Major-General*
7 Feb 1901 - 7 Nov 1907:           Commander, 1st Brigade, 18th Infantry Division
7 Nov 1907:                        Promoted to *Lieutenant-General*
7 Nov 1907 - 2 May 1910:           Commander, 25th Infantry Division

*Major-General* Aleksandr Vladimirovich **Mukhanov** (4 Mar 1874 - 1941)
31 Jul 1916 - 20 Nov 1916:         Chief of Staff, 2nd Siberian Rifle Division
30 Oct 1916:                       Promoted to *Major-General*
20 Nov 1916 - 1918:                Military Attaché, Greece

*Major-General* Fyodor Fedorovich **Mukhin** (6 Feb 1868 - ?)
16 Nov 1915 - 1917:                Chief of Bureau, Preparatory Liquidation Commission
6 Dec 1916:                        Promoted to *Major-General*

*Major-General* Innokenty Aleksandrovich **Mukhin** (1871 - 15 Oct 1944)
13 May 1916 - 1917:                Commander, Borderguard Park Artillery Brigade
1916:                              Promoted to *Major-General*

*General of Infantry* Pyotr Petrovich **Mukhin** (8 Jan 1857 - ?)
28 Nov 1896 - 7 Feb 1903:          Military Judge, Vilnius Military District Court
6 Dec 1900:                        Promoted to *Major-General*
7 Feb 1903 - 1 Nov 1905:           Military Prosecutor, Warsaw Military District
1 Nov 1905 - 25 Feb 1906:          Military Prosecutor, St. Petersburg Military District
25 Feb 1906 - 13 Feb 1907:         Chairman of the Military Tribunal, Vilnius Military District
13 Feb 1907 - 3 May 1909:          Chairman of the Military Tribunal, St. Petersburg Military District
22 Apr 1907:                       Promoted to *Lieutenant-General*
3 May 1909 - 31 Mar 1917:          Member, Supreme Military Tribunal
6 Dec 1915:                        Promoted to *General of Infantry*
31 Mar 1917:                       Dismissed

*Major-General* Vasily Dmitriyevich **Mukhin** (24 Nov 1864 - 1 Nov 1917)
23 Jun 1916 - 30 Apr 1917:         Deputy Commander, 1st Siberian Replacement Rifle

17 Jan 1917:                        Brigade
17 Jan 1917:                        Promoted to *Major-General*
30 Apr 1917 - 1 Nov 1917:     Commander, 1st Siberian Replacement Rifle Brigade

*Major-General* Maksimilian Nikolayevich **Munte von Morgenstyern** (10 May 1846 - ?)
5 Mar 1901 - 11 May 1904:    Commander, 16th Infantry Regiment
11 May 1904:                     Promoted to *Major-General*
11 May 1904:                     Retired
1915 - 3 Oct 1915:                Recalled; Commander, 36th Militia Brigade
3 Oct 1915 - 28 Sep 1916:     Brigade Commander, Infantry Division
28 Sep 1916 - 18 Feb 1917:    Brigade Commander, 101st Infantry Division
18 Feb 1917 - 23 Apr 1917:    Commander, 157th Infantry Division

*General of Artillery* Kuzma Yevstafyevich **Muntyanov** (1 Nov 1856 - 28 Apr 1931)
22 Oct 1911:                     Promoted to *Major-General*
22 Oct 1911 - 28 Dec 1915:    Commander, 4th Siberian Rifle Artillery Brigade
27 Nov 1915:                     Promoted to *Lieutenant-General*
28 Dec 1915 - 11 Feb 1916:    Unassigned
11 Feb 1916 - 10 May 1916:   Inspector of Artillery, XXIX. Army Corps
10 May 1916 - 11 Sep 1917:   Reserve officer, Petrograd Military District
11 Sep 1917:                     Promoted to *General of Artillery*
11 Sep 1917:                     Retired

*Major-General* Semyon Dmitriyevich **Muratov** (24 Apr 1851 - ?)
1 Aug 1909:                      Promoted to *Major-General*
1 Aug 1909 - 25 Sep 1910:    Commander, 1st Replacement Artillery Brigade
25 Sep 1910 - 1 Aug 1911:    Commander, 38th Artillery Brigade
1 Aug 1911:                      Retired

*Lieutenant-General* Vladimir Dmitriyevich **Muratov** (3 Jul 1847 - 1910)
17 Apr 1890 - 1910:             Member of the Artillery Committee, Main Artillery
                                         Directorate
30 Aug 1893:                     Promoted to *Major-General*
6 Dec 1903:                      Promoted to *Lieutenant-General*
16 Nov 1904 - 1910:             Member, Main Fortress Committee

*Major-General* Vladimir Pavlovich **Muratov** (27 Jul 1868 - 1934)
18 Dec 1916 - 1918:             Chief of Lines of Communication, 2nd Army
6 Dec 1916:                      Promoted to *Major-General*

*Admiral* Pyotr Petrovich **Muravyev** (30 Jan 1860 - 12 Jul 1940)
28 Aug 1909 - 15 Nov 1911:    Commander, Mine Training Detachment, Baltic Fleet
6 Dec 1910:                      Promoted to *Rear-Admiral*
15 Nov 1911 - 25 May 1915:   Chief of Main Directorate of Shipbuilding
14 Apr 1913:                     Promoted to *Vice-Admiral*
25 May 1915 - Mar 1917:      Deputy Minister of the Navy
6 Dec 1916:                      Promoted to *Admiral*

*Lieutenant-General* Aleksandr Aleksandrovich **Mushnikov** (6 Sep 1849 - 1909)
| | |
|---|---|
| 7 Jul 1897 – 25 Mar 1901: | Military Judge, Warsaw Military District Court |
| 6 Dec 1897: | Promoted to *Major-General* |
| 25 Mar 1901 - 1906: | Military Judge, Vilnius Military District Court |
| 1906: | Promoted to *Lieutenant-General* |
| 1906: | Retired |

*General of Infantry* Ilya Ivanovich **Mushrub-Shaverdov** (2 Sep 1853 - ?)
| | |
|---|---|
| 1 Jan 1899 - 16 Jun 1902: | Military Prosecutor, Amur Military District |
| 1 Jan 1901: | Promoted to *Major-General* |
| 16 Jun 1902 - 27 Feb 1906: | Military Judge, Moscow Military District Court |
| 27 Feb 1906 - 13 Feb 1907: | Military Prosecutor, Kazan Military District Court |
| 13 Feb 1907 - 10 May 1912: | Chairman, Vilnius Military District Court |
| 22 Apr 1907: | Promoted to *Lieutenant-General* |
| 10 May 1912: | Promoted to *General of Infantry* |
| 10 May 1912: | Retired |

*Lieutenant-General* Sergey Ivanovich **Mushrub-Shaverdov** (11 Oct 1852 - 1907)
| | |
|---|---|
| 23 Jun 1897 - 1905: | Military Judge, Turkestan Military District Court |
| 6 Dec 1899: | Promoted to *Major-General* |
| 1905: | Promoted to *Lieutenant-General* |
| 1905: | Retired |

*General of Cavalry* Count Aleksandr Ivanovich **Musin-Pushkin** (10 Jul 1827 - 19 Dec 1903)
| | |
|---|---|
| 27 Mar 1866: | Promoted to *Major-General* |
| 7 Sep 1866 - 2 Oct 1873: | Commander, Guards Cavalry Regiment |
| 2 Oct 1873 - 18 Dec 1873: | Commander, 1st Brigade, 1st Guards Cavalry Division |
| 18 Dec 1873 - 27 Jul 1875: | Commander, 2nd Guards Cavalry Division |
| 27 Jul 1875 - 21 Mar 1881: | Commander, 1st Guards Cavalry Division |
| 30 Aug 1876: | Promoted to *Lieutenant-General* |
| 21 Mar 1881 - 18 Jul 1887: | Commanding General, V. Army Corps |
| 18 Jul 1887 - 23 Oct 1890: | Deputy Commanding General, Warsaw Military District |
| 30 Aug 1890: | Promoted to *General of Cavalry* |
| 23 Oct 1890 - 19 Dec 1903: | Commanding General, Odessa Military District |

*Major-General* Ivan Levanovich **Muskhelov** (15 Aug 1859 - 1940)
| | |
|---|---|
| 23 Jan 1914: | Promoted to *Major-General* |
| 23 Jan 1914 - 13 May 1916: | Commander, 9th Siberian Rifle Artillery Brigade |
| 13 May 1916 - 5 Apr 1917: | Inspector of Artillery, XIX. Army Corps |
| 5 Apr 1917 - 1917: | Reserve officer, Dvinsk Military District |

*Lieutenant-General* Andrey Robertovich **Musselius** (6 Sep 1854 - 1913)
| | |
|---|---|
| 3 Mar 1904: | Promoted to *Major-General* |
| 3 Mar 1904 - 21 Mar 1908: | Commander, 18th Artillery Brigade |
| 21 Mar 1908: | Promoted to *Lieutenant-General* |
| 21 Mar 1908 - 8 Oct 1908: | Commander of Artillery, XIX. Army Corps |
| 8 Oct 1908: | Retired |

*Lieutenant-General of Naval Engineers* Aleksandr Ivanovich **Mustafin** (5 Dec 1850 - 1912)
| | |
|---|---|
| 18 Apr 1908: | Promoted to *Major-General of Naval Engineers* |
| 3 Sep 1908 - 1909: | Senior Deputy Inspector-General of Shipbuilding |
| 1909 - 1912: | Attached to Naval Shipbuilding Division, Naval Technical Committee |
| 1912: | Posthumously promoted to *Lieutenant-General of Naval Engineers* |

*Major-General* Vladimir Andreyevich **Mustafin** (24 Jun 1867 - 21 Feb 1933)
| | |
|---|---|
| 21 May 1906 - 18 Mar 1911: | Chief of Bureau, Governor-General of Turkestan |
| 18 Apr 1910: | Promoted to *Major-General* |
| 18 Mar 1911 - Jul 1914: | Military Judge, Vilnius Military District Court |
| Jul 1914 - 1917: | Military Judge, Dvinsk Military District Court |
| 1917: | Special Assignments General, Southwestern Front |

*Major-General* Yevgeny Konstantinovich **Mustyats** (22 Feb 1864 - 20 May 1915)
| | |
|---|---|
| 1914 - 20 May 1915: | Commander, 53$^{rd}$ Infantry Regiment |
| 16 Oct 1915: | Posthumously promoted to *Major-General* |

*Major-General* Vladimir Aleksandrovich **Muzeus** (1 Sep 1868 - ?)
| | |
|---|---|
| 1914 - 19 Apr 1916: | Commander, 11$^{th}$ Infantry Regiment |
| 27 Mar 1915: | Promoted to *Major-General* |
| 19 Apr 1916 - 18 Apr 1917: | Commander, Brigade, 3$^{rd}$ Infantry Division |
| 18 Apr 1917 - 1917: | Commander, 3$^{rd}$ Infantry Division |

*General of Engineers* Yakov Konstantinovich **Myaskovsky** (25 Oct 1847 - 1918)
| | |
|---|---|
| 3 Dec 1895 - 17 Dec 1904: | Secretary of the Engineering Committee, Main Engineering Directorate |
| 1 Apr 1901: | Promoted to *Major-General* |
| 17 Dec 1904 - 5 May 1906: | Deputy Inspector of Engineers, Forces Operating against Japan |
| 5 May 1906 - 23 Jan 1914: | Chief of the Engineering Committee, Main Engineering Directorate |
| 4 Sep 1908 - 12 Mar 1914: | Member, Main Fortress Committee |
| 6 Dec 1908: | Promoted to *Lieutenant-General* |
| 12 Mar 1914: | Promoted to *General of Engineers* |
| 12 Mar 1914: | Retired |

*Major-General* Vasily Yemelyanovich **Myasnikov** (19 Feb 1861 - ?)
| | |
|---|---|
| 21 Dec 1911: | Promoted to *Major-General* |
| 21 Dec 1911 - 29 Jul 1914: | Chief of Staff, II. Siberian Army Corps |
| 29 Jul 1914 - 25 Jul 1916: | Commander, 1$^{st}$ Brigade, 7$^{th}$ Siberian Rifle Division |
| 25 Jul 1916 - 7 Aug 1917: | Reserve officer, Petrograd Military District |
| 7 Aug 1917 - Oct 1917: | Deputy Chief of Staff, Omsk Military District |

*Major-General* Nikolai Aleksandrovich **Myasoyedov** (3 Feb 1872 - ?)
| | |
|---|---|
| 1915 - 3 Jun 1916: | Commander, 2$^{nd}$ Battalion, Life Guards 3$^{rd}$ Artillery |

| | |
|---|---|
| | Brigade |
| 18 Jul 1915: | Promoted to *Major-General* |
| 3 Jun 1916 - 1917: | Reserve officer, Petrograd Military District |

*Major-General* Vladimir Alekseyevich **Myasoyedov** (21 Sep 1852 - ?)
| | |
|---|---|
| 16 Apr 1904 - 21 Dec 1906: | Chairman, Main Evacuation Commission, Manchurian Army |
| 22 Oct 1905: | Promoted to *Major-General* |
| 21 Dec 1906 - 13 Dec 1908: | Commander, 1st Brigade, 38th Infantry Division |

*Admiral* Aleksandr Ivanovich **Myazgovsky** (18 Nov 1857 - 24 Oct 1918)
| | |
|---|---|
| 1908 - 22 Oct 1909: | Chief of Staff, Black Sea Fleet |
| 22 Oct 1909: | Promoted to *Rear-Admiral* |
| 22 Oct 1909 - 4 Jul 1916: | Mayor of Nikolayev, Commander, Port of Nikolayev |
| 14 Apr 1913: | Promoted to *Vice-Admiral* |
| 4 Jul 1916 - 1917: | Member, Main Naval Tribunal |
| 1917: | Promoted to *Admiral* |
| 1917: | Retired |

*General of Infantry* Sergey Nikolayevich **Mylov** (7 Sep 1842 - ?)
| | |
|---|---|
| 18 Jul 1881 - 19 Aug 1890: | Deputy Chief of Staff, Caucasus Military District |
| 30 Aug 1885: | Promoted to *Major-General* |
| 19 Aug 1890 - 15 Dec 1894: | Commander, Caucasus Native Reserve Brigade |
| 15 Dec 1894 - 23 Jan 1901: | Commander, 20th Infantry Division |
| 14 May 1896: | Promoted to *Lieutenant-General* |
| 2 Aug 1900 - 23 Jan 1901: | Commanding General, III. Siberian Army Corps |
| 23 Jan 1901 - 7 May 1905: | Commanding General, VIII. Army Corps |
| 17 Apr 1905 - 30 Apr 1905: | Acting C-in-C, 2nd Manchurian Army |
| 7 May 1905 - 1 Jan 1911: | Member of the Military Council |
| 11 Jul 1905: | Promoted to *General of Infantry* |
| 3 Mar 1906 - 20 Jan 1907: | Chairman of the Army Education Committee |
| 1 Jan 1911: | Retired |

*Lieutenant-General* Prince Pyotr Nikolayevich **Myshetsky** (27 May 1858 - 6 May 1925)
| | |
|---|---|
| 4 Feb 1904: | Promoted to *Major-General* |
| 4 Feb 1904 - 2 Dec 1904: | Commander, 1st Brigade, 4th Cavalry Division |
| 2 Dec 1904 - 4 Aug 1908: | Commander, 2nd Brigade, 13th Cavalry Division |
| 4 Aug 1908 - 12 May 1910: | Commander, 1st Brigade, 13th Cavalry Division |
| 12 May 1910: | Retired |
| 19 Jul 1914 - 22 Nov 1915: | Recalled; Commander, 2nd Brigade, 5th Don Cossack Division |
| 22 Nov 1915 - 18 Apr 1917: | Commander, Sibirian Cossack Division |
| 26 Mar 1916: | Promoted to *Lieutenant-General* |
| 18 Apr 1917 - 23 May 1917: | Unassigned |
| 23 May 1917: | Dismissed |

*Major-General* Prince Vladislav Mikhaylovich **Myshetsky** (5 Nov 1851 - 1917)
6 Dec 1904: Promoted to *Major-General*
6 Dec 1904 - 1906: At the disposal of the Commanding General, St. Petersburg Military District

*General of Infantry* Aleksandr Zakharyevich **Myshlayevsky** (12 Mar 1856 - 1920)
6 Nov 1898 - 20 Jan 1905: Professor, General Staff Academy
18 Jan 1899 - 1 May 1903: Chief of the Military Science Archives, General Staff
6 Dec 1900: Promoted to *Major-General*
20 Jan 1905 - 6 Jul 1905: Chief of Section 1, General Staff
6 Jul 1905 - 22 May 1908: Duty General, General Staff
6 Dec 1906: Promoted to *Lieutenant-General*
22 May 1908 - 11 Mar 1909: Chief of the General Staff
11 Mar 1909 - 19 Sep 1909: Chief of the General Directorate of the General Staff
19 Sep 1909 - 24 Dec 1913: Commanding General, II. Caucasus Army Corps
6 Dec 1912: Promoted to *General of Infantry*
24 Dec 1913 - 30 Aug 1914: Deputy Military Governor of the Caucasus
30 Aug 1914 - 31 Mar 1915: Deputy C-in-C, Caucasus Army
31 Mar 1915: Retired
23 Jul 1915 - 7 Mar 1917: Recalled; At the disposal of the Minister of War
25 Nov 1915 - 5 Mar 1917: Chairman, Committee for the Steel Industry for National Defense
7 Mar 1917 - 2 Jun 1917: Commanding General, Caucasus Military District
2 Jun 1917 - Oct 1917: At the disposal of the Minister of War

*Major-General* Nikolai Aleksandrovich **Myuller** (11 Dec 1858 - ?)
7 Nov 1904 - 18 Jul 1905: Commander, 122$^{nd}$ Infantry Regiment
17 Feb 1905: Promoted to *Major-General*
18 Jul 1905 - 12 May 1908: Commander, 2$^{nd}$ Brigade, 31$^{st}$ Infantry Division
12 May 1908: Retired
19 Mar 1916 - 18 Feb 1917: Recalled; Commander, Brigade, 2$^{nd}$ Turkestan Rifle Division
18 Feb 1917 - 10 Apr 1917: Commander, 8$^{th}$ Turkestan Rifle Division

*Major-General* Napoleon Akhilovich **Myurat** (25 Aug 1872 - 14 Jun 1943)
1 Aug 1916 - 1917: Commander, 12$^{th}$ Dragoon Regiment
1917: Promoted to *Major-General*

*Major-General* Panaiot Nikolayevich **Nachev** (15 Feb 1860 - ?)
30 Aug 1912 - 26 May 1914: Military Judge, Kazan Military District Court
6 Dec 1912: Promoted to *Major-General*
26 May 1914 - Jul 1914: Military Judge, Warsaw Military District Court
Jul 1914 - 12 Oct 1914: Military Judge, Minsk Military District Court
12 Oct 1914: Retired

*General of Infantry* Ivan Pavlovich **Nadarov** (3 Jan 1851 - ?)
23 Jun 1897 - 31 Jul 1898: Deputy Chief of Staff, Amur Military District
6 Dec 1897: Promoted to *Major-General*

| | |
|---|---|
| 31 Jul 1898 - 9 May 1901: | Quartermaster-General, Amur Military District |
| 31 Jan 1901: | Promoted to *Lieutenant-General* |
| 9 May 1901 - 12 Apr 1904: | Military Governor of the Trans-Baikal Region, Ataman, Trans-Baikal Cossack Army |
| 12 Apr 1904 - 23 Feb 1905: | Chief of Military District Administration, Manchurian Army |
| 23 Feb 1905 - 25 Apr 1906: | Rear Area Commander, Manchurian Army |
| 25 Apr 1906 - 8 Jun 1908: | Commanding General, Omsk Military District, Ataman, Siberian Cossack Army |
| 8 Jun 1908: | Promoted to *General of Infantry* |
| 8 Jun 1908: | Retired |

*Lieutenant-General* Mitrofan Aleksandrovich **Nadein** (20 Nov 1839 - 1 Jan 1908)
| | |
|---|---|
| 26 Nov 1902: | Promoted to *Major-General* |
| 26 Nov 1902 - 22 Feb 1904: | At the disposal of the Chief of the General Staff |
| 22 Feb 1904 - 15 Oct 1905: | Commander, 2nd Brigade, 4th East Siberian Rifle Division |
| 22 Oct 1904: | Promoted to *Lieutenant-General* |
| 15 Oct 1905 - 21 Feb 1907: | Commander, 7th East Siberian Rifle Division |
| 21 Feb 1907 - 1 Jan 1908: | Member, Committee for Wounded Veterans |

*Major-General* Konstantin Vasilyevich **Nadezhin** (1 Aug 1856 - ?)
| | |
|---|---|
| 7 Dec 1899 - 1913: | Military Commander, Ardahan District |
| 1913: | Promoted to *Major-General* |
| 1913: | Retired |
| 5 Sep 1915 - 1917: | Recalled; Attached to the Chief of Communications, Caucasus Army |

*Lieutenant-General* Dmitry Nikolayevich **Nadezhny** (24 Oct 1873 - 1945)
| | |
|---|---|
| 26 Jan 1914 - 8 Jan 1915: | Chief of Staff, 10th Infantry Division |
| 18 Apr 1914: | Promoted to *Major-General* |
| 8 Jan 1915 - 3 Aug 1915: | Commander, 40th Infantry Regiment |
| 3 Aug 1915 - 20 Apr 1916: | Commander, 1st Brigade, 10th Infantry Division |
| 20 Apr 1916 - 13 May 1916: | Chief of Staff, 69th Infantry Division |
| 13 May 1916 - 7 Apr 1917: | Commander, 10th Infantry Division |
| 7 Apr 1917 - 12 Oct 1917: | Commanding General, III. Army Corps |
| 29 Apr 1917: | Promoted to *Lieutenant-General* |
| 12 Oct 1917 - 1918: | Commanding General, XLII. Army Corps |

*Major-General* Viktor Vladimirovich **Nagayev** (11 Nov 1863 - 3 Feb 1938)
| | |
|---|---|
| 26 Aug 1915 - 3 Feb 1916: | Commander, Brigade, 2nd Finnish Rifle Division |
| 31 Oct 1915: | Promoted to *Major-General* |
| 3 Feb 1916 - 10 Aug 1916: | Chief of Staff, 3rd Turkestan Rifle Division |
| 10 Aug 1916 - 7 Jan 1917: | Chief of Staff, XLVI. Army Corps |
| 7 Jan 1917 - 23 Nov 1917: | Commander, 173rd Infantry Division |

*Major-General* Lev Aleksandrovich **Nagel** (1 Feb 1854 - ?)
| | |
|---|---|
| 13 Dec 1903 - 9 Jun 1907: | Commandant of Kiev |

6 Dec 1906: Promoted to *Major-General*

*Major-General* Ivan Aleksandrovich **Nagibin** (19 Oct 1852 - 1910)
30 Mr 1908 - 1910: Commander, West-Siberian Artillery Battalion
1910: Posthumously promoted to *Major-General*

*Lieutenant-General* Prince Aleksandr Davydovich **Nakashidze** (1837 - 25 Sep 1905)
8 Nov 1877: Promoted to *Major-General*
8 Nov 1877 - 16 Feb 1880: Military Commander, West Dagestan
16 Feb 1880 - 1897: Governor of Elizavetpol Province
30 Aug 1889: Promoted to *Lieutenant-General*

*Lieutenant-General* Prince Ivan Aleksandrovich **Nakashidze** (4 Jan 1848 - 1917)
6 May 1909: Promoted to *Major-General*
6 May 1909 - 31 May 1917: General à la suite
1914 - 31 May 1917: Attached to the Russian Red Cross
31 May 1917: Promoted to *Lieutenant-General*
31 May 1917: Dismissed

*General of Cavalry* Khan Ismail **Nakhichevansky** (5 Jan 1819 - 10 Feb 1909)
8 Mar 1845 - 18 Aug 1908: Attached to the Caucasus Military District
19 Dec 1877: Promoted to *Major-General*
28 Oct 1890: Promoted to *Lieutenant-General*
18 Aug 1908: Promoted to *General of Cavalry*
18 Aug 1908: Retired

*General of Cavalry* Khan Hussein **Nakhichevansky** (28 Jul 1863 - Jan 1919)
4 Jul 1906 - 15 Apr 1911: Commander, Life Guards Cavalry Regiment
31 May 1907: Promoted to *Major-General*
15 Apr 1911 - 18 Apr 1912: At the disposal of the Commanding General, St. Petersburg Military District
18 Apr 1912 - 16 Jan 1914: Commander, 1st Independent Cavalry Brigade
16 Jan 1914: Promoted to *Lieutenant-General*
16 Jan 1914 - 18 Oct 1914: Commander, 2nd Cavalry Division
22 Jul 1914 - 19 Oct 1914: Commander, Cavalry Group, 1st Army
19 Oct 1914 - 25 Oct 1915: Commanding General, II. Cavalry Corps
25 Oct 1915 - 9 Apr 1916: At the disposal of the C-in-C, Caucasus Army
23 Jan 1916: Promoted to *General of Cavalry*
9 Apr 1916 - 15 Apr 1917: Commanding General, Guards Cavalry Corps
15 Apr 1917 - 23 Jun 1917: Reserve officer, Kiev Military District
23 Jun 1917 - Oct 1917: Reserve officer, Petrograd Military District

*Lieutenant-General* Elbert Asmurziyevich **Nalgiyev** (4 Nov 1863 - 1918)
1915 - 14 Feb 1916: Commander, 2nd Brigade, Consolidated Kuban Cossack Division
14 Feb 1916 - 1917: Commander, 1st Brigade, 2nd Caucasus Cossack Division
26 Feb 1917: Promoted to *Major-General*

1917: Promoted to *Lieutenant-General*
1917: Commander, 2nd Caucasus Cossack Division

*Lieutenant-General* Fyodor Aleksandrovich von **Nandelshtedt** (6 Apr 1845 - 3 Mar 1903)
4 Apr 1880 - May 1898: Chief of Bureau, Main Engineering Directorate
30 Aug 1890: Promoted to *Major-General*
May 1898: Promoted to *Lieutenant-General*
May 1898: Retired

*Major-General* Nikandr Petrovich **Naperstkov** (2 Aug 1854 - 28 Dec 1934)
11 Mar 1914: Promoted to *Major-General*
11 Mar 1914 - 29 Jul 1914: Commander, Irkutsk Local Brigade
29 Jul 1914 - 16 Jan 1915: Commander, 2nd Siberian Replacement Rifle Brigade
16 Jan 1915 - 22 Oct 1915: Commandant, 1st Irkutsk Ensign School
22 Oct 1915 - 1917: Commander, Irkutsk Local Brigade
1917: Chief of Infantry Training Schools, Irkutsk Military District

*Lieutenant-General* Aleksandr Aleksandrovich **Narbut** (27 Mar 1840 - 5 Mar 1910)
18 Sep 1899 - 9 Mar 1904: Deputy Intendant, Moscow Military District
1 Jan 1901: Promoted to *Major-General*
9 Mar 1904 - 1906: Intendant, Vilnius Military District
1906: Promoted to *Lieutenant-General*
1906: Retired

*General of Infantry* Mikhail Aleksandrovich **Narbut** (14 Jan 1837 - ?)
19 Jan 1877 - 30 Nov 1882: Attached to the General Staff
1 Jan 1878: Promoted to *Major-General*
30 Nov 1882 - 28 Feb 1897: Deputy Chief, Main Cossack Administration
30 Aug 1888: Promoted to *Lieutenant-General*
28 Feb 1897 - 6 Dec 1903: Member of the Military Training Committee, General Staff
6 Dec 1903: Promoted to *General of Infantry*
6 Dec 1903 - 1 Jan 1911: Member of the Military Council
1 Jan 1911: Retired

*Lieutenant-General* Vasily Aleksandrovich **Narbut** (28 Dec 1846 - ?)
31 Oct 1899: Promoted to *Major-General*
31 Oct 1899 - 1 Feb 1900: Commander, 2nd Brigade, 2nd Infantry Division
1 Feb 1900 - 9 Jun 1903: Commander, Life Guards Kexholmsky Regiment
9 Jun 1903 - 24 Nov 1904: Commander, 1st Brigade, 3rd Guards Infantry Division
24 Nov 1904 - 11 Nov 1907: Commander, 29th Infantry Division
6 Dec 1906: Promoted to *Lieutenant-General*

*Lieutenant-General* Vladislav Andreyevich **Narbut** (26 Jul 1856 - ?)
30 Jun 1900 - 10 May 1906: Commander, Volyn Brigade, Borderguard Corps
2 Apr 1906: Promoted to *Major-General*
10 May 1906 - 1 Dec 1908: Deputy Commander, Amur Borderguard District

1 Dec 1908 - 1917: Commander, 7th Borderguard District
14 Apr 1913: Promoted to *Lieutenant-General*

*Major-General* Vladislav Valerianovich **Narbut** (11 Sep 1859 - 1912)
19 Sep 1907 - 15 Jun 1912: Commander, 1st Uhlan Regiment
1912: Promoted to *Major-General*

*Major-General* Konstantin Mikhailovich **Narkevich** (16 Jun 1854 - 10 Oct 1905)
6 May 1901 - 16 May 1902: Deputy Intendant, Caucasus Military District
6 Dec 1901: Promoted to *Major-General*
16 May 1902 - 10 Oct 1905: Deputy Intendant, Odessa Military District

*Major-General* Pyotr Antonovich **Narkovich** (25 Jun 1865 - Aug 1909)
23 Nov 1908: Promoted to *Major-General*
23 Nov 1908 - Aug 1909: Commander, 35th Artillery Brigade

*Lieutenant-General* Fyodor Aleksandrovich **Narsky** (20 Apr 1826 - 1 Sep 1905)
16 Feb 1874 - 14 Oct 1880: Military Commander, Tomsk
19 Feb 1879: Promoted to *Major-General*
14 Oct 1880 - 31 Oct 1881: Military Commander, Semipalatinsk
31 Oct 1881 - 6 Feb 1883: Transferred to the reserve
6 Feb 1883 - 14 Aug 1889: Military Commander, Tomsk
14 Aug 1889 - 16 Nov 1889: Unassigned
16 Nov 1889 - 26 Feb 1893: Commander, 25th Regional Brigade
30 Aug 1891: Promoted to *Lieutenant-General*
26 Feb 1893 - 1 Sep 1905: Attached to the Commanding General, Caucasus Military District

*Major-General* Semyon Yakovlevich **Narushevich** (3 Feb 1862 - ?)
31 Dec 1913 - 24 Apr 1916: Commandant, Warsaw Military District Arsenal
6 Apr 1914: Promoted to *Major-General*
24 Apr 1916 - 1917: Deputy Chief of Section 3, Technical Artillery Department, Main Artillery Directorate

*Major-General* Kirill Anatolyevich **Naryshkin** (28 Apr 1868 - 1920)
18 Sep 1909 - 6 Dec 1916: Deputy Chief of the Tsar's Military Camp Office
6 Dec 1916: Promoted to *Major-General*
6 Dec 1916 - 31 Mar 1917: Chief of the Tsar's Military Camp Office
31 Mar 1917: Retired

*Major-General* Vladimir Yevgenyevich **Nasekin** (10 Apr 1858 - ?)
17 Oct 1914 - 22 Jan 1917: Commander, 28th Artillery Brigade
16 May 1915: Promoted to *Major-General*
22 Jan 1917 - 25 Aug 1917: Inspector of Artillery, XLVII. Army Corps

*Lieutenant-General* Nikolai Aleksandrovich **Nasledov** (4 Sep 1854 - 5 Apr 1927)
30 Apr 1907 - 3 Jul 1913: Ataman, 2nd Military Division, Orenburg Cossack Army
29 Mar 1909: Promoted to *Major-General*

| | |
|---|---|
| 3 Jul 1913: | Retired |
| 22 Oct 1913: | Promoted to *Lieutenant-General* |
| 12 Mar 1916 - 28 Apr 1917: | Recalled; Deputy Ataman, Orenburg Cossack Army |
| 28 Apr 1917: | Retired |

*Major-General* Sergey Platonovich **Nastavin** (28 Sep 1859 - 1929)
| | |
|---|---|
| 16 Aug 1914 - 1 Oct 1916: | Commander, 296th Infantry Regiment |
| 13 Nov 1915: | Promoted to *Major-General* |
| 1 Oct 1916 - 26 Apr 1917: | Commander, Brigade, 74th Infantry Division |
| 26 Apr 1917 - Jan 1918: | Commander, 74th Infantry Division |
| Jan 1918: | Dismissed |

*Lieutenant-General* Vladimir Aleksandrovich **Nasvetevich** (16 Jun 1829 - ?)
| | |
|---|---|
| 30 Aug 1873: | Promoted to *Major-General* |
| 30 Aug 1873 - 26 Nov 1878: | Commander, 2nd Brigade, 20th Infantry Division |
| 26 Nov 1878 - 30 Aug 1885: | Commander, 1st Brigade, 20th Infantry Division |
| 30 Aug 1885: | Promoted to *Lieutenant-General* |
| 30 Aug 1885 - 24 May 1895: | Commander, 16th Regional Brigade |
| 24 May 1895 - 1898: | Commander, Tambov Regional Brigade |

*Major-General* David Malakhiyevich **Natsvalov** (8 Nov 1859 - 20 Sep 1915)
| | |
|---|---|
| 20 Dec 1912 - 20 Sep 1915: | Commander, 2nd Battalion, 21st Artillery Brigade |
| 27 Jan 1916: | Posthumously promoted to *Major-General* |

*Major-General of the Fleet* Frants Frantsevich **Naturalis** (15 May 1862 - 26 Jan 1935)
| | |
|---|---|
| 28 Mar 1909 - 1913: | Chief Mechanical Engineer, 7th Reserve Division |
| 1913: | Promoted to *Major-General of the Fleet* |
| 1913: | Retired |

*Major-General* Ivan Vasilyevich **Naumenko** (17 Jul 1861 - ?)
| | |
|---|---|
| 22 May 1910 - 1 Jul 1912: | Chief of Warsaw Ujazdowski Military Hospital |
| 6 Dec 1910: | Promoted to *Major-General* |
| 1 Jul 1912 - 23 Mar 1913: | Transferred to the reserve |
| 23 Mar 1913 - 1915: | Commander, Tiflis Local Brigade |
| 1915 - 12 Sep 1915: | Commander, 1st Transcaucasus Replacement Rifle Brigade |
| 12 Sep 1915 - 1917: | Commander, Tiflis Local Brigade |

*Major-General* Aleksandr Dmitriyevich **Naumov** (25 Oct 1853 - ?)
| | |
|---|---|
| 30 Apr 1905: | Promoted to *Major-General* |
| 30 Apr 1905 - 30 Jan 1906: | Commander, 2nd Brigade, 1st Turkestan Cossack Division |
| 30 Jan 1906 - 1908: | Commander, 1st Brigade, 1st Turkestan Cossack Division |

*Lieutenant-General of the Fleet* Aleksandr Nikolayevich **Naumov** (18 Nov 1854 - 1920)
| | |
|---|---|
| 2 Oct 1900 - 28 Mar 1911: | Senior Deputy Commander, Port of St. Petersburg |
| 17 Apr 1905: | Promoted to *Major-General of the Admiralty* |
| 28 Mar 1911 - 1917: | Chief of St. Petersburg River Police |

10 Apr 1911: Promoted to *Lieutenant-General of the Admiralty*
8 Apr 1913: Redesignated *Lieutenant-General of the Fleet*

*Major-General* Nikolai Ivanovich **Navrotsky** (23 Jul 1858 - ?)
23 Jun 1913: Promoted to *Major-General*
23 Jun 1913 - 29 Jul 1914: Commander, 1st Brigade, 39th Infantry Division
29 Jul 1914 - 25 Dec 1915: Commander, Brigade, 71st Infantry Division
25 Dec 1915 - 1917: Commander, 33rd Replacement Infantry Brigade
1917 - 5 Apr 1917: Reserve officer, Petrograd Military District
5 Apr 1917 - 1917: Commander, 33rd Replacement Infantry Brigade

*Lieutenant-General* Sergey Sergeyevich **Navrotsky** (28 Oct 1862 - 1924)
9 Nov 1906 - 29 Apr 1917: Special Assignments General, Ministry of Internal Affairs
6 Dec 1908: Promoted to *Major-General*
6 Dec 1914: Promoted to *Lieutenant-General*
29 Apr 1917: Retired

*Lieutenant-General* Mirza-Gadzhi-Bek **Navruzov** (20 Jul 1832 - ?)
13 Dec 1878: Promoted to *Major-General*
13 Dec 1878 - 24 Mar 1879: Attached to Caucasus Military District
24 Mar 1879 - 1 Mar 1893: Commander, 1st Brigade, 2nd Caucasus Cossack Division
1 Mar 1893 - 1896: Attached to Caucasus Military District
14 May 1896: Promoted to *Lieutenant-General*
1896: Resigned

*Major-General* Ivan Nikolayevich **Nazansky** (22 Jan 1822 - ?)
16 Apr 1889: Promoted to *Major-General*
16 Apr 1889 - 28 Aug 1889: Commander, 2nd Brigade, 30th Infantry Division
28 Aug 1889 - Oct 1897: Commander, 2nd Brigade, 19th Infantry Division

*Major-General* Nikolai Ivanovich **Nazansky** (20 Nov 1868 - Jan 1935)
15 Jan 1910 - 19 Mar 1915: Chief of Bureau, Inspectorate of Rifles
19 Mar 1915: Promoted to *Major-General*
19 Mar 1915 - 1917: Special Assignments General, Inspector-General of Rifles

*Major-General* Foma Ivanovich **Nazarbekov** (4 Apr 1855 - 19 Feb 1931)
14 Aug 1906 - 4 May 1907: Commander, 14th Infantry Regiment
4 May 1907: Promoted to *Major-General*
4 May 1907: Retired
6 Nov 1914 - 24 Mar 1915: Recalled; Commander, Brigade, 66th Infantry Division
24 Mar 1915 - 19 Nov 1915: Commander, 2nd Caucasus Rifle Brigade
19 Nov 1915 - Jan 1917: Commander, 2nd Caucasus Rifle Division
Jan 1917 - 26 Dec 1917: Commanding General, VII. Caucasus Army Corps

*Major-General* Aleksandr Georgiyevich **Nazarov** (7 Oct 1848 - ?)
23 Oct 1897: Promoted to *Major-General*
23 Oct 1897 - 18 Jan 1900: Chief of Staff, South Ussuri Sector
18 Jan 1900 - 14 Dec 1902: Commander, 1st Brigade, 4th Infantry Division

*Major-General* Anatoly Mikhailovich **Nazarov** (12 Nov 1876 - 18 Feb 1918)
6 Aug 1914 - Apr 1915: Commander, 20th Don Cossack Regiment
Apr 1915 - 9 Dec 1915: Unassigned
21 Oct 1915: Promoted to *Major-General*
9 Dec 1915 - 4 Feb 1916: Reserve officer, Petrograd Military District
4 Feb 1916 - 24 Mar 1917: Commander, 2nd Trans-Baikal Cossack Brigade
24 Mar 1917 - 18 Apr 1917: Commander, 8th Don Cossack Division
18 Apr 1917 - 27 Aug 1917: Commander, Caucasus Cavalry Division
27 Aug 1917 - Oct 1917: Chief of Staff, VII. Caucasus Army Corps

*Lieutenant-General* Konstantin Aleksandrovich **Nazarov** (7 Sep 1844 - Jul 1916)
6 Feb 1901: Promoted to *Major-General*
6 Feb 1901 - 2 Dec 1901: Commander, 1st Brigade, 9th Cavalry Division
2 Dec 1901 - 4 Jun 1904: Commander, 2nd Brigade, Caucasus Cavalry Division
4 Jun 1904 - 29 Dec 1906: General for Special Assignments, Kiev Military District
29 Dec 1906: Promoted to *Lieutenant-General*
29 Dec 1906: Retired
23 Apr 1915 - Jul 1916: Recalled; Reserve officer, Kiev Military District

*Major-General* Nikolai Pavlovich **Nazimov** (12 Jan 1840 - ?)
7 May 1884 - 17 Aug 1892: Commander, 36th Dragoon Regiment
17 Aug 1892: Promoted to *Major-General*
17 Aug 1892 - Mar 1901: Commander, 2nd Brigade, 11th Cavalry Division

*Admiral* Pavel Nikolayevich **Nazimov** (9 Jul 1829 - 24 Dec 1902)
1882 - 1884: Commander, 5th Naval Depot
1883: Promoted to *Rear-Admiral*
1884 - 1889: Junior Flagman, Baltic Fleet
1889: Promoted to *Vice-Admiral*
1889 - 19 Feb 1891: Flagman, Pacific Squadron
19 Feb 1891 - 1892: Commander, Pacific Squadron
1892 - 1898: Chief of the Hydrographic Department, Ministry of the Navy
1894 - 24 Dec 1902: Member of the Admiralty Board
1901: Promoted to *Admiral*

*Rear-Admiral* Nikolai Ivanovich **Nebogatov** (20 Apr 1849 - 4 Aug 1922)
13 Sep 1900 - 26 May 1903: Deputy Chief of Training & Naval Artillery, Baltic Fleet
6 Dec 1901: Promoted to *Rear-Admiral*
26 May 1903 - 10 Jan 1905: Commander, Training Detachment, Black Sea Fleet
10 Jan 1905 - 28 May 1905: Commander, 3rd Pacific Squadron
11 May 1905 - 28 May 1905: Deputy C-in-C, Pacific Fleet
28 May 1905 - 1906: POW, Japan

8 Aug 1905: Dismissed

*Rear-Admiral* Arkady Konstantinovich **Nebolsin** (14 Oct 1865 - 3 Mar 1917)
20 Oct 1914 - 4 May 1915: Commander, 1st Battleship Brigade, Baltic Fleet
29 Jan 1915: Promoted to *Rear-Admiral*
4 May 1915 - 3 Mar 1917: Commander, 2nd Battleship Brigade, Baltic Fleet

*Vice-Admiral* Yevgeny Konstantinovich **Nebolsin** (28 Sep 1859 - 1934)
24 Nov 1908 - 1914: Commander, Port of Sveaborg
18 Apr 1910: Promoted to *Rear-Admiral*
1914 - 1915: Admiral for Special Assignments, Ministry of the Navy
1915 - 1917: Vice-Chairman, Naval Fortress Board, Emperor Peter the Great Naval Fortress
1917: Promoted to *Vice-Admiral*

*Major-General* Ivan Yevteyevich **Nechayev** (6 Sep 1842 - ?)
11 Mar 1898: Promoted to *Major-General*
11 Mar 1898 - 12 Oct 1902: Commander, 2nd Brigade, 34th Infantry Division

*Major-General* Izmail Yevlampiyevich **Nechayev** (1837 - ?)
1901: Promoted to *Major-General*

*Lieutenant-General* Nikolai Ivanovich **Nechayev** (24 Nov 1851 - 1919)
19 Dec 1898: Promoted to *Major-General*
19 Dec 1898 - 20 Nov 1899: Chief of Staff, XII. Army Corps
20 Nov 1899 - 13 Oct 1900: Chief of Staff, X. Army Corps
13 Oct 1900 - 1 Jun 1904: Commander, 51st Reserve Infantry Brigade
1 Jun 1904 - 1906: Commander, 51st Infantry Division
17 Apr 1905: Promoted to *Lieutenant-General*
1906: Retired

*General of Artillery* Nikolai Pavlovich **Nechayev** (4 May 1841 - 17 Jul 1917)
3 Sep 1894 - 30 Nov 1901: Professor of Chemistry, Konstantinov Artillery School
31 Dec 1894 - 7 Sep 1903: Member, Class V, Technical Committee, Main Intendant Administration
6 Dec 1897: Promoted to *Major-General*
25 Oct 1901 - 10 Mar 1910: Instructor, Intendant Training Courses
7 Sep 1903 - 14 Oct 1908: Head of Technical Committee, Main Intendant Administration
6 Dec 1904: Promoted to *Lieutenant-General*
10 Mar 1910: Promoted to *General of Artillery*
10 Mar 1910: Retired

*Major-General* Pyotr Stepanovich **Nechayev** (17 Feb 1858 - Mar 1917)
29 Aug 1906 - Mar 1917: Company Commander, Pskov Cadet Corps
20 Mar 1917: Posthumously promoted to *Major-General*

*General of Artillery* Viktor Vasiliyevich **Nechayev** (25 Aug 1822 - 1913)
16 Sep 1864 - 1901: Chief of Nikolayev Rocket Factory
28 Mar 1871: Promoted to *Major-General*
26 Feb 1885: Promoted to *Lieutenant-General*
1901: Promoted to *General of Artillery*
1901: Retired

*Major-General* Vyacheslav Vladimirovich **Nechayev** (1 Mar 1865 - ?)
11 Jan 1916 - 1917: Commander, 9th Heavy Artillery Brigade
22 Dec 1916: Promoted to *Major-General*

*Lieutenant-General* Aleksandr Dmitriyevich **Nechvolodov** (25 Mar 1864 - 25 Dec 1938)
11 May 1909: Promoted to *Major-General*
11 May 1909 - 12 May 1910: Commander, Brigade, 65th Infantry Division
12 May 1910 - 23 Jul 1911: Commander, 1st Brigade, 10th Infantry Division
23 Jul 1911 - 25 Aug 1915: Commander, 2nd Brigade, 4th Infantry Division
25 Aug 1915 - 12 Apr 1917: Commander, 19th Infantry Division
27 Nov 1915: Promoted to *Lieutenant-General*
12 Apr 1917 - Oct 1917: Reserve officer, Kiev Military District

*Major-General* Mikhail Dmitriyevich **Nechvolodov** (10 Feb 1867 - 10 Jan 1951)
21 Jan 1916 - 13 Feb 1917: Commander, 1st Special Infantry Regiment
26 Sep 1916: Promoted to *Major-General*
13 Feb 1917 - 25 May 1917: Commander, Brigade, 45th Infantry Division
25 May 1917 - 1917: Commander, Brigade, 1st Special Infantry Division
1917: Reserve officer, Petrogard Military District

*Lieutenant-General* Platon Platonovich **Nechvolodov** (26 Jan 1856 - 10 Nov 1936)
16 Apr 1900 - 31 Dec 1904: Deputy Head of Affairs Committee, Main Artillery Directorate
6 Dec 1903: Promoted to *Major-General*
31 Dec 1904 - 11 Nov 1910: Deputy Chief of the Main Artillery Directorate
6 Dec 1909: Promoted to *Lieutenant-General*
11 Nov 1910 - 1917: Head of Artillery Committee, Main Artillery Directorate
28 Sep 1914 - 1917: Chief of Technical Department, Main Artillery Directorate
1917: Head of Artillery Technical Committee, Main Artillery Directorate

*Rear-Admiral* Konstantin Konstantinovich **Nekhayev** (25 May 1865 - ?)
10 Apr 1916: Promoted to *Rear-Admiral*
1916 - 1917: Deputy Chief of Main Shipbuilding Directorate

*Major-General* Nikolai Aleksandrovich **Neklyudov** (15 Nov 1866 - ?)
7 Dec 1910 - 10 Jan 1916: Senior Staff Officer for Special Assignments, Don Cossack Army
22 Mar 1915: Promoted to *Major-General*
10 Jan 1916 - 11 Apr 1917: Commander, 30th Don Cossack Regiment

11 Apr 1917 - 1918: Commander, 1st Brigade, 3rd Don Cossack Division

*Lieutenant-General* Georgy Mikhailovich **Nekrashevich** (4 Mar 1865 - 23 Dec 1942)
15 Jan 1909: Promoted to *Major-General*
15 Jan 1909 - 9 Jul 1910: Commander, 1st Brigade, 38th Infantry Division
9 Jul 1910 - 6 Sep 1914: Chief of Staff, VI. Army Corps
6 Sep 1914 - 25 May 1915: Chief of Staff, XXVII. Army Corps
25 May 1915 - 9 Sep 1916: General for Special Assignments, 10th Army
9 Sep 1916 - 22 Mar 1917: Commander, 1st Turkestan Rifle Division
26 Sep 1916: Promoted to *Lieutenant-General*
22 Mar 1917 - Oct 1917: Reserve officer, Kiev Military District

*Major-General* Aleksey Petrovich **Nekrasov** (22 Nov 1852 - ?)
7 Jul 1907 - 1913: Staff Officer for Weapons Inspection, Omsk Military District
1913: Promoted to *Major-General*
1913: Retired
6 Oct 1915 - 10 Oct 1915: Recalled; Staff Officer for Special Assignments, ? Army
10 Oct 1915 - 12 May 1917: Staff Officer for Special Assignments, Western Front
12 May 1917: Dismissed

*Lieutenant-General* Konstantin Gerasimovich **Nekrasov** (15 Jul 1864 - Aug 1917)
10 Aug 1908 - 4 Nov 1914: Commander, Life Guards Pavlovsky Regiment
6 Dec 1908: Promoted to *Major-General*
4 Nov 1914 - 9 Jan 1915: Commander, 1st Brigade, 2nd Guards Infantry Division
9 Jan 1915 - 8 Feb 1915: Commander, 32nd Infantry Division
8 Feb 1915 - 2 May 1916: Commander, 21st Infantry Division
2 May 1916 - 12 Oct 1916: Attached to the Tsar's retinue
12 Oct 1916: Promoted to *Lieutenant-General*
12 Oct 1916 - Aug 1917: Commanding General, XXIV. Army Corps

*Lieutenant-General* Sergey Petrovich **Nekrasov** (26 Jun 1854 - ?)
4 Feb 1904: Promoted to *Major-General*
4 Feb 1904 - 12 Sep 1905: Commander, 1st Brigade, 15th Infantry Division
12 Sep 1905 - 11 Jun 1910: Chief of Staff, VIII. Army Corps
11 Jun 1910: Promoted to *Lieutenant-General*
11 Jun 1910 - 4 Mar 1913: Commander, 11th Siberian Rifle Division

*Major-General* Aleksandr Vladimirovich **Nelidov** (12 Mar 1852 - ?)
18 Apr 1910: Promoted to *Major-General*
18 Apr 1910 - 1917: Attached for Special Assignments to the Main Horse Breeding Directorate

*Major-General* Aleksey Nikolayevich **Nelidov** (28 Jun 1857 - ?)
31 Mar 1899 - 1906: Military Judge, Amur Military District Court
6 Dec 1901: Promoted to *Major-General*

*Major-General* Dmitry Nikolayevich **Nelidov** (29 May 1853 - ?)
| | |
|---|---|
| 4 Jan 1900 - 18 Jan 1913: | Head of Programs, Mikhailovsky Artillery Academy |
| 13 Apr 1908: | Promoted to *Major-General* |
| 18 Jan 1913 - 30 Apr 1917: | Deputy Commander of Artillery, Caucasus Military District |
| 30 Apr 1917 - 1917: | Deputy Commander of Artillery Logistics, Caucasus Army |

*Lieutenant-General* Ivan Antonovich **Nemilov** (19 Sep 1858 - ?)
| | |
|---|---|
| 25 Mar 1907: | Promoted to *Major-General* |
| 25 Mar 1907 - 17 Oct 1910: | Commander, 4th Sapper Brigade |
| 17 Oct 1910 - 29 Nov 1912: | Inspector of Field Engineers, Warsaw Military District |
| 29 Nov 1912 - 1 Aug 1914: | Inspector of Engineers, Warsaw Military District |
| 14 Apr 1913: | Promoted to *Lieutenant-General* |
| 1 Aug 1914 - 13 Nov 1914: | Chief of Engineering Logistics, Northwestern Front |
| 13 Nov 1914 - 1917: | Reserve officer, Dvinsk Military District |

*Lieutenant-General* Otton Iosifovich **Nemira** (19 Aug 1828 - ?)
| | |
|---|---|
| 10 Sep 1877: | Promoted to *Major-General* |
| 10 Sep 1877 - 14 Sep 1877: | Commander, 2nd Brigade, 9th Infantry Division |
| 14 Sep 1877 - 8 Jan 1889: | Chief of Staff, XI. Army Corps |
| 30 Aug 1888: | Promoted to *Lieutenant-General* |
| 8 Jan 1889 - 17 Feb 1896: | Commander, 28th Infantry Division |

*Lieutenant-General* Andrey Afanasiyevich **Nemirovich-Danchenko** (6 Oct 1836 -?)
| | |
|---|---|
| 20 Aug 1890 - 8 Jul 1891: | Deputy Chief of Staff, Kiev Military District |
| 30 Aug 1890: | Promoted to *Major-General* |
| 8 Jul 1891 - 11 Aug 1899: | Commander, 3rd Rifle Brigade |
| 11 Aug 1899 - 1903: | Commandant of Kiev |
| 6 Dec 1899: | Promoted to *Lieutenant-General* |

*Major-General* Yevgraf Yevdokimovich **Nemov** (9 Dec 1868 - 6 Nov 1944)
| | |
|---|---|
| 11 Jul 1915: | Promoted to *Major-General* |
| 11 Jul 1915 - 1917: | Intendant, Western Front |

*Major-General of Naval Artillery* Nikolai Pavlovich **Nemtsov** (9 Apr 1856 - 4 May 1915)
| | |
|---|---|
| Aug 1914 - 4 May 1915: | Chief of Drill Section, Naval Engineering Directorate |
| 6 Dec 1914: | Promoted to *Major-General of Naval Artillery* |

*Major-General* Aleksandr Karlovich **Nemysky** (13 Jan 1843 - ?)
| | |
|---|---|
| 22 Jun 1892 - 1 Nov 1897: | Commander, 35th Infantry Regiment |
| 14 May 1896: | Promoted to *Major-General* |
| 1 Nov 1897 - 14 Jan 1898: | Commander, 2nd Brigade, 19th Infantry Division |
| 14 Jan 1898 - 16 Aug 1901: | Commander, 2nd Brigade, 42nd Infantry Division |

*Major-General* Anton-Yemelyan Voytsekhovich-Adalbertovich **Nemysky** (14 Nov 1844 - ?)
| | |
|---|---|
| 20 Nov 1901: | Promoted to *Major-General* |
| 20 Nov 1901 - 7 Jan 1905: | Commander, 1st Brigade, 11th Infantry Division |

*Vice-Admiral* Dmitry Vsevolodovich **Nenyukov** (18 Jan 1869 - 3 Jul 1929)
Nov 1913 - 25 Jul 1914: Deputy Chief of Naval General Staff for Shipbuilding
21 Jul 1914: Promoted to *Rear-Admiral*
25 Jul 1914 - 1915: Chief of Naval Administration, Supreme Commander-in-Chief
1915 - 1916: Commander, Danube Naval Detachment
1916 - 1917: Commander, Special Naval Task Force
6 Dec 1916: Promoted to *Vice-Admiral*

*Lieutenant-General* Tomas Fridrikhovich **Neovius** (10 Nov 1840 - 14 Sep 1906)
1 Jul 1887 - 25 Jan 1893: Commander of Artillery, Fortress Osovets
25 Jan 1893: Promoted to *Major-General*
25 Jan 1893 - 10 Mar 1893: Commander of Artillery, Fortress Ivangorod
10 Mar 1893 - 14 Mar 1895: Commander of Artillery, Fortress Osovets
14 Mar 1895 - Feb 1901: Commander of Artillery, Fortress Libau
Feb 1901: Promoted to *Lieutenant-General*
Feb 1901: Retired

*Vice-Admiral* Adrian Ivanovich **Nepenin** (21 Oct 1871 - 4 Mar 1917)
17 Jul 1914 - 6 Aug 1916: Chief of Communications, Baltic Sea
1 Sep 1914: Promoted to *Rear-Admiral*
6 Aug 1916: Promoted to *Vice-Admiral*
6 Aug 1916 - 4 Mar 1917: C-in-C, Baltic Fleet

*Major-General* Ivan Vladimirovich **Nepenin** (4 Mar 1851 - 29 Jul 1909)
24 Feb 1905 - 29 Jul 1909: Commander, 14th Artillery Brigade
22 Apr 1907: Promoted to *Major-General*

*Major-General* Pyotr Vladimirovich **Nepenin** (21 Dec 1849 - ?)
16 Mar 1903: Promoted to *Major-General*
16 Mar 1903 - 1 Aug 1906: Commander, 1st Brigade, 45th Infantry Division
1 Aug 1906 - 1908: Commander, 64th Replacement Infantry Brigade
1908: Retired

*Major-General* Sergey Yakovlevich **Nepenin** (3 Jul 1869 - ?)
28 Sep 1916 - 6 Aug 1917: Chief of Staff, 13th Infantry Division
6 Dec 1916: Promoted to *Major-General*
6 Aug 1917: Retired

*General of Engineers* Vladimir Stepanovich **Neplyuyev** (15 Feb 1847 - ?)
19 Jul 1886 - 4 Mar 1898: Commander of Engineers, Fortress Kaunas
17 Sep 1895: Promoted to *Major-General*
4 Mar 1898 - 27 Feb 1903: Commander of Engineers, Vilnius Military District
6 Dec 1902: Promoted to *Lieutenant-General*
27 Feb 1903 - 6 Aug 1905: Commandant of Fortress Ochakov
6 Aug 1905 - 14 Feb 1907: Commandant of Fortress Sevastopol
14 Feb 1907 - 1 Nov 1908: Commandant of Fortress Kaunas
1 Nov 1908: Promoted to *General of Engineers*

1 Nov 1908:                          Retired

*Major-General* Klavdy Pavlovich **Nepokoychitsky** (21 Nov 1857 - ?)
13 Aug 1904 - 4 Jan 1908:            Commander, Baku Borderguard Brigade
4 Jan 1908 - 21 Feb 1912:            Commander, 12$^{th}$ (Kalisz) Borderguard Brigade
10 Apr 1911:                         Promoted to *Major-General*
21 Feb 1912 - 3 Jan 1914:            Commander, 24$^{th}$ (Crimean) Borderguard Brigade
3 Jan 1914 - 1917:                   Commander, 1$^{st}$ Borderguard District

*Major-General* Aleksandr Karlovich von **Nerike** (6 Apr 1876 - 27 May 1934)
1 Oct 1915 - 14 Dec 1916:            Commander, 148$^{th}$ Infantry Regiment
22 Sep 1916:                         Promoted to *Major-General*
14 Dec 1916 - 9 Feb 1917:            Reserve officer, Petrograd Military District
9 Feb 1917 - 1918:                   Chief of Lines of Communications, 7$^{th}$ Army

*Major-General* Vladimir Dmitriyevich **Neronov** (19 Apr 1860 - ?)
3 Aug 1909 - 13 Aug 1914:            Section Chief, Electro-Technical Department, Main
                                     Military Technical Directorate
6 Dec 1913:                          Promoted to *Major-General*
13 Aug 1914 - Oct 1917:              Senior Acceptance Engineer, Main Military Technical
                                     Directorate

*Major-General* Aleksey Vasilyevich **Nesterenko** (8 Feb 1857 - 22 Aug 1915)
15 Jun 1914:                         Promoted to *Major-General*
15 Jun 1914 - 22 Aug 1915:           Commander, 8$^{th}$ Siberian Rifle Artillery Brigade

*Major-General* Aleksandr Yevplovich **Nesterov** (21 Jul 1850 - ?)
20 Jan 1904 - 31 Dec 1913:           Staff Officer for Weapons Inspection, St. Petersburg
                                     Military District
14 Apr 1913:                         Promoted to *Major-General*
31 Dec 1913:                         Retired
17 Jan 1915 - 1917:                  Recalled; Reserve officer, Petrograd Military District

*Major-General* Nikolai Petrovich **Nesterovich** (1 May 1847 - ?)
2 Jun 1892 - 1903:                   Military Judge, Vilnius Military District Court
30 Aug 1893:                         Promoted to *Major-General*

*Lieutenant-General* Aleksandr Ivanovich **Nesterovsky** (23 Mar 1862 - ?)
24 Mar 1909:                         Promoted to *Major-General*
24 Mar 1909 - 26 Feb 1914:           Chief of Staff, Orenburg Cossack Army
26 Feb 1914 - 4 Mar 1915:            Chief of Staff, Fortress Modlin
4 Mar 1915 - 30 Jun 1917:            Deputy Chief of Staff, Minsk Military District
30 Jun 1917 - 14 Aug 1917:           Commander, 7$^{th}$ Siberian Rifle Division
14 Aug 1917 - 27 Oct 1917:           Commander, 7$^{th}$ Turkestan Rifle Division
15 Aug 1917:                         Promoted to *Lieutenant-General*

*Major-General* Aleksandr Sergeyevich **Netsvetayev** (13 Apr 1830 - ?)
19 Dec 1888 - 1898:                  Chief of Mikhailovsk Baronet Villie Clinical Hospital

14 May 1896: Promoted to *Major-General*

*Major-General* Baron Ivan Robertovich **Nettelgorst** (14 Sep 1854 - ?)
9 Feb 1898 - 2 Apr 1916: Head of the Izmailovsky Tsar Nikolai I Invalid Home
6 Dec 1913: Promoted to *Major-General*
2 Apr 1916: Dismissed

*General of Cavalry* Baron Pyotr Robertovich von **Nettelgorst** (13 Dec 1850 - ?)
13 Apr 1902: Promoted to *Major-General*
13 Apr 1902 - 4 Apr 1905: Commander, Life Guards Ataman Regiment
4 Apr 1905 - 19 Jun 1905: Commander, 1st Brigade, 2nd Guards Cavalry Division
19 Jun 1905 - 10 Feb 1907: Commander, 3rd Brigade, 1st Guards Cavalry Division
10 Feb 1907 - 3 Sep 1907: Commander, 2nd Brigade, 2nd Guards Cavalry Division
3 Sep 1907: Promoted to *Lieutenant-General*
3 Sep 1907 - 1 May 1910: Commander, 14th Cavalry Division
1 May 1910: Promoted to *General of Cavalry*
1 May 1910: Retired
11 Oct 1914 - 1916: Recalled; Commanding General, IV. Militia Corps

*General of Artillery* Dmitry Ivanovich **Nevadovsky** (26 Oct 1850 - ?)
4 Jan 1900 - 25 Jul 1906: Commandant, Mikhailov Artillery School
1 Apr 1901: Promoted to *Major-General*
25 Jul 1906 - 26 Jul 1910: Commander of Artillery, III. Army Corps
22 Apr 1907: Promoted to *Lieutenant-General*
26 Jul 1910 - 26 Oct 1913: Inspector of Artillery, III. Army Corps
26 Oct 1913: Promoted to *General of Artillery*
26 Oct 1913: Retired
Jul 1914 - 3 Aug 1915: Recalled; Inspector of Medical Institutions, Petrograd
3 Aug 1915 - 29 Apr 1917: Inspector of Artillery, XII. Army Corps

*General of Infantry* Ivan Fyodorovich **Nevadovsky** (2 Aug 1832 - 18 Mar 1902)
2 Apr 1871 - 21 Apr 1878: Commander, 45th Infantry Regiment
14 Nov 1877: Promoted to *Major-General*
21 Apr 1878 - 10 Nov 1884: Commander, 2nd Brigade, 33rd Infantry Division
10 Nov 1884 - 12 Jun 1891: Commander, 9th Regional Brigade
30 Aug 1886: Promoted to *Lieutenant-General*
12 Jun 1891 - 17 May 1896: Commander, 41st Infantry Division
17 May 1896: Promoted to *General of Infantry*
17 May 1896: Retired

*Lieutenant-General of the Fleet* Nikolai Aleksandrovich **Nevakhovich** (3 Nov 1835 - 21 Aug 1901)
1886 - 1900: Commander of the Guards, Imperial Yacht "Aleksandria"
1889: Promoted to *Rear-Admiral*
1895 - 1900: Honorary Trustee, Board of Imperial Institutions
1900: Promoted to *Lieutenant-General of the Fleet*
1900: Retired

*Major-General* Vasily Ivanovich **Nevrazhin** (21 Jan 1868 - ?)
6 Dec 1916 - 1917: Special Assignments General, Ministry of the Interior
31 Jan 1917: Promoted to *Major-General*

*Major-General of Naval Engineers* Vladimir Ivanovich **Nevrazhin** (16 Sep 1868 - Aug 1918)
1914 - 11 May 1917: Deputy Chief of Mechanics, Shipbuilding Office, Port of St. Petersburg
8 Sep 1915: Promoted to *Major-General of Naval Engineers*
11 May 1917 - Aug 1918: Chief of the Admiralty Plant

*Major-General* Aleksandr Alekseyevich **Nevsky** (13 Oct 1858 - ?)
18 May 1913 - 28 Dec 1915: Commander, 48th Infantry Regiment
13 May 1915: Promoted to *Major-General*
28 Dec 1915 - 1917: Reserve officer, Odessa Military District

*Major-General* Mikhail Ivanovich **Nevtonov** (20 Oct 1830 - 1904)
6 May 1898: Promoted to *Major-General*
6 May 1898 - 17 Aug 1899: Chief of Chancellery to the Commander, Transcaspian Province
17 Aug 1899 - 1904: At the disposal of the Chief of the General Staff

*Lieutenant-General* Vladimir Fyodorovich **Nevtonov** (26 Jan 1856 - ?)
15 Jan 1909: Promoted to *Major-General*
15 Jan 1909 - 29 Jul 1914: Commander, 1st Brigade, 20th Infantry Division
29 Jul 1914 - Sep 1914: Commander, Brigade, 64th Infantry Division
Sep 1914 - 1915: Commander, Brigade, 59th Infantry Division
1915 - 9 Sep 1915: Reserve officer, Dvinsk Military District
9 Sep 1915 - 1916: Reserve officer, Caucasus Military District
1916 - 1917: Commandant, School of Infantry Ensigns, Caucasus Military District
6 Dec 1916: Promoted to *Lieutenant-General*

*Major-General of the Hydrographic Corps* Aleksandr Ivanovich **Neyelov** (1868 - 31 Oct 1918)
1912 - 5 Jun 1918: Member, Commission on the Review of the Finnish Archipelago
1917: Promoted to *Major-General of the Hydrographic Corps*

*Major-General* Fyodor Vasilyevich **Neyelov** (25 Jul 1856 - ?)
20 Sep 1901: Promoted to *Major-General*
20 Sep 1901 - Sep 1905: Chief of Staff, II. Turkestan Army Corps

*Major-General* Iosif Adolfovich **Neygebauer** (24 Mar 1858 - 1911)
1 Jun 1906 - 24 Apr 1908: Chief of Communications, Caucasus Military District
30 Jul 1907: Promoted to *Major-General*
24 Apr 1908 - 1911: At the disposal of the Minister of Railways

*Major-General of Naval Engineers* Tomas Romualdovich **Neyman** (13 Nov 1867 - 1942)
31 Jan 1912 - Oct 1917: Member, Commission for Shipbuilding, Black Sea
6 Dec 1915: Promoted to *Major-General of Naval Engineers*

*Major-General* Stepan Ignatyevich **Nezhinsky** (16 Jan 1856 - ?)
22 Jun 1913 - 1917: Military Commander, Novomoskovsk District
28 May 1915: Promoted to *Major-General*

*Major-General* Aleksandr Aleksandrovich **Neznamov** (10 Oct 1872 - 28 Jun 1928)
27 Apr 1915 - 20 Nov 1915: Commander, 102$^{nd}$ Infantry Regiment
24 May 1915: Promoted to *Major-General*
20 Nov 1915 - 12 Jul 1916: General for Assignments, C-in-C, 7$^{th}$ Army
12 Jul 1916 - 1 May 1917: Quartermaster-General, 7$^{th}$ Army
1 May 1917 - 25 Aug 1917: Chief of Staff, 7$^{th}$ Army
25 Aug 1917 - Feb 1918: Quartermaster-General to the Deputy C-in-C, Romanian Front

*Vice-Admiral* Aleksandr Georgievich von **Nidermiller** (19 Jul 1851 - 21 Mar 1937)
1902: Promoted to *Rear-Admiral*
1902 - 1903: Chief of Staff, Port of Kronstadt
1903 - Feb 1906: Deputy Chief of the Main Naval Staff
Feb 1906 - 1907: Chief of the Main Naval Staff
1907 - 1908: Chairman of the Committee of the Volunteer Fleet
1908: Promoted to *Vice-Admiral*
1908: Discharged

*General of Infantry* Nikolai Yegorovich von **Nidermiller** (6 Dec 1849 - ?)
9 Jul 1887 - 23 Nov 1898: Chief of Troop Movement Section, General Staff
30 Aug 1891: Promoted to *Major-General*
1894: Acting Commander, 2$^{nd}$ Brigade, 37$^{th}$ Infantry Division
23 Nov 1898 - 14 Jun 1906: At the disposal of the Chief of the General Staff
6 Dec 1899: Promoted to *Lieutenant-General*
14 Jun 1906: Promoted to *General of Infantry*
14 Jun 1906: Retired

*Lieutenant-General* Nikolai Yegorovich **Nikiforaki** (4 Jan 1838 - 15 Feb 1904)
18 Dec 1879 - 12 Mar 1887: Commander, Chernomorsk Region
30 Aug 1885: Promoted to *Major-General*
12 Mar 1887 - 15 Feb 1904: Governor of Stavropol
14 May 1896: Promoted to *Lieutenant-General*

*Major-General* Nikolai Konstantinovich **Nikiforov** (21 Sep 1862 - 29 Apr 1934)
9 Nov 1913 - 26 Apr 1916: Commander, 125$^{th}$ Infantry Regiment
16 Apr 1916: Promoted to *Major-General*
26 Apr 1916 - 1917: Commander, Brigade, 47$^{th}$ Infantry Division

*Major-General* Nikolai Nikolayevich **Nikiforov** (11 May 1872 - 30 Mar 1948)
4 Feb 1915 - 1917: Chief of Artillery Section, General Staff, 6$^{th}$ Army

6 Dec 1916: Promoted to *Major-General*

*Major-General* Pavel Nikolayevich **Nikiforov** (21 Feb 1868 - ?)
8 Apr 1915 - 23 Jun 1916: Commander, 3rd Uhlan Regiment
26 Mar 1916: Promoted to *Major-General*
23 Jun 1916 - 1917: Reserve officer, Minsk Military District

*Lieutenant-General* Pyotr Dmitriyevich **Nikiforov** (10 Jul 1846 - 1910)
22 Oct 1884 - 1910: Military Judge, St. Petersburg Military District Court
30 Aug 1892: Promoted to *Major-General*
6 Dec 1909: Promoted to *Lieutenant-General*

*Major-General* Sergey Yakovlevich **Nikiforov** (12 Sep 1857 - 4 Aug 1914)
3 Aug 1911 - 4 Aug 1914: Commander, 2nd Battalion, 40th Artillery Brigade
2 Nov 1914: Posthumously promoted to *Major-General*

*Major-General* Nikolai Kondratyevich **Nikitenko** (24 Dec 1855 - 1928)
25 Aug 1914 - Oct 1917: Commander, 2nd Reserve Artillery Brigade
18 Jan 1917: Promoted to *Major-General*

*Major-General* Aleksandr Vladimirovich **Nikitin** (17 Jan 1865 - 1934)
14 Jul 1910 - 3 Aug 1915: Commander, 1st Battalion, 23rd Artillery Brigade
23 Apr 1915: Promoted to *Major-General*
3 Aug 1915 - 27 Feb 1917: Commander, 11th Artillery Brigade
27 Feb 1917 - 1918: Inspector of Artillery, XI. Army Corps

*Lieutenant-General* Pavel Andreyevich **Nikitin** (15 Aug 1863 - 18 Aug 1916)
2 Jul 1913: Promoted to *Major-General*
2 Jul 1913 - 29 Jul 1914: Commander, 2nd Brigade, 19th Infantry Division
29 Jul 1914 - 30 Sep 1914: Commander, Brigade, 65th Infantry Division
30 Sep 1914 - 15 Apr 1915: Quartermaster-General, 8th Army
15 Apr 1915 - 21 May 1916: Chief of Staff, XXV. Army Corps
21 May 1916 - 18 Aug 1916: Commander, 5th Infantry Division
11 Nov 1916: Posthumously promoted to *Lieutenant-General*

*Major-General* Pyotr Fedotovich **Nikitin** (4 Jul 1874 - ?)
24 Jan 1915 - 1917: Attached to Mikhailovsky Artillery Academy
6 Dec 1915: Promoted to *Major-General*

*Major-General* Semyon Vlasyevich **Nikitin** (24 May 1859 - ?)
25 Aug 1915 - 1917: Commander, 1st Brigade, 2nd Kuban Cossack Division
18 May 1916: Promoted to *Major-General*

*Major-General* Sergey Sergeyevich **Nikitin** (15 Feb 1867 - 1930)
7 Aug 1912 - 18 Jan 1916: Commander, 181st Infantry Regiment
5 Oct 1915: Promoted to *Major-General*
18 Jan 1916 - 26 Mar 1916: Commander, Brigade, 29th Infantry Division
26 Mar 1916 - 1917: Commander, 4th Replacement Infantry Brigade

*Major-General* Vladimir Kuzmich **Nikitin** (24 Aug 1836 - 16 Oct 1898)
30 Apr 1889 - 15 Jul 1892: Commander, 29th Infantry Regiment
15 Jul 1892: Promoted to *Major-General*
15 Jul 1892 - 20 Jul 1895: Transferred to the reserve
20 Jul 1895 - 16 Oct 1898: Commander, 2nd Brigade, 40th Infantry Division

*General of Artillery* Vladimir Nikolayevich **Nikitin** (17 Jul 1848 - 21 May 1922)
29 Dec 1899 - 8 Feb 1904: Commander, 20th Artillery Brigade
29 Dec 1899: Promoted to *Major-General*
8 Feb 1904 - 25 Aug 1905: Commander of Artillery, III. Siberian Army Corps
3 May 1904: Promoted to *Lieutenant-General*
25 Aug 1905 - 11 Apr 1906: Unassigned
11 Apr 1906 - 8 Jun 1908: Commander of Artillery, I. Army Corps
8 Jun 1908 - 11 Mar 1911: Commanding General, I. Army Corps
6 Dec 1910: Promoted to *General of Artillery*
11 Mar 1911 - 13 Jun 1912: Commanding General, Irkutsk Military District
13 Jun 1912 - 19 Jul 1914: Commanding General, Odessa Military District
19 Jul 1914 - 19 Oct 1915: C-in-C, 7th Army
19 Oct 1915 - 16 Mar 1916: Member of the Military Council
16 Mar 1916 - 9 Apr 1917: Commandant of Fortress Petrograd
9 Apr 1917: Retired

*Major-General* Nikolai Dmitriyevich **Nikolas** (4 May 1864 - ?)
28 Jul 1913 - 13 Jun 1916: Deputy Chief of Construction, Tsar Peter the Great Naval Fortress
6 Dec 1913: Promoted to *Major-General*
13 Jun 1916 - 1917: Commander of Engineers, 9th Army

*Lieutenant-General* Aleksandr Nikolayevich **Nikolayev** (24 Dec 1850 - 14 Apr 1916)
11 Jun 1896 - 11 Aug 1896: Commander, 1st Brigade, 15th Cavalry Division
12 Jun 1896: Promoted to *Major-General*
11 Aug 1896 - 17 May 1900: Commander, Guards Cavalry Regiment
11 Jan 1899 - 14 Apr 1916: General à la suite
17 May 1900 - 11 Apr 1902: Commander, 2nd Brigade, 1st Guards Cavalry Division
11 Apr 1902 - 28 Dec 1903: Commander, 1st Brigade, 1st Guards Cavalry Division
28 Dec 1903 - 14 Apr 1916: Reserve officer, Guards Cavalry
18 Apr 1910: Promoted to *Lieutenant-General*
18 Apr 1910: Promoted to *General-Adjutant*

*Major General* Aleksandr Nikolayevich **Nikolayev** (27 Aug 1864 - 1910)
27 Sep 1908 - 1909: Commander, 191st Reserve Infantry Regiment
1909: Promoted to *Major-General*
1909: Retired

*Major-General* Aleksandr Panfomirovich **Nikolayev** (19 Aug 1860 - 28 May 1919)
11 Dec 1914 - 3 May 1916: Commander, 169th Infantry Regiment
23 Dec 1915: Promoted to *Major-General*
3 May 1916 - 1917: Commander, Brigade, 19th Infantry Division

1917:                              Commander, 19th Infantry Division

*Major-General* Aleksey Ivanovich **Nikolayev** (13 Mar 1860 - ?)
1915 - 12 Aug 1915:              Commander, 293rd Infantry Regiment
12 Aug 1915 - 1916:              Reserve officer, ? Army
1916 - 1917:                     Reserve officer, Petrograd Military District
6 Dec 1915:                      Promoted to *Major-General*

*Lieutenant-General* Andrey Mikhailovich **Nikolayev** (18 Jul 1858 - 13 Oct 1926)
2 Jun 1910:                      Promoted to *Major-General*
2 Jun 1910 - 22 Jun 1912:        Commander, 2nd Brigade, 1st Turkestan Cossack Division
22 Jun 1912 - 9 Nov 1913:        Commander, 2nd Brigade, 3rd Cavalry Division
9 Nov 1913 - 14 Nov 1915:        Commander, Trans-Caspian Cossack Brigade
1914 - 1915:                     Commander, Makin Detachment
1915 - 14 Nov 1915:              Commander, Ararat Detachment
21 Jul 1915:                     Promoted to *Lieutenant-General*
14 Nov 1915 - 15 Nov 1916:       Commander, 5th Caucasus Cossack Division
15 Nov 1916 - 1917:              Commander, 2nd Kuban Cossack Division

*Major-General* Konstantin Konstantinovich **Nikolayev** (13 Mar 1859 - ?)
1915 - 1917:                     Commander, 299th Infantry Regiment
26 Sep 1916:                     Promoted to *Major-General*
1917:                            Reserve officer, Minsk Military District
1917:                            Dismissed

*Major-General* Konstantin Mikhailovich **Nikolayev** (22 Apr 1854 - ?)
12 Apr 1906 - 11 Nov 1907:       Commander, Orenburg Cossack Horse Artillery Brigade
6 Dec 1906:                      Promoted to *Major-General*

*Lieutenant-General* Pavel Timofeyevich **Nikolayev** (4 Nov 1862 - 24 Jan 1916)
4 Dec 1907 - 25 Aug 1910:        Commander, Life Guards 1st Rifle Battalion
13 Apr 1908:                     Promoted to *Major-General*
25 Aug 1910 - 27 Sep 1914:       Commander, Life Guards 1st Rifle Regiment
27 Sep 1914 - 24 Jan 1916:       Commander, 45th Infantry Division
30 Sep 1915:                     Promoted to *Lieutenant-General*

*Lieutenant-General* Roman Nikolayevich **Nikolayev** (1 Oct 1844 - 1914)
30 Jan 1904:                     Promoted to *Major-General*
30 Jan 1904 - 1909:              Special Assignments General to the Commanding General, Borderguard Corps
1909:                            Promoted to *Lieutenant-General*
1909:                            Retired

*Lieutenant-General* Vladimir Aleksandrovich **Nikolayev** (28 Jul 1847 - 1917)
21 Nov 1895 - 1917:              Commander, Main Engineering Depot
8 Jul 1906:                      Promoted to *Major-General*
1916:                            Promoted to *Lieutenant-General*

*Major-General* Vladimir Vasilyevich **Nikolayev** (29 Oct 1840 - ?)
| | |
|---|---|
| 1 Sep 1879 - 1908: | Professor, Pavlov Military School |
| 6 May 1905: | Promoted to *Major-General* |

*Major-General* Anatoly Timofeyevich **Nikolenko** (16 Apr 1853 - ?)
| | |
|---|---|
| 23 Jan 1901 - 1916: | Chief of Tambov-Ural Railway Gendarmerie |
| 13 Apr 1908: | Promoted to *Major-General* |

*General of Engineers* Nikolai Mikhailovich **Nikolenko** (17 Jun 1855 - ?)
| | |
|---|---|
| 4 Sep 1903: | Promoted to *Major-General* |
| 4 Sep 1903 - 13 Oct 1904: | Commander, $2^{nd}$ Sapper Brigade |
| 13 Oct 1904 - 7 Dec 1906: | Inspector of Engineers, $2^{nd}$ Manchurian Army |
| 7 Dec 1906 - 3 Jun 1907: | Commander, $6^{th}$ Sapper Brigade |
| 3 Jun 1907 - 17 Oct 1910: | Commander, $1^{st}$ Sapper Brigade |
| 6 Dec 1908: | Promoted to *Lieutenant-General* |
| 17 Oct 1910 - 5 Mar 1911: | Inspector of Field Engineers, St. Petersburg Military District |
| 5 Mar 1911 - 23 Mar 1914: | Commandant of Fortress Kronstadt |
| 23 Mar 1914 - 2 Apr 1917: | Commandant of St. Petersburg |
| 6 Dec 1914: | Promoted to *General of Engineers* |
| 2 Apr 1917: | Retired |

*Lieutenant-General* Iosif Ivanovich **Nikolev** (13 Oct 1838 - ?)
| | |
|---|---|
| 4 Jan 1891: | Promoted to *Major-General* |
| 4 Jan 1891 - 25 Sep 1892: | Deputy Chief of Staff, Warsaw Military District |
| 25 Sep 1892 - 3 Oct 1894: | Duty General, Warsaw Military District |
| 3 Oct 1894 - 3 Mar 1897: | Quartermaster-General, Warsaw Military District |
| 3 Mar 1897 - 13 Jul 1900: | Commander, $2^{nd}$ Rifle Brigade |
| 13 Jul 1900: | Promoted to *Lieutenant-General* |
| 13 Jul 1900: | Retired |

*Major-General* Konstantin Vladimirovich **Nikolsky** (4 Aug 1869 - ?)
| | |
|---|---|
| 20 Jun 1913 - 9 Jul 1915: | Commander, $19^{th}$ Infantry Regiment |
| 16 May 1915: | Promoted to *Major-General* |
| 9 Jul 1915 - 7 Feb 1917: | Commander, $1^{st}$ Brigade, $5^{th}$ Infantry Division |
| 7 Feb 1917 - 28 Apr 1917: | Commander, $2^{nd}$ Caucasus Grenadier Division |
| 28 Apr 1917 - 1917: | Reserve officer, Kiev Military District |

*Major-General* Viktor Ksenofontovich **Nikolsky** (25 Jun 1835 - 8 Jul 1906)
| | |
|---|---|
| 26 May 1890 - 3 Jun 1892: | Commander of Gendarmerie, Omsk Province |
| 30 Aug 1890: | Promoted to *Major-General* |
| 3 Jun 1892 - 1900: | Commander of Gendarmerie, Kostroma Province |

*Major-General* Vladimir Pavlovich **Nikolsky** (14 Aug 1873 - 1960)
| | |
|---|---|
| 14 Aug 1913 - 30 Apr 1917: | Chief of Staff, Corps of Gendarmes |
| 6 May 1915: | Promoted to *Major-General* |
| 30 Apr 1917 - Oct 1917: | Reserve officer, Petrograd Military District |

*Major-General* Vyacheslav Nikolayevich **Nikolsky** (4 Mar 1858 - ?)
| | |
|---|---|
| 1 Sep 1909 - 1914: | Deputy Chief of Okhtenskaya Explosives Factory |
| 6 Dec 1909: | Promoted to *Major-General* |
| 1914 - 1917: | Chief of Okhtenskaya Explosives Factory |

*Admiral* Konstantin Petrovich **Nikonov** (14 Apr 1844 - 10 May 1915)
| | |
|---|---|
| 26 Jan 1898: | Promoted to *Rear-Admiral* |
| 10 Aug 1898 - 1902: | Commander, Port of Emperor Aleksander III (Libau) |
| 1902 - 1903: | Commander, Training Detachment, Baltic Sea |
| 1903 - Apr 1904: | Chairman of Testing Commission for the Cruiser "Aurora" |
| 1 Jan 1904: | Promoted to *Vice-Admiral* |
| Apr 1904 - 16 May 1905: | Senior Flagman, 2nd Naval Flotilla |
| 16 May 1905 - 1 Oct 1908: | C-in-C, Baltic Sea Naval Forces, Military Governor of Kronstadt |
| 1 Oct 1908: | Retired |
| 13 Oct 1908: | Promoted to *Admiral (Retired)* |

*Major-General* Mikhail Pavlovich **Nikonov** (10 Oct 1862 - 6 Nov 1935)
| | |
|---|---|
| 22 Aug 1910 - 27 Aug 1916: | Inspector of Classes, Nizhny Novgorod Cadet Corps |
| 6 Dec 1913: | Promoted to *Major-General* |
| 27 Aug 1916 - Jun 1920: | Director of Kharabovsk Cadet Corps |

*Lieutenant-General* Semyon Ivanovich **Nikonov** (2 Feb 1852 - ?)
| | |
|---|---|
| 10 Mar 1902: | Promoted to *Major-General* |
| 10 Mar 1902 - 28 Apr 1906: | Commander, 2nd Brigade, 2nd Grenadier Division |
| 28 Apr 1906 - 29 Dec 1908: | Commander, 56th Reserve Infantry Brigade |
| 29 Dec 1908: | Promoted to *Lieutenant-General* |
| 29 Dec 1908: | Retired |
| 7 Feb 1915 - 18 May 1917: | Recalled; Commander, 9th Replacement Infantry Brigade |
| 18 May 1917: | Dismissed |

*Major-General* Ivan Andreyevich **Nikulin** (28 Jan 1868 - ?)
| | |
|---|---|
| 5 Jan 1913 - 15 May 1915: | Commander, 8th Uhlan Regiment |
| 15 May 1915 - 10 Nov 1915: | Commander, 1st Brigade, 5th Cavalry Division |
| 27 May 1915: | Promoted to *Major-General* |
| 10 Nov 1915 - 7 May 1917: | Chief of Staff, V. Cavalry Corps |
| 7 May 1917 - 1918: | Commander, Ural Cossack Division |

*Major-General* Nikolai Pavlovich **Nikushkin** (15 Feb 1870 - 3 Apr 1939)
| | |
|---|---|
| 18 Nov 1916 - Apr 1917: | Commander, 18th Sapper Battalion |
| 6 Feb 1917: | Promoted to *Major-General* |
| Apr 1917 - 1918: | Commander, 18th Engineer Regiment |

*Lieutenant-General* Ivan Dmitriyevich **Nilov** (31 Jan 1859 - 19 Oct 1933)
| | |
|---|---|
| 6 Oct 1905 - 21 May 1912: | Commander, 1st Hussar Regiment |
| 21 May 1912: | Promoted to *Major-General* |

21 May 1912 - 25 Aug 1915:        Commander, 2nd Brigade, 1st Cavalry Division
25 Aug 1915 - 26 Apr 1916:        Unassigned
26 Apr 1916 - 18 Apr 1917:        Commander, 5th Cavalry Division
1917:                             Promoted to *Lieutenant-General*

*Admiral* Konstantin Dmitriyevich **Nilov** (7 Feb 1856 - 1919)
1 Jan 1903 - 13 Apr 1908:         Commander, Guards Naval Depot
6 Apr 1903:                       Promoted to *Rear-Admiral*
8 Oct 1905 - 24 Mar 1917:         Flag Captain to the Tsar
6 Apr 1908:                       Promoted to *Vice-Admiral*
5 Oct 1908:                       Promoted to *General-Adjutant*
25 Mar 1912:                      Promoted to *Admiral*
24 Mar 1917:                      Dismissed

*Lieutenant-General* Andrey Aleksandrovich **Nilus** (5 Jan 1858 - 6 Dec 1941)
26 Apr 1905 - 2 Jul 1909:         Extraordinary Professor, Mikhailovsky Artillery
                                  Academy
13 Apr 1908:                      Promoted to *Major-General*
2 Jul 1909 - 25 Feb 1914:         Ordinary Professor, Mikhailovsky Artillery Academy
1913:                             Promoted to *Lieutenant-General*
30 Mar 1913 - Oct 1917:           Head of Sergievsky Artillery School

*Major-General* Count Fyodor Maksimilianovich **Nirod** (20 Jul 1871 - 4 Apr 1952)
14 Nov 1912 - 13 Jan 1915:        Commander, Life Guards Dragoon Regiment
29 Apr 1913:                      Promoted to *Major-General*
13 Jan 1915 - 30 Aug 1915:        Commander, 2nd Brigade, 2nd Guards Cavalry Division
30 Aug 1915 - 11 Sep 1915:        Commander, 2nd Brigade, 1st Guards Cavalry Division
11 Sep 1915 - 15 Aug 1916:        General à la suite
15 Aug 1916 - 1917:               Commander, Consolidated Kuban Cossack Division

*Major-General* Konstantin Nikanorovich **Nishchenko** (19 Jan 1844 - ?)
22 Jun 1892:                      Promoted to *Major-General*
22 Jun 1892 - 1896:               Commander, 2nd East Siberian Rifle Brigade

*General of Artillery* Arkady Nikanorovich **Nishchenkov** (6 Mar 1855 - Feb 1940)
13 Oct 1898 - 20 Jun 1901:        Commander, Guards Rifle Artillery Battalion
26 Feb 1901:                      Promoted to *Major-General*
20 Jun 1901 - 23 Oct 1904:        Commander, Life Guards 2nd Artillery Brigade
23 Oct 1904 - 25 Mar 1906:        Commander of Artillery, XVI. Army Corps
25 Mar 1906 - 29 Dec 1908:        Commander of Artillery, Grenadier Corps
6 Dec 1906:                       Promoted to *Lieutenant-General*
29 Dec 1908 - 26 Apr 1911:        Commander, 2nd Grenadier Division
26 Apr 1911 - 11 May 1912:        Commanding General, I. Siberian Army Corps
11 May 1912 - 7 Aug 1913:         Commanding General, IV. Siberian Army Corps,
                                  Commandant of Fortress Vladivostok
6 Dec 1912:                       Promoted to *General of Artillery*
7 Aug 1913 - 10 Aug 1914:         Member, Committee for Wounded Veterans
10 Aug 1914 - 10 Nov 1914:        Commanding General, Irkutsk Military District

| | |
|---|---|
| 10 Nov 1914 - 31 May 1917: | Commanding General, Amur Military District, Ataman, Ussuri Cossack Army |
| 31 May 1917 - 12 Jun 1917: | Reserve officer, Petrograd Military District |
| 12 Jun 1917 - Oct 1917: | Member, Committee for Wounded Veterans |

*Lieutenant-General* Nikanor Nikanorovich **Nishchenkov** (28 Dec 1853 - ?)
| | |
|---|---|
| 14 Nov 1907: | Promoted to *Major-General* |
| 14 Nov 1907 - 6 Nov 1908: | Commander, 2nd East Siberian Rifle Artillery Brigade |
| 6 Nov 1908 - 26 Jul 1910: | Commander, 9th East Siberian Rifle Artillery Brigade |
| 26 Jul 1910 - 5 Jun 1914: | Inspector of Artillery, II. Turkestan Army Corps |
| 14 Nov 1913: | Promoted to *Lieutenant-General* |
| 5 Jun 1914: | Dismissed |
| 8 Sep 1914 - 18 Apr 1917: | Recalled; Inspector of Artillery, XXVII. Army Corps |
| 10 Jun 1917: | Retired |

*General of Infantry* Vladimir Nikanorovich **Nishchenkov** (7 Jun 1852 - ?)
| | |
|---|---|
| 30 Nov 1894 - 1 Nov 1905: | Military Judge, Warsaw Military District Court |
| 1 Jan 1901: | Promoted to *Major-General* |
| 1 Nov 1905 - 13 Sep 1906: | Military Prosecutor, Warsaw Military District |
| 13 Sep 1906 - 1912: | Chairman, Odessa Military District Court |
| 22 Apr 1907: | Promoted to *Lieutenant-General* |
| 1912: | Promoted to *General of Infantry* |
| 1912: | Retired |

*Major-General* Leonid Vitalyevich **Nishchinsky** (8 Jun 1870 - 3 Dec 1937)
| | |
|---|---|
| 29 Jan 1914: | Promoted to *Major-General* |
| 29 Jan 1914 - 8 Aug 1916: | Commander, 34th Artillery Brigade |
| 8 Aug 1916 - 22 Jan 1917: | Inspector of Artillery, XLIV. Army Corps |
| 22 Jan 1917 - 1917: | Inspector of Artillery, I. Turkestan Army Corps |

*Major-General* Prince Konstantin Konstantinovich **Nizheradze** (26 Sep 1869 - ?)
| | |
|---|---|
| 1915 - 24 Aug 1916: | Commander, 154th Infantry Regiment |
| 16 Jul 1916: | Promoted to *Major-General* |
| 24 Aug 1916 - 1917: | Commander, Brigade, 66th Infantry Division |

*Major-General* Baron Ivan Stanislavovich von **Nolken** (28 Apr 1866 - 1943)
| | |
|---|---|
| 16 Sep 1910 - 18 Mar 1911: | Military Judge, Vilnius Military District Court |
| 6 Dec 1910: | Promoted to *Major-General* |
| 18 Mar 1911 - 28 Mar 1913: | Military Judge, Moscow Military District Court |
| 28 Mar 1913: | Retired |
| 10 Jul 1916 - Oct 1917: | Recalled; Military Judge, Kazan Military District Court |

*Lieutenant-General* Baron Karl Boguslavovich von **Nolken** (25 Jun 1844 - 12 Jan 1913)
| | |
|---|---|
| 20 Dec 1900: | Promoted to *Major-General* |
| 20 Dec 1900 - May 1904: | Commander, 5th Sapper Brigade |
| May 1904: | Promoted to *Lieutenant-General* |
| May 1904: | Retired |

*Major-General* Baron Karl Stanislavovich von **Nolken** (19 Mar 1858 - 1919)
6 Nov 1905 - 16 Sep 1908: Governor of Tomsk
31 Dec 1907: Promoted to *Major-General*
16 Sep 1908 - 1910: Governor of Mogilev
1910: Retired

*Rear-Admiral* Baron Magnus Genrikhovich von **Nolken** (14 Sep 1856 - ?)
?: Promoted to *Rear-Admiral*
1907 - 1911: Commander, Black Sea Training Detachment
1911: Retired

*Lieutenant-General* Vilgelm-Karl Kasperovich von **Nordgeym** (21 Oct 1860 - ?)
20 Aug 1907: Promoted to *Major-General*
20 Aug 1907 - 16 Jun 1910: Chief of Staff, Fortress Warsaw
16 Jun 1910 - 22 Dec 1914: Chief of Staff, XXIII. Army Corps
Nov 1914 - 22 Dec 1914: Acting Commander, 1$^{st}$ Brigade, 4$^{th}$ Infantry Division
22 Dec 1914 - 20 Sep 1916: Commander, 50$^{th}$ Infantry Division
3 Apr 1915: Promoted to *Lieutenant-General*
20 Sep 1916 - 1917: Reserve officer, Petrograd Military District

*Lieutenant-General* Kazimir Dominikovich **Nosarzhevsky** (4 Mar 1836 - ?)
21 Hab 1891 - 5 Feb 1897: Commander, 71$^{st}$ Infantry Regiment
14 May 1896: Promoted to *Major-General*
5 Feb 1897 - 18 Jul 1900: Commander, 1$^{st}$ Brigade, 17$^{th}$ Infantry Division
6 Jul 1900: Promoted to *Lieutenant-General*

*Major-General* Aleksandr Vasilyevich **Noskov** (15 Nov 1870 - ?)
15 May 1915 - 30 May 1916: Commander, 1$^{st}$ Regiment, Kuban Cossack Army
30 May 1916 - 25 Sep 1916: Chief of Staff, 5$^{th}$ Caucasus Cossack Division
25 Sep 1916 - 25 Mar 1917: Deputy Quartermaster-General, Caucasus Army
21 Dec 1916: Promoted to *Major-General*
25 Mar 1917 - 23 Nov 1917: Chief of Staff, IV. Caucasus Army Corps

*Major-General* Pyotr Alekseyevich **Noskov** (11 Nov 1867 - 27 May 1917)
Jul 1914 - Jul 1915: Commander, 239$^{th}$ Infantry Regiment
23 Apr 1915: Promoted to *Major-General*
Jul 1915 - 21 Aug 1915: Commander, Brigade, 71$^{st}$ Infantry Division
21 Aug 1915 - 29 Jan 1917: Commander, Brigade, 60$^{th}$ Infantry Division
29 Jan 1917 - 27 May 1917: Commander, 184$^{th}$ Infantry Division

*Major-General* Aleksandr Dmitriyevich **Nosov** (9 Aug 1869 - 1942)
13 May 1909 - 2 May 1918: Commander, Feldjaeger Corps
6 Dec 1916: Promoted to *Major-General*

*Major-General* Konstantin Dmitriyevich **Nosov** (14 Nov 1863 - ?)
29 Jun 1911 - 7 Oct 1916: Chief of Bureau, Nikolayev Engineering Academy
6 Dec 1913: Promoted to *Major-General*
7 Oct 1916 - 1917: Chief of Projects, Nikolayev Engineering Academy

*Major-General* Vladimir Vladimirovich **Nosov** (26 Sep 1866 - ?)
10 Aug 1912 - Jul 1916: Inspector of Classes, Suvorov Military School
6 Dec 1912: Promoted to *Major-General*
Jul 1916 - 1917: Chairman, Temporary Commission for the Construction of Fuse Production Plants

*Major-General* Count Grigory Ivanovich **Nostits** (23 Jan 1862 - 29 Apr 1926)
3 Aug 1908 - 1 Mar 1912: Military Attaché, France
6 Dec 1909: Promoted to *Major-General*
1 Mar 1912 - 28 Feb 1915: Chief of Staff, Guards Corps
17 Dec 1914 - Mar 1917: General à la suite
16 Aug 1915 - 11 Sep 1917: At the disposal of the Chief of the General Staff
11 Sep 1917 - Oct 1917: Reserve officer, Petrograd Military District

*Major-General* Pyotr Petrovich **Not** (19 Mar 1847 - 5 Jan 1914)
4 Nov 1900 - 27 Jun 1906: Commander, 12$^{th}$ Artillery Brigade
6 Dec 1901: Promoted to *Major-General*
27 Jun 1906 - 1906: Commander of Artillery, III. Siberian Army Corps

*Lieutenant-General* Vladimir Vladimirovich von **Notbek** (9 Jul 1865 - 1921)
15 Sep 1906 - 31 Dec 1910: Duty General, St. Petersburg Military District
13 Apr 1908: Promoted to *Major-General*
31 Dec 1910 - 3 Jul 1915: Commander, 2$^{nd}$ Finnish Rifle Brigade
23 Mar 1915: Promoted to *Lieutenant-General*
3 Jul 1915 - 25 Apr 1917: Commander, 1$^{st}$ Guards Infantry Division
25 Apr 1917 - 9 Sep 1917: Commanding General, VI. Army Corps
9 Sep 1917 - Nov 1917: C-in-C, 1$^{st}$ Army

*Major-General* Yevgeny Ivanovich **Novakov** (31 May 1865 - ?)
14 Jul 1914: Promoted to *Major-General*
14 Jul 1914 - 19 Jul 1914: Chief of Communications, Amur Military District
19 Jul 1914 - 7 Sep 1917: Chief of Economic Section, 4th Army
7 Sep 1917 - 1918: Commander, 48$^{th}$ Infantry Division

*Major-General of the Admiralty* Ivan Mikhailovich **Novakovsky** (20 Oct 1855 - ?)
30 Nov 1909 - 1910: Senior Deputy Commander, Port of Vladivostok
6 Dec 1910: Promoted to *Major-General of the Admiralty*
1910: Commander, Port of Vladivostok

*Major-General* Nikolai Ivanovich **Novakovsky** (22 Nov 1831 - ?)
31 Jan 1887 - 1900: Commander of Gendarmerie, Kaluga Province
13 Apr 1897: Promoted to *Major-General*

*Lieutenant-General* Aleksandr Vasilyevich **Novikov** (2 Feb 1864 - 1932)
24 Feb 1907 - 15 Jun 1910: Commandant, Yelisavetgrad Cavalry School
31 May 1907: Promoted to *Major-General*
15 Jun 1910 - 8 Oct 1913: Commander, 2$^{nd}$ Brigade, 5$^{th}$ Cavalry Division
8 Oct 1913: Promoted to *Lieutenant-General*

8 Oct 1913 - 13 Oct 1914: Commander, 14th Cavalry Division
13 Oct 1914 - 31 Jan 1915: Commanding General, I. Cavalry Corps
31 Jan 1915 - 25 Jun 1915: At the disposal of the Supreme Commander-in-Chief
25 Jun 1915 - 2 Apr 1917: Commanding General, XLIII. Army Corps
2 Apr 1917 - 28 Apr 1917: Reserve officer, Petrograd Military District
28 Apr 1917: Retired

*Major-General* Gennady Rodionovich **Novikov** (18 Aug 1860 - ?)
29 Nov 1912 - 1917: Deputy Inspector of Engineers, Odessa Military District
6 Dec 1912: Promoted to *Major-General*

*Major-General* Iosif Petrovich **Novikov** (11 Mar 1862 - ?)
21 Mar 1915 - 11 Apr 1917: Deputy Chief of Administration, Warsaw Palace
6 Dec 1916: Promoted to *Major-General*
11 Apr 1917: Retired

*Lieutenant-General* Nikolai Petrovich **Novikov** (6 Dec 1851 - ?)
5 Jun 1906: Promoted to *Major-General*
5 Jun 1906 - 26 May 1910: Duty General, Vilnius Military District
26 May 1910: Promoted to *Lieutenant-General*
26 May 1910: Retired

*Major-General* Vasily Ivanovich **Novikov** (25 Jul 1838 - ?)
23 Dec 1891: Promoted to *Major-General*
23 Dec 1891 - Nov 1894: Chief of Izhevsk Arms Factory

*Lieutenant-General* Vladimir Mikhailovich **Novikov** (24 Jan 1851 - ?)
3 Aug 1900: Promoted to *Major-General*
3 Aug 1900 - 12 Sep 1905: Commander, 1st Brigade, 22nd Infantry Division
12 Sep 1905 - 7 Jul 1906: Commander, 22nd Infantry Division
7 Jul 1906: Promoted to *Lieutenant-General*
7 Jul 1906 - 1907: Attached to the General Staff

*Major-General* Fyodor Fyodorovich **Novitsky** (2 Aug 1870 - 6 Apr 1944)
22 Aug 1914 - 2 Oct 1914: Commander, 1st Brigade, 8th Infantry Division
2 Oct 1914 - 25 Apr 1917: Chief of Staff, I. Army Corps
17 Nov 1914: Promoted to *Major-General*
Mar 1917 - 25 Apr 1917: Acting Commander, 22nd Infantry Division
25 Apr 1917 - Dec 1917: Commander, 82nd Infantry Division
Dec 1917 - 28 Mar 1918: Commanding General, XLIII. Army Corps

*Major-General* Konstantin Georgiyevich **Novitsky** (21 May 1862 - 7 Dec 1933)
1 Feb 1911 - 9 Jul 1912: Bureau Clerk, Ministry of War
25 Mar 1912: Promoted to *Major-General*
9 Jul 1912 - 26 Feb 1915: Ministry of War Representative, Military Council, Amur Military District
26 Feb 1915 - 1917: Chief of Sanatory Section, 9th Army

*General of Cavalry* Nikolai Dementyevich **Novitsky** (22 Jan 1833 - 1 Mar 1906)
| | |
|---|---|
| 1 Mar 1877 - 2 Mar 1878: | Chief of Staff, V. Army Corps |
| 19 Aug 1877: | Promoted to *Major-General* |
| 2 Mar 1878 - 7 May 1878: | Commander, 2nd Brigade, 8th Cavalry Division |
| 7 May 1878 - 2 Sep 1878: | Commander, Volyn Cossack Detachment |
| 2 Sep 1878 - 19 Sep 1880: | At the disposal of the Commanding General, Kiev Military District |
| 19 Sep 1880 - 21 Jul 1882: | At the disposal of the Inspector-General of Cavalry |
| 21 Jul 1882 - 6 Apr 1884: | Chief of Staff, Turkestan Military District |
| 6 Apr 1884 - 30 Aug 1885: | At the disposal of the Inspector-General of Cavalry |
| 30 Aug 1885 - 21 Feb 1896: | Commander, 9th Cavalry Division |
| 30 Aug 1886: | Promoted to *Lieutenant-General* |
| 21 Feb 1896 - 29 May 1899: | Commanding General, XII. Army Corps |
| 6 Dec 1898: | Promoted to *General of Cavalry* |
| 29 May 1899 - 3 Jan 1906: | Member of the Military Council |
| 3 Jan 1906: | Retired |

*Vice-Admiral* Pavel Ivanovich **Novitsky** (23 Jun 1857 - 15 Dec 1917)
| | |
|---|---|
| 6 Dec 1909: | Promoted to *Rear-Admiral* |
| 1909 - 1911: | Chief of Staff, Port of Sevastopol |
| 7 Jun 1911 - 8 Aug 1911: | Acting C-in-C, Black Sea Fleet |
| 8 Aug 1911 - 1912: | Commander, Mine Division, Black Sea Fleet |
| 14 Apr 1913: | Promoted to *Vice-Admiral* |
| 20 Jul 1914 - 21 Jul 1916: | Commander of Battleships, Black Sea Fleet |
| 21 Jul 1916 - Feb 1917: | Commandant, Port of Sevastopol |

*Major-General* Sergey Mikhailovich **Novitsky** (7 Oct 1861 - ?)
| | |
|---|---|
| 1914 - 1 Nov 1916: | Battalion Commander, 12th Rifle Regiment |
| 1 Nov 1916: | Promoted to *Major-General* |
| 1 Nov 1916: | Retired |

*Lieutenant-General* Vasily Dementyevich **Novitsky** (3 Jan 1839 - 14 Nov 1907)
| | |
|---|---|
| 24 Jun 1878 - 1903: | Chief of Gendarmerie, Kiev Province |
| 5 Apr 1887: | Promoted to *Major-General* |
| 1903: | Promoted to *Lieutenant-General* |
| 1903: | Retired |

*Lieutenant-General* Vasily Fyodorovich **Novitsky** (18 Mar 1869 - 15 Jan 1929)
| | |
|---|---|
| 1 Aug 1914 - Sep 1914: | Commander, 1st Brigade, 30th Infantry Division |
| 7 Aug 1914: | Promoted to *Major-General* |
| Sep 1914 - 21 Mar 1915: | Acting Quartermaster-General, 1st Army |
| 21 Mar 1915 - 22 Oct 1915: | Commander, 5th Rifle Brigade |
| 22 Oct 1915 - 20 Mar 1917: | Commander, 73rd Infantry Division |
| 20 Mar 1917 - 9 May 1917: | Deputy Minister of War |
| 31 Mar 1917: | Promoted to *Lieutenant-General* |
| 9 May 1917 - 17 Jul 1917: | At the disposal of the Minister of War |
| 17 Jul 1917 - 15 Nov 1917: | Commanding General, II. Siberian Army Corps |
| 15 Nov 1917 - 30 Nov 1917: | C-in-C, 12th Army |

30 Nov 1917 - 16 Dec 1917: Reserve officer, Petrograd Military District

*Lieutenant-General* Yevgeny Fyodorovich **Novitsky** (29 Nov 1867 - 11 Jun 1931)
26 Mar 1910: Promoted to *Major-General*
26 Mar 1910 - 22 Nov 1913: Commander, Life Guards Semyonov Regiment
22 Nov 1913 - 12 May 1915: Commandant, Infantry School
12 May 1915 - 22 Apr 1917: Commander, 48th Infantry Division
10 Apr 1916: Promoted to *Lieutenant-General*
22 Apr 1917 - 14 Jul 1917: Commanding General, XLV. Army Corps
14 Jul 1917 - Oct 1917: Reserve officer, Odessa Military District

*Lieutenant-General* Konstantin Stanislavovich **Novogrebelsky** (13 Jun 1860 - ?)
31 Aug 1908: Promoted to *Major-General*
31 Aug 1908 - 16 Aug 1914: Duty General, Kiev Military District
16 Aug 1914 - 6 Oct 1914: Reserve officer, Kiev Military District
6 Oct 1914 - 23 Jul 1915: Chief of Staff, Governor-General of Galicia
23 Jul 1915 - 30 Aug 1916: Chief of Staff, Kiev Military District
10 Apr 1916: Promoted to *Lieutenant-General*
30 Aug 1916 - 19 Apr 1917: Attached to the Chief of Logistics, Southwestern Front

*Major-General* Stanislav Stanislavovich **Novogrebelsky** (5 Sep 1846 - ?)
11 Jan 1893: Promoted to *Major-General*
11 Jan 1893 - 5 Jan 1898: Chief of Staff, III. Army Corps
5 Jan 1898 - 26 Jul 1899: Chief of Staff, XX. Army Corps
26 Jul 1899 - Jul 1902: Commander, 5th Rifle Brigade

*Lieutenant-General* Nikolai Vasilyevich **Novoselov** (26 Nov 1850 - ?)
6 Jul 1904: Promoted to *Major-General*
6 Jul 1904 - 3 Dec 1910: Commander, 2nd Brigade, 17th Infantry Division
3 Dec 1910: Promoted to *Lieutenant-General*
3 Dec 1910: Retired

*Major-General* Sergey Ivanovich **Novoselsky** (1864 - ?)
3 May 1909 - 1912: Military Judge, Amur Military District Court
6 Dec 1910: Promoted to *Major-General*

*Major-General* Lev Semyonovich **Novosiltsev** (25 Feb 1863 - ?)
30 Jan 1914 - 31 Dec 1916: Commander, 69th Infantry Regiment
31 Dec 1916 - 14 Apr 1917: Commander, 1st Brigade, 18th Infantry Division
18 Feb 1917: Promoted to *Major-General*
14 Apr 1917 - 1917: Reserve officer, Dvinsk Military District

*General of Cavalry* Anton Vasilyevich **Novosiltsov** (17 Mar 1850 - 9 Mar 1923)
8 Mar 1895 - 4 Mar 1899: Commander, Life Guards Cossack Regiment
6 Dec 1895: Promoted to *Major-General*
4 Mar 1899 - 18 Feb 1904: Commander, 3rd Brigade, 1st Guards Cavalry Division
18 Feb 1904: Promoted to *Lieutenant-General*
18 Feb 1904 - 22 Nov 1908: Commander, Consolidated Cavalry Division

| | |
|---|---|
| 22 Nov 1908 - 2 Feb 1914: | Commanding General, IV. Army Corps |
| 18 Apr 1910: | Promoted to *General of Cavalry* |
| 2 Feb 1914: | Promoted to *General-Adjutant* |
| 2 Feb 1914 - 1917: | General à la suite |

*Lieutenant-General of the Admiralty* Nikolai Gavrilovich **Nozikov** (12 Apr 1839 - 1918)
| | |
|---|---|
| 1886 - 1891: | Deputy Chief Inspector of Naval Mechanical Engineers |
| 1887: | Promoted to *Engineer-Mechanic (Flag rank)* |
| 1891 - 1907: | Inspector-General of Naval Mechanical Engineers |
| 1907: | Promoted to *Lieutenant-General of the Admiralty* |
| 1907: | Retired |

*Lieutenant-General* Mitrofan Yefimovich **Nudzhevsky** (22 Feb 1848 - 27 Feb 1933)
| | |
|---|---|
| 1 Jun 1904: | Promoted to *Major-General* |
| 1 Jun 1904 - 18 Jul 1905: | Recalled; Commander, 2$^{nd}$ Brigade, 71$^{st}$ Infantry Division |
| 18 Jul 1905 - 1906: | Commander, 1$^{st}$ Brigade, 1$^{st}$ Siberian Infantry Division |
| 1906: | Promoted to *Lieutenant-General* |
| 1906: | Retired |

*Major-General* Vasily Andreyevich **Nudzhevsky** (16 Apr 1841 - ?)
| | |
|---|---|
| 19 Jul 1890 - 20 Feb 1895: | Commander, 46$^{th}$ Dragoon Regiment |
| 14 Nov 1894: | Promoted to *Major-General* |
| 20 Feb 1895 - Nov 1901: | Commander, 2$^{nd}$ Brigade, Caucasus Cavalry Division |

*Major-General* Otton Lyudvigovich **Nyankovsky-Voynilovich** (22 Dec 1857 - 5 Nov 1940)
| | |
|---|---|
| 19 Jun 1910 - 4 Dec 1913: | Commander, 155$^{th}$ Infantry Regiment |
| 4 Dec 1913: | Promoted to *Major-General* |
| 4 Dec 1913: | Retired |
| 27 Jun 1916 - 5 Jun 1917: | Recalled; Deputy Commander, Airship Squadron |

*Lieutenant-General* Vladimir Lavrentyevich **Ober** (31 Aug 1838 - ?)
| | |
|---|---|
| 16 Jan 1890: | Promoted to *Major-General* |
| 16 Jan 1890 - 23 Jul 1896: | Commander, 1$^{st}$ Brigade, 21$^{st}$ Infantry Division |
| 23 Jul 1896 - 31 Aug 1900: | Commander, 51$^{st}$ Replacement Infantry Brigade |
| 31 Aug 1900: | Promoted to *Lieutenant-General* |
| 31 Aug 1900: | Retired |

*Major-General* Nikolai Mikhailovich **Oberuchev** (24 Mar 1861 - 15 Feb 1915)
| | |
|---|---|
| 29 Jul 1911 - 15 Feb 1915: | Commander, 37$^{th}$ Siberian Rifle Regiment |
| 16 May 1915: | Posthumously promoted to *Major-General* |

*Major-General of Naval Engineers* Viktor Aleksandrovich **Obnorsky** (28 Sep 1860 - ?)
| | |
|---|---|
| 9 Jun 1908 - ?: | Chief Mechanical Engineer, Port of Reval |
| 6 Dec 1911: | Promoted to *Major-General of Naval Engineers* |

*Major-General* Prince Aleksandr Nikolayevich **Obolensky** (24 Feb 1872 - 14 Feb 1924)
| | |
|---|---|
| 20 Jul 1914: | Promoted to *Major-General* |

| | |
|---|---|
| 20 Jul 1914 - Aug 1916: | Mayor of Petrograd |
| Aug 1916 - Nov 1916: | General à la suite |
| Nov 1916 - 18 Sep 1917: | Commander, Infantry Brigade |
| 18 Sep 1917: | Discharged |

*Lieutenant-General of the Admiralty* Prince Ivan Mikhailovich **Obolensky** (11 Feb 1853 - 27 Feb 1910)

| | |
|---|---|
| 14 Jan 1902 - 31 Mar 1903: | Governor of Kharkov |
| 25 Mar 1903: | Reactivated from retirement (1881, *Lieutenant*) |
| 25 Mar 1903: | Promoted to *Lieutenant-General of the Admiralty* |
| 31 Mar 1903 - Jul 1904: | Attached to the Ministry of Internal Affairs |
| Jul 1904 - 6 Dec 1905: | Governor-General of Finland |
| 1 Aug 1904: | Promoted to *General-Adjutant* |
| 6 Dec 1905 - 27 Feb 1910: | Member of the Tsar's retinue |

*Major-General* Prince Nikolai Dmitriyevich **Obolensky** (24 Nov 1859 - Dec 1912)

| | |
|---|---|
| 25 Oct 1902 - 11 Feb 1905: | Comptroller, Ministry of the Imperial Court |
| 1904: | Promoted to *Major-General* |
| 11 Feb 1905 - 13 Aug 1909: | Chief of Cabinet to the Tsar |
| 13 Aug 1909 - Dec 1912: | Attached to Grand Duches Maria Feodorovna |

*Lieutenant-General* Prince Nikolai Nikolayevich **Obolensky** (10 Nov 1833 - 25 Aug 1898)

| | |
|---|---|
| 1 Nov 1876 - 26 Feb 1887: | Commander, Life Guards Preobrazhensky Regiment |
| 12 Nov 1877: | Promoted to *Major-General* |
| 26 Feb 1887 - 16 Sep 1887: | At the disposal of the Commanding General, St. Petersburg Military District |
| 16 Sep 1887 - 20 Jan 1888: | Commander, 1st Brigade, 1st Guards Infantry Division |
| 20 Jan 1888 - 11 Sep 1889: | Commander, Guards Rifle Brigade |
| 30 Aug 1888: | Promoted to *Lieutenant-General* |
| 11 Sep 1889 - 29 Mar 1897: | Commander, 1st Guards Infantry Division |
| 1896: | Promoted to *General-Adjutant* |
| 29 Mar 1897 - 25 Aug 1898: | Commanding General, Guards Corps |

*Major-General* Prince Vladimir Nikolayevich **Obolensky** (24 Jul 1865 - 24 Oct 1927)

| | |
|---|---|
| 26 Aug 1912: | Promoted to *Major-General* |
| 26 Aug 1912 - 12 Jul 1914: | Commander, Life Guards Preobrazhensky Regiment |
| 12 Jul 1914 - 20 May 1917: | General à la suite |
| 20 May 1917: | Retired |

*Major-General* Prince Platon Sergeyevich **Obolensky-Neledinsky-Meletsky** (12 Jun 1850 - 26 Mar 1913)

| | |
|---|---|
| 27 Mar 1881 - 23 Dec 1896: | Aide-de-Camp to Grand Duke Vladimir Alexandrovich |
| 17 Dec 1896: | Promoted to *Major-General* |
| 23 Dec 1896 - 9 Feb 1902: | Transferred to the reserve |
| 9 Feb 1902 - 1908: | Honorary Trustee, Board of Trustees of Empress Maria Institutions |
| 1908: | Retired |

*General of Cavalry* Aleksandr Dmitriyevich **Oboleshev** (23 Aug 1855 - 1918)
16 Aug 1900: Promoted to *Major-General*
16 Aug 1900 - 23 Jul 1902: Chief of Staff, Fortress Novogeorgiyevsk
23 Jul 1902 - 29 Dec 1906: Chief of Staff, I. Cavalry Corps
29 Dec 1906 - Jul 1908: Commander, 3rd Cavalry Division
22 Apr 1907: Promoted to *Lieutenant-General*
Jul 1908: Promoted to *General of Cavalry*
Jul 1908: Retired

*Major-General* Nikolai Nikolayevich **Oboleshev** (13 Oct 1868 - 1920)
1 Sep 1910 - 19 Jul 1914: Chief of Communications, Turkestan Military District
6 Dec 1910: Promoted to *Major-General*
19 Jul 1914 - Feb 1914: Chief of Staff, Moscow Military District
6 Mar 1917 - 22 Apr 1917: Commander, 6th Finnish Rifle Division
22 Apr 1917 - 18 Sep 1917: Acting Commanding General, Kiev Military District
18 Sep 1917 - 1918: Reserve officer, Moscow Military District

*Major-General* Aleksandr Konstantinovich **Obrucheshnikov** (16 Mar 1867 - ?)
4 Dec 1915 - 1917: Commander, 32nd Artillery Brigade
19 Oct 1916: Promoted to *Major-General*

*Lieutenant-General* Nikolai Afanasyevich **Obruchev** (31 May 1864 - 4 Jan 1929)
4 Nov 1909 - 17 May 1914: 1st Quartermaster-General, General Staff
6 Dec 1909: Promoted to *Major-General*
17 May 1914 - 19 Jul 1914: Commander, 1st Finnish Rifle Brigade
19 Jul 1914 - 24 Sep 1914: Acting Chief of Staff, Dvinsk Military District
24 Sep 1914 - 12 May 1915: Commander, 1st Finnish Rifle Brigade
12 May 1915 - 31 Mar 1917: Commander, 1st Finnish Rifle Division
21 Oct 1915: Promoted to *Lieutenant-General*
31 Mar 1917 - 17 Jul 1917: Commanding General, XXII. Army Corps
17 Jul 1917 - Oct 1917: Reserve officer, Kiev Military District

*General of Infantry* Nikolai Nikolayevich **Obruchev** (22 Nov 1830 - 25 Jun 1904)
1 Dec 1863 - 28 Apr 1867: Member, Committee for Military Reforms, General Staff
27 Mar 1866: Promoted to *Major-General*
28 Apr 1867 - 19 Feb 1881: Business Manager, Committee for Military Reforms, General Staff
13 May 1873: Promoted to *Lieutenant-General*
17 Apr 1878: Promoted to *General-Adjutant*
19 Feb 1881 - 10 Jun 1881: Deputy Chief of the General Staff
10 Jun 1881 - 31 Dec 1897: Chief of the General Staff
30 Aug 1887: Promoted to *General of Infantry*
31 Dec 1897 - 25 Jun 1904: Member of the State Council

*Major-General* Sergey Nikolayevich **Obukhov** (16 Nov 1860 - Nov 1916)
25 Mar 1904 - 14 Feb 1907: Commander, 1st Life Grenadier Regiment
14 Feb 1907: Promoted to *Major-General*

14 Feb 1907:                          Retired
11 Aug 1910 - 12 Nov 1915:            Recalled; General for Assignments, Ministry of War
12 Nov 1915 - 9 Dec 1915:             General for Assignments, Moscow Military District
9 Dec 1915 - Nov 1916:                General for Assignments, Ministry of War

*Major-General of the Admiralty* Aleksey Ivanovich **Odintsov**
25 Jun 1908 - 22 Nov 1910:            Junior Inspector of Inland Waterways & Roads
22 Nov 1910:                          Promoted to *Major-General of the Admiralty*
22 Nov 1910:                          Retired

*General of Infantry* Dmitry Aleksandrovich **Odintsov** (12 Jun 1852 - ?)
25 Mar 1897:                          Promoted to *Major-General*
25 Mar 1897 - 21 Sep 1897:            General for Assignments, Caucasus Military District
21 Sep 1897 - 17 May 1898:            Deputy Chief of Staff, Caucasus Military District
17 May 1898 - 20 Jun 1899:            Military Governor, Kars Region
20 Jun 1899 - 25 Jan 1904:            Governor of Baku
25 Jan 1904 - 11 Nov 1904:            Commander, Caucasus Grenadier Division
28 Mar 1904:                          Promoted to *Lieutenant-General*
11 Nov 1904 - 29 Mar 1906:            Ataman, Kuban Cossack Army
29 Mar 1906 - 28 Jul 1906:            Attached to the Ministry of War
28 Jul 1906 - 1909:                   Deputy Commanding General, Omsk Military District
1909:                                 Promoted to *General of Infantry*
1909:                                 Retired

*Major-General* Sergey Ivanovich **Odintsov** (2 Jul 1874 - 1920)
24 Jul 1915 - 24 Oct 1916:            Commander, Primorsky Dragoon Regiment
19 Oct 1916:                          Promoted to *Major-General*
24 Oct 1916 - 16 Apr 1917:            Chief of Staff, Amur Cavalry Division
16 Apr 1917 - Dec 1917:               Commander, 3rd Caucasus Cossack Division

*Major-General* Vladimir Ampliyevich **Odintsov** (12 Jul 1852 - ?)
6 Jul 1907:                           Promoted to *Major-General*
6 Jul 1907 - 7 Dec 1912:              Commander, 1st Brigade, 32nd Infantry Division
7 Dec 1912:                           Retired

*Rear-Admiral* Yevgeny Nikolayevich **Odintsov** (9 Dec 1863 - 1 Mar 1917)
21 Aug 1914 - 1 Mar 1917:             Commander, Artillery Training Detachment, Baltic Fleet
30 Jul 1916:                          Promoted to *Rear-Admiral*

*Lieutenant-General* Ilya Zurabovich **Odishelidze** (25 Mar 1865 - ?)
30 Oct 1909 - 9 Nov 1911:             Special Assignments General, Turkestan Military District
16 Jul 1910:                          Promoted to *Major-General*
9 Nov 1911 - 9 Jan 1914:              Military Governor of Samarkand
9 Jan 1914 - 13 Nov 1914:             Chief of Staff, Turkestan Military District
11 Oct 1914:                          Promoted to *Lieutenant-General*
13 Nov 1914 - 23 Dec 1914:            Chief of Staff, 4th Army
23 Dec 1914 - 16 Jan 1917:            Chief of Staff, 1st Army

| | |
|---|---|
| 16 Jan 1917 - 12 Sep 1917: | Commanding General, XV. Army Corps |
| 12 Apr 1917 - 24 Apr 1917: | Acting C-in-C, 1st Army |
| 12 Sep 1917 - 2 Oct 1917: | C-in-C, 3rd Army |
| 2 Oct 1917 - 28 Feb 1918: | C-in-C, Caucasus Army |

*Major-General* Georgy Fyodorovich **Odnoglazkov** (3 Feb 1871 - 5 Jun 1920)
| | |
|---|---|
| 20 Feb 1911 - 1915: | Chief of Staff, 8th Cavalry Division |
| 1915 - 7 Mar 1915: | Chief of Staff, Orenburg Cossack Division |
| 7 Mar 1915 - 30 Oct 1916: | Commander, 7th Hussar Regiment |
| 30 Oct 1916 - 30 Jul 1917: | Chief of Staff, 7th Cavalry Division |
| 6 Dec 1916: | Promoted to *Major-General* |
| 30 Jul 1917 - 1918: | Chief of Staff, 2nd Orenburg Cossack Division |

*General of Cavalry* Prince Nikolai Nikolayevich **Odoyevsky-Maslov** (24 Jan 1849 - 15 Apr 1919)
| | |
|---|---|
| 8 Jun 1892 - 11 Aug 1896: | Commander, 26th Dragoon Regiment |
| 11 Aug 1896: | Promoted to *Major-General* |
| 11 Aug 1896 - 25 May 1901: | Commander, Life Guards Cavalry Regiment |
| 25 May 1901 - 25 May 1903: | Commander, 2nd Brigade, 2nd Guards Cavalry Division |
| 25 May 1903 - 7 Jan 1904: | Commander, 10th Cavalry Division |
| 7 Jan 1904: | Promoted to *Lieutenant-General* |
| 7 Jan 1904 - 1 Mar 1905: | Commander, 1st Guards Cavalry Division |
| 1 Mar 1905 - 3 Apr 1907: | Ataman, Don Cossack Army |
| 3 Apr 1907 - 19 Apr 1907: | At the disposal of the Minister of War |
| 19 Apr 1907 - Mar 1917: | Chief of Moscow Palace Administration |
| 1913: | Promoted to *General-Adjutant* |
| 6 Apr 1914: | Promoted to *General of Cavalry* |

*Lieutenant-General* Baron Aleksandr Fyodorovich **Offenberg** (12 Oct 1835 - 1900)
| | |
|---|---|
| 26 Jun 1884 - 26 Jan 1885: | Commander, 18th Dragoon Regiment |
| 26 Jan 1885: | Promoted to *Major-General* |
| 26 Jan 1885 - 27 Nov 1889: | Commander, Life Guards Dragoon Regiment |
| 27 Nov 1889 - 22 Apr 1892: | Commander, 3rd Brigade, 2nd Guards Cavalry Division |
| 22 Apr 1892 - Mar 1897: | Commander, 2nd Cavalry Division |
| 14 Nov 1894: | Promoted to *Lieutenant-General* |
| Mar 1897: | Retired |

*Lieutenant-General of the Fleet* Vladimir Khristianovich **Offenberg** (1 Feb 1856 - 8 Nov 1927)
| | |
|---|---|
| 24 May 1910: | Promoted to *Major-General of the Fleet* |
| 17 Jan 1911 - 19 Oct 1911: | Senior Deputy Chief Inspector of Shipbuilding |
| 19 Oct 1911 - Jan 1914: | Deputy Chief of Shipbuilding Section, Main Directorate of Shipbuilding |
| Jan 1914: | Promoted to *Lieutenant-General of the Fleet* |
| Jan 1914: | Retired |

*Lieutenant-General* Dmitry Petrovich **Ofrosimov** (4 Feb 1849 - 5 Jul 1911)
| | |
|---|---|
| 18 Dec 1900: | Promoted to *Major-General* |

18 Dec 1900 - 28 Aug 1907: Commander, 1st Brigade, 5th Cavalry Division
28 Aug 1907 - 15 Jun 1910: Commander, 2nd Brigade, 5th Cavalry Division
15 Jun 1910: Promoted to *Lieutenant-General*
15 Jun 1910: Retired

*Major-General* Mikhail Aleksandrovich **Ofrosimov** (19 Aug 1864 - ?)
1913: Promoted to *Major-General*

*Major-General* Pavel Aleksandrovich **Ofrosimov** (14 Dec 1872 - 24 Feb 1946)
24 Jun 1915 - 22 Aug 1916: Commander, Life Guards Uhlan Regiment
16 Oct 1915: Promoted to *Major-General*
22 Aug 1916 - 1917: Commander, Brigade, 3rd Guards Cavalry Division

*Major-General* Yakov Mikhailovich **Ofrosimov** (15 Sep 1866 - 10 Jun 1924)
8 Oct 1913 - 9 Jul 1915: Commander, 56th Infantry Regiment
11 Nov 1914 - 7 Jan 1915: Acting Commander, 2nd Brigade, 14th Infantry Division
16 Feb 1915: Promoted to *Major-General*
9 Jul 1915 - 7 Aug 1915: Commander, Brigade, 58th Infantry Division
7 Aug 1915 - 1918: POW

*General of Infantry* Pyotr Ivanovich **Oganovsky** (26 Aug 1851 - ?)
25 Mar 1904: Promoted to *Major-General*
25 Mar 1904 - 24 Mar 1905: Commander, 2nd Brigade, 2nd Siberian Infantry Division
24 Mar 1905 - 21 Nov 1906: Quartermaster-General, 1st Manchurian Army
21 Nov 1906 - 18 Apr 1907: Commander, 53rd Replacement Infantry Brigade
18 Apr 1907 - 13 Feb 1909: Commander, 66th Replacement Infantry Brigade
13 Feb 1909 - 24 Oct 1910: Commander, 66th Infantry Division
18 Apr 1910: Promoted to *Lieutenant-General*
29 May 1910 - 24 Oct 1910: Commander, 52nd Infantry Division
24 Oct 1910 - 31 Dec 1913: Commander, 51st Infantry Division
31 Dec 1913: Promoted to *General of Infantry*
31 Dec 1913: Retired
8 Oct 1914 - 24 Jan 1915: Recalled; Commander, 66th Infantry Division
24 Jan 1915 - 19 Dec 1915: Commanding General, IV. Caucasus Army Corps
19 Dec 1915 - 16 Apr 1916: Reserve officer, Kiev Military District
16 Apr 1916 - 11 Sep 1916: Commanding General, III. Army Corps
11 Sep 1916 - 1917: Reserve officer, Minsk Military District

*Major-General* Aleksandr Nikolayevich **Ogarev** (9 Jan 1847 - ?)
28 Nov 1895 - 7 Feb 1901: Commander, Life Guards 1st Rifle Battalion
14 May 1896: Promoted to *Major-General*
7 Feb 1901 - 1902: Commander, 1st Brigade, 1st Guards Infantry Division

*Major-General* Mikhail Dmitriyevich **Ogiyevsky** (14 Sep 1859 - ?)
28 Feb 1908 - 12 May 1914: Military Judge, Irkutsk Military District Court
6 Dec 1909: Promoted to *Major-General*
12 May 1914: Dismissed

*Major-General* Vladimir Mikhailovich von **Oglio** (20 Dec 1862 - ?)
| | |
|---|---|
| 11 Jun 1913 - 26 Sep 1916: | Chief of Gendarmerie, Olonets Province |
| 26 Sep 1916: | Promoted to *Major-General* |
| 26 Sep 1916: | Retired |

*Lieutenant-General* Aleksandr Semyonovich **Ogloblev** (25 Aug 1856 - 1935)
| | |
|---|---|
| 5 Nov 1908: | Promoted to *Major-General* |
| 5 Nov 1908 - 3 May 1913: | Commander, 2$^{nd}$ Brigade, 9$^{th}$ Siberian Rifle Division |
| 3 May 1913 - 19 Jul 1914: | Commander, 2$^{nd}$ Brigade, 3$^{rd}$ Infantry Division |
| 19 Jul 1914 - Jul 1917: | Commander, 59$^{th}$ Infantry Division |
| 26 Sep 1916: | Promoted to *Lieutenant-General* |
| Jul 1917 - 12 Apr 1918: | Reserve officer, Moscow Military District |
| 18 Apr 1918: | Dismissed |

*Lieutenant-General of the Hydrographic Corps* Konstantin Nikolayevich **Ogloblinsky** (29 Nov 1863 - 12 Jun 1933)
| | |
|---|---|
| 27 Jan 1914 - 28 Jul 1917: | Chief of Fleet Navigation |
| 6 Apr 1914: | Promoted to *Major-General of the Hydrographic Corps* |
| 28 Jul 1917: | Promoted to *Lieutenant-General of the Hydrographic Corps* |
| 28 Jul 1917: | Retired |

*Lieutenant-General of the Hydrographic Corps* Nikolai Nikolayevich **Ogloblinsky** (23 Mar 1862 - 2 Oct 1936)
| | |
|---|---|
| 18 Apr 1910: | Promoted to *Major-General of the Admiralty* |
| 21 Aug 1910 - 1917: | Professor of Hydrographics, Nikolayev Naval Academy |
| 4 Feb 1913: | Redesignated *Major-General of the Hydrographic Corps* |
| 6 Dec 1915: | Promoted to *Lieutenant-General of the Hydrographic Corps* |

*Lieutenant-General* Arkady Platonovich **Ogon-Doganovsky** (24 Mar 1854 - ?)
| | |
|---|---|
| 3 Oct 1899 - 20 Mar 1906: | Commander, Warsaw Artillery Depot |
| 6 Dec 1901: | Promoted to *Major-General* |
| 20 Mar 1906 - 19 Feb 1911: | Deputy Commander of Artillery, Warsaw Military District |
| 19 Feb 1911: | Promoted to *Lieutenant-General* |
| 19 Feb 1911 - Jun 1914: | Commander of Artillery, Vilnius Military District |
| Jun 1914 - 11 Jan 1917: | Commander of Artillery, Dvinsk Military District |
| 11 Jan 1917 - ?: | Deputy Commander of Artillery Logistics, Northern Front |

*Major-General* Ivan Platonovich **Ogon-Doganovsky** (15 Nov 1864 - ?)
| | |
|---|---|
| 21 Mar 1908 - 18 Dec 1914: | Military Judge, Odessa Military District Court |
| 6 Dec 1908: | Promoted to *Major-General* |
| 18 Dec 1914 - 13 Aug 1915: | Military Prosecutor, Military Government-General of Galicia |
| 13 Aug 1915 - 1918: | Military Judge, Odessa Military District Court |

*Major-General* Mitrofan Nikolayevich **Ogon-Doganovsky** (10 Jul 1844 - ?)
27 Oct 1892 - 1902: Commander of Engineers, Fortress Mikhailovsk
6 Dec 1895: Promoted to *Major-General*

*Lieutenant-General* Fyodor Yevlampiyevich **Ogorodnikov** (4 Jul 1867 - 3 Mar 1939)
17 May 1911: Promoted to *Major-General*
17 May 1911 - 7 Oct 1913: Chief of Staff, XXV. Army Corps
7 Oct 1913 - 14 Nov 1914: Chief of Staff, XXII. Army Corps
14 Nov 1914 - 28 Mar 1915: General for Assignments, 10th Army
28 Mar 1915 - 25 Aug 1915: Chief of Staff, XX. Army Corps
25 Aug 1915 - 11 Aug 1916: Commander, 26th Infantry Division
9 Aug 1916: Promoted to *Lieutenant-General*
11 Aug 1916 - 2 Apr 1917: Commander, 125th Infantry Division
2 Apr 1917 - 28 Jul 1917: Commanding General, XVII. Army Corps
28 Jul 1917 - 29 Aug 1917: Reserve officer, Kiev Military District
29 Aug 1917 - 9 Sep 1917: C-in-C, Southwestern Front

*Lieutenant-General* Mikhail Aleksandrovich **Ogranovich** (1 Oct 1848 - 27 Jan 1912)
23 Jun 1898 - 10 May 1911: Member of the Artillery Committee, Main Artillery Directorate
26 Jan 1900 - 28 Jun 1901: Commandant, Kiev Regional Arsenal
9 Apr 1900: Promoted to *Major-General*
28 Jun 1901 - 10 May 1911: Chief of the St. Petersburg Pipe Plant
29 Mar 1909: Promoted to *Lieutenant-General*
10 May 1911: Retired

*Major-General* Ivan Fyodorovich **Oguretsky** (28 Nov 1851 - ?)
30 Apr 1910: Promoted to *Major-General*
30 Apr 1910 - 30 Apr 1912: Commander, 1st Artillery Brigade

*Major-General* Genrikh Genrikhovich **Okerman** (26 Oct 1841 - 21 Apr 1919)
29 Jul 1891 - 27 Mar 1899: Chief Intendant, Finnish Military Commissariat
14 May 1896: Promoted to *Major-General*
27 Mar 1899 - 26 Aug 1900: Commander, Kuopio Province
26 Aug 1900 - 1901: Senator, Imperial Finnish Senate
1901: Retired

*Major-General* Vilgelm Khristianovich **Okerman** (25 Nov 1835 - ?)
26 Feb 1894: Promoted to *Major-General*
26 Feb 1894 - 11 Oct 1899: Commander, 2nd Brigade, 12th Infantry Division

*Major-General* Mikhail Ivanovich **Okhotin** (8 Nov 1842 - ?)
1 Jun 1904 - 26 Nov 1904: Commander, 223rd Infantry Regiment
1904: Promoted to *Major-General*
26 Nov 1904 - 1905: At the disposal of the Chief of the General Staff

*Major-General* Stanislav Antonovich **Okulich** (4 Nov 1846 - ?)
26 Nov 1901: Promoted to *Major-General*
26 Nov 1901 - 22 Feb 1904: At the disposal of the Chief of the General Staff
22 Feb 1904 - 19 Jul 1906: Commander, 1st Brigade, 5th East Siberian Rifle Division
19 Jul 1906 - 25 Sep 1906: Attached to the General Staff
25 Sep 1906 - 1908: Commander, Kuban Cossack Infantry Brigade

*Lieutenant-General* Nikolai Fomich **Okulich-Kazarin** (19 Nov 1849 - 26 Apr 1923)
10 May 1895 - 3 Sep 1901: Military Judge, Moscow Military District Court
6 Dec 1899: Promoted to *Major-General*
3 Sep 1901 - Apr 1906: Military Prosecutor, Caucasus Military District Court
Apr 1906: Promoted to *Lieutenant-General*
Apr 1906: Retired

*Major-General* Boris Vladimirovich **Okunkov** (13 Dec 1863 - ?)
31 Dec 1913 - 4 Aug 1916: Military Commander, Moscow District
22 Mar 1915: Promoted to *Major-General*
4 Aug 1916 - 16 Mar 1917: Duty General, Moscow Military District
16 Mar 1917 - 22 Jun 1917: Chief of Staff, Moscow Military District
22 Jun 1917: Retired

*Major-General* Mikhail Karlovich **Oldekop** (16 Feb 1848 - 12 Mar 1908)
24 Oct 1889 - 1904: Staff Officer, VI. Class, Main Intendant Directorate
1904: Promoted to *Major-General*
1904: Retired

*General of Infantry* Prince Aleksandr Petrovich **Oldenburg** (21 May 1844 - 6 Sep 1932)
28 Mar 1871: Promoted to *Major-General*
28 Mar 1871 - 1 Nov 1876: Commander, Life Guards Preobrazhensky Regiment
1 Nov 1876 - 17 Sep 1880: Commander, 1st Brigade, 1st Guards Infantry Division
19 Feb 1880: Promoted to *General-Adjutant*
17 Sep 1880 - 5 Jun 1884: Commander, 1st Guards Infantry Division
30 Aug 1881: Promoted to *Lieutenant-General*
1 Apr 1885 - 11 Aug 1889: Commanding General, Guards Corps
11 Aug 1889 - 14 May 1896: General à la suite
6 Dec 1895: Promoted to *General of Infantry*
14 May 1896 - 3 Sep 1914: Member of the State Council
3 Sep 1914 - 22 Mar 1917: Chief of Sanitation & Evacuation Services
22 Mar 1917: Retired

*Lieutenant-General* Prince Konstantin Petrovich **Oldenburg** (27 Apr 1850 - 5 Mar 1906)
21 May 1869 - 5 Mar 1906: Reserve officer, Life Guards Preobrazhensky Regiment, Attached to the Kuban Cossack Army
5 Aug 1887: Promoted to *Major-General*
1 Aug 1900 - 5 Mar 1906: Member of the Board, Main Directorate of State Horse Breeding
6 Dec 1900: Promoted to *Lieutenant-General*

*Major-General* Prince Pyotr Aleksandrovich **Oldenburg** (9 Nov 1868 - 18 Mar 1924)
| | |
|---|---|
| 6 May 1913: | Promoted to *Major-General* |
| 6 May 1913 - 24 Jan 1915: | General à la suite |
| 24 Jan 1915 - 13 Apr 1917: | At the disposal of the Supreme Commander-in-Chief |
| 13 Apr 1917: | Retired |

*Lieutenant-General* Vasily Vasilyevich von **Olderogge** (22 Aug 1848 - 1911)
| | |
|---|---|
| 14 Apr 1902: | Promoted to *Major-General* |
| 14 Apr 1902 - 1911: | Director of the Imperial Law School, St. Petersburg |
| 6 Dec 1908: | Promoted to *Lieutenant-General* |

*Major-General* Vladimir Aleksandrovich von **Olderogge** (24 Jul 1873 - 27 May 1931)
| | |
|---|---|
| 27 Oct 1914 - 12 Mar 1916: | Commander, 113$^{th}$ Infantry Regiment |
| 30 Jul 1915: | Promoted to *Major-General* |
| 12 Mar 1916 - 7 Jul 1917: | Commander, Brigade, 1$^{st}$ Turkestan Rifle Division |
| 7 Jul 1917 - 1918: | Commander, 1$^{st}$ Turkestan Rifle Division |

*General of Cavalry* Sergey Vilgelmovich **Oliv** (26 Oct 1844 - 28 Jan 1909)
| | |
|---|---|
| 29 May 1878 - 6 May 1884: | Commander, 8$^{th}$ Dragoon Regiment |
| 6 May 1884: | Promoted to *Major-General* |
| 6 May 1884 - 18 Jun 1890: | Transferred to the reserve |
| 18 Jun 1890 - 30 Nov 1893: | Governor of Kherson |
| 30 Nov 1893 - 6 Apr 1900: | Deputy Chief, Main Principalities Directorate |
| 16 Mar 1900: | Promoted to *Lieutenant-General* |
| 6 Apr 1900 - 17 Mar 1903: | Honorary Trustee, Empress Maria Department of Institutions |
| 17 Mar 1903 - 2 Apr 1906: | Deputy Chief Superintendent, Empress Maria Department of Institutions |
| 2 Apr 1906 - 28 Jan 1909: | Chief Superintendent, Empress Maria Department of Institutions |
| 1 Jan 1907: | Promoted to *General of Cavalry* |
| 1 Jan 1909 - 28 Jan 1909: | Member of the State Council |

*Lieutenant-General* Aleksandr Nikolayevich **Olkhin** (4 Oct 1845 - 1 Sep 1915)
| | |
|---|---|
| 23 Nov 1889 - 20 Apr 1893: | Commander, 19$^{th}$ Dragoon Regiment |
| 20 Apr 1893: | Promoted to *Major-General* |
| 20 Apr 1893 - 2 Mar 1894: | Commander, 1$^{st}$ Brigade, 1$^{st}$ Cavalry Division |
| 2 Mar 1894 - 4 Apr 1894: | Commander, 1$^{st}$ Brigade, 15$^{th}$ Cavalry Division |
| 4 Apr 1894 - 24 Oct 1894: | Attached to the Main Horse Breeding Directorate |
| 24 Oct 1894 - 1905: | Council Member, Main Horse Breeding Directorate |
| 1905: | Promoted to *Lieutenant-General* |
| 1905: | Retired |

*General of Infantry* Pyotr Dmitriyevich **Olkhovsky** (26 Jun 1852 - 14 May 1936)
| | |
|---|---|
| 29 Jan 1898: | Promoted to *Major-General* |
| 29 Jan 1898 - 26 Apr 1899: | Chief of Staff, XXI. Army Corps |
| 26 Apr 1899 - 5 Dec 1900: | General for Special Assignments, Finland Military District |

| | |
|---|---|
| 5 Dec 1900 - 15 Sep 1902: | Commander, Finnish Rifle Brigade |
| 15 Sep 1902 - 25 Jul 1904: | Chief of Staff, Finland Military District |
| 25 Jul 1904 - 2 Feb 1908: | Commander, 3rd Guards Infantry Division |
| 6 Dec 1904: | Promoted to *Lieutenant-General* |
| 2 Feb 1908 - 26 Aug 1912: | Commanding General, XXII. Army Corps |
| 6 Dec 1910: | Promoted to *General of Infantry* |
| 26 Aug 1912 - 27 Jul 1914: | Deputy Commanding General, St. Petersburg Military District |
| 27 Jul 1914 - Oct 1914: | Commanding General, St. Petersburg Military District |
| Oct 1914 - 22 Apr 1915: | Commander, Warsaw Detachment |
| 22 Apr 1915 - 2 Jul 1915: | Attached to the Supreme Commander-in-Chief |
| 2 Jul 1915 - 2 Sep 1915: | Commanding General, Moscow Military District |
| 2 Sep 1915 - 12 Nov 1917: | Member of the Military Council |

*Major-General* Vyacheslav Aleksandrovich **Olkhovsky** (1 Jan 1868 - 26 Aug 1914)
| | |
|---|---|
| 22 Jan 1912 - 26 Aug 1914: | Commander, 136th Infantry Regiment |
| 2 Nov 1914: | Posthumously promoted to *Major-General* |

*General of Infantry* Vladimir Apollonovich **Olokhov** (21 Jan 1857 - 14 Dec 1920)
| | |
|---|---|
| 9 Jun 1903: | Promoted to *Major-General* |
| 9 Jun 1903 - 31 Aug 1908: | Commander, Life Guards Lithuanian Regiment |
| 31 Aug 1908 - 13 Feb 1909: | Commander, 2nd Brigade, 3rd Guards Infantry Division |
| 13 Feb 1909: | Promoted to *Lieutenant-General* |
| 13 Feb 1909 - 30 May 1912: | Commander, 22nd Infantry Division |
| 30 May 1912 - 28 Dec 1914: | Commander, 1st Guards Infantry Division |
| 28 Dec 1914 - 1 Jul 1915: | Commanding General, XXIII. Army Corps |
| 22 Mar 1915: | Promoted to *General of Infantry* |
| 1 Jun 1915 - 1 Jul 1915: | C-in-C, Army Group Olokhov |
| 25 Aug 1915 - 8 Dec 1915: | Commanding General, Guards Corps |
| 8 Dec 1915 - 27 May 1916: | Commanding General, II. Guards Corps |
| 27 May 1916 - 1917: | Member, Committee for Wounded Veterans |
| 1917: | Retired |

*Major-General* Roman Slavomirovich **Olshanovsky** (12 Jul 1866 - 24 May 1935)
| | |
|---|---|
| 18 Nov 1915 - 1917: | Commander, 1st Battalion, 60th Artillery Brigade |
| 26 Feb 1917: | Promoted to *Major-General* |
| 1917: | Commander, 14th Heavy Artillery Brigade |
| 1917: | Commander, 109th Artillery Brigade |
| 1917 - 1918: | Commander, 22nd Artillery Brigade |

*Major-General* Slavomir Nikodimovich **Olshanovsky** (24 Oct 1837 - ?)
| | |
|---|---|
| 12 Oct 1892: | Promoted to *Major-General* |
| 12 Oct 1892 - 9 Feb 1898: | Commander, 5th Artillery Brigade |

*Major-General* Kaetan-Boleslav Vladislavovich **Olshevsky** (7 Aug 1858 - 20 Aug 1944)
| | |
|---|---|
| 18 Jun 1910 - 3 Apr 1915: | Commander, 185th Infantry Regiment |
| 31 Dec 1914: | Promoted to *Major-General* |
| 3 Apr 1915 - 19 Sep 1916: | Commander, 2nd Brigade, 1st Grenadier Division |

| | |
|---|---|
| 1915: | Acting Commander, 1st Grenadier Division |
| 19 Sep 1916 - 6 Mar 1917: | Commander, Polish Rifle Brigade |
| 6 Mar 1917 - 7 Oct 1917: | Commander, 153rd Infantry Division |
| 7 Oct 1917 - Apr 1918: | Reserve officer, Kiev Military District |

*General of Infantry* Melenty Yakovlevich **Olshevsky** (11 Feb 1816 - 1 Mar 1895)
| | |
|---|---|
| 1855: | Promoted to *Major-General* |
| 1855 - 1856: | Chief of Staff, Corps |
| 1857 - 1961: | Duty General, Caucasus Army |
| 23 Apr 1861: | Promoted to *Lieutenant-General* |
| 1861 - 1865: | Commander, Caucasus Reserve Division |
| 13 Jun 1866 - 1868: | Commander, 9th Infantry Division |
| 1868 - 1873: | Commander, 15th Infantry Division |
| 1873 - 15 Jun 1881: | Transferred to the reserve |
| 15 Jun 1881 - 1 Mar 1895: | Member, Committee for Wounded Veterans |
| 30 Aug 1881: | Promoted to *General of Infantry* |

*General of Infantry* Vladimir Petrovich **Olshevsky** (30 Aug 1851 - ?)
| | |
|---|---|
| 11 Aug 1900 - 15 Feb 1905: | Commander, 29th Artillery Brigade |
| 6 Dec 1901: | Promoted to *Major-General* |
| 15 Feb 1905 - 21 Sep 1906: | Commander of Artillery, I. Siberian Army Corps |
| 21 Sep 1906 - 3 May 1910: | Commander, 3rd East Siberian Rifle Division |
| 31 May 1907: | Promoted to *Lieutenant-General* |
| 3 May 1910: | Promoted to *General of Infantry* |
| 3 May 1910: | Retired |
| 19 Apr 1915 - 1917: | Recalled; Reserve officer, Kiev Military District |

*Lieutenant-General* Count Aleksandr Vasilyevich **Olsufyev** (30 Mar 1843 - 28 Mar 1907)
| | |
|---|---|
| 24 Mar 1885 - 9 Apr 1895: | Chief of Staff, Main Imperial Apartments |
| 30 Aug 1890: | Promoted to *Major-General* |
| 9 Apr 1895 - 9 Oct 1905: | Deputy Commander, Main Imperial Apartments |
| 1896: | Promoted to *General-Adjutant* |
| 6 Dec 1899: | Promoted to *Lieutenant-General* |
| 9 Oct 1905 - 28 Mar 1907: | Chief of the Moscow Palace Administration |

*General of Cavalry* Count Aleksey Vasilyevich **Olsufyev** (12 Aug 1831 - 9 Jun 1915)
| | |
|---|---|
| 6 Jan 1865 - 17 Mar 1872: | Commander, Life Guards Grodno Hussar Regiment |
| 27 Mar 1866: | Promoted to *Major-General* |
| 17 Mar 1872 - 2 Oct 1873: | Commander, Warsaw Guards Cavalry Brigade |
| 2 Oct 1873 - 18 Dec 1873: | Commander, 3rd Brigade, 2nd Guards Cavalry Division |
| 18 Dec 1873 - 3 Nov 1877: | Reserve status |
| 3 Nov 1877 - 16 Aug 1880: | Attached to the Main Intendant Directorate |
| 1 Jan 1878: | Promoted to *Lieutenant-General* |
| 16 Aug 1880 - 29 May 1884: | Attached to the Ministry of War |
| 29 May 1884 - 9 Jun 1915: | Honorary Trustee, Moscow Board of Trustees, Empress Maria Institutions |
| 30 Aug 1892: | Promoted to *General of Cavalry* |
| 6 Jul 1896 - 9 Jun 1915: | Director, Committee for Wounded Veterans |

*Major-General* Nikolai Ivanovich **Omelyanovich** (10 Feb 1861 - ?)
| | |
|---|---|
| 20 Dec 1911: | Promoted to *Major-General* |
| 20 Dec 1911 - 5 Nov 1913: | Special Assignments General, Turkestan Military District |
| 5 Nov 1913 - 13 Sep 1914: | Commander, 6th Turkestan Rifle Brigade |
| 13 Sep 1914 - 19 Nov 1914: | Special Assignments General, 10th Army |
| 19 Nov 1914 - 7 May 1915: | Commander, 57th Infantry Division |
| 7 May 1915 - 2 Sep 1915: | Unassigned |
| 2 Sep 1915 - 24 Oct 1917: | Commander, 7th Replacement Infantry Brigade |
| 24 Oct 1917: | Dismissed |

*Major-General* Aleksandr Nikolayevich **Onchokov** (4 Nov 1866 - ?)
| | |
|---|---|
| 13 Aug 1912 - 11 Nov 1916: | Commander, 1st Orenburg Cossack Artillery Battalion |
| 3 Oct 1916: | Promoted to *Major-General* |
| 11 Nov 1916 - 1918: | Commander, Orenburg Cossack Artillery Brigade |

*General of Artillery* Aleksandr Vasilyevich **Onopriyenko** (7 Jan 1837 - ?)
| | |
|---|---|
| 8 Nov 1885: | Promoted to *Major-General* |
| 8 Nov 1885 - 7 Aug 1888: | Commander, 23rd Artillery Brigade |
| 7 Aug 1888 - 29 Aug 1895: | Commander, Life Guards 2nd Artillery Brigade |
| 29 Aug 1895 - 12 Aug 1904: | Commander of Artillery, St. Petersburg Military District |
| 6 Dec 1895: | Promoted to *Lieutenant-General* |
| 12 Aug 1904 - 1917: | Member, Committee for Wounded Veterans |
| 6 Dec 1906: | Promoted to *General of Artillery* |

*Lieutenant-General* Viktor Ivanovich **Onopriyenko** (2 Jun 1834 - 31 Mar 1905)
| | |
|---|---|
| 19 Mar 1883 - 28 Jan 1897: | Commander of Gendarmerie, St. Petersburg Province |
| 9 Apr 1889: | Promoted to *Major-General* |
| 28 Jan 1897 - 1 Sep 1899: | Deputy Military Governor of Warsaw |
| 6 Dec 1898: | Promoted to *Lieutenant-General* |
| 1 Sep 1899: | Dismissed |

*Lieutenant-General* Vladimir Vasilyevich **Onopriyenko** (12 Dec 1838 - 1902)
| | |
|---|---|
| 17 Dec 1886: | Promoted to *Major-General* |
| 17 Dec 1886 - 5 Apr 1893: | Commander, 14th Artillery Brigade |
| 5 Apr 1893 - 1 Jan 1898: | Artillery Inspector, Omsk Military District |
| 14 May 1896: | Promoted to *Lieutenant-General* |
| 1 Jan 1898 - 1902: | Commander of Artillery, XIV. Army Corps |

*General of Engineers* Aleksandr Ilich **Oprits** (21 Aug 1843 - ?)
| | |
|---|---|
| 17 Mar 1891 - 2 Feb 1900: | Commander of Engineers, Fortress St. Petersburg |
| 30 Aug 1892: | Promoted to *Major-General* |
| 2 Feb 1900 - 4 Jun 1910: | Commander of Engineers, St. Petersburg Military District |
| 1 Apr 1901: | Promoted to *Lieutenant-General* |
| 4 Jun 1910: | Promoted to *General of Engineers* |
| 4 Jun 1910: | Retired |

*Lieutenant-General* Nikolai Aloiziyevich **Oranovsky** (21 Nov 1869 - 19 Feb 1935)
| | |
|---|---|
| 21 Nov 1907: | Promoted to *Major-General* |
| 21 Nov 1907 - 23 Nov 1908: | Commander, 35$^{th}$ Artillery Brigade |
| 23 Nov 1908 - 24 Jan 1909: | Commander, 3$^{rd}$ Artillery Brigade |
| 24 Jan 1909 - 25 Mar 1914: | Commander, Life Guards Horse Artillery |
| 25 Mar 1914 - 10 Aug 1914: | Commander, 1$^{st}$ Independent Cavalry Brigade |
| 10 Aug 1914 - 24 Jun 1915: | Commander, 1$^{st}$ Brigade, 2$^{nd}$ Cavalry Division |
| 24 Jun 1915 - 14 Mar 1916: | Inspector of Artillery, XXXVII. Army Corps |
| 14 Mar 1916 - 19 Apr 1917: | Inspector of Artillery, XIII. Army Corps |
| 10 Apr 1916: | Promoted to *Lieutenant-General* |
| 19 Apr 1917 - Oct 1917: | Inspector of Artillery, 5$^{th}$ Army |

*General of Cavalry* Vladimir Aloiziyevich **Oranovsky** (7 Jan 1866 - 29 Aug 1917)
| | |
|---|---|
| 20 Apr 1901 - 13 Nov 1904: | Quartermaster-General, Amur Military District |
| 18 Jul 1904: | Promoted to *Major-General* |
| 13 Nov 1904 - 24 Mar 1905: | Quartermaster-General, 1$^{st}$ Manchurian Army |
| 24 Mar 1905 - 3 Mar 1906: | Quartermaster-General, C-in-C, Far East |
| 3 Mar 1906 - 21 Aug 1907: | Chief of Staff, Far East |
| 11 May 1907 - 9 Aug 1907: | Commander, Brigade, 2$^{nd}$ Guards Cavalry Division |
| 21 Aug 1907 - 11 Jul 1908: | Commander, 2$^{nd}$ Independent Cavalry Brigade |
| 11 Jul 1908 - 7 Nov 1909: | Chief of Staff, Inspector-General of Cavalry |
| 7 Nov 1909 - 1 May 1910: | Chief of Bureau, Inspectorate-General of Cavalry |
| 1 May 1910: | Promoted to *Lieutenant-General* |
| 1 May 1910 - 23 Aug 1913: | Commander, 14$^{th}$ Cavalry Division |
| 23 Aug 1913 - 19 Jul 1914: | Chief of Staff, Warsaw Military District |
| 19 Jul 1914 - 31 Jan 1915: | Chief of Staff, Northwestern Front |
| 25 Oct 1914: | Promoted to *General of Cavalry* |
| 31 Jan 1915 - 19 Apr 1917: | Commanding General, I. Cavalry Corps |
| 19 Apr 1917 - 26 Jul 1917: | Commanding General, XLII. Army Corps |
| 26 Jul 1917 - 9 Aug 1917: | Reserve officer, Petrograd Military District |
| 9 Aug 1917 - 29 Aug 1917: | At the disposal of the C-in-C, Northern Front |

*Lieutenant-General* Prince Georgy Ilich **Orbeliani** (26 Oct 1853 - 14 Jul 1924)
| | |
|---|---|
| 6 Dec 1901: | Promoted to *Major-General* |
| 6 Dec 1901 - 25 Mar 1904: | Attached to Prince Aleksandr Petrovich Oldenburg |
| 25 Mar 1904 - 4 Oct 1907: | Commander, Caucasus Cavalry Brigade |
| 4 Oct 1907 - 5 Jul 1910: | Ataman, Terek Cossack Army |
| 5 Jul 1910: | Promoted to *Lieutenant-General* |
| 5 Jul 1910 - 9 Nov 1913: | Commander, Trans-Caspian Cossack Brigade |
| 9 Nov 1913 - 28 Jul 1914: | Transferred to the reserve |
| 28 Jul 1914 - 26 Jul 1917: | Recalled; Attached to the Chief of Sanitation & Evacuation Services |

*General of Infantry* Ivan Ivanovich **Ordynsky** (2 Jun 1833 - ?)
| | |
|---|---|
| 5 Jun 1877 - 22 Aug 1884: | Director, Nizhny Novgorod Military School |
| 30 Aug 1880: | Promoted to *Major-General* |
| 22 Aug 1884 - 1905: | Attached to the Main Directorate for Military Schools |
| 30 Aug 1892: | Promoted to *Lieutenant-General* |

5 Oct 1904: Promoted to *General of Infantry*

*Major-General* Vasily Denisovich **Ordynsky** (12 Apr 1857 - ?)
12 Oct 1900: Promoted to *Major-General*
12 Oct 1900 - 31 Jul 1902: Chief of Staff, XIX. Army Corps
31 Jul 1902 - 1903: Duty General, Warsaw Military District

*Major-General* Aleksandr Andreyevich **Orel** (7 Sep 1861 - ?)
27 Oct 1908: Promoted to *Major-General*
27 Oct 1908 - 29 Jan 1909: Commander, 1st Brigade, 29th Infantry Division
29 Jan 1909 - Sep 1914: Commander, 2nd Brigade, 29th Infantry Division
Sep 1914 - 1918: POW

*General of Artillery* Iosif Andreyevich **Orel** (9 Sep 1841 - 20 Feb 1908)
16 Mar 1887 - 23 Oct 1893: Commander of Artillery, Fortress Vyborg
30 Aug 1892: Promoted to *Major-General*
23 Oct 1893 - 21 Apr 1899: Commander of Artillery, Fortress Modlin
21 Apr 1899 - 9 Apr 1901: Deputy Commander of Artillery, Odessa Military District
9 Apr 1901 - 1904: Artillery Inspector, Kazan Military District
6 Dec 1902: Promoted to *Lieutenant-General*
1904: Promoted to *General of Artillery*
1904: Retired

*Major-General* Vasily Fyodorovich **Orel** (26 Jul 1849 - ?)
21 Jul 1905: Promoted to *Major-General*
21 Jul 1905 - 25 Jul 1906: Commander, 1st Brigade, 17th Infantry Division

*General of Infantry* Ivan Ivanovich **Oreus** (11 Dec 1830 - 22 May 1909)
24 Dec 1880 - 21 Feb 1906: Member, Military-Scientific Committee, General Staff
30 Aug 1881: Promoted to *Major-General*
30 Aug 1891: Promoted to *Lieutenant-General*
21 Feb 1906: Promoted to *General of Infantry*
21 Feb 1906: Retired

*General of Artillery* Mikhail Fyodorovich **Oreus** (2 May 1843 - 1920)
1 Jul 1883 - 8 Apr 1889: Commander, Life Guards Uhlan Regiment
24 Apr 1888: Promoted to *Major-General*
8 Apr 1889 - 3 Jan 1896: Commander, Life Guards Horse Artillery Brigade
3 Jan 1896 - 13 Jan 1903: Commander of Artillery, Grenadier Corps
14 May 1896: Promoted to *Lieutenant-General*
13 Jan 1903 - 19 Jun 1904: Commanding General, XVI. Army Corps
19 Jun 1904 - 15 Mar 1906: Commanding General, Grenadier Corps
15 Mar 1906 - 23 Mar 1906: Attached to the Ministry of War
23 Mar 1906 - 1917: Member, Committee for Wounded Veterans
6 Dec 1906: Promoted to *General of Artillery*

*Major-General* Aleksandr Afinogenovich **Orlov** (26 Oct 1865 - Oct 1908)
9 Oct 1902 - 4 Sep 1907:         Commander, Life Guards Uhlan Regiment
17 Apr 1905:         Promoted to *Major-General*
4 Sep 1907 - Oct 1908:         Commander, 2$^{nd}$ Brigade, 2$^{nd}$ Guards Cavalry Division

*Major-General* Aleksandr Aleksandrovich **Orlov** (9 Feb 1872 - ?)
17 Sep 1914 - 23 Apr 1916:         Commander of Engineers, I. Army Corps
5 Oct 1915:         Promoted to *Major-General*
23 Apr 1916 - 27 Jan 1917:         Commander of Engineers, 10$^{th}$ Army
27 Jan 1917 - 1917:         Senior Engineer, Technical Engineering Training Committee, Main MilitaryTechnical Directorate

*Major-General* Aleksandr Kirillovich **Orlov** (6 Apr 1858 - ?)
2 Jul 1909 - 1911:         Commander of Engineers, Kiev Fortress Depot
18 Apr 1910:         Promoted to *Major-General*

*Major-General* Aleksandr Vasilyevich **Orlov** (14 Nov 1862 - 10 Oct 1914)
21 Jun 1912:         Promoted to *Major-General*
21 Jun 1912 - 29 Jul 1914:         Commander, 2$^{nd}$ Brigade, 25$^{th}$ Infantry Division
29 Jul 1914 - 10 Oct 1914:         Commander, Brigade, 61$^{st}$ Infantry Division

*Major-General* Prince Aleksey Nikolayevich **Orlov** (18 Apr 1867 - Oct 1916)
21 Apr 1901 - Oct 1916:         Attached to the Imperial Embassy, Paris
19 Jul 1909:         Promoted to *Major-General*

*Major-General* Aleksey Vasilyevich **Orlov** (4 Oct 1856 - ?)
22 Aug 1906 - 2 Nov 1911:         Commandant of Helsingfors
18 Apr 1910:         Promoted to *Major-General*

*Lieutenant-General* David Ivanovich **Orlov** (24 Jun 1840 - 11 Aug 1916)
26 Feb 1878:         Promoted to *Major-General*
26 Feb 1878 - 8 Dec 1895:         Member of the Tsar's retinue
9 Mar 1889 - 29 Feb 1892:         Member of the Don Region Council
8 Dec 1895 - 11 Sep 1896:         At the disposal of the Commanding General, Warsaw Military District
30 Aug 1892:         Promoted to *Lieutenant-General*
11 Sep 1896 - 10 Nov 1898:         Commander, 12$^{th}$ Cavalry Division
10 Nov 1898 - 5 Aug 1900:         Commander, 1$^{st}$ Don Cossack Division
5 Aug 1900 - 1910:         Attached to the Don Cossack Army
1910:         Retired

*Major-General* Dmitry Dmitriyevich **Orlov** (13 Jan 1857 - ?)
30 Jan 1908:         Promoted to *Major-General*
30 Jan 1908 - 21 Feb 1910:         Commander, 2$^{nd}$ Brigade, 35$^{th}$ Infantry Division
21 Feb 1910 - 19 Jul 1914:         Commander, 1$^{st}$ Brigade, 35$^{th}$ Infantry Division
19 Jul 1914 - 31 May 1915:         Commander, 72$^{nd}$ Infantry Division
31 May 1915 - 1917:         Commander, 28$^{th}$ Replacement Infantry Brigade

*Lieutenant-General* Fyodor Fyodorovich **Orlov** (10 Aug 1850 - ?)
| | |
|---|---|
| 3 Oct 1904: | Promoted to *Major-General* |
| 3 Oct 1904 - 10 Aug 1910: | Commander, 2nd Brigade, 27th Infantry Division |
| 10 Aug 1910: | Promoted to *Lieutenant-General* |
| 10 Aug 1910: | Retired |

*Major-General* Ivan Davydovich **Orlov** (3 Feb 1870 - 14 Mar 1918)
| | |
|---|---|
| 31 Dec 1913: | Promoted to *Major-General* |
| 31 Dec 1913 - 24 Jan 1915: | Commander, Life Guards Cossack Regiment |
| 24 Jan 1915 - 21 Oct 1915: | Commander, 3rd Brigade, 1st Guards Cavalry Division |
| 21 Oct 1915 - 22 Dec 1915: | Commander, Trans-Baikal Cossack Brigade |
| 22 Dec 1915 - 24 Mar 1917: | Commander, 1st Trans-Baikal Cossack Division |
| 24 Mar 1917 - Jan 1918: | Commander, 9th Don Cossack Division |

*Major-General* Mikhail Ivanovich **Orlov** (3 Nov 1875 - 22 Jul 1944)
| | |
|---|---|
| 30 May 1916 - 17 Dec 1916: | Chief of Staff, 18th Infantry Division |
| 17 Dec 1916 - 19 Apr 1917: | Quartermaster-General, 1st Army |
| 23 Dec 1916: | Promoted to *Major-General* |
| 19 Apr 1917 - 28 Jun 1917: | Commander, 120th Infantry Division |
| 28 Jun 1917 - 7 Aug 1917: | Quartermaster-General, Western Front |
| 7 Aug 1917 - 27 Aug 1917: | Quartermaster-General, Southwestern Front |

*Major-General* Mikhail Nikolayevich **Orlov** (1 Jul 1866 - ?)
| | |
|---|---|
| 20 Sep 1910 - 31 Aug 1915: | Staff Officer for Gunpowder & Ammunition Inventories, Main Artillery Directorate |
| 6 Dec 1914: | Promoted to *Major-General* |
| 31 Aug 1915 - 7 Sep 1915: | Section Chief, Technical Artillery Committee, Main Artillery Directorate |
| 7 Sep 1915 - 1918: | Chief of Section 1, Technical Artillery Committee, Main Artillery Directorate |

*General of Infantry* Nikolai Aleksandrovich **Orlov** (8 Apr 1855 - 1917)
| | |
|---|---|
| 4 Jun 1892 - 5 Dec 1901: | Professor, General Staff Academy |
| 6 Dec 1899: | Promoted to *Major-General* |
| 5 Aug 1900 - 26 Nov 1900: | Commander, Transbaikal Cossack Infantry Brigade |
| 5 Dec 1901 - 1 Jun 1904: | Commander, 54th Replacement Infantry Brigade |
| 1 Jun 1904 - 21 Sep 1904: | Commander, 54th Infantry Division |
| 21 Sep 1904 - 21 Oct 1904: | At the disposal of the Chief of the General Staff |
| 21 Oct 1904 - 11 Jan 1906: | At the disposal of the C-in-C, Far East |
| 1 Nov 1904 - 7 Nov 1904: | Attached to C-in-C, 1st Manchurian Army |
| 25 Sep 1905: | Promoted to *Lieutenant-General* |
| 11 Jan 1906 - 22 Sep 1910: | Commander, 3rd Infantry Division |
| 22 Sep 1910 - 2 Oct 1914: | Commander, 12th Infantry Division |
| 15 Sep 1914 - 16 Dec 1914: | Commanding General, VIII. Army Corps |
| 12 Dec 1914: | Promoted to *General of Infantry* |
| 16 Dec 1914 - 7 May 1915: | Reserve officer, Kiev Military District |
| 7 May 1915: | Retired |

*Major-General* Pavel Aleksandrovich **Orlov** (12 Jun 1872 - Sep 1915)
23 Feb 1914 - Sep 1915: Commander, 7th Finnish Rifle Regiment
22 Oct 1915: Posthumously promoted to *Major-General*

*Major-General* Pyotr Petrovich **Orlov** (15 Jul 1874 - 6 Oct 1929)
24 Jan 1915 - 26 Dec 1915: Commander, Life Guards Cossack Regiment
22 Mar 1915: Promoted to *Major-General*
26 Dec 1915 - 27 Jun 1916: Commander, 3rd Brigade, 1st Guards Cavalry Division
27 Jun 1918 - 2 Oct 1917: Commander, 2nd Brigade, 3rd Guards Cavalry Division
2 Oct 1917 - Jan 1918: Commander, 3rd Guards Cavalry Division

*Lieutenant-General* Vitaly Firsovich **Orlov** (3 Apr 1857 - 27 Jul 1934)
29 Feb 1908 - 29 Mar 1909: Commander, Aleksandrov Borderguard Brigade
1909: Promoted to *Major-General*
29 Mar 1909 - 1917: Commander, 6th Borderguard District
22 Mar 1915: Promoted to *Lieutenant-General*

*General of Infantry* Vladimir Aleksandrovich **Orlov** (10 Jun 1852 - ?)
3 Apr 1897: Promoted to *Major-General*
3 Apr 1897 - 28 Apr 1903: Duty General, Vilnius Military District
28 Apr 1903 - 15 May 1910: Commander, 43rd Infantry Division
28 Mar 1904: Promoted to *Lieutenant-General*
15 May 1910: Promoted to *General of Infantry*
15 May 1910: Retired

*Major-General* Vladimir Alekseyevich **Orlov** (25 Dec 1859 - ?)
17 Apr 1905: Promoted to *Major-General*
17 Apr 1905 - 1906: Special Assignments General, Warsaw Military District

*Lieutenant-General* Prince Vladimir Nikolayevich **Orlov** (31 Dec 1868 - 29 Aug 1927)
26 Aug 1906 - 25 Aug 1915: Head of the Military Office of the Tsar
6 Dec 1909: Promoted to *Major-General*
25 Aug 1915 - 16 Nov 1915: Attached to the Viceroy of the Caucasus
16 Nov 1915: Promoted to *Lieutenant-General*
16 Nov 1915 - 31 Mar 1917: Assistant Viceroy of the Caucasus
31 Mar 1917: Retired

*Lieutenant-General* Count Nikolai Fyodorovich **Orlov-Denisov** (11 Jun 1839 - 18 Nov 1897)
1 Jan 1878: Promoted to *Major-General*
1 Jan 1878 - 10 Aug 1885: General à la suite
10 Aug 1885 - 18 Nov 1897: Attached to the Don Cossack Army
30 Aug 1888: Promoted to *Lieutenant-General*

*General of Engineers* Nikolai Osipovich **Orlovsky** (28 Apr 1822 - 29 May 1895)
29 Jul 1863 - 6 Oct 1873: Commander, Life Guards Sapper Battalion
27 Mar 1866: Promoted to *Major-General*
6 Oct 1873 - 29 Oct 1877: Attached to the Inspector-General of Engineers

| | |
|---|---|
| 29 Oct 1877 - 9 May 1878: | Military Commander, Zimnitskoye-Sistov |
| 1 Jan 1878: | Promoted to *Lieutenant-General* |
| 9 May 1878 - 13 Aug 1889: | Commander, 1st Sapper Brigade |
| 13 Aug 1889 - 3 Dec 1890: | Attached to the Commanding General, St. Petersburg Military District |
| 3 Dec 1890 - 11 Apr 1892: | Special Assignments General, St. Petersburg Military District |
| 11 Apr 1892 - 29 May 1895: | Member of the Military Council |
| 30 Aug 1892: | Promoted to *General of Engineers* |

*Major-General* Aleksey Alekseyevich **Ornatsky** (13 Feb 1842 - ?)
| | |
|---|---|
| 29 Dec 1900 - 1902: | Commander, 5th Reserve Artillery Brigade |
| 6 Dec 1900: | Promoted to *Major-General* |

*General of Cavalry* Pyotr Vasilyevich **Orzhevsky** (11 Aug 1839 - 31 Mar 1897)
| | |
|---|---|
| 25 Dec 1873 - 12 Jun 1882: | Commander, Warsaw Gendarmerie District |
| 29 Jun 1874: | Promoted to *Major-General* |
| 12 Jun 1882 - 6 Apr 1887: | Deputy Minister of Internal Affairs, Commanding General, Corps of Gendarmerie |
| 30 Aug 1882: | Promoted to *Lieutenant-General* |
| 6 Apr 1887 - 31 Mar 1897: | Governor-General of Vilnius, Kaunas & Grodno |
| 14 May 1896: | Promoted to *General of Cavalry* |

*Major-General* Vladimir Vasilyevich **Orzhevsky** (12 Aug 1838 - ?)
| | |
|---|---|
| 13 Jun 1888: | Promoted to *Major-General* |
| 13 Jun 1888 - 2 Nov 1888: | Commander, 2nd Brigade, 9th Infantry Division |
| 2 Nov 1888 - 26 May 1893: | Commander, 2nd Brigade, 24th Infantry Division |
| 26 May 1893 - 23 Jul 1899: | Commander, 2nd Brigade, 22nd Infantry Division |

*Major-General* Georgy Onufriyevich **Oshchevsky-Kruglik** (1 Aug 1855 - ?)
| | |
|---|---|
| 20 Oct 1890 - 10 Aug 1913: | Commandant, Yekaterinoslav Railway Station |
| 10 Aug 1913: | Promoted to *Major-General* |
| 10 Aug 1913: | Retired |

*Major-General* Aleksandr Antonovich **Osinsky** (14 Feb 1870 - 19 Feb 1956)
| | |
|---|---|
| 1915 - 29 Nov 1916: | Commander, 124th Infantry Regiment |
| 18 Jul 1916: | Promoted to *Major-General* |
| 29 Nov 1916 - 30 Apr 1917: | Commander, Brigade, 133rd Infantry Division |
| 30 Apr 1917 - 1918: | Commander, 133rd Infantry Division |

*Lieutenant-General of the Fleet* Mitrofan Grigoryevich **Osinsky** (16 Jul 1857 - 14 Aug 1938)
| | |
|---|---|
| 16 Dec 1902 - 20 Mar 1911: | Senior Deputy Commander, Port of Emperor Aleksandr III (Libau) |
| 6 Dec 1908: | Promoted to *Major-General of the Admiralty* |
| 20 Mar 1911 - ?: | Senior Deputy Commander, Port of St. Petersburg |
| 8 Apr 1913: | Redesignated *Major-General of the Fleet* |
| 6 Dec 1913: | Promoted to *Lieutenant-General of the Fleet* |

1 Jan 1915 - 1917: Member of the Economic Committee, Ministry of the Navy

*Major-General* Aleksandr Stepanovich **Osipov** (24 Aug 1854 - ?)
20 Mar 1908 - 1913: Commander, 156th Infantry Regiment
1913: Retired
1914 - 6 Jun 1915: Recalled; Commander, State Militia Brigade
6 Jun 1915 - 14 Apr 1917: Commander, Brigade, 109th Infantry Division
1916: Promoted to *Major-General*
14 Apr 1917 - 1917: Reserve officer, Dvinsk Military District

*General of Artillery* Georgy Sergeyevich **Osipov** (21 Mar 1860 - ?)
2 Oct 1903 - 14 Jan 1913: Inspector of Classes, Nikolayev Cavalry School
6 Dec 1906: Promoted to *Major-General*
14 Jan 1913 - 10 Jun 1916: Director, Pskov Cadet Corps
6 Dec 1913: Promoted to *Lieutenant-General*
10 Jun 1916: Promoted to *General of Artillery*
10 Jun 1916: Retired

*Major-General* Georgy Vasilyevich **Osipov** (2 May 1857 - May 1906)
4 Jun 1904 - 1905: Commander, 51st Artillery Brigade
1905: Promoted to *Major-General*
1905 - May 1906: Commander, 13th Artillery Brigade

*Major-General* Mikhail Pavlovich **Osipov** (1 Oct 1859 - ?)
12 Feb 1910 - 1913: Chief of Military Topography Section, Irkutsk Military District
25 Mar 1912: Promoted to *Major-General*

*General of Infantry* Nikolai Vasilyevich **Osipov** (2 Apr 1850 - ?)
29 Dec 1899: Promoted to *Major-General*
29 Dec 1899 - 9 Apr 1901: Commander, 37th Artillery Brigade
9 Apr 1901 - 13 Feb 1904: Commander, 22nd Artillery Brigade
13 Feb 1904 - 19 May 1906: Commander of Artillery, IV. Siberian Army Corps
11 Jun 1905: Promoted to *Lieutenant-General*
19 May 1906 - 9 Nov 1912: Commander, 1st Grenadier Division
9 Nov 1912 - 1917: Commandant of Tsarskoye Selo
22 Mar 1915: Promoted to *General of Infantry*

*Major-General* Pyotr Vasilyevich **Osipov** (22 May 1851 - ?)
4 Mar 1903: Promoted to *Major-General*
4 Mar 1903 - 4 Jun 1904: Commander, 34th Artillery Brigade
4 Jun 1904 - 27 Jan 1907: Commander, 23rd Artillery Brigade
27 Jan 1907 - 21 Nov 1907: Commander of Artillery, V. Army Corps

*Lieutenant-General* Yevgeny Matveyevich **Osipov** (6 Apr 1859 - ?)
19 Mar 1908 - 25 Apr 1914: Commander, 10th Infantry Regiment
14 Apr 1913: Promoted to *Major-General*

| | |
|---|---|
| 25 Apr 1914 - 29 Jul 1914: | Commander, 2nd Brigade, 7th Infantry Division |
| 29 Jul 1914 - 20 Mar 1916: | Commander, Brigade, 3rd Infantry Division |
| 20 Mar 1916 - 1917: | Commander, 3rd Amur Border Infantry Division |
| 20 Oct 1916: | Promoted to *Lieutenant-General* |

*Major-General* Pyotr Stepanovich **Osovsky** (29 Jun 1860 - ?)

| | |
|---|---|
| 22 Feb 1915 - 15 Nov 1915: | Commander, 283rd Infantry Regiment |
| 16 May 1915: | Promoted to *Major-General* |
| 15 Nov 1915 - 25 Oct 1916: | Commander, Brigade, 2nd Amur Borderguard Infantry Division |
| 25 Oct 1916 - 22 Apr 1917: | Commander, 13th Siberian Rifle Division |
| 22 Apr 1917 - Oct 1917: | Commander, 1st Amur Borderguard Infantry Division |

*Vice-Admiral* Konstantin Stepanovich **Osteletsky** (11 Mar 1847 - 22 Aug 1904)

| | |
|---|---|
| 1895: | Promoted to *Rear-Admiral* |
| 1895 - 1898: | Junior Flagman, Black Sea Fleet |
| 1898 - 1900: | Chief Inspector of Mines |
| 1900 - 22 Aug 1904: | Commander, Training Detachment, Marine Corps |
| 1902: | Promoted to *Vice-Admiral* |

*Lieutenant-General of the Admiralty* Pavel Stepanovich **Osteletsky** (9 Feb 1845 - 15 Jan 1916)

| | |
|---|---|
| 26 Jan 1898 - 1906: | Captain, Port of Kronstadt |
| 4 Jan 1899: | Promoted to *Rear-Admiral* |
| 4 Oct 1904: | Promoted to *Lieutenant-General of the Admiralty* |

*Major-General* Aleksandr Aleksandrovich Baron von der **Osten-Driesen** (6 Aug 1852 - 18 Jul 1907)

| | |
|---|---|
| 9 Sep 1904: | Promoted to *Major-General* |
| 9 Sep 1904 - 6 Feb 1907: | Commander, 2nd Brigade, 15th Cavalry Division |

*General of Infantry* Nikolai Fyodorovich Baron von der **Osten-Driesen** (27 Sep 1837 - 1911)

| | |
|---|---|
| 27 Sep 1877 - 25 Nov 1884: | Commander, 123rd Infantry Regiment |
| 15 May 1883: | Promoted to *Major-General* |
| 25 Nov 1884 - 17 Apr 1889: | Commander, 2nd Brigade, 16th Infantry Division |
| 17 Apr 1889 - 30 Oct 1890: | Transferred to the reserve |
| 30 Oct 1890 - 8 Apr 1896: | Commander, 2nd Brigade, 25th Infantry Division |
| 8 Apr 1896 - 27 Sep 1901: | Commander, 25th Infantry Division |
| 14 May 1896: | Promoted to *Lieutenant-General* |
| 27 Sep 1901: | Promoted to *General of Infantry* |
| 27 Sep 1901: | Retired |

*Lieutenant-General* Baron Aleksey Alekseyevich von der **Osten-Sacken** (23 Nov 1857 - ?)

| | |
|---|---|
| 26 Apr 1906 - 28 May 1909: | Military Judge, Vilnius Military District Court |
| 6 Dec 1906: | Promoted to *Major-General* |
| 28 May 1909 - 11 Oct 1911: | Military Judge, St. Petersburg Military District Court |
| 11 Oct 1911 - 27 Jul 1914: | Military Prosecutor, Irkutsk Military District |

14 Apr 1913: Promoted to *Lieutenant-General*
27 Jul 1914 - 10 May 1917: Military Prosecutor, Omsk Military District
10 May 1917: Dismissed

*General of Infantry* Baron Ernest Rudolfovich von der **Osten-Sacken** (9 Apr 1846 - Mar 1911)
1 Dec 1883 - 6 Feb 1892: Military Prosecutor, Vilnius Military District
30 Aug 1890: Promoted to *Major-General*
6 Feb 1892- 19 Aug 1894: Military Prosecutor, St. Petersburg Military District
19 Aug 1894 - 13 Sep 1906: Chairman of the Military Tribunal, St. Petersburg Military District
6 Dec 1899: Promoted to *Lieutenant-General*
13 Sep 1906 - 29 Mar 1909: Member, Supreme Military Tribunal
29 Mar 1909: Promoted to *General of Infantry*
29 Mar 1909 - Mar 1911: Chief Military Prosecutor, Chief of the Main Military Justice Directorate

*Major-General* Baron Vladimir Fyodorovich von der **Osten-Sacken** (30 May 1860 - 1920)
25 Nov 1906 - 1915: Chief of Security, Tauride Imperial Palace
6 Dec 1910: Promoted to *Major-General*
1915 - 30 Jun 1916: Commandant of Minsk
30 Jun 1916 - 1917: Reserve officer, Petrograd Military District

*Major-General* Apollon Apollonovich **Ostolopov** (21 Jan 1849 - ?)
31 Jan 1904 - 4 Sep 1905: Commander, 10$^{th}$ Infantry Regiment
13 Jul 1905: Promoted to *Major-General*
4 Sep 1905 - Oct 1906: Commander, 2$^{nd}$ Brigade, 6$^{th}$ East Siberian Rifle Division

*General of Infantry* Aleksey Nikolayevich **Ostrogorsky** (25 Jan 1840 - 2 Oct 1917)
20 Aug 1882 - 9 Apr 1890: Special Assignments Officer (5$^{th}$ Class), Main Military Education Directorate
30 Aug 1886: Promoted to *Major-General*
9 Apr 1890 - Apr 1906: Special Assignments General (4$^{th}$ Class), Main Military Education Directorate
6 Dec 1902: Promoted to *Lieutenant-General*
Apr 1906: Promoted to *General of Infantry*
Apr 1906: Retired

*Major-General* Nikolai Nikolayevich **Ostrogorsky** (5 Mar 1838 - ?)
18 Aug 1875 - 1895: Director, Tiflis Cadet Corps
30 Aug 1882: Promoted to *Major-General*

*General of Cavalry* Vsevolod Matveyevich **Ostrogradsky** (8 Aug 1843 - 16 Mar 1932)
21 Sep 1884 - 7 Jan 1892: Commander, Life Guards Grodno Hussar Regiment
30 Aug 1886: Promoted to *Major-General*
7 Jan 1892 - 9 Nov 1892: Commander, 1$^{st}$ Brigade, 2$^{nd}$ Guards Cavalry Division
9 Nov 1892 - 30 May 1895: Commander, 5$^{th}$ Cavalry Division

| | |
|---|---|
| 30 May 1895 - 14 Mar 1901: | Commander, 2nd Guards Cavalry Division |
| 14 May 1896: | Promoted to *Lieutenant-General* |
| 14 Mar 1901 - 15 Jun 1905: | Deputy Inspector-General of Cavalry |
| 15 Jun 1905 - 19 Jan 1917: | Inspector-General of Cavalry |
| 6 Dec 1906: | Promoted to *General of Cavalry* |
| 19 Jan 1917 - Feb 1917: | Member of the State Council |
| Feb 1917: | Retired |

*Major-General* Konstantin Valerianovich **Ostromentsky** (21 May 1835 - ?)
| | |
|---|---|
| 1 Feb 1895: | Promoted to *Major-General* |
| 1 Feb 1895 - 1899: | Commander, Horse Artillery Brigade, Orenburg Cossack Army |

*Major-General of Naval Engineers* Sergey Vasilyevich **Ostroumov** (23 Jul 1863 - 1931)
| | |
|---|---|
| 1907 - 23 Jul 1912: | Chief of Lighthouse Construction, Baltic Sea |
| 23 Jul 1912 - Oct 1917: | Chief of Construction, Emperor Peter the Great Port |
| 3 Dec 1912: | Promoted to *Major-General of Naval Engineers* |

*Major-General* Iosif Albertovich **Ostrovsky** (20 Mar 1859 - 1929)
| | |
|---|---|
| 12 Jul 1907 - 27 Oct 1908: | Commander, 264th Infantry Regiment |
| 27 Oct 1908: | Promoted to *Major-General* |
| 27 Oct 1908: | Retired |
| 18 Jan 1916 - 1917: | Recalled; Commander, 89th State Militia Brigade |

*Major-General* Nikolai Maksimovich **Ostryansky** (24 Feb 1867 - 24 Nov 1941)
| | |
|---|---|
| 10 Jun 1913: | Promoted to *Major-General* |
| 10 Jun 1913 - 14 Nov 1914: | Chief of Staff, Ural Cossack Army |
| 14 Nov 1914 - 2 Dec 1916: | Chief of Staff, XV. Army Corps |
| 2 Dec 1916 - 4 May 1917: | Commander, 136th Infantry Division |
| 4 May 1917 - 1918: | Reserve officer, Kiev Military District |

*Lieutenant-General* Ivan Karlovich **Otto** (13 Mar 1840 - 9 Jul 1910)
| | |
|---|---|
| 28 Feb 1890 - 23 Jun 1896: | Deputy Intendant, Moscow Military District |
| 30 Aug 1891: | Promoted to *Major-General* |
| 23 Jun 1896 - 1898: | Intendant, Amur Military District |
| 1898: | Promoted to *Lieutenant-General* |
| 1898: | Retired |

*General of Artillery* Yakov Ivanovich **Ovander** (20 Nov 1827 - 30 Aug 1898)
| | |
|---|---|
| 23 Dec 1869 - 19 Mar 1877: | Commander, 3rd Guards Grenadier Artillery Brigade |
| 21 Jun 1870: | Promoted to *Major-General* |
| 19 Mar 1877 - 10 Mar 1880: | Commander of Artillery, I. Army Corps |
| 10 Mar 1880 - 9 Apr 1889: | Commander of Artillery, Guards Corps |
| 30 Aug 1880: | Promoted to *Lieutenant-General* |
| 9 Apr 1889 - 24 Aug 1892: | Commanding General, IX. Army Corps |
| 24 Aug 1892 - 30 Aug 1898: | Member, Committee for Wounded Veterans |
| 30 Aug 1894: | Promoted to *General of Artillery* |

*Lieutenant-General* Aleksey Konstantinovich **Ovchinnikov** (13 Oct 1861 - 1928)
5 Oct 1910: Promoted to *Major-General*
5 Oct 1910 - 18 May 1913: Chief of Engineers, Fortress Brest-Litovsk
18 May 1913 - Oct 1917: Chief of Electrical Engineering Department, Main Military Technical Directorate
6 Dec 1916: Promoted to *Lieutenant-General*

*Lieutenant-General of the Naval Legal Corps* Ivan Aleksandrovich **Ovchinnikov** (11 Nov 1865 - 1 Mar 1917)
18 Jan 1900 - 1916: Professor, Military Law Academy
10 Apr 1911: Promoted to *Major-General of the Admiralty*
8 Apr 1913: Redesignated *Major-General of the Fleet*
6 Dec 1915: Promoted to *Lieutenant-General of the Naval Legal Corps*

*Rear-Admiral* Fyodor Semyonovich **Ovod** (? - ?)
1904 - 1905: Captain, Cruiser "Ochakov"
?: Promoted to *Rear-Admiral*

*Lieutenant-General* Aleksandr Nikolayevich **Ovodov** (30 Mar 1844 - 1901)
13 Jan 1892 - 18 Oct 1895: Commander, 29th Dragoon Regiment
18 Oct 1895: Promoted to *Major-General*
18 Oct 1895 - 23 Jul 1896: Commander, 2nd Brigade, 12th Cavalry Division
23 Jul 1896 - 16 Sep 1896: At the disposal of the Commanding General, Moscow Military District
16 Sep 1896 - 12 Dec 1900: Commander, 2nd Independent Cavalry Brigade
12 Dec 1900: Promoted to *Lieutenant-General*
12 Dec 1900: Retired

*Major-General* Aleksandr Aleksandrovich **Ovsyany** (13 Apr 1856 - 1909)
9 May 1906 - Apr 1909: Commander, 1st Siberian Rifle Artillery Brigade
6 Dec 1906: Promoted to *Major-General*

*Lieutenant-General* Nikolai Romanovich **Ovsyany** (7 Dec 1847 - 16 May 1913)
23 May 1886 - 14 May 1894: Tutor to Prince Daniel of Montenegro
30 Aug 1893: Promoted to *Major-General*
14 May 1894 - 12 Aug 1910: At the disposal of the Chief of the General Staff
12 Aug 1910: Promoted to *Lieutenant-General*
12 Aug 1910: Retired

*Major-General* Aleksandr Erastovich von **Ozarovsky** (14 Aug 1861 - ?)
6 Nov 1915 - 1917: Commander, 1st Finnish Rifle Artillery Brigade
3 Mar 1916: Promoted to *Major-General*

*General of Infantry* Aleksandr Fyodorovich von **Ozarovsky** (4 Apr 1839 - ?)
19 Feb 1890: Promoted to *Major-General*
19 Feb 1890 - 25 Aug 1892: Commander, 2nd Brigade, 17th Infantry Division
25 Aug 1892 - 14 Feb 1894: Commander, 1st Brigade, 18th Infantry Division

| | |
|---|---|
| 14 Feb 1894 - 12 Sep 1897: | Commander, 55th Reserve Infantry Brigade |
| 12 Sep 1897 - 1906: | Commander, Tiflis Regional Brigade |
| 6 Dec 1900: | Promoted to *Lieutenant-General* |
| 1906: | Promoted to *General of Infantry* |
| 1906: | Retired |

*Major-General* Vislav-Tomash Osipovich **Ozemblovsky** (10 Feb 1855 - ?)
| | |
|---|---|
| 29 Sep 1906 - 1911: | Commander, Turkestan Sapper Battalion |
| 1911: | Promoted to *Major-General* |
| 1911: | Retired |

*General of Infantry* Aleksey Fyodorovich **Ozerov** (3 Aug 1839 - 21 May 1907)
| | |
|---|---|
| 24 Aug 1872 - 30 Jun 1884: | At the disposal of the Commanding General, Kazan Military District |
| 15 Jun 1879: | Promoted to *Major-General* |
| 30 Jun 1884 - 27 May 1888: | Commander, 2nd Brigade, 41st Infantry Division |
| 27 May 1888 - 29 Apr 1892: | Commander, 20th Regional Brigade |
| 30 Aug 1889: | Promoted to *Lieutenant-General* |
| 29 Apr 1892 - 8 May 1900: | Commander, 3rd Infantry Division |
| 8 May 1900: | Promoted to *General of Infantry* |
| 8 May 1900: | Retired |

*Major-General* Andrey Sergeyevich **Ozerov** (25 Jul 1845 - 14 Oct 1897)
| | |
|---|---|
| 31 Aug 1881 - 13 Aug 1892: | Adjutant to Grand Duke Mikhail Nikolayevich |
| 30 Aug 1890: | Promoted to *Major-General* |
| 13 Aug 1892 - 14 Oct 1897: | Administrator, Court of Grand Duke Mikhail Nikolayevich |

*Lieutenant-General* David Aleksandrovich **Ozerov** (10 Aug 1856 - 1918)
| | |
|---|---|
| 26 Dec 1896 - 1913: | Chief of Administration, Imperial Palace |
| 1 Jan 1900: | Promoted to *Major-General* |
| 18 Apr 1910: | Promoted to *Lieutenant-General* |
| 1913: | Retired |

*Lieutenant-General* Sergey Sergeyevich **Ozerov** (16 Jul 1852 - 1920)
| | |
|---|---|
| 6 Dec 1899: | Promoted to *Major-General* |
| 6 Dec 1899 - 7 Mar 1900: | General à la suite |
| 7 Mar 1900 - 21 Oct 1904: | Commander, Life Guards Preobrazhensky Regiment |
| 21 Oct 1904 - 11 Jul 1905: | Commander, Brigade |
| 11 Jul 1905 - 9 Sep 1905: | Attached to the Commandant of the Imperial Palace |
| 9 Sep 1905 - 21 Jun 1906: | Commander, 1st Guards Infantry Division |
| 21 Jun 1906: | Dismissed |
| 30 May 1912 - 13 Apr 1917: | Recalled; General à la suite |
| 10 Jul 1916 - 13 Apr 1917: | Chief of Administration, Imperial Palace |
| 13 Apr 1917: | Promoted to *Lieutenant-General* |
| 13 Apr 1917: | Retired |

*General of Infantry* Aleksey Trifonovich **Ozerovsky** (17 Mar 1839 - ?)
| | |
|---|---|
| 41 Feb 1886 - 28 Jul 1895: | Senior Assistant Inspector, Border Guard Corps |
| 9 Apr 1889: | Promoted to *Major-General* |
| 28 Jul 1895 - 1 Jul 1899: | Deputy Commanding General, Border Guard Corps |
| 3 Jan 1898: | Promoted to *Lieutenant-General* |
| 1 Jul 1899 - 16 Feb 1901: | Commanding General, 1st District, Border Guard Corps |
| 16 Feb 1901 - 1910: | Deputy Commanding General, Border Guard Corps |
| 16 Nov 1908: | Promoted to *General of Infantry* |

*General of Infantry* Vladimir Fyodorovich **Ozharovsky** (23 Jun 1848 - 23 Aug 1911)
| | |
|---|---|
| 24 Oct 1899: | Promoted to *Major-General* |
| 24 Oct 1899 - 16 Apr 1903: | Commander, 1st Brigade, 6th Infantry Division |
| 16 Apr 1903 - 7 Dec 1904: | Commander, 58th Reserve Brigade |
| 7 Dec 1904 - 14 Dec 1906: | Commander, 44th Infantry Division |
| 6 Dec 1906: | Promoted to *Lieutenant-General* |
| 14 Dec 1906 - 23 Aug 1911: | Governor of Orenburg, Ataman, Orenburg Cossack Army |
| 4 Sep 1911: | Posthumously promoted to *General of Infantry* |

*Major-General* Dmitry Ivanovich **Oznobishin** (8 Aug 1869 - Sep 1956)
| | |
|---|---|
| 20 Dec 1913 - 1917: | Attached to the Guards Cavalry |
| 6 Dec 1916: | Promoted to *Major-General* |
| 1917: | Deputy Military Attaché, France |

**Primary Sources:**

- Генералитет российской императорской армии и флота (http://www.rusgeneral.ru)
  [*Generals of the Imperial Russian Army and Navy*]

- Генералов, Штабъ и Обер-офицеров, Корпусов Морского Ведомства, Чинов по Адмиралтейству и Числящихся по Корпусам
  [*Generals, Staff- and Senior Officers of the Naval Office, Officials of the Admiralty*]

- Русская армия в Первой мировой войне (http://www.grwar.ru)
  [*The Russian Army in World War I*]

- Список генералам по старшинству 1894 - 1916
  [*Seniority list of generals*]

- Список личного состава судов флота, строевых и административных учреждений Морского ведомства
  [*List of fleet personnel, combat and administrative institutions of the Naval Office*]

- Список полковникам по старшинству 1894 - 1916
  [*Seniority list of colonels*]

- Suomalaiset kenraalit ja amiraalit Venäjän sotavoimissa 1809–1917
  (http://www.kansallisbiografia.fi/kenraalit/)
  [*Finnish generals and admirals of the Russian armed forces 1809 - 1917*]

- Участники первой мировой войны (http://1914ww.ru/biograf/index.php)
  [*Participants of World War I*]

## **ACKNOWLEDGEMENTS**

Of all the writing projects that I have undertaken during the last twenty years, this has by far been the most labor-intensive and time-consuming. I must thank my wife, Rosemarie, for her patience, support and encouragement during this project.

---

Other books by Andris J. Kursietis:

The Fallen Generals
La Regia Marina 1919 - 1945
The Wehrmacht at War
The Armed Forces of Latvia 1918 - 1940
The Hungarian Army & Its Military Leadership in World War II
The Luftwaffe 1935 - 1945
Generals & Admirals of the Spanish Armed Forces 1900 - 1945
A Lifetime for Hungary
The Imperial Japanese Navy (Nihon Kaigun) 1900 - 1945
Under Three Flags